353.976
W 585

D1508329

MESSAGES OF THE
GOVERNORS OF TENNESSEE
1845–1857

Volume Four

MESSAGES OF THE

Governors of Tennessee

1845–1857

by

ROBERT H. WHITE, Ph.D.
STATE HISTORIAN

AUTHOR OF

*Development of the Tennessee State Educational Organization,
1796–1929* AND *Tennessee: Its Growth and Progress*

VOLUME FOUR

Published by

THE TENNESSEE HISTORICAL COMMISSION
NASHVILLE

COPYRIGHT, 1957
BY
THE TENNESSEE HISTORICAL COMMISSION
NASHVILLE

23952

TYPOGRAPHY, PRINTING, AND BINDING IN THE U.S.A. BY
BENSON PRINTING COMPANY, NASHVILLE, TENNESSEE

Ref
J
87
T216
v.4

PREVIEW

OF

VOLUME IV

1845-1857

The twelve-year period from 1845 to 1857 witnessed a continuation of "the golden age" of Tennessee history. Internal Improvements advanced from a relatively paper status to one of real accomplishment. The construction of railroads and turnpikes as well as the improvement of river channels greatly improved transportation systems and opened up means for the marketing of products from farm, forest, and mine.

State services were greatly expanded through the media of enlarged facilities for the care of the mentally afflicted, the establishment of the Tennessee Bureau of Agriculture and the State Library, and the enactment of legislation that provided the first State-dollar for the promotion of Public Education. The divorcement of the Judiciary from the Legislature, as the elective agency, and transferring that power direct to the people marked a significant step forward in democracy. The State Capitol was begun and practically completed during the above twelve-year regime. Within the same span of years, the War with Mexico was fought and won; Slavery—the issue that split the Nation asunder— forged to the forefront in all major political contests within the State; and Religious Freedom constituted the principal issue in one hotly contested gubernatorial race, that of 1855.

The two-party system was really in vogue. In five gubernatorial contests the average majority of the successful candidates was a mere handful of 2,021 votes. Andrew Johnson was the only Governor who was able to succeed himself as Chief Executive. It was an era of interesting and intense movements in the social, political, and economic life of Tennessee, and embraced stirring events of importance and value to the present and future citizenry of the State.

ACKNOWLEDGMENTS

Sincere appreciation is hereby expressed for the support rendered by Governor Frank G. Clement and the Seventy-Ninth General Assembly for provision of funds for research and publication of Volume IV of the contemplated ten volumes of *Messages of the Governors of Tennessee*. Splendid cooperation was given by the State Department of Conservation, the State Library and Archives, the Tennessee Historical Society, and the Nashville Public Library.

R. H. W.

CONTENTS

VOLUME FOUR

ILLUSTRATIONS

VOLUME FOUR

From Portrait by William Cooper. Courtesy of Tennessee State Library, Nashville.

MESSAGES OF THE
GOVERNORS OF TENNESSEE
1845-1857

VOLUME FOUR

CHAPTER ONE

Aaron Venable Brown

Aaron Venable Brown was born August 15, 1795, in Brunswick County, Virginia. He was the sixth child of the Reverend Aaron Brown, a Methodist minister, and his second wife, Elizabeth Melton. With the exception of his very early schooling, young Brown received his education in North Carolina to which place his father had moved. Entered in Westrayville Academy in Nash County, he was placed under the tutelage of John Bobbitt, an exceedingly able instructor. At the end of two years, he transferred to the University of North Carolina, graduating in 1814 as valedictorian of his class. While attending the above institution, his family had migrated to Tennessee, settling in Giles County. The year following his graduation, he began the study of law under the guidance of Judge John Trimble, of Nashville, one of the ablest lawyers of the time. After a brief period of practice in Nashville, Mr. Brown was persuaded to move to Giles County to take over the law practice of Alfred Harris of Pulaski who had accepted a place on the bench. Shortly afterwards, a partnership was formed with James K. Polk which was continued until Polk's public service was commenced.

Despite a lucrative law practice, Mr. Brown at length entered the political arena and was elected in 1821 as State Senator from the counties of Lincoln and Giles and, with the exception of 1825 when he was not a candidate, served continuously through the legislative session of 1827. In 1831, he was elected a member of the lower branch of the General Assembly. Throughout his entire legislative career, his course was marked by active and intelligent espousal of numerous measures designed for the public welfare. Perhaps his outstanding contribution was his masterly effort in behalf of an independent judiciary which would establish a liberal and enlightened system of jurisprudence. By order of the Judiciary Committee, during the legislative session of 1831, his scholarly and philosophical dissertation on capital punishment was submitted to the Legislature and was favorably commented on in practically every quarter of the Nation. His position was not the abolition of capital punishment altogther, but a drastic reduction of the number of causes for which the death penalty was imposed.

In 1839, Mr. Brown was elected to Congress over a formidable Whig, Ebenezer J. Shields, who had served in the two preceding sessions of Congress. In 1843, his Congressional District was altered in such manner as to reduce the usual Democratic majority by which he had previously been elected. Despite the political "gerrymander", he defeated Neill S. Brown who later turned the scales by defeating him in the gubernatorial race of 1847. During the period of his service in Congress, 1839-1845, he championed in his speeches before the Congress the whole Democratic program of the "reannexation of Texas" and the "reoccupation of Oregon", both burning political issues at the time. He was an able member of a number of Congressional Committees and served as Chairman of the Committee on Territories. Of his own volition, he terminated his Congressional services in 1845, thus ending his Congressional career at the very beginning of President James K. Polk's administration.

Having decided to retire from public life, Mr. Brown was on his way home when he received the news at Pittsburgh of his nomination as the Democratic candidate for Governor. He was reluctant to accept the honor, as doing so conflicted with his purposes to retire to private life and resume his law practice. Furthermore, the prospects for success were far from flattering. James K. Polk had twice been defeated for the office, in 1841 and 1843, and had failed to carry his home State in the Presidential race of 1844, losing it by 113 votes.

Contrary to his own personal desires, Mr. Brown accepted the challenge and waged a vigorous campaign which resulted in his triumph over an exceedingly formidable Whig opponent, Ephraim H. Foster. Governor Brown's administration was marked by such constructive measures as the incorporation of numerous male and female academies, the chartering of several railroads, and improvements at the Hospital for the Insane and the penitentiary. He was Governor during the time of the Mexican War and proved himself to be an able and alert administrator during the conflict. His attempt to procure re-election in 1847 to the governorship proved futile, he being defeated by Neill S. Brown, Whig.

In 1850, he was a member of the Southern Convention which met in Nashville. He authored what is known as the Tennessee Platform which opposed the compromise on the slavery question then pending in Congress. The high point in his proposal was not disunion or secession as a remedy, but a sectional *retaliation* which involved a refusal to trade with the North. In short, he proposed an economic boycott. He was a member of the Democratic Convention in 1856, and received twenty-nine votes for the Vice-Presidency. His last official position was that of Postmaster General in President Buchanan's cabinet, in which position he demonstrated much administrative ability by shortening transcontinental mail routes.

His first wife was Sarah Woodford Burruss of Rutherford County who died leaving four children. In 1845, he was married to Mrs. Cynthia (Pillow) Saunders to whom was born one child, a son. Governor Brown died in Washington City, on March 8, 1859, of pneumonia. On March 14, his remains reached Nashville and the whole city was in mourning. After impressive funeral discourses by two eminent divines, the body was interred in Mt. Olivet Cemetery under the auspices of the Masonic Fraternity.

Legislative Messages of
Governor Aaron Venable Brown, 1845–1847

Politically speaking, the Democrats in Tennessee had experienced for four years a famine in the gubernatorial office. "Lean" Jimmy Jones, the Whig, had delivered twice a solar plexus to James K. Polk, once in 1841 and again in 1843. It behooved the Democracy to survey all political angles and plumb all the depths with reference to the selection of a standard-bearer in the forthcoming contest for the governorship. Polk was ensconced in the White House in Washington, and he had taken with him another Democratic stalwart, Cave Johnson, who had been appointed Postmaster General. Moreover, Ex-President Andrew Jackson was in feeble health and only a few months distant from death's door. Absence from the State and inability of a number of strong Democratic leaders to take an active part in the gubernatorial battle was calculated to dim the enthusiasm of aspiring Democratic candidates. The prospects were anything but encouraging.

There was, however, one exceedingly able Democrat who had not laid aside his thinking cap. A. O. P. Nicholson, experienced in "practical" politics both as an office-holder and newspaper editor, had been surveying the scene. It was his judgment that prospects for Democratic success would be greatly enhanced by the nomination of Aaron Venable[1] Brown who was just ending his term in Congress. Accordingly, there is indisputable evidence that Nicholson had contacted Brown

---

[1] Author's note. Numerous Tennessee publications refer to Aaron V. Brown as Aaron *Vail* Brown. The middle name was *Venable* and not *Vail*. See *Speeches, Congressional and Political and Other Writings of Ex-Governor Aaron V. Brown*, Nashville, 1854, 507, in which Brown himself stated that his middle name was *Venable*.

while the latter was yet in Washington in regard to the selection of a candidate to oppose the Whig nominee, whoever the latter might be. Brown's position was set forth by him in the following communication [2] to Nicholson:

"Washington, February 23, 1845

DEAR SIR:

I know not what to say to you in relation to the approaching convention. I have had no agency in connecting my name with it, but on the contrary have, on all suitable occasions, desired my friends to look to some other quarter for a standard bearer of our principles in the coming contest. Those principles lie near to my heart, and I have been and shall ever be proud in doing anything to advance and uphold them. But I cannot but think that the Convention, in casting about, can find others more able than myself and more available to accomplish the great work which now lies before them. If so, I desire most earnestly and sincerely that they may make a different selection, and will cooperate with them by all means and exertions in my power. This desire is predicated on no indifference, nor on any despondence of success. More than twenty years in the public service will disprove the first; and as to the last, he were unworthy of Democratic support who would stop to count the chances. These sentiments I have before expressed to you, and I now desire that you will take charge of my name before that Convention, and not permit it to be used for any purpose of distracting or dividing our Party, nor in a manner to effect a nomination which shall not receive the sanction and approbation of the whole democracy of the State. In any diversity of opinion as to the individual to be selected, I earnestly desire that you yield it up in favor of any other to whom any portion of the convention may indicate a preference.

Writing with some pain from recent indisposition, I remain

Your Obedient Servant,

AARON V. BROWN

A. O. P. Nicholson, Esq."

When the Democratic Convention met in Nashville in early March, two candidates were nominated, Frederick T. Stanton of Memphis and Aaron V. Brown of Pulaski. In the midst of counting the votes, Mr. Stanton's name was withdrawn whereupon the nomination of Mr. Brown was made unanimous. Immediately thereafter, Mr. Nicholson produced and read the letter above mentioned.[3] Hearty approval of the nomination of Brown was proclaimed by the Democratic organ, the *Nashville Union*, which editorialized as follows:[4]

"... Our Whig friends will hardly venture to affect so much ignorance as to ask 'Who is Aaron V. Brown'?"

This editorial thrust, of course, at the Whigs was occasioned by the taunting remarks of Whig papers at the nomination of James K. Polk for the Presidency, "Who is James K. Polk?".

---

[2] *Nashville Union*, March 6, 1845.
[3] *Ibid.*
[4] *Ibid.*, March 8, 1845.

Opposed to Aaron V. Brown was the Whig candidate, Ephraim H. Foster, a veteran of many political battles and a man possessed of real ability. The contest proved to be what all expected—a real battle between giants. The race, relatively speaking, was shorn of much of the banter and ballyhoo which had largely characterized the two contests between Polk and Jones. Political principles rather than individual personalities constituted the bases of the battle. The situation, as viewed by the Editor of the Democratic organ, was summed up in the following comment:[5]

"A FAIR TRIAL OF STRENGTH

The present contest in Tennessee will be the fairest trial of party strength that we have ever had. The candidates for Governor are politicians of age and experience and what is important, they are fully identified with their respective parties. We have no new man on the track to be run because 'he has no political sins to answer for'. To select a candidate for Governor on such grounds is to pay him a very equivocal compliment. But, at present, we congratulate the Whigs upon their repudiation of that doctrine which, at best, is but an attempt to evade a fair race. If Mr. Brown has been guilty of political sins, the Whigs have a career of twenty years in which to find them —if to have been a straightforward and unwavering Democrat be a sin in their sight, then they will find our candidate a great sinner and they will find him ready to answer therefor. If Mr. Foster has committed political sins, we are very certain they will be discussed and placed to his *debit*. That he sinned egregiously when he left the Democratic Party and joined the modern Whigs, is a prevalent notion in our ranks; but Mr. Foster stands ready to answer for this sin as well as all others alleged against him.

We have not heard of any local or state questions which are likely to have an influence in affecting the strength of parties. The Democrats have suffered materially in one or two canvasses from such causes. All remember how much was said in 1843 about the State Bank and its political proposition. That humbug died out when the Legislature assembled. The Thirteen Question was made prominent in that canvass—we suppose some of the small politicians may try this again. But upon the whole, if local questions are to be brought to bear, we are very certain that the advantage is with the Democrats in the present contest. As the canvass advances, we shall have occasion to bring forward such acts of the last Whig Legislature as, in our judgment, are fit subjects for comments and condemnation. Before we turn our attention to this branch of the canvass, we desire to see the general plan of the contest as it may develop within the next few weeks."

According to the then prevailing custom, a long list of appointments for a joint discussion between the two candidates was announced. Contemporary newspapers fairly groan under lengthy editorials and reports relative to the race. Quoting from the *Jackson Republican*, the *Nashville Union* incorporated an extract giving details[6] of the discussion at Jackson:

---

[5] *Ibid.*, March 27, 1845.
[6] *Ibid.*, April 22, 1845.

"Agreeable to appointment, *Governor* Brown and Ex-Senator Foster addressed their fellow-citizens of Madison county on Monday last; and if the democratic triumph in August next was in the least foreshadowed in the triumph of Mr. Brown over Mr. Foster—or if the Whig defeat was foreshadowed in the severe drubbing received by the latter gentleman from the former, the triumph will indeed be glorious, and the defeat a perfect Waterloo case. We do not make this observation for effect; for all who heard the debate will bear witness of the truth of our statement; and we hazard nothing in saying, that since last Monday democratic stock has risen at least ten or twelve per cent., and from a disposition manifested by many whigs of our acquaintance to purchase, we are of opinion it will very soon increase to 20 or perhaps 30 per cent.

Mr. Foster led off in his usual Bombastes Furioso style, dividing his speech into two parts, the Exordium and the Peroration, leaving out the argumentative, and entirely failing in the pathetic part.

After giving in detail the subjects discussed and the positions taken by the speakers, which were similar to those at Clarksville, the Republican closes with the following account of the sparring:—

The debate closed with a spirited display of sparring in the way of wit and levity, in which our noble standard bearer fairly got the ascendency even of the 'immortal Eph;' and though much of the pith and force of their sallies will be lost in an imperfect sketch upon paper, we have thought that a rehearsal of them, even in an imperfect form, would not be uninteresting to some of our readers.

Mr. Brown being the last speaker, closed his remarks by saying that his great object had been to convince Mr. Foster himself of the error of his way, and to draw him back to his old republican principles; and he hoped he had not been altogether unsuccessful; yet if he had, all that he could say, was, in the language of scripture, 'Ephraim! Ephraim is joined to his idols, let him alone,' and he hoped on the 7th of Aug. the people would let him alone.

After the shouts of the multitude had subsided, Mr. Foster rose and replied that there was another passage of scripture, in which a certain man by the name of Aaron was mentioned, who, while Moses ascended the mount to receive the law of God, built a golden calf and worshiped it, and that it was a fat calf, (pointing to Mr. Brown.)

Mr. Brown replied that such was the fact; that Aaron did build a golden calf, but that it was made of gold, whereas he (Mr. Foster) made his God of Clay.

Mr. Foster here found himself in a very disagreeable situation in endeavoring to reply amid the deafening shouts and applause of the democracy, which continued for a considerable time, to the great confusion of Mr. Foster. After the applause had subsided, however, he replied that his Clay God was formed in the image of his creator—that our Creator made Adam of clay, and that it would have been much better had Aaron made his golden calf of clay.

Mr. Brown answered that Mr. Foster's Clay God, like all other false Gods, had been overturned.

Here again the shouts of applause were long and enthusiastic; and supposing the sparring had ended, Mr. Brown observed to the audience, that as he was a stranger to them, he hoped they would give no importance to their wit and levity, but that they would go to their homes and think seriously upon the grave subjects they had heard debated.

Mr. Foster, unwilling to leave the stand thus outwitted, again arose and said his competitor reminded him of a drunken preacher he once heard of, who, at the close of his sermons, always admonished his congregations to do as he said, and not as he did.

Ah, said Mr. Brown, looking Mr. Foster in the face, you are for sermonizing are you? I will not pretend to say what kind of a preacher *you* would make but this much I do know, that you would afford the best *text* for a sermon I know of. With such a text, the most ordinary minister might preach an excellent sermon either for Texas or against Texas—either for the Tariff or against the Tariff—either for a Bank or against a Bank—either for Jackson or against Jackson—either for Clay or against Clay.

Here the audience, no longer able to restrain themselves, not only shouted, but yelled, and Mr. Foster, evidently outwitted, mortified and chagrined, like a dying man catching at a straw, said he would be glad if Mr. Brown could say something about Mr. Buchanan and the Tariff; and with this glorious failure at a retort, yielded up the ghost and the scene ended, leaving the whigs downcast and mortified, while the democrats filled the house with their long and continued shouts of triumph and victory."

But the Whig contingency peered through different political lenses and an altogether different picture was presented, as the opposing candidates swapped political blows at Lexington:[7]

"Yesterday, according to previous appointment, we had the candidates for Governor with us and though it rained pretty much without intermission for two days yet the fire of enthusiasm that burns in the bosoms of the honest freemen of old Henderson was not to be extinguished.

Foster led off in gallant style, making one of the most eloquent exordiums I ever heard. He touched upon the various questions at issue, and handled them with great effect. Upon the distribution question, he was peculiarly forcible and eloquent—he spoke of the advantages to be derived from an equitable distribution of the proceeds of the public lands among the states— the increased facilities of the market by the improvement of our roads and navigable streams, the digging of canals and the like, to which desirable object one portion of the money could be well appropriated, and another portion to the establishment of Common Schools, that the poor man's child, by the fostering care of government, may have extended to him the same advantages that the child of the wealthy man enjoys, or the purse of the aristocrat affords, for the acquirement of knowledge, which enables a man above all other things to truly appreciate the blessings of liberty. I have heard Mr. Foster on several occasions before; but, in all candor, am compelled to pronounce his speech on yesterday, by far the happiest effort I have ever heard him make. Old Henderson was the first county in the district to nominate Foster for Governor, and yesterday the hearts of her gallant Whig sons were made glad by his triumphant response. The Hall where he spoke was crowded to overflowing and it rained nearly all the time— but, standing near an open door, he was enabled to address his attentive audience within the house as well as some several hundred who assembled without unable to effect an entrance, but who patiently stood throughout his entire speech in the rain and mud, listening with delight to the bold and manly display of the highly gifted speaker and statesman. The Democrats even speak well of Foster's effort.

Mr. Brown followed in a speech of the same length. It was the first time

---

[7] *Nashville Whig*, May 13, 1845.

I ever heard him and must confess that I, at least, was disappointed. The
fame of the warrior preceeded him in his onward march. Polk's superior!—
the Ajax of his party! Truly, I was led to believe that Foster might have said,
'A god within me bids me try'.
But no! Mr. Brown is not the superior of Mr. Polk; neither is he anything
like an equal of Mr. Foster. His style of oratory is by far better adapted to
the bar than the stump. I look upon him by no means, however, as a common
man; but, on the contrary, as a politician of ability and some tact. His friends
were evidently disappointed, and it may have been one of his failures; or perhaps it was because he did not have Cheatham along *to cry* for him."

In the course of debate, each contestant indulged in flights of
oratory that intrigued the partisans of each candidate. Perhaps posterity
should not be denied the privilege of ready accessibility to a rainbow-
hued sample of what Aaron V. Brown displayed at Athens and numerous other places. As a peroration, he plucked the feathers from the
eagle's wing and regaled his hearers with this choice *morceau:*[8]

"...America may be the last asylum of liberty for the human family. In
almost every other country the just and equal rights of man have been
cloven down by the sword, or usurped by the kings, princes, and potentates
of the earth. Here liberty has reared her favorite temple. She has laid its
foundations deep and wide. Her bulwarks have been made strong, and the
ministers who attend her altars and the worshippers who throng her gates
should never surrender it but with their lives. Never was there a people who
possessed a finer or nobler country. Go up with me in imagination and stand
for awhile on some lofty summit of the Rocky Mountains. Let us take one
ravishing view of this broad land of liberty. Turn your face toward the
Gulf of Mexico, who do you behold? Instead of one lone star faintly shining
in the far distant south, a whole galaxy of stars of the first magnitude are
bursting on your vision and shining with a bright and glorious effulgence.
Now turn with me to the west—the mighty west—where the setting sun dips
her broad disk in the western ocean. Look away down through the misty
distance to the shores of the Pacific, with all its bays and harbours and rivers.
Cast your eyes as far as the Russian possessions in latitude fifty-four degrees
and forty minutes. What a new world lies before you. How many magnificent States to be the future homes of the sons and daughters of freedom.
Turn now your face to the east, where the morning sun first shines on this
land of liberty. Away yonder, you see the immortal old thirteen, who
achieved our independence; nearer to us lie the twelve or fifteen States of the
great valley of the Mississippi stretching and reposing like so many giants in
their slumbers. O! now I see your heart is full—it can take in no more, who
now feels like he was a party man, or a southern man, or a northern man?
Who does not feel that he is an American, and thankful to Heaven that his
lot was cast in such a goodly land? When did mental vision ever rest on such
a scene? Moses, when standing on the top of Mount Pisgah, looking over
on the promised land, gazed not on a scene half so lovely. O! let us this day
vow that whatever else we may do, by whatever name we may be called,
we will never surrender one square acre of this goodly heritage to the dictation of any king or potentate on earth. Swear it! swear it, my countrymen,
and let Heaven record the vow forever...."

[8] Brown, Aaron V.: *Speeches, Congressional and Political, and Other Writings,*
Nashville, 1854, 202–203.

During the first five weeks of the campaign, the two candidates traveled nearly one thousand miles and addressed the voters in twenty counties. Worn to a frazzle, a joint announcement was made to the effect that a two-week armistice was in order, and that a revised list of appointments would be announced which would include twenty-seven counties.[9] At length, the exhausting campaign came to an end in early August resulting in a victory for Brown over Foster by a majority of 1,623 votes.[10] The *Nashville Whig* carried an epigrammatic statement [11] as to the result of the election,

"Neither party turned out well, but the Democrats went to the polls better than the Whigs."

The total vote was for Brown 58,269 and for Foster 56,646.

On October 6, 1845, the twenty-sixth General Assembly convened in Nashville. The Democrats had a majority of one in the Senate and two in the House of Representatives. Curiously enough, the political complexion in the Senate was an exact duplicate of the two preceding Legislatures, thirteen Democrats and twelve Whigs. The first order of business was the election of Speakers of the respective branches of the General Assembly. Without appreciable difficulty, Brookins Campbell was elected Speaker of the House of Representatives. Campbell, it will be recalled, had defeated Andrew Johnson for Representative in 1837.[12] In the Senate, it was quite another story. Senator Harvey Magee Watterson, representing the counties of Warren, DeKalb, Cannon, and Coffee, nominated for Speaker Senator John A. Gardner from the counties of Henry, Weakley, and Obion. Senator Gardner had been a member of the two preceding Legislatures and was one of the "Immortal Thirteen" who had refused to go into a joint session of the Legislature in 1841 and 1842 for the purpose of electing a United States Senator, thereby depriving Tennessee of representation in the United States Senate for two years. Senator John Trimble of Davidson County nominated for Speaker Senator Abram Poindexter Maury from the County of Williamson. On the first ballot, Senator Gardner received twelve Democratic votes, he himself refraining from casting a ballot. Senator Maury received eleven Whig votes, he himself voting for Whig Senator John D. Tyler from the counties of Robertson and Montgomery. Neither candidate having received a majority vote, the result was declared to be "no election". Twenty more ballots were taken "with precisely the same result as on the first call".[13] For three days the battle over the Senate Speakership continued with unabated

[9] *Nashville Union*, May 20, 1845.
[10] *Senate Journal*, 1845, 86.
[11] *Nashville Whig*, August 16, 1845.
[12] *Messages of the Governors of Tennessee*, Volume III, 158.
[13] *Senate Journal*, 1845, 4.

zeal, and without any election having been made. The principal factors underlying the snarl were set forth in the contemporary press. Here was the Whig version:[14]

"SPEAKER OF THE SENATE

The election of Speaker for the Senate has been attended with much difficulty, some manifestation of feeling and unprecedented delay. One hundred ballotings have taken place and, up to this writing, there is no election. We shall very briefly endeavor to explain the difficulty. Parties stand in the Senate, thirteen Democrats, twelve Whigs. Thirteen votes are necessary to make an election. Mr. Gardner, the Democratic nominee, has uniformly received the votes of his twelve Democratic colleagues; but one more vote is necessary to effect his election—all the members being present and voting. Unless, therefore, Mr. Gardner votes for himself or receives a Whig vote or some Whig Senator retires from the chamber, Mr. Gardner cannot be elected. The Whig Senators are unwilling to aid in his election, directly or indirectly, solely on political grounds. He is a gentleman of talents, second in that respect to no member of the Senate and no doubt is entertained of his qualifications for the station—no apprehension as to his want of courtesy and impartiality. Simply as *Speaker of the Senate*, the Whig Senators, as we understand, have as little objection to Mr. Gardner as to any other Democratic Senator. What they object to is to lend *their* aid in electing him. He was one of the *thirteen* Democratic Senators who, it will be recollected, in 1841 refused to unite with the House in the election of a Senator of the United States. That *political* act of his, the Whig Senators regard as interposing an insuperable obstacle to *their support* of him. They have professed a willingness to unite with their Democratic brethren in the election of Mr. Thomas of Maury, Mr. Fletcher of Franklin and Mr. Williamson of Fayette. But for any one of the 'Thirteen', they say it is impossible consistently with their notions of propriety for them to *vote*. And thus the matter stands."

The viewpoint of the Democrats was set forth as follows:[15]

"THE ELECTION OF SPEAKER IN THE SENATE.

The novel condition in which the Senate was placed during the two first days of the session has excited deep interest in this community:—As the facts become known the sensation will be diffused throughout the State. The announcement that the Senate has spent two entire days and balloted one hundred times without electing a Speaker, cannot fail to excite surprise and elicit a universal inquiry as to the facts connected with so unexpected a state of things.

It becomes our duty, therefore, to present the facts; and whilst we shall not indulge in any language calculated to irritate, we cannot doubt but that the simple statement of the facts will not only fully vindicate the course of the democratic Senators, but produce no little dissatisfaction amongst the people with the course of the whig Senators. The fact that the democrats are known to be in a majority in the Senate, will cause some surprise that they should not be able to organize the body by the election of a Speaker. The first impression likely to be made, would be that the responsibility of a

---

[14] *Nashville Whig,* October 9, 1845.
[15] *Nashville Union,* October 9, 1845.

failure to elect a Speaker must fall upon the democratic majority. To remove this impression, and fix the responsibility where it belongs, makes it necessary that we make a plain statement of the facts.

It is known that in the Senate there are thirteen democrats and twelve whigs—it is also known that the usage in choosing a Speaker heretofore, has been to require the votes of a majority of all voting for some one candidate. In voting the usage has been either that the candidates should not vote, or should interchange their votes. It will be seen at once, that if either of these usages had been followed in the present case, that there could have been no difficulty in making an election. The former usage was followed at the last session of the Senate, and at the present session of the House, and we believe it is considered the more general practice. Indeed some have doubted whether a candidate for Speaker in our State has the right to vote in his own election —upon the ground that he is interested in the result—his compensation being uniformly six dollars per day, whilst that of other members is but four. Without expressing any opinion on this point, it is enough to know that either from this consideration, or one of delicacy, it has been the custom for the candidates not to vote—at least not to vote so as to affect the result.

Another usage, perhaps better settled than the former, is that each political party should select one of its own members as a candidate, and nominate him for election. This usage was followed in the present case. The democrats selected Mr. Gardner as their candidate—the whigs selected Mr. Maury as theirs. These two gentlemen were nominated by their respective friends. When the roll was called and the name of Mr. Gardner reached, he followed the usage and declined to vote. When Mr. Maury's name was called, he cast his vote for some other whig Senator. At a subsequent stage of the ballotings, when Mr. Gardner's name was called, he voted more than once for Mr. Maury—still Mr. Maury declined to interchange the compliment, and voted for some other whig. These are the facts which will strike the public mind, as presenting a departure on the part of the whigs from both the usages which have heretofore governed.

The consequence of this course on the two sides was, that Mr. Gardner received twelve votes, and Mr. Maury either eleven or twelve accordingly as Mr. Gardner did not vote or voted for him, and Mr. Tyler usually received one, the vote of Mr. Maury. There was of course a failure to elect, inasmuch as, according to the usage referred to, Mr. Gardner did not receive a majority of all the votes given.

This statement will show how it happened that although the democrats had a majority, yet they failed to make a Speaker—the responsibility is thrown from them and fixed on the whig Senators, unless some justifiable reason can be found for departing from the usages which have heretofore prevailed. No such reason can be found in the character of the democratic nominee— he is a gentleman of superior talents—of unquestionable integrity—of the most honorable feelings—in every respect highly fitted for the station. His competitor for the Speakership admitted as much in a speech in the Senate.

But it is said that the whigs have a preference amongst the democrats, and they have a right to designate that preference—and of course that they have a right to coerce the majority to acquiesce in their preference! What is this but the assertion of the right of the minority to control the majority and designate for them a Speaker, or of stopping the public business? By selecting Mr. Gardner the democrats have all declared they do not desire any other person to preside over them—yet the minority claim the right of requiring one of those to preside, who have announced that they are no candidates and desire no votes, either whig or democratic! Some of the whigs have voted for Mr. Fletcher—yet he has said to them plainly by his course, if not in so many words, that he does not desire their votes—he is no candidate, and has designated Mr. Gardner as the presiding officer.

In whatever light the subject is viewed, it results in this:—By departing from all the usages in such cases, the minority have the power to say to the majority, '*You have the right to elect a Speaker, but we have the power to designate the individual—you must either yield to our power of selection, and elect the individual we designate, or you must take the responsibility, as the majority, of permitting the public business to be neglected.*' There is nothing in the fact that the minority are willing to designate one of the majority as Speaker—if they can proscribe four democratic Senators and declare them unworthy to preside, they can with equal propriety proscribe the entire majority and designate one of the minority as the Speaker. They may as well say to the majority, 'We have the power to control your action, and we claim the right of stopping the public business until you consent to accept one of the minority as Speaker'—as to say, that the majority must submit to be presided over by any one of their own party, to be designated by the minority. It is the violation of the great fundamental principle, *that the majortiy has the right to govern*, which is involved in the proceeding. This grand doctrine is involved in the controversy, and upon that the public judgment will be made up.

P. S. Since the foregoing was written the Senate have succeeded in making a Speaker. On the 133d ballot on yesterday afternoon, Mr. Gardner rose and made a most beautiful, impressive and eloquent speech, at the conclusion of which he declined a further canvass for the Speakership. This was one of the happiest speeches ever delivered in the Senate, and was received with unbounded applause. Mr. Gardner nominated Mr. Watterson for Speaker, and on the 138th ballot he was elected—having thirteen votes, (Mr. Bradbury, whig, voting for him,) Mr. Maury six and Mr. Thomas five. Mr. Watterson made his acknowledgements in an appropriate address."

Aaron V. Brown having been officially declared elected Governor, legislative arrangements were made for the inauguration on October 15, 1845. The inaugural exercises were held in the Methodist Church, the oath of office being administered by Judge Thomas Maney.[16] Thereupon Governor Brown delivered his Inaugural Address.[17]

"Inaugural Address
Of Hon. A. V. Brown, delivered on the 15th of October, 1845, on his Instalment as Governor of Tennessee.

GENTLEMEN OF THE SENATE
AND HOUSE OF REPRESENTATIVES:

In presenting myself before you on the present occasion, I feel very deeply impressed by the solemnities which we have just wit-

---

[16] *Senate Journal*, 1845, 102.
[17] *Speeches of Aaron V. Brown*, 365–374.
Author's note. Since the Address was directed to the General Assembly, it has been deemed proper to incorporate same in this treatise.

nessed. The transitions of power from one dynasty to another in the old world have rarely been effected without revolution and bloodshed. There, the triumph of the one party is too often the destruction of the other, leaving the great masses of the people but little benefited by the change of dominion. In our own free and happy form of government it is wholly different. Here, the great popular principle is recognized in its full force, 'that all power is inherent in the people, and all free governments are founded on their authority and instituted for their peace, safety, and happiness.' It is a remarkable fact, that this was the first great truth uttered by the illustrious men who framed the Constitution of Tennessee. It seemed to have been uppermost in their minds, and to have burst forth in advance of all their noble and patriotic sentiments.

It is under the influence of this cardinal principle that we have just witnessed the surrender of all the executive power and authority of the State by my distinguished predecessor; a surrender so peaceably and promptly made that it must constitute one of the highest eulogiums on our representative form of government. But in presenting myself before you and this large assembly, for the purpose of assuming the high office from which he has just retired, I must be permitted to express my deep and abiding gratitude to those by whom it has been bestowed. To a station so exalted and responsible I should never have aspired, but for the unanimous call of my fellow-citizens in convention assembled. Most earnestly did I desire the nomination of some other individual more able to vindicate and sustain the great principles involved in the recent election. Not that I then was or ever could be insensible to the high honor of presiding over such a noble and gallant State as Tennessee. She is the land of my youth, the home of my manhood. I have traversed her in all her borders; and I feel to-day a proud consciousness that I love her, not more for her physical grandeur, her lofty mountains, her deep majestic rivers, her wide luxuriant valleys, than for the moral excellence of her brave, and hardy, and industrious people. To preside over such a State, and to contribute any thing valuable to the prosperity of such a people, ought to kindle up the fires of a virtuous ambition in the bosom of any man living. But, gentlemen, whilst I freely admit the full influence of an emotion like this, I trust you will allow me to declare the most unfeigned distrust of my abilities to discharge the duties of the high office which I am about to assume. Fidelity and zeal in the discharge of those duties, and the most anxious and earnest desire to advance the welfare and happiness of every individual member of our beloved Commonwealth, without reference to the party to which he may belong, must be the only pledge which I can offer my countrymen for this distinguished mark of their preference and confidence.

The duties to which I allude are embraced in the comprehensive but solemn oath which you will presently cause to be administered, faithfully 'to support the Constitution of this State and of the United States.' In general terms, to support these, is to support all the high principles of rational liberty and representative government—the liberty of speech—the freedom of the press—the rights of conscience, of property and reputation—the purity of our elections, and the implicit obedience of the representative to the will of his constituents. It is not, however, in relation to these great cardinal principles of government that the practical difficulty of the American statesman may be expected to arise. The oath which you are about to administer to support not only the Constitution of the State of Tennessee, but of the United States, imposes a double allegiance, challenging my most unreserved obedience to both governments. It is the danger of collision between them that constitutes the precise point of difficulty and embarrassment. In anticipation of the bare possibility of such an event, it becomes my duty to declare the principles on which I should feel bound to act—to declare them here in your presence—to declare them now, at the very beginning of my administration, and at the very moment when I contract the obligation of this double allegiance.

Rightly understood and fairly construed, I hold collisions between Federal and State Governments to be utterly impossible. The wise men who framed the former, seem to have studiously and incessantly guarded against such an event. They knew well that in the political as well as in the physical world, where equal powers meet, a fearful and dreadful pause must ensue. They therefore weighed and considered with profound anxiety every line and word inserted into our Federal Constitution. In the States to which this instrument was submitted for adoption, the most distinguished statesmen and jurists employed all their talents and learning in an animated and fearless discussion of its provisions. The result of all this care and patriotic labor, was to throw additional safeguards around the sovereignty of the States, by declaring that 'the powers not delegated to the United States by the Constitution, nor prohibited by it to the States, are reserved to the States respectively, or to the people'.

This amendment should have rendered every thing easy and harmonious in the operations of our political system. It should have established it as a maxim in the creed of every American statesman, never to claim for the Federal Government any power which was not *expressly* granted in the Constitution, or which did not necessarily or properly belong to the execution of an express power. It was for the establishment of this great rule of construction, that Jefferson and Madison, and the Virginia Resolutions of 1798, so earnestly contended.

But unfortunately for the country, another school of politicians rose up co-eval with the Constitution, insisting on an additional class of *implied* powers, with no limitation but the wild discretion of Congress, and guided by no object but the vague and indefinite notion of 'the general welfare.'

It has been this difference of opinion as to the mode of construing the Federal Constitution, that has laid the foundation of all the party struggles of this country. The establishment of a United States Bank, the enactment of a Protective Tariff, without regard to revenue, the distribution of the proceeds of the sales of the public lands, the assumption of the debts of the States, the suppression of the liberty of speech, under the pretext of preserving the freedom and purity of our elections, have all depended on a latitudinous construction of the Federal Constitution. The present occasion will by no means allow of an extensive reference to any of these subjects; but the questions of a Bank and the Tariff enter so deeply into the political discussions of the day, that I may be pardoned for submitting a few observations on them.

In relation to the Bank, the great fact that no power for its creation is to be found in express terms in the Constitution, has often been adverted to. But another fact, scarcely less important, has been strangely neglected. That fact is, that the journals of the convention show clearly that such a power was often asked for and as often refused, in every form in which it could be presented. There is a potency in this recorded fact, second only to the silence of the Constitution, which ought to have long since overthrown all the feeble *implications* so much relied on by the advocates of such an institution. Beside this, a power so vast and mighty as this is, should never have been left to mere implication at all. It should have stood out in advance of all others, and have been rendered undoubted by its boldness and conspicuity.

It was but a poor evasion of the constitutional objection to have located the bank in the District of Columbia. If Congress has the power of exclusive jurisdiction over that District, it must be *for it* as well as *in it*—local in its objects, and territorial in its action.

To seize on a power granted for such limited and special purposes, and expand it over a mighty continent, is a shameless perversion, a fraudulent usurpation—far more wicked than the boldest interpolation of that instrument could be. The pretence so often relied on, that a bank *was necessary and proper*, (and therefore constitutional,) as the fiscal agent of the government, is fully exposed by the fact that the bank never was charged with the collection or disbursement of the revenue at all. The most that could ever have been said of its fiscal agency would have been that it was charged with the simple *custody* of the funds during the brief period between their collection and disbursement. I repeat, therefore, what I have before said in another place, that this alleged fiscal necessity is a false pretence, for the experiment has now been made and the fact tested, that the government has, and can collect, keep and disburse its own revenues, without the aid of any bank whatever—an experiment which Washington adopted by signing the act of 1792, which Mr. Jefferson subsequently recommended and declared to be entirely practicable.

But I forbear any further observations on the subject of a bank. I have referred to it only for the purpose of illustrating my opinions more fully as to the mode of construing one of the constitutions which I am presently to swear that I will faithfully support. I say nothing of the expediency—nothing of its dangerous and corrupting tendencies—nothing of that full and ample refutation, which time and experience have given to the argument, that exchanges could not be regulated, nor a sound, uniform currency be given to the country, without such an institution. All these topics belong not to the occasion, nor is their discussion necessary in order to make known my opinions to my fellow-citizens of the State.

In relation to the Tariff, I have always maintained that its rates were too high, its discriminations unjust, and that it ought to be modified and greatly reduced. The agricultural States have suffered much already, and nothing but the warmly cherished hope that it will soon be repealed or greatly modified has subdued the murmurs of the consuming classes. I am fully aware of the arguments usually employed to prove that the people, so far from being injured, are really benefited by the high duties of the Tariff; but I know not which most to condemn—the impudence which could fabricate, or the credulity which could be imposed upon by them. Strong as this language may seem, I nevertheless entertain no hostility to the manufactures of the United States. I cherish for the valuable and important ones the very highest regard, and would cheerfully give to all any advantage incidental to the collection of our national revenue. I look forward with confidence to the next Congress of the United States to make such modifications and alterations in the present Tariff, as will make the system impartial and honest. That dissatisfaction which is now felt with its provisions in many quarters will then be suppressed, and those deep feelings of attachment which are cherished by nearly our whole population, in favor of the perpetuation of our blessed Union, will then acquire renewed energy and strength.

Passing now, gentlemen, from those subjects on which the Federal and State governments have heretofore conflicted—and which lay too directly in my way to be omitted—I desire to submit a few observations in relation to our State government in particular. The condition of our affairs at home, challenges our most anxious attention. Our legislatures have yet much work to do to enable the people to enjoy all the blessings which a wise use of our free institutions can certainly secure. The preservation of our public credit stands out amongst the foremost of all our duties. Every liability, whether prudently or imprudently contracted, should be met with most scrupulous punctuality. In individual life many apologies may be urged for the want of this virtue which can find no parallel in the public engagements of a great and prosperous State like ours.

To meet these liabilities with ease and without probable inconvenience to the people, I shall, in some future communication to you, invite your attention to the establishment of a sinking fund adequate to the liquidation of our outstanding liabilities at the respective periods when they may fall due. The bank of the State has heretofore been much relied on, by the profitable operations of its concerns to meet these liabilities. However this may be, it cannot be amiss, in my opinion, to bring to its aid all the other means, short of additional taxation, which the State may have at its disposal. Amongst these, none can be more commendable than the most rigid economy in the administration of the government of the State.

Economy in your own expenditures—in the length or duration of your session—in the execution of the necessary public printing—and, in fact, in all the subjects of expenditures which are immediately connected with your legislative deliberations. Economy also in the executive and judicial departments, carried to the utmost extent compatible with the administration of justice and a faithful execution of the laws of the land. It will be a part of my duty under the Constitution, 'to take care that the laws be faithfully executed', and I can assure you that no portion of my duty will be more agreeable than that which shall be performed in sustaining the public credit unimpaired at home and abroad, and in carrying out any system of enlightened and just economy which your wisdom may advise.

For many years the true friends of our liberal institutions have earnestly desired the establishment in our State of a wise and efficient system of public instruction. As friends to religion and pure morals, they cannot repress the hope that the day is not far distant when every individual within our borders shall be capable of reading and understanding the Holy Scriptures, of transacting his own business, and, if necessary, of instructing his own offspring in the rudiments of learning. I rejoice that a salutary feeling like this now seems to pervade our whole population, reaching every hamlet within the limits of our fertile and extensive territory. The patient and meritorious schoolmaster must now go abroad through the land on his errand of labor and love, dissipating the darkness in which so many minds are enveloped. It is on the education of the great mass of the people that our hopes of preserving and perpetuating our liberties must be founded. The knowledge to understand is as essential as the spirit to defend our republican institutions. With a continual and rapid increase of our numbers, what else can be expected but anarchy and misrule, unless we provide that science and literature shall maintain their ascendency over all the sons and daughters of freedom, who are through future time to control the destinies of the republic! In the enlargement and improvement of our present partial system of education, I here offer freely, and with all my heart, my humble and unceasing co-operation.

The present seems to be a suitable occasion to offer you my congratulations on the recent annexation of the republic of Texas to the United States. It has been accomplished by no invasion on the rights of Mexico, and in a manner which can give no just cause of offence to any other nation. It has been effected not by the sword, but a simple covenant or contract between coterminous nations, speaking the same language, accustomed to the same political institutions, and whose common object was more effectually to secure to themselves all the blessings of civil and religious liberty. It ought to be regarded by the friends of freedom every-where but as another triumph of rational liberty and representative government over the degrading despotisms of the old world.

All the forebodings of evil to our country, as likely to occur from the consummation of the deed, have been signally disappointed. As yet we can discover no sign of the displeasure of Heaven in consequence of it. The earth is still putting forth its verdure, and blessing the husbandman with the rich abundance of its fruits, whilst peace, and health, and general prosperity are everywhere smiling upon a great and prosperous people. Our bright and glorious Union, too, whose shattered and broken fragments were everywhere to have met the eye of the heart-stricken patriot, still bespans the continent, stretching, like the rainbow of hope and of promise, from the great inland seas of the North to the Gulf of Mexico in the South. The incredible prophesy, that a convention was to be held in this beautiful city, in order to accomplish the work of national destruction, has failed of its fulfillment, and the illustrious citizen who was to have presided over the guilty assembly has gone down to the grave with his last prayer trembling on his lips for the Union and his country.

With the acquisition of Texas and the successful maintenance of our title to Oregon, the United States will present a spectacle of territorial grandeur and magnificence unequaled in the world. In those who have charge of our negotiations in relation to the latter country, I have unbounded confidence; and I believe they would not retain more of it, if they could, than we are fairly entitled to. I am equally certain they will never surrender one square acre of it to the unjust demand of any nation on the earth. Far distant as it may now seem to be, every revolving year will increase its importance to the hundred millions of freemen, who, at no distant day, will inhabit our continent. In the order of Providence, America may become the last asylum of liberty to the human family. Here then let us rear her loftiest temple. Let us lay its foundations deep and wide for the millions who in after ages may worship at her altars.

I turn now from the contemplation of our wonderful and increasing magnificence, in order to remind you of a great and sad calamity which has befallen our common country since you were last assembled on an occasion like this. But a few months have passed away since you in particular, and the people of the United States generally, were called upon to mourn the departure from our midst of our most illustrious citizen.—The immortal spirit of Andrew Jackson, the patriot, the soldier and the statesman, has passed from time to eternity—devoted, until he breathed his last breath, to the best interests of his country, which he had defended with heroic fortitude and courage, and served with a zeal more fervid with increasing years, he finished the great work which a wise Providence had chosen him to perform, and accomplished his destiny. Clinging to the faith and the hope which sustain the Christian whilst he is 'passing through the dark valley of the shadow of death,' he died at peace with the world, leaving behind him a bright and enduring example, worthy the imitation of future generations. Hereafter, the song of the poet will be heard in praise of his memory—the pen of the historian will chronicle the deeds which he achieved, whilst the painter and the engraver will transmit his image to admiring millions.

Let Tennessee, his own adopted State—Tennessee, whose armies he had so often covered with glory—Tennessee, whom he honored, and loved, and served so long and so faithfully—Tennessee, beneath whose green and hallowed sod his mortal remains have been deposited—let Tennessee rear him a monument lasting as time—let it be planted in or near one of her most beautiful cities, on the bank of the noblest river in the world, where the millions who will pass for ages and ages to come, may pause and gaze upon it with wonder and admiration."

With the inaugural ceremonies of the Governor out of the way, the Legislature turned its attention to further organizational steps by the appointment of sixteen standing committees on the part of the Senate,[18] with a comparable number in the House of Representatives. There now loomed a question of paramount importance for attention—the election of a United States Senator. The term of that office had expired, retiring Ephraim H. Foster who had opposed Governor Brown in the recent gubernatorial contest. But, Foster having failed to triumph over Brown in the gubernatorial contest, the Whigs began maneuvers whereby the thin Democratic majority in the Legislature might be defeated in its effort to elect a favorite to the coveted office. On October 16, the Senate was advised that the House of Representatives had concurred in the Senate resolution fixing October 21 as the day for said election. Being in the minority, a part of the Whig strategy consisted in not nominating any candidate of its own political faith for the office, but to "lie low" and await developments in the Democratic camp. On the appointed day, the Legislature met in joint session and the Democrats nominated three prominent Democrats, A. O. P. Nicholson, Hopkins L. Turney, and W. C. Dunlap. The two latter men were placed in nomination by small minorities of Democrats who were opposed to the caucus nominee, Nicholson. And so, the battle was on!

The first ballot was a precursor of things to come. The caucus nominee, Mr. Nicholson, received ten votes in the Senate and thirty in the House. Mr. Turney, a so-called "independent", received two Senate votes, one being that of his brother, and nine in the House. Judge Dunlap received only one vote in the Senate and a mere half dozen in the House. On the first ballot, the Whigs concentrated upon John Bell, the Tennessee Whig bellwether, who received eleven votes in the Senate and twenty-five in the house.[19] All along, the Whigs knew that neither Bell nor any other Whig could be elected, but a heavy block of votes for Bell would prevent the divided Democrats from piling up a majority vote for the caucus nominee, Nicholson. *This was the essence of the Whig strategy.*

Both the Democrats and the Whigs buckled on their partisan armor

---

[18] *Senate Journal*, 1845, 87–88.
[19] *Ibid.*, 117.

and all knew that a knock-down-and-drag-out battle was a certainty. How long the contest would last, no one knew. The Senate, in its battle for election of a Speaker, had demonstrated that it was a long-winded aggregation. One hundred and thirty-eight ballots were cast before a Speaker was elected,[20] indicating that the members of the Senate were well-stocked with "wind" and would rival a greyhound or a blacksmith's bellows in that category. On October 21, nine ballots were cast for the election of a United States Senator without any decisive results. On the following day, after unsuccessful efforts for a postponement of the election had failed, the balloting resulted in "no election."

On the eve of the balloting for election of United States Senator, the Democratic organ, *Nashville Union*, had made its analysis of the probable Whig strategy in the following editorial:[21]

"THE SENATORIAL QUESTION AGAIN.

The press in different sections of the State are discussing this subject with commendable zeal, and in most instances in the proper spirit. So long as the friends of the various aspirants content themselves with advocating the claims of their respective favorites without attempting to disparage the claims of others, or to confine the selection within prescribed limits, there will be no danger. But should they go beyond this (as we conceive legitimate mode of canvassing the claims of individuals or sections) the consequences may prove disastrous to the democracy; and we deem it proper to caution our friends throughout the State to proceed in this matter with prudence, and to be on their guard against whig tricks. 'Divide and conquer' is now the avowed motto of the whigs, and should the lessons of the past be disregarded by the democrats in the elections that are to be held by the approaching Legislature, we have no expectation that any thing that can now be said will be of any avail.

It will not be forgotten that the Nashville Whig, a few days since, announced the determination (indirectly, to be sure) of casting the whig vote upon some democrat—manifestly for the purpose of defeating the choice of the democratic party. As they are in the minority their only hope of this result is by uniting the whig vote upon some man who can control a few democratic votes, and thereby defeat the Democratic nominee. For this purpose they will endeavor to persuade some section of the State or some particular individual to demand as a right this distinguished honor. We do not believe there is a democrat elected to the legislature who can be influenced by such considerations. They will look first to the certain success of the nominee, whoever he may be, and then with laudable zeal endeavor to secure the nomination for his favorite candidate. This is the spirit we hope to see manifested by all the members when they come up to this important work.

We have men of distinguished talent all over the State who would do honor to the State and station, and who if elected would possess the entire confidence of the Democracy. Let all such submit their claims to the party with a full determination to abide by their choice, and they will receive the merited approbation of the State and nation.

---

[20] *Ibid.*, 33.
[21] *Nashville Union*, September 13, 1845.

We have been led into the foregoing remarks by the language of a correspondent of the Whig, who signs himself 'Shelby.' He says: 'Give us a Senator from the District—if he be a whig. We are entitled to the Senator—and we believe the State, the Democratic party, will accord it to us. Our claims are founded in justice, and we set them up in confidence. Concert secures them to us—without it we fail. The Senator we must and will have—a Democrat if *you* will, but a whig if *we must*.'

Against the assumption of this correspondent, whether he be Whig or Democrat, we enter our protest. This is certainly extraordinary language for a Whig who is in the minority to use, and we have no fears that there is a Democrat holding power in the District who would prefer a Western District Whig to a Middle or an East Tennessee Democrat. They are made of better metal than to prefer the defeat of the party to a rejection of their sectional claims to the Senatorship. We shrewdly suspect the real sentiment of 'Shelby' would have been more truthfully expressed in language like the following: 'A Whig if we *can*—a Democrat if we *must*.' "

After a few preliminary ballots had been cast for United States Senator, excitement increased and rumors of "bargain and intrigue" were bandied about regarding a "trade" between the Whigs and Hopkins L. Turney, one of the Democratic nominee candidates. Representative Powhattan Gordon, Democratic Representative from Maury County (the home county of Judge Nicholson, the Democratic caucus nominee for U. S. Senator) tossed a bomb into the legislative proceedings. A Whig appraisal of the Senatorial situation and of Mr. Gordon's Resolution was as follows:[22]

"NO SENATOR YET—EXTRAORDINARY PROCEEDING.

Up to this present writing there has been no election of Senator, and judging from present appearances, it is difficult to say when there will be one. Meanwhile, the 'agony' is every moment being 'piled up' higher and higher.—The facts of the case are briefly these:

The Democratic party has a majority of one in the Senate and two in the House of Representatives. They would have had a majority of three in the latter, but for the death of the member from Henry. On joint ballot the strict party vote would be—Democrats 51—Whigs 48. Mr. Nicholson, the Editor of the Nashville Union, received the caucus nomination of his party, under the two-thirds rule. There were members of that party, however, who from the beginning refused to go into caucus or to be bound by its decision, on the ground, that as there was to be no Whig candidate, and as it was only a choice between Democrats, a caucus was unnecessary. Accordingly, when the two Houses met in Convention to proceed to an election, three Democratic candidates were presented by the Democratic side of the Convention. We want this *fact* borne in mind. Three *Democrats* were brought forward by three *Democratic* members, and presented to the *Convention* (including, we suppose, the Whig as well as the Democratic members thereof) as suitable persons to fill the office of United States Senator. The candidates were, Mr. A. O. P. Nicholson, Mr. Hopkins L. Turney and Judge Wm. C. Dunlap. The Whigs brought forward no candidate of their

---

[22] *Nashville Whig*, October 25, 1845.

own, and from the beginning have voted scatteringly. In the course of the ballotings, however, in the exercise of their right of choice, they appeared to be gradually concentrating on Mr. Turney, who started with six Democratic votes which have been steadily cast for him. He also received on the first ballot five Whig votes—in all 11. Mr. Nicholson received 40 Democratic votes on the first ballot, which number he has not been able to increase except on one occasion, when he received 41 votes. Mr. Turney on one occasion received 42 votes. It requires 50 votes to make an election.

The friends of Mr. Nicholson, after thirteen ballotings, saw very clearly that if the Whigs united upon Mr. Turney, his election was certain, and they exhibited very manifestly their fears of such a consummation. To prevent this consummation, therefore, has been their object for several days past. The whole of the afternoon of Wednesday was consumed in the effort made by them to procure a postponement of the election. They candidly admitted that there was discord in their ranks and that their object was *time;* and they procured it for the nonce by *speaking against it.* Thus passed the afternoon of Wednesday—Mr. Turney's supporters eager for a ballot— Mr. Nicholson's successfully interposing obstacles to a ballot. In the course of the debate which sprung up on a motion to postpone the election, Mr. Watterson, the Speaker of the Senate, openly denounced Mr. Turney, and charged him, upon the authority of rumor, with having made concessions to the Whigs for the purpose of securing their support.

On Thursday the same state of things continued the whole day—no balloting was had.—In the forepart of that day, Mr. Gordon, a Democratic member, introduced the following resolutions which we consider as without a parallel in the annals of legislation:

MR. GORDON'S RESOLUTIONS.

Whereas, A portion of the members of this House have addressed a letter to the Hon. Hopkins L. Turney and others aspiring to the office of Senator to the Congress of the United States to answer interrogatories propounded therein, touching their votes and course in the Senate in the event of the election, to which an answer was returned by the Hon. A. O. P. Nicholson, but no answer has been received from Mr. Turney; and whereas rumors exist tending to show that Mr. Turney has made concessions to the Whig party with a view to his election to that station; and whereas it is due to Mr. Turney, this House and the country, that a full investigation should be made touching this matter. Therefore,

Resolved, By the General Assembly of the State of Tennessee, that a joint committee be raised forthwith—to wit: five of the House and such number as the Senate may designate, who shall be vested with full powers to take proof, and report on the following points:

1st. Have there been any overtures made by any portion of the whig party of the General Assembly, to induce Mr. Hopkins L. Turney to change any of his avowed principles, or vote for any of the whig measures, or favor the whig party, in the event of his election to the Senate of the United States, and if so, to what extent?

2nd. Has Mr. Hopkins L. Turney made any overtures, either verbally or in writing, either by himself or others for him, by which any concessions were made to the whig party by which he agreed, in the event of his election, to vote against or abandon any of his principles, by which he was to vote for or sustain any of the whig measures; particularly his course to be taken upon the subject of the Tariff of 1842, and the distribution of the public lands? The joint committee shall have full powers to send for persons and papers in aid of the investigation committee to this charge, and make report thereon as soon as possible.

2nd. *Resolved*, That, with the view of giving the joint committee time to make the investigation and report, the joint resolution of this General Assembly bringing the two Houses together for the purpose of electing a Senator to the Congress of the United States be, and the same is hereby rescinded.

3rd. *Resolved*, That the Senate meet the House of Representatives in their Hall on Friday the 31st instant, for the purpose of electing a Senator to the Congress of the United States, in the place of the Hon. E. H. Foster, whose office expired on the 4th of March last.

These resolutions, as unconstitutional as they are inquisitorial, would strike not only at the rights and privileges of the members of the Legislature, but at the very foundation of society itself. Where did the Legislature of Tennessee acquire the right to institute an inquisitorial investigation into the opinions which a candidate before them may have expressed to members on subjects of national policy? But we have neither space nor time to-day for extended comment on these singular resolutions. We shall not, however, lose sight of them, nor of the proceedings which may be had upon them. They will do very well as a hook to hang speeches upon and kill time. It is impossible that they can be adopted, and if adopted, it would be impossible to carry them into effect.

As to the charge of 'bargain and intrigue' between the Whigs and Mr. Turney, they all laugh heartily at it. The Whig members certainly have a right of choice between the three Democratic candidates brought forward by the Democratic members themselves, and for the reasons of any preference which they may feel for one Democratic candidate over another Democratic candidate, they are not responsible to their Democratic brethren of the Legislature who may chance to differ with them in opinion.

Thus stands the state of things at present with regard to the Senatorial election. The Whig members, and the Democratic members supporting Mr. Turney, are anxious to proceed with the election. Mr. Nicholson's friends desire a postponement. The minority (Mr. Nicholson's friends) not having strength enough to carry their point by direct action—by a simple call of the yeas and nays—seek to effect their object by indirect means—by making motions and speeches of one kind or another. It is as clear a case of the *minority* obstructing the prosecution of the public business, when the *majority* are ready and anxious to proceed with it, as was ever presented. On that minority be the responsibility of producing so unnecessary a consumption of the public time and the public money.

Yesterday brought with it but a repetition of the scenes of the day before and of Wednesday evening. First there was a motion made by one of Mr. Nicholson's supporters to take up Mr. Gordon's inquisitorial resolutions (the discussion of which if once begun may last for days, and weeks,) which, happily failing, a motion was made by a Whig member to take a recess a few minutes for the purpose of preparing the House for the reception of the Senate, in order to proceed with the election. But the motion to take a recess for the purpose of receiving the Senate and proceeding with the order of the day—the election of Senator—having been decided by the Chair to be a debatable question, it was of course debated until near dinner time, when motions for adjournment, being always in order, took precedence. Twice did the majority refuse on a call of the Yeas and Nays to adjourn. But what did the minority care for that? They talked and made motions until the House was compelled to adjourn for dinner. This obstruction of the public business—this trifling with the public time—this wanton waste of the public money may be fun to the parties concerned in it, but we apprehend the *people* will take a different view of the subject. What we desire the people—without reference to party—to understand is this:

That since dinner time on Wednesday last a clear, undisputed majority of both branches of the Legislature have been not only desirous, but exceedingly anxious, to proceed with the public business and make an election.

That, in our opinion, an election could and would have been made, in one hour, on Wednesday evening, Thursday or yesterday, had the ballotings been resumed.

That the minority apprehending this result, and fearing to trust the election to the majority, have up to this moment talked and trifled the public time away for the avowed purpose of putting off the election.

That this trifling away of the public time costs a good deal of the public money. As for instance—estimating the expenses of the Legislature at $500 per day.

Wednesday (half the day) $250
Thursday 500
Friday 500
                                                    ————
                                                  $1,250"

A Whig firebrand, Dr. J. W. Richardson of Rutherford County, frankly laid before the House of Representatives the specific reasons [23] for his voting for the "independent" Democratic candidate, Hopkins L. Turney:

"REMARKS OF MR. RICHARDSON

On the motion to suspend the rule requiring all resolutions to lie one day on the table in order to take up and consider the resolutions of Mr. Gordon.

Mr. Richardson said he hoped the rule would not be suspended, because no good could possibly arise from the suspension. It was not the custom of the House to suspend the rule in order for the *immediate* consideration of any resolution, unless the adoption of the resolution was necessary to expedite the public business, or to accomplish some object of paramount importance.

But, he said, there was another, and *better* reason why the rule should not be suspended. We have met here to transact the public business and among other things, to elect a Senator to the Congress of the United States. These resolutions charge bargain and sale between one of the gentlemen, who is a candidate for this distinguished honor, and the whig party. The resolutions ought not to be received by this House, nor ought they to be considered for a moment. Have gentlemen the right to establish a worse than Spanish inquisition here, and demand of honorable members upon this floor the *reason* why they vote for this, or the other man? The Gentleman says it is very strange, why the whigs should vote for Mr. Turney! Sir, there is nothing strange about it. It is the usual course in all parties, and nothing

---

[20] *Ibid.,* October 25, 1845.

more than the democratic party ought to expect. Why sir, what are the facts about this whole matter? A majority of this legislature are democrats—the whigs are the minority, and cannot elect a man of their own party. He had voted for whigs—distinguished whigs—until he was convinced there was no possible chance of electing one, and he was driven then to the necessity of chosing between democrats. It was apparent to every member on this floor that an election would have to be made between *two* distinguished gentlemen of the democratic party, and he, in company with many other whigs had made a choice in favor of Mr. Turney. But, he said, the Gentleman from Maury, contended that there was, and of necessity must be something *wrong* about this matter. Why sir, it is the plainest thing in nature—the very course which every thinking man would have taken and the only course we ought to take. He said, he came here to vote for a whig Senator and had voted again and again for Messrs. Bell and Foster, but no man dreamed that either of them could be elected, and finally he had voted for Mr. Turney, and for this act his motives are impugned, and inquisitorial resolutions are introduced here to ascertain, if possible, whether Mr. Turney has sold himself to the whigs, and whether we have accepted the purchase. He said as many gentlemen had 'given in their experiences' upon this subject he would also give his.—When he came to this city, he ascertained, as he believed, that Mr. Nicholson was the candidate of the President—the man selected by him to represent this State in the Senatorial branch of the United States' Congress. The Legislature met, and he also understood that by the action of the democratic caucus that Mr. Nicholson was the nominee of the caucus, and the candidate of the party. Mr. Turney was an *independent* candidate—running upon his own hook—discarded by the party and relying alone upon his own energies for his election.

He saw him denounced by his own party because he had the courage to suffer his friends to use his name. He looked on him to be as good a man as Mr. Nicholson—carrying with him the endorsement of his party, and he had determined to vote for him in preference to Mr. Nicholson. He did not want to vote for *him*, nor any other democrat, and only chose him as the least of two evils. He did not think that he ever could vote for a democrat, and had hoped never to be driven to that necessity; but the time had come when it was necessary to do so, or to prevent an election entirely. He had finally however, got up to the sticking point, and here, he said, he called on the Clerk as a witness, (asking the speaker if *he could be a witness,*) to testify to the truth of what he was about to say. While the Clerk was calling the vote, he had determined to vote for Mr. Turney, and as he wished to do this thing after democratic style, when the Clerk called his (Mr. Richardson's name) *he shut his eyes*, and went it blind. In order to explain this whole matter he asked the Speaker of the House, suppose sir, that you lived in a whig county and that the whig party were to meet in caucus and nominate a candidate for the Legislature, and suppose, after this, another whig candidate should oppose the candidate of the party, for which one of them would *you*, as a democrat, vote? He said that he would not answer this question for the chair, but he would take the liberty to say that the chair and every other democrat, almost, in the county would vote for the independent candidate. And they would vote for him, not because they liked him better, nor because they had any more confidence in him than they had in the *nominee*, but simply because they wished to defeat the object of the opposing party, and produce confusion amongst them. The democratic party practiced upon this principle, and did endeavor two years ago by this very means to defeat us, but sir, by much labor and severe drilling, we outmanaged them.

Now sir, apply this rule to the present case, and the course of myself and those whig friends who vote with me is explained at once. We can't elect a man of our own choice because we are in the minority—we find Mr. Turney denounced by the democratic party and charged with changing his opinions because he has dared to oppose the candidate of the party, and because some whigs vote for him. We are opposed to Mr. Nicholson and are determined to beat him, if we can, and have no other means of defeating him except with Mr. Turney.

Six of Mr. Turney's Democratic friends have taken him up, and have stood by him all the time.—He saw this—and he sympathized with them.— Truly they are a 'Spartan band,' and merit all praise for their devotion to their friend and a determination to represent the wishes of their constituents. Whether they are acting correctly or incorrectly was for them, and not for him, to determine. He had chosen Mr. Turney because he was the anti-President, anti-caucus, and independent candidate, and with him he wished and desired to defeat the candidate of the Democratic party.

This, sir, is the fairest and most natural conclusion in the world. The conclusion to which the chair, and he, and every other man would come.— It was an honorable mode of warfare, practised by both parties, and approved by all the people. He then appealed to gentlemen to say whether this was not true, and whether it was not the universal practice of both parties to pursue this course. He could not defeat Mr. Nicholson with a whig; but if the whig party would act harmoniously with that Spartan band who had stood by Mr. Turney from the first they could defeat him, and elect a Democratic Senator, objectionable as he was, yet less so than the President's candidate.

He always felt disposed to join with the weak side in a controversy, from motives of humanity, if nothing more, and he had thought as this was a family quarrel between the 'harmonious Democracy,' he could join the weak and independent party, without being subject to dishonest imputations—and without placing the man for whom he voted in a condition to be denounced by his own friends. But it has been charged that there had been a correspondence between Mr. Turney and certain whigs upon this subject, and the gentleman wished to have this correspondence produced. He asked gentlemen if he did not have the right to ask of any candidate who sought office at his hands what his opinions were upon any question? Let us *suppose*, for example, that he did write to Mr. Turney to know what his opinions were upon certain subjects, and suppose Mr. Turney had answered him, was this a subject upon which he ought to be interrogated? He asked honorable gentlemen upon the floor, if they thought this was an honorable and dignified course of proceeding? Two gentlemen present themselves as candidates for Senator, a gentleman in order to satisfy himself of the views of either gentlemen had addressed one of them a note asking his views upon certain subjects—suppose he answers and the answer is satisfactory to the enquirer, or not satisfactory, do gentlemen imagine that they have the right to interrogate the writer upon this subject who had written a private note for his own satisfaction? Why sir, what do you think of such proceedings? What will the country think of it? Indeed, sir, things have come to a pretty pass if a member of this house could not write a letter to any gentleman who may be a candidate for office, without exciting unjust and dishonorable suspicions in the minds of gentlemen.

Suppose the gentleman from Maury should address a note to Mr. Nicholson, and Mr. Nicholson should answer his note, and declare political sentiments satisfactory to the writer, but not in accordance with his opinions as understood by the body of his party, would the gentleman from Maury not practice a fraud upon his party if he concealed these opinions? Certainly he would. But would he practice any fraud upon Mr. Nicholson's *opposers?* —No, sir, no. Then, suppose as strong a case as you please—suppose Mr. Turney (said he,) had written a letter renouncing his opinions to him, would he practise any fraud upon the gentleman who opposed Mr. Turney, by not showing them the renunciation? None at all. *They* are not voting for him— they denounce him, and consequently they cannot be imposed on. But if any gentleman has any communication from Mr. Turney which, if kept private, would practise a fraud upon those who are voting *for* him, then that gentleman ought to expose the communication. He did not understand Mr. Turney as deceiving his friends, but he did suppose that he (Mr. Turney) had deceived his party, and for this he is now denounced by his party. He said he had a right to choose between the gentlemen who were candidates; he had made that choice, because he believed Mr. Turney, the anti-caucus candidate, was more acceptable to his constituents than Mr. Nicholson. At any rate *he* preferred him.

He knew that his *whig* constituents had much confidence in his judg- ment and were willing to leave this matter in his hands; and as for his Demo- cratic constituents he knew that they would not and could not complain, because he had voted for the very man whose political character was in- dorsed by their leaders in 1841, and who was admitted by them to be worthy of all confidence. He hoped the rule would not be suspended in order to consider the resolutions of the gentleman from Maury. They were inquisi- torial in their character, calculated to produce much injury, and bad feeling, and could not by any means get the facts, or establish the charges which gentlemen had preferred.

Whatever Mr. Turney's opinions may be it is impossible that those who are denouncing him and voting against him can be imposed on by them.— His opinions are of no value to them. However, they have endorsed those opinions long ago, and have manifested by many acts that they had the ut- most confidence in his opinions, and were willing to promote him to the Senatorship. He hoped the House would go into convention and settle this vexed question. The Democrats were the majority here, and they were re- sponsible for this delay. He hoped that an election would be effected. The country expected a Democratic Senator to be elected. He knew his party were in the minority and could not elect a Senator, but he was willing to help the majority, and would even vote for a Democrat, but must be per- mitted to select for himself. He was sick and tired of this delay."

For approximately two weeks, October 13-25 inclusive, the Legis- lature had done little except indulge in political sparring and shadow- boxing in regard to the election of a United States Senator. The newspapers were growing critical at the prolonged "playing politics" and frequent outbursts of temper were exhibited in the Legislative Hall. On Saturday, October 25, the Senatorial Gordian knot was cut by the reading of a letter [24] from Judge Nicholson, the leading Democratic candidate.

"THE RESULT—A SENATOR ELECTED.

The two Houses of the General Assembly met in Convention on Saturday morning, and on the first ballot elected the Hon. Hopkins L. Turney Senator in Congress. Before the balloting commenced Mr. Thomas withdrew the name of the editor of the Union as a candidate. His authority for so doing was derived from a letter addressed to him, which was read at the clerk's table, as follows, as near as we can remember it having no copy before us:—

'Nashville, Oct. 25, 1845.

Hon. Jonas E. Thomas:

DEAR SIR: In compliance with the expressed will of a large majority of my political friends in the Legislature, I consented that you might present my name before that body as a candidate for United States Senator. You are well aware, that I never would have accepted that station, except with the sanction of the body of the Democratic members. In the repeated trials which have been made to elect a Senator, I have been gratified to see that so large a majority of my party has deemed me worthy to fill so exalted a station. This manifestation of confidence brings me under a debt of gratitude which I shall never be able to discharge, but which will command my increased exertions in sustaining those political principles which I have always advocated.

I am contented with the honor, which the generous and persevering support I have received, has conferred upon me. You know, (whatever may be the opinion of others) that there never has been a moment, since my name has been connected with the office of Senator, when I would not have cheerfully resigned all pretentions to it to any other person designated by our party. I have yielded the use of my name, thus far, in obedience with the wishes of my friends, and I have stood aloof from any control over it as long as my duty to my party requires me to acquiesce.

In bringing my mind to the conclusion which I am about to announce to you, I must take occasion to set myself right on one point. Those who have been most active and energetic in opposition to my election, have taken much pains to array party prejudices against me, by the allegation that I was the candidate in whose favor the wishes and influence of the President of the United States have been exerted. As far as I know, or believe, there is not the slightest foundation for the allegation. Those who flatter themselves, that, in defeating me, they would inflict pain or mortification upon the President, have been greatly misled.

---

[24] *Senate Journal*, 1845, 139–140.
    Nashville Union, October 23, 1845.
    Author's note. The *Nashville Union* of October 23, 1845, carried the Nicholson letter together with editorial comment on the letter and the subsequent action of the Legislature. Actually, the Nicholson letter bears a date *two days later* than the date of the paper carrying the letter. The newspaper version of Nicholson's letter varies in some detail from that carried in the *official* record, the *Senate Journal*. The letter appearing in the *Senate Journal* is the one incorporated in this treatise.
    If the Nicholson letter appearing in the *Nashville Union* was the *real date* on which the "copy" was handed to the *Union*, of which paper Judge Nicholson was at the time Editor, it is conclusive that he had decided that he could not be elected and that the withdrawal of his name was indicated.

I have devoted my time and energies in defence of the doctrines of the Administration because they were my own doctrines.

I have opposed the doctrines of the Whig party with industry and zeal, because I believed them erroneous, but towards the Whigs, personally, whilst my course has been decided, it has been respectful. I desire them, however, to be fully apprised, that, on the point to which I have referred, they have labored under a total misapprehension.

No consideration could induce me to take a seat in the Senate merely to echo the will of the President, and the bare suspicion that such would be my position (however unfounded it is) makes me the more ready to request that you will withdraw my name as a candidate from before the General Assembly.

In taking this course, allow me to express my sincere gratitude for the generous support which has been given to me by my Democratic friends.

Very Respectfully,
Your ob't servant,
A. O. P. Nicholson

Hon. Jonas E. Thomas,
    Senate Chamber.'

When the clerk was about to call the roll, Mr. Guild rose and alluded to the reasons assigned by the whigs for their opposition to the candidate just withdrawn. He said that it had been charged in debate and urged out of doors that that gentleman was the candidate of the President, and that his influence had been exerted to secure his election. Mr. G. pronounced the charge to be without the shadow of foundation, and he was authorized to make this denial by letters which he had received on the previous night from Washington. The balloting then proceeded without further obstruction, except from explanations given by members, when their names were called, as to their reasons for voting for or against Mr. Turney—several whigs taking occasion to absolve him wholly from all obligations to the whig party, and declaring that they voted for him as a good and true democrat, under no pledges or concessions made to the whigs. When the votes were counted they stood as follows:—

> For Mr. Turney.................................53
> For Mr. Dunlap................................46

Mr. Turney received six democratic votes, viz: Messrs. Fletcher and Turney of the Senate—and Messrs. Turney, Roberts, Garner and Northcutt of the House. He received forty-seven whig votes—that being all, except Mr. Etheridge, who voted for Mr. Dunlap—his other votes were all democratic.

Thus has ended a contest which has excited much interest and consumed much time. The immediate result was highly gratifying to the whigs—particularly to those who had been most active in bringing it about. How long they will continue to rejoice in their victory is yet to be seen. The first feeling of the democrats was one of disappointment and mortification, but 'in the present attitude of things and under the circumtances which surround us' it is possible that this feeling may very soon give way to one of reluctant acquiescence.—Their great object was to elect a democrat—one who would sustain the Administration in carrying out democratic measures. They had a decided preference for another and would have been pleased to elevate him, but under the solemn assurances of honorable whigs, made on the floor, and the equally solemn assurances of Mr. Turney, made immediately after his election, the democrats have reasons to believe that the whigs have elected for them a Senator who will be as ardent and faithful an advocate of their measures as would have been the man of their first choice."

It is impossible, at this faraway time, to determine with any degree of accuracy as to whether or not the rank and file of the Democratic members of the Legislature were taken into the confidence of the Democratic leaders regarding the imminent withdrawal of Judge Nicholson from the race. What is highly probable, though purely conjectural, is that Judge Nicholson, who was politically wise and well-versed in political strategy, saw the handwriting on the wall and acted accordingly. If the Judge kept his own counsel, then the Democratic members witnessed one of the basic axioms of strategy—*expect the unexpected!* At any rate, the hitherto frontal assualt of the Democrats had been repulsed and they were forced to yield to a flanking attack by the Whigs.

Immediately at the conclusion of the reading of the Nicholson letter, the Legislature in joint session proceeded to take the fourteenth ballot, resulting in the election of Hopkins L. Turney as United States Senator. In Turney's election, as also in the election of Watterson as Speaker of the Senate, there was enacted a "first" in Tennessee political history. *In neither instance did the preferred first choice of the Democrats emerge victorious, despite the fact that the Democrats had a majority in each legislative branch.* The Whigs really gave the Democrats a double dose of hoodoo and voodoo. As to just how the "whammy" was executed, let the exposé by a leading Whig organ be presented:[25]

"ELECTION OF U. S. SENATOR

'The long agony is over,' and Mr. Turney is the Senator. He received, on the first and only ballot that took place on Saturday morning last, 53 votes, which, being a majority of all the votes, elected him. Of these 53 votes, 47 were Whig, and 6 of them Democratic votes. Previous to the balloting, a letter was read from Mr. Nicholson, announcing his withdrawal from the contest. His friends then in a body voted for Judge Dunlap. Not *one* of them voted for Mr. Turney, who received every Whig vote, save that of a sterling Whig representing a county in the Western District where there is a considerable Democratic majority.

This has been one of the most highly exciting and arduous struggles we ever witnessed in a Legislative body. Although the Whigs had no candidate of their own, and the choice was obliged to be made between Democratic candidates, three of whom were put in nomination by their own political friends, it was not, so far as the Whigs were concerned, a mere matter of personal preference, on their part, as between Democrats. Grave constitutional questions and great political principles became involved in the issue, in support of which the Whigs rallied and finally triumphed. We congratulate them and the country on the success which has crowned their

---

[25] *Nashville Whig*, October 28, 1845.

efforts. A plain statement of the case in its origin, progress and termination will show its grave importance.

The Democratic majority for Governor at the late election was only 1,470.[26] Out of 100 members, of which the General Assembly consists, the Whigs succeeded in electing 48. Yet even before the Legislature met, it was apparent that the iron despotism of party would be exercised without stint to deprive this large Whig minority—representing, we firmly believe, a majority of the voters of Tennessee—of the poor privilege of exercising a right of choice as between the *Democratic* candidates who might be presented to the Legislature. Rather than permit the *Whig* members to choose and *decide* between the various *Democratic aspirants*—and it was known there were several such—Mr. Nicholson, the Editor of the Nashville Union—himself the most prominent of them, and the one on which it was known the Caucus nomination of his party would fall, and in whose behalf it was believed the potent influence of the Executive at Washington would be exerted—rather, we say, than permit the Whig members of the Legislature—48 in number—to have lot and part in the matter, Mr. Nicholson avowed his readiness, soon after the result of the election was known, to take the Senator from *East Tennessee*, although the Senator in office is from that section of the State. This contemptuous disregard of the feelings, preferences and rights of the minority proceeds from the same party who, in 1841, in the face of a Whig majority of upwards of 3,000 in the State, and of a Whig majority of two members in the Legislature, refused to go into the election of Senators at all, and actually kept the State from being represented in the United States Senate for two years, because a Whig majority of the Legislature representing a Whig majority of the people of the State, would not accord to the *minority* the privilege of selecting one of the two Senators to be elected from the ranks of their own—the minority party!

When the General Assembly convened, as was foreseen and foretold, Mr. Nicholson received the Caucus nomination of his party. He was the regular Caucus nominee and candidate.

The friends of Mr. Turney, on the other hand, refused to go into Caucus. He repudiated its authority. He claimed the right of 'running on his own hook.' He acknowledged no right in the President of the United States to interfere, however secretly, in Senatorial elections. He scorned to bow to Executive dictation.—In short, he stood forward an *independent* candidate —the *anti-Caucus—anti-Executive—anti*-POLK candidate, who, if elected, would not stoop to be the mere instrument of 'the powers that be' at Washington, but would discharge his Senatorial duties unshackled by Executive influence, and in the manner which *he* might think would best subserve the interests of our common country. Such was Mr. Turney's position from the moment the Legislature met.—He took it boldly and openly, and manfully and fearlessly maintained it.

Besides Mr. Nicholson and Mr. Turney, Judge Dunlap, of the Western District, also a Democrat, was put in nomination by a member of his own party, but as he received only four Democratic votes on the first ballot, it was evident that the dominant party, almost in one entire body, had rejected the claims of the Western District and were bent upon the election of Mr. Nicholson at all hazards. With no candidate of their own, and with no possibility whatever of electing one, if they should bring him forward, what were the Whigs to do? We maintain that they owed it to their *principles* and

---

[26] Author's note. The cited figures are slightly erroneous. The actual majority vote was 1,623. See citation, reference 10.

the *public interests,* when a choice of evils was thus presented to them, to choose that which seemed to them the *least*—and if by concentrating their votes upon any one of the Democratic candidates they could vindicate a single Whig principle or successfully resist the exercise of the iron despotism with which the majority of the dominant party in the Legislature had evinced a determination to carry out all their measures, they, the Whig members, were under the highest obligations to their country to do so.—This view of the subject a portion of them took from the beginning—upon others it was forced by the unwarrantable and extraordinary course of their political opponents.

The election began, and after thirteen ballotings it became manifest—

1. That to the feelings and wishes of the Whigs the election of Mr. Nicholson was utterly repugnant. There were several Gentlemen of his party whom they preferred to him.

2. That a very large majority of them would vote, and were voting for Mr. Turney in preference to him, and that if the latter could procure a united Whig vote, or nearly so, it would, with the aid of the six Democratic votes he was receiving, elect him.

Notwithstanding these facts, and although, during thirteen ballotings the highest vote received by Mr. Nicholson was 41, while 50 were required to effect an election, his friends, being in a *minority,* determined if possible to *force him upon the majority!* The means they resorted to for the purpose of effecting this object were characteristic of the party.

All parliamentary law and order were openly set at defiance!

It was decided by the Speaker of the Senate, that the two Houses, when met in convention for the purpose of electing a Senator, were not subject to the ordinary rules of parliamentary proceeding, and that members, when thus in convention, could talk without the slightest restraint as to time or topic!

In the House, motions to *reconsider* a question not debatable under the rules of the House were decided to be debatable, and to open the whole subject for the widest latitude of discussion. Under this decision, the minority had it in their power to postpone an election as long as it suited their convenience, without the slightest regard to the will of the majority!

Although the convention of the two Houses would adjourn to meet at a particular hour, the House would refuse to receive the Senate at the appointed hour, although repeatedly notified by that body that they had taken a recess and were then waiting to unite with the House and proceed with the order of the day!

Hours and days were spent in making and discussing frivolous and unparliamentary motions for the avowed purpose of postponing the election against the wishes of a decided majority of the House; and intimations were thrown out that no election at all would be permitted to take place during the session—unless, we presume, the majority should surrender at discretion to the minority.

As a last resource, the floodgates of defamation and abuse were opened upon Mr. Turney and the Whigs.

The Speaker of the Senate, one of the presiding officers of the convention, left the chair, took the floor and delivered a violent Philippic against Mr. Turney—charging bargain, intrigue and corruption between that Gentleman and the Whigs.

To cap the climax, resolutions were introduced by a friend of the Caucus nominee, providing for the appointment of a committee, with power to send for persons and papers, in order to investigate this charge—made avowedly on the authority of rumor.

Under this most unconstitutional and inquisitorial proceeding, members of the Legislature would have been subject to an examination under oath, as to any opinions which might have been expressed by Mr. Turney to them on subjects of national policy—such as the Tariff, the Distribution of the sales of the public lands, &c.

Member after member of the dominant party, following the example of the Speaker of the Senate, rose and reiterated the insinuations and charges of a corrupt intrigue and understanding between the Whigs and Mr. Turney.

These disreputable proceedings continued for two whole days and a half —during which time the progress of the public business was impeded—the public time was consumed—the public money was wasted, and all for what? Why, that a mere majority of the majority, but, constituting in reality a minority of the whole Legislature, might force upon an unwilling majority their nominee, Mr. Nicholson!

This high-handed proceeding, however, not only failed most signally, but it recoiled on its authors, and materially contributed to the election of Mr. Turney! Those Whig members who, up to that time, had felt reluctant to vote for any Democrat under any contingency—or who entertained strong objections to Mr. Turney—or who, if compelled to vote between him and Mr. Nicholson, might have preferred the latter, hesitated no longer, but expressed a determination to vote for Mr. Turney. The Whig members having now united on Mr. T., *elected him.* In electing him, they have, as we conceive, not only signally defeated their opponents—for it is regarded in that light by the Democrats themselves—but they have successfully vindicated some of the great and vital principles of the Whig party:

They have, on this occasion, successfully vindicated the great Whig principle of uncompromising resistance to Presidential interference and dictation in State elections.

They have elected a Gentleman who openly denounced and resisted such interference and dictation, and who will denounce and resist it on all proper occasions.

They have sent a Senator to Washington who himself will be the sole judge of the course which the public interests require him to pursue, without consulting the *wishes of the Executive.*

They have met and rolled back the tide of violent denunciation, oppression and injustice with which the iron despotism of party attempted to overwhelm one of its own leaders, for no other reason than that he had the spirit and manliness to refuse obedience to its imperious and tyrannical dictates.

They have signally rebuked the unconstitutional, inquisitorial, search-warrant attempt of the minority to investigate the *motives* by which they were actuated in the simple exercise of their constitutional right, as members of the Legislature, to vote for a United States Senator.

They have successfully vindicated the right of a majority of the Legislature, when their will is distinctly ascertained—as it was in the case of U. S. Senator—to carry it out and execute it according to the forms of parliamentary proceeding and the requisitions of the law and the constitution.

They have successfully resisted the tyrannical, anti-Republican attempt of a mere majority of a majority—and constituting, in fact, a *minority* of the members—to dragoon them, the Whigs, into the support, direct or indirect, of the Caucus nominees of such minority.

In accomplishing these results, the Whig members of the present General Assembly of Tennesee, have, in our opinion, acted in strict accordance with Whig principles, and pursued a course calculated to promote the public interests. They will doubtless receive the thanks and congratulations not only of the Whigs of Tennessee, but of their brother Whigs of the Union."

Apparently Mr. Speaker Watterson was nettled by the thrusts delivered by the Whig newspaper in characterizing his action as presiding officer as being "unconstitutional, inquisitoral, and high-handed." With a copy of the *Whig* in his hand, Mr. Watterson proceeded to give his version of what he said relative to Mr. Turney's alleged "selling out" to the Whigs in order to gain the coveted goal—a United States Senatorship. Mr. Watterson's explanations and the *Whig's* rebuttal were set forth as follows:[27]

"SENATORIAL ELECTION—MR. SPEAKER WATTERSON'S DECISIONS AND SPEECHES.

In the Senate, on Tuesday last, another Senator being in the Chair, Mr. Speaker Watterson took the floor, with the 'Whig' of that morning in his hand, and said he desired to call the attention of the Senate to what he was going to read. He then read the following passage from the leading Editorial article in the paper:

'It was decided by the Speaker of the Senate, that the two Houses, when met in Convention for the purpose of electing a Senator, were not subject to the ordinary rules of Parliamentary proceeding.'

Mr. Watterson simply added, that he had made 'no such decision.'

He also read the following paragraph from the same article:

'The Speaker of the Senate, one of the presiding officers of the convention, left the chair, took the floor and delivered a violent Phillippic against Mr. Turney—charging bargain, intrigue and corruption between that Gentleman and the Whigs.'

Mr. Watterson remarked, that he had made 'no such charge.' What he had said was:

'That Mr. Turney had made concessions to the Whigs, he as firmly believed, as he believed there was a God in Heaven, who ruled the universe and governed the destinies of men.'

We give Mr. Watterson's corrections and explanations with pleasure, and sincerely wish we could let them pass without remark. But we told him when, immediately after making them, he came to our table and requested us to publish them, that *we* had made no mistake; and in justice to ourselves we must now proceed to establish the correctness of our allegations with regard to his conduct during the pendency of the late Senatorial election.

The *whole* of the first paragraph of ours which he referred to, is as follows:

'It was decided by the Speaker of the Senate, that the two Houses when met in convention for the purpose of electing a Senator, were not

---

[27] *Nashville Whig*, October 30, 1845.

Author's note. The *Senate Journal* makes no reference whatsoever to the incident as reported by the *Whig*. Apparently, the "personal privilege" prerogative was considered just a "side show" performance and was omitted from the official record.

subject to the ordinary rules of parliamentary proceeding, *and that members, when thus in convention, could talk without the slightest restraint as to time or topic!'*

It is the accuracy of the first part of the paragraph only down to the word 'proceeding,' that Mr. Watterson impeached. The fact stated in the last part of the paragraph, which we have italicised, he did not dispute. He tacitly admitted it was true, then, as stated by us, that he decided that 'members when thus in Convention, could talk without restraint as to time or topic.' And is not the one proposition tantamount to the other? Can the members of any deliberative Assembly, where the ordinary rules of parliamentary proceeding prevail, talk *without restraint as to time or topic?* In admitting the truth, therefore, of the second proposition, Mr. Watterson has admitted the truth of the first. But we are fortunate enough on this occasion to be able to prove, by positive and unimpeachable testimony that Mr. Watterson *did* make the identical decision we attributed to him. The following statement of what occurred, on the occasion referred to, has been drawn out, at our request, by Senator Cullom, and his recollection, we are authorized to say, is confirmed by Senator Henry. Doubtless there are many members of both Houses who will bear witness to its entire accuracy. We have applied to no others on the subject:

STATEMENT:

'The two Houses having met in Convention for the purpose of electing a Senator to Congress, and Mr. Speaker Watterson being in the Chair, a motion was made to proceed with the balloting. Mr. Guild, upon the supposition that that was a debatable motion, was proceeding to address the Convention at length, when Mr. Cullom rose to a point of order, and insisted that the motion was not debatable. The Chair decided that it was, from which decision Mr. Cullom appealed to the Convention. The Chair thereupon decided, that as there were no rules governing the proceedings of the Convention, there could be no appeal, from which second decision Mr. Cullom appealed, urging that in the absence of express rules for the government of the proceedings of the Convention, the rules of proceeding of the two Houses would apply. The Speaker decided otherwise, and refused to put the question of appeal to the Convention. Whereupon Mr. Cullom addressing the Chair, said: Mr. President, are you the Speaker of the Convention or the Speaker of a faction?'

This makes the case still stronger against Mr. Watterson than we stated it. He has made a bad matter worse by noticing it. He not only decided that there were no rules governing the proceedings of the Convention, but he, the President of the Convention, refused to permit an appeal to be taken and decided from his decisions. The presiding officer of a free, representative body, refusing to allow appeals from his decisions to the body over which he presided, on the ground that there were no rules governing its proceedings! We venture to say that a case parallel to this cannot be found in the annals of the British Parliament during the whole of the despotic rule of the Stewarts. It is worthy of remark, also, in this connection, that the very next morning after the decision in question, Mr. Cullom introduced a resolution in the Senate, providing that when the two Houses should be in Convention, its proceedings should be governed by the Rules of the House of Representatives, which resolution has been since adopted by the Senate and is before the House of Representatives.

With regard to Mr. Watterson's denial that he charged the existence of 'bargain, intrigue and corruption' between the Whigs and Mr. Turney, we beg it to be understood that we did not undertake or assume to give the *very words* of Mr. Watterson. We were not *reporting* his speech. We undertook to state a fact in relation to that speech—to give the substance or gist of an allegation made by him. That we did truly give the *substance* and *true meaning* of the charge he made against Mr. Turney and the Whigs, we are perfectly willing to submit to the members of the Convention without respect to party. Curious to see how our contemporary of the Orthopolitan, who was present, understood and reported Mr. Watterson on the occasion referred to, we turned to that paper and found the following:

'When Mr. Watterson's name was called, he asked leave to explain the reasons of his vote. He would not vote for Mr. Turney because he did not believe he was the choice of the democrats of his district—because, not being the choice of the democrats of the Legislature, he believed as firmly as he believed there was a God in Heaven that he had entered into a *corrupt bargain* to secure his election.'

Here, as Sam. Weller would say, is 'a *h*extraordinary coincidence,' to say the least of it, between our contemporary and ourself as to the very words in which each of us undertook to characterize the charge made by Mr. Watterson against Mr. Turney.

The sketch made of Mr. Watterson's speech, by the Reporter for the Banner, is as follows:

MR. SPEAKER WATTERSON'S REMARKS.

I vote against Hopkins L. Turney, Mr. President, I vote against Hopkins L. Turney! because, sir—

(Here cries of 'order!' 'order!' arrested the Speaker, and several gentlemen arose in their places, and called Mr. W. to order.)

Mr. Watterson.—'The election is made, gentlemen, and I ask but five minutes to explain the reasons which will govern me in casting my vote?'

(Cries of 'no!' 'no!' and remonstrances from several members; but upon Mr. W's insisting to go on, cries of 'leave' were heard from several Whig members, and then from others, and Mr. Watterson was permitted to proceed.)

Mr. W.—'I vote against Hopkins L. Turney, because I have seen him urging his claims before this Convention; and because I saw him, when supported by only a small minority of the Democratic party, and unable to unite his own political friends in his support, still persisting in his position of a candidate for Senator; and finally, because I have seen him throw himself in the arms of his political opponents, and cry, 'save me! save me! or I perish.'

I vote against Hopkins L. Turney, sir, because I have seen your Gov. Jones, Hon. John Bell, and Ephraim H. Foster, whipping the reluctant whigs into the support of a political traitor.'

Mr. Senator Cullom.—Mr. President, does the Senator intend to apply these remarks to me?

Mr. W.—I do not allude to the Senator from Smith—(Mr. Cullom.)

Here Mr. Senator Muirhead also asked Mr. W. if he alluded to him?

Mr. W.—'I did not have the Senator from Wilson (Mr. Muirhead) in my mind.'

Mr. Bullock here also rose, and demanded of the Speaker, who he did have in his mind? Here were heard cries of 'order' from various portions of the House, when Mr. Watterson was understood to say that he did not allude to the gentleman from Madison (Mr. Bullock), nor any other gentleman in particular.

Order having been restored Mr. W. continued, 'I vote against Hopkins L. Turney, because Gov. Jones, Mr. Bell, and Mr. Foster attended a whig caucus, and urged them to vote for Mr. Turney. Sir, I believe as firmly as I believe there is a God in Heaven, that Hopkins L. Turney has made concessions to the Whig party—and is now a traitor to his own party. Sir, I know the people of the mountain district. They resisted Whiteism, and they will resist Turneyism. Aye! sir, there is already 'fire in the mountains,' and woe to the luckless wight, who attempts to oppose it. And now sir, I throw my banner to the breeze, and wash my hands from the foul deed, which elevates a traitor, to the dignity of a Senator, and now here in my place, declare eternal war against Hop. Turneyism.'

It will be seen that though the word 'concessions' is used in the above report, the meaning is the same, 'Traitor,' 'foul deed,' 'eternal war against Hop. Turneyism,' &c, &c.,—that will do for our purpose. We are not particular about *words*. We aimed to give the *tenor* and *purport* of Mr. Watterson's denunciation of Mr. Turney, and we think it is now abundantly evident that we gave them correctly, and did Mr. Watterson no injustice."

Frequently, it is a moot point as to whether or not the deliberations in a Legislative Assembly call so much for a display of eloquence as for the ingenious exercise of the powers of disputation. In either case, if the Tennessee Legislative Hall had been the Palace of Truth in 1845 and its members had possessed transparent bosoms, unquestionably one could and would have seen a swarm of corroding passions pervading the breasts of the thirty-one legislators who drafted and signed the following political anathema[28] hurled at the head of Hopkins Lacy Turney:

"AN ADDRESS

Of thirty-one Democratic members of the Legislature to their Constituents, in reference to the late Senatorial Election.

FELLOW-CITIZENS—The result of the late election in our State was hailed as a triumph, which entitled the Democracy of Tennessee to the warmest congratulations of the party throughout the Union. It was regarded with peculiar gratification at home and abroad, because it induced all to expect the election to the United States Senate of some member of the party who would enjoy its confidence, and be thereby enabled to give to the administration an efficient and cordial support. In the reasonableness of this calculation the mass of our political opponents cheerfully acquiesced. They concurred in the sentiment that the Senator should be chosen by his own political friends and enjoy their confidence. In the result which has taken place both parties have been disappointed, and the duty devolves upon the undersigned to explain the means by which the popular will has been defeated.

This duty has been rendered more imperative in consequence of the appearance within a few days past of an address by Mr. Turney, who succeeded in obtaining the office of Senator. Before we proceed, however, to notice the contents of this extraordinary address we deem it proper to state, as succinctly as possible, the facts and circumstances connected with his election.

---

[28] *Nashville Whig*, December 18, 1845.

Upon our assembling at Nashville it was soon found that the names of several prominent democrats were freely spoken of for the office of Senator. The sentiment, however, was generally entertained that their claims ought to be submitted to the decision of the body of the party—that but one candidate should be presented, and that he should be the man upon whom the preferences of the body of the party might be united.

When the day of election was fixed by the Legislature, the democratic members pursued the practice which has long prevailed in both parties— they assembled in Convention to ascertain the will of the party as to the candidate for Senator. Six of the friends of Mr. Turney declined to unite in the movement and refused to acquiesce in its decision.

The names of several prominent democrats were submitted to the Convention—amongst the number was the name of Mr. Turney. It was soon ascertained that more than two-thirds of the entire number of Democrats in the Legislature were in favor of the election of the Hon. A. O. P. Nicholson.—He was accordingly chosen as the democratic candidate. When the two Houses assembled in Convention on the 21st Oct. to make the election, the names of Messrs. Nicholson, Turney and Dunlap were put in nomination.

The balloting continued through the 21st Oct., and down through the forenoon of the 23rd Oct.—Mr. Nicholson usually received through the thirteen ballots which were made, about forty democratic votes—Mr. Turney received six democratic votes, and Mr. Dunlap usually five and sometimes seven democratic votes. On the first ballot the body of the whigs voted for Mr. Bell, whilst the others scattered their votes—a few for Mr. Turney, and a few for Mr. Dunlap. As the balloting proceeded the whigs gradually concentrated their votes on Mr. Turney, until on the 13th ballot he received thirty-three whig votes.

The gradual concentration of the whig votes on Mr. Turney created the impression that it was their intention finally to elect him by a complete combination of all their strength with the six democrats who were voting for him. The ostensible reason or the preference which the whigs manifested for Mr. Turney over Mr. Nicholson was, that the latter was the regular democratic candidate, and was believed to be the choice of the President of the United States. But it was impossible not to doubt the sufficiency of this reason as there was no evidence that Mr. Polk had ever expressed any such preference, *and particularly as the whigs were alike preferring Mr. Turney over Mr. Dunlap against whom no such charge was urged.* This reason was made the more untenable from the fact that it was well known that Mr. Turney had been peculiarly obnoxious to the whigs, and many of them had been heard frequently to avow their determination never to vote for him.

In this state of the balloting and of the public mind a rumor became prevalent in Nashville that Mr. Turney had secured the support of the whigs by agreeing to oppose any modification of the Tariff Act of 1842, to sustain the distribution of the proceeds of the land sales, and to denounce the head of the Administration. The rumor was understood to come so directly from Whigs who were in possession of the action of their party that it produced a strong sensation, and when connected with the singular fact that whigs had been voting for Mr. Turney, who had but shortly before been known to be opposed to him, it was deemed absolutely necessary, in justice to Mr. Turney, as well as out of regard to the known popular will, that the balloting should be suspended until some light could be thrown upon the rumor.

The most speedy and certain mode of ascertaining the truth of the alleged concessions seemed to be to address a letter to Messrs. Turney and Nicholson, propounding interrogatories as to their *present* political opinions. This course was determined on between the adjournment of the Convention at noon, on the 22nd, and its meeting in the afternoon. A letter of interrogations was prepared and sent by a committee of the members to both the candidates, who were then present in Nashville. The letter was immediately delivered and was as follows:

'Nashville, Oct. 21, 1845.

To Messrs. Nicholson and Turney:

GENTLEMEN: Your names now being before the Legislature of this State for the vacant seat in the United States Senate, we, the undersigned respectfully ask categorical answers to each of the following interrogatories:

1. Are you in favor of the re-establishment of a Bank of the United States?

2. Are you in favor of the modification of the Tariff Act of 1842?

3. If elected would you vote to distribute the proceeds of the sales of the public lands amongst the States?

4. Would you vote to receive the Constitution of Texas?

5. Would you extend the laws and jurisdiction of the United States over our citizens in Oregon?

6. Would you obey instructions, or resign?

An early reply is requested.

Your ob't servants,

WM. B. ALLEN,	THOMAS SHAW,
SAM. MILLIGAN,	G. C. TORBITT,
JOHN B. HAMILTON,	T. C. H. MILLER,
JAS. M. HORD,	J. VOORHIES,
ROBT. S. HOLT,	JNO. A. GARDNER,
J. E. THOMAS,	RICH. A. L. WILKES,
P. CRITZ,	MICHAEL DUFFY,
PLEASANT WALKER,	THOMAS M. JONES,
JO. C. GUILD,	N. G. FRAZIER,
BROOKINS CAMPBELL,	A. MARTIN.'
POWHATAN GORDON,	

This letter was delivered to both gentlemen before 2 o'clock on the 22d. Mr. Nicholson immediately responded in a matter satisfactory to the democratic members.

The following is the reply of Mr. Nicholson:

'Nashville, Oct. 22, 1845.

GENTLEMEN:—I have this moment received your letter propounding to me a series of questions on political subjects. In compliance with your request I proceed to answer them in their order.

1. I am opposed to the re-establishment of a Bank of the United States.

2. I am in favor of reducing and modifying the Tariff Act of 1842 to the revenue standard.

3. I am opposed to the distribution of the proceeds of the land sales.

4. I am in favor of ratifying the Constitution of Texas.

5. I am in favor of extending our jurisdiction over the Oregon Territory.

6. I acknowledge the right of the Legislature to instruct Senators, and their duty to obey or resign.

Very respectfully,

A. O. P. NICHOLSON.'

Mr. Turney received the letter and promised to respond in one hour. He afterwards declined responding before the morning of the 23d, and he then declined altogether.

The two Houses met in Convention in the afternoon of the 23d, when a motion was made to suspend the balloting and postpone action for about ten days. This motion was resisted by the whigs and Mr. Turney's six democratic friends. In the discussion which sprung up the importance of the postponement was urged upon the ground that there were rumors prevailing which charged Mr. Turney with having made the concessions before referred to, in order to secure the votes of the whigs. The whigs still resisted the postponement, but made no denial of the truth of the rumors. Mr. Watterson, the Senator from Coffee, stated the existence of the rumor, and that a letter was said to have been written by Mr. Turney in which he had made the concessions, and called upon Mr. Cullom, the Senator from Smith, to state whether he knew any thing about such a letter. Mr. Cullom replied that *he* had no such letter in *his* possession. Upon being asked again whether he knew any thing about such a letter, he evaded the question. The effect of this proceedings, connected with the other circumstances, produced conviction on the minds of many as to the truth of the rumors, and made it still more important that time should be attained for further investigation. The whigs, combined with Mr. Turney's six democratic friends, resisted the motion for time and succeeded in defeating it.

Under the impressions naturally produced by the circumstances to which we have referred, we felt fully justified in availing ourselves of every legitimate expedient to procure time for such developments as would either fix upon Mr. Turney the truth of the charges or relieve his character from all suspicions. In efforts to attain these ends two days (the 23d and 24th) were consumed; resolutions were introduced in the House of Representatives setting forth the existence of the rumors and asking that a committee be appointed with power to take proof and report. Much discussion took place, but no whig ever ventured to deny the charges, (except some few who, on the final balloting, when their names were called arose in their places and declared *their* utter ignorance of any concession having been made by Mr. Turney) but the body of the whig members, by their silence or evasions when interrogated, and their efforts to justify Mr. Turney upon the supposition that the charges were true—indeed, their whole course strengthened and confirmed the belief that he had secured their support by agreeing to make concessions. The resolutions were resisted and defeated by a combination of the whigs and Mr. Turney's democratic supporters.

At the close of the 24th October we became satisfied that the purpose was fixed between the whigs and the six Turney democrats to elect him in the face of the charges resting on his character. We believe that the circumstances were then sufficient to satisfy all reasonable men of the truth of the alleged concessions. We therefore, determined to cease opposition to the resumption of the ballotings, and, to take from the whigs all pretext as to their opposition to Mr. Nicholson on the score of his being the supposed favorite of Mr. Polk, that gentleman voluntarily withdrew his name as a candidate, and left the choice to be made between Mr. Turney and Mr. Dunlap. The vote was taken on the morning of the 25th; every whig except one (Mr. Ethridge) voted for Mr. Turney—every democrat except six (Messrs. Sam Turney, Henry Turney, Fletcher, Garner, Northcutt and Roberts), voted for Mr. Dunlap.

We feel fully satisfied that the just and liberal of both parties will sustain

our course upon the facts as we have stated them. But since the election of
Mr. Turney, other developments have been made, which must forever
settle the question of the existence of an understanding between Mr. Turney
and a portion of the whigs which secured his election. On the same day on
which he was elected, Mr. Turney wrote a card, which was published in the
Nashville Union, in which he requested a suspension of the public judgment
until he could prepare a defence against the charges which had been made
against him pending the election. For this purpose he asked about ten days,
when he promised to make a full defence and vindication of his conduct. In
the mean time he authorized Mr. Glenn, the Representative from Tipton
county, to pronounce the charges false. Whilst the public was waiting for
the promised vindication, several whig members of the Legislature freely
disclosed the facts connected with the alleged concessions, and fully confirmed the truth of the rumors. But as Mr. Turney had asked a suspension
of the public mind, and had authorized a denial of the charges of concession,
we deemed it proper to await his promised vindication before any steps were
taken in our own justification. The address has appeared and has been extensively published and read, and to some portion of it we desire to call the
attention of the people.

The first remark which must strike every man who reads it, is, that although Mr. Turney sets out with the declaration that he was slandered,
abused and misrepresented pending the election, *he has wholly failed to make
any denial of the alleged concessions of principle with which he stood
charged?* He was charged with having secured the support of whigs by
making written pledges which involved an abandonment of certain important
doctrines. To the charge he has failed to make even an allusion, and thereby
leaves the inference to be drawn that the charge was well founded. If any
thing had been needed to justify the efforts of the undersigned to procure
a disclosure of the facts pending the election, this omission of Mr. Turney
to deny the truth of the rumors on which they acted, furnishes an ample
vindication. If the disclosures had been made before the election, a portion
of the six democrats who voted for Mr. Turney stood pledged to abandon
his support. The concealment of the concessions was, therefore, a fraud
upon these democrats, and hence we are fully justified in regarding the election of Mr. Turney as the result of fraud perpetrated upon a portion of the
electors.

The undersigned deem it due to the President of the United States, as
well as to Mr. Nicholson, that we should meet with a prompt and unqualified denial, the charge of Mr. Turney, in reference to the interference of
the former in behalf of the latter.—No such interference, either directly or
indirectly, was known to any one of the undersigned, nor do we believe
that there is the slightest foundation for the insinuation of Mr. Turney as a
mere pretext to excuse an unjustifiable violation of one of the usages of the
party, to which he has again and again gave sanction.

It is not deemed necessary for us to comment upon the reasons assigned
by Mr. Turney for his refusal to answer the interrogatories propounded to
him.—The references which he has made to the doctrines and practices of
Mr. Van Buren and Mr. Polk, furnish no apology for his course. He was
interrogated by members of his own party, and those who interrogated him
knew that in 1841 he had responded to similar questions and had avowed the
doctrine that a *candidate was bound to answer whether interrogated by his
friends or his opponents.* We leave the people to decide whether he would
have 'degraded' himself more by answering than by refusing to answer under
the circumstances which surrounded him.

Those portions of Mr. Turney's address to which we desire to call the special attention of the democracy of the State, refer to his opinions as now expressed on the subjects of tariff and distribution.—These are the leading questions at issue between the two parties, and no doubt was entertained as to Mr. Turney's position until the rumors which prevailed pending the election. In Congress by his votes and addresses, before the people by his speeches, and in the last Presidential contest by his acceptance of the station of elector, and his support of the nominee of the Baltimore Convention, and his advocacy of the doctrines promulgated by that convention, he had been regarded as strictly democratic on those subjects as any member of the party.—To show how fully we are sustained in this declaration, we need only quote a few passages from an address issued by Mr. Turney in conjunction with his democratic colleagues in Congress from Tennessee in 1841. His opinion as to the constitutionality of distribution may be learned from the following passages in that address:

'We have heard the leading members of the Harrison party avow, time after time, in debate, that the measures to be proposed and adopted under the new administration, are

1. A National Bank.

2. A Distribution of the proceeds of the sales of the public lands.

3. An increase of the Tariff, and

4. A law to punish officers for interfering in elections.

The first remark which strikes us as important and singular, is, that there is no one of their measures which is not deemed unconstitutional by a large portion of our countrymen. *No one of them comes plainly within the delegated powers of Congress. No one of them can be adopted without resorting to the federal mode of construing the constitution. These remarks are applicable to all the proposed measures.'*

Mr. Turney's opinion as to the inexpediency and dangerous tendency of distribution may be gathered from the following passage in the same address:

'*We pronounce it one of the boldest grasps after power and one of the most reckless assaults upon the independence of the States, that was ever made. It is but the deceptive beginning of the revival of the old American system. A bribe of five millions of dollars is held out to the States, to induce them to submit without a murmur to the collection of five millions more by an increase of the Tariff.'*

It is then a deceptive proposition to tax the people of the whole country to pay the debts of those States which are unable promptly to pay their own debts. *We feel justified in predicting that it will terminate in a high tariff, and an assumption of the State debts, with a national debt of two hundred millions. This is the system of policy in prospect which is now in its first stage.*

We have already remarked, that not one of the measures chalked out for consummation by the new Administration is free from constitutional difficulties. We now say that there is not one of them that does not tend directly to an increase of federal power.—The Bank—*the distribution of land revenue*—the tariff; the gag bill; we ask you to examine them, one by one, with reference to the honor which they are calculated to add to the Federal Government, either in its Legislative or Executive branches. *Combine them to-*

gether and view them all in operation, and then determine how far our system of government will be removed from a monarchy.'

These were Mr. Turney's views on distribution as avowed by himself, and no change in these opinions was known to have taken place, until the pendency of the Senatorial election, when he entered into a secret arrangement to secure the whig vote, and to effect this end made to them the concessions to be found in his late address. In his address he speaks of distribution as follows:

'I think Congress has the power to distribute the proceeds of the public lands that have been derived from the States, by cession, nor do I perceive any serious objection, in the present state of our finances to the adoption of that policy. General Jackson was of opinion that it was "our true policy that the public lands shall cease, as soon as practicable, to be a source of revenue," and that great and venerated man thought "the most safe, just and federal disposition," would be the distribution of their proceeds among the States.

When I voted against the distribution act of 1841, the country was in debt, and its revenues were unequal to the expenditures of the government. At present, the state of things is far otherwise—the national debt has been paid, and the finances of the country are in a most flourishing condition. In measures of this kind a statesman is not to be influenced by a desire to deserve *that sort* of consistency which would prevent him from supporting at one time a measure he would oppose at another time, regardless of the circumstances of the country—but he must look to all the surrounding circumstances and act with an intelligent and patriotic reference to them.'—*Mr. Turney's Address.*

In justice to the memory and character of General Jackson it is incumbent on us to correct the misrepresentation of his opinions contained in the foregoing extract. It is not true, as stated by Mr. Turney, that General Jackson thought the most safe, just and federal disposition of the proceeds of the public lands would be their distribution among the States. In his message of 1829, 'that great and venerated man,' looking forward to the difficulty of reducing the high tariff then in existence, anticipated from its operation a large surplus revenue, and to avoid the evils of such a surplus, he made the following suggestion:

'To avoid these evils it appears to me that the most safe, just and federal disposition which could be made of this surplus revenue, would be its apportionment among the several States, according to their ratio of representation; and should this measure not be found warranted by the constitution, that it would be expedient to propose to the States an amendment authorizing it.'

In his message of 1832, General Jackson advocated the policy of reducing the price of the public lands and in so doing used the following language:

'It seems to me to be our true policy that the public lands shall cease as soon as practicable to be a source of revenue, and that they be sold to settlers in limited parcels, at a price barely sufficient to reimburse to the United States the expense of the present system and the cost arising under our Indian compacts.'

By comparing these extracts with the garbled quotations of parts of sentences made by Mr. Turney, it will be apparent how gross a misrepresentation of Gen. Jackson's views has been resorted to, and what palpable injustice to him has been attempted. This is the more surprising and inexcusable, because Mr. Turney must have known that Gen. Jackson at a period subsequent to the date of his message of 1832, actually vetoed a bill passed by Congress for distributing the proceeds of the land sales! It is also seen that in neither of the messages from which Mr. Turney has made garbled quotations was *Gen. Jackson* giving his views on the question of distributing the proceeds of the land sales!

If Mr. Turney had been disposed to do justice to Gen. Jackson, he would have stated that in reference to a distribution of a surplus, his opinions afterwards underwent a change, and that this change was frankly avowed in his message of 1836. We cannot presume that one who has professed so much admiration for that 'great and venerated man,' and who has occupied so prominent a position as a politician, could have been ignorant of the following views contained in the message referred to. In that message Gen. Jackson said:

'Without desiring to conceal that the experience and observation of the last two years have operated a partial change in my views on this interesting subject, it is nevertheless regretted that the suggestions made by me in my annual message of 1829 and 1830, have been greatly misrepresented.... In view of the dangers of such a surplus, and in preference to its application to Internal Improvements, in derogation of the rights and powers of the States, the suggestion of an amendment of the Constitution to authorize its distribution was made.... No such appeal (to the States for an amendment of the Constitution) has been taken; and *in my opinion a distribution of the surplus revenue by Congress, either to the States, or the people, is to be considered among the prohibitions of the Constitution.* As already intimated, my views have undergone a change, so far as to be convinced that *no alteration of the Constitution in this respect is wise or expedient.*'

With a full knowledge, as we have no doubt, of these explicit declarations by Gen. Jackson, it is humiliating to see Mr. Turney resorting to a perversion of his opinions in order to justify himself in the means resorted to to reach a seat in the Senate.—We should be wanting in fidelity to the memory of the departed statesman and patriot, if we had failed to expose this insidious attack upon his political reputation.

Although Mr. Turney avows himself for a tariff for revenue, yet his doctrine on distribution shows that he does not mean such a revenue tariff as is advocated by the democrats, but a tariff which shall raise revenue enough, *exclusive of the land fund,* to pay all the expenses of the Government.

These extracts from Mr. Turney's address, connected with the fact, now well ascertained, that during the pendency of the Senatorial election he held secret communications with leading whigs, and his entire failure to deny the charges of his having made concessions in order to secure the whig votes, must forever settle the question that he owes his elevation to the Senate to a fraud successfully practiced upon his own party. It presents a case of political immorality which has no parallel within our knowledge, and calls for a rebuke from the honest of all parties which will show that such political corruption and treachery cannot be practiced with impunity. In our deliberative judgment Mr. Turney has forfeited the respect and confidence of his party, and in this sentiment we have the fullest assurance that we have the entire concurrence of every true democrat. The honor and integrity of the party must be preserved, and this can be effected in no other way than by holding every man as unworthy of membership who shows himself capable of bartering his principles for the support of his adversaries. The facts now laid before the country call for a response from the great body of our party, which we cannot doubt will be made in due season, and when made, will inflict merited punishment upon the guilty, and finally give increased strength to the cause of democracy.

JOHN EUBANK, of Dixon,
J. HEMBREE, of Roane,
JAMES LAUDERDALE, of Bradley,
NICHOLAS G. FRAZIER, of Rhea,
RICHARD A. L. WILKES, of Maury,
AUSTIN MILLER, of Hardeman,
THOS. M. JONES, of Giles,
R. YATES, of Humphreys,
THOS. BLACK, of Bedford,
H. M. WATTERSON, of Coffee,
G. C. TORBITT, of McMinn,
RICHARD WARNER, of Marshall,
P. CRITZ, of Hawkins,
A. G. McDOUGAL, of Wayne,
J. VOORHIES, of Dixon,
ISAAC ROBERTSON, of Bledsoe,

JOSEPH C. GUILD, of Sumner,
LANDON C. HAYNES, of Washington,
ROBT. S. HOLT, of McMinn,
HENRY TROTT, JR., of Cannon,
G. W. L. MARR, of Obion,
JOHN BUCHANAN, of Giles,
T. C. H. MILLER, of Marshall,
C. T. HUDDLESTON, of Overton,
WM. B. ALLEN, of Lawrence,
H. H. STEPHENS, of Monroe,
MICHAEL DUFFY, of Sumner,
SAM. MILLIGAN, of Greene,
JOHN B. HAMILTON, of Sullivan,
JAMES H. HORD, of Hawkins,
THOS. SHAW, of Stewart."

Apparently, the withering attack upon Senator-elect Turney bore fruit through the medium of "merited punishment in due season." In this instance, due season arrived upon the termination of Senator Turney's term of office in 1851. That item was not overlooked, for on October 20, 1851, Senator John W. Wester introduced the following Resolution: [29]

"Resolved by the General Assembly of the State of Tennessee, that the Senate and House of Representatives will meet in the Hall of the House of Representatives on Monday, the 3d day of November, at 10 o'clock, A. M., for the purpose of electing two United States' Senators; one to fill the vacancy occasioned by the expiration of the term of Hopkins L. Turney, and the other to fill the vacancy that will occur before the meeting of the next General Assembly, in the place of the Hon. John Bell;
Which resolution was received and read."

On November 12, the above Resolution was amended whereby only one Senator was to be elected

". . . to fill the vacancy occasioned by the expiration of the term of Hopkins L. Turney, instead of two as contemplated in said resolution."[30]

Two days later the Legislature met in joint session for the purpose of electing a successor to Senator Turney. Former Governor James C. Jones and William Trousdale were the two leading candidates nominated. Andrew Johnson's name was presented, but was withdrawn before any ballot was cast. The name of Hopkins L. Turney did not appear among the list of nominees. Only one ballot was cast, resulting in the

[29] *Senate Journal,* 1851, 84.
[30] *Ibid.,* 199.

election of "Lean Jimmy" Jones by a vote of 55 to 38.[31] Not only had Senator Turney been left out in the cold by his being utterly ignored by the 1851 General Assembly, but he was later defeated in 1851 in his effort to be elected as Representative from Franklin to the Legislature,[32] his opponent, Jesse Arledge, being victorious by a vote of 1,002 to 544. *Sic transit gloria mundi!*

True enough, the Whigs had not been able to elect either John Bell or any other Whig to the United States Senatorship, in 1845. But they had thrown the bulk of their strength to Turney and thereby procured for themselves a large measure of political revenge upon the "Immortal Thirteen" who had wrecked the hopes and plans of the Whigs in the memorable Senatorial battle of 1841, in which there was no election whatsoever of a United States Senator, leaving Tennessee without any such Representative for two years.

On November 7, 1845, Governor Brown transmitted his official message* to the Legislature.

"GENTLEMEN OF THE SENATE
        AND OF THE HOUSE OF REPRESENTATIVES:

In the 11th section of the 3rd article of the Constitution, it is made the duty of the Executive, from time to time, 'to give to the General Assembly information of the state of the government and recommend to their consideration such measures as he shall judge expedient.' The performance of this duty by my predecessor at the commencement of your present session, seems not, in the former practice of the State, to supersede the necessity of a similar communication from me. Whilst it was the evident policy of those who engrafted this provision into the Constitution, to establish the utmost freedom in the interchange of opinion, it wisely left the Legislature at full liberty finally to adopt or reject the recommendations of the Executive.

This fact greatly diminishes the responsibility of the present communication, made at a period so early in my administration, as to furnish ample apology for any errors which it may be found to contain. It has been often found in the history of all popular governments, that every party succeeding to power is too anxious to signalize its triumph by some bold and novel policy calculated to

---

[31] *Ibid.*, 208–209.
[32] *Nashville True Whig*, August 12, 1851.
* *Senate Journal*, 1845, 198–206.
  House Journal, 1845, 152–160.

attract attention, but not always to advance the permanent interest and welfare of the people. Human government, whether of families or communities, should, however, in my opinion, be in few things more distinguished than in its uniformity and stability. It is not within the competency of government to effect such great and sudden, and at the same time salutary improvements in the condition of the people, as many vainly imagine. These are the products of time and experience, aided by all the lights which the history of our race can shed upon the science of jurisprudence. Guided by these lights in the legislation of our own beloved commonweath, I would especially recommend to you to pass no laws in the rash spirit of adventure, and to overturn no settled policy of the State but on full and mature conviction of its propriety.

One of the subjects of settled policy in the State, I consider to be, the almost entire abolition of the punishment of death. It is one which I have long advocated under the most solemn convictions of its propriety, and should witness, with infinite pain, any attempt to recede from the enlightened humanity of the age. The gradual amelioration of the criminal code of Tennessee, effected as it has been, through slow degrees for many years, has added another proof to those drawn from other countries in favor of the abolition of capital punishment. Instead of weakening it has evidently increased the actual strength of the Government, by drawing around it the rational approbation of society, and by the explosion of those ancient barbarities, which are now justly regarded with the deepest abhorrence. Nor has this relaxation tended in the slightest degree to the increase of crimes. The long continued confinements of the prison house and degradation of becoming the humble vassals of the turnkey, that nightly locks them in their solitary cell, has done more in deterring from the commission of crimes than the fear of death, which men always behold in distant obscurity. In all cases authorized by law and justified by their circumstances, I shall, with the greatest pleasure, commute the punishment from death to imprisonment for life in the penitentiary. Closely connected with this subject is the condition and management of our State prison. Of these, it is probable you are already informed by the report of those having charge of the institution, if not by the personal inspection of one of your committees. I have heard much complaint of the unusual mortality of its unfortunate inmates, within the last year or two. If this be owing to its location or the too crowded condition of the convicts, I know well, with what readiness you will apply any corrective in your power.—The idea is a most revolting one, of holding our State prisoners in confinement under circumstances fatal to their lives. Even as to those whose punishment is inflicted for the highest offences, it would be but the mockery of humanity to have saved them from the speedy execution of the halter, only to subject them to the more tedious but fatal visitation of the fever. If the remedy for this unusual mortality is to be sought for in the enlargement of the present buildings, so as to obviate the effects of a too crowded population, I respectfully submit, whether it would not be better to lay the foundation for the establishment of a new institution of the kind in the Eastern portion of the State. When that was done, the two prisons could occasionally relieve each other of any super-abundance, keeping each with only such a number as would be entirely consistent with the preservation of health, and the profitable employment of their labor. Such an instituition, suitably located in East Tennessee, it is believed, could furnish employment for its convicts in iron, marble, &c., which would not bring its products so much in competition with the ordinary mechanical labor of the country as the present one is understood to do. It is confidently asserted by many, that a small appropriation for the building of the walls and erecting some of the cells, for immediate use, would be all that is necessary. After that, by a transfer of a reasonable portion of the present convicts to that point, with the aid of newly arriving accessions to their number, the whole internal structure of the establishment could be completed without much further expense on the part of the State. All these suggestions, will, however, have to be postponed to the now almost universally received opinion that the labor of all the convicts, and the available means of the present institution, will have to be applied for some years to come to the erection of the State Capitol. To the valuable report lately made to the commissioners appointed to superintend the erection of that building, by the Secretary of State, I beg leave to refer you, for much useful information, which it would have been difficult otherwise to have procured.

The erection of the State Capitol, I am happy to learn, is in fine progress, under the superintendence of an accomplished architect, whose correct taste and sound judgment was singularly displayed in the plan which he furnished. It is on a large and commodious scale, well worthy, not only of the present, but the future population of a great and noble State like Tennessee. Whether it was not on a scale *too* magnificent for the present resources of the State, is now, perhaps, too late to enquire. It has been adopted by the board of commissioners appointed at the last session, approved of by my predecessor, and is now in the course of due execution. Beside the aid which can be derived from the labor and means of the Penitentiary, I recommend such additional appropriations, for the purchase of material, &c., as will keep the work in reasonable progress, without, however, producing any serious embarrassment to the Treasury. It is certainly better to take more time for its completion, than to involve the State in taxation by a too liberal application of its funds.

I most earnestly recommend to your favorable regard the Lunatic Asylum and the institutions established by law for the benefit of the blind, the deaf and the dumb. All these were established for the most benevolent and charitable purposes, and appeal directly to the noblest sympathies of the heart for their advancement and promotion. Man, endowed with reason, stands forth the proudest and noblest work of God's creation; but deprived of that faculty, he sinks down into utter helplessness, the pitiable object of commiseration and charity. To provide for the recovery of many and the safety and comfort of all who are so fatally and deeply afflicted, becomes the first duty of every christian community. Nearly in the same condition are all those, who, though possessing the noblest faculty of our species, are yet deprived of some of those great avenues of instruction which so essentially contribute to adorn and perfect it. I have several times lately enjoyed the pleasure of being present at the exercises of one of these institutions, (for the blind), when I found myself unable to decide whether most to admire the wonderful proficiency of the pupils, the skill and perseverance of the preceptor, or the zeal and enlightened liberality of many distinguished persons of both sexes in advancing the best interests of the establishment.

On a recent occasion I seized on the opportunity to advert to the now almost universal sentiment in the State in favor of the establishment of an enlightened and liberal system of public instruction. Not such as one as will pander to the light and dazzling literature of the age, but such as will impart usefulness and solid value to our industrious and hardy people. There can be no necessity for here remarking on the value and importance of such a system if it can be established. We have one already too partial in its operation, and too deficient in its organization, because too contracted in its means to accomplish the above objects. How shall these means be enlarged so as to meet the sanguine expectations and desires of the public mind? The Executive communication of the present session informs us that 'there are more than two hundred and fifty thousand children in the State between the ages of six, and twenty-one years, whilst there are only one hundred thousand dollars to be appropriated to common schools.' This gives us only forty cents per annum for the education of each child of the State within those ages. If you strike off fifty thousand of this number, for those who would not take its benefits, even if the system were established, it would then leave you only fifty cents per head, per annum. The suggestion has often been made that to supply this palpable deficiency of funds, the distribution of the proceeds of the sales of the public lands of the United States should take place.—Estimating these proceeds at two millions per annum, and that Tennessee would be entitled to one-twentieth part of the same, one-half of which could, under the constitution, be appropriated to education, it would only give us fifty thousand dollars per annum, or twenty-five cents to each child to be educated: making in all, with both funds combined, the sum of seventy-five cents for each one per annum. Now it must be evident that this sum is totally insufficient for the purpose of establishing a general and comprehensive common school system in the State, and I am free to acknowledge that I know of no means of materially increasing it at the present time, but by taxation on the people. Public sentiment, I believe, has never yet been pronounced on this aspect of the case. All the popular demonstrations in favor of common schools have been made on the supposition that the funds requisite for their establishment were to be derived from some other source and not by taxation on themselves. Under this decided conviction I cannot recommend the increase of our present fund by a further resort to taxation, but must leave the subject, with such additional remarks upon it, as you will find in another part of this message. The plans and suggestions there made, if they postponed the further enlargement of our present system at this time, may (although at a period more distant than could be desired), ultimately furnish a fund adequate in a good degree to the wants of the country.

In relation to our system of Internal Improvements, I do not know that it is necessary for me to trouble you with many observations.—The able report of the chairman of the committee appointed to settle with the different turnpike companies is already before you, and contains much which should attract your attention, and to commend the zeal, industry and ability of that committee. Beneficial as the present improvements have been, there are others which claim an equal if not a greater degree of public favor and patronage. To say nothing of the improvement of the navigation of several of our rivers, by means of what are generally termed locks and dams, the extension of the South Carolina and Georgia railroad from Chattanooga to Nashville is every day attracting more and more of public attention. However important I consider the latter project, I can by no means recommend the issue of any further State bonds or securities for its execution. To the granting of liberal and wisely guarded charters to individual companies, I think there can be no good objection. It is highly probable that the stocks would be taken by individuals, and thereby several of our most important streams would be greatly benefitted, and the road under consideration be extended to Nashville, passing through a considerable portion of the State, and bringing with it almost incalculable advantages to the country. A connection between the South and the West can no where be more easily and beneficially effected. The project of connecting them by a road passing through the northern portions of Alabama and Mississippi by no means supercedes the propriety of the proposed road from Chattanooga, or near there, to Nashville. I should regret much to witness, in the slightest degree, a spirit of rivalship between the two projects. Both are important in the highest degree, and both are fairly within the range and compass of execution, by individual capital and enterprize. The distance between Charleston and Nashville is about 560 miles. The greater part of the road is now completed, and it will be but a very short time before the cars will be regularly passing from Chattanooga to the first named city. From Chattanooga to Nashville is about 130 miles, over a surface of country remarkably favorable to the making of such a road. The practicability of its construction at a cost of about two millions of dollars, is now almost universally conceded. A very large portion of the labor of construction could be performed by farmers and other persons on the route, who possess no mechanical skill, thereby greatly diminishing the actual outlay of money in its completion. The increased value of property at the two termini of the road in our State, and for many miles on either side of it, would be very considerable, whilst the increase of agricultural productions, suitable for southern consumption would be almost incalculable.

The occasion will not allow of even the briefest enumeration of the advantages of the proposed road to the people of the Eastern and Middle portions of the State, nor of the considerations rendering it highly probable that it would be a profitable investment of capital to the stockholders. I must content myself, therefore, with an earnest recommendation that a most liberal and judicious charter be granted to individuals for its construction.

In the discharge of the duties imposed upon me, the necessity of recommending such measures as will secure the public credit and at the same time avoid the imposition of heavy burdens on the people, has pressed with peculiar force upon my mind. I am gratified to know that in reference to the importance of making ample and certain provisions to meet all our liabilities as a State, there is but one sentiment amongst our constituents. They do not stop to enquire into the wisdom of the original measures out of which their indebtedness has grown, but knowing the existence of the obligation they expect their respresentatives to devise the most effectual and the least oppressive means in their power to maintain unimpaired the high credit which their State has ever enjoyed. With an anxious desire that their reasonable expectations on this subject may not be disappointed, I will proceed to lay before you the result of my deliberations.

The entire indebtedness of the State may be stated at about three millions of dollars—the interest required annually to be paid upon it is about two hundred thousand dollars. To advise the ways and means of paying this debt as it shall fall due, and its interest as it accrues annually, presents the important problems which we are now called on to solve. Of this indebtedness, the bonds of the State to the amount of $500,000, issued to raise the means of paying for stock to that amount in the Union Bank, constitute a part. As the State still owns this stock, considerably increased by the re-investment of our surplus profits therein, and as the Union Bank has heretofore paid punctually the interest on these bonds, I shall confine my attention to the remainder of the debt which is made up as follows:

Bonds issued for capital of Bank of Tennessee $1,000,000
Internal Improvement Bonds at 5¼ per cent 263,166
Internal Improvement Bonds at 5 per cent 1,579,500
          Total $2,842,666

The amount of indebtedness for which it is incumbent on the Legislature to make provision is $2,842,666, bearing an annual interest of $152,790. This debt will become due at different periods, covering a space of thirty years, before the whole becomes payable. To meet these liabilities as they shall respectively be payable, no adequate provision has as yet been made by law. In my judgment, a proper regard for the credit of the State requires at your hands Legislative action on the subject. It is ascertained that a Sinking Fund of $35,000, annually applied can be so managed as to be amply sufficient to meet our whole indebtedness as it becomes due. This estimate, however, is made upon the supposition that the Bank of Tennessee will continue to be relied on as the means of providing for the payment of the accruing interest on the debt. It becomes necessary therefore, that I should call your attention to the present condition and the probable future operations of this institution, together with such suggestions in reference to its re-organization as will make it more available.

By reference to the late Report of the President and Directors of the Bank of Tennessee, the capital of the institution is found to be $3,200,598. It is made up as follows:

State Bonds for Bank Capital $1,000,000
School Fund 847,389
Surplus Revenue 1,353,209
          Total $3,200,598

From the same report it is ascertained that during the last two years the net profits of the Bank have been annually $168,305. By the laws now in force, the Bank is required to distribute annually to Common Schools and Academies $118,000—this amount added to the interest on the Internal Improvement bonds and the bonds issued to raise capital for the Bank, making, as before stated, $152,790, constitutes the burdens imposed on the institution. By the existing laws the Bank is expected and required to pay out of her annual profits the sum of $270,790, when it is now demonstrated that her annual profits amount to only $168,305. I trust that this important fact will not fail to impress itself forcibly on the minds of the members of the General Assembly. The necessity for prompt and efficient action to avoid the consequences threatened by this state of things cannot be overlooked or disregarded by the patriotic representatives of the people.

In looking for the causes which have led to this state of things, the fact cannot escape observation, that whilst the Bank has made within the last two years, less than six per cent net profits on its capital, the amount required to be distributed to Common Schools and Academies is about fourteen per cent on the amount of the School Fund in the Bank. The Bank has the use of $847,389 belonging to the School Fund, and by its use makes a clear profit of about $50,000—yet by law she is compelled annually to distribute for purposes of education $118,000. If the law were so amended as to require the institution to distribute annually the amount of profits actually made by the use of the School Fund, the annual deficit of the Bank hereafter would be about $34,000 instead of about $100,-000 under existing laws.

I am aware that there is a strong aversion in the minds of some to any interference with the distribution now provided for purposes of education. This aversion is felt more sensibly by none than by myself, and if I saw any possible escape from it without a resort to a heavy increase of the public taxes, I should allow my feelings to control and dissuade me from the recommendation. But it has become a question no longer debatable that we cannot continue to make an annual distribution of $118,000 to schools and academies upon any scheme of managing our financial affairs which has yet been suggested. If it be determined that the Bank shall be put into liquidation by vesting the school fund in State bonds, the amount for annual distribution cannot then exceed $50,000. The question resolves itself into this: if the distribution to schools and academies is continued at the present sum the Bank must unavoidably become crippled, its capital consumed, the school fund, itself in all probability, be greatly diminished, and the credit of the State entirely ruined. If the Bank is wound up, the school fund will be vested in State Bonds bearing 5 per cent interest, and will, therefore, only yield about $50,000 annually. But if the actual profits made by the Bank on the school fund are distributed, so much of the burden will be lifted from that institution that the way will be open for its prosperous continuance. As reluctant as I am to make any recommendation which would seem to conflict with the prospects of an extension of our common school system, I feel coerced under the weight of the consideration to which I have alluded, to invite to these suggestions your careful and favorable consideration.

It will be observed that if the suggestions already made should meet your approbation, the profits of the Bank as at present organized, will fall short by the sum of $35,000 in meeting the liabilities imposed upon it. It becomes important, then, to inquire whether the institution can be so re-organized as to increase its profits to an extent to cover this deficiency. After mature reflection, I am fully satisfied that an increase of profits amounting to $35,000 annually, or more, can be secured by such alterations in the number and locations of the branches, and such a change in its system of doing business as will enable its directors to conduct it upon legitimate banking principles. When the Bank was created, our leading object was to afford relief to an embarrassed people by furnishing loans on accomodation paper. That object was attained, and at present the great purpose in continuing the Bank is to make profits to pay the interest on our debt and avoid a resort to burdensome taxation. Reason and experience combine to prove that the business of banking cannot be conducted safely or profitably upon the principle of dealing mainly in accommodation notes, renewable upon small calls. If the question of creating the Bank were now to be settled, the popular voice would at once reject the proposition; but in the present attitude of the question I am constrained to express the opinion that the wisest course that can be devised would be to give to the directory of the principal Bank the power to take steps for the gradual discontinuance of all such branches as are found to be unprofitable and to transfer their capital to some three or four points where commercial advantages hold out certain prospects of affording better profits. This recommendation, I am aware, may encounter strenuous opposition, but under the solemn obligations imposed upon me, and under the most thorough convictions as to the necessity of the course indicated, I cannot withhold the expression of a strong hope that I shall have your final co-operation in the suggestions. If the course indicated shall be adopted by you, I have every reason to believe that the increased profits of the Bank would enable it in a very short time to increase the annual distribution to the cause of education and give assurance that the common school system could be permanently maintained.

In the suggestions which I have already made, it has been my object to devise the means of securing the payment of the interest on our State debt without any resort to the Treasury. If upon investigation of the operation of the revenue laws, as they now stand, it shall be found that any considerable aid can be derived from that source, it will enable you to increase by so much the annual distribution to schools beyond the actual profits made on the school fund. If it shall be found that by a system of rigid but just economy in the public expenditures, and by the use of any surplus in the Treasury derivable from taxes, you can not only distribute to schools the profits on the school fund, but also the profits on one half of the surplus revenue on deposit with the State, everything demanded at your hands by the strictest principles of justice and equity in behalf of education will have been achieved. But my convictions are so strong that I cannot refrain from again remarking that no resort to the Treasury for aid can weaken the force of the high considerations which demand a re-organization of the Bank according to the principles I have suggested.

When you shall have made ample provision for the payment of the interest on the State debt, your duties will be but imperfectly discharged until you also provide a sinking fund for the liquidation of the debt itself. I have already remarked that a sinking fund of $35,000 can be so managed as to pay off our entire debt by the time it becomes due. I am gratified to learn that through the valuable and efficient labors of the commissioners appointed by the last Legislature to settle with the Internal Improvement Companies, the means have been made available, with a small annual appropriation from the Treasury, to effect this most desirable object. If provision shall be made setting apart the dividends derivable from our road stocks, together with an amount from the Treasury, making a permanent annual fund of $35,000, and it be made the duty of the President of the Bank or some other officer to vest the same annually in State Bonds, and if to this sum be added each year any surplus profits of the Bank, after paying its liabilities, it will be found that when our State debt falls due, it would have been liquidated and our bonds cancelled without any further resort to taxation. Our whole interest in internal improvement companies, amounting to over one million seven hundred thousand dollars, together with the surplus revenue on deposit, amounting to over $1,353,000, can be added to the school fund, making in all a school fund of nearly four millions of dollars. In view of a result so ardently desired by every patriotic citizen, I cannot too strongly urge upon your consideration the adoption of all necessary means for its effectuation.

AARON V. BROWN.

Executive Office, Nov. 7, 1845."

Legislative Message, November 7, 1845

As will be noted in the second paragraph of Governor Brown's Message, a spirit of moderation and conservatism was inculcated upon the Legislature. Time and experience, said Governor Brown, were vital determinants in the enactment of laws, and he especially recommended that "no laws be passed in the rash spirit of adventure." On the whole, the Legislature heeded Governor Brown's advice and, after the bitter partisan battle over the United States Senatorship had been settled, the remainder of the session was relatively calm. Occasionally, there was a sporadic outburst of partisan politics, but the general tenor of the deliberations was without rancor or petty bickering.

An overall summary of the Governor's recommendations may be catalogued under the following seven headings:

1. Opposition to capital punishment.
2. Prison management.
3. Building of State Capitol.
4. Lunatic Asylum.
5. Education.

6. Internal Improvements.

7. State Debt.

In all probability, no Governor of Tennessee ever felt more keenly in regard to capital punishment than did Governor Brown. Fourteen years before he became Governor, he prepared a scholarly and masterful treatise in support of a bill to abolish the death penalty. This able report [33] was by order of the Judiciary Committee of the Legislature printed and distributed.

Governor Brown's attitude, both personal and official, regarding capital punishment was set forth in his message, to-wit:

"In all cases authorized by law and justified by their circumstances, I shall, with the greatest pleasure, commute the punishment from death to imprisonment for life in the penitentiary."

The Legislature, however, enacted no law bearing upon the question of abolition of the death penalty.

With reference to the unwholesome conditions at the penitentiary, as affecting health and even life itself, the most authoritative analysis of actual conditions was that contained in the report [34] of the attending physician, Dr. Felix Robertson. An epidemic of measles involving approximately one hundred convicts left after-effects that resulted in numerous "chronic affections". According to Dr. Robertson, the lack of adequate sanitary facilities and the overcrowded condition of the prison were the two basic factors responsible for much illness and the upward trend in the deathrate of the prisoners. Dr. Robertson's recommendations were not followed at the time, due largely to the fact that a large number of the convicts were to be employed in helping build the State Capitol which was just being started. Governor Brown, while deprecating the conditions existing at the penitentiary, recognized the stern realities confronting the State in regard to the erection of the Capitol building:

"All these suggestions will, however, have to be postponed to the now almost universally received opinion that the labor of all the convicts, and the available means of the present institution, will have to be applied for some years to come to the erection of the State Capitol."

Two minor regulatory measures were enacted that related to the convicts; one measure provided that no corporal punishment was to be

---

[33] *Speeches, Congressional and Political, and Other Writings, of Ex-Governor* Aaron V. Brown (Nashville, 1854), 557–606.

Author's note. There is internal evidence in Governor Brown's thesis of his tremendous research into the question of Capital Punishment. He displayed a penetrating knowledge of the works of Montesquieu, Beccaria, Rush, Livingston, and other noted authorities. His Biblical citations of specific cases are interesting and illuminating.

[34] *Senate Journal*, 1845, 324–325.

inflicted upon any prisoner except under the written authority of the Penitentiary Inspectors; the other item provided that

"It shall be lawful for the agent of the Penitentiary to furnish each convict one pint of coffee each day."[35]

Governor Brown's recommendations regarding the construction of the State Capitol constituted the second communication by a Chief Executive of the State dealing with the topic. On October 10, 1845, just five days before he retired from the gubernatorial chair, Governor James C. Jones gave a brief resumé of the initial steps looking to the erection of a State House.[36] Governor Jones, in his Message to the Legislature, recited the chief provisions of an Act [37] relating to appointment of Capitol Commissioners, employment of an architect, and utilization of convict labor in erecting the building. As will be noted, Governor Brown was "happy to learn" that the work was in progress under the superintendence of "an accomplished architect", though he was a bit apprehensive as to the "magnificence" of the building in view of the State's resources. If necessary, Governor Brown advised the taking of plenty of time rather than involve the State Treasury in any serious embarrassment. In no event, did he desire a resort to taxation for the erection of the structure.

Had Governor Brown, like Hamlet, been blessed with a "prophetic soul", he would have seen that the following decade and even more would be concerned with the construction of the State Capitol. Reports galore from the Capitol Commissioners, the Capitol architect, and legislative committees will be incorporated in this volume in order to give a full and accurate account of the State Capitol and its construction. The first such account [38] is herewith submitted:

"REPORT
of the
COMMISSIONERS, APPOINTED TO SUPERINTEND THE CONSTRUCTION OF THE STATE HOUSE.

To the Hon. Speaker of the House of Representatives:

The Commissioners appointed to superintend the construction of the State House, submit the following report:

That shortly after their appointment they met together and organized themselves into a board by the appointment of the late Gen. W. Carroll, Chairman.—The two subjects which first presented themselves to the atten-

---

[35] *Acts of Tennessee,* 1845, Chapter 129.
[36] See Volume III, *Messages of the Governors of Tennessee, 1835-1845,* 740-742.
[37] *Acts of Tennessee,* 1843, Chapter 205.
[38] *Senate Journal,* 1845, Appendix, 52-64.
House Journal, 1845, Appendix, 52-64.

tion of the board, were the selection of an architect and the procurement of a place for the building.

The Act of the General Assembly creating the board, prescribed the employment first of a suitable architect 'who shall lay down a plan for the Capitol'—and precluded the board from the privilege of advertising for plans and of offering a premium for the one that might have been selected, which would have called forth not only the best architectural talent in the country, but also a great variety of plans.

Under these circumstances, the board determined to move cautiously, at the risk of delaying the commencement of the work, and if possible not to make a mistake in this first and most important step to its future progress —to wit: the selection of the architect.

After various enquiries and much correspondence with persons in the northern and eastern cities—we learned that the services of Wm. Strickland Esq. of Philadelphia could be secured as the architect—a gentleman who had devoted a life, now somewhat advanced, to this profession—that he had commenced it on the Capitol at Washington under La Trobe, its architect; had superintended many of the public buildings in this country, and had personally visited and examined the most remarkable public edifices in Europe.

That while on all occasions he had displayed the utmost good taste in the buildings erected by him, he never sacrificed solidity for show—the useful, for the merely ornamental; and that his estimates of cost were to be implicitly relied on. The board at once determined to employ him at a salary of $2500 per annum, and invited him to repair to Nashville. He arrived here about the 1st of May last, and commenced the preparation of plans. The one suspended in the office of the Secretary of State was finally selected;—For a full and detailed description of which, with estimates of cost of construction made out by the architect, we beg leave to refer you to the papers, herewith submitted, marked A, as part of this report.

In regard to the plan, the Commissioners may be allowed to add a word, particularly as the impression is entertained by some that it is too large in dimensions, and beyond the present or future wants of the State.

The building from out to out, exclusive of the porticos, is 109 by 206 feet 10 inches, and contains under its northern end a cellar so constructed as to light and ventilation, as to afford a most safe and suitable depository for the arms of the State. The cellar under the southern end is intended for fuel.

In the northern end of the basement story, rooms are provided for the Supreme Court of the State and Federal Court, and in the southern end are the office for the Secretary of State, and rooms adjoining for the reception of the books, papers, maps &c., connected with that office, which already require much space and are rapidly accumulating:—as well as offices for the Governor, Comptroller, Treasurer and Superintendent of Public Instruction.

On the main floor are the Halls for the Senate and House of Representatives, a Library room and small rooms for the Speakers, Clerks and Committees of the two Houses and Librarian.

It is the opinion of the commissioners that all the rooms in the house can be put to some useful and appropriate purpose, and that if error has been committed at all in the dimensions of the house, it is on the safe side. For its exterior, in the body of the building, the Ionic order has been adopted—an order which is equally removed from the elaborate and too costly Corinthian on the one hand, and the too plain and common place Doric on the other.

There is nothing about the building to offend the taste of a plain and

Memorandum of an agreement made and entered into between William Strickland of Philadelphia Architect of the first part and "The Commissioners to Superintend the Construction of the State house" — under an act of the General Assembly of the State of Tennessee passed the 30th Janry 1843 — of the other part. —

The party of the first has been employed by the party of the second part as architect in the Construction of the State House for the State of Tennessee to be erected in the City of Nashville. — —

The party of the first part agrees and undertakes to prepare and furnish drawings of the plans, elevations and sections for the said State House, subject to the adoption and approval of the party of the second part and the Executive of the State of Tennessee. He also agrees to make accurate copies of the plans, elevations and sections so approved & adopted to be deposited in the Office of the Secretary of State. — The party of the first part also agrees to superintend and direct all the artizans, Mechanics & laborers that may from time to time be employed by order of or under the directions of the party of the second part in & about the Construction of said building — to select & Judge of all the materials that may be required for said work, and if required by the party of the second part, to make Contracts for materials for the execution of said work, and generally during the progress of the said work to give his personal attention & Supervision both as to the preparation of materials & putting the same together — so that the said building shall progress with all reasonable rapidity & be executed in the most Substantial & workmanlike manner. —

The party of the second part agrees to pay to the party of the first part for the services aforesaid the sum of Twenty five hundred dollars per annum, payable ~~quarterly~~ monthly out of any monies that may be from time to time appropriated by the General assembly of the State for the erection of the State House

William Strickland

Nashville
June 18 1845.

Morn Batt chairm
of Board of Commrss

In Legal Parlance, "There Was a Meeting of Minds."

Requisition for the necessary tools to commence the quarrying and excavation of the scite
and cellar of the building of the State Capitol.

✓ Viz 6 Crow bars 5 feet in length,
Thus,

3 of these   3 f.

3 of these   2 f.
5 ft.

1 inch pointed

✓ 6 picks and Mattocks
✓ 8 Wheel Barrows without sides, extra strong for
     Wheeling stone &c. —
✓ 12 Spades and Shovels.
   6 Gangs of Wheeling plank 2^{in} in thickness and
        from 16 to 18^{in} wide by 18 & 20 ft. in length,
     say, 1400 super^{l} feet
✓ 4 Carts & Horses. Hand
✓ 2 Wood Axes,— 2 Saws, & 2 hammers.
✓ 4 Buckets. & 4 Churn Augurs, pruning wires &c
                              W. Strickland

Nashville 16th May/45.

To/ John M. Bass Esqr

A Modest Request for Undertaking a Mammoth Job.

republican, but enlightened people—nothing too elevated or too grand for the State of Tennessee, whose population ere long will reach two million, and whose resources, agricultural, mineral and manufacturing, place her in the front rank among her sister States.

Shortly after the organization of the board, its attention was drawn to the importance of adding to the Capitol grounds, the two lots on the east side of High Street and between the Capitol and the public square. It was ascertained that a row of houses erected on the east side of High Street of ordinary height, would most materially obstruct the view of the Capitol and grounds, besides subject them to other inconveniences from too close proximity to a crowded population.

A committee was appointed, who concluded a negotiation with the owners for the conditional purchase of those two lots at a cost of $8,500 with interest from date, subject to the ratification of the General Assembly on or before the 1st of January next.

It is proper to say that the gentlemen from whom this purchase was made, Messrs. F. B. Fogg and David Craighead of Nashville and Jesse Blackfan of New York, acted with praiseworthy liberality in this transaction, as it is known that by subdividing these lots, a higher price could have been obtained from individuals. The title papers for this ground are already executed and in the hands of the commissioners to be delivered to the State on the ratification of the contract.

The commissioners cannot too strongly express their individual conviction of the importance of this purchase, and would respectfully suggest that the grounds be examined by the General Assembly, or a committee appointed for the purpose.

It is probably expected of the board to make some suggestions as to the mode of progressing with the work, and the amount of means necessary to carry it on.

A building of that magnitude should progress at such a rate only as will afford the materials the necessary time to settle and consolidate, but beyond this requirement sound economy forbids us to go, for the reason that the work already executed will be injured more or less by exposure to the weather, besides the additional amount of salary paid for superintendence and care of the building if the work is necessarily prolonged. Under these circumstances it is fortunate that the State has under its control a band of operatives, by means of whose labor for the next few years, with moderate appropriations of money, the work may be carried on with all desirable rapidity—we mean the convicts in the Penitentiary. In confirmation of our views more at large on this subject, we beg leave to refer to the very able letter of Dr. J. S. Young, Secretary of State, and ex-officio Inspector of the Penitentiary, herewith submitted, marked B, as part of this report.

While on this subject it is proper to say, that by this gentleman and his co-Inspector, and the agent of the Prison, every facility has been afforded the commissioners for carrying on the work and for making the Prison an important auxiliary in its progress, while our intercourse with these officers has been of the most harmonious and satisfactory kind.

Of the sum of $10,000 appropriated by the last General Assembly, $8,000 have been paid over to the commissioners—of this latter, the sum of $6,000 has been expended, leaving on hand in the Bank of Tennessee to the credit of the commissioners, the sum of $1,400.

The accounts and vouchers for this expenditure are ready for the inspection of the General Assembly, or any committee that may be appointed, as are also the minutes of the proceedings of the board, and all contracts, correspondence and all other papers relating to the subject matter.

Jno. M. Bass, *Ch'm.*
Sam'l. D. Morgan
Morgan W. Brown
J. T. Elliston
Allen A. Hall
James Woods,

\} Commissioners

Nashville, October 10th, 1845.

A

To the Commissioners for the erection of a Building for the State Capitol at Nashville, Tennessee.

Gentlemen:—I have the honor to submit to you a design for a Building for the State Capitol at this City, consisting of plans and a perspective elevation, which are drawn in conformity with the following specification:

In plan it is to have a crypt or cellar and two stories.—The basement 17 feet in height, and the principal story 38 feet, containing a Representative chamber, Senate, Library, committee rooms and Halls of approach. The dimensions of the Hall of Representatives are 95 feet by 70 over the Galleries —of the Senate chamber, 70 by 35 feet. The Library opposite the Senate chamber, is of the same size and separated from it by a Hall 20 ft. in width, which intersects with a great central passage of 32 feet in width, and extends to the chamber of Representatives. From these longitudinal and transverse Halls, you approach the Porticos on each front and flank of the Building, as well as from the floors of the Senate and House.

In the central Hall there are to be two great flights of stairways for the public use, and four smaller stair cases on each side of the Hall, for the use of the members of the Senate and House. These stairs also lead from the basement story to the galleries, to the roof and cupola of the Building, as well as to two rooms of 32 feet square, immediately over the central hall, and a room of 20 feet by 70 ft. over the longitudinal Hall, between the Senate chamber and the Library.

On two of the sides of the Hall of Representatives, there are to be eight committee rooms, connected immediately on the same floor with the Hall. These are 16 feet square, and support the Galleries on the right and left of the body of the House. The Senate and Library have also appropriate retiring rooms on the same floor of the principal story.

In the basement story, the building is intersected by the same sized Halls as above described, running through from the centre of each front, which not only communicate with the stairways and Porticos, but with all the rooms of the story, which may be appropriated to the uses of the Governor, Supreme Court, Secretary of State, Treasurer, Librarian, Comptroller, Clerks, etc. Four of these rooms are 36 by 34 feet, and eight of them 36 by 16 feet. The whole dimensions of the building, including the Porticos, are 232 by 124 feet, surrounded with a flagged Terrace or platform 18 feet in width.

The architecture of the building consists of a Doric basement, four Ionic Porticos, two of eight and two of six columns four feet in diameter, surmounted by a Corinthian Tower in the centre of the roof, the whole height of which is to be 170 feet from the summit of the site. The Porticos are after the order of the Erectheum, and the tower from the choragic monument of Lysicrates at Athens.

The whole structure to be composed of the best cut and chisseled compact Limestone, from the neighborhood of Nashville and Marble from East Tennessee. The various chambers, halls and porticos to be arched throughout. The columns of the Hall of Representatives and Senate Chamber to be variegated marble, as well as all the decorative parts of the interior of the building.—The rafters of the roof to be constructed of cast and wrought Iron and covered with sheet copper. The window frames and sash of cast Iron, and the floors of all the Halls, Lobbies and Porticos to be flagged with stone or otherwise, so as to be thoroughly fire proof in all of its various compartments.

Furnaces to be constructed in the crypt to generate and diffuse warm air in the Halls and Chambers, as well as fire places in all the rooms, for the purpose of burning wood or coal and ventilating the building.

The whole estimate of the cost of the building as above described, and according to the prices of materials and labor in Nashville, is calculated at $340,000 if done by contract, but which amount may be reduced from $85,000 to $100,000 by the employment of Prison labor, leaving from $240,000 to $260,000, as the entire cost of the building, with the addition of 7½ per cent for contingent expenses—Hoisting Machinery, Tools, etc.

The cellar story or crypt, which is 10 feet in height, is to be appropriated to the purposes of an armory, and as a depository for fuel. The armory to be approached from an arched way, some distance from the northwest angle of the building.

In conclusion I beg leave to refer you to the plans and drawings which have been made, and which accompany this specification, for the better understanding of the design. Respectfully submitted by

Your obedient servant,
WILLIAM STRICKLAND, <i>Arch't.</i></div>

Nashville, May 20th, 1845.

B

Nashville, September 10th, 1845.

To Doct. John S. Young, Secretary of State.

DEAR SIR:—Will you be kind enough to answer the two following interrogatories at your earliest convenience.

1st. From your knowledge of the State Prison, (having, as we know devoted much attention to its operations for the last two years as one of its Inspectors) do you not think that the whole labor of it can be profitably devoted to the work of constructing the State Capitol?

2nd. Are you not of opinion that the plan adopted by the last General Assembly, of applying the surplus labor only, to that object, is inefficient, and incapable of producing decided results?

Very respectfully,
Your obedient servants,
Signed
JOHN M. BASS.
S. D. MORGAN.
JOSEPH T. ELLISTON.
Committee.

Nashville, September 15th, 1845.
To Jno. M. Bass, S. D. Morgan, and J. T. Elliston, Esqrs.:

GENTLEMEN:—I have received your note dated the 10th inst. propounding to the two following interrogatories:

1st. From your knowledge of the State Prison as an Inspector, do you not think that the whole labor of the Prison could be profitably directed to the work of constructing the Capitol?

2d. Are you not of the opinion that the plan adopted by the last General Assembly, that of applying the surplus labor only, is inefficient and incapable of producing decided results?

To both of your interrogatories, I answer in the affirmative; and shall without further preliminary remarks, endeavor to elucidate the position I have assumed, by arguments founded upon facts, which my official connection with the Prison has placed within my reach; and in order to be more clearly understood, I will reduce the first subject of inquiry presented by you, to a detailed form, by proposing the following plan of operations, viz:

That from and after the 1st day of Jan. or Feb. next, all the existing operations in the Prison be suspended, and that from and after that time, the whole labor of it be directed to the work of preparing materials for the Capitol; and that from and after the same period, the victualing and clothing of convicts, together with the salaries of the officers, be assumed and paid directly out of the Treasury of the State, upon quarterly estimates to be furnished to the Comptroller by the Agent, and to be accounted for by him, in quarterly settlements with the Comptroller, which settlements shall exhibit, by receipts and vouchers, the manner in which each dollar has been disbursed.

In demonstrating what I conceive to be, the practicability of the plan proposed, I will rest nothing on an assumed state of facts, which require for their support theoretical deductions, the correctness of which may be doubted or denied; but will base all my calculations upon *data* which cannot be controverted, and for which I may safely claim as much accuracy, as if they were intended to be presented under the sanction and responsibility of an official name.

The whole number of convicts at present in the Prison is 190.—In my estimates I shall assume 180 as the average number. Of this number, 45, or 25 per cent may be set down as infirm, diseased, and superannuated, and therefore unfit for active labor, which would leave 135 as the number of picked and reliable men.

The books and vouchers of the Prison show, that nine dollars is the amount required to clothe a convict for one year, and eighteen dollars and twenty-five cents, the amount required to victual a convict for the same time.

The following exhibits the annual expenses of the Prison.

Clothing 180 convicts at $9 each......................	$ 1,620
Victualling convicts at 18 25 cts......................	3,285
Salary of Physician and medicines...................	700
Fuel and lights,..	1,500
Officer's and guards' salaries,........................	5,872
Horses and hire of Drayman,........................	500
Contingent expenses, ...	300
Total,	$13,777

The experience of the last four years proves that the above sum will cover the expenses of the Prison. Should the change I have contemplated, be made, I feel assured that it could be reduced to $13,000, which would make the amount to be placed by the Comptroller, at the disposal of the Agent, at the commencement of each quarter, $3,250—nearly all of which would be reimbursed to the Treasury for the first three years, as I shall be able to show in the sequel.

Taking former years as the guide in making estimates the probable value of manufactured articles and materials, which will be on hand on the first day of October next will be $24,000, exclusive of $3,550 in tools and shop furniture. I have not the means at hand, of ascertaining with entire accuracy, the probable amount of money and uncollected debts on solvent persons, which will be on hand at the same period; but it is within the range of safe calculation to estimate them at an amount, which added to the $24,000, in manufactured articles and materials, would make the *assets* of the Prison $40,000, a sum nearly sufficient, as you will perceive, to reimburse to the Treasury, the amount annually required to meet the ordinary expenses of the Prison for the next three years, provided there is no considerable increase in the number of convicts.

The collection of the debts, and the sale of the manufactured articles &c., could be confided to the clerk of the Prison, under the direction and supervision of the Agent, and the funds arising from such collections and sales, could be paid into the Treasury by said clerk, at the end of each month or quarter; and when articles were exchanged for provisions and clothing for the convicts, the accounts thus created, could be adjusted by proper credits in the quarterly settlements between the Agent and Comptroller.

From the foregoing view of the statistics of the Prison, in adopting the plan proposed the State would have nothing to risk, and indeed, so far from the danger of loss, it would in my view be a measure of economy, from which compensating advantages might be expected.

I have stated 135 as the number of picked and reliable men, to be employed in the work of cutting stone for the Capitol; 10 of the number are good stone cutters, and more than 20, have had some experience in the business. The larger proportion of the work to be performed, is plain stone work, requiring in its execution, a small amount of skill. I am assured by the head of the stone department in the Prison, that fresh hands set at the business, will in the course of six months, become average workmen, in the execution of plain work.

There may be some difference of opinion as to the daily or annual value of the labor of the 135 men. I will fix the annual aggregate value of their labor at $33,000, being a shade under 75 cents per day each, for the 125 men who are not practised in the business of cutting stone, and $1.25 each per day for the 10 good workmen. Considering the Building Commissioners in the light of contractors or undertakers, and having the control of the 135 operatives mentioned, after paying for their labor the amount specified above, the question arises, 'how much profit would they make on the labor of each hand?' Under the best advice, I set down the aggregate profit at $10,000 per year, being 24 cents per day for the labor of each man. Add $10,000 to $33,000, gives $43,000 as the aggregate annual amount of labor the State would derive from the Institution, out of which would have to be paid $13,000 for expenses, which would leave the nett profits $30,000 per annum in labor upon an important public work. If these calculations are vague and indefinite, there is certainly no rule for estimating the value of labor.

It may be asked: 'If the Prison is capable of producing in labor upon the Capitol $30,000 annually, why have not large profits accrued from present pursuits?' The answer is plain, and the reason most obvious. If you direct the whole of its labor to preparing material for the Capitol, you create at once an active demand for its labor. The State becomes the purchaser of its products at adequate prices, and it would receive each day remunerating benefits and possess all the attributes of a successful enterprize, based upon a safe and profitable investment of capital.

Its present system of operations comprises a variety of pursuits, trades and occupations. Could you secure to it in the exercise of each of them, the state of things alluded to above; that is create for it an active market, which would insure daily cash sales of its products, the consequence would be, that a large per cent upon its capital would be realized, and it would become a highly fruitful source of revenue to the State. But let us glance at the real state of things as they have existed, and do exist, at present. Notwithstanding, the Prison has been ably, honestly, and intelligently managed by the gentlemen who have been charged with the immediate administration of its affairs, and all its arrangements judiciously planned and ordered, and its pursuits and avocations conducted with spirit, energy and skill, it has made small profits. The reason of this is found in the fact, that the demand for the articles of its manufacture, has not corresponded with its ability to produce them, which has resulted in a heavy loss of interest upon its capital; added to which has been a loss of interest, produced by vending its articles upon credit. It has no mart at which to vend its products except within its walls; its remoteness from the banks of the Cumberland River throws it out of line of active commercial intercourse, which has forced it to engage in the most of the smaller trades, and to depend chiefly upon neighborhood patronage for support in competition with the mechanics in its vicinity, who make it the cause of much complaint, and its officers the subjects of undeserved censure. They view it as privileged labor, commanding and exercising capital and skill against skill alone, and therefore, an unfair competitor. Being considered a grievance by so respectable a portion of our fellow-citizens, it comports with the spirit of wise legislation to redress it; provided that in doing so, no principle or right is violated and no legal obligation contravened.

That which has operated most against the Prison is the selection of its present location. Had it been placed upon the banks of the Cumberland River, contiguous to a wharf, it would have proved to be an enterprise, possessing in comparison, fourfold energies, and one, upon which a far different field for operation would have been opened. With the facility to use steam power to an unlimited extent, it could have engaged in pursuits fully capable of eliciting and turning to account, its ample powers and resources. Its contact with the navigation and commerce of the River, would have caused its products to have found their way to the Southern market; its facilities would have increased, whilst its expenses would have diminished. Situated as it is at present, it has to derive a large portion of its fuel and materials from the river, upon which it has to pay transportation, and is forced to incur the additional expense of delivering its manufactured articles at the city of Nashville. There is another consideration deserving great weight, to which I would barely advert, viz: that the Prison grounds do not afford the means for the adoption of successful measures for preserving the health of large bodies of men. There is not, and there can never be, a *sewer* constructed, through which the accumulating offensive matter of the Prison, can make its escape. All attempts at its construction would create a nuisance, against which legal remedies would be successfully opposed. During the summer months, there is an inadequate supply of water for the purposes of cleanliness; moreover, the water to be used for drink at that season, is highly impregnated with lime, so much so, as to be capable of disturbing the healthful operations of the system, and producing disease. With the increase of population, we may expect an increase of crime, and can look forward to the day, not far distant, when the number of convicts will greatly exceed the present number. When that day arrives, I now venture the *prediction*, and claim for it almost *prophetic* certainty, that unless the evil is anticipated an amount of mortality will occur, from the causes I have mentioned above, which will have to be arrested by the benevolent interposition of the legislative arm. If the change I have proposed, be made, it will give sufficient time to wind up the concerns of the Prison, preparatory to *ulterior action* in regard to it, which would best consist in limiting the number of convicts in the Prison, to a small number, and sending the residue to a Branch to be established in East Tennessee or the Western District. If to East Tennessee, it would afford the means of developing the wealth she possesses in her marble quarries; if to the Western District, the advantages of the Southern trade would ensure success to the measure.

Some may object to directing the whole labor of the Prison to a single pursuit, on the ground that moral influences would be lost, in not teaching convicts different trades. To such I would reply, that the work of preparing materials for the Capitol, would be temporary; those already in the Prison would not lose their trades, whilst those who would enter the Prison during the progress of the work, could not learn a better trade than that of stone cutting.

I am entirely sceptical on the subject of reforming convicts by teaching them mechanical trades—little or no good results from it. When the *convict* leaves the Prison, he lays down his *cap*, and with it his *trade*. He looks back upon both as the *badges* of his disgrace, and the companions of his imprisonment; he aims to something else which he considers better than his trade, or returns to the re-commission of crime. The trade in most instances, as I believe, serves to better quality the *villian*, without reforming the *man*. Those who would attempt the moral reformation of the *felon* must employ other means. They must bear in mind, that three fourths of those who are stained with crime can neither read nor write. The mind must be cultivated in order to produce those genial influences, which are calculated to remove vicious inclinations and base propensities, and give place to proper sensibilities and corrected feelings, from which altered intentions and virtuous actions must spring.

Whilst the convict is suffering punishment for his crime, it does just as well to employ him at one thing as another. That which best subserves the interest of the State, whose laws he has violated, is, in my estimation, the most proper.

In recurring to the plan I have proposed, there is one important consideration, which highly commends it, that it would give to the work of building the Capitol, a more systematic, economical and better organized plan of operations, than could be derived from any other source. The work shops of the Prison would afford ample accommodation for the whole force, without the necessity of extending the walls; the work would move steadily on; there would be no clashing interests and discordant views to reconcile; the architect would only have to hand to the agent his drafts, to be certain that they would be faithfully executed; concert of action would be established between the Architect and the Agent, and they would become valuable co-adjutors in promoting the work.

There is another consideration of paramount importance. It is this, that in carrying out the details of the plan, no change in the present police regulations of the Prison would be necessary. The convicts could be worked within the walls of the Prison, just as they have been heretofore, which is the only safe and proper method. I am aware that the opinion is entertained by some, that it would be safe to carry the convicts in large bodies, beyond the limits of the Prison, to be worked in open fields. Some knowledge of the temper and dispositions of the convicts in the Prison, has brought my mind to a far different conclusion. It would, in my estimation, be attended with great difficulty, and if continued any length of time, would most probably lead to disagreeable consequences. It would render necessary a system of discipline which would add rigor to the punishment of the convicts, for which no adequate reason or justifying cause could be urged; and being a measure wholly extrajudicial in its character, it could not be expected that the Legislature would legalize it, or that public opinion would approve it. There is generally a very small number of convicts that can be worked without the walls of the Prison, but with the *mass*, in order to secure subordination, you require the potency of the stone wall, and the bolts and bars of the cell at hand. These are found to be sufficient within the walls of the prison. To accomplish the same ends beyond their limits, the right to use chains and fire arms would have to be tolerated; two dangerous instruments, except when confided to cautious and responsible hands; and I think it would comport best with sound views of humanity, and a judicious dispensation of authority, not to adopt a system which could be so easily abused. If the convict can be best controlled within the walls of the Prison, it is certainly the place where his labor can be rendered the most available.

The labor required at and around the building, must be derived from some other source. It might be obtained in a very economical manner, by authorizing the purchase of fifteen or twenty likely, active, and intelligent negro men, to be quartered on the public grounds, under the general direction of the Building Commissioners, and the immediate control of some individual selected by them. With them might be purchased horses, carts, and other necessary appliances. During five years, they would be worth to the State more than fifty per cent upon their cost, and could, at the end of that time, be passed into the hands of kind masters, at, or near, rates corresponding with their original cost. I believe it is admitted that in the South it does not succeed well to mix white and black labor for menial purposes, and that of the two, the black is the best.

In closing the first subject of enquiry presented by you, I will urge the very strongest argument in favor of the adoption of the plan—viz: that it would prevent the necessity of large appropriations from the Treasury, to carry on the work.

In answering the second subject of enquiry contained in your note, I will endeavor to show that the plan adopted by the last session of the General Assembly, that of applying the surplus labor only, is not only inefficient, but full of difficulty and embarrassment to those charged with its execution. To decide what the surplus labor of the Prison *is*, is a problem wholly incapable of solution, and all attempts at its solution are calculated to produce differences of opinion, and discordant views unfavorable to the advancement of the public service. If the same plan is continued by the next session of the General Assembly, the Prison will be found to be but a feeble auxiliary in the work of constructing the Capitol; whilst under the arrangement of things I have proposed, it would become an active, energetic and efficient agent, because it would possess the organization, power, physical force and skill, capable of producing results proportioned to the magnitude of the enterprize in which it would be embarked.

The idea of the Prison becoming a charge on the Treasury, has been the subject of peculiar dread with some persons. I am at a loss to understand the philosophy, or to perceive the force of the reasoning, upon which this fear is founded. In my humble judgment, the Institution should never have separated from the Treasury. So far from it, its accounts from the first, should have been settled and adjusted at the desk of the Comptroller. It should have been considered as a means of profit or loss to the State in a revenue point of view. If it made profit, that profit would have passed as revenue into the Treasury—if it failed to meet its current expenses, the Treasury would of course be bound to make up the deficit. The further you remove the Institution from the Treasury, in the same degree you place it beyond the reach of strict accountability, and impose upon the officer at its head unnecessary responsibility, and subject him to imputations for mal-management, without affording him the means of vindicating himself, except through legislative committees which will not take the time, or have not the inclination to examine a mass of books and papers as voluminous as those of an extensive mercantile establishment.

If the Prison were brought strictly within the fiscal operations of the State, and its accounts settled and adjusted at short periods, with the proper revenue officer, the state of its finances could, at all times, be well understood, and be by that officer communicated to the General Assembly, in a form as tangible and correct, as the accurate calculation of figures could make them.

If the change I have contemplated be adopted, the affairs of the Institution would be placed precisely upon that basis, one of certainty and unerring calculation. The Prison would cease to be that sort of *riddle* it is viewed to be by many who end all their calculations as to its resources, in speculations as to whether or not, it may become a charge upon the Treasury. *Apply,* (says the highest authority) the surplus labor of the Prison to the work of constructing the Capitol, but be cautious that you do not thereby make it a charge upon the Treasury. I am unable to discover any reason or argument to support a line of policy so undefined. It certainly cannot lead to determinate action, and its results must be uncertain. If the Prison can be made an active agent in carrying on an important public work, why not make it so? Instead of being considered a source of danger to the Treasury, it would become a safeguard.

The work of preparing material for the Capitol would probably occupy two or three years. As the time would draw to a close, if it were desired, the Prison could, by an easy movement, fall back upon its former pursuits; or what would be better, the changes I have suggested in regard to it, could be made greatly to its advantage, and without the danger of loss.

I have witnessed with pleasure your personal efforts aided by those of the able and intelligent Architect selected by your Board, in carrying forward the work of building the State Capitol, and desiring for you, success ¨n the work so auspiciously commenced.

ᴵ am, very sincerely and respectfully
Your friend and servant,

JNO. S. YOUNG
Secretary of State.

P. S. I have not alluded to the fact, that amongst the one hundred and thirty-five men mentioned, there are a number of good blacksmiths, who could keep in order the tools, and do a great deal of the work in iron, which will be required on the Capitol. This would give their labor an increased value over the estimate I have fixed it at. I will further add, that if the change I have suggested be made in the operations of the Prison, the materials on hand will consist chiefly of the timber used in manufacturing articles of wood, and the largest amount, that used for wagons, which could be sold at a profit, or it might be kept on hand, until the prison would resume operations, after it had performed the work for the Capitol, as it would improve by keeping; and if during the progress of the work on the Capitol, there should be found to be any surplus labor, it could be employed in the manufacture of wagons, that being the most profitable pursuit. By the forty-five infirm men, could be performed all the menial duties of the Prison, cooking, washing, and the duties of what are termed *shop tenders;* and in addition, they could keep going the carding of wool. They would be found to be worth what it would take to clothe and feed them.

J. S. Y."

In the above first report of the Capitol Commissioners there was a succinct but relatively detailed sketch of just what was being projected by the Commissioners regarding the Capitol Building itself. Only one faint tone of discontent was heard—that the law prohibited the Commissioners from seeking competition among architects for a suitable plan for the Capitol Building. Fortunately, that prohibition was more than compensated for in wise selection of perhaps the most famed architect of those times, William Strickland. The architect's brief but cameo-like sketch [39] of the proposed building is self-explanatory. To a nine-line letter of inquiry from the Capitol Commissioners, the Secretary of State indulged himself in the luxury of submitting a document of eight printed pages. Dr. Young must be credited, however, for the most sensible attitude exhibited by any of the public officials—that the cost of building the Capitol should have been a direct charge upon the State Treasury which would have been good business procedure. Misunderstandings, bickerings, and legislative repercussions resulted later on account of rather loose and uncoordinated machinery under which all concerned were compelled to function. A sample of the unsound business basis upon which the Commissioners at first were forced to operate was specified in the original act [40] providing for the construction

---

[39] Author's note. There has been a great deal written, *pro* and *con*, concerning the cupola or "tower" on the Capitol Building, the question being as to whether or not Strickland included in his original drawings (which unfortunately have been lost) the cupola or whether it was added at the order of the Capitol Commission. There can be no question but that Strickland in his first report referred to the "cupola." Moreover, there is no question but that Strickland was "tower-minded," for confirmation of which see *William Strickland,* by Agnes Addison Gilchrist, (Philadelphia, 1950) wherein is shown a picture of "the Tower of Independence Hall, plate 22, in Philadelphia," designed by Strickland in 1828.

[40] *Acts of Tennessee,* 1843, Chapter 205.

of the Capitol Building, namely, that the appropriated sum of ten thousand dollars must come from collecting the debts due the penitentiary and from the sale of surplus products manufactured by the convicts therein! A more sensible approach to providing funds for the project was exhibited by the 1845 Legislature which directed that the appropriation of sixteen thousand dollars was to come direct from the State Treasury.[41]

After a brief homily upon the misfortunes of those afflicted with mental illness, Governor Brown admonished the Legislature to give favorable consideration to the institution erected for their benefit. The status of facilities for the mentally afflicted was presented in a Report of the Joint Committee on the Lunatic Asylum. An epitome of previous legislation in behalf of these unfortunates was set forth and appropriate recommendations were outlined for improvements:[42]

"REPORT.

The Joint Committee on the Lunatic Asylum, to whom were referred sundry bills and resolutions touching the affairs and management of said Institution, have had the same under consideration and have directed us to make the following report:

By an Act passed on the 19th October, 1832, for the benefit of that unfortunate portion of our fellow citizens who are afflicted with insanity, six individuals of the city of Nashville, were appointed Commissioners to purchase a site upon which to erect an Asylum sufficient for the care and safe keeping of at least two hundred persons, and the sum of *ten thousand dollars* was appropriated for that purpose.

Your committee have not been able to procure the report of those commissioners, but a site was obtained, and it will be seen by reference to the act of the 20th of January, 1838, that commissioners were appointed to superintend the construction of the building and that *fifteen thousand dollars* were appropriated for the work subject to their control and management.

On the 6th of January, 1840, an act was passed authorizing the Governor to appoint seven suitable persons to act as Trustees of the Asylum for the period of two years, from and after the date of this Act, who were also authorized to elect a Physician to the Institution, who was to have the general superintendence of all matters relating to the Asylum, and who was required to visit the inmates at least twice in every week.

For his services the Physician received by the provisions of this act *five hundred dollars annually,* commencing from the 1st of March 1840, and continuing until otherwise provided by law. The Trustees were also authorized and required to appoint a Keeper and Matron of the Hospital who were to reside in the buildings, and give their attention to all such orders and regulations touching the Hospital and its inmates as the Trustees might direct and command; and for their services, the Keeper was to receive a salary of *five hundred dollars,* and the Matron a salary of *four hundred dollars* per annum. For the improvement of the Asylum and the grounds belonging

---

[41] *Ibid.*, 1845, Chapter 49.
[42] *House Journal*, 1845, Appendix, 285–294.

thereto, for the furnishing of the same, and for the benefit and accommodation of the inmates, the sum of *four thousand five hundred dollars* was also appropriated by this act.

On the 15th January, 1842, the Legislature appropriated *two thousand nine hundred and forty-six dollars and twenty-eight cents*, to discharge outstanding liabilities, and declare that all debts thereafter contracted by the Trustees over and above the sum appropriated by law, should be on their own personal responsibility.

The Legislature appropriated also, by the act of the 5th of February, 1842, *six thousand dollars* to be expended by the Trustees according to the provisions of the laws then existing, for the payment of the salaries of the officers of the Asylum, maintaining lunatic paupers, and furnishing the building, &c., &c.

It is also provided that the Board of Trustees, should, at the next and every subsequent time of its appointment, be so organized that it should comprise *three Physicians* known to the Governor of the State to be men of good report in their profession.

This arrangement continued in operation until the 26th of January, 1844, when the Legislature altered and amended the previous regulations of the Institution, in the following manner:—For the support and benefit of the Asylum and its inmates, the Legislature appropriated *six thousand dollars* annually, and made it the duty of the Legislature, by a joint vote of both Houses, to elect the Physician, for two years, whose wife should be Matron, who, together, should reside in the Asylum, and perform all the duties of superintendent and Matron, in addition to those of Physician; and for their services they should receive the sum of *fourteen hundred dollars* annually.

The Legislature also authorized the Trustees to make a special contract with the Physician, or any other person to feed, clothe, and render every necessary attention to not less than fifty pauper patients, for a sum less, or equal to, but not to exceed the amount specified for the annual support of the Institution. The Physician was also authorized, as superintendent, under the direction of the board of Trustees, to employ assistants, hire servants, and purchase all such articles as might be required.

The same act also provided, that no boarding patient should be received into the Institution without paying six months board in advance, and giving bond and security for the payment of board every six months in advance after the first six, or for any shorter period said patient may remain after the first six months; and that each Senatorial district in the State should be entitled to send two pauper patients to the Asylum.

The Committee have reported all the appropriations which they have been able to collect from 1832, to 1844, inclusive; and such facts touching the management of the Institution as they deem important. They are not apprised of any other appropriations, though it is suggested by two members of the Committee that a portion of the taxes of Davidson county were appropriated to the Institution by some one of the Legislatures intermediate to those of 1832 and 1837. Your committee, however, have not been able to find the act.

Having given a condensed account of the several appropriations—the manner in which they were to be applied, together with an epitome of the organization of the Asylum, the committee will now proceed to report, as specifically as they are able, upon the interrogations. And in order that the whole subject may be presented to the Legislature, they have prepared a table, and annexed it to this report, in which will be seen at a glance the results of their investigation upon most of the subjects submitted to them.

The construction of the table has cost us much labor owing to the difficulty in obtaining the data, and the confused manner in which the facts have been recorded. The committee believe, however that the table is correct, or at any rate as nearly so as it can be made under the circumstances. It will be seen by referring to this table that the cost of keeping paupers in the Asylum is equal to about $400 for each patient. In this calculation the term of *two years* is included, and consequently the cost *per annum* is just half that sum for each patient, or equal to about $200, supposing the average number of pauper patients for the last two years to be 24, which is the number according to the best estimate the committee have been able to make.

The entire sum appropriated (exclusive of the taxes of Davidson county,) by the State for the Asylum, is only $56,046.28. This sum includes all the appropriations, of every description running through a period of eight years, and will be found upon a comparison with the appropriations made by other states to similar institutions, to be very small.

It seems from the act of 1832, in which the provision is first made for the construction of the Asylum, that a building was contemplated which would be sufficiently large to accommodate two hundred patients. And indeed when we take into consideration the number of lunatics in the State, it appears that the Legislature ought to provide for the accommodation of at least 200. But when we take, also, into consideration the condition of the State Treasury, and the State liabilities, and that the keeping of 100 paupers would cost, according to the present rates of keeping them, $20,000 annually, the committee cannot recommend an enlargement of the building at this time. That the building ought to be enlarged is apparent to all who have examined it, and understand the wants and necessities of lunatics; for an absolute necessity exists for such alterations in the building, and additions thereto, as will admit of a natural and scientific *classification* of patients. The committee are thoroughly convinced of the importance of classing lunatics, and of having an apartment for each class; for it will often be found that by throwing the insane together indiscriminately that many cases will be aggravated, and some of them rendered incurable. The committee would therefore recommend that the board of Trustees for the ensuing two years take this subject, with such other improvements as they may deem advisable, into careful consideration, and report their investigations, including the cost of the contemplated improvements to the Legislature at its next regular session.

The great object intended to be accomplished by erecting and sustaining Lunatic Asylums, is not only to divest society, the friends and relations of the mad-man of the trouble, expense and terror which he may be to them, but to restore *his* reason, and prepare him for the enjoyment of his friends, and enable him to discharge the ordinary duties of life. If the latter *cannot* be effected, *any* expenditure of money which this, or any other State may have made, or shall make for the erection of Asylums for the insane, is useless, save only so far as may be necessary to provide for their annual wants and protect the community against their depredations.

It cannot be necessary that the committee should go into an argument to demonstrate to this General Assembly that *insanity*, though the most terrible disease to which the human family are liable, *is curable*, when treated by the skilful and scientific physician; for instances have fallen under your own observation to prove this assertion. But they do assert that recent investigations on insanity, its causes and pathology, together with the successful treatment of the disease in Europe and America, have proved conclusively not only that insanity is curable, but that a much larger proportion

	No. of paupers	No. of pay patients	Restored & Discharged	No. of deaths	No. of escapes	Appropriation State	Rec'd from pay patients	Expenditures of Asylum
Appropriations of 1832 and 1833.						$25,000.00		$25,000.00
No. of patients received from 1st of March, 1840, to 22d October 1841........33	12	21	15	2	3	$7,300.00	$1,739.00	$5,493.26
No. of patients received from 22d of Oct. 1841, to 1st Oct. 1843 45	13	30	15	3	5	$8,946.28	$2,183.72	$8,520.83
No. of patients received from 1st of Oct. 1843, to 1st of Oct. 1845 57	23	33	24	7	2	$14,800.00	$4,507.43	$15,907.19
Total	48	84	54	12	10	$56,046.28	$8,430.15	$54,921.26

NOTE.—In the second term there were two patients received, the history of which the Committee are not informed as to their being paupers or pay patients; and one in the third term. There were also received, nine in the second term and two in the third, of which the Committee have no information as to their history, restoration, discharge or death.

of the cases can be cured than are generally supposed. In England, and particularly in France, great discoveries have lately been made on this subject. And instead of amusing the insane by charms and incantations—frightening them by ghostly apparitions—punishing them by starvation and flagellations, or burning them for witchcraft, they are treated upon principles of sound medical philosophy, and thousands of them have been restored, and become useful in life. The fact has been clearly demonstrated that lunatics are susceptible of moral discipline, that they are capable of being brought under the influences of motives similar to those which govern the actions of other persons. We have discovered that the insane, like the sane, have distinct characters, they have their own peculiar trains of thought, peculiar habits, and pursuits. And hence it has become as important to study the philosophy of the human mind, its eccentricities and peculiarities, as it is to study the anatomy and physiology of the human body, its organs and their diseases, in order to qualify an individual to treat insanity successfully.

The committee will not undertake to report to this legislature, an article upon the *medical* treatment of the insane, for such a report would be only proper for medical men and physicians. But the committee feel that they will not have discharged the responsible duty imposed upon them by the Legislature, and the obligations which they owe to the insane, unless they speak freely on the subject and with an earnestness commensurate with its importance.

Our Asylum is but yet in its infancy. Like some other benevolent institutions in Tennessee, it has scarcely excited the attention of our people. It is true that *much* good has not resulted from it as yet, but it is also true that it has not had the means of accomplishing much. Some good, however, has resulted, and the committee cherish the fond hope that when the attention of the people is directed to it, and when they become alive to the responsibility which rests upon them, that this unfortunate and miserable class of our fellow-citizens will receive from them a kind and liberal support. Justice, humanity and every principle of our moral nature calls upon us to provide for them, and no virtuous and intelligent community can, or will be satisfied until the provision is made.

In all public institutions it is the duty of those to whom the public liberality is entrusted, to see that it is faithfully and advantageously applied. And it is the duty of those who make appropriations to specify as nearly as they can, the objects for which the appropriations are made. If this is not done, it matters not how judiciously the guardians of the fund may have applied it, there will often be murmurings and suspicions; the propriety of this expenditure, or the necessity of that will be themes of conversation with many who find it much more agreeable to scrutinize the liberality of others, than to be liberal themselves. Your committee would therefore recommend that the appropriations which may be made by this Legislature to the Asylum for the next two years, and indeed, by all subsequent Legislatures, shall be as specific in their nature as possible; and that a correct and faithful account of the expenditures, under such appropriation, be kept by the particular officer who may be entrusted with this charge.

If the appropriation which may be made for any specific purpose, or purposes, shall prove to be inadequate, future legislation can increase it; and if on the contrary it should prove to be larger than was necessary, the Legislature can reduce it. Great exactness ought to be observed, and the stewart ought to be required to keep a day-book in which he should set down the precise sum expended daily, and the number of pauper and pay patients in the Asylum every day through the year. It is an easy matter, and might be of some value to him as a testimony of his faithfulness.

In order to show the propriety of the course recommended by the committee as to keeping a correct account of the expenditures under each appropriation, it is only necessary to recur to the third section of the Act passed 26th January, 1844, in which it will be seen that it was contemplated by the Legislature, the sum of $6,000 per annum would be sufficient to support *fifty pauper patients*, and that if a contract should be made with any individual to feed, clothe, &c., not less than fifty paupers, said contract should not be for a larger amount than $6,000 per annum; and if the number of paupers at any time should fall below *fifty*, then a *pro rata* deduction should be made from the sum total contracted to be paid. That is to say, if there were only twenty-five paupers, a deduction of one half of the amount should be made; and consequently the Legislature thought that $120 would feed and clothe a pauper for twelve months, and pay all his expenses. It appears, however, from information furnished the committee by the board of Trustees that the amount appropriated by the State, was not more than sufficient to support 29 paupers, after deducting the sum applied to improvements.

The most important subject, however which demands the attention of the Legislature is the selection of the principal officers of the Institution and the manner of selecting them.

At the last session of the Legislature the law requiring the Trustees to elect the Physician was repealed, and this duty was devolved upon a joint vote of the two Houses of the General Assembly. The question arises, is this a salutary change in the law? The committee have no hesitation in saying, that it is not so.

The qualifications for a Physician to the Asylum are necessarily foreign to those upon which legislative bodies are called to decide, and although by the present law the office is opened to competition, yet applicants, especially from a distance, find it difficult to authenticate any other claim than popular favor, which is in the estimation of the committee the least important, and very often deceptive itself.

In saying that the Legislature is not competent to judge of the qualifications of the applicants, the committee do not allude to those high intellectual and moral qualifications—that pure and enlightened philanthropy—sound mental philosophy—dignity, firmness and peculiarity of address, all of which are so indispensably necessary for the Physician and Superintendent of an insane Asylum, but they allude particularly to his *medical* qualifications. The latter should be of the first order, and yet *they* are insufficient unless happily blended with the former. Without enlarging upon this topic, for surely there can be no necessity for it, before this intelligent and virtuous body, the committee must frankly declare that the Legislature is wholly incompetent to make a good selection, and in making this declaration the committee hope and believe that they will be sustained by the unanimous voice of the General Assembly. It is a fact known to every member of the Legislature, that owing to the divisions of parties in our State for several years, that it not unfrequently happens that men are promoted by one or the other party to offices of importance and great responsibility, who, to say the least of them, are not more highly qualified than they ought to be. The committee do not pretend to plead exemption for themselves from this charge, and knowing the influence which political relationship has had upon them, they can be suffered to allude to this subject without exciting any suspicions unjust in themselves.

The prospect of profit alone will often induce many ignorant and uneducated men and women to seek the offices of Physician and Matron, and keeper of the Asylum; and these elections coming off biennially, the poor, unfortunate inmates will be transmitted like stock in trade from one keeper to another, until the character of the medical profession will become degraded, and the Asylum despised by all sensible men.

It is not only necessary that the Superintendent and Physician should be a gentleman in all the relations of life, but it is also necessary that he should understand the *pathology* and treatment of insanity, and of these qualifications the Legislature cannot judge. The committee therefore recommend that the election of 'Physician and Superintendent for the Asylum' be placed forever hereafter in the hands of a board of trustees, nine in number, six of whom, at least, shall be physicians, known to be of high moral character, and good report in their profession, which board of Trustees shall be nominated biennially by the Governor, subject to confirmation or rejection by the Senatorial branch of the State Legislature, and who shall hold their offices for two years, and until their successors are nominated, and qualified to enter upon the discharge of their duties. Or that the Legislature would incorporate a board of Trustees for a number of years, giving the board the privilege of filling vacancies, and doing all other such things as the Legislature may at present or hereafter direct.

The committee would most earnestly recommend the adoption of the one or the other of these propositions, believing it will be productive of much good to the Institution. And authorize the board to require of each applicant for the office of Physician and Superintendent, good and sufficient evidence of his moral and medical qualifications, before his election.

The Committee would also recommend that the Physician to the Asylum should have no other duties to perform save only those which peculiarly belong to him as Physician, and the *general* superintendence of all things belonging to the Institution. To the Stewart should be committed all the duties peculiar to his office; he should attend to furnishing all articles directed by the Physician; with the consent of the board of Trustees—keep a daily account of all the expenditures, the number of pauper and pay patients which he may feed each day, and discharge all such other duties as belong to his office, and may be defined by the Trustees.

The Committee would likewise recommend that the Trustees be authorized to elect a visiting, or consulting Physician at the same time that they elect the resident Physician, or as soon thereafter as possible, for the term of two years; who shall be required to visit the Asylum at least once every week —who shall have no control, nor direction in the Asylum, but shall advise and consult with the attending Physician in all such cases of lunacy, and other matters touching the condition and management of the institution as he may deem advisable. He shall also attend the monthly meetings of the board, and make such suggestions and give such information as the Trustees may require of him; and for his services, we recommend that he be paid a salary of two hundred dollars per annum.

After a careful examination of the Asylum, the Committee have decided that there are many improvements necessary to make the Institution as useful as it ought to be. There is not land enough—rooms enough, nor water enough in and about the Asylum to answer the wants of the inmates nor the necessities of the Institution. There is no dining room for the female lunatics, and the one used by the males is not one fourth as large as it ought to be. There is not land enough to give many of the male inmates that labor, and healthful exercise which some of them need very much, nor is there a sufficiency of water about the premises to extinguish a fire should one occur in the buildings.

Many of the rooms are so situated (to say nothing of the cells which are so constructed that they cannot be made comfortable even for brutes,) that they are almost entirely useless.

The object, however, most desirable at present, and the one most needed, is *fire*. It will not do to put lunatics in rooms where there is fire, and permit them to be alone; neither is it possible to give each patient an attendant through the night, to prevent him from doing mischief with the fire; consequently you are compelled (as is the custom at our Asylum,) to huddle some twenty or more together in one room—build up a large fire and place an attendant with them to guard them through the night. This is all wrong, and the Committee recommend that the Trustees be requested to proceed immediately to employ some person or persons to construct some plan, either by furnaces or some other preferable means, by which every apartment in the building occupied by the insane can be made comfortably warm.

The Committee would also recommend that the ground on the female department should be levelled and planted with shade trees and shrubbery. This will afford them some amusement and exercise through the spring and summer in cultivating their flowers, and will be a pleasant retreat for those who frequently wish to get clear of the noise and bustle often made in madhouses.

We have prepared a Bill in which are incorporated such provisions as the Committee deem most important for the present; with the hope, however, that, from time to time, such improvements and additions may be made as shall appear necessary to make the Institution useful and capable of affording that good which was no doubt anticipated by those who first engaged in its construction.

All of which is respectfully submitted, by
John H. Tyler,
Chairman of the Committee of the Senate.
John W. Richardson,
Chairman of the Committee of the House."

A forward step was taken by the enactment of legislation empowering the Governor and the three constitutional officers to sell the wholly inadequate existing institution and with the proceeds to purchase a tract of land containing not more than four hundred acres in some Middle Tennessee county for the erection of a suitable building thereon for the care and comfort of the inmates.[43]

In his legislative message Governor Brown, like his predecessors, discussed the value and importance of education. He pin-pointed the important defect existing in the so-called public educational system by pointing out the pathetically inadequate fund for the education of the children of the state. He cited the fact that there were in the State some quarter-million of children between the ages of six and twenty-one years for whose education there was available the sum of only $100,000 exacted annually from the earnings of the Bank of Tennessee. This

---

[43] *Acts of Tennessee*, 1845, Chapter 183.

sum, he sharply pointed out, yielded the pitiable sum of only forty cents per annum for the education of each child. He reminded the Legislature that the long-hoped-for distribution of funds arising from the sales of the public lands of the United States would give to Tennessee in all probability only about $50,000 per annum, and that the State and Federal funds when combined would amount to about seventy-five cents per annum for each child within the educable age. And then the Governor remarked:

"Now it must be evident that this sum is totally insufficient for the purpose of establishing a general and comprehensive common school system in the State. . . ."

At this juncture in his Message, Governor Brown remarked that he knew of no method for increasing the school fund except by a resort to taxation. But he hastened to add quite explicitly and emphatically that

". . . I cannot recommend the increase of our present fund by a further resort to taxation. . ."

Like most of his predecessors, Governor Brown bewailed the tragic lack of any public educational system worthy of the name, but he too tossed the ball to the Legislature with the almost certain knowledge that nothing would be done in the premises. Anyway, that's exactly what happened. The only legislation relating to public education that was enacted by the Twenty-Sixth General Assembly was a slight amendment to a previous law governing the sale of school lands.[44] A bill "to promote popular education" was, upon the recommendation of the Committee on Education and Common Schools, rejected.[45]

Examination of the original bill [46] discloses that its author was a rampant Whig, William Cullom, later a two-term Congressman from Tennessee. Defeat of the farcical measure is evidence that a majority of the Legislature was not wholly bereft of ordinary common sense. Here was Senator Cullom's proposed panacea:

"A bill to promote popular Education
Be it enacted by the General Assembly of the State of Tennessee that the common school Commissioners shall attend the first day of Each Term of the Circuit Court in their respective Counties and the Judge of the Court or some other person by his procurement shall address them on their legal powers and duties and the means of promoting popular Education provided however said Commissioners shall not be indictable for failing to attend."

Unquestionably, Governor Brown's remarks upon Internal Improve-

[44] *Ibid.*, Chapter 121.
[45] *Senate Journal*, 1845, 338.
[46] Mss. bill in State Archives, Nashville.

ments were tempered by the facts disclosed in the legislative committee's Report on Internal Improvements to which findings the Governor referred. The above Report[47] consisted of fifty-two printed pages in the Appendix of the *Senate Journal*. A break-down was made regarding two railroads and twenty-three turnpike companies, to all of which the State had contributed financial aid through the issuance of State Bonds. An abbreviated summary disclosed the following items: Total amount of bonds issued by the State, $1,738,416; Deficit of Individual Stockholders, $74,605.33; Defalcation of Companies, $70,107.82; and Indebtedness of Companies not properly chargeable to proceeds of State Stock, $111,352.92.

In the main, the legislative investigating committee ascertained that the indebtedness of the various companies was largely attributable to a failure of stockholders to pay in their subscriptions or to the construction costs exceeding the capital stock subscribed. A loophole through which funds had been poured seemed to have been related to the manner of letting construction contracts, to-wit:

"... The interest of the State has been compromised in several instances by the manner of *letting* the respective roads to contractors. Several of the companies having done this in such a manner as, in the opinion of the committee, was calculated to preclude competition in bidding. In some instances by letting the entire route in one contract, and in others by requiring successful bidders to become stockholders and to receive one half the consideration for construction in stock of the company.—Consequently in all cases where speculation was the primary, and the general utility or necessity of an improvement scarcely a secondary consideration in organizing a company, the contracts were confined for the most part to the original corporators, and their bids were made in reference to the amount derivable from the State upon their respective contracts—the stock in such cases being wholly unproductive.

A capital defect therefore in our system was the failure to constitute at its inception, an effectual police to protect the interests of the State by exercising such general supervision over the contracting and reception of the roads and adjudication of the accounts of the several companies, as would have ensured the *bona fide* payment and *actual expenditure* of the amount subscribed by individuals.

In the absence of such police, by a mere compliance with the *forms* of the law, the companies have been enabled to obtain bonds upon the State's subscription; and consequently from their general *direction* under existing laws, the subscription of individual capital in those enterprises has not operated to protect the State against unproductive investments.

Where roads were let to or bid off by contractors at six thousand dollars per mile for construction, the committee have simply stated the *reported* cost. This being a subject matter over which the directory have entire control, the State is consequently concluded by their act in the premises. (See Humphreys, State vs. Jefferson turnpike co.) ..."

---

[47] *Senate Journal*, 1845, Appendix, 1–52.

In an effort to tighten up the legal provisions and policies governing the State's participation in aiding internal improvements, the Secretary of State was empowered to visit and examine into the condition of the respective companies with a view of determining the financial status of each respective enterprise and to collect any funds due the State. A report was to be submitted to each Legislature setting forth the financial status of the various companies, and certain powers were defined whereby the said official was to have access to all records and could require persons to be examined under oath.[48]

Governor Brown's immediate predecessor, in his parting Message to the Legislature at the beginning of the session, had opposed strongly the indiscriminate issuance of more State Bonds in behalf of internal improvements. Governor Jones, although out of office when Governor Brown's Message was transmitted, nevertheless had considerable influence with the Legislature in which the Whigs were a minority party by only some three or four votes. Moreover, Governor Brown was in substantial agreement with the position outlined by Governor Jones relative to issuance of additional State Bonds.[49] Said Governor Jones:

"... Of the importance of a well regulated system of Internal Improvements, I entertain no doubt. That such a system would afford great facilities to the enterprise and industry of the country developing its resources and stimulating its energies, is certainly true. No one estimates its benefits more highly than I do, and no one would rejoice more than I would, to see a gradual and permanent system engrafted on the policy of the State. Gladly would I contribute by all proper means to its establishment. That such works are greatly needed in many portions of the State, no one will doubt. In the Eastern division, from its insulated position, and the very imperfect and uncertain navigation of its streams, such facilities would be of great value and utility. But great as these benefits are conceded to be, their importance does not in my judgment justify a resort to that most destructive financial policy, of raising means by an extension of the credit of the State in the issuance of its bonds. The bonds that have already been issued, have been sold at a discount of from twenty to fifty per cent, and yet the State is bound to redeem them at their nominal or par value. This objection to a further issue of the bonds of the State, is a formidable one, yet there are others of far greater magnitude. Any policy that contemplates an enlargement of the debts of the State at the present time, I should consider of dangerous tendency. In the name of Justice and Honor, let us issue no more Bonds, let us create no more debts, until we have either paid those we owe, or made some certain provision for them as they come to maturity. If inequality in the distribution of the means already vested in these works exist between the different divisions of the State, if injustice has been done, correct the error by all the honorable means at your command; if needs be, correct it by a resort to the Treasury of the State, to any means that you have—but in the name of the honor of the State, *issue no more Bonds*. To create debts without possessing

48 *Acts of Tennessee*, 1845, Chapter 23.
49 *Senate Journal*, 1845, 70–71.

or providing some certain means for their redemption, is to trifle with the credit of the State; it is to sport with its honor ..."

Aside from the authorization of the issuance of bonds to the amount of four thousand and nine hundred dollars in favor of the Franklin and Columbia Turnpike Company and six thousand dollars for the Lebanon and Nashville Turnpike Company, no additional State Bonds for Internal Improvements were authorized by the 1845 Legislature.[50] A definite halt had been made on the matter of ladling out State funds to Tom, Dick and Harry who may have corralled a group of men for the alleged purpose of building a turnpike or railroad, always provided that the generosity of the State Treasury was made available to them.

Perhaps no Governor prior to Governor Brown had made a clearer-cut analysis of the State's financial status as of the time the customary Message to the Legislature was transmitted. Assuredly, no legislator could truthfully allege that he was in the dark as to the State's financial condition, for Governor Brown had gone into almost meticulous detail regarding same. From the various suggestions and recommendations of the Governor, the Legislature saw fit to act upon only one item. The President and Directors of the Bank of Tennessee were directed and required to discontinue the branch banks located at Athens, Clarksville, and Columbia.[51]

Obviously, the inadequate school fund remained inadequate, and the so-called Common School System remained a skeleton organization on the statute books without any life-blood in its veins in the form of revenue. Granting charters of incorporation to private schools, however, was done on a lavish scale, inasmuch as not one dollar was appropriated from the State Treasury for the erection and maintenance of such institutions. No less than twenty-two such institutions were awarded articles of incorporation by the 1845 Legislature. They ranged all the way from Black Oak Grove School to the University of Memphis. As a rule, the Board of Trustees was vouchsafed "perpetual succession," but in the case of Sylvan Academy the tenure was limited to one hundred years! In one instance, twenty men requested and received a charter for the establishment of Orean Institute "to be located at such place as the Board of Trustees may direct." If so disposed, one might be a bit facetious regarding the action or inaction of the Twenty-Sixth General Assembly. Little constructive legislation was enacted by that body; much of its time was consumed in party strife and in the enactment of trivial laws. Apparently lacking any real interest in the educational welfare of the children of the State, the Solons were content with exempting from taxation any person exhibiting "the skeleton or

[50] *Acts of Tennessee*, 1845, Chapter 24.
[51] *Ibid.*, Chapter 131.

fossil remains of animals found within the limits of Tennessee," said tax-exemption being based upon the premise that

"...Such exhibitions tend to improve the knowledge and taste of a people, and ought not to be discouraged and prohibited...." [52]

In all fairness, however, it should be added that exhibitors of specimens of "fine paintings and sculpture" likewise escaped the tax collector's clutches. Why, it may be asked, was the Legislature reluctant to enact some remedial legislation regarding public education, the real foundation of democracy?

A thumbnail sketch of the industrial, economic, and social life of Tennessee at this period will supply most of the basic facts as to why public education was so grossly neglected. First of all, the industrial revolution had begun to operate in Tennessee. Railroad charters were being granted, turnpikes were being extended, manufacturing enterprises were being increased and enlarged and agriculture passed from the "truck patch" stage to that of the broad plantation worked by multitudes of slaves. The invention of machines for spinning and weaving and making cloth was being reflected in the increased acreage devoted to "King Cotton." The landlord was in the heyday of his social glory and financial success. Tennessee was no exception to the general rule. With a soil fertile, a climate inviting with a long-growing season, with an abundance of timber and minerals, and with plenty of slave labor, why should not material progress have been the order of the day? Amid such conditions, what of education?

With extreme difficulty, the Constitutional Convention of 1834 had incorporated an educational "plank" in the 1835 Constitution. That belated recognition consisted largely of a glowing eulogy on the importance of "knowledge, learning and virtue." With solemn assurance the Constitution decreed that "the common school fund shall remain a perpetual fund," but overlooked the fact that the fund was practically inconsequential and that there was no real public school system in operation. In 1836, the Legislature created the office of Superintendent of Public Instruction. The first superintendent, Robert H. McEwen, became entangled in his accounting of the school funds entrusted to his administration. A legislative investigation was ordered and a report charged a shortage of about $120,000; a terrific legislative battle ensued, accompanied by a bitterly contested lawsuit. McEwen finally emerged from the battle by paying approximately $11,000 and calling the matter settled. The alleged mishandling of the funds gave both political adversaries and the opponents of public education an opportunity to berate the whole theory and practice of trying to provide mass educa-

---

[52] *Ibid.*, Chapter 10.

tion at public expense. One result was that the office of Superintendent of Public Instruction was abolished in 1844.

Aiding and abetting the inadequate school fund was the prejudice against common schools themselves, two formidable factors that delayed and for a long time prevented the development of facilities for mass education at public expense. One basis for such prejudice was due to "pauper school" laws enacted in 1815 and 1823;[53] the other basis was traceable to the institution of slavery. Many members of the 1834 Constitutional Convention from Middle Tennessee and West Tennessee, large slave-holding sections, had opposed public schools. The landed aristocrats, many of whom were influential political leaders in their respective communities, sent their children to private or denominational schools, or employed private tutors. Obviously, those property-owners were the main taxpayers and they displayed no enthusiasm about imposing taxes upon themselves for the support of schools which they did not propose to patronize. All along, the earlier efforts of the State had been primarily concerned with the establishment of colleges and academies, and as a result the common schools had been unable to compete with the favored institutions. Such a condition had made it difficult for the common schools to win the confidence and respect of even the lower and middle classes of society. It all boiled down to this: without adequate funds, deprived of any responsible supervisory authority, a victim of the social and economic handicaps imposed by slavery, and bereft of any appreciable public sentiment, the wonder is that there existed even a skeleton system of public education.

Although both Governor James C. Jones and Governor Aaron V. Brown had registered opposition to the further issuance of State Bonds for internal improvements, yet there was much public interest in the development of transportation systems, both by land and water. Each of the above Governors, however, had expressed keen interest in bettering transportation systems and Governor Brown emphasized his viewpoint by stressing the importance of connecting Chattanooga and Nashville by a railroad, and said in his Message to the Legislature

"To the granting of liberal and wisely guarded charters to individual companies, I think there can be no good objection."

On November 3, 1845, on motion by Senator Montgomery Thornburg

"The Senate took up the consideration of a Message from the House of Representatives, transmitting the report of Dr. Gerard Troost, Mineralogist and Geologist of the State, on the practicability of constructing a Rail Road

---

[53] *Acts of Tennessee*, 1815, Chapter 49.
Ibid., 1823, Chapter 49.

from Chattanooga to Nashville, and a dissertation on the mineral resources over which said road is proposed to pass. . . ." [54]

Five hundred copies of the Troost Report [55] were ordered to be printed. In that Report, Dr. Troost stated that he was not "skilled in the business or science of civil engineering," yet he admitted that the enthusiasm of citizens of Nashville and of those living along the supposed route of the railroad had induced him to make some "cursory examinations" as to the practicability of the proposed enterprise. In considerable detail Dr. Troost sketched the general topography of the country through which the road would pass, not failing to indicate with meticulous detail the various types of rock underlying the earth's surface. He pointed out three tentative routes, each of which "would have to ascend and descend the steep declivities of the Cumberland Mountain." Such ascension and descension could, said he, "be obviated by a *tunnel*." He suggested a fourth route, but even then the Cumberland Mountains would present a barrier to be overcome. But, said Dr. Troost, the base of the Cumberland Mountains is composed of "Oolitic limestone" and can be more easily penetrated than the rock which Montgomery Bell had already penetrated at the Narrows of the Harpeth when he constructed ironworks on that stream.

How to get over the Mountain was the enigma that had to be resolved if the proposed railroad were to become anything more than an idle dream. Moreover, that question would be in the forefront when and if the promoters of the road applied to the Legislature for a charter. It should be recalled that this was before the day of dynamite, high explosives, power drills, and bulldozers. Picks, shovels, hand drills, and black gunpowder were the only available aids at the time. On one occasion, when promoters of the road were addressing an audience on the advantages of such a line, a heckler wanted to know how anybody expected to build a railroad over Cumberland Mountain. "Bore a hole through it," Dr. John Overton of Nashville replied.[56] Dr. Overton's retort must have convinced some of the doubting Thomases, for a charter [57] was granted by the Legislature on December 11, 1845, and the actual work of construction began. The provisions of the charter, consisting of forty sections, were rather liberal in that all employees of the railroad were exempt from military service except in cases of actual invasion or insurrection, the company was empowered to purchase slaves, and its capital stock "forever exempt from taxation."

Much stimulus to the railroad movement in Tennessee was generated by a convention held in Memphis in November, 1845. The primary consideration before the convention was the linking together of

[54] *Senate Journal*, 1845, 166.
[55] *Ibid.*, Appendix, 65–75.
[56] *Tennessee: Old and New*, Volume I, 143.
[57] *Acts of Tennessee*, 1845, Chapter 1.

the Atlantic seaboard and the Mississippi Valley region by means of a railroad. Legislative recognition of the forthcoming convention was noted by Senator Jacob Voorhies on November 7th, when he introduced the following resolution:[58]

"*Whereas,* the recent appointment of delegates to a Convention about to be held in Memphis, has been so connected with the official character of the members of this Legislature, as to give to said Convention all the impulse which the State can yield through her Legislative character, unless said appointment should be divested of official influence, by a distinct announcement coming from this body. It is, therefore,
Resolved by the General Assembly of the State of Tennessee, That no action in Convention, tending to solicit the General Government to open its treasuries for the purpose of promoting a system of Internal Improvements, will be recognized as an expression of the will of the people of said State."

A four-day session of the Southern and Western Convention, of which John C. Calhoun of South Carolina was President, was held in Memphis and wide-spread interest was created throughout the South for increasing the movement for building railroads. Unquestionably there was a carry-over from this Convention that helped influence the Tennessee Legislature to grant a charter to the Memphis and Charleston Railroad on February 2, 1846. In the law,[59] which embraced forty-one sections, were incorporated generous provisions exempting the officers and employees from military service and from serving on juries and working on public roads. Other provisions empowered the railroad company to purchase slaves and to have its capital stock exempt from taxation "forever."

From the standpoint of legislative intent, it was made clear that internal improvements were not to be restricted to *land* transportation solely. The "water boys" had not gone to sleep at the switch. On January 31, 1846, the Cumberland Navigation Company was incorporated for the purpose of improving the navigation of the Cumberland River below Nashville.[60] The provisions of the charter, however, were not so generous as those dealing with the railroads. When the dividends exceeded six per cent on the paid in capital stock, a tax of ten per cent was levied on such excess dividends. The company was also required to complete its improvements to the Kentucky State Line within seven years, or its charter would be revoked and all rights, privileges, and franchises would revert to the State.

For the improvement of Duck River from Columbia to the Tennessee River, a concern was incorporated under the title of the Duck River Slack Water Navigation Company.[61] The company was em-

---

[58] *Senate Journal,* 1845, 193–194.
[59] *Acts of Tennessee,* 1845, Chapter 182.
[60] *Ibid.,* Chapter 159.
[61] *Ibid.,* Chapter 57.

powered to erect locks and dams and to sell water power for "propelling machinery of all kinds." The life of the charter was fifty years, provided the improvements were completed within twenty years from the passage of the act. Various and sundry laws were enacted dealing with such minor streams as Caney Fork, Obion, Tellico, Forked Deer, and Wolf, none of which amounted to very much in the improvement of water transportation facilities.

With reference to the State debt, Governor Brown in his message had given a bill of particulars. In round numbers, the indebtedness amounted to three millions of dollars, requiring an annual payment of about two hundred thousand dollars for interest. To maintain the high credit rank of the State, Governor Brown earnestly requested the Legislature to provide for the State's obligation regarding this matter. In compliance with Governor Brown's plea, a law was enacted for providing a sinking fund "for the gradual extinguishment of the Public Debt." [62] The dividends accruing to the State on behalf of State stock in Internal Improvement Companies plus the State whiskey tax were the sources of revenue designated to take care of the State's obligations regarding its debt. Apparently, these provisions handled the matter, for later on the Report of the Comptroller of the Treasury disclosed that the annual interest on the State debt had been met, leaving a residue of approximately $32,000 which, in his opinion, "probably makes a sinking fund." [63] This specific action by the Legislature denoted that Governor Brown's emphatic and insistent recommendation had received favorable indorsement.

Almost without exception, every Legislature notes the various recommendations of the Governor and acts, either favorably or unfavorably, upon them. Occasionally, certain recommendations are permitted to die a lingering death without the Legislature's having assumed any responsibility by any direct action thereupon. On the whole, Governor Brown fared very well at the hands of the 1845 Legislature, insofar as his recommendations were concerned. True enough, his first recommendation went for naught, inasmuch as no legislation was enacted softening up the death penalty. The other six recommendations may be said to have been favorably received, even though the legislative action in some cases was indeed mediocre. This was certainly true in regard to the all-important subject of Education.

Though not a specific recommendation, yet Governor Brown made an eloquent and emphatic reference in his Inaugural Address to the desirability of erecting a monument to the memory of Andrew Jackson who had died some four months previous to Governor Brown's inauguration as Chief Executive. In conformity with Governor Brown's

---

[62] *Ibid.*, Chapter 154.
[63] *Senate Journal*, 1847, Appendix, 180.

90 MESSAGES OF THE GOVERNORS

suggestion, Representative Jos. C. Guild of Sumner County "enjoyed the honor of introducing a bill on the subject." The bill, as originally drafted and introduced, called for a State appropriation of ten thousand dollars, five thousand for the erection of a marble statue to be placed in the State Capitol and five thousand for a monument to be erected in Memphis. But partisan politics raised its slimy head, as is evidenced by speeches made in the House of Representatives on the anniversary of the Battle of New Orleans. Herewith are incorporated the remarks [64] made by Representative William B. Allen of Lawrence County:

"REMARKS OF MR. ALLEN,

On the 8th of January, 1846, on the bill proposing to erect a Statue and Monument to Gen. Jackson.

MR. SPEAKER:—When the proposition was first made to erect a statue of 'imperishable bronze,' to be placed in the Capitol of the State when finished, and a monument in accordance with the recommendation of the Governor in his inaugural address, to be planted on the bank of the 'noblest river in the world, where the millions who will pass for ages and ages to come, may pause and gaze upon it with wonder and admiration,' in perpetuation of the memory of Gen. Andrew Jackson, I did not intend to say one word upon the subject. I do not *now* rise for the purpose of discussing the merits of the bill, nor to pronounce a studied and inflated panegyric upon the life and character of Gen. Jackson. He needs none at my hands. The country he contributed so largely and freely to defend is vocal with his praise. His public acts from the time he entered the councils of the nation (to say nothing of his military prowess,) to the day he retired with dignity to the shades of private life, are sufficient and enduring testimonials of his greatness.—These have been portrayed to us in the most eloquent language by the gentleman from the county of Sumner (Mr. Guild,) who enjoys the honor of introducing the bill, and by the rich oratory of the representative from Washington (Mr. Haynes). They have expressed the hope which I here take occasion to renew, that the bill will pass by acclamation—that however widely and materially certain members may differ with Gen. Jackson upon political questions, they will illustrate their magnanimity by awarding to his memory its just deserts—That a portion of his political enemies in this body will do this we have the most convincing and satisfactory testimony.

It is a cherished desire by members on this side of the House that nothing of a party character shall enter into our deliberations upon this question. Such a feeling and disposition on such an occasion, should animate every bosom. It is a state of things most 'devoutly to be wished.' These expectations and hopes may yet be realized. No person would rejoice at it with more

---

[64] *Nashville Union*, February 3, 1846.
The Life and Character of Capt. Wm. B. Allen, 172–180.
Author's note. Mr. Allen was the youngest member of the House of Representatives, being only twenty-two years of age. He had defeated by only six votes a former Speaker of the House, Franklin Buchanan, a veteran campaigner. Eight months after the delivery of his speech *re* the Jackson Statue and Monument, Captain Allen was killed at the battle of Monterey, Mexico. His last words were, "Boys, I am dying, but charge the fort." *Ibid.*, 150.

unfeigned satisfaction than myself. Who wishes to see the glorious 8th of January dessecrated by the representatives of the people, in widening the breach between the two parties when an identity of interest should make them more united? If there be such an individual, I can only say that I do not envy his feelings. After premising these remarks, it is due to candor and truth, that I should say, from the indications made, we will not act together with that unanimity and concert so ardently hoped for. Already has the demon of party been aroused from its lair. Its tendency is to frighten members from the support of such measures as they conscientiously approve. To those who are aiding in fanning the flame, I would say with becoming respect, beware unless you suffer by the conflagration you are instrumental in creating. Those few choice spirits whose political identities are adverse to my own who have the independence and moral firmness to sustain the bill will be greeted and cheered by the plaudits of the liberal men of all parties. But with the course honorable gentlemen may think proper to pursue upon this question, I have nothing to do.—They, like myself, are responsible to their country for their acts.

I will not, however, disguise the fact that I was not a little surprised at the introduction of the amendment to the bill by the representative from the county of Madison (Mr. Bullock). Knowing that there was an inkling towards opposition to the bill as it was first introduced on the part of some of our whig friends, and in order that they might be reconciled to vote for it, by general consent, we agreed to strike out the two first sections of the bill which made an appropriation from the Treasury.—After doing this we had the assurance that they would cease their hostility to the measure. But, sir, we were mistaken. It pains me to make this announcement, but it is *true*. What now do we hear? A voice of opposition coming up by way of amendment, after previous concessions and compromises. And by whom has it originated! By a leading member of the whig party as personated in the representative from Madison (Mr. Bullock). The amendment, to say the least of it, is an insidious attack upon the bill. This may be strong language, but not stronger than the occasion will justify.—The gentleman may be sincere when he expresses a hope that the bill will pass. I don't stand up here to impeach his sincerity. But, sir, we will try men's faith by their works. Here is a Procrustean standard by which the member may regulate his friendship for the bill. It may be found in the proposition made by the gentleman from Washington (Mr. Haynes). I now call upon my friend from Madison, for whom I cherish none other than the kindest feelings, to unite with us upon this question.—What is the object of the amendment offered by the gentleman from Madison? It proposes also the erection of a statue to the memory of George Washington, 'the defender of his country, the founder of liberty, the friend of man.' To the amendment, if it had been offered as a substantive proposition, and in good faith, no individual could reasonably object. Every Tennessean, *especially*, who is proud of his 'own, his native land,' would be glad to see such a statue to the memory of the greatest man that ever lived, who 'in the annals of modern greatness, stands alone, and the noblest names of antiquity lose their lustre in his presence.' But serious fears are entertained that it will have a tendency to embarrass the passage of the bill. If satisfied that such will not be the case, I would gladly see it incorporated as a part of the bill. So far, however, as the perpetuation of his fame is concerned, no monument need be erected. He has built his 'monument in the hearts of his countrymen,' and his fame is co-extensive with civilization itself. But it has been an immemorial and time-hallowed custom to erect such monuments to the distinguished dead in all ages of the world. The United States is no less proud of her great men than other nations. She will ever embalm in grateful recollection the invincible defenders of her liberty.

> 'Patriots have toiled, and in their country's cause
> Bled nobly. And their deeds as they deserve
> Receive proud recompense. We give in charge,
> Their names to the sweet lyre. The historic muse,
> Proud of her treasure, marches with it down
> To latest times; and sculpture in her turn
> Gives bond, in stone, and ever-during brass,
> To guard them, and immortalize her truth.'

The erection of a statue to the father of his country would seem to be more appropriately a national object which every citizen of the Union, however, humble and obscure, may contribute his free will offering. In the Capitol at Washington stands in unmutilated and unsullied grandeur his sculptured form. It belongs to the whole nation. If gentlemen are sincere in what they profess, and I impeach the purity of no man's motives, the time may not be far remote when the Capitol of our own proud and chivalrous State will be ornamented and adorned with living, speaking and eloquent statues of Washington and Jackson. As their names are to be linked together in connection with whatever is virtuous, chivalrous and great in the history of the country they fought to sustain, it may not be inappropriate that a statue be erected to each and placed side by side in the Capitol of the State. Like Washington, Jackson needs no monument so far as the perpetuation of the memory of his great deeds are concerned. As long as the 8th of January is remembered, he will be heralded as the greatest captain of the age in which he lived. While the great father of waters continues to roll by the monument to be planted on its bank, bearing upon its ample and majestic bosom the wealth of the surrounding country, it will murmur his deathless praise. To use the language of another 'his fame is eternity and residence creation.' Being 'first in war, first in peace, and first in the hearts of his countrymen,' he was second to none in the social relations of private life. But I shall not dwell upon those virtues so admirably illustrated in his character. I wish to see erected on yonder hill a magnificent edifice—one that will be highly creditable to the State we represent. When completed, I am willing to see the statuary forms of Washington and Jackson within it as guardian angels to preside over the deliberations of future Legislatures for all time to come. And when the madness of party shall disturb the harmony so essential to the administration of wholesome laws, by these images they may be reminded of their councils while living. Let them read the prophetic language that is addressed to them to avoid against the baneful effects of party spirit. Among the ancients it was a saying that

> 'While stands the Coliseum, Rome shall stand.'

Let this kind of feeling animate our people and nerve their arms to action. Let them resolve that as long as that edifice shall endure, *aye* as long as the hill upon which it rests shall remain, our country with her free institutions shall stand, as the proudest monument of human wisdom. And let them constantly bear in mind that those inestimable privileges which they enjoy under the auspices of such institutions, have been transmitted of them unimpaired through the instrumentality of Washington and Jackson.

Transatlantic nations may speak in terms derogatory to our people and government—they may attempt a depreciation of the merits of our great men, but when an impartial verdict shall be rendered, as it WILL be, it will appear that for all the elements of true greatness there are Americans who can honorably compare with those of any other country. In saying this I am not ignorant of the impression that prevails that it is impossible for the United States to produce, in the strict sense of the term, genuine statesmen, that her politicians are numerous, her statesmen none—that we cannot point to them in the exultation of our hearts and exclaim, 'here stand the choicest spirits of their age; the greatest wits, the noblest orators, the wisest politicians, the most illustrious patriots. Here they stand, whose hands have been raised for their country, whose magical eloquence has shook the spheres, whose genius has poured out strains worthy the inspiration of the gods, whose lives were devoted to the purity of their principles, whose memories were bequeathed to a race grateful for benefits received from their sufferings and their sacrifices.' Such an insinuation is as illiberal as it is untrue. However invidious may be the fault-finders and hypercritical writers of the old world, they are constrained to award to Genl Jackson a high niche in the temple of renown. With the gentleman from Sumner (Mr. Guild), it may be said that he has emphatically 'filled the measure of his country's glory' and his name will *never die*.

> 'Rear strong the vast memorial high,
> That Freedom's future sons may come to bless
> His memory, and breathe new spirits there.
> And at that altar-shrine, like mighty sons
> Of Hannibal of old, most proudly swear
> Like him to fight, like him to nobly die
> The deathless foes of fading tyranny—
> That down from age to age the truth may live,
> *Republics not ungrateful are*, and wreaths can weave
> And monuments upraise for patriots true,
> Arising, like their deeds, from common dust,
> O'er common men, and pointing to the skies,
> To note that, *as the stars*, they glitter there!'

His deeds of matchless daring and his inflexible devotion to his country stand like a tower pointing magnificently to Heaven exciting the envy and admiration of the world. His faults, from which no man can claim exemption, it is hoped, have descended with him to the oblivion of the tomb. Peace be to his manes! is the patriot's prayer.

His resplendent virtues, and he had many, should be emblazoned upon the pages of history and left as a rich heritage to the millions of freemen who are to succeed him in all time to come. As the patriot, the soldier and sage, full of years and full of honors, has gone down to his grave in peace with the world and his God, let his virtues be resurrected—let them continue to live in the song of the poet and eulogium of the orator. Let ingenious youths as they assemble together around one national altar on the annual return of the jubilee of the 8th of January, herald forth his admirable traits of character. They will never cease to emulate those Socratic virtues of which he was the representative—that they will never forget the obligations they are under to promote the cherished interest of their country and advance the 'symbols of her triumph'—and that no consideration of personal aggrandizement will ever be the cause of an abandonment of those great and important principles for which he fought, is confidently and ardently hoped. If there be any thing on earth calculated to disturb the patriot's repose and cause his great spirit to rise up and condemn it, it is a base and treacherous attempt to sever this glorious Union. *Never, never*, may our people be so blind and insensible to their interests and the happiness of those who are to succeed them as to consent to have it 'rent asunder.' If our government is ever to be free, prosperous and happy—if the sun of her greatness is not to set in the starless night of despotism—if our brightest hopes and anticipations are to be realized in reference to the continued security and welfare of our country, our people must be *virtuous, enlightened and brave.* They should adopt the favorite maxim to 'ask nothing that is not right, and submit to nothing that is wrong.' They should watch with distrust that public servant or diplomatic functionary who would consent to an abandonment of one inch of our territory where our title is 'clear and unquestionable.' With such a determination our country is secure. 'Esto perpetua', is written in characters of light upon her destiny. When the monuments of her glory shall have fallen to decay, her peerless form will still stand up like a giantess full of proportion, animated with life, and buoyant with lofty anticipations. But I shall not pause to weave visions about the future in reference to the perpetuity of our republican institutions.—May the memory of his deeds who has reflected a radiance of glory around Tennessee and the Union be eternal! May every youth like the young Carthagenian swear upon the altar of his country never to forsake her, and with the defender of the emporium of the west, at all events and under every circumstance 'Our Federal Union, it *must* be preserved.' "

The astute Speaker of the House, Brookins Campbell, who had in 1837 unseated Andrew Johnson for a legislative seat, was determined to unmask the Whigs by showing the purpose of their crippling amendment to the Jackson statue and monument bill. His speech, also delivered on the anniversary date of the Battle of New Orleans, was as follows:[65]

"SPEECH OF MR. CAMPBELL, OF WASHINGTON

Delivered in the House of Representatives on the 8th of January, 1846, in favor of a bill providing for the erection of a Statue to be placed in the State Capitol, and a Monument to be raised on the banks of the Mississippi river, at Memphis, in honor of GEN. ANDREW JACKSON.

Nothing was farther from my intention than to have troubled the House with any remarks on this occasion, nor would I now act in a way differing from that intention, had not the two last sections of the bills as introduced by Mr. Guild, the chairman of the committee, been stricken out. My purpose is, simply, to show that the object of the bill is defeated, and the means by which its defeat has been produced. But it will be proper in the first place to show the design of the subject under consideration.

The friends of General Andrew Jackson believe it to be due to his public services to erect a monument to his memory, commensurate in magnitude and quality with the greatness of his deeds; and hence it is, that this bill was offered, which proposed for the State in conjunction with individual contributions, to erect a monument on the banks of the great Mississippi river, at the city of Memphis, in honor of this illustrious man; also to place a marble statue to his memory in the rotunda of the Capitol of the State, at a cost by the State of five thousand dollars to each.

This proposition was submitted for our reflection some weeks since, and

[65] *Nashville Union,* February 3, 1846.

referred to a select committee with instructions to report to this House on the EIGHTH DAY OF JANUARY.—A day more propitious for its consideration than all others, because it is the anniversary of that eventful day, which covered our army with undying glory on the plains of New Orleans, and won for its Commander-in-Chief, a position in military fame towering far above ancient heroes, and fixed his name in the highest rank of modern conquerors.

When this bill was introduced all parties seemed to approve its object— all seemed to agree that it was due to his character, on account of the many valuable and extraordinary services which he had rendered to his country through a long and 'eventful life,' that monument as high as human hands could build it, should be erected on the banks of that noble stream (the Mississippi), to perpetuate his memory, and point to the future traveler through all time to come, our appreciation of his services and to show foreign countries as well as our own people that he lives, though dead, in the hearts of his countrymen.

But, sir, strange to tell, notwithstanding it has been openly avowed on the other side of this House (whig), that they desired to vote for the bill, and wished its friends to agree to amend it, so that all can unite in its support. In this spirit it has been amended—they have begged its friends to agree to strike out all from the bill which appropriates any thing to the erection of these trophies. This has been done, *wrongfully done*. Notwithstanding all this —how are we now met? Do gentlemen now tell us they will vote for the bill since they have accomplished their design? No, sir, instead of uniting as we expected and passing it by acclamation, amendments are offered, intended for no other purpose but to embarrass, and if possible defeat the whole object of the original proposition.

This bill as it now stands is a nullity. It proposes to erect a statue and monument to the memory of General Jackson, but appropriates not one cent for its construction. How is it expected the work will be completed unless you provide some means for its erection? It is answered—the people will voluntarily contribute enough. That may be true, and should it so turn out, the State will not be called on according to the bill for the amount proposed to be given for this very laudable object. But on the other hand, suppose the amount of individual contributions should be insufficient to accomplish them, and this bill as it now stands should be referred to as giving assistance from the State, would it not be a beautiful reliance—*a grand spectacle*, for the world to dwell upon—that the Legislature of Tennessee had passed an act, making provisions for the erection of these memorials to the memory of this departed, and illustrious hero, and statesman, without appropriating anything for their construction? Why talk about legislation, if you will give nothing? You say the people will build them—I say according to this bill they will receive no assistance from the State.

I hope this day, so memorable in the annals of American history, will not be desecrated to a design so unholy as to be spent in doing *mock honor* to the most distinguished captain general of the age in which he lived.—He was not only the most distinguished at home, but pre-eminently so throughout the civilized world—his name carries with it the impress of his country's *genius* to every *ocean* and *sea* over which the American flag now floats; and wherever the '*stars and stripes*' of our beloved country are hailed by the patriot and philanthropist as the insignia of liberty, then Jackson's name is lisped by every tongue, as the unconquerable defender of human rights and human liberty. I do not intend to speak of the Roman courage that marked his early actions in the revolutionary struggle for independence, nor the valiant part which he bore in the war of 1812—nevertheless the House will indulge me in reminding it of the eventful crisis in which our country's institutions, her hopes, and her destinies were involved in the events of the morning of the memorable EIGHTH OF JANUARY—. Thirty-one years ago, of which this is the joyful anniversary return, where I ask, was he on that occasion, whose body lies cold in death, and, whose spirit has ascended to God who gave it? I answer, upon the fate of war our country and our liberty were staked, and upon the plains of New Orleans that day the two belligerent armies met in fearful battle array? Where, I repeat, was he, whose memory we now seek to perpetuate? I answer, at the head of his columns! What must have been the feeling when he left the city to meet this daring and veteran foe—a foe already rich with spoils and gray with victory—a foe, a part of which had met upon the plains of Waterloo the hitherto invincible Napoleon, and conquered that great conqueror. Who does not imagine with the warmest sensibility the deep suspense, which must have pervaded every bosom, and the still more aching pain which must have pierced the hearts of every woman, whose father, or son, or husband, or brother formed a part of the American line. No tongue can describe with proper force the scenes which really occurred as the OLD HERO passed through the city on his way to the *battlefield*. The time had come to try men's souls, and to test the love and patriotism of woman. The latter met him in the streets, and would not let him pass, *weeping, and crying, 'save, O save the city, or we perish!!'—* Save us from a mercenary foe, whose watch word is the *'beauty and booty of New Orleans!!'* Save our old men and our children, they cried, O save the city! Nor would they let him pass until they had the promise. He then *swore* by his reliance IN HIM *'who lives forever and forever'*—that by the *'eternal God,'* the foe should never enter the city until it had first trampled over his *dead body!* This was enough, the promise was made—their tears were dried up—the General proceeded—the armies met—the din of arms and the roar of artillery as it struck the earth and rung through the air increased their fears, lest in a moment, their husband, their son, or their sire should be hurried to the tomb. This deep suspense could not be quieted—their agonies increased as the battle roar went up; terror and horror sat upon every heart, until the *'Lion'* cowered beneath the *'Eagle's talons.'* It was then and there the Eagle's flight was loftiest—the shadow of her wings in her triumphant ascent, announced to the city *victory and peace*. Think you, sir, the Ladies of New Orleans would withhold the poor pittance of ten thousand dollars to raise a monument to the memory of Gen. Jackson, to be reared upon the banks of that great river which flows by their proud and prosperous city? Or do you believe, when the news of that brilliant triumph, unsurpassed in the annals of warfare, reached Tennessee, if it had been asked to give ten thousand dollars by the State, to prepare some suitable insignia to his memory, that it would have been denied. No, sir, I answer no! Then every Tennessean's heart beat high with gratitude—all were proud of being his fellow-citizen, and who would not proudly own the distinction of being a citizen of the same State with him? Then we were all of one mind in giving thanks to the Almighty, who always crowns the cause of justice with victory, and in our praises too of *him*, who was the master spirit of that *eventful day*. But, alas! how things have changed!! Then we would have raised a 'triumphal arch' by our united power to the very heavens, as a mark of our gratitude and respect to the Chief who terminated the war in such a *'blaze of glory'*. But now, when his body lies cold beneath the clods of the valley, and when the descendants of his soldiers in arms, and of victory, ask a small pittance to be paid by the people of his own gallant State, to raise a monument to his memory, it is refused—I fear on political accounts.

I appeal to gentlemen for once to lay party feelings down; let us rise above its storms, and in justice to the memory of the illustrious dead, award to his services such an appreciation as we would were we untrammelled by party fetters. It is not pretended that Gen. Jackson was faultless. The Father of his country had his faults. It is the lot of man to err. But now that he is gone to that bourne from whence no traveler returns, I trust his faults will be overlooked, and that we will show to the world that we appreciate his virtues as citizens of the same great State.

But gentlemen on the other side of the House, urge as an objection to the appropriation, that the people did not send us here to appropriate money to the erection of statues to our heroes. Sir, the people sent us here to do justice to the living and to the memory of the dead. What will the appropriation be to each voter in the State?—There is about 120,000 voters in Tennessee—we ask $10,000 from them by the bill, which would be just 12 cents per voter. Where is the man I ask, who would not be willing and anxious to give that sum, as a last tribute of respect to the memory of this departed Hero and Statesman? Where is the *Tennessean,* who would refuse to contribute the small sum of *twelve cents* to keep green in the memory of succeeding generations, the distinguished military and civil services of this most devoted friend of human liberty, both civil and religious, any where to be found in the history of man? Surely such an one is not in Tennessee—in chivalrous Tennessee! We proudly boast of this appellation, which was won and secured to us by *him,* whose name to-day we seek to honor, upon the plains of New Orleans. Who is it, and to what party does he belong, that is not proud of being a Tennessean? If you are proud of your State, as you surely are, for the high and elevated station which she as a sovereignty of this great confederacy occupies, then to whom, it may be properly asked, do you owe most for your distinction? The answer is too obvious for a reply. All agree that Jackson led our soldiers in arms to victory, and impressed upon the world the idea of our chivalry. Hence we derive the enviable preeminence of unrivalled valor. Superadded to this may be appropriately connected our exalted Statesman-like position among the sovereignties of this happy Union. Then, if Tennessee stands as high as we suppose among our sister States, and as we all admit, this pre-eminence proceeded from the genius and the generalship of our own illustrious Jackson, why then is it, that we refuse the pittance proposed by the bill? It should be remembered that such calls are seldom made. We have existed as a State about half a century, and it has never before entered into the minds of our people to erect such trophies as these to the memory of any man. It is also reasonable to suppose, judging of the future by the past, that we will not be called upon soon again to render this kind of tribute to the memory of any man. Indeed it seems to me, that we should seize the moment as being the first and perhaps the last for ages, that presents us with a man upon whose character a tribute so meritorious could be bestowed.—The nation boasts of his exalted worth, and the people everywhere are anxious to do honor to his name; and will Tennessee show indifference in her admiration of the man who has contributed more to elevate her character than any man has been able to do by his connection with any State or government in any former age or country?

The proposition to erect a monument to the memory of Gen. Jackson who now sleeps with his fathers highly honorable and strongly endeared to the whole nation, should not excite surprise. Such procedure is not without precedent in the world; even families mark the spot where a departed friend is laid, by the erection of something visible and durable. The nation is his family. In a national sense this is only true—true in the acceptable expression everywhere admitted, that he is the second Father of his country, associated in all the great concurrent efforts for human liberty with that illustrious man, who is emphatically styled the 'Father of his country.' To his enduring name monuments have been reared, statues erected, biographies written—deeds consecrated by the most solemn rites under the nation's auspices. Surely such faint monuments of regard offered to the immortal Washington by a nation's munificence, will not detract from her honor or her wealth. Nor will it detract from the honor or wealth of the nation to rear trophies to the memory of the distinguished Jackson, equal in every respect to those which have been erected to the memory of Washington. Virginia did not forget her immortal son when his body was laid in the tomb, but as a dutiful and grateful State statues of marble and of brass, to show future ages, after generations had passed away, her appreciation of the man, and her exalted sense of his undying deeds. Will Tennessee, proud and chivalrous Tennessee, who owes so much for her present high position to the eventful life and extraordinary energies and power of her own Jackson, not erect similar statues and monuments of marble and of brass, to point to future ages, and the teeming millions yet to populate this happy land of ours, that he was the competitor of tyrants, the antagonist of aristocrats, and the pure, fearless and unconquerable defender of the equal rights of man?

Mr. Speaker, I am sure if party, and all our acquaintance with it could be forgotten but for one moment, the appropriation asked would be granted without one dissenting voice. But party often prohibits us from acting in obedience to our convictions of right and wrong. I appeal again to gentlemen to unite with us in this last tribute of respect we will ever be called upon to give to our illustrious departed fellow citizen,—it is but the obsequies of mourning friends at the sepulchre of the dead.

The amendment offered by the gentleman from Madison, (Mr. Bullock) which has been adopted by the friends of the bill; is a proper one, and the only regret connected with it is, that it was proposed with a view of embarrassing the bill; although it has failed to accomplish its intended object, it nevertheless develops with unerring distinctness the design of its mover. The gentleman proposes to erect a statue to the memory of Genl. George Washington to be placed in the Rotunda of our State Capitol, long-side of the statue we propose to place there to the memory of Genl. Andrew Jackson. We accept the association, and thank the gentleman for his high appreciation of our illustrious fellow citizen. While we congratulate ourselves upon an association so apt, so fit, and so proper as marble statues of Washington and Jackson to be placed together in the Capitol of our State, we nevertheless painfully regret to hear the mover (Mr. Bullock) avow that he will not vote one cent for the erection of either. The only reasonable inference to be drawn from the intention of his amendment is, that he hopes to defeat the bill with it. He may succeed in arraying his political friends (or most of them) in opposition to it, but he never can defeat it. Gratitude and duty to the departed worth of those illustrious men, will force its passage against all opposition. He talks of raising a statue to Washington and declares at the same time, he will not vote anything to erect it. If he desires it to be placed in the Capitol, how I ask does he expect to get it there—it will cost money—he refused to give it—he is therefore against the bill and his own amendment.

Mr. Speaker, I call upon the friends of George Washington and Andrew Jackson—I care not of what political faith they may be, to come up and vote for the bill. It provides for the erection of a statue to each, that their memories may be perpetuated together, as great and good men whose lives have both been spent in the same glorious cause, the extension of human liberty, and whose spirits we trust, are now associated in a more exalted employment in a better and brighter world than this.—Under these circumstances, it seems to me, every voice should be raised in favor of carrying out the design of the bill, by appropriating a reasonable amount to place their statues side by side in our State capitol. Fear not the consequences of this vote—our country-women will pay it from the profits of their gardens and their looms, if your constituents should shrink, which I am sure they will not do. It is well known that I vote appropriations with a sparing hand, and I am on that account, sometimes charged with being too penurious. But when I am called upon, as at present, to speak to future ages my honest opinion of the lives and services of George Washington and Andrew Jackson, in conjunction with other representatives of Tennessee, although it may be at a cost of a few thousand dollars, I am willing to cast the vote and assume the responsibility.

Where is the Tennessean, who would not pay twelve cents, to place in the capitol of our State marble statues of these illustrious personages, that we may show to present and future generations the images of these two most distinguished Generals and Statesmen known to this or any former age of the world? And where is the Tennessean, who would not delight to know that he assisted in rearing to the memory of General Jackson a monument at Memphis on the bank of the Mississippi, a city destined in a short time to rival if not excell the most prosperous in the great Mississippi valley. It seems to me that our people, in conjunction with the State, will never hereafter be able to ratify so perfectly the high esteem in which we are held abroad, unless at this time we embrace the favorable opportunity of doing honor to the *man*, who in days gone by has done honor to us. An account will be given of this day's proceeding, if we refuse to sustain the object of the bill; such an account will sound badly abroad, most mortifying indeed abroad as well as at home; to be denounced with the shameful epithet of penury and cold ingratitude to the man who hazarded his life in the battlefield, and exhausted all his energies in council and statesmanship for the public good. It becomes this gallant State, and in this there should be no division, for the people to unite in their consent to erect a monument at Memphis as high and as grand as the sculptor and architect could rear it, towering so high in the air, that it would look down, as it were, upon the rising and setting sun, and throwing its shadow alternately upon the Atlantic and Pacific oceans. It must be magnificent in its plan and construction or it will but dishonor him whom it is intended to honor."

On next to the last day of the legislative session, the Jackson Monument bill was acted upon in the Senate. Even with the insertion of amendments designed to placate the hostile Whigs, the bill was still opposed by nine Whig Senators among whom were the fiery William Cullom and the able Abram Poindexter Maury, each representing counties bordering upon Jackson's home county of Davidson.[66] In the

---

[66] *Senate Journal*, 1845, 560.

House of Representatives, party lines were disregarded in considering the bill. Stalwart Whig leaders like Richardson and Pepper opposed the bill, while Emmerson Etheridge supported the measure.[67] On the final day of the legislative session, all quibbles were ironed out and the emasculated bill finally emerged in the following law:[68]

"An Act to erect a statue and monument to Genl. Andrew Jackson and Genl. Washington

Whereas, since the adjournment of the last session of the General Assembly of Tennessee, the life of General Andrew Jackson terminated on the 8th of June, 1845, at the Hermitage. In the death of Andrew Jackson, we recognize the loss of the most illustrious and distinguished citizen of the State. In early youth, the enthusiastic friend of liberty, he consecrated his devotion to the principles of the revolution, by pouring out his blood in their defence. In the second war of Independence, by his skill and courage, his profound sagacity and unparalleled energy, the fairest, richest and noblest portion of the republic was protected, preserved and secured. In peace, all his councils were directed to the advancement of the welfare and prosperity of his country. Whatever difference of opinion may exist as to the measures and policy of his civil administration, while he was at the head of the National Government, the general voice of his countrymen proclaims that he was honest and patriotic; that in his policy as a public man, and in his conduct as a private citizen, he sought to promote the honor and glory of his country, that he sought to perpetuate the liberties for which he had shed his blood and exposed his life, that he sought to extend and spread the blessings of freedom to his fellow-men in every quarter of the globe, that he was the inflexible advocate and defender of the great principles upon which human freedom is based, the preservation of the union of these States; that as the chief executive of the union, he elevated the national character and dignity in his intercourse with foreign nations, claiming all that was our right and submitting to nothing that was wrong. That the age in which he lived was illustrated by the action of his life; the memory of which will last as long as the history of this union of free states is preserved among men; that he was a patriot, a philanthropist, a benefactor to his country; that while in peace as in war he was the master spirit of his times, he practiced the sacred precepts of the Divine Redeemer of man, and finally yielded up his soul in the confidence of immortality and happiness beyond the grave. The high reputation which attaches to the name of Tennessee throughout the civilized world is identified with the greatness and glory of this deceased patriot, sage and hero. In doing honor to the memory of Andrew Jackson, we elevate the character and standing of our beloved country.

And whereas, the name of George Washington is intimately blended with whatever belongs most essentially to the prosperity, the liberty, the free institutions, and the renown of our country, a name of power to rally a nation in the hour of thick thronging public disasters and calamities; a name that shone amid the storms of war; a beacon light to cheer and guide the country's friends; it flamed too like a meteor to repel her foes; a name in the days of peace; a loadstone attracting to itself a whole people's confidence; a whole people's love, and the world's respect, a name descending with all

---

[67] *House Journal,* 1845, 435.
[68] *Acts of Tennessee,* 1845, Chapter 199.

time, spreading over the earth and uttered in all languages belonging to the tribes and races of men; a name which will ever be pronounced with affectionate gratitude by every one in whose breast there shall arise an aspiration for human rights and human liberty.

SECTION 1. *Be it enacted, by the General Assembly of the State of Tennessee,* That a marble statue shall be erected to Andrew Jackson, and located at the capital of the State of Tennessee.

SEC. 2. *Be it enacted,* That the citizens of Tennessee are called upon to unite and raise by voluntary contribution a sum sufficient to erect this memorial to the memory of the hero and patriot; and to effect this purpose, the Governor of this State shall appoint proper and responsible commissioners in the counties of this State, who shall open books and receive contributions for the purpose of aiding in the construction of said statues, and the moneys so subscribed and paid, shall be by said commissioners forthwith deposited in some one of the banks of this State, and shall take duplicate receipts of said deposits from the cashier of the bank, one of which he shall envelope in a sheet of paper addressed to the comptroller of the treasury, and shall put the same in the post office. The cashier of the bank with whom deposits shall be made, shall keep a separate account of the said fund so deposited, to be denominated the Jackson Monument fund, and which shall only be drawn upon the check of the treasurer.

SEC. 3. *Be it enacted,* That the commissioners for contributions shall make quarterly returns of the amount of the Jackson monument fund contributed and deposited, to the comptroller, commencing upon the first day of March, 1846, and the comptroller shall quarterly publish the amount of the fund so contributed.

SEC. 4. *Be it enacted,* That as the fund shall accumulate upon deposit in any of the banks of this state, the comptroller shall make arrangements with said banks to pay 6 per cent interest per annum thereon, and in case of any of said banks refusing to pay said interest, then the comptroller shall issue his warrant to the treasurer, who, by his check, shall withdraw said fund from such bank refusing to pay said interest, and shall forthwith deposit said funds with the bank of Tennessee or branches, which shall pay 6 per cent per annum interest thereon until withdrawn.

SEC. 5. *Be it enacted,* That the commissioners for contributions, and cashiers of said banks having any of said fund on deposit, shall on the 1st day of October, in each and every year, report to the comptroller of the treasury the amount of the said Jackson monument fund, and where deposited, and when. The comptroller shall examine, adjust and ascertain the amount of said fund and report its state and condition to the General Assembly.

SEC. 6. *Be it enacted,* That Felix Robertson, John M. Bass, Vernon K. Stevenson, Andrew Ewing, John N. Esselman, Francis B. Fogg, Joseph Vaulx and Samuel D. Morgan, be and they are appointed commissioners to contract with some American sculptor or artist, and to direct, and superintend the construction of said statue to Jackson to be located at the capitol of the State of Tennessee. The said commissioners shall form themselves into a board, a majority of whom shall transact business, and shall have the power to receive from time to time the warrant of the comptroller, requiring the treasurer to check on the Jackson monument fund, to be applied towards the erection of said statue, and who shall report to the General Assembly.

SEC. 7. *Be it enacted,* That for the purpose of raising funds to aid in the construction of a suitable monument or statue to General Andrew Jackson, to be erected upon the bank of the Mississippi river, at or near Memphis, the

Governor of this State shall appoint proper and responsible commissioners as required in the second section of this act, who shall have the same power, and be required to perform the same duties, as is therein prescribed to said commissioners, and the fund raised by them, and deposited in bank, shall be denominated the Memphis river monument fund, and the same duties prescribed to the comptroller, treasurer, governor and cashiers of banks, touching the Jackson monument fund, are prescribed to them touching the Mississippi river monument fund, which fund shall by all of said persons be kept separate and apart, and applied to the respective objects prescribed in this act.

SEC. 8. *Be it enacted,* That Nat. Anderson, W. W. Hart, Robertson Topp, James M. Walker, Joseph W. Watkins, H. Van Pelt, Robert H. Petillo, E. F. Watkins, F. P. Stanton, George W. Smith, Peter Gaines, Charles G. McClain, M. B. Winchester, William Armour, George W. Murphey and I. G. Harris, be and they are hereby appointed commissioners to contract for the construction of said monument or statue to Andrew Jackson, to be located upon the bank of the Mississippi river, at or near Memphis, and superintend the erection of the same, the said commissioners shall form themselves into a board, a majority of whom shall transact business, and shall have the power to receive from time to time the warrant of the comptroller, requiring the treasurer to check upon the Mississippi monument fund so deposited, to be applied towards the erection of said monument or statue, and shall report to the General Assembly.

SEC. 9. *Be it enacted,* That the commissioners for contributions to the Jackson monument fund, and the commissioners for contributions to the Mississippi monument fund, shall keep separate lists, showing the names, residences and occupations of all persons paying money, with the amount subscribed by each: inducing subscribers, as far as practicable, to write their own names, and shall transmit the original list to the office of the Secretary of State upon the first day of October, in each and every year, which shall be preserved by the secretary in his office.

SEC. 10. *Be it enacted,* That the commissioners to superintend the construction of said statue or monument shall have the power to sue in the name of the president of the board, for the use of the State, upon any contract, obligation or duty, touching said funds or their application, and to enforce the performance of the various duties, or any of them, prescribed by this act, before any jurisdiction having cognizance thereof.

SEC. 11. *Be it enacted,* That no one of the commissioners, or officers specified in this act, shall receive any compensation for their services; and all vacancies which may occur, shall be filled by the Governor.

SEC. 12. *Be it enacted,* The Governor of the State shall in like manner appoint commissioners to open books for subscriptions for the erection of a statue of George Washington, the Commander in Chief of the Armies of the United States during the Revolutionary War, and first President of the United States, to be placed in the capitol of the State when the same shall be completed.

SEC. 13. *Be it enacted,* That the faith of the State is hereby pledged for the appropriation of the sum of fifteen thousand dollars to the erection of the statues and monument contemplated in this act to the memory of George Washington and Andrew Jackson, to be equally divided between said statues and monument, when a sufficient sum shall be subscribed by the people, in connection therewith, to complete said statues and monument.

SEC. 14. *Be it further enacted,* That this General Assembly respectfully invoke the aid and co-operation of the ladies of Tennessee in advancing the several objects contemplated in this act; and they are hereby earnestly solicited to aid in raising the fund, to be applied as aforesaid, by fairs, concerts and such other means as their ingenuity may suggest; and said fund, so raised, to pay over to the commissioners herein appointed to receive the same.

SEC. 15. *Be it enacted*, That the name of each officer and soldier slain in the battle of New Orleans, be engraved upon the base of said statue.

> BROOKINS CAMPBELL,
> *Speaker of the House of Representatives.*
> H. M. WATTERSON,
> *Speaker of the Senate.*

Passed February 2, 1846."

As is quite obvious, the "catch" in the law was embodied in Section 13 where it was provided that the State appropriation was available

"when a sufficient sum shall be subscribed by the people, in connection therewith, to complete said statues and monument."

Here is a classic example wherein a Legislature, torn by partisan strife, erected a monument to its own folly. To make a State appropriation contingent upon public subscription, the latter to be aided by the ingenuity of women conducting fairs and concerts, was so manifestly farcical that the whole movement lapsed into utter futility. Even four years later, the Legislature displayed no appreciable judgment as to how to provide funds for so meritorious a project. The act of 1845 was so amended as to allow "agents" a commission of 5% on all amounts collected by them.[69] Here we had a forerunner of the present-day menace, the "five per center"!

The real story of the resuscitation of the movement to erect an appropriate statue to the memory of the life and services of "Old Hickory" may be found by referring to the official records of the *Tennessee Historical Society*. Anybody who reads the report [70] of Judge John M. Lea on the Jackson Monument, as transmitted by him to the above *Society*, can not but be grateful that such an organization was both alive and alert, and that the laudable action of the Society saved the citizenry of the State from positive humiliation and disgrace. Let's read Judge Lea's analysis, and at this late date, chide a Legislature that was riddled and made ridiculous by its own petty partisan politics!

"Hon. John M. Lea presented the following report in relation to the Jackson statue, which was received and ordered to be spread on the minutes, to wit:
The committee appointed at a meeting held the 20th day of January, 1880, for the purchase of Mills' equestrian statue of Gen. Andrew Jackson respectfully report:
That so long ago as the session of the General Assembly of 1845-6, the

---

[69] *Acts of Tennessee*, 1849, Chapter 217.
[70] *Tennessee Historical Society Minute Book* for 1880, page 183.

idea was conceived of erecting at the Capitol in Nashville a statue in honor of Gen. Andrew Jackson, whose death took place the 8th day of June, 1845; and an act was passed the 2d day of February, 1846, appropriating the sum of $7,500, 'when a sufficient sum shall be subscribed by the people in connection therewith to complete said monument.' Commissioners were appointed in the sixth section of said act to receive any voluntary contributions, control the disbursement of all funds, contract with an American sculptor or artist, and superintend the erection of said statue. The passage of the act seemed a dismissal of its provisions from the public attention. The indifference to the performance of a duty so manifest and obvious was, however, more apparent than real, and the feeling that such an honor would some day be accorded to the name and fame of the illustrious hero and statesman, though quiescent, was nevertheless imminent in the breast of every Tennessean. The times were not favorable for the inspiration of patriotism or any expression of it in works of art designed to commemorate important wants in our public history. The first ten years succeeding Gen. Jackson's death were marked by an interest in material development and a devotion to the accumulation of wealth so absorbing that there was scarcely time or opportunity for the entertainment or discussion of any other subject. The next decade witnessed an excitement on political subjects so fierce and violent that the apprehension of impending peril caused a temporary forgetfulness of all the recollections of the glorious past in war with all its attendant horror. The next decade brought peace, but to a people with crippled fortunes, who with a courage as undaunted as that exhibited by them upon the field of battle, entered upon the noble task of repairing the evils, moral, political, and financial wrought by the destructive energies of military force.

The General Assembly soon after the re-establishment of civil authority, with laudable pride, vested commissions with authority to lay out and ornament the Capitol grounds, and in obedience to the general but passive sentiment, the space so long vacant—now we are happy to say adorned by the statue—was, we presume, designed for the reception and erection of this or some other imposing monument significant of men or events connected with Tennessee history. The severe ordeal through which the people passed, for a few years succeeding the declaration of peace, forbid attention to this or any other subject not bearing directly upon the interests of the passing hour.

Early in the month of January, 1879, Gen. Marcus J. Wright, of Washington City, addressed a letter to the Vice President of the Society, suggesting that Clark Mills' equestrian statue of Gen. Jackson was on sale, expressing the hope that Tennessee would be induced to make the purchase and tendering his services to aid in the negotiation. A correspondence ensued between Gen. Wright and the Vice President, and those papers, with a letter from Mr. Mills, stipulating the price, were laid before the Society. There was a discussion of plans for obtaining the requisite funds to make the purchase but nothing definite was agreed on, and the Vice President was instructed to communicate further with Gen. Wright, and also to confer with the Governor of the State as to the policy of applying to the General Assembly for an appropriation. There was a conference with the Governor, and also with some members of the General Assembly—letters also passed between the Governor and Gen. Wright—but after due deliberation the time was not deemed opportune to invoke the assistance of the State, and we did not care to have any future prospect clouded by a denial of favorable legislation. The facts were duly reported to the society, and notwithstanding all obstacles in our path, so great was our earnestness, that the subject was again brought up and discussed in connection with the celebration of the centenary at a meeting held the 1st day of July, 1879. Various plans for raising the money were proposed, none of which, however, commanded that assurance of success which warranted immediate action, and the measure was indefinitely postponed with a firm conviction that under more favorable auspices our cherished desire might some day be gratified.

On the 14th day of March, 1878, resolutions were passed by the Society contemplating the celebration of the centenary of Nashville. At subsequent meetings the proper committees were appointed, reports made, etc., the entire proceedings to be conducted under the supervision of the Society. Further reflection induced a change of purpose and it was determined at a meeting held the 4th day of November, 1879, to ask the people of the city to unite with the Society and make a combined effort to mark the centenary of Nashville as an event in our local history. A committee with this view was appointed to wait upon the Mayor and City Council, and, an affirmative answer being given, invited the Mayor to a general meeting of the citizens, for consideration of the subject, on the 16th day of December, 1879. The attendance was large, and from the incipient action of the meeting on that evening has resulted a success beyond anticipation in any and every department connected with the celebration of the centenary. A glow of enthusiasm at once seized the entire community. There was a pause in the pursuit of individual interests and the moment given to unselfish and patriotic inspiration. Memories of the past seemed to rise spontaneously in the public mind, and it doubtless occurred to more than one that the conjunction of circumstances was favorable for the acquisition of the Jackson statue. Such a thought did certainly occur to a venerable and patriotic citizen of Nashville—Maj. John Lewis Brown—who, early after the meeting in December, expressed his intention to try to raise by voluntary subscriptions the money necessary for its purchase.

He wrote to Senator Harris and Maj. Blair, of Washington City, to make inquiry of Mr. Mills as to the cost of the statue. Maj. Blair replied on the 23d of January, 1879, that the statue was for sale but Mr. Mills declined to state the price, giving as his reason that Col. Bullock, of Tennessee, then sojourning in Washington City, was negotiating for the purchase. Afterwards, ascertained that the object of Col. Bullock and Maj. Brown was identical—the procurement of the statue for Tennessee—the 'figures were given at $5,000 as the lowest price.' About this time an admirable letter, written by Col. Bullock on the subject of the purchase was printed in the *American* of this city, and from that moment so forcibly were the facts put forth, the public mind was impressed with the idea that our celebration would be incomplete if we could not present to the thousands of people who would throng our streets the grand spectacle of the unveiling of the statue.

Much credit should be awarded to Col. Bullock for the impetus which his letters gave to the movement, and especially is it to be cited that it was through his negotiation the price was reduced from $12,000 to $5,000, thus placing the object within probable reach of our pecuniary ability. Our acknowledgments are certainly due, and are most cheerfully rendered to our esteemed fellow-citizen, Col. Bullock, for the zeal and interest thus displayed by him. Pending these negotiations at Washington, our fellow-citizen, Maj. Brown, was tireless in forming plans for devising ways to secure the necessary amount of money. He appeared before the Historical Society and stated that if he were armed with their recommendation and allowed to work under their name, he would guarantee success, counting alone upon the liberality and public spirit of the people. Previous to this time, however, without recognized authority from any society or association, he had secured some subscriptions, but after his appointment with the Vice President and Secretary, at a meeting held the 29th day of January, 1880, 'as a committee for the purchasing of the statue for the State of Tennessee,' he set to work vigorously, earnestly and systematically. He addressed letters to leading citizens in the different counties, made personal application and used every means and appliance to further the enterprise, the success of which lay so near his heart. There were difficulties in his way. There had been heavy drains upon the people for subscriptions to the Exposition, and the public liberality had been strained to its utmost tension. In this emergency a suggestion was made that the 'Exposition' should buy the statue and count for its remuneration upon the increased receipts to be derived from this additional feature of its attractions. To this intimation Maj. Brown strenuously objected, contending that if time were given, the $5,000 could be raised. He redoubled his energies, appointed agents, and the list of subscribers so increased that on the 18th of March, 1880, success being within sight, the Centennial Board of Directors 'incorporated as one of the regular committees of the Board, Gen. Jno. F. Wheless, Mr. A. J. Adams, Mr. Jo. L. Weakley, Judge John M. Lea, Gen. G. P. Thruston, Mr. Anson Nelson and Maj. John L. Brown, to be known as the committee for the purchase and dedication of the Equestrian Statue of Gen. Jackson.' On account of his onerous duties as commanding officer during 'Military Week,' Gen. Wheless resigned and Gen. Thruston was appointed to the chairmanship of said committee. The subscriptions soon aggregated an amount, finally reaching near or quite $5,500, which justified a consummation of the purchase. The naked price was not, however, the only expense. Transportation had to be secured, a temporary pedestal constructed and a vexatious litigation was set on foot in Washington likely to retard the delivery of the statue in time for the unveiling during 'Military Week.'

Further expense was thus necessarily incurred, but the difficulty was obviated by an agreement on the part of the Centennial Board to make good the deficiency, provided there should be a surplus of that amount (after the repayment by the Military Committee of the award loaned) realized at the Fair Grounds during military week. The deficiency, upon settlement, amounted to $630, and our obligations are due to the Military Committee—not only for this substantial aid but also for the éclat which was given to the occasion of the unveiling of the statue by the presence of the citizen soldiery from this and other States.

It is the province of the committee, of which Col. G. P. Thruston is chairman, to set forth the particular items of expense connected with the transportation, removal from the depot to the capitol grounds, construction of the temporary pedestal and mounting of the statue; but we take pleasure in stating that we owe much to his good management for the safety which attended this delicate work and the economy with which it was performed. No accident happened in the transportation, and the statue stands on the pedestal as perfect as in its state of original completion.

The statue was unveiled on a bright, beautiful day, the 20th of May, 1880, in the presence of a vast assemblage of people from this and other States, a full account of which, the erection and military display, will, doubtless, appear in the proceedings of the Directors of the Centennial Board, to whom the Society, on the determination of a joint celebration, resigned the conduct of all ceremonial observances.

Mr. Clark Mills was an invited spectator, and his bosom must have swelled with pardonable pride in knowledge of the admiration bestowed upon the workmanship of his hands.

The unveiling of the statue was the grandest feature of the celebration—a red-letter day in the annals of Nashville—an event worthy to link the past with the succeeding centenary of our beautiful city.

The list would be long, indeed, if thanks were especially expressed to all who have aided the Society, but it is a simple act of justice, in the opinion of this committee, to declare that the zeal, energy and patriotism of Maj. John L. Brown put in motion the machinery which brought about this grand result, and to him more than to any other person are the people of Tennessee indebted for the magnificent work of art which adorns our beautiful grounds —a monument which symbolizes alike the greatness of the departed hero and the devotion of the people of Tennessee to his debtors.

> Respectfully submitted,
> JOHN M. LEA, *Ch'm,*
> ANSON NELSON."

In regard to honoring the memory of another distinguished Tennessean, the 1845 Legislature was more generous and sensible than was true in the case of Andrew Jackson. The man who thus far served as Governor of Tennessee longer than any other had died in 1844. On the closing day of the legislative session, February 2, 1846, a resolution was passed calling upon the Governor to designate some suitable person to supervise the erection of a suitable monument to the memory of former Governor William Carroll, and to direct the State Comptroller to issue a warrant to cover the cost of such memorial.[71] In the Report of the State Comptroller in 1849, there appeared the following entry,

"Monument to William Carroll..............$2,500." [72]

Once more, the liquor question arose in the General Assembly of 1845. It will be recalled that the "quart law", or anti-tippling act, had been enacted in 1837 whereby it was made illegal to sell spirituous liquors in quantites less than one quart.[73] That law had been subjected to eight years of actual experience and had resulted in a divided camp. In some portions of the State, the law had been enforced; in other sections, the law had become a notoriously dead letter statute. Despite the provisions of the 1837 liquor law, tippling houses had increased and were doing a land-office business. There was strong sentiment for elimination of wide-spread liquor-selling, but there was great diversity of opinion as to how best to attain that objective. Petitions, *pro* and *con,* were filed with the Legislature. Advocates of the existing law argued that it was a good law and needed only to be enforced. Opponents maintained that the "quart law" was an invasion of human rights, and

---

[71] *Acts of Tennessee,* 1845, Resolution XXXI, 361.
[72] *Senate Journal,* 1849, Appendix, 143.
[73] See *Messages of the Governors of Tennessee,* Volume III, 242–255, for a resumé of legislative action *re* liquor control.

that its non-enforcement was evidence that morals could not be legislated into people.

On November 3, 1845, Senator James M. Williamson representing the counties of Hardeman, Fayette, and Shelby introduced the following resolution [74] which was passed:

"*Resolved*, That the Committee on the Judiciary be instructed to enquire into the expediency of repealing the present law for the suppression of the offence of retailing spirituous liquors, and enacting such other law as will more effectually restrain or regulate the traffic in spirituous liquors by the small measure."

For nearly two months, November 3-December 30, the liquor bill received but mediocre attention by the Legislature. On the above latter date, at the morning session, Senator Jonas E. Thomas representing the counties of Maury and Giles laid before the Senate

"Three memorials from sundry ladies and citizens of Maury County, praying to retain the present law prohibiting tippling and tippling houses, and to amend it by repealing the laws which prohibit the punishment of public drunkenness—to make the retail of wine punishable as the retail of spirituous liquors; and to give grand jurors the powers in relation to tippling and tippling houses that they have in relation to gaming and gaming houses." [75]

At the night session, Senator Richard Warner representing the counties of Bedford and Marshall offered a rather unique resolution that authorized

"any person or persons in the State to sell spirituous and vinous liquors by the quart, or in any larger quantity, and the same may be drunk on the premises when sold; *provided*, the person or persons vending said spirituous or vinous liquors shall be subject to an indictment or punishment for any disorderly or improper conduct that may take place when said spirituous or vinous liquors may be sold and drank." [76]

On January 21, 1846, the Senate took up the liquor bill and, after the adoption of a minor amendment by Senator Thomas, the bill was placed on third and final reading. The bill was passed by an eye-lash majority, the vote being 13 for and 12 against. [77] The House, after concurring in sundry amendments, passed the bill without recording the aye and nay vote. [78] On January 23, the Senate was notified that the bill had been signed by the Speaker of the House and was being transmitted to the Senate for the signature of the Speaker of that body. Mr. Speaker Watterson signed the bill and it was now the law of the land. [79]

---

[74] *Senate Journal*, 1845, 167.
[75] *Ibid.*, 361.
[76] *Ibid.*, 367.
[77] *Ibid.*, 465.
[78] *House Journal*, 1845, 540.
[79] *Senate Journal*, 1845, 480.

Now, that the "quart law" of 1837 had been repealed, what sort of liquor law had been cooked up by the Solons? The very caption itself of the new law [80] indicated that *revenue* was a dominant feature of the new measure, in that the purposes were declared to be

"To tax and regulate Tippling and Tippling Houses, and to increase the Revenue."

Section I of the new law indicated quite clearly that the State was returning to a general licensing system. It was made lawful for any person to sell spirituous or vinous liquors in "any quantity the purchaser or purchasers desired," provided certain conditions were observed. The vendor was required to obtain a license, paying an annual tax of twenty-five dollars on a stock of goods amounting to two hundred and fifty dollars plus an additional tax, not exceeding the State tax, that might be levied by any county or incorporated town. If the stock of liquors exceeded two hundred and fifty dollars in value, an additional tax of ten dollars was assessed on each one hundred dollars worth of liquors. The applicant for a license was forbidden to sell liquor to slaves or to vend his wares on Sunday, nor could he sell liquor to Free Persons of Color. On the whole, the provisions of the new law differed from the old law chiefly by imposing a higher tax for a license and by prohibiting liquor sales on Sunday.

Contemporary opinion as to the new liquor law was expressed by two Nashville newspapers of opposite political complexion. The Democratic organ [81] viewed the matter as follows:

"THE LICENSE LAW.

After an animated struggle of eight years duration the friends of legalizing the retail of spirituous liquors, under a license system, have at length achieved a victory. The law of 1837, which prohibited the retail traffic in liquor, and which has at length been supplanted by an act which authorizes any person to retail who will pay a specified tax, give specified bonds, and take specified oaths. A law has seldom been enacted with so many restrictions and guards and penalties thrown around it—and if it shall be administered with half the rigor with which its friends expect it to be executed, it may well be doubted whether the friends of temperance will have much cause to regret its passage. The late law effected much good in some sections, whilst it was a dead letter in others. If the same result shall follow with the present law, as we fear will be the case, it were better that the old law had remained. There are features in the present law which will make it the object of bitter assault by those who are in favor of a license system. If it is executed with rigor by grand juries and Circuit Judges, it will become an odious law —if it is not so executed the advocates of the late law will clamor against it— in any event it will play a conspicuous part in the future political contests of the State.—We have no expectation that the law will stand more than

---

[80] *Acts of Tennessee*, 1845, Chapter 90.
[81] *Nashville Union*, January 24, 1846.

two years—many of its provisions are of a character so obnoxious to the attacks of demagogueism that they will hardly remain in force long. The danger is that the restrictions now in the law will be removed one by one until the retail of liquors shall become as free as in former times. We shall take an early occasion to publish the act that all may see its provisions."

Three days later, the Whig journal [82] through its editorial column gave expression to its views:

"The object of both parties was the same—*To put down tippling houses as far as practicable;* but they differed as to the most efficient means of effecting this object. The effect of the Act of 1838 was to prohibit, under strong penalties, the sale of spirituous liquors in less quantities than a quart under any circumstances, and likewise in quantities over a quart if to be drank at the place where sold. The intention of the framers of this law was undoubtedly praiseworthy—their object was to *abolish tippling houses* entirely. But seven years experience showed that the operation of the law had not answered the expectations of its authors. In some sections of the state the effect was highly beneficial, undoubtedly. In those sections, tippling houses *were* put down. In other sections, however, the operation of the law was directly the reverse. In them, the law was notoriously a dead letter. Public opinion mocked at its execution. It became a mere nullity, and openly and notoriously and in increased numbers tippling houses sprung up and prospered in defiance of the law. It was this difference in the operation of the law in various parts of the state that produced a difference of opinion and views that existed among the members of the Legislature. Those members who represented counties where the old law had proved beneficial were naturally in favor of letting it remain as it was. On the other hand, those members who represented counties where the law was notoriously a mere nullity and where its effect so far from being salutary was considered to be absolutely mischievous were in favor of repealing it and substituting in its place the license system guarded by proper restrictions. A majority of both houses of the Legislature being of this latter class, the Act of 1838 has been repealed, and the act which we published today substituted for it. Unquestionably the principal reason which operated on them in voting to repeal the old law and in favor of the present act was a conscientious belief on their part that the present act will more effectually suppress the evils of tippling than the old law. Those who voted to repeal the old law are in *theory* and in *practice* as much the friends of temperance as those who voted to retain it. Time alone can decide which view of the subject was the correct one. For ourselves, we shall be greatly surprised if the evils, tippling and intemperance, shall be found to increase under the operation of the strongest regulation of the law which has just been passed."

The enactment of the liquor law of 1845, like all previous laws on the subject, gave only limited satisfaction. Ten years later, "prohibition" was thrust into the gubernatorial campaign. Almost every legislative session had to deal with the problem in one form or another. Despite the fact that the liquor law of 1845 was only partially effective, yet it had a rather long life, considering the life-span of liquor laws in general. The 1845 law, with the exception of just two years, remained the

---

[82] *Nashville Whig,* January 27, 1846.

law in Tennessee until after the termination of the War Between the States.

There is ample evidence throughout the deliberations of the 1845 Legislature of much interest in regard to the status of transportation and commerce in Tennessee as of that time, and transportation facilities were a *must*. Tennessee was admirably adapted, both by climate and soil, for producing agricultural products. In 1840, Tennessee was the largest corn-growing State in the Union; in 1850, more hogs were grown in Tennessee than in any other State. In addition, cotton was a great money-crop, and wheat was being exported to other States. Tobacco was another ready money-crop. It is no wonder that the need of transportation facilities occupied the attention of the Legislature. In recognition of that fact, four railroad charters were granted; four laws relating to improvement of river channels were enacted; seven laws were passed regarding navigation; and twenty-nine turnpike laws were passed. Industry, however, received but scant legislative attention, there having been only one law enacted dealing specifically with that topic, namely, to incorporate the Port Royal Manufacturing Company. Privileges were granted for

"... carrying on the manufacture of all goods which cotton, wool, hemp, and flax form a part, and for the establishment of a flour mill or paper mills. ..." [83]

However, a Joint Select Committee submitted a rather comprehensive report [84] on the manufacturing advantages possessed by Tennessee, to-wit:

"The joint select committee of the two houses of this General Assembly whose duty it was to elicit all the statistical and other information which they can obtain respecting the Manufacturing advantages of this State ask leave to report on the same. The late period of the session at which the committee was raised preclude the possibility of giving a detailed account of the facilities to manufacturing which each section of the State affords. It is a fact too palpable for demonstration that but few if any States in the Union transcend Tennessee in the natural advantages for manufacturing. Her water power is never failing. The Iron ore imbedded in her hills is boundless and inexhaustible. It is an important fact that Tennessee Iron is inferior to none in the world.

The Geologist of the State in his last report to this General Assembly gives publicity to the following facts.

English imported iron is not to be compared with our Tennessee iron, to the honor of which I beg leave here to mention that none of the steam boilers made of Tennessee iron, out of which I am informed several have been constructed in Cincinnati and Pittsburgh, have burst, of course therefore our iron masters are free from any blame of having contributed to the sacrifice of the hundreds of lives that have been lost by those accidents.

For the purpose of obtaining information satisfactory upon the subject of Tennessee Manufactures the committee addressed a letter propounding

---

[83] *Acts of Tennessee*, 1845, Chapter 125.
[84] *House Journal*, 1845, 594–597.

various interrogatories to one of the most intelligent and extensive manufacturers in the State who has favored us with a reply answering the questions propounded which letter we have incorporated as a part of our report and reads as follows:

Nashville, December 25th, 1845.

GENTLEMEN:

I am requested by your note of yesterday's date to reply to several interrogatories relating to the Manufacturing Interests of Tennessee.

In replying to it, it is proper for me to apprise you, that owing to the want of all reliable data and the difficulty of obtaining the information sought for, that my answers (so far as statistics are concerned) must be taken for nothing more than mere approximations, as such they are offered.

To your first question relating to the amount of capital which is invested in manufacturing operations in Tennessee, I answer that I estimate the capital so employed *at certainly not less than five million three hundred and eighty three thousand dollars*—divided thus viz:

In the production of Iron in its various forms................$4,100,000
In Cotton and Woolen Mills................................ 900,000
In the manufacture of Hemp and other less important articles 380,000
                                                            ──────────
                                                            $5,380,000

In the foregoing estimate I feel convinced that I rather underrate than overrate the amount.

In arriving at the amount of investments in the iron business, I availed myself of the aid of several of the most eminent and intelligent iron masters of the State.

As to the quantity of raw material which is annually consumed by our manufacturers (to which your second interrogatory applies,) I have made no attempt to arrive at any conclusion, because I have no means at hand sufficiently reliable to found an estimate upon.

Your third like your second interrogatory is one very difficult of solution; inasmuch as in the southern and western States few if any of the manufacturing operations are conducted by corporations or joint stock companies, as is almost universally the case in the eastern and northern States. Hence there is no necessity for publicly declared dividends, and by which the public are enabled to arrive at the profits of any such company; therefore the impossibility of an answer on any such reliance should be placed.

So far, however, as I am enabled to judge of the profits of manufacturing in our State, I am inclined to the belief that capital judiciously invested and carefully, energetically and prudently managed, will yield a very fair return in profits—perhaps greater than in any other industrial pursuit pursued in the State.

These remarks are intended to apply more especially to the production of iron and the more common descriptions of woolen and cotton goods. To other branches of manufacturing, I have not had my attention particularly directed, therefore decline any expression of opinion—not, however, because I have reason to suppose other branches may not be as profitably entered into as those alluded to.

Your fourth interrogatory which asks: What is the probable difference in supporting operations engaged in manufacturing in Tennessee and the northern States? is more readily answered—and I reply: That in Tennessee the cost of such maintenance will not certainly exceed one-half (and most probably less) of what it does in the New England States. This will be made manifest to all who may take the trouble of comparing a Boston prices current with one of the same date issued at Nashville.

In Tennessee the average values of corn and pork are for the former twenty cents per bushel, and for the latter two and a half cents per pound; whereas, in Boston and Lowell the usual price of the former is fifty-five to sixty cents, and for the other, less than six cents per pound is seldom asked and obtained.

You ask in your fifth interrogatory what are the advantages or disadvantages attending slave labor compared with white labor employed in manufacturing?

In answering this the most important of your questions, I am aware of having to encounter the old and deep rooted prejudices of most persons who have not investigated the subject for themselves, but who have rather adopted opinions expressed (perhaps interestedly) by others. To such an extent has this opinion that slave labor cannot successfully compete with free labor in manufacturing operations taken possession of the public mind, that it has become in a manner a proverb, and like all other old maxims is most difficult to eradicate.

In some of the more delicate and intricate operations, where there is much exercise of the mind requisite, I admit that *it may be true*—but to an extent beyond this I deny its truth; and I appeal to all whose experience qualify them as judges to bear me out in the assertion—that in all operations, where patience, care, application and strength are the chief requisites, that the slave is found in all respects competent. He is patient of toil, submits readily to discipline, and unencumbered with cares of the mind; hence it is more entirely brought to bear on the operation he may be performing. To this may be added his physical ability of enduring the heat of the iron-furnace or of the spinning room decidedly better than the white man.

Again: The employer of the slave operative is not deprived of his services from having him called off to sit on juries; to attend musters and elections; and many other such drawbacks on labor.

Nor is he found uniting in combinations 'to strike for higher wages' or for 'shorter hours of work' at that particular juncture of time, too, when his services are most needed.

And yet another reason still more cogent is at hand, to prove that to the manufacturer, *who is the owner of the slave,* his services are doubly valuable. It is this; when the owner has taught him the art of manufacturing he is not called on from time to time, as improvement in skill take place, to increase his wages, as is always the case with the white laborer, who becoming more and more expert, demands and is certainly entitled to higher pay, because the instruction he has acquired, enables him to make for his employer more money.

But great as I view the advantages resulting from the use of slave labor in manufacturing, I am unwilling to believe that the success of manufacturing in Tennessee depends solely on it. For let me assure you that there exists in Tennessee no inconsiderable amount of free white labor, which can most readily be availed of by those who from prejudice or supposed interest prefer it.

In conclusion of this branch of the subject I will remark, that what I have written relative to the adoption of slave labor to manufacturing, is not a mere hypothesis, for it has been *fairly* and *fully* tested in many instances.

There is now, and has been for many years, in *full* and *successful operation,* in North Alabama, an extensive establishment, where large amounts of woolen and cotton goods are daily produced, and of a quality too, much superior to the same description made in the New England States. This concern is in Madison County, owned by Patton, Donegan & Co. and operated *exclusively by slaves in every department,* save only the manager, a clerk, a dyer and a watchman.

Nor are the goods thus produced confined alone to the coarse fabrics, but they embrace many articles of the finer descriptions; to produce which in perfection (as their goods are) requires much skill on the part of the operative.

In Tennessee there are also several establishments at which the same description of goods are made, but none that I am aware of where the laborers are exclusively slaves, as is the case with the Alabama factory.

To these advantages which Tennessee possesses as a favorable point for manufacturing profitably, may be added her excellent water power; a superabundance of the best and cheapest building materials; the mildness and salubrity of our climate, having our cotton, wool, hemp and other raw materials produced in abundance at our very doors, with excellent river navigation as an outlet for our productions. These advantages added to that of possessing in inexhaustible quantities the very best of iron ore and stone coal, tend, as I conceive, to point to Tennessee as decidedly the most desirable point in the Union at which capital and manufacturing skill may be most profitably used—and they are advantages, too, which cannot certainly much longer be overlooked by those possessing the requisites for embarking in such enterprises.

Respectfully, yours, &c.

S. D. MORGAN

To A. G. McDougal, and
    Wm. B. Allen, Chairmen, &c.

The Committee deem it unnecessary to comment upon the very able letter embraced in their report. It will be found upon examination, that it contains facts highly interesting and important to our State, and augurs for a bright and prosperous future.

A. G. McDOUGAL,
Chairman of the Senate Committee.

W. B. ALLEN,
Chairman of the Committee of the House."

Two rather minor Messages from Governor Brown are herewith inserted, not so much because of their importance as for the purpose of the record. On November 20, 1845, the Senate received the following Message:

"GENTLEMEN OF THE SENATE,
    AND OF THE HOUSE OF REPRESENTATIVES: *

In pursuance of the provisions of the Act 'to establish a State Bank, to raise a fund for Internal Improvements, and to aid in the establishment of a system of Education,' passed January 19th, 1838,

* *Senate Journal,* 1845, 240.
  House Journal, 1845, 211.

I nominate the following named gentlemen to be Directors of the Bank of Tennessee, viz:

A. O. P. Nicholson,
C. Connor,
Andrew Ewing,
Wm. E. Watkins,   of the County of Davidson.
John Waters,
Isaac Paul,
Hardin P. Bostick,

Robert C. Foster, of the County of Williamson.
H. D. Lester, of the County of Wilson.
James C. Moore, of the County of Rutherford,
George Allen, of the County of Smith.
J. R. A. Tompkins, of the County of Sumner.
EXECUTIVE OFFICE,
Nashville, Tennessee, 19th Nov., 1845.
                                        AARON V. BROWN."

Two days after the reception of the above Message, the Senate confirmed all of the nominations by a vote of 22 to 3.[85] The action of the House of Representatives was favorable by a vote [86] of 51 to 9.

On January 19, 1846, the Legislature called upon Governor Brown to nominate three persons to act as Inspectors of the Penitentiary.[87] In response to the request, Governor Brown dispatched the following Message on January 31, 1846:

"GENTLEMEN OF THE SENATE: *

In pursuance of an Act passed at your present session, I hereby nominate to your body the following named persons, as Inspectors of the Penitentiary of this State, the next two years, to wit:—Wm. B. Sheppard, Dr. John N. Esselman, and John Thompson.

                                        Respectfully,
                                        AARON V. BROWN."

---

[85] Senate Journal, 1845, 247.
[86] House Journal, 1845, 219.
[87] Acts of Tennessee, 1845, Resolution XI, 343.
* Senate Journal, 1845, 559.

Without delay, the *Senate Journal* records the following action: [88]

"Mr. . . . . moved a concurrence in said nomination.

And the question being had said motion of concurrence was decided in the affirmative."

The House took no action whatsover in regard to the confirmation of the nominees, inasmuch as the Senate alone had been by a recent statute [89] vested with the power to confirm or reject.

A few minor items, not incorporated in any Executive Message from Governor Brown, seem to deserve brief mention. A digest of the general statutes of the State and of the Supreme Court Reports had appeared desirable, and the Legislature of 1843 provided for the appointment of two persons to attend to that duty. A report [90] on the topic was submitted to the Legislature of 1845 on November 21, portraying a thumbnail sketch of the procedure followed and of the difficulties that had been encountered, to-wit: [91]

"REPORT
of
MESSRS. FOGG AND MEIGS.

To the General Assembly of the State of Tennessee:

Under the resolution passed by the last General Assembly that two persons should be appointed by the Judges of the Supreme Court, whose duty it should be to revise and digest the general statutes of the State of Tennessee, and the Reports of the Supreme Court and report the same to the present session of the General Assembly,—the undersigned beg to state to your Honorable Body, that they were appointed to prepare these works by the Judges of the Supreme Court on the 5th day of February 1844. And they now proceed to report, that they have to regret that they are under the necessity of stating that neither of the contemplated works is ready to be laid before your Honorable Body.

As soon as their necessary attendance upon the Supreme Court would permit, they applied themselves to the arduous task before them, and a short examination convinced them of the advantage, if not necessity of first publishing the digest of the decisions of the Court, before even beginning the revisal of the statutes. The reason of this will be obvious to professional men, when they reflect that nearly one half of all our reported decisions relate to the construction of the statutes of the State, and that, without a careful collation of the decisions, an attempt to reconstruct the statutes must be attended with great hazard of error. For, it has been well observed by a professor of law in England, that it is often impossible, even for lawyers, to

[88] *Senate Journal*, 1845, 561.

[89] *Acts of Tennessee*, 1845, Chapter 129.

[90] *Senate Journal*, 1845, 244.

[91] *House Journal*, 1845, Appendix, 340–341.

form any opinion of the meaning and effect of statutes, until the decisions of the courts have given them a definite construction, and reconciled them not only with each other, but with themselves. Hence, in revising the statutes, it becomes necessary, as the same professor remarks, to engraft the exposition of the courts upon the statute, a method, indeed, pursued in the several States of the Union whose laws have been revised. We, therefore, immediately began the digest of the decisions, and the plan pursued in the preparation of the work has been to read every case, beginning with the most recent volume of Reports, and digest the principles of law found to be decided in each case under appropriate alphabetical heads.

By beginning with the latest decisions, we obtain the benefit of all the modifications, limitations and criticisms, to which the earlier cases have been subjected, and all the new lights that the most mature investigation has shed upon decided principles. And by reading every case, we shall be enabled to give assurance, when we shall have completed the work, that it is really a digest of *all* the decisions. We might easily have published this work long ago, had the usual plan of digesters been followed; that is, of trusting alone to indexes and merely arranging under general titles the matter found in them. And indeed had we consulted our own pecuniary interests, we ought to have adopted that method, for doubtless, the utility of even such an index to the profession, would have ensured for it as ready a sale, and as great a price as will probably be obtained for that, which so far, has been very painfully elaborated. But fidelity to the trust committed to us, and a proper regard for our own reputation determined us to perform our work upon the plan already indicated, however tedious and irksome in the execution.

As we are not entitled to any compensation till the books have been completed, it is scarcely necessary to observe, that we can only bestow upon them the time that is left to us by our professional pursuits, which we are obliged to prosecute with as much diligence as if we were not engaged in these great public works. It will, therefore, be seen, that in addition to our ordinary practice,—which with lawyers whose services are no more sought for than ours, would usually be deemed enough to demand the devotion of one's undivided attention,—we have taken upon ourselves, labors, of themselves sufficient, to occupy all the time allowed us for the preparation of these works, without any other avocation.

We are, therefore, only able to report, that the digest of the decisions is in such a state of forwardness, that if two months of exclusive attention of one of us could be devoted to it, we could have it ready for the press. We had flattered ourselves that this work would have been printed before your present meeting, but an indisposition of some continuance, which happened to one of us, produced a suspension of the work.

For the revisal of the statutes, we have only collected materials, but have not made any important progress in the composition of the laws. Should our health be spared, we pledge ourselves to make every possible exertion to have the digest of decisions printed in a short time, and to lay the Manuscript Revisal before the next General Assembly.

FRANCIS B. FOGG
R. J. MEIGS."

It was three years later before Volume I of the Digest appeared, and not until 1850 did Volume II come from the press. The work had been delayed because of the enormous amount of detail involved, plus the death of one of the digesters, Francis B. Fogg. In the preface to Volume I, Mr. Meigs stated that he had labored

"...faithfully in accomplishing a task at once profitless, slavish, and inglorious." [92]

Posterity has not agreed with all of the self-diagnosis made by Mr. Meigs. Doubtless the work was "profitless and slavish," but his Digest was a monumental piece of almost interminable research. An able legal writer bestowed upon Mr. Meigs the following richly deserved tribute: [93]

"...His work has never been equalled by any similar work in the State, and probably never surpassed anywhere.... The Digest shows a broad and thorough comprehension of the spirit of our jurisprudence as a whole.... It is the work of a scholar and a philosopher, as well as a profoundly learned lawyer...."

On January 7, 1846, Senator Jacob Voorhies laid before the Senate the petition of Mary Hunt, praying that the bequest of her husband, Spencer T. Hunt, be relinquished to her instead of being bequeathed to the State, as provided in the last will of her husband.[94] Her request was denied by the Legislature.[95] Two years later, a legislative resolution decreed as to how the bequest to the State should be handled.[96] In his last will and testament, Spencer T. Hunt, a citizen of Humphreys County, willed that a certain portion of his estate, consisting of land and slaves, should at his death be sold and the proceeds placed with the State Comptroller for the use of the Common Schools of Dickson and Humphreys counties. The land and slaves were sold, and the value [97] of the bequest to the State was later evaluated at $4,545.92. This money is still held in trust by the State, and for more than a hundred years every regular session of the Legislature appropriates a sum of money sufficient to pay interest on the above bequest. The accrued interest is then allocated to the above two counties for the benefit of the public schools in those counties.

On February 2, 1846, the Twenty-Sixth General Assembly adjourned *sine die*. Just prior to adjournment, Mr. Speaker Watterson spoke briefly on a "personal privilege" matter. Calling a fellow Senator to the Chair, Speaker Watterson had this to say: [98]

"MR. SPEAKER:

I understand from some of my friends, that on Saturday evening last, in

---

[92] Meigs, Return Jonathan: *Digest of all Decisions of the Former Superior Courts of Law and Equity and of the Present Supreme Court of Errors and Appeals in the State of Tennessee*, Volume I, Preface V.

[93] Caldwell, Joshua W.: *Bench and Bar of Tennessee*, 92–96.

[94] *Senate Journal*, 1845, 394.

[95] *Ibid.*, 412.

[96] *Acts of Tennessee*, 1845, Resolution 27, 439.

[97] *Appendix* (Legislative Documents), 1857, 150.

[98] *Senate Journal*, 1845, 565.

the heat of the moment, on the passage of the bill for the management and government of the Lunatic Asylum, that I charged fraud upon the Senate. Such, certainly, sir, was not my intention. I could not, sir, intentionally, so remarked as to charge fraud upon the Senate, when I well know that on the passage of bills through the Senate, no fraud can be perpetrated. I have nothing more to say."

Upon the conclusion of his little *amende honorable*, the Senate adopted unanimously a resolution of thanks to Mr. Speaker Watterson

"... for the ability and impartiality with which he has discharged the duties of Speaker the present session."

With appropriate decorum, the other legislative branch brought its deliberations to an end. Mr. Speaker Brookins Campbell addressed the following remarks to his fellow members: [99]

"Gentlemen of the House of Representatives:

The resolutions which you have this moment unanimously adopted, bring me under renewed obligations to each and every member of this House. I confess myself wholly unable to express adequately the gratitude I feel. Nevertheless, I must advert briefly to our relations for the last four months. At the commencement of the present session, I was, by your unsolicited kindness, elevated to the chief office of this House. Notwithstanding my high appreciation of the distinction of presiding over the deliberations of the Representatives of a great State like ours, I accepted the honor with much diffidence and doubt lest my inexperience in parliamentary law might in some degree forfeit your confidence, injure the public interest and dishonor myself.

I embraced the first moment to implore your constant assistance in aiding my humble efforts to discharge the arduous and intricate duties devolving upon the station. To know that I have received your kind and unremitting aid through every vicissitude is a truth which gratitude requires me to acknowledge.

To withhold the announcement, that I have on all occasions been kindly and magnanimously sustained by both political parties, would be a cold hearted indifference of which I hope never to be guilty.

When I remember the exciting scenes through which we have passed; the angry political controversies into which we have sometimes fallen, and the nearly equal divisions of political parties on this floor, which have so often in the heated debate of party questions, aroused all the animosities consequent upon the circumstances and relations which we respectfully bear to the country and our own opinions.—In view of these opposing elements, to receive the approval of all my associates, is gratifying beyond my power of utterance. An additional source of unfeigned pleasure is found in the rare fact, although in the progress of our deliberations, many points of order have been raised, often involving the most intricate and complex questions of parliamentary law, requiring always the prompt opinion of the chair, from which decisions a few appeals have been made to the House and the opinions of the chair have in every instance been sustained, mostly by very large majorities.

A respect so kindly shown for my decisions, and so magnanimously

---

[99] *House Journal*, 1845, 628–629.

maintained throughout the session, demands an additional acknowledgment from a heart already overflowing with gratitude.—This indisputable evidence of your kindness and respect is impressed upon my heart as undying as memory or thought, and will be regarded through after life as the proudest in my humble history.

GENTLEMEN:

Our separation is near at hand; the thought of parting with friends even for a time is painful; but how much more so for us to be separated when we know our separation must be forever, especially after having cultivated the ties of friendship with so much intimacy and kindness, until they have become indissolubly strong in all our personal relations and intercourse. But it is the lot of man—we must part—in all probability to meet no more, either here or elsewhere on any earthly stage; my prayer is that your several destinies may be peace, and your pursuits prosperity, and that the rewards of your present labors may be the public good and an approving constituency.

And now that the curtain which will separate us must soon drop, I avail myself of the moment to bid each of you an affectionate farewell; therefore but one thing now remains but to adjourn this House of Representatives without day.

> BROOKINS CAMPBELL,
> *Speaker of the House of Representatives.*
> McDONOUGH J. BUNCH,
> *Principal Clerk of the House of Representatives."*

Approximately three and one-half months after the adjournment of the 1845 General Assembly on February 2, 1846, there developed a war between the United States and Mexico. The causes of the war, its progress, and the results have been ably discussed by various historians and will not, therefore, be rehearsed in this treatise. Since the war broke out during Governor Aaron V. Brown's administration as Governor of Tennessee, it is proper and fitting to see how he handled the situation as Chief Executive of a sovereign State. The first important action on the part of Governor Brown was the issuance of a proclamation in May, 1846, setting forth the official communication [100] from the War Department at Washington, and Governor Brown's report as to his own response:

"PROCLAMATION

Of Gov. Brown, raising the three first Regiments of Tennessee Volunteers for the Mexican War, May, 1846.

———

WHEREAS, I have received the following communication from the Department of War at Washington:

WAR DEPARTMENT }
Washington, May 16, 1846. }

SIR: I have the honor to enclose a copy of an act of Congress, entitled 'An

---

[100] Brown, Aaron V.: *Speeches, Congressional and Political, and Other Writings* (Nashville, 1854), 388–393.

act providing for the prosecution of the existing war between the United States and the republic of Mexico,' which authorizes the President to accept the services of volunteers.

It will be perceived that all the officers, with volunteers, taken into the service of the United States under this act, are to be appointed and commissioned, or such as have been appointed and commissioned in accordance with the laws of the State from whence they are taken, and that the volunteers received into the service of the United States, are to have the organization of the army of the United States. For this exact organization, so far as relates to companies and regiments, please see the memorandum appended to the law herewith, to both of which particular attention is requested; but, under the discretion allowed him, the President has decided that the number of *privates* in all volunteer companies shall be limited to eighty.

On the part of the President, I have to request your Excellency to cause to be organized, at the earliest practicable period, the following corps of volunteers:

One regiment of cavalry, or mounted men, and two regiments of infantry, or riflemen.

Your Excellency is requested to designate, and to communicate promptly to this Department, some convenient place of rendezvous for moving towards Mexico, for the several companies, as fast as they shall be organized, where they will be further organized into regiments.

The several corps will be inspected and mustered into the service of the United States, as far as practicable, by an officer or officers of the United States Army. When this cannot be done, you are requested to designate the inspecting and mustering officer, who will in every case be instructed to receive no man under the rank of commissioned officers, who is in years apparently over forty-five or under eighteen, or who is not in physical strength and vigor; nor the horse of any volunteer not apparently sound and effective, with the necessary horse equipments or furniture.

It is respectfully suggested that public notice of these requirements of law, may prevent much disappointment to the zealous and patriotic citizens of your State, multitudes of whom the President cannot doubt will be eager to volunteer.

Should there be any difficulty or considerable delay in obtaining the amount and description of the force proposed to be received from your State, you will give the earliest notice of these to this Department, that proper steps may be taken to receive them from other sections of the country. Memphis is suggested as the place of rendezvous for the mounted regiment, and Nashville for the regiments of infantry or rifle.

Very respectfully, your ob't serv't,

W. L. MARCY, *Sec'y of War.*

His Ex'cy A. V. Brown, Gov. of Tenn.

In compliance with the communication aforesaid, I have caused the requisition therein made to be apportioned amongst the military divisions of this State in the following manner:

To the first division, (East Tennessee,) seven companies, four of which to be infantry or riflemen, and three to be cavalry or mounted men.

To the second division, eight companies, six of infantry or riflemen, and two of cavalry or mounted men.

To the third division, nine companies, six of infantry or riflemen, and three of cavalry or mounted men.

To the fourth division, (Western District,) six companies, four of infantry or riflemen, and two of cavalry or mounted men.

An infantry company, according to the directions of the Secretary of War, accompanying said requisition, will consist of one captain, one first lieutenant, one second lieutenant, four sergeants, four corporals, two musicians, and NOT MORE than eighty privates—the minimum is not mentioned by him, but I will add, NOT LESS than sixty-four rank and file. A company of cavalry or mounted men will consist of one captain, one first lieutenant, one second lieutenant, four sergeants, four corporals, two buglers, one farrier and blacksmith, and not more than eighty privates, and not less than sixty-four rank and file.

The Major Generals commanding said Divisions are hereby required to furnish the quota of volunteer companies above specified, and according to the organization aforesaid.

In raising said volunteer companies, the Major Generals will duly observe the 44th section of the militia laws of this State, passed in the year 1840, which is in the following words, viz: 'Be it enacted, that each volunteer company which shall receive the arms of the State, shall be held in readiness and subject to the FIRST call for service of the State or of the United States.'

Under this act all volunteer companies which have received the arms of the State since the passage of said act, and which have not returned the same to the State, and continued their existence until the receipt of the requisition aforesaid, viz: the 22d day of May, 1846, will, on application, be entitled to priority. Next to these, all old companies which have been revived, and new ones which have been formed since the date of order No. 1, issued by R. B. Turner, Adjutant General of the State, viz: since the 13th instant, and up to the date of this proclamation, and which have been reported to me or to the Adjutant General, (including all cases in which reports may have been started by mail or private conveyance, whether the same have yet come to hand or not,) shall be entitled to priority over companies formed since the date of this proclamation.

If a greater number of companies formed between the periods aforesaid shall tender themselves to any of the Major Generals, than will fill up the requisition on their divisions, it shall be the duty of such Major General forthwith to determine fairly by ballot, which shall be received, (holding separate ballotings for infantry and cavalry,) and notify such companies, as soon as possible, in their respective neighborhoods; and said companies, on learning such acceptance, shall take up their march in time to reach the place of rendezvous as hereinafter stated. And where a sufficient number of the two last described class of companies shall not be presented, any volunteer company, formed since the date of this proclamation aforesaid, viz: the 24th instant, may be received, unless so many of such companies shall apply as shall make it necessary to resort to a ballot, in order to determine between them.

In no case is it expected that any volunteer company shall leave its neighborhood until it shall have received notice of its acceptance or successful ballot, and thereupon it will be expected to repair to the place of rendezvous hereinafter mentioned.

All volunteer companies in the first division, (East Tennessee,) will report themselves as soon as possible after seeing this proclamation, to Major General Brazelton, at Knoxville, who is hereby requested to make that place his headquarters, for the purpose of giving greater dispatch to the service.

When he shall have waited ten days from the receipt of this proclamation for volunteer companies to tender their services, he shall make his acceptance, or determine by ballot, (when too many companies are presented,) and notify by express, when necessary, the companies accepted, and order the cavalry companies to repair forthwith to the general rendezvous at Memphis. All infantry companies to be ordered by the most approved route to the same place, unless he shall find it practicable and expedient to cause them to be transported on the Tennessee River from any point thereof to Memphis as aforesaid; and he is hereby directed and authorized to make all suitable and reasonable contracts for such mode of transportation, and to appoint an agent to act as Quarter Master and Commissary for the purchase of supplies, and to draw on any disbursing officer of the United States sent to this State, or on the Executive Department of this State. If, after the expiration of fifteen days from the receipt of this proclamation, he shall not be able to furnish the number of companies required from his division, he will report the deficiency to the Executive, that the same may be received from some other division of the State.

Volunteer companies from the second division, will make return and report forthwith after this date to Major General Campbell, who is requested to make his headquarters at Nashville, for the greater convenience of the companies of his division, who will accept their services in the manner and on the principles specified in a former part of this proclamation.

Those of the third division, will report to Major General Bradley, at Franklin, who will likewise give due attention to this order in the manner pointed out. All letters announcing the existence and formation of companies tendering their services, in the event of a requisition, which have been received by me, or the Adjutant General of the State, will be handed over to the Major General of the proper division, in order to enable him to give to the companies, in whose behalf they were written, the full benefit of their patriotism and zeal.

Volunteer companies from the fourth division, (Western District,) will report themselves to Major General Hays, at Jackson, who will accept of their services by the rules and on the principles herein stated, and notify by express, when necessary, such companies; and on receiving such notice, all the companies (infantry and cavalry) will march to Memphis, the place of their rendezvous and further organization, on the 15th June. Any deficiency which may occur in raising the required number of companies from his division, the Major General will report to the Executive, that the same may be received from some other portion of the State.

The seven infantry companies from the second and third divisions (Middle Tennessee,) will be expected to be at Nashville by the 8th of June, where suitable and proper arrangements will be made for their transportation to Memphis, the place of general rendezvous, on the 15th of June, where the whole force will be further organized into regiments as prescribed by the laws of the State. The cavalry companies, from every part of the State, will proceed by land to Memphis.

Gen. Levin H. Coe, Inspector General of the State, is hereby instructed, unless superseded in that duty by some officer charged with the same by the United States, to select a suitable encampment in or near Memphis, and cause an adequate supply of rations and supplies to be engaged for the subsistence of said troops whilst at that place, and employ suitable assistance for that purpose.

Volunteer companies, after they have been accepted by the Major Generals, will be at liberty to arm themselves with 'Hall's rifles,' or muskets, or other arms, at the depots in the several divisions of the State, either in whole or in part, so as to go to the field with arms in as good condition as possible, and the keepers of the public arms are hereby directed to deliver such arms to the Captain of any ACCEPTED COMPANY, taking his receipt for the same.

All companies from the second and third divisions will be mustered into the service of the United States at Nashville, and all others at Memphis.

The East Tennessee troops will arrive at Memphis as soon after the said 15th of June as practicable.

The Executive has witnessed, with the proudest satisfaction, the zeal and alacrity with which the citizens of Tennessee have rallied to the standard of the country. He has endeavored to give all parts of the State an equal chance to engage in the service, and has gone into all the above details, in order to save time and to give the utmost possible expedition to the departure of the troops.

In testimony whereof, I have hereunto set my hand, and caused the great seal of the State to be affixed, on this the 24th day of May, 1846.

AARON V. BROWN

By the Governor
Jno. S. Young, Sec'y of State.''

In a message to Colonel William B. Campbell, who five years later was elected Governor of Tennessee, Governor Brown analyzed the procedure [101] followed by him in mustering into service the volunteers of Tennessee:

"ADDRESS

Of Gov. Brown, transferring the third Regiment of Volunteers
to the United States.

EXECUTIVE DEPARTMENT, }
Nashville, June 3, 1846   }

To COL. WM. B. CAMPBELL:

SIR: The first regiment of the Tennessee Infantry Volunteers, which you have the honor to command, being now fully organized and mustered into the service of the United States, in pursuance of a requisition made on me by the Secretary of War, dated 16th May, 1846, you will proceed with it, by means of the steamboats chartered for that purpose, to the city of New Orleans as speedily as practicable, and report yourself to Major General Edmund Pendleton Gaines, for further orders.

In surrendering the State authority, and passing you over, during the term of your service, to that of the United States, I cannot permit the opportunity thereby afforded to pass by, without submitting a few observations to you and the brave and gallant men under your command. You have been called on at a moment of great emergency to engage in the service of the country. The requisition on me arrived by one mail; mine on you was sent forth by the next. In the short space of one week you nobly responded to my call, and are now here from the different portions of a widely extended country with a promptitude and alacrity which has never been surpassed in

101 *Ibid.*, 394–397.

the volunteer service of the country. It would have been impossible to have given greater celerity to the movement, without having taken the requisition from a few of our principal towns and nearest counties of the State, without giving the balance of it any opportunity to participate in the glorious privilege of defending the country. This I could not consent to do; and in order to give all parts of the State over which I preside an equal opportunity, I caused the requisition to be apportioned among the different military divisions established by law. But such has been the patriotic ardor of my countrymen, that at least five times as many companies offered themselves as it would take to fill up the requisition. I could not take *all*, for reasons hereafter mentioned, and I therefore directed the four Major Generals of the State to select, according to the rules laid down, the companies to be received from their respective divisions. It would have been impossible for me to have made the selection with propriety amongst companies formed all over the State, with which the Major Generals may well be presumed to have much better acquaintance than anybody else. I directed them to receive the old armed companies under the fortieth section of the militia laws of the State, and wherever there was a conflict between other companies described, *to decide the same fairly by ballot*. I know of no mode more equitable than that. The Major Generals of the second and third divisions have reported to me that they have selected you (the twelve companies now present) as the fortunate ones on whom the glorious privilege of defending the rights and honor of the country has finally devolved.

Others, no doubt, may feel some disappointment and mortification, that they, too, cannot share with you at this time in the toils, and dangers, and honors of the present campaign.—Many have petitioned and entreated me to take them also into the public service. Most heartily would I have consented to do so, if it had been in my power. But the requisition was expressly limited to three regiments, and no more. Besides this, the Secretary of War, after learning that Gen. Gaines had called for a much larger requisition, and when he knew every thing known to us, as to Gen. Taylor's condition, expressly and promptly *required* me not to comply with it. Moreover, after the requisition was made, authorizing companies to contain as many as *eighty* privates, the Secretary of War desired that they should be reduced so as not to exceed *sixty-four* privates, thereby considerably diminishing the number of the first call. Under these circumstances, I felt constrained to decline accepting more than would fill the requisition. The requisition from which all my authority is derived, was against it. The letter of the Secretary of War, commanding me not to comply with the larger requisition of Gen. Gaines, was against it.—His letter to reduce the *size* of the companies, if not too far advanced in organization, was against it,—and nothing in favor of it, but the patriotic eagerness of my countrymen to repel the insolent invader of our soil.

The letter of Gen. Gaines was one of *advice*, in anticipation of a call, and not a requisition at all. If considered as *mandatory*, it was void for want of authority. If (as it declares in express terms) it is regarded as *advisory* only, it turns out that I acted precisely in accordance with the wishes of the general government, in not complying with it. And more than all, suppose I had yielded to the enthusiasms of the moment, and instead of two thousand or three thousand men, I had sent five thousand or six thousand, what assurance have we that any more than the requisition would have been received? None, whatsoever; and we might have been doomed to see or hear of hundreds and thousands of our fellow-citizens rejected in New Orleans, without provisions, and many without money, to grope their way back to

Tennessee, cursing the folly of her Governor, in having disobeyed all the orders and admonitions of the constituted authorities of the general government.

And now, Sir, having explained to you and the regiment under your command, and to our fellow-citizens at large, the principles on which you have been selected rather than others, to bear the time-honored standard of Tennessee to the field of battle and of glory, I have only to say, Go, gallant sons of gallant fathers, go and join with others of your countrymen, in driving back, if not already done, the insolent invader of our country, and if need be, to carry home the war into the very heart of his territory. Go, under that beautiful banner, which innocence, virtue, and beauty have presented to you. Never permit it—and I know you will not—never permit it to be lowered in the face of the enemy, whilst your regiment has one soldier left to hold it proudly floating to the breeze. Go, and may a kind Providence attend you, and bring you back in health and safety, the pride of an admiring and grateful country.

AARON V. BROWN,
Governor and Commander in Chief."

The zeal and alacrity with which Tennesseans answered Governor Brown's call to arms constitute one of Tennessee's proudest honors. To the call for twenty-eight hundred men, thirty thousand tendered their services.[102]

---

[102] Author's note. The author, along with most Tennesseeans, had long believed the traditional story concerning the origin of the term "Volunteer State," until, in the course of writing volume four of the *Messages of the Governors of Tennessee,* he sought to identify, if possible, the person who first applied the term to Tennessee. If the specific object of his research was not attained, the work was nevertheless productive. For out of the newspapers of the period emerged conclusive evidence that the state nickname originated, not in the Mexican War but in the War of 1812.

Although a survey of readily available newspapers published during the War of 1812 does not reveal the specific term, "Volunteer State," numerous references are to be found to "the volunteers from Tennessee," "the volunteers and militia of the State of Tennessee," and "The Tennessee Volunteers." Such references create a strong supposition that the term "Volunteer State" also was in use at the time.

More specific references are to be found in editorials which appeared in papers of the Mexican War period, some extracts of which are printed below.

Tri-Weekly Nashville Union, May 16, 1846.

" . . . As a state, the measure of our military glory is full—our fathers have bequeathed to us their own immortal honor won on many a battlefield. We cannot expect to eclipse the lustre of their glorious deeds, but we are bound to emulate their example and to cherish the rich inheritance of military renown handed down to us. They achieved for Tennessee the proud title of the 'Volunteer State.' We are bound to maintain the distinction thus won for us. . ."

Tri-Weekly Nashville Union, June 2, 1846.

" . . . Without multiplying words, we can truly say that the call has been most gallantly met—the result has proved that we are proud of the title of the '*Volunteer State.*'"

Nashville Daily Union, May 17, 1847.

" . . . and the VOLUNTEER STATE, to the utter confusion of federal politicians, again shows herself ready to vindicate the country's rights. . . ."

Nashville Daily Union, July 26, 1847.

" . . . It brings back the days of the last war with England, when the volunteers flocked to the standard of Jackson, and Carroll, and Coffee, and by their numbers, in proportion to our sparse population, and gallant bearing, won for their State the enviable and deserved reputation of *the Volunteer State.* . . ."

While Tennessee's volunteer soldiers were fighting their country's battles in Mexico, Tennessee politicians were contesting bitterly the battle for State offices. Some of those battles were waged in the National Congress, and a representative sample of attempted political scalping was a speech in the House of Representatives on December 16, 1846, by Congressman Meredith P. Gentry of the Seventh Congressional District. Gentry's speech, bristling with ridicule, satire, and political attacks upon a near-by neighbor, President James K. Polk, was intended for home consumption, inasmuch as the Whigs were already girding their loins for an all-out battle in Tennessee for the governorship in the election of 1847. A number of prominent Tennessee Whigs were preparing to toss their hats into the ring, among whom were Gentry, Neill S. Brown, Gustavus A. Henry, and Ephraim H. Foster. Gentry possessed a vast store of political knowledge, and was an eloquent speaker and a formidable opponent in political debate, as the following extracts from his speech [103] will corroborate:

"SPEECH OF MR. M. P. GENTRY,
of Tennessee,
In the House of Representatives,
Wednesday, December 16, 1846.

...Lest I should be suspected of being alarmed into silence, I speak now, to show I am not afraid to speak. These are terms which the Constitution employs to define treason, and, in my opinion, the President, in fulminating that denunciation, imputes that crime to a majority of the people of the United States. I am one of those who believe that the war was brought about by the President—by a violation of the Constitution—for the purpose of conquest, and that it has been prosecuted by him with a view to that end. Entertaining these opinions, I feel it to be my duty, under existing circumstances, to give utterance to the convictions of my mind. The imputation which the President has thought proper to make, in his official communication to Congress, was echoed and reechoed, upon this floor, by his liegemen yesterday, in a way which raises a strong presumption that there is a concerted purpose to frighten us, with a storm of denunciation, from the independent discharge of our duties as representatives of the people. We are called upon to assert our rights, or basely succumb to Executive intimidation. Our moral courage, as well as our patriotism, are thus put on trial. I choose, therefore, to speak *now*, although unprepared for the debate, merely to exhibit my defiance of these denunciations, and express the contempt in which I hold them. I choose to present myself as a mark for them—to offer myself as a victim, if indeed it be in the power of the President, and the remorseless majority which sustains him, to victimize those who claim to maintain freedom of thought and freedom of speech, rights 'dear to freemen, and formidable only to tyrants and usurpers.' I speak to announce my opinions upon the subject of the Mexican war, and assume all the responsibility which ought to attach to the maintenance of such opinions.

---

[103] *Congressional Globe*, Second Session, Twenty-Ninth Congress, Appendix, 56–61.

When the nation is engaged in a constitutional war, waged for constitutional purposes, I would deem it proper to waive all discussion as to the propriety of beginning the war, and, by united and harmonious efforts, bring the war to an honorable conclusion, and then hold the public functionaries to a proper account. But this Mexican war is of a character, as I will endeavor to show, which ought to make it an exception to this general rule. 'Our country, right or wrong,' is a noble and patriotic sentiment, when rightly understood and properly applied. It is most grossly misapplied when it is used as a sanction for the principle that a patriotic devotion to the country implies, necessarily, a servile devotion to the President. On the contrary, a state of things may arise—in my opinion has arisen—when, to be true to the country, patriotism demands opposition to the President. Yes, sir, I contend that we may be loyally and faithfully devoted to our country, and yet opposed to its President. But gentlemen have proceeded in this debate upon the assumption that the *President* of the United States is the *Government* of the United States, which is an assumption utterly at war with the Constitution, and of most dangerous tendency. They have read copious extracts from the Law of Nations, defining the rights of belligerent governments, to prove that the President has not been guilty of lawless usurpation in overrunning, with the armies of the United States, vast territories; organizing therein civil governments; absolving the citizens thereof from their previous allegiance—declaring them, by proclamation, citizens of the United States; and, by the same summary process, annexing the territories thus conquered to the United States. The law of nations is but a set of rules or maxims, to which nations, by their acquiescence, have given binding force. Many, indeed most of these rules or maxims, had an existence before the Government of the United States existed; and, in so far as they define the rights and powers of the chief rulers of nations, they apply, for the most part, to monarchies or despotisms, whose sovereignty rests in a single individual. The Government of the United States is a republican Government, the powers of which are defined by a written Constitution. That Constitution, and the laws made in pursuance thereof, confer upon the President all the power which he possesses. He does not imbody the sovereignty of the United States. He is not, as gentlemen would seem, from thir conclusions in this debate, to assume, the *Government of the United States*. Therefore, the public law which defines the powers and rights of monarchal rulers, when engaged in war, do not apply to the President of this constitutional republic. Justly to claim and exercise such powers and rights, he must act with the sanction, and under the authority of the Congress of the United States, the legislative branch of the Government. He has audaciously assumed thus to act without the sanction or authority of Congress. He has, by his own acts, as I will presently show, involved the nation in war; whereas, for wise reasons, the power of declaring war is vested, by the Constitution, in Congress; and he has prosecuted that war for purposes not sanctioned or authorized by Congress. He is, therefore, in the fullest sense of the term, a lawless usurper. Yet, in view of these palpable truths, men, forgetting that there are higher and more sacred obligations than mere party allegiance can impose, stand up here, in this Hall, consecrated to liberty, and justify and defend these flagrant usurpations, arguing that the *President* is the *Government*, claiming for him the powers of an absolute monarch, and joining with him in denouncing those who protest against his usurpations as advocating and adhering to the cause of the enemy, and thus giving him aid and comfort. Although, when, by the act of the President, a collision had been brought about between the army of the United States and that of Mexico, we voted, on this side of the House, with remarkable unanimity, for a bill authorizing the President to receive fifty thousand volunteers, and appropriating ten millions of dollars; although, when he called for volunteers, the Whigs rallied by thousands around the standard of their country, conscious that none of the honors of the war would be conferred upon them; although a large majority of the officers of the regular army and navy—your commanders, by sea and land, are Whigs; although they have, in obedience to the commands of the President, braved danger and death in every possible form, and done all that brave men could do to uphold the honor of the nation; although thousands of them have died in battle; or by the diseases of that climate into which they were prematurely marched by his orders; yet, because we will not fall down and worship him; because we will not crouch, with spaniel-like humility, at his feet, and whine an approval of *all his acts*, we are met, at the beginning of the session of Congress with the grateful compliment from the President that we are traitors to our country; and his liegemen on this floor catch up the foul and false imputation, and echo and reecho it through these Halls.

It would seem that those who would win the commendation of the President and his supporters, must rely upon deeds of mean servility, rather than deeds of patriotism. They must serve the *President*, instead of the *country*. They must conform to that maxim of monarchical loyalty which affirms that 'the King can do no wrong.' If they dare to express a doubt of executive infallibility, they must expect to encounter the thunders of executive vengeance. This is the state of things to which we are required to conform ourselves. Let those whose servility of soul qualifies them for a task so mean, go and truckle to the President. On this side of the House we think we have higher duties to perform, and a nobler destiny to fulfil. One of those duties is to inquire how it happens that the United States are at war with Mexico? By whose act that war has been brought about? For what purpose is it waged? Is it to conquer a peace? What are to be the conditions of that peace? How much of Mexican territory does the President intend to annex permanently to the United States? Will Congress sanction such annexations? What are to be the consequences of the war? How will it affect the union of these States and the destiny of this Republic? How many millions of public debt will it impose? These are high and grave questions, which the free representatives of a free people must inquire into. To speak out fearlessly upon these questions is the imperative duty of the representatives of freemen; and to act firmly, wisely, and patriotically, so as to put a limit to executive discretion and usurpation, is a duty which they are bound to discharge. And he who will shrink from its performance, is better qualified to be the slave of an Asiatic despot, than to be a Representative in the Congress of this free Republic.

I hold it to be the duty of Congress, so long as the army of the republic is in the field by the sanction of the Government, to do all that is necessary to sustain it, that its victories may maintain the glory of the national arms. But it is a yet higher and more sacred duty to guard and preserve with sleepless vigilance the Constitution of the republic. I repeat, that we may be loyal to our country and yet oppose its President, whose ambitious schemes, whose lawless usurpations, may make him a more dangerous enemy to public liberty, than an hundred well-appointed invading armies; for these would be met on every plain, at every mountain pass, and driven back from our borders. But who will restore to us our Constitution and liberty, when they shall be wrested from us? History tells of nations that have been free, and that have lost their freedom; but it tells us also of exertions and privations—

of noble deeds of daring, in resisting the encroachments of tyranny; it tells us that they were enslaved only when might prevailed over right—numbers over valor and patriotism. Shall we, the descendants of the Whig patriots of the American Revolution, tamely and silently yield up the Constitution of our country, the guarantee of our liberty, to be violated and trampled upon by a petty usurper, whose nomination for the Presidency was a *political accident;* which was met with sneers of contempt by the most distinguished men of his own party; and who, being President, possesses not the high qualities, either of head or heart, to command the *real* respect of the meanest minion that shouts in his train? No, sir; no. We would dishonor the glorious name which constitutes our designation as a political party if we were thus to act. Our veneration for our fathers, our duty to ourselves and posterity, our devotion to liberty—every glorious recollection of the past, every high hope of the future, forbid a course of conduct so unpatriotic, so inglorious. In defiance of calumnies and denunciations, from whatsoever quarter they may come, we will struggle to maintain the rights of the Legislative branch of the Government, and resist the encroachments and usurpations of the Executive. We will, to the utmost of our power, uphold the Constitution of our country, which we contend has been violated by the President, in making war of his own will, by his own acts, without the authority or advisement of Congress, upon which alone the Constitution confers the power of declaring war. . . .

Mr. Chairman, I do not believe this declaration of the President of the United States, and I feel it to be my duty to express my disbelief unequivocally. If any one thinks that, in making this declaration, I am withholding the proper deference and respect which ought to be extended to the Chief Magistrate of the nation, I hope I will be excused when I present the array of facts which, in my opinion, justifies my distrust of his sincerity; and if these should fail to plead my acquittal, I am sure I will be pardoned for my doubts, when I refer to another important transaction in which the President bore rather a conspicuous part: I allude to the difficulty between this Government and England upon the subject of the Oregon territory.

Every member of this House will remember the vehement earnestness with which the President, in his message at the beginning of the last session of Congress, asserted the right of this Government to the whole of Oregon, and the determination of the Executive branch of the Government, to maintain that right. He recommended Congress to adopt measures in conformity with his views, and his partisans denounced those who faltered or hesitated, as wanting in patriotism. Distinguished members of this House and the Senate, thus assured by the President, zealously took position with him for the 'whole of Oregon or none.' During the session, and, as I suppose, after it had been satisfactorily ascertained that England was willing to adjust the controversy upon the basis of the 49th parallel of latitude, a Democratic Senator from the State of North Carolina, (Mr. Haywood,) rose in his place, and gave an exposition of his views of the President's position, which was in direct conflict with the idea that the President intended to insist upon the extreme claim put forth in his message; for he gave the Senate very clearly to understand, that the President was willing to compromise upon the 49th parallel of latitude. . . .

Thus are we informed, that the annexation of the Californias, by conquest, *is to be the great question of the age.* Not because the President desires it; not because my colleague desires it; not because the people desire it; nor yet because Congress has sanctioned it; but because there is, in '*the pres-*

ent circumstances, a state of things which must inevitably lead to that result.' Who, but the President of the United States, created *the state of things* which imposes upon us this result, which, according to my colleague, is inevitable? The President, in his message, congratulates Congress upon the acquisition of territory greater in extent than the original thirteen States of the Union. But the conquest and annexation of this vast territory is not yet complete. To an usurper, an independent legislature is a very inconvenient thing; and a refractory Congress might, possibly, interpose some obstacles to the consummation of the President's grand scheme of conquest and annexation. But it is obvious that this difficulty has been foreseen, and that the President is armed with a resource against it. The honorable gentleman from Illinois, (Mr. Douglas), who, I suppose, may be justly regarded as an accredited exponent of the views of the Administration, oracularly announced to us a few days ago, that by the law of nations, if the Government of the United States makes peace with Mexico, without specifying a boundary, all the territory which may have been conquered by our arms will be in fact annexed to the United States, and will forever constitute a part of its territory, unless reconquered or ceded away by the United States. This, I suppose, is the plan of the President; and Congress will, as in the case of making war with Mexico, be called upon, one of these days, not *to annex* the vast territories overrun by our armies, but *to recognize their annexation.* These are the rapid strides which usurpation is making in this free republic. Shall we tamely submit? Will nobody come to the rescue of the Constitution? On this side of the House we are in a minority, and without aid we can effect nothing. I call upon gentlemen on the other side of the House to throw off the shackles of party, and cooperate in vindicating the outraged law. I call upon the Representatives of Virginia and South Carolina to come to the rescue of the Constitution, and I beg to remind them, that the glory of those ancient commonwealths was not won by subserviency to power, but by brave and patriotic resistance to its usurpations. Our fathers would have been astounded by the idea, that any President of the United States would have the temerity and audacity to attempt such usurpations as those which the President evidently contemplates, and has partially consummated.

'Fools rush in where angels fear to tread.'

The President has been rendered sensitive, I suppose, by the question, 'Who is James K. Polk?' so often asked when he was a candidate for the Presidency, and he desires to create a sensation in the world; or, perhaps, envying Mr. Tyler the glory of annexing Texas to the United States, he strikes for the Californias and New Mexico, that his administration may be signalized by an achievement equally glorious. Let Congress and the people sanction his usurpation, and he will no doubt have imitators in the future. Every ambitious President will aim to make his administration more brilliant than those of his predecessors, and the republic will be continually engaged in wars of conquest—wars of ambition and aggrandizement; and with a vast national debt, and a people morally debauched and ground into the dust by oppressive taxation, our Presidents will be Presidents no longer, but despots, wielding unlimited power; and our Union, our Constitution, and liberty, will perish forever. The executive power of this Government is vested by the Constitution in the President, and although it makes him the commander-in-chief of the army and navy, he is nevertheless but the chief executive officer of the Government; and as the Constitution confers upon Congress the power to declare war, the President, as commander-in-chief of the army and navy, has no right to wage war for objects and purposes not contemplated and sanctioned by Congress. Where does the President find a sanction of the national will for his vast conquests and annexations? There has been no such expression of the national will, either by the Representatives of the people, or by the people themselves. The President involved the nation in war, and has waged the war for purposes not sanctioned by the national will. In the origin and prosecution of the war he has violated the spirit of the Constitution. It is the duty of Congress, and I invoke the performance of that duty, to limit and control the discretion of the President in relation to the further prosecution of the war. If Congress believes it to be expedient and just to wage a war of conquest for the acquisition of territory, let that fact be declared; and if Congress believes it to be inexpedient, let it assert the constitutional right of the legislative branch of the Government, by saying to the President, 'Thus far shalt thou go, and no farther.' If Congress shall decide for a war of conquest, though I may be individually opposed to it, all the support in my power shall be given to my country; but I confess that I could not but entertain the belief that my country had chosen a career which must lead to disastrous results.

Mr. Chairman, I solemnly believe that the present Administration has already brought upon this nation manifold evils, which can only be remedied by years of patriotic effort and wise administration; and I believe that the President is now driving this republic into a position fraught with so much of danger to our Union and liberty, that he can never hope to be forgiven by the present or future ages, except by the exercise of that principle of charity which actuated our Saviour, when He prayed for those who crucified Him: 'Father, forgive them, they know not what they do.' There is not, I believe, mind and patriotism in the Administration to comprehend and appreciate the alarming dangers into which they are recklessly driving the republic. It is moral cowardice, when the great interests of the republic are in peril, to shut our eyes and shrink from a contemplation of the dangers with which we are threatened. A learned and profound French author, in speculating upon our institutions, remarks: 'The most formidable of all the evils which threaten the future existence of the Union, arises from the presence of a black population upon its territory; and in contemplating the causes of the present embarrassments, or of the future dangers of the United States, the observer is invariably led to consider this as a primary fact.' Our experience conforms with the opinion of the author from whom I have quoted. The existence of slavery in a portion of the States of this Union, was a disturbing element in the convention which formed the Constitution of the United States, and a very great obstacle to its formation. Fortunately there were patriotism and wisdom sufficient to overcome the obstacle then. When Missouri applied for admission into the Union, this difficulty again presented itself, more formidably than before. It arrayed the nation in sectional parties, which, with passions and prejudices violently inflamed, struggled for mastery, until the intensity and force of that struggle shook the Union to its deepest foundations. At various periods of our history, since that time, the same cause has interrupted the fraternal feelings between the different sections of the Union, and balefully disturbed the harmony of our legislation. The annexation of Texas to the Union, which added a large territory to that section of the Union in which slavery exists, thereby changing the relative political strength of the slaveholding and non-slaveholding States, has, to a considerable extent, requickened and revitalized this disturbing element. This fact was developed at the last session of Congress, when an honorable member from Pennsylvania (Mr. Wilmot)—the bill appropriating two millions of dollars to enable the President to negotiate a treaty with Mexico being under consideration—moved an amendment, *which was adopted by the House*, providing that slavery should never be permitted in any territory which the United States might acquire from Mexico. He must be blind to all the signs of the times who does not perceive that there is a fixed and almost universal determination in the Northern States not to acquiesce in a further extension of territory without attaching to such extension the prohibition to which I have referred. How shall we overcome this difficulty, when the question shall come before Congress permanently to annex the conquests of the President? We have already seen, by a vote of this House, that the non-slaveholding States will insist upon prohibiting slavery in those territories. Will the Southern States consent to the admission of free States south and west of Texas? What will Texas say? What will Louisiana say? What will the whole South say? All the dangers growing out of this question of slavery, which we have met and overcome heretofore, are as nothing compared with those which will arise when that question shall come up as the consequence of Mr. Polk's conquests and annexations.

Mr. Chairman, in my opinion, there are bad men in the North and the South, who desire a dissolution of the Union, and who, without avowing their object, are laboring diligently to produce that end. The President is driving the ship of state into a most stormy and dangerous sea; and if Congress fails to act in the lofty spirit of patriotism which the occasion demands—if it fails to assert the constitutional rights and perform the constitutional duties which properly belong and attach to the legislative branch of the Government, by putting a limit to executive discretion in the further prosecution of this war with Mexico, in my opinion the day is not distant when it will require all the virtue, intelligence, and patriotism of the country, to preserve the Union, and save the public liberty."

But Congressman Gentry did not have the political field all to himself. There was a member of Congress from the First Congressional District of Tennessee who "marched breast forward" when a political showdown was at hand. One never to seek cover nor to dodge the issue, Andrew Johnson took his colleague to task for his (Gentry's) inconsistent position regarding the cause and conduct of the Mexican War, and Johnson's speech is credited with having played a significant part in Gentry's defeat for the Whig nomination for Governor at the Whig Convention in March, 1847. The "Great Commoner" hammered away at Gentry, and undoubtedly to the discomfort of the latter:[104]

"Substance of
THE SPEECH OF MR. A. JOHNSON,
of Tennessee,
In the House of Representatives,
January 5, 1847.

In Committee of the Whole on the state of the Union, the Bill to increase the Army of the United States being under consideration—
MR. ANDREW JOHNSON addressed the committee as follows:
He said, in presenting himself before the committee that morning, he did not intend to discuss so much the bill immediately before them, as the

---

[104] *Ibid.*, 86–90.

general questions connected with the war, and the policy of the Administration with regard to it. It appeared to him that a very strange position had been taken by one of the speakers, and not so strange either; but, at all events, he thought that the gentleman was very bold in taking that position. He (Mr. J.) could not but admire the spirit, frankness, and candor, of the gentleman in taking that position. Great complaint had been found with the President for the use he had made in his message of the words 'aid and comfort.' Yesterday, however, a position had been assumed, which he thought fully authorized the inference that any individual, or any party, or *clique*, who assumed that position, were, whether they intended it or not, extending 'aid and comfort' to the enemy of the country. Yesterday they were told by the gentleman from Indiana (Mr. McGaughey) that he did not intend to vote for the bill under consideration—that he did not intend to vote in favor of raising any more armies—that he intended to vote against all measures which might be introduced into that House for the purpose of prosecuting the war, unless there was a certain provision that the army was to be withdrawn within the legitimate boundaries of the United States. Well, if that was an indication, to any extent, of the feelings or opinions of the party with whom the gentleman acted, it seemed to him (Mr. J.) that there was a fixed and settled purpose—at least, he had a right to infer that there was a purpose of extending 'aid and comfort' to the enemies of the country. To what was such a declaration equivalent? Was it not virtually proclaiming in the ears of Mexico that there was a powerful party in the United States that had taken the ground that they would neither vote supplies, nor in any way assist their own Government in the prosecution of the war? That they would vote for nothing, unless the army in the field, and the squadron in the gulf, were withdrawn clearly within the limits and jurisdiction of the United States? Did not all that indicate a resolute determination to paralyze the arm of the Government of the United States, and protract the war by every possible means, until a change in the Administration could perchance be effected? It was holding out a powerful inducement to the Mexican Government to resist our arms to the last; protract the hope that in the next Congress majorities would be changed, and thereby supplies to the invading army would be stopped, and the whole force withdrawn within the legitimate boundary of the United States, and the existing difficulties between the Governments would be settled on terms the most favorable to Mexico. It was understood—the position had been taken before the country—that the Democratic party, with the present Administration at its head, intended to prosecute this war until an honorable peace was made. But if the opposite party took the ground that they would resist the grant of any supplies, would it not afford a powerful stimulant to the enemy? Yet that was certainly a fair deduction from the repeated declarations made yesterday by the gentleman from Indiana, to whom he had alluded, and who had expressly stated that if the opinions he had uttered were not those of the Whig party, then he was no longer a Whig. It was, then, for his party to declare whether he was really a Whig or not. But it was not his (Mr. J's) design to occupy much of his time in any reply to the gentleman from Indiana.

A few days since they had been favored with a speech from one of the 'immortal fourteen' who voted against the bill authorizing the President to receive into the United States army fifty thousand volunteers, and appropriating ten millions to defray the expenses. Yet now that same gentleman, with bold and unabashed front, stood up before the House, and resisted all supplies! The gentleman declared that he intended to persist in that opposition; and in the effort to establish and maintain a plausible position for himself and his party, the gentleman had attempted to impose upon the country, proof which was nowhere to be found. He (Mr. Hudson) assumed the position that the troops of the United States had invaded Mexico; and attempted to maintain his position by reference to documentary evidence. As he (Mr. J.) did not wish to occupy much time in paying his respects to the gentleman from Massachusetts, he would ask their attention to one item only of the evidence adduced by him in support of his position, in order that the House might discover how the gentleman has mutilated his authority. The gentleman quoted in his speech what purported to be an extract from one of the letters of the American charge' d'affaires in Texas. The gentleman said:

'Mr. Donelson, writing to Mr. Buchanan, from Galveston, under date of June 2, 1845, says: "It is believed that Mexico is concentrating troops on the Rio Grande, *where Texas as yet has established no posts.*" '

That was thrown in by the gentleman, in connexion with other items, for the purpose of proving an admission, on the part of Mr. Donelson, that the country was Mexican territory; that Texas had established no posts there as yet. But when the House came to the paragraph from which that garbled quotation had been made, they would perceive the monstrous injustice to Mr. Donelson—the shallow artifice upon that House, which had been attempted by the honorable gentleman from Massachusetts. What did Mr. Donelson say? He said:

'It is believed that Mexico is concentrating troops on the Rio Grande, where Texas has as yet established no posts. *If this be so, it is possible that Texas may send a force there to remove intruders.*'

They would be 'intruders' upon the soil of the State of Texas, of course! After that sample of the honorable gentleman's *suppressio veri*—after that specimen brick of the fabric which he had reared, the House would be enabled to judge of the integrity of the structure. That gentleman had talked a great deal about Caesar, and usurpers, and all that sort of thing—the usual staple of declamatory opposition. In the introduction of his speech he had quoted a remarkable passage from 'Cato.' They all knew—and he (Mr. J.) made the remark in no disrespect—they all knew the singular air of sincerity with which the gentleman was accustomed to deliver his speeches, and which at once stamped them with the impress of honesty. When he read that paragraph from Mr. Donelson's letter, it was not at all strange that he (Mr. J.) should have been disposed to allow it to pass without questioning it, though it did sound rather oddly. But in running over the correspondence, he (Mr. J.) happened accidentally to discover the great discrepancy presented. Now, he knew not what system of ethics the gentleman had honored with his homage—he did not know in what school of morality he had been educated—but certainly this he would say, that an individual who could deliberately and wilfully suppress a material portion of a paragraph, and employ the balance of it to establish a proposition wholly unauthorized by the paragraph when taken together, placed himself in a position of which that House and the country were fully competent to judge. He (Mr. J.) was not accustomed to inquire into the private character of relations of members of that body; but it did strike him with no little surprise, when he came to reflect that this thing had been done by one who had been solemnly dedicated to the service of God—whose business was the care of souls—who held a commission from the skies to reform men, and qualify them for a future state,—he did think that it was a singular thing, and entirely irreconcilable with his

(Mr. J.'s) ideas of sound morals, to make use of a paragraph in that way, in order to establish a proposition directly the reverse of that enunciated in the paragraph itself. Yet the air of extreme candor and sincerity with which the thing was done, was quite irresistible! It reminded him very much of a picture which he (Mr. J.) had seen hanging on the fireplace in a certain gentleman's room which he once happened to visit. The picture represented Diogenes bending downward, and, with lantern in his hand, apparently engaged in studying the head of an individual. He (Mr. J.) approached a little closer and read the lines—

'Diogenes his lantern needs no more
An honest man is found—the search is o'er!'

And when he came to examine to whom the very complimentary couplet was meant to apply, lo, and behold—Daniel Webster was the man! Now, he thought that, after the interesting little specimen of the gentleman's ingenuity, to which he had just directed the attention of the House, nobody could doubt the propriety of directing the lantern of Diogenes to the countenance of *another* honorable gentleman from Massachusetts! But the gentleman, while speaking of the President, the war with Mexico, and the army of the United States, had applied to the President the reply of Cato to the emissary sent by Caesar, while in the Senate at Utica:

'Bid him disband his legions;
Restore the Commonwealth to liberty;
Submit his actions to the public censure,
And stand the judgment of a Roman Senate:
Bid him do this, and Cato is his friend.
Nay, more: though Cato's voice was never raised
To clear the guilty or to varnish crimes,
Myself will mount the rostrum in his favor,
And strive to gain his pardon from the people.'

How remarkably appropriate the words of the honest Cato in the mouth of one who had discovered himself to be capable of so mutilating—so distorting from its true sense, by suppressing an essential portion of it—the declaration of another. The voice of Cato

'Never raised to varnish crimes!'

If he (Mr. J.) remembered the run of the play from which the gentleman had, with so much propriety, made the quotation, there was a Sempronius who performed a prominent part in the drama. He pretended to be Cato's best friend, and, to use his own language—

'I'll bellow out for Rome and my country,
And mouth at Caesar till I shake the Senate;'

whilst at the same time he was engaged in a conspiracy with Caesar to perpetuate his usurpation, and, in the sequel, the base conspirator was found openly arrayed with the enemies of Cato. It is for the House and the country to determine which of the two characters, Cato or Sempronius, is the most applicable, in the present condition of our public affairs, to the member from Massachusetts. But he (Mr. J.) was proud to boast that, in that government, they had no Caesar, and needed no Cato to ask his pardon from the people. They had no need of a Pompey to meet him on the plains of Pharsalia. There was no need of a Brutus to assassinate him in the Senate chamber.

Mr. J. said he should devote the remainder of his short hour to some extraordinary passages in a speech delivered by one of his colleagues a few days since (Mr. Gentry.)

MR. I. E. HOLMES. I call the gentleman to order.

THE CHAIRMAN. The gentleman will state his point of order.

MR. HOLMES. He is out of order in alluding to the gentleman by name.

MR. JOHNSON. Suppose my colleague to whom I refer is not in the House, how is the proper reference to be known? I followed the rules of common sense—a commodity in which some gentlemen do not appear to deal.

THE CHAIRMAN. The Chair recognises the rule, but does not conceive that in this case its spirit has been violated.

MR. JOHNSON. The gentleman from South Carolina will now please come to order.

MR. HOLMES. Has the Chair called me to order?

THE CHAIRMAN. Certainly not.

MR. JOHNSON. The Chair ruled that I was not out of order—that's all. Mr. J. proceeded. He would go on with his remarks as briefly as possible. His colleague (Mr. Gentry) had commenced his speech on matters and things in general, as follows:

'But his course had been changed: changed in part by the remarks of gentlemen in the debate yesterday, and in part, and indeed chiefly, by the denunciations contained in the message against those who belonged to the same political party with himself. The language held by the President in the part of his message alluded to, had induced him to alter his purpose, and to speak now. And he spoke now more for the purpose of showing that he was not afraid to speak than for anything else.

'The President of the United States in his message to both Houses of Congress had descended from the dignity of his high station, and violated the propriety of his office by assuming that all who dared to call in question the propriety of his acts in originating and continuing the present war, were guilty of affording "aid and comfort" to the enemies of the United States: terms which seemed purposely taken from the legal definition of *treason:* and his friends in the debate of yesterday, if not called upon, had volunteered to reiterate the same charge against every independent American freeman, who should have the temerity (and as they seemed to think the insolence) to call in question the conduct of the Chief Magistrate.'

That was the purpose, then, of his colleague—to show that he was not afraid to speak. They all remembered the passage in the message of the President to which his colleague had alluded, and which had prompted him to make such a bold manifestation of his determination not to be intimidated. His colleague, therefore, was such a brave man that he would afford aid and comfort to the enemy, in order to show that he was not afraid of the denunciations of the President! But Mr. J. preferred calling the attention of the House to the passage in the President's message, so much complained of by his colleague. He then read as follows from the message:

'I deem it to be my duty to present to you, on the present occasion, a condensed review of the injuries we had sustained, of the causes which led to the war, and of its progress since its commencement. This is rendered the more necessary because of the misapprehensions which have to some extent prevailed as to its origin and true character. The war has been represented as unjust and unnecessary, and as one of aggression on our part upon a weak and injured enemy. Such erroneous views, though entertained but by few, have been widely and extensively circulated, not only at home, but have been spread throughout Mexico and the whole world. A more effectual means could not have been devised to encourage the enemy and protract the war than to advocate and adhere to their cause, and thus give them "aid and comfort." '

He (Mr. J.) could not see why his colleague had become so fired at this portion of the message. If his colleague was not one of the small number alluded to in the paragraph, he had no right to complain; but my colleague has taken high ground upon the allusion by the President to giving 'aid and comfort' to the enemies of the country. It seems from his language that he has joined the enemy of the country for the purpose of being in opposition to the President of the United States. He makes use of the following emphatic language:

'Mr. G. said he had chosen to express his sentiments now, simply in order to bring himself within range of these denunciations. He chose to identify himself with those who were thus accused.'

It was to bring himself within the range of these denunciations—to unite himself with those thus accused! In order to discover his independence, the gentleman had voluntarily joined in with the enemies of his country! Whether he could sustain himself with his constituents, it was not for him (Mr. J.) to say. But as a representative from the State of Tennessee, he (Mr. J.) regarded it as his duty to place this matter in its true light fully before the country. His colleague went on and said, in reply to a remark from Mr. KENNEDY, that 'his object had been to show how much he despised and scorned the President.' Was not that a patriotic speech from the mouth of a representative from the State of Tennessee? Could no explanation be afforded of the course and conduct of his colleague? He (Mr. J.) thought he had a right in this case to look to the combination of circumstances, and draw his own conclusions. The people of the State of Tennessee had been canvassing, or were preparing to canvass the claims and pretensions of various aspirants to the gubernatorial chair, amongst whom was his colleague. Another gentleman—a distinguished Whig who had been at the storming of Monterey, where he had rendered signally important service—had also been brought into the canvass. That gentleman had been probably regarded as likely to command popularity from his services with the brave volunteers; and his (Mr. J.'s) colleague, it somehow appeared, did not now entertain the same views with regard to the war and the propriety of conducting it with vigor, that he entertained during the last session of Congress. Now he seemed to have a holy horror of the war. He seemed to be monstrously opposed to the acquisition of territory. How far that gentleman might be swayed by a conviction that some of those who had gained laurels in the war might stand in his way, he (Mr. J.) would not say.

MR. GENTRY. Will you gentlemen allow me to make one remark?

MR. JOHNSON. I cannot give way, as it would consume my time, which is now rapidly passing away.

MR. GENTRY. I want to correct the gentleman as to facts.

MR. JOHNSON. Of the facts, there can be no doubt. I may be wrong in my inferences; but I think, after all, I am fully sustained by my premises. He knew (Mr. J. went on to say) that frequently men rushed eagerly into a campaign in order to fight a little and get a shot and a scar, and then return home to claim great credit for their bravery and patriotism. Well, he could not say that he had much approbation to bestow on such personages, and was inclined to concur in the opinions expressed by one greater than he ever hoped to be—that most of these wars got up a brood of heroes which it took an age or two to get rid of. But his colleague appeared to entertain some dread of running even odds against an individual who had distinguished himself at Monterey.

But the gentleman went on, and characterized the President as a despot, and all that sort of thing:

'But who would give us back our lost liberties, our violated Constitution? When a petty usurper had come into power without the will of the people of these States, and almost without the wish or knowledge, even of his own party, and without qualities in his own character to command the respect even of the meanest persons in the country.'

It would seem from the extract just read from his colleague's speech, that the great American chart of liberty had been dragged from its high place, torn in pieces and trampled under foot. That we were now walking amid the fragments of a ruined and violated Constitution. Not content with making the charge of a petty 'usurper,' &c., he condescends to make a low personal fling at the Executive of the nation, to gratify, he (Mr. J.) supposed, some private grievance. That was certainly courteous from one Tennessean to another! It was highly respectful language to apply to the President of the United States. He said that the President had come into power 'without the will or consent of the people, and almost without the wish or knowledge of his own party.' Now, if the gentleman applied that to himself, he would not be so far mistaken. He (Mr. J.) thought that there was one Mr. JONES, formerly Governor of Tennessee, and many other distinguished Whigs, who were opposed to the gentleman's occupying a seat in that Hall. The case was entirely parallel; and indeed there were very few individuals, perhaps, on that floor who had not encountered opposition from distinguished men of their own party. But there was evidently a personal feeling of hostility against the President of the United States, although in making a personal explanation, his colleague had disclaimed any personal feeling. The gentleman had declared that he entertained no unkind feelings to the President, and that he had been accustomed to meet him on terms of gentlemanly courtesy. What ideas the gentleman entertained of courtesy it was not for him (Mr. J.) to say, but certainly the language he had applied to the President sounded rather oddly in the mouth of one professing feelings of kindness and courtesy. But the gentleman proceeded and said:

'The President was going to conquer a vast region of country, larger than all the old thirteen States, and add it to this Union.'

Where did the gentleman find a shadow of authority for such a bold assertion? Let them hear the President himself on that subject. Let them refer to the passages in his message, (which were too long to read there,) alluding to the acquisition of Mexican territories, and then judge how his colleague was sustained.

(The following are the passages referred to by the honorable speaker:)

'I congratulate you on the success which has thus attended our military and naval operations. In less than seven months after Mexico commenced hostilities, at a time selected by herself, we have taken possession of many of her principal ports, driven back and pursued her invading army, and *acquired military possession* of the Mexican provinces of New Mexico, New Leon, Coahuila, Tamaulipas, and the Californias, a territory larger in extent than that embraced in the original thirteen States of the Union, inhabited by a considerable population, and much of it more than a thousand miles from the points at which we had to collect our forces and commence our movements. By the blockade, the import and export trade of the enemy has been cut off.'

'Whilst the war was in a course of vigorous and successful prosecution, being still anxious to arrest its evils, and considering that, after the brilliant victories of our arms on the eighth and ninth of May last, the national honor could not be compromitted by it, another overture was made to Mexico, by my direction, on the twenty-seventh of July last, to terminate hostilities by a peace just and honorable to both countries. On the thirty-first of August following, the Mexican Government declined to accept this friendly overture, but referred it to the decision of a Mexican Congress, to be assembled in the early part of the present month. I communicate to you, herewith, a copy of the letter of the Secretary of State proposing to reopen negotiations, of the answer of the Mexican Government, and of the reply thereto of the Secretary of State.

The war will continue to be prosecuted with vigor, as the best means of securing peace. It is hoped that the decision of the Mexican Congress, to which our last overture has been referred, may result in a speedy and honorable peace. With our experience, however, of the unreasonable course of the Mexican authorities, it is the part of wisdom not to relax in the energy of our military operations until the result is made known. In this view, it is deemed important to hold *military possession* of all the provinces which have been taken, until a definite treaty of peace shall have been concluded and ratified by the two countries.

The war has not been waged with a view to conquest; but having been commenced by Mexico, it has been carried into the enemy's country, and will be vigorously prosecuted there, with a view to obtain an honorable peace, and thereby secure ample indemnity for the expenses of the war, as well as to our much-injured citizens, who hold large pecuniary demands against Mexico.'

Was it not apparent (Mr. J. continued) that his colleague had made assertions entirely unsustained?

But his colleague had charged, in bold, emphatic terms, that the war now existing between the United States and the republic of Mexico, was an Executive war—was a war brought on by the President to enable him to carry out his own ambitious purposes. Mr. J. then read the following extracts from Mr. G.'s speech:

'But the first question Mr. G. desired to ask was, How did this war come into existence? By whom had it been made?' * * *

'It was the war of the President, commenced and carried on for his own objects, without the consent of the body to whom exclusively the Constitution had committed the warpower in this Government.' * * *

'The President was an executive officer, but whose will did he execute? The will of the people? Mr. G. had heard no such expression of their will; they had nowhere declared it to be their wish to annex half a dozen Mexican provinces to this Union. No—no such thing. The President had rushed forward on his own mere motion. He was a usurper, a violator of the Constitution; and it would be treason, moral treason, not to denounce him.'

Mr. J. continued. Bold assertions, truly! It was, indeed, rather a decided position which the gentleman had assumed. The inquiry, then, fairly came up, Whose war was it? Had the President of the United States involved the country in that war? Did the President begin the war? His colleague flatly asserted that the President rushed into the war 'on his own mere motion.' Let them now appeal 'to the law and to the testimony.' In 1845 there was a struggle in that House between the two great political parties as to who should have the honor and credit of introducing a resolution there that would be most acceptable to the country, and best secure the annexation of Texas to the United States. That struggle was between the Whigs and the Democratic party. Several propositions were brought forward, but all were voted down. Who concocted—who matured the proposition that was accepted? Was it the President of the United States? Was it a Whig or a Democrat? Why, it was his (Mr. J.'s) worthy colleague (MILTON BROWN) who introduced the measure there, after the various democratic propositions had been voted down; and that resolution, introduced by a good Whig of the State of Tennessee, was voted for by the whole delegation, both Whigs and Democrats of the State of Tennessee. The resolution he referred to prescribed all the necessary steps to be taken for the admission of Texas into the Union as one of the sovereign States.

The resolution was approved by the President of the United States on the first day of March, 1845. Immediately after the approval of this resolution by the President, Almonte, who was then Minister Extraordinary from Mexico to the Government of the United States, on the 6th day of March, protested against annexation, and declared that it was just cause of war on the part of his Government. Mr. J. then referred to the following part of the protest alluded to:

'For these reasons, the undersigned, in compliance with his instructions, finds himself required to protest, as he does in fact protest, in the most solemn manner, in the name of his Government, against the law passed on the 28th of the last month by the general Congress of the United States, and approved on the 1st of the present month by the President of these States, whereby the province of Texas, an integrant portion of the Mexican territory, is agreed and admitted *(se consiente y admite)* into the American Union. The undersigned moreover protests, in the name of his Government, that the said law can in nowise invalidate the rights on which Mexico relies to recover the above-mentioned province of Texas, of which she now sees herself unjustly despoiled; and that she will maintain and uphold those rights at all times, by every means which may be in her power.'

He (Mr. J.) continued, by saying, that after this protest was entered by the Mexican Minister, (Almonte,) the republic of Texas went on and complied with all the requisitions of the resolution prescribing the manner and the mode of annexation—forming her constitution, which was republican in its character, and presented to the Government of the United States. In due time (on the 29th day of December, 1845) the resolution admitting the republic of Texas into the Union as a sovereign State, was approved by the President of the United States; his colleague, (Mr. Gentry,) with the whole Tennessee delegation, voting for the passage of the resolution.

The passage of the resolution by this Government on the 29th of December, 1845, admitting the republic of Texas into the Union, the Government of Mexico assumed and considered a consummation of the cause of *war*, and refused to receive our Minister, Mr. Slidell, in consequence of the passage of the two resolutions by this Government.

Mr. J. said he would read one or two passages from the correspondence had with Mr. Slidell and the authorities of Mexico, which is as follows:

'NATIONAL PALACE, MEXICO
March 12, 1846.

Considering the time as having come for carrying into effect the annexation of Texas, the United States, in union and by agreement with their natural allies and adherents in that territory, concerted the means for the purpose. The project was introduced into the American Congress. It was at first frustrated, thanks to the prudential considerations, the circumspection, and the wisdom with which the Senate of the Union then proceeded. Nevertheless, the project was reproduced in the following session, and was then approved and sanctioned in the form and terms known to the whole world.

'A fact such as this, or, to speak with greater exactness, so notable an act of usurpation, created an imperious necessity that Mexico, for her own honor, should repel it with proper firmness and dignity. The Supreme Government had beforehand declared that it would look upon such an act as a *casus belli;* and, as a consequence of this declaration, negotiation was by its very nature at an end, and war was the only recourse of the Mexican Government.

J. M. De Castillo Y Lanzas.

His Excellency John Slidell.'

Mr. J. said, after this reply to Mr. Slidell, all hope of negotiation having ceased, he returned home. On the 18th of April, 1846, General Paredes, who had recently come into power by revolution, and who, in *fact,* was the Government absolutely at the time, addressed a letter to the commander on that frontier, in which he stated to him, 'at the present date, I suppose you at the head of that valiant army, either fighting already, or preparing for the operations of a campaign; and supposing you already on the theatre of operations, and with all the forces assembled, it is indispensable that hostilities be commenced, yourself taking the initiative against the enemy.'

Orders had been issued as early as the 4th of April to attack the army of the United States by Parades, who was then dictator.

On the 11th of March, the army of the United States, under the command of General Taylor, took up the line of march, and on the 28th of the same month, encamped on the left bank of the Rio Grande, opposite Matamores, within the legitimate boundary of the State of Texas. On the 24th of April, 1846, General Arista, who was then in command of the Mexican forces, informed General Taylor that he considered the hostilities 'commenced, and should prosecute the same.' On the same day, a company of sixty-three dragoons, men and officers, were sent from the American camp up the left bank of the Rio Grande, to ascertain whether the Mexican army had crossed over into the United States. The dragoons were attacked by a large body of the Mexican troops, and sixteen of them were killed and wounded, the remainder taken prisoners. On the 8th and 9th days of May, the bloody battles of 'Palo Alto' and 'Resaca de la Palma' were fought on the left bank of the Rio Grande, and within the boundary of the United States—the American army obtaining a signal victory over the Mexican forces. On the 11th of May, Congress recognised the existence of the war between the republic of Mexico and the United States. Mr. J. said he had commenced with the assumed cause of the war by Mexico, and traced its steps until the first blow had been struck by that republic, for the purpose of showing how utterly groundless the charges were, that had been made by his colleague, that it was the President's war, &c.; but for the purpose of making his conclusions perfect and complete, he would call the attention of the House and the country to the preamble of the law passed by Congress recognising the existence of the war between the two Governments. He then read the preamble to the law, as follows:

'*Whereas,* by the act of the republic of Mexico, a state of war exists between that Government and the United States.'

Mr. J. continued by saying that his colleague (Mr. Gentry) had voted for the preamble while acting under the solemn sanction of an oath, and at the same time appropriated ten millions of dollars, and authorized the President to receive into the service of the United States fifty thousand volunteers, to enable him to '*prosecute*' the war with vigor and effect. The House, the country, and his colleague himself, must see the glaring inconsistency, the ridiculous contradiction, the inextricable labyrinth in which he had involved himself in making those bold untenable charges against the President of the United States, and particularly a citizen of his own State. He (Mr. J.) thought that the statement of facts connected with the Mexican war was so clear and overwhelming in their character as to nail the groundless charges made by his colleague against the President of the United States to the counter, as spurious coin of the baser sort. And now he would leave this portion of his subject.

But he (Mr. J.) would not be understood as admitting the cause of war as assumed by Mexico as being well founded or just—very far from it. In April, 1836, Texas, by successful revolution, achieved her independence, and was acknowledged by Santa Anna himself, who was then the Government *de facto*. Texas then proceeded and organized a republican form of government. On the 19th of December, 1836, Texas, acting in her highest political attitude, laid down and defined the boundary of the republic of Texas as follows:

'Beginning at the mouth of the Sabine river, and running west along the Gulf of Mexico, three leagues from land, to the mouth of the Rio Grande; thence, up the principal stream of said river, to its source; thence, due north, to the forty-second degree of north latitude; thence, along the boundary line as defined in the treaty between the United States and Spain, to the beginning.'

Mr. J. said, this was the Texas he was talking about, and no other; not the ancient province of Spain—the cession by France of Louisiana or any of the departments or States of Mexico as delineated by any particular set of lines anterior to the 19th of April, 1836. He could know of no other boundary at this time than the one defined by herself. With that boundary her independence and sovereignty had been acknowledged by Great Britain, Belgium, France, the United States, and even by Spain. It was some three years after Texas achieved her independence, and had exercised all the functions pertaining to an independent nation, before Spain acknowledged the independence of Mexico herself.

After Mexico, by revolution, had succeeded in separating from old Spain, and after Texas had succeeded by the same means in separating herself from Mexico, the Government of Spain acknowledged the independence of both as separate and distinct nations. After this, Mexico proposed to acknowledge the independence of Texas if she would not annex herself to the American Union. The republic of Texas, after achieving her independence with her treasury and her blood—after that independence was acknowledged by many of the principal powers of Europe and the United States—after maintaining that independence and exercising all the functions of a separate and distinct sovereignty for some nine years, she thinks proper to associate or to blend her sovereignty and her fortunes with the States of the American Union, their kindred and their blood; and this union of the two Governments, begun and consummated as before alluded to, Mexico assumed as just cause of war, and actually commenced hostilities.

Texas, on the 29th of December, 1845, was admitted into the Union upon an equal footing with the other States of the Confederacy; and for this act of admission on the part of the Federal Government, Mexico commenced the war, not upon Texas particularly, but upon the Government of the United States; not for the establishment of any particular boundary on this side of the Rio Grande, but for the purpose of avenging a conceived wrong inflicted upon her by the Government of the United States for admitting Texas into the Union.

Texas is now, and was when Mexico commenced hostilities, a member of this confederacy of States, and the Government of the Union is bound to 'guaranty to her a republican form of government, and protect her against invasion.' In protecting Texas against invasion, the Government of the United States can know no boundary except the old laid down by Texas herself, unless a question of boundary should arise between the State of Texas and 'other Governments.' In that event, the Government of the United States has reserved to itself the right of 'adjustment.' But (Mr. J. said) no question of boundary had arisen between the State of Texas and any other Government. Mexico had raised no question of boundary; Mexico had never fixed upon the Nueces as the line between the Governments, or any other line; hence the folly and futility of debating about the territory lying between the Nueces and the Rio Grande.

Mr. J. said the attempt by his colleague and others to make the territory debatable on the frontier of Texas was not even plausible, and was not entitled to be dignified with the appellation of argument. The United States could recognize no difference in any other portion of Texas over another. Every inch of soil embraced in the entire area of Texas lying within the boundary he (Mr. J.) had before alluded to, was alike known to belong to that Government. It was within the sovereign limits of Texas, and that Government was bound to regard it as such.

Mr. J. said, the fact that there being here and there a spot or section of country over which the sovereignty and jurisdiction of the State of Texas had never been exercised, did not affect her claim to the whole country in the slightest degree. Suppose, (said Mr. J.,) when peace is made, the people of Santa Fe are willing and desirous to submit to either the laws of the United States or the laws of the State of Texas, is there any one bold enough to say that the Federal Government can step in and exercise jurisdiction over the country to the exclusion of the authority of the State of Texas? There were cases (Mr. J. thought) illustrative of the point now under consideration; take, he said, any one of the old States—North Carolina: she claimed all the territory lying within her limits; yet there were large portions of it, now Tennessee, she never did exercise jurisdiction over to the hour of her cession of the territory to the Federal Government. There were portions of territory lying in one or the other of the States of Tennessee or North Carolina from the organization of the Federal Government, till the year 1833, that neither of those States exercised jurisdiction over; yet, when the obstacle was removed, the right to exercise jurisdiction was never disputed by any one. The obstacle alluded to was the existence of a powerful nation of Indians within their borders; during the existence of this powerful tribe in the State of Tennessee, which was from 1796 till 1835, the sovereignty and jurisdiction of the State remained in a state of abeyance—this tribe exercised all the functions of a government while in the State.

There may be portions of the State of Texas, over which it may not be good policy, or even convenient at this time to exercise jurisdiction; but that does not impair her right to do so, when she may deem it most expedient and proper. Mr. J. said, he had merely alluded to this case, to show that there was nothing in the argument so much relied on by many in the debate. He declined trespassing further with details upon this point.

But he (Mr. J.) would now call the attention of the committee to one or two other points in his colleague's speech. There is one paragraph in that speech which condemned all the balance of it. Mr. J. then read as follows:

'The President next undertook to give a history of the outrages of Mexico on the people of Texas, from the first existence of that State to the present time; and this was done with a view *to create the impression that these were the causes of the war*. But no man of sense could admit such an idea; it was intended for fools, and for fools only. Mr. G. did not controvert the position, that for these outrages we had had good cause for war against Mexico long ago; and if the President had openly brought them before Congress, and recommended war on that ground, Mr. G. did not know but he might have been in favor of it; but the case was otherwise, and the Executive had not consulted Congress in the matter, till he was urged by imperious necessity.'

It seemed that his colleague had misunderstood the message entirely. The President had not, so far as he (Mr. J.) could understand the message, attempted to make the impression upon the country that the cases he had enumerated had been the cause of the war with Mexico. The President had enumerated all of the many wrongs inflicted upon the people and Government of the United States, to show there was just cause of war on the part of this Government, yet we had forborne to declare war. The President, in his message to the Congress of the United States, of May the 11th, 1846, says, in so many words, 'that war exists by the act of Mexico herself;' but he (Mr. J.) said, because Mexico begun the war upon this Government, does not prove that there was no cause of war on our part. But as Mexico continued to persist in the series of outrages committed upon this Government and people, and now to consummate the work of wickedness and folly by an act of war, it was but justice to have a final settlement of all the difficulties existing between the two Governments, and teach her a lesson in the school of experience, that will be of service to her in all future time.

Thus it would seem, that out of the gentleman's own mouth he stood condemned. In these few sentences the gentleman had refuted his own speech. He admitted the justice of the war. He recognised the truth of the position assumed by the President. The war was right, but the President had got into it wrong—that was all! Then the gentleman proceeded:

'The general rule was, that it was expedient and wise, when the nation was engaged in a war constitutionally made, that all debate about the expedience or propriety of the war should cease, and that all should unite to bring it to an honorable conclusion, and, when that was accomplished, then to hold the public functionaries engaged in originating and prosecuting it to a strict responsibility. That was the general rule.'

That was all right. The gentleman had himself voted for the war—voted for it at every step, and yet now, in open and most extraordinary violation of his own rule, thus gravely set down, he denounced the war! He (Mr. Gentry) wanted to know what they were to do with the new acquisitions of territory. That was, indeed, a strange inquiry, coming from him. It was hardly to be expected that that gentleman would have introduced such an element into the discussion. He (Mr. J.) regretted that his hour was so nearly out. He had not had time to do more than glance at the gross inconsistencies and erroneous and entirely gratuitous assertions of his colleague. He could have wished to allude also to the speech of the gentleman from Indiana, (Mr. McGaughey,) who desired the troops to be withdrawn; and to that of the gentleman from Ohio, (Mr. Root,) who declaimed so feelingly about the price to be paid for the brave men who had perished on the field. He (Mr. J.) would ask, were those gentlemen willing that the bones of those heroic patriots should be exposed to the indignity of Mexican hate? Were they prepared to yield up their graves to Mexican desecration?

Are we now prepared to adopt the position of the member from Indiana, (Mr. McGaughey,) that is, to withdraw our troops from the field, and our squadron from the Gulf, without reparation for the long list of wrongs inflicted by Mexico upon the property, the honor, and the rights of the American people? Are we prepared to turn our backs upon the bones and the graves of the two thousand patriotic spirits who fell victims to the disease peculiar to that climate, and take up the retrograde march, leaving them to sleep beneath the enemy's soil, without even a stone with the initials of their names rudely carved, to indicate to the inquiring stranger the *spot* that contains their mortal remains? Are the American people willing now, after having obtained such brilliant triumphs and signal victories in a cause so just, to retrace their footsteps without ample indemnity for the past and full assurance of peace in the future? Are the American people, whose souls swell with animation and pride at the unfurling of their country's flag, who admire the majestic eagle's flight, and love to hear his screams of triumph and bold defiance, to take so humiliating and degrading a position as the one proposed by the opposition to the war? Are they, while standing in full view of the formidable heights of Monterey, of the noble deeds of daring and chivalry performed on the 21st, 22d, and 23d days of September, of the soil made *fat* with their countrymen's blood, to abandon all to the advancing tyrant? Is my colleague willing to surrender the twenty-eight gallant sons of Tennessee who fell in the fierce and bloody conflict at Monterey, and who now repose in silence in a foreign land, as trophies to a perfidious and half-civilized nation, or would he rather include them within the broad, protecting circle of our glorious Union, and erect to their name and memory a cenotaph as enduring as time itself, and engrave upon its most conspicuous tablet—

> 'Twice hath the sun upon their conflict set,
> And risen again, and found them grappling yet,
> While streams of carnage in noontide blaze
> Smoke up to Heaven.'

He (Mr. J.) said, if the aegis of his country was not extended over them now, he trusted in God, that in our midst would rise up some crusading Peter, with a holy zeal and eloquence like that which characterized them in olden times, and inspire the people of the Union to go forward and rescue from the impious tread of the marauding myrmidons of Mexico, the sepulchres of their kindred and their blood."

The election in 1847 turned out disastrously for the Democrats in Tennessee. Governor Aaron V. Brown was defeated for re-election by his Whig rival, Neill S. Brown, and each branch of the Legislature had a Whig majority, with a majority of ten on joint ballot. This setback was a blow to President Polk's personal and political prestige, inasmuch as only six Tennessee Democratic Congressmen survived the Whig upsurge in Tennessee. In Tennessee, the Democrats had temporarily reached the end of the row; at the convening of the Legislature on October 4, 1847, Governor Aaron V. Brown transmitted his message to the Legislature on October 6.

Legislative Message, October 6, 1847

"GENTLEMEN OF THE SENATE
    AND OF THE HOUSE OF REPRESENTATIVES:

Assembled as you now are, as the representatives of the people, you cannot fail to observe in the circumstances which surround you, increased cause of gratitude and reverence to that Supreme Being, who presides over the destinies of Nations.

The two past years have been signalized by unnumbered blessings and benefits. The labor of the husbandman has been crowned with abundance, whilst fair and remunerating prices have been received for the rich productions of his fields; our commerce has been greatly increased, and our domestic industry of every variety has flourished in the most remarkable degree. Tranquility and good order have been maintained, and the supremacy of our laws acknowledged throughout all our borders.

In the full enjoyment of these blessings, to which may be added that of almost uninterrupted good health, the people of Tennessee have been steadily advancing in knowledge, in virtue, and indeed in all the elements of national greatness. It must be a pleasing duty to serve such a people, and a delightful task to add any thing valuable to the legislation of such a noble State.

When the reports of the various branches or departments of the State Government shall have been made to you, I doubt not that you will find, that all the duties of them have been performed with a promptitude and fidelity in perfect harmony with the other pleasing circumstances under which you have assembled.

The benevolent institutions of the State, (the Lunatic Asylum, and those for the education of the Blind, the Deaf and the Dumb) will be found to have realized, in a good degree, the expectations of the public. They will, however, continue to appeal to the noblest sympathies of our nature for still further advancement and promotion.

The sale of the Lunatic Asylum and its location in the country, for reasons which will be communicated in another form, has not been effected; and I recommend a reconsideration and amendment

---

  * *Senate Journal,* 1847, 24–42.
  House Journal, 1847, 26–44.

of the law directing its sale. During the past two years, I have many reasons to believe, that the institution has been well and faithfully managed, especially the female department of it, which has been superintended by a lady of singular energy, skill and ability for such a station.

From the Penitentiary, I anticipate a very satisfactory report to you. The convicts generally have been in the enjoyment of good health, and have manifested no spirit of rebellion or disobedience. The Keeper, his deputy and the other officers, having great skill and experience in such matters, seem to have blended the stern rigor of discipline with all the kindness and humanity which such a situation will admit of. The greater portion of the efficient labor of the convicts has been directed to the building of the State Capitol, under the law directing it so to be done; a most beautiful edifice is slowly rising up, likely to attract the admiration of the country and to outstrip in magnitude, convenience, durability and elegance, the capitol of any other State in the Union.

I have no reason to recommend any change in this policy, nor any material ones in the details of the law on this subject.

There is no subject upon which I desire to hold communion with you more freely than on that of Education.

Our Universities and Colleges are, in the general, meeting the just expectations of their friends. Some new ones have been recently established in the State, founded chiefly, if not entirely, on the enlightened liberality of individuals, which promise soon to rival their older predecessors in the diffusion of a sound and wholesome intelligence among the people. Among these it may not be considered invidious to mention the one at Lebanon, whose rising reputation gives fine promise of its future usefulness to the State.

Our County Academies may also be said, in the general, to be doing well; but besides all these, we must have a full and complete system of common or primary schools, dispensing their benefits to all those whose means do not enable them to send off their children to distant seminaries of learning.

No system can be compared to this latter description of schools. They secure to the great mass of society an education, if not highly finished and polished, yet commensurate with the every day wants and necessities of the people. We should never relax our exertions on this subject until we could send the gratifying intelligence abroad, that not one native born son or daughter of Tennessee could be found who could not read the Scripture of Divine Revelation, and likewise the laws and constitution of the country. How such a blessed and happy result is to be attained, is a question constantly addressing itself to the friends of education throughout the land.— That Legislature which shall be able to answer it in the establishment of such a system, with adequate funds to support it, will have well entitled themselves to the gratitude of the present, and the blessings of future generations.

For the reasons formerly given by me to your immediate predecessors, I cannot recommend a present resort to taxation, until by some unequivocal expression of public sentiment, it is made manifest that such a measure would be cheerfully acquiesced in.—How far it might answer a valuable purpose, to authorize such counties, whose population might be willing to do so, to levy and collect a school fund, for their own county purposes, to be applied in the same manner as the other school funds furnished by the State, and the propriety of such a law, is respectfully submitted, both as to its constitutionality and expediency, to your consideration. Such legislation should be carefully guarded, both as to its amount and application.

If but a few counties should set the example of self-taxation for so noble an object, the beneficial effects resulting from it might open the way to its imitation by other counties, until public sentiment, although slowly and cautiously developed, might demand the measures as one of great policy, eminently calculated to improve the minds and elevate the morals of the whole community.

If, however, the wisdom of your honorable bodies should find insurmountable objections to this limited and experimental mode of eliciting an expression of public opinion, I know of no better plan than to husband the resources of the State Bank; and by establishing liabilities and leave the whole capital and funds of that institution, amounting to several millions of dollars, as a permanent endowment of common schools. Taxation is, therefore, the immediate and direct mode of establishing the system. Through the agency of the Bank is the more remote and contingent one, and the wisdom of the Legislature must decide between them, or devise a better one than either.

With a mind fondly lingering over this subject, and unwilling to leave it, I beg permission to trouble you with another suggestion in aid of those already made.

We have no 'Superintendent of Public Instruction.' The examples of other States, and the very nature and importance of the subject would seem to rebuke the omission. Even if such an officer were of temporary appointment, with no power over the funds, he might be of great advantage in rousing up and directing the sleeping energies of the people. He should be a man eminent for his attainments in science, and for his devotion to the moral and intellectual welfare of the rising generation. He should commune freely with the learned and the pious of the land. He should visit every county in the State. He should organize county committees of such zealous and patriotic citizens as might agree to visit the school districts of their respective counties, and by suitable appeals and lectures impart new vigor and energy to the present system. He should excite the acting school commissioners of each county to renewed exertions in raising and increasing the present school fund by voluntary individual subscription. In short, such a man, by traversing the State, addressing his fellow-citizens at suitable times and places, and finally reporting to the Legislature a full account of his labors, and the result of his best opinions, might well render a service to the cause of education, which would outweigh a thousand fold, the $1500 or $2000 which might be paid him. It cannot be necessary in this communication to elaborate the duties and advantages of such an officer, and I suggest his creation, because I earnestly desire you to do everything—I had almost said anything—for the advancement of so great and so good a cause.

The laudable anxiety exhibited by your predecessors to foster and encourage internal improvements in the State, gives assurance that that subject will engage much of your attention. Through the agency of the committee (members of the Legislature) appointed by the Legislature in 1843, and that of the commissioners appointed at the last session, settlements have been made with the several internal improvement companies, by which all the difficulties in the intercourse between the State and the companies have been obviated. The solvent and insolvent companies have been ascertained. With the former nothing remains to be done, but to receive the dividends due the State, semi-annually, on the first of January and July, whilst from the latter, nothing is to be expected. I therefore regard the continuance of a special agent as a mere collector of the State's dividends, as an unnecessary expense, as the duty could be performed by the cashier of the Bank of Tennessee, or by the Treasurer of the State. The officers from all the companies from which the State will receive dividends, reside in or so near Nashville, that the payments could be so made without trouble or difficulty. The cashier or treasurer, however, should be required to file statements with the comptroller, exhibiting the receipts or disbursements of the roads, together with the duplicate receipts of the cashier or treasurer, for the inspection and approval of the internal improvement board. The duty of collecting dividends during the last year has been performed by the Secretary of State, together with the other duties pertaining to his appointment as commissioner, which have now ceased, for which he was allowed five hundred dollars as an addition to his salary, the continuance of which I look upon as an unnecessary expense, as the mere collection of dividends can be performed by the treasurer or cashier of the Bank without additional compensation.

The completion of the Georgia Railroad to Chattanooga, an event now soon to be expected, will constitute a new and important era in the commercial and agricultural history in the eastern portion of our State. It unlocks the door, which for so many years has been closed against the profitable exchange of her mineral and agricultural productions with the other States which surround her. If nothing more were done, her people might well exult in such a vast improvement in their condition. But the Hiwassee Railroad, extending as it will, the benefits of this improvement to a much higher point on the Tennessee at Knoxville, makes the completion of the whole line a matter of intense, and almost vital interest to the whole of that large and interesting portion of the State. We have now good reason to expect the completion of this latter portion of the road. The company has been newly organized, its old liabilities have been, to a considerable extent discharged, and the present excellent directory have exhibited a laudable determination to push forward the work with vigor and earnestness.

From Knoxville, if a well built McAdamised road extending in the proper direction to the Virginia line, could be constructed, and the principal obstructions in the Tennessee river could be removed to the flourishing village of Kingsport—East Tennessee, reposing amid her lofty mountains, would be surpassed by no portion of our State in the abundant means of wealth and general prosperity.

If these grand projects cannot be carried on successfully by individual capital and enterprise, it will devolve upon you to determine whether any and how much assistance can be furnished by the State. The objects are of sufficient importance to engage in their behalf as full a share of State encouragement as her present liabilities and means would render prudent, and to this extent I earnestly recommend the subject to your attention.

In Middle Tennessee we are every day receiving the richest rewards from many of the improvements already made. The eye strikes at once on the map and traces out the many great roads stretching across the State, and centering at Nashville, a convenient point of the navigation of the Cumberland. So too, it glances along another road striking from Columbia, situated in the very heart of this middle region, and terminating on the Tennessee, in its Northern sweep through the State. Further North is to be seen a fine road coming in from Kentucky, terminating at Clarksville, and destined to contribute largely to the prosperity of a beautiful town now rapidly improving and bidding fair to become one of the most important commercial places in the State. Still the most superficial observer cannot fail to perceive the immense advantages to be derived by an extension of the Georgia road from Chattanooga to Nashville—advantages not to Chattanooga or Nashville alone, nor to the counties through which it would pass, but to almost every county in the middle portion of the State. This truth is every day becoming more manifest, in the increased anxiety every where displayed in favor of its construction. The corporation of Nashville has been authorized by the popular vote of the city, to subscribe for half a million of the stock, and many individuals of acknowledged sagacity and shrewdness in all that relates to the profitable investment of their funds, are known of, who intend to embark freely in the enterprise. In connection, however, with this work, the improvement of the Cumberland ought not to be lost sight of. A charter to individuals for this purpose was granted at the last session of the General Assembly, singularly defective in some of its provisions.—I earnestly recommend its supervision and amendment in such a manner as to insure the speedy removal of those obstructions, so detrimental to the commerce and trade of the middle portion of the State. When the Chattanooga and Nashville Railroad shall have been completed, and the obstructions in the Cumberland, the Elk, the Duck and the Caney Fork, shall have been removed, it would be difficult to find any region in the world possessing more advantages than Middle Tennessee. With a soil remarkable for its fertility—a climate happily exempt from the sickness of the South, and the intense protracted cold of the North—a population proverbial for its industry, sobriety and enterprise—with an easy accessibility by her roads and rivers to the markets of New Orleans, and through her proposed railroad to those of Charleston and Savannah, she may well challenge comparison with the most favored regions of the Union.

The Western District of our State is happily situated, in reference to natural facilities for carrying off her agricultural productions.—Lying nearly in a square, she is surrounded on three sides by two of the noblest rivers in the world, while the Hatchee, the Forked Deer, and the Obion, all navigable for small boats, penetrate into many of her richest and most populous counties. A project has however been started in the south proposing to extend to her further facilities by the construction of a railroad from Mobile to the Mississippi, near the mouth of the Ohio.

The engineer, Mr. Lewis Troost, son of the accomplished Geologist of the State, gives the following description of the route and the surface of the country over which it is proposed it should pass:

'Commencing at the city of Mobile, the route projected is in nearly a North direction, diverging slightly to the West, on the comparatively level lands dividing the waters of the Mississippi from those of the Tombigby and Tennessee rivers, through the South-western portion of Alabama, the Eastern and North-eastern of Mississippi, the Western District of Tennessee, and the Southwest corner of Kentucky, to the Mississippi river, at or near the junction of the Ohio. At this point it is suggested to cross the Mississippi river by a steam ferry; similar to that over the Susquehana, on the line of railroad between Philadelphia and Baltimore, and to extend the road on the West bank of the Mississippi to the city of St. Louis.

'The distance from Mobile to the junction of the Mississippi and Ohio rivers on this line, would be about four hundred and forty miles, and from the mouth of the Ohio to the city of St. Louis, about one hundred and fifty miles, making the total distance from the city of St. Louis to the city of Mobile, equal to about five hundred and ninety miles.

'A glance at the map of the States through which this route is projected, will indicate that from Mobile to the mouth of the Ohio, there is not a river or stream of any magnitude to cross, and that on the West bank of the Mississippi river, up to the city of St. Louis, there is only one river, the Maramec, to overcome.

'In the present communication it is proposed to say nothing of that part of the route between the city of St. Louis and the mouth of the Ohio. There can be no doubt that as soon as a continuous line of railway exists from the waters of the Gulf of Mexico to the Mississippi, at the junction of the Ohio, the citizens of St. Louis, anxious to partake of the advantages of railroad communication, will be ready to meet it with a railroad from their city to the West bank of the Mississippi .

'St. Louis is the great depot of the vast productions of the Upper Mississippi and Missouri. She receives and distributes supplies for an immense extent of territory, exceedingly fertile in the production of articles which must be transported to markets other than those afforded at home. Her navigation to these markets is at all times dangerous, interrupted frequently by the shifting of channels and the accumulation of snags, and for weeks in the winter season entirely closed by ice. Her interests will, at no distant period, even if they do not now, point out the necessity of having constant intercourse with the South, uninterrupted by low water, by ice, or by the numerous dangers of river navigation.

'For eighty or one hundred miles, the country North of Mobile, through which the railroad will pass, is described to be a comparatively level sandy region, very favorable for railroad making, and covered with yellow pine of matchless height and straightness, affording timber of excellent quality, in sufficient quantities to construct the road in its progress through it.

'Thence through Mississippi and Tennessee and Kentucky, where the line will run, the natural surface of the soil is said to offer no obstacles to obtain a straight route of easy grades, without heavy excavations or embankments. The character of the grading will be of the easiest description, there being no rock to encounter except at the northern termination of the route, near the Tennessee and Ohio rivers. Through the Eastern part of Mississippi the route will pass over prairies from five to ten miles wide, and from twenty to thirty miles long. From surveys made for railroads through the Western District of Tennessee, the natural level of the country is represented to offer so many desirable routes in this respect, that the chief difficulty will, perhaps, be in selecting the most favorable. Parallel to the Mississippi and Tennessee rivers are two ridges of highlands, on either of which the road might be located to advantage.

'The main line can be made to form a junction with the Tennessee river, at or near Savannah, or at Perryville, which is in the vicinity of extensive beds of iron ore. At either place it would intercept the trade of the valleys on both sides of the Tennessee river, which now has to perform a tedious voyage around by the Tennessee, Ohio, and Mississippi rivers, of from four to five hundred miles, before it arrives at the same parallel of latitude as the point of departure. From either Perryville or Savannah, at the great elbow formed by the Tennessee river, a branch might be made to Nashville, avoiding altogether the Cumberland Mountains, which present many obstacles of a serious kind to any other approach to Nashville from the sea-ports on the South Atlantic coasts. This branch to Nashville will form a link of the great chain of railroads now being projected to connect the Eastern and Middle with the Southern States, by running a line of railroads to the South and East of the Ohio river, and of which the Baltimore and Ohio railroad is the commencement. By the proposed route, Nashville can have a much more direct and expeditious communication, with a better sea-port for her purposes, and by far, over a more favorable route than by the route she is now seeking to establish, via. Chattanooga. That this branch to Nashville, considered as a part of a line which must be formed at no distant day to connect the Northern, Eastern and Middle and Southern States together, is of great importance, there can be no question, when it is considered that it will run through some of the richest agricultural portions of the Union.

'Through the Western District of Tennessee are inexhaustible beds of marl cropping out at the surface. This valuable material for agricultural purposes will form a great article of transport.

'There is no route for a railroad in the Union, to compare with this. Here is a main continuous line of 440 miles in length, running, without crossing navigable rivers or mountains, through the richest portions of three of the most productive States, where they are in a great measure deprived of all kinds of communication, where it can command the trade and travel of eight States and the Western Territories, with lateral branches extending by short distances into the richest and most varied agricultural and mineral region, which although passing through different State governments will be governed throughout by the same laws, subject to the same institutions, and will be under the same management and responsibility.'

If this Mobile project be too vast for early or eventful execution, the sagacity of those who have charge of it, will not fail to discover how much better it would be to make the Northern terminus on the Tennessee river, where it makes its great bend through the State, than to permit it to fail altogether. This would reduce its magnitude to a size entirely practicable, and be to the city of Mobile scarcely less profitable. To that point at or below the town of Waterloo, the Tennessee is easily navigable at all seasons of the year by most of the steamboats that ply on our Western waters.— Such a terminus would therefore be perfectly accessible to all the commerce of the Cumberland, the Ohio, the Mississippi, and Missouri, which might seek an outlet through the Bay of Mobile.— Much of the Western District would still be deeply interested in its success, and the State would doubtless aid and encourage the project presented in either form by all the means which could at any time be fairly and justly appropriated to its advancement.

The present period, however, is much more favorable to the execution of internal improvements by the enterprise and capital of individuals, than by the direct appropriations of the States. There are but few of them, who have not, on former occasions, either for banking or improvement purposes, contracted as large a public debt, as they now have any ability to meet. This is certainly so with regard to the State of Tennessee. So far, she has been entirely able to save herself from the reproach of having failed to meet her liabilities. A proper sense of pride, justice, and honor should restrain her from now creating against herself any new liabilities which she may have no means of meeting, even for the accomplishment of the most inviting projects of prospective usefulness. On the other hand, the people, unlike the States, are less involved in debt at this time, than at any recent period. They have been blessed generally with good crops for several years, which have commanded remunerating prices. Other pursuits are understood also to have been eminently successful, so that all classes of the community have more ability than usual to patronise and encourage all safe and profitable projects that may be presented.

It is to this individual ability, and to the well known sagacity of our people, prompting them readily to engage in all safe and profitable investments, that we ought mainly to look, at least for the present, for the further extension of our system of Internal Improvements.

In the discharge of the various duties which devolve upon you, none will require more earnest investigation and patient deliberation, than those connected with the important interests which the people have in the successful management of the Bank of Tennessee. You cannot exercise too much care in looking into its present condition and its past management, with the view of discovering any defects that may exist in its present organization, and of devising the best measures for increasing its usefulness and prosperity. When it went into operation it was regarded by many as an experiment which would inevitably terminate disastrously at an early day. The absence of the grand conservative principles of individual interest was the alleged capital defect in its organization, on which these predictions were based of its early failure. To this suggestion it was answered, that the combination of the interests of Internal Improvements and Education, with Banking, would furnish a substitute for individual interest equally as efficacious in securing a faithful and successful administration of its affairs. The experiment has now been on trial for nine years, a period sufficiently long to enable you to form a reliable opinion as to the probable success or failure of the experiment.

If a careful investigation into its past operations and its present condition, shall satisfy you that it has failed to accomplish in a reasonable degree the important objects of its creation, and that it is destined unavoidably to end in ruin and disaster, it will become your imperious duty to avert the threatened blow by an immediate provision for the gradual settlement and liquidation of its affairs. If, on the contrary, such an investigation shall produce the conviction, that the experiment has proved reasonably successful, and that the public interest would be promoted by its continuance, the duty of exerting the utmost possible vigilance in guarding it against future mismanagement and misfortunes, will devolve upon you.

Without assuming to pass sentence on the wisdom of establishing the Bank at all, or of uniting in one system the interests of Banking, Internal Improvement and Education, I have no hesitation in announcing to you that my investigations into its past transactions and its present condition, have disclosed to my mind no satisfactory reason for recommending its discontinuance and abandonment.—So far as the Bank was designed to furnish a sound and safe circulating medium, it must be admitted that it has been thus far successful. Its influence in mitigating the pressure of the pecuniary embarrassment which prevailed during the several years of its existence has been universally acknowledged.

The friends of education have abundant cause to be well pleased with its promptness and fidelity in the fulfillment of its obligations to Common Schools and Academies, whilst the present high credit enjoyed by our State securities fully attest it successful management of that branch of our financial affairs which has devolved upon it. Within the last nine years the Bank has paid an aggregate sum of more than two millions of dollars, which has been appropriated by the State in diffusing the benefits of education and in the payment of the accruing interest on her debt. Within the same period the net profits of the institution have fallen but little short of two millions of dollars, showing an annual average profit of two hundred and sixty thousand dollars, an amount equal to nearly eight per cent on its actual capital.

These results would seem to go very far towards proving that the experiment has been successful, and must have a strong tendency to dissipate the fears of those who have looked to its failure as inevitable—unless it shall be found upon investigation, that the losses sustained have been unreasonably large.

In the examination of this point, it will become material to ascertain at what period of time the largest portion of the losses have occurred; and if it shall be found, as it is believed to be true, that they occurred at an early period, and before certain important amendments were made to the charter, and that very little has been lost since that time, it will rather furnish a reason for an increased diligence in seeking for other defects, than for the total abandonment and annihilation of the system. The main ground on which it has been unsuccessful in accomplishing the objects of its creation, is furnished by the fact that its annual profits are not sufficient to meet the annual payments required to be made. This objection should have but little weight, if the burdens imposed upon it are unreasonably great, and that this is the case, will admit of no doubt, when it is recollected that the payments required to be made annually, amount to about two hundred and seventy thousand dollars—an amount equal to more than nine per cent on its actual capital.

In coming to the conclusion that the Bank ought not to be discontinued and wound up under existing circumstances, (whatever my opinions about Banks of paper issue may be), I have not failed to be duly impressed by the unavoidable pressure in our monetary affairs, which would be produced by the withdrawal of so large a portion of our circulating medium, as is now furnished by it, and by the collection of so large an amount of debts as are due to it.— This pressure might be greatly mitigated, but could not be entirely avoided, by adopting a liberal policy in the gradual liquidation of its affairs; nor have I overlooked the difficulties and embarrassments which would be encountered in providing the means of meeting the liabilities imposed upon the Bank during the time required for its liquidation.

Influenced by these considerations, I cannot recommend the discontinuance of the Bank, but instead thereof, your attention is most earnestly invited to the investigation of such measures as shall promise to increase its profits, and render them sufficient to meet its liabilities. In view of the fact that for several years past the profits made at most of its Branches have been greater than those made at the principal Bank, in proportion to the capital respectively employed by them, I submit to you whether the three Branches now in a state of process of liquidation, may not be advantageously restored. In making this suggestion it is proper for me to remark that it is founded on information not possessed at the former session of the General Assembly, and is not intended as a condemnation of the Act by which these Branches were discontinued—that Act might well be justified under the impressions which prevailed at the time of its passage.

It is now believed, however, that the progress made in settling their affairs will shew that these impressions were materially erroneous, and that the losses sustained ought not to prejudice the claims of those interested to the restoration of these Branches—being fully satisfied from a careful view of the character of the population interested, the anxiety which exists amongst them for additional banking facilities, (whilst the present form of the banking system continues), and the increasing commercial interest at each of the places, I am constrained to recommend to you that these Branches be restored. In connection with this subject, I feel it also my duty to call your attention to the claims of the city of Memphis to an increase of its banking facilities. The rapid growth of this flourishing city, based on its proper commercial interests and advantages, would indicate it as one of the most eligible points in the State for profitable banking, and under this conviction, if you determine in favor of the continuance of the principal Bank, I recommend the establishment of a Branch or Agency of the Bank of Tennessee at Memphis, with such capital as can be advantageously furnished by the institution. But I cannot indulge the hope that the adoption of these suggestions would enable the Bank to increase its profits to such an extent as would meet all of its liabilities—the necessity would therefore still exist for an investigation of the best means of diminishing the present liabilities of the Bank. These liabilities at present amount to about two hundred and seventy thousand dollars annually, whilst the annual average profits, heretofore, have been about two hundred and sixteen thousand dollars.

By an Act passed in 1844, the Treasury is required to make up the deficiency unavoidably occurring on account of the inability of the Bank to make profits sufficient to meet the liabilities chargeable upon it. I submit to you whether a sinking fund could not be set apart by the Treasury, without any increase of taxation, to be annually vested in the purchase of State Bonds at their current value, as a means of gradually reducing the liabilities of the Bank to a sum that would not exceed the amount of its profits. This suggestion will receive additional weight from the consideration, that under existing circumstances, the deficiency may be permanent, and therefore constitute a permanent drain upon the Treasury. It is believed that a sinking fund of one hundred thousand dollars furnished by the Treasury for five years, would so far reduce the State debt, and consequently the liabilities of the Bank, as would enable the institution after that time to meet all burdens imposed upon it.

It gives me great pleasure to express to you the belief, that the Bank has been faithfully and satisfactorily managed during the last two years.

The Report of the President and Directors will contain all the information necessary to enable you to understand its present condition and to devise the proper measures for rendering it more useful and profitable in the future, whilst it will exhibit a very large increase of the profits during the last two years.

Since the last session of the General Assembly, a war has been declared to exist between the United States and the Republic of Mexico. The circumstances which led to this declaration were such as to extort it from the Congress of the United States by an almost unanimous vote; Abolitionary Fanatacism alone stood out against it. Every Representative from Tennessee of both political parties voted for it. Ten millions of money, and authority to call into the public service fifty thousand volunteers, for the purpose of prosecuting the war to a safe and honorable peace, were voted by Congress and placed in the hands of the President. Under this Act, a requisition was made on this State on the 16th of May, 1846, for one regiment of calvary or mounted men and two regiments of infantry or riflemen.

On the receipt of this requisition, I issued my proclamation dated 24th May, 1846, apportioning the call equally and fairly

among the three grand divisions of the State. It was nobly responded
to.—Instead of three thousand, about thirty thousand rushed forward with eager anxiety to engage in the service of their country.
The call was met so promptly, that the troops assembled in advance of any officer of the United States, either to muster them into
service, or to make those usual advances of money so necessary to
troops, suddenly called on to leave their home on so long and
distant an expedition. To remedy this circumstance, I appointed
suitable officers to inspect and muster them into service in their
respective quarters of the State, rather than subject them to the uncertainty of being rejected after they had gone to a distant place of
rendezvous.

To make a suitable advance of money to each officer and soldier,
to defray all the expenses incident to their encampment at Knoxville, Nashville and Memphis, and also to subsist the East Tennessee
troops in their march to the latter city, required the negotiation of
large sums of money.

The Union and Planters' Banks, with a patriotism which cannot
be too highly extolled, promptly stepped forward and proposed to
lend any sum of money, not exceeding one hundred thousand dollars each, which might be demanded by the occasion. Without any
law authorizing me to borrow money for this or any other purpose,
but unwilling to submit to any delay, I took the responsibility of
negotiating with the Union Bank for some sixty or seventy thousand dollars, which were applied to the above objects of expenditure.—So soon, however, as our troops were gone, and the state of
my official business would allow of it, I repaired to Washington
City, whilst every item of expenditure was fresh in my recollection
and those of my officers, and presented my accounts for settlement,
and I am happy to say they were promptly but thoroughly examined and allowed by the proper Department, with perhaps the
single exception of interest, for which no existing law of Congress
was supposed to provide, but which I doubt not, will be hereafter
adjusted satisfactorily to the Bank. It is with pleasure, therefore,
that I inform you that in going beyond the law, and assuming the
responsibility of raising this sum of money as the Chief Magistrate
of the State, no debt was incurred by which the State can be in any
wise injured.

The advances that made this unauthorized negotiation necessary, were indispensable to the comfort of the troops. Volunteers suddenly called on to leave their homes on such a campaign, could not well afford to equip themselves out of their own private means and to support themselves in their respective encampments until the arrival of the officers of the United States, who had no idea of so prompt and early a movement, for such had been unknown before in the volunteer service of the United States; nor could the East Tennessee volunteers, suddenly called on to march four or five hundred miles to Memphis, be expected to be prepared with ready means of their own to bear their expenses.

But whilst I took on myself as the Executive of the State to make this negotiation, I endeavored to consult the most rigid economy and to make only such accounts as the United States would recognize as just, and to appoint only such officers as they would think to be absolutely necessary. Under this view of a just and proper economy, I left the troops, (except those of East Tennessee, on account of their distance), to subsist themselves on their travel from their respective neighborhoods to the places of rendezvous, precisely as is done by the laws and regulations of the United States. But I established encampments at Knoxville, Nashville and Memphis, for the reception of them, as fast as they should arrive, where they were attended to by one or two suitable officers, and supplied with the same rations as are allowed by the United States to their own troops. These arrangements I am happy to believe, proved entirely satisfactory, not only to the United States, but to the troops themselves, with perhaps a solitary exception, which, as it relates to my Executive action in carrying out the requisition on this State, is here submitted for your consideration.

On the 6th of June, 1846, I received the following communication, recently found, after diligent search, and which I had supposed might have been thrown aside, as not important to be preserved:

'Camp Brown, June 5th, 1846.

To the Hon. A. V. Brown, Gov'r &c.

DEAR SIR: On to-morrow evening I will have the honor of leading ninety-four of the gallant sons of Giles county to an encampment on Brown's Creek. By the request of the company I have the honor to ask of you the favor of selecting us a proper and judicious place of encampment, where we can have water and rest on Sunday. We have camp equipage and a wagon, and will be prepared to take care of ourselves in soldiers' style. We expect to be ready to be mustered into service on Monday morning.

I have the honor to be, very respectfully,
Your obedient servant and friend,
(Signed)   MILTON A. HAYNES,
Captain Giles County Mounted Riflemen.'

This communication was not addressed to me as a private individual—it was addressed to me as Governor of the State, and delivered to me at my office as such. It spoke nothing of one night, but of several nights, and the greater part at least of two days.

It made no allusion to going at all to the general encampment. It asked no privilege of encamping on my grounds, nor did it in the slightest degree, in form, or manner, call up the question of my individual hospitality. It avowed the intention to encamp on Brown's Creek, a small stream of excellent water directly on the road, which had borne that name from the earliest settlement of the country, and on which I had no lots or grounds at all. Regarding it, therefore, as an application to me as the Executive of the State, for the selection of a public and additional encampment to the one already at Nashville, I returned the following answer, in accordance with the advice of the Adjutant General of the State and of my own sense of duty and propriety:

'Nashville, June 6, 1846.
I have no opportunity to procure an encampment in the neighborhood you mention, and no officer to send to attend you. My encampment at Nashville is at the Rack Track, where some of the troops are yet encamped, where you and company can have provisions and horse-feed provided.

In haste, yours, &c.
(Signed)   AARON V. BROWN.'

This reply was predicated on the idea, that to furnish, as I had done the three encampments at Knoxville, at Nashville and at Memphis, with suitable officers to attend them, was all that a just sense of economy, and the practice in all such cases, both in and out of the State, would allow of; besides, I was by no means confident that the United States would settle the accounts made at two separate encampments so near Nashville.

No other volunteer company had received any such special accommodation, and I desired to mete out the same measure of justice to all. To avoid all difficulties and complaints, and to enable the company to reach a better and more comfortable encampment than it was possible to furnish at Brown's Creek, I threw open the doors of my general encampment, and invited them, by a march of an hour longer, to partake, with their brother soldiers, of its ample supplies and accommodations.

I lay these precise facts before you, that they may go upon the permanent records of the country, repelling, as they do, every idea of Executive inhospitality to these brave and gallant men.

To my Quartermaster General, G. W. Rowles, and to Major General Brazelton, and to Inspector General Coe, and Major General Hays, I am under, and the volunteer service of the State is under, many obligations for the promptitude, skill, and energy with which they conducted the operations in the respective divisions of the State.

In the transactions of the middle portion of the State, I cannot withhold from Major General Bradley, and Adjutant General Turner, equal expressions of gratitude for the services which they rendered.

Early in the month of June, the three regiments, (two only fully organized), were handed over to the United States. They were the flower and chivalry of the State. The sons of those worthy sires who, under Jackson, Carroll and Coffee, in former days, had shed so much lustre around the name of Tennessee. Would these, their descendants, prove themselves worthy of such illustrious ancestors?

I did not doubt it—no one doubted it—they went forth in a just cause. Not one of them felt that it was an unjust one, or they would not have gone. They went forth, and on every battle-field, at Monterey, at Vera Cruz, at Cerro Gordo, they performed deeds of heroic valor, worthy of Tennessee in the proudest days of her glory.

But it was not on the battle-field alone, that your regiments bore your banner so high and so proudly. In the toilsome march, beneath the burning sun, in the pestilential encampment, everywhere, and under all circumstances, your volunteers well sustained the honor of the State. In behalf of our whole people, I recommend the strongest expression of public gratitude and admiration for their heroic services, and that a full register of the names of every soldier of the three regiments be made out and safely deposited in the new capitol, when completed, that posterity may know who they were that contributed so largely to the honor and glory of the Commonwealth. Let the State contribute largely to the erection of some lofty monument to the memory of those who fell either in battle or by disease, in the prosecution of a war, which could not have been avoided without a sacrifice of national honor, dignity and character.

But the patriotic devotion of our fellow-citizens has been tested by another requisition, recently made, for two more regiments of infantry from the State. It is with no common degree of pride that I announce the pleasing fact to you, that, not withstanding the many appeals made to the people of the State, through a portion of the public press, and the debates and discussions of the past Summer, against the justice, propriety and necessity of the Mexican war, the chivalrous sons of Tennessee have responded to the call, with a noble enthusiasm.

Five companies were called for by my proclamation from each Major General's division in the State, thereby giving, as on the former occasions, a fair and equal chance to the citizens of every portion of the State.

Many more companies reported themselves than could be selected to fill the requisition, whilst many others were known of who were in a forward state of completion, when the time arrived for making selections. It cannot, I hope, be considered invidious to mention that East Tennessee was peculiarly chivalrous on the occasion, having furnished not only the five companies called for, but tendered ten other companies besides, composed of her brave and hardy sons. The officers of the United States having learned, by experience, something of the promptitude and celerity with which the citizen soldiers of Tennessee always rush to the standard of their country, have promptly repaired to the State to aid in carrying out the movement, exempting the Executive from much of the labor and responsibility of a former occasion. The volunteers are now on their way to their respective encampments at Nashville and Memphis, where they will be regularly organized into regiments, and pass over to the command and service of the United States.— If the war continues, the whole community cannot but feel the deepest interest in the future destination and fortunes of these brave and gallant men.

The career of their predecessors in this war has been so distinguished—for their patience under fatigue, for their ready obedience to the commands of their officers, for their undaunted courage in the face of the enemy—that it would be difficult to emulate their bright and glorious example. But I hazard nothing when I assure you that these regiments will go forth nerved to new energies by that high example, and firmly resolved, living or dying, to add new lustre to the name and character of Tennessee.

But at the moment when I am writing down these proud and pleasing assurances, the news may be brought to us that a treaty should hail with rapture and delight the bright and beautiful Goddess of Peace, at whose shrine the American people have always delighted to worship. Her return would be more welcome, because she will doubtless bring with her all that was ever demanded—'indemnity for the past, security for the future.' This was all that the Administration at Washington—the President and his friends in Congress, and throughout the Union—all that the Commanding General in his Proclamation in the earliest stages of the war ever demanded. The territory she is expected to bring will be stained with no blood unjustly shed, in the proud and lustful spirit of conquest. She will bring it as the only indemnity Mexico can offer against the expenses we have incurred in the prosecution of a war, which Mexico herself was the first to proclaim, and first to commence. A war originating in Mexico's unjust attempt to reconquer a territory which had been, under all the forms of our Constitution, made one of the States of the Union; a war which she wantonly and wickedly provoked by an invasion of that part of Texas lying east of the Lower Rio Grande, to which our title extended (whatever might be said of the Upper Rio Grande) without a shadow of a doubt. But I cannot shut my eyes to the great fact, that there are many persons, of this State and elsewhere, who, in anticipation of a result such as we are now considering, have labored hard to convince the people that, if indemnity in land against the expenses of this war, and for the purpose of paying the millions that are due to our citizens, should be willingly offered by Mexico, such an indemnity should be scorned and rejected. Whether the infatuation of party will persist in such doctrine, remains to be seen. But I most earnestly recommend to this General Assembly, never to adjourn until you have instructed your Senators and requested your Representatives not to vote against a treaty of peace, or refuse the necessary appropriation to carry it into effect, only because it may contain a cession of territory to the United States.—Indemnity against the war, I hold to be clearly right—Mexico herself, I doubt not, will so consider it. Shall the United States reject the indemnity because it may be in land, and not in money? She has not the latter to pay, and the former constitutes her only remaining resource. It will therefore be indemnity in land or nothing.—*I repeat, in land or nothing*. What wise or sensible man, in the management of his private affairs, would reject a payment in land, when his debtor had no other resource left, with which to satisfy his demand? The plea that our country is large enough already, takes no account of the future millions of freemen who are to inhabit it. The natural increase of our own population—the amazing emigration to the United States, from the starving and oppressed nations of the old World—the genius, industry, and enterprise of the Anglo-Saxon race—all unite in demanding that our country should be extended from ocean to ocean—widened out in all her borders, whenever it can be done consistently with the dictates of national honor and justice. Such an opportunity will now be offered freely to us, and perhaps for the last time in the history of our country.

The pretext that any new accession of territory, may endanger the perpetuation of our glorious Union, is only a shallow device for alarming the timid and deceiving the ignorant.

The same cry was raised when Louisiana, extending from the Gulf to the Northern Lakes, was acquired—the same when Missouri was admitted—when Florida was purchased—when Texas, neither conquered nor purchased, walked into our Union by sovereign compact and agreement. The Union dissolved!! dissolved by the growth and enlargement of our free and happy Republic!! No.—It grows stronger and stronger by it, the very elements of perpetuation being increased in the exact proportion of its contemplated magnitude. The spirit of modern Abolitionism, if it existed at all in the early days of the Republic, stood rebuked by the Constitution. It stood equally rebuked in the Missouri Compromise, which was but a virtual continuation of that of the Constitution. So it will be in the extension of the same line of latitude 36 deg. 30 min., through the newly acquired territory of California. What a beautiful harmony in our national action would then be exhibited! Our Revolutionary Fathers, in adjusting the proportion of the free and slaveholding States, substantially fixed it on latitude of 36 deg. 30 min. The next generation (for the Revolutionary one had nearly departed), then extended that line through the newly acquired territory from France, and now it is proposed (and to this I give my assent, and earnestly recommend that you give yours), to extend this line Westward, through the territory which may be ceded to us by Mexico, to the shores of the Pacific. This being done, the great strife and contention about slavery, we may hope, will be settled and ended forever. Then no 'Wilmot Proviso' will break upon our repose, like a fire-bell by night. The line of separation will be fixed. All men would understand it and conform to it, in the formation of States. Nor need the conscientious and sincere friend of the black race, (for there are many such), be in the slightest degree apprehensive that slavery, though permitted to exist South of that line, would ever be in fact established in any one of the States of California. The character of the country—the nature of its resources —the insecurity of such property on many accounts, would deter any slaveholder from taking that description of property with him. The question about slavery, therefore, loses much, if not all, its practical importance in relation to the territory now to be acquired from Mexico, as has been truly said by one of our greatest statesmen, and said too, at a most auspicious moment for the peace and harmony of our country. The Union therefore, I hold to be in no danger from any new accession of territory. I believe that, under the Providence of God, it is destined to last and endure forever, stretching, like the beautiful rainbow of Hope and of Promise, until it bespans this whole continent.

A vacancy has occurred in the Supreme Court, by the resignation of Judge Reese, now on file, to take effect from the first day of the present month, which places it in the power of the General Assembly to fill it, without the intervention of the Executive. Another vacancy occurred in the 4th Judicial Circuit, by the death of Judge Cannon, which was temporarily filled by George W. Rowles, Esq. Vacancies in the 4th, 8th, and 10th Solicitorial Districts have been filled by the appointment of Mr. Joseph G. Pickett, of Carthage; Mr. J. P. Campbell, of Columbia; and Mr. T. P. Scurlock, of Jackson—whose commissions will expire with the close of the present Legislature. Mr. Nelson, Register of the Mountain District, having resigned, the vacancy was filled by the appointment of Mr. J. H. Minnis, and subsequently, on his resignation, by the appointment of Mr. J. F. Brown, of Sparta.

It will also be your duty to elect a Senator to Congress, to supply the place of the Hon. Spencer Jarnagin, whose term of service expired on the 4th of March last. I need not anticipate, by a single remark, the care with which you will select some individual, eminent for his ability and patriotism, to fill this exalted station, at a crisis so important to the honor and welfare of the nation.

I have now presented to your consideration, all the subjects which I desire to present before you, and close this communication with the sincere and confident hope that your deliberations may be distinguished for their harmony, and may result in the advancement of the best interests and welfare of the State.

I have the honor to be,

Your obedient servant.

Aaron V. Brown

Executive Office, October, 1847."

The above Message was a State paper of real statesmanship caliber. Few, if any, Executive Messages have thus far carried more constructive suggestions and recommendations. The following editorial fairly summarized the contents of the Message,[105] and that epitome was as follows:

"GOV. BROWN'S MESSAGE

The message of Gov. A. V. Brown to the General Assembly is spread before the country, and either has been, or will be, read with that interest which such a document necessarily excites. We doubt whether any Chief Magistrate of Tennessee has ever been so fortunate in securing the approbation of the people in the discharge of his duties as Gov. Brown. Although

---

[105] *The Daily Union* (Nashville), October 8, 1847.

these duties have been of a character unusually delicate and responsible on some occasions, his clear head and pure heart have enabled him to meet every emergency with a wisdom and patriotism which have disarmed the opposition of his bitterest political enemies, and extorted from all a ready acquiescence in his fidelity and ability as Governor of the State. With a single exception, he passed through the late animated contest without being required to vindicate any act of his administration. His successful opponent paid a high compliment to the administration, wisdom, and fidelity of Gov. Brown, inasmuch as he made no issue with him in regard to any act connected with his official duties. The people every where, and of all parties, freely expressed their satisfaction as to his conduct as Chief Magistrate, and freely conceded to him talents of the highest order.

These considerations, in connexion with the fact that he surrenders his official power at a time when the people over whom he has presided are enjoying unexampled prosperity, cannot fail to afford him solid and enduring grounds of gratification under his defeat.—Under such circumstances, he can and does bow to the apparent will of his countrymen, without complaint or mortification—we say *apparent* will of his countrymen, because we do not suppose that any candid man, of any party, doubts that he is the choice of a majority of the voters of Tennessee, and that his defeat was entirely owing to accidental causes. In laying down the office which he has filled with so much credit to himself and honor to the State, he might well refer, in eloquent terms of gratification, to the high state of prosperity with which the whole people are blessed. He might well congratulate them upon the successful administration of the government in all its departments, and upon the bright prospects which are held out for the future.

Gov. Brown's remarks on the subjects of education, internal improvement, and banking, will be read with peculiar interest—they contain suggestions, reflections, and recommendations which show how anxiously he has investigated the subjects, and how solicitous he is for the advancement of these great interests.

His remarks as to the manner in which he has discharged the responsible duties which devolved upon him in consequence of the war with Mexico, and his reflections upon the justice of that war, are worthy of the man and of the occasion. His vindication of the only act of his administration which has been made the subject of attack, is triumphant and conclusive. We allude to the contemptible charge in reference to his refusal to allow a company of volunteers to encamp on his grounds.—Every man who has been instrumental in using this vile slander to the prejudice of Governor Brown, will feel ashamed of his conduct when the facts contained in the message are seen.

The sentiments expressed by Gov. Brown in reference to the war and the manner of its prosecution, will find a hearty response in the bosoms of the patriotic portion of all parties, whilst his sound views as to the policy of acquiring new territory and the terms of its admisson, will be found worthy of ready approval.

We doubt not that the whole message will be received with feelings of satisfaction, and even admiration, by the candid and impartial of both parties. It is a paper worthy of Gov. Brown, and worthy of the Chief Magistrate of a great State."

On Saturday, October 16, 1847, Governor Aaron V. Brown laid down the reins of government at the inaugural services of his successor,

Neill S. Brown. Without a trace of bitterness over his recent defeat, the retiring Governor delivered his Valedictory Address [106] which was appropriately addressed to the General Assembly:

"GENTLEMEN OF THE SENATE
    AND OF THE HOUSE OF REPRESENTATIVES:

I present myself before you to-day, that I may lay down, in your presence, all the power and authority appertaining to the Executive Office of the State—to lay them down at the feet of the Constitution, that you may presently confer them in due form, on my honorable successor; such has been the declared will of my fellow-citizens, and to their decision I bow, without murmur or regret.

In the two years, during which I have filled the exalted office from which I am now retiring, events of the greatest magnitude have been crowding upon us. The annexation of Texas, although commencing before, has been consummated, adding an Empire to the Republic; an Empire, large as modern France, with a soil rich as that of Egypt, and a climate soft and delicious as that of enchanting Italy. The settlement of the Oregon question confirmed our title to another Empire, larger than the first, and extended the now undisputed boundaries of the Republic to the shores of the Pacific.—When these two great events are contemplated together, what an amazing spectacle of territorial grandeur does our country at this day exhibit!!

At first we had but thirteen States, stretching in narrow, but dazzling brightness, all along the shores of the Atlantic. In a few years, our population scaled the eastern mountains—poured itself into the great valley of the Mississippi, felling its ancient and unbroken forest, building up towns and cities, rearing halls of science, and Temples of Religion, until what in the old World, would have required a long succession of ages for its accomplishment, is here presented as the magic work of a single generation.

But, in addition to all this, what do we now behold? Yet another Empire, large as Texas and Oregon both put together, subdued by our arms, subjected by the law of nations to our military government, and destined, as I believe, and hope are long to constitute an integral portion of our great Republic. Wonderful nation!! Stretch-

---

[106] *Ibid.*, October 18, 1847.

ing from ocean to ocean, and from the Gulf of Mexico to the great inland seas of the north!! Millions yet unborn, the sons and daughters of freedom, who are hereafter to inhabit this continent, will bless, and honor the memories of those illustrious statesmen and patriots, who have made or confirmed these amazing accessions to our country.

But it is not the physical grandeur of our country alone, which should challenge our patriotic emotions. After a long period of profound peace, when her old and renowned warriors, who used to adorn her camps, and her history, had all been 'gathered to their fathers', she has raised and set forth a new race of heroes, whose gallant deeds at Monterey, at Buena Vista, at Vera Cruz, at Cerro Gordo, and at the late great battles before the city of Mexico, have filled America with joy and the world with admiration.

Nor yet is it her amazing expansion, nor the heroic deeds of her warriors, that should challenge our highest degree of patriotic ardor.—No, it is not these, great and dazzling as they may be,—it is from our sacred constitution, securing to us our civil and religious liberties, and from our glorious Union protecting us in their enjoyment against all foreign enemies, that the patriot should draw his deepest and holiest emotions. By these he should be chiefly inspired, humbly to supplicate, that they might last and endure forever—

'Till wrapt in flames, the realms of ether grow,
And Heaven's last thunder shakes the world below.'

Turning from this bright and animating picture of national greatness, let us look to the no less cheering and happy condition of our own beloved and honored Tennessee.

You and I (turning to the Governor-elect) have lately traversed her in all her borders; we have scaled her eastern mountains; we have penetrated her rich luxuriant valleys; we have reposed on the banks of that mighty river which marks her western boundary; every where we have seen a contended, happy, and patriotic people —a people exempt from debt—their industry crowned with abundance—their institutions of learning crowded with the votaries of science, whilst religion is ministering to them her consolations in all her consecrated temples. Such are the people, and such their condition at the moment when you are called to preside over their destinies. I congratulate my fellow-citizens that such *is* their condition in spite of all the prophetic annunciations of approaching ruin. The ocean and the lakes have become no vast solitudes. The husbandman has not been driven from his home by the stench of the rotting productions of his farm. The industrious manufacturer has not been doomed to abandon his loom and his work-shop for the already too much crowded pursuits of agriculture. No. Thanks to the kind and overruling Providence. Thanks to the industry, sobriety, and enterprise of our people.—Thanks to the wisdom and patriotism of our rulers, however much they have been reviled and persecuted.

Thanks to all these that prosperity like an angel, is still hovering and smiling over our State and nation.

I should have rejoiced, gentlemen, if on my retiring from office, I could have congratulated you and my fellow-citizens at large on the return of peace.

That beautiful goddess is yet standing on the confines of Mexico, holding out the olive-branch to our deluded and obstinate enemy. Our victorious arms have wrested from her city after city, and province after province, until our Star Spangled Banner is this day proudly waving over the Halls of the Montezumas, but let it be ever recorded, let all Christendom know, let posterity know, that not a gun has been fired, not a city has been taken, not a province has been invaded, without our having first tendered to her the terms of a just and honorable peace. 'These terms were indemnity for the past and security for the future'—indemnity for the millions due to our citizens—indemnity for the millions, which we have expended in the prosecution of a war, which she was the first to declare, and the first to commence—security against any further invasion of territory, which has been made a part of our Union under all the forms of the Constitution, and to which she has no shadow of right, by the solemn declaration of every civilized nation in the world. This indemnity and security we will have—she may fly from her capitol to her mountains, but our victorious Eagles will pursue her to their loftiest summit, and the thunder of our cannon will extort it from her.

With the return of peace with Mexico, with no cause of future irritation with any foreign nation, with all the elements essential to national greatness, what prophetic spirit can anticipate the future growth and progress of our nation—all that the heart can desire—all that the imagination can conceive of—lies before us. How brilliant, how animating the prospect! If we are true to ourselves, true to the constitution, true to our bright and glorious Union, Earth has no happiness, Heaven has no blessings, which may not belong to the people of the United States.

But gentlemen, pleasing and delightful as are these meditations, I must not and will not forget that the chief honors and ceremonies of this occasion are intended for another, I therefore conclude, by tendering, to you all, the homage of my profound respect."

CHAPTER TWO

Neill Smith Brown

Neill Smith Brown was born in Giles County, Tennessee, on April 18, 1810. In the preceding year, his father had emigrated to this State from North Carolina. The parents were of Scottish descent and were Presbyterians. The life of a typical small-time farmer was the pattern followed in the youth of Neill S. Brown who acquired the rudiments of elementary education by the firelight at home after a day of hard toil. When seventeen years of age, young Brown attended two sessions at a neighboring academy and then taught school to obtain means for entering Jackson College, an institution near Columbia in Maury County, in which he completed his formal academic training. After another turn at teaching school, he then placed himself under the tute-lage of Chancellor Lunsford M. Bramlett as a student of the law. The "Go West" fever was in evidence at the time, and the young lawyer decided to try his fortunes in Texas then a province of Mexico. But a short stay at Matagorda convinced him that he had made a mistake by locating in a country then largely wild and unsettled, a situation that did not appeal to a young man of ambitious but peaceful nature. He returned to his native county and opened a law office in Pulaski. As with many bright young lawyers of the time, he was lured into the political arena in 1836 as an elector on the ticket of Hugh Lawson White who had broken with Andrew Jackson and was a candidate for the Presidency to succeed General Jackson. In this way Neill S. Brown became an adherent of the Whig Party and may be regarded as one of the founders of the Anti-Jackson Party in Tennessee. In 1837, he was elected a member of the State Legislature and was an earnest sup-porter of the measure chartering the Bank of Tennessee and of the law which marked the beginning of the movement for building turn-pikes and railways.

In 1843, he was brought out as the Whig candidate for Congress against a veteran who had held the office for two terms. Although the

176

From Portrait by Washington B. Cooper. Courtesy of Tennessee Historical Society, Nashville.

District was Democratic by some 1,600 votes, he reduced the majority of his victorious rival, Aaron V. Brown, to about four hundred votes, thereby acquiring a reputation as an impressive speaker and logical debater. In the following year, 1844, he was again on the electoral ticket and cast his vote for Henry Clay whom he esteemed highly and followed with an almost knightly devotion.

In 1847 he was nominated as the Whig candidate against his former antagonist, Governor Aaron V. Brown, who was the Democratic candidate for re-election. In an exciting and exhausting contest, the Whig candidate emerged victorious by a small majority, and at the age of thirty-eight Neill S. Brown was inaugurated as the thirteenth Governor of Tennessee. Two years later, he was defeated for re-election by William Trousdale.

In 1850, President Zachary Taylor appointed Ex-Governor Brown as Minister to Russia where he remained at the Court of St. Petersburg until 1853 when he returned to his native State and located in Nashville for a resumption of the practice of law. Five years later (1855), he was elected to the House of Representatives and became Speaker of that body. In the following year he headed the ticket in the Presidential race as an elector on the Know-Nothing ticket with Millard Fillmore as the standard bearer of that party which went down to signal defeat.

In 1860, he supported John Bell as candidate of the Constitutional Union Party for the Presidency. At the outbreak of the War Between the States, former Governor Brown was appointed a member of the Military Board by Governor Isham G. Harris with the responsibility of organizing the provisional army in Tennessee. In 1870, he was a member of the Constitutional Convention over which his brother, John C. Brown (later elected Governor) presided as President. This was the last public service of Neill S. Brown.

In 1839, Neill S. Brown was united in marriage to Miss Mary Trimble, a daughter of Judge John Trimble. Several children were born of the union. His name is identified with numerous measures which redounded to the welfare of the citizenry of his native State. His career is an inspiring illustration of the opportunities, when grasped, for making a real contribution to his age and generation through the medium of public service. His public life, in every phase and through trying periods of stress and strain, partook of the virtues which were the bases of his personal character. In all relationships, both public and private, he was candid, honest, and sincere. Full of years and honors, he died in 1886 and was buried in Nashville.

Legislative Messages of
Governor Neill S. Brown, 1847–1849

When Neill S. Brown and Governor Aaron V. Brown locked horns in the gubernatorial battle of 1847, neither was a stranger to the other. They were fellow townsmen, and had been opposing candidates in a Congressional race in 1843 wherein Aaron V. Brown had emerged victorious. The gubernatorial campaign of the two Browns from Pulaski followed the usual pattern. A joint campaign was agreed upon, speaking dates were announced in advance in the newspapers, and from mid-April until the election in August the candidates toured the State but discussed largely National political issues. From time to time, the candidates regaled the audience with anecdotes and occasionally took friendly "pot shots" at each other. As illustrative of these friendly jibes, Neill S. Brown said he proposed to do to Aaron V. Brown what "Lean Jimmy" Jones had done to James K. Polk—pave the way for him to the Presidency by defeating him for Governor! On numerous occasions, Neill S. Brown "fell into poetry," and recited the following paraphrase:

> "That day shall come, that great avenging day,
> When Polk's proud turrets in the dust shall lay;
> And Aaron's power, and Aaron's self shall fall,
> And one prodigious ruin swallow all."

A Whig organ,[1] in reporting on the joint debate between the two Browns at Clarksville, asserted that Governor Aaron Brown had

"...replied in which he exercised much wit, much sophistry, many tears, strange gestures, some eloquence, a little tragedy and a little comedy. He didn't try to debate (could, we reckon, if he had been disposed)."

As to Neill S. Brown, the Whig candidate, the same Whig paper stated that

"The General (Neill S. Brown) read copious extracts from 'the Epistle of Aaron the Apostle of Polk to the Athenians'."

The reference to the Athenians was an allusion to Aaron V. Brown's speech at Athens, to which speech Neill S. Brown referred repeatedly throughout the gubernatorial campaign.

---

[1] *Nashville Whig*, July 9, 1847.

Local political issues were largely lost sight of in the vigorous campaign, the bull's-eye being the Mexican War. The Whig candidate leveled his barrage upon James K. Polk, charging that the President was responsible for an unjust and an unnecessary war in that a unit of the United States Army had been sent into a section of Mexico that had not been a portion of Texas. It was, he declared, "Jim Polk's war, waged for the glorification of his administration." Aaron V. Brown, on the other hand, firmly asserted that it was a just war because it was a war of self-defense. He wore to a frazzle a map which he carried throughout the campaign, pointing out the spot of ground where the first blood was shed, alleging that the Mexicans had invaded the United States and had launched an attack. After his map demonstration, the Governor would appeal to a spirit of patriotism and then throw at his opponent a rhetorical question, "Would Tennesseans engrave on a monument the names of those who had given their lives in behalf of their common country—

'Died at Monterey, in a War of Conquest and Plunder'."

More so than in many subsequent gubernatorial campaigns in Tennessee, party lines were drawn closely and tightly. Candidates might change and political issues shift ground, but most of the voters voted the ticket straight—either Whig or Democrat. On the whole, men voted *for* their party or *against* the opposing party. A change on the part of a few, or the failure of only a few to go to the polls and vote might determine the outcome of the contest. Personal appeals were made, political hysteria was generated, and every effort put forth to win the election. The result was close, but in 1847 the Whigs were victorious in Tennessee.

As the scattering election returns were coming in, the Editor of a strong Democratic newspaper was decidedly "blue" over the signs of the times. The news from Bedford County distressed him very much, "because the Whigs are making the village ring with shouts." At the end of his editorial column, the ardent partisan penned the following:

"SINGULAR COINCIDENCE—A hearse passed by our office yesterday shortly after the arrival of the mail from Bedford." [2]

On Friday, October 8, 1847, the General Assembly met in joint convention for the purpose of counting the votes and comparing the polls in the recent gubernatorial election. In tallying up the vote,[3] it was disclosed that Neill S. Brown had received 61,372 votes and Governor Aaron V. Brown 60,004. It also appeared that the official vote of Fentress County had not been reported. That "missing link" put a stop to official proceedings for that day. On the following day, how-

---

[2] *Nashville Daily Union*, August 7, 1847.
[3] *Senate Journal*, 1847, 46–47.

ever, the Legislature resumed its action relative to the official vote received by each candidate for the office of Governor. Thereupon, Senator John A. Minnis, who represented Fentress County in the Senate, proposed the following resolution: [4]

"*Whereas*, no returns have been made by the Sheriff of Fentress county, of the official vote cast in that county for Governor as required by the Constitution of the State of Tennessee; and whereas, without the vote of Fentress county, the votes as compared by the Houses in convention stands for Neil S. Brown 61,372, and for Aaron V. Brown 60,004, leaving the majority of Neil S. Brown 1,368 votes; and whereas, the official vote of said county of Fentress is reported in the newspapers for Neil S. Brown 97, and for Aaron V. Brown 450, and which is corroborated by the statement of John A. Minnis, who represents the said county of Fentress in the Senate, and Jabez G. Mitchell, who represents the same in the House of Representatives, as being the true statement of the official vote of said county; therefore,

Resolved, That said vote of 97 for Neill S. Brown and 450 for Aaron V. Brown be permitted to go on the Journal as the official vote of Fentress county; provided that said vote shall not be calculated in the official aggregate vote for Governor; and provided nothing herein contained shall be taken as a precedent for the future action of any similar convention; which resolution was read and adopted."

According to the provisions of the second paragraph of the Minnis resolution, the *official* majority of Neill S. Brown was 1,368 votes. But when the Fentress County vote is considered, the *actual* majority of Neill S. Brown was reduced to 1,015 votes. But the end-result was the same—the election of Neill S. Brown as Governor over Aaron V. Brown.

When the formality of counting the vote and officially announcing the result had been transacted, the inauguration date of the Governor-elect was fixed as Saturday, October 16, 1847. Upon that date, the General Assembly met at the First Presbyterian Church in Nashville for the inaugural ceremonies.[5] The invocation was pronounced by the Reverend C. D. Elliott of the Methodist Church followed by the Valedictory Address of Governor Aaron V. Brown. The oath of office was then administered by Honorable Nathan Green, one of the judges of the Supreme Court of Tennessee, and thereupon the newly-installed Governor, Neill S. Brown, delivered the following Inaugural Address:[6]

"Gov. Brown's Inaugural Address

FELLOW-CITIZENS: I have been honored with the confidence of the people of Tennessee; and by their kindness I am about to assume the duties of the chief Executive office of the State.

[4] *Ibid.*, 49-50.
[5] *Ibid.*, 77.
[6] *Nashville Daily Union*, October 18, 1847.

For this distinguishing mark of their partiality, I feel a sincere sense of profound gratitude; and here tender, as the pledges of my fidelity, an identity with them of interest, of feeling, and of destiny.

But before I proceed to take upon myself the vows of office, it becomes my duty in conformity to usage to present a brief and general outline of my principles. And here a striking exemplification of the beauty of our form of government, and the harmony of its constituent members, at once presents itself and challenges our highest admiration. It is the calmness and dignity which so soon succeed the conflict of public opinion, however highly excited, and however eager for the elevation of respective favorites. Each successive election, however it results, furnishes but another evidence of the capacity of man for self-government. No popular disorders, no civil convulsions, mark the races of our elective franchise, or the transfer of power from one hand to another. And although party conflicts do occasionally engross the people, and excite a high degree of interest in behalf of opposing political principles, yet even the unfortunate party finds in the strength and endurance, and stability of our institutions much cause of consolation; the country is still safe, whether a favorite system of political expediency has triumphed or not.

Our form of government is propitious, liberal, and strong; yet it is not in these elements that the duration of the Government itself so much consists, but rather in the virtue and intelligence of the people. There lie our main guaranties, for when these fail, force becomes the great substitute, and there liberty ends and despotism begins. To no other causes than the want of these virtues, can be attributed the fate of our South American neighbors. Their cultivation then, upon which so much depends, should constitute the cardinal point of our legislation. Much, in this respect, has been accomplished, I trust, by the wisdom of the past, but much still remains to be done. A boundless field presents itself, fertile in expedients, for the offices of patriotism and philanthropy. No State in the Union contains more natural resources than Tennessee. Her Agricultural and Manufacturing facilities are happily blended, and in inexhaustible abundance. And blessed also with a healthy climate, we may fairly boast of the finest country on earth. The highest amount of human prosperity and happiness may here be attained.

To do this, however, requires the application of art, the fostering hand of legislation. Rivers must be opened to the entrance of our commerce, and roads constructed to connect the markets of the world with our great interior. When this is accomplished, private enterprise will unlock the mountains and pour out their hidden stores of mineral wealth, and render subservient our thousand streams and waterfalls.

Of superior importance to this, but of kindred rank, is the cause of Education; a cause, which enlightened statesmanship never overlooks, and to which true patriotism ever renders its warmest homage. Internal improvements have their great offices to perform (and their benefits are invaluable) but it is rather as arteries and veins of the body politic and body commercial, while education is the heart where noble enterprises are generated, and whence the moral life-blood of the country pulsates.—On this subject, it is especially the duty and the interest of the State to bestow its countenance, and patronage, and all the means within its power. Upon both these great questions we may learn important lessons from our New England brethren; and while we are not called upon to adopt some of their peculiar views on other subjects, in these at least we may feel honored in following their example.

The same spirit of internal improvement and education which has blessed, and encircled, and adorned New England, would make Tennessee the first State in the Union and in the world. Here is the seed in profusion, and here is the soil in boundless extent, and under the genial beneficence of Heaven, combined with well directed labor, we may claim as rich a harvest as ever bloomed and ripened on the bosom of the earth.

These questions, though local in their character, are of much more importance to us as a people, and as a state, than all the abstractions drawn from political disquisitions. Within their scope, and spirit, and effect, lies the true destiny of man—one to which nature has annexed her unerring index, and around which Christianity has thrown her noble sanctions.—Their true import is still further manifested, by contrasting our condition and prospects as a nation, with those of our miserable neighbors of the South-West. That ill-fated people have had no trade but arms, no music but the fife, and no inspiration but the drum. The railroad car, and the Steam Boat, and the Common School, are as rare with them as their seasons of peace; and nature walks in the same, and even deeper solitudes, as in the days of the Incas. Let science then erect her observatories upon our heights, and then may we expect to see the stars of general literature breaking out in all their native splendor. Under these influences, public sentiment will become enlarged and invigorated, and too enlightened to be surprised by any emergency; too virtuous to be decoyed by any temptation, and too strong to be shaken or terrified by any power.

Men have usually sagacity and enterprise enough to prosecute their own individual interests, and provide for their own individual wants. But in the great relative connections, in the social and political relations, in all the great schemes for the promotion of commerce and elevating public opinion, the concurrence of state authority and state patronage, is indispensable—all history proves this. Philosophy in her secret walks, and science in her lonely retreats—may accomplish much, in enlightening the public mind and in furnishing theories or practical enterprises, but they constitute rather pioneers to penetrate the wilderness of thought and of action; to open forests and select sites, while legislation must follow on to confirm the possession, and to erect and maintain the superstructure. The strong impulse now manifested throughout the State in behalf of these great questions augurs well for their advancement; and from this we may derive assurances, that our legislation will not be in arrears, in paying the full measure of its great tribute. This is not the place, however, or the occasion for details. But I sincerely congratulate you on the growth and vigor of public sentiment on these subjects, and hail it as the harbinger of great good to the State; and I shall be found cooperating with those who go furthest in their behalf; restrained only by a prudent regard to the capabilities of the State.

But while I feel a decided zeal for all measures that may conduce to the developement of the State, morally, physically and intellectually, I have not less zeal for the preservation of the public faith. The obligations of the State are paramount, and must be promptly met, 'without sale, denial, or delay.'

And who that reflects upon the force of the term public faith— what Tennessean, born upon the soil of this noble Commonwealth, but feels a glow of inspiration and pride, as he contemplates her present character and past history? No other State has yielded more promptly to every appeal made to her confederate allegiance, or given more signal evidence of devotion to the Federal Union, that great moral superstructure, in which liberty maintains her only throne upon earth. The drums of Tennessee have echoed to every call upon her military strength—while her deep-toned thunder has reverberated upon many a glorious battle field. The trophies of her renown already decorate the galleries of American chivalry—and not a star that twinkles in the bright constellation of States, burns more brightly, than that which shines upon her own noble destiny—while her legislative council is here, to deliberate on the domestic weal, her streaming columns, in patriotic obedience to the public authority, are wending their way to the distant West, to new fields of conflict and of danger, and I trust, it may be, to new scenes of glory. The conquering Eagles of Tennessee will proudly hover, wherever the standard of the stars and stripes is erected. These considerations are high, and animating, and inspiring and kindle a flame of State pride in the bosom of every Tennessean.

But there is another chapter in the history of Tennessee, replete with high moral renown and entitled to no less of our admiration. The public history of the State, has been hitherto untarnished by a single act of delinquency, in her pecuniary engagements; and from this has arisen, much of her reputation and that of her people, and this is a just source of pride and exultation to every Tennessean. A reputation for strict prompt justice, is worth more in the great moral scale of the civilized world, than all the loud trumpet notes of heroism, and the enchanting plaudits of renown. And without arraigning the action of some other States (for it is no business of mine) I fervently trust that repudiation will never find a lodgement among the people of Tennessee, or enter into the night dreams or visions. It is a doctrine founded in bad morals; dictated by a false and unwise policy; destructive and ruinous in its consequences; behind the present age; unworthy of the American character, and beneath the dignity of the Anglo-Saxon race. It is one to which I can find no vindication in the philosophy or common sense of the age; and at which Christianity revolts.

And as anxious as I feel for the happiness and prosperity of the people of Tennessee, and their freedom, as far as consistent with the public interest, from burdens and exactions, yet I would sooner see them doomed for a season to the toils and tributes of the ancient Israelites than to see them bearing and transmitting the withering curse of repudiation.

Claiming as full an exemption from superstition as most men, I firmly believe, and take pleasure in announcing it, that no State can prosper in a long career of true glory, in the disregard of the claims of justice, and the injunctions of the Christian religion. A flood tide of apparent prosperity may come, filling for the time the avenues of trade, and satiating the cravings of taste and curiosity, yet sooner or later it has its ebb, and either cloys with its abundance or leaves the void greater than before. History is a silent but eloquent witness of this truth, and from her undying lamp, sheds a stream of unceasing light along our pathway. The fabrics of ancient greatness, built by injustice and consecrated to ambition, are now flitting shadows before us, starting up from behind the broken pillars and falling columns, that were reared to perpetuate the genius by which they were wrought.

Within the points then, of exerting the highest capabilities of the State for these great and beneficent ends, and of disregarding the public resources of the State, lie the duty of the wise, and the danger of imprudent legislation.

The restraints of law and order under our system of jurisprudence, have vindicated the wisdom in which they were framed, by their happy results on society, and exemplify that just medium between licenciousness and oppression. No where else, perhaps, has liberty been required to make fewer surrenders. Our laws are mild, restricting capital punishments to few extreme cases, that stand beyond the reach of moderate correctives, and without the pale of human sympathy—and in this have we signally illustrated the triumph of civilized freedom and religion over barbarism and superstition. But we can only approximate perfection in this, as in every other branch of civil policy. The golden age has not yet come, nor the perfectibility of man been attained.—These, alas! are the dreams of the poets; and let them dream on. It is a happy delusion.—Unfortunately, the legislator, the practical jurist, and the man of business, finds this spell of the imagination dissolving under every contract with society; still proving the necessity of laws and their penalties, to restrain the vicious and to protect the good. Society is much more interested in the certainty than in the severity of punishment. Certainty and uniformity in the administration of the law, inspire the virtuous with confidence and security; while the vicious and outbreaking are powerfully deterred.

I forbear any allusion to the questions of Federal policy that has divided and agitated the country; not because I am without definite and fixed opinions, but because I feel bound by what is due to this occasion. The Union and harmony of both parties are necessary to the best interest of the State, in her local well being.

The prompt and efficient execution of the laws will constitute the chief duty of the office upon which I am about to enter. I am deeply sensible of the high responsibility of this department; and in this, to me a solemn moment, I feel its pressure exceedingly. I cannot hope to meet all the difficulties incident to such a task, with the approbation of every one. But I have searched in vain the springs of motive that animate my bosom, if I am not impelled by a leading and ardent desire to promote the best interests of all the people of the State. And to this great end, I here in the presence of this large assembly, solemnly dedicate myself—and I invoke to my aid the whole people of Tennessee, in a common cause, a common interest, and common glory! trusting that this rising commonwealth, endeared to me by the ties of birth, and by this signal manifestation of confidence and regard, may long enjoy the light and beneficence of that Providence, without which all human effort is abortive."

Prior to the transmission of the usual Executive Message to the Legislature, there were two important matters on the legislative agenda, the election of three Supreme Court Judges and one United States Senator. On Saturday, October 30, 1847, the resolution "to elect three Supreme Court Judges" was taken up, but any action thereon was promptly halted on motion of John Bell, a Representative from Davidson County, to adjourn the joint-convention meeting.[7] It should be remembered that John Bell was a Whig leader of tremendous influence, both locally and nationally. He had served seven consecutive terms in Congress, and had been appointed Secretary of War by President Har-

---

[7] *Senate Journal*, 1847, 159.

rison. In addition, he had served as Speaker of the House of Representatives in the National Congress. When the Tennessee General Assembly convened on October 4, a Whig caucus preferred him for the Speakership of the Lower House, a position that he could have had easily, inasmuch as the Whigs were in a majority. But Bell had other things in view. He declined the proffered honor by declaring that he preferred not to be "tongue-tied" in the legislative deliberations. He well knew that there was an important political matter to be resolved by the Legislature—the election of a United States Senator.

At an evening session on November 1, the joint convention took up the election of a Supreme Court Judge "to reside in the Western District." [8] After five indeterminate ballots, the convention postponed the election of a Supreme Court Judge from the Western District and proposed to go into the election of a Judge of the Supreme Court from Middle Tennessee.[9] This proved to be an easy task, for Judge Nathan Green was elected on the first ballot over A. O. P. Nicholson by a vote of 96 to 1.[10] Incidentally, Judge Green had been first elevated to the Supreme Court in 1831, remaining on the bench until his voluntary retirement in 1852.

On the following day, November 2, the joint convention again resumed the unfinished business—that of electing a Supreme Court Judge from West Tennessee. The names of the same four candidates in the preceding ballots were again before the convention, namely, Milton Brown, William B. Turley, George W. Gibbs, and one William T. Brown, the latter never receiving on any ballot more than one vote. At the end of the twelfth ballot, the vote stood: Milton Brown 38; Gibbs, 15; and Turley, 46. No election was declared, and the convention adjourned.[11] At an evening session, the convention agreed to take up the election of a Supreme Court Judge from East Tennessee. Four men were immediately nominated, Spencer Jarnigan, whose term as United States Senator had expired on March 3, 1847; Robert H. Hynds, Thomas C. Lyon, and William H. Sneed. Though not formally nominated, Robert J. McKinney received two votes on the first ballot.[12] At the end of the fourth ballot, no election having taken place, the convention adjourned its session.

On the evening of November 3, the fourteenth ballot was taken for the election of a Judge from West Tennessee, the result being as follows: Milton Brown, 39 votes; George W. Gibbs, 11 votes; and William B. Turley, 51 votes, the latter being declared duly and constitutionally

[8] *Ibid.*, 163.
[9] *Ibid.*, 165.
[10] *Ibid.*, 166.
[11] *Ibid.*, 170.
[12] *Ibid.*, 171.

elected for the term of twelve years.[13] On the following day, November 4, on the thirteenth ballot, the result of the balloting for a Judge from East Tennessee was as follows: Hynds, 2 votes; Jarnagin, 2 votes; Lyon, 38 votes; and McKinney, 53 votes, the latter being declared elected for a term of twelve years.[14]

Mixed in with the balloting for Supreme Court Judges was another election that held high priority with many members of the Legislature, that of United States Senator. Even prior to the convening of the Legislature, it was widely rumored that the incumbent Whig Senator, Spencer Jarnigan, was scheduled for retirement on account of his having voted for a tariff law obnoxious to many Whigs. Be that as it may, Jarnigan was never in the race, although he received ONE VOTE ONLY 36 times in the balloting gamut that ran to 48 ballots before an election was made.

Almost a month prior to the convening of the Legislature, a militant Democratic newspaper rather joyfully sketched the impending battle over the election of Senator. Sectionalism had raised its head, and it was predicted that the Senatorial fight would array East Tennessee Whigs against West Tennessee Whigs. In support of the predicted fight, the Democratic editor quoted from Whig organs in the two respective sections of the State: [15]

"WHO SHALL BE SENATOR, AND WHERE SHALL HE COME FROM!

These are very important questions just now to our whig friends. There are plenty of answers, but the answers do not agree. The Knoxville whig papers are demonstrating the fact that East Tennessee has always had a Senator, save for the brief space of two years; and they draw from this fact a conclusive reason that she ought to continue to have one. *Per contra:* the West Tennesseans say that East Tennessee has always had a Senator, and it is now the turn of the West. Thus it will be seen that different conclusions are drawn in the extreme divisions of the State from the same admitted fact.

East Tennessee says, (we quote from the Tribune:)

'We would ask of our *party* friends in Middle and West Tennessee, if it shall, in future, become at any time necessary and proper to set aside or disregard the claims of East Tennessee, would it be *well-timed at present?* Would it be *liberal* and in *good taste*, to say the least? East Tennessee, always triumphantly whig, has, in the late election, prominently distinguished herself. Largely more than one-third of the gain in the Gubernatorial canvass has been hers. The legislative gains in the whole of Middle and West Tennessee have been *three*; in East Tennessee alone they have been *four*, one more than in the whole balance of the State; and it is owing greatly to her, that this present debate could have arisen between whigs. We repeat,

---

13 *Ibid.*, 179.
14 *Ibid.*, 188–189.
15 *Nashville Daily Union*, September 13, 1847.

therefore, is it *well-timed* and in *good taste* now, to seek to take from her a *political honor*, if that were all, which has been heretofore conceded to her?'

On the other hand, West Tennessee says, (we quote from a communication in the Memphis Enquirer:)

'The subject of a U. States Senator is attracting much attention—far more than I had anticipated. Middle Tennessee having one Senator—and having always had one—besides the Governor and her due share of legislative honors, it seems to be universally admitted, that she will put forward no candidate for the office of Senator. The particular friends of Messrs. Bell and Foster here, who are supposed to know their feelings, say that under no circumstances will they come before the Legislature for any office. Indeed, some go so far as to state, that it will blast the reputation of any man in Middle Tennessee who will offer for Senator. It seems to be generally conceded that East Tennessee—always greedy—will again claim the Senator as an *ancient right*. The names of Reese, Jarnagin and Netherland are spoken of as candidates from East Tennessee. The last named gentleman is believed to be the strongest. Christopher H. Williams and Robertson Topp are generally spoken of as the candidates from West Tennessee. The better informed say that Mr. Topp will be the man, as he will be able, in addition to his district influence, to bring to bear a large influence in his behalf from Middle Tennessee. This opinon is strengthened from the fact that in 1843 when he was evidently stronger than Jarnagin, he withdrew from the contest, rather than produce discord in the whig ranks. The unprejudiced men, not politicians, from every part of Middle Tennessee, say without hesitation, that the District is entitled to the Senator. Tell our friends to stand up to their rights and all will be safe.'

Fight it out, gentlemen! You shall have none of our help in settling the quarrel."

For almost a month, October 28 to November 22, intermittent balloting for United States Senator held sway in the legislative halls. When the Legislature met in joint convention on October 28, nominations for United States Senator were declared to be in order. William B. Reese and John Netherland from East Tennessee and Robertson Topp of West Tennessee, all Whigs, were placed in nomination. Middle Tennessee, like Brer Rabbit, "laid low" and presented no candidate at the time. On the first ballot, the vote stood: Topp, 17 votes; a non-nominee, John Blair, 13 votes; Netherland, 12 votes; and Reese, 12 votes.[16] Seventeen other men received a scattering vote, among whom were John Bell with 7 votes. During the day, five ballots were taken, with the following results on the fifth ballot: Topp, 19 votes; Netherland, 16; and Reese, 15 votes. John Bell received 3 votes. Middle Tennessee was scattering its vote, being indicative that the mid-State Whigs were not yet ready to show their hands. For some three weeks the deadlock remained intact. On November 10, the twenty-first ballot was conducted, with a change in the West Tennessee strategy. Christopher H. Williams, of Henderson County, was placed in nomination by Senator Hezekia Bradberry, representing the counties of Henderson, Perry,

[16] *Senate Journal*, 1847, 140.

and McNairy. The newcomer received 34 votes, while Topp toppled down to only 4 votes. The stalemate, however, continued. Just prior to taking the twenty-fourth ballot, the name of Williams was withdrawn, whereupon John Bell leaped forward with 25 votes, just one vote shy of Netherland who lead with 26 votes.[17] Incidentally, Bell did not receive a single vote on the twenty-second and twenty-third ballots.

But the Bell strategy was now being revealed. A deadlock, however, continued to hold sway, for no candidate received a majority vote. The public was becoming restless. Various newspapers became critical over the consumption of time and money in the hitherto fruitless effort to elect a Senator. Despite all criticism, the well-greased skids of political shifting, maneuvering, and shadow-boxing continued to be utilized. At length, "Parson" Brownlow, Editor of the *Jonesborough Whig*, was joined in his ardent support of Bell by a Memphis Whig newspaper which editorially declared that four-fifths of the people in West and Middle Tennessee now favored the election of Bell.[18]

On November 20, the thirty-ninth ballot was taken and Bell made his most significant gain, picking up 9 additional votes, thereby placing him in the lead of all candidates with 31 votes.[19] In the remaining nine ballots to be cast before an election was made, Bell never fell lower than 32 votes. On the forty-seventh ballot, Bell received 42 votes, while his nearest opponent, Joseph L. Williams of Knox County, had 25 votes. At this juncture, the ancient maneuver was invoked, but in vain; the joint convention refused to adjourn by a vote of 70 to 27.[20] Another maneuver was then resorted to by withdrawing the name of Williams of Knox County and re-nominating Robertson Topp of Shelby County. But again the maneuver was in vain. On the forty-eighth and final ballot, Bell received a total of 51 votes, whereupon the Speaker of the Senate, Josiah M. Anderson,

"... declared him (John Bell) to be duly and constitutionally elected Senator to the Congress of the United States for the ensuing six years." [21]

When it came to political strategy, John Bell's votes throughout the Senatorial battle verify the assertion that he was neither neophyte nor nincompoop. Realizing that the newly-inaugurated Governor Neill S. Brown possessed real political power, Bell cast his first two votes for Governor Brown for Senator. On four occasions, Bell voted for the strong West Tennessee favorite, Robertson Topp. East Tennessee, a stronghold of Whiggery, presented two able candidates for the Senatorship, William B. Reese and John Netherland. Bell cooperated with

---

[17] *Ibid.*, 236.
[18] *Weekly American Eagle,* October 27, 1847.
[19] *Senate Journal,* 1847, 281.
[20] *Ibid.*, 281.
[21] *Ibid.*, 291.

the partisan supporters of each by voting thirteen times for Netherland and nineteen times for Reese. When the name of the redoubtable Whig orator, Gustavus A. Henry of Middle Tennessee, was presented on the thirty-third ballot, Bell gave his support to Henry for five successive ballots. A charitable view of Bell's hop-skip-and-jump voting for Senator would be that he was State-minded rather than sectional-minded! Another view—and more probably correct—would be that Bell was currying political favor with all three sections of the State as a means of winning the plum for himself in the final showdown.

While the Democrats enjoyed the dissension within the Whig ranks over the Senatorial contest, it was the general consensus of opinion that the most outstanding Whig leader in Tennessee had been chosen. Perhaps a dyed-in-the-wool Democratic paper, the *Columbia Beacon*, summed up in cryptic fashion the prevailing opinion of the Democrats:

"We had rather combat with the Eagle than bandy blows with the pigmy sparrow." [22]

To the East Tennessee sectional-minded partisans, Bell's election was "the most unkindest CUT of all," to quote Shakespeare's oft-quoted grammatical error in his *Julius Caesar*. Shortly after Bell's election, the over-the-mountain boys gave vent to their abundant spleen and keen disappointment: [23]

" 'INDIGNATION' IN EAST TENNESSEE.

The Knoxville papers furnish us with the proceedings of an 'indignation meeting' in that place, held on receipt of the news of the election of Mr. Bell to the Senate. We publish these proceedings below. They are accompanied, in the Tribune, with a column and a half of equally indignant remarks. Our friends of the Standard indulge in a quiet laugh at these proceedings. We hint to them, aside, that they will have still greater occasion for laughing before six months pass by:

The chair appointed Messrs. Wm. G. Swan, Dr. Wm. J. Baker, and Hugh L. McClung, said committee, who after a few moments retirement, presented the following report, which was read and received:

The crisis has arrived when East Tennessee would prove recreant to every principle of dignity and honor, and even of self-preservation, were she passively and quietly to yield her concurrence in what has recently been done by the Legislature of the State in the election of a U. States Senator. This declaration is not the hasty impulse of a factious spirit, but is founded upon considerations far more important than any that are involved in *party* attachments.—While a sense of patriotic duty reminds us that we are whigs, we do not and *will not* forget that we are East Tennesseans. While we rejoice at the triumph of the *principles* of our party, we will not repress an indignation which a flagrant outrage upon our most cherished sectional interests may prompt. We hold the dignity and prosperity of East Tennessee as dearer to us than our party: and whenever we shall be constrained to aban-

[22] Quoted in the *Politician and Weekly Nashville Whig*, December 3, 1847.
[23] *Nashville Daily Union*, December 6, 1847.

don the one or the other, we cannot hesitate to determine which we shall forsake.

The time was when what is now East Tennessee was the entire State, and *then* it was that it became a proud distinction to be called a Tennessean. In the councils of the nation she could number among the wisest her own sons. Ever responding with alacrity to 'the call of the country,' she sent forth 'to the fight'—when the barbarity of the Indian was to be avenged, or the haughty Briton repelled—her hundreds of men, 'and each one a hero.' *Then* honors came thick upon her. *Then* Legislative acts contemplated the happiness and prosperity of her people. But how changed are the times! Though East Tennessee is indeed the RIGHT ARM of the whig party in the State—though in the last party contest she secured for the State a whig Governor and a whig Legislature, and thus maintained the proud political reputation of TENNESSEE—though, while the Western portion of the State utterly failed to furnish its quota of men under recent requisitions of the War Department. East Tennessee, with a promptitude unparalleled, not only met the requisition, but furnished a Regiment besides, and thus maintained the *chivalrous* character of Tennessee! Yet what has all of this profited her?—Nothing. Absolutely nothing. On the contrary, while she has thus contributed so liberally to form and sustain the honor of the *entire State,* she has received from those whom she has aided to exalt 'injury and insult.' She has asked and is now imploring at the hands of the Legislature the means to develope her vast resources of wealth, yet the very scantiness which has been bestowed has caused Legislators who reside west of the Mountains to boast that they have been liberal. Besides, others whose friends thought them pre-eminently qualified for the station, she presented to the Legislature upon the *last and decisive balloting,* as a candidate for the exalted and responsible post of Senator, one whose 'qualifications and pretensions,' eminently fitted him for the office—one who, in the language of the Bar, with which he was most intimately associated, has contributed greatly to build up the present high juridical character of the State—one whose political orthodoxy could not be questioned—one whose sound judgment, well cultivated mind and unsullied moral character, constitute him what a Senator should be. Yet by the voice of *a Whig Legislature,* he has been precluded from the office because he is an East Tennessean. In view of these facts, therefore,

Be it Resolved—That while we properly appreciate the worthiness of the Hon. John Bell, we cannot but regret that by his election East Tennessee has been deprived of the Senator.

Resolved—That conformity to a 'time honored custom'—*the rights of East Tennessee,* and the highest interests the Whig party demanded the election of an East Tennessean."

Legislative Message,* November 3, 1847

"EXECUTIVE DEPARTMENT,

Nashville, Nov. 3, 1847.

GENTLEMEN OF THE SENATE AND
    HOUSE OF REPRESENTATIVES,

By the provisions of the law, establishing the Bank of Tennessee,

---

* *Senate Journal,* 1847, 182.

it is made the duty of the Governor to nominate at each regular session of the General Assembly, twelve persons to serve as Directors for two years. In conformity with the provisions of the law, I submit the names of the following persons, as such Directors, to wit: Thomas L. Bransford, William Ledbetter, Jas. Morton, J. W. Hoggett, John Shelby, M. M. Monohan, John Waters, George C. Allen, Benjamin R. Howard, Wm. B. Shepherd, R. W. H. Bostick, E. A. White; all of which is respectfully submitted.

N. S. BROWN."

The above Message received delaying action on the part of the Legislature for almost a month. The cause of the delay may have been due to three factors: (1) the Message came during rather hectic days occasioned by the pending election of Supreme Court Judges; (2) the election of a United States Senator; and (3) various other elections involving Attorneys-General, Circuit Judges, State Treasurer, Secretary of State, and other officials. With the whole judicial system, so far as its functionaries were concerned, always involved and often embroiled in bitter legislative battles, it is a wonder that any sort of judiciary existed. The twelve persons nominated by Governor Brown were confirmed [24] unanimously by the Senate on November 29.

On November 16, Governor Brown transmitted another minor Message to the Senate:

Legislative Message,[*] November 16, 1847

GENTLEMEN OF THE SENATE:

I hereby nominate Thomas S. King, John D. Kelly, and William E. Watkins, all citizens of the County of Davidson, and State of Tennessee, as Inspectors of the Penitentiary.

N. S. BROWN."

The three nominees were confirmed by the Senate,[25] the only opposition vote being cast by Senator Isaac J. Roach representing the counties of Gibson, Carroll, and Dyer.

The major Message from Governor Brown was transmitted to the Legislature on November 5, and was as follows:

---

[24] Senate Journal, 1847, 315.

[*] Senate Journal, 1847, 254.

[25] Senate Journal, 1847, 315.

Legislative Message,* November 5, 1847

"EXECUTIVE DEPARTMENT,
Nashville, Nov. 5, 1847.

GENTLEMEN OF THE SENATE AND HOUSE OF REPRESENTATIVES:

You are now in the active exercise of the high trusts committed to you by the people of Tennessee; and no doubt anxiously deliberating, for the best interests of the State. Participating in this spirit, and willing to contribute any thing in my power to aid you in your councils, I beg leave to submit a few considerations on some of the more prominent subjects before you.

In taking a survey of the State, we are not without many causes of rejoicing. General health, domestic peace and tranquility, and an abundance of the necessaries of life, are striking characteristics of our present condition. And upon these blessings I sincerely congratulate you and our common constituents. It is not your misfortune to have to legislate under the goadings of any pressing exigency, or amid the influences of any domestic calamity. Hence, your task is much alleviated, and your responsibility diminished. But it is not to be concealed, that there are some questions of high importance, which, while they are not immediately afflicting, demand your sober and serious consideration, in reference to the future.

It appears that no provision has been made to meet the first instalment of $125,000 on the bonds issued for stock in the Union Bank, and which is soon to fall due. Doubtless none was practicable. It now remains to be considered what means can be devised to make the payment. In addition to this, is the deficiency in the profits of the Bank of Tennessee, to meet its liabilities—amounting on the 1st of July, 1847, to $115,243.49—making together the aggregate sum of $240,243.49, to be supplied by the Treasury, or in some other mode. I do not hope for any increase of the profits of the Bank for the next two years, under any new organization of that institution, or any new policy for its administration, however wise. The last two years have been marked by an unusual state of things—one propitious to banking operations, but not likely to occur soon again. On

---

* *Senate Journal,* 1847, 201–216.
  House Journal, 1847, 307–321.

the contrary, difficulties are to be apprehended, tending rather to depress than to enlarge the operations of any Bank. These, however, I will refer to hereafter.

Assuming, then, that we cannot, upon any reasonable calculation, rely upon the Bank for the means to meet this growing exigency, we must look to other resources. And we may rely with some confidence upon a considerable increase of profits in the Internal Improvement Companies: the amount, however, is conjectural. Another resource may be found, in furnishing some adequate remedy for the present defects in the mode of valuing property subject to taxation. Much complaint exists on this subject, in many parts of the country, and there is abundant reason to believe that it is well founded. It is certainly right, that every article made subject to taxation, should be valued *at its cash rate in the market at the time*. Of this no honest man could complain—and by this, and only by this, can the public burdens be equalized, and justice done to the State. In my opinion, this can be accomplished without creating the office of Assessor, and with but little if any additional expense. Let the commissioner who takes the list of taxable property, be required, first, to take an oath, that he will take such list, at the cash value of the property in the market. And when he returns it, let him be required to swear, in the same terms, that he has taken such list. The commissioner, of course, can employ what means he pleases to arrive at the value of property, and if he chooses, content himself with his own judgment. I, therefore, recommend an amendment of the present law in this particular. It is for you to determine whether the suggestion is wholesome and proper, or whether any better expedient can be devised. I do not hesitate to declare, as my opinion, if all the complaints on this subject are true, that if the true valuation of taxable property were attained, it would increase this species of revenue at least one-half, or perhaps more. I can see no objection to the cancellation of the Bonds which have been purchased, the discount on which, amounting to $50,816.55, will be, by so much, a reduction of the deficit referred to.

The sale of the stock owned by the State in the Union Bank, ought still to be made, if it can be done without too great a sacrifice. That stock was not taken at the time, it is presumed, with any view to speculation, but merely to aid in the creation of an Institution, that it was believed at the same time, would be useful to the people. If the State is the owner of any other stocks, which could be sold without sacrifice, it might be well to authorize the sale of them, at least to such extent as will meet the present emergency.

By a fair and reasonable calculation of receipts and expenditures, for several years past, and with a moderate reliance on present resources, I think we may safely assume, that the means on hand and to accrue within the ensuing fiscal year, will be sufficient to meet the ordinary expenses, including appropriations for the Capitol, and also the deficit in the contingent fund. We have then to be provided for, the $125,000 for stock in the Union Bank alone. This I believe can be fully met by the increased profits from works of Internal Improvements, and from the additional revenue arising from taxes on property, by amending the mode of valuation as before mentioned. To avoid any possible failure, provision might be made for a contingent loan, to be effected in the event of a deficiency of means in the Treasury at the time this instalment falls due: and which can be repaid at maturity out of any accruing funds. I think this view of our resources is correct, and it is one upon which I feel willing, on my part, to risk the experiment. But from the short period of time since my induction into office, I have had less opportunity than many of your honorable body, to make a full and thorough research into these questions. I, therefore, submit these views with the most entire deference; hoping they may aid you in some degree, but earnestly desirous that they may mislead no one.

I need not impress upon you the duty of promptly providing for all the public engagements, and of maintaining inviolate the public faith; for such an appeal might seem to imply some distrust. I feel no distrust. Our past history foreshadows what will be our future policy. The honor of the State has never made its silent but eloquent appeal in vain, to any of our predecessors; and the same noble vindication, I doubt not, will be awarded at your hands. But if in your judgment, the resources here indicated shall be deemed insufficient to meet the demands upon the Treasury, there remains but one other resort, and that is, increased taxation. And in such an event, I do not hesitate to recommend it; for I shall not shrink on my part, from any responsibility that relates to the public honor, or the public interest. Such a resort is always disagreeable, and ought not to be made but upon clear necessity. This being apparent, I have no fears of the ready approval of an honest people. Any increase of taxes that may be found necessary, might be greatly mitigated in its effect, by issuing the bonds of the State for the amount required, payable at such dates as would make them approximate par value; and then adopt a rate of taxes commensurate with that amount, according to the time. The revenue thus raised would constitute a Sinking Fund, to be applied each year to the payment of the bonds as they fell due—and the rate of taxes in this way be comparatively moderate. This view commends itself, not as an evasion of present payment and its attendant burdens, but on account of the probable increase of profits on the stocks belonging to the State, and the enhanced value of some of the stocks themselves, which it is fair to anticipate.

Further appropriations for the construction of the Capitol will of course be necessary—what amount, it will be for you to determine. But I respectfully suggest, that a considerable sum might be saved to the State, by hastening the completion of that building. The salary of the Architect, and, perhaps, some other stated annual allowances, would be curtailed in the aggregate. Besides, it is desirable that that noble edifice should be in the use and enjoyment of the State as early as practicable. This view contemplates heavier appropriations, and the employment of additional labor.—Economy in the end, dictates this course, if the present resources will justify it.

Some change, it is obvious, is necessary to be made in the Lunatic Asylum. Whether that shall be in its entire location, or by additions to the present buildings, is submitted to your consideration.—The Report of the Physician of that Institution is before you; and I shall not attempt to amplify or improve upon the sound views which it presents. Much benefit has, doubtless, arisen from this Institution already. And it is the duty, as well as the interest of the State, to render its means as efficacious as possible. The voice of humanity is continually making its appeal in behalf of that unfortunate class of our countrymen, and against it there is no argument.

Some change in the present organization of the Bank of Tennessee, seems to be demanded in many quarters of the State. This is a subject, to me at least, of no small magnitude; and I doubt not, it will receive at your hands, the most patient consideration. It is

now too late to discuss the policy of creating such an institution.—
Our only duty is, to make the best use of it we can, for the interest
of the State. The great evil connected with the Bank, and one which
was developed early in its history, is the heavy demand upon it. It
has been tasked beyond its ability. Hence it is continually subject
to the temptation of overaction, in order to meet the charge upon
it; and at the same time, liable to a full share of reproach and want of
confidence, for failures that are unavoidable. The policy of putting
the whole institution in a state of liquidation, was urged at the last
session of the Legislature, as you know, and rejected, with the exception of the discontinuance of a few of the Branches. The question of liquidation, whatever reasons existed in its favor (and there
were many) I consider as settled for the present, and so far as public
sentiment has been indicated, it is in favor of the continuance of the
Bank, and to some extent at least, of the restoration of the Branches.
Independent of this, the proposition now is, how can we make the
most money, to meet the various demands that have been and may
be, created? I believe it can be done by the continuance of the Bank
for the present, and the restoration of the Branches. Aside from
the opinion urged by many, that the whole capital of the institution
can be safely used, a large sum has been invested in real estate
for the use of the Principal Bank and its Branches, which cannot be
converted except at great sacrifice, and which, from the peculiar
character of the buildings, would be in the main, unproductive. And
in a course of liquidation, there would be an annual expenditure,
for several years, in the shape of salaries, stationery and other items,
if not equivalent, at least not far short of the present rate. This
latter view, applies in like manner to the suspended Branches, and
the policy of restoring them. Experience has proved in the main,
that greater profits have been made by the Branches, in proportion
to their capital, than by the Principal Bank. This remark is not intended to imply any censure upon the administration of the Principal Bank at any period, or to make any disparagement. The absence of competition, gives to the Branches their only advantage.
There are many points in the State, where banking capital is scarce,
and the demand bottomed upon real resources, that are compelled
to seek foreign accommodations. And this may be said of most of
the locations that have been hitherto selected. Whether all the

points now or heretofore occupied by Branches, are the most suit-able, I have not the means within the power of many of you, of knowing. No Branch ought to be restored, or even continued, upon the mere ground of local accommodation, as desirable as that might be to our feelings, if experience has demonstrated that it can-not be profitably employed. To make profits is paramount, and is the great desideratum at present. I would not, however, have the Bank in any state of circumstances, peddling for patronage, or forcing its accommodations: advantages thus sought, must ever be short-lived, and the consequences, both to the Bank and the coun-try, disastrous.

The view here intended to be inculcated, is addressed to things as they are, and not as they have been, or might have been. If the proposition were now pending to create this institution, I could find a hundred reasons against it. Its relative connection with other interests, or rather their dependency upon it, invest the question with its chief importance; and hence the ground of deep public solicitude. If, however, you are satisfied, according to the opinion of some, that the Bank cannot be safely administered, and that it is destined to ultimate disaster, the sooner it is put in liquidation the better. The great interests, which it would now only retard by a gradual cessation, it would absolutely destroy by a permanent exis-tence, if indeed it carries within it the elements of decay. Posterity has an inheritance in this Bank, involving in a good degree the fate of our systems of Common Schools and Internal Improvements as at present organized. Our task is therefore a delicate one, and our duty sacred. I am not satisfied that it would be good policy to multiply the Branches in any event. Some of the reasons which vindicate the restoration of Branches, do not apply to the creation of new ones. The proposition involves a new train of expenditures, and increased difficulties in the way of liquidation, should that be found desirable in any short period of time hereafter. The advan-tages, however, to be derived to the institution and the State, should settle this, as it should the whole policy. I concur with my imme-diate predecessor, if a new Branch is created, in fixing it at Memphis, a point which presents, perhaps, the most profitable field of opera-tion. In such event, I suggest that it might be wise policy, to give to the principal board, discretion upon the subject of buying ground and building, or of erecting a house for the accommodation of such Branch.

I would respectfully urge upon you an examination into the condition, not only of this but of the other Banks. I am persuaded the result would not only be advantageous to the Banks themselves, but to the country at large. This suggestion carries with it no suspicion of them, nor is it so intended; but those institutions and the people are mutually interested in maintaining well-founded confidence, and I know of no means so well calculated to inspire it in the latter, as through the inspection of their own Representatives. If their condition is really safe, as I trust and believe it is, it cannot be too well known; and if otherwise, equal reason exists for its full development. Their Reports are severally before you, and need no comment at my hands. The necessity of the inquiry here indicated finds an additional reason in several surrounding circumstances. The downward tendency in the prices of some of our principal staples, coupled with the unparalleled commercial failures abroad, are well calculated to excite distrust and alarm. Added to this, is the drain of specie from the United States to Mexico, to maintain our army, which has taken place to a considerable extent, and must still continue while the war lasts. It is not to be disguised that these agencies will have some effect upon our commerce, and, of course, upon the Banks themselves. These considerations are well worthy of reflection, in devising any plan of policy in reference to the Bank of Tennessee.

The subject of education, always important, but especially so at this juncture, demands a large share of your consideration. I know it has become, in the estimation of many, a hackneyed theme, but that does not affect its merits. This is because so little has been done for it. A long period has elapsed since the State of Tennessee, in a spirit that promised great results, and which excited high commendations, began a system of Common Schools. Time has waned, and almost a new generation has come upon the stage. The authors of the system have, most of them, gone down to the tomb, with all their hopes and wishes for its success; and their successors have come; but alas! how little do they find to admire in the accomplishment of this great undertaking. The State has almost been transformed from a wilderness; fields, and cities, and towns, and roads, mark her great physical progress; her population has doubled; her wealth has greatly multiplied, and what is gratifying to our pride, her character has reached the highest places of renown. Yet this effort for popular education has slumbered, and languished, and pined, and exists now rather as a momento of the past than as a living system for future growth and expansion.—Many ardent friends of education throughout the State, begin to despair of any effective public aid, and the labors of your present session are looked to by a large portion of the people with no ordinary interest. It is a maxim with men of all parties, that virtue and intelligence among the people are indispensable in every free government to its well being and security; and no other maxim perhaps can be found as often in the journals of our legislation. If it be once admitted that it is the duty of the State to establish and maintain, at public expense, some system of education by which every child may attain the elementary branches of learning, (and this ought to be taken for granted), the only remaining question is one of means. We have not got the means! But can we not raise the means? Most assuredly we can, and without oppressing or injuring a single individual in the State. The people have all along been in advance of us on this subject, and in many parts of the State there is a deep feeling, a burning ardor in favor of it. They will in my opinion, submit to a moderate tax for this purpose, most readily and cheerfully, and praise the authors of it. There are about one hundred and twenty-two thousand voters in the State: an increase of taxes so as to make an average of one dollar to each voter, would furnish a sum greater than our annual appropriations for Schools. Would the people murmur at such a tax as this? levied for the sole benefit of their children, to elevate them morally and intellectually? To sustain a system that comes to them like the bread of life, appealing to their noblest nature, and addressing in behalf of their own offspring, the tenderest sensibilities of humanity? A system which seeks the humble shepherd boy, who watches his father's flocks in the gorges of the mountain, and elevates him from his lowly inheritance, to higher and nobler pursuits; perhaps to thunder in the national Forum, or to lead his country's armies to battle and to victory!

With every other appeal (and there are a hundred) patriotism blends her soft harmonious notes; and whose ear will be deaf to her enchanting music? It is here, in behalf of this and every other laudable means of promoting education, that patriotism in a free country, pays the offerings of her full homage; and she will linger, and still linger around every temple consecrated to learning, and there find the true shrine of her devotions long after the cause of education shall have been scouted from the halls of legislation. It seems to me, that no man who has the soul of a Tennesseean can object for a moment, and when it is remembered by every father who educates his children at all, that all the appropriations made to Common Schools, operate as a credit upon his account for tuition, all sense of burden vanishes at once.

The system, as at present organized, is inefficient, more, doubtless from the want of adequate means, than from its own inherent defects. Though I feel certain, that much improvement can be made upon the present plan, especially if adequate means are furnished— I wholly disagree with those, who would suspend the Common School fund for a season, with a view to its accumulation, and with the hope of great ultimate blessings from it, when it shall be restored. I am unwilling to see it abstracted for a single day; for if it is, I shall not expect to see its return; new demands upon it will multiply, as new emergencies may arise, until the whole fund is lost in the vortex of change and speculation, and thousands of children in the State will thus lose the only inheritance they have. If I knew the fund could not now be increased, I would say preserve it, in its practical use: keep it alive, like the vestal fire upon the altar: a flame may yet be kindled from it, whose incense Heaven will approve and posterity will bless.

But there is no necessity, in my judgment, for delay. The time has come for prompt vigorous exertions upon the subject; the people need it, and I believe their hearts are in it. Let the County Courts of each county be required to raise by taxes from the people, a sum at least equal to that which shall be appropriated to the county each year. The sum thus raised could be paid into the hands of the County Trustee, who should be regarded as the county superintendent, and compelled to give bond accordingly. There should also be a board of county examiners, appointed by the County Courts, or by some other competent tribunal, whose business it should be to examine every applicant as teacher of a Common

School. And no man should be allowed to be employed by the district commissioners or trustees, without a certificate of competency from the board of examiners. This would avoid imposition by men of no qualification, whose tuition is worse than useless. In this connection, I respectfully urge the appointment of a general superintendent for the State, with a competent salary. He should be a man of talents and learning, and if possible, of commanding character—and required to traverse the State, and obtain and impart information connected with the system and education generally, and report to each succeeding legislature.

These suggestions are drawn from the plan in operation in New York; the success of which is familar to all who are conversant with the history of that State. The amount of the annual appropriations in that State were not greater than ours, and like we, they had experimented with the exclusive use of the public fund, and with like effect. The present results there, are highly propitious, and furnish the most animating assurances of what we may accomplish by following the example. Education there has flourished, until, I suppose, fewer children can be found in that great State, within the scholastic ages, who are destitute of learning, than in any other in the world of equal population.

The policy of maintaining education in some form, at the public expense, is as old as civilization: originating in some States in a motive of interest, which expected more revenue and better service from an enlightened people; in others, arising from a magnanimity, which sought the good of the people for their own sakes. And we are not without examples at this day, even among the despotic governments, of a most striking character. In Austria, where power finds its security in bolts and bars and dungeons, and not in the intelligence and virture of the people, it is a law of the Empire that no person is allowed to marry who cannot read, write and cypher.— This rule will ill suit the genius of our people, but we may imagine what a powerful incentive it would present to that portion of our gallant young countrymen who have not yet attained these branches of learning. We find also, by the new Constitution of Republican Colombia, it is ordained that after 1840, no person shall enjoy the rights of citizenship who is unable to read and write.—These examples deserve to stimulate us, though we will not adopt the policy from which they arise—we can accomplish the good work, without holding up the terrors of disfranchisement, or the evils of perpetual celibacy.

The necessity for liberal exertions on this subject, in some form is even great in Tennessee, amid all her glory and prosperity in other respects—I refer you to the census table—it speaks in the language of mute, but solemn eloquence—I will not detail its figures. The reference is made with no pleasure, nor in a spirit of reproach upon that portion of our fellow-citizens, young and old, who from want of opportunity, and from poverty and misfortune, are destitute of education. I am endeavoring to plead their cause, and that of posterity: and I am in deep earnest. I would rather participate in the honor of devising and putting on foot, some scheme, which would diffuse education to every family in the State, which would kindle up intellectual bonfires on the mountains and all along the valleys, than to hold any office within the gift of any people. I ask, (and it is without invoking the aid of invidious distinction between classes and conditions, for I would scorn it), how does the poor man of humble lot, expect to elevate his children to the level of the more favored and wealthy, except through the medium of their mental improvement? There is no other way. And this is the only mode to ensure practical republicanism among us—and to realize those theories of equal rights and equal privileges, which we have written in our constitutions. Here are the means, under which crime diminishes, morals improve, intellect expands, public sentiment ripens and strengthens, property multiplies, revenue increases, and the State attains true glory. Can we not then signalize this session by acts of beneficence, that will be felt and cherished by those who are to come after us: that your children and mine, when they shall assemble in the halls of yonder rising Capitol, may find in this year's journal, the origin of a system which shall excite their gratitude and inspire a noble emulation, and to which they may trace perhaps the means of filling those same honorable seats. Thousands of our fellow-citizens are gone to pour out their blood in a distant land, and to gather laurels with which they will decorate the brow of this commonwealth. Can we not weave some noble chaplet, to add to the adornment, and let these twin emblems of public honor repose side by side, to be freshened by the breath of coming generations, as the evergreen that blooms upon the summit of the mountain, is fertilized with perpetual verdure, by each returning shower?

I may be allowed to express my deepest regrets, at the failure of one great question of national policy, I mean Distribution—because it involved a rich treasure to the State of Tennessee. Had that fund been realized, how easily could we now establish a complete system of Education throughout the land! How much also could we not do for the cause of Internal Improvement, without drawing upon the credit of the State! The Chattanooga and Hiwassee Railroads could be completed, and other improvements in the Eastern and Western rivers accomplished. These means would have formed the lightning of the steam-car, to illuminate many a dark mountain waste, and the thunder of the steam-boat, to awaken the silence of many a solitary stream. But regrets are unavailing, and will not supply what is wanting.

I therefore recommend an increase of the Common School Fund, to at least double the present annual appropriations—and so far as it cannot be done with present resources, I recommend that it be done by taxes. If anything can justify taxation, it is the Education of the children of the State.

I regret that nothing can be done at present for the different Colleges and Academies, that are making a noble struggle in another department of learning. They deserve the regard, and if it were possible, the patronage of the State. All we can do, is to commend them to their own private efforts, and to express our approbation, which I do most cordially *to them all, without any distinction.*

In connection with the subject of Education, I suggest the propriety of granting a charter of Incorporation, to a society to be called, 'The Washington Education Society of Tennessee'; the object of which will be to aid in the promotion of learning, by funds to be raised by private contribution. Such an association, endowed with the ordinary powers, would constitute a potent auxiliary to other means. The spirit of private liberality on this subject is at present diffused—this would enable it to embody. The Society might exist in every section of the State, and thus derive its means, as well as impart its benefits, here and there, over the whole surface—sustaining and aiding institutions of learning, and assisting individuals of both sexes, who are unable to educate themselves. I am indebted for the suggestion to public spirited individuals in private life, and cannot too much commend its objects. It will cost nothing at least to make the effort, and may be, and I believe will be, the foundation of much good.

The question of Internal Improvement demands also a large share of your consideration. I might content myself with simply declaring my earnest wish for the success of all useful projects of Improvement, consistent with the resources of the State; but I beg leave to specify to some extent. The Hiwassee Railroad, already in a state of progress, and upon which a considerable sum has been expended, commends its claims for additional aid. I believe this road, when completed, will add greatly to the wealth and prosperity of a large and fertile region of country, covered by a vigorous and enterprising population. It will form a noble highway to market for a heavy produce, that is now in a great degree excluded; and there is every reason to believe that the stock would yield a fair dividend. The people of that section of the State feel a very lively interest in the completion of this work; but it is rendered evident, that it cannot be done without additional appropriations by the State. How much aid is required, and how much can be granted, I leave to your wise deliberations. I do not hesitate to recommend this as a fit subject for further public expenditures. The removal of the obstructions in the French Broad and Holston rivers, forms another subject of deep interest, to a large portion of the people of East Tennessee. The expenditure of a few hundred thousand dollars, it is believed, would carry the navigation of these rivers to the highest practicable points, and open up enlarged commercial facilities.

The construction of a road from Knoxville through upper East Tennessee, to some point on the Virginia line, is greatly desired, and I can safely say, much needed. The line of such a road passes through an extensive country, of fine capabilities, but unfortunately peculiarly hemmed in by hills and mountains, and not penetrated, I believe, but in part by a single navigable stream. The only hope of much of that population to attain a market, is in the construction of this work. What character of road is most suited to that region of the State, is best known to those representing it. A Railroad is desired by many. Whether this is practicable at present, depends upon the amount of stock which could be taken by private individuals, and the extent to which the State should embark her credit. I do not hesitate to recommend at least the granting of a charter for it, as a graded road, adapted to become a Railroad as time and circumstances shall dictate—the State taking one-half of the stock. If nothing more can be done at present, I am persuaded that even this would be of signal benefit to that portion of the State, and greatly alleviate the evils under which it labors.

Obstructions also exist in the Tennessee river between Knoxville and the Alabama line, which materially interfere with navigation, especially at low water. Their precise extent and character are better known to many of your honorable body than to me. It cannot be expected that appropriations to the full extent of this demand can now be made; but if I am correctly informed, an appropriation of even ten thousand dollars would give material relief, and greatly enhance the navigation of that river, between those points. I respectfully recommend all that can be done on this subject; and I deem it of sufficient importance, not only to the region immediately contiguous, but in its relative bearing on other sections of the Union, to urge a memorial to Congress for appropriations from that body. Tennessee has been but a small beneficiary of the Federal Government, in the way of Internal Improvements. It has received less than any other State of the same age, and has needed and merited more.

These, I believe, embrace all the subjects of Internal Improvement now agitated in East Tennessee; and I sincerely regard them all as worthy of your liberal consideration, and of whatever aid you may deem it safe to render. A recent survey of that end of the State, has forcibly impressed me with the necessity of these improvements. Indeed, I know no country which would be so much benefitted by them. East Tennessee possesses great natural resources, fertile soil, boundless mineral wealth, and extra-ordinary water power, while her air is as pure as her own mountain springs. It is capable of the highest grade as an agricultural and manufacturing country. And the only drawback upon all these fine resources, is in the stern ramparts with which nature has environed it—the want of outlets to market.

The Nashville and Chattanooga Railroad is another project of high and commanding importance to which private enterprise is now being vigorously directed. A glance at the map, it seems to me, settles its value. It addresses itself directly to Middle Tennessee, and a large portion of East Tennessee, and indirectly to the whole State. It is destined to be the great artery to connect the body of the State with the Southern Atlantic—thus giving to our staples of every description a choice of markets. I have no hesitation in believing that a subscription by the State, for stock in this road, would not only be safe, but profitable. The advantages otherwise to our commerce and general intercourse, are to me incalculable; while socially and politically speaking, they are not less important. This road in its present and probable future extent, would tend to unite more closely the three divisions of the State, and to break down those distinctions that now exist—an end which every Tennessean ought earnestly to desire; while its influence as a medium of communciation with several other States, would have a happy effect upon our external political relations, strengthening the bonds of union and fellowship, by the great ties of reciprocal interest. To what extent the State should embark in this great enterprise, is a subject for discussion and forecast, and belongs more appropriately to you. I think though, that much can and ought to be done; and I will only remark further, that I feel earnestly desirous for its completion.

Much improvement is also needed in the Western District. The growing importance and constantly increasing commerce of that end of the State, entitle it to the highest consideration. Much inconvenience is experienced, during the Winter season, for the want of good roads. The roads during much of that season are miserable and often impassable. From the character of the soil and general face of the country, the ordinary means of improving these roads are unavailing; and in the absence of stone for McAdamizing, and the great distance in many places to gravel as a substitute, I have been at much loss what other attainable material would be adequate. It is well worthy of inquiry, whether charcoal would not suffice, or at least answer a very valuable purpose. I have endeavored to obtain some *data* on this subject, and have been informed that in some parts of Ohio the experiment has been made with success. If the fact be so, it is within your reach, and deserves consideration. A road commencing at Savannah, or some point lower down the river, to connect with the Central Turnpike, and terminating at Memphis, would be of incalculable benefit to that section of the State. Also, one commencing at Jackson and terminating at the same point—and another commencing at some point still further North and converging in the same direction.—These would not supply all that is wanting, but they would certainly cover the main ground. One department of expense in building roads, I mean grading, would, in that section of the State, be inconsiderable. And I have no doubt any one, or all these enterprises, would meet a ready co-operation by the people. Their means would enable them, in many places, to do much, and their necessities, I imagine, would prompt them to vigorous exertions.—All these projects, in whatever form they may be presented, are respectfully submitted to your consid-eration, with an earnest wish that if they cannot all be promoted, they may receive a share at least of that patronage which it may be in your power to bestow.

I have thus briefly glanced at all the prominent species of In-ternal Improvement in the different parts of the State, which have come to my knowledge—I believe them all practicable, useful, and highly desirable. And I wish I could see the means for their accomp-lishment, as readily as I can conceive their importance. I know and appreciate the difficulties which lie between the preservation of the public faith and the construction of great works dependent on ad-ditional pledges of State credit. I have felt their force in all my re-flections on the subject. My reliance for the support of these great enterprises is on the spirit of the people, which I think is fully awakened to their importance. They have the ability and the patri-otism to encounter temporary evils, for measures that must ultimate-ly ensure their own interest. Education and Internal Improvement, I regard, in a financial view, as *the ways and means*, aside from the paramount general benefits to be derived.

Taxation ought never to be resorted to, except to discharge existing obligations, and for objects which guarantee, at least, cor-responding advantages. With these, I am never afraid to appeal to an honest, public-spirited people. And what are present honors and public stations worth, if they are not worth even a sacrifice at the

shrine of public interest? For my own part, without claiming unusual disinterestedness, I acknowledge no medium between a sense
of public duty, and a fear of personal responsibility. Without depreciating the importance of Federal politics, I regard these two
great questions, in their effect upon our local well-being and prosperity, present and prospective, as worth infinitely more than all the
Federal politics on both sides. And we have to lament those distrac-
tions and divisions upon national questions, which have preoccupied
the people of Tennessee, to the exclusion, too much, of our own
immediate interests. And may I exhort you, without the imputation
of arrogance, to let us close up for once, in the breach, upon ground
that is common to us all. Here is a field fruitful in happiness, prosperity and glory, in which we can all labor. Here is a cause, rife with
blessings and benefits, which, if cultivated, will outlive all our present divisions, and shed a radiance and a lustre upon the destinies
of this growing commonwealth, long after we shall cease to participate in its strifes, or mingle in the aspirations of the hour.

In the Military Department I have but little additional information to communicate, which you did not learn from my immediate
predecessor. I am happy to inform you, that the previous and late
calls for Volunteers upon Tennessee are near being filled. The 5th
Regiment, now in rendezvous at Memphis, I trust is complete. And
the 6th is nearly made up, and will be ready to embark by the 16th
instant, for the seat of war. These brave men deserve great credit
for enlisting in so arduous a service upon an indefinite term of time,
and for the promptness with which they have responded to the call.

I would gladly forego the indulgence of any remarks upon questions of Federal policy, because they are foreign to your deliberations; and if I trespass a little upon what I conceive to be a rule of
propriety, my apology is to be found in usage upon like occasions,
and which, in the estimation of many, may make it my duty not
to be wholly silent. It is not to be disguised that the war now raging
between the United States and Mexico, is a question of deep and
vital interest to every American, because its effects upon the nation
and upon the people are to be universal in a greater or less degree.
While we all rejoice at the triumph of our arms and participate in
the glory which is won to the national character, by the bravery of
our officers and men, we have to regret its indefinite duration, and

the heavy cost at which every advantage is gained. We certainly have the same right to pass judgment upon the policy which led to a war and that upon which it has been prosecuted, as we have upon the policy of any thing else. There is nothing magical or sacred in the question of war, that should seal the lips of discussion, or silence or terrify the spirit of comment. I acknowledge no such orthodoxy in politics, or any thing else. And the spirit which demands a blind compliance, or an unwilling acquiescence in this or any other question, is itself at war with all that is sacred in the rights of the freedom of thought and of speech. I believe, and believing it, I have dared to proclaim, that this war might, could and ought to have been avoided; that the rights and dignity of the nation could have been vindicated by a little more forbearance upon the questions immediately at issue; by time, by temperate counsels, and without an appeal to the last resort of nations. I believe that this war is a national blunder, a great calamity, the full effects of which, upon the peace and happiness of the country, no human sagacity can foresee. It is becoming an absorbent of a nation's blood and treasure—a canker to a nation's repose. What, no calamity, when ten thousand brave men have already been sacrificed upon its altars, and the god that presides over it is still unappeased! No calamity, when the list of expenditures has swelled to near or quite a hundred millions, and the end is not yet! Peace, like the treasures of the rainbow, still recedes and eludes our anxious grasp. I am aware that these sentiments, in the estimation of some, imply a want of patriotism, a sort of new-fangled treason; and such charges have been preferred, but oftener insinuated, by sources not wanting in respectability. Be it so.—With all due respect to those who differ with me, such charges deserve to be loathed, detested and defied. They are unworthy of the spirit of republicanism—indeed, they have no affinity with that noble creed. The spirit which prompts them is one of rank intolerance, and grossly despotic; and in other ages, and under other circumstances, would have proscribed Martin Luther as a heretic and sent Hampden to the scaffold. I arraign the patriotism of no man. It is a maxim with me that all men love their country and desire its prosperity and its glory, whatever their political views may be—self-interest is generally an adequate motive, even when true integrity fails. And to those who differ with me, I freely accord the existence of the same high and noble motives. And I may ask here, what could not have been accomplished by the U. States, in her commerce and trade, in the arts and in every element of happiness and prosperity, by the use of the vast sums which have and will yet be expended? They would have raised the smile of joyous life, the bustle of business, and the hum of civilization, in many a region where nature still reigns in all her darkness and solitude. Does this view form no subject of regret? Is there no loss in this, to say nothing of the loss of that invaluable, living, human capital, which cannot be restored? The sober sense of the country will settle all these questions.

But while I have no concurrence with those whose policy I conceive led to and precipitated the country into this war, I feel as little concurrence and sympathy with others, who are opposed to the prosecution of the war. That I believe to be a false position, in any and every view of the national rights, and national dignity and authority. The nation is committed to the war by its constitutional authorities—and the voice of the nation is imperative upon the people. I feel and appreciate the obligation in its fullest extent.—The nation desires peace, but peace can be attained now only through war. And whatever might have been done in the earlier stages of it, by withdrawing the army and establishing a line of posts, according to the advice of great and good men, I fear that time has past. This policy now, I fear, would only heighten the exasperation of the Mexican people, and make the consequences still more disastrous by rendering the attainment of any permanent peace indefinite. In my judgment, the motto, 'to conquer peace,' is now made indispensable; there is no other alternative. Then let the nation's power be summoned to a mighty effort, and let it break upon that devoted country, peal after peal, in one unceasing note of thunder! Let the public right arm be made bare, and the sword remain unsheathed until peace is extorted. The public interest requires this—commerce, both domestic and foreign, demands it—our currency, which must be affected by such a powerful continuing cause, claims it—quite and repose, business and thrift of every description now begin to make their loud appeal. I am satisfied that economy, both of blood and treasure, dictates this policy. And it is to be regretted, and with me the regret has been coeval with the war itself, that a large force was not called into prompt requisition at the beginning. Peace would have crowned the effort, as I verily believe, long since. Had the volunteer force of 50,000 men been called into service immediately upon their grant by Congress, the moral effect at that juncture might have induced peace. And what could not such a force, added to the regular army, have done in the posture of affairs then in Mexico? The whole country could have been overrun long since, and peace extorted, and at less than half the present loss of life and treasure. Our army, though equal to Roman legions, has been too small to follow up its victories, as has been proven at every stage of the war. As to the questions that lie behind the attainment of peace, they are to my mind full of difficulty—speculation alone can now reach them. I trust that all ground of apprehension may disappear under the influence of wise and harmonious counsels.

These views are submitted with the profoundest respect towards that portion of you who I know differ with me. And having presented, as well as I have been able, all that I have deemed important, I close this communication with the tender of my best wishes for the success of your labors, and your personal and individual well-being; hoping that the results of the session may meet the approbation of your constituents, and the smiles and approval of an all-wise Providence.

N. S. Brown."

Approximately three weeks after his inauguration, Governor Neill S. Brown transmitted to the General Assembly the above Message. The high points in the Message fall into seven categories:
1. Status of State finances.
2. State Capitol Building.
3. Lunatic Asylum.
4. Bank of Tennessee.
5. Education.
6. Internal Improvements.
7. Mexican War.

Under a provision in the 11th section of the Charter of the Bank of Tennessee, the President of the Bank was required to furnish the General Assembly at each regular session a statement showing the condition of the institution. On October 1, 1847, only two weeks after the convening of the Legislature, President A. O. P. Nicholson submitted a report embracing fifteen printed pages.[26] This report, it will be noted,

---

[26] *Senate Journal*, 1847, Appendix, 53–69.

A TABLE

Showing the annual dividends of the Bank; the contingent fund each year; the total of dividends and contingent fund each year; the annual interest paid on State bonds; the annual distribution to schools and academies; the annual expense account, and the deficiency of profits to meet liabilities:

Year ending	Annual Dividends	Contingent Fund	Total Contingent Fund and Dividends	Interest Paid on State Bonds	Paid to School and Academies	Total Paid in Interest and to Schools	Annual Expense Account	Deficiency
July 1, 1839	$129,319.76	$99,810.49	$229,130.25	$45,035.62	$118,000.00	$163,035.62	$42,266.68	
" 1840	139,436.02	53,009.71	242,445.73	92,443.39	118,000.00	210,443.39	30,331.82	
" 1841	209,650.97	19,806.39	229,457.36	98,752.04	118,000.00	216,752.04	21,901.09	
" 1842	191,305.81	15,542.20	205,848.01	121,207.14	118,000.00	239,207.14	25,062.20	
" 1843	175,035.61	5,802.81	180,838.42	137,788.96	118,000.00	255,788.96	23,288.17	
" 1844	243,578.48	4,036.24	247,614.72	134,934.91	118,000.00	252,934.91	24,808.59	
" 1845	149,152.06	14,440.10	163,592.10	123,820.97	118,000.00	241,820.97	21,647.89	76,589.97
" 1846	213,247.99	18,756.89	232,004.88	143,316.10	118,000.00	261,316.10	24,137.53	108,867.60
" 1847	204,113.45	61,223.53	265,336.98	153,712.87	118,000.00	271,712.87	22,970.45	115,243.49
	1,704,840.15	292,928.36	1,997,768.51	1,051,012.00	1,062,000.00	2,113,012.00	236,413.42	

was transmitted to the Legislature more than a month before Governor Brown sent his regular Message to the law-making body. The Governor, therefore, had opportunity of familiarizing himself with the condition of the bank prior to any recommendations that he desired to make. Likewise the Legislature had before it the same information for its consideration. President Nicholson, a capable man with long legislative experience, went into rather meticulous detail in his report, for he knew that the report would be subjected to close scrutiny by the Whig Governor and a Whig Legislature. In the preparation of the lengthy report, Nicholson submitted a tabular analysis showing the condition of the bank throughout its nine-year existence.[27]

Further on in his report, President Nicholson pointed out that the specific liabilities of the bank consisted of an annual payment of $118,000 for Common School and County Academies and of approximately $150,000 for interest on State Bonds. In view of past earnings and the above required payments, the bank could not avoid, so Nicholson declared, an annual average deficit of about $54,000. "The only practicable remedy, therefore, must look to a diminution of the liabilities of the Bank" was Nicholson's conclusion.

Early in his Message, Governor Brown revealed that he had read the Nicholson Report, inasmuch as he referred to the deficit of $115,243.49 as of July 1, 1847, the exact amount specified by President Nicholson. Moreover, Governor Brown apprehended that the following two years would likely decrease rather than increase the net earnings of the State Bank. No doubt reluctantly but nevertheless specifically, the Governor screwed his courage up to the sticking point by pointing out that the evaluation of property subject to taxation was lax and inequitable, and that the remedy lay in correcting that defect. And with that, he hit the nail squarely on the head by recommending that the law be amended in that regard.

On November 16, Whig Senator John W. Richardson from Rutherford County dropped a bill[28] into the legislative hopper for the purpose of regulating and equalizing taxes. Senator Richardson's bill proved unacceptable and, on January 12, his bill along with eight other bills on the same subject were ditched in favor of a bill drafted by the Committee on the Judiciary.[29] Whig Senator Return Jonathan Meigs of Davidson County, a member of the Judiciary Committee, submitted the Committee's bill which dragged along until final and favorable action was taken just three days before the end of the legislative session, February 7, 1848. Illustrative of the tendency of the Legislature to higgle and haggle over details was an unsuccessful effort by Democratic Sen-

---

[27] *Ibid.*, 59.
[28] *Ibid.*, 252.
[29] *Ibid.*, 473.

ator Landon C. Haynes who wanted to strike out "one mill and insert three-fourths of a mill" on each dollar as the proposed increase in taxes upon land.[30]

A yearly tax of one mill on each dollar was levied upon land, town lots, slaves, jewelry, pianos, pleasure carriages, and various other small items. License fees were increased on peddlers, auctioneers and race tracks. Unsuccessful parties in law-suits were subjected to further losses by having to pay specified fees. An annual tax of fifteen cents was levied upon every white male between the ages of twenty-one and fifty years.[31] The loophole in the law was that the local revenue commissioner should "estimate all real and personal property at its full value", such evaluation being subject, of course, to favoritism, kinship, and a horde of other intangibles.

At any rate, the new revenue law brought in more money than was true of the preceding biennium. For the biennium, 1845-7, the State Treasury received from all sources $710,907.61 and expenditures for the same period amounted to $642,314.32.[32] For the next biennium, 1847-9, collections from all sources amounted to $790,693.53. But expenditures for the biennium amounted to $802,436.66, leaving a deficit of nearly $12,000.[33] Even then, "things were going up"!

The second recommendation of Governor Brown had reference to the building of the State Capitol which had its beginning two years previous. "Hastening of the building" was not effected to the degree anticipated and desired, for more than a decade later the completion of the structure was still on the agenda of the General Assembly. In compliance with the request of the Governor, an annual appropriation of $50,000 was made by the Legislature for the ensuing biennium.[34] Since that amount of money in the State Treasury was not anticipated, the Governor was authorized to issue State Bonds bearing six per cent interest. The surplus revenues of the State Penitentiary were appropriated for the purpose of paying the interest and also for retiring the bonds.

In order that the Legislature might be fully informed as to the exact status of the progress made on the erection of the Capitol, the Building Commissioners and the architect, W. Strickland, submitted near the opening date of the Legislature reports showing just how matters stood. Those two reports are herewith incorporated for the purpose of disclosing just how the early work on the Capitol Building was transacted:[35]

---

[30] *Ibid.*, 519.
[31] *Acts of Tennessee*, 1847, Chapter 161.
[32] *Senate Journal*, 1847, Appendix, 172.
[33] *Ibid.*, 1849, Appendix, 132.
[34] *Acts of Tennessee*, 1847, Chapter 79.
[35] *Senate Journal*, 1847, Appendix, 17–22.

"REPORT OF THE BUILDING COMMISSIONERS

To the General Assembly of the State of Tennessee:

The Commissioners appointed to superintend the erection of the State Capitol, state, that since their report to the last General Assembly, the work under their charge has progressed with as much rapidity as the limited means under their control would permit.

They refer to the report of the Architect herewith submitted, for full details of the work done, and his estimate of its value, the out door force employed for quarrying, cutting and setting stone, &c. &c.

The whole amount of money received by the Commissioners for the prosecution of the work since its commencement is $41,271.60 cents.

The whole amount expended to 4th inst., $40,681.31 cents, leaving a balance to their credit on that day in the Bank of Tennessee $592.29 cents.

A full statement of these receipts and expenditures, is appended to this report. The vouchers and receipts for payments are in the custody of their Secretary, Mr. Edward G. Steel, and subject to the inspection of the General Assembly or any Committee of that body.

The State has been most fortunate in its selection of quarries, not only on account of their convenience of situation which is a great saving in transportation, but because they continue to yield, now that they have been opened, a building material of so satisfactory a character, not surpassed in durability and beauty, by granite or marble.

The Building has been planned, and thus far executed with a strict regard to stability and taste, while nothing has been sacrificed to useless ornament.

The Commissioners cannot but congratulate themselves and the State on their choice of an Architect, combining as he does, experience, judgment and taste, which eminently qualify him to conduct such a work.

To Mr. James Birth, the Superintendent of the Stone department in the prison, the State is much indebted for the highly accurate and satisfactory manner in which the prison work has been executed by the convicts under his charge.

Whatever may be said of the past policy of the State in its limited appropriations to this object, it occurs to the Commissioners that there are considerations which should induce an abandonment of this policy, by making such appropriations as will secure the early completion of the work.

Now that the quarries have been opened; a good McAdamised road constructed from them to the prison; an architect and all necessary superintendents appointed; an efficient and well drilled working force organized within the prison, and a body of stone cutters collected together from the neighboring towns—in fact, a system established for carrying on the work; it can be conducted with much greater advantage than heretofore.

The present policy will prolong the work through an indefinite series of years, and it may well be doubted whether the State will be acting wisely or justly, in confining so large a number of the convicts to one branch of business or one mechanical calling. One object of prison labor is to furnish the convict with a trade, by which he can earn an honest livelihood after his enlargement.

So limited is the demand for the business of Stone cutting in this new country, that it may well be feared, that out of so large a number sent forth from the prison walls, all will not be able to obtain employment. It is desirable then, as the Commissioners think, that a sufficient amount of out door labor in conjunction with that of the convicts, should be employed to finish the work within a reasonable time.

Should the state of the Public Treasury not admit of an appropriation of one hundred thousand dollars per annum for the next two years, the same object might be accomplished, by the issuance of short bonds of the State, to fall due within the next ten years, say twenty thousand dollars each year. —If these bonds should be made to bear an interest of six per cent payable semi-annually, and a law should be passed authorizing guardians and others having trust funds, to make investments in them, they could be readily cashed at par within the State, and the principal and interest be thus kept at home. Such bonds might be issued by the Governor, only as fast as in his opinion they might be needed in the progress of the work.

No money has been received from the prison by the Commissioners under the 1st section of the act of 29th Jan., 1846, entitled 'an act to better organize the State prison &c.'

The deeds for the two lots of ground in front of the Capitol purchased by the Commissioners under the law of the last General Assembly, have been duly executed, registered and deposited in the office of the Secretary of State. By the terms of the contract made with the owners of these lots, and as reported by the Commissioners to the last General Assembly, interest on the purchase money, was agreed to be paid from the date of the purchase, which was conditional, to the time of its ratification by the General Assembly.—The contract was fully ratified and confirmed by an act passed 5th Jan. 1846, entitled, 'an act to authorize the Commissioners of the State Capitol to continue and complete the construction of the State House &c.' Under this law the Comptroller declined to pay any amount beyond the principal of the purchase money (say $8500) and the Commissioners had either to let the purchase fail altogether, or to appropriate the sum of $409.53 cents for interest accrued on the purchase money as above stated, out of money in their hands for the construction of the building. They, without hesitation, adopted the latter alternative. If the construction placed upon the above act by the Comptroller was correct, as not authorizing him to pay beyond the sum of $8500, then there was no law for the payment of this interest by the Commissioners, and some action of the General Assembly may be required to legalize such payment.

You will learn from the report of the Architect, that there are two sets of hands employed in quarrying rock, the one consisting of negroes hired under the direction of the Commissioners, the other of convicts from the prison, under the keeper and his deputies. It would seem to be bad economy to have these two sets of hands employed on the same object, with the expense of separate overseers, tools, cooking departments &c., when the same labor might be performed by increasing the number of convicts, at but little additional expense of guards and superintendents.—As this kind of labor requires the smallest amount of mechanical skill, the convicts with short terms of service might be very appropriately employed in this way, and the expense of hiring be dispensed with. When the Commissioners first determined to employ an out door force of stone cutters, application was made to Mr. McIntosh, the keeper to increase the number employed in the quarries in order to supply this out door force, as well as that within the prison, with raw material.—A compliance with this request was declined, for the reason that the 8th section of the act of 29th Jan. 1846, entitled, 'an act to better organize the State prison &c.,' required 'that the convicts shall be worked within the walls of the prison under the existing police regulations.'—

Whether the General Assembly really intended in this section such a prohibition as would prevent the State from quarrying its own rock with convict labor, or whether it was not rather intended to prevent the undertaking
of work for individuals outside the prison, in town and country, are questions which need not here be inquired into; the Commissioners however,
would suggest the repeal or modification of this law, so as to leave no doubt
on the subject, and to authorize the employment of at least thirty of the
convicts at the quarries, should such a number be required to supply the
stone cutters.

All of which is respectfully submitted,

JOHN M. BASS, *Chr'm.*
JOS. T. ELLISTON,
SAML. D. MORGAN,
MORGAN W. BROWN,
JAMES WOODS,
ALLEN A. HALL.

Nashville, October 19, 1847.

REPORT OF THE SUPERINTENDENT

To the Commissioners for building the State Capitol:

GENTLEMEN:

It is now twenty-seven months since the corner stone of this building
was laid upon a rocky eminence, 197 feet above the low water mark of the
Cumberland River, and situated nearly in the centre of the Corporate limits
of the city of Nashville. The building occupies a space or area of three quarters of an acre on the very summit of the hill, its dimensions being 240 feet
in length by 130 feet in width.

Upwards of 3600 perches of rock excavation has been made and the
stone laid in the foundation walls of the crypt, together with 5000 supl.fft.
of chisselled blue rock in the piers and buttresses necessary for the support
of the various arches and vaults throughout the area of the building. All of
which material has been quarried out on the side.

The arches have been laid in hydraulic cement and their spandrils built
up with solid masonry to the height of the floor line of the basement story.

The cut stone ashler of the sub-basement and the various steps rising
between the piers of the porticos, on all the fronts, are laid and completed.

Five courses of the basement story, rusticated and tooled on the outside
and finished with rubbed stone on all the interior walls, which, together
with the cut stone of the sub-basement and piers, make upwards of 13 feet
in elevation about the rough stone foundations all around the building.

The gang of men allowed us by the Superintendent of the Penitentiary
to work in quarrying rock, was found to be inadequate to supply the stone
cutters with material enough to employ them and keep the setters going at
the building, and early in May last an additional force of from 20 to 30 negroes were hired, and placed at the quarries under the charge of an overseer.

Early in June last, 24 stone cutters were employed in order to facilitate
the progress of the cut work:—Sheds were built at the Quarries for their
accommodation, and with a view of saving labor in the loading, unloading,
and hauling in and out of the Penitentiary.

Since last May the negro force have quarried nearly 7000 cubic feet of
rock, and now the quarries are in such a state that all the stone cutters, both
in and out of the Penitentiary, are kept supplied, and by the 1st of Decem-,

ber next a similar quantity will be quarried so as to keep the cutters at work during the whole of the coming winter.

The following is an estimate of the work and its value, if executed by measurement up to the present day, viz;—

Rock excavation, the building up of the foundation walls, piers, buttresses, &c.	14,000
The brick arches, centreing plank, joist for platforms, hoisting machinery, rigging, &c.	6,500
Cut rock Ashler, wrought by the cutters at the quarries together with the setting of the same at the building and including that from the Penitentiary	12,600
Turnpike round the building, sand, lime, cast iron water pipes, wheeling plank, stationery, Architect's salary, &c.	8,000
	$41,100

The cut stone work done at the Penitentiary equals 49,000 superficial ft. of Ashler, *which is estimated at what it would cost in any of the Eastern cities,* including a large Ionic capital, as a specimen of those that are intended to crown the columns of the porticos, and which was carved in the Penitentiary under the care and supervision of Mr. James Birth, the superintendent of stone cutters, $49,620, which makes the value of the building, by Penitentiary and other workmanship, in its present stage, including the finished cut stone in the Prison and that unset at the Capitol Hill, $90,720, which amount would be the actual cost of the work now done, if it were altogether executed by good stone cutters hired for the purpose.

The progress which has been made in the building so far, may seem to have been slow, but when the magnitude and permanent character of its workmanship is taken into consideration,—the walls being faced with heavy blocks of stone on all sides, together with the great amount of labor in blasting out the rocks to form the crypt, and the massive foundations of the structure, you are well aware, that with the means we have had, no time has been lost in its advancement so far. The limited amount of our funds has prevented us from employing an adequate number of hands upon so large a work. If a liberal appropriation be made by the Legislature, such as would enable us to engage an adequate number of hands, say in all, 150 stone cutters, inclusive of those now at work in the Penitentiary, the building could easily be completed in the course of the next 3 years.

Respectfully submitted,

By your obedient servant,

W. STRICKLAND, *Arch't.*

To Messrs. Bass, Morgan, Elliston, Woods, Brown, and Hall,
    Building Commissioners.

Nashville, October 4, 1847."

Apparently the Building Commissioners and the architect knew how captious and caviling a Legislature can be, if so disposed. To obviate any just grounds for unwarranted criticism, twenty-five printed pages [36]

---

[36] *Ibid.,* 24–51.

in the official record were utilized in portraying day by day expenditures, including such items as

"For coins to deposit in Corner Stone.................$ 19.40
  W. Coleman, for hire of boy 2½ days 83
  A. A. Adams, for patterns for pipes.................. 6.00
  Bill for engraving drawing of Capitol............... 137.72
  R. Stewart, for oil for blocks.......................   1.75
  W. Strickland, for 1 month's salary................. 208.33
  C. M. Holt, for bricks............................ 466.93
  Fanning & Embry for mule........................ 90.00
  James Irwin, for spirit level........................   2.50
  Dr. W. D. Dorris, medical services to boy............ 11.00
  Freight on 2 bbls. sand from Memphis............... 2.00"

At the very end of the itemized Report, there appeared the omnious statement, "Balance on hand, $592.29."

In his regular Message to the Legislature, Governor Brown submitted rather general observations concerning the Lunatic Asylum. Well-intentioned but rather half-hearted efforts on the part of the Legislature during a preceding five-year period had resulted in average annual appropriations for the support of the Lunatic Asylum of only some $5,600. The 1847 Report of the Joint Select Committee on the Lunatic Asylum attempted to give a resumé of past legislation and appropriations, but its chief concern seemed to be to show that expenditures had exceeded "legislative intent." [37] As a rule, references to the mentally ill at that time classified such persons as "lunatics," implying that their ailment was in some way tied up with the moon! Diagnosis of mental illness was crude and almost wholly unscientific, and most legislation was on a parallel with the faulty diagnosis.

Early in the legislative session there was presented to the Legislature a lengthy but searching analysis of the conditions prevailing at the Hospital for the Insane. On December 1, the Senate acknowledged receipt of a message from the House of Representatives of

"... a memorial, No. 104, of Miss D. L. Dix, soliciting enlarged and improved accommodations for the insane of the State of Tennessee, by the establishment of a new Hospital." [38]

Miss Dorothea Lynde Dix, it should be stated, was a maiden lady who was born in Maine, in 1802, had fallen heir to considerable property, and afterwards had devoted her time, talent, and fortune to the alleviation of the mentally ill. She visited almshouses, prisons, and hospitals in nearly every State in the Union, as well as in Europe, and by her efforts contributed greatly to the establishment of some thirty hospitals for the insane in the United States. This philanthropic lady paid Tennessee a visit in the fall of 1847 while the Legislature was in session.

---

[37] *Ibid.*, 342–345.
[38] *Senate Journal*, 1847, 320–321.

It was not just a casual tour. Her "sight-seeing" activities included several trips to the pathetically inadequate "Lunatic Asylum" where, with notebook in hand, she jotted down numerous defects and deficiencies which were incorporated in her memorial to the Legislature.

Despite the length of the memorial, it deserves recognition and incorporation in this treatise. There can be no question but that the broad observations, keen analyses, and overall recommendations embraced in the memorial had a tremendous impact upon the Legislature which, for the first time in the history of Tennessee, took serious steps toward alleviating the distressing conditions that had prevailed for altogether too long a time. Let us see and read what Miss Dix had to say, a lady whose services to humanity were rewarded in 1903 by an appropriation of $10,000 by Congress for the erection of a monument to her at her birthplace. Here was the Memorial [39] which she drafted and presented to the Tennessee Legislature:

"MEMORIAL
of
MISS D. L. DIX,
Soliciting Enlarged and Improved Accommodations
For The
INSANE OF THE STATE OF TENNESSEE
By the Establishment of
A NEW HOSPITAL

To the Honorable,
  the General Assembly of the State of Tennessee.

GENTLEMEN:
  I ask to lay before you, briefly and distinctly, the necessities and claims of a numerous, and unfortunately, an increasing class of your fellow-citizens —I refer to the Insane of this State; the various distresses of whose various condition can be fully appreciated only by those who have witnessed their miseries. Pining in cells and dungeons, pent in log-cabins, bound with ropes, restrained by leathern thongs, burthened with chains—now wandering at large, alone and neglected, endangering the security of property, often inimical to human life; and now thrust into cells, into pens, or wretched cabins, excluded from the fair light of heaven, from social and healing influences— cast out, cast off, like the Pariah of the Hindoos, from comfort, hope, and happiness, such is the present actual condition of a large number of your fellow-citizens—useless and helpless, life is at once grievous to themselves, and a source of immeasurable sorrow to all beside.

  In some cases, indeed, pitying friends strive to procure comforts, and exercising consoling cares; how little, under the cloud of this malady, these avail, many can bear sorrowful testimony. The only remedy or alleviation is to be found in *rightly organized Hospitals* adapted to the special care the peculiar malady of the Insane so urgently demands.

  Made conversant with the cruel sufferings and measureless distresses of which I speak, by patient investigations, reaching through long and weary

---

[39] *Senate Journal*, 1847, Appendix, 148–170.
  House Journal, 1847, Appendix, 259–280.

years, over the length and breadth of our land, I represent the existence of troubles no imagination can exaggerate, and I have come now to Tennessee, as the advocate and friend of those who can not plead their own cause, and for those who have no friend to protect and succor them, in this, the extremity of human dependence.

I appeal confidently to the Legislature of Tennessee, in which is vested the power, by the will of a whole people, to interpose relief, and timely to apply a remedy to heal, or at least to mitigate, the ravages of their cruel malady.

This subject, gentlemen, is not new to you. Good, humane, and liberal men in this State, more than eight years since, discerned the necessities of the Insane, and applied their energies to the establishment of a Hospital, in which it was hoped and designed these should find relief through the application of physical remedies and moral treatment. Why the just and liberal spirit of the Legislature which first acknowledged in Tennessee, the claims of the Insane to become wards of the State, and through its generous guardianship to find healing influences, has not been practically carried out, it is not my province to search into and declare.

The intention on the part of the public was correct, and the means ample; but that the experience of other States in the construction of the Hospital, and in its internal organization, was not consulted, or, if consulted, not made instructive, is evident, even to an uninformed and casual observer.

Most of the essential defects of the present edifice, which is immediately on the confines of the city, do not admit of repair or remedy; and even if this was not a demonstrable fact, the location, so singularly ill chosen, would present a cogent objection to the permanent establishment by repairs and extended hospital buildings, upon the present site.

But again—though it might have been conceived by those entrusted with the responsibility of determining the extent of accommodations that the present edifice was of sufficient capacity for the then understood wants of the patients, it is quite certain that now it cannot receive within its walls *one fourth* of all who are suffering immediately within your own borders, for such remedial treatment as a well established Institution ought to afford.

I am not able to state the whole number of Insane, epileptics, and idiots in Tennessee, but it is certain that they are no longer to be numbered by *tens*, but by *hundreds*. Some calculators, predicating their estimates on the basis of ascertained facts in most other States, give an amount of from *ten to twelve hundred, in all*. I think this an excess, but allowing that there are but one-half or one-fourth of the above number, the need of much enlarged accommodations is not the less urgent.

There is less insanity in the Southern, than in the Northern States proportioned to the inhabitants of each; for this disparity several causes may be assigned; there is, in the former, comparatively but a small influx of foreigners, while they throng every district of the latter. In the Boston City Hospital for the Insane poor, were (in 1846) 169 patients, 99 of which were *foreigners*, 35 natives of other States, and 44 alone residents of the city. Of the 99 foreigners, 70 were Irish. In the New York City Hospital for the Insane poor, on Blackwell's Island, were (on the first of January, 1846), 356 patients; of whom 266 were foreigners: at present the number exceeds 400. At the Philadelphia City Hospital for the Insane poor, and connected with the Alms House, there were received in one year 395 patients. The above Hospitals were established for the treatment of the Insane poor alone. But a more obvious cause is found in the fact of the much more numerous colored population here than there. The negro and the Indian rarely become subject to the malady of insanity, as neither do the uncivilized tribes and clans of European Russia and Asia. Insanity is the malady of civilized and cultivated life, and of sections and communities whose nervous energies are most roused and nourished.

Upon careful inquiry, it will be discovered that great suffering is experienced in every county of this State, from the want of a suitable Hospital for the Insane poor, as well as for those who are in moderate or affluent circumstances. This proposition admitted, it is clearly a duty to adopt such measures as shall effectually remedy the evil.

Successive Legislatures have, biennially, for a considerable period, made such appropriations from the Treasury as have been found to meet the most obvious wants which have been revealed. The people at large, therefore, are aware that Hospital care for the Insane is desirable, and that it is sustained at least to a limited extent. I apprehend that the insufficiency of this support for present necessities is not widely known and appreciated. It will require no subtle arguments to show that much more is to be done, and it is not Tennessee which will offer the example of slighting the claims of her afflicted children. *Here,* you will not reveal yourselves less true, less honorable, less just than are your sister States on every hand. Tennessee, which in population and productions ranks fifth in the Union, will not allow her younger or her senior sisters to excel her in what is liberal and humane. She is abundantly able to do this good work—she *will* do it, and she will do it, *now,* freely, unitedly, and well!

Allow me to state briefly the most prominent defects of the Hospital, at present devoted to the treament of the Insane.

1st. The interior construction:—the wards in each wing are ill-arranged for the proper classification of the patients; the excitable, the noisy, the sick, the languid, and the convalescent, are frequently associated in such sort as to prevent comfort, destroy quiet, and retard recovery. The highly excited patients shut into those wretched cells in the cellar, damp, cold, and unventilated as they are, are not fit for any human creature, much less for the treatment of the sick; and these patients are beneath apartments occupied by others requiring repose, and every comforting and cheering influence. Your superintendent in his last report anticipates my statements, declaring that 'the cells belonging to this institution being under ground, and not susceptible of ventilation, are wholly unfit for the habitation of human beings; and even supposing them to be of value as places of temporary confinement, they are nevertheless utterly useless for any remedial purpose.' On a late visit at the Hospital, I found these cells occupied, and the most vehement excitement prevailing, unquestionably stimulated and protracted by the unfortunate circumstances surrounding the patients. The lodging rooms above are of sufficient size, indeed might without disadvantage be made smaller, but they are either not warmed at all, or insufficiently heated, and not ventilated. In fact, the proper ventilation of the whole building appears to have been entirely overlooked in its construction, and it is not possible to preserve a pure and wholesome atmosphere throughout.

A new warming apparatus, lately introduced at a large cost, is apparently a complete failure; and by its defective construction, allowing the escape of deleterious gasses, the patients are in worse condition than before the introduction of the furnaces. In no way, at present apparent, can the temperature either of the day-rooms or the lodging apartments be properly regulated for the feeble or more vigorous patients.

There are in the Hospital no bath rooms; and thus a most important remedial agent is not to be had, except under circumstances of great exposure, and unreasonable extra labor. Convenience is not consulted, nor personal cleanliness attainable in any special department. There are no clothes room, no store rooms, no labor saving arrangements of any description whatever— no convenient dining-rooms, with labor saving dumb-waiters, &c. &c.

The kitchens and laundry are so amazingly defective that the surprise is to witness the accomplishment of daily work in any manner so as to secure the order of domestic economy. There is no bakery, no meat house, no smoke-house, no ice-house, no corn-crib nor meal-bin, no spring-house, milk-house, nor sheds for storing coal, wood, &c., &c.

There are no cisterns, and no wells which afford a supply of water— there is never, I am told, at any season a sufficient supply for culinary and domestic purposes, much less for the preservation of personal cleanliness. The superintendent informs me that they are often 'mainly dependent on the quantity they can haul from the river with one horse, over a distance of a mile and a half!' Wood being used for fuel, a large, if not ample supply' might be saved from the roofs, but *there are no cisterns*, and the casks used are *so few* and so small, that water collected in this way of course fails to meet the demand. The superintendent states in his report, 'that during a considerable portion of the year, they have not water even to drink,' (see report, page 7.) It would require but a moderate outlay to construct cisterns and tanks, and so furnish *without delay*, what appears indispensably requisite, a supply of wholesome, pure water. To this plan it is indeed objected, that wood costs more than coal used as fuel—the next remedy then seems to be to economise in fuel, and conduct water through a sub-surface channel from the city water-works, or from the river by horse power and a water-wheel. This should be a first care; for, finally, suppose the occurrence of a conflagration—no improbable event—there at your Institution, and no water at hand to check the progress of the destroying element—suppose it probable that the patients could be removed, (and this is doubtful when the number of care-takers is remembered,) why peril the loss of a valuable edifice, quite suitable to serve many uses, unfit though it is for the residence and proper treatment of the Insane.

There is another want too prominent not to attract notice. It is stated that for a number of patients, varying from *fifty* to *sixty* and *seventy*, there are but 'three attendants or nurses.' Incredible as this seems, I am assured it is the fact—indeed, a reference to the Report previously quoted, *(see page 4,)* exhibits at once *the fact and the assigned cause* in juxtaposition. '*The means at the disposal of the Institution,*' writes the superintendent, 'enable it to employ *only two male attendants and one female.*' This admits an effectual and immediate remedy. Reference to the Treasurer's Report of the present year opens the following exhibit for the last two financial years: (see page 16.) 'Attendants $2,066.73;' and directly following, 'Servants hire $1,546.58.' Perhaps the first charge embraces the salary of the physician, matron and steward. There is no table of officers, and it is not shown in either of the documents referred to, that there ever has been any organized body of this sort, as is usual in other Hospitals. I am sure that the Legislature do not purpose that the patients should suffer for lack of necessary care, nor that the Physician should be charged with a responsibility so great as that of guarding the patients from harm, and treating them remedially, without adequate means.

That present legislation is not requisite for authorizing remedy for many actual wants, is apparent in the Statutes for 1839-40: (see page 208, Chap. cxx, sec. 4.)

'*Be it enacted*, That said Board of Trustees shall have power to make such orders and regulations as may be necessary for the government of their patients in the Hospital, its internal police, the supply of provisions, fuel, *water, clothing, books, and whatever else may be deemed necessary for the health, comfort, cleanliness, and security* of the inmates.'

This act is certainly benevolent in its aim, and sufficiently full and explicit upon the subject treated.

In most of our State Hospitals, the *average* of nurses and attendants is one nurse to every ten patients. Sometimes the number of patients in charge of one nurse is larger, sometimes fewer, according to the state of the patients and other circumstances. (See numerous Hospital Reports.) Paying patients may, according to the choice of friends, have special nurses wholly devoted to their service. The night-watch nurses are always chosen with great care.

Too much caution cannot be taken in the choice and selection of nurses for the Insane. Comparatively, the number is not large who are suited to fulfil these duties. Yet they can be found here as elsewhere. They must possess correct principals and self-control: they must be patient, enduring, and forbearing; firm but kind; never requiting injurious language and violent acts with passionate words or vehement demonstrations. To return good for evil must be the invariable rule. No excitement should be exhibited under the wayward conduct and ungracious speech of an intractable patient. Nor must the smallest deviation from truth and sincerity be permitted. The conscientious nurse, and no other, should approach the dependent insane. None should accept this responsible and careful office, alone for the means of self-support, but because they may, while laboring for their own subsistence, be at the same time rendering a priceless benefit to their fellow-beings. Money alone can never compensate a faithful nurse; an approving conscience must supply the deficiency. It is a rule closely laid down, as far as I have witnessed, in all well-ordered Hospitals, that no attendant shall, under any circumstances, strike a patient. No blow shall ever be inflicted upon those patients, who are so eminently unaccountable through the malady under which they suffer—they must be guarded with fidelity, guided with firmness and kindness, and respected in their misfortunes. No attendant should be retained in office one hour, after being known to offend by manifesting any form of violent speech or act towards his patients. I would never make one exception to a rule so necessary to be enforced, and of so searching obligation.

I have represented chiefly the interior defects of the State Hospital, except one deficiency which exists to the same extent in no kindred establishment: I refer to the want of moral means to aid the skill of the Physician in procuring the mental health and bodily vigor of his patients. They have neither suitable occupations nor recreations. There are no exercise grounds, no gardens, no fields, where productive and healthful labor in the open air may be carried on. There is no carriage for the use of the feeble patients, when daily exercise abroad would be highly beneficial. There is no Library, no supply of periodicals fitly selected, for use and entertainment; no musical instruments; no sets of simple games, no workshops—in short, life in the Hospital seems necessarily, under present circumstances, to be one dull unvarying round of like uninteresting events from day to day, and month to month. Under the head of Moral Treatment, the Physician of Bloomingdale Hospital renders the following exposition, which in general corresponds with all the best organized and most successful Institutions of the country. I must somewhere abridge the statement:

'We have religious worship on the Sabbath; a school in the men's department during the cold season; lectures on scientific and miscellaneous subjects, by the Superintendent, illustrated by experiments and painted diagrams. The Library which contains a thousand volumes; with current newspapers, magazines and reviews, furnishes reading for all who are disposed to use them, and the number is not small. Most of the patients walk out or ride daily in suitable weather.

'Some of the men work in the carpenter's shop, upon the farm or about the grounds. Many of the women wash and sew, and assist in keeping their apartments in order. We use also ninepins, quoits, bagatelle, chess, chequers, dominoes, a swing in the grove, &c. We have social parties, from the different wards, but strictly within our own household of course, once a week. There is no undue exposure of the patients, or repetition of their insane conversations abroad. These are our chief moral means.'

'Labor,' remarks the superintendent of the Hospital at Utica, 'especially gardening and farming, are to the men, in most instances, the favorite amusement. In addition, they resort to reading, writing, ninepins, battledore and ball. The women walk and ride abroad; quilt, complete all sorts of plain work, and almost every kind of fancy article that taste can desire.

'The school is beneficial to those who are convalescent, those who are melancholy, and to those whose mental powers seem sinking into dementia; their memories are thus improved, and they become more active and cheerful. Musical parties for those for whom a little excitement is good, are formed often at evening.

'The want of proper *mental* occupation has, till of late years especially, been much felt in Hospitals for the Insane; this end may now be supplied every where to a great extent.'

The choir of singers at evening prayers, and at service on Sundays, is, in most Hospitals, composed of the patients aided by some of the attendants.

Very similar are the moral measures employed by Drs. Bell, Kirkbride, Awl, Allen, Brigham, Butler, Parker, Chandler, and others, as *remedial* means, too valuable to be dispensed with. Mere medical treatment, after the first few days, is usually altogether subordinate to diet, exercise, occupations, and amusements, employed of course always with discrimination.

In the Ohio Asylum, the ladies find great pleasure in cultivating their flower gardens in Summer, and their house-plants in Winter, and in the use of the needle in plain and fancy work. The most dull, inert, demented patient, may, with kind perseverance, be induced to take part in some work or sport. Dr. Allen, in Kentucky, has been eminently successful with this class.

Dr. Ray, who is high authority, and well known in Europe, as in our own country, for his excellent work, the 'Jurisprudence of Insanity,' remarks in one of his Reports, while yet he was superintendent of the Maine State Hospital, that 'he would be a bold man, who would venture to say that Pinel and Espuirol, whose medical treatment was confined chiefly to baths and bitter drinks, were less successful in their cure of mental diseases, than those numerous practitioners who have exhausted upon them all the resources of the healing art. Strictly medical means has less to do than some others, with treatment of the Insane. In chronic disorders, especially those which are of a nervous character, the means on which the intelligent practitioner chiefly relies with most confidence, are *proper diet and exercise, change of air and scene, useful and agreeable* occupation of the mind, and various employments.

Yet much must be done to prepare the system, by the *judicious* application of proper medical remedies, for the efficient action of moral means.'

Dr. Trezevant, formerly of the South Carolina Hospital at Columbia, in a clearly written and valuable Report, remarks, that 'there is not a year in which I do not see in patients brought to our Hospital, cases of constitutions shattered, and the recuperative energies of the brain entirely destroyed by the free use of the lancet and depleting remedies, before the patient is removed to our care.'

In corroboration of these sensible views, I might proceed to adduce other opinions in accordance with them, from the highest authorities in our own country, in England, and in France; this is not here and now requisite but allow me to direct your inquiries to your State Institution, so deplorably destitute of moral means for the benefit of the patients.

It appears to be universally conceded, that manual labor is eminently desirable for a large class of patients. To this end, it is important that at least one hundred acres of land be attached to the Hospital for cultivation, and other purposes.

The productions from the small farm attached to the Bloomingdale Hospital, at their fair market value, were estimated at $3,872.99—no inconsiderable sum in the item of table expenses, &c., in the Institution.

A careful, intelligent Physician will be cautious in giving active out-door work to recent patients, whose malady has been of short duration. All cannot be indiscriminately tasked, or rather employed: neither can the same patients, day by day, do an equal amount of labor. These things will always call for daily supervision, as do all things relating to the hygienic treatment of the patients.

Incurables who are able and willing to work, are more contented, and enjoy better health when employed. The following examples given in a Report of the Bloomingdale Institution, will pleasantly illustrate the benefits of employment for the curable patient. 'Two farmers, each of whom possessed a good farm, were admitted into the Asylum, one about a week after the other. They were laboring under the most abject form of melancholy, and had both attempted suicide. In less than a month, their condition, being already somewhat improved, they expressed a willingness, and one of them a strong desire, to work out of doors. Being furnished with implements, they daily went out together, and worked upon the farm with as much apparent interest as if it belonged to themselves. Under this course they both rapidly improved, and both were discharged recovered, one at the end of six weeks, and the other three months, from the time their respective admissions.

'Another man was brought in the spring, in a state of active mania, his appetite was poor, and his frame emaciated. He was careless of his personal appearance, ruthless, turbulent, and almost incessantly talking in an incoherent manner upon the delusions attending his disease. When out of doors, he was wandering to and fro, talking to himself or digging the earth with his hands, without end or object, and generally having his mouth filled with grass.—For some months there was but little change in his condition: at length, having become somewhat less bewildered, his attendant succeeded in inducing him to assist in making beds; shortly after, he was employed with the painters and glaziers upon the green-house, and then went to the carpenters' shop, where he worked regularly for several weeks. Meanwhile his bodily health improved, his mind gradually returned to its former integrity, and he was discharged cured of his mental order, and weighing more than at any previous period of his life.'

In the New York Hospital, a violent patient, after a few weeks special care and medical treatment, was invited to visit the carpenters' shop; he gazed round listlessly, but on a sudden seized a saw and declared he would make a sleigh and explore the frigid zone: he was allowed to carry out his fancy, worked laboriously with the carpenter for several hours daily, till his sleigh was finished—then declaring that there was not yet snow enough for good travelling, he resolved to commence another, and gave the first specimen of his skill to his fellow worker, the carpenter. It was soon observed that his mind was resuming a healthful tone; his zeal in sleigh-making effectually diverting him from his delusions, and in a few months he returned to his family perfectly restored.

At another Institution, one lady quite recovered her health first diverted from her delusions by an interest in making work baskets of pasteboard and silk for her friends. Another was earnest to make a present for a friend, who was a student of natural history, and betook herself so zealously to copying birds from Audubon's Ornithology, that she forgot her troubles and recovered the use of her reason.

These cases are fair examples of the efficacy of a combination of medical and moral means.

Before the establishment of the City Hospital for the Insane poor, in Boston, Mass., that department of the Alms-House assigned for their occupation, was a place of utter abomination. Scenes too horrible for description might be daily witnessed. These madmen and madwomen were of the most hopeless cases of long standing; their malady confirmed almost, by early adverse circumstances, and following gross mismanagement.

The citizens at length made sensible of great abuses, and conscious of the great injustice of herding these maniacs together, where day and night their shrieks and wild ravings destroyed the least appearance of repose, and where reigned all that was most loathsome and offensive,—resolved on establishing on correct principles, and at large cost, a special Hospital for their residence and treatment. The most sanguine friends of this measure hoped nothing more for these most wretched beings than to procure for them greater decency and comfort; recovery to the sound exercise of reason not being, under these circumstances, anticipated. The new Hospital was opened and its government declared. The Insane were gradually removed from the old department, disencumbered of their chains, and freed from the remnants of four garments; they were bathed and clothed, and placed in cheerful, decent apartments, under the superintendence of Dr. Butler—since made superintendent of the Retreat at Hartford, Conn. Thereafter, visit the Hospital when one might, at neither set time nor season, these hitherto most wretched beings would be found well clad, usually tranquil, and capable of various employments in the gardens and within doors, which were advantageous in the economy of the Institution. Some might always be found abroad, exercising under charge of an attendant, or busy in the vegetable and flower gardens; others were in the laundry, in the ironing-room, in the kitchen, &c. Care was had not to allow fatigue by over labor, and the visitor would see amongst those busy ones many of the incurables who had worn out years of misery in a dreary abode; and though of this once miserable company, less than one-sixth were restored to the right use of the reasoning faculties, with but few exceptions they were capable of receiving pleasure from employments and recreations, and of being present in the chapel during religious service, where they were serious and orderly. Than their's no condition could be worse before their removal from the old Institution; afterwards none could be better for creatures of impaired faculties, incompetent as they were to guide and govern themselves, yielding to beneficent influences, and gentle, kindly cares.

In former times, it was judged that severity alone was the power for governing the unfortunate beings who should become subject through bodily ailments, to loss of capacity for self-care and self-government. It is true, indeed, that, according to early writers, the priests of ancient Egypt received to their charge, persons drooping under deep melancholy, and languishing under nervous diseases, the symptoms of which were marked by deep depression or strange delusions. These were conducted to gay pavilions, charming gardens, surrounded by all that was cheerful and animating in nature, or captivating in art, and under a choice diet, often recovered, and went their way to their near or remote abodes! Not such was the discipline in the middle ages and later; no limit was placed before the terrors of the harshest treatment. The first radical reforms are traced to France, from thence have England and America brought the examples which now, in their practical results, bless humanity; restoring, through the exercise of benignant cares, and wise treatment, hundreds and even thousands to health, to usefulness, and all the blessings and benefits of domestic endearments, and social intercourse. With what blessings upon the name of the good Vincent de Paul do we learn of his self-sacrificing efforts to ameliorate the hard lot of the Insane, and then long years following we see Pinel, the benevolent, good man, the enlightened and skilful Physician, apply his noble mind to a thorough reform of those heretofore dreaded receptacles, the Hospitals of France. 'It was,' said the son of Pinel, in a memorial before the Academy of Arts and Sciences in Paris, 'near the close of 1792, that Pinel, after reiterated importunities, induced government to issue a decree, permitting him to unchain the maniacs at Bicetre. After the most vexatious delays, he at last, by every skilful argument, induced Mr. Couthon, member of the Commune, to meet him at the Hospital, there to witness his first experiments. Couthon himself first proceeded to visit the patients, and to question them, but in return only received abuse and execrations, accompanied by terrible cries, and the clanking of chains. Retreating from the damp and filthy cells, he exclaimed to Pinel, 'Do as you will, but your life will be sacrificed to your false sentiment of mercy.' Pinel delayed no longer; he selected fifty, who he believed might be released from their chains without danger to others. The fetters were removed, first from twelve, using the precaution of having ready for use, jackets with long continuous sleeves, and closing behind.

'The experiments commenced with a French Captain, whose history was unknown, save that he had been in chains forty years! He was thought to be dangerous; having with a single blow of his manacles at one time killed one of his keepers, so that ever after he was approached with caution. Pinel entered his cell unattended. 'Ah well, Captain, I will cause your chains to be taken off: you shall have liberty to walk in the court, if you will promise to behave like a gentleman, and offer no assaults!' 'I would promise,' responded the maniac, 'but you deride me, you are amusing yourself at my expense; you all fear me.' 'I have six men,' replied Pinel, 'ready to obey my orders; believe me, therefore, I will set you free from this duresse, if you will put on this jacket.' The Captain assented; the chains were removed, the jacket laced, the attendants withdrew, but left the door unclosed. He raised himself, but fell: this effort was repeated again and again: the use of his limbs so long constrained, nearly failed: at length trembling, and with tottering steps, he emerged from his dark dungeon. His first look was at the sky! 'Ah,' cried he, 'how beautiful!' The remainder of the day he was constantly moving to and fro, uttering continually exclamations of pleasure. He heeded no one: the flowers, the trees, above all, the sky, engrossed him. At night he voluntarily returned to his cell, which had been cleansed, and furnished with a better bed, his sleep was tranquil and profound. For the two remaining years that he spent at the hospital, he had no recurrence of violent paroxysms, and often rendered good service to the attendants in conducting the affairs of the establishment.

'The next person released after the Captain, was Chevigne, a soldier of the French Guards, who had been in chains ten years, and was always difficult to control. Pinel, entering his cell, announced, that if he would obey his instructions he should be chained no longer. He promised, and executed the directions of his liberator with alacrity and address. Never in the history of the human mind was exhibited a more complete revolution, and this patient, whose best years had been sacrificed in a gloomy cell, in chains and misery, soon showed himself capable of being one of the most useful in the establishment. During the horrors of the Revolution, this man repeatedly saved the life of his benefactor.

Next were released three Russian soldiers, who had been chained together for many years, but none knew when, why, or how they had been committed.

An aged priest next followed, who for twelve years had been a martyr to the most barbarous treatment. In less than a year, Pinel witnessed his entire recovery. He was discharged cured.

In the short period of a few days, this heroic and judicious Physician released more than fifty miserable maniacs: men of various rank and conditions, merchants, lawyers, priests, soldiers, laborers—thus rendering the furious tractable, and creating peace and contentment to a wonderful degree, where had for so many years reigned without interruption the most hideous tumults and outrages.

The efforts of Pinel were not limited to the Bicetre. At La Salpetriere, a ward bears his name, continually reminding the visitor of what France and the world owe to this great Philanthropist.

This rule of kindness displacing violence and abuse, soon extended to England. The Retreat at York, founded by the Society of Friends, was the first so distinguished, as in this country was their Hospital at Frankford the first to recognize and adopt humane laws. In England, the Middlesex Hospital, at Hanwell, under Sir William C. Ellis, first attained celebrity through the humane methods of treatment. His successor, Dr. Conolly, has advocated in his practice and through his published works, an enlarged liberality and kind treatment.

In Germany, the principles of Pinel, and of his distinguished co-adjutor, Esquirol, were established by the lamented Heinroth. The high rank of the Hospital at Leigburg, on the Rhine, under the direction of Jacobi, whose law and practice was 'firmness and kindness,' is every where known by all who are interested in the ameliorations I have described.

I might adduce innumerable examples witnessed in our Hospitals, and familiar to my own experience in poor-houses, jails, and private dwellings, where the exchange of kindness for severity; care and nursing for abuse and neglect, have been attended and followed with the happiest results. I do not know of a Hospital bearing the least reputation or trusted with confidence, where chains, severe restraints, or any sort of abuse of act or language are permitted.

Dr. Conolly, connected with the celebrated Institution at Hanwell, in England, for so many years, in a recent letter, published in the October number of the Westminster Review, expresses his idea of the obligations of the resident Physician in a Hospital, while wisely objecting to the very serious disadvantages of subjecting these Institutions to the control of a 'visiting, consulting Physician.'

'The resident medical officer of an Asylum is, and must always be, the most important person in it. No regulations, no caprice of committees, no appointments of other officers, lay or medical, or however designated, can alter his real position in this respect. He is constantly with the patients; their characters are intimately known to him; he watches the effects of all the means of cure to which he resorts, and his own character gives the tone to the whole house. The patients look to him as their friend, protector and guide. They know that he has authority to control them, and power to confer many indulgences upon them; he is always at hand to be appealed to, and his moral influence is complete. No arbitrary or prospective rule of treatment can be followed among the Insane, from day to day, or even from hour to hour, their varying modes require constant consideration.'

Skilful Physicians, of enlarged minds and liberal attainments in our country, spend the best strength of their best years, in conscientious and diligent exertions for the relief of patients entrusted to their care. Most of these men, profoundly impressed with their great responsibilities, devote themselves without reservation to mitigate, by their skill and their cares, the sufferings of the disabled mind. Their interests, their labors, their lives are spent within the Institutions over which they preside, with an earnestness of self-devotion, which, so far as I can discern, bears fair comparison with no other labors in any of the liberal professions.

It is knowledge of this fact which inspires me with confidence in the treatment of the Insane, in every correctly governed, rightly organized Hospital. Insanity requires a peculiar and appropriate treatment, which cannot be rendered while the patients remain at their own homes, or by even skilful Physicians in general practice. I confide in Hospital care for remedial treatment, and in no other care. One might quote volumes to show, that, however able the patient or his friends may be, to provide in private families every luxury and accommodation, it is hazarding final recovery to make even the experiment of domestic treatment.

Dr. Brigham, in one of his early reports of the New York State Hospital, remarks, that 'when sufficient time has elapsed to show clearly that the case is Insanity, unaccompanied by acute disease, then *no time should be lost,* in adopting the most approved remedial measures, among which, as has often been stated, is *removal from home,* to a place where the exciting causes of disease are no longer operative.' 'Let the friends *fully satisfy themselves that the patient will receive kind treatment,* then, forbear all untimely interference with the remedial measures adopted in the Hospitals of their choice.' An individual being Insane, *all ordinary considerations* should give place to the aim of recovery; and this should be steadily adhered to, however discouraging the circumstances, till it is entirely established that the case is beyond the reach of all available means of cure.

But, granting the patient *incurable,* hospital care and protection is hardly less necessary, whether we study the real comfort of the patient, the security and quiet of his family at home, or the safety of society. There are patients sunk into a state of low dementia, who may be considered under all ordinary circumstances harmless, but a numerous portion of those permitted at

large, are liable to sudden access of vehement excitements, in which condition, depredations, assaults, suicides, murders, and arson, are committed, and
not seldom under the most pitiable circumstances. Within the last *four* weeks
I have seen the record of *thirteen* cases of self-destruction, homicide, and
arson by the Insane, recorded under authority. I was induced to visit the ill-
conducted jail at Pittsburg, three weeks since, and amidst a throng of disorderly prisoners of all ages, colors, and conditions, found an insane woman
charged with the murder of her mother. The poor mother took care of her
as best she could, for there was no Hospital within the reach of her means
where to place the mad girl in safety, but ordinarily, I was told, she was
'looked on as harmless;' in a sudden and unexpected paroxysm she murdered
her mother in a horrible manner; an attempt, strange to say, was made to
bring the well known irresponsible creature to trial, but 'she was too crazy
for management in the court-room,' and so was remanded to prison.

Your own Penitentiary, on the outskirts of this city, has one inmate,
charged with the compound crime of murder and arson. The details are too
sickening and horrible to relate. It is a most undoubted case of moral insanity,
from which no recovery can possibly be expected.

More than two years since, a convict was sent to the Cherry Hill prison,
under a long sentence, charged with assault and battery, with intent to rob on
the highway; it was evident to every officer, that the man was insane; this
was confirmed by the Physician on his first visit, but his sentence had been
pronounced, he was legally committed, and could be discharged only by gubernatorial clemency. Some weeks went by, he grew worse, his friends traced
him, his history was ascertained; he was a respectable operative in a neighboring manufacturing district; had sickened and became insane upon the
sudden decease of a favorite son; his watcher slept, the excited patient
escaped half clad, and after running some miles, suddenly leaped into a market wagon which was entering the city; the terrified owner gave the alarm—
arrest followed, &c. Finally a pardon was obtained, he was restored to his
family, and in a few months was perfectly recovered, and returned to his
usual employments.

I might weary you with successive details; but I doubt not your own
knowledge reaches in many instances to cases corroborative of my position.
It is not safe, nor is it humane, to leave the Insane, *whether curable or incurable*, to roam at large, or abide in families, unguarded, unguided, and uncon-
trolled. For their own sake, for that of their friends, for that of the community, they should be tendered to the *kind, skilful, intelligent, judicious watch*
of Hospital protection.

Beside the propriety and general obligation which I assert of placing
patients in good Hospitals, there is the great probability of ultimate recovery
of the healthy functional action of the brain.

Dr. Bell, of the McLean Hospital at Somerville—whose name commands
a respectful confidence rarely exceeded, the skilful Physician, wise friend, judicious superintendent, the good man, he whose cares have restored so many
sufferers to their homes, and the blessed affections centering there—has stated,
in an early report, and repeated the proposition in succeeding documents,
that, '*in* an institution *fully provided with attendants*, there may be afforded
to all except a few highly excited patients, any comfort to which they have
been accustomed at home, *and all cases certainly recent*, whose origin does
not date directly or obscurely back more than one year, *recover under a
fair trial*. This being the general law, the cases to the contrary counting as the
exceptions.'

In the Hospital at Lexington, in 1845-46, of 19 *recent* cases, 16 were discharged cured.

That must indeed be an indiscreet State policy which forfeits the happiness of its citizens to fill its treasury, and even still more reprehensible, when a well defined economy suggests a contrary course. Legislators have not the leisure, as but seldom the opportunity to enter upon suitable investigations of this subject, and therefore facts are collected and placed at their disposal, giving them opportunity of pursuing an enlightened and *just* course.

Dr. Allen, the excellent and successful superintendent of the Kentucky State Hospital, at Lexington, after the experience of several years, concurs in the opinions quoted above, and urges in eloquent language, the *early* care of the Insane by qualified persons; recommending as the best economy as well as humanity, that a State can practice, prompt and entire provisional care of the Insane.

No fact indeed is better established in all Hospital annals than this; that it is cheaper (we now set aside the plea of humanity) to take charge of the Insane in a curative Institution, than to support them elsewhere for life.

In the Massachusetts State Hospital, at Worcester, then in charge of Dr. Woodward,

in 1843, twenty-five old cases had cost	$54,157.00
Average expense of old cases	2,166.20
Whole expense of twenty-five recent cases till recovered	1,461.30
Average expense of recent cases	58.45
In the Maine State Hospital at Augusta, in 1842 twelve old cases had cost	25,300.00
Average expense of old cases	2,108.33
Whole expense of twelve recent cases	426.00
Average expense of recent cases	35.50
In the Ohio State Hospital at Columbus, in 1844, thirty-five old cases had cost the counties and State	35,464.00
Average expense of old cases	1,418.56
Whole expense of twenty-five recent cases	1,608.00
Average expense of recent cases till recovered	64.32
In the Western State Hospital at Staunton, Va., twenty old cases had cost	41,633.00
Average expense of old cases	2,081.65
Whole expense of twenty recent cases	1,265.00
Average expense of twenty recent cases till recovered	63.25

It appears unnecessary to multiply examples derived from other Hospitals, whether in locations near to or remote each from the other; but reference to other records may be made, if additional evidence is needed to prove the economy both to citizens individually, to counties, or to States, of establishing curative Institutions for the Insane.

I have endeavored to show that your State Hospital is defective for the objects which should be held in view, the care and comfort of its inmates. I have tried to exhibit the unfitness of treatment in private families; a few lines will illustrate the only three remaining methods by which the insane are brought under treatment or disposed of. I mean in the State prison, in the jails, and in the poorhouses.

First, the State prison is a totally unfit place of detention for the Insane, since there, they cannot be cured, if not incurable; they are not fit subjects of discipline; they are not amenable to the rules of a Penitentiary; they are not accountable for violent speech or criminal acts. Danger to officers, danger to convicts, and injury to themselves, accompanies their imprisonment. It is not many years since the Penitentiaries of Massachusetts, of Connecticut, of New York, of Pennsylvania, &c., &c., gave terrible examples to show how easily human life could be taken by the madman, and of the madman, in their workshops, in their corridors, and in their cells.

The criminal jurisprudence of insanity has of late years engaged the careful consideration of some of our ablest jurists and most enlightened citizens. In Europe, France led the way to this wholesome reform, declaring with equal justice and perspicuity, *'that there is no crime nor fault when the party accused was in a state of insanity at the period of the act.'* 'Ill n'y a ni crime, ni delit losque le presence etait en etat de demence au temps de l'action.'

In the penal code of Louisiana, compiled by Honorable Edward Livingston, the same declaration appears, though less precisely worded. The penal code of New York lays down the same principle; and Massachusetts more recently and quite effectually protects this case, and declares in addition, (but it is since the murder of a warden in the prison,) that a convict becoming insane while serving out his term of sentence, shall, when the insanity is fully proven, be transferred to the State hospital.

If a State penitentiary is an unfit place of custody for a maniac, surely a county jail is not less so; here exist the same objections as above advanced, only in much increased force; but it is not always the supposed criminal insane man or woman who is liable to be committed to the custodial charge of the jailors: we find too often those unfortunates incarcerated in dreary cells or loathsome dungeons, and this for 'safe keeping alone!'

Upon this monstrous abuse of human rights I need not pause to comment.

Finally, in the poor-houses are frequently found the poor who are insane, as well as other afflicted cases, there most inappropriately bestowed. If violent, their phrensied ravings disturb the members of the household, and disquiet especially the sick, the infirm, and the aged, who should find in these institutions a comfortable asylum and tranquil home. If blasphemous and unruly, their presence is demoralizing, as well as dangerous to the personal security of other inmates. On the other hand, the insane are continually exposed to injudicious treatment, to careless oversight, to abuse and insult, nay more, as I have had too much opportunity to know, to gross outrages.

A very large proportion of the insane of the United States, are either in narrow circumstances or absolutely dependent. In poor-houses they rarely recover the exercise of the reasoning faculties; especially where rigorous discipline is employed. Poor-houses should have every arrangement for the comfort of the aged, the helpless, the cripple—those who are altogether dependent on the public for support, who are unable to care for themselves, or incapable of laboring for their own subsistence, but not including in this class the insane, whether tranquil or violent.

I submit the question, gentleman, whether the poor-houses of Tennessee are fit asylums for the curable or incurable insane. If any doubt through want of knowledge from personal observation, I suggest that the poor-house of Davidson county, which I visited last week, and which I am assured is 'one of the best in Tennessee'—be visited for purposes of positive information. The insane will be found there, in ill-repaired out-houses and cold, cheerless cells, though 'some' lately inmates, I was told, were 'dead, and others had run away.' In inclement weather the patient must suffer severely.

Gentlemen, the object of this memorial is accomplished if I have succeeded in showing you, that you are destitute in this State of that which it has also been my aim to convince you that you need, *a suitable curative Hos-*

pital for all classes of the insane, and attached thereto a department for such as are considered *incurable*.

'Incurable cases,' writes an experienced superintendent, 'instead of being immured in jails and county poor-houses, without employment or comfort, where they are continually losing mind and becoming worse, should be placed in good asylums, and have employment on the farm or in shops. In this way they would be rendered much happier, and their existence, if in one sense a blank to themselves, would not be useless to others.'

Look over our country at the large class of incurables, oftenest made so by neglect and ill-treatment, see these wretched beings wearing out a mere animal existence through long and dismal years; place yourselves, if you have courage, only in imagination, and for but few hours in their condition, then ask what would you, that, in such circumstances, your fellow-men should do for you? In *act*, let your reply be—'do even so unto them.'

Were I to recount but briefly, a hundredth part of the shocking scenes of sorrow, suffering, abuse, and degradation, to which I have been witness—searched out *in jails, in poor-houses, in pens, and block-houses, in dens and caves, in cages and cells, in dungeons and cellars;* men and women in chains, frantic, bruised, lacerated, and debased—your souls would grow sick at the horrid recital. Yet have all these been witnessed, and for successive years shocking facts have been patiently investigated; and why?—in order to solicit and *procure a remedy* for such heart-rending troubles; the only remedy—*the establishment of well constructed curative hospitals.* I desire not to nourish morbid sensibilities, nor to awaken transient emotions. The ills for which I ask relief, in the name of all who are suffering, are too real, too profound for transient emotions to work a remedy, or for sudden sensibilities to heal. I ask you, gentlemen of the Legislature, men of Tennessee, to think, to ponder well, to discuss fairly this subject; then you will not need that I urge other arguments to secure effective action. Fathers, husbands, brother, friends, citizens—you will require no more earnest solicitations to incite to the accomplishment of this noble work of *benevolence*, of *humanity*, and of *justice*.

Go—look in the dreary cell—behold there the phrensied, helpless maniac! —go thence, and look into the well-disposed wards of a hospital—or, rather, go to the home made happy—and behold the Insane *'clothed and in his right mind!'*

You will be prompt to admit that the sentiment of patriotism, whether in its broadest or most limited interpretation, is not to be associated with narrow views, selfish desires, or aims after mere personal aggrandizement. You are here to act from noble motives, pure and exalted principles of integrity. Upon the fidelity with which the representatives of a people discharge the duties of their grave and responsible office, depends the honor, and ultimately the prosperity of our States, and of the United Republic.

That all the affairs of government ought to be administered with regard to a just and well-directed economy, none can doubt. That a high moral courage should actuate those who control public affairs, is undeniable, if those affairs are to be administered so as to secure the *greatest good for the largest numbers*.

In promoting the establishment of beneficent institutions, the State discharges a just debt to society. The admitted *claims* of the Insane, of the Blind, and of the Deaf and Dumb, are almost universally acknowledged. And let it be remembered, this is not the exercise of *charity*, but the enactment of *justice;* and I repeat a previous affirmation, that efficient provision for the Insane in State institutions, is the truest *economy*.

Shall I, in conclusion, gentlemen, anticipating the results of your legislation upon this question, state briefly what is needed to remedy existing necessities, and what will, at the same time, be rendering justice to the humane sentiments, the obligations, the high-mindedness, and to the Federal rank of the State of Tennessee?

The *first* step must be to secure a farm of from one to two hundred acres, a considerable portion of which has been reclaimed by cultivation. It is not desirable that there should be any buildings upon that property, as they would not be available, or in a very unimportant manner. Office buildings must be adapted to a hospital, not the hospital conformed to the standing buildings. In the choice of a farm, care must be had that it be reached over good roads, that it be in such vicinity, say within a mile and a half or two miles of the city, as to afford ready daily communication with the markets, shops and post-office, and other accommodations affecting the comfort of the inmates and convenience of the officers: also it should not be too remote from the steam-boat landings, and stage-coach offices, as the transfer of patients would be more expensive and inconvenient. A primary consideration in the choice of a farm, having determined the distance from the town, is, that it furnish an ample, never-failing supply of wholesome water for all domestic, agricultural, and general uses. There must be no oversight here. If coal is to be used for fuel, you must rely on springs and wells; in this country it seems desirable to avoid the vicinity of creeks or any streams subject to overflow their banks. The Ohio Hospital is supplied by cisterns and wells, as are most others; but at the hospital in charge of Dr. Kirkbride, near Philadelphia, they have on the premises, in addition to those, a pure stream of soft water, affording unfailing supplies to the laundry and farm.

Your commissioners will be instructed to build for *use* and *comfort*, not for display and needless ornament. Every thing which can minister to the recovery and accommodations of the patients should be supplied; all modern improvements in plan, in ventilation, in building, in labor-saving arrangements should be studied, compared, selected from, and such adopted as are best suited to your *climate*, and to the entire provision for not less than two hundred, nor more than two hundred and fifty patients. Let every thing pertaining to the construction of your hospital be carefully estimated, only do not suffer wise economy to degenerate into meanness. All appropriations for State charities, or uses lavishly applied, is but robbery of the poor and needy, and brands the vice of extravagance as yet more vicious, through misapplication of the public monies. In building raise the walls of the edifice of brick rather than of stone; save some thousands of dollars by burning the brick upon your own grounds if you have at hand clay of good quality, and this, first, that the cost of transportation is saved, second it may be equally well made at much lower rates. It is the best economy to employ the best workmen in each branch of labor. It is well in all buildings, but especially is it important in the construction of hospitals, to give the basement its chief elevation above the surface; otherwise dampness occasions many evils not needful to dwell upon here. The lodging-rooms for the patients should be well ventilated by flues and transom windows, and the outer sash so constructed as to be raised or closed without the patients interference. Hot air furnaces, full evaporation of water being secured in the air-chambers, are preferable for heating these buildings throughout, to steam apparatus, being less liable to get out of order if properly constructed than the other, and less liable to injurious accidents if the conducting pipes through any flaw in their make cause explosion.

Avoid in the construction of the hospital windows, every thing giving the *appearance* of a prison. Build the wings of the hospital three stories above the basement, thus giving advantages of light, and dry air, and another sound reason for adopting that elevation in preference to an extended area, is, getting the choicest aspects for the greatest number of rooms. I might add that it is better economy, as there is much less roofing to keep in repair.

An English writer remarks that 'there is no doubt that the average atmosphere is purer and better adapted for humane breathing at a height of from fifty to one hundred feet above the surface of the earth, than it is at the surface, whether that surface be composed of clay or gravel;' if of vegetable mould it is yet more important to gain elevation for lodging rooms. The air is drier as you rise above the line of surface evaporation, and poisonous or unwholesome gases are less prevalent.

The washing establishment, especially in a climate like this, should not be in the *main building,* but removed to a considerable distance, for reasons too obvious to require to be specified.

The bath rooms as usual in all hospitals, should be adopted to the accommodation of each class of patients upon each floor of the several wings.

There is another very important point to secure, that the building should be so placed as that the sun's direct rays, at all seasons, may, during some portion of the day reach all occupied apartments. It is not needful to discuss here the soundness of this position, sustained by philosophy and plain reason as it is.

Perhaps I am tedious, but all these things are more important in securing health than is commonly estimated. And while we are seeking physical health for patients, through which perfect mental health alone can be ensured, we certainly do most wisely to adopt all those rules of hygiene which modern science and intelligence supply.

Tennessee has been called 'the Mother of States!' Shall she not, by the *promulgation of wise laws,* the liberal encouragement of *schools* of *learning,* and the substantial *support of beneficent institutions,* offer an example for the young States she has so largely and widely colonized? Embalming her memory in the hearts of her grateful children, they hereafter, reverting to their mother-land, with fond veneration and pride shall declare, how noble her example, and hasten to emulate her exalted aims!

Respectfully submitted,

D. L. DIX."

Nashville, November, 1847.

Senator John W. Richardson, representing the counties of Rutherford and Williamson, was a physician and voiced doubts as to the advisability of printing the Dix Memorial. His objections [40] were answered by Senator William P. Rowles, representing the counties of Hickman, Lawrence, Wayne, and Hardin. Fortunately, the wishes of Senator Rowles prevailed and the Memorial was printed in full in the Appendix of the *Senate Journal.*

------

[40] *Nashville Daily Union,* December 9, 1847.

Author's note. The original manuscript also of Miss Dix's Memorial is in the State Archives, Nashville.

"Remarks of Mr. Rowles, on the motion to print the memorial of Miss Dix in reference to the Lunatic Asylum.

Mr. Rowles (replying to the Senator from Rutherford, Dr. Richardson,) said: The senator from Rutherford is opposed to printing this memorial; he thinks few will read it, and those few, being mostly professional gentlemen, are already in possession of the facts comprised in the memorial, 'if they have kept up with the advance of their profession.' Mr. Speaker, the clearness and courtesy with which the senator from Rutherford delivers his sentiments on this floor, is sure to win the respect, if not the assent, of his opponents. He is one of those who

> With temper calm and mild,
>   And words of soften'd tone,
> He seeks to sink my doubtful cause
> And recommend his own.

From a position taken by that gentleman, especially on this subject, I dissent with sincere reluctance. He is one of the committee on the Lunatic Asylum, and I well know will favor all feasible means to improve its condition. But he has not read this memoir, and cannot but guess its contents to be, as he supposes, nothing more than we have in our medical and law books. This is a great mistake, sir: those books cannot possibly contain a relation of observations made by Miss Dix, on a late tour over a large part of several states. The books contain no appeal in behalf of the ten thousand insane of Tennessee to this General Assembly. But the memoir does contain such an appeal. It comes from the heart of one whose standing in society would enable her to confine her means and mind to the promotion of her own individual welfare. But she has chosen, nobly chosen, to traverse the length and breadth of this broad land at her own expense. Alone and unprotected by any save the hand of Him who, I doubt not, has prompted her to the labor, she has for years devoted her time to the search of human misery in dens, pens, caves, prisons, hospitals, and wherever found, and bringing the wants of the wretches to the notice and sympathy of the wise and good, who have it in their power to have pity on those who have none to care for them. This memoir contains information that ought to go to the people of this State. It is the voice of ten thousand mindless men who, amid their chains, darkness, filth and woe, clank their shackles in our ears and call, in the name of Him who made men, to have pity on the down-trodden, and raise them up. I will not believe that any senator on this floor, will refuse his aid to restore those bereft of reason—to restore to its soundness the

> Eternal spirit of the chainless mind:
> That wonderful part of our nature
> Which knows by retrospect through time to range,
> And *forward*, time's great secret to survey.

This memoir contains a survey of the subject and will enable those who read it to engage in the work all admit should be done, and all desire to see done understandingly. By knowing the extent of the labor, the means by which others have succeeded, we can measure our own means and proceed in the light of experience. Then, sir, no contracted, pent up, premises shall mark the measure of our taste and liberality, but a noble structure, with ample space and means suited to the purpose, will arise, such an institution as shall be an honor to the state and a blessing to the unfortunate. I beg to be indulged in the remark that I have been so far behind the books that until I looked into this picture I did not suppose it possible that in this pleasant land, the proud and happy home of freemen, there was any part of our people so miserably abject, so ill provided and cared for, as the insane. They have claims on our sympathy. But they have none on this floor to speak for them. In their present condition, they are lost to themselves, to society and the country. It seems to me a solemn duty to come to their rescue. What has been done is wholly inadequate. In devising further methods for their relief and restoration, I am persuaded this memoir will be of essential service by diffusing correct information among the people and giving a right impulse to popular action on the subject. I hope, therefore, the recommendation of the Committee to print will be concurred in, and the memoir be printed."

On the last day of the legislative session, save one, the final touches were placed upon Senate Bill No. 131 providing for the establishment of a Hospital for the Insane, when the Senate concurred in sundry amendments that had been added by the House of Representatives.[41] In addition, a vote of thanks and a highly complimentary resolution were tendered to Miss Dix. Now that the bill had been enacted into a law, what were the provisions of that law?

First of all, the law [42] had real substance in it. Makeshifts and temporary expedients were eliminated and real basic facts were recognized and incorporated into the statute. The Governor was authorized to appoint seven Commissioners who were directed

"... to superintend the construction of said Asylum, and to select and purchase a tract of land at a fair price, embracing not less than one hundred acres, capable of cultivation..." [43]

The law furthermore directed the Commissioners to construct the building

"in the most approved manner, after the most approved recent and accepted plans embracing all improvements and accommodations for institutions of this description..."

Funds for the building were provided by setting up forty thousand dollars to be raised by increasing the tax upon all taxable property for a period of three years. A further provision of the law was that the Governor should nominate and the Senate confirm nine trustees who constituted the governing board, with power to select the Superintendent of the Hospital for a term of eight years. This procedure, had it been followed, would have put an end to legislative logrolling in the selection of a physician as superintendent of the Hospital! Another salutary provision was that the Trustees would elect and fix the compensation of all officers and employees of the institution.

A site about six miles from Nashville on the Murfreesboro pike was selected. Plans for the institution were modeled in the main after those of the then famous Butler Asylum at Providence, Rhode Island. This

---

[41] *Senate Journal*, 1847, 650–651.
[42] *Acts of Tennessee*, 1847, Chapter 205.
[43] *Ibid.*

marked the beginning of the Central State Hospital, an institution now occupying a charming site of more than 800 acres with commodious buildings and employing the latest scientific methods of care and treatment for the mentally ill.

Governor Brown's recommendations concerning the Bank of Tennessee received scant consideration by the Legislature. There was enacted no basic reorganization as suggested in the Governor's Message. The branch banks at Athens, Columbia, and Clarksville were ordered to be continued, but with the curious proviso that "the branches are not restored at the present session of the Legislature." [44] In addition, Governor Brown pointed out that

". . . Posterity has an inheritance in this Bank, involving in a good degree the fate of our systems of Common Schools and Internal Improvements. . . . "

All along, the Legislature at its various sessions had exhibited more concern about "safeguarding" the meager and wholly inadequate School Fund than in passing any measures that would increase significantly the revenue for the promotion of public education. In accord with that type of philosophy, a law [45] was enacted that made the Directors of the Bank of Tennessee the Board of Commissioners of Common Schools.

In one respect, Governor Neill S. Brown had at his finger tips more specific information regarding the status of education in Tennessee than was true of any of his predecessors in the Executive Department of State Government with the exception of Governor Aaron V. Brown. That information was embodied in a memorial drafted at a Common School Convention which met in Knoxville, April 19, 1847. In his final communication to the Legislature, under date of October 6, 1845, Governor Aaron V. Brown incorporated a number of the recommendations contained in the above memorial. Governor Neill S. Brown also availed himself of the facts set forth in the convention of the schoolmasters. That Memorial [46] represented the most comprehensive view of education in Tennessee ever presented up to that time, and deserves to be preserved for posterity:

"*To the Honorable, the Senate and House of Representatives of the State of Tennessee in General Assembly convened.*

The undersigned, your memorialists, would humbly represent to your honorable body that, at a common school convention, composed of delegates from the counties of Greene, Cocke, Hawkins, Claiborne, Jefferson, Blount, Knox, Roane, Marion and Anderson, which convened in Knoxville on the 19th day of April, 1847, they were appointed a committee to memorialize your honorable body upon the subjects embraced in the proceedings of said convention. In discharging the duty assigned them, your memorialists would respectfully call the attention of your honorable body to the following resolutions adopted by the convention:

---

[44] *Ibid.*
[45] *Ibid.*, Chapter 175.
[46] *Senate Journal,* 1847, Appendix, 388–395.

I. *Resolved by this Convention,* That it be recommended to the Legislature at its next session, to appoint a superintendent of public instruction for the State.

II. *Resolved,* That the duties of said superintendent, shall be,

1. To preside over a department called the department of public instruction.

2. To control, regulate and give life and efficiency to all the parts of the common school system.

3. To distribute the laws, instructions, decisions, forms, &c., through the agency of the board of education in the several counties.

4. To decide all controversies under any of the laws relating to common schools.

5. To keep up a constant correspondence with the several chairmen of the board of education.

6. To exercise a liberal discretionary power on equitable principles, in all cases of inadvertent, unintentional, or accidental omissions to comply with the strict requisitions of the law.

7. To report annually through the medium of ...., the condition, prospects, resources, and capabilities of the common schools, and such suggestions for the improvement of the system as may occur to him, and vigilantly to watch over, encourage, sustain and expand to its utmost practicable limit, the vast system of common school education throughout the State.

8. And lastly, to visit personally, all the counties in the State at least once a year, and as often as practicable, to lecture on the educational interests of the State.

III. *Resolved,* That this convention recommend to the next legislature, to provide for the appointment of a board of education for each county, to be composed of three gentlemen of known literary acquirement, whose duty it shall be to examine applicants for the office of teacher in our common schools, and that no teacher shall be employed by the district trustees without a certificate of recommendation from said board, and that said board shall have power to recall, on just grounds, such certificate; that it shall moreover be the duty of the chairmen of said boards to make and transmit to the superintendent, at certain prescribed times, reports stating:—

1. The whole number of school districts and neighborhoods separately set off within their counties.

2. The district or districts from which reports by trustees have been made to them or their immediate predecessors in office.

3. The length of time a school shall have been kept in each of said districts or parts of districts, distinguishing what portion of time the school shall have been kept by qualified teachers.

4. The number of children taught in each, and the number of children over the age of six and under twenty-one, residing in each.

IV. *Resolved,* That in the opinion of this convention, these boards of education should be chosen by the county courts of each county.

V. *Resolved,* That this convention recommend to the Legislature, the publication of a monthly State Journal, devoted exclusively to the cause of education throughout the State.

VI. *Resolved,* That this convention recommend to the Legislature at its next session, as a plan for increasing the common school fund, that they require each county to raise annually a sum equal to the amount of the present school fund appropriated to the respective counties, to be assessed and collected in the same manner as the State and county taxes are assessed and collected.

VII. *Resolved,* That this convention recommend to the Legislature, to provide for the election of one trustee for each school district in the place of the school commissioners under the present law, whose duty shall simply be to take charge of the house and furniture belonging to the district school, and to provide such articles as fuel, &c., that may be necessary for the comfort of the school; to employ such teacher or teachers as he may think will give satisfaction to the community: Provided, in all cases, that such teacher or teachers has been examined, or will stand an examination satisfactorily before the board of education for that county; and that this trustee shall make a report once annually to the county board upon the state of education in this district.

Your memorialists, after giving the resolutions, deem it entirely useless to invite your calm, serious consideration of the subjects upon which your action is invited, believing that you will properly appreciate the importance of extending to the rising generation an education that will fit them for the several stations they are destined to occupy in this Republic, and that you will be found ready and willing, in the capacity of Legislators, as well as private citizens, to co-operate in this great and important work. Your memorialists cannot believe that you will refuse your assent and cordial support to any measure or measures, the object of which is to perfect that system by which the rising generation is to be instructed in the elementary principles of education, and to make it more thorough and extensive in its operations, and they, therefore, approach you in the fullest confidence, not only in the justice and importance of the cause for which they plead, but in the belief of your willingness to hear and act as becometh men charged with guarding and advancing the interests of a great and growing State.

The first resolution recommends the appointment by the Legislature of a superintendent of public instruction, whose duties are prescribed in the second resolution. The duties of this officer make it a responsible station, and it will require to be filled by a man of no ordinary talents. He must be an able, intelligent, zealous and faithful officer, who will properly appreciate the importance and responsibility of his trust, and who will make it his business to traverse each county, inspect the schools, recommend improvement where his experience would suggest as necessary, address the people, and arouse them to action. Such an officer would impart great energy to the system. Much of the effective operations of any system of common schools, however perfect, depends upon the people, and it will be the duty of the superintendent to arouse them upon the subject of education, and to inspire in them a zeal worthy themselves and the cause, and to see to it that those whom the system is designed to benefit, are the recipients of its blessings. In other States, the superintendent of public instruction is considered of invaluable service in carrying out the provisions of the common school law, and in making the system what the wants of those interested demand. The appointment of a superintendent of public instruction cannot be too strongly urged upon your attention. Without supervision, active, zealous, and unremitting, as we have abundant evidence both in our own and other States, any system will gradually decline, and finally cease to be of service. Your memorialists would, therefore, respectfully, but earnestly recommend to your consideration whether such an officer would not greatly facilitate the objects of common schools.

The third resolution recommends the appointment of a board of education for each county. The duties of this board are important, and will exert a healthful and invigorating influence upon the system. Upon them will devolve the duty of examining, as to the literary and moral qualifications, those who seek employment in the capacity of teachers, and it will be their duty to recommend to the people none except such as are qualified for that responsible station. It is essentially necessary to have good teachers—men of undoubted moral character, and of literary acquirements amply capacitating them for the responsible duties they assume in taking charge of the school in which the youthful mind is to receive that impress which will be its shape in age. To the want of good teachers, in a great degree, may be attributed the failure of those children who are sent to school to acquire a knowledge of even the elements of an education. It cannot be expected that incompetent teachers can impart instruction to youth, and yet it is too often the case that such men are employed in this vocation, and why? Because they will teach cheap, and interested individuals are ready to foist them upon the people. It, therefore, becomes the duty of the State, contributing as she does of her money to the education of her youth, to adopt such measures as will secure competent teachers. One good teacher is worth a score of such as are 'fit for nothing else and willing to teach cheap,' for his qualifications enable him to impart instructions to children with greater facility. Put a worthless, ignorant man to preside in a school, and you pay him nearly as much as if his qualifications were of the best order, while your children derive little or no benefit from his *attempt* to instruct them. Of the great importance of selecting good teachers and even of preparing them at the expense of the State, for that responsible office, you cannot fail to be satisfied that no laborious examination, no pecuniary consideration, should outweigh it. The matter of preparing teachers expressly for the work in other States, has proved highly beneficial, and it is earnestly recommended to the consideration of your honorable body, whether such a course should not be adopted among us. To secure such instructors, trained among us, accustomed to our people and institutions, and sympathizing with those whose children they are to instruct and train for future usefulness, no effort, no pecuniary expense should be spared. The judicious selection of teachers, however, will entirely depend upon the board of education, and those, who compose this board, should be selected for their virtues and intelligence, and their devotion to the cause of education. Give us good teachers, and a higher and more perfect grade of education will be introduced into our common schools, and parents will imbibe greater confidence in them, and more cheerfully and promptly entrust their children to be educated in these schools. It is, therefore, earnestly but respectfully recommended to your honorable body to give to this resolution that consideration its importance demands.

The fourth resolution recommends that the board of education be appointed by the county court, which is thought to be very judicious, and accordingly recommended by your memorialists.

The fifth resolution recommends the publication by the State, of a Monthly Periodical devoted to the cause of Education. Such a publication properly conducted, would be an invaluable auxiliary, and is very much needed in this State, inasmuch as the papers published in the State do not devote much of their space to this important subject. But whether it would not be best to leave it to private enterprise, with some encouragement from the State, is for your honorable body to decide.

The sixth resolution recommends a plan for increasing the common school fund. This fund ought to be increased, and largely, too, and it will devolve upon your honorable body to devise some measure whereby this desirable end may be accomplished. If the plan suggested by the convention be the better one, adopt it; if not, let us have that which in the judgment of your honorable body, will the more effectually meet the wants of the people in this matter. In all countries where common schools have been successfully established, the principle of taxation has been adopted, and to that is to be attributed much of the efficiency of such schools. The experience of several of our States sustains this view of the case. In those where the common school system has accomplished the most good, the fund set apart for that purpose has been largely increased by taxes; while, on the contrary, in those where the aid of the government alone was depended upon, the common school system has accomplished comparatively little in educating the mass of the youth. The principle laid down by the convention in this resolution is that common schools being a common benefit, should constitute a common burden. It is for your honorable body to decide whether this be practicable. If not, it will be your duty—a duty you owe to your constituents—to increase the common school fund by some means, so as to place the operations of the system within the reach of *all*—the poor as well as the rich. The system was in its inception designed to benefit all, but the fund set apart for that purpose in our State is entirely too small to meet the wants of the people. There are large numbers in every portion of the State who are almost entirely dependent upon the provision made by the State for the education they receive, and under the present operations of the system, this must of course be limited. The experience of those States in which the common school system, is most efficient, goes to establish the fact that these schools ought to be accessible to every white child of proper age. This is the desirable end in our State, to the accomplishment of which your memorialists would earnestly invite your attention, in the fullest confidence that you will think and *act* as becometh men guided by wisdom and the most exalted patriotism.

The seventh resolution recommends the appointment of one trustee for each school district, in the place of the commissioners under the present law. In the event the other changes in the system, suggested by the convention, be adopted, this one will be desirable for several reasons.

Two of the other resolutions subsequently adopted by the convention, are also embraced in the duty assigned your memorialists. They are as follows:

Resolved, That this convention recommend to the Legislature the propriety of empowering the county courts so to district the several counties in the State, according to the scholastic population, as to embrace only one school house.

Resolved, That it be recommended to the next Legislature to pass a law providing that all fines collected for failure to discharge military duty, be added to the common school fund for the county where such fines are collected.

The recommendation in the first of these resolutions is worthy the consideration of your honorable body. One school house is enough in each district, and by this you will be the more apt to have a school in each neighborhood and within the reach of every child, and this is a consideration of no slight importance in this great matter.

The recommendation in the second is very good, and your memorialists sincerely hope it will meet the approbation of your honorable body.

In submitting to your honorable body the foregoing resolutions, and asking your favorable action thereupon, your memorialists cannot refrain from indulging in a few reflections upon the state of education in Tennessee.

At no period, perhaps, in the existence of our State, and by no event was the pride of our people, of all parties, denominations and classes, more deeply wounded than when the returns of the census of 1840 were promulgated. The revelations of that census relative to the ignorance of a large portion of our people, from which every one who feels an interest in the prosperity and elevation of our State, or is possessed of one spark of generous pride, must recoil with shame and dismay. That census exposed our ignorance in strong and humiliating contrast with the superior intelligence of other of our sister States, many of which have been admitted into our union since our own. Where is the Tennessean whose heart is not pained at the comparison? The sons over twenty years of age who could neither read nor write, was heralded over this broad union, and made the subject of sneering remark in almost every newspaper in the country. Our State stood within *one* of the bottom of the list in point of universal intelligence—the number of the ignorant in North Carolina being a fraction greater, according to population, than in Tennessee. It is with a view of calling the attention of your honorable body and of the people of the State at large, to these facts that we now repeat them, hoping thereby to awaken in both legislators and citizens, an interest upon the subject of education that will not rest until it has accomplished what the character and position of the State imperiously demand—the education of her entire white population. That is a noble cause which imparts to the people a sufficiency of knowledge to enable them to discharge their duties to their country in the capacity of private citizens, with credit to themselves and honor to their State; and surely a recurrence to the educated condition in which the census of 1840 presented Tennessee, will have the desired effect of uniting all in giving life and activity to a cause upon which depends in so pre-eminent a degree the destiny not only of our own State, but of the whole union—the 'paragon republic of the nineteenth century.'

According to the last census, the total number of white persons in this State in 1840, was 640,797; of this number 249,008 were over twenty years of age. According to the same document, there were in this State, in the same year, 58,531 white persons over twenty years of age who could neither read or write, being one in every *eleven* of the entire white population, and one in *four and one fourth* of those above twenty years of age. This is truly a gloomy picture of the intelligence of a State occupying the position that Tennessee does in point of population and wealth. Only think of it, that nearly one-fourth of the white population of our State above twenty years of age, are unable to read or write! And why is it that Tennessee is thus shrouded in ignorance? Has she no capital, or resources of wealth, no facilities for the education of her people? These surely are not the causes.—We have the wealth and we have the facilities, and it needs only the proper application of both to secure a desirable result. What a waste, what a deadly waste of uncultivated intellect there is in this State. What a loss to the present and to future ages!—Think of this, ye legislators of Tennessee, and blush for the pride of your State! How long shall we bear this reproach? It appeals to your pride, your State pride, with an eloquence to which words can add no force, to arrest the dark tide in its onward progress, and roll back its turbid, sweeping billows, and leave the pure, unsullied stream of intelligence to roll on in moral grandeur and beauty. And shall the appeal go unheeded? No—spurn the very thought. Gather up, we pray you, all your energies and bring all your wisdom and influence to bear upon this important subject, and devise some means whereby all within the broad limits of our State shall receive the inestimable benefits of education —aye, make Tennessee a model, that she may say to other States of the Union —'FOLLOW MY EXAMPLE.'

It is not at all improbable that 25,000 of those who cannot read and write, in this State, are legal voters—more than *one-fifth* of the voting population!

What a field for political fraud and corruption! According to our constitution, the votes of these unlettered men will, in any election, have as great a weight as an equal number of the most intelligent citizens of which our State can boast. How important then that all should be well informed. This is a consideration of no ordinary importance in a State where the voice of the majority is and ought to be the supreme law. But there are other and weighty considerations which urge upon your honorable body the importance of devising means for the education of all, and we can not believe you will permit them to pass unheeded.

We lay down as an axiom that the blessings of a sound and useful education cannot be too widely diffused among the people of our State. In our youth, those upon whom we desire to see the benefits of education bestowed with no sort of stint, are centred the hopes and destiny of our State, since upon them will devolve, in the course of a few years at farthest, the duty of guarding her sacred rights and maintaining her honor inviolate, and their education we deem worthy any cost. Our common schools stand pre-eminent among the agents to be employed in giving our youth that sort of an education which will enable them to discharge their respective duties to themselves and to their county with honor to both. They constitute the mighty engine which is to bear our country onward and upward in her career of glory, and they are to mould the moral and intellectual energies of the people. Upon no branch of our whole system of instruction depends so much as upon our common schools, and yet they are, in comparison with their importance, the least effective, the most wretchedly managed. Every effort should, therefore, be made to perfect this system, that its operations may be more *effective* and reach *all*. Place it within the reach of every one to furnish himself with at least elementary education, and if he does not properly exercise it, let all the blame rest upon his own shoulders, not upon the State. And your memorialists will, as in duty bound, ever pray, &c.

> Samuel B. Boyd,
> Wm. G. Swan,
> John Miller M'Kee."

Although his earnest pleadings in behalf of education came to naught, insofar as remedial legislation was concerned, yet Governor Neill S. Brown in his legislative communication did not only the usual thing, but he did also a very unusual thing. Like all his predecessors, from the days of Governor John Sevier, Governor Brown pursued the customary procedure of eulogizing the importance of education and deploring the glaring deficiencies of the system. So far, that was "old stuff." At this juncture, however, he did a very unusual thing—he recommended an increase in the Common School Fund, to at least double the then annual appropriation of $100,000, and he recommended that the increase be made by TAXATION! Here was the first instance of a Tennessee Governor recommending *direct taxation* for the support of a public educational program. One or two previous Governors had hinted vaguely about taxation, but had hastily refrained from making any affirmative commitment on the matter. Despite the urgency with which Governor Brown pleaded in behalf of bettering educational facilities, the Legislature turned a leaden ear to his suggestions, even declining to enact any law relative to partial maintenance of the school system through local taxation.

It can be only conjectural as to what caused the change in Governor Neill S. Brown, between 1847 and 1849, concerning his requests for the improvement of the educational system. His 1847 Message was strongly worded regarding the necessity of doing something worthwhile for public education, but his "educational fever" had cooled off by 1849 when, in his parting Message to the Legislature, he reversed his former position by stating that

" . . . I do not believe a system of direct taxes expedient or proper." [47]

Was the change of heart due to the Legislature of 1847 refusing to follow his recommendations? Or was the shifting in position due to his defeat for re-election to the governorship in 1849? Or was the right-about-face attitude due to a combination of the above two factors, or to other causes not apparent at that or this time? The query must, perhaps, remain unanswered.

With reference to internal improvements, Governor Brown specified certain railroads and rivers which, if put into practical operation, would prove beneficial to trade and commerce. Eight laws, dealing with incorporation or revising previous incorporations of railroads, were enacted, the most important one being the Nashville and Chattanooga Railroad.[48] Practically nothing of importance was done in regard to Governor Brown's suggestion that obstructions in such important rivers as the French Broad, Holston, and Tennessee should be removed, thereby opening up these river channels for better water transportation facilities. On the contrary, the Legislature contented itself with enacting minor laws permitting the building of draw bridges over such small streams as the Hatchee and Caney Fork, and making it lawful to build fish traps in such streams as the Pigeon and Little.[49]

If number had any real significance, the "turnpike boys" were in tall clover. Fifty-four laws were passed dealing with that number of turnpikes. As a rule, the law provided for incorporation, amending a previous charter, or granting an extension of time in which to complete the turnpike. Inasmuch as the State in previous years had taken stock in numerous turnpike enterprises, the redemption of such bonds depended in part upon the revenues taken in by the several turnpikes. As a control measure over this sort of business, a law was enacted setting up the toll to be charged for various sorts of conveyances. For example, a loaded wagon passing over a Macadamized turnpike in which the State was a stockholder was required to pay as follows:

"At each toll gate, for all loaded wagons drawn by three horses, mules, or

<hr/>

[47] *House Journal*, 1849, 45.
[48] *Acts of Tennessee*, 1847, Chapters 14, 70, 118, 120, 150, 169, 187, 195.
[49] *Ibid.*, Chapters 11, 153, 208.

oxen, twenty cents; and when unloaded they shall collect (10) ten cents; for all loaded wagons drawn by four horses, mules, or oxen, they shall collect at each gate twenty-five cents, and when unloaded they shall collect ten cents; for all loaded wagons drawn by more than four horses, mules, or oxen, they shall collect five cents for each additional horse, mule, or oxen attached to and drawing said wagons; and they shall collect for all unloaded wagons, drawn by more than four horses, mules, or oxen, fifteen cents at each gate." [50]

Of the fifty-four turnpikes, only five can be identified with West Tennessee. Abundance of rock in large areas of both Middle and East Tennessee facilitated the building of turnpikes. West Tennessee had no such material within its boundaries. Aware of that fact, Governor Brown in his Message rather naively suggested that the denizens of that realm might do well to consider the use of charcoal as a substitute for rock and gravel!

Governor Brown concluded his Message to the Legislature with an expression of his views regarding the War with Mexico which was still raging at the time. Since the Mexican War had been the chief issue in the gubernatorial campaign in which he had defeated Governor Aaron V. Brown, doubtless Governor Neill S. Brown thought that he might be accused of "dodging" had he not referred to the conflict in his major communication to the General Assembly. He faced the issue squarely, and displayed neither hesitation nor fear in expressing his convictions on the topic. Neither comment nor interpretation seems to be indicated, for no ambiguity lurked in his crystal-clear enunciations. It was his belief that "This war might, could, and ought to have been avoided ..... that this war is a national blunder." Being in the war, however, Governor Brown declared that "the public right arm should be made bare, and the sword remain unsheathed until peace is extorted."

Shortly after the War with Mexico had begun, President James K. Polk requested $2,000,000 from Congress with which to negotiate terms of peace, the general understanding being that territory would be acquired from Mexico. A bill to appropriate that sum was introduced in the Lower House of Congress, but David Wilmot of Pennsylvania sought to tack on an amendment that proposed to eliminate slavery from any portion of territory thus acquired. Debates over the Proviso sprang up throughout the Nation, and sectional animosity was greatly increased. Within a week after the convening of the 1847 Tennessee Legislature, Senator Isham G. Harris from the counties of Henry, Weakley, and Obion proposed the following Resolution,[51] to-wit:

"*Whereas*, a series of aggressive movements, originating with the repeal of the 21st rule, and terminating of late in one of a more systematic, mature, and practical form, as evidenced by the twice repeated passage through the House of Representatives of the Congress of the United States, of what is

---

[50] *Ibid.*, Chapter 194.
[51] *Senate Journal*, 1847, 56–57.

termed the 'Wilmot Proviso,' and the combined affiliated resolutions in approbation of the same, by ten of the Sovereign States of this Confederacy, discloses the alarming and startling fact, that the Abolition party, having completed their work of organization, have at last agreed upon a basis which, combining and arraying in its support all the various elements of hostility to slavery, is calculated to give to their operations in future, a unity of purpose and energy of action, which, if not opposed in a spirit of prompt and wise resolve, and a corresponding unanimity of opinion and union of effort, must inevitably produce consequences the most fearful to contemplate; and, whereas, in the opinion of this General Assembly, it is believed to be a duty which they owe to the people of the State which they represent, not only to warn them of the danger which, in the present case, so imminently presses, but to devise, adopt, and announce in their name and by their authority, such measures as, by firmly and fearlessly vindicating the guarantees of the constitution, will be most efficacious in averting it.

Resolved, therefore, by the General Assembly of the State of Tennessee, That the four following resolutions, as recently adopted by the Legislature of the State of Virginia, be, and they are hereby declared to contain the views and opinions entertained by this General Assembly.

Resolved, That the Government of the United States has no control, directly or indirectly, mediately or immediately, over the institution of slavery, and that in taking any such control, it transcends the limits of its legitimate functions, by destroying the internal organization of the sovereignties which formed it.

Resolved, That under no circumstances will this body recognise, as binding, any enactment of the Federal Government which has for its object the prohibition of slavery in any territory to be acquired, either by conquest or treaty, south of the line of the Missouri compromise; holding it to be the natural and independent right of each citizen of each and every State of the Confederacy, to reside with his property, of whatever description, in any territory which may be acquired by the arms of the United States, or yielded by treaty with any foreign power.

Resolved, That this Assembly holds it to be the duty of every man, in every section of this Confederacy, if the Union is dear to him, to oppose the passage of any law, for whatever purpose, by which territory to be acquired may be subject to such a restriction.

Resolved, That the passage of the Wilmot Proviso by the House of Representatives of the United States, makes it the duty of every slave-holding State, and the citizens thereof, as they value their dearest privileges—their sovereignty—their independence, and their rights of property, to take firm, united and concerted action in this emergency.

Resolved, further, as the sense of this General Assembly, That no candidate for the Presidency of the United States ought to be supported, who does not, unconditionally, clearly, and unequivocally, declare his opposition to the principles and provisions of the Wilmot Proviso."

After much delay, the Legislature on January 20, 1848, took up the Harris Resolution which was toned down somewhat by a proposed amendment by Whig Senator John D. Richardson of Rutherford County. Richardson's proposal was suffered "to lie on the table" for a week, whereupon the original Harris Resolution, subjected to a committee revision, was boiled down to the following three propositions,[52] namely:

"*Resolved*, That it is inexpedient for this Legislature to define the duties of the General Government, because those duties are already defined by the Constitution of the United States.
Ayes, 14; Noes, 11.
Resolved, That it is impolitic for the Legislature to declare that it will not recognise the acts of the General Government, because this would be nullification in advance.
Ayes, 15; Noes, 10.
Resolved, That this Legislature is opposed to the 'Wilmot Proviso' in every shape and form; they believe that its adoption by the Congress of the United States would produce great discord in our Union, and that no possible good would ever grow out of it.
Ayes, 25."

According to the official record, the Resolution was then engrossed, but no mention was made to the effect that the Resolution was transmitted to the House of Representatives.[53] At any rate, the Resolution did not appear in the 1847 *Acts of Tennessee*, thus indicating that affirmative action was never taken by the House of Representatives.

Seven communications from Governor Neill S. Brown to the 1847 Legislature are omitted in this treatise, inasmuch as they dealt with extremely minor details involving nominations for Bank Directors, Penitentiary Inspectors, notification of the resignation of a Judge, and a letter from General Zachary Taylor acknowledging an invitation to visit Nashville. Should anybody desire to read those brief messages, they can be found by consulting the indicated references.[54] Just two days before the Legislature adjourned, however, Governor Brown rushed the following Message* to the Legislature:

"EXECUTIVE DEPARTMENT,
Nashville, Feb. 5, 1848.

GENTLEMEN OF THE SENATE AND
    HOUSE OF REPRESENTATIVES:

I trust I will be pardoned even at this late hour, for intruding upon your consideration a few suggestions connected with the public interests. There is much reason to fear that the State will be unable to meet all its liabilities for the ensuing two years without additional resources. Frankness compels me to state, that, in my

---

[52] *Ibid.*, 561.
[53] *Ibid.*, 561.
[54] *Senate Journal*, 1847, 181, 254, 392, 464, 509, 631, 649.
  * *Senate Journal*, 1847, 652–653.
    House Journal, 1847, 1039–1040.

opinion, the failure to increase the revenue at the present session, will make it my duty to convene a called session before the period of your next regular meeting, such an alternative is to be deprecated, and it seems to me, might now be avoided, with a great saving to the State.

Let it be borne in mind, that the present state of commerce and trade is very unpropitious to the operations of the Bank of Tennessee, and upon the success of that institution, depend your homes and mine, for meeting the engagements of the State. I have no idea that the profits of that Bank can equal for the ensuing two years, what they have been for the corresponding period past. It is impossible, with the continual depression in the prices of the great staples of the country, and if this turns out to be so, it requires no great forecast to see the condition in which it would place the credit of the State. The ability of the State to meet the accrueing interest on her bonds, will be diminishable in the proportion of the failure of profits from the Bank. To provide then against all contingencies seems to me, to be dictated by good faith, and by economy itself. The course is due to the character of the bonds that have been and will be issued and to the vigorous prosecution of the two great enterprises to which the faith of the State has been pledged at the present session, that no ground may exist for even a suspicion. To insure all that is desirable will, in my judgment, require but little beyond a certain and full valuation of taxable property; a burden which can oppress no one, but the benefits of which may, in the end be of the highest importance. These suggestions are submitted with the profoundest deference, and I confess with some reluctance, for I appreciate to the fullest extent, your feelings, with your eyes turned towards your homes and families. But from a due sense of duty, allow me earnestly to recommend, that you will not adjourn without providing, beyond all doubt, the ways and means, to meet all the public engagements.

Beyond this subject I have nothing further to communicate to your honorable body. And beg leave to tender you my congratulations upon the approaching termination of your arduous labors, with my best wishes for the welfare and happiness of each individual member.

N. S. Brown."

On February 5, a Joint Committee called upon Governor Brown to inform him that the Legislature was on the point of adjourning. Whig Senator John W. Richardson of Rutherford County, a member of the committee, brought back with him the above Message which was submitted to the Senate. The only official action of the Senate was to receive the Message

"... Which was read; and, on motion of Mr. Richardson, *Ordered,* That it be transmitted to the House of Representatives." [55]

The "Macedonian call" had come too late! Already the Legislature had increased taxes by levying an additional one and one-half mills on each one hundred dollars of taxable property, and doubtless that was the basic reason for giving the Governor's eleventh-hour request for more revenue short shrift.

The Twenty-Seventh General Assembly had within its ranks some men of outstanding ability. Among the Senators were the brilliant Landon C. Haynes, one of the State's most eloquent orators and later a Senator in the Congress of the Confederate States; Isham G. Harris, later Governor of Tennessee during the War Between the States, and for twenty years United States Senator and regarded as an able parliamentarian; and Return Jonathan Meigs, one of the most scholarly men and able jurists within the confines of the State. In the House of Representatives were John Bell, a statesman of real ability who served with distinction in such capacities as Congressman, United States Senator, Secretary of War, and candidate for the Presidency of the United States; and John M. Bright, a brilliant orator who served five successive terms in Congress. But Governor Brown's recommendations, dealing with the two most important topics of the times—Education and Internal Improvements—received scant attention and no basic remedial legislation. Likewise, the law enacted with reference to the Bank of Tennessee was inconsequential. Only two of the Governor's recommendations really bore any fruit—enlargement of facilities for the mentally ill, and an increase in taxes for improved operational costs of State activities.

Out of a veritable medley of miscellaneous legislation, characteristic of practically all legislative sessions, one finds a mixture of good, bad, and indifferent laws. Right here and now, the writer of this treatise proposes to pay tribute to Senator William R. Rowles who, on October 28, 1847, introduced the following Resolution: [56]

"*Resolved by the General Assembly of the State of Tennessee,* That the Clerk of each House shall prepare and furnish to the public Printers, an index to their respective Journals, which index shall contain an alphabetical list of the proceedings, had on each bill, motion, resolution, report, or other pro-

---

[55] *Senate Journal,* 1847, 653.
[56] *Ibid.,* 146.

ceedings, acted on with reference to the pages of the Journals respectively, on which such action from day to day, and from time to time, is printed, so that the progress of any measure may be traced, in the Journals, from its inception, to final disposition thereof."

Despite the violence to punctuation, grammatical and rhetorical syntax, every person doing historical research in the Tennessee legislative Journals will and must feel deeply indebted to Senator Rowles for the inestimable service which his Resolution initiated. On January 15, 1848, Senator F. S. Heiskell submitted a Resolution [57] upon the same subject, to-wit:

"*Resolved*, That the Clerk prepare an index, in alphabetical order, to the Journal of the Senate, on the plan of the index to the journals of Congress, to accompany the journal of the present session."

Mr. Heiskell did not go to sleep at the switch, for on the day preceding final adjournment, he moved successfully to amend the general bill covering the expenses of the legislative session

". . . so as to allow the clerk of the Senate $50—for preparing an index to Senate's journal." [58]

This is the story of how, for the first time in the history of Tennessee, the first *indexed* legislative Journal came into being. Not one of the seventy-five members of the House of Representatives displayed any similar interest in having an index prepared for the *House Journal*, with the result that that official document, like every preceding Tennessee legislative journal, both Senate and House, contains neither an index nor table of contents. If you want to find some specific item in the Legislative Journals of Tennessee, 1796 to 1847, just start thumbing the pages and scanning the paragraphs! That's the only way it can be done! !

Two weeks after the convening of the 1847 Legislature, an Act [59] was passed on October 18 incorporating the New Orleans and Ohio Telegraph Company. This was the first telegraph company to be incorporated in Tennessee. The incorporators were Samuel F. B. Morse, John M. Bass, G. M. Fogg, James A. Porter, J. J. Gill, James Woods, John Kirkman, C. Connor, James Johnson, and James A. McAlister who were authorized to build side lines, and to organize the company by passing appropriate by-laws for proper management of its property. The company was given the power to cross roads, streets, and watercourses with their lines without being subjected to the charge of being a public nuisance. Two other companies were also incorporated, namely, the Huntsville, Pulaski, and Columbia Telegraph Company, and the Nashville and Memphis Telegraph Company.

---

[57] *Ibid.*, 486.
[58] *Ibid.*, 645.
[59] *Acts of Tennessee*, 1847, Chapter 10.

TO THE HONORABLE LEGISLATURE OF TENNESSEE.

The undersigned, citizens of *Marshall County* Tennessee, would respectfully call the attention of your honorable body to the propriety of revising the Tippling laws of the State.

They believe that it is morally wrong for any free State to have laws that tempt men to do wrong, and that tend directly to the increase of crime. This, they believe, the present Tippling laws of Tennessee do. The law of 1846 has wholly failed as a revenue measure. The statistics of each county, and the reports of the proper money agents of the State, show an increase of crime that more than absorbs the revenue collected by the State and the counties under the law. They know its tendency, in this county, has been to multiply crime, and consequently costs, and to increase poverty and suffering. What it has occasioned here has, no doubt, been seen and felt in other places.

Tennessee justly boasts of her high character. They believe it to be unbecoming her proud position to carry on a partnership with men, whose very business can flourish only by corrupting the public morals, and by multiplying widows and orphans in the land.

They do not call upon you to pass any act of prohibition. They believe that the public wants might be met, at this time, by repealing the whole of the act of 1846, except the 13th and 18th Sections, and by reviving the act of 1838—making it a misdemeanor, in all cases, to sell vinous or spirituous liquors by a smaller measure than the quart, and retaining the principle of the old act of 1779, authorizing every body to sell by the quart, with a provision that it should, in no case, be drank on the premises, or place where sold.

In this way the respectability of Tippling will be broken down, and the snares and temptations which are now thrown before the sober and the young will be removed, and those who claim the right of getting drunk, as one of the hereditaments in the charter of their liberty, can still gratify their appetites to their heart's content.

They believe that your honorable body ought to act efficiently upon this subject. They can see no good reason why Tennessee should license Tippling any more than any other crime. It is, they believe, not only a crime itself (if a public nuisance and immorality can be called such,) but it is the fruitful parent of others, the most revolting and terrible in their character.

With all due respect, they are your fellow citizens.

Some "Grass Roots" Work!

What would have been an exceedingly valuable law was embodied in House Bill No. 318 [60] which was passed by that body on February 4, 1848. The bill provided for the registration of births, deaths, and marriages throughout the State. On second reading in the Senate, the bill encountered fatal opposition in the person of Senator John W. Richardson, a physician, who moved successfully that the bill be rejected.[61]

The ever-recurrent liquor control question did not make any appreciable headway in the 1847 legislative session. Less than a dozen petitions on the subject were filed with the Legislature, none of which resulted in any change whatsoever in the existing statute. Sixteen hundred ladies residing in East Tennessee requested that the *sale or no sale* of spirituous liquors should be submitted to a popular vote of the people.[62] The Judiciary Committee, to which the petition had been referred, asked to be discharged from further consideration of the subject, as considerable time had already been spent upon its discussion, and that it would be fruitless to revive it. What may be considered as a herald of the later four-mile law was the petition of a business concern, Wood, Stacker & Company,

"... praying the Legislature absolutely to prohibit the sale of spirituous liquors within three miles of any forge, furnace, or rolling mill." [63]

Three days before adjournment, the Legislature voted an appropriation of five hundred dollars

"... to preserve the place of interment, where the remains of Gen. Meriwether Lewis were deposited." [64]

A committee, composed of Robert A. Smith, Honorable Edmund Dillahunty, and Barclay Martin of Maury County, and Dr. Samuel B. Moore, of Hickman County, was appointed to carry into execution the provisions of the law and report to the next General Assembly. The Report, an exceedingly interesting one, will be presented in the following chapter.

This chapter, dealing with the Messages and the administration of Governor Neill S. Brown will now be terminated. It is appropriate, however, to conclude with his Message of October 5, 1849, his last official communication to the General Assembly, except his Valedictory Address a few days later. He had been defeated for re-election but, like his predecessors, he fired a "parting shot."

[60] *Senate Journal*, 1847, 625.
[61] *Ibid.*, 645.
[62] *Ibid.*, 418–419.
[63] *Ibid.*, 360.
[64] *Acts of Tennessee*, 1847, Chapter 135.

Legislative Message,* October 5, 1849

"GENTLEMEN OF THE SENATE,
     AND HOUSE OF REPRESENTATIVES:

You have assembled at the seat of Government to discharge the trusts with which you have been invested, under the Constitution and laws of the State. And it is gratifying on such an occasion to be assured of the general health and prosperity which now mark the condition of our community. For these blessings we are laid under a new tribute of gratitude to the Great Disposer of all human events.

The reports from the different Departments of the State, and from the institutions under its control, will acquaint you with their condition respectively, and the manner in which they have been administered. I am happy to believe they have all been managed with fidelity, and that their operations have been reasonably successful.

The Bank of Tennessee has at all times, since its creation formed a subject of deep interest to the State. Much depends upon it. It is the great paymaster for all the public obligations. So far, it has certainly met all demands against it—has in the main, been well conducted; and its profits have been equal to those of most other banking institutions of the day. But I think it can be demonstrated that there has been a loss of the capital of the Bank to the amount of near eight hundred thousand dollars, if not more. I mean it has taken that much, together with its net profits, to discharge the obligations that have, from time to time, been imposed upon it. If this be so, the result sooner or later, and at no distant day, cannot be mistaken— it must end disastrously.

To determine whether there has been this loss of capital we need only refer to the history of its operations, and the reports made from time to time. Whether the amount of loss upon the capital of the Bank is correctly stated or not, it is certain there has been a loss, and that on the 1st of January, 1848, it amounted to $777,360.69 according to the report of the joint select committee of the last session of the General Assembly. This is a state of things that ought not

---

* *Senate Journal*, 1849, 44–53.
  House Journal, 1849, 42–51.

to be permitted to continue. The evil arises from the fact that the Bank has been required to do impossibilities. It has made an average profit of about seven per cent, taking the whole term of years since it was organized; but to meet all the liabilities imposed upon it, would require a profit of about ten or eleven per cent. This it cannot and ought not to be expected to accomplish. If the present line of policy is continued, we must look forward to the time when the whole capital of the Bank shall have been expended. That capital, as is known, embraces the Common School fund, and the surplus revenue fund deposited with the State by the General Government. If the latter should ever be called for it would present to us a melancholy alternative—while there is but little probability that the former would ever be supplied, however solemnly it has been pledged by the Constitution, and however ardently it has been cherished by the friends of education. The real capital of the Bank at present, does not exceed two millions and a half; and if we assume that the nett profits will hereafter amount to seven per cent per annum, we would realize an aggregate profit of $175,000 per annum. With this sum, according to the stated liabilities in 1847, we would have to meet $271,712.87, which shows a deficit at that date of $96,712.87. This calculation allows nothing for the increased liabilities of the Bank for the last two years, nor for the reduction in the capital by the current drain. The Bank began its operations on the 1st of July, 1839, with a capital of $3,226,976.82, and by the 1st of July, 1840, has lost the sum of $800,000, as is believed. Now, at this rate of loss, it can be demonstrated that in 16 years the whole capital will have been expended. No man who wishes well to the prosperity of the State, desires such a result. And yet it is to me most manifest, if the Bank is continued with the present encumberences upon it. The policy of gradual liquidation has heretofore been tested by your predecessors and was zealously advocated by many. Others there were, who, while they conceded the evils connected with the institution, were deterred from fixing a period to its duration, by the fear of what they deemed greater evils. The Bank then, as now, with its numerous Branches, furnished a large portion of the circulating medium of the country, and is convenient for many purposes—both to the State and to the people. The public mind was not then prepared for its withdrawal. Whether it is now, you will determine. A more intimate acquaintance in the last two years, with the history and operations of the Bank, has satisfied me, that the public interest requires that it should either be discontinued, or that it should be so far relieved from its obligations as to save its capital from further reduction.

Indisposed at all times to favor a radical change upon questions of mere domestic policy, while any reasonable ground of success remains, I would be willing to see the Bank continued for the present, if the relief indicated, is extended to it. This I think can be accomplished by making the Treasury chargable with all the liabilities which now rest upon the Bank; and responsible for any deficit in the means of payment. In this way, whatever profits the Bank may realize, will go into the Treasury for its profits, and upon accounting with the Treasury for its profits, let the Bank be discharged from further obligation. Under the present system, if the profits of the Bank are inadequate, as they have been, the capital is made to supply the deficit; and thus we are presented with a policy, which, in the case of an individual in private life, would be universally condemned, and lead inevitably to poverty and bankruptcy. This policy is also recommended by its simplicity, irrespective of the condition of the bank. It would render the state of our resources less complex, and manifest at all times, without dispute or cavil, the precise amount of available means. And what objection can be taken to this course of policy? Let us not be startled at the idea of an increase of taxation to make up any deficit. I believe no such necessity will arise. But if it does, we ought to know it in due time, and not wait until the whole capital of the Bank is expended—until necessities multiply upon us to an extent beyond our ability to meet.

If the Bank is put in a state of liquidation, it should of course be so gradual as not to impair the business of the country, or lesson the circulation. As the vacuum is formed it would be supplied from other Banks now in existence, or such as you may choose to create.

I am then prepared, and do earnestly recommend, that the Bank be either discontinued or disencumbered. Either policy is decidedly preferable to the present. Either would be safe to the best interests of the State, while the present is destined, in my judgment, to be disastrous.

The subject of Common Schools, will, of course, engage your

considerate attention. It is evident to every one that the present system is far from being satisfactory to the people. And in many places, either from its defects, or from improper management, it has become odious. Doubtless many improvements could be made on the present plan without reference to the increase of the fund, by which the administration of the whole could be rendered more easy and certain. But it is an increase of the fund which is most desired, and without which, no other innovation or improvement would be of any great practical utility. But how is this to be attained? Upon this subject there is a variety of opinions. I think our present revenue system will be found to furnish a surplus over and above the ordinary wants of the State, and probably beyond all contingencies. If so, how could it be better applied, than to common school purposes? If this addition to the present fund be insufficient, I know no other mode of enlarging it, but by taxation. Whether this should be resorted to in any shape, you, who represent the immediate interests and wishes of the people, will determine. I beg leave, however, to state, that I do not believe a system of direct taxes expedient or proper. Some counties are unable to bear additional burdens—while others are indisposed to do so. And experience has shown that a voluntary tax is much more conducive to the success of common schools, than one to be enforced by a general law of the State. By a voluntary tax, I mean, to confer, by law, the power upon the county courts of the different counties, to levy an amount within certain limits, for common school purposes—provided, that before such tax can be laid, the voice of the voters of the county shall be taken, and the exercise of the power be under the control of a popular majority. And whatever sum may be raised in this way, will be added to the proportion of the State fund annually received by the county, and expended for school purposes within the county. In this way each county will control the matter for itself, and the people will or will not tax themselves, as they please. I think this plan is practicable, and so far as I have been able to perceive, it will be acceptable to the people. Something ought to be done to advance a subject of so much importance. We owe it to the character of the State, and we owe it as an act of justice to the children of the State. I need not enlarge on the inestimable benefits of a general and diffusive system of education. It lies at the foundation of our form of government—giving strength both to the ballot-box and to the cartridge-box—and furnishing guarantees for the maintenance of law and order not to be found in pains and penalties. And from it we are to expect the origin and support of all great enterprises, that tend to develope our country and elevate our people. I sincerely trust you may find it in your power at the present session to advance this great cause, so that every child in the State, within the scholastic ages, may be enabled to learn the elements of education free of expense.

The subject of Internal Improvement is one which is exciting more interest at present, than any perhaps which will enter into your deliberations. And it is gratifying to witness the spirit which now pervades the different sections of the State with regard to it. The Nashville and Chattanooga railroad, and the East Tennessee and Georgia railroad are in a state of vigorous progress, and furnish assurances of their completion at no distant day. Much interest is also felt in Upper Tennessee, in favor of a road from Knoxville to the Virginia line, chartered at your last session. These enterprises are all rendered more important by the policy of the State of Virginia, which promises the construction of a route from the Tennessee line to Lynchburg, thus presenting the prospect of a line of railroad, almost unbroken from Nashville to the Eastern Atlantic. While, by the enlightened policy and liberal enterprise of the people and State of Georgia a continuous line is opening to us, to the Southern Atlantic. The vast advantages presented by these works, appeal to your enlightened policy for all the aid in your power to bestow, to ensure their completion. Although the State debt is now considerable, yet it is not such in my opinion, considering the amount of our means, as to deter us from still further appropriations of the public credit in aid of specific objects, I say in aid of specific objects, for I hope never again to see the indiscriminate policy of the act of 1837-8 resorted to by the State. Such a policy, if persevered in, would bankrupt any State in the world. The tendency was to construct any and every sort of road, without reference to its importance or value. The Upper East Tennessee route, viewed both in its local bearing upon the interests of that section of the State, and as a part of the great chain connecting us with the Eastern Atlantic, becomes an enterprise of the highest value. Indeed, it is indispensable, and I have no hesitation in recommending it as deserving a liberal partronage at the hands of the State. How much may be needed, remains to be seen; and how much should be granted, you will determine. It is not to be expected that private enterprise alone can build the road—it is a work of too much magnitude. The advantages of this branch of improvement to East Tennessee are apparent. No man can contemplate her condition and natural resources, without being impressed with it. But these works, though directly connected with East and a portion of Middle Tennessee, are important to the whole State. They form the basis of other and similar enterprises already in agitation, and destined at no distant day, I trust, to be carried out. Looking at the spirit of the day upon such subjects, and the necessity of multiplying outlets to market, no one can believe for a moment that the Nashville and Chattanooga railroad will be limited to its present terminus. And to all, who indulge an enlarged view of the interests of the whole State, it must be a desirable object to see this road extended from Nashville, or some intermediate point, west to Memphis. The Western portion of the State, is interested in such a communication to the East and Southeast. And so are the other sections of the State, in a speedy approach to the Mississippi and the South-west. The extension of this route West, would complete the chain from one end of the State to the other. And besides the commercial advantages to flow from it, it would bring into constant and close communication, the people of all portions of the State: a result greatly to be desired, in every view of our social and domestic well-being. I trust you may concur with me in the importance and practicability of the route from Nashville to Memphis, and grant a charter with such pledges of aid from the State as you may deem safe. I do not doubt but the greater portion of the stock, at least, would be taken, as the line would pass through many counties of great wealth and resources, and deeply interested by their locality in the attainment of such a road. I need not employ arguments or facts to enforce the incalculable benefits of such a line of railroad to the people of Tennessee. Remote from the ocean and lakes, and limited, and, to a great extent, excluded from water communication, this State, with all its vast resources, has been kept in the rear of improvements which now mark the age. Our growth in numbers and wealth, though considerable, has been slow, compared to our capabilities. This is a question which addresses the interest of every farmer and mechanic in the land, more especially, they being producers and directly concerned in the enjoyment of a speedy and certain market. The interest of all others compared to theirs, is but secondary. But there is another inducement, which appeals alike to all. The construction of such a road throughout the length of the State, would conduce to the growth of manufacturers in all their variety. Besides its influence in enticing the capital of our own people into that department of industry, it would not fail to bring into our midst the capital and enterprise of other States. Our natural resources, argicultural, mineral and manufacturing, are well known and appreciated. Development ought to be the order of the day, at least in the politics of Tennessee. The property-holder and the non-property-holder are equally interested: the former in the increased value of what he has, and the latter in the acquisition of means for the attainment of property.

And, if we need the stimulus of example upon this subject, we have it in the policy of our sister State of Georgia. That State has the honor of being foremost, among all the Southern States, in this great branch of enterprise. Though bounded on her Southern limits by the Atlantic shore, and enjoying many navigable rivers, yet, not content with these natural advantages, far superior to ours, her public undertakings for railroads already amount to about six millions, while private enterprise has incurred an equal sum, on the same account. The results so far, have been propitious, and promise the certainty of a new era in the wealth and commerce of that State.

One difficulty, always encountered in any specific work of this kind, is the opposition of those sections not directly addressed by it. This ought not to be. All portions cannot at once be supplied with these facilities. It must be done in detail, and with a steady and cautious calculation of the public and general, as well as local advantages to arise.

But there is still another reason that ought of itself to enforce the extension of this railroad to some point on the Mississippi river —and that is the probable construction of a route to the Pacific— to be built by the General Government out of the public lands. This latter enterprise, if carried on, may connect itself with some

point on our Western border—if so, it would form but the continuation of the line above recommended. And why may we not expect the route from Tennessee to be selected? It is recommended by the very enterprises I have been urging—now in progress and in contemplation—and the character and resources of the countries through which they will pass—forming altogether an inducement in favor of this point. And from every observation that has been made, it will be shorter, cheaper in its construction than any other yet indicated, and will not encounter the impassible snows, that are to be found, at least in winter, on the other routes. This great national project, so important to the nation at large, and especially to the Mississippi valley, will, doubtless, receive your earnest countenance and favor, as it is now receiving much attention and regard by the people of the Southern and Western States. To have the Atlantic and Pacific connected by one great highway, and Tennessee enjoying an intermediate portion of it within her own territory, is well worthy of a vigorous demonstration on your part at the present session, independent of all other local considerations and interests.

The Mobile and Ohio Railroad, will no doubt be pressed upon your consideration, either in its main route across the State, or in one or more diverging branches. It is destined, if completed, to be of immense value to a large and growing portion of our State, and proposes to add to other advantages another Southern market for our produce. I respectfully bespeak for this, as well as every other substantial project of improvement that may be presented, your liberal and enlightened regard. In this connection, the further improvement of our rivers, ought not to be overlooked. Many lasting advantages can be attained by the expenditure of small sums, in the removal of specified obstructions, that now interfere materially with the navigation of many of our streams. The details of these, their locality, and estimated cost, are best known to yourselves.

But while I am the earnest advocate of every thing that tends to develop the resources of the State; to quicken and advance her growth, in agriculture and the mechanic arts, in commerce and manufactures; I am not a friend to rash and improvident expenditures. The faith of the State ought not to be impaired, or endangered for any improvements however desirable. And it is gratifying to our pride of character as a people, that hitherto all our public engagements have been promptly and faithfully met. The credit of the State has hitherto escaped any reflection, either at home or abroad, and this may assure the world that repudiation will never find a lodgment within our limits, as I trust it may never find an advocate.

I beg leave to call your attention to that portion of the revenue law, passed at the last session, which relates to the tax on merchants. It is, in my judgment, unequal and oppressive, and I respectfully recommend its modification. It was no doubt the result of oversight in its framers. As the law now stands, it is a great hardship on that class of men.

Some amendment might be made to advantage, in our penal code, so far as relates to the punishment of slaves. The present law, conferring power on the Executive, to commute the punishment of death to imprisonment for life in the Penitentiary does not, in my judgment, extend to slaves. And cases will often occur, where the pardoning power ought to be exercised, but where some punishment short of death, would be gladly inflicted if authority existed for it. Now it is death or no punishment at all, in all capital convictions of slaves. What additional mode of punishment should be adopted in such cases, is difficult to determine. The choice, perhaps, is limited between confinement in the common jail and in the Penitentiary. The punishment now inflicted on a slave for larceny, is a mere farce, and has no sort of terror connected with it—since he receives the same at the hands of his master for every day delinquencies. I submit to you, whether there is any remedy for these defects in the law, consistent with sound policy.

A vacancy has occurred in the Third Solicitorial District, by the resignation of Samuel A. Smith, Esq., which was temporarily filled by the appointment of James B. Cocke, Esq., of Athens. A vacancy occurred in the office of Register of the Ocoee District, by the resignation of J. C. Tipton, and was supplied by the appointment of F. W. Lea, of Cleaveland. A vacancy also occurred in the office of Register of the Mountain District, by the death of Jacob A. Lane, and was supplied by the apointment of John F. Voss, of Sparta. The office of Comptroller of the State became vacant by the resignation of F. K. Zollicoffer, and was filled by the appointment of

Benjamin H. Shepherd. The office of Physician and Superintendent of the Lunatic Asylum, became vacant by the death of Dr. John S. McNairy, and was filled by the appointment of Dr. Boyd McNairy. Hon. Jas. Scott, Judge of the 14th Judicial Circuit, recently resigned his office to take effect on the 29th ult. This vacancy has not been filled by me, but is reserved for your election. These embrace all the vacancies, that have occurred since your last adjournment, the appointment of which is vested in your Honorable body.

Here I might close this communication, as all the principal subjects of State interest proper to be presented, are embraced. But the question of slavery, or rather the questions connected with it, have of late assumed such importance, as to demand my notice and some consideration at your hands. This institution, in my opinion, belongs exclusively to the States, where it exists, and neither the General Government, nor the other States of the Union, have any right to interfere with it, directly or indirectly. And if such right did exist, the subject is of too delicate and agitating a character to justify its exercise. I also deny the power, claimed by many, in the General Government, to exclude slavery from the new territories where it does not exist. That power is at least questionable, and it will be time enough to yield its existence when it is settled, by the graver tribunals of the country. In short, it seems to me that slavery in any aspect of it, does not properly admit of legislation by Congress, either to determine where it shall or shall not go, or to abolish, limit, or impair it where it is. And certainly the repose of that section of the Union, where slavery exists, is best consulted by total silence on the part of Congress upon this delicate subject. While this is so, the termination of slavery, if it is to have a termination, is deeply involved in the prudence and forbearance of those, who are desirous to witness such an event. Every attempt to limit or interfere with it, by direct or indirect means, tends but to perpetuate it, and what is more, to weaken, and alienate the feelings and affections of one section of the Union towards the other. Let the people who shall inhabit the new territories, determine the question for themselves, when they meet to establish a State government. Their right to do this is admitted by all, but to exclude slavery from the territories in advance, by the adoption of what is called the Wilmot Proviso is, in effect, to foreclose the whole question. I am happy in the belief, that all difficulty on the subject will be obviated at an early day, by the establishment of State governments, both in California and New Mexico; and whether they adopt or exclude slavery, is a matter for themselves, in which we have no concern, and about which, I am sure, I feel no solicitude. All lovers of the Union; all friends to peace and harmony, will rejoice at such a consummation. And it can neither injure nor disappoint any class, unless it be a few political agitators, both in the North and South, who have found in this question a prime element for commotion and disturbance. I have no sympathy with the threats of violence and disunion, that have been but too often heralded forth, on both sides of the question, as the ultimate remedy. This is not the proper mode of vindicating rights, between two great sections of the country—bound together by so many glorious recollections—and inspired by so many brilliant hopes and expectations as belong to the future. I see nothing in the present aspect of this question to justify either a resort to violence or disunion, or to threaten them as remedies. If it should present a graver feature, in its progress, let the emergency dictate the remedy. In the meantime, let us insist on our rights by all constitutional means, and also resolve to maintain the Union 'at all hazards and to the last extremity.' I am willing to yield the honor of present or probable evils, to arise from the question of slavery. Upon them will rest the responsibility (and a fearful one it will be) of calculating the value of the Union, and cheapening its dignity and duration, in the estimation of any portion of the American people. With the Union, we have every thing to inspire the hopes and impel the energies of patriotism, amid the vast field of improvement that lies before us. Without it, we have nothing worth maintaining—worth living for—worth dying for! Clouds and darkness rest upon such a future—sectional jealousies—border forays—endless collisions—the patriotism of trade and commerce, and the ruin of American liberty, fill up the baleful picture. Against such a contemplation, all men of all parties, ought to turn with instinctive horror. The Union ought to be deemed invaluable—as when it was formed it was deemed indispensible. It is invaluable: and deserves to be the last of human institutions that shall fade before the trumpet of retribution.

Whether slavery is right or wrong—founded in good or bad

policy, it will run its course, and maintain its place. And whenever slave labor ceases to be profitable, the institution will no doubt be dispensed with, in the same way and from the same motives, which terminated it in the North-Eastern States, where it formerly existed. It asks for no protection, but simply demands to be let alone. It cherishes no spirit of propagandism, but acknowledges the right and power of those who dispense with it to do so.

For the purpose, therefore, of vindicating our rights, as well as to allay existing agitation, I recommend, that you memorialize Congress in a firm, vigorous and temperate appeal, against all legislation on the subject, and leave the evil, if it be an evil, to correct itself under the auspices of local public sentiment, and local legislation—and allow the blessing, if it be a blessing, to be enjoyed unmolested, under the sanctuary of State authority.

In closing this communication, I beg leave to tender the assurance of my best wishes for your success, in the discharge of the high duties which surround you, and for the lasting prosperity and happiness of our beloved State.

N. S. Brown."

CHAPTER THREE

William Trousdale

William Trousdale was born in Orange County, North Carolina, in 1790. His father, James Trousdale, was a Revolutionary War soldier and attained the rank of Captain. While the present Tennessee was the Southwest Territory, Captain Trousdale came to the new country and settled on the site of the present Gallatin where he resided until his death. Young William was a pupil of the celebrated Reverend Gideon Blackburn, one of the first pioneers of education in the State. When the Creek War broke out in 1813, the youth volunteered as a private but was soon advanced to the grade of Lieutenant. He fought by the side of General Coffee and was in the battle of Talladega under General Andrew Jackson. When the National Capitol was burned in 1814, once more William Trousdale responded to the call of duty as a private. Later, he distinguished himself for his gallantry at the Battle of New Orleans.

Upon his return home in the spring of 1815, the former soldier resumed his studies and was admitted to the bar in 1820. Fifteen years later, he was elected State Senator. At the outbreak of the Seminole War, he was elected a Major General of a regiment of mounted men and proceeded to Florida where on one occasion for three successive days he displayed a degree of bravery that amounted almost to rashness. Upon his return home, he was nominated as the Democratic candidate for Congress, but was defeated by his Whig opponent. In 1840, he was a Democratic elector in the Presidential contest. He served with unusual distinction in the Mexican War, taking a leading part in some of the fiercest battles of the conflict, especially so at Chepultapec where he was wounded twice but refused to resign his command until he had captured an enemy battery. At the close of the war, he was assigned to the command of the Third Division of the army on its homeward march. With such a notable military record, it is no wonder that he was affectionately known as "the War Horse of Sumner."

In 1849, he became the Democratic candidate for Governor against

From Portrait by Washington B. Cooper. Courtesy of Tennessee Historical Society, Nashville.

the Whig incumbent, Neill S. Brown. To the surprise of some of his strongest supporters, he was elected and served with satisfaction to his party. He was renominated in 1851, but was defeated by one of the most popular Whigs in the State, William B. Campbell.

Ex-Governor Trousdale was appointed Minister to Brazil by President Franklin Pierce. One inducement for him to accept the appointment was the hope that the climate would prove beneficial to his health. He had become a victim of chronic rheumatism which plagued him for many years, ultimately reducing him to the status of an invalid confined to his home. In fact, for the last ten or twelve years of his life, he rarely left his home. In his enfeebled condition, he fell a victim of pneumonia which was the immediate cause of his death. He died March 27, 1872, at the ripe old age of eighty-two and was buried in Gallatin.

Legislative Messages of
Governor William Trousdale, 1849–1851

As preliminary to citing and discussing the administration of Governor Trousdale, it might be advisable to take a hasty survey of Tennessee's situation at or near the mid-point of the nineteenth century. Unlike the States of the "Deep South," slavery had not become deeply intrenched in Tennessee's social and political life. Prior to the Brown-Trousdale gubernatorial race of 1849, slavery as a political issue had rarely been even a minor issue in local political campaigns. But the Mexican War and the Wilmot Proviso brought into the forefront the issue of slavery, the South's "peculiar institution" as it was designated by its friends. A protest against the Wilmot Proviso failed of passage in the 1847 Tennessee General Assembly, thus indicating that Tennessee was far from being "wedded" to the peculiar institution at the time.[1] But shortly after the termination of the War with Mexico, sectional controversy over the status of slavery in the newly-acquired territory increased both in frequency and in intensity, and ere long Tennessee joined up with the "cause" espoused by her sister States.

As a sort of paramount issue in the gubernatorial campaign of 1849, the question of resistance to the possible exclusion of slavery in the territory acquired from Mexico forged to the forefront and occupied a place of prominence in public speeches of the respective candidates. There can be no question but that the Democratic Party in Tennessee was on the anxious seat, having witnessed Whig triumphs in the State

---

[1] See Chapter II, pages 249–251.

in the past four consecutive races for President of the United States, Hugh Lawson White in 1836, William Henry Harrison in 1840, Henry Clay in 1844, and Zachary Taylor in 1848. Fresh in the Democratic memory also was the defeat of Aaron V. Brown for re-election to the governorship in 1847 by the Whig candidate, Neill S. Brown. Politically speaking, it was no time to just "play favorites" in selecting a man to be pitted against the incumbent Whig Governor Neill S. Brown who doubtless would seek re-election. Picking a candidate who could win the governorship was the *sine qua non* confronting the apprehensive Democrats.

Early in 1849, it became evident that the Democrats were girding their political loins for a battle royal with their formidable political foe. One of the true and tried Democratic organs [2] put forth its diagnosis of the political factors involved in the selection of a candidate to carry the Democratic banner:

"CANDIDATE FOR GOVERNOR.

The *Knoxville Standard and Reformer* contains the following article:
'Candidates for Governor—In our paper of to-day will be found the proceedings of a democratic meeting held at Athens on the 5th inst. The name of Gen. Trousdale seems to have been the choice of the democracy of McMinn. The General seems also to be the choice of the Nashville *Union*. In fact it has been thought by many that the Union has been paving the way for the nomination of Gen. Trousdale by proposing that the candidates for Governor should remain at home, and not make speeches. We are in favor of doing away with any speeches from our gubernatorial candidates, and cannot say that we are now against it. But, if Gen. Trousdale is our candidate for Governor, he, of all others, will have to undergo a canvass throughout the State.— Even the bare mention of his name, in connection with the office, has furnished one of the whig papers in East Tennessee (the Tribune) with an excuse for throwing out hints of a want of capacity as an officer in the late war. False and slanderous as the charges are, they must be met from the stump. The readers of the whig papers do not generally read democratic papers, and for this reason it may be necessary for the democratic party, in convention, not to make any pledges as to the course of their candidate. The Centre-State American is in favor of letting the candidates arrange the plan of the canvass. This seems the better policy.

We do not pretend to know the opinions of the democracy of East Tennessee. We do know, however, that Gen. Levin H. Coe has a vast number of friends in our section of the State, and we believe if there is a man in the State who can make a successful run without the canvass, he, more than all others, is the man. He is known to be able and eloquent on the stump, and no whig will be anxious for speaking in the various counties of the State, if General Coe is to travel with him as his opponent; and then General Coe is well known all over the State, and no one can more readily unite the democratic party.

Gen. Trousdale may be an able speaker, and may, if nominated, run successfully. We are certainly not against him, and if he is the candidate of the

---

[2] *Nashville Daily Union*, February 20, 1849.

party we will support him as cordially as any other man in the State. We are for the democratic party, and for no particular man or set of men of that party. *We, certainly,* 'have no friends to reward,' and in serving our party, we know we are serving our country.

The subject of the next canvass has frequently been referred to in our presence, and never without bringing up the name of Gen. Coe as one every way qualified to lead the democracy in the coming contest.

It will be our pleasure to publish the proceedings of the democracy, and it is to be hoped that some plan may be devised by which a union of our party can be effected. The democrats who voted for Gen. Taylor, and who were silent in November, will rally to our standard if the proper man is brought forward as our leader in the approaching canvass. Coe will do without speaking. Trousdale may answer just as good a purpose; but when we speak of Coe, *we write what we know.'*

We have no fault to find with but one expression in the foregoing article. We are said to have proposed that the candidates shall not canvass the State. The Standard must remember that it was the Gallatin Tenth Legion which *proposed* this course; and that *the Knoxville Standard* endorsed the Legion's article much more strongly than the Nashville Union did. These facts ought not to have been forgotten by the Standard; and if it is necessary for that paper to refer to the course of the Union at all, we must ask it to represent us correctly, and, least of all, not find fault with us for committing its own sin. If the Knoxville Standard may approve a suggestion of a staunch democratic contemporary, surely the Knoxville Standard cannot object to our course in approving the same suggestion.

We do believe the practice of canvassing the State by candidates for Governor a bad one. We are in favor of leaving such canvassing to candidates for Electors, for Members of Congress, and of the State Legislature. These are our private opinions, honestly entertained, as a citizen of the State. As editor of a paper, we shall not force these views on the attention of our readers, nor attempt to lead public opinion to adopt them. We care very little whether they are adopted or not. We never expect to be a candidate for Governor ourself, and therefore have no personal interest in the matter. If candidates choose to speak, they will continue to have the right to do it. *Let them!* We shall interfere no farther. We have expressed an honestly entertained opinion; and, having done so, take leave of the subject.

So much for *that!* We trust it will do away with the possibility of our being farther misunderstood by our Knoxville friends, or misrepresented by pretended democrats, who wear the outside garb of our party only that they may stab it the more deeply.

As this is an article of explanations, we will add here, that while *we are not* paving the way for the nomination of any man as the candidate of our party for Governor, leaving, as we do, the nomination *to the untrammeled action of the State Convention,* we have yet said not one word in praise of Gen. WILLIAM TROUSDALE which we wish unsaid. We only regret that we cannot infuse into our language additional strength, when speaking of his talents, his courage, his patriotism, his services, and his virtues. No public station can honor such a man. We have mentioned his name only with the gratitude which, as a citizen of the State whose character his acts have exalted, we owe him. We will repeat these honest praises on all suitable occasions, while our Maker vouchsafes to continue to us a spark of national pride, or a feeling of gratitude to the bravest of our country's defenders. And should the time ever arrive when scheming politicians, from selfish considerations, shall attempt to stifle those praises, by the blessing of God we will resist their efforts, and throw ourselves into the arms and hearts of THE GREAT AND HONEST PEOPLE OF THE STATE, certain of a support and a sympathy warm, true, and abiding. We refer to General Trousdale as *a man*. For Governor, we will support the nominee of the State Convention with our best powers.

Most ridiculously idle is the idea which has got abroad that we advocate an abandonment of the practice of canvassing the State on Gen. Trousdale's account. He is a good speaker—*better* than N. S. Brown—a man of education and talent—is rapidly recovering his health, and is the last man of our party who, if a candidate, we should wish to have stay at home. *Let this fact be re-: membered*. We have honored a man for acts which deserve honor. We have done nothing more. We will do this on all proper occasions hereafter. Into this explanation we have been forced by an interested misrepresentation of our course, (*not* by the Knoxville Standard.) We have written *plainly*, and hope to be understood.

That there is a feeling, in some sections of the State, in favor of Gen. Trousdale as our candidate, is unquestionable. He has been nominated in McMinn county; and we have also heard him spoken of in other quarters. But this feeling is, as yet, far from being unanimous.—Other men have earnest and ardent friends; and the task of selecting a candidate, by the State Convention, may not be a very easy one. East Tennessee has not, for many years, had a Governor. The whig party in the last Legislature took from her the Senator who has heretofore been accorded to her; and it might be good policy for the democracy to give her a chance to have the Governor. Then, she has men every way worthy and deserving of the office—men who have distinguished themselves in the hot conflicts of past years: The eloquent and indefatigable HAYNES, who possesses more of Polk's peculiar energy and eloquence than any man we recollect; the self-made statesman and orator, ANDREW JOHNSON, whose giant blows upon the fortress of our opponents we have been accustomed to hear ringing clear above the din of the conflict from the first moment of the battle until its close; the clear-headed and able ROWLES, so long the bulwark of our party in Lower East Tennessee; and the accomplished and popular SMITH whose services in the third district have entitled him to the gratitude of our whole democracy.

Nor is our own division of the State without its men of mind and merit. The question is every day asked if AARON V. BROWN would again canvass the State; and, if the question is answered affirmatively, a rush of that old enthusiasm, which has ever attended his canvassings, would greet the announcement at once. Not only in our division of the State, but East and West, JOHN M. BRIGHT, of Lincoln, has hosts of friends. As a popular orator, we have never listened to his superior; and there is no man in whose hands we would sooner entrust a defence of our principles. Besides, OLD LINCOLN, (God bless her!) deserves all honor. In the worst of times she never falters; and there is now a very strong disposition throughout the State to honor her by selecting as the Gubernatorial candidate her eloquent son. A. O. P. NICHOLSON has friends every where among the friends of democracy. He is one of the chief ornaments of our party, and reflects honor upon it, whenever he consents to receive its votes. We have already mentioned Gen. Trousdale's name; and although the list is far from being exhausted, we have room here only to add the name of one other soldier, who is deserving of the highest honors of our democracy, not only for a gallantry in battle as brilliant as that which won knighthood on the proudest fields of ancient chivalry, but because he was made the object of one of the foulest conspiracies, by our opponents, ever devised to blacken the honest fame of a patriot soldier. We need not say that we allude to Gen. PILLOW, whose fame as a General is written in the history of the best battles of the war with Mexico, and whose capacity is shown in his triumphant defence of himself against Scott's conspiracy.

The West, too, has its claims and its talents. We yield neither to the Knoxville Standard, nor to any other paper, in admiration for the talents or gratitude for the services of Gen. Coe. In the ten long years which we have spent in the service of the democracy of Tennessee, we have felt and seen how often and how largely the party has leaned on his strong arm and brave heart for support in days of trial. The experience of the ten years to which we have referred, has enabled us to teach young laborers how deep is the debt which our party owes Gen. Coe, and supersedes the necessity of their attempting to teach us this lesson.—There are thousands of democrats in the State with whom Gen. Coe is the first choice, for Governor, and no man would bring out the democratic strength more fully. Judge WILLIAM T. BROWN, HON. F. P. STANTON, D. M. CURRIN, Esq., and JOHN A. GARDNER, Esq. have also been named in connexion with the office. All have warm friends, all are sound democrats, and the nomination of either would be received with cordial good feeling throughout the State.

We have thus mentioned the names of some of those gentlemen who will probably have friends in the State Convention. But we apprehend no serious difficulty in making a selection, and have no doubt that the nominee of that convention, be he who he may, or from what section, will receive a cordial and united support.

This article is a long one, and it has been forced from us by an interested misrepresentation of our course, more malignant than any to which we have ever before been subjected as editor of a newspaper. We have now set ourselves right, beyond the possibility of farther misrepresentation. We shall continue to do equal justice to all our prominent men. The day will never come with us when we shall turn our weapons against our friends. When we have no longer enemies to fight, we will sheathe our sword. We thank our friends of the Knoxville Standard for the courteous tone of their article, and for the opportuniy they have given us of setting ourselves right. We hope they will oblige us by copying this article, and we will reciprocate the favor, should opportunity offer.

We are *done* with the subject."

Imbued with more pugnacity than polish, ardent supporters of prospective candidates for the Democratic gubernatorial nomination were in danger of cutting each others' throats with their fusillades of personal invective. Like Milton's character in *Paradise Lost*, blind and fanatical partisans

"... also erred in overmuch admiring."

As an antidote to the political poison being dished out in the warm-up period preceding the forthcoming State Democratic Convention in April, a dyed-in-the-wool Democratic editor issued a serious and valid warning to the "friends" of the two most formidable rivals for the nomination:[3]

---

[3] *Nashville Daily Union*, March 12, 1849.

"CANDIDATE FOR GOVERNOR–DUTY OF THE DEMOCRATS

We have witnessed with deep mortification and sorrow the course that has been pursued by some of the friends of two distinguished and honorable democrats, whose names have been prominently connected with the gubernatorial canvass. We allude to Gen. Trousdale and Gen. Pillow. These gentlemen have served the State with honorable distinction, and shed increased lustre upon the fame and chivalry of Tennessee.

We need not at this time recount their heroic deeds, nor point to their noble daring on fields of strife and in the hour of danger. With their gallant exploits, our readers are familiar. Their claims upon the affection and gratitude of their countrymen no one will dare dispute.

That they are eminently qualified in all respects to discharge the executive duties, and every way worthy of executive honors, is universally admitted. Why then, we ask, in the name of the democracy of the State, into whose keeping their reputation is measurably intrusted, should the friends of these honorable competitors, if competitors they may be called, indulge in criminations and recriminations, which can only serve to wound their own feelings, and to divide and distract the party of which they are distinguished ornaments.

Mistaken, indeed, are the friends of these gentlemen, if they suppose the claims of either can be advanced with the democracy of the State by depreciating the merits or popularity of the other.

Democrats are not in the habit of permitting their distinguished men to be slandered with impunity even by their political foes, and the democrat who indulges in a course of detraction of our war worn veterans may not hope to escape the strong indignation of a just and generous public opinion. That the shafts of calumny and ridicule will be hurled at the candidate selected by us for political honors, by the reckless press of the opposition, is to be expected. But the democracy of Tennessee will never permit her valiant sons who have freely shed their blood in defence of her exalted fame, to be 'stabbed in the house of their friends' with impunity.

So long as the friends of any man content themselves with a presentation of his claims or merits to the consideration of the party, no one has a right to complain, but when they attempt to advance his pretensions by depreciating the services of others, they inflict an injury upon the party which it is not in their power to repair. If they are not disposed to prepare themselves with arms and ammunition with which to fight our opponents before the battle commences, let them not spend their time in forging weapons with which our enemy may be the better able to contest the field when the battle rages. It is gratifying to KNOW that in this spirit of disparagement and detraction neither of these gentlemen in the slightest degree sympathizes. None but the kindest feelings of friendship and esteem exist between them, and we feel entirely confident, that upon a little reflection their *real* friends will not further indulge in unkind remarks or invidious comparisons. We believe that with a united, energetic and well organized support, either of the gentlemen above named can be elected Governor of Tennessee in August next. Without such support no democrat may hope for success. The duty then of every democrat in the State, from this time until the nomination is made, in our estimation is, to ascertain as far as practicable who can command the greatest strength, and to assist in effecting an organization of our forces that will bring every man to the poles [polls] on the day of election. This is the time to effect such an organization, and if it is neglected till the canvass opens, we shall be too much engaged with our adversaries to effect it at all. We again appeal to the democrats in every civil district in the State to commence this work at once, if it has not already been attended to. If a democratic meeting could be held in every precinct in the State before delegates to the convention are selected, the right man would be certain to receive the nomination for Governor, and the party would then be prepared to give him a harmonious and enthusiastic support. Remember that the time for organizing is short. In five weeks our candidate will be in the field. Are our friends every where determined that but one candidate for each office in the State shall be supported, and that they will make one decisive effort to give him the full strength of the party? If so we shall succeed in redeeming the State. If not, we shall assuredly fail and defeat will be merited."

The skirmishing among the Democratic hopefuls came to a showdown on April 19, 1849, when the State Democratic Convention convened in Nashville for the purpose of nominating a candidate for Governor and adopting a platform for presentation to the voters of the State. The morning session was devoted to organization, resulting in the selection of A. O. P. Nicholson as President, with seven Vice-Presidents and five Secretaries to aid him. At two o'clock in the afternoon, nominations for Governor were declared to be in order. Colonel John Savage nominated General William Trousdale of Sumner County, and Landon C. Haynes of Washington County was the other nominee. Balloting by the county delegates resulted as follows: Trousdale, 34 votes; Haynes, 9 votes. On motion of Andrew Ewing, General Trousdale was declared "unanimously nominated."[4]

At the evening session, General Levin Coe of the Platform Committee presented the following resolutions or "planks" which were adopted, to-wit:

"1. *Resolved,* That in General William Trousdale, of Sumner, we recognize the hero, the patriot, and the statesman—a man of pure and spotless character, of great devotion to his country in peace and in war, and one who, we have assurances from his past life, will stand by her interests with a firm and unflinching hand, in every emergency. From the division of parties in Tennessee, he has been the warm and consistent advocate of democratic measures, though courteous and respectful to his political opponents; and, as the democratic candidate, we unanimously recommend him to the people of Tennessee as a man eminently qualified to fill with honor and usefulness to the State the Gubernatorial chair.

2. *Resolved,* That the democracy of Tennessee, unappalled by their recent defeat in the Presidential election, have again united their energies in favor of their principles and of the cause of human freedom; that they adhere, with undiminished faith and unabated zeal, to the fundamental doctrines heretofore adopted in their public assemblies and conventions, and that they never cease their efforts in this glorious cause, until the doctrines of the country are once more committed to their guidance.

3. *Resolved,* That we approve of the great measures of policy adopted and carried out by the late administration of the General Government; that we have seen with pride its resistance to aggression from foreign powers—its

---

[4] *Ibid.,* April 20, 1849.

defence of the rights of our country in a foreign war—the passage of the Independent Treasury—the revenue tariff of 1846—the warehousing system—the adoption of the treaty with Mexico—the acquisition of new territory, and the other measures of administrative policy for which the gratitude of the nation is due to the Ex-President and the other members of the Government.

4. *Resolved*, That the Government of the United States has no control directly or indirectly, mediately or immediately, over the institution of slavery, so to impair the rights of the slaveholder, and that in taking such control it transcends the limits of its legitimate functions by destroying the internal organization of the sovereignties who created it.

5. *Resolved*, That all territory acquired by the arms of the United States, or yielded by treaty by any foreign power, belongs to the several States of this Union, as their joint and common property, in which each and all have common rights; and that the enactment by the Federal Government of any law, which should directly or by its effects, prevent the citizens of any State from emigrating, with their property, of whatever description, into such territory, would be a discrimination unwarranted by and in violation of the rights of the States from which such citizens emigrated, and in derogation of that perfect equality that belongs to the several States as members of this Union and would tend directly to subvert the Union itself.

6. *Resolved*, That if in disregard alike of every consideration of justice, of constitutional right and fraternal feeling, the fearful issue shall be forced upon the country, which must result from the adoption and attempted enforcement of the Wilmot proviso as an act of the General Government, we can have no difficulty in choosing between the only alternatives that will then remain of abject submission to aggression and outrage on the one hand, or on the other, by the adoption, at all hazards and to the last extremity of such measures as will vindicate our constitutional rights.

7. *Resolved*, That we hold it to be the duty of every man in this confederacy to oppose the passage of any law by which our newly acquired territory may be subject to such a restriction.

8. *Resolved*, That the passage of the above mentioned proviso makes it the duty of every slaveholding State and of the citizens thereof, as they value their dearest privileges, their sovereignty, their independence, their rights of property, to take firm, and concerted action in this emergency.

9. *Resolved*, That we regard the passage of a law by the Congress of the United States abolishing slavery or the slave trade in the District of Columbia, as a direct attack upon the institutions of the southern States.

10. *Resolved*, That in the recent movements of a large portion of the people of the north, in Congress, in the legislatures of the States, in the civil courts, in the primary assemblies of the people, in their continued efforts to abolish slavery in the District of Columbia, in the establishment of the principles of the Wilmot proviso, and in the protection of fugitive slaves, we perceive a total disregard and a reckless violation of all their pledges in the constitution: and a design not only to prevent the extension of slavery into the newly acquired territory, but to abolish it forcibly, at no distant day, in all the States of the Union where it now exists.

11. *Resolved*, That we view with admiration the noble stand taken by the States of Virginia, N. Carolina and Florida in the resolutions which have passed their respective Legislatures.

12. *Resolved*, That in the event of the passage by Congress of the Wilmot proviso, or any law abolishing slavery or the slave trade in the District of Columbia, we are ready, heart and soul, with a united front, to join Virginia, the

Carolinas, Florida, and other southern States, in taking such measures for the vindication of our rights, and the preservation of ourselves and those whom we hold dear, as the highest wisdom of all may, whether through a southern convention or otherwise, suggest and advise.

13. *Resolved,* That the President of this convention appoint a State Central Committee of five persons, residing in Nashville; and that this committee appoint central committees of five in each Congressional District, to cooperate with the State Central Committee in effecting a thorough organization of the party in the State.

14. *Resolved,* That the State Central Committee, to be appointed under the foregoing resolution, be, and are hereby, instructed to prepare an address to the people of Tennessee."

Two days after the nomination of General Trousdale for Governor, the Nashville *Daily Union* floated from its masthead the following: [5]

"For Governor
GEN. WM. TROUSDALE
The Veteran of Three Wars

The Soldier of Tallashatchee, Talledega, Pensacola, the Glorious Night of the 23rd December, 1814; the 8th of January, 1815; of the Forks of Withlacoochie; the Three Battles of the Wahoo hummock, 17th, 18th, and 21st November, 1836; of Contreras, of Cherubusco, of Molino del Rey and of Chepultepec, in 1848."

The same newspaper carried a resumé of the proceedings of the Convention which had formulated and adopted a ringing declaration regarding the "slavery question" which had seriously raised its head for the first time in Tennessee in a gubernatorial campaign, an issue that was precipitated by the Mexican War and the Wilmot Proviso, to-wit: [6]

"... In relation to the selection of a candidate for Governor, the finest spirit of 'union, harmony and concession' prevailed. The delegates freely interchanged views; and while others had warm and earnest friends, the majority thought Gen. Trousdale to be the first choice of the largest portion of the democracy, and he was accordingly nominated.

Col. Haynes, of East Tennessee, was warmly supported by several friends. A strong feeling in his favor also pervaded the entire convention, and there was a general desire to honor East Tennessee with the nomination in the person of a son who has shown himself devoted to her interests, as well as one of the most able advocates of our cause. It was thought, however, by the majority that Gen. Trousdale would probably at this time, more thoroughly unite the whole party, including the many who were Taylor democrats, than any other member of our party, and this opinion gave him the nomination by a decisive vote on the first ballot.

A debate on the resolutions relative to the slavery question sprang up during the evening session, between Andrew Ewing, Esq., and Gen. Coe, which was characterized with extraordinary ability. Mr. Ewing doubted the expediency of passing one of the resolutions, and made, what he always makes when he speaks, a powerful and brilliant speech in opposition to its adoption. Gen. Coe spoke in favor of the resolution, and, with a degree of

[5] *Ibid.,* April 21, 1849.
[6] *Ibid.,* April 21, 1849.

eloquence and a strength of argument which we had never heard surpassed, advocated its passage. The majority of the convention agreed with Gen. Coe, that the time for a firm declaration of our purpose to resist the encroachments of northern fanaticism, when pushed to the extremity, had arrived; and the resolution, as reported by General Coe, was adopted.

We have no doubt that the action of the convention will meet with general approval by the democracy of the State. That the nomination for Governor will be hailed with enthusiasm by all the democrats and thousands of the whigs of the State, we think certain. There is no abandonment of principle involved in voting for a candidate for Governor who may not agree with the voter in politics, because the Governor of Tennessee has no control over any of those questions which divide our people into parties. The 'honesty and capacity' of Gen. Trousdale cannot be questioned. And, what *must* conciliate the support of the Taylor men, he is, as a soldier, the man who has seen more service than any other man in the State, and who stands, among the volunteers of the Volunteer State,

'The noblest Roman of them all.'

The Taylor democrats of the State, united with those who voted for Cass, are a majority of the voters of the State; and we therefore look upon the election of Gen. Trousdale as a fixed fact. We need scarcely urge our friends to rally to his support. They will do it 'by spontaneous combustion.' No party drill which the whigs may be able to get up can prevent THE PEOPLE of Tennessee from voting for WILLIAM TROUSDALE."

In a vein of rather sarcastic irony, the Whig organ called the hand of its competitor and political opponent in the following editorial:[7]

"GENERAL WILLIAM TROUSDALE

Was on Thursday last nominated as the Locofoco candidate for Governor of this State. General Trousdale has the reputation of a courteous gentleman. Some of the most ardent of his friends in the Convention urged that his services in the wars and his acts and wounds would speak for him, if he was not so able a debater as some of the Democrats spoken of for the candidate. Gen. Coe of the Western District and Mr. Helm, of Knox, did not think him the most available man—they and others preferred an able debater, but Gen. Trousdale prevailed by the following vote, taken by counties, as represented in the lower House of the Legislature—several of the counties voted by proxy, or had held meetings and expressed preferences, which preferences were counted as votes. . . .

Will the Union do Gen. Trousdale the justice to correct the table of battles thrown out at the head of its columns? We don't want to see our old fellow-soldier, (we were in several of those battles, but don't claim a nomination for Governor, and don't claim to be a 'veteran' of even 'one war,') Gen. Trousdale placed before the country as being in battles where he was not present. Gen. Trousdale will claim nothing more than having done his duty in those battles, where he was present, and we intend to give him full credit for all the services he has rendered his country. We think it unkind in our Democratic friends to put our old fellow-soldier in the political breach to fall again as he did in 1837. When Gen. Trousdale had been the 'veteran of two wars,' on his return from Florida, in 1837, where he had, as Colonel, com-

---

[7] *Nashville True Whig*, April 21, 1849.

Whereas, it is the duty of this General Assembly, in its deliberation, to observe strict rules of economy + justice: And as many daily newspapers are placed upon the table of each member; containing nearly the same report of Legislative proceedings. — There=fore, that no inconvenience may be experienced or injustice done to the state or individuals —

Resolved by the General Assembly of the state of Tennessee That the Public printer of this General Assembly be authorized & required to cause to be laid on the table of each member, — every morning — One Copy of some of the daily newspapers, published in the city, containing the reported legislative proceedings of the preceding day — that the same may be provided for in the general appro-=priation bill. — And in the selection of such daily paper, the wishes of members shall be regarded. —

A Proposal for Obtaining Personal Information at Public Expense.
(See *Senate Journal*, 1849, pages 83-84)

manded a regiment, his Democratic friends brought him out as a candidate for Congress, and one of the Captains, who had served under him in his regiment, (the gallant Wm. B. Campbell,) ran against him, and, if we recollect correctly, beat him about 1700 votes, in the then Sumner Congressional District.—When there was a Brigadier General to appoint, Mr. Polk passes over our old fellow-soldier and then 'veteran of two wars,' and appoints Gen. Pillow, who had not then 'smelt battle' even afar off, a Brigadier General and gave our old fellow-soldier the office of Colonel. But now, when Tennessee has crushed modern Democracy by the overwhelming majority of more than six thousand, Gen. Pillow yields the 'honor and profits' of a defeat to Gen. Trousdale! This is unkind."

On April 23, 1849, the Whig State Convention convened in Nashville for the purpose of nominating a candidate for Governor. The Organization Committee, "after a short absence," reported and recommended Return Jonathan Meigs as Chairman, together with three recommendations for Vice-Presidents and five Secretaries, all of whom were elected without opposition. There followed immediately the following resolutions which were unanimously adopted:[8]

"WHEREAS, it appearing by the action of primary meetings throughout the State, that the present distinguished incumbent of the Gubernatorial Chair, Gov. NEILL S. BROWN, is the first choice of the Whigs of Tennessee for the same elevated post: Therefore,
Resolved, Unanimously, that he be and is hereby nominated the Whig candidate for re-election to the office of Governor of the State of Tennessee.
R. W. H. Bostick, Esq., then offered the following resolution, which, on motion, was unanimously adopted:
Resolved, That a Committee of three be appointed to notify Gov. Brown of his nomination by this Convention, and request his presence in the Hall.
The President then announced the following named gentlemen as such Committee:
Messrs. R. W. H. Bostick, John Muirhead, and Thos. A. Pasteurs.
The Committee having retired soon returned with Gov. Brown, whose appearance having been greeted with loud acclamation, he proceeded to address the Convention, thanking it for the confidence expressed in him and pledging renewed efforts in behalf of Whig principles.
At the close of the Governor's address, Gen. F. K. Zollicoffer, of Davidson, offered the following Resolutions, which were unanimously adopted—
Resolved, That as full and free discussion is eminently favorable to the promotion and ascendancy of Whig principles: Therefore
Resolved, That the members of this Convention are gratified to learn that the Rough and Ready newspaper and other Campaign papers are to be renewed by our enterprising Whig Publishers in Tennessee, and that we pledge ourselves to do everything in our power to promote their circulation and usefulness.
On motion of H. L. Davidson, Esq., of Bedford, it was
Resolved, That the Whig papers throughout the State be requested to publish the proceedings of this Convention.
On motion of Col. Muirhead, it was further
Resolved, That the thanks of the Convention are due and are hereby ten-

---

[8] *Ibid.*, April 24, 1849.

dered to the officers thereof, for the able manner in which they have discharged the duties devolving upon them.

On motion of Russell Houston Esq. the Convention then adjourned *sine die*.

R. J. MEIGS, *Pres't.*

S. W. MITCHELL,
A. M. ROSBOROUGH,
W. WALES,
W. HY. SMITH,
JNO. E. GARNER, *Secretaries.*"

Prior to the meetings of the Democratic and Whig State Conventions, the editor of the Gallatin *Tenth Legion* had advocated the abandonment of joint speakings by the respective gubernatorial candidates. His proposal received support from a limited number of newspapers, both Democratic and Whig.[9] Urged as reasons for the discontinuance of such a practice were the long and exhausting journeys to distant parts of the State, inimical to both health and comfort, and the financial expenses of such campaigns. But the time was not ripe for the abandonment of the face-to-face contests; the public relished the slugging exhibitions and each contestant was required by the spirit of the times to "take the medicine" administered by his opponent and the opposing press. And so the old-time procedure was continued, and the blow by blow battle was waged vigorously with no holds barred.

The newspaper columns were filled with partisan accounts of the campaign. Taking the "reports" and the "sketches" of the speeches with *cum grano salis* (with a grain of salt) is not adequate; a barrel of salt would prove insufficient in many instances! Lack of space prevents the inclusion of such prejudiced accounts, and the reader will have to be content with a mere statement as to the one vital issue discussed. Towering above all other questions was that of slavery, the paramount issue in this gubernatorial campaign. It was an issue of such gigantic implications that each political party found within its own ranks a division of sentiment. Many Memphis Whigs, for instance, vehemently denounced anti-slavery measures which "justified resistance on the part of the Southern States." On the other hand, some strong Democrats like Congressman Cave Johnson viewed with distrust any movement that might endanger the Union. And so, the gubernatorial candidates, attempting to sail safely between Scylla and Charybdis, were forced to give professional exhibitions of some fancy tight-rope walking. The Ides of August ultimately arrived, and General Trousdale squeezed through by a narrow margin and landed in the gubernatorial chair.

The Twenty-Eighth General Assembly convened at Nashville on Monday, October 1, 1849. As indicative of how "tight" the political

---

[9] Hamer, Philip M.: *Tennessee—A History*, Volume I, 474.

battle lines were drawn, the Senate had a Whig majority of three, while the House countered with a Democratic majority of the identical number. On joint ballot, when various public officials were to be elected, there was politically a tie vote. Among the Whig personnel were Felix Zollicoffer, the first Confederate General to be killed in the West, and General William B. Stokes, a four-term Congressman and unsuccessful candidate for Governor on the Radical ticket in 1869. The Democrats had among their number General William B. Bate, later Governor of Tennessee and United States Senator; the silver-tongued orator, Landon C. Haynes, later a member of the Confederate Congress; E. L. Gardenhire, also a member of the Confederate Congress. Whig Senator John F. Henry of Knox County was elected Speaker of the Senate and Democrat Landon C. Haynes was the choice for Speaker of the House of Representatives. Rival candidates for legislative officers were legion. In the Senate, fifteen candidates vied for the position of Engrossing Clerk, and the election required forty-four ballots.[10] Twenty candidates were presented for Doorkeeper, requiring fifty-three ballots before an election was made. In the House of Representatives, twelve candidates aspired to the position of Assistant Clerk, necessitating thirteen ballots.[11] Nine ballots were required before there was an election of a Doorkeeper,[12] ten gentlemen having let it be known that they desired to guard the portal of entry.

With the organizational preliminaries attended to, Whig Senator M. Thornburg proposed to notify the retiring Whig Governor, Neill S. Brown, that the Legislature was ready to hear from him, to-wit:[13]

"*Resolved*, That a committee of three members of the Senate be appointed to join such committee as shall be appointed by the House of Representatives, to wait upon his Excellency the Governor of the State of Tennessee, and inform him that the two Houses of the General Assembly are now organized, and ready to receive any communication he may think proper to make."

In response to the legislative invitation, Senator Thornburg advised the body that

"... the committee have performed the duty assigned them and received for answer from his Excellency that he would instantly transmit a message in writing to the General Assembly."[14]

To the joy of the Democrats and to the dismay of the Whigs, it was necessary to take official action relative to the election of a new Governor. At an afternoon session, October 10, the Legislature met in joint

[10] *Senate Journal*, 1849, 20.
[11] *House Journal*, 1849, 17.
[12] *Ibid.*, 1849, 24.
[13] *Senate Journal*, 1849, 35.
[14] *Ibid.*, 44.
Author's note. Governor Brown's Message was duly incorporated on pages 256–267.

session to count the vote for Governor as cast in the August election. Upon examination, it appeared that out of the then seventy-four counties three counties had made no official returns, namely, Cannon, Bedford, and Bradley. An agreement was reached that the statements of the Representatives from the delinquent counties be received and counted, whereupon it was disclosed that William Trousdale had received a total of 61,740 votes, and Neill S. Brown 60,350 votes, giving Trousdale a majority of 1,390 votes.[15] Thereupon, Mr. Speaker Henry declared William Trousdale duly and constitutionally elected Governor of the State of Tennessee for the ensuing two years. The next step was to fix the day of inauguration which was attended to in the following manner;[16]

"The Committee appointed to wait upon the Governor-elect and to enquire of him when and where it will suit his convenience to be inaugurated, have performed that duty, and beg leave to report,

That his Excellency appoints Tuesday the 16th instant, at half past two o'clock as the time, leaving the place discretionary with the committee; and the committee have selected the Methodist (McKendree) Church as the place of performing the ceremony."

On October 13, Governor Neill S. Brown transmitted the following brief Message to the Legislature:[17]

"EXECUTIVE OFFICE,
Nashville, October 13, 1849

GENTLEMEN OF THE SENATE AND
    HOUSE OF REPRESENTATIVES:

I herewith transmit to you the Report of the Board of Commissioners of Common Schools recently made to me.

Respectfully,
N. S. BROWN."

The official account of the inaugural ceremonies, conducted on October 16, 1849, was as follows:[18]

"Mr. Speaker Henry and the Gentlemen of the Senate repaired to the Representative Hall, for the purpose of proceeding to the inauguration of Wm. Trousdale, the Governor elect of the State of Tennessee.

The two Houses being in convention, the Speaker of the Senate directed the clerk to announce the order of procession, which being done;

Was as follows, to wit:

1. Governor and Governor elect in front.

---

15 *Ibid.*, 1849, 75–76.
   House Journal, 1849, 72–73.
16 *Senate Journal*, 1849, 92.
17 *Ibid.*, 96.
18 *Ibid.*, 104–105.

2. Ministers of the Gospel.
3. Judges of the Supreme, Chancery and Circuit Courts.
4. Members of Congress in the city.
5. Speaker of the Senate and House of Representatives.
6. Members of the Senate in double files and officers.
7. Members of the House in same order and officers.
8. Ladies.
9. Citizens generally.

And thereupon the two Houses of the General Assembly in procession, in accordance with the above order, repaired to the Methodist (McKendree) Church in this city, where the ceremony of inauguration took place in presence of both Houses of the General Assembly.

Prayer being offered by the Rev. C. D. Elliott of the Methodist Church, his Excellency Neil S. Brown delivered his valedictory address; after which Wm. Trousdale delivered his inaugural address. The several oaths prescribed by the Constitution and laws of the State were then administered to his Excellency Wm. Trousdale, Governor of the State of Tennessee, by the Hon. Wm. K. Turner, one of the Judges of the State of Tennessee; when prayer was again offered up by Mr. Smith of the Cumberland Presbyterian Church.

Whereupon, the members of the General Assembly returned in the same order of procession to the Hall of the House of Representatives.

On motion of Mr. Kyle,

The Speaker and Gentlemen of the Senate returned to their chamber and resumed their session."

Governor Brown's Valedictory Address and Governor Trousdale's Inaugural Address, curiously enough, were carried in a local church paper and were as follows:[19]

"GENTLEMEN OF THE SENATE AND HOUSE OF REPRESENTATIVES:

You have assembled in pursuance of past usage, to witness the Inauguration of the Governor-elect of the State. And I am here at the close of my term of service to deliver up the seals of office which I have held for the last two years.

In retiring from this station, I am gratified in the belief, that the State over which I have presided, is in the enjoyment of a full measure of prosperity and happiness; and every indication now presented augurs well for the future. Prominent in view is the spirit of improvement which marks the tone of public sentiment and public action, and which, if unchecked by adversity, nor palsied by over action, promises a rich harvest to the State. Few portions of the Union, require more improvement, or contain more abundant elements to tempt the spirit of enterprise than Tennessee. Many a rugged mountain, across whose summit the hardy emigrant has passed for half a century, teems with native material far more valu-

---

[19] *Presbyterian Record* (Nashville), October 20, 1849.

able, than even the spreading vallies, that enticed his eye. Within the memory of those now living, the region of our metropolis was but the green home of the pioneer amid the wild music of nature; now a growing city with its accompanying train, the arts and sciences, looms up to view and challenges admiration. To what art has already done will soon be superadded a great highway to market, sustaining a rapid communication between the interior and the Atantic. In a few years, the humblest man in Tennessee, at small expense and a brief journey, may behold the capitol of the nation and witness those great intellectual struggles that sway the public mind, and of which he now only hears at a distance. The emporiums of commerce will be rendered accessible to all classes of commodities, without the delay and uncertainty that now mark the ranges of trade. These ends will be accomplished by railroad communication which leaves behind in the distance all other modes of conveyance. Neither the ship that swims the sea, nor the steamboat that plies the river can vie as an agent of commerce with the great land car, either in speed or economy; while the concomitant advantages in the growth and settlement of the country; in the establishment of manufactures and the improvement of the arts, distinguish it as the rapid messenger of glad tidings. Although our borders are washed by no wave of the ocean, and no bright lake glitters on our surface, or swelling sails gladden our prospects, yet the dawn of that day is upon us, which will witness our commercial enfranchisement, and introduce us through the avenues of art to the great commercial theatre of nature.

There are portions of the State of the highest capabilities in all the varied enterprizes of the day, but which are surrounded by the frowning battlements of nature, beneath whose shadows, the energy of man has toiled in vain for half a century. Is it not the policy of the State, to bring into requisition all her elements of wealth and strength? To break the icebergs that enclose the fleet of her power and greatness? It can be done! It will be done! Public sentiment is ripening for it, and will soon be upon it like an avalanche. Public sentiment that makes and unmakes goverments—that depresses one dynasty and elevates another, is competent to the task.

Enlightened, invigorated public opinion is the great magic

wand, beneath whose mighty strokes bleak mountains can be made to pour forth the tribute of their long hidden treasures, and rivers that never felt the pressure of navigation, be made to acknowledge the propeling power of steam and the dominion of man. In this bright train will be found the growth of manufacturers and the improvement of the arts; while education in all its grades, from the common school to the university, will flourish and prevail.

This may now be deemed fancy; but it will soon be fact. And in the space of ten years, some honored successor in this department, on retiring from his term of service, will be able to point to the bright reality, not in the faltering language of prophecy, but in the bolder notes of fulfillment.

Tennessee is capable, above every other State, from the character of her soil, climate and mineral wealth, of sustaining all classes of American pursuits in full vigor and harmony. And from this will arise that commercial independence in reserve for us, without which no State can be eminently prosperous, happy, or great. Nature has lavished in our midst her golden bounties, and prescribed in legible characters the task to be performed by the hand of art. There are valleys, and mountains, and streams, and waterfalls.—There, agriculture in all its variety, and manufactures, and the mechanic arts may flourish in the fullest perfection. They will flourish. And soon the ear of the passing traveller will be regaled by other sounds than the wild notes of the forest and the roar of the cataract. The music of the spindle will mingle with the sturdy tones of husbandry. The loud blows of the forge-hammer will echo to the thunder of the passing steam car; while the commercial genius of a great and growing commonwealth will smile in the plenitude of her own acquired strength and supremacy.

Tennessee occupies a central position in the Union, geographically speaking. Why may she not be made the centre of its strength and greatness—the real keystone of that sublime arch that now bespans the continent? Secure from the ultra passions that play in the extremes; safe in her own resources, self-poised, she can stand in the evil day of discord, if it should ever come, like a mighty tower of strength, and say to the angry waves on either side, 'Peace! be still!' Happy in her own position; conscious of her own prowess; holding in one hand the tie of this great sisterhood, and in the other

the sword of its defence, with all her unconquered eagles cluster-
ing around her, I trust her destiny will be as glorious as her responsibility, her power and her advantages are great!

With these hopes, and to these ends, have I dedicated whatever
of influence belonged to my late public employment. But too
conscious am I, however, at this moment, of the little I have been
able to accomplish, and into that retirement on which I am about
to enter, I shall carry with me the same solicitude for the State that
gave me birth; by whose confidence I have been honored, and with
whose fortunes I am identified.

The voice of public sentiment, two years ago, called me from
my retreat to preside in this department; that same voice now summons me to retire. I heard the former, I trust, with a chastened and
just sense of the honor implied in it, and I have heard the latter without a murmur or complaint. And whatever imputations, either of
motive or conduct, I may have been the subject of, in the heat of
strife and the collission of opinions, (and no public man can be
wholly exempt,) I this day write them upon the sand; let them fade
into forgetfulness!

While I shall cherish in fond remembrance, the generous support I have received in the discharge of official duty, and my attempts to serve the public, I shall cherish with not less fondness the
principles at large, of my choice of which I have been the humble,
but zealous and honored advocate. And so long as a thread or patch
of the glorious flag which proclaims them, floats upon the breeze, I
shall rally to it—stand by it—sustain it, through good and through
evil report; neither vaunting in victory, nor repining in defeat! For
Tennessee and for the Union in undivided fortune and glory! ought
to be engraved upon every heart and every banner, and heralded
from every platform. I trust the last light that gilds the earth, may
shine upon this noble confederated structure, unimpaired, majestic,
as in the days of its first consecration and that every element which
conspires to break its proportions or mar its beauty, may be scattered by the strong arm of true American patriotism.

I trust the State is destined to enjoy wiser counsels than mine,
an abler supervision and more fortunate auspices; and that every
instrumentality to be employed by my distinguished successor may
redound to the interest, the happiness and the glory of Tennessee."

"Gov. Trousdale's Address

GENTLEMEN OF THE SENATE,
AND OF THE HOUSE OF REPRESENTATIVES:

Your Committee have informed me that I have been chosen by the people of Tennessee to the Chief Executive office of the State, and we are here assembled for the purpose of transferring the duties of that office from the hands of one individual into those of another. In this transaction, the beauty and harmony of our system of government, contrasted with that of other Nations, most clearly appears. When power, in most other countries, passes from one man to another, the transit is generally the result of war, blood-shed, and misery; but under our happy form of government no such precursions attend a change. The struggle for office, while the contest is in progress, may be fierce and violent; but when the result has been told by the ballot box, the contest is ended and the troubled elements become calm. This glorious system of government was not the acquisition of a day, it cost our fathers a war of eight years, in which was expended much blood and treasure. In this war many individuals met privations, hardships, and death under circumstances which would move the sympathies of any human being who has a soul which can feel for the sufferings of others. We now stand as the representatives of those patriots, and the duty of administering the government which their strong arms hewed out, devolves upon us. They have left us the rich legacy. Shall we permit tyrants to rob us of this rich boon, and rivet upon us the shackles burst asunder by the American Revolution? Is it not the wish of every American citizen that our free and happy institutions may move hand in hand with time, and disseminate blessings to benighted Europe and every other country which man inhabits! Custom has made it necessary for me, before I take the solemn pledge of office, briefly to indicate the principles on which I intend to administer the government. In relation to State policy, the subjects which most vitally interest the public, are those of Education and Internal Improvement. Our Common School system does not disseminate the blessings of Education to all who need the fostering care of the government.

A proper system by which education can be extended and brought to a greater degree of perfection, will receive my sanction.

Education is of vast importance every where, but in the republic of the United States, where one of the fundamental principles of the government is knowledge, it is essential to properly qualify man for citizenship. Argument to prove the importance of Education before this enlightened community, is wholly useless, and doubtless any well digested legislation which might be enacted, would meet the approbation of your constituents.

The subject of Internal Improvements by the State government is now to some extent agitating the public mind. This is a subject well worthy of mature consideration. Nature has done much for our beloved Tennessee, in soil, climate, rivers and many other particulars, but the hand of art is necessary to aid the natural advantages, and to develope the resources of the country. It would seem to be the true policy of every government, at the earliest practicable period, to develope the resources of the country by such improvements as may be necessary to accomplish the object. A course of this kind would enable the present generations, could it be done now, to enjoy advantages which might be kept back for ages. But the system should be practicable before it is attempted. It would be bad policy, by a system of Internal Improvement, to contract a debt beyond the ability of the State to pay. The government instead of being benefited by such a course would be greatly injured, and the real progress of the State much retarded. But before a great enterprise of this kind should be adopted, a thorough investigation of the means and the liabilities of the State should be made, and the cost of the intended enterprise well understood; and if upon such examination it should fully appear that the State had the means of making the improvement, then the work should be undertaken and pushed to a consummation as soon as practicable.

On the subject of federal relations, although we can take no direct action, yet we are most vitally interested in what may be there transacted. We constitute a portion of the people of the United States; we live under the federal as well as the State government, and it is our imperious duty to guard our rights under the constitution of the United States. The great question with politicians and with the people of the United States is, what construction shall be given to the Federal Constitution. Some contend for a liberal—and others for a strict construction of that instrument, and this difference constitutes the foundation of parties in the United States. Those who contend for a liberal construction can thereby make the constitution sanction almost any thing which they may wish to do. This construction would render the constitution a dead letter, and substitute the will of man as the fundamental rule of action. The party which insists upon a strict construction, say that the federal Government is limited in its powers, and can exercise no power which is not expressly given by the constitution, or such as result from an express gift. To this last construction of the constitution, of the United States, I most heartily subscribe and shall stand prepared at all times to meet and repel to the best of my ability any departure from that rule of construction.

I cannot hope in the discharge of the duties upon which I am about to enter, that my course of action will be approved by all; such success seldom falls to the lot of man. There is one thing, however, within my own control and that is, to direct my best energies to the faithful discharge of all the duties resulting from the office.

I acknowledge my gratitude to you, gentlemen, and to the people of the State at large, for distinguished honor conferred on me, by selecting me as the Chief Magistrate of this high minded, patriotic, chivalrous State, and shall endeavor to merit the confidence thus manifested, in all my public acts."

Two days after his inauguration, Governor Trousdale transmitted the following brief Message to the Legislature:

Legislative Message,* October 18, 1849

"EXECUTIVE OFFICE
Nashville, Oct. 18, 1849

To the Senate and
    House of Representatives:

I herewith nominate and appoint as directors of the Bank of Tennessee, the persons named in the accompanying list.

W. Trousdale.

---

* *Senate Journal*, 1849, 124.

Author's note. The *Senate Journal* contains two typographical errors as to dates. The Message was transmitted on October 18 and not October 8; the year was 1849 instead of 1848.

Davidson—A. O. P. Nicholson, John B. Johnson, Jno. Waters, Jas. Morton, L. B. Fite, R. C. McNairy, Isaac Paul 7
 Sumner—Benj. R. Howard 1
 Smith—Geo. C. Allen 1
 Wilson—E. A. White 1
 Robertson—A. G. Green 1
 Macon—Thos. A. Williams 1
 Rutherford—Wm. Ledbetter 1
 Maury—B. Martin 1
 Williamson—Robt. C. Foster, Sen. 1
 Lawrence—Richard Allen 1
 Hickman—Jas. D. Easley 1
 Dixon—Robt. McNeely 1
 Cannon—Wm. D. Gower 1
 Humphreys—Levi McCollom 1

              20"

More than a week prior to the inauguration of Governor Trousdale, the Democratic Speaker of the House, Landon C. Haynes, had appointed seventeen Standing Committees, one of which was the Committee on Banks.[20] The Committee on Banks was composed of seven members, distributed politically as follows:

Name	County	Politics
Bate, Humphrey R.	Tipton and Lauderdale	Democrat
Buford, Thomas	Giles	Democrat
Searcy, Granville D.	Shelby	Whig
Blair, John	Washington	Democrat
Allen, Beverly S.	Carroll	Whig
Strayhorn, William J.	Maury	Democrat
Harrell, George A.	Montgomery	Whig

Apparently, this "4 to 3" ratio was a bit too thin, for subsequently additional members were appointed, to-wit:

Name	County	Politics
Gantt, George	Maury	Democrat
Atkins, J. D. C.	Henry	Democrat
Bate, William B.	Sumner	Democrat
Adams, Nathan	Lincoln and Giles	Democrat
Benton, John W.	Wilson	Whig
Nance, C. W.	Davidson	Whig

---

[20] *House Journal*, 1849, 54–55.

Thus, it will be seen, that the over-all House Committee on Banks consisted of thirteen members of whom eight were Democrats, a sufficiently large majority.

On October 6, the same day on which the House Committee on Banks had been appointed, the Whig Speaker of the Senate, John F. Henry, named eighteen Standing Committees. The Committee on Banks was as follows:[21]

Name	County	Politics
Bostick, R. W. H.	Rutherford and Williamson	Whig
Zollicoffer, Felix K.	Davidson	Whig
Wilkes, Richard A. L.	Maury and Giles	Democrat
Harris, W. S. S.	Henry, Weakley, and Obion	Democrat
Kyle, Gayle H.	Madison, Haywood, Tipton, and Lauderdale	Whig
Gillespie, James W.	Hamilton, Marion, Bledsoe, Rhea, and Meigs	Whig
Britton, James	Greene and Hawkins	Democrat

Since each branch of the Legislature was divided politically, it will be noted that the Whig Senate did not overlook giving its party a majority on the powerful and dynamite-loaded Bank Committee, a point equally recognized by the Democratic House Speaker when he placed the majority of the Bank Committee in the hands of Democrats. In all probability, no other legislative committee was picked with more caution than the Banking Committee, for the very good reason that the Bank of Tennessee was all along a powerful political machine and its support or opposition was a potent factor in numerous gubernatorial contests.

At the time of Governor Trousdale's inauguration, the President and a majority of the bank's Directors were Whigs. President William Ledbetter of Rutherford County was a Whig of outstanding ability and had had a lot of experience in public life. Although Ledbetter was retained in the list recommended by Governor Trousdale in the above Message, yet the list contained the name of A. O. P. Nicholson, a militant Democrat with previous experience as President of the Bank of Tennessee, United States Senator, and Chairman of the recent State Democratic Convention that had nominated William Trousdale for Governor who had defeated for re-election the Whig candidate, Governor Neill S. Brown. Moreover, the list recommended by Governor Trousdale contained a majority of Democrats, and it was almost axiomatic that Ledbetter would be replaced in all probability by Nicholson as President of the institution.

---

[21] *Senate Journal*, 1849, 55.

The Whig Senate's opposition to the nominees by Governor Trousdale for Directors of the Bank of Tennessee prevailed. Delay after delay in regard to considering the nominees was the procedure adopted. Immediately after receiving the Governor's recommended list, Whig Senator Bostick moved successfully

"That said message and accompanying list do lie upon the table until the 15th of November next."[22]

On the appointed day, Whig Senator Thornburg moved successfully that the Message remain on the table another thirty days, thereby granting a respite of another month.[23] Once again, another delay of thirty days, or until January 15, was ordered by the Senate by the close vote of 13 to 12.[24] When the appointed day rolled around, Whig Senator Samuel Pickens picked up the ball and postponed the date until February 4, again by a vote of 13 to 12.[25] On the latter date, the matter received no consideration despite the fact that a specific date had been determined. On February 9, just two days prior to adjournment *sine die*, another postponement until the day of adjournment was made by a vote of 11 to 10.[26] On the last day of the legislative session, Democratic Senator J. W. Whitfield moved to take up the confirmation of the Bank Directors nominated by Governor Trousdale, but his motion failed for lack of a quorum vote.[27] Thus, procrastination won its long-drawn-out battle, the Message and its recommendations having been before the Legislature from October 18, 1849 to February 11, 1850.

How had Governor Trousdale's Message and recommendations for Bank Directors fared in the House of Representatives? The following Message from Governor Trousdale revealed that the Whig Senate had not been content with instituting delaying tactics in its own body, but that the Senate had delayed for two months transmitting the Message of October 18 to the House of Representatives. Here was the Governor's reminder of that fact.

---

[22] *Senate Journal*, 1849, 124.

[23] *Ibid.*, 255.

[24] *Ibid.*, 407.

[25] *Ibid.*, 530.

[26] *Ibid.*, 768.

[27] *Ibid.*, 780.

Author's note. The printed *Senate Journal* covering this last item contains a significant typographical error. Senator Whitfield's motion was "that the Senate do *now* take up and consider the Governor's Message nominating Directors for the Bank of Tennessee." The printed *Journal* carries the word "*not*" instead of the word "*now*."

"EXECUTIVE OFFICE
Nashville, Dec. 18, 1849.

TO THE SENATE AND HOUSE OF REPRESENTATIVES: *

GENTLEMEN:—Having in my message of the 18th of October, submitted to your body through the Senate, the following list of names, as a board of Directors of the Bank of Tennessee, for the confirmation of the Legislature, in conformity with the law of 1845, chapter 9, section 1, and the said message not having as yet been transmitted to the House of Representatives, I herewith again nominate as directors in the said Bank, the persons named in the following list.

W. TROUSDALE

A. O. P. Nicholson, John B. Johnson, John Waters, James Martin, L. B. Fite, Maj. R. C. McNairy, Isaac Paul, Benj. R. Howard, B. M. Moore, E. A. White, A. G. Greene, Thomas A. Williams, Wm. Ledbetter, B. Martin, R. C. Foster, sr., George C. Allen, James D. Easley, Robert McNeeley, Wm. D. Gowan, Levi McCullum and John McDougal."

At an afternoon session of the House of Representatives on December 18, the day of the reception of the Governor's Message, Whig Representative P. G. S. Perkins of Williamson County attempted to ape the delaying action of the Whig Senate by proposing the following resolution, to-wit: [28]

"*Resolved*, That all action upon the confirmation of the State Bank directory nominated by the Governor shall be postponed until an investigation into the conduct of the directory of said Bank for the past six years can be had and reported to this House."

But the Democratic House of Representatives differed from the position assumed by their Whig colleague by defeating his resolution. Thereupon, on motion, the Directors nominated by Governor Trousdale were confirmed by a vote of 46 to 26.[29]

The whole question of banking, confirmation of Bank Directors

---

* *Senate Journal*, 1849, 421.
    House Journal, 1849, 452.
[28] *House Journal*, 1849, 454.
[29] *Ibid.*, 454.
    Author's note. In Governor Trousdale's Message of December 18, the name of Richard Allen had been dropped from the original list of nominees and three other names added to the revised list, namely, Richard Allen, B. M. Moore, and John McDougal. For some reason unknown to the writer, McDougal was confirmed by the Senate, the only nominee thus honored out of the twenty-one nominees submitted by Governor Trousdale. See *Senate Journal*, 1849, page 701.

et cetera was intensified in the early part of the legislative session by the passage of a resolution [30] directing the Committee on Banks

"... To enquire and report whether there has been any violation of the charter of the Bank of Tennessee, within the last six years, by extending loans or accommodations to a director or directors or otherwise; and, if so, to report when, where, and to whom such loans or accommodations were made."

As might have been expected, with a Legislature split closely along political lines, a prolonged investigation resulted in the filing of both Majority and Minority Reports.[31] These Reports embrace 104 printed pages in the *Senate Journal* and 145 printed pages in the *House Journal*, 1849. The Majority Report of the Senate was signed by Whig members of the Banking Committee, while in the House the Majority Report bears the names of Democratic members of the Banking Committee! Curiously enough, the Majority and Minority Reports, both in the Senate and in the House, differ from each other, there being no repetition in any case. The Reports, quite contradictory in many respects, include the testimony of a large number of persons, exhibits of loans made by the bank and its branches, the political affiliation of the Bank Directors, both the parent and branch banks, and a lot of detail wholly irrelevant to the specific issue itself. In the main, it was just another instance of each political party attempting to put the *onus* on the other, with neither succeeding to any marked degree.

As heretofore pointed out, only one of the men nominated for Director of the Bank of Tennessee was confirmed by the Senate, the other twenty nominees remaining in "cold storage." The Whig Senate was satisfied as to the status quo of the bank directorate, inasmuch as a majority of the incumbent Directors were Whigs.[32] Failure of the Senate to act upon the Executive recommendations as of October 18, 1849, gave rise to many rumors and expressed fears regarding the legal status of the State Bank. So impressive were the mooted points that Governor Trousdale felt impelled to transmit a special message to the Legislature upon the matter, though he had carried out his part of the legal responsibility almost three months earlier. Consideration of that special message will be noted shortly in this chapter.

One week after his inauguration, Governor William Trousdale transmitted to the General Assembly his chief Message.

---

[30] *Senate Journal*, 1849, 117.

[31] *Senate Journal*, 1849, Appendix, 257–361.
House Journal, 1849, Appendix, 275–420.

[32] Author's note. In the course of the Bank of Tennessee investigation by the Banking Committee, evidence was introduced to show that upon the recommendation of William Ledbetter, a Whig and the President of the Bank of Tennessee, all the branch banks were Whig-controlled. The allocation was as follows: Sparta Branch; 9 Whigs, and 5 Democrats; Rogersville Branch; 10 Whigs, and 5 Democrats; Trenton Branch; 10 Whigs, and 5 Democrats; Somerville Branch; 8 Whigs, and 4 Democrats; Shelbyville Branch; 8 Whigs, and 4 Democrats. (See *House Journal*, 1849, Appendix, 284–286.)

Legislative Message,* October 22, 1849

"GENTLEMEN OF THE SENATE, AND
      OF THE HOUSE OF REPRESENTATIVES:

It is made my duty by the Constitution, from time to time, to give to the General Assembly information of the state of the government, and recommend to their consideration such measures as I shall judge expedient. The reports already submitted to you by the several officers in charge of the different branches of the government, will convey to you the information necessary to enable you to understand its condition. In discharge of my duty, I commend these several reports to your careful examination, and with as much brevity as I can command, I will proceed to submit to you such suggestions as seem to me to be expedient in regard to some of the more important subjects connected with your legislative duties.

At the threshold you will allow me to impress upon your minds the importance of instituting a rigid scrutiny into the condition of the different departments of the government, and the several institutions in any way connected with them, as well as into the official conduct of the several functionaries who have been entrusted with their administration.—Such a scrutiny will enable you to discharge your own responsible duties, with satisfaction to yourselves and profit to your constituents. In the same spirit, I trust I may commend to your approval the virtues of industry and economy in executing the high trust which has been committed to your hands.

Prominent amongst the subjects which will engage your earnest attention, is the Bank of Tennessee. I cannot too strongly urge upon you the importance of examining thoroughly into the condition of this institution, with a view to the adoption of such measures as will insure its continued safety and efficiency. I am satisfied from the Report of its presiding officer, that the burthens and liabilities imposed upon it by existing laws, are greater than it can bear without such inroads upon its capital as must greatly impair its usefulness, if not terminate in its ultimate prostration. These are results which cannot be avoided except by your interposition. It is required by

---

* *House Journal*, 1849, 142–150.
  Senate Journal, 1849, 133–140.

existing laws to meet liabilities to an amount much larger than it can realize in the way of profits by any system of prudent and safe management. In this state of things, it becomes your imperious duty either to provide for its gradual liquidation or to come to its relief by a timely removal of its burthens.

I cannot discover the necessity for the liquidation of the Bank. This process would inevitably be attended with a large amount of pecuniary embarrassment and commercial derangement. The withdrawal of its circulation would create a vacuum which would be filled by the paper of other Banks, incorporated by our own or other States. The currency furnished by it has been at all times as good as that of the other institutions in our State, and I see no reason to suppose that it is not as good as that which could be furnished by any other Bank that might be hereafter created. I see no reason to expect that any other Bank in our State would be better managed or would yield better profits. When compared with the management of the other institutions in the State, I have no reason to doubt that it has been conducted with equal skill, prudence and profit.

If the Bank of Tennessee were wound up it would devolve upon the Legislature to invest that portion of its capital made up of the Common School Fund, and the amount deposited by the General Government in our Treasury. These funds are now yielding more than legal interest under the operations of the Bank. It would be difficult, if not impossible, to find any safer or more profitable investment of these funds. If they were invested in the purchase of the State Bonds, the interest on so much thereof as might be purchased with the School funds would necessarily have to be provided out of the State Treasury. These are some of the obstacles to liquidation, which strike my mind as insuperable, and induce me to invite your serious consideration to the necessity of relieving the Bank of some of its burthens.

My examination of this subject has satisfied me that the true policy to be adopted in regard to the Bank, is to require the profits made annually to be paid into the Treasury, to constitute part of the revenue of the State, and to be disbursed by the Treasury in meeting the liabilities of the State, in the same manner that the other revenue of the State is now disbursed. If this were done, and the liabilities now imposed upon the Bank were transferred to the

Treasury, the Bank would be entirely relieved, and our financial system would be reduced to entire simplicity. The Bank would continue to be the depository of the public revenue, as at present, and might act as the agent of the Treasury, as it now does, in paying the accruing interest on the State Bonds, which are held at distant points. The Comptroller's report each year would then exhibit a full and intelligible view of our financial condition, and our system would be relieved of that complication which now makes it somewhat difficult of ready comprehension. I submit these suggestions to your attentive consideration, and indulge the anxious hope that if they fail to meet your approval and adoption, your own wisdom will devise some other efficient plan for giving relief to the Bank. In connection with this subject, I invite your consideration to the propriety of resuscitating the three branches which are now in a process of liquidation. These branches were all located at important commercial points, surrounded by rich country and an enterprising population. In such locations banking operations are usually carried on with profit, and I know no reason to doubt a similar result if these branches were restored and placed under prudent management.

In calling your attention to the subject of popular education, I have most sincerely to regret that I am unable to recommend for your adoption any specific measure for the improvement of our present system of common schools. Of the great value of an efficient system of common schools, I am strongly convinced; and I am equally well satisfied of the utter incapacity of our present system to meet the reasonable wishes of the people. This incapacity, I doubt not, arises mainly from the limited amount of the fund for annual distribution. It may be true that there are defects in the system itself, which your wisdom can remedy, but with the present amount of annual distribution, I cannot indulge the hope that the system can be so amended as to be made efficient.

The importance of popular education in the preservation and perpetuation of our invaluable institutions, is so palpable and so universally felt and admitted, that it is matter of regret and surprise that more progress has not been made in securing its benefits. It is manifest to my mind that these benefits can never be secured without a large increase of the common school fund. I know of no mode

of attaining this end, except by a resort to taxation for school purposes. None will doubt that the purposes of education furnish a
legitimate object for the exercise of the taxing power. Indeed, it
would be difficult to conceive of an object more appropriate for the
exercise of the taxing power, than that of training up the rising
generation to become useful and valuable citizens.—The claims of
patriotism, philanthropy and religion, all combine in a strong appeal in behalf of so noble an object. If I felt authorized to recommend for your adoption my individual wishes and opinions on this
interesting subject, I would urge upon you the exercise of the
power vested in you; but in my extensive intercourse with our own
common constituents, I have seen no evidence to justify me in supposing that such a recommendation would be in accordance with
their convictions or expectations. Your more intimate acquaintance
with the sentiments and wishes of the people will enable you to
judge more accurately on this subject than I can do; and into your
hands I commit the subject, with the ardent hope that your labors
may be successful in advancing the great cause of popular education.

I know of no subject which is entitled to more of your deliberations than that of a system of Internal Improvements.—Nature has
been liberal in bestowing upon our State the elements of prosperity
and happiness, but until these resources are developed by a liberal
system of Internal Improvements, our real advantages can never be
fully understood and appreciated. Without facilities for commercial
communication, our citizens are not presented with inducements to
exert their industry and enterprise in bringing to light the hidden
treasures within their reach. Some portions of our State in which
nature has been most lavish in her agricultural and mineral bounties,
are so completely cut off from commercial facilities by surrounding
mountain ranges, that little or no advancement can be made towards
wealth and prosperity.—I regard it to be the duty of the State to
exert her power in removing the barriers to commercial intercourse,
and so far as she has the means, to enable all of her citizens to have
easy access to the best markets for the products of their labor.

Upon looking at the geographical position of our State, the
mind is strongly impressed with the necessity of a railroad communication extending from the eastern to the western boundary, as

nearly through its centre as practicable. Such an improvement would place every portion of the State within an accessible distance of the line of road, and would give a universal impulse to industry and enterprise which could not fail in a short time to make ours one of the richest States in the Union. Such a line of railroad is the more strongly recommended from the fact that, at our eastern boundary it would promise direct communication with the Atlantic, through simular works in progress by Virginia, and at the western boundary it would make the communication easy with the projected railroad to the Pacific. Upon the completion of these several projects in connection with the Georgia improvements which are rapidly approaching our borders, our State would become the great thoroughfare, in its whole length, for the immense travel and transportation which such a line would command. If our State possessed the necessary means of constructing such a work, I should have no hesitation in recommending its adoption as a system worthy of our enterprise. All, however, who are acquainted with the extent of our means and the amount of our present indebtedness, will at once agree that the system indicated is impracticable on account of its great magnitude.

If we cannot accomplish so great an undertaking it is a matter of duty to inquire whether we can safely embark in any portion of it, and to what extent.

With this view, I invite your attention to four projects already occupying a large share of the public mind. I allude to the proposed railroad from the Virginia line to Knoxville—the Tennessee and Georgia road already in process of construction, connecting Knoxville with the Georgia road, and the Nashville and Chattanooga, in a rapid progress of construction, connecting Nashville with Chattanooga, and that portion of the Mobile and Ohio railroad proposed to be extended from South to North through the Western District of our State. The three first may all be regarded as sections of the general system to which I have already directed your attention. The two proposed roads in East Tennessee are of incalculable importance to that portion of the State.—Their completion, (particularly if the Virginia road is constructed to our eastern border), would remove the barriers which have heretofore prevented the development of the rich resources of that division of the State. The

Tennessee and Georgia road presents particularly strong claims upon your consideration, from the fact that the State has already sunk a large amount on this work and its completion furnishes the only hope of any return for the expenditures already made. Of the importance of the Nashville and Chattanooga road to the interests of the middle portion of the State, I need not speak—the work will at once commend itself to your consideration as one of the noblest enterprises of the age. The advantages of a road running through the Western District, between the Tennessee and Mississippi rivers, will at once occur to all who examine the subject.

I recommend each of these projects as well worthy of all the aid which the State can safely render to them. But in determining whether you will extend the aid of the State to all or either of them, and to what extent, there are certain considerations of great moment, which, in my judgment, ought to be kept constantly in view. It is certain that the State can furnish no aid to these or any other projects of Internal Improvement except by the use of her credit. In deciding whether her credit can be safely resorted to or not, it will be incumbent on you to look carefully into the present indebtedness of the State and our means of meeting promptly its principal and interest. If you shall come to the conclusion that our present debt cannot be increased without affecting the credit of our bonds, this ought to be an insuperable barrier to any action on the subject. We are bound by the highest obligations to preserve the credit of the State inviolate and untarnished. If you should be satisfied that our credit would not suffer by an increase of our debt, I cannot too strongly impress upon your minds the importance of providing with certainty for the payment of the accruing interest at the same time that you provide for contracting the additional debt. I feel it my duty also to recommend that before embarking the credit of the State in any work you satisfy yourselves fully that the work when completed will yield a fair profit upon the capital invested, and as the best guarantee on this point that the State shall only come forward with her aid after individual capital has been embarked to such an extent as to insure the State against ultimate loss. These principles I regard as fundamental in connection with this subjct, and I commend them to your adoption, whether you are about to embark the State in the works I have specifically designated or any others in which the aid of the State may be invoked.

It will be your duty to look carefuly into the revenue laws to detect any defects which may exist and to make such amendments as may be needed. Complaints have been made as to the unequal operation of the revenue laws as they affect the mercantile community. These complaints appear to me to be well founded, and I recommend the subject to your consideration, for such amendments as will remove all just grounds of complaint.

Your attention has been no doubt already directed to the progress made towards the completion of the beautiful capitol building now in progress of erection. The magnificent scale on which this structure was originally projected, necessarily requires much time and money for its completion, but when completed, it will be a State House of which we may well be proud. I deem it proper to recommend this work to your especial examination, with a view of determining whether it would not be sound policy and good economy to provide the means for a more early completion of the building than can be attained without providing additional force.

The reports of the Superintendent of the Penitentiary and of the Physician to the Lunatic Asylum are already before you, and from these you will learn the present condition of those institutions, and the management for the last two years.—Their great importance will call for a full share of your attention and deliberations in determining whether any and what improvements can be made in their internal management and police.

I concur fully in the sentiment that the fundamental law of the State should not be subjected to frequent and inconsiderate changes. But experience may develop defects even in our Constitution, and when clearly developed it becomes our solemn duty to apply the necessary correction. Our Constitution has now been in operation for about fifteen years, and it is matter of congratulation that its provisions have proved so satisfactory that few attempts have been made to disturb them by amendment. At the present time, however, there is a strong conviction pervading the public mind, that the best interests of the State demand a change in the mode of electing the several officers connected with the administration of justice. In this conviction my own mind fully concurs, and I avail myself with pleasure on this occasion, to recommend the subject to your most thoughtful consideration. The evils attending the present mode of electing judges and attorneys general, are too palpable to escape the attention of the most careless observer. It is probably true that no mode can be devised which would be entirely free from objections; but upon a survey of all the considerations connected with the question, I am satisfied that the election of these officers directly by the people is liable to fewer objections than any other plan, whilst it is strongly recommended by its strict conformity to the general spirit and genius of our institutions. Of the capacity of the people to make wise and judicious selections, none can well doubt, whilst we have the lights of experience in other States, showing that the fears which in former times prevailed on this subject have proved groundless. Our Constitution wisely prohibits hasty and rash amendments of the fundamental law, but with equal wisdom it provides a safe and satisfactory mode of securing necessary reforms. Fully satisfied that the reform indicated is demanded as well by the true interests of the State as by the popular will, I recommend that you take the necessary steps for securing the desired amendment at as early a period as may be practicable under the Constitution.

According to the structure of our federal and State governments, certain specified powers have been delegated to the former, whilst all others have been reserved to the latter. The preservation of the line thus drawn between them, calls upon us for constant vigilance in guarding against encroachments on either side. You will not fail to feel sensibly the high responsibility which rests upon you to maintain the rights reserved to your constituents in all their fullness and vigor.

A deep conviction is rising upon the minds of many, and in this conviction I participate, that a disposition prevails among a large portion of our northern brethren to give such a direction to the action of Congress, as will ultimately interfere with the rights reserved to us, in connection with the institution of slavery. It becomes our duty to our best interests to meet this disposition at the threshold, and to assert and maintain our rights with unflinching firmness. It will be readily conceded by all, that Congress has no power to interfere directly with slavery in the States. Such an interference would be so gross a violation of our constitutional rights, that we cannot anticipate that any one will have the hardihood to propose it. Our danger does not lie in open and direct assaults upon our rights, but in covert and indirect measures, whose ultimate purpose and tendency will be to effect results which could not be attained by direct means. If Congress can be induced to adopt a series of measures, which would encircle the slaveholding States with free territory, would abolish slavery in the District of Columbia, and would prohibit the transfer of slaves from one State to another for sale, it is apparent that the permanency of our rights would be seriously endangered. Against such measures as these, as well as against direct attempts to infringe upon our rights, it is our solemn duty to protest. I hold that Congress can exercise no power but such as has been delegated by the Constitution. In that instrument, I find no warrant for any action by Congress on the subject of slavery in a territory; and hence I stand upon constitutional ground in denying the power of Congress either to establish or prohibit slavery in our newly acquired territories. These territories are the common property of the several States of the confederacy, won by the joint blood and treasure of our brave countrymen. Each State and each citizen has the same rights in this property as any other State or citizen. An attempt by Congress to make distinctions on this subject, by attaching conditions to the enjoyment of this common property, would be an outrage upon justice and principle, which would justify prompt and efficient resistance by all the means known to the Constitution.

Entertaining these sentiments, and being fully satisfied that the true place to meet and arrest danger is at the threshold, I deem it to be our duty as a State to proclaim to our nothern brethren, in terms of respectful frankness and firmness, our unalterable purpose of maintaining our rights, at all hazards and to the last extremity. With this view, I recommend that you adopt and forward to Congress a remonstrance expressive of the sentiments of our constituents on this exciting question.

I submit these suggestions to your wise consideration, with an ardent hope that your deliberations will be characterized by harmony and energy, and that your labors will redound to the lasting happiness and honor of our State.

W. TROUSDALE."

In the above Message, nine topics were singled out for specific mention, namely:

1. Bank of Tennessee
2. Education
3. Internal Improvements
4. Revenue Laws
5. State Capitol Building
6. Penitentiary
7. Lunatic Asylum
8. Judiciary
9. Slavery

The Bank of Tennessee had been saddled with the burden of providing $100,000 annually for the support of the Common Schools and $18,000 annually for the maintenance of eighteen County Academies. This drain upon the assets of the Bank had proved to be very heavy, and the Bank had requested some relief at the hands of the Legislature. Governor Trousdale joined in this request and, at the same time, voiced opposition to liquidating the institution. At the time of the transmission of the above Message, he was not aware that his nominations of a new Board of Directors would meet such stubborn and ultimately successful opposition on the part of the Whig Senate. But delay on the part of a hostile Senate for nearly three months, regarding the confirmation of the nominees for Directors of the Bank of Tennessee, forced the Governor to investigate the legal status of the Bank's present situation. Quite appropriately and sensibly, he called upon the Attorney-General of Tennessee for his opinion. Along with that opinion, the Governor transmitted the following special message.

"EXECUTIVE OFFICE,
14th January, 1850.

TO THE GENERAL ASSEMBLY OF THE STATE OF TENNESSEE: *

The Constitution of this State has made it the duty of the Executive to take care that the laws be faithfully executed, and from time to time to give to the General Assembly information of the state of the government and recommend to their consideration such measures as he shall judge expedient.

---

* *House Journal*, 1849, 568–577.

The amended charter of the Bank of Tennessee, passed 3d December, 1845, 'makes it the duty of the Governor to nominate the board of Directors of the Bank of Tennessee to the General Assembly for confirmation within thirty days after the meeting of the same, and that said Board of Directors shall be organized to enter upon their duties by the first of January succeeding their confirmation, at which last named time the term of service of the former board shall terminate.'

Shortly after I came into office, and within the time limited by the act of 1845, a Board of Directors for the Bank was nominated by me and sent to the General Assembly, and I am advised that up to this time there has been no final action upon that nomination.

The term of service of the old board of directors of the Bank of Tennessee terminated on the first day of January, 1850; and since that time the Bank has been wholly without a board of directors, or any other person legally authorized to take charge of the effects of the bank.

The Bank of Tennessee is the fiscal agent of the State. In it, the public funds are kept, and the interest on the bonds of the State and other liabilities are paid by it. It is, therefore, a matter of deep interest to the State that this institution should be well guarded, and not permitted long to remain in the perilous condition in which it has been since the first of January last.

Considering the bank without a directory, and the public funds in great danger, I called the attention of the Attorney-General of the State to the subject, and asked his written opinion as to the present condition of the Bank—whether that institution was or was not now in existence, and what was its present condition. The Attorney-General has examined the question, and has furnished me with his opinion, which is hereby transmitted for your deliberate consideration, and for such action upon the same as in your wisdom the impending danger may demand.

I might here suggest a host of evils likely to result to the public should the present state of things be permitted long to exist; but reflections of this kind force themselves upon the mind of every legislator, and need not be here enumerated.

W. Trousdale."

(DOCUMENT ACCOMPANYING GOVERNOR'S MESSAGE
OF JAN. 14, 1850)

"SIR:—I received your note of the 5th inst., in which you state that the facts which have transpired in relation to the Bank of Tennessee create a doubt in your mind whether that institution has a corporate existence or not; and in which you request me, as Attorney-General of the State, to give the subject a careful examination, and furnish you with a written opinion thereupon.

I have acted on your request, and, in accordance with the duty imposed on me by law, proceed to give you the result of my examination.

I assume that you allude, in your note, to the fact that no board of Directors were confirmed to take charge of the bank on the first day of January last. On this state of things, the following questions arise:

First. Is there in existence any Board of Directors, authorized to take charge of the institution?

Second. What is the legal effect of the non-existence of a lawful directory?

The act of 1837-8, ch. 107, chartered the Bank of Tennessee, and pledged the faith and credit of the State to its support. Its capital consists of the school fund; of moneys deposited by the General Government on loan, and of other funds raised on the credit of the State. The institution is the property of the people of the State; it is subject to the control of the legislature. It is therefore, a municipal or public corporation.—4 *Wheaton* 518. *Dartmouth College* vs. *Woodard*.

The second section provides that the Governor shall nominate and appoint twelve persons to act as directors, while nomination and appointment shall be subject to confirmation or rejection by the General Assembly, and the twelve persons so nominated and confirmed, shall constitute the directors. The 7th section provides that the president and directors shall continue in office for two years, and until their successors are nominated and confirmed.

This custom continued to be the law governing the appointment of the directory till the year 1845—a period of seven years—when a law was passed, entitled 'An act to amend the charter of the Bank of Tennessee.' The first section of this act declares that 'it shall hereafter be the duty of the Governor of this State to nominate the board of directors of the Bank of the State of Tennessee to the General Assembly for confirmation, within thirty days after the meeting of the same, and that said board of directors shall be organized to enter upon their duties by the first day of January succeeding their confirmation, at which last named time the term of service of the former board shall terminate.' The second section provides that the directors then in the bank should continue till the first day of January, 1846, and that their acts should be valid to that period; and that the board nominated and confirmed at that session should enter on their duties on the first day of January, 1846; and that within thirty days after the first day of January, the boards of the branches should be appointed in each and every year.

The question now arises, Did the Legislature, by the passage of the act of 1845, intend to repeal the 7th section of the act of 1837-8, so far as it authorizes the directors to hold over till their successors are nominated and confirmed? Did the Legislature intend that the term of service of the old board should expire on the first day of January, and that they should go out? and did the Legislature intend to impose on subsequent Legislatures the necessity of confirming a new board, to take charge of the bank on the termination of the service of the old board? And if such was the intention of the act of 1845, was the purpose accomplished by the passage of the act?

The will of the Legislature expressed according to the forms of the constitution is the law of the land; and the intent in the passage of the act must be ascertained and carried out. All rules which have been established for the construction of statutes, are only so many aids in arriving at the true intent and meaning of the Legislature. The intent, says Kent, is to be collected from the context—from the occasion and necessity of the law—from the mischief felt, and the objects and remedy in view. It will be seen that between the passage of the act creating the charter of the bank and the amendatory act of 1845, a period of seven years had elapsed; and the first matter which will occur to all intelligent minds is the question, What was the occasion and necessity of the last law, what the mischief felt, and the remedy in view? It is most evident that if the administration of the bank had moved on slowly and harmoniously under the operation of the 7th section of the bank charter —if no 'mischief' had been felt—there would have been no occasion for the passage of the act of 1845, and the act would not have been passed.

What was the mischief which produced the act of 1845? The supreme court of the United States, in the case of Browder vs. Preston (1st Wheaton, 115,) says: 'It is frequently necessary, in the construction of statutes, to recur to the history and situation of the country, in order to ascertain the reason, as well as the meaning of many of the provisions in them, to enable a court to apply correctly the different rules for construing statutes.' If this were not so, it would frequently be impossible to ascertain what occasioned the passage of a law, and what mischief the Legislature intended to remedy. When a statute is passed to remedy a particular mischief, that construction shall be put on it, says Coke, which will redress the mischief intended to be remedied, guard against all subtle inventions and evasions for the continuance of the mischief for private convenience, and give life and strength to the remedy for the public good, according to the true intent of the makers of the law.'— 7 *Bacon*, 462.

We ask, then, what was the mischief which produced the act of 1845? There is a prominent fact in the history of the administration of the Bank of Tennessee which occurred previous to the passage of the act of 1845, which involved a prolonged discussion of the seventh section of the act of 1837-8. That fact is to be found recorded on the Journals of the Senate, to wit: that the Senate of the State rejected the nomination of a board of Directors for the Bank, and in consequence thereof the board which had held the custody of the Bank for the two previous years held over under the 7th section of the charter and controlled the institution the period of four years. This gave birth to much heated and prolonged discussion in the halls of legislation and throughout the State. These facts are a part of the legislative history of the State and are to be found recorded in the Journals of the Senate, in the archives of the Bank and in the productions of the periodical press. These facts, then, that a nomination was rejected, that in consequence thereof the board held charge of the Bank for four years and that angry and violent collisions of opinion took place in consequence of it as to the true intent and meaning of the seventh section of the charter are authentic and well ascertained. I, therefore, refer to these facts in accordance with the opinion of the Supreme Court of the United States in the case of Browder vs. Preston, as constituting the ground-work of the amendatory act of 1845; and there is no reason to suppose that such an act ever would have passed if the facts alluded to had not occurred. It was believed necessary to incorporate in the charter of the bank, in reference to the duration of the terms of service of the directors, that great principle in modern representative governments, to wit: short terms of service, subject to renewal by the appointing power. This was no doubt thought particularly necessary in the case of agents having the custody of public money which was subject continually to the attacks of private cupidity, without the guard of private interest to protect it and where the change of agents might become necessary to eviscerate frauds and expose misconduct. The power of selecting new agents every two years was vested in the Governor. His range of selection was large. This selection was open to the examination of the General Assembly, and subject to rejection or confirmation according to their judgment of the fitness or propriety of the nominations. This power was never given, in my judgment, to enable the Legislature to compel the continuance of the old board in office for four years, or for an indefinite period of time. The declaration that the Governor should make such nominations every two years is conclusive with me that this view is correct. It is most evident that the provision that the board should continue until their successors were confirmed, was only intended to guard against contingencies, and not to lengthen their term of service and permanently instal a board of directors in office. This was not the spirit and intent of the act of 1837. It is a well known fact in the history of English and American legislation, that the provision for holding over has been usually inserted in municipal and private corporations with no view of installing permanently in office the officers, but simply to guard against temporary contingencies. The use of this provision is, therefore, for any other purpose, altogether illegitimate. I therefore assume, upon well known historical facts and well established principles, that the continuance of a board of directors for four years, contrary to the spirit of the charter, produced the act of 1845; and that the continuance of the same directors in the bank for an indefinite period, without a re-nomination, was a mischief intended to be remedied. If the act of 1845 be construed to legalize a holding over of the old board, it does not remedy the mischief which produced it, and the Legislature has not accomplished what it intended to accomplish. If it be construed to prohibit a holding over for four years then it suppresses the mischief the Legislature intended to suppress. This act directs that the Governor shall make a nomination within thirty days after the meeting of the General Assembly. His duty is thus prescribed. It directs that the General Assembly shall act on such nomination before the first day of January succeeding. The duty of the General Assembly is thus prescribed. It directs that the new board shall be organized and ready to enter on their duty by the first of January, and that they shall appoint the Directors in the Branches within thirty days thereafter. Thus it prescribes the duty of the new Directors. It directs that on the first day of January the term of service of the board shall terminate. Thus the old board has definite information as to the period of the cessation of its functions.

The act of nominating a Board of Directors is an Executive function, and the act of confirming or rejecting such nomination is an Executive function also; and the act of regulating the discharge of this duty is in conformity with the practice of legislative bodies. Every legislative body prescribes rules for the government of its own proceedings and those of future legislatures. This is particularly necessary, so far as the discharge of Executive functions is concerned, so that there shall be a rule in existence at the time, when collisions of opinion demand such rule for the control of the violence of excited passions. Therefore the legislature chose to declare that the Governor should make his nomination within thirty days after the meeting of the General Assembly; therefore it chose to declare that the legislature should act on the nominations by the first day of January; therefore it chose to direct the old board that they should go out on the first day of January, and that on the same day the new board should take charge of the bank. They assume absolutely that these duties will be performed, and they create an absolute necessity that they should be performed. This statute is utterly incompatible with the seventh section of the charter, and accomplishes what it was intended to accomplish, to wit, its repeal as to the right to hold over. Both statutes cannot stand together, and the last statute repeals the former. *Rex* vs. *Caton;* Burrow's Rep.

If on the 1st day of January last the term of service of the old board terminated that board ceases of course to have official existence or power. If their term of service expired on that day, then it is absurd to contend that their term of service continues. It is most clear that there is a positive, direct and explicit negative on the right of the old board to hold over after the 1st day of January. The charter says the directors shall be elected for two years, and shall hold till their successors shall be nominated and confirmed. The amendment of the charter declares that on the first day of January, the new directors shall enter on the discharge of their duties, and that on that day the term of service of the old board shall terminate. How can these two statutes be reconciled? The thing is preposterous on the face of the statutes, but doubly so when the legislative history of the State demonstrates most conclusively, that if the last act did not prohibit a holding over it did not accomplish the object the legislature had in view in the passage of the act.

It may be supposed that the act of 1845, is, what is called a directory statute, that is that it prescribes duties to the governor and to the legislature, and that if those duties are not discharged the board may hold over. That that part of the act which directs that the Governor shall perform his duty within thirty days after the meeting of the General Assembly is to be considered as directory is unquestionable; that is, if he do not perform his duty within the thirty days, he may do it afterwards, and the nomination would be valid; and that that part of the act which requires the General Assembly to act upon the nomination by the 1st day of January is directory to that body is also unquestionable; and if it does not confirm a nomination before that date, it may lawfully confirm a nomination afterwards. But how in any legal sense is the last clause in the first section directory? The act says, 'at which last named time [1st day of January,] the term of service of the former board shall terminate.' This informs the Governor, the legislature, the new board, and the old board, in terms as explicit as the English language can furnish, that the old board can no longer have legal control over the funds of the bank, and that they are to go out and that their places must be supplied by that time. If the legislature in prescribing a rule for the government of future legislatures and board of directors, had said that 'on the confirmation of the new board of directors the term of service of the old board shall expire,' then the term of service of the old board would have continued till there was a confirmation. But the holding over was the very mischief the Legislature intended to prohibit, and therefore it directs the governor and the legislature to put the bank in the control of a new directory, and that on that day the old board without reservation should go out.

These are the reasons which induce me after a careful examination of the subject, to express the opinion, that since the first day of January last, the Bank of the State of Tennessee is without a board of directors.

It is evident that this question depends on the legislative history of the times, and the peculiar features of the act for its elucidation and decision. But I propose to examine very briefly the progress of the law in Great Britain and in the United States on the subject to show that there is nothing to contradict, but much to support the conclusion which I have arrived at.

The case of the corporation of Banbury was an information in the nature of a *quo warranto* in the King's name against A. B. calling on him to show by what authority he held the office of Recorder. It appeared that the corporation having omitted to elect a Mayor on the charter day that integral part was gone. The court held that he was not legal recorder, because the corporation was dissolved, and *Parker, Ch. J,* said, 'If a mayor is not chosen by the time prescribed by the charter, and that there is no provisions of the charter for the mayor to hold over till a new mayor is chosen, the corporation is dissolved and consequently cannot proceed to a new election.' *Pet. Ab.*

The case of the King against Pole was a *quo warranto.* It appeared by the charter that the election was to be held on the 18th day of October, and no provision was made for holding over. On the 18th day of October the corporation met and proceeded to the election, but before the poll was closed the Mayor adjourned the election to the following day, when a new Mayor was elected. It was objected that there being no provision by the charter for the Mayor to hold over, his functions had ceased, and therefore, an election after such time was void. To which it was replied the II George I was passed to remedy such inconvenience, but the court held the case was not within the act, and therefore the election was void. *Pet. Ab.*

These decisions rest on the ground that without a provision in the charter for the Mayor to hold over in the event there was no Mayor elected on the given day, no election could be held; and the corporation was, therefore, destitute of Magistrates. This was the view of the law taken by Blackstone. He says (Com. Vol. I, page, 404:) 'Because by the common law corporations elected on the day appointed by the charter, it is now provided that for the future no corporation shall be dissolved on that account, and ample directions are given for appointing a new officer in the event there be no election on the charter day.'

These decisions go to establish the generally recognized doctrine that the duration of the terms of service of corporate officers depends on the charter that corporations have no powers but those derived from the charter, and that it was believed to be the policy of the law to enforce strictly a compliance with charter provisions.

There are cases in which it is decided that if it is declared in general terms that the officers shall be annually elected, they may hold over.—*See Strange, 625.*

One of the leading cases in opposition to the general tenor of the English cases, is the case of the People *vs.* Runkle, 9 Johnson. In that case the courts say that in the charter 'neither a precise day of election nor of entering upon office is given'—and even on that state of facts, Johnson gives the result of the case in the following manner: '*It seems* that where officers are required to be elected annually, they may continue in office till others are elected.'

Chancellor Kent says: 'It is a question, not definitely settled, whether the officers of a corporation who are to be elected annually, can continue in office after one year, and until others are elected in their stead, where the time of the election has elapsed through mistake, accident or misfortune'— and says it is a usual provision in charters, which direct the election of officers annually, most such officers shall continue till others are elected in their places.

The Supreme court of Tennessee used the following language on the subject: 'Although we incline to the opinion that the tendency of the cases in the absence of terms, respecting or enlarging the powers of a corporation is to maintain the authority of the officers to hold over without an election, still we cannot but feel that after all, as Chancellor Kent declares, that it is not definitely settled.'—3d *Humphrey's Rep.*, 529.

It may well be remarked on the state of the law on this subject, that the struggle has arisen in the courts between the overthrow on the side of the general doctrine in regard to charter powers, and on the other, the inconvenience which would result in special cases, from deciding that a corporation had no officers.

How, then, does this state of the law apply to the facts of this case? In the first place, then, there is a wide distinction between the provisions of a charter which declares in general terms, that elections shall be held annually, and the provisions of a charter which fixes the duration of the terms of service of the other officers, prescribes the time when one set shall go out and another shall take their places—*(See People vs. Runkle, 9 Johnson.)* If the question of a right to hold over be doubtful, in a charter which uses open, vague and general directory terms, how can it be at all doubtful when it is declared that the directory shall hold their stations for two years; that the term of service of the old board shall terminate on the first day of January, and that the new board shall enter on the discharge of their duties on that day? These are positive restricting words on the right to hold over; and, how could it be doubtful, in addition to all this, when it is a known historical fact that it was the intention of the legislature to prohibit the right to hold over?

I feel, therefore, bound to declare, both on reason and authority, that the Bank of Tennessee is without a lawful directory.

The next question is as to the legal effect of the non-existence of a lawful directory. Does it work a dissolution of the corporation? I am clear that it does not, so far as to endanger the security of debts and credits. In 1735, Seaber executed a bond to the Mayor and Alderman of Colchester. They were ousted by judgment, and from 1710 to 1763, the corporation remained without magistrates. The charter was revived by sovereign authority, and suit was brought by them against Seaber on the bond. Lord Mansfield said: 'many corporations for want of legal magistrates have lost their activity and obtained new charters, and it has never been disputed but that the new charter revived and gave activity to the old charters. Where the question has arisen on any remarkable metamorphosis, it has always been held that they remain the same as to debts and credits. We are clear upon principles of law, that the old corporation was not dissolved and annihilated, though it had lost its magistrates, and that by the new charter it was so revived as to be entitled to the credits and liable for the debts of the old corporation.—3 *Burrows, Rep.* 1866.

Wilcock, an English author on municipal corporations [page 179] says: 'a municipal corporation is a body which does not depend for its existence on its having magistrates capable of transacting its business. Its constitution remains and it is suspended but not dissolved.'

Angell and Ames, American authors on corporation says: 'the non-existence of managers does not suppose the non-existence of a corporation. The latter may be dormant; its functions may be suspended for want of means of action; but the capacity to restore its functions by means of a new election may remain. There is no reason why the power of action may not be revived by a new election of officers and managers, competent to carry on the affairs of the corporation agreeable to the charter.'

It is decided on several American cases that an omission to elect the officers and managers of a corporation at the time appointed by the charter, will not dissolve the corporation. It suspends its functions which may be restored by a subsequent election.—*See 5 Watts, 66: 4th Rowle 9 1 page 290–2 Kent, 310: 3 Dess. 557.*

WEST H. HUMPHREYS."

Despite the cameo-like remarks of Governor Trousdale relative to the perilous situation challenging the continuance and operations of the Bank of Tennessee, coupled with the clear-cut analysis and opinion of the Attorney-General of Tennessee, yet the *Senate Journal* (1849) contains no record as to whether Governor Trousdale's Message and the opinion of the Attorney-General were ever received and read. Moreover, the *Senate Journal* did not include the above Message in its official proceedings. It is highly questionable whether any Governor of Tennessee, prior to this date, had ever received more ignoble treatment than that administered by the Whig Senate to Democratic Governor William Trousdale, who was merely calling the recalcitrant Senate to a sense of its duty and responsibility to the citizens of the State. Unfortunately, political animus had been allowed to reach such a pitch as to be a disgrace to any deliberative body guilty of such tactics.

To cap the climax, no more farcical caption could have been pasted upon a law than the one entitled "An Act to relieve the Bank of Tennessee." [33] The alleged "relief" consisted in giving the bank directorate power, if approved by the Governor, to sell its stock in the Union and Planters' Banks and use the proceeds for the purchase of State bonds, and to use any surplus money in the State Treasury in the purchase of outstanding bonds! There was not a word in the law that gave the Bank of Tennessee any relief whatsoever.

On the subject of public education, neither Ex-Governor Neill S. Brown nor Governor William Trousdale had any specific or progressive measures to advocate. In his farewell Message to the Legislature on October 5, 1849, Ex-Governor Brown in discussing the need for improving educational facilities took a "run out powder" on the question of taxation for education by making one *positive* statement regarding his *negative* position,

"I beg leave, however, to state that I do not believe a system of direct taxes expedient or proper." [34]

In this same Message, public confession was made by him that the existing system of public education was unsatisfactory and had become "odious." In concluding his remarks upon the subject of education, he indulged himself in a bit of "wishful thinking" by expressing the hope that the Legislature would find some means "to advance this great cause"! His immediate successor, Governor William Trousdale was, in

---

[33] *Acts of Tennessee*, 1849, Chapter 115.
[34] *Senate Journal*, 1849, 47.
    House Journal, 1849, 45.

regard to education, an exact facsimile of his predecessor. His message, too, indicated that the common school system had another well-wisher for its ultimate triumph in the eradication of illiteracy in the State, but that he was at a loss to make any official contribution in the matter of recommendation for an increase of funds. After he had expressed the opinion that the "incapacity of the present system to meet the reasonable wishes of the people" was due to the inadequacy of the funds, he uttered these words: "I have most sincerely to regret that I am unable to recommend for your adoption any specific measure for the improvement of our present system of common schools." Further on in his message, he admitted that he knew of no mode of increasing the school fund "except by a resort to taxation for school purposes"; but he quickly added that his own extensive intercourse with his constituents did not warrant his believing that they would approve of such a policy. And with this note of resignation, to the Legislature he "committed the subject with the ardent hope that their labors might be successful in advancing the great cause of popular education."

The outgoing and incoming Governors Brown and Trousdale could not have been uninformed as to the pitifully inadequate school fund; for on October 13, 1849, the President of the Commissioners of Common Schools, William Ledbetter, informed their Excellencies and the Legislature just what the situation was by submitting a detailed Report. For the year, 1848, there were 272,235 pupils over six and under twenty-one years of age, for whose "education" there had been available the annual sum of 41¾ cents per pupil.[35] For 1849, there was an increase in number of 5,814 children, while the per capita expenditure fell to 40¾ cents per pupil.

Without any Executive guidance or even worthwhile suggestion on the matter of public education, it is no wonder that the Legislature found itself floundering about in a veritable quagmire of uncertainty. Evidence of the fact is to be found in the seventeen educational bills introduced by various members of the Legislature. These bills were of diverse nature, devoid of any real educational vision, and on the whole were "void and without form, darkness moving upon the face of the deep."

One such bill proposed to suppress usury and thereby increase the school fund; another bill advocated amending the tippling law so as to augment the school funds; another proposed to tax bachelors, such tax to inure to the school fund; and still another bill offered better protection to sheep-raising, and by so doing enhance the school fund. What must have been regarded as a sure-shot measure was a bill providing that any person dying intestate, "leaving no widow or legitimate children," six per cent of his estate would go to the common school fund.

---

[35] *House Journal*, 1849, Appendix, 79.

Undoubtedly, the most incoherent and impossible suggestion came from an East Tennessean who attempted to enlighten the Legislature by giving them a "one world" viewpoint in a memorial,[36] to-wit:

"To the Senate of Tennessee

GENTLEMEN:

As it appears you do not think it proper that the one quarter million dollars on hands of the Patent Office should be divided amongst the State that the people might know & see what is in it & that the people might be enabled to know what vast quantities of useful models is there will you please tell Congress what disposition they had better make of it.

There is one or two other matters I would respectfully suggest might be worth your notice one is that probably thirty years since an Englishman by the name of Smithson left about six or seven hundred thousand dollars to the United States for the purpose of establishing at the seat of Government a siminary of learning for the purpose of diffusing information amongst men now do inquire in what manner this money as a disposing of it might amuse you to read the accts of it

Another by the treaty with England establishing the North Eastern boundary this nation bound itself to keep on the coast of Africa an armament of not less than eighty guns to prevent Brazil & the Spanish possessions in the West Indies from bringing people from Africa to open & cultivate their lands this armament costs over one half million yearly have we any business or right to do so supposing this nation wants fifty thousand European to dig her canals & railroads has any other nation the right to stop them on the high seas & send them back to where the started from

England is now paying interest on one hundred million dollars to the people of West India Islands for their negroes the surface when within a circle reaching out ten miles distance from St. Pauls Church London there is one hundred thousand of her own white population in a worse state of degradation than these slaves she set free, made slaves of her own people to set her negroes free this is statesmanship England is understood to be willing to withdraw her fleet & let France & this country off with continuing theirs France has notified England that she will withdraw hers now supposing you say to congress let ours be withdrawn too that money would educate many people here & make some good roads yet another the reduction made in 1846 of the duties on foreign goods was done believing it would induce France & England to keep quit whilst we were engaged in prosecuting the war against Mexico that is now over & I would respectfully suggest that you say to Congress to reinstate the duties as laid in 42 or something near them so that our own people may be put to work in place of English & Frenchmen or the people of any other nation on earth I am always for home first

The great Western Armory so long talked of Tennessee is now prepared to put in her claim for the rail road south through Georgia & across from it to Nashville gives her lines of communication everywhere necessary she has water power stone coal & iron ore equal to any quarter of the earth do Gentlemen ask Congress to examine your situation for such an establishment

Well Gentlemen what will you do with Liberia you have been nursing her for sometime she is now an independent nation acknowledged by France & England & she is knocking at the door of the White House in Washington to be acknowledged there that she may send a representative as other inde-

---

[36] Original document in State Archives, Nashville.

pendent nations does says she has a sea coast of 700 miles & inland not known now look at the poor white population, who pays money to send them where land is got for settling on none no not one such humanity mongring I am sick of it I am for my own folks in preference to negroes or any other folks

By a treaty with England made last winter letters from any distance can pass to New York or Boston on their way to England for five cents whilst to an individual if over three hundred miles ten cents does not this appear to be strange legislation at the incoming of our President Polk 27 Senators drew nearly twenty four thousand dollars charging for going home & returning whilst the never left the city at the incoming of Genl. Taylor all drew but three Cass, Calhoun & Benton amount over forty thousand this last the ac-counting officers of the Treasury refused to allow in settlement with Mr. Dickinson clerk Senate last fall the members drew over seventy thousand dollars mileage more than the were entitled to now Gentlemen here is a case for your committee to act, & report on I hope the will act & do with it as Tennesseans ought to do & if so your constituents will greatly rejoice & say well done the honest & faithful & amongst them will certainly be your Hum-ble Servant

SAMUEL MARTIN
Campbells Station, 18th January, 1850"

The memorial was referred to the Senate Committee on Federal Relations whose Chairman, Senator Samuel M. Fite of Smith and Sum-ner Counties, reported as follows:[37]

"... The memorial (No. 66) of Samuel Martin, of Campbells Station, upon the subject of the Patent Office, the Smithsonian Institute; the squad-ron kept on the coast of Africa; the paupers of England; the negroes of the West Indies; the tariff; Liberia; the postage on letters, extra mileage of mem-bers of Congress, and other subjects not necessary to enumerate,

Reported, that the committee had had the same under consideration, and had instructed him to report, that the above are proper subjects for the action of congress and the British Parliament, and recommend the petitioner to send his petition to those august bodies; the committee ask to be discharged from the further consideration of the petition."

On January 4, 1850, with more than two-thirds of the legislative session already passed into history, Whig Representative R. D. Allison of Smith County decided to try his hand in drafting an "educational measure" which he laid before the Lower House for consideration. His proposed remedy[38] for the educational welfare of the children of the State was a classic example of how to dodge the real issue—that of taxation for support of public education. Here was his idea:

"SECTION 1. *Be it enacted by the General Assembly of the State of Ten-nessee,* That whenever three or more citizens of this State desire to form a corporate society for the purpose of establishing a school or literary club, or of promoting education in any other way; they may form such articles of association as they shall think best adapted to effect their object and report the same to the Circuit Court of the County in which the association is

---

37 *Senate Journal,* 1849, 656.
38 Original Manuscript document in State Archives, Nashville.

formed, and if the Court shall be of opinion that it is really the design of the association to promote education science or literature, and that none of the articles of association are inconsistent with the constitution and laws of the State or of the United States, a certificate of those facts shall be made by the Court, a copy of which articles of association and the certificate of the Court shall be spread on the minutes of the Court and a copy thereof certified by the clerk of said Court shall also be filed in the office of the Secretary of State; and from the date of filing said copy in the office of the Secretary of State, said society shall be a body corporate in the name they have assumed in their articles of association.

SECTION 2. *Be it enacted*, That the societies so incorporated shall have power to sue and be sued, make bye-laws and contracts, buy, hold and sell property real & personal, for the purposes for which they are organized, and all other usual powers of corporations for said purposes.

SECTION 3. *Be it enacted*, That the societies which may be organized under this act shall cooperate as far as practicable with the educational officers of the State, and they may at any time be required to report to the Legislature or to any officer of the State designated by law or by Resolution of the General Assembly.

SECTION 4. *Be it enacted*, That the Societies so organized may form such connexions with each other or with any existing chartered educational societies or Institutions of learning, as they may deem expedient."

On January 19, 1850, the Allison bill was referred to the Committee on Education and Common Schools which reported the bill two days later without amendment and recommended its passage. The House obliged its author by passing the bill by a vote of 44 to 13.[39] With the addition of a minor Senate amendment, allowing the leasing of mineral rights on school lands in Polk County, the Allison bill became a law carrying the extravagant title of "An Act to promote popular Education by the formation of Societies and Institutions of Learning." [40]

A more serious but fruitless effort to do something in behalf of public education was the introduction of a bill on December 21, 1849, by Whig Representative G. D. Searcy of Shelby County. His bill[41] carried such proposals as (1) the election of a Superintendent of Public Instruction at a salary of $2,000; (2) the outlining of his duties and responsibilities; (3) delegating the power to County Courts to levy a tax, provided the voters of the county approved of said tax, not less than the amount received from the State; (4) appointment of a Board of Examiners to pass upon the qualifications of teachers; and (5) to prescribe the minimum curriculum to be taught in the schools. Sufficient interest was manifested in the bill that five hundred copies were ordered printed for the use of the House. As might have been expected, quite a bit of haggling arose as to the proposed salary of the Superintendent, the figure being reduced to $1,600. Thereupon, the first section of the bill, which included the above office and salary, was eliminated by

[39] *House Journal*, 1849, 623–624.
[40] *Acts of Tennessee*, 1849, Chapter 181.
[41] Original manuscript in State Archives, Nashville.

a vote of 43 to 29.[42] On February 5, 1850, the bill was up for the third and final reading. After an unsuccessful effort to postpone the bill until the next General Assembly, the bill was "laid on the table." [43]

After a routine first and second reading of the Searcy bill in the Senate, final action on the bill was taken on February 4, 1850, said action being short but sweet. The bill was "indefinitely postponed."[44]

Had the Legislature enacted the Searcy bill into law, even with its manifold weaknesses, such action would have given the deliberative body far more credit than it will ever receive as regards public education. Admittedly, the mere delegation of power to the County Courts of laying a tax for educational purposes was a vulnerable spot in the proposed law. With the Chief Executive and legislative leaders viewing with disapproval public taxation for public education, no clairvoyant powers are necessary to predict what the County Courts would have likely done. From the standpoint of the public, Caesar's famous maxim *(Veni, vidi, vici)* would have been reversed as to the last phrase. It would have read, "We came, we saw, *but we were conquered.*"

Despite the "do nothing," and apparently "care nothing" attitude demonstrated by the 1849 General Assembly regarding education, yet there was exhibited some concern in various parts of the State as to the pathetic condition of public education. In all candor, the petitions of citizens in behalf of public education exhibited more real concern and common sense than any of the miscellaneous abortions perpetrated by the Legislature in the name of education. Typical of such expressions of public sentiment was the following memorial [45] from Jefferson County:

"MEMORIAL
To the Senate and House of Representatives, of the State of
Tennessee
In General Assembly Convened,

The Memorial of the undersigned, citizens of the county of Jefferson, in said State, respectfully sets forth—That the Common School System of the State is admitted, on all hands, to be greatly defective. To your memorialists this appears to result, not so much, perhaps, from any large inadequacy of the general Common School Fund, as from the want of an auxiliary fund, annually contributed by the people of the State, and from imperfect organization and non-superintendence. Your memorialists beg leave respectfully to state, that the duty and the interests, the honor and the pride of Tennessee strongly urge the adoption of prompt and effective measures, that may render our Common School System equal to the wants, and worthy of the character of

---

[42] *House Journal*, 1849, 701.
[43] *Ibid.*, 765.
[44] *Senate Journal*, 1849, 699.
[45] Original Manuscript document in State Archives, Nashville. (68 signatures) Author's note. There are a number of similar 1849 memorials in the State Archives, all of which are in printed form, leaving a blank for name of county to be inserted and space for individual signatures. Somebody had done some "grass roots" work in various communities!

the State. Eminently distinguished for gallantry in war, it is time that Tennessee should win some of the victories of peace, and no longer lay ingloriously behind the foremost of her sisters, in the cause of imparting cultivation and knowledge to the masses of the people. To his end the undersigned, a portion of her citizens, invoke legislative action. Two modes, as it seems to your memorialists, present themselves: The first, perhaps the best, is to levy, by operation of a general law, a school-tax, throughout the State, upon property, privileges and polls, in aid of the general Common School Fund, and, like that fund, to be distributed according to the scholastic population of the State; and the other is, to authorise the several county courts, if a majority of the voters of the county shall so direct, to assess, and cause to be collected, a county tax, adequate to the purpose, withholding from any county, refusing to make the assessment, any portion whatever of the original general fund —in the confident belief, that paternal duty, and social honor and pride, would, in a short time, leave no county in the State, in such disgraceful recusancy. And whether legislature may, in its wisdom, super-add such school rates, upon the actual scholastic population, within any district, as may be adequate, and at the same time just and equitable. The undersigned believe, that these provisions, with a good general and local superintendence, to be established by law, will go far to make the system such as it ought to be.
   All of which is respectfully submitted."

So far as education was concerned, the Legislature had before it the Message of retiring Governor Neill S. Brown and the incoming Governor William Trousdale, in which communications each Chief Executive expressed his position on the subject. Despite their opposing views in the hotly contested race for the governorship, their legislative Messages were in "sweet harmony" as regards education. Each delivered a fulsome eulogy upon the benefits and advantages of educational facilities for the citizenry of the State. Said out-going Governor Brown:

"Something ought to be done to advance a subject of so much importance. We owe it to the character of the State, and we owe it as an act of justice to the children of the State. I need not enlarge on the inestimable benefits of a general and diffusive system of education. It lies at the foundation of our form of government—giving strength both to the ballot-box and the cartridge-box. . . ."

But the above eulogistic phrasing of words possessed about as much bite as a calico cat when placed in juxtaposition with another statement of his appearing in the same State paper regarding financial support for public education:

"I beg leave, however, to state that I do not believe a system of direct taxes expedient or proper!"

Some two weeks after the transmittal of the above Message, the incoming occupant of the gubernatorial chair felt it expedient to express his sentiments upon the same question. And so, another panegyric on education was forthwith delivered. Said Governor Trousdale:

"The importance of popular education in the preservation and perpetuation of our invaluable institutions is so palpable and so universally felt and admitted, that it is a matter of regret and surprise that more progress has not

MEMORIAL.

TO THE SENATE AND
HOUSE OF REPRESENTATIVES,
OF THE STATE OF TENNESSEE,
IN GENERAL ASSEMBLY CONVENED.

The Memorial of the undersigned, citizens of the county of *Jefferson*, in said State, respectfully sets forth—That the Common School System of the State is admitted, on all hands, to be greatly defective. To your memorialists this appears to result, not so much, perhaps, from any large inadequacy of the general Common School Fund, as from the want of an auxiliary fund, annually contributed by the people of the State, and from imperfect organization and non-superintendence. Your memorialists beg leave respectfully to state, that the duty and the interests, the honor and the pride of Tennessee strongly urge the adoption of prompt and effective measures, that may render our Common School System equal to the wants, and worthy of the character of the State. Eminently distinguished for gallantry in war, it is time that Tennessee should win some of the victories of peace, and no longer lay ingloriously behind the foremost of her sisters, in the cause of imparting cultivation and knowledge to the masses of the people. To this end the undersigned, a portion of her citizens, invoke legislative action. Two modes, as it seems to your memorialists, present themselves: The first, perhaps the best, is to levy, by operation of a general law, a school-tax, throughout the State, upon property, privileges and polls, in aid of the general Common School Fund, and, like that fund, to be distributed according to the scholastic population of the State; and the other is, to authorise the several county courts, if a majority of the voters of the county shall so direct, to assess, and cause to be collected, a county tax, adequate to the purpose, withholding from any county, refusing to make the assessment, any portion whatever of the original general fund—in the confident belief, that paternal duty, and social honor and pride, would, in a short time, leave no county in the State, in such disgraceful recusancy. And whether the one mode or the other be adopted by your honorable body, your memorialists suggest that the legislature may, in its wisdom, superadd such school rates, upon the actual scholastic population, within any district, as may be adequate, and at the same time just and equitable. The undersigned believe, that these provisions, with a good general and local superintendence, to be established by law, will go far to make the system such as it ought to be.

All of which is respectfully submitted.

"Vox Populi, vox Dei"!

been made in securing its benefits. It is manifest to my mind that these benefits can never be secured without a large increase of the common school fund. I know of no mode of attaining this end, except by a resort to taxation for school purposes."

And then, seemingly fearful of what interpretation might be put upon such bold language, perhaps exacting some sort of political reprisal, Governor Trousdale hastened to add the following "escape" clause:

"... but in my extensive intercourse with our common constituents, I have seen no evidence to justify me in supposing that such a recommendation [taxation] would be in accordance with their convictions or expectations ... and into your hands I commit the subject with the ardent hope that your labors may be successful in advancing the great cause of popular education."

Governor Trousdale's "ardent hope" must have been in the same category as that of the Negro preacher called upon to preach the funeral of a "bad" Negro. After quoting all the "merciful" passages of Scripture that came to mind, for the consolation of the bereaved, he concluded his sermon with the following anthitetical observation: "We hope he hab gone, whar we know he ain't."

Newspaper comments upon the two above Messages were so gangrened with political bias as to render such appraisals practically worthless. As an example of their unreliability, let two brief excerpts from the *same newspaper* be introduced as confirmatory evidence. In extolling retiring Governor Brown's Message, an uncomprising Whig journal stated that

"... his ardent advocacy of popular education ... will doubtless be read with approving interest by the great body of the people." [46]

As to Governor Trousdale's position regarding public education, although identical with that of Governor Brown, the *True Whig* soundly condemned the Democratic incumbent:

"And yet the Governor of the State, the accredited guardian of the public weal, says 'I am unable to recommend for your adoption *any specific measure* for the improvement of our common school system,' though 'well satisfied of its *utter incapacity* to meet the reasonable wishes of the people.' Upon this subject, it seems, he has *nothing to say*, and emphatically *he said it.*' " [47]

Public education was stymied in the doldrums, for not a single progressive step was taken by either the executive or legislative departments of the State government.

Like several of his predecessors, Governor Trousdale emphasized the importance of increasing transportation facilities in the State so as to facilitate the moving of agricultural and mineral products. On the whole, stress was placed upon the development of railroads, while river

---

[46] *Nashville True Whig*, October 6, 1849.
[47] *Ibid.*, October 27, 1849.

and dirt road transportation methods were practically ignored in his Message. Quite properly, Governor Trousdale pointed out that serious consideration ought to be given to the State's financial ability to pay for such improvements, and he warned that it was imperative that the State's credit should be preserved "inviolate and untarnished."

With reference to Internal Improvements, the Legislature was decidedly conservative in regard to piling up additional financial obligations on the State. In the main, legislation dealt largely with the incorporation of railroads and turnpikes, or the amending of existing charters. Eighteen such laws were enacted. Particular attention, it seems, was paid to the East Tennessee and Georgia Railroad, the State subsidy of $350,000 being rigidly restricted to the purchase of iron rails and equipment as completion of segments of the railroad were completed in sections of forty miles or more.[48] Curiously enough, all such restrictions and limitations upon the above railroad were incorporated in a law whose caption related to a minor Williamson County turnpike to be chartered under the name of the Owen and Winstead Turnpike Company. What came to be a very important railroad, the Louisville and Nashville, was granted a charter [49] and the Nashville and Chattanooga Railroad's charter was amended by a requirement that the bridge across the Tennessee River should be at least "thirty feet above extreme high water mark." [50]

Provision for the removal of obstructions in certain river channels and the declaration of the navigability of others constituted the bulk of the legislation concerning water transportation. Two thousand dollars was allocated for improving the navigation of the Tennessee River, five hundred of which would be used for constructing a pier above the Suck and "of a size sufficient for a windlass to operate by horse power, so as to wind up steamboats over the Suck."[51] In the same law, Big Emery and Big Indian Creek were declared to be navigable streams. The commissioners having control of the fund for improvement of Forked Deer River were commanded to submit a report as to how said fund had been handled by them, and failure or refusal to comply with said requirement subjected each commissioner to indictment and fine, if proved guilty.[52]

In a general law entitled "An Act to improve Public Roads," County Courts were authorized to provide overseers "such a number of small hammers, for breaking stone, as may be deemed necessary by the Court."[53] In case the overseer misused "said small hammers," he was

---

[48] *Acts of Tennessee*, 1849, Chapter 42.
[49] *Ibid.*, Chapter 118.
[50] *Ibid.*, Chapter 266.
[51] *Ibid.*, Chapter 239.
[52] *Ibid.*, Chapter 239.
[53] *Ibid.*, Chapter 101.

warned that he would be liable to the same penalty as provided in a law of 1807 designed to prevent the misuse of said implements, said penalty not to exceed a fine of five dollars for each offense. Seven thousand dollars, being the unexpended sum appropriated heretofore for improvement of the Clinch and Powell Rivers, could now be used for the improvement of dirt roads from Tazewell to Knoxville and from Jacksborough to Knoxville.[54] As may readily be inferred, river transportation and dirt road hauling did not appeal to the Legislature, if appropriations of public funds for improving such facilities be the criterion. And all of this despite the fact that improved dirt roads, at the time, were a *sine qua non* if a fog in summer and a bog in winter were to be avoided.

But when it came to turnpikes, erected out of private funds, the Legislature was generous minded in granting charters. A total of one hundred and twenty-three such charters were granted at the 1849 legislative session.[55] Among the names were Canoe Branch, Port Royal, Sycamore Mills, Brick Church, Bear Creek, and so on *ad infinitum*.

A sort of blanket law was enacted which dealt specifically with "the formation of turnpike companies."[56] Meticulous details were covered in the law as related to by-laws, election of officers, number constituting a quorum, time of meetings, failure to pay for stock, *et cetera*. In case the proposed turnpike passed through lands owned by the State, the turnpike company was privileged to avail itself of the free use of timber, stone, gravel, earth, and a fifty-foot strip of land.

A rather comprehensive bird's-eye view of just how the State and the Railroad and Turnpike Companies were transacting business may be gleaned from the Report of the Secretary of the State Internal Improvement Commission:[57]

"REPORT OF THE INTERNAL IMPROVEMENT COMMISSIONER.

Department of State. ⎫
Nashville, November 12, 1849. ⎭

To the General Assembly of the State of Tennessee:

In obedience to the law of the 26th of January, 1846, imposing the duties of Internal Improvement Commissioner upon the Secretary of State, I have the honor of submitting the following report of my proceedings under the provisions of that law. Since I came into office nearly, two years ago, I have collected, and promptly paid into the Treasury of the State, the following sums of money, collected from the following companies, viz:

Lebanon and Nashville turnpike company..................$ 4,300.00
Nashville, Murfreesborough and Shelbyville turnpike company   9,122.97
Columbia, Pulaski, Elkton and Alabama turnpike company...   3,447.39

---

[54] *Ibid.*, Chapter 261.
[55] For a list of turnpike names, See Index, *Acts of Tennessee*, 1849, 618–622.
[56] *Acts of Tennessee*, 1849, Chapter 72.
[57] *Senate Journal*, 1849, Appendix, 167–170.
    House Journal, 1849, Appendix, 167–170.

Nashville and Charlotte turnpike company................... 2,100.00
Nashville and Kentucky turnpike company................. 2,031.61
Franklin and Columbia turnpike company.................... 2,385.90
Lebanon and Sparta turnpike company...................... 1,729.83
Clarksville and Russelville turnpike company................ 1,461.42
Columbia Central turnpike company........................ 782.98
                                                          _____
                                                          $27,362.10

Making an aggregate of twenty-seven thousand three hundred and sixty-two dollars and ten cents, all of which is the dividends of toll accruing upon the State stock in said companies.

This aggregate would have been much greater, if it had not been for the destructive effects of the freshets in the winter of 1847-8, and the prevalence of the cholera in Nashville, and some of the contiguous counties, throughout a large portion of the last year. By the freshets occurring in the winter of 1847-8, the bridge over Duck river, on the Franklin and Columbia turnpike road, was entirely swept off, and a new one has been erected at a cost of five or six thousand dollars to the company—during its re-construction the collection of a portion of the tolls was suspended. By the same freshets, the bridges over Stone's river, Browns and Mill Creeks, on the Nashville and Lebanon road, and the bridges over the east and west forks of Stone's river, on the Jefferson turnpike, were either entirely swept off, or so damaged, as to require heavy outlays to re-construct or repair them. During the actual or reported prevalence of cholera in Nashville for six months of the current year, the travel and transportation were greatly diminished, and, for a portion of that time, wholly suspended, on all the lines of road leading into Nashville.

From the 'Nolensville company,' I have received no toll. By its undertaking to construct one mile of the 'Mill Creek Valley' road, its tolls have been mostly absorbed; but according to its last report, all of its liabilities will have been discharged by the first of January next, and an overplus of $600 or $700 will at that time be paid into the treasury of the State.

From the 'Gallatin company' no tolls have been received, and probably will not be for several years. The creditors of this company, some years ago, filed a bill to subject the stock to the payment of their claims—the court refused to sell the stock, but decreed that the whole dividends of toll should be paid over to the creditors in discharge of their claims—about $3000 a year has been thus paid, and the residue of the debts amounts to about $20,000.

The Big Hatchee, Forked-Deer, Ashport and Fulton turnpike companies are paying no dividends, and probably never will—all the tolls collected are expended in such temporary repairs as will keep these roads in a passable condition. By an act of the last General Assembly the Board of Internal Improvement was authorized to sell the State's interest in the Big Hatchee road, but no sale has been made.

The 'Harpeth company' has as yet, paid no dividends. The original construction of the road was imperfect, and the company has given a lease of its tolls for three years to have it repaired in a substantial manner; two years of which lease have yet to expire.

The 'Pelham and Jasper' road by compromise has passed into other hands, and the State sustained an entire loss of the fund expended in its original construction.

By an act of the last legislature, the time for the completion of the 'Murfreesborough and Manchester' turnpike road was extended for one year from the passage of the act. At the expiration of the year, I visited the road and found some portions of it wholly impassable, and but little of the macadamized part completed as the charter requires. This, together with all the other necessary facts in relation to the road, were reported to the Attorney General of the State, who has instituted suit against the company, which is now pending.

The 'East Tennessee and Georgia Railroad Company,' since its re-organization by the last Legislature, has received $40,000 in State Bonds, being a part of the original subscription of the State to that improvement. The whole of this road, as I understand, has been put under contract; in the prosecution of which five or six hundred hands are now at work on the lower end, and unless some unlooked for event retards the progress of the work, seventy-five miles will be in readiness for the superstructure in some short time.

The 'Memphis and LaGrange Railroad,' on which the State has expended $216,000, has been for some time considered as a total loss of the whole sum; but from the growing commerce of Memphis, some line of Railroad communication will be pushed from that point into the interior, either directly to Charleston or to meet the Nashville and Chattanooga Railroad, probably at Nashville; in either of which events the bed of the Memphis and LaGrange Railroad will fall within the general route of these new improvements; and the State in granting either of these new charters, will be exercising but a just regard for her own vested rights, to require in the charter, that the new company shall take the present improvement of the Memphis and LaGrange road at a reasonable valuation, either as stock in the new improvement, or in cash. In this way the State, without doing injustice to any one, may reimburse herself to some extent, the funds she has expended.

At different periods during the last two years, I have inspected as many of the roads as absence from other official duties would allow; found them, generally, in good condition, and the companies efficiently administered. The original tollbooks at the several gates were carefully examined, and compared with the reports made to me, and I had the satisfaction to find that the full amount appearing on the books had been, in every instance, faithfully and honestly reported by the companies.

Before closing this report, I trust it will not be considered intrusive to direct the mind of the Legislature to what is evidently a defect in the existing legal provisions connected with these turnpike companies. In granting the charters, it was no doubt the intention of the Legislature to invest the companies with the right of exacting and receiving from each individual using the road a certain compensation for such use, proportionate to the distance. As a means of defining and collecting these dues, a system of tolls and of toll-gates was established, at prescribed points on the road. This system, where the roads are regularly traveled through, and each gate passed as it occurs, is very simple and efficient in doing equal justice to all concerned. But there is a disposition in the minds of many, who use the roads, to evade the payment of tolls wherever it can be done without incurring the existing legal penalties. Many pass along the intermediate portions of the road without passing through any of the gates, and of course without the payment of any toll. And, as it is the *use of the road*, and not simply a passing through the, gates, which creates the obligation to pay, many of these just obligations remain undischarged, and the companies have no legal means of enforcing them. Thus, the system of toll-gates, as the only instrument of the law, fails to attain the ends of justice, and requires some auxiliary remedy to accomplish that object. If a law were passed authorizing the companies, in all cases where the gates are not passed through, and the regular tolls not paid, to sue for and recover from the person using any portion of a road, a sum not exceeding the regular rates of toll on said road, a remedy would be furnished broad enough to meet the full equity and justice of every case. Under such a provision as this, I doubt not, the State's revenue from these roads would be increased some thousands of dollars annually, and the existing temptations to evade the payment of tolls be entirely removed.

Respectfully submitted,

W. B. A. RAMSEY,

Secretary of State and Internal Improvement Commissioner"

The fourth recommendation of Governor Trousdale had reference to an examination of the revenue laws, giving especial attention to the complaints registered by merchants. In compliance with the Governor's suggestion, the Legislature passed an act [58] entitled "to reduce the tax on merchants' licenses." The revised tax scale called for payment of seventy-five cents on each hundred dollars of merchandise handled by wholesale, retail, and commission merchants with the exception of articles grown and manufactured within the State. An exception was also made to the sale of spirituous liquors. The tax on salt, iron, sugar, coffee, molasses, spun cotton, and garden seeds was to be levied "only upon persons introducing them into this State for sale."

According to a Report of the Comptroller of the Treasury, filed with the Legislature on October 15, 1849, the chief sources of revenue were a State tax of fifteen cents on each hundred dollars of taxable property, and a special tax of one and one-half cents on each hundred dollars, for a term of three years, to provide funds for the erection of the State Hospital for the Insane; and certain miscellaneous sources of revenue such as fees from entry takers, privilege licenses, and bonuses from banks and insurance companies. For the preceding year, 1848, the Comptroller's Report [59] disclosed the following breakdown on the sources of State revenue:

Value of Land	Value of Slaves	Value of Town Lots	Value of White Polls
$66,414,771	$46,740,829	$11,458,429	$14,904

Money & Stocks
$4,896,014

In addition to the above State sources of tax revenue which yielded in 1848 the sum of $166,394, there was collected by sheriffs and revenue commissioners the sum of $270,212 in the form of fees and licenses, all of which went to the State Treasury. It will be noted that two principal types of taxable property consisted of land and slaves. Even so, expenditures for the preceding biennium, 1847-1849, had exceeded receipts by the sum of $11,743.13.[60]

In alluding to the State Capitol then in the early state of erection, Governor Trousdale suggested in his Message that it might be sound

[58] *Acts of Tennessee,* 1849, Chapter 22.
[59] *Senate Journal,* 1849, Appendix, 154–165.
[60] *Ibid.,* 132.

economy to provide "additional force" for hastening the completion of the structure. In the preamble to a law providing for the continuation of "the building of the Capitol," it was declared that the heavy draft made upon convict labor from the penitentiary for the preceding four years had made it impossible for that institution to meet its ordinary operating expenses.[61] An appropriation of $15,000 for the ensuing biennium was requested by the Agent of the penitentiary. The request was granted, although provision was made that all such items as were requested by the Agent must receive the approval of the inspectors of the penitentiary before the Comptroller should issue a warrant for same. Section 2 of the above law provided the sum of $150,000 and a continuation of the same Capitol Commissioners for the ensuing two years. The Commissioners were instructed to investigate the question of whether or not the employment of outside labor would be conducive to the shortening of time and the reduction of expenses in regard to carrying forward the work on the building.

In a project of such proportion as the State Capitol, quite naturally there arose in the minds of some of the legislators the question as to whether or not the most economical means were being employed in its construction. One such legislator was Representative B. S. Allen of Carroll County who, on November 12, 1849, submitted the following resolution [62] which was adopted:

"*Resolved,* That the committee on capitol buildings and public grounds, be instructed to inquire whether or not the work upon the capitol has been prosecuted with reasonable dispatch and economy, and to this end, that they be empowered to send for persons and papers, if deemed by them necessary, to arrive at a full knowledge of the same.

Resolved, That said committee be directed to inquire into the expediency of employing an Architect for a stipulated price to complete the building, in lieu of an annual salary as allowed now by law; and that they report by bill or otherwise."

On January 5, 1850, Representative George D. Crosthwait of Rutherford County from the Committee on Capitol Building and Public Grounds submitted the following report:[63]

"The Committee on the Capitol Building and Public Grounds, to whom was referred House resolution (No. 77) have had the same under consideration, and beg leave to report:

That although the committee cannot say that in their opinion the erection of the capitol has been prosecuted with the utmost possible despatch and economy, still they cannot but say that a moderate degree both of despatch and economy have been used in its erection thus far. The committee, if the present architect would consent to finish his contract for a specific sum, would think it best so to employ him. But as he is unwilling to contract in that way, and a law requiring that arrangement would therefore necessarily involve a

---

[61] *Acts of Tennessee,* 1849, Chapter 219.
[62] *House Journal,* 1849, 274.
[63] *Ibid.,* 513–514.

change of the architect, the committee respectfully recommend that the present arrangement be continued. The committee report further, that whilst it is probable that fifty thousand dollars per annum is as large a sum as will be necessary for carrying on said building, it is possible that circumstances may favor a larger expenditure. True economy would dictate that the largest amount which can be judiciously expended, should be; and they therefore recommend that the sum of seventy-five thousand dollars per annum for the ensuing two years be placed at the disposal of the board of commissioners. With such an appropriation, it is calculated that the capitol will be so far completed at least as for the next session of the Legislature to be held in it. They therefore have instructed me to report the accompanying bill, and to recommend its passage.

    All of which is respectfully submitted.

GEO. D. CROSTHWAIT, Chm."

The above Report indicated that a minor squabble had arisen between the above legislative committee and the architect, William Strickland. The committee wanted Strickland to agree to a lump sum as his fee for supervising the construction of the building. To this proposition Strickland would not consent. He probably reasoned that there were too many contingencies involved in such a matter, such as convict labor, and supply of various materials which included some highly specialized products.

    Knowing that the Legislature would demand a strict accounting of the work covering the preceding two years, the Capitol Commissioners were prepared to meet such a request. Accordingly, two weeks after the convening of the General Assembly, there were placed before the body detailed reports from both the Capitol Commissioners and the architect. The two Reports [64] were as follows:

"REPORTS OF THE COMMISSIONERS AND ARCHITECT
OF THE BUILDING
of the
STATE CAPITOL,
12th October, 1849.

To the Honorable, the General Assembly of the State of Tennessee:

    The Commissioners to superintend the erection of the State Capitol, report that at the date of their report to the last General Assembly, 1st of October, 1847, they had on hand an unexpended balance of........$ 592.29
Received since that period from the sale of State Bonds
and other sources 102,000.50

Making the sum of...$102,592.79
Within the same period they have expended the sum of......... 115,811.29

Showing excess of expenditures over receipts of...............$ 13,218.50

64 *Senate Journal*, 1849, Appendix, 322–326.
   House Journal, 1849, Appendix, 258–262.

Which has been advanced to the Commissioners by the Bank of Tennessee. As the General Assembly was soon to convene, the Commissioners thought it more advisable thus to exceed the appropriations than to diminish the force employed, or arrest the work altogether for a time.

The account shewing the details of the receipts and expenditures to 1st inst., signed by H. A. Gleaves, Secretary, is herewith transmitted as part of this report. The original vouchers or receipts, on which these payments have been made, are in the possession of the Secretary, and await the examination of the General Assembly or any Committee they may appoint.

This sum of $115,811.37
Added to amount previously expended, say................... 40,679.31

Makes the whole expenditure in money on the Capitol,
    since its commencement...................................$156,490.68

The Commissioners were enabled to sell the hundred thousand dollars of State Bonds, having ten years to run, at par, according to the provisions of the act of the last General Assembly.

Should that mode of raising funds be continued, the Commissioners would suggest such a modification of the law, as will authorize bonds of the denominations of $1000, to be issued instead of confining the issue to those of $250.

For full details of the work done, the present condition of the building, the force employed &c., &c., they refer to the able and satisfactory report of the Architect, hereunto appended.

They moreover invite a personal and thorough examination of the building by the members of the General Assembly.

All which is respectfully submitted.

JNO. M. BASS, Ch'n.

By order of the Board of Commissioners.
Nashville, October 12th, 1849."

"REPORT OF THE ARCHITECT.

To John M. Bass, Esq.,
President of the Board of Commissioners for building the State Capitol.
SIR:

Since my last report to the Commissioners, dated the 4th October, 1847, upon the progress then made in the building of the State Capitol, the cut stone ashler of the basement story, together with the Cornice and Plinth courses have been completed and set all around the building, both inside and out.

The Basement Story has been subdivided in its interior with rubbed or polished stone, forming the Halls, stairways and chambers for the accommodation of the Supreme and Federal Courts, and the various offices connected with the State. The whole of this story has been arched over entirely, and the stairways carried up to the platforms of the principal story.

The Principal Story, on the outer walls have been raised to the height of about 9 feet above the basement, and all the interior subdivisions of the walls, forming the Hall of Representatives, Senate Chamber, Committee rooms and Library have also been founded in stone to the height of the Plinth course on the inside of the building, while the exterior walls are considerably advanced toward their destined height of 43 feet to the ceiling of the interior Entablature. In the course of the next season the walls will be up and ready to receive the cornice, and preparations will be made to roof in the body of the building as soon thereafter as practicable.

The arches are now all completed, with the exception of those over the Committee rooms of the House, these will be vaulted so as to form all the side galleries and seats for spectators both here, and over the Committee rooms of the Senate, which will be situated on each side of the Library room on the N. W. division of the building.

The original act of the General Assembly authorizing the contruction of a State Capitol, defines that the whole structure should be built '*with cut or hewn stone*,' and with this view the Board of Commissioners, have, from time to time, instructed the Architect to carry out the law for the work to be done accordingly, in a substantial and workmanlike manner.

The material used in the building is of the most durable kind, quite equal in texture and compactness to any of the Northern and Eastern marbles, and as far as regards the rubbed or polished surfaces of the interior stone walls, there are no examples of any buildings in the United States, either public or private, in which the walls are constructed of rubbed or polished stones on the interior; indeed, there are very few buildings in Europe of this handsome and permanent class.

The body of the building may now be considered to be about half up to its height, so far as regards its crypt and cell, that is to say, exclusive of the Porticos and roof. It is necessary that the sixteen interior columns of the Hall of Representatives, should be wrought as soon as practicable, in order that the roof may be sustained and the building covered in. These columns are already quarried, each in one block of 21 feet in length, including their capitals and bases.

The materials for the division walls of the great Hall, extending North and South and separating the Senate Chamber from the Library and Committee rooms, are in a great state of forwardness, and the developments at the quarries, since the last report to you, gives an assurance of an abundant supply of rock, and that of the very best quality. The amount of stone now quarried is sufficient to keep the stone cutters employed all this winter at the quarries, and in the Penitentiary.

The following is an account and average estimate of the number of men daily employed, and material wrought, within the last two years, viz:

The hired hands at the sheds on the quarry bed will average about 50 men at cutting and rubbing stone.

95   Laborers rolling, loading wagons, and quarrying—45 men.

112   *The Penitentiary force* averages about 47 convicts cutting and rubbing stone, 45 sawing and rolling stone, quarrying, 20 men diminished much during the prevalence of the cholera.

26   At the building, stone setters, trimmers, riggers and masons— average 26 hands.

233   Men of all descriptions as Mechanics and Laborers, who have wrought and set stone in the building, to the amount of superficial feet 144,000 of stone.

Bricks.—The arches have taken 643,130, including the filling of walls, spandrils &c., all of which has been laid by 13 bricklayers, 40 tenders and mortar makers, employed from May to July in the present year.

Respectfully submitted by

Your obedient servant,

W. STRICKLAND, *Architect.*

State Capitol, Nashville, October 12th, 1849"

Governor Trousdale's abbreviated comments in his Message upon the Penitentiary and the Lunatic Asylum shed no light upon many interesting features concerning those institutions. If one desires any specific information, recourse has to be made to the official reports embracing some sixty-three printed pages in the Appendix of the legislative *Journals*.[65] It is regrettable that space limitations preclude the inclusion of these reports, for they exhibit many items and data of much interest to sociologists, psychiatrists, penologists, lawmakers, and the general public.

As of the date of October, 1849, there were 192 inmates in the penitentiary, of whom only three were women. One hundred and twenty of the convicts were employed in quarrying and cutting stone for the State Capitol. Convicts on the "inside" were engaged in nineteen other occupations, such as blacksmithing, mattress making, and harness making. Larceny headed the list of crimes for which twenty-nine men had been convicted; twenty-one were in for second-degree murder; nine for "Negro stealing"; two for "seducing" slaves; one for stealing a sheep; one for polygamy; one for persuading slaves to leave their owners, while another was there because of "special act of the Legislature." Fifteen of the convicts were "lifers"; other sentences ranged from twenty-one years to one year and eight months. Four of the inmates were of ages between 60 and 70, while twenty-one were under 20 years of age. Thirty-two of the convicts were from Davidson County, and Shelby came next with twenty. Eighty-four were Tennesseans; thirty-one were from North Carolina; twenty from Virginia; fourteen from Kentucky; while England and Prussia were represented by one convict each. One hundred and fifteen were married men, and one woman was single. Prior to conviction, ninety-eight were listed as intemperate drinkers, and seventy-four were moderate drinkers. Forty-seven could neither read nor write, and thirty-eight were recorded as "uneducated."

In his Report[66] to the Legislature, Dr. Felix Robertson who was the Prison Physician attributed, in part, the increase in mortality to the lack of a hospital at the penitentiary. Eighteen deaths had occurred during the past two years, but in the opinion of Dr. Robertson the prevalence of cholera in Nashville had contributed to the uptrend in mortality.

Annexed to the Penitentiary Report is a brief statement[67] addressed to the Agent of the Penitentiary, J. McIntosh, to-wit:

---

[65] *Senate Journal*, 1849, Appendix, 3–28; 55–77; 179–192.
   House Journal, 1849, Appendix, 3–28; 55–77; 179–192.
[66] *Senate Journal*, 1849, Appendix, 74.
[67] *Ibid.*, 75–77.

"REPORT OF PROF. J. H. INGRAHAM.

To J. McIntosh, Esq.; Agent of the Tennessee Penitentiary:

Sir:—As you are about to make your report, I feel it is duty owed to you and to the Penitentiary to furnish you with a brief report of the result of my Sunday labors, during the last two years, among the prisoners under your charge.

A casual visit to the Penitentiary in the fall of 1849, made me acquainted with the fact, that no stated religious services, as in other State prisons, were provided by *law* for its inmates, and that they were dependent wholly upon the occasional and infrequent visits of ministers, for all the religious instruction which they received. I learned, further, that in default of these chance services on the Lord's day, they were shut up in their cells, thus suffering more severely on that day than any other, the irksome weight of their imprisonment. The two-fold desire to afford them stated religious instruction, and to open the doors of their cells for a few hours on Sunday, prompted me to ask permission of you to visit them regularly as a teacher. Your obliging compliance with my request, I here acknowledge with pleasure, and, also, your courtesy and attention up to this time, as well as the politeness of your officers, whose duties and responsibilities have been greatly augmented by the increased watchfulness necessary when the convicts assemble in a body in the Halls, but which have been borne by them always with cheerfulness and alacrity.

During the period in which I have been a regular Sunday visitor to the prison, I officiated the first year but once a day; but by your request last summer, I since then officiated twice a Sabbath.

The Experience which my labors have given me, convince me, that religious instruction produces upon the minds of convicts the most beneficial results. Knowing, in the outset, that seventy out of the two hundred men could not read, I assumed that they were *wholly* ignorant of the Bible; and of the remainder, I suspect few possessed much knowledge of it, or they would not have been there.

Upon this ground I began my teachings with the first chapter of Genesis, and pursued a systematic course of bible teaching with them, which occupied seventeen months to the Revelations. By this means I brought before their minds all the great outlines and prominent points of revealed truth, from the fall of man to the ascension of Christ. As it is impossible for a man to hear the Bible read through without being benefitted, I trust that some good has been effected.

The constant attendance of the prisoners, (it being voluntary with them to attend or not) their eager, earnest attention, their deep interest in listening to the word of God, (hitherto to most of them a sealed book) has been a source of gratification to me that has amply rewarded all my pains-taking. At your request, I give you some results: Four months ago eleven gave their names to you for baptism; and shortly afterwards four more were applicants, and last Sabbath, one additional one handed his name to an officer for the same sacramental rite. Of these, fifteen, after due examination, were baptised by my brother, the Rev. Mr. John Ingraham, Rector of St. Paul's: besides this there are about twenty who wait to be admitted to the Holy Communion.

Whether the general character of the prisoners has been improved by religious teaching, you have better opportunity of judging than I possess. If you are satisfied that religious teaching does really elevate the standard of moral character in the prison, I trust that you will exert your influence towards having a regular chaplaincy appointed by the Legislature, in order that so large a body of men may not be left without constant Sunday services. A prison of two hundred men is a parish in itself, and requires for the sick, the dying and the penitent, the regular visitations of a clergyman. Certainly no more responsible charge could be committed to a minister of God.

I think a convenient chapel should be erected over the workshops, so that the prisoners can all be brought together in a body, and not be divided as they now are, one half having service in its wing only in the morning, and the other half only in the evening. A hospital ought, also, to be provided instead of the small, inconvenient apartment now used for the purpose, and for which it is wholly unsuited. Both the chapel and hospital could be under one roof; and might be erected at a very light cost.

Before closing my report, I desire to embrace this opportunity to bear testimony to the admirable and efficient discipline which I have witnessed within the prison: Strict yet parental, humane yet vigilant, quiet yet efficient, it appears to be all that can be desired. The office you hold, sir, is one of peculiar responsibility, and calls for qualities of character that do not meet together in every man. Severity tempered by kindness, decision by mildness, justice by pity should characterise the governor of a prison; and these qualities, I well know, you have eminently shown in your government of the penitentiary. Most of those who are discharged call upon me as soon as they come into the city, to thank me for teaching them on the Sabbath, and invariably they have spoken of you with affection and respect. They speak of the admirable order of the prison regulations, the kindness of the officers, the goodness of the food, and the absence of all cruelty of punishment. As I have ventured to express a hope that a chapel and hospital may be provided, I also cherish the hope that some alteration may be effected in the construction of the cells. They are far too small for *men* to be confined in. Being but three feet wide and nearly filled up by the cot, the prisoner must of necessity lie down when locked in. It is to be hoped that our enlightened Legislature will take this subject into serious consideration.

I have the honor to be, sir,

Your obedient servant,
J. H. INGRAHAM."

Nashville, Oct. 1, 1849.

Apparently Professor Ingraham's communication was responsible for a legislative movement dealing with the spiritual welfare of the inmates of the penitentiary, for on December 15, 1849, Senator Felix K. Zollicoffer of Davidson County introduced

"A bill to provide Sabbath teaching to the convicts in the Penitentiary." [68]

On the third and final reading in the Senate, on January 25, 1850, the Zollicoffer bill was passed by a vote of 19 to 5.[69] Two days before adjournment of the session, the House of Representatives passed the bill without amendment by a vote of 54 to 4.[70] The law [71] authorized the inspectors of the penitentiary to appoint

---

[68] *Senate Journal*, 1849, 409.
[69] *Ibid.*, 610–611.
[70] *House Journal*, 1849, 850.
[71] *Acts of Tennessee*, 1849, Chapter 188.

some competent person, who should be a minister of the gospel, to act as prison chaplain, at a salary of one hundred dollars per annum. The inspectors were empowered, however, to discontinue such service if, in their judgment, the service was "without remunerating good effect."

Two Reports [72] were submitted to the Legislature concerning the New Lunatic Asylum, one by Dr. Boyd McNairy the physician in charge of the care of the inmates and the other by the Commissioners who were responsible for the construction of the proposed buildings. Difficulty had been experienced in getting men to serve as Commissioners, but finally a full Board of Commissioners was consummated by the appointment and acceptance of the following: Lucius J. Polk of Maury County; John J. White and Daniel S. Donelson of Sumner County; Henry S. Frazier of Wilson County; Samuel D. Morgan, Andrew Ewing, and Alexander Allison of Davidson County. The Board employed Dr. John S. Young and Major A. Heiman "at moderate salaries" who were actively in charge of the supervision of the buildings to be erected on a two hundred and fifty acre farm, six miles from Nashville, located on the Nashville and Murfreesboro pike. This marked the beginning of the present-day Central State Hospital. Dr. Young made extensive investigation of similar plants in the Eastern States and returned with a wealth of information which was utilized by Major Heiman, the architect, in drafting plans for the new buildings. In his report to the Board, Dr. Young pointed out a serious restriction that had been imposed by the Legislature, namely, that the whole establishment including the cost of the land should not exceed forty thousand dollars. Quite frankly, he stated that the lowest estimate was between ninety thousand and one hundred thousand dollars, and that it was up to the Legislature as to whether or not the plans would be modified and the cost reduced or provision made to "carry out the magnificient intentions of your predecessors."

Dr. McNairy's Report dealt largely with the care of the inmates, adequate "care" being impossible under the limitations of the old plant, crowded conditions, and deficient equipment in all particulars. There were in the institution at the date of his Report, October 1, 1849, one hundred and forty-four inmates of whom one hundred and two were men. Ages "when insanity commenced" ranged from nine years to sixty-one. Sixty-one of the men had been farmers and forty of the women housewives. Included also were six school teachers, seven lawyers, and two clergymen. Listed as "supposed causes" of insanity were intemperance, jealousy, family afflictions, disappointed love, religious and political excitement, abuse of step-father, and mumps. During the preceding two years, 1847-1849, there had been seventeen deaths from various causes, such as consumption, dropsy, marasmus, and effects of

---

[72] *Senate Journal*, 1849, Appendix, 3–28; 179–183.

insanity." Dr. McNairy pleaded for additional recreational features, and he recommended earnestly the employment of a regular chaplain to conduct religious exercises on the Sabbath.

When Governor Trousdale emphasized in his Message the importance of amending the Constitution in regard to the method of electing Judges and Attorneys-General, he was subscribing to a wave of public sentiment favorable to such reform in the judicial system. An effort had been attempted in 1847 to effectuate such a change, but the movement went down to defeat in that session of the Legislature. Credit for the initial step, whereby the election of the above officials would ultimately be taken from the Legislature and placed in the hands of the people, must be given to Major David W. Ballew, Representative from McMinn County in the 1847 General Assembly. On October 18, Representative Ballew submitted the following proposition:[73]

"Proposed amendments to the Constitution of the State of Tennessee, to be acted on by the present General Assembly in the manner prescribed in the eleventh Article, and third Section thereof, of the Constitution of the State.

First Proposed Amendment. In Section the third, of Article the 6th, of the Constitution, strike out the words, 'the General Assembly shall, by a joint vote of both Houses, appoint Judges to the several Courts of Law and Equity,' and insert in their room and stead, the following words: 'The Judges of such inferior Courts as the Legislature may establish, shall be elected by the qualified voters residing within the bounds of any District or Circuit to which such inferior Judge, or Judges, either of Law or Equity, may be assigned, by ballot, in the same manner that members of the General Assembly are elected.'

The said third Section, when amended, to read in the following words and figures:

'SEC. 3. The Judges of such inferior Courts as the Legislature may establish, shall be elected by the qualified voters residing within the bounds of any District or Circuit to which such inferior Judge, or Judges, either in Law or Equity, may be assigned, by ballot, in the same manner that members of the General Assembly are elected. Courts may be established to be holden by Justices of the Peace. Judges of the Supreme Court shall be thirty-five years of age, and shall be elected for the term of twelve years.'

Second Proposed Amendment. In Section the 5th of the 6th Article of the Constitution, strike out the words, 'The Legislature shall elect Attorneys for the State by a joint vote of both Houses of the General Assembly,' and insert in their room and stead, the following words: 'The General Assembly shall, by joint vote of both Houses, appoint an Attorney for the State; and the Attorney for the State for any Circuit or District to which a Judge of an inferior Court may be assigned, shall be elected by the qualified voters residing within the bounds of such Court or District, in the same manner that members of the General Assembly are elected.'

Said 5th Section, when amended, to read in the words and figures following:

'SEC. 5. The General Assembly shall, by joint vote of both Houses, appoint an Attorney for the State; and the Attorney for the State for any

---

[73] *House Journal*, 1847, 108–109.

Circuit or District to which a Judge of an inferior Court may be assigned, shall be elected by the qualified voters residing within the bounds of such Circuit or District, in the same manner that members of the General Assembly are elected; all which Attorneys shall hold their office for the term of six years. In all cases where an Attorney for any District fails or refuses to attend and prosecute according to law, the Court shall have the power to appoint an Attorney, *pro tempore.*

SCHEDULE TO AMENDMENTS.

SECTION 1. And that no inconvenience may arise from the proposed amendments, should the same be adopted by the people, it is declared that all Judges of Courts and Attorneys, contemplated in the proposed amendments, shall continue to hold their offices and exercise the duties and functions thereof, according to the true existing Laws and Constitution, until the election of their successors by the people, to be held and made under a law to be passed by the General Assembly next elected after the ratification of the proposed amendments by the people; which law shall prescribe the times and places of holding said election, and which shall be passed without delay, and in strict pursuance of said amendments."

On January 28, 1848, the Ballew resolution was passed in the House of Representatives by a vote of 35 to 32.[74] Three days later, when the measure reached the Senate, Senator Thomas M. Jones from the counties of Giles and Maury

"moved that the further consideration thereof be postponed till the 1st October, 1849, which was agreed to. Ayes, 13; Noes, 12." [75]

But the tiger cub had received its first lap of blood. During the ensuing year, numerous newspaper editors kept the judicial reform movement before the people. Some six months prior to the convening of the Legislature in October, 1849, the *Daily Union* called attention to the matter in the following lengthy editorial: [76]

"THE ELECTION OF JUDICIAL OFFICERS BY THE PEOPLE

We understand that the proposition to amend our State Constitution so as to give the election of judicial officers directly to the people, is undergoing discussion by the candidates as well as by the papers in different parts of the State. When this reform was proposed by the talented representative of Mc-Minn county, in the last Legislature, (Maj. Ballew,) we expressed our hearty concurrence in his movement, and predicted for it complete success at no very distant day. Judging from present indications, we shall be disappointed, if the next Legislature does not determine to submit the question to the people in accordance with the requisitions of our Constitution.

Our observation of the evils attendant upon the present mode of electing judicial officers, has long since satisfied us that of all the modes that could be adopted, that, which gives the election to the Legislature, is the most objectionable. If the whole people could witness the proceedings which frequently characterize these elections in the Legislature, we are confident that there

---

[74] *Ibid.*, 846.
[75] *Senate Journal*, 1847, 596–597.
[76] *Daily Union* (Nashville), March 16, 1849.

would be no division of opinion as to the necessity of a reform. All might not arrive at the conclusion that these officers ought to be chosen by the people, but we believe all would agree that the present is the very worst mode that could be adopted.

The only reason besides a distrust of popular capacity, that could have induced the convention to submit the election of Judges to the Legislature, must have been the belief that this plan would be more convenient and economical than that of a general popular election. There was prevailing an old prejudice against submitting judicial officers to popular choice, based upon the idea that the Judges ought to be independent, which induced the convention to suppose that the representatives of the people would make the choice with more convenience and economy than the people themselves do. The experience of twelve years, however, in our own State, has demonstrated the error of this reasoning, whilst the experience of other States has demonstrated with equal clearness that the prejudices against popular elections of Judges is without any just foundation.

We can conceive of no spectacle more humiliating than that of a candidate for Judge lounging for months about the lobbies of the Legislature, dogging members in their seats and in their rooms, seeking to make arrangements and combinations, and resorting to all the usual appliances and intrigues which mark the Legislative elections. The very fact that there are only one hundred voters, furnishes facilities and temptations for this species of electioneering which could not exist in popular elections—and experience has proved that it frequently results in protracted ballottings, costing the State heavy amounts of money, obstructing the legitimate business of the Legislature, and by no means necessarily terminating in the choice of competent officers. These evils are increased in proportion to the number of elections to be made—for it is a well known fact that all the elections from doorkeeper to Senator in Congress, become interwoven with each other by the appliances of electioneering, so that the whole system has degenerated into a species of *log-rolling* and *bargaining*, which makes the result in any election, more a matter of chance or luck than anything else. We are sure that no one who has spent a whole session in attendance on the Legislature, will accuse us of having colored the picture too highly. We do not charge that the result has been the election of incompetent officers—on the contrary, in general, we believe that our State has been fortunate in having good judicial officers—but this result has arisen from the fact that the materials out of which the elections have been made, have been so good that bad selections could hardly have been made. If the system, however, continues, it must degenerate until bad materials will be presented, and when that occurs high-minded and talented men will be deterred from *such scrambles* with *such competitors*.

It will be readily conceded that, according to the theory of our government, the people ought to choose all their officers, legislative, executive and judicial. On account of certain prejudices which have long existed, it has been a prevalent opinion in times past, that this principle could be applied with safety only to legislative and executive officers. This prejudice has arisen in part from a misapplication of an old English maxim, which asserts the necessity of an independent judiciary, and in part from a distrust of the popular judgment. An independent judiciary is essential in a monarchy, where the king makes the appointment, and is considered the source of all power. But the principle can have no such application in a government where the people are the source of all power. In a monarchy, an independent judiciary is necessary to protect the people against the encroachments or oppressions of the ruler; but in a republic, the people themselves rule, and therefore they do not need an independent judiciary to protect themselves. We need an *honest, intelligent,* and *firm* judiciary, to expound the laws and protect the constitution; but we do not need one that is *independent of the people,* to secure these ends.

The whole question resolves itself into an inquiry as to the competency of the people to choose their judicial officers. It is strange that it should be conceded, that they are capable of choosing those who *make* and those who *execute* the laws, and yet that it should be denied that they are capable of choosing those who *expound* the laws! It surely requires no more capacity to choose a man competent to *construe* laws than one competent to *make* them. The people have as much interest in having the laws well constructed and expounded, as they have in having them well made. In each case it is their own interest that is involved, and in each case there is the same guaranty for honesty and fidelity in the choice. But it may be supposed that there is more difficulty in choosing a good judge than a good legislator. We deny this proposition. Judges are necessarily to be chosen from the lawyers, and we assert that the characters of the lawyers are better understood by the people than any other class in society. Take the case of a supreme judge. Suppose the people were called on to elect a supreme judge from middle Tennessee. Can it be said that the people are ignorant of the character of those lawyers who would be selected for this office? Is there a county in middle Tennessee where the talents and acquirements of our most eminent lawyers are not well understood amongst the people? Are not the peculiar traits of character of such men as Fogg, Meigs, Ewing, Washington, Nicholson, and others in Nashville and out of it, fully known and appreciated throughout the State? How much more true is our remark, when applied to circuit judges and chancellors! The people see and hear the lawyers at the courthouses—they discuss their merits and their characters in their neighborhoods; and they are fully as competent to tell who would make good judges and who would not, as they are to tell who would make good legislators.

But there is a kind of dread in the minds of some, of the corruption and demoralization arising from, and attendant upon popular elections. This is a dread which presupposes some degree of distrust of the people, either on the score of their want of intelligence or virtue. It is a dread which might be as reasonably entertained in regard to the election of representatives or governors as of judges. It is a dread, however, which has no real foundation for its existence. How could a candidate for circuit judge corrupt the voters in a judicial circuit? Why should demoralization be expected at an election of judges more than of legislative and executive officers? Who will compare the chances of corruption and demoralization in an election in the legislature, with an election throughout a judicial circuit? But it is not now necessary to reason on this subject; we have facts in abundance to rest upon. We have the experience of many of our sister States, and that experience has established the competency of the people to make for themselves better judges than the legislatures made. We have also the experience of our own State. Our magistrates are judicial officers, transacting much the largest portion of the judicial business of the country; they are chosen by the people, and no man will maintain that the system has not proved entirely satisfactory. Every reason that can be assigned against the proposed reform, is met and refuted by the experience which we have had in our State as well as in other States. We trust, therefore, that the next Legislature will carry out the proposition commenced in the last, and that in a few years we shall be living under a truly republican constitution."

Just on the eve of the convening of the Legislature, on October 1, 1849, the same newspaper expressed a keen desire to see the movement resuscitated, but noted with regret that only one Whig journal had come outright for the constitutional amendment that would make such a reform possible.[77]

"ELECTION OF JUDGES BY THE PEOPLE.

We have frequently brought this important measure before our readers, and urged the propriety of abandoning the existing practice of leaving to the Legislature the choice of judges of our several courts; and we have the gratification of finding the entire democratic press of the State with us in this great object of reform. The whig press have not shown the same unanimity, and we are sorry for it. If we remember right only one, the Memphis *Enquirer* or the *Eagle*, has taken ground in its favor. Whether their reluctance to embark in this reform in our law originated in an inherent distrust of the capacity of the people, or springs from a desire to oppose the measure because the democratic press has advocated it, we have no means of determining. We had hoped that both parties might be induced to harmonize, and go forward, hand in hand, in effecting a change which is imperiously demanded by the reforming spirit of the age. We have, at no time, had the disposition to seize the question as an instrument to advance party interests—we would not appropriate it as a party hobby—we regard it as a measure above mere party and upon which whigs and democrats can cheerfully unite. It is a platform upon whose broad surface we can all stand—the platform having the intelligence and wisdom of the people as a basis—republican in its structure and sustained by a perfect confidence in the capacity of the great masses for self government.

We trust that the members of both parties will, during the coming session of our Legislature, take up the question and examine its merits with an impartiality entirely devoid of party prejudice. We deem it hardly necessary, at this time, to bring forward the impregnable arguments which are found to be in its favor, as we have urged them at length on several occasions and have been sustained in every section of the State by the able assistance of our contemporaries. It might be well, however, to advert, in a brief manner, to several of the main points in favor of judicial reform.

There is one principle which is so sound in a republican government, and so applicable to the present question, that we would be willing to rest its success upon its truth:

No person should be allowed to hold an office contrary to the wishes of those upon whom the power is to operate.

This principle, if true, should, at once, decide the minds of every one who is republican in his instincts. It is the corner stone of a free government and implies the natural right of every citizen, to have a voice in the selection of those who wield the power conferred upon them by their office. It presupposes an inherent and absolute right in the governed to choose, as executors of the power they have created, such agents, as to them may seem most fit. Starting then with this correct principle as our guide, we will have no difficulty in following the true faith of republicanism. We had better, by far, plant ourselves upon correct principle as a basis in our laws than pursue the uncertain and deceptive track of temporary expediency. Principle is ever the

---

[77] *Ibid.*, September 27, 1849.

best test of a measure, and should never be made the victim to any consideration of present policy—no matter how attractive and seemingly wise at the
moment. That the principle of the election of judges by the people is correct,
is a matter of no question, and there only remains to be considered the policy
of abolishing, at once, an old practice and falling in with the tide of reform
which is sweeping over the length and breadth of the whole Union. We have
not time to-day, even to mention the various points involved in the question.
We might sustain, successfully, the assertion that the people are the *better*
judges of the qualification and fitness of their candidate for office. That the
Legislature, from its very nature, is an improper forum to try the merits of
aspirants to the bench; that the members are necessarily almost entirely ignorant of their character and capacity; that the legislative hall invariably becomes the theatre of a system of *logrolling* which operates as a buying and
selling—a trading and bartering of the several offices within their gift; that
the will of the people is frequently defeated and individuals are elevated to
office directly contrary to their wishes.

We might refer to the fact that the system has been *successfully tried* in
several States; that Connecticut has for more than two hundred years elected
her judges in this manner, and is unsurpassed in the purity and ability of her
judiciary; that Mississippi has for many years tried the system, and triumphantly vindicated its superiority: that their citizens are almost in a body
satisfied with its operation: that the great State of New York, renowned for
the intelligence and education of her citizens, has swept from her statute
books her ancient practice, and substituted this feature of modern improvement: while Pennsylvania, Wisconsin, and other States, are taking steps to
lop off from their laws this relict of an age which reposed too little confidence
in the wisdom and capacity of the people for self-government. We do hope
that our legislature will, at an early day, take up the matter and give it a fair
and frank investigation. We are satisfied that the public voice is clearly in
favor of reform, and calls for immediate action in the premises. In various
counties of the State, during the late canvass, most of the candidates declared
in favor of an elective judiciary, and they were sustained, almost without a
dissenting voice, and we confidently believe that the passage of a bill by the
Legislature to amend the constitution in this particular, would be ratified by
the people with unprecedented unamity. Who will take the lead in the
matter?"

Within ten days after the convening of the Legislature, Whig Senator Abraham Tipton from the counties of Johnson, Carter, Sullivan,
and Washington introduced the following [78]

"*Proposed amendments to the Constitution of the State of Tennessee*, To
be acted upon by the present General Assembly in the manner prescribed in
the 11th article and 3d section thereof of the Constitution of this State:

1st proposed amendment—in section the 3d, of article the 6th of the Constitution strike out the words: 'the General Assembly shall by a joint vote of
both Houses appoint judges to the several courts of law and equity,' and insert in their room and stead the words: 'the judges of such inferior courts as
the legislature may establish shall be elected by the qualified voters residing
within the bounds of any district or circuit to which such inferior judge or
judges, either of law or equity may be appointed by ballot, in the same manner that members of the General Assembly are elected.'

---

[78] *Senate Journal*, 1849, 63–64.

The said 3d section when amended to read in the words and figures as follows:

SEC. 3d.—The judges of such inferior courts as the Legislature may establish, shall be elected by the qualified voters residing within the bounds of any district or circuit to which such inferior judge or judges, either of law or equity, may be appointed by ballot in the same manner that members of the General Assembly are elected. Courts may be established to be holden by justices of the peace—judges of the Supreme court shall be thirty-five years of age and shall be elected for the term of twelve years.

2d proposed amendment—in section the 5th of the 6th article of the Constitution, strike out the words: 'the Legislature shall elect Attorneys for the State by joint vote of both Houses of the General Assembly' and insert in their room and stead the following words: 'The General Assembly shall by joint vote of both Houses appoint an Attorney for the State and the Attorneys for the State, for any circuit or district to which a judge of an inferior Court may be assigned, shall be elected by the qualified voters residing within the bounds of such circuit or district in the same manner that members of the General Assembly are elected.'

Said 5th section when amended to read in the figures and words following, to wit:

SEC. 5.—The General Assembly shall by joint vote of both Houses appoint an Attorney for the State; and the Attorneys for the State for any circuit or district to which a judge of an inferior court may be assigned shall be elected by the qualified voters residing within the bounds of such circuit or district in the same manner that members of the General Assembly are elected, all which Attorneys shall hold their offices for the term of six years. In all cases where an Attorney for any district fails or refuses to attend and prosecute according to law the court shall have power to appoint an Attorney *pro tempore.*

3d. proposed amendment—in section 1st of the fourth article of the Constitution. Strike out the word 'county' and insert in its room and stead the word 'district.'

Said 1st section when amended to read in the figures and words following:

SEC. 1. Every free white man of the age of 21 years, being a citizen of the United States and a citizen of this district wherein he may offer his vote six months next preceding the day of election, shall be entitled to vote for members of the General Assembly and other civil officers for the county or district in which he resides; *Provided,* that no person shall be disqualified from voting in any election on account of color, who is now by the laws of the State a competent witness in a court of justice against a white man; all free men of color shall be exempt from military duty in time of peace and also from paying a free poll tax.

SCHEDULE TO AMENDMENTS.

SEC. 1st.—And that no inconvenience may arise from the proposed amendments, should they be adopted by the people, it is declared that all courts and attorneys contemplated in the proposed amendments shall continue to hold their offices and execute the duties and functions thereof according to the then existing laws and constitution until the election of their successor by the people, to be held and made under a law to be passed by the General Assembly next elected after the ratification of the proposed amendments by the people, which law shall prescribe the time and place of holding said elections, and which shall be passed without delay, and in strict pursuance of the spirit of said amendment."

On the same day on which Senator Tipton introduced his measure, October 9, 1849, Democratic Representative Jacob Adcock from Cannon County introduced in the House of Representatives a measure almost identical with that of Senator Tipton.[79] On the following day Democratic Senator A. Northcutt from the counties of Warren and DeKalb introduced a resolution which was almost a *verbatim* copy of the Tipton resolution.[80] On October 15, the Chairman of the Judiciary Committee, Representative Edwin Polk of Hardeman County, submitted the following report of the Judiciary Committee;[81]

"REPORT OF THE COMMITEE ON THE JUDICIARY
on the subject of the
ELECTION OF JUDGES
By the People

The Committee on the Judiciary to whom was referred Resolution No. 21, proposing amendments to the Constitution of the State, so as to throw the election of Inferior Judges and Attorneys General before the people, have had the same under consideration, and beg leave to report, that they recommend that the said Resolution do pass.

The committee can see no bar to the passage of the Resolution from the fact that a resolution passed the last Legislature of Tennessee, on the 4th February, 1848, proposing an amendment to the Constitution so as to admit new counties with less territory than that fixed by the Constitution. The 3d section of the 11th article of the Constitution provides the mode of the amendment of that instrument. The amendment must be proposed and pass the Legislature by a majority. At the succeeding Legislature, and after publication, it must pass by a majority of two-thirds, and then be submitted to the people; and if a majority of the voters vote for the amendment, it is adopted, and the Constitution is amended. The same section further provides that the 'Legislature shall not propose amendments to the Constitution oftener than once in six years.' It is clear that the proposition contemplated in this clause means a proposition from the Legislature to the people. That it is not a proposition by the Legislature until it goes to the people. It does not mean that the mere entertaining a proposition in the Legislature shall bar all other proposed amendments for six years. If that were the case, all amendments to the Constitution might be forever barred by frivolous resolutions to amend, made designedly.

There, then, being no constitutional barrier, the committee would urge the passage of the resolution upon the strongest grounds of expediency. We are aware that any effort to change our judicial system must combat prejudices of the strongest character. Precedent and established usage in every thing connected with the law, exercise a powerful influence on the public mind, and experience teaches us that the human mind is slower in adopting an enlightened policy of judicial reform, and in throwing off the shackles of established precedent, than in any other work of improvement which has marked the gradual stages of human progress.

---

[79] *House Journal*, 1849, 60–61.
[80] *Senate Journal*, 1849, 77–78.
[81] *House Journal*, 1849, 95–97.
  Senate Journal, 1849, Appendix, 29–32.

Legal forms and proceedings which existed centuries ago, and were suited to the day, still exist, and though the reason has ceased, the law yet remains.

In adopting the common Law of the mother country, we also adopted the usage of appointing judicial officers by executive authority. But the state of things is entirely different here. There, it is the policy of the government to be as little responsible to the people as possible; and the very fact of the people being so much restricted in their political privileges, incapacitates them, in a great degree, from being the repositories of such an important power. But here, there is a more diffused intelligence—the masses are more enlightened—enlightened by the impulse that free institutions always give to the human intellect. They are the repositories of all political power, and are aware that upon their use of that power depends their own weal or woe. They are accustomed to grave responsibilities, and *that* enables them to meet responsibilities successfully.

If the people are competent to elect their Presidents, who hold in their hands such vast power and important interests; if they are competent to elect their Governors, Congressmen and Legislators, surely they are competent to elect their Judges and Attorneys General.

It is believed that the present is the worst possible mode of electing those officers. The electing body is small, and there is great inducement for combinations and influence to operate, and that, too, with the best intentions, frequently at war with what should be the true tests in such elections—the merit and qualifications of the aspirant.

Besides this, from the marked geographical divisions of our State and the few facilities of intercourse, it is impossible for members of one division of the State to know as much of the qualifications of the candidates for these stations, who reside in another division, as well as the people among whom they reside, and in the hurry of the elections and amidst business of importance frequently vote at perfect random. Merit then is not always rewarded, and many men who have toiled and struggled to some eminence in the rugged path to legal distinction, frequently find in their canvass before the Legislature, their talents unrewarded and that they must bear the 'spurs which patent merit of the unworthy takes.'

But it is objected that you degrade the dignity of the Bench by throwing these elections before the people, and subjecting the candidates to the exciting influence of a partizan contest. We have no fear of the purity of the ermine being contaminated by popular contact. The minds of the people would be turned to those persons best qualified to fill those stations, and party influences or ties which so often bind in adamantine chains the minds of men, would become to be disregarded in a great degree where the dearest interests of the people would be involved. Abuses there would doubtless be at first. They exist where all new systems are adopted and old ones overthrown; but these abuses would soon give way to a just public sentiment. A well regulated public opinion always rises in this country with the necessity for it. Would it be a party contest before the people? We believe not so much so as a contest before the Legislature. It is clear that in small electing bodies, party lines are more apt to be drawn than where the electing bodies are more numerous. Nor can it be urged that the decisions of the Bench would be influenced by considerations of an interested character or personal friendships. All members of the Bench now have their personal and political friendships, and if such considerations would operate in the one case they would in the other. Nor can it be urged that elections will be too frequent, for it is believed that in those States where elections are annual, less excitement prevails than where they occur biennially. Their very frequency has a tendency to dull the excitement.

The elections of these officers by the people would be more in unison with our system of government. The framers of that system launched it forth to buffet the waves of deep rooted prejudices and long established theories, with no guide but the moral and intellectual capacity of the people to steer it through a troubled sea. The result has proved their wisdom, and the fact that power entrusted to the hands of an intelligent people will be used for the best interests of the country. Other States are taking the lead in the cause of judicial reform. Mississippi has adopted the system with entire success. The great State of New York elects all judicial officers by popular suffrage. Pennsylvania at the last session of her Legislature commenced the alteration of her Constitution for that purpose—a similar provision with regard to its alteration prevailing there that we have here. Other States are moving on this subject, and we hope that ere long Tennessee will take her stand among the foremost in the work of judicial reform. And it is certainly a gratifying spectacle when we behold in the old world the cause of liberty follow, beneath the arm of despotism, and arbitrary Governments wresting from the people the free privileges which an advancing State of civilization had taught them to assume, to turn to our own land and see that we are extending the privileges of the masses, and peacefully widening the foundations of popular power.

The Committee entertaining the views here expressed do urgently recommend the adoption of the proposed amendments to the Constitution.

E. Polk, Ch'n.''

As might be expected of any measure of such major importance, various and sundry amendments were introduced from time to time. For example, one such amendment by Senator John W. Whitfield from the counties of Hickman, Wayne, Lawrence and Hardin would have included the State Treasurer and the Secretary of State in addition to the Judges and the Attorneys-General,[82] all such officials to be elected by the people. With the Tipton, Adcock, and Northcutt bills on the same subject referred to the House Committee on the Judiciary, the said committee settled upon the Adcock bill as the bill containing all the features deemed essential in the proposed amendment of the Constitution. In the singling out of the Adcock bill for consideration (Resolution No. 21), it is conceivable that a tinge of political favoritism may have been displayed. The Chairman of the House Judiciary Committee was Edwin Polk, a Democrat. The author of Resolution No. 21 was Jacob Adcock, the Democratic Representative from Cannon County. Moreover, the House of Representatives had a majority of three Democrats. On the other hand, the Senate bill had been introduced by Whig Senator Abraham Tipton, and the Senate had a Whig majority of three. At any rate, the Judiciary Committee stated specifically that its deliberations and recommendations related to "Resolution No. 21," and said resolution was the Adcock resolution.[83]

---

[82] *Senate Journal,* 1849, 467.
[83] *House Journal,* 1849, Appendix, 901.

The final showdown on the proposed amendment of the Constitution was reached in the House of Representatives on December 3, 1849. On third and final reading, the bill was passed by a vote of 52 to 16.[84] On December 20, Whig Senator H. S. Kimble from the Senate Judiciary Committee reported that his committee was giving consideration to the Adcock Resolution.[85] For more than a month, the Senate allowed the matter to "lie upon the table." Finally, on January 29, the Senate took up the Adcock Resolution. Some half dozen amendments were proposed, but the only significant one was that of Senator M. Thornburg whose motion was that the Senate strike out the words:

"The judges of the Supreme court shall be elected by the qualified voters of the State...." [86]

Senator Thornburg's motion was defeated by a vote of 18 to 7. With one or two minor amendments tacked on, the Senate passed the bill and transmitted it to the House of Representatives requesting concurrence in the amendments. On the following day, the House refused to concur in the Senate amendments and notified the Senate accordingly.[87] On February 1, 1850, at a night session, the Senate brought to a close legislative action upon the measure that had been before the Legislature since October 9, 1849, by taking up and considering

"... The message from the House announcing their non-concurrence in Senate's amendment to House resolution (No. 21) proposing certain amendments to the Constitution of the State of Tennessee; when
On motion of Mr. Fisher,
The Senate agreed to recede from their amendment to said resolution,
Ordered, that the Clerk acquaint the House therewith, and that said resolution be returned to the House for enrollment." [88]

The first step in the emancipation of the election of Judges and Attorneys-General by the Legislature had been accomplished. Two more steps were necessary before complete emancipation could be procured, namely, the passage of the same resolution by the next General Assembly by a two-thirds majority and then ratification by a majority vote of the people. These two items will receive proper consideration in the next Chapter.

The Resolution [89] as passed in final form was as follows:

"NUMBER VI.
Proposed Amendments of the Constitution of the State.
Proposed amendments of the Constitution of the State of Tennessee to be

---

[84] *House Journal*, 1849, 371.
[85] *Senate Journal*, 1849, 427.
[86] *Ibid.*, 644.
[87] *House Journal*, 1849, 704.
[88] *Senate Journal*, 1849, 676–677.
[89] *Acts of Tennessee*, 1849, Resolution VI, 566–567.

acted on by the present General Assembly, in the manner prescribed in the eleventh article and third section thereof of the Constitution of the State.

The third section of the sixth article of the Constitution shall be so amended as to read as follows:

Sec. 3. The judges of the supreme court, shall be elected by the qualified voters of the State at large, and the judges of such inferior courts as the legislature may establish, shall be elected by the qualified voters residing within the bounds of any district or circuit to which such inferior judge or judges, either of law or equity, may be assigned, by ballot in the same manner that members to the General Assembly are elected. Courts may be established to be holden by justices of the peace. Judges of the supreme court shall be thirty-five years of age, and shall be elected for the term of eight years.

The fifth section of the sixth article of the Constitution shall be so amended as to read as follows:

Sec. 5. An attorney general for the State, shall be elected by the qualified voters of the State at large, and the attorney for the State for any circuit or district to which a judge of an inferior court may be assigned, shall be elected by the qualified voters within the bounds of such circuit or district in the same manner that members to the General Assembly are elected, all said attorneys, both for the States and circuits or districts, shall hold their offices for the term of six years. In all cases where an attorney for any district, fails or refuses to attend and prosecute according to law the court shall have power to appoint an attorney, *pro tempore*.

SCHEDULE TO AMENDMENTS.

Section 1. And that no inconvenience may arise from the proposed amendments, should the same be adopted by the people, it is declared that all judges of the courts and attornies, contemplated in the proposed amendments, shall continue to hold their offices and exercise the duties and functions thereof, according to the true existing laws and constitution, until the election of their successors by the people to be held and made under a law to be passed by the General Assembly next elected after the ratification of the proposed amendments by the people, which law shall prescribe the times and places of holding said election, and which shall be passed without delay and in strict pursuance of said amendments: *Provided*, The legislature shall appoint a day for holding the election of judges and attorneys general separate and apart from the days already prescribed or hereafter to be prescribed by the legislature for holding the elections for State and county officers.

LANDON C. HAYNES,
Speaker of the House of Representatives.
JOHN F. HENRY,
Speaker of the Senate.

Adopted February 1, 1850."

The ninth and last major topic mentioned in Governor Trousdale's Message, of October 22, 1849, dealt with slavery. On this subject, both Governor Trousdale and his predecessor, Neill S. Brown, maintained substantially the same position in their Messages to the Legislature. Each deplored the then prevalent agitation by abolitionists, and each maintained that slavery was an institution recognized by the Federal Constitution and that Congress had no right to attempt to legislate upon its retention or elimination. In each Message was a recommendation that the Legislature memorialize Congress in a firm but temperate appeal to leave the matter alone, subject to the will of the sovereign States themselves.

On November 23, 1849, Democratic Representative William B. Bate of Sumner County (later Major General in the Confederate Army, Governor of Tennessee, and United States Senator) offered a series of resolutions on the subject of Southern rights with reference to domestic slavery. The resolutions were as follows:[90]

"We the members of the General Assembly of the State of Tennessee, feel that we should not have fully discharged the duty imposed on us by our position, if we were not to solemnly protest against the unfounded pretentions assumed, that Congress has power to prevent the introduction and existence of domestic slavery in the territories, and other powers of a kindred nature.

It is asserted, that Congress has this full power over all the territories belonging in common to the people of the United States. That the exercise of this power is expedient and necessary—with rare and patriotic exceptions, this seems to be the settled design by the people of the northern States. The pulpit, the ballot box, the Hall of Legislation have all become tributary to this fanatical hostility to the South. For a series of years we have stood upon the defensive. Devoted to the Union we have shrunk from the agitation of a question so fearfully calculated to estrange us in feeling from our northern brethren. Relying upon the truth of our cause, we have presented the calm front of a patient forbearance to every aggression. We have appealed to them by every reason that could move the noble emotions of an American citizen—to their patriotism, their devotion to our common union; we have invoked the recollection of the past; we have appealed to the hopes of the future. It has all been of no avail. We are forced to the painful conclusion, that it is vain to hope for an abandonment of this subtle design. Submission to a series of wrongs has but provoked further aggression, and it is wise in States as in individuals to resist encroachments. In this unfortunate controversy, should the people of the northern States persevere in their present avowed intent, there are but two alternatives left us; the one is resistance; the other submission. To the one we cannot, we will not consent; the other we are reluctant to adopt.

In the name of our constituents, we solemnly deny the existence of the power claimed. We assert, it will violate the constitution, and tend to a dissolution of the Union. We again remonstrate in feelings of consiliation with our northern brethren.—We warn them of the consequences of perseverance. They have disregarded the most solemn compromises in which we yielded too much. Their course indicates a determination to decide by the force of numbers. There is no common arbiter, and we too must decide for ourselves. That decision is made. We take our stand on the plain principles of the constitution, and intend to maintain it, or sink in the effort.

We assert that these States by the revolution; by the declaration of independence; and by the treaty of peace, become separate and independent sovereignties, with all the political power of separate and distinct nations; that they are still so except so far as they have expressly delegated part of their power to the General Government. They have not delegated their sovereignty. The Federal government is not sovereign. It is a limited federative system possessed only of such powers as have been expressly granted to it

[90] *House Journal*, 1849, 327–331.

by the constitution, with such implied powers as are absolutely necessary to carry out the express grants. We maintain that the system of slavery was recognized by the Constitution; slaves were recognized as property; the full right to which was guarded, protected and guarantied by the compact with more especial care than other species of property. Congress has no power over such property to abolish, or prohibit or impair its usefulness. The right of property preceded the constitution; it is coeval with the history of man; it exists by a paramount law of nature; it is subject of control by state sovereignty only. This Union never would have been formd, but for the guaranty contained in the constitution on the subject of slavery.

We assert that the territory acquired by the late treaty with Mexico, is the common property of all the people of the United States, and all have the right to move to it, and take with them their property, their religion and liberty. Congress did not create property in slaves, nor can it say they shall cease to be property. To abolish slavery in the territories is to diminish their value and limit their usefulness in the States. It is an appropriation of the territories to the people of one portion of our country to the exclusion of another whose blood and treasure flowed freely in the war which acquired it. The power of Congress to legislate for the territories is to protect the citizens and property, not to declare what is property.

The efforts of the great body of the people of the North to pass the Wilmot Proviso upon the territories, to abolish slavery in the District of Columbia, the slave trade between the States and prohibit their employment in our southern navy-yards and dock-yards, added to the violence and bitterness with which slavery, slave States, and slave owners are in every manner and at all times abused and denounced, together with the aid given by their emissaries to our fugitive slaves to escape from their owners, and refusal to surrender them up in direct violation of the plain injunction of the constitution, all evidence a settled design on their part at no distant day to abolish slavery in the states themselves.—Therefore.

1. *Resolved,* That we continue to entertain a devoted and cherished attachment to the Union, but we desire to have it as it was formed and not as an engine of oppression.

2. *Resolved,* That all attempts by Congress or others directly or indirectly to interfere with the subject of slavery in the southern States, are in violation of the constitution, dangerous to the rights and safety of the South and ought to be promptly resisted.

3. *Resolved,* That Congress has no power to abolish slavery in the District of Columbia, or to prohibit the slave trade between the several States, or to prohibit the introduction of slavery into the territories of the United States, and that the passage by Congress of any such law, would not only be a dangerous violation of the constitution, but afford evidence of deliberate and fixed design on the part of that body to interfere with the institutions of slavery in the States.

4. *Resolved,* That we would regard the passage by Congress of the 'Wilmot Proviso' which would in effect deprive the citizens of the slaveholding states of an equal participation in the territories acquired more than equally by their blood and treasure, as an unjust and insulting discrimination to which these states cannot without political degradation, submit; and to which this assembly representing the feelings of the people of Tennessee, solemnly declare they will not submit.

5. *Resolved,* That it is the duty of Congress without delay to enact such

laws as in their operation will give all the aid which the General Government constitutionally possesses, to the owner to secure his fugitive slave.

6. *Resolved,* That the Missouri Compromise was originally adopted by a large majority of northern votes in Congress, as a dividing line between slave and free States, but although then as now regarded by the people of the southern States as an invasion of our constitutional rights, we have at all times acquiesced in good faith to the surrender therein of our rights north of that line, because we viewed it as a compromise settlement of an exciting question which seriously threatened to destroy the fraternal feeling between the people of the north and south—perhaps the Union itself. In view of the fact that the equity of said compromise, as well as the safety of the south, requires that the entire region of country south of that line to the Pacific Ocean, be surrendered to southern institutions without opposition from the northern States—we therefore declare that the war made upon us in regard to said territory even before it was acquired by treaty from Mexico, followed by the getting up of the pretended Constitution, which without regard to the forms of law, or requirements of the constitution lately emanated from a self-styled convention of a part of those styling themselves people of California, is a fraud upon the south as palpable and dangerous as a direct application of the Wilmot Proviso itself, and that it is our duty to resist the acceptance and enforcement of the same by Congress as promptly and to the same extent as the Wilmot Poviso in express words.

7. *Resolved,* That we recommend to the people of this State to take into consideration the proposed mode of the late convention held at Jackson, in the State of Mississippi, in October last, 'that a convention of the slaveholding States should be held at Nashville, in this State, on the first Monday of June, 1850, to consider, devise and adopt some mode of resistance to these aggressions,' and recommend, should they see proper to meet in said proposed convention, that the people of each Congressional District appoint two delegates and two alternatives to represent them in said convention.

8. *Resolved,* That, in the language of an eminent Northern writer and patriot, 'the rights of the South in African service, exist not only under but over the Constitution. They existed before the Government was formed. The Constitution was sanctioned by them, then they by the Constitution. Had not that instrument admitted the sovereignty of those rights it never would itself have been admitted by the South. It bowed in deference to rights older in their date, stronger in their claims, and holier in their nature than any other which the Constitution can boast. Those rights may not be changed, even by a change of the Constitution. They are out of the reach of the nation, as a nation. The confederacy may dissolve and the Constitution pass away; but those rights will remain unshaken, will exist while the South exists—and when they fall the South will perish with them.'

9. *Resolved,* That the passage by Congress of the 'Wilmot proviso,' or a law abolishing slavery in the District of Columbia, or prohibiting the slave trade between the States, would of itself be such a breach of the federal compact, as, in that event, would make it the duty, as it is the right, of the slaveholding States to take care of their own safety; and, upon the passage by Congress, of either of these laws, the Governor of this State is requested forthwith to convene the General Assembly to consider of the mode and measure of redress."

On November 28, Representative Bate's resolutions were referred to the Committee on Federal Relations where they remained in cold storage until February 5, 1850, at which time they were recommended for passage by the above Committee.[91] On the following day, however, Majority and Minority Reports on Slavery were reported to the House of Representatives by the Committee on Federal Relations. The two Reports[92] were as follows:

"REPORT OF THE MAJORITY OF THE COMMITTEE ON FEDERAL RELATIONS, BY MR. POLK, CHAIRMAN PROTEM, DURING THE SICKNESS OF MR. GANTT.

The Committee on Federal Relations to whom was referred resolution No. ...., on the subject of slavery, beg leave to report: That the time has arrived when the State of Tennessee should occupy a decided position on the great question at issue between the North and South. It is a question far above party, and we should bring to its consideration a spirit of calm and dispassionate enquiry unmingled with party prejudices worthy of its great importance, and that may lead to a just conclusion. The peaceful settlement of this dangerous question is a consummation that must be desired by patriotic men of all parties; every man of patriotic feelings must deeply regret the existence of a question that involves in its agitation so many consequences dangerous to this confederacy of States. It is one of those trials that every nation must undergo as the price of its safety, and we must not shrink from the test.

The great importance of the crisis at hand demands that Tennessee, one of the great States of this confederacy, should assume a position. The question is, what shall that position be, whether a conciliatory policy shall be adopted, or whether we shall present to the world our opinion of our constitutional rights and resolve to stand to them.

For years upon years this question of slavery has been growing in importance. From a mere agitation on the part of a few mad fanatics, in the progress of time it became connected with party controversies gathering strength at each succeeding session of Congress until it has assumed a position alarming in its character, and threatening the most disastrous consequences. All efforts to establish a provisional government for the territory of California on account of the Wilmot proviso, excluding slavery being attached to it, failed at the last Congress. The proposition to abolish slavery in the District of Columbia, and in all these places, even the bosom of the southern country under the control of the General Government, and the refusal of the northern States to deliver up fugitive slaves, show the determined purpose on the part of the abolitionists to make war upon the institution wherever it exists. They confine themselves mostly at present to the agitation of the question as to new territories. This is the outwork to be overcome before they strike at the main fortress. It must be evident to every unprejudiced mind that the object of the abolitionists is to abolish slavery in the States of the Union. To say that they will cease their opposition should they succeed in excluding slavery from the territories, would argue a strange ignorance of the nature and elements of moral and political fanaticism, with renewed violence, they would raise the standard of exterminating war, and urge it on with blind fatality, even though the Union should go down.

We consider that this controversy involves relations which the States are

---

[91] *Ibid.*, 759.
[92] *Ibid.*, 788–797.

to bear to the General Government whether the States are to remain equal and independent in the sphere of their reserved powers and rights or whether they are to become mere dependencies to the will of a consolidated government. If we are to be excluded from the new territories, we are no longer equal members of this confederacy and the constitutional barriers limiting the action of the General Government, within the sphere of specific powers would be broken down, and our dearest rights thrown at the feet of overshadowing central power. This subject engaged the attention of the framers of our constitution; slavery was recognised as property under the control of State authority. Let it be borne in mind, that the States were the original governments, holding their local institutions to which they were attached and among them was slavery. To pay off the public debt, and to regulate the commerce of the States, with foreign nations among themselves, which was in a confused state, on account of the existence of so many separate communities, mainly induced the states jealous and repugnant as they were to parting with any of their powers to make our present constitution.

We speak of this because the objects and necessity of the formation of the constitution, will go far to show the extent of power intended to be given by the States. We speak of it to show that the States never could have intended to give Congress the power to interfere with their property, recognized as such by their own laws. That the States never intended to cede away power by which there would be a conflict of dominion over that property between State and Federal authority. It was entirely foreign from the object of framing the Constitution, to give to Congress the power to depreciate and limit the enjoyment of property recognised by State authority, and then owned by the States as such. It is evident that it was intended that the States should be the sole great repositories of all the powers necessary to preserve individual rights, and we firmly believe that on the true understanding of this by the people of this country, depends the permanency of our system as it is, and the liberties and happiness of the people.

Slavery being recognized at the formation of the constitution, as a local institution belonging to the States, the States never could have ceded to Congress the power to forbid its introduction to any place unforbidden by State authority, or to territories the common property of all the States.

The clause in the constitution giving Congress the power to regulate the territories belonging to the United States, never intended to create in Congress, a supreme power over the territories. The very fact that the territories are permitted to throw off their territorial form, and merge into State sovereignties, shows that Congress is only trustee for the benefit of all the States, and was given the power to regulate and protect the territories in their inchoate state, its power mostly ceasing when the State gains admission in the Union. The constitution recognises slavery as property by various provisions and of course assumes the attributes of all property without any limitation to the exercise of the rights of ownership. The exclusion then of them from the territories by Congress would be equivalent to a denial of the right of property in slaves. For the advocates of exclusion, nor any one else ever thought of preventing the introduction of any other property into the territories. We consider that the intention was to give Congress the power over the territory as property to make such regulations in their territorial government as would preserve law and order. To give Congress unlimited power, would be at war with every true conception of the position of the State and Federal Government. Congress has no more power to prohibit slavery there than it has to enact that slavery should exist there; suppose that Congress should pass a law refusing to admit the state unless slavery were permitted there by the State authority, would any doubt its unconstitutionality? This surely is as much an attribute of the unlimited authority claimed for it, as the right to exclude slaves. If it has the right to exclude slavery, it has the right to establish it. The power cannot be divided. But it has no such power—if such a proposition had have been advanced it would have met the united opposition of every southern member. The constitution never could have been framed with such a provision.

It is well known that the constitution would not have been agreed to if the proposition to stop immediately the odious African slave trade, carried on by the cupidity of our British ancestors could have succeeded, which was at last compromised by fixing the limitation of such trade at the year 1808, by the combined votes of four northern and four southern States. With such sentiments as these existing among the States on this subject, they never could have given Congress power to interfere with slavery. But it is urged that we are debarred from denying the constitutionality of this power, because we have heretofore recognized the right of Congress to exercise this power. The question, as to the admission of Missouri, was placed, perhaps more on the grounds of expediency than of constitutionality. It was a compromise necessary, it was believed, to save the Union. A difference of opinion existed as to the constitutionality. The constitutional question was then waived, and the compromise agreed upon. It was shown that slave labor could not be profitable north of the compromise line, and that local legislation would prevent its existence. It was an agreement between the north and south, brought about by necessity that rose above the constitution. The south has inviolably observed the compact; not objecting to the restriction as to slavery being engrafted in the constitution of the States applying for admission north of thirty-six degrees and thirty minutes. But now the north has violated the compact made by the Congress of 1819-20. The question has become of vital importance because the restriction is sought to be imposed on territories south of the compromise line, and where the slave-labor is profitable. We have held up to the north the compact agreed upon, but they disregarded its injunctions. We throw ourselves on our constitutional rights and are determined to stand on them. Concession only invites aggression. We cannot yield our equality with the northern States, nor can we permit the Federal Government to encroach upon our reserved rights. The maintenance of our reserved powers can alone preserve the Union of these States. Yield to the encroachments of Federal power, and soon the States become mere dependencies to a consolidated government. We confidently believe that a bold, decided stand by the south is the only course to save the Union. A continued conciliatory policy produces ceaseless aggression; and those who advise such policy, unintentionally take such a position that will lead to the result as much deprecated—disunion. We can have no possible motive to desire disunion. Every consideration which can move the human mind, impels us to preserve and cherish the union of these States. We know and feel the great benefits *that* union has conferred upon the people within its limits and upon mankind. We look with pride upon its past history. We ardently hope for its future glory. We know that its cheering light has fallen upon other nations and taught oppressed man to hope. We know that its grave would be the common receptacle of the hopes of man for free government throughout the world. But we desire it as it has been, and as it is. Let it become an engine of oppression; let it trample upon our rights; let it destroy the equality of the States, and the objects for which it was formed will have ceased, and with them will cease our obligations to preserve its integrity. We believe that a firm stand taken by the southern States will preserve the Union a blessing to us, to prosperity, and to the world. Entertaining these views, the committee recommend the adoption of the resolutions.

E. POLK, *Chm.*

PREAMBLE.

We, the members of the General Assembly of the State of Tennessee, feel that we should not have fully discharged the duty imposed on us by our position, if we were not to solemnly protest against the unfounded pretensions assumed, that Congress has power to prevent the introduction and existence of domestic slavery in the territories, and other powers of a kindred nature.

It is asserted that Congress has this full power over all the territories belonging in common to the people of the United States. That the exercise of this power is expedient and necessary. With rare and patriotic exceptions, this seems to be the settled design by the people of the northern States. The pulpit, the ballot box, the halls of legislation have all become tributary to this fanatical hostility to the South. For a series of years we have stood upon the defensive. Devoted to the Union we have shrunk from the agitation of a question so powerfully calculated to estrange us in feeling from our northern brethren. Relying upon the truth of our cause, we have presented the calm front of a patient forbearance to every aggression. We have appealed to them by every reason that could move the nobler emotions of an American citizen, to their patriotism, their devotion to our common union. We have invoked the recollection of the past; we have appealed to the hopes of the future. It has all been of no avail. We are forced to the painful conclusion that it is vain to hope for an abandonment of this subtle design. Submission to a series of wrongs has but provoked further aggression, and it is wise in States as in individuals to resist encroachments. In this unfortunate controversy should the people of the northern States persevere in their present avowed intent, there are but two alternatives left us, the one is resistance, the other submission. To the one we cannot, we will not consent; the other we are reluctant to adopt.

In the name of our constituents we solemnly deny the existence of the power claimed. We assert it will violate the contitution and tend to a dissolution of the Union. We again remonstrate in feelings of conciliation with our northern brethren. We warn them of the consequences of perseverance. They have disregarded the most solemn compromises in which we yielded too much. Their course indicates a determination to decide by the force of numbers. There is no common arbiter, and we too must decide for ourselves. That decision is made. We take our stand on the plain principle of the constitution, and intend to maintain it or sink in the effort.

We assert that these States by the revolution, by the declaration of independence and by the treaty of peace, become separate and independent sovereignties with all the political power of separate and distinct nations; that they are still so except so far as they may have expressly delegated part of their power to the General Government. They have not delegated their sovereignty. The federal government is not sovereign. It is a limited federative system possessed only of such powers as have been expressly granted to it by the constitution, with such implied powers as are absolutely necessary to carry out the express grants. We maintain that the system of slavery was recognized as property, the full right to which was granted, protected and guaranteed by the compact with more special care than other species of property.

Congress has no power over such property to abolish or prohibit or impair its usefulness. The right of property preceded the constitution; it is coeval with the history of man; it exists by a paramount law of nature; it is subject of control by State sovereignty only. This Union never would have been formed but for the guaranty contained in the constitution on the subject of slavery.

We assert that the territory acquired by the late treaty with Mexico, is the common property of all the people of the United States, and all have the right to move to it and take with them their property, their religion and liberty. Congress did not create property in slaves, nor can it say they shall cease to be property. To abolish slavery in the territories, is to diminish their value and limit their usefulness in the States. It is an appropriation of the territories to the people of one portion of our country to the exclusion of another whose blood and treasure flowed freely in the war which acquired it. The power of Congress to legislate for the territories is to protect the citizens and property, not to declare what is property.

The efforts of the great body of the people of the north to pass the Wilmot proviso upon the territories, to abolish slavery in the District of Columbia, the slave trade between the States, and prohibit their employment in our southern navy-yards and dock-yards, added to the violence and bitterness with which slavery, slave States and slave owners are, in every manner and at all times, abused and denounced, together with the aid given by their emissaries to our fugitive slaves to escape from their owners, and refusal to surrender them up in direct violation of the plain injunction of the constitution all evidence a settled design on their part, at no distant day, to abolish slavery in the States themselves. Therefore,

1. *Resolved*, That we continue to entertain a devoted and cherished attachment to the Union, but we desire to have it as it was formed and not as an engine of oppression.

2. *Resolved*, That all attempts by Congress, or others, directly or indirectly, to interfere with slavery, or its institutions in the southern States, are in violation of the constitution, dangerous to the rights and safety of the south, and ought to be promptly resisted.

3. *Resolved*, That Congress has no power to abolish slavery in the District of Columbia, or to prohibit the slave trade between the several States, or to prohibit the introduction of slavery into the territories of the United States, and that the passage by Congress of any such law, would not only be a dangerous violation of the constitution, but afford evidence of a deliberate and fixed design, on the part of that body, to interfere with the institutions of slavery in the States.

4. *Resolved*, That we would regard the passage by Congress of the 'Wilmot proviso,' which would in effect deprive the citizens of the slaveholding States of an equal participation in the territories acquired more than equally by their blood and treasure, as an unjust and insulting discrimination, to which these States, without political degradation cannot submit; and to which this Assembly, representing the feelings and wishes of the people of Tennessee, solemnly declare they will not submit.

5. *Resolved*, That it is the duty of Congress without delay, to enact such laws as in their operation will give all the aid, which the General Government constitutionally, possesses, to the owner to secure his fugitive slave.

6. *Resolved*, That we view the Missouri compromise as a settlement of an exciting question which was likely to destroy the fraternal feeling between

the North and South the result of mutual concession, deriving its sanction and validity from the most solemn obligations of honor and patriotism.

7. *Resolved*, That the unprecedented manner of forming the organic law of California, the peculiar character of her population and her extraordinary boundaries are questions which should undergo rigid scrutiny by our Representatives in Congress, but we will not attempt to prescribe a rule of action for their government, but leave them to take such steps as may be necessary to vindicate southern rights.

8. *Resolved*, That all territory acquired by our General Government, is the joint property of all the States of this Union.

9. *Resolved*, That the 4th article of the 3d section of the constitution, in giving to Congress the power to dispose of, and make all needful rules and regulations respecting the territory or other property belonging to the United States, was never intended to delegate to Congress the power to specify the particular kind of property that should exist in the territories.

10. *Resolved*, That we request the Governor to appoint two delegates from the State at large, and two from each Congressional district irrespective of party, and we recommend to the people of each county, to appoint one or more to attend the convention to be held at Nashville on the first Monday in June, 1850."

"REPORT OF THE MINORITY OF THE COMMITEE ON FEDERAL RELATIONS, CUT OFF BY THE PREVIOUS QUESTION.

The minority of the Committee on Federal Relations to who were referred a series of resolutions respecting the introduction of slavery into the territories belonging to the United States and abolishing it in the District of Columbia, ask leave to report—We do not believe that we are called upon at this time to give any other than a remonstrance against this assumption of right in Congress. It is not our design in this report, to enter into any argument upon a want of necessity requiring any threats upon the part of this body; but simply to assume that no practical good can result from such a course, prior to an action of Congress upon the subject. We entertain a sacred regard for the preservation and prosperity of the Union, and being based upon the virtue and intelligence of its citizens in connection with our free institutions, we believe it is destined in the providence of God to be perpetual —Therefore,

1. *Resolved*, That we deprecate the passage by Congress of the Wilmot proviso, as being an unjust and insulting discrimination in which the South cannot acquiesce, and against which we remonstrate in the name of the people of this State.

2. That California with suitable boundaries, under her present application, ought to be admitted as one of the States of this Union, and that appropriate territorial governments should be established by Congress in all such territories as have been acquired by the United States from the Republic of Mexico, not included in the boundary of the State of California, without any condition or restriction on the subject of slavery with regard to either.

3. That it is inexpedient and unjust in Congress to abolish slavery in the District of Columbia without the consent of the State ceding the same and the people of said District, and also a just compensation to the owner of the slaves thus emancipated; and that we remonstrate against and resist the same by all means recognized by the constitution.

4. That more effectual provision ought to be made by Congress for the restitution of slaves who may escape into any other State or territory of this Union, from either of the slave States.

5. That the admission or exclusion of slavery, or its sale or transfer from one State to another depends exclusively upon their own particular laws; and any act of Congress prohibiting or obstructing the same, would be unconstitutional, unjust and oppressive, to which the South could not submit without political degradation, and which should be promptly resisted.

6. That we leave it to the people of this State, to take into consideration the proposed convention to be held at Nashville, in this State, on the first Monday of June, 1850, to consider, devise and adopt such measures as they may deem right and proper under the circumstances; and they appoint such delegates from each Congressional district as they may deem expedient to represent them in said convention.

All of which is respectfully submitted.

P. G. STIVER PERKINS.
A. G. SHREWSBURY."

The Democratic House of Representatives had now before it for consideration three separate documents upon the subject of slavery, namely, (1) the Majority Report of its Committee on Federal Relations; (2) the Minority Report of its Committee on Federal Relations; and (3) the militant Resolutions on Domestic Slavery by Representative William B. Bate. The Senate, with its Whig majority, had skirted along for four months without taking any decided stand upon the topic of slavery which was now assuming both form and substance, not only in the Tennessee Legislature but in other States as well. On Monday morning, February 4, 1850, Democratic Senator E. L. Gardenhire from the counties of Fentress, Overton, Jackson, and White challenged the Senate's chalk-and-water attitude on slavery by the introduction of the following Resolutions,[93] to-wit:

"*Whereas,* This General Assembly has witnessed with deep and painful emotion, the continued agitation of the slavery question, both in and out of the Congress of the United States, and believing that a most dangerous crisis in the action of the Federal Government is approaching in relation to this subject, feel constrained by the most solemn sense of public duty, to make known to the world our opinion and determinations in relation to it; therefore,

Resolved, 1st. that we continue to entertain a devoted and cherished attachment to the Union, that we desire to have it as it was formed and not as an engine of oppression.

Resolved, 2d. that Congress has no power to interfere with the subject of slavery, and all attempts on the part of Congress to interfere with it, are in violation of the Constitution, a usurpation and abuse of power by the Federal Government, destructive to the rights, safety, and sovereignty of the Southern States and ought to be promptly resisted.

Resolved, 3d. that Congress has no power to abolish slavery in the District of Columbia, to prohibit the slave trade between the states, or to prohibit the introduction of slavery into the territories of the United States; and the passage by congress of a law to this effect, would not only be a dangerous violation of the Constitution, but afford evidence of a deliberate and settled design on the part of that body, to interfere with the institution of slavery.

---

[93] *Senate Journal,* 1849, 690–691.

Resolved, 4th, that we would regard the passage by Congress of the 'Wilmot Proviso' which would in effect deprive the citizens of the slave holding states of an equal participation in the territories acquired equally by their blood and treasure, as an unjust and insulting discrimination, to which those States cannot submit, without political degredation and to which this General Assembly representing the feelings of Tennessee solemnly declare they will not submit.

5th. *Resolved,* That it is the duty of Congress without delay, to enact such laws as in their operation will give all the aid which the General Government constitutionally possesses to the owner to recover his fugitive slaves.

6th. *Resolved,* That the Missouri compromise was originally adopted by a large majority of Northern votes in Congress, as a dividing line between slave and free States, and although then as now regarded by the people of the Southern States as an invasion of their constitutional rights, they have at all times acquiesced in good faith to the surrender therein of their rights north of that line, because it was regarded as a compromise settlement of an exciting question, which seriously threatened to destroy the fraternal feelings between the people of the north and south, perhaps.

7th. *Resolved,* Finally, that with a view of preserving the Union, and with the further view of devising the best means of preventing and defeating the above mentioned wanton wicked and dangerous aggressions on the rights of the South, and if that cannot be done to deliberate with our sister States of the South, as to the means and measures of redress, this General Assembly hereby authorize, and request the Governor of this State to appoint two wise and discreet men from each Congressional district without distinction of party; and each of the counties in this State is requested to send such a number of delegates as they may think proper to represent this State in the convention proposed to be held in the city of Nashville, on the 1st Monday of June next."

Under the rule of the Senate, the Gardenhire Resolutions were "read and laid upon the table." On February 9, Whig Senator Samuel M. Fite from Smith and Sumner counties, a member of the Committee on Federal Relations, reported to the Senate that both House and Senate documents on slavery had been considered by the Committee, but that in lieu of the other bills and resolutions on the same subject the following action by the Committee had been recommended for adoption, to-wit:[94]

"1st. *Resolved by the General Assembly of the State of Tennessee,* That 'under the constitution, every State has the right of establishing and from time to time altering its municipal laws and domestic institutions independent of every other State and of the General Government, subject only to the prohibition of the United States.'

2nd. *Resolved,* that slavery being a domestic and local institution, it should be left to the control solely of those amongst whom it exists; and that any interference therewith by Congress, or the northern States should be met by the people of the south, with such remedies as may be called for by the emergency, and such as shall be fully adequate to the protection of our rights.

3d. *Resolved,* that whilst we are fully resolved to protect southern rights, we declare our unshaken attachment to the Union, 'connected as the Union

---

[94] *Ibid.,* 758-759.

is with the remembrance of past happiness, the source of present blessings, and the hope of future peace and prosperity, every dictate of wisdom, every feeling of duty, and every emotion of patriotism tend to inspire fidelity and devotion to it and admonish us cautiously to avoid any unnecessary controversy which can either endanger it or impair its strength, the chief element of which is to be found in the regard and affection of the people for each other.

4th. *Resolved*, 'that more effectual provision ought to be made (by Congress) for the restitution and delivery of persons bound to service or labor in any State, who may escape into any other State or territory of the Union.'

5th. *Resolved*, that this General Assembly recognize the right of the inhabitants of a territory in forming a constitution preparatory to an application for admission into the Union as a State, to regulate the subject of slavery as to them shall seem proper; but do most solemnly protest against any congressional legislation upon this subject and do deliberately declare, that such legislation prohibiting slavery, would be unjust and oppressive upon the south, and that therefore Congress ought to establish governments for the new territories without any restrictions as to slavery.

6th. *Resolved*, that as 'it is understood that the people of the western part of California have formed a plan of a State Government, and will soon submit the same to the judgment of Congress and apply for admission as a State, if the proposed constitution shall when submitted to Congress, be found to be in compliance with the requisitions of the constitution of the United States' she should be admitted as one of the States of the Union with suitable boundaries.

7th. *Resolved*, that it is no part of our delegated trusts, as members of this General Assembly, to aid in organizing a southern convention, or any other convention of the people; and that if such convention be desired by the people, it belongs to them in their primary assemblies to select the delegates, and not to this General Assembly, or the Executive of the State.

8th. *Resolved*, That the Governor of the State be requested to forward to each of our Senators and Representatives in Congress copies of the foregoing resolutions, as an expression of the sentiments of this General Assembly."

Immediately upon the conclusion of the reading of the report and the recommendations of the Committee on Federal Relations, Democratic Senator Gardenhire pulled out of his pocket

"... the following preamble as an amendment to said resolutions:[95]

We, the members of the General Assembly of the State of Tennessee, feel that we should not have fully discharged the duty imposed on us by our position, if we were not to solemnly protest against the unfounded pretensions assumed that Congress has power to prevent the introduction and existence of domestic slavery in the territories, and other powers of a kindred nature.

It is asserted, that Congress has this full power over all the territories belonging in common to the people of the United States. That the exercise of this power is expedient and necessary—with rare and patriotic exceptions, this seems to be the settled design of the people of the northern States. The pulpit, the ballot box, the Halls of legislation have all become tributary to this

---

[95] *Ibid.*, 759-763.

fanatical hostility to the South. For a series of years we have stood upon the defensive. Devoted to the Union we have shrunk from the agitation of a question so fearfully calculated to estrange us in feeling from our northern brethren. Relying upon the truth of our cause, we have presented the calm front of a patient forbearance to every aggression. We have appealed to them by every reason that could move the nobler emotions of an American citizen—to their patriotism, their devotion to our common Union; we have invoked the recollection of the past; we have appealed to the hopes of the future. It has all been of no avail. We are forced to the painful conclusion, that it is vain to hope for an abandonment of this subtle design. Submission to a series of wrongs has but provoked further aggression, and it is wise in States as in individuals to resist encroachments. In this unfortunate controversy, should the people of the northern States persevere in their present avowed intent, there are but two alternatives left us; the one is resistance; the other submission. To the one we cannot, we will not consent; the other we are reluctant to adopt.

In the name of our constituents, we solemnly deny the existence of the power claimed. We assert, it will violate the constitution, and tend to a dissolution of the Union. We again remonstrate in feelings of conciliation with our northern brethren. We warn them of the consequences of perseverance. They have disregarded the most solemn compromises in which we yielded too much. Their course indicates a determination to decide by the force of numbers. There is no common arbiter, and we too must decide for ourselves. That decision is made. We take our stand on the plain principles of the constitution, and intend to maintain it, or sink in the effort.

We assert that these States by the revolution; by the declaration of independence; and by the treaty of peace, became separate and independent sovereignties, with all the political power of separate and distinct nations; that they are still so except so far as they may have expressly delegated part of their power to the General Government. They have not delegated their sovereignty. The Federal Government is not sovereign. It is a limited federative system possessed only of such powers as have been expressly granted to it by the constitution, with such implied powers as are absolutely necessary to carry out the express grants. We maintain that the system of slavery was recognized by the constitution; slaves were recognized as property; the full right to which was guarded, protected and guaranteed by the compact with more special care than other species of property. Congress has no power over such property to abolish, or prohibit or impair its usefulness. The right of property preceded the constitution; it is coeval with the history of man; it exists by a paramount law of nature; it is subject of control by state sovereignty only. This Union never would have been formed, but for the guaranty contained in the constitution on the subject of slavery.

We assert that the territory acquired by the late treaty with Mexico, is the common property of all the people of the United States, and all have the right to move to it, and take with them their property, their religion and liberty. Congress did not create property in slaves, nor can it say they shall cease to be property. To abolish slavery in the territories is to diminish their value and limit their usefulness in the States. It is an appropriation of the territories to the people of one portion of our country to the exclusion of another whose blood and treasure flowed freely in the war which acquired it. The power of Congress to legislate for the territories is to protect the citizens and property, not to declare what is property.

The efforts of the great body of the people of the North to pass the

Wilmot Proviso upon the territories, to abolish slavery in the District of Columbia, the slave trade between the States and prohibit their employment in our southern navy-yards, added to the violence and bitterness with which slavery, slave States, and slave owners are in every manner and at all times abused and denounced, together with the aid given by their emissaries to our fugitive slaves to escape from their owners, and refusal to surrender them up in direct violation of the plain injunction of the constitution, all evidence a settled design on their part at no distant day to abolish slavery in the states themselves.

Mr. Thornburg moved that said preamble do lie upon the table; and the question, upon agreeing thereto being put, was decided in the affirmative. Ayes—11, Noes—9. . . .

Mr. Gardenhire offered the following in lieu of the first resolution reported by the committee, viz:

Resolved, that the Missouri Compromise was originally adopted by a large majority of northern votes in Congress, as a dividing line between slave and free States, but although then as now regarded by the people of the southern States as an invasion of our constitutional rights, we have at all times acquiesced in good faith to the surrender therein of our rights north of that line, because we viewed it as a compromise settlement of an exciting question which seriously threatened to destroy the fraternal feeling between the people of the north and south—perhaps the Union itself.

Which was read. On motion of Mr. Thornburg, *Ordered*, that said amendment do lie on the table. Ayes—11, Noes—9. . . .

Mr. Gardenhire then offered the following in lieu of the second resolution reported by the committee:

Resolved, that it is the duty of Congress without delay to enact such laws as in their operation will give all the aid which the General Government constitutionally possesses, to the owner to secure his fugitive slaves.

Which was read, and on motion of Mr. Thornburg, *Ordered*, that it do lie on the table. Ayes—11, Noes—9. . . .

Mr. Gardenhire then offered the following in lieu of the third resolution reported by the committee:

Resolved, that we continue to entertain a devoted and cherished attachment to the Union, but we desire to have it as it was formed and not as an engine of oppression. Which was read, and on motion of Mr. Thornburg, *Ordered*, that it do lie on the table. Ayes—11, Noes—9. . . .

Mr. Gardenhire then offered the following in lieu of the fourth resolution reported by the committee:

Resolved, that with a view of preserving the Union, and with the further view of devising the best means of preventing and defeating the wanton, wicked and dangerous aggressions on the rights of the south, and if that cannot be done, to deliberate with our sister States of the south, as to the means and measures of redress; this General Assembly hereby authorize and request the former to appoint two wise and discreet men from each Congressional District without distinction of party, and each of the counties of this State is requested to send such a number of delegates as they may think proper to represent this State in the Convention proposed to be held in the city of Nashville, on the 1st Monday of June next;

Which was read, and on motion of Mr. Fite, *Ordered*, that it do lie on the table. Ayes—11, Noes—9. . . .

Mr. Gardenhire then offered the following in lieu of the fifth resolution reported by said committee:

Resolved, that Congress has no power to interfere with the subject of slavery, and all attempts on the part of Congress to interfere with it, are in violation of the Constitution, a usurpation and abuse of power by the Federal Government, destructive to the rights, safety and sovereignty of Southern States, and ought to be properly resisted.

Which was read, and on motion of Mr. Fite, *Ordered,* that it do lie on the table. Ayes—11, Noes—9."

With the various Gardenhire resolutions "upon the table," the question recurred upon the adoption of the Resolutions as reported and recommended by the Committee on Federal Relations. Whig Senator James W. Gillespie demanded a division of the question, in order that each resolution might be voted upon separately. Each resolution was thereupon submitted to a vote of the Senate, with the following results:

Question. Will the Senate agree to the first resolution?
Ayes 11; Noes 9

Question. Will the Senate agree to the second resolution?
Ayes 13; Noes 7

Question. Will the Senate agree to the third resolution?
Ayes 13; Noes 7

Question. Will the Senate agree to the fourth resolution?
Ayes 14; Noes 6

Question. Will the Senate agree to the fifth resolution?
Ayes 13; Noes 7

Question. Will the Senate agree to the sixth resolution?
Ayes 11; Noes 9

Question. Will the Senate agree to the seventh resolution?
Ayes 11; Noes 9

Question. Will the Senate agree to the eighth resolution?
Ayes 12; Noes 8.[96]

Upon the completion of the balloting upon the eighth resolution, it was then ordered that

"The Clerk acquaint the House therewith and request a concurrence therein."

The requested "concurrence" on this particular slavery item did not take place. Time was coming to be of the essence, for only one more day remained on the legislative calendar, as adjournment *sine die* was set for Monday, February 11, 1850. As if three slavery resolutions were not already too much—the Majority and Minority Reports, and the sizzling Bate Resolutions—now, the hitherto lackadaisical Senate (that is, lackadaisical so far as action on the slavery issue was concerned) was shuttling over to the House the categorical resolutions of the Senate Committee on Federal Relations which had been used as a foil to

---

[96] *Ibid.,* 764–766.

ward off the impact of the Bate Resolutions. It was apparent that time would not permit of any extended discussion or argument of even one of the Reports or Resolutions on Slavery, let alone *THREE!* Perhaps it was a situation that led Whig Representative Beverly S. Allen of Carroll County to seek to cut the Gordian Knot by introducing a sort of "Save, Oh, Save the Union" Resolution which omitted altogether any reference whatsoever to the real issue at hand—*SLAVERY.* The Allen placebo [97] was as follows:

"*Resolved by the General Assembly of the State of Tennessee,* That the chief source of happiness and prosperity of the people of the United States, both as individuals and as a nation has been conferred by and through the union of the States and the adoption of our sacred Constitution, the adoption of which was effected by the compromises and concessions of our patriotic sires, both of the North and South; And,

Resolved further, That the continuation of that happiness and prosperity and even liberty itself depends upon the perpetuity of the Union, 'one and indivisible;' that the destruction of the cause of liberty in our own beloved land, will not confine its effects to the borders of the home of Washington, but that it would sound the death knell of liberal government in every part of the civilized world.

Resolved further, That the patriotic people of the State of Tennessee deprecating the sad effects of a disunion of these States to themselves and to their children and the world, and also feeling a sacred regard to the memory and services of their revolutionary fathers, will stand by and defend the Union at all hazards and to the last extremity."

On February 11, 1850, the last day of the legislative session,

"Mr. Allen moved to take up the resolution introduced by him on Saturday, on the subject of the Union." [98]

Representative William B. Bate offered the following amendment which was adopted:

"And that the only method by which the Union can be preserved in the original purity, so as to secure to the several states their constitutional rights is by resisting at all hazards and to the last extremity any and all attempts to violate the spirit and intent of the provisions."

The amended Allen resolution was then ordered to be engrossed and transmitted to the Senate.[99] A report from the latter body stated that "the resolution on the subject of the Union" had been signed by the Speaker of the Senate.[100] Here was the "Union" preservative:[101]

"NUMBER XIII

Resolved by the General Assembly of the State of Tennessee, That the chief source of happiness and prosperity of the people of the United States,

---

[97] *House Journal,* 1849, 834.
[98] *Ibid.,* 858.
[99] *Ibid.,* 858.
[100] *Ibid.,* 860.
[101] *Acts of Tennessee,* 1849, Resolution XIII, 572.

both as individuals and as a nation, has been conferred by and through the union of the States and the adoption of our sacred Constitution, the adoption of which was effected by the compromises and concessions of our patriotic sires, both of the North and South; and

Resolved further, That the continuation of that happiness and prosperity, and even liberty itself, depends upon the perpetuity of the Union, one and indivisible; that the destruction of liberty in our own beloved land will not confine its effect to the borders of the home of Washington, but it would sound the death knell of liberal government in every part of the civilized world.

Resolved further, That the patriotic people of the State of Tennessee, deprecating the sad effects of a disunion of these States to themselves, to their children and the world, and also feeling a sacred regard to the memory and services of their revolutionary fathers, will stand by and defend the Union at all hazards and to the last extremity; and that the only method by which the Union can be preserved in its original purity, so as to secure to the several States their constitutional rights, is by resisting, at all hazards and to the last extremity, any and all attempts to violate the spirit and intent of its provisions.

LANDON C. HAYNES,
Speaker of the House of Representatives,
JOHN F. HENRY,
Speaker of the Senate."

Passed February 11, 1850.

A rather conservative Whig journal [102] summed up the current legislative inertia on the slavery question in this wise:

"... The lesser lights took the shine out of the greater.... The slavery question fell between the two Houses. The House passed a series of resolutions of an inflammatory nature, calculated rather to fan the flame of excitement than to exert a beneficial influence. These were lost in the Senate, and a milder and more conservative series passed that body. In the House, Mr. Allen's resolution expressive of attachment to the Union and declaring the intention to maintain it 'at all hazards and to the last extremity' were adopted with but one or two dissenting voices, thus showing that however great may be the desire of members to make political capital out of the slavery question, they do not put on record a desire to destroy the glorious edifice of Freedom erected by their Revolutionary sires. The passage of these resolutions was a glorious close to the proceedings of the House...."

On Monday, February 11, 1850, the Twenty-eighth General Assembly was officially adjourned *sine die,* after a session of approximately four and one-half months. As noted at the beginning of this chapter, the Legislature was split politically, the Senate being Whig by a majority of three and the House of Representatives being Democratic by the same narrow margin. Consequently, the Democratic Governor, William Trousdale, was faced with a "divided house" which, Scripturally speaking, "can not stand." Partisan politics, at times, rode rough shod over items that deserved careful and non-partisan consideration. The two

---

[102] *Nashville Gazette,* February 12, 1850.

paramount issues, Education and Internal Improvements, received but mediocre attention, with the result that no significant remedial legislation was enacted on either of the two topics. In that particular, the 1849 Legislature failed to measure up to a high standard of excellence.

On the other hand, every legislative session is confronted with a host of miscellaneous matters that frequently constitute a sort of barometer that measures the social philosophy of the deliberative body. A number of such items are of importance, though not of major proportion. Other items are frequently trivial and comprise mere driftwood. Still other matters prove to be stumbling blocks that blocked progressive legislation. Let us turn our attention to some of the miscellaneous questions that consumed a large portion of legislative time.

First of all, the 1849 Legislature reached perhaps an all-time "low" in regard to one item which should have received unanimous support from each political faction. Four days after the convening of the Legislature, on October 1, 1849, Representative William B. Bate of Sumner County introduced the following resolution:[103]

"*Resolved by the General Assembly of the State of Tennessee*, that the members of the Senate and House, have heard of the death of James K. Polk, late Governor of Tennessee and President of the United States, with profound sorrow; that his eminent virtues as a private citizen, and his illustrious services as a public servant have adorned each station he has occupied, and elevated the character of our State and Nation.

Resolved, That a joint select committee be appointed to select some person to deliver a eulogy on the life and character of Mr. Polk on the last Thursday in October.

Resolved, That the city authorities be invited to participate in the ceremonies of the occasion, and that the Clerks of the Senate and House of Representatives be instructed to furnish said authorities with a copy of these resolutions.

Resolved, That a committee of arrangements consisting of five members of the House and three of the Senate be appointed to select a place for the delivery of said eulogy."

On October 8, upon motion of Whig Senator Felix K. Zollicoffer of Davidson County the House Resolution was amended by striking out the first section and inserting in lieu thereof the following:[104]

"*Resolved by the General Assembly of the State of Tennessee*, That the members of the Senate and the House having heard of the death of James K. Polk, late Governor of Tennessee, and President of the United States, with profound sorrow, regard this as a proper occasion to declare that his eminent virtues as a private citizen and his distinguished services as a public servant have adorned each station that he occupied, and largely contributed to the honorable fame of our State and nation."

The Zollicoffer amendment was adopted by a strict party vote, 14

---

103 *House Journal*, 1849, 52.
104 *Senate Journal*, 1849, 60–61.

Whigs for and 11 Democrats opposing. The Joint Select Committee appointed to make arrangements for the delivery of the eulogy on the life and services of James K. Polk agreed upon the following program:[105]

"That the Eulogy is to be delivered at the McKendree church, in this city, at 11 o'clock, A. M., on Thursday, the 25th inst., by the Hon. A. O. P. Nicholson. The procession is to form on the Public Square, at 10 o'clock, A.M., under the direction of Col. S. R. Anderson, Chief Marshal, who is authorized to appoint as many Deputy Marshals as he may deem proper.
The order of procession is as follows:

Mayor and Aldermen of the City,
The Governor and his Staff, and Ex-Governors,
Members and Ex-Members of Congress,
All Ministers of the Gospel that may be in the City,
The President, Faculty, and Trustees of the Nashville University.
Orator of the Day, accompanied by the Speakers of the Senate and
House of Representatives, Members and Officers of the Senate.
Members and Officers of the House of Representatives.
Judges and Bar of the Supreme, Chancery, Circuit, and Criminal Courts.
Masons—of which Order the late President was a member;
Odd Fellows,
Sons of Temperance.
Fire Companies of the City,
Citizens generally.

The course of the procession through the streets of the city will be arranged by the Chief Marshal and his deputies, and published before the morning of the procession. The church bells will be tolled from 10½ till 11 o'clock, A.M. The Speakers, Members and Officers of the Legislature are requested to wear the usual badge of mourning on the occasion, and for thirty days thereafter.
19th Oct., 1849.

A. L. R. WILKES,
Chairman of the Senate Committee."

On Thursday, November 1, 1849, the *Eulogy on the Life and Character of JAMES K. POLK* was delivered at the McKendree Methodist Church in Nashville by A. O. P. Nicholson in accordance with the Resolution passed by the General Assembly.[106] On the day following the Polk Memorial Services, Representative William B. Bate introduced the following resolution,[107] to-wit:

"*Resolved*, That the committee on the part of the House, appointed to select an orator to pronounce a eulogy on the late James K. Polk, be instructed to request a copy of said eulogy for publication; and that 7,500 copies be printed for the use of this House."

---

[105] *Senate Journal*, 1849, 125.
House Journal, 1849, 128.
Author's note. The date for delivery of the eulogy was changed to November 1, 1849.
[106] *House Journal*, 1849, Appendix, 424–443.
Author's note. The all-encompassing eulogy was a masterful production and deserves to be incorporated in this volume.
[107] *House Journal*, 1849, 223.

The resolution was passed by a vote of 47 to 23.

"EULOGY.

Gentlemen of the General Assembly and Fellow-citizens:

We have assembled together to pay the merited tribute of respect to the virtues of one of our deceased fellow-citizens, whose brief career was rendered illustrious by the magnitude of his public services, and whose name will adorn the pages of public history as one of the distinguished benefactors of his country. It is a truth, not unmixed with cause for regret, that posterity is the only tribunal on earth whose judgment as to the characters of distinguished men can be impartial and consequently infallible; but posterity must rely for the materials of its judgment upon the evidence of cotemporaneous witnesses, and on that account, it is due alike to the living, the dead and the unborn, that the important events in the lives of public benefactors should be honestly collected and carefully preserved by their cotemporaries. In discharging this duty in reference to the life and character of James K. Polk, I can, without affectation, express my regret, that the choice did not fall upon one better able to do justice to the dead, and to meet the legitimate wishes and expectations of the living. At the same time, it is but candid in me to say, that the choice could not have fallen on one more willing than myself to dedicate what little ability I possess in attempting to execute the mournful task. In the countless throng of his personal acquaintances there is scarcely one, outside of his family, who has had better opportunities of learning and understanding the true character of the deceased than myself; and if I possessed the power to delineate it, I should hope even to anticipate the judgment of posterity and present before you the picture of James K. Polk as it will be viewed in after times, when all who now hear me will sleep with him in the silent dust. His father and mine emigrated from the same State, about the same time, and actuated by the same spirit of enterprise pitched their tents side by side, as deep in the then western wilds as civilized men could venture to live. They were neighbors and friends whilst they lived. My personal knowledge of the deceased embraces the whole period of my life—but being my senior by several years, our association together commenced after my majority. From that period we were close neighbors, belonged to the same profession, were members of the same political family, and closely identified in the political conflicts of each successive year. I trust, therefore, that I speak but naked truth when I lay claim to a thorough knowledge of the true character of him of whose life and public services I am called upon to speak.

Since our government went into operation under its present glorious constitution, twelve of our distinguished patriots have been called to fill the office of Chief Magistrate. Of these, nine have paid the last debt of nature and are now sleeping with their fathers; and amongst these our own beloved State numbers two of her distinguished sons. Many who now hear me stood around the pulseless forms of both of them as they lay locked in the icy arms of death, and followed them, with broken hearts and tearful eyes, to their silent tombs. In life they were devoted personal and political friends, united by bonds of attachment which no change of time or circumstances could break or weaken. Their judgments concurred as to the means of securing and perpetuating the prosperity and glory of their country—for these they counselled together and labored together—the names of Jackson and Polk will illustrate the same bright pages of history and be embalmed, side by side, in the hearts of all true patriots as joint benefactors of their country and joint contributors to its lasting fame. It is, therefore, fit that the last resting places of two such patriots should be so near to each other, that when the pilgrim shall visit the banks of the beautiful Cumberland to catch fresh inspirations of patriotism at the tomb of Jackson, he can turn hard-by for confirmation of his impressions to the tomb of Polk.

When I call to your recollection the fact that from the time when Mr. Polk closed his educational preparation to play his part in the busy affairs of life, until his death, there elapsed less than thirty years, and that of this period he was engaged twenty-four years in the public service, it will at once occur to you that such unparalleled success as attended his career necessarily pre-supposes more extraordinary endowments than you may have been in the habit of awarding to him. In 1821, we see him a clerk to the General Assembly; in 1823, he was a member of that body; in 1825, he was a member of Congress and continued so until 1839; in 1835, we see him Speaker of the House of Representatives in Congress and again filling the same office in 1837; in 1839, we see him Governor of the State of Tennessee; in 1844, we see him President of the United States. Such rapid elevation, step by step, from the private station to the highest honor which can be conferred on man, has no parallel in this or any other country! If any period of his life had been rendered illustrious by some brilliant feat of military prowess, we would at once say he owed his extraordinary success to the characteristic gratitude manifested by our countrymen towards their military chieftains—but Mr. Polk was purely and exclusively a civilian and statesman, and of course must have risen without the help of mere adventitious circumstances. Looking simply to the various stations which he filled, without stopping to consider the manner in which he filled them, it may well be doubted whether his merits have heretofore been appreciated by those who supposed that they knew him best. Two causes suggest themselves in explanation of this circumstance: He was the acknowledged leader of one of the political parties in our State for many years. This circumstance arrayed against him in determined opposition the members of the other political party. That he should be underrated and depreciated by partisan opponents, was to be looked for, if indeed it was not a natural and legitimate mode of warfare. His political friends were devoted to him as their champion and leader, but it was not the devotion which we feel for men of distinguished talents who are unknown to us except by reputation. We all knew Mr. Polk personally, associated with him freely, admired and loved him as our leader, and had every confidence in his intellectual endowments, but our appreciation of his talents lacked the 'enchantment which distance lends;' and hence, though we loved him the more from our personal knowledge of his virtues, we estimated his talents less than others who knew him only by his public career. If it be true that the standard of appreciation applied only in his own State to the character of Mr. Polk has hitherto been too slow, it becomes now the more important that the error should be made manifest, and that complete justice should be awarded to the real merits of the dead. His reputation is national property—it constitutes a part of the honor and glory of our country—its faithful protection and preservation devolve upon us as patriotic duties.

James Knox Polk was the eldest of ten children and was born on the 2nd of November, 1795, in Mecklenburg county, North Carolina. His ancestors were emigrants from Ireland in the early part of the eighteenth century. They settled upon the eastern shore of Maryland, where some of their descendants still reside. They brought with them from their native land the characters of energetic, intelligent and liberty-loving men. That branch of the family from which James K. Polk descended, removed from Maryland into Pennsylvania, and from thence, about the middle of the eighteenth century, to North Carolina, where they were residing when our Revolutionary struggle commenced. The character of his ancestors will be best illustrated by reference to a well authenticated historical fact connected with our revolutionary struggle. It is now well ascertained that the first formal and solemn act of separation from the mother country that occurred, was the work of the people of Mecklenburg county, on the 20th of May, 1775. Amongst the most conspicuous actors on that memorable occasion were two brothers—Thomas Polk, the great uncle, and Ezekial Polk, the grand-father of James K. Polk. By their resolutions this noble band of pioneers in the cause of Independence declared their eternal separation from the British Crown, and their purpose to maintain their freedom and independence at all hazards. They proclaimed every man a traitor who would accept a commission from the crown, and closed their declaration of Independence with this significant resolution:

'Resolved, That Col. Thomas Polk and Dr. Joseph Kennedy purchase 300 pounds of powder, 600 pounds of lead, and 1000 flints for the military of this country.'

These incidents will serve to show the devotion to civil liberty and the energy of character which animated and distinguished the ancestors of the late Ex-President. How much of this spirit descended to him, or how much influence the frequent narration of these interesting events around the fireside may have made upon his tender mind in the formation of his character, we can best judge when we have reviewed his own eventful career.

In 1806, when James K. Polk was a little over ten years of age, his father, Maj. Samuel Polk, actuated by that indomitable love of enterprise and adventure which was characteristic of the family, emigrated from Mecklenburg, and sought a home in what was then the remotest western frontiers. He located upon the rich lands of Duck River, and there spent the remainder of his life. He was a farmer of small means, but intelligent, active, energetic, persevering and devoted to the acquisition of a fortune for his rising family. He turned his attention to securing the rich lands in his neighborhood, and in executing his plans, his son, James K., was required to share with him in the toils and exposures incident to a surveyor's life in a wild border country. It was in the wild woods attending to the drudgery of a camp life that James K. Polk first became inured to the endurance of severe toil and hardships. Until his feeble physical constitution was likely to give way under the labor, he was the companion of his father in securing the handsome estate which he left to his children. The idea of educating him for one of the liberal professions, was not entertained by his father, until the earnestness with which it was pressed by his son, induced him to yield as a matter of duty. The University of North Carolina, then and ever since a favorite seat of learning throughout the south, was selected for his collegiate education. He entered that institution in 1815, at the age of twenty, and graduated at the end of three years, in 1818. His successful career in college, was but the foreshadowing of the success which crowned his efforts in after life. The reputation which he left at Chapel Hill, was not that of a brilliant college genius—the expectations created by such a reputation are seldom realized—but he owed the honors, which were conferred on him at each successive examination, to the untiring diligence and industry with which he applied himself to the duties assigned to him. During the three years he was never known to be absent from a recitation, nor from the morning and evening prayers in the Chapel at sun-rise and sun-set. He took delight in the mathematical branches of education, and never tired in the details of the most abstruse and complicated investigations. His mind was trained and methodised and systematised by his close attention to mathematical investigations, whilst it was beautified and softened by the less severe, and usually more attractive influences of classic literature. At the close of his course he bore away from his *Alma Mater* the highest honors of the institution, and along with them the ardent attachments of his preceptors and associates.

Having finished his collegiate education, he immediately chose the Law for his profession, and prepared himself to enter upon its duties, under the patronage and superintendence of the late Felix Grundy.

At this stage in the life of Mr. Polk, when he is standing upon the threshold, prepared to enter upon the busy scenes of the world, we may pause profitably for a moment to see if we can collect and group together those peculiar excellencies in his character which formed the substratum on which he afterwards reared his splendid superstructure. I have said that at college, he did not enjoy the reputation of a *brilliant* genius—brilliancy was not one of the distinguishing characteristics of his mind—of imagination he had but little. In writing he used no ornaments derived from fancy—in speaking his flights of fancy and figures of rhetoric were few, and these the productions of others. He was lively and sociable in his disposition, and interspersed his conversation with much wit, humor and anecdote. His perception was quick, and his apprehension ready. His memory, particularly as to dates, names and faces, was extraordinary—he never forgot the name or face of a person he had seen and conversed with. He retained dates with equal tenacity. He comprehended the force of facts at a glance, and could wield or parry them with an adroitness of which those only are capable whose reasoning faculties are highly cultivated. In his early life he learned to read men from the book of nature. He observed closely the impelling motives of human action, and was thoroughly versed in the science of human nature. He possessed the rare talent of infusing his own ardor into his friends. His mind had been so fully trained to investigation that his judgment was clear, and rested on sound reasoning. No subject was too comprehensive or too complicated for the analysing process of his mind. Nature did not endow him with a great mind, but nature did better by him—she endowed him with a good mind, in which the several faculties were well balanced. By his habits of application he secured for himself all the advantages of a great mind. If nature did not enable him by intuition to arrive at correct conclusions, he cultivated the faculties which nature did give him, so assiduously, that he enabled himself to arrive at correct conclusions by reasoning. Without a liberal education, he would have become a man of great wealth, but as a man of mind could never have attained eminence. Nature planted in his bosom a desire for distinction—the precepts and example of his father impressed him with the excellence of economy and industry—had he not been well educated, these impressions would have directed his devotions to money as to the road to distinction. Fortunately for him and for his country he succeeded in inducing his father to extend to him the ennobling benefits of a liberal education. With habits of promptness, punctuality and industry, which he formed under his parental education, sustained by his high regard for virtue and morality, and impelled by that ardent desire for distinction, which he manifested in boyhood, it would have been strange if he had not distinguished himself during his collegiate course. With the same habits confirmed, with virtue, morality and a reverential regard for religion in all his conduct, with his mind thoroughly trained and disciplined, with a native energy of character always found in a pioneer life, with a capacity for the endurance of mental and physical labor almost without parallel, with the genius of distinction beckoning him onward, it would have been equally strange if James K. Polk had failed to fill a large space in the world's eye.

The body of his character was composed of those peculiar elements which distinguish the hardy, enterprising intelligent pioneer: native shrewdness, closeness and quickness of observation, disregard of hardships or dangers, firmness and steadiness of purpose, promptness in deciding, and rapidity in executing, scrupulous devotion to personal integrity and indomitable energy and perseverance. These are the prominent features exhibited in the lives and characters of that noble band of enterprising patriots, who cut themselves loose from the endearments of friends and homes in the old States, about the beginning of the present century, and penetrated our western wilds in search of larger liberty, and wider fields of enterprise. All that they wanted to constitute them the best republican population on earth, was the mollifying and refining influences of liberal education. Mr. Polk possessed all these noble pioneer traits of character, but they were modified and reformed of their roughnesses, and reduced to symmetry and beauty by the hand of education. They still, however, constituted the body and substance of his character. Education had done for his character just what the chisel of the artist does for the marble block—it gave it form, proportion, symmetry and beauty.

With the traits of character and the previous preparation which I have endeavored to describe, Mr. Polk took his place on the stage of action in the year 1820, as a practitioner of law, in the county of Maury. His career as a lawyer was short, but eminently successful. He occupied a prominent position at the bar from his first appearance, and continued to have an extensive and lucrative practice, until he withdrew to devote his whole time to his public duties.

The political career of Mr. Polk commenced in 1823, by his election to the General Assembly of the State. In that body, he acquired the character of a prompt, attentive, practical, business member, and a ready, efficient and forcible debater.

At the election in 1825, he was chosen a member to Congress, after a most arduous and warmly contested canvass. In this canvass the peculiar traits of his character were prominently developed. His competitors were men of age, experience and intelligence. He was young and comparatively inexperienced and unknown. It was a contest to be decided mainly upon personal popularity. The people were not then divided into two great political parties. The candidates all professed the same general political faith. The chances at the outset were decidedly against him, but he had set his heart upon success, and he resolved to attain it. The district was large, but he traversed and canvassed it again and again. Before the canvass was half over he had displayed so much activity and energy in his movements, and had instilled into his supporters so much of his own ardent zeal that he was regarded by each of his competitors as the most formidable opponent. In his public speeches there was always an earnestness and sincerity of manner which was peculiarly impressive. He seemed ever to feel what he said, and to speak with an animation and ardor, which flowed from his heart. This was the secret of his success as a popular orator. He was persuasive, because he spoke from his heart as well as from his head. His superior tact in illustrating his positions by numerous anecdotes, of which he had stored away in his capacious memory very many, whilst he was always courteous and mild, and respectful, aided him to win the predilections of his hearers. As the canvass approached its termination, he displayed all the skill of a veteran general in marshalling his forces for an impending battle. He dashed from point to point over his district, with a rapidity which struck his opponents with surprise, and paralyzed them with despair. He infused into his own friends the same ardor and energy which actuated himself.

When the election came on, he was triumphantly successful.

In 1827, he was re-elected to Congress after another severe contest with a single competitor. In this canvass he was opposed by a gentleman of distinguished legal attainments and extensive talents. The result, however, proved that Mr. Polk had imbedded himself too deeply in the hearts of his constituents to be successfully opposed.

He continued to be re-elected with little or no opposition until 1833, when he was subjected to another arduous contest. In the preceding year as a member of the committee of ways and means, Mr. Polk had made a minority report to the House of Representatives against the United States Bank as a depository of the Public Revenue. In this report he had exposed the precarious condition of that Institution, particularly as connected with the operations of its western branches. In the spring of 1833 he had announced himself as a candidate for re-election and had gone to the western portion of the State on private business. In his absence one of the newspapers at Nashville charged him with having slandered and injured western credit in his report to Congress. The charge was scattered industriously throughout his district and a strong feeling of indignation was aroused against him. The charge was made with so much confidence and urged with so much feeling and plausibility that the excitement swept over the district and his final prostration seemed inevitable. In the midst of the excitement two gentlemen of distinguished abilities and great popularity became candidates in opposition to him. Some of his friends, knowing the time when he would return, announced that he would make his vindication against the charge on the first day of the April Circuit Court at Columbia. The announcement brought together an immense crowd from all quarters of the district. The excitement had grown in strength and intensity until the whole crowd seemed to be animated with one feeling of indignation. At the appointed hour Mr. Polk took the stand. He met the charge with boldness, maintained the truth of his report, vindicated his own motives and character and denounced with crushing power the injustice done him by his assailants. The appeal made by him to his old friends and constituents was irresistible—it was the eloquence of the heart and it met a responsive sympathy in every bosom. Tears of joy trickled down the cheeks of many of his old supporters, whilst the countenances of the whole audience were bright with gladness. His vindication was complete, his triumph was signal, and the tide of popular indignation was rolled back upon his accusers. His two competitors continued to struggle on for victory, but the struggle was in vain—he was re-elected by an overwhelming majority. From this time until he voluntarily retired from Congress in 1839, he had no further opposition.

A full exposition of the congressional services of Mr. Polk would require a complete review of the entire administrations of John Quincy Adams and Andrew Jackson and two years of Mr. Van Buren's term. During all this period he was an active and during most of the terms a prominent participant in the consideration and discussion of all the great questions which engaged the deliberations of Congress. To review these at full length must be the work of the historian—it will be sufficient for me merely to glance at some of the more important of these questions so as to exhibit Mr. Polk in his true position.

With the accession of Mr. Adams to the Presidency the spirit of party, which had slumbered during the Administration of Mr. Monroe, was again wakened, and from that period it has continued ever since to reign over the deliberations of Congress. The exceptionable manner of Mr. Adams' election as well as the character of the doctrines promulgated in his first annual message caused the new party division which followed his election. Mr. Polk took his position in opposition to the administration and during its whole term was an active, vigilant and efficient opponent. He regarded the election of Mr. Adams as a defeat of the popular will, and to avoid a similar occurrence he advocated an amendment of the Constitution by which the election of President and Vice President should be made directly by the people. His speech on this question was among the earliest made by him in Congress, and although he was with probably one or two exceptions the youngest member in the body, his effort will not suffer by comparison with those of the oldest and most talented members who engaged in the discussion. The fundamental principles of our government were involved in the proposition. Whoever reads the speech of Mr. Polk will find it abounding in deep research into the origin and history of the constitution, in profound statesman-like views of the relative powers of the different departments of the government, and in powerful arguments in favor of giving efficiency to the popular will. At the same session the discussions in regard to the celebrated Panama Mission, and the right of the House of Representatives to withhold supplies for carrying out a treaty made by the Executive and Senate took place. The investigation of these questions engaged the first talents of the body. They involved principles of international and constitutional law, which were of the most difficult solution. Mr. Polk took a prominent part in this investigation and discussion. By his efforts on the questions, he secured the high respect of the House and established for himself a character for profound abilities. This was manifested at the commencement of the next Congress by his appointment as chairman of the important committee on Foreign Relations.

Most of the questions which became the subject of zealous party contention, during the administration of Gen. Jackson had originated or been subjects of action, during the administration of Mr. Adams. This is particularly true as to the power of Congress to appropriate money for works of Internal Improvement in the States, and to impose tariff duties, for the purpose of protecting and building up domestic manufactures. Both of these objects were favored by Mr. Adams, and both received the sanction of Congress, during his administration. These together with the questions connected with the currency constituted the leading subjects of public excitement, during the administration of Gen. Jackson. On all of these questions, Mr. Polk's position was distinctly defined, during the administration of Mr. Adams. His opposition to the administration was based in no small degree upon what he regarded the consolidating tendencies of the power yielded to Congress by Mr. Adams, in regard to Internal Improvement, whilst he regarded a system of high protective duties as necessarily unjust and oppressive to the great agricultural interests of the country. The question of re-chartering the Bank of the United States did not arise during Mr. Adams' administration, and therefore Mr. Polk in his official capacity did not take his position on this subject, until it was brought forward by Gen. Jackson. It is a fact within my own knowledge, that before Gen. Jackson had communicated any message to Congress, and before the re-charter of the Bank was agitated in the public mind, Mr. Polk had been called on through the press at Columbia, and had frankly avowed his opposition to the re-charter of the Bank, both upon grounds of expediency and constitutionality. It is therefore true, and it is due to the memory of the dead that the truth be distinctly stated, that on all the leading measures of Gen. Jackson's administration, in sustaining which Mr. Polk was so prominent, and so efficient, he was maintaining his own principles taken in advance of their being brought forward by General Jackson.

Gen. Jackson entered upon the discharge of his Executive duties with a profound conviction, that the permanent prosperity and happiness of his country, demanded a radical reformation of the existing administrative policy of the government. His great mind, which comprehended the most momentous subjects at a glance, and arrived at its conclusions almost by intuition, was thoroughly convinced that a system of measures, then in full operation would ultimately result in the complete overthrow of the substantial principles of representative freedom, leaving nothing standing but the mere name and forms of our splendid structure of Republicanism. He regarded the Bank of the United States, the construction of works of Internal Improvements in the States by the General Government, and the imposition of Tariff duties, for the protection of domestic manufactures, as three measures so intimately connected as to constitute one grand system, which was destined to sap the foundations of the Constitution, and end in disaster and ruin. Whether his views were correct or not, it is not now necessary or proper to be examined. He entertained them strongly and honestly, and he felt it to be his solemn duty to carry them out during his administration. The reforms which he contemplated, involved no less than a total revolution in the financial policy of the government. That policy was so intimately connected with the commercial and monetary interests of the country, that the contemplated revolution could not fail seriously to affect the private interests of a most influential and numerous portion of the community. To understand fully the magnitude of the reforms proposed, and of the obstacles to their execution, it must be remembered that the whole surface of the country, was chequered over with projected lines of roads and canals, for the construction of which the general government was expected to provide the means. It is impossible even to conjecture the amount of individual interests, thus enlisted in favor of the system. When I state to you that the estimated cost of the various projects, which had received the virtual sanction of the government, was over one hundred millions of dollars, you will at once discover that hundreds of thousands of individuals must have been flattered with pleasing visions of increased wealth to be derived from the immense amounts of public money, which was expected to be expended. What an amount of disappointment and dissatisfaction would follow upon the abandonment of all these projects was clearly foreseen by Gen. Jackson, but his unbending purpose was fixed, and he resolved to encounter all in the discharge of a high and solemn duty.

It would require a man of more than ordinary decision and firmness of purpose to encounter the opposition, which would naturally array itself against the defeat of the contemplated projects of internal improvement. But when it is borne in mind, that an equally fierce and powerful opposition was to be encountered in proposing to bring down the tariff duties to an economical revenue standard—and that in combination with both another still more violent and potent opposition in consequence of the proposition to defeat a re-charter of the United States Bank, was to be encountered, we

372

MESSAGES OF THE GOVERNORS

are lost in wonder and admiration of the man, who had the moral courage to enter upon so stupendous an undertaking. Men of ordinary stature would shrink back in despair before such obstacles, but impelled by a high sense of duty, and looking alone to the ultimate glory and happiness of his country, Andrew Jackson cheerfully 'took the responsibility' and put opposition at defiance.

The result has proved that the reforms proposed by Gen. Jackson were not impracticable—the extravagant schemes of internal improvement in contemplation, were arrested by the veto of the Maysville Road-bill—the Bank of the United States sunk to rise no more under the veto of the bill for its re-charter—and the protective tariff policy was forced to yield to the compromise of 1833. These results were attained through eight years of intense and uninterrupted public excitement. From the commencement to the close of his administration, the spirit of party, and not unfrequently of faction, raged throughout the union. Our entire population became warm politicians and active partisans. The eyes of the whole country were fixed with deep solicitude upon the Halls of Congress. There the warfare of parties was waged with fiercest fury. The highest talents of the country were engaged in the conflict. Prominent in all these collisions of intellectual gladiators was Jas. K. Polk. He concurred cordially in the several reforms proposed by Gen. Jackson—they were reforms, which his own judgment had approved before Gen. Jackson succeeded to power. He had then been a member of Congress four years, and had established a reputation for superior abilities. He was the devoted personal as well as political friend of Gen. Jackson. It was therefore natural that General Jackson should repose peculiar confidence in him, and that he should become his most conspicuous supporter in the House of Representatives. With every discussion that took place his reputation increased until by common consent, he was regarded as the leader of the Jackson forces in the House of Representatives. Whenever Gen. Jackson was attacked, (and the attacks were daily,) Mr. Polk was prompt, bold and efficient in his vindication. No matter from whose stalworth arm the blow came, he was there to return it with equal power. His antagonists in these conflicts were no pigmies—they were intellectual giants in debate—amongst them were the McDuffies, the Adamses, the Binneys and a host of others, whose splendid talents have given lustre to American eloquence. How he acquitted himself in these high intellectual encounters, may be best determined from the success which crowned his efforts, and from the fact that many of the distinguished men, who were his antagonists in these discussions, sought every opportunity in after life to testify their appreciation of his talents. The people looked on as witnesses of these exciting, and sometimes angry debates—their judgment as to his abilities was manifested in 1844, by the alacrity and enthusiasm with which they received and supported his nomination to the Presidency. How he was appreciated by his political friends in Congress, was clearly shown in his election by them, on two occasions to preside as Speaker over their deliberations.

Mr. Polk filled the office of Speaker of the House of Representatives during four years of high party excitement. In his own language, this was 'at all times an office of great labor and responsibility.' It was peculiarly so during his administration of the office, but the united judgment of all parties had long since decided that he met its labors and responsibilities with ability, dignity and impartiality. More points of parliamentary law and order were made during his two terms of service than had been made from the beginning of the government. He decided them all with promptness, and on every occasion was sustained by the judgment of the House without distinction of parties. He retired from the Speakership and from Congress in 1839, carrying with him the respect of his political opponents and the warm attachment and admiration of his political friends, throughout the Union.

After retiring from Congress, Mr. Polk canvassed our State three times as a candidate for Governor. In his first contest he was successful—in the last two he was unsuccessful. His speeches in these canvasses have been admired by all as amongst the finest specimens of popular oratory ever witnessed in our State. Without disparagement to other distinguished gentlemen who have canvassed the State for Governor, I may be permitted to remark that the discussions between Gov. Jones and Gov. Polk were distinguished on both sides for their ability and eloquence.

Mr. Polk closed his gubernatorial term of service in 1841, and from that period to his elevation to the Presidency, in 1844, he was assiduously and successfully engaged in the practice of law.

The nomination of Mr. Polk to the Presidency by the Democratic National Convention, in the spring of 1844, was unexpected to him. His name had been freely used for several years in connection with the Vice Presidency, but for the Presidency the public attention had been directed to the names of older members of the party. Mr. Van Buren would, in all probability, have received the nomination but for his exceptionable views on the annexation of Texas—a question which was then a prominent subject of discussion before the public. By way of securing the harmonious co-operation of the democratic party, the delegates wisely determined to go outside of the names to which public attention had been attracted, and to select a nominee whose known principles and distinguished services would command the cordial support of the entire party. The name of James K. Polk was suggested and approved. He became the nominee of the convention, and by the voice of his countrymen was elevated to the Presidency.

It is impossible within the limits of an address, to do justice to the brilliant succession of important measures which have rendered illustrious the administration of President Polk. His four years of service stand without a parallel in this or any other government, for the number and magnitude of the measures matured and consummated. Almost every legitimate subject of either foreign or domestic policy came up for consideration and received final action. In a government like ours, where unrestrained freedom of thought is cherished as the main conservative of national liberty, there will be necessarily a diversity of opinion as to the ultimate wisdom of some of these measures. Whilst we freely concede to each other entire sincerity and honesty in our respective opinions, no just exception can be taken to a frank and distinct avowal of the grounds on which those who concur in the wisdom of his measures believe that the last Ex-President is entitled to the gratitude of his countrymen.

In sketching the congressional career of Mr. Polk, I have given you some idea of the distinguished part which he bore in overthrowing the measures of finance, revenue and currency which then prevailed. From the date of the overthrow of those measures until the accession of Mr. Polk to the Presidency, the policy of the government was unsettled and vascillating. Upon him who had achieved so much distinction in prostrating the old system devolved the duty of rearing upon its ruins a new structure. The new system of finance and revenue recommended by him have now been in successful operation for several years, and each additional year's experience but increases the admiration of those who concur in the wisdom and skill with which it was constructed. Our revenue system now rests upon the basis of *taxation according to value*—a principle of eternal justice, as its advocates believe, which ought to commend itself to universal support. Thus far it has proved entirely practicable and eminently successful. Experience may and doubtless will suggest modifications of the relative rates of some of the duties, but it is sincerely hoped by its friends that the great fundamental principle on which the system rests will never be disturbed.

In connection with our present revenue policy the commercial interests of the country are rejoicing in the benefits derived from the adoption of the warehousing system. This measure has broken up the monopoly in the import trade heretofore enjoyed by large capitalists, and has opened up the channels of commerce to free and advantageous competition. It is but another step in the progress towards free trade which is characteristic of our age.

The fiscal system adopted by President Polk's administration has proved equally as successful as his revenue system. The immense revenues derived from taxes and other sources are no longer mingled with the funds of banking corporations as part of their trading capital; but under the simple operations of the independent treasury law are kept, disbursed and transmitted by the government's own agents. Although this measure encountered the most violent and determined opposition when it was first proposed, its operation for several years has been so simple, silent and salutary, that its wisdom has almost ceased to be questioned in our political discussions.

The policy adopted and recommended by President Polk in regard to our public lands was characterized by views of liberality, humanity and patriotism, which must ever command respect. He regarded our vast public domain as valuable less as a source of revenue than as furnishing cheap homes to the hardy enterprising pioneers. In his first annual message he said: 'Experience has proved that no portion of our population are more patriotic than the hardy and brave men of the frontier, or more ready to obey the call of their country, and to defend her rights and honor, whenever and by whatever enemy assailed. They should be protected from the grasping speculator, and secured, at the minimum price of the public lands, in the humble homes which they have improved by their labor. With this end in view, all vexatious or unnecessary restrictions imposed upon them by the existing pre-emption laws, should be repealed or modified. It is the true policy of the government to afford facilities to its citizens to become owners of small portions of our vast public domain at low and moderate rates.'

These are noble sentiments—worthy the statesman, the patriot and the philanthropist. He was in favor of opening wide the door and inviting emigration from the old and densely populated portions of the country to the fertile regions of the far west. He regarded our public domain as valuable in the preservation of our republican institutions, because it serves as an asylum for all who may feel themselves oppressed by the power of associated capital and overgrown wealth in the old and densely populated States. He regarded it as equally valuable in rearing up a race of sturdy republicans who never fail to rally to the standard of their country whenever their services are needed. Relying with unshaken confidence upon the security furnished by the federative character of our Union, Mr. Polk discarded and repudiated the antiquated doctrine that the territorial limits of a republic could not be enlarged without endangering its strength and perpetuity. He had no fears of seeing the 'area of freedom' extended too far—he believed that our glorious constitution was broad enough to embrace a confederacy of sovereignties extending from ocean to ocean, and that by its extension the Union would lose nothing in strength or durability.

In regard to our intercourse with Foreign Nations, President Polk adopted the principle promulgated by one of his illustrious predecessors—*to demand nothing that was not clearly right and to submit to nothing that was wrong.* Early in his administration, he had occasion to apply this principle, in regard to a pending difficulty with Great Britain as to the Oregon Territory. This had been a subject of frequent, but fruitless negotiation between the two governments for more than half a century. Our government claimed the territory as its own property, but under the arrangement for a joint occupation of the country, it had become in effect, a British Province, governed by British laws. Three propositions to compromise the questions of title and boundary, had been made and rejected. In deference to the action of his predecessors, President Polk renewed one of the propositions of compromise, but it met with its former fate. In this state of things, he determined to infuse into our Diplomacy, a degree of energy which it had not exhibited for years. Upon the rejection of the proposed compromise, he ordered the proposition to be immediately withdrawn, and our title to the whole of Oregon to be distinctly asserted to the British government. He communicated his proceedings to Congress, and recommended that the notice for the cessation of the joint occupation of the territory should be immediately given. There was a promptness, openness and directness in this policy to which the British government had not been accustomed in her late diplomacy. Mr. Polk was resolved to be no longer delayed or baffled in the settlement of the question by diplomatic evasions or procrastinations. Our citizens who had settled in Oregon, were calling for the protection of their government—they had been neglected already too long—Mr. Polk determined to bring the difficulty to an immediate and direct issue. The result proved the wisdom of his statesmanship. By the firmness, frankness and directness of his policy, the settlement of the question could no longer be evaded by British counsels without assuming the high responsibility of a rupture between the two governments. Mr. Polk is entitled to the credit of great sagacity in selecting the time for pressing this question. British pride might well be expected to meet his policy in a tone and spirit of defiance, but British statesmen could not but know that such a response would be tantamount to a declaration of war. Great Britain was in no condition for such a declaration of war, and hence concluded upon the principle, that 'discretion is the better part of valor,' to concede what she had so long and so pertinaciously denied to us. Thus ended an international difficulty which had baffled the ablest diplomatists for more than twenty-five years. In its settlement our national honor was preserved, and our national domain was greatly enlarged. Thousands upon thousands of bold adventurers, the brave pioneers will find homes in the territory, thus rescued from British usurpation, and under the benign influence of our constitution and laws will pour out their grateful hearts in commendations of the wisdom and firmness of the President, whose policy has added such an empire to the national domain.

In the final adjustment of the Oregon question, by which a government was provided for the territory, it became the duty of Mr. Polk to take his position on the subject of slavery, as connected with our territorial governments. The bill presented for his action contained a clause prohibiting slavery in the Oregon Territory. He approved the bill, but to avoid any misconstruction of the act, he accompanied its return to Congress with a special Message, in which he recognized the obligatory character of the Missouri Compromise line, and on that basis rested his approval of the law. He did not place the obligatory character of the compromise upon its force as an act of Congress, passed in pursuance of the Constitution, but as a covenant entered into by the two divisions of our Union, for the observance of which, the sacred honor of the contracting parties was pledged. He regarded the Oregon Territory as embraced within the spirit of this compromise, and on that account that a disapproval of the bill would be obnoxious to the imputation of a violation of the solemn pledge. At the same time he distinctly avowed his purpose to disapprove any act which might attempt to interfere with this compromise by prohibiting slavery in territory south of the line—thereby adopting and recognizing this compromise line, as the true basis for the settlement of this agitating question. Time must prove whether any other basis can be found better calculated to harmonize the conflicting views on this exciting subject.

No subject has taken stronger hold upon the public mind within the last few years than did the measure of the annexation of Texas to the United States in 1844. It exerted a controlling influence upon the selection of a democratic candidate for the Presidency, and during the excited canvass which followed, it was the most agitating topic of popular discussion. Mr. Polk was an early and ardent advocate of the proposed annexation. His warmest sympathies were enlisted in behalf of the citizens of Texas. Many of them had been his early and devoted personal friends. He had watched with interest their noble resistance of Mexican oppression, and rejoiced sincerely in the splendid victory of San Jacinto, which secured their independence. He was also the advocate of annexation upon high principles of national policy. He believed that the acquisition of the vast fertile territory of Texas, would add greatly to the commercial and agricultural wealth of the nation. He considered it as a part of the great Mississippi Valley, which had been improperly torn asunder by the Florida Treaty, and that its restoration was essential to the security of the vast interests which were constantly freighted upon the bosom of the Mississippi. He saw evidences of a purpose on the part of Great Britain to secure a controlling influence over the counsels of Texas, and he saw the dangers which threatened the interests of the great Mississippi Valley from such an influence. His views on this subject harmonized freely with the peculiar sentiment of the country, and his election was universally regarded as a verdict of the popular mind in favor of annexation. The moral influence of this result upon Congress, was so decided, that the passage of the annexation resolutions was precipitated previous to Mr. Polk's inauguration as President, leaving to him the work of consummating what had already commenced.

The duties which devolved upon President Polk in perfecting the measure of annexation, were of a character of delicacy and responsibility that called for the highest order of statesmanship. Two days after his inauguration, the Mexican Minister, resident at Washington, protested against the resolutions of annexation, as violative of the rights of his government, and abruptly demanded his pass-ports. This protest was based upon the assumption, that Texas was still a Mexican Province, and was a denial of her existence as a separate and independent republic. It was a repudiation of the right of revolution, to which Mexico herself was indebted for her national existence, and to which our government appeals as the basis of our independence. Texas had exercised this right and had maintained it so triumphantly that for nearly nine years no hostile Mexican foot had trod upon her soil. Most of the leading powers of Europe as well as our own government, had acknowledged and recognized her claim to separate nationality. She was *de jure* and *de facto* a free and independent government. The denial of her rights in the manner which characterized the conduct of the Mexican minister was an insult to our national honor, which would have justified measures of redress far more prompt and stringent than those adopted by Mr. Polk. Actuated, however, by a sincere desire for peace, and sympathising cordially with a feeble sister Republic, he sought to overcome the infatuation of Mexico by the exercise of forbearance and conciliation. He remonstrated earnestly, but respectfully, with the Mexican minister upon the absurdity of his positions, and having failed to make an impression on him, Mr. Polk despatched an Envoy to the Mexican government, with full powers to adjust and reconcile all questions of dispute. The Mexican government met this noble offer of conciliation with renewed insult, and prepared to reclaim Texas at the point of the bayonet. It was not the Texas between the Rio Grande and the Neuces that she sent her army to re-conquer and re-claim, but Texas from the Rio Grande to the Sabine. It was not a mere question as to the boundary of Texas, for which Mexico appealed to arms, but her claim to the whole of Texas, was to be thus vindicated. Impelled by an infatuation which bordered on absolute madness, they resolved to put in issue the sacred principle involved in the right of revolution, and to submit its decision to the arbitrament of war.

Whilst Mr. Polk was seeking to avoid a hostile collision by measures of forbearance and conciliation, he was not unmindful of the high responsibility which rested upon him, to be prepared to meet the threatened invasion of our soil. When the Mexican forces concentrated on the Rio Grande, they found there our gallant little army of regulars, prepared to meet them on the threshold. Whatever contrariety of opinion may exist as to the commencement of hostilities, there can be none as to the skill and energy with which the war was prosecuted after it was commenced. The summons to arms was responded to with an alacrity and enthusiasm which characterize none but freemen. Army after army was raised, concentrated, organized and marched from the remotest quarters of the Union to different points of the Mexican territory with so much rapidity and in so short a space of time, that we are at a loss which most to admire, the energy and promptitude of the executive officers of the government, or the courage, skill, perseverance and patriotism of the officers and soldiers of the several divisions of the general army. In quick succession after the first brilliant victories in the valley of the Rio Grande, village after village, town after town, city after city, province after province, surrendered to the irresistible power and courage of our brave troops, until the complete conquest of all of Northern Mexico was consummated in the ever-glorious victory won on the field of Buena Vista.

It was hoped and believed that the signal display of our power and prowess in overrunning the northern provinces of Mexico in the first campaign, would humble the pride of this stubborn and infatuated enemy and induce him to sue for peace. This expectation was not realized and the necessity of striking a decisive blow at the very heart of Mexico became apparent. To Mr. Polk himself is due the high credit of having originated, planned and arranged the expedition which was to strike this decisive blow. His plans met the approval of his cabinet and the General-in-Chief and were executed with a promptness, energy and skill which challenge the admiration of the world. The march of our troops from Vera Cruz to the city of Mexico was marked by a series of hard-fought battles and splendid victories which scarcely find a parallel in ancient or modern warfare. With the fall of the Capitol, fell the pride and power and spirit of Mexico. She was subdued, peace was conquered,

and along with it a treaty which recognized our title to Texas and transferred to us the vast territory embraced by New Mexico and California.

This is but a meagre sketch of the more important measures which were
crowded into the four years during which President Polk sat at the helm of
the government. Time alone can develop their influence upon the future
destinies of our country and of the world. We may be permitted, however,
with becoming diffidence to lift the curtain that veils the future and look for
a moment down the vista of time to see how some of these measures will
probably affect the future history of our beloved country.

In glancing the eye over the eventful administration of President Polk
the mind is arrested by two features in it which stand out in bold relief—
the Mexican War and the immense accessions of territory to our national
domain.

Need I stop to calculate or measure the amount of national glory won by
our gallant armies on the battle fields of Mexico? The voice of an astonished
world has already pronounced our eulogium. What corner of the earth, or
what isle of the ocean is so remote that it has not heard of Monterey—of Buena
Vista—of Vera Cruz—of Cerro Gordo—of Contreras—of Chepultepec—of Molino del Rey! Each one of these names is a tower of strength, resplendent
with halo of our victories, on which the eyes of freedom's votaries throughout the world are gazing with longing admiration, whilst tyrants every where
look upon them and tremble. They are so many lofty bulwarks of national
defence whose bright beacon fires proclaim to crowned heads that our sacred
honor can never be insulted with impunity. The exhibitions of moral and
physical power displayed by our countrymen, have dispelled a delusion,
under which foreign powers had long labored. They were ready to concede
that on our own soil and in defence of our homes and family altars, our
power could set invasion at defiance, but they denied to us the capacity or
the willingness to redress our wrongs, to avenge our insults and to vindicate
our national honor by seeking our enemies and meeting dangers in a foreign
land. Henceforth they will concede that although we are a patient, long-
suffering people, slow to anger and devoted to peace, yet that in vindicating
our national honor, our power is as terrible in prosecuting as in resisting an
invasion. This conviction fastened upon the foreign mind by the memorable
events of the Mexican war, will in future constitute our 'shield and buckler'
against insult or aggression, even more effectual than strong walls or frowning battlements. As the mind of the patriot runs over the long catalogue of
glorious achievements, his heart beats with quicker and stronger devotion to
his country, and his bosom swells with a loftier pride in being an American
citizen. He feels that in all the elements of national strength, national grandeur and national glory, his country stands upon an elevation which it never
before occupied. Whilst he sheds a tear to the memory of the gallant dead,
whose bones are mouldering in a distant land, his heart overflows with gratitude to the patriotic wisdom of the Statesman, and to the heroic courage and
chivalry of the officers and soldiers who accomplished so much for their
country.

But this is no more than the beginning of our national destiny—the mere
rosy tints of the early dawn, bespeaking the transcendent effulgence of the
rising sun of day. When Mr. Polk ascended the Executive chair, the march
of freedom's empire westward was bounded by the Rocky mountains. There
sat the genius of liberty on the craggy summit of this lofty battlement of nature, gazing down upon the broad Pacific, anxious to bathe her feet in its
smooth and peaceful waters. To the northwest lay Oregon, subject only to

the laws of savage Indians, and of usurping Britons. To the south-west lay New Mexico and California, in which Mexican despotism maintained a precarious dominion over the semi-barbarous tribes of mixed nations. To the south-east lay Texas, where freedom had erected her altar, but where Mexican infatuation was threatening to carry indiscriminate destruction and extermination. Four years roll away, and how changed the scene! By the magic operation of two treaties, these four empires of territory are born into the Republican family. What an acquisition! Give wings to your minds and trace around its boundaries! See it extending along the Gulf of Mexico from the Sabine to the Rio Del Norte—then westward spanning the continent, and looking upon the Pacific through seventeen degrees of north latitude, embracing the entire western slope of the Rocky Mountains and encircling with an empire of wealth and power, the mouth of the great Mississippi. Throughout this vast region nature has deposited in abundance the means of agricultural, mineral and commercial wealth, but there they were valueless for the great purposes for which God created them, until they were brought within the influence of the enterprise and industry of a free people under the wise policy of our late illustrious Ex-President. Already the tide of emigration, quickened by the miraculous accounts of mineral wealth, which reach us by every arrival, has commenced the work of peopling and reclaiming this immense territory. We may well pause to look with astonishment upon our stupendous structure of Republicanism, when this vast empire shall be filled with an industrious population, when its unbounded resources shall be developed, when State after State shall have knocked and received admittance into our Union, until our mighty Republic shall present the grand spectacle of a confederacy of sovereign States, spanning the continent from ocean to ocean. What nation upon the face of the earth will then dispute our pre-eminence in moral and physical power, in national grandeur and happiness!

But the picture of our national destiny is not yet fully drawn. In securing the long line of Pacific coast, with its noble harbors, President Polk has snatched the sceptre of commerce from the Old World, and transferred to it the New. He laid the foundation of a total revolution in the trade of the world. Henceforth we command the wealth of the Pacific and Indian Oceans. He has procured the key that will unlock the boundless treasures of the East. When the indomitable perseverance and enterprise of our countrymen shall have connected the Atlantic with the Pacific by railroad communication, (and who now doubts such a connection,) we become at once masters of the commerce of the world.—Our position will insure to us a virtual monopoly of the vast oriental trade, and in all ages this trade has carried along with it wealth and dominion. A distinguished statesman of our country has traced its history and value with an eloquence, which cannot but excite our admiration. 'Look at its ancient channels and the cities which it raised into kingdoms, and the population which upon its treasures became resplendent in science, learning and the arts. Tyre, Sidon, Balbec, Palmyra, Alexandria, among its ancient emporiums, attest the power of this commerce, to enrich, to aggrandize, and to enlighten nations. Constantinople, in the middle ages, and in the time of the Crusades, was the wonder of Western Europe; and all because she was then a thoroughfare of Asiatic commerce. Genoa and Venice, mere cities, in later time became the match of kingdoms, and the envy of kings, from the mere divided streams of this commerce of which they became the thoroughfare. Lisbon had her day, and Portugal her pre-eminence during the little while that the discovery of the Cape of Good Hope put her in communication with the East. Amsterdam, the city of a little territory rescued from the sea, and the seven United Provinces not equal in extent to one of our lesser States, became great in arms, in letters, in wealth and power—and all upon the East India trade. And, London—what makes her the commercial mistress of the world—what makes an Island no larger than our first class States, the mistress of possessions in the four quarters of the globe—a match for half of Europe and dominant in Asia? What makes all this, or contributes most to make it, but this same Asiatic trade. In no instance has it failed to carry the nation or the people, which possessed it, to the highest pinnacle of wealth and power, and with it the highest attainments of letters, arts and sciences.'

With a proper appreciation of the inestimable value of this trade, you will understand the motives which actuated British statesmen in their efforts to hold on to Oregon, and to prevent the success of our policy in the acquisition of Texas and of California. You will understand also, why they are now straining every nerve to obtain a foothold on the western continent. Great Britain was struggling to maintain the mastery over the commercial world, which she had enjoyed with undisputed sway for ages. She saw a gigantic rival rising up in the west, and she saw with consternation that that rival was guided by counsels of statesmanship, which would win from her the sceptre of commerce, unless thwarted by her active interference. The same superior statesmanship which fixed its eye upon the trade of the East, as the grand object of its policy, saw that to make that policy completely successful no further European colonization should be tolerated on the western continent. Time will attest the sagacity of President Polk in proclaiming this noble doctrine to the powers of Europe. If it shall be maintained with unshrinking firmness in the future policy of our country, our government will stand the acknowledged colossus of nations, dispensing commercial law to the world, radiating the benign influence of its free institutions to every quarter of the globe, and securing its own citizens in the enjoyment of unexampled prosperity and happiness. Each succeeding sun will rise and set upon the freest, the happiest and the most powerful people on the face of the earth—a people in whose hearts will be forever embalmed the name and memory of James K. Polk, as one of the purest patriots, wisest statesmen and greatest benefactors of our country.

The Administration, of which I have attempted to give a mere outline, came to a close on the 4th of March, 1849. The entire work chalked out for execution in Mr. Polk's Inaugural Address, and even more, had been accomplished—nothing that he had undertaken was left unfinished or incomplete. Our difficulties with foreign nations had all been amicably or honorably adjusted, and we were at peace with the world, whilst prosperity and happiness prevailed throughout our own country. With the witness of a good conscience attesting that he had faithfully discharged his whole duty, Mr. Polk with unaffected cheerfulness resigned the insignia of office, surrendered the helm to his illustrious successor, and descended into the ranks as a private citizen. His journey homeward was marked by a succession of enthusiastic demonstrations of popular approbation and attachment, which gave to it more the appearance of a victorious military chieftain returning home covered with laurels than of a private citizen seeking the retirement of a quiet home.

No man ever sought the happiness of private life with better prospects of finding it, than did Mr. Polk. With ample means to command every comfort, he had the society and companionship of a wife whose superior intellectual endowments, combined with the choicest graces and virtues of female excellence, qualified her to shed lustre upon public station or to infuse contentment and happiness into the domestic circle. How great an accession he would have been to our immediate society, where he had determined to spend the evening of his life, all who have appreciated his eminent private virtues will readily understand. Plain and simple in his manners, mild and forbearing in his temper, kind and sociable in his dispositon, liberal and tolerant in his opinions, accessible and easy in his intercourse, free and lively in his conversation, he was eminently fitted to adorn and enliven the social circle, whilst his habitual and conscientious regard for virtue and morality in all his conduct combined with his uniform reverential respect for the Christian religion, were well calculated to give weight to the influence of his example. He was a regular reader of the Bible, and a constant attendant upon divine worship. As illustrative of his private habits and opinions in connection with religious subjects, I may be indulged in quoting entire a memorandum made by him on his fiftieth birthday and left amongst his papers. It is as follows:—'Sunday, Nov. 2, 1845. Attended the Methodist church (called the Foundary Church,) to-day in company with my private secretary, J. Knox Walker. It was an inclement day—there being rain from an early hour in the morning—and Mrs. Polk and the ladies of my household did not attend church today. Mrs. Polk being a member of the Presbyterian Church, I generally attend that church with her, though my opinions and predilections are in favor of the Methodist Church.

This was my birth-day—being fifty years old—having been born according to the Family Register in the Family Bible, corroborated by the account given me by my mother, on the 2nd of November, 1795.

The text to-day was from the Acts of the Apostles chap. 17, verse 31: "Because he had appointed a day in the which he will judge the world in righteousness by the man whom he hath ordained." It was communion day in the church and the sermon was solemn and forcible. It awakened the reflection that I had lived fifty years, and that before fifty years more would expire, I would be sleeping with the generations which have gone before me. I thought of the vanity of this world's honors—how little they would profit me half a century hence, and that it was time for me to be "putting my house in order." '

In addition to the enjoyment which he anticipated in the domestic and social circle in his retirement, he had determined to employ his leisure hours in literary pursuits and in arranging, digesting and preparing the ample materials in his possession for a historical review of the political events of his own times. With such hopes and anticipations he had looked forward with pleasure to the termination of his public career as the commencement of a new era of domestic and social happiness in his retirement. To the enjoyment of such a retirement he was strongly invited by the precarious condition of his physical constitution, which had been greatly enfeebled and shattered by the excessive labors and cares of public life. When he returned amongst us we were all struck by the marks of premature old age in his personal appearance. Four years before we had seen him standing erect in our midst, in the prime and vigor of manhood, receiving the warm congratulations of his neighbors and friends upon his elevation to the highest office in the world. It was my fortune to be the organ through whom these congratulations were tendered to him. How little did I then suppose that at the end of four years I should see him return with locks vieing in whiteness with the snow and his body bending as if under the age of many years! Much less did it occur to my mind that in so short a time I should be called to stand at his tomb and recount the virtues and services of his life! But such has been the will of an all-wise Providence and we bow to it with becoming submission. He returned among us literally worn out in the service of his country, and instead of finding the years of happiness which he sought in his beautiful retreat, he returned only to mingle for a few days with his friends and then find an early grave. The dread summons, however, was not unexpected to him, nor was he unprepared to meet it. The conviction fastened upon his mind on his fiftieth birthday had never been erased, nor had he abandoned the resolution then formed—he had 'put his house in order' and through faith in the blood of a Redeemer he had made his peace with his God and was prepared to pass through the dark valley of the shadow of death without fear. After attaching himself to that branch of the church for which he had long cherished and expressed his predilection, he waited with calm resignation and composure the approach of death. Watched over and consoled in his expiring moments by the partner of his bosom, whose society for more than twenty years had thrown around his life its purest enjoyment, and by the venerable mother who gave him birth, whose prayers then as during a long life were ascending to God for his choicest blessings on her son, together with many other near and dear relatives and friends, he sunk gently and quietly to sleep on the 15th of June, 1849, to wake no more until the morning of the Resurrection. He had lived the life of an honest man, a pure patriot and a virtuous statesman—he died the death of a true Christian. For the former he has his reward in this world—for the latter a far richer reward in the world to come.

> He's gone to his home, like a well ripen'd sheaf,
> The ear in its fullness, and sear in its leaf;
> The angels have borne him with joy to the skies,
> The portals of Heaven have closed on their prize.
>
> He's gone, like the sun at the dying of day,
> When shades veil the earth as its light fades away,
> In greatness he ruled, and in glory he rose,
> When call'd by the Saviour from this world of woes.
>
> He's gone like the waters in brightness that flow,
> While verdue and flowers clothe their banks as they go,
> Till forth to the deep, in their grandeur they roll;
> He's gone to the ocean, the home of the soul.
>
> He's gone! and the nation in sackcloth is dressed;
> We mingle our tears round the place of his rest!
> Like a widow, who deeply doth mourn in her weeds,
> We linger in love round the scene of his deeds.
>
> He watch'd o'er the nation, he saw her bright form
> Arise in its beauty 'mid battle and storm;
> Our sighs, like an orphan's, are heavily drawn,
> While speaks the cold marble—He is gone! he is gone!"

Apparently, the passage of the resolution by the House of Representatives to print the Eulogy provoked quite a bit of feeling on the part of certain members of the Legislature, for a few days later Whig Representative Jo. Parsons of Knox County felt impelled to place on permanent record his position on the printing of the Nicholson eulogy on Polk:[108]

"A resolution was introduced in the House of Representatives on the 2d inst., for the purpose of having the eulogy pronounced by the Hon. A. O. P. Nicholson, relative to the life and public services of Hon. James K. Polk, late President of the United States, published, for which I voted. A reconsideration was moved, against which I voted. When voting for the resolution, and against the motion to reconsider, I was actuated by motives of courtesy, without believing the resolution to be strictly in accordance with Legislative usage. Nor did I believe it in strict accordance with the duties devolving on us as members of the General Assembly. Yet, from motives of delicacy, respect and courtesy towards the memory of a departed Chief Magistrate of our great republic, I voted to have the funeral oration delivered on his memory printed. I did not feel disposed by voting against the resolution to display what I feared might be construed as the mere opposition of an embittered partisan. I do not wish to impugn the motives of gentlemen, and hope that mine will meet with equal respect. My reasons for voting for the resolution were pure and honest. My motives for now dissenting are equally so. I therefore respectfully but earnestly beg leave to have this my dissent to the resolution, entered upon the Journal of the House of Representatives.

Jo PARSONS."

On November 12, five days after Representative Parsons had put himself on record regarding the printing of the Nicholson Eulogy on Polk, a routine resolution was introduced in the Senate directing that a strict audit be made of the accounts submitted by the public printers who were charged with the printing of the various proceedings of the Legislature.[109] Here was the opportunity for partisan politics to be invoked, and an uncompromising Whig Senator, Abraham Tipton from the counties of Johnson, Carter, Sullivan, and Washington, seized Time by the forelocks and moved to amend the routine resolution by adding the following:

"*Provided*, that the printing of the eulogy on the late President be not included in said accounts." [110]

A laconic sentence tells the story of the action of a Whig-controlled Senate—"Which amendment was agreed to." Just a few days before final adjournment of the Legislature, Senator Tipton demonstrated that there had been no political repentance on his part. While considering the bill for defraying the expenses of the legislative session, Senator Tipton moved

"To amend the sixth section of said bill by adding thereto the following, to-wit: '*Provided*, the eulogy upon the life and public services of the late James K. Polk, delivered by A. O. P. Nicholson, shall not be included'." [111]

Senator Tipton's political prejudice prevailed, with the result that

---

[108] *Ibid.*, 246–247.
[109] *Senate Journal*, 1849, 239.
[110] *Ibid.*, 239.
[111] *Ibid.*, 688.

only the *House Journal* contains the Eulogy on James K. Polk. Perhaps Shakespeare hit the nail on the head in *As You Like It:*

"... TIME is the old justice that examines all such offenders!"

In contrast to the petty politics played regarding the printing of the Eulogy on James K. Polk, there was exhibited some evidence of recognizing the desirability of Tennessee's being placed on record in regard to the erection of a monument to President George Washington. Whig Representative Elijah Thompson of Williamson County introduced the following resolution:[112]

"*Whereas,* the commissioners of the great Washington monument at Washington city have suggested the propriety of each of the States of this great confederacy placing within said monument some slab of marble or other memento, with the proper insignia or inscription to designate it; and,
Resolved, That the Governor of the State of Tennessee be and he is hereby requested to appoint some suitable person to select from the finest specimen of marble in the State, a slab with the name of the State and any other inscription deemed prudent, and have it placed within said monument."

Without any delay, quibbling, or revision of the original, the Thompson resolution was adopted on December 13, 1849.

On December 21, 1849, Democratic Senator J. W. Whitfield from the counties of Lawrence, Hickman, Wayne, and Hardin introduced the following resolution:[113]

"*Whereas,* the patriotic citizens of this State have, by private contribution, caused to be erected a suitable monument to the memory of the citizen soldiers of Tennessee, who gave their lives a willing sacrifice for their country's honor in the late war with Mexico, at a cost of $2500, with suitable inscriptions thereon; and whereas, about $100 of said contribution have been collected; therefore,
Resolved, That the sum of $1500 be, and the same is hereby appropriated out of the treasury, not otherwise appropriated, for the purpose of completing the payment for erecting of said monument; and that the Comptroller issue his warrant to Thomas D. Davenport, Solon E. Rose, Frank Buchanan, and Wm. P. Rowles, monumental commissioners at Lawrenceburg, and that they pay said money out for the erection of said monument; and that they be required to take receipts for all sums so paid by them; and that they report to the next General Assembly of this State."

The Senate, by a vote of 19 to 4, adopted the above resolution. In the House, the vote was in favor of the resolution by a vote of 59 to 5. A day or so later, Democratic Representative Jacob Adcock of Cannon County attempted to have the House reconsider its action, but he was overwhelmed by the lopsided vote of 56 to 10.[114]

---

[112] *House Journal,* 1849, 388–389.
[113] *Senate Journal,* 1849, 438.
Author's note. The item, $100, is a typographical error; the figure should be $1,000, as may be verified by comparing with Resolution No. XVIII, as finally adopted.
[114] *House Journal,* 1849, 528.

It will be recalled that the 1847 Legislature appropriated the sum of five hundred dollars for the erection of a monument to Meriwether Lewis under the supervision of Honorable Edmund Dillahunty, Dr. Samuel B. Moore, and Barclay Martin.[115] It was expressly provided in the law that the above agents should submit their report to the next ensuing Legislature, that of 1849. The report, bearing internal evidence of careful research on the part of the committee, was as follows:[116]

"REPORT OF THE LEWIS MONUMENTAL COMMITTEE

To the General Assembly of the State of Tennessee:

By the 9th section of an act, passed at the last session of the General Assembly of this State, entitled an act to establish the County of Lewis the sum of $500 was appropriated, or so much thereof as might be necessary, to preserve the place of interment where the remains of Gen. Merriwether Lewis were deposited; and the undersigned were appointed the agents of the General Assembly to carry into execution the provisions of the act, and report to the present General Assembly.

Looking upon the object to be accomplished to be one highly honorable to the State, the undersigned entered upon the duties assigned them most cheerfully and with as little delay as possible. They consulted with the most eminent artists and practical mechanics as to the kind of monument to be erected, and a plan being agreed upon they employed Mr. Lemuel W. Kirby, of Columbia, to execute it for the sum of five hundred dollars.

The entire monument is twenty and a half feet high. The design is simple, but is intended to express the difficulties, successes and violent termination of a life which was marked by bold enterprise, by manly courage and devoted patriotism.

The base of the monument is of rough, unhewn stone eight feet high, and nine feet square where it rises to the surface of the ground. On this, rests a plinth of cut stone four feet square and eighteen inches in thickness, on which are the inscriptions which are given below. On this plinth stands a broken column eleven feet high, two and a half feet in diameter at the base, and a few inches smaller at the top. The top is broken to denote the violent and untimely end of a bright and glorious career. The base is composed of a species of sandstone found in the neighborhood of the grave. The plinth and shaft, or column, are made of a fine limestone, commonly known as Tennessee marble. Around the monument is erected a handsome wrought iron rail fence.

Great care was taken to identify the grave. George Nixon, Esq., an old Surveyor, had become very early acquainted with its locality. He pointed out the place; but to make assurance doubly sure the grave was re-opened and the upper portion of the skeleton examined, and such evidences found as to leave no doubt of the place of interment. Witnesses were called and their certificate, with that of the Surveyor, prove the fact beyond dispute. The inscription upon the plinth was furnished by Professor Nathaniel Cross, of

---

[115] *Acts of Tennessee*, 1847, Chapter 135.

[116] *House Journal*, 1849, Appendix, 238–240.

Author's note. Two errors appear in the Committee Report, the given name of Lewis and the place of his birth are spelled incorrectly.

the University of Nashville. It is beautiful and appropriate. It is placed on the different sides of the plinth, and is as follows:

MERRIWETHER LEWIS,
Born near Carlottesville, Virginia, August 18, 1774,
Died October 17, 1809; Aged 35 Years;

An Officer of the Regular Army—Private Secretary President
Jefferson—Commander of the Expedition to the Oregon
in 1803-1806—Governor of the Territory of Louisiana—
His Melancholly Death Occurred where this Monu-
ment now stands, and under which rest his
Mortal Remains.
In the language of Mr. Jefferson:
'His Courage was undaunted; his Firmness and Per-
severance Yielded to Nothing but Impossibilities;
A Rigid Disciplinarian, Yet Tender as a
Father of those Committed to his Charge;
Honest, Disinterested, Liberal, with
a Sound Understanding and a Scru-
pulous Fidelity to Truth.'

Immaturus obi: sed tu felicior annos
Vive meos, Bona Republica! Vive tuos.

ERECTED BY THE LEGISLATURE OF TENNESSEE, A. D., 1848.

In the Latin distich, many of your honorable body will no doubt recognize as the affecting epitaph on the tomb of a young wife, in which, by a *prosopopocia*, after alluding to her immature death, she prays that her happier husband may live out *her* year and his own.

'*Immatura peri: sed tu felicior annos*
Vive meos, conjux optime! vive tuos.'

Under the same figure, the deceased is represented in the Latin distich as altered, after alluding to his early death, as uttering as a patriot a similar prayer, that the republic may fulfil her high destiny, and that her years may equal those of time. As the distich now stands, the figure may be made to apply, either to the whole Union, or to Tennessee that has honored his memory by the erection of a monument.

The impression has long prevailed that under the influence of disease of body and mind—of hopes based upon long and valuable services—not merely deferred, but wholly disappointed—Gov. Lewis perished by his own hands. It seems to be more probable that he died by the hands of an assassin. The place at which he was killed is even yet a lonely spot. It was then wild and solitary, and on the borders of the Indian Nation. Maj. C. L. Clark, a son of Gov. Clark of Missouri, in a letter to the Rev. Mr. Cressey, of Maury county, says: 'Have you ever heard of the report, that Gov. Lewis did not destroy his own life, but was murdered by his servant, a Frenchman, who stole his money and horses, returned to Natchez, and was never afterwards heard of? This is an important matter in connection with the erection of a monument to his memory, as it clearly removes from my mind, at least, the only stigma upon the fair name I have the honor to bear.'

The undersigned would suggest to the General Assembly, the propriety of having an acre of ground, or some other reasonable quantity, around the

Meriwether Lewis Monument, near Hohenwald in Lewis County.

grave secured against the entry of private persons. This can be done, either by reserving the title in the State, or by directing a grant to issue in the name of the Governor and his successors in office. The first mode would perhaps be the best.

All of which is respectfully submitted,

EDMUND DILLAHUNTY,
BARCLAY MARTIN,
ROBERT A. SMITH,
SAMUEL B. MOORE."

In support of the committee's report as to the difficulties encountered in attempting to locate with certainty Lewis' grave, the following letter is of interest, since the letter [117] was from the man who dug the grave in which Lewis was buried.

"Feliciana Graves County Ky.
31st Januy. 1848

*To the honorable the legislator of Tennessee
at the capital in Nashville seting*

Gent. in looking over Leighs Commercial Standard published at Hickman Foulton Co. Ky I then noticed a bill which had passed a second reading in relation to the discovery and erection of a monument over the remains of Col. Lewis. I am of opinion beyond a doubt that I can find his remains for the very good reason that I am the man that dug the grave with my own hands and there are some peculiar circumstances connected to the place that I cannot be mistaken there were six of us present when the General was buried and four of them are to my knowledge dead persons not acquainted with the above peculiar circumstances would be liable to be mistaken for there are other graves since the time the General was buried at or near the same spot. I lived within 5 miles of the place at the time the Col was buried and several years afterwards and am of opinion that it would not be a suitable place to erect a monument for the very good reason the situation of the place is such no person save huntsmen would ever see it.

Respectfully yours
JOHN McFALL"

In 1925, the Federal Government established the Meriwether Lewis National Monument to commemorate the notable services of the intrepid leader and explorer who carried the flag of his country across the Rocky Mountains and ushered in the later gigantic expansion of the Great Westward Movement of the United States. The Lewis Monument is in the Meriwether Lewis National Park located near Hohenwald in Lewis County.

A futile effort was made to erect a monument to another famous Tennessean whose patrotic fervor was sealed with his life's blood at the immortal Alamo. On January 5, 1850, Whig Representative M. J. Clay of Gibson County introduced the following resolution:[118]

"*Resolved,* that the sum of one thousand dollars be and the same is hereby appropriated out of any money in the Treasury for the purpose of erecting

[117] Original manuscript document in State Archives, Nashville.
[118] *House Journal,* 1849, 520.

a monument, with appropriate devices, to the memory of David Crockett, in the county of Gibson."

The movement seems to have died a-borning, for the official records disclose no further action on the resolution.

A progressive step was embodied in a bill introduced by Whig Representative William Heiskell of Monroe County, said bill providing for the registration of births, deaths, and marriages.[119] But vital statistics were not at the time regarded as being vital, for the bill was rejected [120] by the House of Representatives on January 23, 1850, the bill not even reaching the Senate.

Apparently Whig Representative Hawkins P. Murphy of the counties of Carter and Johnson became peeved about something, for a week before final adjournment of the Legislature he introduced the following resolution: [121]

"*Resolved by the General Assembly of the State of Tennessee,* that the committee on federal relations be, and they are hereby instructed to report a bill as early as practicable to cede that portion of the State of Tennessee known as East Tennessee, to the General Government, preparatory to its being admitted into the Union as a separate State."

His legislative confreres were of an entirely different opinion, for immediately after the introduction of his resolution it was on motion "indefinitely postponed."

For a number of years, mechanics had registered complaint about the teaching of trades to convicts in the penitentiary, alleging that such a procedure tended to degrade the mechanical professions. In an effort to relieve the odium, if any, Senator Zollicoffer introduced a bill

"To relieve the mechanic trades of Tennessee from moral, pecuniary, and social degradation." [122]

The legislative committee to which the above bill had been referred submitted the following report: [123]

"The committee to whom was referred 'the bill to relieve the mechanic trades of this State, from moral, pecuniary and social degradation' beg leave to report, that they have had the same under consideration. They have not been able to resist the conclusion, that the present penal code of Tennessee virtually wages war upon a great number of useful and thrifty mechanic arts among us. The Penitentiary is, in effect, a great manufactory, in which the dregs of every other class of society are converted into the mechanic class—in which felons degraded with infamous crimes, men even *branded* as 'infamous' by the statutes—disfranchised and outlawed for their enormities, are steadily being converted from every other pursuit in life into mechanics, and sent out to compete with, to mingle and work with, socially to connect

---

119 *Ibid.,* 530.
120 *Ibid.,* 637.
121 *Ibid.,* 752.
122 *Senate Journal,* 1849, 353.
123 *Ibid.,* 603–605.

themselves with, and to degrade our honest and toiling mechanic citizens. This is unjust. It is impolitic and incongenial with that equality of right and position which is at the foundation of popular government. To break down the independence and respectability of one class of the people for the supposed good of others, is a policy leading to the putting the feet of one class upon the neck of another, and can only be supposed worthy of a monarchy or a despotism. To suppress and socially degrade with felon labor and association, a variety of valuable industrial pursuits, and the millions of freemen who follow them, is unworthy a republic, where independent industry and independent suffrage are the bulwarks of popular liberty and prosperity. The legislation of a well regulated popular government can certainly never tend deliberately to degrade and humble one class, and a large and useful one of the people whom elevation and self respect are essential to the preservation of the government.

In Tennessee, your committee are of opinion that there are too few mechanics, and too few mechanic trades. We have among us only the simple mechanic trades, carpenters, blacksmiths, &c. whilst millions of money are taken out of Tennessee annually to pay for the products of the more complicated mechanic arts and manufactories of Pennsylvania, New York, Massachusetts and other States of the Union. Instead of depressing and socially degrading by our laws, we should endeavor to encourage the introduction of new mechanic arts and thousands of additional laborers. Perhaps, fifty thousand Collins' axes from Massachusetts are sold annually in Tennessee; steam engines and machinery for cotton and wool factories, cabinet ware, fine marble work; hats, boots and shoes, carriages, upholstery, glass and porcelain ware, cutlery, saws, chisels, hoes, and almost a thousand other things in daily use among us, are manufactured in the eastern States, and imported in large amounts, running up our importations to some $10,000,000 per year, when our whole exportations to pay for them do not exceed $8,500,000. This is a heavy drain upon us, when no State in the Union could more cheaply feed and better support the manufacturers of these articles than Tennessee. In Pennsylvania the products of the mechanic and manufacturing arts are equal to the whole products of agriculture. In New York, they are nearly as great, and in Massachusetts they are much greater; but in Tennessee whilst the agricultural crop in 1848 is estimated at $40,000,000, the products of manufacturers and mechanic arts amount to but $5,000,000. In Massachusetts there is a consumer for nearly every producer; but in Tennessee, where we so much need consumers for our vast agricultural surplus, where we so much need the products of these handicrafts, and where we have all the elements of their employment, and could feed them so cheaply, we have only about one consumer for every five producers among our industrial classes.

Your committee are earnestly impressed with the belief, that the Penitentiary system tends to perpetuate this condition of things in socially degrading the mechanic arts and driving away or deterring from coming among us men who are adding wealth and strength to other commonwealths where mechanic arts are not so oppressed with that degradation of felon labor. The very sparseness of our mechanic population, your committee believe, renders the penal system in Tennessee more invidious and injurious to mechanics as a class. Farmers would not be so injuriously affected by such a system because of their great number. But from the great body of farmers and citizens of every pursuit the felons are taken and converted into mechanics, who, being few in number are thereby seriously affected as a class.

Your committee would not, however, recommend any sudden or violent change in our Penitentiary system. They have conferred with the keeper of the penitentiary, and found that some modifications are admissable without conflicting with any interest of the State, and in view of the high considerations to mechanics above mentioned, and much to be desired.

The bill under consideration leaves much to the discretion of the keeper within certain narrow limits. It proposes certain slight modification which, in the opinion of your committee will not in any respect prejudice any public interest whatever. It is a step in the right direction. The bill is so guarded as to permit the keeper to carry the proposed change so far, and no farther, than the work upon the Capitol and other public interests will allow in safety. They therefore respectfully recommend the passage of the two first sections of the bill.

M. THORNBURG, Chairman."

The bill was passed in the Senate [124] by a vote of 18 to 4, but ran into a snag in the House of Representatives which rejected the bill by a vote of 35 to 26.[125] Two days before final adjournment of the Legislature, the bill upon reconsideration was again defeated by a vote of 33 to 24.[126]

Perhaps Alexander Jackson, Representative from Madison County, had read or heard at some time the address of Governor Aaron V. Brown on capital punishment in which was incorporated this statement:

"If the hanging of a fellow being produce no good effect on the profligate and abandoned, what impression does it make on the minds of the virtuous and orderly part of the community? From some motive, which it is perhaps impossible to specify or define, great crowds will always assemble to witness the terrible and solemn spectacle. At the appointed hour, the condemned victim, seated on his coffin, and surrounded by the swords and spears of the guard, is seen approaching on the slow-moving car of death: he is carried forward in this condition through the immense assembly until he reaches the scaffold. Here, standing on that narrow isthmus, which separates time from eternity, he makes his last and solemn appeal to the world!" [127]

At any rate, Representative Jackson believed that executions should not be public spectacles and, to help quell morbid curiosity on such occasions, he introduced the following resolution:[128]

"*Resolved,* That the judiciary committee be instructed to inquire into the expediency of requiring sentence of death to be executed within the walls of the prison, and report by bill or otherwise."

The House Judiciary Committee asked to be discharged from any further consideration of the matter which was granted.[129] A Senate bill on the subject, however, was prepared and introduced concerning

[124] *Ibid.,* 622.
[125] *House Journal,* 1849, 809.
[126] *Ibid.,* 849.
[127] *Speeches and Other Writings of Ex-Governor Aaron V. Brown,* 594–595.
[128] *House Journal,* 1849, 260.
[129] *Ibid.,* 366.

A Bill to make Capital punishments private.

Sec. 1 Be it enacted by the General Assembly
of the State of Tennessee:

That from and
after the passage of this act, that all
persons convicted of a felony which
by the laws of this State, is punished
Capitally, shall be executed privately
in the jail or jail yard, in the
presence of such persons not exceed-
-ing five, and including one or more
Ministers of the gospel, if desired by
the person to be executed, as shall be
appointed by the Court pronouncing
Sentence of death upon such felon.

Sec 2. All felons that may be hereafter
punished Capitally, shall be
executed in the County where
the offense for which they are hung,
was committed.

Public Curiosity Prevailed over Private Opinion.

which the Senate Judiciary Committee reported through the Chairman of the Committee, Senator H. S. Kimble:

"To which had been referred Senate's bill No. 172 to make capital punishment private, reported that the committee had had the same under consideration and had instructed him to report its rejection. The committee are of opinion that capital punishment by hanging or otherwise should be public, and not private, as proposed by this bill. That our progress has not yet attained that point of necessity; nor can they the committee suppose it charitable to deprive our Yankee curiosity of the luxury of seeing felons die. Besides, when defeated and baffled, would soon run into suspicion that something was wrong. When the thing is done in secret, it would tend to excite mobs and riots." [130]

The recommendation of the Senate Judiciary Committee was carried into effect on January 7, 1850, by the above bill's being rejected.[131] It appears that Senator Jackson was a bit premature, for a third of a century had to roll by before the provisions of his 1849 bill were enacted into law.[132]

Representative Samuel B. Moore of Hickman County felt that some consideration should be given to providing a suitable home for the Governors of Tennessee. With that object in mind, he introduced a resolution to the following effect:[133]

"*Resolved*, that the committee on public buildings be and they are hereby required to inquire into and report the propriety of purchasing a residence to be kept and held for the use of the Governors of Tennessee."

The official records are silent as to any further notice of the above resolution which seems to have been "chloroformed" and put quietly to sleep without even the formality of being postponed or rejected.

Thomas Snodgrass, Representative from White County, evidently thought a biennial session of the Legislature was too often; accordingly, he proposed to have it convene every four years as his resolution disclosed:[134]

"*Resolved*, That the committee on the judiciary be requested to inquire into the expediency of so amending the constitution as only to require the legislature of this State to meet once every four years, unless expressly called together by the Governor of the State for special purpose."

The House was not in agreement with the proposition, for the resolution was rejected without a record vote.[135]

Usually every Legislature has before it at least one "fool bill"; the 1849 Legislature was no exception to the general rule. Representative Seburn W. Senter from Grainger County introduced

---

[130] *Senate Journal*, 1849, 427–428.
[131] *Ibid.*, 485.
[132] *Acts of Tennessee*, 1883, Chapter 112.
[133] *House Journal*, 1849, 536.
[134] *Ibid.*, 230.
[135] *Ibid.*, 249.

"A bill to tax bachelors and increase the common school fund." [136]

On second reading, an amendment was adopted whereby "all gentlemen over the age of twenty-five years shall be declared bachelors within the meaning of this act." [137] Upon the recommendation of the Committee on Education, the bill was rejected.[138]

On the day before final adjournment of the Legislature, Democratic Senator E. L. Gardenhire made a desperate but futile effort to have adopted a resolution imploring the people of the State to select delegates to attend what was called a Southern Convention to be held in Nashville in June, 1850. The purpose of the Convention was to discuss the burning issue of the day, the slavery question. By a vote of 11 to 9, the Whig Senate refused to suspend the rule requiring a resolution to lie over one day before any action was taken.[139] This technique doomed the Gardenhire resolution, inasmuch as it was not called up on the closing day of the session.

Governor Trousdale informed the Legislature that he had nothing further to communicate, and thereupon the Legislature adjourned *sine die* on Monday, February 11, 1850. The alabaster box of ointment was opened by the respective Speakers of each House, and Mr. Speaker of the House of Representatives regaled his hearers with this parting salute: [140]

"The last official duty which I am called upon to perform, gentlemen of the House of Representatives, is to pronounce the adjournment of this body without day. But before I proceed to the discharge of this official duty, I may be permitted to present to you, individually and collectively, my sincere acknowledgments for the flattering terms of the resolution in which you have been pleased to express your approval of my official conduct. Entering upon the duties of this office, I was aware of the delicate nature of its responsibilities. I knew that no Legislative body could be entirely exempt from those feelings of excitement which are always incident to conflicting opinions in regard to all questions of State policy. But I am glad to learn that, whatever of ill feeling may have been engendered in this body, has passed away with the moment that gave it birth; and that now, upon our separation, we all feel like brothers.

Much has been done, gentlemen, during the session of the present General Assembly, for the benefit of the State at large, whilst other propositions of a general character, and interesting to many, have failed. But it is a duty, which, I presume, you all understand, to bow to the authority of the State with respect and submission. Much has been done in the way of granting charters to the public institutions of the State and much in the way of reform. Resolutions have been passed to give the State an elective judiciary, by which any citizen may find his way through the ballot-box up to the highest stations of judicial trust. You have opened a liberal hand to all the charitable institutions of the State. The deaf, whose ears have never been saluted with the

136 *Ibid.*, 243.
137 *Ibid.*, 351.
138 *Ibid.*, 445.
139 *Senate Journal*, 1849, 766.
140 *House Journal*, 1849, 861–862.

voice of harmony; the blind, who have never seen a mother's face, nor a star of the heavens; and the insane, whose reason has shot from its place like a falling star: these all have been provided for. You have taken these children of misfortune, with the fondness of a mother, you have drawn them to the bosom of the public charities and made them to feel that they have a home and an abiding place in their own native State.

Gentlemen, it is painful with me to part with you, because I know that we shall never meet again in this world; but I trust we shall meet in another and better world—in a more beautiful city where life is endless. But I feel that the pain of separation is to a great extent modified by the pleasing reflection that we are soon to return to the sweet circles of home, where wife and children have their empire—where the fires of domestic bliss burn on the altar of wedded love—where those reside whose office it is to wipe away the tears of sorrow and smoothe the blow of care, and bring back to the heart the sunshine of the spirit and point with the hand of Hope to a brighter Future.

Gentlemen, I now return, once more, my heartfelt thanks for the indulgence and support which I have constantly received from every member of the House of Representatives. Whatever may be my destiny, wheresoever I may be driven, on the tide of the future, I shall ever turn to the recollections of this day as

'The greenest spot in mem'ry's waste.'

I now pronounce the adjournment of this House without day.
So the House adjourned *sine die.*

LANDON C. HAYNES,
Speaker of the House of Representatives.

Elbridge G. Eastman,
Clerk of the House of Representatives."

The Twenty-eighth General Assembly had passed into history. Governor Trousdale's next and last Message to a Legislature was transmitted to the Twenty-ninth General Assembly which convened on October 6, 1851. That Message was as follows:

Legislative Message,* October 9, 1851

"EXECUTIVE DEPARTMENT,
Nashville, October 9th, 1851.

GENTLEMEN OF THE SENATE,
AND OF THE HOUSE OF REPRESENTATIVES:

Assembled as you are, at the seat of government, to discharge the duties with which you have been invested, it is gratifying to be assured of the health and prosperity now prevailing in our community.

---

* *House Journal,* 1851, 43–49.
  Senate Journal, 1851, 50–56.

For these blessings we are under renewed obligations to the Great Ruler of the Universe, who has watched over us, and at all times contributed with a bountiful hand to our wants.

Reports will be laid before you from the different Departments of the government of the State, and the Institutions under its control, from which you will learn their respective conditions, and the manner in which they have been conducted.

The subject of Internal Improvements is more exciting than any other likely to occupy your attention during the session. The people in each division of the State, are aroused upon this subject, and have their plans of improvement, some in progress and others in contemplation. You will be asked to extend the aid of the State, to a large amount, in building railroads and opening rivers. Beginning at the West, a railroad is in progress, or soon will be, from Memphis to Charleston, South Carolina, a portion of which is located in this State. I am not advised that any aid will be asked for that road from your body. From Memphis by Jackson to Nashville a railroad is contemplated to unite with the Nashville and Chattanooga road; this we all know would be a work of vast interest to the people, and should receive every aid the State can give it.—The Mobile and Ohio railroad, should it be made, will cross the State from South to North, west of the Tennessee river, and would be of no small importance to the people in that section of the State, affording them an additional market for the sale of their produce. The utility of a continuous railroad from the Mississippi river to the Atlantic, traversing the entire length of our State, cannot be denied. In Middle Tennessee, the Nashville and Chattanooga railroad, a most noble enterprise, a portion of which is now in operation, and the East Tennessee and Georgia railroad, now partly in operation, and nearly completed, a most admirable road, constitute an important part of the road above indicated, and guarantee the construction of the whole line of road from the Mississippi to the Eastern boundary of the State, there to unite with the road now building from Petersburg, Virginia, to the Tennessee line. The road from Knoxville to the Virginia line has been chartered and a portion of it placed under contract; this road calls loudly for the assistance of the State, both on account of its National importance, and the many local advantages which would result from it to the people of that division of the State. This road would develope the vast sources of wealth which have been concealed for ages in the mountains of East Tennessee. This delightful division of our State, abounding in all the native elements of wealth, but hemmed in on all sides by ledges of lofty mountains, which seem to forbid its intercourse with other parts of the earth, demands artificial assistance to remove the obstructions which so long have kept back the streams of wealth which would fertilize the country were those barriers removed. The line of road above mentioned would pass diagonally through the State from South-west to North-east, affording railroad communication with the Atlantic, East and South by the Virginia and Georgia roads.

This improvement would secure the travel and transportation for a large scope of country from the Valley of the Mississippi to the Atlantic, and would be a source of great profit to the stockholders in the road, besides the wealth and population it would bring into the State. The completion of this line of road would be an inducement, should the General Government determine to build a railroad to the Pacific, to make its Eastern terminus unite with the Tennessee road.

Thus our State would become the highway of nations, and the traffic between Europe on the one hand, and the East Indies and China on the other, would be conducted along this road.

Many other rail roads are in contemplation, some of which would be highly useful. The road from Nashville to Jefferson City in the State of Missouri, called the Central Missouri Railroad, would cross the Tennessee river not far from the Kentucky line, and would furnish railroad communication to the people occupying the northern section of Middle Tennessee with the Atlantic. Also the Cincinnati Railroad from Nashville through Frankfort, Kentucky, to Cincinnati, thus uniting with the north-eastern railroads and the lakes, and onward to the Atlantic; likewise the Louisville and Nashville Railroad. These roads, or at least one of them, would be of great utility, and may require the aid of the State in their construction. In addition to these, other railroads have been mentioned as likely to pass over some portion of our State. But having already treated this subject at some length, I shall particularize no others.

We are all satisfied of the benefits which would result to the

State, from a well organized system of railroad communication. But the great question is, can the State safely extend such aid to individual enterprise, as will accomplish this desirable object? This is a question alone for the determination of your honorable body. Experience has shown that partnerships between the State and individuals, in works of internal improvement, result badly. Perhaps the better plan would be, to grant liberal charters to companies composed of individuals, for the construction of railroads. Let them by their money and labor prepare the road for the rails and fixtures, and then call upon the State for aid. Should it appear from investigation that the improvements thus made, when furnished, would be profitable, let a lien be taken by the State, upon the whole stock of the company in the road as completed, and upon the rails and fixtures, to save the State from loss; then let the State loan her credit in State bonds payable at a distant day, say fifty years or less, bearing an interest of six per cent, payable semi-annually, at some commercial point in the United States. Should the credit of the State not be impaired by the issue of bonds to an amount beyond which it can safely go, the bonds will sell in market for a premium, which might be applied in the payment of interest. In this way, works of internal improvement may be constructed and put in operation, which would defray the expense of building, and enrich the individual stockholders, and the State be subjected to no cost, and but little risk in the aid she affords in the construction. I recommend to your favorable considerations, each of the roads specified above, as meriting all the aid the State can safely give, while at the same time, the interest of the State should be strictly guarded, and all necessary steps taken to secure her against loss.

A portion of your attention will be given to the subject of popular Education. This is a matter that well deserves your consideration. The system of Common Schools now in use, in many particulars may not be the best which can be devised. But I regret that I have no other plan to recommend. The amount of the fund for annual distribution is too small to meet the demands upon it, under any system that can be devised.

Upon examination, it will be found difficult to suggest a mode by which the fund can be increased, except by taxation. Are your constituents prepared to submit to a tax for Common School purposes? A more intimate knowledge of their views may enable you to judge with greater accuracy than I can do. But the indications which have come under by observation, induce the belief that such a tax would not meet the approbation of a majority of the taxable population of the State.

Impressed with this conviction, it would be improper to recommend that method of increasing the School Fund; we must wait till public sentiment shall require it, which ultimately must be the case, if ever the indigent children in our midst are to be educated at public expense.

It would be wholly useless to urge the utility of popular Education, in preserving and perpetuating our free institutions; this proposition is universally admitted, yet how little progress has been made in securing its blessings.

I commit the subject to your consideration, hoping your wisdom may devise some plan by which this desirable object may be attained.

The Bank of Tennessee is a subject in which the State is deeply interested. It has at all times been the duty of your body to examine thoroughly into the condition of this institution. At no period in its history has such an investigation been more necessary than at the present.

You remember that in this Bank is vested the whole of the Common School Fund, and the surplus revenue of deposits with the State, together with the unexpended interest thereon; and in addition to these amounts, a sum was ordered to be raised on the faith of the State, sufficient to make the whole capital five millions of dollars; yet the capital of the Bank has never reached that amount. The annual revenue of the State is likewise deposited in this Bank. The Bank of Tennessee is also used as the great fiscal agent of the State. These facts show the deep interest which the people of the State have in the faithful administration of this institution, and indicate the vigilance which should be exercised by their agents over its administration. What its present condition is, and how it has been conducted for the last two years, you will learn from a report to be made by its presiding officer.

I commend to your consideration the various acts of Assembly pertaining to this institution, for such amendments as the nature of the case may seem to require.

I am no advocate for frequent changes in the fundamental law of the State, but when defects become apparent, it is the part of wisdom to remove them, and to adopt something in their stead, more likely to answer the original design.

The interest of the State, combined with public sentiment, demand a change in the mode of electing Judges, and Attorneys General. The incipient steps were taken by the last Legislature to so amend the Constitution, as to give the election of those officers to the people direct. To consummate the measure requires the action of this General Assembly.

I commend to your favorable consideration this subject.

Complaints have been made as to the unequal operation of the revenue laws, as they affect the mercantile community. It will be your duty to look carefully into this subject, and should defects be found to exist, to apply the proper remedy.

I recommend the subject to your consideration, for such amendments as may be thought necessary.

A vacancy occurred in the office of Chancellor, in the Middle Division of the State, by the death of the Hon. Terry H. Cahal, which was filled temporarily by the appointment of Hon. A. O. P. Nicholson, who after holding the office some time resigned, and S. D. Frierson was then appointed, who now holds the office. Also a vacancy occurred in the seventh judicial circuit, by the death of the Hon. M. A. Martin, the temporary appointment was tendered to Alfred Robb, Esq., who declined it, and the Hon. Cave Johnson was then appointed, and is now in office. In the fourth judicial circuit a vacancy was made by the resignation of the Hon. W. B. Campbell, which was filled temporarily by the appointment of the Hon. Alvin Cullom. Likewise a vacancy occurred in the common law and chancery court of the city of Memphis, by the death of the Hon. W. B. Turley, which was temporarily filled by the appointment of the Hon. William R. Harris.

The office of Attorney General in the eleventh judicial circuit was vacated by the resignation of D. M. Leatherman, which was filled by the appointment of John D. Goodall, Esq. Also a vacancy exists in the office of Attorney General in the twelfth district by the resignation of J. W. Carter to take effect from the first day of October, 1851. In this last case no appointment has been made. No other vacancies have come to my knowledge, which your Honorable body can fill, since your last adjournment.

In compliance with an act of the General Assembly, passed January 30th, 1850, I appointed Doctor J. G. M. Ramsey, of Knox county, East Tennesse, Agent, to control the bonds of the State, authorized and required to be issued, in behalf of the East Tennessee and Georgia Railroad company, I caused to be issued and placed in the hands of the agent for the benefit of said company, coupon bonds of the State, to the amount of three hundred and fifty thousand dollars, payable forty years after date, bearing six per cent per annum interest, payable semi-annually in the city of New York. Doctor Ramsey has made a report, now on file in the office of the Secretary of State, which shows the able manner in which he has in part executed his trust, the law authorizing the appointment is silent on the subject of compensation to the agent, whether the compensation and expenses of the agent should be paid by the State, or by the company is not determined by the law. I would respectfully call your attention to the subject for such action as you may deem proper. The trust has been one of great responsibility, and attended with some difficulty in the execution, and should be well rewarded.

On application of the President and Directors of the Memphis and Charleston Railroad company, and in obedience to an act passed 25th January, 1850, I appointed three Commissioners to wit: William B. Grove, R. F. Mackin and James A. Rogers, qualified as the act requires, to assess the value of the interest of the State, in the Lagrange and Memphis Railroad company, and to report the same to the Governor. The Commissioners have made their report, fixing the amount at fifteen thousand dollars, which is filed with the Secretary of State. But owing to some defect in the bond for the payment of the purchase money the title has not been conveyed, but full assurance has been given that the whole matter will soon be adjusted.

In obedience to an act of the General Assembly, passed 4th February, 1848, and at the request of the President and Directors of the Nashville and Chattanooga Railroad Company, and after being satisfied that all provisions of the law had been complied with, I endorsed and guaranteed, in the name and on the behalf of the State of Tennessee, the bonds of the Nashville and Chattanooga Railroad Company, to the amount of two hundred and fifty thousand dollars, bearing interest at the rate of six per cent per annum, and payable thirty years after date. These bonds when endorsed and guaranteed, were delivered to the President of the Nashville and Chattanooga Railroad company, to the amount of two hundred and fifty thousand dollars, bearing interest at the rate of six per cent per annum, and payable thirty years after date. These bonds when endorsed and guaranteed, were delivered to the President of the Nashville and Chattanooga Railroad company.

The beautiful State Capitol now in progress of construction has, since your last adjournment, made rapid advances towards completion, owing in part to the fact that a larger amount had been appropriated for that object than on former occasions. I submit to your honorable body the propriety of making still greater allowances and completing the building with as little delay as practicable. This course would doubtless result in the benefit of the State, by relieving it from the high salary of officers employed to superintend its construction.

I congratulate your honorable body that the new State Hospital for the Insane in Tennessee is now ready, or nearly so, to be occupied. It will be for you to direct and control its management by special law. This edifice and its benevolent objects do honor to the humanity of our Legislature in behalf of many, deserving both our pity and tender care.

The General Assembly by resolution passed 13th December, 1849, made it my duty to appoint some suitable person to select from the finest specimens of Marble in the State, a slab, on which the name of the State, and any other inscription deemed prudent should be made, and to have the same placed within the great National Washington Monument, at the City of Washington. I appointed the late Girard Troost to make the selection, who after entering upon the duties, but before much progress had been made departed this life. I then appointed the Hon. Dan'l Graham, who made the selection from the quarry of Orville Rice, Esq., of the county of Hawkins. The slab is four feet long, two feet thick, and eighteen inches deep, of a dark chocolate color, highly finished, and with the following inscription: 'Tennessee—The Federal Union. It must be preserved.' The slab has been sent to the City of Washington, and the expenses paid, which amounted to three hundred dollars.

I have now touched briefly upon the subjects of State policy which I wished to lay before you, and might here close this communication. The subject of Federal relations, now occupies a very equivocal position. The first session of the last Congress was chiefly occupied in discussing the points of controversy between the different sections of the Union, and after a lengthy, heated debate, they passed a series of laws called the Compromise measures, which were intended to finally settle all the points of controversy among the different sections of the Union. Should this adjustment have the desired effect, it will be a matter of general joy throughout the Union. I deem it the duty of every good citizen to give this attempted adjustment a fair trial, and to endeavor by all honorable means to reconcile the disturbed elements, and to restore peace and harmony to the country. My views upon the subject of Federal politics have been recently freely expressed all over the State, in the presence and hearing of the assembled multitudes. I therefore deem it wholly useless, as they remain unchanged, here to express them.

In closing this communication, permit me to tender my best wishes for your success, indulging the hope that your labors may result in the adoption of such measures as will promote the lasting prosperity and happiness of the State.

W. TROUSDALE."

CHAPTER FOUR

William Bowen Campbell

William Bowen Campbell was born February 1, 1807, on Mansker's Creek in Sumner County, where his father owned a farm on which young Campbell grew up. He was the eldest child of David and Catherine (Bowen) Campbell. He completed his education at Abingdon, Virginia, where he studied law under a relative, Governor David Campbell, supplemented with law lectures by the celebrated Henry St. George Tucker. Upon his return to Tennessee, he located at Carthage in 1829 for the practice of his profession. Here he married Frances Owen, in 1835, to which union there were born seven children.

William B. Campbell came from a family distinguished for military service. In 1836, he volunteered for the Seminole War and fought with unusual bravery under Colonel William Trousdale, later a political opponent in several contests. When war with Mexico was declared, he was elected to command the First Regiment of Tennessee Volunteers, an outfit that won and merited the title of the "Bloody First." At Monterey, Vera Cruz, and at Cerro Gordo he and his men fought with a courage that rendered their leader a popular hero. Campbell's slogan at Monterey, "Boys, follow me," became well-known later when Campbell entered the political arena where he likewise won numerous victories.

In 1831 he was elected Attorney General of the Fifth District. He resigned within the year, moved to Sparta but returned to Carthage shortly, and in 1835 was elected to the Tennessee Legislature as a member of the House of Representatives. Two years later, he defeated his former military commander, William Trousdale, in a race for Congress, and repeated in 1839. At the end of his second term in Congress, he voluntarily retired to private life, resuming his law practice. In 1847, he was again called into public service, being elected Circuit Court Judge of the Fourth District by the Legislature, not a single vote being cast against him.

Three years later, 1851, he was unanimously selected as the Whig

From Portrait by Washington B. Cooper. Courtesy of Tennessee Historical Society, Nashville.

candidate for Governor. Once more, his old political adversary was pitted against him, William Trousdale who was the incumbent Democratic Governor and who was seeking re-election. For the third time, Trousdale was defeated by Campbell. At the end of his term, he declined to stand for re-election and again retired to private life. In 1853, he moved from Carthage to Lebanon and accepted the presidency of the Bank of Middle Tennessee.

In 1861, he canvassed the State in opposition to secession. A year later he was commissioned a Brigadier General in the Union army but served only a short time on account of ill health. In the fateful campaign of 1861, he had supported John Bell as the Union candidate for President. But with secession an accomplished fact, he remained the most distinguished of those few Middle Tennesseans who still remained loyal to the Union. When the war was ended, as a "conservative unionist" he worked for the return of Tennessee to the Union. He was elected as a Democrat to the Thirty-Ninth Congress and took his seat on December 3, 1866, having won out over Dorsey B. Thomas who unsucessfully contested the election of Campbell. In his short service in Congress, he gave support to the conservative policies of President Andrew Johnson. His health had been precarious for quite a time, and on August 19, 1867, he died at Lebanon and was buried in Cedar Grove Cemetery.

Governor Campbell was a man of courage and unquestioned integrity. All who knew him respected him highly. His private life was without reproach, and his public career was such as to be envied. Thomas Jefferson's characterization of James Monroe might be truthfully applied to William B. Campbell, the last Whig Governor of Tennessee: "A man whose soul could be turned inside out without disclosing a single blemish."

Legislative Messages of
Governor William B. Campbell, 1851–1853

A mere glance at the status of political parties in Tennessee in 1851 will suffice to show how delicately poised were the political scales between the Democratic and Whig parties. Most assuredly it was a case of tweedle-dum and tweedle-dee. A Tennessee political wiseacre, Cave Johnson, diagnosed the situation by saying

"Our State is the most nearly balanced in the Union, success depending mainly on the organization and activity of the party; the party out being generally successful because the more active." [1]

[1] Letter from Cave Johnson to James Buchanan, September 15, 1851. Original in possession of the Pennsylvania Historical Society.

The seven-term Congressman and Postmaster General of the United States under President James K. Polk was no neophyte in politics and knew whereof he spoke. From 1836 to 1852 inclusive, Tennessee's electoral votes in presidential campaigns had gone against the Democrats, though the Democrats generally won a majority in Congressional elections. From 1845 to 1853, it was tit for tat in the gubernatorial races. Within that period, no Governor was able to succeed himself in office. In no race for the gubernatorial chair was the differential more than 4,000 majority for either party, and more than once the successful candidate squeezed through with scarcely more than a thousand votes in his favor. In those gubernatorial campaigns, personality counted. In discussing the gubernatorial campaign of 1849, in which William Trousdale had defeated Governor Neill S. Brown for re-election, it was maintained that

"Trousdale's reputation for courage cramped the energy and vigor of his opponent . . . Neill S. Brown evidently quailed beneath the fierce look and hard face of Trousdale, and hence he failed to sustain his reputation as an orator." [2]

The 1851 election in Tennessee was regarded by both political parties as one of major proportions insofar as each party was concerned. A Governor was to be elected, and a Legislature as well. And this Legislature would have before it the election of a United States Senator to succeed Hopkins L. Turney. And, too, the State would have to be redistricted from the standpoints of congressional and State legislative representation. The political cauldron began to boil early, and a lot of "steam" was generated even before the campaign opened. Toward the middle of January, the Democrats were casting about for a man most likely to defeat the Whig candidate whoever he might be. As is nearly always the case, more than one name rose to the top of the political waters. A strong Democratic paper gave an over-all perspective in the following editorial: [3]

"THE GUBERNATORIAL CANDIDATE

We give place in our columns to-day, to a communication from Maury, advocating the claims of the Hon. Andrew Johnson as the candidate of the democratic party for Governor of the State. We have heretofore inserted a communication from Hickman, suggesting the name of Hon. Cave Johnson in connection with the same office. We have also published letters in favor of Gov. Trousdale's renomination, and have expressed ourselves editorially to the same effect. As a public journal of the democracy, we have felt it our duty to throw our columns open to the friends of all those who stand prominent before the democracy. We the more cheerfully insert the communication from our Maury correspondent, as we cordially agree with him,

---

[2] Letter from Cave Johnson to James Buchanan, August 12, 1849.
[3] *Daily Nashville Union*, January 18, 1851.

in the preliminary remarks with which he has so happily prefaced his sugges-tion. We cannot forbear saying, however, that the great body of the demo-cracy throughout the State are in favor of again elevating to the gubernatorial chair, our present able and worthy chief magistrate, the hero of three wars, who so bravely bore our banner to victory in the last canvass against one of the strongest men of the whig party. That his renomination by the convention which is soon to meet, is certain, we entertain not a doubt, and that it will be unanimous we feel equally confident. Gov. Trousdale has performed his official duties to the entire satisfaction of the people. He has claims upon his party and on the people of the State, which they are anxious to satisfy. More than all, he has always occupied strong and constitutional ground upon the great questions which have lately shaken our country to its very centre. He was among the first to occupy the platform laid down by the Georgia con-vention, and which all parties at the South seem now to occupy. The people honor him for his foresight and firmness. And their minds are made up to reward him according to his deserts."

The State Democratic Convention met in Nashville, February 25, with Ex-Governor Aaron V. Brown presiding and apparently largely determining the outcome of the proceedings. Without difficulty, Gov-ernor Trousdale was nominated for re-election and a party platform adopted. A strong appeal was made by championing the South's interest in slavery as opposed by threatened aggression on the part of the North. The provisions of the Wilmot Proviso were again condemned, but there was a somewhat timid reluctance to accept the Compromise of 1850 as a solution of the slavery controversy. The platform also contained the oft-repeated assurances of a desire for the improvement of "popular education," development of the State's natural resources, and State-aid to railroads with carefully guarded restrictions to protect the State from financial loss or impairment of its credit.

Approximately a month later, the Whig Convention met in Nash-ville on March 20, with a number of prospective candidates being boomed for the gubernatorial nomination. Among the most prominent were Gustavus A. Henry, Thomas A. R. Nelson, Robert L. Caruthers, and William B. Campbell. A brief survey of the delegates in attendance disclosed that Campbell was by far the most strongly supported of any of the candidates and, following the withdrawal of the other hopefuls, Campbell was enthusiastically nominated by acclamation. As a rebuff to past assertions by the Democrats that the Whigs were afraid or ashamed to publish a declaration of Whig Party principles, the Conven-tion formulated and published in the public press perhaps the longest "platform" ever announced by the Whigs in Tennessee, to-wit:[4]

"ADDRESS TO THE PEOPLE OF TENNESSEE
By the Whig State Convention.

FELLOW CITIZENS: The chosen delegates of the Whig party, having this day assembled in convention, to select from the body of their fellow

---

[4] *The True Whig*, (Nashville), March 21, 1851.

citizens one worthy of your confidence and support for the high office of
Governor of the State, deem it proper that you should not for one moment
misunderstand what they regard as the essential principles of our government, and consequently those by which they are guided. They would feel
that an exposition of those principles was almost superfluous, but for the
ungenerous imputations by a recent assemblage, claiming to speak for their
political opponents, that they have heretofore withheld an open and manly
avowal of them.

The Whig party of Tennessee glory in their time-honored republican
principles. For sixteen years they have spread them fairly before you, amid
oft recurring and animated political contests, and you have deliberately given
them the sanction of your hearty approbation. They are the principles which
animated the people of Tennessee in the memorable contests of 1824 and 1828,
elevating Andrew Jackson to the Presidency of the United States. Boldly
standing upon them in 1836, against the powerful name and influence of that
venerable man, who, under the then alluring counsels of Martin Van Buren,
as we verily believe, had lost sight of some of the brightest landmarks of
republicanism, which had so plainly characterized his earlier administration,
the Whigs of Tennessee fought their first great battle for *principle*, against
those who chose to follow *men* rather than measures; and you, fellow-citizens,
unswayed by power, unseduced by names, covered yourselves with a world
wide honor by adhering to your cherished principles, those borne upon the
banners of the Whig party, even against the honored Hero who had led you
to victory on so many glorious battle fields. In 1840—in 1844, and in 1848, you
again had them presented to you, upon the same Whig banners, on every
mountain, and in every valley of the State, in every mode of free and full
discussion, and against a powerful array of talent and influence, both on the
stump and in the press; and again, your judgment approved and your suffrages
triumphantly sustained the well-known principles of the Whig party. In no
national contest since 1824—nay, since the organization of your State government, have a majority of the people of Tennessee voted *adversely* to those
who became, and have been known as, the Whig party of Tennessee. In support of Mr. Jefferson, Mr. Madison, Mr. Monroe, and the earlier administration of Gen. Jackson, we were *all united*. But when, in 1836, New York
politics had obtained too great an ascendancy, and were sought to be trans-
planted upon Tennessee soil—when Martin Van Buren was presented to us
an exponent and personification of Republican doctrines, we *divided;* and a
majority of the people of Tennessee stood firmly upon the doctrines they
had been taught to venerate. Those doctrines being identical with those of
the Whigs of the Revolution, they became to be known as a part of the great
Whig party of the country. From that day to this, in no single Presidential
contest, have the principles and opinions of both political parties failed to be
thoroughly exposed and scrutinized, and in no such contest have the people
of Tennessee failed deliberately to endorse and support the principles of the
Whig party. The imputation that you have been deceived, and have voted for
principles which you did not understand, or have sustained a party which
habitually concealed its real character, cannot but imply a want of confidence
in the capacity of the people, or in their political honesty, which is truly
unworthy of any political party claiming to support the principles of popular
government, and must be legitimately interpreted, as insulting to a free and
intelligent people. If it is shown, as every citizen of Tennessee will testify,
that for sixteen years, in every Presidential contest, a majority of the people
of the State have sided with the Whig party, and our opponents declare that

during that long period the Whigs have withheld an open and manly avowal of their principles, how can we resist the conclusion that our adversaries, who call themselves Democrats, imply the charge against the people that they are ignorant and have been grossly deceived, or are debased, and have knowingly given their countenance to this gross fraud upon republican institutions.

Whigs spurn and disclaim such conclusions.—They believe in the capacity of the people for self-government. They have faith that the public judgment will correct such false assumptions upon a hearing of both parties.

Whigs believe that majorities should rule under the Constitution—that that Constitution, framed by the wisdom of our sages, should be held inviolate —that the State governments should be sustained in all their rights, as the most competent administrations for our local concerns, and the surest bulwarks against anti-republican tendencies—that the General Government should be preserved in its whole constitutional vigor, as the sheet anchor of our peace at home and safety abroad—that the Union should be revered and watched over as the palladium of our liberties—that nullification, or forcible resistance to the Constitution and laws of the land, is unsanctioned by patriotism and incompatible with the preservation of the Union—that the extreme doctrine of States' Rights, which maintains that the General Government has no right to employ force to sustain the Fugitive Slave law, should be sternly discountenanced, whether advocated by Mr. Rhett, or Mr. Niles, by Southern or Northern fanatical leaders—and that the open advocates of Secession and Disunion, whether to be found among the Garrisons, the Hales and the Tappans of the North, or the Cheveses, the Rhetts and Quittmans of the South, should be watched as formidable conspirators, deliberately plotting the destruction of the greatest and wisest government ever formed for the happiness of man.

Whigs, fellow-citizens, can point you with pride and satisfaction to a WHIG PRESIDENT and administration now at Washington, as the practical, every-day exponents of Whig principles and policy. They firmly believe that a high character for national morality—for maintaining a strict neutrality with foreign powers—for acting towards other nations as we wish them to act towards us, are essential to the permanent well being of a great popular government, such as ours. They are proud to believe and to know that this character conspicuously distinguishes the present Whig administration.

Whigs believe that the LAW is the only sure protection to the weak, the only efficient restraint upon the strong—that when trampled under foot, all government is at an end, and anarchy, tyranny and bloodshed, may be expected legitimately to follow. They are proud to point you to a Whig administration which, in the darkest perils of our country, will shrink from no responsibility, but firmly encounter every adverse event, in faithfully enforcing the execution of the laws.

The Whigs of Tennessee regard the series of laws recently passed by Congress for the compromise and adjustment of the Slavery issues, which have excited so much anxiety in the public mind, as the best which, under the circumstances, could have been adopted. They regard them as a settlement which has, thus far, saved the country in a dark and perilous crisis—a *final settlement*, if ever they are to be settled, of the dangerous and exciting subjects which they embraced. As such, they must heartily support them.

But if, contrary to this understanding, the people of the Northern States should continue to obstruct and prevent the execution of the Fugitive Slave Law—a law guaranteed by a plain provision of the constitution—the Whigs of Tennessee, whilst pledging themselves promptly to rally to the support of the constituted authorities of the country in the enforcement of its faithful observance, must warn their Northern brethren, in that spirit of hope and kindness which must subsist to preserve this Union, that a repeal, or general refusal to enforce its provisions, will at once unite all the South, and tend to a train of deplorable consequences, from which a dissolution of the Union will be the most probable dreadful result.

They will not, however, anticipate certain other outrages and insults by the North of a grade so enormous that they cannot believe the North will ever attempt to perpetrate them, and upon such mere conjectural and improbable premises, make threats of what violences they will in turn commit.

They do not believe that in such spirit the Union is to be preserved.

They do not believe that Congress will ever perpetrate the outrage of abolishing slavery in the District of Columbia against the wishes of its inhabitants, much less of attempting to abolish it in the States—or of changing the present basis of slave representation—or of prohibiting the transportation of slaves from one slave State to another—or of rejecting new States because they tolerate slavery. But should a dominent majority in Congress ever effect the diabolical work of breaking down the constitution, of palpably, intolerably and unconstitutionally oppressing any section of the people, we hold it to be their inherent right forcibly to resist such usurpation and oppression; but such resistance would be revolutionary in its character, and there is no present cause for the exercise of such a right, justifiable only in the last extremity, and when constitutional and peaceful remedies are exhausted.

Whigs believe in law—and order—and well-regulated constitutional liberty. Whigs believe in an honest and economical administration of the National and State governments. Whigs believe in a proper limitation of the power and patronage of the Federal Executive, and, in connection therewith, a wholesome restraint upon the arbitrary and unlimited exercise of the Veto power, but not in abolishing that power. Whigs believe that the country has been subjected to great inconvenience and loss in not adopting their opinions in relation to a sound, uniform currency, but they acquiesce in giving a fair trial to the experiments which are being made, content that their glorious country is prospering, as it will continue to prosper, by reason of its inherent energies, despite of less wise legislation. Whigs believe that, when, in the more prosperous periods of the Republic, the revenues of government are adequate, the proceeds of the sales of the public lands may be beneficially distributed among the States, to aid in promoting general education among the people, and perhaps other legitimate purposes. Had this policy been adhered to, it would have been of vast benefit to Tennessee. But in the present condition of the Treasury, with a heavy National debt, the result of a different line of policy, they regard the discussion of this measure, for the time being, as without practical utility.

Whigs believe that a well regulated system of Internal Improvements, embracing works of a general and national character, is eminently promotive of the public interests; and that by these operations, easy channels of communication will be opened between the States, the lines of separation will disappear, their interests will be identified, and their Union cemented by new and indissoluble ties.—They believe that our great interior Lakes and rivers are as much entitled to the public care as the harbors and coasts of our extensive seaboard—that the great valley of the Mississippi, with its large rivers upon which our vast products are floated to market, full of perils to life and property, can never have justice done it, until we are united on this subject—and that though the present heavy national debt must greatly restrict such improvements, and the hostility of our political opponents for the last few years has completely cut them off, yet, confiding in the general intelligence and public spirit of the American people, we cherish the hope that, at no distant day, this policy will be made to prevail under circumstances more auspicious to its successful prosecution than those which now exist.

Whigs are misrepresented when said to approve a high prohibitory Tariff, but they do most heartily approve a tariff for revenue and reasonable protection to domestic industry. They regard 'free trade' as an impracticable theory. We must ever expect selfish legislation in other nations, and are therefore compelled to adapt our own to their regulations, in the manner best calculated to avoid serious injury, and to harmonize the interests of agriculture, commerce and manufactures. The great mass of articles imported are foreign luxuries, and may well be taxed with moderate duties to maintain our great interests at home, and counteract a hostile policy abroad. Whigs believe that the present extraordinary inundation upon the country of foreign fabrics, will, as it did prior to 1837, prove the sure precursor of a revulsion of the monetary affairs of the country, similar to that which we had at that period. They believe it desirable at all times to provide at home a market for our own products, by promoting a policy which shall tend to build up manufacturing establishments, as consumers of our vast agricultural surplus. This they regard as especially the policy of the South, which has too long depended upon purchasing from abroad what ought to be manufactured by consumers of our own produce at our own doors.

They have therefore witnessed with the greatest satisfaction, 'the growing disposition' recently manifested by both parties in the State to encourage home manufactures, and were not less surprized than rejoiced to find this sentiment, placed in the most *recent* 'platform' of their political adversaries. They earnestly trust that henceforward no more opposition to liberal charters and whatever other reasonable incidental encouragement and countenance it may be in the power of the State to afford, to so desirable a division of labor among us, may be apprehended from that quarter. Heretofore, manufacturing charters have been again and again refused, unless encumbered by unreasonable and oppressive restrictions, such as are imposed, as we believe, in no other State in the Union. At the last session of the Legislature, a general charter was granted, which augured a more commendable appreciation of manufacturing facilities, but it is believed that in some of its provisions, less stringency is admissable, without endangering any interest of the State whatever.

Whigs have been the old and ardent advocates of an efficient system of public schools. They have endeavored to enforce the idea, that 'the grand lever which shall move the world is popular education.' They have felt regret, that our school fund has, as yet, been productive of no more decided beneficial results. They feel that it should be still enlarged; and are of opinion that had a just proportion of the proceeds of the sales of the public domain, a portion of which has recently been acquired in part by Tennessee valor, been set apart to the education of her sons and daughters, it would have been better than to waste it in paying the salaries of government officers, and other government expenses, which should be met out of the proper current revenues of the government arising from duties on those foreign fabrics which come in competition with the infant manufacture we are now trying to build up among us.

Prominent among matters of domestic policy, now attracting public attention, is the present mode of electing judges, and perhaps some other officers, by the Legislature. This mode is believed to be unsatisfactory to the popular mind, and in itself liable to objections. Respect for the intelligence and virtue of the people has ever been a cardinal point in the creed of the Whig party. Though there may be some diversity of sentiment among Whigs, yet it is believed that a large majority desire to bring the election of these officers directly before the people, who are, after all, the safest depositories of power, in every free and enlightened age or country.

Prominent, also, as matter of State policy, and deeply interesting to the people, is the subject of Internal Improvement. The Whigs believe that a well regulated system of Internal Improvement is calculated to develope the resources of the State, and promote the happiness and prosperity of her citizens, and ought, therefore, to be encouraged by the General Assembly—that the State may safely and prudently grant efficient aid to the construction of important works which are demanded by the Commercial, Agricultural, and Manufacturing interests, promoting thereby not only the interest of the people individually, but also of the State, multiplying their industrial resources, stimulating productive enterprize, and enhancing the aggregate value of property. We hail with pride the bright prospect of the final success of this cherished principle.

Such, fellow citizens, is a brief exposition of the principles of the Whig party of Tennessee. They glory in the consciousness of their rectitude. They would inscribe them upon their banners, and proudly bear them aloft in the sunlight of a great conflict. They stand before you the true friends of the South and of the Union—true to the Constitution—true to the laws under it —true to the reserved rights of the States, and true to the clearly expressed powers of the General Government.—They are poised on the medium ground of a dispassionate constitutional liberty—decided but conservative—firm but reasonable—fearless but full of chaste and well-balanced patriotism. They trust to the intelligence of the people, and labor to promote Education, Public Improvements, and a wise Division of Labor, as great popular interests. They have ever stood upon these impregnable grounds.—Your judgment has often sanctioned their patriotic opinions, and we have an abiding confidence will do so again. The conflict is with a party embracing every diversity of sentiment on some of the most vital questions involved in discussion, and with whom it is now uncertain what particular positions will ultimately obtain ascendency. The times, in our judgment, admit of no uncertain light. The perils of the country demand that parties and politicians should not only take great care to be right, but should show, by their unity of action, and clearness of expression, that they are not afraid to stand together and to show precisely where they stand."

The Compromise of 1850 was the major issue in the gubernatorial race, while important State issues relative to education and internal improvements were forced into a secondary role. Each candidate had "smelt gunpowder" in actual combat and, in that respect, neither possessed any advantage over the other. The Whig newspapers adorned their editorial page with the name of CAMPBELL and his shout to his soldiers at Monterey, "Boys, Follow Me!" In a similar vein, Democratic newspapers carried in box-car type the name of "General WILLIAM TROUSDALE, the Veteran of Three Wars." At Springfield, on April 28, the two military heroes threw down the gage of battle and entered upon a speaking tour that was planned to cover sixty-four

announced places for face-to-face discussion. The canvass, however, was interrupted by Campbell's falling victim to an acute attack of dysentery at McMinnville where the disease had reached epidemic proportions. Trousdale was forced "to go it alone" until he reached Jonesboro where T. A. R. Nelson substituted for Campbell who was unable to fill any more engagements until just two or three days before the close of the campaign.

Well, the Ides of August rolled around and disclosed that William B. Campbell had defeated Governor Trousdale for re-election, the official vote later being announced as follows: William Trousdale, 61,673; William B. Campbell, 63,333.[5] That small majority of 1,660 votes enabled Senate Speaker M. R. Hill to declare officially on October 11, 1851, that

"William B. Campbell, of the county of Smith, having received a majority of the votes cast for Governor at the recent election, was duly and constitutionally elected Governor of the State of Tennessee for the ensuing two years."[6]

Incidentally, William B. Campbell was the last Whig to be elected Governor of Tennessee.

"What beat Governor Trousdale for re-election?" was a current question on par with the hoary inquiry, "Who killed Cock Robin?" Some political commentators attributed the defeat to Governor Trousdale's rather aggressive position on "the Southern question"—slavery. Other observers thought that a wide-spread "rumor" on the part of Trousdale and some of his over-zealous supporters was a factor that helped ditch the incumbent Democratic Governor. It will be recalled that General Campbell became ill and was unable to continue the joint canvass for a considerable time. It seems that the rumor soon became current that Campbell was merely "playing 'possum," and that his illness was largely a feigned one. On that point, an ardent Whig newspaper fired a hot shot at the insinuation that Campbell was "a fraidy cat" and was seeking an alibi for not continuing the joint debate with Governor Trousdale, as originally planned and agreed upon. A blazing editorial, accompanied with a signed statement of the two *Democratic* physicians attending General Campbell, might well have been the turning point in the campaign which tipped the political scales through a "sympathy and fair play" attitude on the part of some voters. Here was the scorching challenge:[7]

"A SLANDER BEHEADED—JUSTICE TO CAMPBELL.

Gov. Trousdale, as we have been informed from various highly respectable sources, has been throwing out the impression quite broadly that Gen.

---

[5] *Senate Journal*, 1851, 59.
    House Journal, 1851, 54.
[6] *Senate Journal*, 1851, 59.
[7] *The True Whig* (Nashville), July 15, 1851.

Campbell was not too unwell to accompany him, and participate in the canvass, leaving it to be inferred that he was *afraid* to meet *him*, even in that stronghold of whiggery. 'Hearing of this slander' says the Knoxville *Register*, 'a gentleman of this city addressed a friend at McMinnville on the subject, who has procured and forwarded to his correspondent the following certificate from Gen. Campbell's attending physicians, remarking that 'Drs. Hill and Smartt are *both Democrats*, but gentlemen of high character for truth and integrity.'

'How unfair in Gov. Trousdale to give currency, by a broad insinuation, to a rumor which men of his own party over their own proper signatures pronounce '*false and unfounded.*'—Will the Democracy sustain Gov. Trousdale in such a disreputable course. Will they sacrifice their reputation for high-minded and honorable bearing by conniving at such base resort to injure a brave soldier who never quailed before an enemy of his country, or turned his back upon a sick or disabled companion in arms? Read the certificate below and then let the headless slander stalk through Tennessee to haunt those who would propagate it.'

McMinnville, July 3, 1851.

We, the attending Physicians of Gen. Campbell, having been informed that it has been rumored in East Tennessee, to his prejudice, that he was not much indisposed—that he was not disabled by disease from prosecuting the canvass—or that he was merely feigning disease to avoid the contest, take great pleasure in pronouncing all such rumors or insinuations *false and unfounded*. We have been in constant attention on the General for the last two weeks, during the greater portion of which time he has been, not only unable to go on with the canvass, but utterly unable to leave his room at all, and barely able to leave his *bed* for a moment at a time.

His disease is acute dysentery or flux—a disease than which none is more painful or effectually disables the patient from active exertion. We know that he has been and is now, unable to get about, nor do we think it at all probable that he will be able, before the election, to resume the canvass with any safety, and we shall so advise him.

M. HILL
THOMAS C. SMARTT."

A dyed-in-the-wool Democratic paper attributed Democratic defeat to apathy, indifference, and a failure of certain hitherto Democratic counties to do their duty on election day:[8]

"The Legislature.

The whigs will have a majority on joint ballot of ten—seven in the Senate and three in the House.

For this result they should pour out their most fervent thanks to the *democracy* of

Maury and Giles.
Of Giles.
Of Humphreys and Benton.
Of Jackson, Overton, Fentress, White and Van Buren.
Of Monroe, McMinn and Polk.

[8] *Daily Nashville Union*, August 19, 1851.

Of McMinn.
Of Bradley.
Of Hawkins.
Of Hawkins, Greene and Washington.
Of Washington, Sullivan, Carter and Johnson.

In each of these Representative and Senatorial Districts, there is a decided democratic majority, yet strange to tell, whigs have been elected! Verily, verily,—it is too bad to talk about.

The Governor's Election.

The 'Banner' and 'True Whig' have counted up the votes for Governor in all the counties, but Carter and Johnson. Here is the result:

Campbell 61,065
Trousdale 60,459

Campbell's majority, ... 606
The whig majority in Carter and Johnson two years ago, was. . 724

Supposing it to be the same now,
Campbell's majority in the State will be. 1,330

Why didn't you count them yourself?—says a friend at our elbow. Couldn't afford it—indeed we couldn't . . ."

A further Whig diagnosis regarding Governor Trousdale's defeat was as follows:[9]

"THE LATE CANVASS.

Some of our democratic contemporaries are speculating upon the *causes* of Gov. Trousdale's defeat. They attribute it to various causes, in part or in whole, none of which, in our humble judgment, is the *true* one. The main cause, as it appears to us, may be summed up in few words. The active, leading members of the Democratic party, Gov. Trousdale among them, took a position upon the great, exciting question of the day, in which the masses of their party did not concur. And though Tennessee is whig by a small majority upon leading party issues, and the battle might have been won by us upon these issues, if they had been fairly brought out, and the public mind excited to action upon them, yet the ultra tactics of our opponents threw the burden of controversy necessarily, in the main, upon the merits or demerits of the PEACE measures of the last Congress—the relative propriety of yielding to the Compromise a hearty, uneqivocal, EFFICIENT support, or a complaining, reluctant, *enduring* 'acquiescence,' calculated to engender anew the elements of sectional strife, and re-open a dangerous and unprofitable sectional controversy. The great body of the masses of the Democratic party in Tennessee, as we have ever maintained, are like the masses of the whig party, conservative to the core—firmly resolved to maintain *at once* the integrity of the Union, and the rights of the south, against all assaults, from whatever quarter—standing immoveably upon the old Republican basis of conservative, Constitutional rights. Hence, it could not be expected, that they would *labor* cordially and *unitedly* together, for the success of those who could see nothing wrong in the proceedings of the first Southern Convention, which embodied

---

[9] *The True Whig*, (Nashville), August 21, 1851.

the abstract doctrines of old South Carolina nullification, directly at war with every principle of Republican conservatism.

The victory is most auspicious and important. We render the homage of our devout thanks to a beneficient Providence for the additional evidence we have of the preservation in its integrity of our peerless and thrice happy American Republic, in this signal triumph of a wise and pacific policy, over the policy of inflamatory, sectional, partizan agitation. To Gen. Campbell, too much praise cannot be awarded for the part he acted in the brilliant campaign by which it was won. Acting under the guidance of his eminently sound and practical judgment, his ardent, generous, patriotic impulses, and his intrepid resolution that invariably pursues the *right*, in whatever direction it leads, his positions and arguments were thoroughly sound and conservative, in hearty and efficient support of the Constitution, and the laws enacted in pursuance thereof, and at the same time unyielding in the maintenance of Southern rights upon the recognized basis of the compromise; and but for some untoward features in the canvass, resulting from the infatuated and impracticable policy of those in other States calling themselves whigs, (but who, if they insist upon making these impracticable abstractions the rule of their action, cannot continue to be regarded as whigs,) his majority would doubtless have been two or three times as large as it is.

We may again advert to this feature of the canvass, and the Jessuistical policy of the Democratic party in connection with it. Suffice it, now to say, that free-soil and anti-slave law agitators will find no more formidable and determined adversary, in the prosecution of their infernal and disorganizing schemes, than is Gen. Campbell."

On October 6, 1851, the Twenty-Ninth General Assembly convened in Nashville with a Whig majority in each legislative branch. Without difficulty, Whig Senator M. R. Hill from the counties of Gibson, Carroll, and Dyer was elected Speaker of the Senate and Whig Representative Jordan Stokes of Wilson County was elected Speaker of the House. It was a different story, however, when the election of minor officers of the Senate were to be made. It required fifty-seven ballots to elect the Engrossing Clerk, Charles E. Ready,[10] and forty-nine ballots to elect a Principal Clerk,[11] H. H. Harrison. Fifteen candidates were nominated for Doorkeeper, requiring thirty-six ballots before a choice was made in the person of Isaac C. Lane.[12] A similar situation existed in the House of Representatives. It required thirty-three ballots to elect Richard B. Cheatham as First Assistant Clerk of the House of Representatives[13] and thirty-six ballots to elect Pleasant M. Senter as Second Assistant Clerk.[14] Twenty-one hopefuls put in their bids for Doorkeeper, and on the eighteenth ballot G. W. Turk was named.[15]

On October 11, 1851, in joint convention the Legislature declared

---

[10] *Senate Journal*, 1851, 33.
[11] *Ibid.*, 19.
[12] *Ibid.*, 45.
[13] *House Journal*, 1851, 18.
[14] *Ibid.*, 28.
[15] *Ibid.*, 36.

that General William B. Campbell had defeated Governor William Trousdale by a majority of 1,660 votes for the governorship of Tennessee.[16] A joint committee worked out details for the inauguration which took place, on October 16, at the McKendree Methodist Church, with the oath of office being administered by Honorable Judge Thomas Maney.[17] On the day following the inaugural exercises, Whig Representative R. E. Thompson of Wilson County introduced the following resolution:[18]

"Resolved, by the General Assembly of the State of Tennessee, that in the procession attending the inauguration of the next Governor of Tennessee, the Governor shall walk, and the members of the Legislature shall ride in open carriages."

The Inaugural exercises followed the usual procedure characteristic of such occasions. Retiring Governor William Trousdale delivered the following valedictory:[19]

"Gov. Trousdale's Valedictory

GENTLEMEN OF THE SENATE,
    AND OF THE HOUSE OF REPRESENTATIVES:

Two years ago I assumed, in obedience to the express will of the people of Tennessee, the discharge of the duties of their Chief Executive officer.

In cheerful obedience to the same will, I am now here to surrender to those who gave it, all the authority with which I have been invested in that capacity.

I rejoice in the conviction that the people with whom I have thus been connected, are in the enjoyment of the highest prosperity and the greatest happiness, and that they are rapidly accomplishing a glorious destiny.

The time has come when they must develope their immense mineral and agricultural riches; when they will encourage manufactures, and perfect the organization of their society by adding to the devotees of the plough, those of the loom and the anvil. The soil of Tennessee is so fertile, and her geographical boundaries so large, that her interests will be, in my humble opinion, best promoted by an extensive and efficient division of her productive labor.

---

[16] Senate Journal, 1851, 59.
[17] Senate Journal, 1851, 75.
    House Journal, 1851, 76.
[18] House Journal, 1851, 78.
[19] The True Whig (Nashville), Oct. 17, 1851.

It has become our duty to retain, if we can, within our limits, all those who are born and reared amongst us, by furnishing them with the means of honorable and comfortable subsistence—by affording to the rising generation sound religious, moral, and intellectual instruction—in a word, by enabling the successive generations to better their condition, and to gratify all their reasonable aspirations.

Even a partial system of Internal Improvements will, I am very sure, if put into successful operation, soon act benignantly throughout our whole State. The millions of persons within our borders cannot remain stationary. Their watch-word must, and I doubt not will be 'onward.'

Scarcely three quarters of a century have passed away since the savage and the beast of the forest bore sway over the spot on which we now are assembled, in perfect security—over yonder lofty eminence that is adorned by an edifice which would have commanded the admiration even of the masters of Grecian and Roman architecture—over this whole city, now having its churches, academies, schools and public charities; its warehouses, filled to overflowing with rich and precious merchandize—over its splendid private residences, adorned with taste, and filled with comforts and luxuries.

Every patriot will fervently pray that these blessings may be perpetuated to our descendants until time shall be no more! They are the offspring mainly of our peculiar form of government, embodied into a written constitution, and adopted by the people. We are now a confederation of thirty-one free, sovereign, and independent States. Our federal constitution secures the enjoyment of certain rights to each of these States, and to every citizen thereof.

It is my solemn conviction that a sacred regard for all these rights will preserve our Union wholly unimpaired to the most distant ages. An infringement of these rights by any one of these states, or strong combination of citizens thereof, will engender discontent, and at last beget distrust and alienation in the rest; and if obstinately persisted in, may induce large numbers even seriously to question the value of the Union. Whilst, therefore, we should look upon even a possible dissolution of our Union with horror, we ought tenderly, earnestly, and almost sternly to admonish all those whose fanaticism, folly and treason are leading them estray, to beware, how they disturb or impair the clearly defined constitutional rights of others, especially where they are left in the full enjoyment of their own.

Many years have elapsed since I first became connected, in an humble way, with the affairs of our beloved country. Most of my contemporaries have passed from the public stage. At intervals throughout this protracted period, I have been employed in her service, with a heart always full, I trust, of devotion to her honor—to the perpetuity of our Union—to the security of the rights of the people, and to the increase of their wealth and power, and the public interest.

All those who are most dear to me on earth are clustered around me upon the soil of their native Tennessee.

In my earliest manhood, and riper age, I gave my small service, with a willing heart, to our common country. I shall scarcely forget my youthful affections in my declining years.

Permit me to express the earnest wish which I cherish, that my distinguished successor may discharge the duties which will be devolved upon him, with satisfaction to himself and with signal benefit to his patriotic and generous constituents."

At the conclusion of Governor Trousdale's farewell remarks, the newly-installed Governor, William B. Campbell, delivered his Inaugural Address:[20]

"GOV. CAMPBELL'S INAUGURAL ADDRESS

About to enter, fellow citizens, upon the discharge of the duties of the office to which I have been elected by the votes of the people of Tennessee, custom makes it incumbent upon me to foreshadow on this occasion the policy by which I shall be governed in the administration of its affairs. Unaffectedly diffident of my own abilities, I can only promise, in the outset to apply with moderation and firmness whatever of experience and judgment I may possess to the promotion of the best interests of the State, relying upon the legislative department for cordial co-operation, whenever my recommendations may be deemed salutary and judicious.

In this country, the people are, as we all know, the source of all political power, and the constitution and laws of the General Government and of the several States are but the reflex of their will. How all important is it, therefore, that their opinions should be intelligent and enlightened! I shall not pretend to assert that the effect of education is to exempt a people altogether from crime, or sin, or weakness. Educated men are very often wicked men, and enlightened nations are not always free. But I do insist that in a government

[20] *Ibid.*

of liberty and equality—liberty, restrained by law, add equality of political rights—the surest way to perpetuate both, is to place the means of education within the reach of every citizen. It has been so much the custom of speakers and writers, candidates for office and incumbents of office in this State, to prate about education and its importance, that the people are apt to listen or to read, with an incredulous smile, or a half suppressed sneer. But let us, gentlemen of the Legislature, endeavor to accomplish something that will remove their doubts, and turn their ridicule into approbation. I sincerely trust that it will be your fortune to signalize your names and labors by the establishment of a liberal, effective and general system. The object is by no means unattainable. Other States have succeeded in their efforts, and profiting by their example, why may not Tennessee achieve a like result? *That* will be a proud day in her annals, when no man shall be found within her limits who is unable to read or write; and, to be instrumental in accomplishing so great an object, may well satisfy the ambition of the most distinguished amongst you.

The progress which has been made by several of our sister States, within the past few years, in railroads—that most important branch of internal improvements—is astonishing; and if we do not bestir ourselves in earnest, and speedily, we shall be left far in the rear in this noble contest. We have made a highly creditable beginning, it is true, but much remains to be accomplished to place us in the front rank, to which we belong from our position and resources.

If any one will take up and examine a map of our country, he will be struck with the commanding locality of Tennessee.

Situated not far from the centre of the representative population of the Union, and in her whole length occupying almost one-third of the distance from Albemarle South on the Atlantic, to the north western portion of Arkansas, her borders are touched by six States, and separated from two others only by the Mississippi River. To travel from the colossal North-west to the South-east, or from Texas and Louisiana to New York or Massachusetts in a direct line, you will be obliged to pass through her limit. Engineers are beginning to discover that the cheapest routes for railroads are those which approach as near as possible to an air-line, and when this rule comes to be generally adopted, our State will be found in the way to almost every important portion of the Union. She is placed, moreover, just between the provision-raising and the cotton-growing regions, uniting in herself many of the advantages of both; and thus central in position, and temperate in climate, escaping the rigors of a northern winter, and exempt from the diseases of a southern summer, she seems marked out for a great and glorious destiny. But as if to take away all excuse for failing to secure this destiny, she possesses, in addition to the advantages of her geographical position, natural resources within her borders, unsurpassed by those of any other State in the Union. Her coal beds are abundant; her iron ore inexhaustible, and equal in quality to any in the world, while her timber, of the most valuable kinds, cannot be consumed for centuries to come. These advantages she has too long neglected; these resources are, in a great degree, yet undeveloped. While her character stands high in the estimation of the country for her military prowess and political intelligence, she has been outstripped in the construction of railroads—so important in their social, moral and commercial effects—by several of her younger sisters. The *sixth* State in point of population, and amongst the *first* in natural advantages, she is yet only the *eighteenth* in respect to the number of miles of railroads within her borders—a kind of Internal Improvement almost absolutely necessary to her, as many of the most valuable and productive portions of her territory are shut out from profitable markets by the want of the means of transportation.

Your constituents, gentlemen of the Legislature, are giving much of their attention to this great subject; and I am satisfied that they will approve and ratify any measure you may adopt, which shall be liberal and judicious. After much reflection I have arrived at the conclusion, that the people of Tennessee would be willing to see the credit of the State brought to the aid of individual capital and enterprize, whenever it can be done without serious danger of loss, and in undertakings of a public character, which are calculated, beyond doubt, to develope the resources of the State, and to increase the general prosperity. To adopt the best plan to carry this object into effect will require deliberation and care on your part, but I sincerely hope that something may be done, bearing at least, a reasonable proportion to the extent and position, the advantages and resources, the prospects and destiny of our beloved Commonwealth.

In the successful establishment and the subsequent career of the government of the United States, a phenomenon has been presented without a parallel in the history of the world. A weak and wide spread colony, the offspring of a higher and holier motive than the mere spirit of adventure, found itself, after years of filial affection and devotion, compelled to submit to continued and heartless aggressions, or 'to take up arms' for the maintenance of those rights to which they were entitled even under the British constitution, and which had not been shorn of a jot or tittle of their sacredness or importance, by the habits and trains of thought of a young, vigorous and distant dependency. The struggle was unequal, but with justice and Heaven on our side, it was ultimately decided in our favor; and novel in its form, and the result of the *compromise* of conflicting opinions, a Republic sprang into existence, unrivalled by all governments either ancient or modern bearing a similar appellation.

It is well for the desponding patriot to recur, now and then, to 'the clouds and darkness' which rested not only upon the pathway of those who in a civil and military capacity brought about, and successfully prosecuted, and terminated the revolution of 1776, but also upon the efforts of the true hearted, who labored unceasingly to shape its results into the form and consistency of a Government of Union and of Law. In the one case they had to contend, with a comparatively small force, scantily clothed and fed, and poorly armed, against the bristling battalions of a mighty empire; and in the other, with timid counsels, open or secret opposition, and opinions as various as the different tints of a Northern winter and Southern autumn. The unnatural foe—the victors in a hundred European battles, were beaten in many an ensanguined field, and finally overcome, while in the civil contests the irresolute, the desponding and the treasonable yielded to the power of persuasion, of argument, and truth, or slunk away to more congenial scenes.

Even after the establishment of our Government, and especially during the administration of the older Adams, the fears of many good men were excited for its efficiency and continuance. The spirit of party assumed almost a fiendish aspect, and in the bitterness of crimination and recrimination, went far beyond the epithets and slang of modern political warfare. But the patriotism and good sense of the American people carried them safely through this portentious period, as well as through subsequent and alarming trials, and until recently the whole country had come to believe that a smooth and easy path was before us to perpetual peace, prosperity and renown.

I have referred to these epochs in our history, fellow citizens, with a two fold object—to show that even our Government—Heaven favored as it was— did not come into existence, or continue for any length of time, without difficulty, danger and trial, and that through all, we passed safe and united, by the aid of Providence, and the good sense and patriotism of the people themselves, who being the rulers as well as the governed, are the persons to suffer from anarchy, discord and disunion.

Another epoch of danger and difficulty has been upon us.

It would ill become any man of sense and observation to deny, that in the last two years, a momentous crisis has arisen in our country, one which has caused the heart of the patriot to sink within him, and was well calculated to dampen the ardor of even the most hopeful. Excitement and apprehension pervaded the land, and the 31st Congress assembled amidst despondency and gloom. But fortunately for us and our children, a band of thoughtful, patriotic and wise statesmen was found in that body, who gave their days and nights to the work of evoking from the discordant and alarming elements around them, a spirit of reflection and conciliation, which might spread abroad its benign influence, and rescue our beloved country from the horrors that threatened it. The celebrated compromise measures were the result of their labors; and we in Tennessee, whose citizens yield to no portion of the country in devotion to the Union, should be ready to render all honor to the statesmen and patriots who projected and carried them through; and to the present Executive of the United States who has so nobly sustained them. He has proved to be the man for the crisis. Calm and thoughtful, firm and decided, he rose above the exciting scenes by which he was surrounded—above all sectional considerations, and guided by the polar star of his political faith— the constitution of the United States—and looking alone to the great interests of the whole country, he announced his adherence to the 'Compromise' in terms which could not be mistaken, and which were unpalatable alike to the 'higher law' men of the north, and the secessionists and disunionists at the south, but which poured gladness and joy into the hearts of the moderate and patriotic every where. All honor, therefore, to Millard Fillmore, and his able and distinguished cabinet!

I rejoice to find, that since the passage of those measures, reason is again resuming her throne, and that the people are evincing the intention to maintain the constitution and the Government as they were established by their forefathers. And how could this be otherwise, when their calm judgment has had time and opportunity to act? Who are to be the sufferers by disunion and anarchy and civil war? Not a royal dynasty, from whose cruel and oppressive hands a sceptre is to be wrested—not a reigning monarch, whose crimes are to be punished, or whose inefficiency or weakness is the cause of existing evils—not a hereditary nobility, whose offices and honors are beyond the hope of all not belonging to their favored class—no, no—but it is the people themselves. It is upon their heads and the heads of their wives and children that the structure must fall—if fall it should—whose foundation was laid amidst privations and trials, by the forethought and firmness of their ancestors, and which has since attained such magnificent proportions and so towering a height, as to attract the attention and admiration of the whole world.

When we look calmly and thoroughly at the matter, it must strike us as idle and insane to talk about seceding from or dissolving the Union, in quiet and in peace, by consent. *This is impossible.* Civil war will inevitably and naturally follow the one or the other. Secession is separation, and, disguise it as you may, it implies and intends separate organization and a separate government. Should one State prove successful, others would seek to follow the example, and, in the course of time, we should probably have thirty or more petty republics, wrangling and quarreling and fighting—for our people cannot quarrel long without fighting—until some ambitious leader taking advantage of the universal disorder, might succeed in consolidating the dissevered parts into a central and unrepublican government.

Pregnant with evils as great if not more disastrous would be the establishment of two confederacies—the Northern and Southern Republics—even if they could be established peaceably and by mutual agreement. The very cause of separation would prove a constant source of irritation, and being fomented and aggravated by conflicting interests and dissimilar habitudes and modes of thought, would soon bring about the usual results of fraternal discord, jealousy, hate and mutual wrongs, and terminate in a bitter and bloody war, alike melancholy and deplorable for the victors and the vanquished.

But the details of such a state of things would be painful, and let us draw the curtain, therefore, upon the horrors which lie beyond the time, but which will follow close after, when this great and united people, as if tired of happiness, prosperity and renown, should consent to pull down the pillars of the Constitution and the Union, and pass, infuriate and insane, over the shattered fragments, to dip their hands in each others' blood.

The 'compromise measures' have averted these evils from our heads, and I am convinced they will continue to exert a beneficial influence the more they are discussed, and the more the sound sense and patriotism of the people are appealed to. While I have the honor to occupy the position of Chief Magistrate of Tennessee, I shall support and sustain them by all the means in my power, because I believe that their continuance on the statute book will promote prosperity and harmony, while an interference with them will inevitably produce agitation, mischief and misery.

I have thought it not inappropriate, fellow-citizens, to devote a large portion of my remarks, on this occasion, to this important subject, especially as my conviction is strong that, an overwhelming majority of the people of Tennessee, are earnestly opposed to either dissolution or secession, and that they would expect, therefore, an expression of opinion from the man who is about to assume the office of their Chief Magistrate, so soon after the excitement and trial through which the country has passed.

I regret, fellow-citizens, that it was my fortune to be brought into conflict upon the political arena with my worthy competitor—especially with one so distinguished in the military history of our country, who by his gallant conduct in war has won distinction for himself, and shed honor upon the escutcheon of Tennessee, already bright with the deeds of her illustrious chieftains. I honor him, as I doubt not do the people of our State, for his virtues as a citizen, and his gallantry as a soldier.

In conclusion, fellow citizens, allow me to express my gratitude for the honor which has been conferred upon me by my native State, and to say that I shall strive strenuously to prove worthy of it, and to obtain that best reward of a public servant, the approbation of my constituents."

After the delivery of Governor Campbell's Inaugural Address and previous to the transmission of his regular message to the Legislature, the latter body marked time by the proposal of various resolutions, the appointment of the usual committees, and the introduction of numerous bills upon various and sundry topics. Two weeks after his induction into office, Governor Campbell transmitted to the Legislature his formal Message which was as follows:

Legislative Message,* October 28, 1851

"FELLOW-CITIZENS OF THE SENATE AND
HOUSE OF REPRESENTATIVES:

The message of my predecessor at the commencement of the session, has placed before you very fully, official information of the state of the government. Yet, in deference to the usages of the State, I submit for your consideration such views as I entertain in respect to the important matters of legislation to which the public good would seem to invite your attention.

You wield the whole legislative power of one of thirty-one sovereign States, united in the most powerful republican confederacy on the face of the earth. In discharging your duties as legislators, your action will necessarily have relation in some degree to the National as well as to the State Government; for such is the structure of our institutions, that both the National and State Governments, endowed with sovereignty within their respective spheres, derive their powers from the same great people, in whom at least rests the real, the ultimate and the supreme sovereignty.

In such a government, and one which has grown to be of vast extent and diverse interests—the injunction of the Constitution of the State 'to encourage knowledge, learning and virtue,' and 'a well regulated system of Internal Improvements'—as 'being essential to the preservation of republican institutions,' and 'calculated to develop the resources of the State, and promote the happiness and prosperity of her citizens,' cannot but be regarded as wise and patriotic. It is by all conceded to be the obvious duty of the legislature to promote and encourage education. A faithful observance of the constitutional provision, making the common school fund a 'perpetual fund, the principal of which shall never be diminished by legislative appropriations,' may doubtless be expected at your hands. I would, however, invite your careful examination into the best mode of carrying out another portion of the same fundamental law, which requires that 'the interest thereof shall be inviolably applied to the support and encouragement of common schools throughout the State, and for the equal benefit of all the people thereof.' It is

---

* *Senate Journal*, 1851, 124–131.
  House Journal, 1851, 147–154.

deeply to be regretted that the fund is not larger or more effective. It is much to be desired that some plan could be devised by which its benefits could be so distributed as to secure an education to all who are really unable to procure one. But, coming as you do fresh from the different counties, and fully enlightened as to the sentiments of your respective constituencies, I submit the question of a modification of the present school system to your decision, merely begging to impress on you the propriety of a free interchange of opinion, and an attentive consideration of the whole subject.

No State has more to promise itself from 'a well regulated system of Internal Improvement' than Tennessee, geographically placed in a vast interior, far distant from ocean and lakes, and the great marts of commerce, the heavy products of our labor slowly wend their way to distant markets, burdened with great costs, risks, and delays of transportation, while the fabrics of other countries reach us in return, taxed with the profits of a hundred hands through which they must pass before they touch our borders.

We possess in a remarkable degree the elements of wealth; but being cut off from commercial intercourse, they remain comparatively undeveloped. The soil teems with a superabundance of agricultural products; emboweled in the earth lie inestimable mineral treasures; the water power of the streams, the timber of the forests, the variety of staples, and the excellence of the climate combine to give us a capacity for population and wealth, rarely to be met with elsewhere. But it is worthy of remark that other States less favored appear to have outstripped us. Why is this so? The last census returns show that our increase of population within the last ten years has been twenty-one per cent., whilst the average increase for the United States has been thirty-five per cent. It would seem that where Railroads have been built, there has been a rapid development of population and resources. Within the period above referred to, Georgia has increased in population thirty per cent; New York twenty-seven per cent; Pennsylvania thirty-one per cent; Ohio forty-one per cent; Indiana forty-four per cent; Illinois sixty-eight per cent, and some other States still more largely.

Rivers and Railroads beyond our borders turn the currents of travel around and from us, diverting to other fields masses of capital and skilled labor in search of employment. A Railroad from Louisville to Nashville, affording a passage in six hours, at a cost of from three to five dollars, would introduce thousands of sturdy and skillful laborers from the teeming thoroughfares of the North-west, who now, encountering a stage passage of thirty-six hours, at a cost of fifteen dollars, turn aside from what they regard as an impenatrable interior. And so it would be at each end of the great thoroughfare from central Virginia through East Tennessee to the Mississippi river at Memphis, or one from the sea board at Charleston and Savannah through Middle and West Tennessee to the Madrid Bend; or from Mobile or New Orleans through West Tennessee to the Ohio river and the lakes.

Our vast coal fields, which lie undisturbed, while our pig iron seeks founderies and rolling mills erected upon the coal fields of Pennsylvania and other States, and while our cotton and wool are transported to still more distant manufactories, would then be thrown open to the purpose for which they were designed, and our mountains and valleys would resound with the busy clang of hammers, looms and spindles. A wise division of labor would ensue; consumers of the farmer's produce would take at good prices all his surplus products at his very door. Every portion of the State would be brought into close proximity with good markets, and the value of lands would be greatly enhanced. The results as shown by other States, which have constructed such roads, and to the details of which I invite your attention, are no less astonishing than cheering to the friends of Internal Improvements.

The public works indicated are invited by the approaches of the neighboring States of Virginia, South Carolina, Georgia, Alabama, Mississippi, Louisiana, and Kentucky, all of whom it is gratifying to observe, are pointing their great roads towards Tennessee. South Carolina and Georgia, as you are aware, have already penetrated our borders; Virginia is pushing work rapidly to the line; Kentucky, Alabama, Mississippi and Louisiana, are earnestly moving in the same great system of public works. We shall have but a small part to be accomplished in the immense network of Railroads of which Tennessee will become the centre; but this small part will be sufficient to tax very greatly the energies of our people. It will require many years and large expenditures to accomplish it; but when done it will return the expenditures ten-fold, fully develop our vast resources, and ultimately render Tennessee one of the most prosperous and powerful States in the confederacy.

Individual enterprise, assisted by the credit of the State, has already accomplished much towards it, and show how the remainder may in the main be effected. Without demanding a dollar from the State Treasury, or requiring any guarantee without the most ample indemnity, the Nashville and Chattanooga company have raised abundant means for completing that road, more than forty miles of which are already finished, and the remainder expected to be completed in another year, a total distance of about one hundred and fifty miles. Individual enterprise, assisted by the State, has already completed about forty miles of the East Tennessee and Georgia road, and the work is rapidly progressing. Individual enterprise has also taken the lead, and thus far without the aid of the State has made a commencement upon the East Tennessee and Virginia road, another great link in the important chain through the valleys of East Tennessee. About $2,600,000 have been subscribed to the Memphis and Charleston road. Over $2,000,000 to the road from Louisville to Nashville, and about $150,000 to the road from Nashville to Columbia.

All these works deserve the countenance of the State, and some of them will, to a greater or less extent, no doubt, require in some form a loan of the credit of the State. Individuals should in all such enterprises take the lead. They are entitled when the works promise to be of public utility, to liberal charters. The State ought not herself to engage in them, but when it is manifest that the works are important to the public interest, promising fair profits on investments, and the citizens have already taxed themselves liberally, but are not able to accomplish their heavy undertakings, it does seem to me to be a high duty of the State to loan her credit, at least towards ironing and equipping the roads after they have been prepared for the iron, upon ample indemnity by the individual stockholders against loss, and to any needed extent which will not seriously embarrass the State Treasury or cripple her credit.

These principles are regarded as fundamental, and ought never to be lost sight of or departed from. It will be your duty carefully to examine into, and determine upon the ability of the State to grant the aid which may be asked for. I would also suggest to you the great propriety of securing for the State an intelligent and careful supervision of such work as she may feel called upon to give her aid to, at least to the extent of seeing that the condition upon which such aid is to be granted, shall in good faith be complied with.

Connected intimately with this subject is an examination into the resources and liabilities of the State. The report of the Comptroller, and those of the different Banks in which the funds of the State have been invested, which reports are already before you, furnish data for determining their true character and amount.

I recommend a careful and thorough examination into the various offices and institutions, having the custody of public funds.— Economy and a faithful discharge of duty on the part of ministerial functionaries, are the better insured by constant habits of vigilance, in the supervision of government authorities, on which they are dependent. Under various changes in the laws, making disposition of special funds of the State, some obscurity is liable to arise in relation to the character and amount of certain funds, if not accounted with care, and with proper distinctness. I observe that the stock of the State in the Union Bank is reported by the Bank, and by the Comptroller at $625,094. The item of $38,494, which is not included by the Bank, and which is mentioned as county school funds by the Comptroller, is a portion of the funds made common school funds of the State, and which has been so strictly regarded by the act of 1827, ch. 64—the act of 1831, ch. 16—the act of 1835, ch. 23, and the act of 1844, ch. 159. The $146,000 item of stock in the Union Bank, is school fund stock of the State, and the interest arising from this and other school fund stocks, is directed by law to be paid into the contingent fund of the Bank of Tennessee, whilst the dividends arising from the original stock of the State in the Union Bank, becomes principal of common school fund, and the bonus paid by the Bank constitutes part of the annual distributive school fund. After meeting the accruing interest upon the Union Bank bonds, the surplus of these profits, should be separately accounted, as directed by law, that no confusion may hereafter arise as to their identity or amount.

It appears that the proceeds of the sales of school lands belonging to school districts of certain of the counties of the State, as provided for in the act of 1844, have accumulated, in the Bank of Tennessee, to the amount of $301,965.12. As these sales were made on the terms of ten annual payments, it is probable that the whole proceeds collected, and uncollected, amount to a much larger sum. With so important a fund, it is worthy of inquiry, what amount of lands have been sold; what are the whole proceeds of the sales; what portion, whether due or undue, remains uncollected; what portion, if any, is not well secured; and to what extent each school land district is entitled to interest, on the funds raised on securities running to maturity?

In connection with the public revenues, it will doubtless arrest your attention, that the average value of land for taxation in the State, has again receded nearly to the low point of depression attained in 1846, which caused the modification of the law at the next ensuing session of the Legislature. The supposed remedy then provided, would seem to have lost its force; and it behooves you to enquire what further change is necessary to enforce just valuations. It is certain that the actual value of lands have generally advanced instead of receded. Yet the average assessment value for the whole State is now reported to be but $3.25 per acre.

It will be your duty at this session, to make provision for the payment of the second instalment of the Union Bank bonds, amounting to $125,000, which fall due on the first day of January, 1853. It appears to me probable that this payment may be safely spared out of the present large surplus in the Treasury; but this you will be better prepared to determine after providing for other unavoidable demands upon the Treasury.

It would seem that about fifteen thousand dollars of the revenue raised for the building of the new Lunatic Asylum, remain in the Treasury unexpended. This building has been completed in a style highly creditable to the commissioners, who superintended its construction, and will, I doubt not, answer the humane and benevolent purposes for which it was designed. It yet remains to be enclosed and furnished, and otherwise fitted up with the conveniences for the reception of patients. I refer you to the report of the commissioners for particulars, and would respectfully recommend that an early appropriation be made for this purpose, out of the funds provided by law.

The net profit, exhibited by the Bank of Tennessee, within the last two years, of $416,799.18, on an actual capital of $2,389,652.54, is large; and it is gratifying to notice that the suspended debt of the Bank has been reduced $94,628.75. I am not aware that any change of the law as respects this important institution, is required at the present session. But a careful, vigilant, and thorough examination into its affairs, is no doubt expected by your constituencies and demanded by the true interest of the State, and should not on your part be omitted or neglected.

I regard it as highly expedient that you should make a liberal appropriation towards the completion of the State Capitol, that it may certainly be finished within the next two years.

Convinced as I am of the great propriety of making serious and important changes in our system of jurisprudence, I cannot pass by that subject without specially calling your attention to the necessity and importance of simplifying the practice and pleadings in our courts of justice, or of altogether abolishing the whole system of special pleading, and of uniting in the same tribunal and administration of both Equity and Law. The improvements of the age in which we live, the genius and spirit of our republican institutions, and an enlightened public opinion, based upon a long and careful consideration of the subject, demand that the reform should be made. Some of the oldest and most enlightened States in the confederacy, on whom were also entailed those antiquated English forms of actions and practice, regarding them as an excrescence injurious to a pure and just administration of the law, have lopped them off, and adopted far more simple and plain procedure in their courts. I sincerely hope you may adopt such measures as will remedy the evil complained of.

I regard the recent expressions of popular opinion with reference to the mode of electing Judges and Attorneys General, as creating a strong implication of duty upon your Honorable body, fully to sanction the act passed upon at the last session of the General Assembly, and which now awaits your action. The present mode of election is justly liable to objections. The fundamental theory of our government consists in reliance upon the virture and intelligence of the people. Who will doubt, that they who have so long been the safe depositories of higher powers, will exercise, with reference to these offices, that wisdom and purity and patriotism which have been the characteristics and the glory of the American people?

I have said that, in discharging your duties as legislators, your action will necessarily have relation in some degree to the National as well as State Government. Among the duties of this class devolving upon you at this session, is that of laying off the State into Congressional districts, in which you will be guided by the late census returns and the regulations of law provided by the government of the United States. Connected with this duty will also be that of laying off the State into Senatorial and Representative districts for the State Legislature, in which you will be aided by the enumeration of votes taken under the constitution within the present year.

The term of the Hon. Hopkins L. Turney, late a Senator in the Congress of the United States, expired on the third day of March last, and the duty devolves upon you at this session to fill that vacancy.

In view of the great interest taken in the subject by the people of the United States, it is my opinion that you should reflect in some form of public expression, the sentiments of the people of our State, in connexion with the great questions which have so recently disturbed the peace, the harmony and safety of the Union. Tennessee is not without a powerful influence in the confederacy—an influence to which the valor of her sons in war, and their wisdom and moderation in peace, have justly entitled her. Her voice should be fully and fairly heard. Her people are patriotic, devoted to the Union, true to the peculiar rights of the South, faithful to the Constitution, obedient to the laws, and ever steadily loyal to the true glory and greatness of this country. They have stood as a mighty rock amid the surges of the sea, whether the tempests of passion have come from the North or South, sternly repelling the threatening tide of abolition on one side, and the angry billows of disunion on the other. The peace and glory of the Republic may yet depend upon a proper observance of moderate and patriotic counsels, such as it is your honored privilege to give utterance to, as the chosen representatives of the people of Tennessee. The series of laws passed by the last Congress, known as the 'compromise measures,' I regard as a great final settlement of the questions connected with slavery. Under the circumstances existing at the time of the passage of these measures, I believe that settlement the best that could have been effected, both for the North and the South—that in no other way could the peace of the country and the integrity of the Union have been so certainly preserved; and that any attempt now to disturb it, if successful, would tend to the extreme peril of the Union, and of that peace, prosperity and happiness which we so eminently enjoy under it. My sentiments are directly at variance with those, whether in the North or in the South, who are dissatisfied with, and would peril the stability of the Union, on account of the enactment of this great adjustment. I rejoice to witness, from day to day, increased evidence, that the American people will sustain this signal achievement of wisdom and patriotism, and thus secure its complete and ultimate triumph over the mischievous purposes of designing politicians, both at the North and the South. I do not doubt that its provisions will be strictly and rigidly enforced by the patriotic administration now in control of the Government; and I am strongly persuaded that a sound public opinion will firmly maintain them inviolate on the statute book.

In conclusion, I can only assure you of my earnest desire, that you shall adopt such measures as will redound to the honor, the prosperity and glory of our beloved State, and of my cordial cooperation in whatever you may devise, that tends to promote the general welfare.

                                                 W. B. CAMPBELL."

Nashville, Oct. 28, 1851.

Governor Campbell's ten-point Message fell into the following categories:
1. Education.
2. Internal Improvement.
3. Custodial care of Public Funds.
4. State Financial Obligation.
5. Lunatic Asylum.
6. State Capitol.
7. Judicial Reform.
8. State Reapportionment, Congressional and Legislative.
9. Election of United States Senator.
10. "Compromise Measure."

In his Inaugural Address, directed to his "fellow citizens," Governor Campbell chided the perennial custom of speakers, writers, and candidates for or incumbents of public office who for decade after decade had yielded to the exigencies of the occasion "to prate about education and its importance." Let the Legislature, he admonished, endeavor to accomplish something that will remove the doubts and apprehensions of the citizenry of the State and turn former ridicule into approbation. In his formal Message to the Legislature, Governor Campbell however lapsed into the usual gubernatorial bromide by submitting to the Solons, "fresh from the different counties," the responsibility of remedying the existing and wholly inadequate "system" of so-called public education. It will be observed that the Governor had no specific recommendations to offer in regard to alleviating the pathetic condition of school finances. The State Treasurer's Report to the Legislature some two weeks prior to the transmission of Governor Campbell's major Message disclosed that the 281,370 school children of the State had each received the sum of 41 cents per annum with which to "purchase" their education![21] After the above distribution of school funds to the various counties, there remained a balance in the State Treasury of only $15.81. Since the annual disbursement and the balance on hand amounted to the total sum of $114,674.08, it was as clear as the noonday sun that the lifeblood of the public school system— PUBLIC REVENUE—was pathetically anemic.

When the General Assembly of Tennessee convened in 1851, there was little or no comfort to be derived from the returns shown by the United States Census with reference to illiteracy in Tennessee. The statistical information indicated that from a total white population of 316,409 persons over twenty years of age, there were 77,522 illiterates.[22] This was an increase in illiteracy over that reported by the same agency in 1840. The increase should not have caused any wonder, inasmuch as the office of State Superintendent of Public Instruction had been abolished by a non-progressive Legislature in 1844, leaving the educational interests of the State without any guidance in the person of an official delegated that specific duty. The "educational ship" was without pilot or rudder, and was merely a drifting hulk.

The Twenty-Ninth General Assembly, 1851-2, had introduced for its consideration at least seventeen bills that related, oftimes very remotely, to some phase of the common school system. About one-half of the bills never advanced beyond first or second reading. With one or two exceptions, the laws that were enacted were of decidedly minor nature. For example, one such law authorized the establishment of a High School at Gallatin.[23] An analysis of the law disclosed that the legislators were possessed with grandiose ideas, for the trustees were empowered

---

[21] *House Journal,* 1851, Appendix, 85.
[22] *Compendium of U. S. Census,* 1850, 145.
[23] *Acts of Tennessee,* 1851, Chapter 46.

to "elect a chancellor, president, or principal of said High School" and were further given authority for "conferring all the degress of literary distinction which can be conferred by other institutions in the United States!" Shades of Harvard and Yale! Another law [24] authorized Common School Commissioners to employ female teachers upon the same terms as "other teachers."

Amid the welter and chaos that appeared to exist in the gubernatorial and legislative minds, in 1851, with regard to remedying the defective school system, Representative Gustavus A. Henry of Montgomery County introduced a communication from a private citizen, Edward McMillan, concerning "A Plan to Make the Common School Fund More Effective." [25]

The author of the above communication [26] stated in the introductory paragraph that the common schools at the time were accomplishing little or nothing towards the advancement of the education of the people. One cause of this was attributed to the employment of "young men equally destitute of education and experience as teachers." Many of these young men were said to have been using the teaching positions merely as stepping stones toward the completion of their own education which, when acquired, enabled them to "go into other professions already filled with practitioners." Due to overcrowded conditions in the schoolroom, Mr. McMillan maintained that the teachers could not do justice to the pupils, that consequently the time of the children was lost, and that many who would do something for the education of their children were depending upon a fund inadequate to meet the wants of the people. Among the topics discussed and recommendations submitted by Mr. McMillan were these: professional training for the teacher, whose qualifications for teaching depends upon his ability "to communicate instruction to the uneducated in an easy, agreeable, and intelligible manner"; teaching will become "as honorable as other learned professions" when the teachers are professionally trained; a recognition of the importance of health education; the necessity of providing professional schools for the special preparation of teachers; teachers for the common schools must come from among the State's citizens, as "the North cannot furnish a sufficient number"; that school commissioners be empowered to grant from the school funds a subsidy to one pupil for each scholarship provided from their funds in the amount of forty dollars; that the youth so trained in accordance with the above plan shall agree to teach a free school in his own district under the jurisdiction of the school officials for a term equal to one-fourth of the time that he enjoyed the subsidy of said district, "provided the people of the dis-

[24] *Ibid.*, Chapter 133.
[25] *House Journal*, 1851, 518.
[26] Original Manuscript document in State Archives, Nashville.

A Plan to make the Common School System more effective

Preliminary facts and principles — 1. The common-school system of this state as at present employed, accomplishes little or nothing toward the advancement of education among the people. The teachers employed, however meritorious in other respects, are generally young men equally destitute of education and of experience as teachers. Many of them are young men of merit, who honor their avocation more completely in receiving wages and means to complete their own education than in exacting efficient aid to the cause of education among the people; and when they have acquired thorough education, they cease to be teachers, and go into other professions already filled with practitioners — They are usually so provided in their schools, that had they the requisite qualifications as teachers, they could not, no justice to their pupils. — And the public money is squandered, the time of the youth is lost, and many who would do something for the education of their children, are depending wholly on a fund, which is inadequate to the wants of the people, even if it were judiciously expended.

2. It is equally the duty and the interest of the state to provide as far as practicable the means of instruction for all the youth. — It enables them to understand their rights and their duties as citizens, to calculate the advantage of every enterprise, to convert the avenue of energy; and thus improves their virtue and extends their means of enjoyment.

An Educational "Blue Print" that "Faded Out" at the time.

trict furnish him with boarding and pay twenty-five dollars to replenish his wardrobe for every session of five months he may teach said free school"; a proposed curricula for professional training of teachers, which curricula were such as would "effectually bar out inferior institutions"; and the requirement of an annual report from institutions "having a common school teacher's department."

Mr. McMillan's "plan" did not share the fate of many similar communications. The memorial was actually read and referred to the Committee on Education and Common Schools. On January 22, 1852, Representative Joseph R. Mosby of Fayette County, a member of the above Committee, reported

"On the communication from E. McMillion [McMillan], and on sundry memorials on the subject of Female Education,
The Committee ask to be discharged from further consideration of said communication and memorials; and on motion the committee was discharged." [27]

On October 27, 1851, Representative Edwin Polk of Hardeman County introduced "House Bill No. 70, entitled, A bill to establish a system of Common Schools." [28]

The above bill was up for legislative action nineteen times, covering the period from October 27, 1851 to March 1, 1852.[29] Inasmuch as this particular education bill received far more consideration than all the other education bills combined, its provisions seem to deserve analysis and comment.

The main provision of the Polk bill was authorization for holding an election in the several counties for ascertaining whether or not a majority of the qualified voters favored the levying of a school tax upon all taxable property, said tax not to exceed fifteen cents on the hundred dollars of taxable property and not more than fifteen cents on each poll. Another provision was that the County Court should elect annually a board of examiners empowered to issue certificates to those adjudged to be of good "moral character, learning, and ability to teach and govern a school," reserving the power to revoke any certificate "for sufficient cause." The bill contained no provision for the election or appointment of a Superintendent of Public Instruction, either State or county.

The tax feature of the bill, which was left to each county for determination, provoked heated discussion and undoubtedly contributed to the ultimate defeat of the measure.

Whether partisan politics played any part in the consideration of the Polk bill may be a mooted point that will likely remain unanswered.

---

[27] *House Journal*, 1851, 573.
[28] *Ibid.*, 130.
Original Manuscript in State Archives, Nashville.
[29] *Ibid.*, Appendix, 970.

The author of the bill was Edwin Polk, a sterling Democrat who was destined to serve as Speaker of the Senate at the succeeding legislative session of 1853. It will be recalled that the 1851 Legislature had a Whig majority in each legislative branch. Polk's educational bill was reported on favorably by the House Education Committee on November 13, 1851, and one hundred and fifty copies were ordered to be printed for the use of the House.[30] On January 20, 1852, four bills on education, including the Polk bill, were replaced by a committee bill "in lieu of all said bills."[31] After considerable haggling, Whig Representative H. H. Hubbard of Jefferson County offered to amend the committee bill by providing for the appointment of a General Superintendent of Common Schools. Democratic Representative Barclay Martin of Maury County did not subscribe to such a provision and accordingly called for the previous question. The committee bill, in lieu of the Polk bill, was then passed on third and final reading on January 23, 1852, by a vote of 43 to 29.[32]

Although the Polk bill, No. 70, had been supplanted by a committee bill, yet the legislative *Journals* continued to refer to the bill by the number originally given to the Polk measure. On February 16, 1852, the above bill was referred to the Senate Committee on Education and Common Schools.[33] On February 20, the Senate indulged in a number of parliamentary maneuvers, among them being amendments proposing to eliminate the office of General Superintendent of Common Schools, a motion to postpone the bill indefinitely, an amendment carrying a tax of five dollars for each marriage license to be added to the school fund, with a further proposed amendment that the proposed tax should be imposed only upon bachelors and widowers.[34] Thereupon the bill was rejected by a tie vote, 12 to 12.

After a few days delay, the Senate reconsidered its action in rejecting the measure[35] and passed the bill on second reading with "sundry additional sections" by a vote of 15 to 8.[36] Finally, a battered and much-amended bill passed and was ordered to be transmitted to the House of Representatives by a vote of 14 to 7.[37] On the day before adjournment of the session, Whig Representative John W. Richardson of Rutherford County moved successfully that the House refuse to concur in the Senate amendments.[38] But the Senate was hard-headed

---

[30] *Ibid.*, 230.
[31] *Ibid.*, 557.
[32] *Ibid.*, 579.
[33] *Senate Journal*, 1851, 630.
[34] *Ibid.*, 661–662.
[35] *Ibid.*, 673.
[36] *Ibid.*, 715.
[37] *Ibid.*, 755.
[38] *House Journal*, 1851, 931.

and refused to recant, still insisting upon its amendments.[39] Whereupon a conference committee, composed of members of both branches of the Legislature, was requested and granted in an effort to iron out the kinks that had developed. On the final day of the session, shortly before *sine die* adjournment,

"Mr. Polk from the committee on Conference on House Bill No. 70, to establish a system of common schools in this State, reported
That said committee could not agree;
And, on motion, the report and subject matter thereof, was laid on the table." [40]

And so, all attempts to revise and vitalize a dead or dying school system went down the drain so far as the Twenty-Ninth General Assembly was concerned.

Before wholesale condemnation be passed upon the Executive and Legislative Departments of State Government in 1851, for failure to provide any reasonable facilities for public education, perhaps the general public should also receive a sharp reprimand. Evidence in legislative documents at the time discloses that the public evinced considerably more interest in other matters than in public education. Of one hundred and forty-three petitions submitted to the Senate direct, forty-six were on matters relating to the regulation of tippling houses alone. If the number of petitions filed with the Senate be valid evidence as to what constituted public interest, then there was interest in a sleight-of-hand performer, in a charter for a plank road through the Sequatchie Valley, and in Porter's self-loading rifle. On the whole, Governor Campbell and the Legislature, so far as education was concerned, had a lot of say-so but not much do-so!

Governor Campbell had specific recommendations to submit to the Legislature regarding the development of Internal Improvements, especially as applied to railroad construction. The "railroad mania," as it was sometimes called, had been intensified in Tennessee as a result of the great commercial convention held in Memphis, in 1845. The "fever" was increasing its tempo in 1851, and Governor Campbell's Message carried evidence of that fact. Of the pressing need for railroad construction there was no doubt. The question was how could the State aid in the movement without placing the credit and financial resources of the State in jeopardy? Governor Campbell's suggestion was to let individual enterprise prepare the road for the placing of rails and fixtures, and then "call upon the State for aid." The Legislature acceded to the recommendation by enacting a sweeping law that incorporated the essential features embodied in the Governor's Message.

On December 5, 1851, Democratic Representative D. M. Currin

---

[39] *Ibid.*, 938.
[40] *Ibid.*, 945.

from the counties of Hardeman, Fayette, and Shelby introduced a bill

"To encourage a well regulated system of Internal Improvements, and to develope the resources of the country." [41]

The House Internal Improvement Committee recommended the rejection of the Currin bill, but a motion to non-concur with the committee's report prevailed. Immediately thereafter, the committee introduced a bill (No. 219) of its own "to establish a system of internal improvements in this State" which bill ultimately was passed.[42] In the meanwhile, fellow-Democratic Representative Barclay Martin of Maury County was quite apprehensive as to the State's "involving her credit for millions without a reasonable remuneration for its aid in return." [43] His apprehension was quite likely due to the introduction of a bill by Representative Brookins Campbell of Washington County proposing the grant of $300,000 to the East Tennessee and Virginia Railroad Company, a bill carrying the recommendation of the Committee on Internal Improvements after certain alterations in the bill had been made by the above committee. A minority of the committee, however, felt impelled to issue a note of warning as to what might happen in case the State embarked upon granting wholesale subsidies in the aid of railroad projects. Their dissent,[44] mild but based somewhat upon sectional prejudice, was as follows:

"The undersigned, a minority of the committee on Internal Improvements, constrained by a sense of duty to their constituents, and by a wholesome regard for the public weal, do dissent from the report of the majority, recommending the passage of the bill granting three hundred thousand dollars of extra aid to the East Tennessee and Virginia Railroad, ask leave, most respectfully, to present the following reasons for their dissent:

The State of Tennessee, from an overweening regard for her credit, has for years permitted her fear of debt to restrain the spirit of enterprise which has characterized many States of this Union, she has been too long torpid and indifferent to the objects of her true interest, but under the wholesome influence of the examples of her more spirited and enterprising sisters, by the arguments and persuasions of her most gifted sons, and by the sober second thought of her yeomanry, she is at length aroused, and through the Messages of the late and present Governor declares to us that she is now disposed to see her Legislature devise and adopt a liberal and judicious system of Internal Improvements, and that she is disposed, when individual means and enterprise have gone ahead and prepared the local work of important lines of Rail-way, passing through her territory, enhancing the value of her soil, swelling her revenue, and contributing to the comfort and prosperity of her citizens, as a generous sovereign, enjoying the eminent domain of this fruitful land, loan her credit to enable such companies to iron, equip, and set to immediate and profitable work, the various important roads, which may be deemed by Legislative sagacity and prudence, worthy of such aid, and by their prospect

[41] *House Journal*, 1851, 205.
[42] *Ibid.*, 342.
[43] *Ibid.*, 261.
[44] *Ibid.*, 305–306.

of profit, and proposed mortgages, will secure the State against liability to loss.—Acting upon this as a governing principle, the undersigned with a full appreciation of the East Tennessee and Virginia Railroad, as one of our great projected thoroughfares, eminently worthy to be included in the provisions of a General Bill, have been unwilling to favor this or any other application for extra aid, out-side of that contemplated for important lines which may be embraced in the General Bill.

For it is the local work done by individual means and enterprise in the preparation of the road-bed for the reception of iron and equipments, that constitutes the basis of security for the advancement of State aid, and if the means of the State are to be asked and obtained to assist in this preliminary work, the security is lessened, and for this reason the example should be avoided.

The majority of this committee who recommend this measure to the House with the exception of two members, are from that division of the State, which feels naturally the deepest interest in this important work, and in the exercise of a very common and excusable partiality for home interests, have urged this proposition with great zeal and assiduity before the committee, and it may be anticipated that the Representatives of other sectional interests encouraged by the success of this precedent, and indulging a like desire to gratify their constituents, will apply for similar bounties. When these various applications for special aid are footed up with the liabilities contemplated in the General Bill, the undersigned fear that the sum total will excite fearful apprehensions in the minds of sanguine and ardent friends of Internal Improvements, and will furnish the opposition with a most potent and formidable weapon of attack.

The undersigned, actuated by the kindest feelings for the East Tennessee works, and with an eye steadily directed to the paramount importance of devising a judicious system, which will be readily endorsed and sustained by the great mass of the State, would most earnestly and respectfully ask the House to ponder well before sanctioning this measure; all of which is respectfully submitted by—

> ALEXANDER JACKSON,
> G. C. HURT,
> J. D. C. ATKINS,
> M. B. KING,
> L. POPE,
> E. A. FERGUSON."

November 26th, 1851.

Whig Representative F. Hardeman of Williamson County was an individual of an inquisitive nature and wanted some facts regarding the proposed State aid for railroad construction. Accordingly, he introduced the following resolution:[45]

"Resolved that the committee on Internal Improvements be instructed to report as soon as practicable, for the information of the house, *the number of miles of Railroad* proposed to be assisted by a bill now before the House, to establish a system of Internal Improvements in this State, specifying the number of miles in length of each road within this State."

The Hardeman resolution was adopted, but no report on same was

---

[45] *Ibid.*, 367.

ever submitted to the Legislature so far as the legislative *Journals* disclose.

For approximately two months, December 5, 1851 to January 30, 1852, the committee bill No. 219 was bandied about in the House from time to time, with proposed amendments galore. With a number of amendments accepted, the bill finally reached the third reading and was passed by a vote of 46 to 22.[46] On February 7, the Senate added a number of amendments to the House bill, some of which proposed to strike out certain railroads and insert others instead.[47] On February 11, a rash of amendments broke out in the Senate, resulting in the acceptance of some and the rejection of others.[48] At an afternoon session, on February 11, the much-amended House bill was passed in the Senate by a vote of 15 to 9.[49]

The law,[50] designed as a panacea for inadequate transportation facilities, authorized the issuance of State bonds for aiding in the building of railroad lines, including a number of restrictions both precedent and subsequent. Prior to the issuance of any bonds, the railroad company was required to show that (1) *bona fide* subscription of stock offered assurance that the company was in position to grade, bridge, and prepare the road bed for the reception of the iron rails; (2) that a specified number of miles (usually thirty miles) were actually ready for the laying of the rails; (3) that no prior lien upon the road existed; and (4) that bonds would be issued in piecemeal as each required section of the road was made ready for the rails to be laid. A summary of the subsequent conditions was that (1) the bonds were not to be sold under par; that (2) the loan constituted a first lien upon the road; that (3) interest on the bonds was to be paid fifteen days before due, and failure to do so gave the Governor power to seize and operate the road until the arrearage was satisfied; and that (4) five years after completion of the road the company was obligated to pay annually two per cent of the loan for providing a sinking fund for retirement of the bonds. In addition to the East Tennessee and Virginia Railroad Company, thirteen other rail roads were included in the expanded statute which provided a loan of $10,000 per mile with additional funds for the building of bridges when necessary. Thus was established a system of railroad building in the belief that none of the financial load would ever fall upon the shoulders of the taxpayers. But the sponsors and supporters of the law did not and could not foresee that within ten years the Nation would be split asunder and that four years of internecine strife and struggle would usher in such chaotic conditions that the roseate dreams of railroad

---

[46] *Ibid.*, 643.
[47] *Senate Journal*, 1851, 578–580.
[48] *Ibid.*, 595–599.
[49] *Ibid.*, 600.
[50] *Acts of Tennessee*, 1851, Chapter 151.

builders would be shattered by the results of four years of bitter military conflict known as the War Between the States. During the decade preceding the above conflict, approximately fifteen million dollars of State-aid bonds were issued to the several railroad companies. In the post-war period under the Brownlow regime, nearly fourteen million dollars of additional State-aid bonds were issued for the same purpose. Ultimately over thirty-four million dollars of State-aid bonds were issued and turned over to the various railroad companies, a number of which were in or shortly went into bankruptcy and left the State "holding the bag." Here was laid the foundation of the larger part of the State debt which has not as yet (1957) been fully liquidated. Shocking details of fraud, chicanery, and "sharp" practices of railroad lobbyists and bribed legislators will comprise a portion of a lurid chapter in a subsequent volume of the *Messages of the Governors of Tennessee*.

With railroad construction largely in a "paper" status, advocates of river transportation called for a report concerning expenditures for the improvement of rivers. On December 1, 1851, the Senate adopted House Resolution No. 69 calling upon the President of the Bank of Tennessee to furnish the Legislature with a statement as to expenditures made for the above purpose. The Whig President of the Bank, William Ledbetter, submitted the following reply to the legislative inquiry, to-wit:[51]

"BANK OF TENNESSEE
Nashville, Jan. 24, 1852

To the General Assembly of the State of Tennessee:

In obedience to your resolution of 1st ultimo, the following statement showing the amount that has been expended upon the several rivers of East Tennessee and the Western District, under the acts of 31st Jan., 1842, and 7th Feb., 1850, is respectfully submitted; which includes ten thousand dollars paid by the principal Bank on the warrant of the commissioners for East Tennessee on 6th May, 1843; but it does not appear to what particular river or rivers this sum was appropriated.

I am, very respectfully
Your obedient servant,
WM. LEDBETTER, *President*.

Statement of the amount expended upon the rivers of East Tennessee and the Western District, under the act of 31st Jan. 1842.

Amount paid by principal Bank on warrant of Commissioners	
of East Tennessee	10,000.00
Amount paid—Holston river	24,238.22
" Watauga	9,999.48
" French Broad	10,485.28
" Nolechucky	10,816.12
" Lick Creek	2,000.00
" Clinch	9,959.72
" Powell's	6,932.78

[51] *Senate Journal*, 1851, 488.

Amount Paid—Sequatchie	5,000.00
” Hatchie	24,564.36
” Obion	30,233.14
” Forked Deer	30,659.23
” Big Sandy	5,920.06
” Hiwassee and Ocoee	5,000.00
” Tellico	3,000.00
” Little River, Blount county	2,000.00
” Big Poplar Creek, Roane county, under the act of Feb. 7th, 1850	1,800.00
” Tennessee, under the act of Feb. 7th, 1850	2,000.00

$194,608.39”

The railroad fever was raging, and charters were granted or revised in the case of sixty-three companies. The “water boys”were in almost total eclipse during the session of the Twenty-Ninth General Assembly. Altogether the small sum of only three thousand dollars was appropriated for the improvement of the navigation of two small streams, the Obed and Caney Fork.[52] Two other minor acts[53] were passed that related to rivers, one law dealing with the navigability of Wolf River and the other decreeing that New River be declared navigable to the mouth of Buffalo Creek in Scott County.

Of the tripartite sponsors of transportation systems—railroad, river, and road—seventy-six turnpike companies had charters granted, extended, or modified in some particular, while charters for thirty-nine turnpike roads were likewise granted or revised.[54] On the whole, the railroad advocates were easily in the ascendancy and made financial hay while the legislative sun shone.

As for Governor Campbell's recommendation for further safeguarding public funds, an act[55] was passed to make embezzlement of public funds a felony not only in the case of certain bank officers, but also to include “all other clerks, officers, and agents having possession of the money of the State.” Moreover, the railroad companies and the officers of “other corporations” were also included in the revised statute.

With reference to the State's obligation respecting the Union Bank bond payment of $125,000, the Legislature merely directed the State Treasurer to receive the “bonus” and the dividends arising from the State stock in said bank and apply same on the obligation. In case this amount were deficient, then the balance was to be paid out of the State Treasury.[56] Inasmuch as the Reports of both the State Treasurer and

[52] Acts of Tennessee, 1851, Chapter 271.
[53] Ibid., Chapters 272 and 342.
[54] Ibid., see Index, 776–780.
[55] Ibid., Chapter 182.
[56] Ibid., Chapter 94.

State Comptroller showed a balance [57] in the Treasury as of October, 1851, in the amount of $222,771.80, for once at least the Legislature rested upon its oars and ceased to trouble itself about the payment of the forthcoming obligation.

The legislative *Journals* exhibit no evidence of controversy regarding continued financial support for the new State Hospital for the Insane. Curiously enough, the institution, rapidly nearing completion, was referred to in official documents by three names. Governor Campbell's Message denominated it "new Lunatic Asylum"; the biennial report of the physician in charge and the State Treasurer called it the "State Lunatic Asylum"; while the Board of Commissioners referred to the institution by the name of the State Hospital for the Insane. Inasmuch as the Institution owed its origin largely to the interest exhibited by Miss Dorothea Dix in 1847 in behalf of the mentally ill, the Board of Commissioners recommended that the name of the Institution be changed to the "Dix Hospital for the Insane in Tennessee." [58] The suggested change in name went unheeded, however.

In his detailed Report [59] to the General Assembly, Dr. Boyd McNairy, Physician and Superintendent, gave meticulous attention to various items connected with the operation of the Institution. Statistical tables presented facts as to age of inmates, supposed causes of insanity, number and causes of death, and the marital status of each individual. Two of the most prominent causes of the affliction were attributed to loss of sleep and ill health. The Report [60] from the Board of Commissioners dealt chiefly with the physical plant, although one recommendation was strongly urged for favorable consideration. The law of 1847 required that the Superintendent should be a married man, that the duties of matron should be performed by his wife, and that both reside within the Asylum. Of this rather rigid requirement, this observation was made:

"We do not doubt that if all the requisites of a good Superintendent and Matron could be easily found united, as required by the law, it would be a fortunate combination, and that the Trustees would readily avail themselves of such a providential union; but we think that there is no absolute necessity in requiring that a Superintendent should be married, or that if married, his family should reside within the Asylum."

The Board of Commissioners estimated that there was an unexpended balance of between ten thousand and fifteen thousand dollars

---

[57] *House Journal*, 1851, Appendix, 52 and 84.
[58] *Ibid.*, 1851, Appendix, 47.
[59] *Ibid.*, 131–149.
[60] *Ibid.*, 44–48.

arising from a special tax levied for the erection of the Hospital for the Insane, all of which would be needed for furnishing the institution. In addition to this residue, an annual appropriation of six thousand dollars was made "to defray the current and ordinary expenses of the Asylum." [61]

The State Capitol, begun six years before, was still incomplete. Governor Campbell called for "a liberal appropriation" in order that the building "may certainly be finished within the next two years," a consummation that was not fulfilled. There is evidence in the official records that some dissatisfaction had arisen regarding the pace at which the building was being constructed. On November 1, 1851, the following resolution [62] was adopted:

"Resolved, That the Commissioners to superintend the erection of the State Capitol, be requested to report to this House:

1st. The progress that has been made in the erection of the said Capitol up to the present date.

2d. The cost of the building up to the present date.

3d. All the different items of expense in the erection of the building, the salary of the architect, the salaries of the different officers engaged in superintending the work, the number of hands employed in the work, the prices paid said hands for labor, etc., etc.

4th. What length of time it will take to complete said Capitol.

5th. The amount of appropriations that will be required to complete said building."

About one week prior to the above House resolution, the Senate had made a general inquiry about the same matter but did not get down to specific inquiries as embodied in the House resolution.[63] The Capitol Commissioners made reply to the legislative inquiry, basing their answer [64] upon a report made to them by the architect:

"*To the Commissioners for building the State Capitol:*

GENTLEMEN:

In compliance with a resolution of the Senate directed to you, requesting to know the probable amount that will be required to complete the building of the State Capitol, I have the honor to report to you an estimate founded upon the present state of the work and the time required to finish the main body of the building.

The estimate is founded upon the quantity of materials quarried, and now in the hands of the workmen of the quarries and at the Penitentiary. The time required without any augmentation of force will, I am confident, not exceed two years from this date, and the funds required will be from $200,000

---

[61] *Acts of Tennessee*, 1851, Chapter 348.
[62] *House Journal*, 1851, 175.
[63] *Senate Journal*, 1851, 108.
[64] *Ibid.*, 137.

to $250,000 to complete the building, ready for its occupancy by the next meeting of the Legislature.

Respectfully submitted by
Your obedient servant,
W. STRICKLAND, <i>Architect.</i>

To John M. Bass,
    James Woods,
    S. D. Morgan,
    M. W. Brown,
    James T. Elliston.
Capitol Hill, 29th Oct., 1851."

Apparently, the Senate was far from being satisfied with Mr. Strickland's statement, for Senator William C. Dunlap from the counties of Hardeman, Fayette, and Shelby propounded the following resolution [65] which was adopted:

"*Resolved,* That the Committee on Public Buildings be instructed to inquire into the expediency of employing a different architect for building the Capitol of the State."

A second resolution from the Senate still exhibited dissatisfaction with the status of the Capitol building and the following resolution [66] was forwarded to the Capitol Commissioners, calling for "down to brass tacks" information:

"*Resolved,* That the trustees of the State Capitol shall make a specific report, in a plain and clear manner, to the Senate of this General Assembly, of all the cost thereon up to the present time, including the yearly salary of the architect, the number of penitentiary and other hands yearly employed, the price of said labor, the yearly cost and progress of said building, what yet remains to be done, and a definite calculation (not a conjecture) of all necessary expenses to complete the same."

Finally, the various resolutions directed to the Capitol Commissioners were referred to the Committee on Public Buildings for investigation and report. This Committee presented the following report [67] on January 13, 1852, to-wit:

"REPORT OF THE COMMITTEE ON PUBLIC BUILDINGS AND GROUNDS.

The Committee to whom were referred the various resolutions relative to the State Capitol, and the bill to provide for continuing its construction, beg leave to report on the same: that it has conferred with the chairman of the board of commissioners and other members of that body, by whom the committee have been afforded all necessary information with regard to the building and to the prosecution of the work, with a free examination of the

[65] *Ibid.,* 144–145.
[66] *Ibid.,* 157.
[67] *House Journal,* 1851, Appendix, 221–224.

accounts and vouchers arising out of the expenditures of money appropriated by the last Legislature.

From an examination of the accounts and vouchers thus exhibited, and a free conference with the commissioners, your committee are fully satisfied that the entire amount of the appropriations heretofore made have been legitimately and scrupulously applied to the erection of the Capitol, in accordance with the plan at first adopted and approved; and in the manner directed by the joint Act of the Legislature, authorizing the erection of the building—and that the work has been urged to a completion with as much diligence and expedition as its nature would admit, with the means within the control of the commissioners; and as confirmatory of this conclusion, it is only necessary to state that in addition to the amount furnished by the last Legislative appropriation, rather than see the erection of the building retarded in any degree, the commissioners have, upon their own personal responsibility, borrowed the sum of about seventy thousand dollars, which has been applied and accounted for in like manner. For the repayment of which, provision will have to be made, besides what may be appropriated for the continuance of the work. And on this latter point the committee would here remark, that the most liberal appropriation for the earliest completion of the building will not only be the best economy, but is demanded by every consideration of policy and convenience.

When it is considered that the building was directed by Legislative enactment, to be constructed in a peculiar manner and of a particular material; and that the plan adopted, after much deliberation and investigation by the board of commissioners, and approved by the proper authorities, has been rigidly pursued with slight exceptions, which have rather lessened the expenses. It is obvious that its cost, although it may not be possible to say exactly what it will be, is yet fixed and certain, and cannot be increased or diminished by any change of, or departure from the original plan, without the most ruinous consequences to the architectural proportions, the beauty, the solidity and security of the structure—all primary considerations in the erection of such a building. Therefore the question can be only one of time, which is readily decided by the consideration that the Legislature has always been in this State, and is now carried on with much inconvenience, and under somewhat humiliating circumstances, and the most valuable public archives, papers, and books of every description subject to imminent danger of total and irremediable destruction, for the want of such an edifice as the Capitol will be when completed. Besides, in an economical point of view, it should be considered that a saving of expenditures to some amount will be effected by dispensing, as soon as possible, with the services of an architect and others who are necessarily employed under a fixed annual salary; and when it is further considered that the money to be appropriated does not come immediately out of the Treasury of the State, but is obtained upon bonds running for many years, and are only made and put into market as the money is needed, it seems that no objection can exist to the most liberal appropriation to obtain so desirable an object as the speedy completion of the building, which the committee are assured by the board of commissioners can be accomplished by the next session of the Legislature. It is recommended, therefore, that an appropriation of two hundred and fifty thousand dollars be made, which is deemed to be not only sufficient to complete the house, but to meet the debt already incurred.

With regard to the propriety of employing another Architect, a matter referred to the committee for examination and report, it can only say that

upon enquiry it finds that the present board of commissioners are fully satisfied with the skill and diligence of the present Architect; and as he was the
designer of the edifice, and it has been thus far executed under his immediate
direction and superintendence, it is not thought advisable to make any change
at this time, and at the present advanced state of the building. Any such
change might be productive of some danger and retardment in the work and
its satisfactory execution: and as the Architect is entirely under the control
and employment of the commissioners, in whom this committee has the fullest
confidence, it is deemed that no legislation on this subject is necessary.

In conclusion, the committee will state that from the fullest enquiry and
examination, it is satisfied that the work has been prosecuted with as much
energy and rapidity as the means in the hands of the commissioners, and the
nature and plan of the building would allow or justify, and with every regard
to economy and strictness of account; and although it may be admitted that
a cheaper building might have been erected in much shorter space of time,
yet the first act of legislation on the subject was specific in its directions, and
seemed to contemplate no common or ordinary structure; and well it might
when it is considered that this great State, with now more than one million
of inhabitants, had never from its origin spent one cent towards the erection of
any description of building of the sort, and its legislation had been carried
on in county court houses, or other buildings temporarily procured for the
purpose, and wholly unfit therefor; and that its most valuable papers, records
and archives had been kept in offices of no more accommodation or security
than the common business offices of the country used by private individuals;
with these facts before them, it is not at all doubtful but that it was contemplated by the Legislature that at this late day, and when the question of locality had been permanently fixed, that a Capitol building should be provided
affording every convenience for legislation, and that perfect security which
the public interest demands.

In conformity to this obvious intention of the Legislature, the board of
commissioners have proceeded in the erection of the building now approaching its completion; a building which, in architectural beauty, solidity of structure, and in its perfect security from the destructive power of time and the
elements of nature, is unsurpassed by any other in the Union, and in the latter
most valuable qualities, by none in any age or country. Your Committee
would therefore reiterate its recommendation for the most liberal appropriation for its immediate completion.

It is due to the commissioners who have had the superintendence of this
important public work, that public testimony should be borne to their energy,
fidelity and disinterested conduct in discharging their duty. When public
agents discharge their duty promptly and faithfully for a sufficient consideration, the meed of praise is their due reward; but when gentlemen accept the
position of public agents in an important capacity, with no other expectation
of reward than the consciousness of having done a public service and benefit
to the community and State of which they are citizens, the tribute of public
gratitude from the Representatives of that State should be recorded for posterity to see that States are not ungrateful to their benefactors.

J. W. WHITFIELD, Chairman."

It is highly probable that certain items in the regular Report of the
Capitol Commissioners somewhat irked some of the members of the
Legislature, particularly the over-expenditure of more than fifty thou-
sand dollars and a request for another appropriation of not less than

$200,000 for the continuance of the erection of the Capitol Building. As per the biennial custom, rather detailed reports [68] were submitted to the Legislature, to-wit:

"REPORT OF THE COMMISSIONERS AND ARCHITECT OF THE STATE CAPITOL,

REPORT OF THE COMMISSIONERS

To the General Assembly of the State of Tennessee:

The Board of Commissioners to superintend the erection of the State Capitol, beg leave herewith to submit a statement of the receipts and disbursements made during the last two years, as prepared by their Secretary, H. A. Gleaves, Esq. It will be seen that the amount received from the sales of State Bonds at par, under the act of the last General Assembly, is $150,000.00
And from other sources (useless lumber, &c.).................   440.10

$150,440.10

While the disbursements for the same period, (including the
balance due the Bank of Tennessee, at the date of the last
report, $13,218.58) amount to........................... 201,776.93

Shewing an excess of expenditures over receipts of..............$ 51,336.83
Which sum has been advanced by the Bank of Tennessee upon the personal responsibility of the Commissioners. In addition to this excess, the Commissioners have purchased all the iron and copper necessary for covering the building. The former, which cost $15,790.57, was purchased of Messrs. Woods, Stacker & Co., and by contract is to be paid for out of appropriations yet to be made by your Honorable Body. The copper has been paid for, and appears in the statement. The whole amount expended since the commencement of the building is as follows:

Received from the Treasury under different appropriations.....$ 41,000.00
From sales of State Bonds.................................... 250,000.00
Interest on Bonds, accrued between date and sale of Bonds....... 1,946.00
Advanced by the Bank of Tennessee........................... 51,336.83

$344,282.83

The vouchers for all the disbursements are in the hands of the Secretary, and ready for examination by the General Assembly, or a committee thereof.

The commissioners need not urge on so intelligent a body the importance of a vigorous and energetic prosecution of the work. To enable them to accomplish which, and to discharge the liability already incurred, they would respectfully suggest that an act be passed *at an early day* of the session, appropriating a sum not less than $200,000 for these objects.

In regard to the progress which has been made within the last two years, the commissioners cannot do better than refer to the building itself.

The corner stone was laid with appropriate ceremonies on the fourth of July, 1845, and although it may seem to have progressed slowly, yet, when the magnitude of the building, the massiveness of its materials—the necessity

---

[68] *Senate Journal*, 1851, Appendix, 161–164.
    House Journal, 1851, Appendix, 161–164.

for their thorough settlement and consolidation are considered, it is doubted whether a more rapid progress would not have diminished to some extent its solidity.

The Commissioners are unwilling to close this communication, without bearing testimony to the ability, zeal, and good taste, of their accomplished Architect, William Strickland, Esq., whose report is herewith submitted.

When completed, the building will be an enduring monument worthy of his well earned reputation, and of the enlightened liberality of the great State of Tennessee.

All of which is respectfully submitted,

> JNO. M. BASS, *Prest.*
> S. D. MORGAN,
> M. W. BROWN,
> JOS. T. ELLISTON,
> JAMES WOODS.

Nashville, Oct. 17th, 1851."

"REPORT OF THE ARCHITECT OF THE STATE CAPITOL

To John M. Bass, Esq., President of the Board of Commissioners for Building the State Capitol.

SIR:—I have the honor to report to you the progress which has been made in the building of the State Capitol during the last two years, and, although you are conversant with all the movements and details of the labor and workmanship of which the building is composed, it is proper for me to call your attention to the principal portions of the items, already embodied in the structure, and those which have been prepared toward its final completion.

Since my last report to the Commissioners, dated October 12th, 1849, upon the progress then made on the State Capitol, the principal story has been carried up nearly to its destined height, the cornice is prepared and ready to be placed upon the walls, as soon as the iron rafters are put together, which will be in the course of three weeks from this time.

The iron for the rafters of the roof, consists of flat and round bars furnished from the Cumberland Iron Works, and prepared with all the necessary drillings, screw bolts, &c., now delivered on the hill and ready to be put together; this work has been skillfully done at the Penitentiary.

The amount of the Iron bill is about 210 tons, cost $15,790.

All the Copper necessary for the covering of the roof has been delivered on the site, and ready to be grooved and put together; this copper has been procured from Pittsburgh, amounting to 54,520 lbs. at 22 cts. which is at a cheaper rate than has been charged heretofore in the west; the whole amount being 27¼ tons; cost $12,267.

All the column blocks for the Porticos are quarried and ready to be worked in the course of this winter, when a sufficient force will be put upon each pillar to complete them in the course of next season.

The four Porticos of the building will be composed of 28 columns, 4 feet 6 inches in diameter, and 36 feet in height, and so soon as the stone cutters can be spared from the working of ashler, or plain work, which be in a short time, the whole force of laborers and mechanics will be put upon the shafts and capitals of the exterior Porticos.

The whole of the exterior cornice, which is the boldest and most prominent feature in the structure is already wrought, and ready to be placed as a Cyma and Corona to the top of the walls, or square of the roof; this member of the building cannot be set in its place, until the iron rafters have been put in their places.

The design which is intended to form the screen and speaker's chair out of East Tennessee marble, now in your possession, should be forwarded to the quarries as soon as practicable, so that no time ought to be lost in its execution; if the variegated stone can be had in the rough and sent down here, we can work it here, perhaps much better than at these quarries.

The number of laborers and mechanics, has not been increased since my last report two years ago; the whole amount of force being about 240 men, including the Penitentiary convicts.

The Stone wrought and set in the building is estimated at about 280,000 superficial feet, together with a large amount of rough stone already quarried out and ready for the chisel.

It affords me much satisfaction to state, that with a moderate increase of force, the building may be put in a condition to receive the Legislative body of 1853, a liberal appropriation will secure this desirable object, beyond all doubt; the rapid progress which has been made within this last year, both in cutting and setting stone, is a sufficient guarantee, that 'our hands are in,' and the work will be assuredly accomplished at that time, so far as regards the occupancy of the building.

The Superintendent of Stone Cutters and Quarriers, Mr. James Birth, deserves great commendation for his industry and skill in the management of the Stone Cutting department, as well as the vigilant co-operation of the Superintendent of the Penitentiary, Mr. McIntosh.

Respectfully submitted by your obedient servant,

WILLIAM STRICKLAND, *Architect.*

Capitol Hill, October 17th, 1851."

Despite dissatisfaction and some petulant inquiries by various legislative members as to what was considered "dragging out" procedures on the part of the architect, the Report of the Committee on Public Buildings seems to have convinced the majority of the Legislature that genuine progress had been made in the construction of the building. At any rate, an appropriation of $250,000 was voted for a continuance of the work with a provision that "the same commissioners be continued for the ensuing two years with the same powers as they now possess." [69] Obviously, this could only mean that Mr. Strickland would continue as the architect.

Whether the militant Whig Representative from Rutherford County had been "tipped off" by Governor Campbell as to the latter's forthcoming recommendation concerning a simplification of court procedure, the fact remains that Representative John W. Richardson introduced the following resolution [70] five days prior to the transmittal of Governor Campbell's Message:

"*Whereas,* there are many absurdities, foreign barbarisms, and useless technicalities, in the practice and pleadings of our courts which ought to be corrected—therefore,

---

[69] *Acts of Tennessee*, 1851, Chapter 94.
[70] *House Journal*, 1851, 105.

Resolved, by the General Assembly of the State of Tennessee, That the Governor of the State be requested, and he is hereby authorized to appoint, with the advice and consent of the Senate, three persons learned in the law, whose duty it shall be as soon as practicable, to prepare a code of practice, both civil and criminal, for this State, by abridging and simplifying the rules of practice, and the laws in relation thereto; to abolish the present forms of action, and pleadings in cases at common law; the distinctions between legal and equitable remedies, substituting a uniform course of proceeding in all cases; and whose duty it shall be to report at as early a day as practicable, the result of their labors to the General Assembly for their adoption or rejection.

And be it further resolved, That the persons so appointed shall receive an adequate compensation for their services, to be fixed by the General Assembly, and to be paid out of the public treasury."

The proposal of Representative Richardson, who was a physician, did not meet with approval, for the Legislature contained a number of lawyers who doubtless felt that judicial reform was a matter completely divorced from the realm of medicine. Consequently, certain changes in court procedure were embodied in two laws dealing with the "regulation of the course of practice of the Courts of Law in this State" [71] and "to regulate Chancery Practice and to expedite the hearing of causes in Chancery Courts." [72] The first law provided that the forms of writ attachment, and actions should remain as heretofore, except as altered by the act in question. The altered statute still retained numerous specifications that doubtless remained so much Greek to Dr. Richardson and other non-legal members of the General Assembly, and are too technical and tedious to be enumerated in this treatise. The second law, relating to chancery practice, still remained wedded to a number of "foreign barbarisms" such as *pro confesso, scire facias*, and furthermore decreed that "multifariousness shall not be a sufficient cause for the dismission of a bill in equity, unless an objection is made by demurrer. . . ."

Governor Campbell's recommendation to the Legislature with reference to a change in the mode of electing Judges and Attorneys-General was based, he said, upon "recent expressions of public opinion." The public press had been agitating a change from election by the Legislature to the people, and in the recent gubernatorial campaign there had been no difference of opinion on this topic between the contending aspirants. Furthermore, Governor Campbell certainly could not and did not advocate the change for any personal reasons, inasmuch as he had been elected Judge of the Fourth Judicial Circuit by the Legislature in 1847 without a dissenting vote.[73] Moreover, the 1849 Legislature had passed a resolution proposing to amend the Constitution so as

---

[71] *Acts of Tennessee*, 1851, Chapter 152.

[72] *Ibid.*, Chapter 365.

[73] *Senate Journal*, 1847, 45.
   House Journal, 1847, 48.

to place the election of the above officials in the hands of the people. It was now the duty of the 1851 Legislature to vote upon the same proposition.

The Legislature lost no time in giving consideration to Governor Campbell's recommendation. Just one week after the Legislature had convened, Democratic Representative Edwin Polk of Hardeman County introduced

"The following Amendments to the Constitution of the State of Tennessee, to be acted upon by the present General Assembly of the State of Tennessee, in the manner prescribed in the eleventh article and third section thereof

The third section of the ninth article, shall be amended so as to read—

Proposed Amendments of the Constitution of the State of Tennessee, to be acted on by the present General Assembly in the manner prescribed in the eleventh Article, and third Section thereof of the Constitution of the State.

The third section of the sixth Article of the Constitution shall be so amended as to read as follows:

SECTION 3. The Judges of the Supreme Court shall be elected by the qualified voters of the State at large, and the Judges of such inferior courts as the Legislature may establish, shall be elected by the qualified voters residing within the bounds of any district or circuit to which such inferior Judge or Judges either of Law or Equity may be assigned by ballot, in the same manner that members of the General Assembly are elected. Courts may be established to be holden by Justices of the Peace. Judges of the Supreme Court shall be thirty-five years of age, and shall be elected for the term of eight years.

The fifth Section of the sixth Article of the Constitution shall be so amended as to read as follows:

SEC. 5. An Attorney General for the State shall be elected by the qualified voters of the State at large, and the Attorney for the State for any circuit or district to which a Judge of an inferior court may be assigned, shall be elected by the qualified voters within the bounds of such circuit or district, in the same manner that members to the General Assembly are elected; all said attorneys, both for the State and circuit or district, shall hold their offices for the term of six years. In all cases where the Attorney for any district fails or refuses to attend and prosecute according to law, the Court shall have power to appoint an attorney PRO TEMPORE.

SCHEDULE TO AMENDMENTS.

SECTION 1. And that no inconvenience may arise from the proposed Amendments, should the same be adopted by the people, it is declared that all Judges of the courts and Attorneys contemplated in the proposed amendments, shall continue to hold their offices and exercise the duties and functions thereof, according to the true existing laws and Constitution, until the election of their successors by the people, to be held and made under a law to be passed by the General Assembly next elected, after the ratification of the proposed amendments by the people, which law shall prescribe the times and places of holding said elections, and which shall be passed without delay and in strict pursuance of said amendments; Provided, The Legislature shall appoint a day for holding the election of Judges and Attorneys General separate and apart from the days already prescribed, or hereafter to be prescribed by the Legislatures, for holding the elections for State and County officers." [74]

Approximately one month later, November 12, Whig Senator Paulding Anderson of Wilson County introduced an identical resolution [75] in the Senate. So far as the sponsorship of the resolution was concerned, there was a bi-partisan approach to the proposed amendment to the 1835 Constitution.

Representative David Whitaker of Haywood County was interested in amending the Constitution in regard to the erection of new counties by providing that the six proposed counties might consist of less than 350 square miles and that the county lines of the proposed counties might run nearer than twelve miles of the old county seats. [76] Representative Frank Hardeman of Williamson County also had some ideas that he desired to have incorporated in the proposed amendment to the Constitution. His proposal was that the boundary line of the new county might approach to within nine miles of the county seat of any older county. An additional idea was that the Constitution be so amended as to provide for the election of members of the General Assembly only once in four years and for the Governor for a four-year term. Neither of the proposals offered by Messrs. Whitaker and Hardeman had been considered by the previous Legislature and consequently would have, if adopted, constituted amendments to the original resolution as passed by the 1849 General Assembly. A real constitutional question had been raised by the Whitaker and Hardeman resolutions, the solution of which was passed on to the Judiciary Committee which reported as follows, to-wit: [77]

"The Judiciary Committee, to whom was referred Resolutions proposing to blend the Resolutions passed at the last session, proposing to amend the Constitution, beg leave to report:

That the Constitution provides that amendment or amendments may be proposed once in six years. It matters not how many amendments are proposed, it is only necessary that they be submitted to the people at the same time. The propositions must be passed by one Legislature by a majority, and at the next session by two-thirds—after passing at one session of the Legislature, they cannot be amended at the next, for the reason that if amended, the propositions would not be the same, and if amendable, there could be no limitation to the amendments, and the identity of the original proposition be entirely destroyed, which carried out to its legitimate result, would make the constitution amendable by the action of one session of the Legislature, and thus make entirely null and void that article of the Constitution providing the mode of its own amendment.

Nor can two separate propositions, passed at one session, be joined together at the next, for the reason that the two are blended into one, and one

[74] *House Journal*, 1851, 56–57.
[75] *Senate Journal*, 1851, 198–199.
[76] *House Journal*, 1851, 84.
[77] *Ibid.*, 251; see Appendix, 305.

must operate as an amendment to the other. Besides when the two propositions are entirely distinct in their features, it would be highly unjust to compel the people to vote upon both or neither. The method to be pursued to attain both objects is plain and easy, and that is only one, as passed at the last session. Let both amendments be voted upon as they now stand, and the only way they can be constitutionally voted upon. Let them, if both are passed, be submitted to the people on the same day for their approval, and let the people vote for or against both or either as they choose.

For the reasons stated above, the committee recommend the rejection of the Resolution."

With the exceptions above noted, the resolution to amend the Constitution as introduced by Messrs. Polk and Anderson had easy sailing through both branches of the Legislature. On November 18, the House passed the measure by the overwhelming vote [78] of 72 to 1. The sole dissenting member was Representative Humphrey R. Bate of Tipton County. Three days later, November 21, the Senate passed the resolution unanimously, all twenty-five Senators voting affirmatively. Far more than the required two-thirds majority had been obtained, and now the legislatively-approved measure was ready for submission to a vote of the people. The proposed amendment, which had now received legislative sanction twice as provided by the Constitution, was as follows: [79]

"RESOLUTION NUMBER III.

The third section of the 6th article of the Constitution shall be so amended as to read as follows:

SECTION 3. The Judges of the Supreme Court shall be elected by the qualified voters of the State at large, and the Judges of such inferior courts as the Legislature may establish, shall be elected by the qualified voters residing within the bounds of any district or circuit to which such inferior Judge or Judges, either of Law or Equity may be assigned by ballot, in the same manner that members of the General Assembly are elected. Courts may be established to be holden by Justices of the Peace. Judges of the Supreme Court shall be thirty-five years of age, and shall be elected for the term of eight years.

The fifth section of the sixth article of the Constitution shall be so amended as to read as follows:

SEC. 5. An Attorney General for the State shall be elected by the qualified voters of the State at large, and the Attorney for the State for any circuit or district to which a Judge of an inferior court may be assigned, shall be elected by the qualified voters within the bounds of such district or circuit, in the same manner that members to the General Assembly are elected; all said attorneys, both for the State and circuit or district, shall hold their offices for the term of six years. In all cases where the Attorney for any district fails or refuses to attend and prosecute according to law, the Court shall have the power to appoint an Attorney *pro tempore*.

---

[78] *Ibid.*, 259.
[79] *Acts of Tennessee*, 1851, 722–723.

SCHEDULE TO AMENDMENTS.

SECTION 1. And that no inconvenience may arise from the proposed Amendments, should the same be adopted by the people, it is declared that all Judges of the Courts and Attorneys contemplated in the proposed amendments, shall continue to hold their offices and exercise the duties and functions thereof, according to the true existing laws and Constitution, until the election of their successors by the people, to be held and made under a law to be passed by the General Assembly (next elected, after the ratification of the proposed amendments by the people,) which law shall prescribe the times and places of holding said elections, and which shall be passed without delay and in strict pursuance of said amendments.

Provided, The Legislature shall appoint a day for holding the election of Judges and Attorneys General separate and apart from the days already prescribed or hereafter to be prescribed by the Legislatures, for holding the elections for State and county officers.

JORDAN STOKES,
Speaker of the House of Representatives.
M. R. HILL,
Speaker of the Senate."

Passed, November 21, 1851.

The next step in the process of amending the Constitution was by providing a method for submitting the proposal to a vote of the people. On December 3, Representative Edwin Polk introduced a bill entitled

"To prescribe the mode of submitting the proposed amendments to the Constitution to the vote of the people." [80]

In a routine manner the above bill passed first and second readings, and was referred to the Judiciary Committee which filed its report [81] before the legislative body:

"REPORT OF THE COMMITTEE
ON THE BILL TO PRESCRIBE THE MODE OF SUBMITTING
THE PROPOSED AMENDMENTS TO THE CONSTITUTION
TO THE VOTE OF THE PEOPLE.

The committee on the Judiciary to whom was referred, Bill No. 209, entitled 'A Bill to prescribe the mode of submitting the proposed amendments to the Constitution to the vote of the people,' with instructions to enquire into the expediency of submitting said amendments for ratification by the people, on some day earlier than the first Thursday in August, 1853. And also, the constitutional mode of ascertaining the number of voters, voting for representatives, beg leave to make the following

REPORT:

That the committee are of opinion that the vote upon the ratification should be taken at the general election for Governor, members of Congress, and Representatives and Senators in the Legislature in this State, which by law is fixed on the first Thursday in August, 1853. It will be seen by reference to

[80] *House Journal*, 1851, 328.
[81] *Ibid.*, 538; see also Appendix, 289–290.

Art. 11th, sec. 3rd, of the Constitution of this State, that the mode of amending the same is provided for by that instrument. The committee will herein quote enough of the said Article, as will be necessary to illustrate the position assumed by them, it reads as follows: 'And if the people shall approve and ratify such amendment or amendments, by a majority of all the citizens of the State, voting for Representatives, voting in their favor, such amendment or amendments shall become part of this Constitution.'

From the foregoing it will be seen, that before the amendments can become part of the Constitution, they must receive the sanction of a majority of the citizens of the State voting for Representatives. The committee are of opinion, that the proper, and perhaps the only certain mode to ascertain the fact, as required by the Constitution, is to submit said proposed amendments to the vote of the people, at the same time that the election takes place for Representatives. This course will insure a full popular vote. The committee are further of opinion, that by submitting the amendments at an earlier day, that their adoption will be endangered, as the confidence felt by many, as to the favor with which the amendments were met, will keep many voters from the polls, from the belief that there will be a large majority without them, and in that way a majority of the citizens will fail to vote, by which the amendments will not be adopted, and the renewal of the proposition cannot be effectually made to the popular vote for six years.

The committee entertaining these views, are unwilling to endanger the fate of measures that seem to be so universally approved by the public sentiment, especially when there is no necessity for requiring the popular vote at an earlier day, than proposed, for the reason that the amendments cannot be carried out until the next session of the Legislature, and therefore, that a vote at an earlier day will be unnecessary.

The constitution does not provide, in detail, the mode of ascertaining the fact of a constitutional vote, but leaves that to be provided for by legislative enactment. The committee are of opinion that the bill referred to them, provided amply for ascertaining the constitutional vote. Which is respectfully submitted,

JNO. NETHERLAND, *Chairman.*"

On January 21, 1852, the bill was re-referred to the Judiciary Committee which reported [82] as follows on January 26:

"The committee make the same report heretofore made without change."

After an ineffectual attempt to substitute "1852" for "1853" was made by Representative David Whitaker of Haywood County, the bill was passed in the House by a vote of 65 to 1, the lone dissenter being again Representative Humphrey R. Bate of Tipton County.[83] After a slight amendment offered by Senator Francis B. Fogg of Davidson County and accepted by the Senate, plus the rejection of two other minor proposals, the bill was passed by unanimous vote, 25 to 0.[84] With the acceptance by the House of the Senate amendment, the bill became the law.

[82] *House Journal,* 1851, 328.
[83] *Ibid.,* 594–595.
[84] *Senate Journal,* 1851, 537.

A preamble stated that the law [85] had been enacted in accordance with constitutional requirements, and the Governor was directed to issue a proclamation at least sixty days before the first Thursday of August, 1853, at which date the people would vote upon the proposed amendments to the Constitution. The result of that election will be noted later on in this volume.

Along with other duties devolving upon the Legislature, Governor Campbell reminded the body in his formal Message of October 28 of its responsibility for laying off the State in Congressional, Senatorial, and Representative Districts. In a sense, his notification was superfluous. On October 13, two weeks prior to the transmission of the Governor's Message, the flaming Whig Representative from Montgomery County, Gustavus A. Henry, introduced the following Joint Resolution,[86] to-wit:

"*Resolved*, that a joint select committee of thirteen on the part of the House be appointed to act in conjunction with such committee as may be appointed on the part of the Senate, to which shall be referred all resolutions, bills and papers, pertaining to the subject of apportioning and re-districting the State of Tennessee into Congressional, Senatorial, and Representative Districts."

Nine days later, Mr. Henry himself moved to amend the resolution by striking out 13 on the part of the House and substituting 9, and to fill up the blank for the Senate by inserting 6. The amendment was accepted, and the resolution as amended was adopted.[87] In the meanwhile, Whig Senator Michael Carriger had proposed that the Secretary of State should furnish both branches of the Legislature a report showing the number of free white males twenty-one years old and upwards, an item that would "facilitate the districting of the State." [88]

Inasmuch as this redistricting of the State had violent repercussions in later political campaigns, it may be advisable to list the personnel of the Redistricting Committee:

Name	*County*	*Politics*
	House Members [89]	
Henry, Gustavus A.	Montgomery	Whig
Martin, Barclay	Maury	Democrat
Richardson, John W.	Rutherford	Whig
Netherland, John	Hawkins	Whig
Campbell, Brookins	Washington	Democrat
Hubbard, H. H.	Jefferson	Whig

---

[85] *Acts of Tennessee*, 1851, Chapter 121.
[86] *House Journal*, 1851, 56.
[87] *Ibid.*, 103.
[88] *Senate Journal*, 1851, 84.
[89] *House Journal*, 1851, 112–113.

Name	County	Politics
Currin, D. M.	Hardeman, Fayette, Shelby	Democrat
Mosby, Joseph R.	Fayette	Whig
King, M. B.	Gibson	Whig
	Senate Members [90]	
Anderson, Paulding	Wilson	Whig
Whitfield, John W.	Hickman, Lawrence, Wayne, Hardin	Democrat
Bradbury, H.	Henderson, Decatur, Perry, McNairy	Whig
Rogers, James A.	Madison, Haywood, Tipton, Lauderdale	Whig
Ball, John	Greene and Hawkins	Democrat
Gillespie, James W.	Hamilton, Marion, Rhea, Bledsoe, Meigs	Whig

As is self-evident, the Redistricting Committee was heavily "loaded" in favor of the Whigs, the party representation being ten Whigs and five Democrats. With a Whig Governor and a Whig majority in each branch of the Legislature, no political soothsayer's services were needed to predict as to what would be the final outcome in partitioning the State into Congressional and Legislative Districts. Among the Whig membership were two of the most influential Whigs in the State, Gustavus A. Henry and John Netherland, both of whom made gubernatorial races later on but were narrowly defeated by Andrew Johnson and Isham G. Harris, respectively. Other Whig bellwethers on the Committee were Dr. John W. Richardson and Paulding Anderson.

Since National issues frequently constituted the main issues in Tennessee gubernatorial contests in the late 1840's and throughout the 1850's, the Whigs were anxious to keep a majority of the Tennessee Congressional Districts "safe for the Whigs." For that reason, the forthcoming redistricting bill was one of supreme concern to the dominant Whig Legislature of 1851. No more militant or brilliant Whig leader in Tennessee could have been chosen to head up the redistricting measure than the "Eagle Orator," Gustavus A. Henry of Montgomery County. In drafting the bill, particular attention had to be paid to the political complexion of the House, inasmuch as the Whig majority was only two votes. The Senate gave no similar concern, for the Whig majority in that body added up to a majority of 7.

Perhaps it was deemed "expedient" to try out first the political pulse of the House on the proposed redistricting bill. The Joint Committee on redistricting the State had been completed on October 27, 1851, by the appointment of the Senate members of the committee. After a period of three months, lacking only two days, Chairman

---

[90] *Senate Journal*, 1851, 120.

A Bill to apportion the Representation in the Congress of the United States

Be it enacted by the General Assembly of the State of Tennessee, That the Counties of Johnson, Carter, Sullivan, Washington, Hawkins, Greene, Cocke, Jefferson, Hancock & Sevier shall compose the first Congressional District

The Counties of Grainger, Claiborne, Campbell, Scott, Anderson, Knox, Morgan, Hendess & Overton shall compose the second Congressional District

The Counties of Blount, Monroe, Polk, McMinn, Meigs, Rhea, Bledsoe, Bradley, Hamilton & Marion shall compose the Third Congressional District

An Exhibit of Legislative Legerdemain.

Henry of the House Redistricting Committee introduced on January 21, 1852,

"A bill No. 401 entitled a bill to apportion the Representation in the Congress of the United States." [91]

One principal target of the redistricting bill was the First Congressional District. For five successive terms, 1843-1851, inclusive, Andrew Johnson had been invincible in as many races for Congress. Pitted against him had been such Whig stalwarts as Oliver Perry Temple in 1847 and Nathanial G. Taylor, the father of Bob and Alf, in 1849. Temple had been defeated by a mere 316 votes, while Taylor had tasted defeat by a little over one thousand votes. If Johnson were to be headed off from becoming a permanent "fixture" from the First District, some drastic remedy had to be devised. So, a little shuffling up of counties in the district seemed to be *apropos* as a preliminary to later Whig success. Consequently, Chairman Henry and his Whig majority on the House Committee reshuffled the deck and came forth with a panacea designed to cure the Whig ills in the First Congressional District.

Under the Apportionment Act, of 1842, the following counties comprised the District, namely, Johnson, Carter, Sullivan, Washington, Hawkins, Greene, and Cocke.[92] The Henry bill merely proposed to add the counties of Jefferson and Grainger to the list. It was just as simple as that! For some reason undisclosed in the legislative record, the Senate on the very same day introduced also a bill to redistrict the State into Congressional Districts. The Senate original bill,[93] No. 216, which in reality supplanted the House bill, proposed to add to the First District the counties of Jefferson, Hancock, and Grainger. Apparently, the past voting record of Grainger County was considered a bit hazardous for the Whigs, and accordingly Grainger was stricken from the list and Sevier inserted in its place. The First Congressional District was to be composed of the following counties, to-wit: Johnson, Carter, Sullivan, Washington, Hawkins, Greene, Cocke, Jefferson, Hancock, and Sevier. In this form the revised Senate reapportionment bill was passed in the Senate on February 10, 1852, by the tight squeeze of 12 to 11.[94]

When the Senate-approved measure came over to the House, it passed a routine first reading and was set for special order two days later.[95] When action on the bill was resumed on February 18, two amendments affecting the 7th, 9th, and 10th Congressional Districts were "laid on the table" on motion of Representative Henry. There-

---

[91] *House Journal*, 1851, 562.
[92] *Acts of Tennessee*, 1842, Chapter 7.
[93] Original Manuscript Bill in State Archives, Nashville.
[94] *Senate Journal*, 1851, 588.
[95] *House Journal*, 1851, 781.

upon, Democratic Brookins Campbell of Washington County moved to take Sevier County from the First District and place it in the Third District. His proposed amendment was also laid on the table.[96] Whig Representative Seburn W. Senter of Grainger wanted Grainger in the First District and Sevier in the Second District, but his efforts were in vain.[97] Various and sundry amendments were proposed, affecting several Districts, but pending action on the several amendments an effort to force a vote was defeated by a margin of 36 to 35.[98] Thereupon, Representative Henry moved successfully for setting the bill for special order on February 20. On the appointed day, amendments galore were offered for placing certain designated counties in specified districts. But the Whig juggernaut prevailed. Finally, Democratic Representative W. M. Simpson of Fentress proposed an amendment that would have shaken up the counties embraced in the first five Congressional Districts. Such a sweeping proposal must have alarmed the sponsors of the "ripper" redistricting bill, for immediately a dyed-in-the-wool Whig, G. W. Mabry of Knox County, called for the previous question and won out by a vote of 35 to 30.[99] The next move was self-evident—"Shall the bill pass on its third reading?" The vote for passage stood 35 affirmative, and 32 negative.[100] The hilarious Whigs were beside themselves with joy, for Andrew Johnson's residential county of Greene was now in a Congressional District calculated to be predominatly Whig. That legislative Whig maneuver, though it ended Johnson's five-term service in the Lower House of Congress, proved to be a sort of Pyrrhic victory. Conceivably, that gerrymandered bill paved the way as a stepping stone to the White House for the "Great Commoner." [101]

The Legislature of 1851, like many preceding and succeeding it, needed no reminder from Governor Campbell that a vacancy existed

---

[96] *Ibid.*, 800.
[97] *Ibid.*, 801.
[98] *Ibid.*, 803.
[99] *Ibid.*, 823.
[100] *Ibid.*, 823.

[101] Author's note. Johnson was exceedingly bitter over the redistricting law and declined to stand for re-election in what appeared a hopeless situation—his Congressional District having been "Henrymandered," as Johnson expressed it, by placing Greene County in a group of counties that practically assured a Whig victory. Being barred from re-election to Congress, as Johnson viewed the situation, he began laying plans for capturing the Democratic nomination for Governor in 1853. In that memorable contest for the governorship in 1853, ironically enough, Gustavus A. Henry, who was the Whig manipulator of the re-districting bill in the 1851 Legislature, was the Whig candidate for Governor against Johnson. Johnson was elected, re-elected, and then won the United States Senatorship in 1857. From Senator he advanced to Vice-President of the United States and, upon Lincoln's death, found himself ensconced in the Presidential Chair. Although wholly conjectural, had the Whigs let Johnson's Congressional District alone in 1851, it is highly probable that he would have been content to remain in Congress. It is conceivable that the "redistricting trick" did the trick!

in the United States Senatorship that the Legislature should fill. A week prior to Governor Campbell's Message to the Legislature, Whig Senator John W. Wester representing the counties of Campbell, Anderson, Roane, and Morgan introduced the following resolution:[102]

"*Resolved by the General Assembly of the State of Tennessee*, That the Senate and House of Representatives will meet in the Hall of the House of Representatives on Monday, the 3d of November, at 10 o'clock, A. M., for the purpose of electing two United States Senators; one to fill the vacancy occasioned by the expiration of the term of Hopkins L. Turney, and the other to fill the vacancy that will occur before the meeting of the next General Assembly, in the place of Hon. John Bell."

Senator Wester's double-barreled proposal may have been suggested by an editorial in an East Tennessee Whig newspaper which had attracted the attention of a staunch Democratic newspaper of Middle Tennessee:[103]

"SHALL TWO SENATORS BE ELECTED:

This question stands at the head of an editorial article in the last Knoxville Register, and is affirmatively answered in the same article. The next question is—

Who shall they be?

Of course one must hail from East Tennessee. This point being settled to the entire satisfaction of the Editors of the Register, they at once bring forward their favorite—Colonel John Netherland—and pronounce him 'emphatically *the* man for the position, having done more, perhaps, for the whig party, at greater sacrifice than any other man in East Tennessee.' Then follows a history of the 'services' for which he should be 'rewarded' with a seat in the Senate of the United States.

In 1833, it appears, that Col. Netherland represented the 'Sullivan' Senatorial district in our legislature. What 'services' he rendered to the *whig* cause, *at that period*, we are left to conjecture. But it is stated, that, as Senator, 'he exhibited those abilities in course of vigorous development, which have distinguished him in subsequent years as a statesman of the highest order.'

In 1835, he was chosen a Representative in the Legislature from 'Sullivan county.' During the session of that year, he was instructed by his constituents to give 'aid and comfort' to Col. Benton, who was calling for help to roll his celebrated 'ball.' But Col. Netherland's 'whig principles' and 'consciousness of right' would not permit him to engage in such unholy work—and consequently 'he resigned his seat.'

In 1836, he was a White Elector, and did 'yeoman service' in the advancement of *White* whiggery.

In 1840, 'he was a sub-elector in the county of Hawkins on the Harrison ticket' and bent all the energies of his mind to the furtherance of *Harrison* whiggery.

In 1841, 'he ran for the lower branch of the Legislature, in Hawkins county,' when he knew he couldn't make the *landing*—his only object being to assist James C. Jones in his Gubernatorial race against James K. Polk.

---

[102] *Senate Journal*, 1851, 84.
[103] *Daily Nashville Union*, October 7, 1851.

In 1844, he was not a candidate for Elector, but 'did efficient service' for Mr. Clay in the capacity of 'high private.'

In 1848, 'he was upon the Taylor electoral ticket for the State at large,' and traveled from Carter to Shelby speechifying the sovereigns.

In 1851, 'he was the only whig in Hawkins county that could beat the democratic candidate' for the Legislature, and his whig friends determined to bring him into the field. Although 'it required a sacrifice on his part' he 'readily' yielded to their demands.

The Register's conclusion from the foregoing facts, is, that Col. Netherland is the best timber in all East Tennessee for the making of a United States Senator, and ought to be immediately hewn out by the Legislature.

No doubt that many will be glad to learn from the Register that 'East Tennessee concedes to the other divisions of the State, the right to furnish the other Senator;' and it may be that Gov. Jones will be peculiarly gratified to hear from the same source that a 'very large majority of the people of East Tennessee prefer' him 'for that position as between Middle and West Tennessee men.'

It is due to the truth of history to state, however, that the Knoxville Whig tells a very different story in regard to whig sentiment in East Tennessee—especially in reference to '*the* man.' The Whig says that T. A. R. Nelson, Esq., is '*the* man'—certain."

Whig Representative William H. Wisener of Bedford County was less greedy than his Whig compatriot in the Senate. On the same day, October 20, of the introduction of the Wester resolution in the Senate, Wisener introduced a joint resolution in the House calling for the election of only one U. S. Senator. The formulating of expedient political strategy called for a lot of huddling and juggling, resulting finally in a showdown on November 14, 1851, when the two legislative branches met in joint convention for the purpose of electing a United States Senator. It appears that the overall Whig strategy [104] called for the election of just *one* Senator rather than two, as proposed by the Wester resolution.

Three names were placed in nomination for United States Senator, to-wit: Ex-Governor James C. Jones by Representative Joseph R. Mosby of Fayette County; Ex-Governor William Trousdale by Representative Levander Pope of Warren County; and Andrew Johnson by Senator John Ball from the counties of Greene and Hawkins. Before a ballot was had, Senator Ball withdrew the name of Johnson. Only one ballot was necessary, as "Lean Jimmy" won by a vote of 55 to 38, with six scattering votes for three other persons among whom was Representative Gustavus A. Henry who received one vote. [105] Elected as a Whig, Senator Jones during his term had a change of heart politically,

---

[104] Author's note. A carefully documented account of the Whig "huddles," in 1851, relating to the various Whig legislative caucuses for determination of their choice for United States Senator, is found in Chapter Four of *Thomas A. R. Nelson of East Tennessee*, by Thomas B. Alexander, Nashville, 1956, published by the Tennessee Historical Commission.

[105] *House Journal*, 1851, 240.

and in August, 1856, in a speech on the floor of the United States Senate, declared that

"The Democratic Party affords the best, if not the last hope of safety and security to the South."

The slavery issue had wrought the political transformation.

But Whig Representative Hawkins P. Murphey from the counties of Carter and Johnson was not satisfied with what he regarded as "half a [Whig] loaf." He wanted the "whole hog,"—TWO *Whig* United States Senators. Accordingly, on December 1, some two weeks after the election of Jones to the United States Senate, Representative Murphey introduced the following resolution:[106]

"Whereas, it was clearly indicated in the address delivered here by Col. Gentry, in the Whig Convention which assembled in March last, to nominate a candidate for Governor, that two United States' Senators would be chosen at this session of the Legislature.

And whereas, the Whig papers throughout the State, and the great body of the Whig candidates, and people also, took the ground that two ought to be elected.

And, whereas, the papers and orators of both political parties, before the August election, urged the importance of the contest, on the ground that two Senators were to be elected.

And, whereas, both political parties in Tennessee, have elected Senators two years in advance, as for instance, in the case of Judge Grundy, Judge White and Col. Foster.

And, whereas, from the adjournment of Congress, on the 4th of March, 1853, to the close of the extra session of the Senate, called by the new President, Tennessee will be represented by only one Senator, therefore,

Be it resolved, by the General Assembly of the State of Tennessee, that the Senate will meet the House in the Hall of Representatives, on Monday the 8th inst. to elect a United States Senator, to fill the vacancy which will occur on the expiration of the present term of the Hon. John Bell."

On the following day, Representative Murphey called up his resolution and demanded a roll call so as to determine its fate. Apparently, the House membership was dominated by "mixed emotions," for a sufficient number of Democrats and Whigs joined together to defeat the motion by a vote of 45 to 21.[107] And thus, the impending battle over the election of another United States Senator was resolved into a "delaying action" for two years.

The tenth and final recommendation of Governor Campbell dealt with the most explosive topic current at the time,—"*The Compromise of 1850.*" Lack of space forbids even a thumbnail sketch of the movement, but its essential features related to the principles of the Wilmot Proviso which the Southerners opposed vigorously, Southerners insisting upon the recognition of the Calhoun doctrine that under the Federal

[106] *Ibid.*, 320.
[107] *House Journal*, 1851, 326.

Constitution all the territories should be deemed open to slavery.[108] It was quite proper and to be expected that Tennessee's position would be made known through its General Assembly, and to that all-absorbing topic the legislative body gave attention early in its 1851 session.

On the day following Governor Campbell's Message to the Legislature, Whig Senator John W. Wester from a tier of East Tennessee counties introduced the following resolution:[109]

"*Whereas*, the Congress of the United States, on the .... day of September, 1850, passed a series of laws known as the compromise measures, by means of which a most alarming agitation of the public mind of the nation was quieted, in a manner that should be satisfactory to all political parties, and to each of the great sections of the Union,

And whereas, the people of Tennessee have witnessed with the strongest emotions of approbation, the wise and prompt execution of those laws by the patriotic Chief Executive of the Republic; therefore,

Resolved by the General Assembly of Tennessee, That our Senators in Congress will be instructed, and our Representatives requested, to resist to the utmost every effort which will be made, come from what source it may, either to repeal, amend, or otherwise change in any essential particular, that series of laws usually denominated the compromise laws.

And be it further resolved, in view of the decisive and efficient manner in which Millard Fillmore, as President of these United States, has enforced these laws, that he merits the enduring and grateful remembrance of his fellow countrymen. And as a tribute to his wisdom and patriotism, they should, in the opinion of this General Assembly, select him as the Chief Magistrate of the nation for the next ensuing Presidential term."

On November 7, Whig Representative Robert E. Thompson of Wilson County introduced a resolution which terminated in a burst of stump oratory, to-wit:[110]

"Whereas, our government having just passed through a crisis which was calculated to try men's souls, and fill the most devoted patriots and wisest statesmen with alarm; and whereas, the patriotism of our country, always triumphant, gave birth to a number of measures denominated the Compromise, which has proved to be the great destroyer of the wild elements of discord and fanaticism, which brooded over our happy country, sowing in their pathway ruin and distruction, and as certain disaffected spirits of the South, held a convention at the capital of this gallant and patriotic State for the purpose of disseminating their sacrilegious and hellish doctrine of disunion, and as we feel that it was a desecration of our sacred soil of the graves of our fathers;

---

[108] Author's note. Readers interested in the specific provisions of the "Compromise Measures of 1850" should consult some authoritative History of the United States. What is usually referred to as the *Nashville Convention* is unquestionably the most important of all the local meetings held throughout many of the States regarding a question that rocked the country from "center to circumference." A scholarly and well-documented article on the topic is *Tennessee, the Compromise of 1850, and the Nashville Convention*, by Dr. St. George L. Sioussat, printed in the *Mississippi Valley Historical Review*, Volume II, December, 1915, 313–347. Reprinted in *Tennessee Historical Magazine*, December, 1918, 215–247.

[109] *Senate Journal*, 1851, 134–135.

[110] *House Journal*, 1851, 206–207.

and that it is right that the legal voice of Tennessee should declare her position, so that her sister states may know how to class her—therefore

Be it resolved, by the General Assembly of the State of Tennessee, that we regard the measures denominated the Compromise as the great palladium of American liberty, and ought to be preserved, and we hereby instruct our Senators and request our Representatives in Congress to do any thing in their power to sustain those measures.

Resolved further, That the repeal or alteration of any material or important feature of any of those measures, especially the fugitive slave law, will be equivalent to a dissolution of this Union, and we hereby warn our brethren of the North, of the fatal consequences that must follow.

Resolved further, That we rejoice in the fact that whilst in the hour of peril, Rome had her Cato, her Cincinnattus; Greece her Pericles, her Aristides; that America had her Fillmore, her Cass, her Clay, Webster and Foote, whose sublime devotion to country preserved the institutions of our fathers, and that these noble patriots, for their pure, disinterested patriotism, deserve the richest meed of praise, the gratitude of their country, the admiration of posterity."

On January 7, 1852, the Committee on Federal Relations announced that the Committee had prepared a report on the Compromise Measures in lieu of two resolutions then pending before the body, namely, the Thompson resolution of November 7, 1851, and the Mosby resolution[111] of January 1, 1852, the latter of which was not printed in the official record at the time of its introduction. However, the Mosby resolution embraced a number of the essential points in the resolution on Federal Relations as enacted eventually by the Legislature.[112]

The report of the Committee on Federal Relations was not unanimous. The majority report[113] was presented by Whig Representative R. B. Brabson of Hamilton County:

"MAJORITY REPORT BY MR. BRABSON.

Whereas, Opinions have been advocated at the North and at the South, in reference to the Compromise measures passed by the last Congress, and the question growing out of slavery in the United States, which, if persisted in, are calculated to bring the General Government in conflict with the States of the Union, and threaten the destruction of the Constitution and the liberties of the country; and the people of Tennessee, through her Legislature, desire distinctly to state their views on these questions.

1. Resolved, therefore, by the General Assembly of the State of Tennessee, that the people of this State feel, and ardently cherish an abiding devotion to the Union and Constitution of the United States.

2. Resolved, That the Constitution of the United States does not recognise the right of secession on the part of any of the States of this Union, and the people of the United States, in the adoption thereof, did ordain and estab-

111 The original document could not be located in the State Archives.
112 Compare "Resolutions on Federal Relations" (*House Journal*, 1851, 473–474) with Resolution Number 1 as enacted by the Legislature, *Acts of Tennessee*, 1851, 719–721.
113 *House Journal*, 1851, 468–469.

lish a government of limited powers, and not a confederacy merely, and that it proceeds upon the idea that it is to be perpetual like other forms of government, subject only to be dissolved by revolution.

3. Resolved, That the State of Tennessee maintains the right of the people of the States, whenever palpably, intolerably and unconstitutionally oppressed by the government of the United States to resist its illegal action by force, if necessary; but this right is, in its character, revolutionary, and that there is no cause at present for the exercise of such right.

4. Resolved, That this State will aid the Executive of the United States, whenever necessary, by all legal means, in executing the constitutional laws of the United States. But in that spirit of hope and kindness which must exist between the States to preserve the Union, she warns her sister States at the North, that a repeal, or failure to enforce the provisions of the fugitive slave bill, or any modification of it, so as to destroy its efficiency, will tend to a train of deplorable consequences, from which a dissolution of the Union will be the most probable result; and she hereby gives utterance to her unqualified condemnation of the agitation of the subject of slavery in the Northern States, and all the steps taken and the movements set on foot by the fanatics and abolitionists, to resist the execution of the law for the reclamation of fugitive slaves.

5. Resolved, That the laws passed by the last Congress for the Compromise of the slavery question, meet with the approbation of Tennessee, as being the best which, under all the circumstances, could be adopted—that their passage was not a triumph of either party or section, and they are regarded as a settlement in principle and substance, a final settlement of the dangerous and exciting subjects which they embraced; and the State of Tennessee hereby pledges her hearty support in their enforcement.

6. Resolved, That the President of the United States has placed himself high in the great work of pacifying the country, and has received the meed of approbation from political friends and political foes. That the people of Tennessee partake of this sentiment, and with pleasure render him justice in the great matter of the salvation of the country, and rejoice that we have in this crisis, a patriot and a statesman, at the head of affairs, who knows his duty and dares to perform it.

7. Resolved, That the course of the President of the United States, in the management of our foreign relations—in maintaining our good faith with all nations—in his determination to enforce the laws of the United States, and in his administration of the affairs of the nation generally, meets with the hearty approbation of the people of Tennessee.

8. Resolved, That duty and patriotism enjoin upon the United States' government carefully to avoid alliances with foreign powers, and to have with them as little political connection as possible.

9. Resolved, Finally, in the language of the Father of the Constitution, that 'ours is a government which avoids intrusion in the internal repose of other nations, and repels them from its own,' and that a departure from this time honored policy, would in the opinion of this General Assembly, endanger its independence, if it did not become the immediate precursor of its downfall.

10. Resolved, That the Governor is hereby requested to transmit copies of these resolutions to our Senators and Representatives in the Congress of the United States."

On the same day, Democratic Representative David M. Currin

from the counties of Hardeman, Fayette, and Shelby presented a minority report [114] from the Federal Relations Committee, to-wit:

"MINORITY REPORT BY MR. CURRIN.

The undersigned being the minority of the committee on Federal Relations, and unable to concur with the majority in their report upon Resolutions No. .... and No. ...., beg leave to submit the following, as containing some of the reasons of their non-concurrence, and beg leave to submit it as their report in lieu of the report of the majority.

1. Resolved, By the General Assembly of the State of Tennessee, That although the acts lately passed by Congress, commonly called the 'Compromise bills' fall short of that measure of justice to which the South, in our opinion are fairly entitled, yet, as the same have become the laws of the land, and for the purpose of giving the highest proof of our attachment and devotion to the Union, this legislature hereby declares its willingness to abide by them, with that fidelity which has distinguished the citizens of our State on all former occasions.

2. Resolved, That this determination to abide by said 'Compromise bills' is predicated on the express condition that the North shall faithfully carry them out on her part according to the spirit and true meaning of the same.

3. Resolved, That this General Assembly does distinctly understand that, according to the true spirit and meaning of said legislation, it embraces all the action which the North proposes to take in relation to slavery.

4. Resolved, If contrary to the above understanding of said compromise measures, the people of the Northern States by voluntary association or otherwise, shall continue to obstruct and prevent the execution of the fugitive slave bill, or if congress shall at any time repeal, or so alter or amend it as to make it less efficacious than it now is, or if it should pass any bill abolishing slavery in the District of Columbia, or abolishing it directly or indirectly in the States, or if the transportation of slaves from one slave-holding State to another be prohibited, or if new States shall be rejected because they may tolerate slavery in their constitutions—in any or in all of these cases, this General Assembly feel constrained to declare that they should hold the same to be such a breach of plighted faith and a violation of the constitution so palpable and wilful, as well to justify the Southern States to resort to any and to every means of self-preservation, which their peace, safety, and honor might demand.

5. Resolved, That whilst expressing the foregoing sentiments in relation to the 'compromise measures,' this General Assembly is free further to declare the unabated attachment and devotion of themselves and their constituents to the Constitution, and the Union; an attachment which they have never failed to evince in all times of peril and danger to the Republic.

The principles involved in the foregoing resolutions which the undersigned submit in lieu of the report of the majority of the Committee, will indicate some of the reasons which restrain them from concurring in said report.

Respectfully submitted,

DAVID M. CURRIN."

At this stage of the controversy, Whig Representative James B. Cook of McMinn County moved successfully

---

[114] *House Journal*, 1851, 471–472.

"That 150 copies of Resolution No. 93, offered by Mr. Mosby on Federal Relations, embracing the subject matter of the compromise, be printed for the use of the House." [115]

The Report [116] was as follows:

"RESOLUTIONS ON FEDERAL RELATIONS.

Whereas, Opinions have been advocated in both sections of the Union, in reference to those measures of the last Congress, known as the 'Compromise Measures of 1850,' which are calculated to destroy the rights and institutions of the South on the one hand, and on the other threaten the existence of the constitution and the perpetuation of the Union;—and whereas, the people of Tennessee, through her Legislature, desire to state distinctly their views on these various questions, Therefore,

Resolved, By the General Assembly of the State of Tennessee, That the people of this State feel and ardently cherish a devoted attachment to the Union and constitution of the country.

Resolved, That the constitution of the United States recognizes no right of secession as existing in the people of any one State or States, or in any number of States; that this is not a pure confederacy, but a perfect government of limited powers; that it proceeds upon the idea that it is to be perpetual, like other forms of government, subject only to be dissolved by revolution.

Resolved, That the State of Tennessee maintains the right of the people of the States to meet oppression from whatever source it may come, when it is grievous, intolerable and oppressive, by forcible resistance if necessary to redress; but, this right is in its character revolutionary, and there is no present cause for its exercise.

Resolved, That this State will sustain the Executive of the United States, in the execution of the constitutional laws of the Union.

Resolved, That the laws passed by the last Congress for the settlement of the slavery question, meet with the approbation of the people of Tennessee, as being right and just in themselves, and honorable to both parties to the controversy.

Resolved, That Tennessee regards said settlement as final and conclusive; to the observance of whose provisions the faith of both sections of the Union stands pledged; and while she is prepared to abide it, and to give a faithful and perfect execution to its provisions, she feels that she has a right to demand of her brethren of the non-slaveholding States, a like faithful observance and perfect execution of its provisions; and in the spirit of fraternal kindness to them, and of unshaken devotion to the Union, she warns her brethren of the non-slaveholding States, that a repeal of the fugitive slave bill, or any modification of its provisions impairing its efficiency, or a failure to execute its provisions, or a failure to execute any other of the material provisions of the said settlement, will be regarded by her as a proclamation from the non-slaveholding States, that they have determined to break the bonds of the Union, and it will be regarded as such an evidence of infidelity to their plighted faith, and of wanton disregard of the rights and honor of the South, as would justify her in resorting for redress to any means which in her wisdom she might adopt.

---

[115] *Ibid.*, 473.
[116] *Ibid.*, 473–474.
Author's note. The "Report" is unquestionably the Mosby Resolution, No. 93.

Resolved, That the President of the United States has placed himself high in the great work of pacifying the country, and has received the meed of approbation from political friends and foes; that the people of Tennessee partake of this sentiment, and with pleasure render him justice in his patriotic efforts to save the country; and rejoice that we have in this crisis a patriot and a statesman at the head of affairs, who knows his duty, and dares perform it."

Next, a second minority report [117] from a member of the Committee on Federal Relations was filed by Democratic Representative F. M. Davis of Sullivan County:

"MINORITY REPORT BY MR. DAVIS.

The undersigned, a member of the Committee on Federal Relations, to whom were referred resolutions No. . . . ., and No. . . . ., most respectfully asks leave to hereby express his dissent from the report of the majority of said committee, which consists in resolutions reported in lieu of said resolutions referred as aforesaid.

By the 2d resolution of said report, I understand the doctrine to be declared, that the government of the United States is not a confederacy, merely, but that it is perpetual, and subject only to be dissolved by revolution. To this doctrine I am unwilling to subscribe. For I hold that a constitutional government, formed and adopted by a free pople, as is the case with the government of the United States, can and may be amended, altered or dissolved by the people at pleasure. It certainly is inconsistent with the idea that all sovereignty is in the hands of the people, to suppose that they are perpetually bound by a government which they have once adopted, and that they cannot dissolve the same without resorting to a revolution. Most certainly the power that creates a government can dissolve it. Now the people having all the power, and in their sovereign capacity governing, and in their individual capacity being governed, the idea of a revolution can have no place in the common understanding. For when they revolt they must revolt against themselves. An event too unnatural to suppose it can ever happen. But when the power of the people is usurped either by their representatives or by any other person, a revolution is then the only resort to restore their power. Until their power is wrested from them by usurpation, they may peaceably dissolve their own government, and cannot, for so doing, be termed revolutionists. That there is or ever has been any danger of a dissolution of this Union, I do not believe. For I have never noticed that the people, to any considerable extent, have agitated the question; and until the people who rule in this Union take up the question, there can be no danger, unless it be done by usurpation. All this cry of dissolution that we have heard for the last few years, has proceeded mainly from ambitious political aspirants, together with what few of the people they could excite. Whenever the question has been voted upon by the people, overwhelming majorities have been for the Union; showing conclusively that the only power that can dissolve the Union, have ever been opposed to its dissolution. The continued agitation of this question of slavery might endanger the Union, but as yet there has been no danger.

The 3d, 4th, and 5th resolutions of said report meets with my approval, as they substantially express my sentiments. And therefore I concur with the majority of the committee in recommending their passage.

---

[117] *Ibid.*, 474–476.

The 6th resolution is expressive of the warmest and most flattering approbation of the course of the President of the United States, because he knew his duty, and dared to execute the fugitive slave law—one of the compromise measures adopted at the last session of Congress—which I cannot approve. I have yet to learn that the Executive officer of any government is entitled to any credit for having merely executed a law, which, by his oath of office, he was bound to do. Mr. Fillmore has done nothing but his sworn duty. He was bound to execute the fugitive slave law or render himself liable to the merited censure of the people who placed him in office. It was not a matter of discretion with him. No matter what were his private views as to the justice or constitutionality of the fugitive slave law, as the Executive of the Union, he was bound to execute it. The adoption of this resolution, it seems to me, would, by express implication, acknowledge that the President of the United States had a right to refuse to execute any law passed by Congress if it did not meet his private approbation. I am unwilling to make any such acknowledgment. I do not for a moment, suppose the President would approve of it. For if there be no error or mistake in the public journals and many of the distinguished men of the day, that are friendly to the President, and that opposed the passage of this law, solely upon the grounds, that as he was the Executive officer of the Government, he had no discretion, but was bound to see that the law was executed. Many of his abolition friends with whom he had acted previous to his election to the Vice Presidency have deserted him because he would not carry out his private views, and refuse to execute the law. The adoption of this resolution would plainly signify that we did not expect that the President would do his sworn duty, and therefore we are so agreeably surprised, that we must signify it by a resolution of praise. Certainly the President would not thank us for this.

The 7th resolution, in general terms, expresses an unqualified approval of the administration of the President of the United States, as regards his foreign and domestic policy. Without adverting to anything more, I beg leave simply to disapprove of this resolution, because I did not approve of the course of the administration of Mr. Fillmore in connection with the late Cuba invasion. I cannot think the laws of nations will justify the appellation of Pirates, to those unfortunate citizens of the United States, who took part in that affair, as they have been denominated by the President. And from what has come to light as to the action of the government in behalf of those American citizens who are now confined within the mines of Spain, there is much cause of regret and complaint. Certainly that promptness which formerly characterized the government in asserting and enforcing the rights of her citizens, has not been made manifest on this occasion. Until we are more fully and officially advised of the action of the government in this matter, as well as the position of England and France, in connection therewith, we should withhold an unqualified expression of approval of the course of the administration.

The 8th, 9th, and 10th resolutions are in the main all proper, and I concur with the majority of the committee in recommending their adoption.

The foregoing is most respectfully submitted as my own views, and are not expressed with any party feeling or at the suggestion of any person other than myself—I alone am responsible for them. I never have and hope I never will be governed by any other than by principle.

F. M. DAVIS."

At the conclusion of the filing of the Davis resolution, the Whig Representative from McMinn County, James B. Cook, moved a concurrence in the report of the Committee on Federal Relations. Quick as a flash, Democratic Representative Currin moved that the minority report as submitted by him be adopted in lieu of the majority report of the Committee. At this juncture, Whig Cook availed himself of a parliamentary move by calling for the previous question, a maneuver that was sustained by a vote of 38 to 31. [118] And so, in the language of the official record,

"The House concurred in the report of the committee, and the resolution offered by the committee was adopted in lieu of resolutions Nos. 54 and 93." [119]

Far from being satisfied with the action of the House on the ticklish questions of slavery and State Rights, Democratic Barclay Martin of Maury County with what Shakespeare's Hamlet called his "prophetic soul" delivered himself of his feelings regarding the future steps necessary to preserve "the integrity of this Union": [120]

"REPORT BY MR. MARTIN

Resolved, by the General Assembly of the State of Tennessee, that whilst this State deeply sympathises with her 'sister States of the South,' in the feelings excited by the unwarrantable interference of the non-slaveholding States with our common institutions, and whilst diversity of opinion exist among the people of the Southern States in regard to the wisdom, justice and constitutionality of the measures of the late Congress, of the United States, taken as a whole, and commonly known as the 'Compromise Measures,' yet the Legislature of Tennessee, deems it a duty to declare to her sister States of the South, that the people of this State are unwilling to take any action, (in consequence of the same,) calculated to destroy the integrity of this Union.

Resolved, That regarding the said acts of the Congress of the United States, taken together, as an adjustment of the exciting question to which they relate, and cherishing the hope that if fairly executed, they will restore to the country that harmony and confidence, which of late has been so unhappily disturbed. The Legislature of Tennessee, do therefore resolve, that believing the constitution of the United States, if faithfully administered, provides adequate protection to the rights of all the States of this confederacy, and still looking to that instrument for defence, within the Union, warned by the experience of the past, the dangers of the present, and the hopes of the future, invoke all who live under it, to adhere more strictly to it, and to preserve inviolable, the safeguards which it affords to the rights of individual States, and the interests of sectional minorities.

Resolved, That whilst Tennessee acquiesce in the late acts of Congress known as the Compromise, that she feels it to be her imperative duty to declare to her sister States of the North, 'that all legislation, or combination, designed in any way to effect the Institutions peculiar to the South, deserves the most unqualified reprobation, is derogatory to the rights of, and peculiarly offensive to the Southern States, and must, if persisted in, inevitably defeat the restoration of peaceful and harmonious sentiments in these States."

---

[118] *Ibid.*, 477.
[119] *Ibid.*, 477.
[120] *Ibid.*, 477–478.

The highly controversial subject of the Compromise Measures had been bandied about in both branches of the Legislature since October 29, 1851. Resolutions, *pro* and *con*, had been introduced in both the House and the Senate, from time to time. Throughout the spirited discussions in the Legislature and the press, there prevailed on the whole a deep underlying desire to avoid disunion with its inevitable calamities. A diagnosis of the situation was proffered by Democratic Senator Wilson P. Davis of Bedford and Marshall counties on February 23, 1852, apparently in an effort to bring the long-standing question to an end. Accordingly, he drafted and offered the following legislative panacea which he doubtless had based upon rather profound convictions:[121]

"*Whereas*, it is the opinion of this General Assembly that the several laws passed at the last session of the last Congress, usually denominated the compromise measures, originated in an anxious desire to avoid the dangers of disunion which were threatened in consequence of a long course of aggression upon the constitutional rights of the southern people:

And whereas, their passage was the result of a patriotic sacrifice of sectional sympathies, and of a cordial union of members of the two opposing political parties for the sake of our federal union, embracing all the elements and solemnities of a sacred covenant between the north and the south, to the faithful and enduring maintenance of which, in its spirit and letter, the honor of each section was pledged:

And whereas, it is the deliberate judgment of this General Assembly that the scrupulous observance of the terms of the covenant by the north and the south will give peace, harmony and permanence to our beloved union, and that an attempt by either section to evade, repeal or modify any of the provisions of the compromise laws without the consent of the other, would be a palpable breach of faith, and a reckless abandonment of constitutional as well as honorable obligations, amounting to the worst species of treason to our beloved confederacy, and thereby inviting the aggrieved party to seek redress by its dissolution; therefore,

Resolved by the General Assembly of the State of Tennessee, That the people of Tennessee will stand to, abide by and faithfully execute the terms and provisions of the several compromise measures; and that they will cordially acquiesce in them as a final and permanent settlement of the agitations which have heretofore disturbed the harmony and endangered the union of the States; and to this end, their Senators in Congress are instructed and their Representatives are earnestly requested to discountenance and oppose all attempts that may be made in Congress to evade, modify or repeal said several laws.

Resolved, That the gratitude of the country is due to the several distinguished patriots and statesmen who have aided in originating and passing said compromise measures, and the same is hereby freely and cordially tendered to them by the members of this General Assembly.

Resolved, That the Governor of Tennessee transmit a copy of this preamble and resolutions to each of our Senators and Representatives in Congress."

Democratic Representative Brookins Campbell of Washington

---

[121] *Senate Journal*, 1851, 690.

County did not forego the opportunity of firing a parting shot in behalf of the Democrats of Tennessee to join "their political brethren of the other States" for the purpose of getting their political house in order prior to the forthcoming National Democratic Convention which would nominate candidates for the Presidency and Vice-Presidency of the United States. His resolution [122] was as follows:

"Whereas, we regard the Union of the States as established by the Federal Constitution, the most certain guaranty for the liberties of the people and the independence of the States. It has heretofore commanded the respect of foreign nations, and been our chief reliance against internal discord—the liberty of conscience, the freedom of the press, our personal liberty and present prosperity have been protected, whilst it has afforded more prosperity and happiness to the citizens of the United States than have fallen to the lot of any other people; under its broad shield, we expect the perpetuation of the independence of the States, and the preservation of the rights and liberties of the people, and a continuance of the prosperity and happiness with which we have been heretofore so signally blessed. Therefore, in the language of the great Jackson:
Resolved, that 'the Federal Union must be preserved.'
Resolved, That the Democrats of Tennessee are ready to meet their political brethren of the other states in National Convention for the purpose of nominating candidates for the Presidency and Vice Presidency of the United States, to be supported upon the platforms adopted by our party at the Baltimore Convention in 1844 and 1848, with a distinct understanding, that the measures passed by the last Congress for the adjustment of the questions connected with slavery shall be faithfully adhered to and acquiesced in as a final settlement of these questions."

On the following day, Whig Senator Francis B. Fogg of Davidson County moved successfully that the Davis resolution be referred to the Committee on Federal Relations.[123]

In the meanwhile, the Compromise Measures had come before the House for action. Once again, Democratic Representative David M. Currin attempted to revive his resolution of January 7 by introducing another resolution [124] substantially the same as that of the former one which had been relegated to the legislative "cooler." On motion of Whig Representative R. B. Brabson, Chairman of the House Committee on Federal Relations, the Currin resolution was laid on the table by a vote of 35 to 26.[125] The "cooler" was still operating under Whig guidance! Thereupon, the fiery Whig Representative from DeKalb County, William B. Stokes (later four-term Congressman and unsuccessful candidate for Governor in the hectic campaign of 1869) called for the previous question which was sustained. And now came the momentous query,—Shall the Resolutions be adopted? By a vote of 36 to 27 the

[122] *House Journal*, 1851, 904.
[123] *Senate Journal*, 1851, 706.
[124] *House Journal*, 1851, 901.
[125] *Ibid.*, 902.

House Resolutions, based upon the Majority Report of the Committee on Federal Relations and the Mosby resolution, were passed and then transmitted to the Senate.[126]

On a special order assignment, the Senate took up on February 28, the House Resolutions on the Compromise Measures. A lot of parliamentary maneuvering took place during which a temporary filibuster occurred. In the midst of the confusion, Democratic Senator Wilson P. Davis from the counties of Bedford and Marshall sought to pour oil on the troubled waters by eulogizing the sponsors of the Compromise Measures of 1850, to-wit:[127]

"*Whereas,* It is the opinion of this General Assembly, that the several laws passed at the last session of Congress, and usually denominated the 'compromise measures,' originated in an anxious desire to avoid the dangers of disunion, which were threatened in consequence of a long course of aggression upon the constitutional rights of the Southern people;

And whereas, Their passage was the result of a patriotic sacrifice of sectional sympathies, and of a cordial union of members of the two political parties for the sake of the Federal Union, embracing all the elements and solemnities of a sacred covenant between the North and the South, to the faithful and enduring maintenance of which in its spirit and letter the honor of each section was pledged;

And whereas, It is the deliberate judgment of this General Assembly, that the scrupulous observance of the terms of the covenant by the North and the South, will give peace, harmony and permanence to our beloved union; and that an attempt by either section to evade, repeal or modify any of the provisions of the compromise without the consent of the other, would be a palpable breach of faith, and a reckless abandonment of constitutional as well as honorable obligations, amounting to the worst species of treason to the Union, and thereby inviting the aggrieved party to seek redress by its dissolution; therefore,

Resolved by the General Assembly of the State of Tennessee, That the people of Tennessee will stand to, abide by, and faithfully execute the terms and provisions of the several compromise measures, and that they will cordially acquiesce in them as a final and permanent settlement of the agitations which have heretofore disturbed the harmony and endangered the Union of the States; and to this end their Senators in Congress are instructed, and their Representatives are earnestly requested, to discountenance and oppose all attempts that may be made in Congress to evade, modify, or repeal said several laws.

Resolved, That the gratitude of the country is due to the several distinguished patriots and statesmen who have aided in originating and passing the compromise measures, and the same is hereby freely and cordially tendered to them by the members of this General Assembly.

Resolved, That the Governor of Tennessee transmit a copy of this preamble and resolutions to each of our Senators and Representatives in Congress."

But the Senate, like the House, evidently wanted to end the mara-

---

[126] *Ibid.,* 902.
[127] *Senate Journal,* 1851, 772–773.

thon which had been running for approximately four months. Accordingly Senator Davis met a sudden and decisive rebuff, for his resolution was defeated by a vote of 15 to 8.[128] Then the final showdown came; the House Resolutions were adopted by the Senate by a vote of 15 to 8 without the change of a single vote on the part of any Senator.[129]

One version of the ancient proverb had now been carried out:

> "The mills of the gods grind slowly,
> Yet they grind exceeding small."

In its final form, the adopted Resolution [130] was as follows:

"RESOLUTION NUMBER I

Whereas, opinions have been advocated at the North and at the South, in reference to the compromise measures passed by the last Congress, and the questions growing out of slavery in United States, which if persisted in, are calculated to bring the general government in conflict with the States of the Union, and threaten the destruction of the constitution, and the liberties of the country. And the people of Tennessee, through her Legislature, desire distinctly to state their views on these questions:

1. *Resolved, therefore, by the General Assembly of the State of Tennessee,* That the people of this State, feel and ardently cherish an abiding devotion to the Union and Constitution of the United States.

2. *Resolved,* That the Constitution of the United States does not recognize the right of secession on the part of any of the States of this Union, and the people of the United States, in the adoption thereof, did ordain and establish a government of limited powers, and not a confederacy merely, and that it proceeds upon the idea that it is to be perpetual, like other forms of government, subject only to be dissolved by revolution.

3. *Resolved,* That the State of Tennessee maintains the right of the people of the States, whenever palpably, intolerably, and unconstitutionally oppressed by the Government of the United States, to resist its illegal action by force, if necessary; but this right is, in its character, revolutionary, and that there is no cause at present for the exercise of such right.

4. *Resolved,* That this State will aid the Executive of the United States, whenever necessary, by all legal means, in executing the constitutional laws of the United States. But in that spirit of hope and kindness which must exist between the States, to preserve the Union, she warns her sister States of the North, that a repeal, or failure to enforce the provisions of the Fugitive Slave bill, or any modification of it, so as to destroy its efficiency, will tend to a train of deplorable consequences, from which a dissolution of the Union will be the most probable result, and she hereby gives utterance to her unqualified condemnation of the agitation of the subject of slavery in the Northern States, and all the steps taken, and movements set on foot by the fanatics and abolitionists, to resist the execution of the law for the reclamation of fugitive slaves.

5. *Resolved,* That the laws passed by the last Congress for the compromise of the slavery questions, must meet with the approbation of Tennessee, as being the best, which under all the circumstances, could be adopted. That their passage was not a triumph of either party or section, and they are

---

[128] *Ibid.,* 733.
[129] *Ibid.,* 774.
[130] *Acts of Tennessee,* 1851, 719–721.

MESSAGES OF THE GOVERNORS

regarded as a settlement in principle and substance—a final settlement of the dangerous and exciting subjects, which they embraced, and the State of Tennessee hereby pledges her hearty support in their enforcement.

6. *Resolved,* That the President of the United States has placed himself high in the great work of pacifying the country, and has received the meed of approbation from political friends and political foes. That the people of Tennessee partake of this sentiment, and with pleasure, render him justice in the great matter of the salvation of the country, and rejoice, that we have in this crisis, a patriot and a statesman at the head of affairs, who knows his duty, and dares to perform it.

7. *Resolved,* That the course of the President of the United States in the management of our foreign relations—in maintaining our good faith with all nations—in his determination to enforce the laws of the United States, and in his administration of the affairs of the nation, generally meets with the hearty approbation of the people of Tennessee.

8. *Resolved,* That duty and patriotism enjoin upon the United States Government, carefully to avoid alliances with foreign powers, and to have with them as little political connection as possible.

9. *Resolved,* Finally, in the language of the father of the Constitution, that 'ours is a government which avoids intrusion in the internal welfare of other nations, and repels them from its own,' and that a departure from this time honored policy, would in the opinion of this General Assembly, endanger its independence, if it did not become the immediate precursor of its downfall.

10. *Resolved,* That the Governor is hereby requested to transmit copies of these resolutions to our Senators and Representatives in the Congress of the United States.

JORDAN STOKES,
Speaker of the House of Representatives.

M. R. HILL,
Speaker of the Senate."

Passed, February 28, 1852.

A summary of the legislative action on the ten recommendations submitted by Governor Campbell yields the following conclusions. Education received fulsome praise from both legislative and executive Departments of State, but no improvement in legislative directives was made; public taxation for public education was shunned to a degree reminiscent of the ancients fleeing from the plagues of Egypt. Interest in Internal Improvements was centered almost wholly upon the authorization of State aid to railroad development. Custodial care of public funds was further safe-guarded by providing penalties for all persons who mishandled such funds. Appropriations for operation of the Lunatic Asylum were provided, and liberal funds were made available for the continuation of the erection of the State Capitol Building. Significant reform was made in the judiciary by transferring the power from the Legislature to the people in electing Judges and Attorneys-General. Reapportionment of congressional and legislative districts was made, but the Whig balance of power in the Legislature was exercised in keeping with a campaign utterance two years later of the Whig wheel-horse, Gustavus A. Henry, who said that

"... The voters by electing a Whig Legislature in 1851 had instructed him to give the Whig party 'a decided ascendancy in the apportionment'." [131]

The election of a United States Senator resulted in elevating former Whig Governor "Lean Jimmy" Jones to the office. The extended battle over the Compromise Measures of 1850 was finally resolved in a manner largely in harmony with Governor Campbell's pronouncement on that explosive subject.

Almost without exception, every Legislature proceeds "upon its own" and enacts laws upon its own initiative. The Legislature of 1851 followed this usual pattern by enacting what was called the "Free Banking Law," first tried out in New York State in 1837. With slight modifications, the Tennessee law [132] was a duplicate of the New York act. In substance, the law authorized banks to be chartered upon a capitalization of only fifty thousand dollars. State bonds, or bonds indorsed by the State, were to be deposited with the State Comptroller who in turn was authorized to turn over to the corporation an amount equal to such notes "for circulation of different denominations." Quite a number of banks were organized under this law on fictitious capital, with the result that "wildcat" banks multiplied figuratively speaking with the rapidity of grasshoppers. The issuance of ornate and highly embellished bank notes became the order of the day, and ere long a ridiculous system of "banking" was in vogue. Upon "easy" capital, the volume of currency was greatly expanded, the credit of the older and more stable banks became impaired, and legitimate profits substantially reduced. Within seven years, the banking situation had become demoralized to such an extent that the Free Banking Law of 1851 was repealed, the repealing act [133] specifying that no new banks could be created under the previous law.

Two Senators of the 1851 General Assembly were endowed with a rare sense of historical perspective, Stephen C. Pavatt representing the counties of Dickson, Stewart, Humphreys and Benton, and Francis B. Fogg of Davidson County. On October 24, 1851, Senator Pavatt introduced the following resolution: [134]

"*Resolved*, That a select committee of five be and the same is hereby appointed to take into consideration a bill to provide for the complete history of the State of Tennessee."

On October 30, the Speaker appointed as members of the above committee Senators Stephen C. Pavatt, William C. Dunlap, Francis B. Fogg,

---

[131] Hamer, Philip M.: *Tennessee—A History*, Volume I, 491.
[132] *Acts of Tennessee*, 1851, Chapter 113.
[133] *Ibid.*, 1857, Chapter 25.
[134] *Senate Journal*, 1851, 144.

James W. Deaderick, and Paulding Anderson.[135] Eight days prior to the appointment of the select committee, Senator Pavat had introduced

"A bill to provide for a complete history of the State of Tennessee." [136]

On November 10, Senator Pavatt, Chairman of the select committee, reported that the above bill was under consideration and that he had been instructed to recommend a sum of $1000 for carrying into execution the purposes of the bill.[137] On January 28, 1852, the bill was passed by a vote of 19 to 4, ordered to be engrossed, and then was transmitted to the House together with the report of the select committee.[138] The excellent report [139] prepared by the select committee deserves recognition and incorporation in this treatise:

"REPORT

The Select Committee to whom was referred 'a bill to provide for a complete History of the State of Tennessee' have had the same under consideration, and after mature deliberation they have directed me to return the bill, with an amendment proposing to fill the blank in the section with $1000, and to recommend its passage. They have also instructed me to submit to the Senate the following Report in favor of the passage of the Bill.

The committee cannot but feel some degree of humiliation in being compelled to admit that no complete and authentic History of the State of Tennessee has yet been written and published. It is true that for some years it has been understood that one or two highly intelligent and enterprizing gentlemen have been engaged in collecting together materials for such a work; but as no specific time has been designated at which the public can calculate upon its completion, the committee feel justified in concluding that the collection of necessary materials for a *complete History of Tennessee*, and their proper arrangement and preparation for publication, is a work of too much labor and expense to be overcome by unaided private enterprize within any reasonable period of time. Indeed it appears manifest to the committee that a very cursory view of the magnitude of the undertaking would at once satisfy any intelligent mind that its accomplishment, by mere private or individual resources, within any reasonable time, would be next to impracticable. Our State is not deficient in that species of intellectual enterprize and talent requisite for the undertaking, nor is there any dearth of uninteresting historical materials, and yet since our existence as an independent State, more than half a century has passed by, and we are still without a standard work to which we can refer as the authentic record of our advancement in all the elements of national prosperity and greatness. How else can we account for this fact than upon the supposition that the undertaking is too onerous for individual enterprize? and how else can we expect to overcome the obstacle than by the liberal aid of the State?

The committee would feel that they were reflecting upon the intelligence and patriotism of the Senate if they were to enter upon an argument to shew

---

[135] *Ibid.*, 138.
[136] *Ibid.*, 95.
[137] *Ibid.*, 186.
[138] *Ibid.*, 511.
[139] *House Journal*, 1851, Appendix, 91–96.

the importance of such a work as is contemplated by the bill. We are all justly proud of the elevated position assigned to our State by the united voice of our countrymen; but when we are called upon for the record of our title to greatness we are forced to make the humiliating admission that *our record is yet to be written! our greatness dwells* 'IN TRADITION'S SIMPLE TONGUE.' If it were profitable or necessary we might find reasons why those who have preceded us in the halls of legislation have not chosen to embark in this enterprize. Perhaps it would be found that the hope has been indulged that the work could and would be accomplished by individual labor and individual means. We are satisfied that it is not wise longer to indulge this hope, and now the question addresses itself in all its practical importance whether the State has such an interest in her own history as to justify her representatives in making the proposed expenditures?

It may be well questioned whether any State in the Union abounds in an equal amount of interesting and valuable historical materials as Tennessee. The period of her existence, prior to her admission into the Union as an independent State, is peculiarly rich in the most thrilling incidents. A faithful record of the various expeditions into the territory, by hunters and pioneers, when the Indian and the wild beast alone disputed its dominion, would possess all the charms of romance, and the *'distance'* of time would *'lend an enchantment to the view'!* Whilst it would illustrate to the philosophic mind some of the noblest traits in the character of our present population. Much of this portion of our history has been lost, and can never be reclaimed, but much has been preserved, and by prompt and diligent research much more may be found. Upon perusing such a record, the present generation would be astonished to find how little they know now of the early history of their own State. Thousands would learn, to their surprise, that they have been born and reared on ground consecrated by the blood of our forefathers, shed by them in rescuing this rich inheritance from the dominion of the Savage. How few within the limits of the beautiful city in which we are assembled, have any correct idea of the toils, dangers, sufferings, battles, victories and deaths of those who first pitched their tents upon this rock bluff! And there are hundreds of spots similarly consecrated within our borders, of which the records live only in the recollection of a few old pioneers who are lingering on the brinks of the grave, or in the dim and declining pages of tradition. Is the State interested in having these consecrated spots made luminous by the putting on record the thrilling incidents which gave permanence to the early settlements on her territory? Is it not due the memory of those bold pioneers in civilization that the State should step forward to rescue their names from oblivion? We delight to honor those who have fallen bravely in battle, and we build monuments on which to inscribe imperishably their names. Why not then also honor the names and the memory of the enterprising band of hunters and pioneers who endured prodigies of suffering and performed prodigies of valor in preparing the way for the tide of safe emigration which followed the track they had marked out with their blood? May we not ask if the State of Tennessee does not owe a debt of gratitude to these noble patriots? which would be but poorly paid in rescuing their deeds from forgetfulness? On what do we rest the solid fame of our State? Is it upon her inexhaustible mineral wealth and her fertile valleys and plains? These were all secured by the bravery, the toils, the sufferings and the blood of the old pioneer! Is it upon the chivalry and gallantry of our soldiers in fighting the battles of our country? These soldiers were the sons of the old pioneers and inherited their chivalry from them! Surely then, our State is interested in dispelling the mists which obscure her early records and in having the heroic deeds of the conquerors of the aborigines spread out in living light upon the faithful pages of history. It may be conceded that such a development of the incidents connected with the first settlements in our State, as is proposed, would not result in the practical benefits which would flow from an authentic history of the State since her admission into the Union. But the bill contemplates a '*complete*' history, and *none* could be '*complete*' which did not trace our rise and progress as a political community from the time when the old hunters from the States traversed the territory in quest of game and carried back the intelligence which excited the adventurous spirit of emigration that resulted in rescuing the rich lands of Tennessee from the dominion of the Indians and wild beasts. Such a history would gratify an intelligent curiosity, whilst it would abound in valuable lessons of wisdom connected with the characters of the permanent actors in the scenes described, and give to us a clear view of the value of perseverance, energy, fortitude and courage in the march of civilization. But the committee feel that it is not necessary to multiply considerations in favor of a liberal expenditure, so far as it may be required to secure the materials for that portion of our history whilst our fathers were laying the foundation for their admission into the Union as a State.

As early as 1784 our mother State manifested a disposition to be relieved of the responsibilities of exercising jurisdiction over and giving protection to the settlers west of THE MOUNTAINS. She passed an act ceding the territory now Tennessee to the General Government, provided the cession should be accepted within two years. To the settlers this act had the appearance of an abandonment on the part of the mother State, and it resulted in the establishment of an independent little REPUBLIC called the State of FRANKLAND. No chapter in our history will present subjects for more interesting reflection, than that which shall detail the events connected with the brief story and existence of '*The State of Frankland.*' They SECEDED from North Carolina because they felt themselves abandoned by her, and they *asserted* their independence because the federal government failed to listen to their appeals for protection. The citizens of Frankland were imbued with the true spirit of freemen, and deserved neither to be regarded or treated as outlaws. The common toast in an adjoining State is said to have been 'Success to the State of Frankland, His Excellency Governor Sevier and his virtuous citizens!' Soon after the dissolution of this little republic, the cession to the General Government took place, and in 1790 a territorial government was provided by Congress. This form of government continued until 1796, when the State of Tennessee was admitted into the Union.

The Committee feel proud that they have it now in their power to present to the State (which will be done in another form), a record of the proceedings of the first legislature, in 1794, that convened under the territorial government established by Congress. It presents the striking characteristic of our forefathers, and should descend to the latest posterity as a monument of their valor, virtue and wisdom. From 1769, when the first permanent settlements were made, the materials are abundant for an authentic and deeply interesting history; but it will require industry and labor to collect them together and prepare them for use. The history of Tennessee as a STATE proper, commences in June, 1795, when the Governor convened the territorial legislature to take into consideration the expediency of applying for admission into the Union as a State. The population of the State was then 77,262, scattered over ten counties, that is: Blount, Davidson, Sullivan, Green, Jefferson, Sevier, Hawkins, Sumner, Washington and Tennessee (now Robertson and Montgomery). A convention assembled at Knoxville on the 11th of January, 1796, *and in less than thirty days* a constitution was agreed upon for the State of Tennessee, upon which she was admitted into the Union as an independent State.

Fifty-five years have passed by, and her ten counties have increased to more than seventy, and her 77,262 population has gone to nearly a *million!* The announcement of such a wonderful growth in population would naturally indicate that the history of such a people must abound in deeply interesting events. The territory of Tennessee covers an area of about 45,000 square miles, or 28,000,000 of acres. At the date of her admission as a State, the title of a large portion of this territory was in the Indians. The settlements were confined to a comparatively small portion of the State. To examine and ascertain the natural resources of this territory, to investigate the legislative policy by which these resources have been developed, to understand the agricultural, mineral and manufacturing facilities of the State, these, together with the general legislative policy of the people, as well as their political relations to other States, and their military engagements at home and abroad, their advancement in morals, science and literature, become subjects for the investigation of the historian, in developing the causes which have produced the astonishing revolution in the condition of our State. When it is remembered that the materials for such an investigation are scattered through hundreds of volumes of legislative journals and acts and as many executive journals and documents, and that these are to be examined, collected and arranged for historical purpose, some idea as to the magnitude of the undertaking may be formed. No one who has taken any interest in the past events of the State can have failed to feel the necessity for such a work as is contemplated by the Bill. The history of our State at present is an undigested mass of confusion. Our legislative journals have been made up as if the object was to make their contents a sealed book. The man who can take hold of this *chaos,* and bring system, method and authentic records out of it, by his researches and his labors will prove a benefactor to his country. It is too much to expect any individual to execute such an undertaking without an assurance that his labors will be properly appreciated and rewarded. The Committee are satisfied that the Senate should give such a guaranty, and under this conviction they recommend the passage of the bill, with the amendment already indicated. The Committee are satisfied that the value of such a work as the bill contemplates is so apparent, that the people of the State will give to the measure their prompt and hearty approval. In the proper execution of the work the State is directly interested, and on that account it is peculiarly appropriate that she should have a voice in designating the person into whose hands is to be committed the important trust of preparing her history. Before the work is sent forth as the authentic record of her existence, she should have the right to see that full justice is done to her character; and when it goes forth it should carry with it the high sanction of her approval. A History of the State thus executed and thus endorsed, will prove to be of incalculable value at the present interesting period of her existence. The time has arrived when the further development of our agricultural, mineral and manufacturing resources must depend mainly upon our legislative policy. Hitherto our advancement in population and wealth has been the result in a material degree of the native fertility of our soil, and the inviting salubrity of our climate. To these we owe much more of our rapid progress as a State, than to the character of our legislation. The proposed History will illustrate this important fact fully, and impress upon our people the necessity of correcting such errors as have marked our past policy. It will also exhibit in the strongest light our inexhaustible natural resources, and demonstrate the advantages to be derived from adopting a more liberal line of policy in their future development. The strong tide of immigration from our State must have attracted the serious attention of our citizens, and must have induced the inquiry into the best means of counteracting the result. A faithful history of the State will establish the fact that our resources are unbounded, and that their development will be the surest means of checking the spirit of immigration, which is now carrying our citizens by thousands to the far west.

But the Committee cannot believe it necessary to dwell upon the benefits to be derived from the contemplated history, and therefore they conclude by an earnest recommendation of the bill to the favorable consideration of the Senate.

S. C. PAVATT, *Chairman*"

On February 3, 1852, the bill routinely passed the first reading in the House of Representatives. Two days later, when the bill came up for second reading, the official record carried the following statement [140] which sounded the death knell of the measure:

"No. 23, to provide for a complete history of the State of Tennessee.
On motion,
Was indefinitely postponed."

It is regrettable that the official record omitted the name of the representative who made the motion and the names of those who supported it. Those representatives, possessed of the vision of a ground mole, robbed posterity of much valuable and interesting history of Tennessee that only contemporary historians could have interpreted and recorded. Since the names of the obstructionists are unknown, perhaps they will always receive what they justly deserve—OBLIVION.

Another member of the select committee on Tennessee History fared better than did Senator Pavatt. On November 5, 1851, Senator Francis B. Fogg introduced the following resolution: [141]

"*Resolved by the General Assembly of the State of Tennessee*, That the Secretary of State be and he is hereby authorized to make a contract for printing .... copies of the Journals of the Territorial Legislature in 1794, 1795, and the State Legislature of 1796, and the Journal of the Convention that formed the first Constitution of this State, and it is
Further resolved, That .... copies be distributed with the Journals of the present General Assembly amongst the several counties of this State."

On November 17, Senator Fogg's resolution was amended by inserting 1,000 as the number of copies to be printed, with five copies to go to each county, provided the cost did not exceed $750. The amended resolution was passed by a vote of 13 to 7. [142] Accompanying the Senate-approved resolution was the following interesting and illuminating report: [143]

---

[140] *House Journal*, 1851, 693.
[141] *Senate Journal*, 1851, 165.
[142] *Ibid.*, 218.
[143] *Senate Journal*, 1851, Appendix, 307–308.

"REPORT.

The Select Committee to whom was referred resolution No. 55, in regard to the re-printing of certain journals of the Legislative Council of the Territory South of the Ohio, and of the Convention by which the original Constitution of Tennessee was framed, have had the same under consideration, and have instructed me to submit to the Senate the following report:

The committee find that the book containing the journals referred to them, contains about four hundred pages; they are informed by an intelligent practical printer that *one thousand copies* of the work, printed and bound in the usual style of legislative acts, will cost about *seven hundred and fifty dollars.*

To enable the Senate to determine upon the propriety of the proposed expenditure, it is proper to give a brief summary of the contents of the several journals.

The first is the journal of the proceedings of the Legislative Council of the Territorial Legislature, which commenced at Knoxville on the 25th of August, 1794.

The second is the journal of the House of Representatives of the Territorial Legislature, which commenced at Knoxville on the 25th of August, 1794.

The third is the journal of the Legislative Council, which commenced on the 29th of June, 1795.

The fourth is the journal of the House of Representatives, which commenced on the 29th June, 1795.

This was a special session of the Territorial Council, for the purpose of determining the expediency of asking admission into the *Union.*

The fifth is the journal of the proceedings of the Convention, which was held at Knoxville on the 11th of January, 1796, and which framed the original Constitution of Tennessee.

The sixth and seventh are the journals of the Senate and House of Representatives commencing their session on the 28th of March, 1796. This was the first session of the General Assembly of Tennessee.

The eighth and ninth are the journals of the Senate and House of Representatives of the Tennessee Legislature, convened in special session on the 30th of July, 1796.

From the foregoing summary of the contents of the book referred to the committee, the Senate will see that these journals contain the authentic legislative history of the State from the 25th of August, 1794, to the 30th of July, 1796, embracing the proceedings of the Convention which formed the first Constitution of the State. The committee do not deem it necessary to make special reference to these proceedings, to satisfy the Senate of their value.— They only deem it proper to remark that they have found the several journals *to abound in the most interesting and valuable materials connected with the early history of the State.* Indeed, it is the only reliable source from which we can learn with accuracy the steps by which our forefathers advanced from one form of government to another, until they secured admittance into the Union as a sovereign State. Here we can find the NAMES of those who participated in building the governmental structure of which we are so justly proud; and from these proceedings we might derive many valuable lessons of wisdom connected with the economy and dispatch of legislative business. Without these journals, the legislative history of our State would be incomplete, and for all practical purposes we are without them. The committee, from the most careful enquiry, are satisfied that the journals here presented, are now in all probability, the only record remaining of our legislative proceedings from 1794 up to 1796, embracing such an interesting era in our history. They would further state, that the book has been preserved by Mrs. .... Beckwith, the daughter of George Roulstone, the printer of the journals, as an invaluable legacy; and if the Senate should not feel disposed to adopt the resolution under consideration, the book must go into private hands, and probably in a short time, the only authentic history of those times *will be lost, and lost forever.*

The committee cannot refrain from recommending that, in case the Senate should adopt the resolution, a copy of the aforesaid journals be procured to be neatly bound and presented to Mrs. .... Beckwith, Jas. G. Roulstone, of Lebanon, and any other of the children of George Roulstone, deceased, by whose hand the type were set up that printed this book.

The committee therefore seriously recommend the re-printing of such number of the journals as will insure a liberal diffusion of the work to the citizens of the State.

All of which is respectfully submitted.

S. C. PAVATT, *Chairman.*"

When the Fogg resolution reached the House on February 24, 1852, its rejection was recommended by the Ways and Means Committee. After an amendment by Representative Edwin Polk was accepted, on motion by Mr. Polk the House non-concurred in the report of the committee.[144] Thereupon Representative Thomas Dean from the counties of Marshall and Bedford attempted to amend the resolution so as to

"Allow the Secretary [of State] to purchase the copy now in print, instead of contracting for its re-publication." [145]

Fortunately for posterity, the mole-like vision of Representative Dean did not prevail. Thereupon, another penny-pincher, Representative J. D. C. Atkins, moved successfully to reduce the number of reprints of the *Journal of the Territorial Legislature* to five hundred copies. Another watch-dog of the Treasury, Representative Robert Farquaharson of Lincoln County, was successful in reducing the number of copies for each county from five to three.[146] With the pruning operations terminated, the amended resolution was then passed by a vote of 37 to 26.[147] The resolution [148] in its final form was as follows:

---

[144] *House Journal*, 1851, 862.
[145] *Ibid.*, 862.
[146] *Ibid.*, 863.
[147] *Ibid.*, 863.
[148] *Acts of Tennessee*, 1851, 748.

Author's note. Posterity is assuredly indebted to the foresight of Senators Pavatt and Fogg for their efforts in preserving the history of our territorial existence just prior to our becoming a State. We shudder when we think that there was *only one known copy* in existence of the proceedings of our territorial Legislature, and of the difficulty encountered in having that one copy reprinted. The author has never seen an *original* copy of the proceedings. What a tragedy had not the Roulstones possessed that one copy! Even with the 500 reprint copies, very few copies are now extant. The author of this volume is the proud possessor of one copy.

"A Resolution directory to the Secretary of State.

Resolved by the General Assembly of the State of Tennessee, That the Secretary of State be and he is hereby authorized to make a contract for printing 500 copies of the Journals of the Territorial Legislature, in 1794-1795, and the State Legislature of 1796, and the Journals of the Convention that framed the first Constitution of this State. And it is

Further resolved, That three copies be distributed with the Journals of the present General Assembly, amongst the several counties of this State. *Provided,* That it does not cost over seven hundred and fifty dollars.

JORDAN STOKES,
Speaker of the House of Representatives.

M. R. HILL,
Speaker of the Senate.

Adopted, February 24, 1852."

The liquor question, which had been rather quiescent since the enactment of a tippling law [149] in 1845 purporting to regulate the traffic, raised its head repeatedly in the 1851 legislative session. A total of seventy-three petitions regarding the liquor business were filed with the Legislature, twenty-three of which were presented by one member alone, Senator Stephan Pavatt, who was accused by sundry citizens of Humphreys County as having been dilatory in pressing the anti-tippling requests. A special committee was appointed to investigate the charges against Senator Pavatt who, according to an extract from the committee's report,

"... had pursued a high minded and honorable course ... endeavoring at no time to suppress or stifle the will of a majority, but at all times presenting such petitions as were addressed to his care on the subject of tippling ... and the charge against this honorable Senator from Benton, as acting anti-republican on this subject, is wholly without foundation." [150]

The anti-liquor movement in Tennessee at this time had undoubtedly been greatly stimulated by the enactment of the "Maine Law," early in 1851, which statute prohibited the manufacture and sale of intoxicating liquors. Agitation for a "Maine Law" for Tennessee was now launched, and prohibition two years later played a prominent part in the gubernatorial and legislative campaigns. But so far as the 1851 Legislature was concerned, the only legislation on the subject was the enactment of a minor law [151] which provided

"That no person shall receive a license, or be a clerk or assistant in any licensed establishment for the retail of spirituous or vinous liquors, who is not a competent witness in a court of justice against a white man."

A bit of legislative concern was manifested regarding the living quarters of the Governor of Tennessee. A salary of only two thousand

---

[149] *Acts of Tennessee,* 1845, Chapter 90.
[150] *Senate Journal,* 1851, 583–584.
[151] *Acts of Tennessee,* 1851, Chapter 60.

dollars per year did not permit the Chief Executive to live in style without drawing upon his own private resources. Democratic Representative Levander Pope of Warren County proposed an investigation of the matter by the appointment of a committee

"... to ascertain what a suitable residence for the Governor of the State of Tennessee can be purchased for in the city of Nashville, or to ascertain whether it would be most expedient to purchase suitable grounds and erect buildings at the public expense." [152]

On December 3, Senator Ephraim R. Osborne from the counties of Maury and Giles submitted the following report [153] from the select committee:

"Your committee beg leave to say that they have performed the duty assigned them, by examining various houses and lots which have been offered them in the city of Nashville, their prices, location, &c., and would say that a house and lot proposed to your committee by Mr. Player, located on Broad Street near the Franklin turnpike, is the cheapest and best property offered them. Mr. Player asks twenty-five thousand dollars for his house and lot. The lot contains two acres. The houses are beautiful and commodious. Your committee would respectfully recommend the purchase of this property for the Governor's residence."

When the bill appeared on the Senate calendar on January 20, 1852, Senator James T. Dunlap of Henry County offered the following amenment,[154] to-wit:

"Strike out the words 'twenty-five thousand dollars' and insert the words 'twenty thousand dollars,' and to insert in lieu of the words 'Mr. Player on Broad Street' the words 'Mr. Campbell on Cedar Street'."

At this juncture, Senator William C. Dunlap of Shelby County moved successfully that the bill and proposed amendment be laid on the table. A week later, the Senate tackled the proposition again. The two Dunlaps, both of whom were Democrats, did not appear to relish the idea of ensconcing the incumbent Whig Governor in a palatial residence. Accordingly, Senator Dunlap of Henry County proposed a purchase price of twenty-two thousand and five hundred dollars, but his proposal was rejected. Thereupon Senator Dunlap of Shelby moved that the bill "be indefinitely postponed." By a vote of 19 to 6, the first legislative effort to purchase a residence for the Governor of Tennessee went down to defeat.[155]

With the Governor left to shift for himself, so far as a residence was concerned, the Legislature became a bit more lenient and eventually passed a law [156] raising the salary of the Chief Executive to three thou-

---

[152] *House Journal*, 1851, 66.
[153] *Senate Journal*, 1851, 279–280.
[154] *Ibid.*, 463.
[155] *Ibid.*, 508.
[156] *Acts of Tennessee*, 1851, Chapter 336.

sand dollars per year. Legislative generosity in this matter was not over-whelming, for the bill squeaked through the Senate by the eye-lash vote of 11 to 10.[157] And even so, Governor Campbell was not a beneficiary of the increase, for it was specifically provided that the increase in salary would become effective "from and after the expiration of the term of office of the present Governor."

Perhaps every legislative session is punctured here and there with some sort of effort to display a sample of alleged humor or originality. In this category falls a resolution [158] by Whig Representative R. W. McClary from the counties of Polk, Monroe, and McMinn:

"Resolved, that the speeches hereafter to be made in this House, that are intended for Buncombe, shall be delivered at Night Sessions, and that Night Sessions be kept for that purpose expressly. And those speeches intended for the benefit of the people shall be delivered in the day time, and

Be it further resolved that Night Sessions be kept up for the express pur-pose of letting our constituents know how very industrious we are, in order to save time and money."

Akin to the McClary resolution was one offered by Democratic Representative F. M. Davis of Sullivan County, to-wit: [159]

"Whereas, in a free and representative government, it is of the most vital importance that the constituent have an opportunity to investigate the con-duct of the representative and to judge for himself as to the faithfulness of the discharge of the trust confided to his representative; And whereas also it is nothing but justice that the representative should have an opportunity to be correctly represented to the constituent—therefore

Resolved, by the House of Representatives of the State of Tennessee, that the committee of Ways and Means be and are hereby instructed to in-quire into and report, by bill or otherwise, for the information of this House, as well as for the information of the public:

1st. What is requisite to secure a puff from the city papers and whether or not the puffs heretofore made by said papers were made in good faith, or merely to bring upon a common level merit and demerit.

2nd. What papers are to be relied upon for a faithful exposition to the public of the conduct and speeches of the members of this House; and in view that the public may not be misled, and be informed what journal they may rely upon for this important information, the said committee are hereby authorized to send for persons and papers."

At times, a serious bill is killed by attempting to weld to it harmful or ridiculous amendments. Such was the case with a bill to render seduc-tion a felony. When the bill came up for second reading, the following amendment [160] was offered:

"Be it enacted, That any female who, by soft looks, sweet smiles, or otherwise seduce or excite any gallant youth, shall be guilty of a felony, and

---

[157] *Senate Journal*, 1851, 606.
[158] *House Journal*, 1851, 437.
[159] *Ibid.*, 586.
[160] *Ibid.*, 587–588.

on conviction thereof be confined in the Penitentiary for not less than two nor more than five years."

As if the above proposed amendment were not sufficient to insure the defeat of the measure, an amendment [161] in lieu was offered:

"Provided the person it is alleged has been so seduced, shall not be a competent witness in any trial under the provisions of this act."

Among the constituents of Representative R. M. Bugg of Giles County were some "do-gooders" who wanted a law enacted to prohibit "Circus exhibitions."[162] Some Hardeman County citizens presented through Representative Edwin Polk a petition urging the suppression of ten pin alleys.[163]

On March 1, 1852, the five-month session of the Legislature came to a close. The Speaker of the Senate, M. R. Hill, in a brief address summarized the accomplishments of the lawmakers. As to the verdict of posterity, he wisely and safely had this comment [164] to make:

"Experience and circumstances must try them; and time, austere and impartial time, will record their just judgment."

Brevity was not a characteristic of the closing remarks of the Speaker of the House, Jordan Stokes. In a panegyric saturated with Fourth of July oratory, he ultimately pronounced the two words— SINE DIE—but not until after he had delivered himself of the following eulogium: [165]

"GENTLEMEN: I rise to perform the last duty incumbent on me as the presiding officer of this House. The complimentary language of the resolution that you have adopted with such unanimity, and apparent cordiality, demands from me a few words expressive of my deep sense of gratitude. I accepted the distinguished position which your kindness and partiality assigned me at the beginning of the session with great distrust of my qualification and fitness for its arduous and delicate duties. I entered upon the discharge of those duties with an honest and sincere desire of demeaning myself in the manner that would best secure your good opinion, and with the humble, yet ardent hope, that the honor and dignity of the high trust would not be lowered in my hands. To this end, I have at all times endeavored to treat every member with the utmost courtesy and respect, to award to each one all his rights and privileges on this floor without partiality or prejudice, and to enforce mildly yet promptly an observance of the rules of parliamentary law. I am truly gratified to know by the terms of your resolution that my official acts have met with your hearty approval. Without this endorsement on your part, the distinguished honor of the position would have covered me with shame and confusion; with it, my humble and imperfect labors are crowned with all the distinction that my ambition aspired to accomplish. I am not able

---

[161] Ibid., 588.
[162] Ibid., 562.
[163] Ibid., 421.
[164] Senate Journal, 1851, 786.
[165] House Journal, 1851, 946–950.

to command language properly to express the emotions of gratitude and thankfulness that swell my bosom in view of this crowning compliment.

I think it is due alike to candor and to truth to say that few legislative bodies have ever convened in this State, possessing so much talent, patriotism and enlightened public spirit. Your deliberations have been characterised by a dignity and manly bearing in harmony with the distinguished character of the body. Great and interesting questions of public policy have come up for free and close investigation, giving rise to much feeling and excitement; yet your debates, at all times full of wit, humor, argument, and commanding eloquence, have been conducted with the greatest decorum and self-respect. While you have not been destitute of ardor and enthusiasm in the advocacy of the particular interest of your constituents, that ardor and zeal have been tempered and dignified by a noble and respectful bearing, alike honorable to the head and heart. Few, very few, occasions have arisen when it has been my painful duty to remind honorable members that they were wandering upon forbidden ground, and it is just to say that in every such instance their high sense of propriety and dignity of character have uniformly checked them in their violation of parliamentary usage. Doubtless passion has been evolved in these conflicts of argument and opinion; but it may be truly said that it has passed away, like the bead in the vial of pure water, with the occasion that produced it, leaving no sediment behind. I have watched with pride and intense pleasure your gallantry and adroitness in the intellectual tournaments of which this hall has been the theatre. It may be that now and then a youthful knight, full of chivalry and adventure, has lost his spurs and helmet, perhaps laid prostrate on the ground, in splintering a lance with some older champion; but no sooner than the conflict is over; than the victor is seen binding up the wounds and laying on the 'flattering unction.' Let no one indulge in gloomy or unkind feelings on account of such a disaster, if indeed any such has befallen him; but let him take fresh encouragement, buckle on his armor anew, and experience will teach him how to wield his lance more adroitly in future conflicts. You have used no shafts, corroded with covert malice and revenge; you have let fly from the quiver of wit and repartee no arrow dipped in gall and wormwood; but while the points of your weapons have sparkled with the brilliancy of careful polish, they have left no rankling in the bosom, no poison in the pure waters of the heart.

I will not presume to pronounce judgment on the various measures which have been passed into public laws at this session. This high prerogative belongs under the genius of our free institutions to the great body of the people. You have transacted an unusual amount of local business, embracing charters of incorporations for almost all purposes—you have made many changes in the laws, simplifying the practice and pleadings in the courts and explaining and removing obscurities and defects in the statute and common law—you have been liberal and generous in appropriations to the institutions of charity, thereby alleviating the misery and gloom of the Insane, and shedding the light of the outward world in the darkened intellects of the Deaf and Dumb and the Blind—you have set apart a Homestead, where the wrecked in fortune and the humble poor can retreat from the wintry blasts of penury and want, and cultivate and enjoy the virtuous endearments of a permanent home—you have passed the apportionment bills without endangering that rancour and bitterness of party-feeling that sometimes break up the harmony and peace of legislative bodies—you have created a scheme of Banking, under which capital can be made to realize reasonable profits and the note holder amply indemnified in the honor and credit of the State, and you have projected a system of railroad improvement, extending liberal aid in the loan of State bonds to the construction of near nine hundred miles of road. Time alone can fully develop the results that will follow your labors, and to this great exponent of truth and error, the wisdom and policy of your acts must be submitted. If the public mind approves the system of improvements which you have created and projected in a broad and very liberal spirit, and the capital of the country co-operates with the bounty of the State in the construction of the main roads, looking to the great channels and avenues of commerce and travel, your legislation will constitute an era in the annals of our prosperous and growing commonwealth, and your names will go down to generations unborn, honored and esteemed as benefactors of your race. A new impetus will be given to the development of the vast resources of the State—the industrial energies of the laboring population will be awakened from its lethargy—the stores of wealth hitherto locked up in mountains and valleys, will be tapped and their incalculable riches made subservient to the wants and comforts of man; cities and thriving villages will spring up as if touched by the wand of enchantment—the beat of the loom and the clinking of the hammer will answer in stirring harmony to the whistle of the steam car—an interchange of wealth, of thought and of friendship will be established with the citizens of sister States, and the Federal Union itself linked together as with hooks of steel and bars of iron in one common destiny. No one will deny but that a system of railway connection tends to bind the Union in closer bonds. The growth in wealth and the advancement in intelligence, consequent on the increased facilities of commerce and personal intercourse, brings about a kind of community of interest, thought and feeling, and as you bring the purses, the views of the hearts of the people closer and closer together you thereby strengthen and endure to them the bonds of the Union. If political madmen, who are engaged in unholy plots to overturn the Constitution and the Union, would get out of the way until the spirit of this progressive age could make its full impress on the intellect and commerce of the country, they could not accomplish their wicked purpose, were they masterworkmen in the strategems of treason, and numbered in their ranks all the traitorous spirits on earth.

Gentlemen you are all Union men—you are Tennesseans in feeling and sentiment. This day the noble theme—the Union falls, enkindling and alive, on your hearts as if it were a coal of fire from off the altars of Heaven. Tennessee owes too much to this glorious Union ever to falter in doing all she can to make its bonds indissoluble, or to abandon its stars and stripes in the hour of danger. Did not the flag of the Union spread its wings over her in the wilderness, when the war-hoop of the Red man awakened the slumbers of her wives and babes? Did not this bright flag wave many a graceful welcome on her admission into the sisterhood of States? Has not its broad shield protected and defended her infancy and riper years from storm and tempest? Have not her liberties and interests flourished and prospered beneath the shadow of its expanded wings? Have not her gallant sons, in days gone by, followed this glorious flag through the gloom and smoke of battle to glory and the grave, and so long as the Union is for Liberty and the Constitution, accursed be the recreant who will not follow this glorious flag wherever its light may lead the way. Tennessee will go on in this great work of strengthening and preserving the bonds of the Union. Should disaster overtake the Republic and the Union be doomed to go down in the blood of civil war, God grant that it may be recorded in that day of gloom, as the chief glory of Tennessee, that *here* the sun-light of American liberty shed its departing beams—that *here* the stars and stripes, every where else stricken down and abandoned, were borne aloft in defiance of its foes—that *here* the fires of patriotism were kindled the last time on the altars of the Union. But this day will not come soon, our country has passed through its darkest hours, the clouds that so recently overspread the land with gloom, have drifted away and the light of the future opens up a brighter and more cheering pathway. The lovers of our free institutions may now indulge the confident hope that the Union will not be rent asunder, the Constitution will not be trodden under foot, that the temple of our liberties will still lift its dome in the 'clear blue sky,' and the Star Spangled Banner ever 'wave o'er the land of the free and the home of the brave.'

Let us not be lukewarm in our devotion to the Union—let not those who come after us blacken our memories with indifference to its perpetuity. Let us look to the flag of our common country, as did Israel of old to the pillar of cloud by day and the pillar of fire by night; let us look to the Union as the smitten rock from which gushes up the living waters of our national and domestic happiness—let us venerate the Constitution as the broad and firm foundation of our liberties at home and our dignity and greatness abroad— let us ever feel that if the light of our example were put out, it would leave the horizon of human freedom without a star to relieve the thickening gloom.

You will pardon me for detaining you so long. I have only a few more words to add. The public duties, which have kept you here are now discharged; the links that have bound you together as one body, will soon be broken. You met a few months ago comparatively strangers, you will part to-day as familiar friends. So long as life endures and memory holds her seat, it will be a pleasant reminiscence to recur to the friendships and attachments here formed, and may it be your purpose as it shall be mine, to keep ever bright as now the links that unite us as friends. Sad, indeed, would be the scenes of the separation that will now take place, were they not alleviated and brightened by the thought that you will soon be welcomed into a circle, whose members are nearer and dearer to you than the ties of personal friendship. Who does not feel his bosom swell with joyful emotions as his imagination catches a glimpse of the hallowed light that burns on the family altar? Who among you will not in this hour endorse the beautiful sentiment of Burns—

> 'To make a happy fire-side chime,
>   To weans and wife,
> That's the true pathos and sublime,
>   Of human life.'

We will meet no more in this Hall—we separate in all human probability never to meet again as legislators. Let your lots be cast wherever they may, whether you pursue the alluring phantoms of political ambition, or repose in the calmer and sweeter shades of private life, you carry with you the humble assurance of my highest regard, and my warmest wishes for your success and happiness.

I thank you again for the complimentary resolution you have adopted. I thank you members and officers of the House, for the kind and courteous manner with which you have uniformly treated me. I thank those members, whose long experience in legislating has made them familiar with parliamentary law, for the prompt and efficient assistance they have rendered me in delicate and difficult questions of order.

I thank most sincerely those gentlemen, who have so often and cheerfully relieved me from the labors of the chair. I beseech you at parting to draw over my many errors and imperfections the mantle of charity. I go from hence to the humbler but happier walks of private life. If I am called away from the scenes of the living before you, and chance or inclination should bring you by the side of my resting place, I ask you as the most acceptable tribute of respect, to bedew the green sod with the tears of a sincere friendship. I would bestow this humble tribute with a full heart to the memory of any honorable member on this floor. May you leave this Hall with the full consciousness that you have discharged your duty to yourselves, your country, to your God. Go, and may the richest blessings of Heaven attend you. I bid you, one and all, an affectionate farewell.

I now declare that this House stands adjourned SINE DIE.

JORDAN STOKES,
Speaker of the House of Representatives.

John H. Leuty,
Clerk of the House of Representatives."

With the adjournment of the Twenty-Ninth General Assembly on March 1, 1852, official relations, from a practical standpoint, between the General Assembly and Governor William B. Campbell were terminated. The next and the last communication that he would transmit to a General Assembly would be to the Thirtieth General Assembly which convened on October 3, 1853. Having declined to be a candidate for re-election, doubtless he felt free and unencumbered when he drafted his parting message and transmitted same to the Legislature just five days after it had convened. That Message,* which will be noted in the succeeding chapter, was as follows:

"GENTLEMEN OF THE SENATE AND HOUSE OF REPRESENTATIVES:

It is with great satisfaction, that, in the exercise of the privilege allowed me, as the Chief Magistrate of the State, of addressing you on this occasion, and so near the close of my official term, I am able to congratulate you upon the auspicious circumstances under which you are assembled. The period is one of general and unparalleled prosperity especially in all the material elements of improvement in condition of the country. The earth has given forth its fruits in the unwonted abundance; and if some of the great agricultural staples are likely to be diminished by the autumnal rains, all the more important and indispensable products of the soil are plentifully distributed. Industry is stimulated by new enterprises. The artizan

---

* *Senate Journal*, 1853, 34–44.
  House Journal, 1853, 37–47.
  Author's note. Ten minor messages of Governor Campbell have been omitted in this treatise. In the main, the messages announce the resignations of a Judge, a trustee of the Lunatic Asylum, and the nomination by the Governor of an inspector of the penitentiary, and bank directors. The ten messages omitted in this volume may be seen by referring to the *Senate Journal*, 1853: 116; 153; 168; 172; 215; 269; 302; 385; 523; 618.

and the laborer find ready employment with increased and remunerating wages, and every where within our borders the comforts of life are being more equally and generally diffused. The facilities of inter-communication have been greatly increased. Our civil and religious institutions and privileges are extended to all classes of our people, and contribute greatly to their happiness and welfare. General good health has pervaded our land, and it becomes us to acknowledge, with grateful hearts, our obligations to an all-wise and beneficent Creator for the blessings he has bountifully conferred upon us. But in congratulating you upon the general prosperity and happiness, I am pained to be compelled to state that there has been some drawback. Though we have abundant cause to be grateful for the blessings of general health, yet within some localities of limited extent in our own State, sore disease has brought mourning into the dwellings of many worthy families—while our sympathies have been deeply moved by the destroying pestilence with which an all-wise Providence has thought proper to afflict our brethren and countrymen of the great Commercial Metropolis of the South, and of many other cities and towns upon the Gulf and lower Mississippi. It is most gratifying, however, to witness the generous sympathy that has been manifested for the sufferers, in the material aid that has been raised and sent foward from various portions of the Confederacy.

It is not my purpose, nor do I deem this a proper occasion, to point out all the causes which have contributed to the present unparalleled prosperity of the country; but I may be allowed to state that, by far the most important and influential of these causes is to be found in the inventions and discoveries by which the power of steam has been successfully applied in the rapid transmission and interchange of all the varied products of industry, both by sea and land. While the locomotive, the river, and the lake have multiplied the facilities and profits of internal trade and intercourse to an incalculable extent, the same power has successfully contended with the winds and tides of the great ocean, and in a proportionate degree extended the advantages of our foreign commerce. The discovery of the gold mines of California, and the sound basis afforded by the abundant yield to our monetary system, may be justly regarded as having had a powerful agency in bringing about the present extraordinary activity and success in our commercial and industrial enterprises. The increased tide of foreign emigration, supplying thousands of skillful artizans to be employed in the various branches of manufacturing industry, and of laborers to carry on the public works, has doubtless had an important and quickening influence in the same direction. These causes, aided by the invigorating spirit of a free system of government, fostered and promoted by the prevalence of universal peace, combined with other causes of less importance which might be enumerated, have created a new era, and enabled the country in the last few years to take a spring forward which has astonished the nations of the old world.

What is to be the duration of this rapid movement in the road to a still higher prosperity, I will not undertake to conjecture or calculate. Some limitation there must be—some proportion to existing means and resources must, in the nature of things, be observed in the steps or degrees by which any country can safely advance to wealth and power; but unless we shall become intoxicated by past success, and rush recklessly into new, ill-considered and impracticable enterprises—unless the national councils shall depart from the long-established policy of the country, in securing the blessings of peace without compromising the national honor—unless a sound discretion shall cease to control the spirit of enterprise and the cord by which the credit system, invented to anticipate future and contingent resources, is suspended, shall be overstrained, and above all, while we continue in the unalterable faith and determination to uphold the Federal Constitution and the Union, I do not see that we may not hope, under Divine Providence, to enjoy a long career of continued and still increasing prosperity in all that constitutes the true glory and happiness of a people.

But it is my more appropriate province to address you upon the condition and prospects of the State of Tennessee. Many of the sister States of the Union have been more upon the alert in availing themselves of the advantages and facilities of railroad communications, and may, therefore, justly claim a pre-eminence in the scale of progress; but by the enlightened policy of your predecessors in the encouragement and patronage extended to incorporated companies, each of the three natural divisions of the State may justly look forward to the time when, by the completion of our projected system of internal improvements, they will be put in connexion by railroad with every State in the Union, save only California, and even with that remote State, when the Pacific railroad shall be constructed—a project which may well be regarded as the grandest of the age, and one not less important and essential to the protection of the Pacific coast, in a military point of view, than to the successful and full development of the resources of the whole country. In the mean time, and when but a small proportion of the railway connexions contemplated within our limits is completed and in operation, and their benefits but partially developed, it is pleasing to observe the effect of the fresh stimulus thereby imparted to every branch of industry and enterprise. It is well known that the State of Tennessee, setting aside its insular position, possesses natural resources and elements of prosperity in its fine medium climate, its fertile soil, its incalculable mineral riches, inferior to none, and superior to most of the States of the Union; and when her progress from the first feeble but daring settlement of the white man in her borders, not dating further back than the ordinary limit of human existence to the present moment, is considered—when she can number more than a million of inhabitants, it may well excite our pride, and challenge general admiration. Yet much remains to be done in amending and perfecting her institutions when they are found by experience to be defective, in providing the means of educational and intellectual advancement, and in sustaining and completing her system of internal improvements already begun, by providing against future embarrassment, and establishing the public credit upon a sure foundation. These are great trusts. They are now committed to you as the constituted representatives of the people, and whether we look to the preservation of the elevated position which the State already enjoys—a position achieved by the wisdom of those who have gone before us, or to what may be rightfully expected in providing by proper guaranties, for the onward and prosperous course of the State, in future, it may be truly affirmed, that at no prior period of our history have the members of the Legislature met together to consult for the common weal, under circumstances imposing obligations so high and responsible.

The state of the finances and the public debt will doubtless attract your early attention. The receipts derived from all sources for the two years terminating on the 1st of October, 1853, were $1,202,046.30; while the expenditure for the same period amounted to $1,218,387.28, showing an expenditure greater than the receipts. It will be for you to inquire, after full reports shall be made to you by the Comptroller, whether any deficit shall appear, and, if any, what measures it will be expedient to adopt in order to supply it.

The total value of the taxable property of the State, reported to the Comptroller, as assessed by the Revenue Commissioners for the year 1852, is stated to be $186,620,119, exhibiting an average value of lands at $3.84 per acre, and of slaves, at $547.25. Although these rates of value are above those of former years, yet there is much reason to apprehend that the returned value, of both slaves and lands, in many sections of the State, are far below their actual values, and as these constitute the principal sources of revenue, I recommend that your earnest attention be given to the subject, and that proper measures be adopted to enforce the faithful execution of existing laws. Independent of the effect upon the revenue, this inequality of taxation, as between the tax payers in the different counties and sections, which is exhibited, is not proper to be tolerated, and calls for correction.

The public debt, exclusive of current charges, and the evidences of which consist of bonds issued by authority of the State, and bonds endorsed by the State, of certain companies, amounts to $5,746,856.-66. These bonds were issued, bearing various rates of interest, that is to say, five and one-fourth per cent internal improvement bonds amounting to $213,416.66; five per cent bonds issued on same account, $1,838,440.00; six per cent bonds issued to the Bank of Tennessee, $1,000,000; five per cent bonds issued to the Union Bank, $250,000: being $125,000 less than the last statement—this last amount having been redeemed by payment since the last session of the Legislature; six per cent bonds issued for building the Capitol, $500,000; six per cent bonds under the act of 1849-50, and under the acts of the last Legislature, and loaned to various rail and plank road companies, $1,095,000.00; six per cent bonds of the Nashville and Chattanooga Railroad Company, endorsed by the State, $850,-000. I refer you to the report of the Comptroller for information as to the periods at which the above bonds respectively become due. It is proper to state that of the above amount of bonds there have been issued since the last session of the Legislature to the Memphis and Charleston Railroad Company, under the act of the 11th February, 1852, $500,000.00; to the plank road company from Dyersburg to the Mississippi river, $25,000.00; to the East Tennessee and Virginia Railroad Company, under the act of the 15th January, 1852, to aid in the construction of bridges on the road, $300,000.00; to the East Tennessee and Georgia Railroad Company, under the acts of the 4th and 26th February, 1852, to aid in the completion of the road, $20,000.00; for completing the State Capitol, $250,000.00; and that the bonds of the Nashville and Chattanooga Railroad Company, within the same period, have been endorsed under the act of 1847-8, to the amount of $250,000.00—an equal amount having been endorsed by my predecessor, under the same act. Bonds of the same company have been endorsed under the act of the last session of the Legislature to the amount of $250,-000.00.

It is proper, also, to observe that, although for the payment of the interest on, and for the ultimate redemption of, a considerable portion of the bonds above stated, as constituting the public debt, the State is only contingently liable, yet that the public credit may in no possible event sustain a check, it will be the part of wisdom to make ample provision against such a result.

To meet the liabilities of the State, of every description, including existing and accruing charges, in addition to the balance now on hand in the Treasury, amounting to the sum of $206,431.86, the means and sources of revenue belonging to the State are, in the Bank of Tennessee, $1,000,000, of stock and $1,353,209.55 of the surplus revenue deposited by the United States Government with the State, which may be properly regarded as means of the State, and $625,600.00 of Stock in the Union Bank. Each of these Banks pay semi-annual dividends of about four per cent, and the stock of each is regarded as at par value. The Bank of Tennessee appears to have been successfully managed during the last two years, and it is believed to be in a sound condition; but as the State owns the entire amount of the capital stock in this bank, and has a very large amount invested in the stocks of both the Union and Planters' Banks, I recommend that a careful and rigid scrutiny be instituted into the condition and management of each of them.

Besides Bank stock, the State owns stock in Turnpike Companies, and in the East Tennessee and Georgia Railroad Company to the amount of $2,028,856.66. Several of these pay dividends. For information as to what extent this source of revenue is available at the present time, I refer you to the report of the Comptroller.

As a further support to the public credit, it should be stated that for the whole amount advanced by the State in the way of loans in bonds of the State issued to Railroad Companies, or by endorsement of bonds of the Companies, amounting altogether to the sum of $1,945,000, and constituting a large portion of the whole amount of the public liabilities, ample indemnity and security are provided by mortgages upon the entire roads and property of the respective companies.

By an act of the former session of the Legislature, authority was given to the Bank of Tennessee, with the advice of the Governor, to sell the stock held by the State in the Union and Planters' Banks. It was not deemed advisable, or for the public interest, that the sale should be made.

All questions connected with Banks and Banking operations are of difficult solution, but it appears to me that the principle upon which free banks, or voluntary associations for banking purposes, under certain regulations, were authorized by the act of the last session of the Legislature, is a sound one, and that its provisions should be further sanctioned and continued. It gives to the note holder—the class of persons most likely to suffer—a perfect security against loss, while other creditors are on no worse footing than the creditors of other banks. So far, the experiments under the late banks, upon the above principle, are now in operation: The Exchange Bank of Murfreesborough, with a capital in bonds filed with the Comptroller, as directed by law, of $89,583; the Bank of Knoxville, with a capital of $50,000; the Bank of Nashville, with a capital of $70,000; and the Bank of Memphis, with a capital of $50,000.

In view of the great advantage, social and commercial, of railroads on great lines of communication between this and other states of the Union, and believing that the credit and resources of the State will be ample to meet any increased liabilities which you in your wisdom may think proper to authorize, I recommend to your particular and favorable consideration the projected Blue Ridge, the Nashville and Henderson, and the Tennessee Central Railroad, and that the same encouragement be extended to these enterprizes which has been afforded to other companies in the State. The Blue Ridge Road contemplated, is upon the route of the old Charleston and Cincinnati Railroad. Since that road was originally projected, the experience of twenty years has but served to strengthen the views then entertained of the expediency and necessity of that connexion.

The importance to the well being of the whole community of the establishment of a system of Common Schools upon a broad and firm basis, one which shall secure to the children of every citizen the benefits of a judicious course of instruction, is so obvious, and I trust at this day, so generally appreciated, that it is unnecessary for me to press the subject upon your consideration.

In connexion with this subject, I would suggest that a rigid inquiry should be made into the present condition of the school lands and the disposition of the proceeds of them in the several counties; also, whether the laws authorizing the sale of them have been faithfully complied with.

It is not alone in a material or physical point of view, that the State may be said to be in a prosperous condition. The highest and most satisfactory evidence exists that there is a more general diffusion of knowledge, and that it has its influence upon the moral sentiments and affections of the people. Nothing could be more conclusive upon this point than the liberal patronage which by legislative grants has been bestowed of late upon those noble charities of the State, the institutions for the Deaf and Dumb and for the Blind; but more especially the Hospital for the Insane. Those are objects which in every enlightened community commend themselves to universal favor and support; and we find, so far as I am informed, not a murmur of complaint against the policy pursued by your predecessors in sanctioning them.

The institution for the education of the Deaf and Dumb at Knoxville is successful and prosperous. For more particular information in regard to the application of the fund appropriated by the last Legislature for the completion of the buildings and enlarging the grounds, and its condition in other respects, I refer you to the report of the Board of Trustees to be made to your body.

Since the last session of the Legislature, a handsome and commodious structure has been erected at Nashville for the Blind, and well adapted to its object. The original design of the building has not, however, been fully carried out, and I recommend that an adequate appropriation be made for that purpose, and for the support of this Institution and the Deaf and Dumb Institution at Knoxville, for the next two years.

The Hospital for the Insane does credit to the State. Under the superintendence of the present humane, skillful and able Physician, assisted by the counsels of an enlightened Board of Trustees, this institution may be compared favorably with the best conducted establishments of the kind in other States. When the buildings are completed upon the original plan, it will accommodate two hundred and fifty patients. Now, only about one hundred can be admitted to its benefits. By the last census it appears that there are four hundred and fifty lunatics in the State, and it is believed there are many more not enumerated, and I therefore earnestly advise that further provision be made for extending the accommodations of this most interesting establishment according to the original plan; and in addition to the amount required for its ordinary support, an increased appropriation be made for the support of a larger number of indigent patients than are now provided for. The employment of a Chaplain, under a liberal salary, to visit the patients, especially on the Sabbath day, and to impart to such of them as may be in a condition to receive it, religious instruction, would be an appropriate extension of the plan of this great public charity.

I invite your attention to the importance of some alterations and additions in the modes now in operation for the punishment of crime.

Under the admirable management of the present humane and gentlemanly Keeper of the Penitentiary, its profits have been increased; and its condition is in every respect improved and excellent so far as the present extent and capacity of the building will admit. It was originally projected upon a scale sufficient only for the admission of two hundred inmates, but upwards of two hundred and forty are now crowded into it. The large number of convicts now employed upon the work about the capitol will, in no great length of time, have to find labor within the walls of the prison, and there will not be room for them. It seems, therefore, that it will be necessary to establish a new or second Penitentiary, or to enlarge upon the plan of the old one. If a new one be thought advisable, I would recommend that it be established in some other section of the State —in the Eastern or Western division of it. I further recommend that a department be provided, or that some addition be made to the existing Penitentiary buildings, for the admission and accommodation of female convicts. Now, no separate apartment exists for females, nor can they be employed usefully, or kept without great expense until such provision shall be made. Nor can I forbear to urge upon your consideration the propriety of so directing interest of that large and most respectable class of our citizens who are employed in the mechanic arts.

The excess of convicts might be relieved, to some extent, if provision were made for the punishment of petit larceny, by confinement in the county prisons. The discipline of these prisons might be greately improved if they were required to be so constructed, or enlarged, as to furnish suitable apartments, or grounds, for the employment of the inmates in some useful labor—the labor to be compulsory in the case of petty offenders not admitted into the Penitentiary, and voluntary on the part of those whose imprisonment is upon accusation only, and to receive their persons for trial. There can be little doubt that all the prisoners would prefer to labor. The profits of the labor of such of the inmates as should be acquitted of the offences with which they were charged should, of course, be paid over to them on their discharge; while the profits of others would go to diminish the expense of the prison.

There is another defect in our system of criminal punishment, which, it seems to me, calls for correction. Persons, both male and female, of tender years, are often convicted of crimes of some enormity, but it has been generally deemed expedient to pardon them for the first offence, rather than pen them up in the State prison with the most depraved adult felons—trusting to their voluntary reformation; but it too often happens that, in the absence of proper paternal interest, many of them, having no parents living, enter again into the practice of crime. To remedy this evil, I sug-

gest the propriety of establishing a house of correction for such offenders, male and female, in which they can be kept employed in
learning some useful trade, and under proper supervision and instruction, their morals be more likely reformed.

I suggest for your consideration, whether the interests of Agriculture and Mining in this State, especially in view of the many late
discoveries of properties in a great variety of soils not known to
agriculturists generally, would not be greatly advanced by an agricultural and geological survey of the State to be made by a competent geologist appointed for that purpose.

Some new provisions of law are necessary for the preservation
of the Public Arms. They are likely to become wholly worthless by
the careless manner in which they are kept. Your special attention
is respectfully called to this subject.

The amendments to the constitution voted upon at the recent
election, will demand your attention. The amendments proposing
the establishment of several new counties, failed to receive the
requisite number of votes. The amendment in relation to the election by the people of Judges and Attorneys General, although some
doubts have been expressed, has, it is believed, received the required
sanction of the people. In that event, it will be your duty to consider
of the proper time and mode of carrying this new provision of the
constitution into effect.

In connection with this subject, it seems to be a most auspicious
and appropriate time for increasing the salaries of the Judges of
the Supreme, Chancery and Circuit Courts. Their salaries are inadequate to the responsible and important services they perform.
The bench should be filled by the ablest and most experienced
members of the bar and salaries given that would command their
services. The price of property and wages of labor of every kind
has greatly advanced, while the salaries of our Judges have been
stationary for near twenty years. The salary of the Governor was
increased to three thousand dollars by the last Legislature without
any addition to his labors; the law, however, does not go into operation until my successor shall be qualified. The labors of the
Judges are far greater than those required of the Governor; in
truth, they are twenty-fold more onerous—requiring far higher
qualifications. Yet the Judges of the Supreme Court receive but

one thousand eight hundred dollars a year, and the Chancellors and Circuit Judges but one thousand five hundred dollars a year, and it seems to be but sheer justice that the salaries of these most valuable officers, should be increased.

I was directed by an act of the last Legislature, to cause certain bonds of the State to be renewed, that were issued without coupons attached, and in conformity with that law there have been renewed one thousand one hundred and thirty-four bonds bearing interest at five per cent, and one hundred and fifty-four bonds at $5\frac{1}{4}$ per cent interest, each of one thousand dollars with coupons attached. The old bonds in lieu of which these were issued, are cancelled and on file in the office of the Secretary of State. The sum of six hundred and sixty dollars has been paid by the State for engraving the plate and for blank bonds, and there has been received from those having their bonds renewed the sum of three hundred and fifteen dollars.

The vacancy in the Senate of the United States occasioned by the expiration of the term of the Hon. John Bell on the fourth of March last, it will be your duty to fill by election.

Since the last session of the Legislature, the Hon. Nathan Green resigned his office as one of the Judges of the Supreme Court of the State, and I appointed Robert L. Caruthers to fill the vacancy. Hon. Thomas Maney, Judge of the Circuit Court for the sixth Circuit, also resigned his office, which I filled by the appointment of Nathaniel Baxter. On the resignation of William L. Martin, as Attorney General for the fifth District, I appointed James L. Scudder to fill the vacancy, and George Bradford to fill the vacancy in the office of Attorney General of the sixth District, caused by the resignation of Robert C. Foster, 3d. Thomas H. Calloway having resigned the office of Register of the Ocoee District, I appointed James S. Bradford to fill the vacancy.

The Hon. Charles F. Keith, Judge of the third Judicial Circuit, resigned his office, to take effect on the 3d day of October, 1853. This vacancy I have not filled, because it will occur during the session of your body, and I refer it to your consideration, for such action as you shall deem proper.

Having pointed your attention to a few of the subjects which appeared of sufficient importance to receive a special notice from me, it might be expected that before closing this communication, I would, according to a usage, not uncommon of late, briefly explore the field of national politics; but I shall not do so. Our admirable political system is such—the respective powers and duties of the State and National Governments being so wisely separated and divided, assigning to the one the regulation and control of all the great interests which concern the States combined in a Federal Union, and to the other, the regulation of the interests equally, and, if possible, of still greater importance, connected with their respective, separate and distinctive internal policy—their laws, their judicatures, their internal improvements and educational systems, their charitable and all other institutions and objects of State concern—that at the present period, there is no sufficient cause to invoke your special attention to any subject other than those over which, by the Constitution you have the exclusive control. Those subjects, I am persuaded, you will deem of sufficient interest and magnitude to give full scope to your faculties and fill up all your time. There have been times, and they may again arise, when it may be not only proper, but an imperative duty, for the State Legislatures to discuss, with freedom, and to boldly announce their opinions and sentiments on national questions, but I perceive no occasion at present for the exercise of this right and privilege. The storm of sectional passion and agitation which swept over the country, and, for a time, created some alarm for the safety of our institutions, has happily subsided. It is true that factions still exist in the country, which continue to plot the overthrow of the Federal Constitution, or to change, or render abortive some of its most essential guarantees; but such factions, whether headed by fanatical reformers, or political aspirants, who, under the simulation of honest sympathy, but without any principle, are ever ready to sacrifice their country to their ignoble ambition, will always exist. They are the inevitable attendants of every system of government. Sectional interests and prejudices may, under our system, occasionally impart to them a formidable aspect; but they will be successfully resisted until the great body of the people shall no longer possess the intelligence to discern their own true interests, and become reckless and insensible alike to the prosperity and glory of the country.

Fortunately, there exists in Tennessee no such sectional feeling, no such divisions of sentiment upon the great questions which have of late disturbed the councils of some of the other States, as will be likely to interrupt your deliberations, or divert your attention from the ordinary and more legitimate subjects committed to your charge. Every attendant circumstance seems propitious to a patriotic and successful prosecution of your labors. The inauguration of the new Capitol—a structure doing equal honor to the skill and genius of the Architect, and to the public spirit inspired by free institutions—is appropriately celebrated by the assembling of the Legislature for the first time within its spacious halls. All around, you have daily presented to your view and contemplation models of all that is pure and beautiful in architectural taste, combined with utility—all that is orderly, harmonious and proportionate—all that is durable and grand—fit types of all that is pure, wise and excellent in legislation.

May your proceedings be characterized by similar order, harmony and dignity, and all that you shall accomplish in the discharge of the important duties assigned you by your constituents, be equally useful and durable in elevating the character and advancing the prosperity of your country.

WM. B. CAMPBELL."

October 8, 1853.

CHAPTER FIVE

Andrew Johnson

Andrew Johnson was born in Raleigh, North Carolina, December 29, 1808. He was the son of Jacob Johnson who was poor and unable to provide Andrew with even the rudiments of an elementary education. Jacob Johnson died when Andrew was only four years of age, leaving his subsequently famous son destitute of property, education, or apparently even a "Chinaman's chance" for success and distinction. If one were to speculate a bit, it might be asserted that the adverse stroke of fate served to develop the faculty of self-reliance which never deserted Andrew Johnson through many years of tempestuous political activity. Born, as he was, in poverty and obscurity, the ten-year-old lad became a "bound apprentice" to a local tailor for a specified number of years. Before the end of his term of indenture, Andrew became involved in a boyish misdemeanor and went to Laurens, South Carolina, where he continued his work in another tailoring establishment. Later, Andrew sought his former employer, apologized for his misconduct, and tendered payment for his unperformed period of service. This commendable offer was refused, whereupon the proud spirit of the youth revolted with the result that he and his widowed mother resolved to seek a new home "across the mountains."

Late in the year 1826, the eighteen-year-old boy and his mother arrived in Greeneville, Tennessee. Here he opened a tailor shop which became historically famous, for in this modest establishment the busy tailor applied himself by day with his "goose" scissors, and thread. At night, and during slack intervals in the day, he applied himself to mastering the alphabet and learning to read and write under the faithful tutelage of a devoted wife. Thrift in his vocation and studious habits soon attracted attention, and in 1828 he was elected alderman and two years later was elected mayor. In 1835, he was elected to the House of Representatives but, two years later, was defeated for re-election. In 1839, he was returned to the Legislature and in 1840 was a State-at-large candi-

From Portrait by William Cooper. Courtesy of Tennessee Historical Society, Nashville.

date for Presidential Elector on the Democratic ticket. With experience in legislative sessions, he had developed into a formidable public speaker and made a deep impression upon the crowds who gathered to hear the current political issues discussed face to face by notable speakers of opposite political faith.

After one term in the State Senate, 1841, Andrew Johnson was elected a member of Congress in 1843 and served continuously until 1853. In 1851, the Whig Legislature redistricted the State and, by adding two Whig counties to Johnson's Congressional District, gerrymandered Johnson out of Congress by rendering his re-election in 1853, if not impossible, at least highly improbable. During his ten-year tenure in Congress, Johnson took part in the discussion of such leading issues as the annexation of Texas, the War with Mexico, tariff revision, and various other measures. During this period, he initiated and advocated the enactment of a law granting homesteads out of the public lands to citizens occupying and cultivating such bounties for a specified time. His efforts, thwarted for a time, ultimately culminated in the granting of his objective, and the opening up of the Great West to thousands upon thousands of immigrants stands as a monument to his interest in and concern for "the common man."

In 1853, Johnson was the Democratic candidate for Governor against the "Eagle Orator," the redoubtable Gustavus A. Henry. He emerged from the contest victorious and during his first administration espoused the cause of public education with such earnestness that there was enacted the first law in Tennessee levying a public tax for the support of public education. Two years later (1855), in the gubernatorial race he was pitted against another strong opponent, Meredith P. Gentry who was backed by the Know-Nothing Party. In the first race, Johnson "broke the back" of the Whig Party in Tennessee; in the second race, he devastated the Know-Nothings. In all probability, these two gubernatorial contests were the most spirited and the most bitterly contested of any similar contests in the annals of Tennessee history. Employing both ridicule and sarcasm, Johnson drove the Know-Nothings from the intrenchment of secrecy and oath-bound obligations, while upholding the fundamental bases of his own political creed— liberty of thought and conscience, and the maintenance of free institutions under the sanction of the Constitution.

Approximately three weeks before the end of his gubernatorial term in 1857, Johnson was elected United States Senator over Ex-Governor Neill S. Brown. Before the end of his term, dissensions in the Democratic Party regarding the status of slavery in the territories resulted in the election of a sectional President, Abraham Lincoln, in 1860. Immediately thereafter, the Federal Union began to dissolve. At this juncture, Johnson delivered in the United States Senate the ablest speech of his life—opposition to the doctrine and policy of secession. But secession followed, and the land heaved as with an earth-quake. In March, 1862, through appointment by Lincoln, Johnson became Military Governor of Tennessee, a position as anomalous and distasteful to him as it was irritating and vexatious to a majority of the people over whom he was to rule.

In 1864, the re-election of Lincoln was considered questionable, he himself expressing doubt on that point. To bolster his prospects, Johnson who had been the leading Tennessean opposing secession was placed on the ticket with Lincoln. This was the compelling motive that resulted in the nomination of Democratic Andrew Johnson for Vice-President on the ticket with Lincoln. But in doing so, the distinctive name of *Republican* was dropped, and Lincoln and Johnson were candidates of the *National Union* Party. It was as a candidate of the latter party that Johnson accepted the nomination, though he clearly set forth in his letter of acceptance that in principle he was still a Democrat.

Within a few weeks after he had taken the oath of office as Vice-President, the tragical death of Lincoln catapulted Johnson into the Presidential chair. Never, perhaps, did any President of the United States assume the reins of power under responsibility more delicate and tremendous. For four long and weary years a divided Nation had waged war with large numbers and insatiable fury. The clash of arms had ceased, but civil strife was rampant. To calm the tumult, to rebuild faith and confidence in the Nation's institutions, to re-establish in form and spirit civil government—these were the tasks to which President Johnson addressed himself. The retention of Lincoln's Cabinet; a general amnesty, with certain reservations, was proclaimed; and the work of establishing provisional civil governments in the lately insurgent States was begun with a view of restoring their just autonomy and proper relations to the Federal Government.

In a message to Congress then assembling, Johnson reviewed the *status quo* of the States lately at war with the rest of the Nation, and presented an able exposition of the principles involved and the measures which he had pursued. His message met with a vindictive and vituperative rebuff, both to himself and to the peaceful work of restoration. Under the name of "Reconstruction" the dominant majority of Congress enacted a series of measures whose baneful effects have as yet scarcely disappeared. In rapid-fire order were passed a so-called Civil Rights Bill, Freedman's Bureau, Enforced Enfranchisement of Negroes by the States; the instituting of Military District Government, and the Tenure-of-Office Act, all of which President Johnson vetoed. Promptly, a highly partisan Congress overrode the Presidential veto. Then came the straw that "broke the camel's back,"—the removal by President Johnson from the Cabinet of a stubborn and unreliable member, Edwin M. Stanton, who had in fact been disloyal to Lincoln. At this juncture, the Congress descended to depths of bitter partisanship comparable to the worst features of England's "Long Parliament." Articles of impeachment were lodged against President Johnson, charging him with having committed "high crimes and misdemeanors." Conscious of his innocence and defending his own integrity, the President's intrepid courage did not fail him in the crisis, and a conviction could not be obtained even before a prejudiced tribunal. No trial exceeded this ordeal in our entire history, and none ever carried consequences of a more pernicious import. The period of his Presidency was tempestuous, but his tenure was illustrated with wisdom, honesty, and administrative vigor. He retired from his exalted station with credit and his niche in the temple of fame assured.

On March 4, 1869, Johnson departed from Washington for his home in Tennessee. He had just turned three-score years, but his stamina was in evidence and his strong nature was yet dissatisfied with the results of his battle with his fierce antagonists. He desired to re-enter the United States Senate Chamber which had once been a court of judgment to him. But the political atmosphere of his State had not cleared, and he was defeated. Some two years later, he was defeated in his effort to be elected Congressman at large. In 1875, in what must have been to him the crowning event of his forty years in public service, he was elected United States Senator. He must have felt that his election was a reversal of any sentence ever passed upon him by his beloved State. His last and only appearance in the Senate Chamber after his election was at the extra session in March, 1875. Curiously enough, the pending measure was the vexed question of Louisiana affairs, a condition brought about by little less than anarchy through the domination of its Legislature by the Federal military forces. Against this invasion and usurpation of States' Rights, Johnson spoke with his characteristic power and logic. This proved to be his last effort in the public service.

In the summer of 1875, he was busily engaged at home arranging his voluminous papers. While on a brief sojourn with a relative in Carter County, the "insatiate archer" paid him the inevitable visit. He was spared any prolonged suffering, for a paralytic stroke produced death in a few hours, on July 31, 1875. On an overlooking hill, near the chartered limits of his beloved Greeneville, his body was laid to rest. Over his grave stands a twenty-seven foot monument whose pedestal is ornamented with a scroll Constitution immediately above an open Bible. Below his name and the dates of his birth and death may be seen a simple sentence that epitomizes the life and career of Andrew Johnson,—

His faith in the People never wavered.

Legislative Messages of
Governor Andrew Johnson, 1853–1857

Before dealing with the administration of Governor Andrew Johnson, it is highly desirable to give a thumbnail sketch of the status of each political party's situation in Tennessee as of that period. First of all, it should be recalled that for almost twenty years, from 1835 to 1852, the Whig party was largely dominant in Tennessee. During this period Tennessee had been carried by the Whigs in five Presidential elections. Out of nine successive gubernatorial contests, the Whigs had triumphed six times. The margin of victory each time was small, but on the whole the Whig party was the victor. William B. Campbell, the last Whig Governor of Tennessee, had led the Whig party to victory in the gubernatorial contest of 1851, but internal dissensions cropped out during his administration. The election of United States Senator constituted the "rock" that helped alienate political leaders which led to a split of the party. The term of Hopkins L. Turney had expired on March 3, 1851, and the election of his successor stirred to a white-heat the ambitions as well as the animosities of aspiring Whigs. With a Whig Governor and a Whig Legislature, the political waters appeared to be "fine," and there were prominent Whig leaders who desired to "swim." Prominently mentioned for the prize political plum were such worthies as Ex-Governor James C. Jones, Thomas A. R. Nelson, Meredith P. Gentry, and Gustavus A. Henry. "Lean Jimmy" emerged the victor, but that triumph helped split the Whig party in Tennessee. Whig Congressman Meredith P. Gentry, able and spirited, had developed a hostile feeling toward Jones and seems to have strayed from the fold when the political pot began to boil early in 1852. He was ardently attached to the candidacy of Millard Fillmore, and in the Congressional Whig caucus of April, 1852, he bitterly opposed the nomination of Winfield Scott. Two months later, Gentry regarded himself as an excommunicated Whig and on the floor of Congress gave utterance to an expression[1] that became famous in the political history of Tennessee, to-wit:

"I will go home. In a sequestered valley in the State of Tennessee there is a smiling farm, with bubbling fountains, covered with rich pasturage, and fat flocks, and all that is needful for the occupation and enjoyment of a man of uncorrupted tastes. I will go there and pray for 'Rome'."

In November, 1852, Gentry delivered a lengthy speech to his constituents, at Franklin, Tennessee. Later, he reduced his speech to writ-

---

[1] *Congressional Globe, Appendix, First Session, Thirty-second Congress,* Volume XXV, 712.

ing which embraced 30 pages in small type. He boldly admitted in his pamphlet that he had withheld his support from General Scott, and his appraisal [2] of Ex-Governor (now United States Senator) James C. Jones was far from flattering:

"... according to my estimate of his past career and present position, there is nothing in either to excite my envy; and so far as his political future is involved, I think it need not excite the envy of *any man;* because it is my opinion that when he shall have exhibited his meager talents and vaulting ambition upon the theatre of national politics, during the remainder of his senatorial term, under the scrutiny of the great men of the nation, it will become a national jest that such a man was ever considered or thought of for the Presidency. . . ."

Congressman Gentry's speech at Franklin did not go unnoticed by U. S. Senator James C. Jones. A Washington correspondent of a Nashville newspaper gave confirmatory evidence [3] of the strained relations between Gentry and Jones:

"... Another matter of interest here concerns Mr. Gentry and Gov. Jones. A duel between these gentlemen has been confidently expected by those who have a very faint personal knowledge of the latter. Some little time ago, Gov. Jones addressed a note to Mr. Gentry making enquiry about the purport of a certain speech made at Franklin by the latter. The reply was that the speech was in the course of preparation for the press, and that when published a copy would be furnished as the best answer to the inquiry. About eight days ago a copy *was* furnished, accompanied by a brief note. Since which time nothing more has been heard from his Excellency. Rumor says that Col. Gentry had prepared himself for an immediate answer—had selected his friend, and was ready for a short trip in the cars at a moment's notice. Eight long days have passed, however, and not the slightest desire has been manifested for 'pistols and coffee,' by the man who felt himself so valorous at New York, and boasted that he would cut off the buttons of the now President-elect. None, however, have the hardihood to doubt his courage. It is supposed only that he has an aversion to coffee, not to pistols, and that if the code of honor recognized 'pistols and tea' or 'pistols and buttermilk,' Col. Gentry would have been food for worms before now. It is very fortunate for the public peace that the nomenclature of the code is so limited, and the taste of our honorable Senator so peculiar."

Gentry's charge that "Lean Jimmy" was angling for "big fish" in the form of nomination for President or Vice-President at the Whig National Convention in 1852 is supported by a statement [4] from quite

---

[2] *Speech of M. P. Gentry, of Tennessee, Vindicating his Course in the Late Presidential Election, Delivered to his Constituents at Franklin, Tennessee, November 20, 1852.*

Author's note. It is possible that personal animosity between Gentry and Jones may have originated in their rivalry for a seat in Congress years prior to their present "unpleasantness." In alluding to that contest, Gentry stated in his pamphlet that Jones had "organized and encouraged a most unjust and illiberal war against me." See page 23 of Gentry's pamphlet.

[3] *Daily Union* (Nashville), March 1, 1853.

[4] Letter from Andrew Johnson to S. Milligan, July 20, 1852. Johnson Papers, Congressional Library, Washington.

another source, none other than the then Congressman Andrew Johnson:

"... Since his [Jones] arrival here [Washington], has been trying to play a bold game for either the first or second place on the ticket, but without doubt has most signally failed.... Bell, Gentry, and Watkins were dead against him in Washington; Brownlow and Nelson and others at home."

But hostilities had also broken out in the ranks of the Democrats. Two of the strongest leaders had become estranged as a result of the fight in the Nashville Convention of 1850 over the Tennessee resolutions. A. O. P. Nicholson and Ex-Governor Aaron V. Brown buckled on their armor and went after each other in a spirited and bitter battle. The schism between these two giants, in the opinion [5] of an eminent historian, proved disastrous for the Democratic party in Tennessee:

"This hostility between the two leading Democrats of Middle Tennessee was augmented by the desire of both men to be elected Senator. The effect of the quarrel was to lose the State to the Whigs who consistently denounced the convention and fastened upon the Democrats the charge of plotting disunion."

In the Presidential election of 1852, the Whig party went down to defeat in the triumph of Franklin Pierce over Winfield Scott, but Scott carried Tennessee by a majority vote [6] of 1,880. The loss of the State to the Whigs left the Tennessee Democrats with a lean hope for any Federal "pie" in the shape of cabinet positions or other political patronage. As for the Whigs, Governor Campbell declared that the party was "broken to pieces." [7]

In Tennessee, whether viewed from the Whig or the Democratic viewpoint, the forthcoming gubernatorial contest of 1853 was all but inviting, for the situation was reminiscent of Colonel John Donelson's closing remarks upon his arrival in 1780 at the site of the present Nashville—"our prospects at present are dreary!" Whig prospects became dreary indeed when the following announcement [8] was made public:

"Gov. Campbell's Declension.

We share in the regret which will be felt by his many friends throughout the State, upon the publication of the following letter from Gov. Campbell, declining to be a candidate for re-election. The editor of the Banner, to whom it is addressed, has politely furnished us a copy for publication:

Nashville, January 5, 1853.

Gen. Zollicoffer: The frequent and unexpected calls that have been

---

[5] *Tennessee and National Parties, 1850–1860*, by St. George L. Sioussat, in American Historical Association, 1914, Volume 1, 243–258.

[6] Miller, Charles A.: *Official and Political Manual of the State of Tennessee*, 167.

[7] Letter from William B. Campbell to David Campbell, March 22, 1853. In Campbell Papers, Duke University, Durham, North Carolina.

[8] *Nashville True Whig*, January 12, 1853.

made upon me through the newspapers to become a candidate for re-election, require that I should at once make known to the people of our State, in some public manner, my determination not to be a candidate for re-election to the office of Governor.

The reasons which have impelled me to this conclusion are of a personal character, and with which the public would have but little concern. But I will state that my private affairs, together with the welfare and happiness of my family, now large and entirely dependent upon my personal exertions for support and education, demand from me my devoted and undivided attention.

It is well known to many of my friends that I not only reluctantly consented to become a candidate at the last election, but that I then declared that I would not run a second time. The success which has attended my efforts, in connection with those of the whig party in our State, has satisfied me for the sacrifice I then made, and I shall ever remember, with grateful pride, the kindness and confidence of my fellow-citizens, regretting only that I have not accomplished more in advancing their prosperity, their glory, and their happiness. Among the many honest and talented men with which the whig party abounds, one can be selected who will lead us to victory in the approaching contest, and who will serve the State more advantageously than I can hope to do. For the generous support you, sir, and the whig press of our State have given me, I tender my sincere acknowledgments.

W. B. CAMPBELL."

With Governor Campbell's positive declaration that he would not seek re-election, confusion and consternation invaded the Whig political wigwams and a "hunt" for a formidable candidate became a *must* on the Whig agenda. About a week after news of Governor Campbell's declination to stand for re-election had been noised about the State, agitation in behalf of Major Gustavus A. Henry was set in motion by a Whig journal. On January 21, Major Henry's home town newspaper, the *Clarksville Chronicle,* declared unequivocally that "Major Henry's fixed determination is that under no circumstances would he accept the nomination if tendered to him." [9] For approximately two months, the Whigs kept fishing about in the political pool and public sentiment seemed to be settling upon General William T. Haskell of Jackson as perhaps the most formidable candidate that the Whigs could produce. General Haskell declined with thanks the prospective nomination. But he dispatched a letter to Felix K. Zollicoffer, editor of a Whig newspaper in Nashville, that an accidental meeting with Major Henry on a steamboat trip down the Cumberland River had offered opportunity for a discussion of the "impending crisis" and that he (Haskell) had implored and entreated Major Henry to reconsider his recent declination of the honor of heading the Whig ticket at the coming election. According to General Haskell, Henry yielded to the solicitation and gave assurance that he would abide by General Haskell's "discretion." [10]

---

[9] *Ibid.,* January 21, 1853.
[10] *Ibid.,* March 15, 1853.

And thus it came about that Major Henry's "fixed" determination became unfixed!

All was "peaches and cream" when the Whig State Convention assembled on April 25 at Nashville. Major Henry was nominated by acclamation as the Whig candidate for Governor, "his nomination being received with entire unanimity and hearty enthusiasm." [11]

Two days after the State Whig Convention had met, the Democratic State Convention convened in Nashville on April 27 for the purpose of selecting a standard bearer to wage a contest with the Whig nominee, Gustavus A. Henry. As is customary on such occasions, varying opinions were in evidence as to the most strategic choice for nomination for Governor. On the night of April 26, just preceding the meeting of the Convention on the following day, a prolonged caucus was held. The name of Andrew Ewing was presented accompanied by a motion that he be declared the nominee by acclamation. Objection was immediately raised on the ground that a majority of the counties were not represented at the caucus. Notice was served that the name of Andrew Johnson would be presented to the Convention as a candidate for the nomination. A delegate from Marshall County thundered away to the effect that he was for no man in particular; he was for the man who could be elected—he was for "Mr. Availability." [12]

Curiously enough, the Nashville Democratic papers carry a very skimpy account of the Democratic Convention. Perhaps a controlling factor in giving only an abbreviated sketch was a desire to keep the "family fuss" from being bruited around by the Whig press of the State. The inner workings of the Convention were thus described by a Whig organ: [13]

"The Secretary here commenced to call the counties for votes, Johnson and Ewing being the candidates. He was interrupted immediately however, and at this juncture Hon. Andrew Ewing appeared in the Convention, and took a prominent position to make a speech. His appearance had the effect to quell commotion—the 'lesser lights' incontinently hid their diminished heads —and

> 'Silence, like a poultice, came
> To heal the blows of sound.'

Mr. Ewing proceeded to define his position. He stated in substance that he occupied an unfortunate attitude. A few months ago he had been spoken of in connection with the nomination for Governor, and he then declined. Soon after he had received a letter from Washington stating that Andrew Johnson would probably be brought out as a candidate, and giving reasons which he deemed sufficient to constrain him to give Mr. J. his support, and he had so replied to the letter, and authorised his correspondent to show his letter to

---

[11] *Ibid.*, April 26, 1853.
[12] *Ibid.*, April 29, 1853.
[13] *Ibid.*

Mr. Johnson. Since that time he had received a letter from a friend of Mr. J. in East Tennessee, advising as to the best means of bringing his (Mr. J.'s) name before the Convention. He had also received a letter from Mr. Johnson himself, who had entrusted his name to his keeping to do with it as he deemed best. He had fought for him in the caucus to the last. But in a moment of excitement and confusion in that caucus, they having failed, after balloting to a late hour, to make a nomination, his friend from Wilson, had offered his name, and it was accepted. His first impulse was to decline, but upon consultation with his friends, and feeling assured that the caucus would fail to agree on that night, he concluded to wait until morning before giving his answer. He did answer in the morning that he could not allow his name to be run in competition with that of Mr. Johnson. But, had Mr. Johnson fallen behind in the balloting, and had he (Mr. Ewing) been nominated, he would have accepted the post, buckled on the armor and fought the enemy from Carter to Shelby.

Hereupon Mr. David of Marshall withdrew the name of Mr. Ewing, and only Mr. Johnson was before the Convention. Gen. Hickman of Davidson nominated Hon. I. G. Harris of Henry. The Secretary commenced calling the counties, but was again interrupted by Mr. Adkins of Henry who requested the gentleman from Davidson to withdraw the name of Mr. Harris, which was done. Mr. Waggoner of Williamson here obtained the floor and said he would nominate a man who was a head and shoulders above any one heretofore spoken of, but before he could name his man, he was significantly pulled by the coat tail. After conference, he stated that he had been informed that Mr. Nicholson would not run, and he therefore would decline nominating him, but, he remarked, as the play book would say, *aside*, 'he would vote for him any way.' One of the delegates from Knox county then withdrew the name of Andrew Johnson, but he was immediately renominated by Mr. Howard of Montgomery. Somebody then nominated Judge Dunlap.

A motion to adjourn was lost. Mr. Adkins, of Henry, regretted to see the feelings that were uppermost in the Convention. There appeared to be no two men agreed upon any one proposition. He was sorry to say it to the enemy, but he might as well be candid. He was disposed to nominate Mr. Nicholson, but one of the Maury county delegation declared that he would not accept. Mr. Bate, of Sumner thought to pour oil on the troubled waters by nominating John M. Bright. The Maury county delegation here withdrew the withdrawal of Nicholson. A delegate from Bradley defended Johnson against the embittered feelings of the Convention, and withdrew his name. Nicholson and Bright were then alone before the Convention, and the latter was withdrawn. Objection was made to the withdrawal of Johnson, and he was again re-nominated. The Chair here explained that the candidates before the Convention were Johnson and Nicholson. One of the delegates here announced that he was just from the bedside of Mr. Nicholson, who was ill, and that he was authorized to say that in no event would he (Mr. Nicholson) allow his name to be brought in competition with that of Mr. Johnson. Johnson was then alone before the Convention. At this point Mr. Wagoner, of Williamson, who had stood out against Johnson, with a Roman fortitude, seeing his favorites withdrawn one by one, seemed suddenly to 'cave,' and declared that it appeared to him that Andrew Johnson was strong enough to run every locofoco out of the Convention, and he reckoned he could run Henry out of the State. With this the hostility to Johnson suddenly disappeared, and the Convention proceeded to vote upon him without any competition, and he was unanimously nominated.

According to our observation the nominee was the third choice of a majority of the Convention, and the 'last resort' of many. The opposition to him was intense, and his opponents fought with a determination to kill. All that saved him was the circumstance that Andrew Ewing, Esq., was his first friend, and neither he nor Mr. Nicholson would contend with him for the nomination.

The speeches during the evening session were characterized by much warmth. After the nomination had been effected, speeches were made of which we may give some account hereafter.

All that is necessary to insure his signal defeat, is an organized and determined EFFORT of the whig party in Tennessee."

Certain factors entered into the placing of the name of Honorable Andrew Ewing before the Convention as the nominee for Governor. He was an eminent lawyer, and a man of exalted character. He was very popular and had been elected to Congress in 1849 from the Nashville District which had sent a Whig to Congress every session since the retirement of James K. Polk in 1839. A Democrat who had been elected to Congress from a strong Whig District was not a man to be cast aside lightly; consequently Ewing's name was one to conjure with. But Ewing's high and noble concept of honor and integrity would not permit him to appear as a betrayer of a trust that he believed had been committed to him. By his own declaration, he put himself out of the contest and left the field to Andrew Johnson. And so, the race was on, and what a race!

A partisan press carried long articles on the merits, demerits, and careers of the respective candidates. Gustavus A. Henry was born in Kentucky in 1803, graduated from Transylvania University, took up the study of law in the office of the Chief Justice of the Supreme Court of Kentucky, was a member of the Kentucky Legislature in 1832, married a lady from Montgomery County, Tennessee, in 1833, and shortly thereafter moved to Clarksville where he opened a law office. In 1836, 1840, 1844, and in 1852, he stumped the State as a Whig Presidential elector and by his fiery eloquence won the title of "The Eagle Orator." In 1851, he was elected to the Legislature from Montgomery County, and was a recognized leader in that body. His only political setback thus far was in 1843 when he contested unsuccessfully for a seat in Congress, being defeated by Cave Johnson, the incumbent Democratic Congressman from that district.

Andrew Johnson's biographical sketch gives most of the pertinent data regarding his humble beginnings, his struggle with poverty, his *will* to advance, and evidence of his personal and political courage. Repetition of those facts here would be superfluous. In the 1853 gubernatorial race, there was the contrast of a delightful and charming orator pitted against sledge-hammer blows delivered with force, logic, and adroitness.

The customary procedure in gubernatorial races was adopted. A list of speaking engagements was announced throughout the State by the public press, and the two contestants "made the welkin ring" from Carter to Shelby. National issues were touched upon in the joint debates; but local and rather personal issues rose to the forefront in nearly every instance when the competitors met face to face, from day to day, through fair weather and foul. The Whig speaker and the Whig press chided Johnson for his early legislative record wherein he had opposed internal improvements. He was savagely attacked for his role in the "Immortal Thirteen" in 1841-2 whereby Tennessee failed to elect United States Senators, thereby depriving the State of representation in the Senate of the United States for practically two years. Johnson was furthermore attacked for his efforts to change the basis of Congressional apportionment in the 1842 Legislature whereby the free population plus three-fifths of the slaves would be altered in such manner that the free population alone would be counted.

But Johnson's legislative record was not the only legislative record resurrected and aired throughout the State. The Democratic press of the State, particularly the *Nashville Union and American*, carried lengthy editorials in which were cited Major Henry's political "sins" as committed by him when a member of the Kentucky Legislature. Fifteen such "sins" were listed by the opposition press,[14] and Johnson never suffered any lapse of memory when he pounded away upon these "omissions and commissions." Among the derelictions, as viewed by the Democratic press and speakers, were the charges

"That Major Henry voted against giving the mechanics of Kentucky a lien for their pay on work done;

That Henry while a member of the Tennessee Legislature, in 1851, voted against extending the provisions of the Mechanic's Lien Law of Tennessee;

That he voted against a resolution requesting the Governor of Kentucky to fire a National salute on the 8th of January 'in honor of the officers and soldiers who so bravely defended the cause of freedom in New Orleans';

That he voted against declaring confidence in the patriotism of ANDREW JACKSON...."

In support of the allegations specified in the Democratic press, readers were cited to the specific pages of the Kentucky legislative *Journals* where Henry's votes were a matter of official record. "To elevate a man with such a past record," editorialized the Nashville organ, "to her chief magistracy, Tennessee must be false to her past fame and regardless of her present interests."

The political gladiators squared off for the opening contest at Sparta, on June 1. Major Henry led off with a speech of one and one-half hours. Johnson replied in a speech of equal length. Since this was the opening round, each contestant sought to "feel out" his opponent. Major Henry devoted the greater part of his speech to National policies,

14 *Daily Union and American* (Nashville), June 15, 1853.

dwelling upon President Franklin Pierce's "free-soil and secession appointees to office." [15] Johnson, at the very beginning of his speech, was quoted as saying that

"He did not run upon the merits of General Pierce or any body else—that he was running on his own merits—and that he wanted to discuss questions legitimately belonging to the executive office." [16]

In his speech, Johnson outlined what he conceived to be the fundamentals of democracy, and epitomized what he later expanded in his Inaugural Address into what was ridiculed by the Whigs as the "Jacob's Ladder" address. According to the Whig newspaper correspondent,

"The Whigs were delighted with Henry, and the democracy seemed to be pleased with their candidate."

During the course of his speech, Johnson alluded to the reapportionment law passed by the Whig Legislature of 1851. In that law, the First Congressional District (which Johnson had represented for ten successive years) was changed by adding two strong Whig counties, Jefferson and Sevier. In commenting on the change, Johnson said

"... The recent Legislature had parted his garments, and for his vesture his opponents were now casting lots." [17]

The one local issue that overshadowed all others was what Johnson and the Democratic press termed the "Henrymander" reapportionment law. With the campaign approximately only three weeks old, the Democrats opened up their heavy artillery against Major Henry, the legislative chairman of the Whig reapportionment bill. In defense of the reapportionment laws as passed by the 1851 Whig Legislature, Major Henry has been reported as saying

"... The voters, by electing a Whig Legislature in 1851, had instructed him to give the Whig party 'a decided ascendancy in the apportionment'." [18]

Just how that "ascendency" was to be obtained was the subject of a devasting editorial by one of the leading Democratic newspapers: [19]

"THE HENRYMANDER.

We are written to almost daily for copies of a statement published about the time of the adjournment of the last Legislature, dissecting in detail the Congressional and Legislative apportionment bills. We find that we cannot supply this demand for copies, and have therefore concluded to republish the

[15] *Nashville True Whig*, June 4, 1853.
[16] *Ibid.*
[17] *Daily Union and American*, June 4, 1853.
[18] Hamer, Philip M.: *Tennessee—A History*, Volume I, 491.
[19] *Daily Union and American*, June 21, 1853.
Author's note. The newspaper tabulation covered all of the Congressional Districts in the State, but only the First and Second District tabulations are germane to the gubernatorial race of 1853.

document. Each reader will study this document for himself. The vote given is that of 1851, as we have not time to revise the tables and give the vote| of 1852.

We give first the Congressional districts. Our tables show the representative population of each district, and the vote for Governor in 1851. They show an excess of representative population in some districts as high as from six to eight thousand, and a deficiency in one district of eighteen thousand five hundred. Let the reader compare this table with the map, and he will find that this excess or deficiency was not rendered necessary by the size of the geographical position of the counties, but that in nearly every instance it was the result of the effort to make whig districts. The whigs had the majority in the Legislature, and we should have uttered no word of complaint had they, in laying off the districts, after first making them compact and convenient and as nearly as possible of the same population, have then taken as many of them as they could get. What we complain of is—and our whig contemporaries will please notice this—that geography and population were both disregarded in the apportionment. Maj. Henry seems to have consulted *only* the election returns in arranging the districts. Population seems to have been only a secondary consideration. He consulted Greeley's election tables in his apportionment but we doubt if he either looked at the census or the map of the State. If any one doubts this, let him now look at the figures:

THE CONGRESSIONAL APPORTIONMENT OF 1852

Showing the Federal (the entire free and three-fifths of the slave) Population of each County and District, and the vote for Governor in 1851.

FIRST DISTRICT

	Federal Representative population	Vote for Governor in 1851 Trousdale	Campbell
Johnson	3,623	84	495
Carter	6,156	202	777
Sullivan	11,841	1459	383
Washington	13,489	1151	969
Hawkins	12,694	1313	1236
Greene	17,418	1684	1144
Cocke	8,013	245	890
Jefferson	12,554	346	1606
Hancock	5,578	New County	
Sevier	6,760	165	897
	97,626	6649	8397
Ratio	90,684		6649
Excess	6,942	Whig majority	*1748

* The fraction of Claiborne county taken to form the new county of Hancock, contains about 50 democratic majority, and will reduce the whig majority in the first district to about 1700.

SECOND DISTRICT.

	Federal Representative population	Vote for Governor in 1851	
		Trousdale	Campbell
Grainger	11,956	675	110
Claiborne	9,105	849	655
Campbell	5,942	497	494
Scott	1,890	New County	
Anderson	6,735	327	659
Knox	17,879	623	2223
Morgan	3,389	267	232
Fentress	4,104	498	184
Overton	10,785	1258	471
	72,175	5014	6018
Ratio	90,684		5014
Deficiency	18,509	*Whig majority	1004

... Whoever carefully studies the foregoing tables will be struck with an inconsistency in the whig arguments of this canvass. They object to the white basis and claim that *slaves* shall be represented. Yet it does not shock them at all to see from six to eight thousand *white people* disfranchised, when their disfranchisement is called for by the whig policy! Maj. Henry had no scruple whatever, when he wanted to deprive Andrew Johnson of a seat in Congress, to give 72,175 federal population in the second district the same relative power as is possessed by 97,625 population in the first district. *Whig convenience* must first be consulted!—It is bad, in Maj. Henry's opinion, to divide the Representatives in Congress among the white people of the State. But it is *just right* to divide them among the whigs. Bad, says Maj. Henry, to disfranchise the negroes. Just right, says the same Major—just what we came to the Legislature to do—to prevent the democrats from electing a member of Congress! Very wrong, says the Major, to give fifty thousand white people in the mountain country as much power as fifty thousand wealthier people in the rich counties. But just right, because Andrew Johnson could not otherwise be kept out of Congress, to give seventy-two thousand people in one district, the same power as is given to ninety-seven thousand in another district! As there are but few slaves in the second district, we suppose that, had the white basis been adopted, its population would have been about right. So that Maj. Henry in fact attacks the white basis as wrong in principle, and yet violated his principle as well as defranchised and oppressed his opponents, when he legislated Andrew Johnson out of Congress."

The gubernatorial campaign was waged vigorously by the two candidates. Despite numerous and keen thrusts on the part of each, it does not seem that either contestant lost his sense of good taste and propriety. Perhaps the climax in repartee was reached in the joint discussion at Knoxville, on July 30, the last meeting of the doughty war-

---

* Scott county was taken from other counties in this same district. A part of Claiborne has been taken off to form the county of Hancock, the fraction giving about 50 democratic majority; which will increase the Whig majority in the district to about 1050.

riors. As Johnson was concluding his speech, he turned toward his competitor, "The Eagle Orator," and said

"That the Bald Eagle has neither blood upon his beak nor flesh upon his talons. To which Henry in his rejoinder replied that Mr. Johnson must resume his studies upon ornithology. That the Bald Eagle was a noble bird; and if there was neither blood upon his beak nor flesh upon his talons, it was because he disdained to prey upon the carcass of the dead." [20]

All pre-election claims, counter-claims, bombast, and political soothsayers' predictions were finally reduced to the cold logic of election returns on the Ides of August. When the votes were counted and summed up, the verdict was rendered in favor of the "Great Commoner," Andrew Johnson. He had defeated a man who was unquestionably the most eloquent Whig orator in the State, a chip off the old block, his distinguished grandfather, Patrick Henry of the "Give me Liberty or give me Death" fame of Revolutionary War days.

Perhaps a fair analysis [21] of the characteristics of the two men was made by a distinguished Whig who had heard the two candidates speak, who was well-versed in Tennessee politics, and who himself had been defeated by Johnson for Congress:

"Johnson's Whig competitor for Governor was Gustavus A. Henry. He was decidedly the most delightful orator as well as one of the most elegant men in the State. At mass meetings, where oratory was needed, he was always the hero of the day. Frank and manly, in person he was grand, in countenance fascinating, in manner electrical, with a voice of surpassing melody.

But when it came to logic, facts, and hard licks, in daily debates, with his adroit competitor, Henry's best friends could hardly say he was Johnson's full match...."

On October 3, 1853, the Thirtieth General Assembly convened in Nashville. The Senate was composed of twelve Whigs and thirteen Democrats, while the political complexion of the House consisted of forty-four Whigs and thirty-one Democrats. On the second ballot, Democratic Edwin Polk of Hardeman County was elected Speaker of the Senate, but it required one hundred and two ballots to elect a chief clerk of the Senate.[22] The House, predominantly Whig, elected on the first ballot Whig William H. Wisener of Bedford County as Speaker.[23] After some three or four days spent in routine organizational matters, the retiring Governor transmitted his final Message to the Legislature on October 8, said Message being heretofore duly noted.[24]

---

[20] *Nashville True Whig*, August 4, 1853.

Author's note. Oliver Perry Temple, in his *Notable Men of Tennessee*, page 380, gives a slightly different version: "They call my competitor 'The Eagle Orator.' The eagle is a bird of prey. Where is his prey? I see no blood on his beak; I do not feel his talons in my flesh." "No," said Henry as quick as thought, "the eagle is a royal bird, and never preys on carrion."

[21] Temple, Oliver Perry: *Notable Men of Tennessee*, 380.

[22] *Senate Journal*, 1853, 19.

[23] *House Journal*, 1853, 5.

[24] See pages 490–503.

Two days after the reception of Governor Campbell's parting Message, the Legislature met in joint session for the purpose of comparing the votes cast for Governor in the past August election. All the election returns had been sent in according to law, and when the votes were officially counted it was declared that Andrew Johnson had received 63,413 and Gustavus A. Henry 61,163. Whereupon, the Speaker of the Senate declared

"Andrew Johnson, having received a majority of all the votes was declared duly and constitutionally elected Governor of the State for two years, and until his successor is qualified." [25]

In view of the heated campaign, it may be of interest to insert the votes of the various counties as cast for Governor, thus showing the political alignments of the several counties as of that date: [26]

VOTE FOR GOVERNOR IN THE ELECTION OF 1853

Counties	No. of Votes Cast for Henry	No. of Votes Cast for Johnson
Anderson	648	379
Bedford	1,359	1,257
Benton	396	465
Bledsoe	469	303
Blount	1,146	734
Bradley	562	1,085
Campbell	356	445
Cannon	445	803
Carroll	1,469	663
Carter	721	294
Claiborne	620	707
Cocke	867	383
Coffee	274	824
Davidson	2,597	1,963
Decatur	408	285
DeKalb	632	610
Dickson	357	743
Dyer	476	383
Fayette	1,010	1,006
Fentress	166	504
Franklin	356	1,224
Gibson	1,514	1,024
Giles	1,301	1,468
Grainger	998	767
Greene	902	1,915
Grundy	58	374

[25] *Senate Journal*, 1853, 47.
[26] *Senate Journal*, 1853, 45–47.
   House Journal, 1853, 48–50.

Counties	No. of Votes Cast for Henry	No. of Votes Cast for Johnson
Hamilton	786	972
Hancock	221	532
Hardeman	651	1,025
Hardin	671	827
Hawkins	805	1,180
Haywood	726	785
Henderson	1,301	593
Henry	891	1,496
Hickman	263	812
Humphreys	341	501
Jackson	1,154	995
Jefferson	1,396	630
Johnson	392	184
Knox	2,279	770
Lauderdale	319	252
Lawrence	523	731
Lewis	66	182
Lincoln	617	2,322
Macon	553	341
Madison	1,261	795
Marion	476	357
Marshall	671	1,282
Maury	1,238	1,731
Meigs	118	561
Monroe	739	900
Montgomery	1,309	1,004
Morgan	229	260
McMinn	799	965
McNairy	1,016	984
Obion	547	792
Overton	431	1,282
Perry	387	329
Polk	249	527
Rhea	270	358
Roane	912	755
Robertson	1,183	763
Rutherford	1,407	1,243
Scott	186	182
Sevier	824	133
Shelby	1,454	1,435
Smith	1,735	546
Stewart	479	718
Sullivan	361	1,407

Counties	No. of Votes Cast for Henry	No. of Votes Cast for Johnson
Sumner	806	1,425
Tipton	284	527
Van Buren	110	205
Warren	402	1,093
Washington	967	1,069
Wayne	709	430
Weakley	733	1,279
White	974	634
Williamson	1,502	710
Wilson	2,241	995
	61,163	63,413
		61,163
Johnson's majority,		2,250

On October 17, the joint legislative committee appointed to make suitable arrangements for the inauguration of the Governor-elect reported as follows:[27]

"While they have been deeply impressed with the fitness of the State House, as regards the design for which it has been erected, and as its vast structure, its imperishable material, its lofty position, its neatness and symmetry, its destined duration, all so appropriately emblem the virtue, wisdom, and patriotism of our distinguished fellow citizen, the Mechanic Statesman, Andrew Johnson, the spectacle would doubtless have been more imposing at this time, than at any other place. But as its unfinished condition at this time will not admit of the conveniences necessary on the occasion, we have preferred to select the McKendree Church, at which place the inauguration will occur..."

The Legislature recessed and proceeded to the McKendree Church for the inaugural exercises. In the meanwhile, Governor Campbell called at the hotel where Johnson was and informed him that he (Campbell) was ready to escort him in his carriage to the place of the inaugural ceremonies. According to a well-informed citizen, this was what took place:[28]

"Mr. Johnson replied, as was correctly reported, that he did not want a carriage, that he was going to walk with the people. And walk he did!"

As was the custom, retiring Governor Campbell delivered the following Valedictory Address:[29]

---

[27] *Senate Journal*, 1853, 63.
[28] Temple, Oliver Perry: *Notable Men of Tennessee*, 381.
[29] *Daily Union and American* (Nashville), October 19, 1853.

"Gov. Campbell's Valedictory Address

GENTLEMEN OF THE SENATE, AND
    HOUSE OF REPRESENTATIVES:

The term of my official duties having expired, I come voluntarily to resign my authority through you into the hands from which
I received it.—While no one can be insensible to the honors of office,
it equally occurs to me that none can fail to experience a certain
relief, in laying aside its responsibility at the same time that he parts
with its authority. Two years ago, it pleased the people of Tennessee to call me to the executive chair of their government, and when I
reflected upon the high position achieved by the arms, the intelligence, and the integrity of the State, I have not been able to place
too high an estimate upon the honor thus conferred. It were needless, perhaps unbecoming in me now to refer to the manner in which
I have discharged the duties of the position. Suffice it to say, that I
have ever entertained a sacred regard for the honor, the constitution, and the fidelity to the Federal Union, of the State of Tennessee, and it will be my highest satisfaction and reward, if it may be
said, that I resign my connexion with its Government leaving all
these in the pure and unsullied condition in which I found them.
It will then be with no regret, that I commit them to the guardianship, in some measure, of another, who has been called by the
sovereign voice of the people to the executive chair, and whose best
efforts, I feel assured, will be exerted to increase the power, preserve the harmony and promote the prosperity and happiness of the
State.

We live in an age where social privileges and political freedom
have attained a height, which the world has never witnessed before.
The governments of the Old World exist in a perpetual struggle,
resulting from habitual allegiance to old customs, on the one hand,
and the feeble but growing impulse to imitate the example set them
this side the water, on the other. While we witness with anxious interest every popular movement there, as involving to a large extent
the progress and eventual condition of the race, we have abundant
cause to felicitate ourselves as Americans, in the fact, that we have
already attained and enjoy what other nations are struggling so
doubtfully to achieve. With us liberty is the substantial reality of

every day life. We enjoy a government which at once possesses the most efficient federal strength, and allows the amplest exercise of State and personal freedom. There is no people on earth, who feel so little the weight and authority of government. In fact, it is by the benefits and protection it affords, that we are made conscious that we owe allegiance to a power beyond our State limits. And yet, this general government sitting so lightly upon the people, who are the subjects of it, is strong enough to maintain peace throughout our domestic territory, and to inspire respect for its power wherever our name is known.—Since my term of office began, one administration has retired, and another succeeded at Washington, and still all is quiet at home and respected abroad, showing the ready obedience of our people to the law, and that foreign nations regard the spirit and nationality of the Republic, rather than the citizen, who may be called for a time, to preside at the helm of public affairs.

We have no standing army guarding the outposts of the country, and no fleets hovering about our domestic ports or darkening the face of foreign seas; yet we feel conscious of our internal strength more formidable than standing armies, while our commerce, where-ever wave and tide may carry it, is secure as if every merchantman were convoyed by a navy. It is the glory of the Republic that her strength is in the freedom of her people, in the spirit of her institutions, in the humanity of all her laws and dealings, in the truth in which her foundations repose; and these cannot fail to carry power and conviction whenever she has a cause to vindicate, a right to maintain, or a principle to establish. Is it not then with just reason, that I say, we are a favored people, and entitled to rejoice in all that constitutes the greatness, the glory and the happiness of a nation?

If we have so much reason to felicitate ourselves as Americans, as Tennesseans we have no less ground for self-gratification. Nature has been bountiful in the distribution of her favors among us, and Tennessee is beginning to exhibit her gratitude for such bountiful-ness, by a systematic enterprise which promises to develope all her resources, and to advance her social and commercial position among the States of the Union. Her insulated position demanded artificial outlets for her commerce and external intercourse, and these are to be supplied by the invention, the wealth, and the public spirit of her people. As the result of this necessity we witness the construction of railroads in many directions, and the projection of others in many more. We may look to these public works as the source of a great variety of public benefits. The question has been fairly settled in other States, and their rapid growth in wealth, population and intelligence, amply establish the sound policy of such investments. One can scarcely have a just appreciation of these improvements, who has not been an eye-witness of their practical workings. If rail roads are essentially needful in New York and other States upon the seaboard; how much more useful and necessary would they be where there are but limited facilities for trade and commerce, and in regions which possess no natural highways. How else are the untold treasures of our mountains, and the products of our inland valleys to be made available in promoting the prosperity of the State? Our mines of iron, copper, coal, and almost every variety of minerals, can be brought to the markets and observation of the world, only by affording convenient access to them, and in a way to bear off their rich deposits. Now let it be supposed that this is the only advantage to be anticipated. A new impetus will be given to every department of business. The increased activity will afford additional encouragement to labor, the ordinary result of which is increased population.

At present many hundreds of our citizens annually leave their homes to seek fortunes elsewhere as imagination, enterprise or information may lead them. It should be the policy of the State to check this continued stream of emigration by affording encouragement to labor in all the industrial pursuits. It has been said that population is wealth, and that is certainly true when that population is characterised by intelligence, industry and enterprize. The diffusion of knowledge and an elevation of the moral standard are immediate effects of such physical improvements, as has been shown by the history of countries where they exist. There are a thousand avenues by which knowledge approaches the human intellect, besides the school house and the college. The intercourse of distant portions of the country by means of travel, the interchange of thought, the contact of mind with mind, are as the seeds of knowledge cast at random over the surface of society. Though many of these may fall in stony places, many will take root where we would scarcely dream that they could find soil to grow. This is the ample school house of the world in which the poorest and most friend-forsaken may obtain an education for the actual conflict of life.

It is deeply to be regretted that the advantages of education among us are not equal and universal. I may take this occasion, however, to congratulate you, upon the growing appreciation of education, and the increased facilities for obtaining it in all parts of the State. The youth of the country are the hope of the country; they are the treasures of the commonwealth. The generous young men of the State are among the bravest patriots of the State, ready to do battle for her in whatever field. I would have their patriotism an enlightened, as well as a brave patriotism. With increase of population and trade, will increase the necessity of intelligence, and the erection of school houses and colleges will be the answering product of this demand.

But I have been led too far from the proprieties of the occasion, by the interesting suggestion of this period of our history. It now remains for me to return, through you, my profound thanks to the people of this my native State, for the honor done me, in conferring the office which I now resign into their hands. I sincerely pray that a Benign Providence will continue his bountiful blessings to them and their posterity forever; that their virtues may be preserved, and their liberties be perpetual."

Upon the conclusion of Governor Campbell's valedictory remarks, Governor-elect Andrew Johnson delivered the following Inaugural Address,[30] and took the oath of office administered by Judge W. K. Turner.

"GENTLEMEN OF THE SENATE,
    OF THE HOUSE OF REPRESENTATIVES,
        AND FELLOW CITIZENS:

It has long been the established custom in this State, upon the Inauguration of the Chief Executive Officer, to shadow forth, in what is termed an Inaugural Address, such opinion as he may entertain in reference to the leading measures and policy of the State and General Governments.

In obedience to this custom and to public expectation, without

---

[30] *Ibid.*, October 18, 1853.

further prelude, I will proceed, in as brief and concise a manner as the nature and the importance of the subjects will permit, to give such views as I may entertain in relation to some of those measures and principles, which I believe lie at the foundation of the two great parties, in this country, and involve the existence of the Government itself. The differences of opinion which have arisen in this are, as in the Governments of the other quarters of the globe, fundamental in their character, and such as have existed ever since men were first formed into social communities. The beginning point of these differences was, as to where the proper lodgment of the Supreme power should be made—whether in the hands of one, or a few men, or whether it should be continued in the possession of the great mass of the people, where it, of right, belongs. Between the interested and designing few, on the one hand, and the laboring many, on the other, political power has been vibrating, as the pendulum, from the origin of man's social condition to the present period of time. Division of sentiment upon this great problem, in this country, made its most remarkable development in the Convention which framed the Constitution of the United States. In that Convention there were two parties—one of them headed by Mr. Alexander Hamilton, who contended for that form of Government which was strongest and farthest removed from the mass of the people, and based upon the old monarchical, or kingly notion, that man was made for government, he not being capable of governing himself. The ardent contest, or struggle, between the advocates of a popular form of government, vesting the sovereign power in the mass of the people, and those who stood opposed to it, resulted in the formation of the Constitution of the United States as it now stands—less republican, in many of its leading provisions, than was desired by those who had confidence in the integrity, honesty and capability of the people to govern themselves. By this reference to the history of our country, it will be at once perceived when and where this division of parties took its rise and had its origin.

It is most manifest that the difference of opinion between parties, or, more properly speaking, the leaders of parties, (for the great mass of the American people are Democratic in sentiment), does not consist in name merely, but has a deeper foundation in the United States, and dates its origin anterior to any appellation by which parties are known and designated in modern times. After the ratification of the Constitution of the United States by the several States, and when the Government had been put into successful operation, these same parties made their appearance in another form, and under another and more imposing name; one of them contending for the exercise of all those powers which had been sought as express grants, and refused in the formation of the Constitution, by implication or a latitudinous construction of the Constitution—the other contending for a Government of limited and defined powers, and for a rigid and strict construction of the Constitution. One of these parties was called the Federal party—the other, the Republican or Democratic party.

The Federal party, from the formation of the Government down to the moment when I stand before you, have contended for the exercise of all doubtful powers on the part of the General Government, without any restraint or limit as to the Constitution. The Constitution of the United States has most generally been viewed by them as a paper wall, through which they could thrust their fingers at pleasure, or a piece of gum elastic that could be expanded or contracted at the will and pleasure of the Legislature.

The Democratic Republican party hold, that this Government is one of limited and fixed powers; and that no power can or should be exercised, unless it is expressly granted; and the incidents necessary and proper to carry it into full and fair effect.

I presume, at this period of my public life, it is hardly necessary for me to state where I stand in reference to these questions on limitations of Constitutional power. My past public course has given, as I conceive, the most conclusive evidence that I have always favored a strict yet liberal construction of the Constitution. I hold that no power should be exercised of doubtful character, either by the State or General Government. If the exercise of doubtful powers by the State or the Federal Government are acquiesced in by the people, and persisted in on the part of the law maker, the whole organic law of the land becomes virtually repealed, and the discretion of the usurping legislator becomes the measure and only limit of his power. Our only hope and safeguard against a consummation of the fearful tendency of Federal policy, on the part of the General Government, in all questions of doubtful power, is in a direct appeal to the States for an enlargement of such power, or such an expression of opinion on their part, as provided in the Constitution of the United States, as will settle all doubt or ambiguity in relation to the exercise of such doubtful power. And if the people of the several States are convinced that the additional grant of power asked for is for the public good, it will be most readily conceded; and if, on the contrary, they are not well satisfied that it is for the public good, it should be withheld, and the Government rigidly confined within its prescribed orbit.

In this connection, I do most solemnly declare that, at this very period of time, I believe that the heavy and weighty responsibility rests upon the great Democratic party of this nation, of recurring once more to first principles—to the original design of the Government—and, if possible, to bring it back to its primitive republican simplicity and economy; and also to confine it within the ancient landmarks as laid down by Jefferson and his patriotic associates, in the earlier and purer days of the Republic.

If there are divisions of the Democratic party, I claim to belong to that division of it which will stand firmly by the combined and recorded judgment of the people, until changed or modified by them; and which will, if it has the power, carry industry, economy, reform and rigid responsibility into every department of the Government. I belong to that division of Democracy proper, which is progressive, not in violation of, but in conformity with, the law and the Constitution, and which holds that man is capable when it *becomes necessary*, of altering or amending the law and the Constitution, so as to conform to his advanced and constantly advancing social and intellectual condition. I am well aware that there are some whose fears are easily aroused, and who become greatly alarmed whenever there is a proposition to change the organic law, either of the States or General Government, which I apprehend, proceeds from a want of confidence, on their part, in the integrity and capacity of the people to govern themselves. To all who entertain such fears, I will most respectfully say, that I entertain none, and with due deference to their fears and opinions, will ask the question, If man is not capable, and is not to be trusted with the government of himself, is he to be trusted with the government of others? Who, then, will govern? The answer must be, Man—for we have no angels, in the shape of men, as yet, who are willing to take charge of our political affairs. Man is not perfect, it is true, but we all hope he is approximating perfection, and that he will, in the progress of time, reach this grand and most important end in all human affairs.

I have not deemed it improper, nor out of place, on this occasion, to make a single allusion to the young men of our country. Many of them, while at our academies and colleges, and when in the study of their profession, imperceptibly imbide notions prejudical to Democracy. Their wealth, and too frequently their preceptors—many of whom are biggotted and supercilious on account of their literary attainments, and assumed superior information on most subjects—inspire their students with false ideas of their own superiority, mixed with a superabundance of self-esteem, which causes them to feel that the great mass of mankind were intended by their Creator to be 'hewers of wood and drawers of water,' that it is in this Government, as it was in olden Rome, between the Patricians and Plebeians; where, in fact, the people never enjoyed for one moment, that pure liberty and freedom of thought and of action which is enjoyed by the people of the United States. To this class of our young men I have a few remarks to make, in reference to the great principles of Democracy, the scope and design of which, I greatly fear, they have, as yet, wholly failed to comprehend, and if comprehended, not duly appreciated. And in doing so, I do not intend, on this occasion to enter into any analytical or metaphysical disquisition upon the great principles of Democracy. At the present I shall content myself by assuming, and taking it as a conceded fact, that *Democracy*, or man's capability to govern himself is a *principle that exists;* That it is *inherent* in the very nature of man; that it is that ingredient in the compound called man, which enables him to determine between right and wrong, in all political affairs, to this principle, called Democracy, consists his capability of self-government. It is that which enables him to reason correctly, and to lift himself above all animal creation. It is this principle that constitutes the intelligence of man; or, in other words, it is that in Man which partakes most highly of the nature and character of Him in whose image he is made—which I term the *Divinity of Man*. And in proportion as this Divinity is enlarged, the Man becomes more and more capable of self-government, and still more elevated in his character. I will also assume, what I know none will venture in reason to deny, that this *Divinity of Man can be enlarged*, and that man can become more God-like than he is. It is the business of the Democratic party to progress in the work of increasing this principle of Divinity, or Democracy, and thereby elevate and make man more perfect. I hold that the Democratic party proper, of the whole world, and especially of the United States, has undertaken the *political redemption of man*, and sooner or later, the great work will be accomplished. In the political world, it corresponds to that of Christianity in the moral. They are going along, not in divergents, nor in parallels, but in converging lines—the one purifying and elevating man religiously, the other politically. Democracy progressive corresponds also to the Church Militant: both fighting against error—one in the moral, the other in the political field. At what period of time they will have finished the work of progress and elevation, is not now for me to determine; but when finished, these two lines will have approximated each other—man being perfected, both in a religious and in a political point of view. At this point it is that the Church Militant will give way and cease to exist, and the Church Triumphant begin; at the same point, Democracy progressive will give way and cease to exist, and Theocracy begin.

The divinity of man being now fully developed,—it may now be confidently and exultingly asserted that the *voice of the people is the voice of God;* and proclamation be made, that the millenial morning has dawned, and that the time has come, when the Lion and the Lamb shall lie down together; when the 'voice of the turtle' shall be 'heard in our land;' when 'the sucking child shall play upon the hole of the asp,' and the 'weaned child put its hand upon the cockatrice's den,' and the glad tidings shall be proclaimed throughout the land of man's political and religious redemption, and that there is 'on earth, peace, good will toward men.'

It will be readily perceived by all discerning young men, that Democracy is a ladder, corresponding in politics, to the one spiritual which Jacob saw in his vision; one up which all, in proportion to their merit, may ascend. While it extends to the humblest of all created beings here on earth below, it reaches to God on high; and it would seem that the class of young men to which I have alluded, might find a position somewhere between the lower and upper extremes of this ladder, commensurate, at least, with their virtue and merit, if not equal to their inflated ambition, which they could occupy with honor to themselves and advantage to their country.

Internal Improvements by the General Government is a subject that is attracting much public attention, and no doubt will continue to do so for sometime to come. How far the General Government can go in constructing works of Internal Improvement, without an infraction of the Constitution of the United States, and an encroachment upon the reserved rights of the States, is a question that has long been discussed by the ablest and wisest statesmen of the age, without coming to any satisfactory conclusion. The precise line at which the national character of a work of Internal Improvement ceases, and the local one begins, approximate so closely, that it is difficult to determine, even by those who are disposed to construe the Constitution fairly, where to fix the limit.

A public work, which is considered national in its character by one class of politicians, is considered local by another; hence, much perplexity and great difficulty is felt in the exercise of this power, on the part of the General Government, over any work of Internal Improvements. Having now, however, in view, the many important works, about which there is so much solicitude on the part of a large portion of the people of the United States, and which is now occupying the attention of the General Government, my own deliberate opinion is, that before the General Government advances another step in works of Internal Improvement, at least those of a doubtful character, there should be an appeal made to the several States composing the compact, to definitely fix and accurately describe the utmost boundary of power intended to be exercised by the General Government in the construction of works of Internal Improvement. The Government, on a subject so grave and deeply important as the one now agitating the public mind, should move within limits well ascertained, both as to power and the amount of money to be raised by taxes, and to be expended in the various projects of Internal Improvements, which may hereafter be projected. If the States intend that the General Government shall embark in a gigantic scheme of Internal Improvements, let the power be conferred as provided in the Constitution of the United States. If not, let the General Government at once be arrested and confined within the written command of the States who spoke it into existence.

The subject of Internal Improvements by our own local authority, has also excited a deep and lively interest among our people, in many portions of the State. A well regulated and judicious system of Internal Improvement, intended and calculated to give all reasonable facilities to the Mechanical, Agricultural, and Commercial pursuits of the country, ought to receive such aid and encouragement from the State as will come clearly within the financial ability of the people. If such aid has to be given by the creation of State indebtedness, the Legislature that creates the indebtedness should never fail to provide the means to meet the annually accruing interests and the principal as they fall due.

In connection with the Internal Improvements of this, as well as other States, there is a question of much importance, which has not, hitherto, very generally attracted the attention of the people in this State. It is one that involves the first principle of free government itself; and will no doubt ultimately come before the sovereign people, for action and final adjustment. How far the Legislature can go in granting the right of way to all companies, which may be authorized to construct works of Internal Improvements, through the real property of individuals, without their consent, is the question referred to; and it is one not well defined in the public mind, nor distinctly understood by the people.

The right of *Eminent Domain* does not, in this State, authorize the Legislature to go beyond, in appropriating the property of the citizen, what is absolutely *necessary* for the public good, and not then without just compensation being made therefor. To set apart so much of the real property owned by the citizens, as may be desired by every company which assumes that it is constructing a work or works of Internal Improvement, for the public good, would be destroying one of the great guarantees in the Bill of Rights, which secures the people in the enjoyment of their real and personal property.

At as early a day as may be practicable, there should be some *boundary fixed*, by the judicial tribunals of the country, or the people themselves, as to the extent this all-important principle is to be exercised by the legislative department of the State; and that boundary should be, when fixed, the *public necessity*, and not the

mere assumption of *public convenience*. All companies incorporated for Internal Improvement purposes, may claim that they were
created for the public good; and under the plea of public good,
claim the right of way, and, consequently, the property condemned,
and the rightful owners compelled to part with the title to it, and
that, too, without their consent. This, among a people calling themselves free, and who claim to have guarantees which will protect
them in the enjoyment of life, liberty and property, is a question of
no ordinary magnitude, and is entitled to their mature and profound
consideration.

The best policy to be adopted by the General Government, in
regard to the future management of our immense public domain,
has, for some time, engaged the public attention, and will continue
to do so, until some permanent disposition be made of it by the
General Government. There is a class of persons in the United
States, more properly denominated land-mongers, or land-monop-
olists, who desire to have the public lands thrown into market in
large quantities, in the shape of land warrants, and grants to incorporated companies, so as to enable them to become the purchasers at
reduced prices, and then to realize immense fortunes from the landless thousands, who emigrate to the new States and Territories, and
settle upon them. This spirit of speculation and plunder, in the
homes of the great mass of toiling thousands, ought at once to be
arrested, and stifled to death, by timely and judicious legislation.
After some experience, and much reflection, as to the best mode of
disposing of the public lands, I have come to the conclusion, that the
General Government ought, and that without delay, to set apart
the entire public domain, by enactment, permanently, as homes for
the people. The Homestead policy ought to be fully carried out,
and the further sale of the public lands confined to actual settlers,
and to them only in limited quantities.—The public lands should be
unalterably fixed and set apart as a heritage, for our children's children in the far distant future. They should at once be consecrated to
this high and beneficial purpose and never thereafter be disturbed.

The Homestead policy—the great *idea* of providing homes for
thousands now living, and the millions that are yet to come after
we have passed and gone—is one that has occupied much of my
time and anxious thoughts for many years past, and I have not yet

abandoned the confident hope of its final consummation. The American mind has been aroused to the consideration of this great scheme of every head of a family in the United States being provided with a home he can call his own. It is based upon the eternal principles of Justice, and is replete with all that is noble and good in our nature and sooner or later, must become the settled policy of the Government. I never recur to this great theme, without an expression of all the nobler qualities of the soul. It is one upon which I delight to dwell, and contemplate the future good that is to flow upon the coming generations. I will refrain, however, from saying more, on the present occasion upon a subject which is interwoven with the dearest sympathies of my soul.

The true policy of the Government, both State and General, consists in the education and diffusion of general information among the great mass of the people, and at the same time, employing all means by which the toiling, producing labor of the country can be elevated to its proper position. Our children should be made thoroughly acquainted with the genius and spirit of our beautiful, though complex, form of government. The Constitution of the United States, and of the States, with their commentaries, should be made one of the principal books to be studied, and understood, in all the schools of the country—and thus a thorough knowledge of the genius and character of our free institutions acquired. And if it shall be the pleasure of Divine Providence to exempt this, so far, favored nation from all wars, for the next fifty years, and it be permitted to go on as it has been—cultivating the arts and sciences of peace—it will have no superior, if an equal, throughout the civilized or Pagan world. If Agriculture, Mechanics, Internal Improvements, with all their legitimate incidents, are permitted to approximate any thing like perfection, we will be the most powerful and formidable people on God's habitable globe. Why not, then, pursue that line of policy which will enable us to attain this great and important end, making this people the wonder and admiration of the enlightened nations of the earth? We should adopt, as a rule for our future action, that which was laid down by the immortal Jefferson, on the 4th of March, 1801:

'Equal and exact justice to all men, of whatever state, or persuasion, religious or political—peace, commerce, and honest friendship with all nations—entangling alliances with none.'

Within the last few years—not to go farther back—the American people have given to all nations, with whom they have any intercourse, the most incontestible proof of their prowess, and military skill and power on the field of battle, which has caused, and will continue to cause the rights of our citizens to be respected abroad. Let our people go on, rivalling each other in all the pursuits of peace; let them acquire renown in the civil, equal to that which they have acquired on the field of military glory, and which is much more valuable and honorable than all the glare of the military world combined.

I would be doing great injustice to my own feelings, were I not, in this connection, to declare—though it may be considered by some as being in bad taste—that I would rather wear upon my garments the dinge of the shop and the dust of the field, as badges of the pursuits of peace, than the dazzling epaulet upon my shoulder, and the sword, with its glittering scabbard, dangling by my side—the insignia of honorable and glorious war.

The Army and Navy in this, as in most of the nations of the earth, are the great absorbants of the people's substance. They are the two great arteries that will, unless confined within proper limits, bleed this, as they have some of the other governments, well nigh to a state of exhaustion. Even here, where we seem to have a fixed prejudice against large standing armies, and extensive navies, it is almost startling to announce the aggregate amount the people have to pay for the support of their Army and Navy, in time of profound peace. According to the most recent estimate made out by the late Secretary of the Treasury and submitted to the Congress of the United States, it will require, during the present fiscal year, twenty-one millions of dollars to sustain our Army and Navy; which is a tax of nearly one dollar per head, for every man, woman and child in the United States. The entire amount collected from the American people, by the General Government alone, in the shape of taxes, and expended since the 4th of March, 1789, to the 4th March, 1840, is $1,428,000,000, in round numbers. Of this amount $513,000,000 has been paid out in the shape of a national debt, contracted for the purpose of carrying on our various wars, at home and abroad, which will leave $915,000,000. Out of the last named sum, there has been paid, for the support of the Army and Navy, six hundred million dollars, exclusive of all pensions, which is sixty-two millions, and is properly chargable to the Army and Navy. It will be very readily perceived from this simple statement of facts, that two-thirds of the whole amount of revenue collected from the people has been appropriated for the support of these two branches of Government. It is not my purpose, in making this allusion to this vast amount that has been expended *in the name* of our little Army and Navy, to detract aught from their high character; but to show that they are costing the American people more, in proportion to the number employed in the naval and military service, than any other government in the world; and for the further purpose of showing, that naval and military glory is not without cost, even in this republican form of government of ours, and that too, where most of the *fighting, in time of actual war,* is done by the citizen soldier. While I make these remarks, I am not to be understood as being opposed to the Government keeping in readiness a sufficient physical force to maintain the honor, dignity, and rights of our country, at home or abroad, upon the ocean or upon the land. But I must be permitted, incidentally, to recur once more to that great scheme, the Homestead Policy, as being better calculated in all its bearings, if faithfully and successfully carried out, for building up the most reliable physical force for this country in time of war. If this scheme is once established, and carried out in good faith, it will build up a standing army, in the character of the citizen soldier, that will, by its own productive power support itself in time of peace, and will be in readiness to defend the country in time of war. It is one that will protect your frontier settlements against any disturbance growing out of unfriendly or hostile relations with our numerous Indian tribes. And in the event of war with any foreign power that dare invade the soil of freedom, it would be the first to obey its country's call, and after having participated in the heat and strife of battle—the benignant star of peace once more resuming the ascendent—the citizen soldiers who compose it would, with alacrity, return to their homes and their firesides, to their wives and their children, and there renew the avocations of peace. This would be a standing army composed of the citizen soldier in fact, that would go when war came, and come when war went, and is the only kind of an army, that can be safely relied upon and trusted by a republican or a Democratic form of government, either in peace or in war.

At as early a day as may be deemed practicable, I will prepare and transmit a communication to both branches of the legislative department, presenting for their consideration such measures of public policy as may seem to require legislative action.

There is a high and solemn duty imposed upon the Executive, to 'take care that the laws be faithfully executed' which are in conformity with the Constitution of the State. In all questions of difficulty, which may arise in regard to the faithful execution of the Constitution, and the laws made in pursuance thereof, the Executive will confidently expect the willing co-operation of the other two departments of the Government.

In discharging the various and responsible duties imposed on me as the Chief Executive Officer of the State, by law and the Constitution, I may often, from defect of judgment, go wrong, and when right, will no doubt be censured and condemned by the fault-finding portion of those who may differ with me in political sentiment, which almost precludes the hope that general satisfaction will be given to all, by any one occupying the position to which I have just been elevated. The entering upon the discharge of duties so responsible and delicate in their character, in reference to which there is such a great variety of opinions, must necessarily be embarrassing to one who feels so forcibly his own incompetency to the performance of so arduous a task. But replying, as I do, upon that great principle of right, which lies at the foundation of all things, I shall repair to the post assigned me by the soverign people, with a fixed and unalterable determination to do my whole duty, in compliance with the laws and the Constitution of my country, and the honest dictates of my own conscience,—trusting in *God* for help, and looking to an honest and confiding people for an approval of my official course.

It is with no ordinary degree of pleasure, that I avail myself of this occasion to tender to the people of my adopted State, the sincere thanks of a heart filled to overflowing with gratitude for the distinguished honor they have conferred, in elevating me to the position I now occupy. This additional manifestation of their confidence in me, as a man and a public servant, inspires me with a deep sense of that true humility which 'is before honor,' and which I trust will characterize me through my whole public life, as giving some proof that I feel what I profess, REVERENCE and *profound* respect for the *high behest* of a *free* people, who have so far never deserted me, and *God* being willing, I will never desert them."

In the annals of Tennessee political literature there is probably no official pronouncement by a Governor that has provoked more widely divergent views than Governor Johnson's Inaugural Address. Certain portions of the Address dealt with practical problems, while other portions essayed to draw an analogy or indicate a parallelism between religion and democracy. To the practical part of the Address a strong political supporter paid the following tribute:[31]

"GOV. JOHNSON'S INAUGURAL

We publish to-day the Inaugural Address of Gov. Johnson, which was delivered yesterday in the presence of the members of the General Assembly and an immense concourse of citizens. It is an able and patriotic document, and will command the attention and consideration of the people of Tennessee independent of party considerations.

We have not space, this morning, for an extended review of the address, and must content ourselves with a bare summary of its leading features:

1st. Governor Johnson believes it the duty of the democratic party, at the present momentous crisis, to recur once more to *first principles,* and confine the government within the ancient landmarks, as laid down by JEFFERSON, and the other great founders of the democratic party. He insists upon a strict construction of the Federal constitution, and an appeal to the States, in all cases of doubtful power, for an express grant of such power, if deemed compatible with the public interests.

2d. He favors a well regulated and judicious system of Internal Improvements by the State, 'intended and calculated to give all reasonable facilities to the Mechanical, Agricultural and Commercial pursuits of the country.'

3d. On the important question of the power of the Legislature to grant the right of way, through the real estate of individuals, to companies authorized to construct works of internal improvements, Gov. Johnson suggests that, at an early day, some boundary should be fixed by the Judicial tribunals, or the people themselves, and that such boundary, when fixed, should be the *public necessity,* and not the mere assumption of *public convenience.*

4th. The education of the great mass of the people, and the elevation and remuneration of the laborer, are subjects which have long engrossed Gov. Johnson's attention and enlisted the best wishes of his heart. In this paper these subjects are recurred to, and enforced with eloquent ability.

5th. On the subject of the Public Domain, Gov. Johnson believes it should be consecrated to the high and beneficent purpose of providing homes for the People. This policy would augment the national happiness and wealth in time of peace, and in time of war it would raise up the only kind of a stand-

---

[31] *Daily Union and American,* October 18, 1853.

ing army which can safely be relied upon and trusted in a republican government.

Such are the leading topics discussed in this first paper of the new Governor. They are handled with uncommon ability and in that earnest spirit which is characteristic of its author. The whole document should be attentively read and pondered upon. We may have occasion again to refer to it, and discuss at length some of its suggestions."

A brief extract from a lengthy excoriation of Governor Johnson's Inaugural remarks contained the following observations: [32]

"All this absurd jargon, about Federalism and democracy is substantially what others have said, time and again, before Governor Johnson, and usually in much better style. It has become unspeakably 'stale, flat and unprofitable,' from long and fruitless use, and is altogether beneath the dignity of a grave State paper, marking the advent of a new administration of the State Government; and we can hardly conceive why the Governor should wish to place in the archives of the State a re-hash of his stump harrangues during the past summer upon this subject.

To the simple proposition, which he labors at length, that man is capable of self-government, whigs, no less than democrats, yield their ready and hearty assent. But when the Governor speaks of 'democracy' or the 'democratic principle,' as the 'Divinity of man,' it would be interesting to know how far he thinks the so called 'democratic' administrations in this country, in modern times, have successfully illustrated this 'Divinity of man' by their acts—especially that of Martin Van Buren, which has been expressly designated as 'the era of peculation;' when, of sixty-eight land receivers, sixty-three were said to be defaulters, and when Swartwout and others embezzled the public revenue by the wagon load—if the amount had been counted in gold and silver.

But we find we are exceeding our limits, and must close for to-day."

Just what Governor Johnson had in mind regarding the "converging lines" is certainly unknown to the author of this treatise. Likewise his comments upon the "Church Militant" and the "Church Triumphant," which merger it was alleged would usher in the reign of "Theocracy," leave much clarification desired. It is possible that Johnson had read Plato's *Republic* and Sir Thomas More's *Utopia* but had not sufficiently digested them. If so, Johnson failed to realize that even those ideal forms of government were to be located on this earth; Johnson's ideal form of government, it seems, was to be attained by scaling a "Jacob's Ladder" where could be located "a position somewhere between the lower and upper extremes of this ladder." Johnson's empyreal commonwealth was some sort of enchanting vision which his deficient information, concerning its location and attainment, forced him into uttering vague and inconclusive deductions. For a usually logical and fact-pounding speaker, such as Johnson, it remains a mystery as to why he lapsed into such a farrago of political nonsense upon such an important occasion.

---

[32] *Nashville True Whig*, October 20, 1853.

On the day following Governor Johnson's Inaugural Address, Democratic Representative W. P. Chambliss from the counties of Lincoln, Giles, and Marshall introduced a resolution [33] providing for a committee

"To wait upon his Excellency, Gov. Johnson, and know if he has any communication to make to this General Assembly."

Two days later the committee reported [34]

"That at present the Governor has nothing to communicate, but may have at some future date."

Two months rolled by before Governor Johnson transmitted his regular Message to the Legislature, the deliberate body in the meanwhile being compelled to mill around with miscellaneous matters until Governor Johnson saw fit to submit his recommendations for consideration. It can be only conjectural at this time as to why such an unprecedented delay occurred, for ordinarily the newly-installed Governor transmitted his regular Message promptly after inauguration. Perhaps the "panning" which Whig newspapers administered the Governor regarding his Jacob's Ladder, converging lines, and ideal republic located in the celestial regions—all of which were vaguely shadowed forth in his Inaugural Address—caused the Governor to deliberate and concentrate on State matters not so far distant and of immediate concern to the citizenry of the State. At any rate, with more than one-third of the legislative session already gone, Governor Johnson finally transmitted to the Legislature his regular Message.

Legislative Message,* December 19, 1853
"EXECUTIVE DEPARTMENT,
Nashville, December 19, 1853.

FELLOW-CITIZENS OF THE SENATE AND HOUSE OF REPRESENTATIVES:

The Constitution of the State requires the Executive, 'from time to time, to give to the General Assembly information of the state of the government, and to recommend to their consideration such measures as he shall judge expedient' and proper. In compliance with this requisition of the organic law of the land, without any long or unnecessary exordium, I shall at once proceed to discharge the high and responsible duties thus imposed.

In the first place, the attention of the General Assembly is most respectfully invited to the present and prospective indebtedness of the State.

---

[33] *House Journal*, 1853, 75.
[34] *Ibid.*, 90.
* *Senate Journal*, 1853, 293–307.
  House Journal, 1853, 452–467.

The liabilities of the State, as they are termed by the Comptroller of the Treasury, were, in October last, three million, eight hundred and one thousand, eight hundred and fifty-six dollars, ($3,801,856). The credit of the State has been loaned to various railroad companies, and the bonds issued to the amount of one million, nine hundred and forty-five thousand dollars, ($1,945,000) which should be added to the present liabilities; making them, in the aggregate, five million seven hundred and forty-six thousand, eight hundred and fifty-six dollars, ($5,746,856).

To this amount there might be very properly added the surplus revenue which was received on deposit, and the faith of the State pledged for the safe keeping and repayment of the same, which now constitutes a part of the capital of the Bank of Tennessee; and the common school fund, which is made a perpetual fund by the constitution. These two sums make one million, five hundred and twenty thousand, three hundred and twenty-five dollars, ($1,520,-325), which makes the liabilities of the State, up to this time, seven millions, two hundred and sixty-seven thousand, one hundred and eighty-one dollars, ($7,267,181).

The prospective liabilities which are authorized by an act to establish a system of Internal Improvements in this State, passed on the 11th day of February, 1852, and various other acts to aid in the building of bridges, will, if carried into full and successful operation, create an additional debt of about eight millions dollars more; which, when added to the liabilities already referred to, will make the whole liabilities of the State fifteen million, two hundred and sixty-seven thousand one hundred and eighty-one dollars, ($15,-267,181). And if the internal improvement bill now under consideration before the Legislature, should become a law, it will increase the prospective liabilities near six million four thousand dollars, ($6,400,000) which will make the grand total of the present and prospective liabilities of the State twenty-one million six hundred and sixty-seven thousand one hundred and eighty-one dollars, ($21,667,181). While on the subject of State indebtedness, it will not be out of place, nor improper, to refer to the probable amount owed by the counties and corporations throughout the State, which has been created by the issuance of county and corporations bonds, which cannot be less than five million dollars, ($5,000,000,) probably much more, making the whole liabilities of the people of the State, present and prospective, twenty-six million, six hundred and sixty-seven thousand one hundred and eighty-one dollars, ($26,-667,181).

Of the present liabilities, the State has at this time vested in various turnpike roads, one million, two hundred and thirty thousand eight hundred and fifty-six dollars, ($1,230,856) for which State bonds have been issued, and now pays interest on them, amounting to sixty-one thousand, nine hundred and sixty-nine dollars, ($61,-969). The entire amount received into the treasury annually from this investment in turnpike roads, is $15,106, making a net loss to the State, annually, of $46,763. It is to be hoped, however, that the profits arising from the investments made in these turnpike roads by the State, is not a correct indication of investments to be made in future in any works of internal improvements. Eleven of these roads, as yet, have never declared a dividend, and the prospect of their ever becoming profitable to the State, is exceedingly doubtful from present indications.

INTERNAL IMPROVEMENTS.

The constitution of the State declares that 'a well regulated system of internal improvements is calculated to develope the resouces of the State, and promote the happiness and prosperity of her citizens, therefore it ought to be encouraged by the General Assembly.' Internal Improvements is a subject that has been for some time back, and is now, exciting a deep and lively interest among the people, in many portions of the State. The questions, how far the State should be involved in constructing works of internal improvements, and what works shall be first undertaken and completed, must be determined by the wisdom and sound discretion of Senators and Representatives, who have been selected on account of their superior knowledge of the local and general interest of the whole State. 'A well regulated system of internal improvement' would seem to indicate that the leading and most prominent works calculated and intended to connect the three grand divisions or the State, should be first selected and completed. Such other works should then be undertaken as experience and the interest of the country might suggest. It should be the great and primary object of the

General Assembly to bind the State together from Johnson to Shelby, by railroads or other improvements which would accomplish the great end, making us one and the same people in commerce, agriculture and mechanics. A system like this, connecting itself with other important works beyond the limits of the State, would seem to accomplish the design of the constitution. While it is the duty of the Legislature, under the constitution, to foster and encourage 'a well regulated system of internal improvements,' it should be extremely careful in not undertaking too many works at the same time, and thereby dividing the energies of the State and individuals to that extent which would cause delay and failure in many of them, and at the same time result in great loss and useless expenditure of the people's substance. The system should always be so regulated as not to involve the State in heavy liabilities beyond what can at all times be met when they fall due, by the treasury, with promptness, without having to resort to heavy and oppressive taxation on the great mass of the people. The General Assembly should, and no doubt will, be exceedingly careful in not giving legislation, which is connected with the internal improvements of the country, that direction which will have a tendency to lessen or impair the public credit and honor of the State at home or abroad.

The duties imposed on the Executive by the laws which have been heretofore passed, or which may be hereafter passed, by the legislature, extending the aid of the State to works of internal improvement, will be discharged by him with strict fidelity.

PUBLIC ROADS.

Our whole system of public roads is exceedingly defective, perhaps more so than in any other State in the Union, imposing the burden of keeping it up upon that portion of our fellow-citizens least able to bear it, and who have the least use for it after it is kept up. Many persons are compelled to work on the public roads many days in the year, who have not the time to spare to do so, without pay, and the necessities of whose families need the proceeds of their entire labor for their support; while on the other hand there are many who are exempt by law from working on the public roads, who are either able physically to work them, or pecuniarily to pay for having it done, and who derive the greatest benefit from good roads when they are made, by the enhanced value good roads impart to their property, and by increasing the comforts and facilities of travelling over them. In view of changing or modifying our present system, I most respectfully call your attention to the system of keeping up public roads in the States of Ohio and Pennsylvania, where property and other taxes are levied for the purpose of keeping up the public roads and highways, and thereby carrying out the principle, that the individual who derives the greatest benefit from having them kept up, and in proper condition for the traveling public, shall pay correspondingly for the benefits thus conferred. All persons should contribute to the support of the government under which they live, in proportion to the protection they may receive from it. Our present road system, it must be conceded by all, operates most unjustly and unequally upon the great mass of the people, and ought to be changed. I therefore recommend to your consideration the propriety of so changing or modifying the present system as to conform it to the requirements of the public judgment and wants of the country, and that it be done during the present session of the Legislature.

EDUCATION.

The members of the General Assembly and the Executive of the State, in entering upon the discharge of their official duties, engaged to perform and obey the solemn obligations imposed on them by the constitution of the State. The framers of the constitution, from a high sense of their moral obligation to the whole people, and with a thorough knowledge of the great importance and the want of an efficient system for educational purposes, declared, in 1834, in the most emphatic language, that 'knowledge, learning and virtue, being essential to the preservation of republican institutions, and the diffusion of the opportunities and advantages of education throughout the different portions of the State, being highly conducive to the promotion of this end, *it shall be the duty of the General Assembly, in all future periods of this government, to cherish literature and science.*'

It must be apparent to all, that our present system of common school education falls very far short of coming up to the imperative commands of the constitution. If the law establishing our system of common schools had been perfect in all its details, the common school fund has been heretofore wholly inadequate to put it into practical and efficient operation throughout the State. At the present period, and for a long time past, our common schools have been doing little or no good, but, on the contrary, have, in many instances, and in different parts of the country, been rather in the way than otherwise, preventing the people from getting up and having schools upon their own responsibility, and at their own expense. The time has surely arrived when the Legislature and the people should lay hold of this important subject with a strong and unfaltering hand. All very readily concur in the opinion that something ought to be done to promote the cause of education, and still there are no effective steps taken. All who entertain any personal and State pride must feel deeply wounded when they are told by the recent census that Tennessee, though the fifth State in the Union, in many of the great elements necessary to make her one of the proudest and most respected, stands last and lowest on the list of education, save one, of all the States composing this confederacy. The great difficulty that seems to have been in the way, and the excuse for doing nothing more than we have done, is, that we have had no means, and that our school fund was too small to do more than we have done. If we are sincere in what we profess for the cause of education, we should, without hesitation, provide means to accomplish it. There is one way, if *no other*, that the children of the State can be educated, which is obvious to all, and that is, to levy and collect a tax from the people of the whole State, or to authorize the county courts, separately, to do so in their respective counties, in such manner as may be deemed by them most acceptable to the people, sufficient in amount, when added to our present school fund, to give life and energy to our dying or dead system of common school education. We should at once make such additions to our school fund as will make it large enough to vitalize the cause of common schools, and thereby make its influence felt in every family throughout the State.

While there are millions being appropriated to aid in the various works of internal improvement, can there be nothing done for education? While we are erecting magnificent State edifices, with niches and rotundas accommodated to the reception of fine statues and gorgeous paintings—the exterior presenting all the grandeur of carved and massive columns which architectural ingenuity can invent or display—the base of the building to be finished with a suitable terrace, together with public grounds, handsomely enclosed and laid out in promenades, as taste and extravagance may suggest, and then to be studded over with monuments and works of statuary, in imitation of oriental splendor and folly, and which will, in all, when completed in a corresponding style to the main structure, cost the people of the State not less than a million and a half or two million of dollars—I repeat the inquiry, while all these things are being done by the legislature, and that, too, at the public expense, *can there be nothing done to advance the great cause of education?*

Upon the increase and diffusion of education among the great mass of the people, and the elevation of labor, depends, to a very great extent, the perpetuity of our free institutions. I feel that I cannot too strongly and too earnestly press the importance of this subject upon your consideration. Let us now, if possible, commence the work in good faith, and carry out the high behest of the constitution, and the rising generation will realize the benefits that will necessarily flow from it. It will develop, in its benign operations, the intellect of our children, and qualify them for all the useful pursuits of life. It will be worth far more to them than the accumulated wealth of the world combined.

In concluding my remarks upon this important subject, I will call to my aid the language of another, which much more fully and forcibly expresses the value and importance of education than anything that may or can be said by me: 'Education is a companion which no misfortune can suppress—no clime destroy—no enemy alienate—no despotism enslave. At home, a friend; abroad, an introduction; in solitude, a solace; in society, an ornament. It lessens vice, it guards virtue, it gives at once a grace and government to genius. Without it, what is man? a splendid slave! a reasoning savage! vascillating between the dignity of an intelligence derived from God, and the degradation of brutal passions.'

The cause of education is now submitted to the Senators and Representatives of the people, to be disposed of as they, in their best judgment, may deem most conducive to the public good.

TAX ON MERCHANTS.

There is some complaint with the mercantile interest, in consequences of the unequal and discriminating operation of our revenue laws regulating merchants' license. The complaint is not without some foundation and good cause on their part. The law, as it now stands, requires all wholesale and retail dealers in merchandise in this State to first pay into the Treasury of the State one-half of one per cent on the invoice cost of all goods vended by them. The main cause of complaint, as I understand it, is, that in the first place, the wholesale merchant, by the revenue law, is required to first pay into the treasury the half of one per cent, or fifty cents on the hundred dollars. After the tax is paid by him into the treasury, the retail merchant then purchases the same goods of him and takes them to another establishment, in or out of the county where purchased, as the case may be, and vends them again; for which he is required to pay one-half of one per cent, or fifty cents on the hundred dollars, into the treasury; which is one per cent paid to the State for the goods thus sold. By this process it will be perceived that the State lays a double tax on the goods purchased from the wholesale dealer within the limits of the State. The business retail dealer has no difficulty in understanding the operation, and finds it to his interest to go beyond the limits of the State to make his purchases, and become the customer of the foreign wholesale dealer, instead of the wholesale dealer at home; and to that extent operates against our own commercial cities and commercial men.

It is most manifest to my mind that the practical effect of the revenue law, as it now stands, regulating merchants' license, is to discriminate against the merchant at home and in favor of the one abroad. The subject is, therefore, submitted to your consideration, with the hope that the law will be so modified as to place the mercantile interest of the State on an equal footing and in a field of fair competition with a like interest of the other States of the Union.

BANKS.

The Bank of Tennessee is represented, in a report made by the President to the General Assembly on the 10th day of October last, as being in a sound and prosperous condition. While the Bank is undergoing an investigation by a committee appointed by the Legislature for that purpose, I will refrain from expressing any opinion in regard to its present condition, or making any definite recommendation as to what course the General Assembly ought to take in reference to its future management, more than, however, barely to suggest that the present would be a very auspicious time to put the principal and all the branch banks into gradual liquidation; giving ample and reasonable time to all persons who are indebted to the institution to make arrangements for paying the amount they owe. The process of winding it up at the present time can be made so gradual and easy as not to embarrass the indebted portion of the community in the smallest degree.

A number of Banks have gone into operation under a law passed by the last General Assembly, and others, no doubt, will soon commence; which will more than supply the vacuum created by the withdrawal of the Bank of Tennessee, and furnish all the banking facilities needed by the whole business portion of the country. As the capital of the Bank is withdrawn, it can be profitably invested in the bonds of the State, bearing an interest of six per cent per annum, which will be the safest and most judicious investment that can be made with the common school and other funds which are now in the Bank of Tennessee and under the control of the State.

If the State can, in any reasonable time, dispose of the stock owned in the Union and Planters' Banks upon good terms, or all other stocks owned by the State, it would be equally wise, safe and judicious to make a like investment with the proceeds of such stocks in the six per cent bonds of the State. The number of internal improvement works which have been commenced, and which are entitled to aid by law from the State, and the great number of others that are to be commenced, which will require the issuance of a large amount of State bonds, amounting to many millions of dollars, will absorb the entire capital of the State Bank and all the stocks owned by the State, if they are invested in the bonds of the State, as already indicated; which investment, in my judgment, will be far safer and more profitable in the end, than in any bank, State or private.

PENITENTIARY.

This institution has, so far, failed in all the leading objects of its creation. The confinement of persons within the prison-house or prison walls of a penitentiary, with the view of reforming them in their moral character, has been proven by all experience to be a great error, and it is not now contended for as a reforming institution by any one who has become at all familiar with the subject. There is not one in every thousand convicts whose moral condition is improved by such imprisonment; but, on the contrary, most of them if not all, are made worse than they were before, and become more confirmed in crime.

Upon the subject of convicts becoming reformed by penitentiary imprisonment and association, Dr. John S. Young, former Secretary of State, in an able and elaborate report made on the 15th of September, 1845, to the Commissioners of Public Buildings, and by them submitted to the Legislature, used the following language: 'I am entirely skeptical on the subject of reforming convicts by teaching them mechanical trades; little or no good results from it. When the *convict* leaves the prison, he lays down his *cap*, and with it his *trade*. He looks back upon both as the *badges* of his disgrace, and the companions of his imprisonment; he aims to something else which he considers better than his trade, or returns to the re-commission of crime. The trade, in most instances, as I believe, serves to better qualify the *villian* without reforming the *man*. Those who would attempt the moral reformation of the *felon* must employ other means. They must bear in mind, that three-fourths of those who are stained with crime can neither read nor write. The mind must be cultivated in order to produce those genial influences which are calculated to remove vicious inclinations and base propensities, and give place to proper sensibilities and corrected feelings, from which altered intentions and virtuous actions must spring.'

The trial, conviction and sentence by the court of persons to the penitentiary for violation of the laws, has had no restraining influence whatever on immorality, and carries little or no terror to the mind of the evil doer. The announcement in the court-house yard that such a person has been sentenced for so many years' imprisonment, is received with no alarm, but, on the contrary, with great indifference; and it is the frequent remark that it is better for the individual who has just been sentenced to so many years' confinement—it will be far better for him. He will, while there, be enabled to learn a good trade, and will live better there than he ever did before. The Sheriff then prepares with his guards and starts with the convict for the penitentiary, making rather the impression, as he leaves, upon the mind of many spectators, that the prisoner has done well in obtaining a traveling trip of pleasure and a money-making business for the sheriff and his escort, and he in the end to be made one of the mechanics of the country. In fine, on these two points, it will be readily perceived, the penitentiary reforms no one after he is confined within its walls; and the sentence of the court and confinement together, deters no one from a violation of the laws of the land.

In the next place, the system has fallen far below the expense incurred in the erection of the establishment, and the annual cost of carrying it on, up to the present time. Upon a close examination of all the items properly chargeable to the institution, after giving full credit for all that it is entitled to, there will still be found a deficit of not less than one hundred thousand dollars—probably much more. I have obtained sufficient data from Mr. Love, the principal bookkeeper, who has appeared very accommodating and much disposed to afford every facility in his power to remove all difficulty in getting all the true financial condition of the institution, together with a report recently made by the Comptroller to the Senate, showing how much has been paid out of the treasury for the conveyance of convicts to the penitentiary, to satisfy my mind that the State has incurred a heavy loss by the penitentiary. It will take but little investigation of this subject to satisfy any discerning mind that the penitentiary system exerts no beneficial moral influence on society, in or out of the penitentiary, and that it is now, and has been, an incubus on the treasury, and will most likely continue so, unless the whole establishment undergoes a thorough change.

While the institution has failed in all the leading objects of its creation, the manner in which it has been conducted has been made to operate injuriously upon the mechanical interest of the country.— It has been made practically a *State mechanic institute*, fostered and sustained by the treasury of the State, and brought into direct competition with the mechanics of the country to the extent of its entire operation. The conditions upon which persons are admitted into this *State mechanic institute*, are very discriminating and invidious in their character. Before the candidate can obtain admission to the high privilege of being employed in this institution, at any one of the branches of business carried on there, he must first commit the horrid crime of murder, arson, larceny, rape, or some other one of the offences violative of law. He must then stand a trial in some of our courts of justice, and then receive a certificate from the presiding judge that these facts are all true, and in addition to this, he must be accompanied by the high sheriff of the county and his retinue to the *State Mechanic Institute*. Having arrived, his credentials are presented, and such other evidences as may be required, that he is a fit and worthy candidate, having passed through the ordeal necessary and proper to his qualification for admission, he is then received by the proprietor of the institute, and safely conducted to the stone mason's, sculptor's, or some other department, and there begins his new vocation of reducing the rough and unpolished marble to shape and fashion. The hands that are yet crimson with the blood of the unoffending, are made to ply the mallet and chisel, as did Socrates, the Grecian philosopher and statesman—perhaps, too, in the course of his servitude, with the same guilty hand, to engrave upon the tomb of the departed and illustrious dead, the lines which are intended to indicate to the inquiring living their many virtues and exalted worth. And so, also, with all the other departments that are carried on in this institution; there might be similar illustrations made in reference to tailors, shoemakers, hatters, blacksmiths, wagon makers, &c. &c.

The State, by the establishment of this institution, and the passage of laws to sustain it, gathers from every county in the State all the incorrigible offenders who are known to the law, and after collecting them within the walls of the penitentiary, embarks in all the branches of mechanism, and openly enters the field of competition with the mechanics of the country. The mechanics outside of the penitentiary are required, by all the obligations of good citizens, in peace as well as war, to submit to taxation to sustain the government under which they live, and at the same time compete with the State in their own branches of business. This policy of the State, in carrying on the branches of mechanism, and the employment of all felons of the country at them, has a direct tendency to degrade the mechanics of the country as a body. Felon and mechanic, crime and mechanism, from their close association, become corresponding terms in the public mind. The felons, after having served out their time, are turned loose upon the country, to mix with the mechanics as best they may, and perchance to become inmates of their families, and companions in their shops. Is it right that this description of our population should be thrown upon, and associated with, the honest and industrious mechanics of the State, either in person or profession? There is an instinctive repugnance in the bosom of all honorable men, and it is reduced to practice by nearly all those who have charge of our cemeteries, by excluding the felon from being associated with us even in the grave. If it is degrading to be associated with a felon after we are dead, it must be much more so to be associated with him while we are living.

In conclusion, upon this subject, I must be permitted to make one earnest appeal, and that is, for the legislature to so direct the future management of the affairs of the penitentiary, by their legislation, as to protect this large and respectable portion of our fellow-citizens from this degrading association and competition, by excluding all the branches of mechanism from the penitentiary.

JUDICIARY.

The true foundation of our Judiciary is to be found in the Bill of Rights, which was adopted by the sovereign people in the year 1796, and was, in the year 1834, re-affirmed. In the 17th section, they have declared in the most emphatic manner, 'that all courts shall be open, and every man for an injury done him, in his lands, goods, person or reputation, shall have remedy by due course of law, and right and justice administered without sale, denial or delay.' 'Right and justice' is to be administered without 'sale, denial or delay'—this is laid down as the basis, as the foundation of our whole system of jurisprudence; and it is imperative on the legislature in the organization of our courts to conform them to the principles herein laid down. To a correct understanding of the kind of courts to be established, we should first determine what is meant by the terms 'right and justice,' as used in the bill of rights. The most approved authors define the term *right:* 'Conformity to human laws, or to other human standards of truth, propriety or justice.' '*Justice*— the constant and perpetual disposition to render every man his due,'

&c. In this connection we might consider the meaning of *equity* also. In an enlarged and legal view, 'Equity, in its true and genuine meaning, is the soul and spirit of the law.' In this, 'equity is made synonymous with justice.' Right, justice and equity, according to common sense, and the best authorities, mean the same thing. When it comes to establishing a court or a tribunal, or it may be called by any other name, which is intended as a standard by which the precise difference can be determined between the contending parties, it is imperative on the legislature to establish that standard which will accomplish the great end as designed in the bill of rights, and if it were possible to so organize our courts, that when parties came into them to have their differences adjusted, for the court and jury to ascertain what is the precise equity between the parties, and then to determine that as the law of the case, 'equity being the soul and spirit of the law'—in other words, making the equity of the case, *the law of the case.* Taking the bill of rights as the foundation for our courts, the inquiry very naturally arises as to whether our courts, as now established, under the sixth section, first article of the constitution, are in conformity with the principles herein laid down. This article says, 'the judicial power of the State shall be vested in one supreme court, in such inferior courts as the legislature shall ordain and establish.' This provision of the constitution would seem to give great latitude to the legislature in the organization of the courts. But the exercise of this power by the legislature must be in strict conformity with the principles laid down in the bill of rights. The bill of rights, being the better part of the constitution, is paramount.

In all questions of apparent conflict between the bill of rights and the constitution, they should be reconciled and made to harmonize, if possible; but where there is a final repugnance, the constitution must give way, it bearing the same relation to the bill of rights that a law does to the constitution. Hence, in the organization of the courts, the legislature has no authority under the sixth article, to depart from this great and fundamental principle, as laid down in the bill of rights, or the better part of the constitution.

Under the constitution of 1796, judges of the supreme and inferior courts were appointed by the legislature to office, during good behavior. The legislature conferred upon the courts chancery and law jurisdiction, which was exercised by them for thirty-eight years, or till 1835. The people, after making this experiment, became well satisfied that our judicial system was exceedingly defective, falling far short of carrying out the great principles, as contemplated in the bill of rights.

In 1834, the people again, in convention, so changed the constitution as to make it more in conformity with the great idea of right and justice, by changing the tenure of all judicial officers from that of life to a term of years, and at the same time referring back many other elections to themselves which had been given up in the constitution of 1796.

These changes in the constitution have been effected, in part, for the purpose of conforming the courts of the country, in their whole structure, to the wants and necessities of the people. There has been evident dissatisfaction with the courts of the country for a number of years past. The people find fault with the judges, complain of lawyers, and sometimes condemn jurors, affording conclusive evidence that there is a wrong somewhere: Delay, expense and perplexity of mind on the part of the litigants—confidence in the courts much impaired in the public estimation. Under our present system, an individual goes into what is termed a court of law, to obtain justice in some matter of controversy, and after much time is spent and expenses incurred, he comes out of law with a long bill of costs to pay, and if he complains of the proceeding, he is told that his case was a good one, but he was unfortunate in bringing his action in the wrong court; that his remedy is not in law, but in chancery. Another individual brings his suit in a court of chancery, and after a like delay of time and trouble in filing bills and hearing answers, he is turned out of court with a long bill of cost and charges to pay, and he is consoled in the same way by telling him his case is a good one, but his remedy is not in chancery, but in a court of law, there being no equity in his case; and in this way parties are kept oscillating from a court of chancery to a court of law, and from a court of law to a court of chancery, until, in the end, if the end ever comes, the substance of the parties is, in many instances consumed, and the gainer of the suit is frequently the loser, and the unfortunate party goes into immediate bankruptcy.— This is the manner in which law and equity is administered under our present system of jurisprudence, which, in fact, is the great cause of complaint of the parties who go into our courts to obtain justice and a want of confidence on the part of the people in the courts of law and chancery.

Upon this subject I shall take high ground, and assume that the courts can be so organized, that law and equity can be administered by the same court, by the same judge and jury, and at the same time, and that, too, without 'sale, denial or delay.' Let the courts of law and chancery be blended or converted into one court, (it is not material by what name you call it)—or, in other words, let the law and the equity of the case be heard by the court and jury at the same time—let the parties, if necessary, be examined in open court— let all the restraints and barriers be removed—all false issues and collateral questions be thrown aside, and the cause tried upon the naked merits involved, and thereby administer 'right and justice' to the contending parties, and let them go hence without delay.

I feel well assured that the people, throughout the State, expect legislative action upon this subject before the close of your session. This is a most propitious time for bringing about the change in our judiciary, as indicated, the people having removed all constitutional difficulties that were in the way, by the adoption of the recent amendments to the constitution. There is now a bill before your honorable body, entitled a bill, 'To abridge and simplify the pleadings, practice and proceedings in the courts of justice in this State,' which will, if passed into a law, accomplish much in conforming the practice in the courts to the requirements of the bill of rights and the wants of the people. In recommending this bill to your favorable consideration, or some one very similar in its provisions, I am not recommending a new and untried experiment, but one which has been tried and approved by many of our sister States. It will and can succeed with us as it has with them, if the experiment is fully and fairly made, and will, no doubt, give general satisfaction here, as it has there, by simplifying, cheapening and shortening the process by which litigants may obtain 'right and justice'.

That the bill referred to has been prepared, by its originator with great care and much labor, is manifest to all who will give it a careful examination; and it is believed, after passing the legislative ordeal will be so improved as more closely to approximate the intentions and design of those who framed the constitution. The leading principles of the measure now recommended to your favorable consideration, have been advocated by me since my first entrance into public life, in the year 1835; and my reflection and observation together with the successful experiment which has been made in other States of the Union, have tended to confirm me in the opinion that it ought to be adopted in this State, and that, too, before the adjournment of the present Legislature.

In connection with this subject, I would recommend that, at the earliest moment practicable, ample provision be made for bringing on all the elections as contemplated by the amendments to the constitution.

WEIGHTS AND MEASURES.

Under the provisions of the Federal Constitution, Congress has adopted a standard of Weights and Measures, and by a resolution in 1836, deposited with the several States a set of those weights and measures. A portion of this set has been sent to the State of Tennessee, and is now in the Secretary's office; the remainder can probably be had upon application. But this provision, to establish a uniform standard of weights and measures, is wholly insufficient under the existing laws on that subject. Indeed, no law has been passed since this standard was adopted, or since the distribution of the weights and measures among the States, and of course there is nothing in our State law requiring our standard keepers to conform to this general standard. It seems to me that a law ought to be passed requiring the standard keeper for each county to have his weights and measures compared with, and tested by, the standard furnished by Congress. And that there should be some responsible functionary, known to the law, whose duty it should be to make inspection of this comparison and test, and when fairly and accurately made, to seal or mark the weight and measure so tried, with some official and authoritative brand or stamp—without some provision of this kind, the provisions of the act of Congress are nugatory, and no authoritative assurance is given that there will be any uniformity in the weights and measures throughout the State. Without a conformity to this common standard, great and constant injustice may be done to our own citizens, or unintentionally practiced by them, in all our interchange of commodities with other States, or among themselves.

CONSULAR CONVENTION.

There has been transmitted to the Executive department, by the Secretary of State of the United States, a copy of a 'Consular Convention between the United States of America and his majesty the Emperor of the French,' concluded on the 23rd February last, between the United States and France, accompanied with a circular, which will explain the object of its transmission; both of which are herewith submitted for your consideration.

AMENDMENTS TO THE CONSTITUTION OF THE UNITED STATES.

I will most respectfully call the attention of the General Assembly to the fifth article of the Constitution of the United States, which prescribes the mode and manner of amendment to that instrument, and, also, three propositions to amend the Constitution of the United States, which are appended to and made a part of this message, which is respectfully submitted for consideration and action by the General Assembly. In submitting this subject, I shall make no long or labored argument to the Legislature, or the country, to prove the importance and necessity of adding these three amendments to the Constitution of the United States. All who are in favor of popularizing our free instiutions as far as may be practicable, and bring the general government nearer to the people, will receive and treat them as self-evident propositions.

I will conclude, by adding, that they were the doctrines of Jefferson, of Jackson, Macon, and a number of other statesmen and patriots, whose opinions are at all times entitled to the respect and consideration of the American people.

NATIONAL HOMESTEAD.

I feel that I cannot conclude this message without urging upon your consideration the importance and propriety of instructing our Senators in the Congress of the United States, and requesting our Representatives to use all reasonable exertion to procure the passage of a bill granting to every head of a family, who is a citizen of the

United States, a 'Homestead' of one hundred and sixty acres of land, out of the public domain, upon condition of settlement and cultivation for a number of years. This is a measure of no ordinary consideration to the American people, and the correctness of its policy has been settled in the public judgment, and would have been the law long before this time, had the popular will been carried out by the Congress of the United States. I therefore hope that you will take such action as will reflect the popular sentiment of the sovereign people of this State, and thereby contribute the weight of your influence to the consummation of this great measure.

Gentlemen of the Senate and House of Representatives: I have now brought to your favorable notice, in as brief a manner as the nature and importance of the subject would permit me to do, such measures and suggestions as have been deemed worthy of your consideration, and entitled to receive legislative action. And I have done this with the earnest hope that they may meet your cordial approbation, and that they be given that direction which you, in your better judgment, may consider most conductive to the public good; and, further, I would most fondly indulge the hope that I have neither in the measures submitted to your consideration, or the manner of submitting them, transcended the limits of that courtesy which is due from one co-ordinate branch of the government to another, and which should be preserved at all times inviolate.

In conclusion of this, my first message to a deliberative body, permit me to invoke, in aid of your deliberations, the guardian-spirit of an over-ruling Providence, and that all your legislative acts may be so thoroughly imbued with patriotism and wisdom, that when you have closed your arduous and perplexing labors as Representatives of a sovereign State, and shall have returned home to the circle of your families and friends, you will receive the welcome salutation of an honest and confiding constituency, of 'well done, thou good and faithful servant.'

ANDREW JOHNSON"

What a contrast in Governor Johnson's regular Message and his Inaugural Address! The former document contains not a single impracticable suggestion; *facts* and a candid presentation of those facts by the Governor entitles his Message to receive favorable comparison with any preceding Message transmitted by any of his predecessors. No longer, as in his Inaugural Address, are present any half-baked theories or vague generalities; current situations were stated, evaluated, diagnosed, and appropriate remedies prescribed. The legislative Message was conveniently divided into sub-heads, each topic being dealt with specifically and unaccompanied with a melange of other unrelated items. If Governor Johnson spent all or a major part of the two and one-half months since his inauguration in the preparation of his regular Message, it was time well spent. Evidence that the Message was a major contribution may be assumed by the absence of any vitriolic criticism from the Whig press which had fought Johnson's election with vigor, persistence, and unrelenting political antagonism.

The Message was divided into twelve topics, namely:

1. State Finances
2. Internal Improvements
3. Public Roads
4. Education
5. Tax on Merchants
6. Banks
7. Penitentiary
8. Judiciary
9. Weights and Measures
10. Consular Convention
11. Amendments to the Constitution of the United States
12. National Homestead

Undoubtedly Governor Johnson's analysis of State finances and obligations served to put the brakes upon legislative appropriations hitherto handed out with a lavish hand for various and sundry items. When attention was called to the State investment of approximately one and one-quarter million of dollars in turnpikes on which investment the State was sustaining an annual loss of nearly $47,000, that cold fact unquestionably caused the Legislature to pause and ponder a bit. That it was a "pause that refreshes" may be deduced from the fact that out of one hundred and twenty-one turnpike companies whose charters were amended in some respect during the legislative session, only a total of $94,000 was appropriated to such enterprises in the form of State bonds, and in those causes a first lien was secured upon the companies as a safeguard to the State for its loan. In pointing out that "the whole liabilities of the people of the State, present and prospective" amounted to approximately twenty-six and one half million dollars, Governor Johnson had presented a solid fact that could not be lightly waived aside, no matter how pressing or persuasive the argument might be. A realistic presentation of the situation was both needed and heeded.

With reference to internal improvements, Governor Johnson cited the constitutional encouragement in the developing of a well regulated system, but he wisely suggested that the State should not go beyond its ability to provide the means without having to resort to heavy and oppressive taxation. As a safeguard on behalf of the State, a law [35] was passed authorizing the Governor to appoint a commissioner of roads whose duty it was to check into the actual condition of railroads applying for State aid. A further provision of the law was that the Governor had to be satisfied that the railroads had complied with the law before he could lawfully issue State bonds for the use of such roads. Any officer of any railroad mishandling any of the funds derived from the sale of the bonds was to be charged with having committed a felony and was liable for a sentence to the penitentiary from five to fifteen years if proved guilty.

Governor Johnson's recommendation that a change be made in regard to keeping the public roads in repair did not receive legislative approval. Apparently his suggestion that the plan operating in Ohio and Pennsylvania, which involved public taxation, be considered did not appeal to the legislators, for no effort to enact such a law was attempted. The only movement that even squinted in the direction of the Governor's recommendation was initiated ten days prior to the Governor's regular Message. Whig Senator Jacob M. Bewly from the counties of Hawkins and Jefferson introduced a bill to exempt students, while at home, from working on the public roads.[36] When the bill came up on second reading, an amendment was proposed for making the law inapplicable to students who did not pay for board and lodging. Another proposed amendment would have exempted all young men under twenty-one years of age from working on the roads and from attending musters. After the rejection of both proposed amendments, Whig Senator Hugh Robertson from the counties of Robertson, Montgomery, and Stewart offered the following amendment [37] which was in line with Governor Johnson's recommendation:

"That hereafter all persons shall be exempt from working on county or public roads, and it shall be the duty of the County Court to make such an appropriation as may seem necessary, out of the county treasury for the purpose of keeping said roads in repair, and it is hereby made the duty of each district constable to keep the said roads in the several districts in good repair, out of such moneys as are appropriated by the County Court, and shall receive such pay as the County Court may deem necessary for performing such duty."

Senator Robertson's amendment was defeated, whereupon the bill was then rejected by a vote of 19 to 5.

The high spot of Governor Johnson's first administration was the enactment of the first law in the history of Tennessee providing for public taxation for public education. Prior to Andrew Johnson, no

[35] *Acts of Tennessee*, 1853, Chapter 131.
[36] *Senate Journal*, 1853, 257.
[37] *Ibid.*, 287.

other Governor of Tennessee had ever come out specifically and unreservedly for public taxation for the support of public education—just
another link in the chain of evidence that Johnson's courage was always
equal to his concept of public duty. When convinced that he was right,
he became the embodiment of Shakespeare's famous dictum:

> "I DARE do all that may become a man;
> Who dares do more, is none."

In the preparation of his regular Message to the Legislature, there
can be no reasonable doubt but that Andrew Johnson had familiarized
himself with one particular item in the State Treasurer's Report as submitted on the opening day of the legislative session. That item, both a
shame and a disgrace, disclosed that for the preceding year each of the
271,139 wards of the State over six and under twenty-one years of
age had received the pitiful sum of thirty-nine and one-half cents *per
annum* for his "schooling!" [38] For more than half a century, Tennessee
Governors and legislators had fiddled and piddled around on the paramount question of public education, but their myriads of resolutions on
the subject were always resolved into penny contributions. True
enough, Governor Neill S. Brown in the early part of his administration recommended taxation for support of public education. But before
his retirement from office, he reversed his position on the issue by saying:

> ". . . I do not believe a system of direct taxes expedient or proper."

With an adroitness that amounted to inspiration, he capitalized upon
a local project which he utilized as a sort of springboard for expressing
clearly and fearlessly his profound convictions on the question of education. He had noted the massive State Capitol nearing completion,
with its towering cupola, its chiseled columns, its graded landscape,
together with its promenade and statuary. That building, he reflected,
had been built with public funds supplied out of the pockets of taxpayers. It is worth our while to review that portion of his Message:

> "...While we are erecting magnificent State edifices, with niches and
> rotundas accommodated to the reception of fine statues and gorgeous paint-
> ings—the exterior presenting all the grandeur of carved and massive columns
> which architectural ingenuity can invent or display—the base of the building
> to be finished with a suitable terrace, together with public grounds, hand-
> somely enclosed and laid out in promenades, as taste and extravagance may
> suggest, and then to be studded over with monuments and works of statuary,
> in imitation of oriental splendor and folly, and which in all when completed
> will cost the people of the State not less than a million and a half or two mil-
> lion of dollars—I repeat the inquiry, while all these things are being done by

---

[38] *Senate Journal*, 1853, Appendix, 227.
House Journal, 1853, Appendix, 227.

the Legislature and that, too, at public expense, can there be nothing done to advance the great cause of education?"

Andrew Johnson had raised a fundamental question when he asked; "Can nothing be done to advance the great cause of education?" Unlike all of his predecessors in office, Johnson did not leave his question unanswered. He did not swerve to some easy political vantage point and shift the responsibility to some sort of legislative hocus-pocus that would have accomplished exactly nothing. Boldly and unreservedly, Andrew Johnson exclaimed in thunder-tones what no preceding Governor of Tennessee had ever advocated and remained steadfast in his position. Listen to his very words on what proved to be a turning point in the educational history of Tennessee:

"There is one way ... that the children of the State can be educated ... and that is to levy and collect a tax from the people of the whole state ... sufficient in amount, when added to our present school fund, to give life and energy to our dying or dead system of common school education."

These were the words uttered by a courageous Governor whose deep conviction and unswerving sense of duty due the childhood of Tennessee entitle him to be known as The Father of Public Education in Tennessee! He closed his earnest plea for educational legislation and financial support with burning and passionate words that glow even today "like apples of gold in pictures of silver":

"Education is a companion which no misfortune can suppress—no clime destroy—no enemy alienate—no despotism enslave. At home, a friend; abroad, an introduction; in solitude, a solace; in society, an ornament. It lessens vice, it guards virtue, it gives at once a grace and government to genius. Without it, what is man? A splendid slave! a reasoning savage! vacillating between the dignity of an intelligence derived from God, and the degradation of brutal passions."

Two months after the delivery of his address to the Legislature on education, Andrew Johnson saw the fruits of his courage and labor culminate in the passage of a law [39] on February 28, 1854, that marked the first milestone in public education in Tennessee. The inalienable rights of childhood had been recognized and then ratified by a law that placed a tax of twenty-five cents on polls and two and one-half cents on each $100 of taxable property for public education. This was the first such law ever enacted in the history of the State. "The Rubicon had been crossed!" This constituted the first milestone in public education in Tennessee.

Despite Governor Johnson's plea for a more equitable tax to be levied on merchants, no relief to this class of citizens was provided by the Legislature. The existing law, as viewed by the Governor, entailed a hardship on resident wholesale merchants in that the local retail mer-

---

[39] *Acts of Tennessee,* 1853, Chapter 71.

chant could purchase his goods outside the State and thereby escape the tax of one-half cent on each one hundred dollars of goods if and when purchased within the State. Apparently the relatively small number of resident merchants was too small to enable them to make any "big noise" among the legislators.

Governor Johnson's suggestion that the present time was an "auspicious" one for putting the Bank of Tennessee and its branches "into gradual liquidation" likewise went unnoticed by the Legislature. Actually, the Bank of Tennessee was not liquidated until 1866, when the reconstruction Legislature passed a law [40] to wind up the business of the Bank of Tennessee.

For many years, the mechanics of the State had filed protest after protest against the general policy being pursued at the State Penitentiary wherein various mechanical trades were being taught the convicts. The swelling opposition to the practice had apparently caught the ear of Governor Johnson who always had been keenly sympathetic to the welfare of "the common working man." Shortly after the transmission of the Governor's regular Message to the Legislature, the question of teaching trades to convicts was revived and numerous petitions against the practice poured into the members of the Legislature. Various methods designed to handle the problem were suggested, one being the introduction of a bill [41] by Whig Representative J. Morris of Wayne County "to farm out the penitentiary." The Penitentiary Committee recommended the rejection of the bill, and on February 21, 1854, the bill was indefinitely postponed.[42]

Of all the manifold memorials [43] protesting against teaching trades to convicts, perhaps the following was representative of the attitude of the mechanics at large:[44]

"MEMORIAL.

State of Tennessee
McMinn County

To the Honorable House of Representatives and Senate of the State of Tennessee:

Your Memorialists, being a Committee appointed by the Mechanics of the State of Tennessee, would most respectfully represent to your honorable body, that the practical operation of a State Institution, known as the 'Jail and Penitentiary House,' conflicts both with the interest and honor of the great body of Mechanics of this Commonwealth. They would respectfully call the attention of your honorable body to the following facts: That, while the number of Mechanics at the present time in the Institution, amounts to one hundred and seventeen, in gross, yet the number of Mechanics *de novo*,

[40] *Acts of Tennessee*, 1866, Chapter 28.
[41] *House Journal*, 1853, 698.
[42] *Ibid.*, 913.
[43] *Ibid.*, 654.
[44] Original manuscript document in State Archives, Nashville. (37 signatures)

or those who were such at the time of their admission was thirty-seven, only. The overplus, therefore, of eighty have been created by the Institution! This number of Mechanics, created out of the most abandoned of our population—condemned felons—when released from confinement, are to be incorporated with and become a part and parcel of the Mechanics of the State. It is unnecessary to inform your honorable body, that, however scornfully we may repudiate any association with them, yet, being of the same calling, and engaged in the same pursuit, it is impossible to prevent the public mind from identifying them with us and, to that extent, as they cannot be elevated, to degrade us to their dishonorable level. Your honorable body, furthermore, need not be informed, that while the State not only ceases to regard or protect a great industrial interest, but upon the contrary, humbles and degrades it, in vain may it hope to elevate itself by the individual effort of those whom it embraces. In other States the mechanic interest, by institutes and circulating libraries, is making giant strides to elevate itself in popular estimation. The arts which it involves are receiving light and illustration from the sciences which guide, direct and develope them, and already does it number many of the most exalted genius and learning. It is science to which the art must look for dignity, and elsewhere does her cheering smile encourage the weary Mechanic to renewed diligence. But here, when the eye of the Mechanic rests upon the Penitentiary, hope is converted into despair, and the struggle which would elevate seeks repose in lethargy. We therefore pray your honorable body to remove this barrier to our progress to usefulness and respectability. This is said to be an age characterized by progress, and if this be so, how unenviable is the condition of him, who sees the world sweep by him while State fetters chain him to the spot. Thus hedged in, the Mechanic, void of offence to man or State, is almost as much a prisoner as the felon in his cell, whom the State is preparing for his future associate.

It is not our province to suggest to your honorable body the proper means for removing this grievance, having an abiding confidence in your justice and wisdom, not shaded by a doubt that you will devise the means and apply the corrective.

And your Memorialists, as in duty bound, &c."

The pleas of Governor Johnson and the mechanics fell upon leaden ears. No legislation even remotely connected with the object of their remonstrances was enacted. Actually, a law [45] was passed directing the utilization of the labor of convicts for building any additional facilities needed at the penitentiary. Democratic Representative W. E. Travis of Henry County apparently was a bit peeved at Governor Johnson's strong recommendation regarding the elimination of the teaching of mechanical trades in the penitentiary, for he presented a resolution [46] which may have been based upon petulancy and irritation:

"Resolved, That His Excellency the Governor be, and he is hereby requested to furnish the General Assembly with some plan by which the evils of the penitentiary, of which he so seriously complains, can be eradicated."

The Travis resolution was adopted by a vote of 45 to 26, and a motion to reconsider the action of the House was defeated.[47]

---

[45] *Acts of Tennessee*, 1853, Chapter 26.
[46] *House Journal*, 1853, 540.
[47] *Ibid.*, 542.

Before dismissing the penitentiary topic, attention should be called to the provisions of a bill "to provide for building a public jail and Penitentiary" by Senator Robert Farquharson from the counties of Franklin and Lincoln. A report [48] from a select committee to which had been referred Senator Farquharson's bill was as follows:

"The select commitee of the Senate, to whom was referred Senate's bill, No. 177, entitled 'A bill to provide for building a Public Jail and Penitentiary in this State, and to aid in establishing a system of Internal Improvements;' have had the same under consideration and instruct me to report:—That owing to the press of public business in the Senate since the bill was referred to them, they have not had time to give the subject that careful examination which the importance of the objects of the bill would seem to demand. From the reflection which they have been able to bestow upon it, however, they have become satisfied that the project is entirely practicable, and only requires to be put in execution, to secure to the State many benefits and advantages, and they have reason to believe that in relieving the honest and industrious mechanics from an odious and degrading competition with convict labor—in developing the mineral resources of the commonwealth and in aiding the establishment of a system of Internal Improvement, upon a firm basis, by preserving the credit of the State—any expenditure required for the establishment and support of the institution, would, in a very few years, be amply and certainly repaid to the treasury.

While the present Penitentiary system has failed in all the leading objects of its creation, the manner in which it has been conducted has been made to operate injuriously upon the mechanical interest of the country, and had your committee no other reason urging them to recommend the passage of this bill, but a desire to redress the wrongs of a class, so every way meritorious as the mechanics—this of itself, would be deemed sufficient.

The language of Governor Johnson upon this subject in his late annual message to the Legislature, is so forcible, clear, and appropriate, that your Committee hope they will be pardoned for adopting it:

'The Penitentiary has been made practically a *State Mechanic Institute*, fostered and sustained by the treasury of the State and brought into direct competition with the mechanics of the country, to the extent of its entire operation.

'The State by its establishment and the passage of laws to sustain it, gathers from every county in the State all the incorrigible offenders who are known to the law, and after collecting them within the walls of the penitentiary, embarks in all the branches of mechanism, and openly enters the field of competition with the mechanics of the country. The mechanics outside of the penitentiary are required, by all the obligations of good citizens, in peace as well as in war, to submit to taxation to sustain the government under which they live, and at the same time compete with the State in their own branches of business. This policy of the State in carrying on the branches of mechanism, and the employment of all the felons of the country at them, has a direct tendency to degrade mechanics of the country as a body. Felon and mechanic, crime and mechanism, from their close association, become corresponding terms in the public mind. The felons after having served out their time, are turned loose upon the country to mix with the mechanics as best they may, and perchance to become inmates of their families, and companions in their

---

[48] *Senate Journal*, 1853, 506–511.

shops. Is it right that this description of our population should be thrown upon and associated with the honest and industrious mechanics of the State, either in person or profession? There is an instinctive repugnance in the bosom of all honorable men, and it is reduced to practice by nearly all those who have charge of our cemeteries, by excluding the felon from being associated with us even in the grave. If it is degrading to be associated with a felon after we are dead, it must be much more so to be associated with him while we are living.'

The Governor says further:

'In conclusion, upon this subject, I must be permitted to make one earnest appeal, and that is, for the Legislature to so direct the future management of the affairs of the penitentiary, by their legislation, as to protect this large and respectable portion of our fellow citizens from this degrading association and competition, by excluding all the branches of mechanism from the penitentiary.'

The bill under consideration expressly provides, that the convicts shall only be employed in such labor as slaves usually perform in coal mines and iron manufacturing establishments—that no branch of mechanics shall be taught in the institution, and that no article except railroad iron shall be sold or offered for sale outside of the walls of the prison, and that no article shall be manufactured there except such as shall be intended for the use of the prisoners—thus affording redress of the just complaints of the mechanic, and making the labor of the convicts available at once. There being no time lost in learning a trade, every able bodied convict, on the day he enters the institution, will be as well qualified to perform the service required of him, as those who may have served an apprenticeship of twenty years.

Your committee are of the opinion that this is a very important consideration. It has long been the subject of complaint on the part of the agents or keepers, and your committee consider it one of the most glaring defects intended to be remedied by a change of the labor in the prison,—that convicts placed in the institution for the shortest term, cost the State as much to deliver them there, as those put therefor the longest; while the labor of the short-term convicts, is always unprofitable, and sometimes expensive; because, after having served an apprenticeship for a year or two, at some useful trade, about the time their labor is becoming of some value to the State, their time expires, and they are dismissed from the institution. For the reasons above stated, and for others, nearly, if not equally important, your committee recommend that no branch of mechanism shall be taught in the penitentiary, and that the whole force of the institution be hereafter directed to the manufacture of railroad iron, as proposed in the bill.

From information, the safest and most reliable, that your committee have been able to collect, the usual number of convicts, estimated at two hundred and fifty, performing slave labor, with from thirty to forty workmen, or overseers, skilled in the manufacture of iron, it is estimated, that the institution could manufacture, on an average, at least twenty tons per day, or more than six thousand tons in a year of three hundred working days.

This number of tons, if the T rail is used, will be sufficient to iron sixty miles of road, and if the U rail is used, the same quantity will iron seventy-five miles.

After much reflection, your committee have come to the conclusion, that six thousand tons per annum would be sufficient to supply the reasonable demands of all the companies engaged in the construction of such works; but should the supply be inadequate, and some companies have to wait a few months, the foreign markets will still be open to them as heretofore; but it is confidently believed that the inducements offered to companies to purchase their iron at home, if accepted, will more than compensate them for any delay that may occur in obtaining the quantity necessary.

At the ruling prices in the English and American markets, six thousand tons of railroad iron delivered in Tennessee, is worth four hundred and fifty thousand dollars, and the prospect for the future is decidedly in favor of the home manufacturer.

Congress has recently refused to reduce the tariff, or extend time to the importer, for the payment of duties on railroad iron imported. This will operate against the importers, and in the same proportion it will aid the home manufacturer by excluding foreign competition, and thereby keeping up the price. Had we individual enterprise in Tennessee and capital sufficient to compete successfully in the manufacture of railroad iron, with foreign capital, and the pauper labor of Europe, your committee would not recommend that the State should enter the field against it: but it is a fact to be deplored by every patriotic Tennessean, that, ever since embarking in the construction of railroads, we have been sending over to England for iron bars to be laid down through and over iron mines, and coal fields, richer by far, than any to be found in Queen Victoria's extensive dominions. With an abundance of material, of a quality unsurpassed by any on the globe, and so convenient that, with one hand we may grasp the ore, and with the other the coal required to refine it; with the judicious protection offered by the liberal tariff policy of the General Government; with all the recent improvements in machinery, and with the labor of two hundred and fifty or three hundred hands, who cost us nothing but their clothing and food, may we not with confidence embark in the project, and undertake to supply our own enterprising companies with the iron necessary for their roads? Without considering the relief to mechanics before referred to, and estimating only the amount of profits to be derived from the manufacture of railroad iron, it seems proper that the State Government (having the capital and labor at command, which individuals have not,) should set an example, worthy to be followed, in developing the mineral wealth of the State.

At the last session of the General Assembly, the aid of the State was pledged to railroads to an amount not far short of ten millions of dollars. But few of the roads then chartered have yet been able to bring themselves within the provisions of the law, and therefore only a small amount of bonds under that law has yet been issued; but the amount issued, whatever it may be, so far as your committee know or believe, has been sold abroad, and is now a debt outstanding against Tennessee. No doubt a large amount of bonds will yet be issued under the Internal Improvement act of 1851-2, and your committee apprehend that, unless some plan is devised by which we can supply the demand for railroad iron, (for which these bonds are issued,) those to be issued hereafter will follow in the wake of their predecessors, and find a foreign market. It is true that the companies receiving the bonds are liable to the State for the payment of six per cent interest on them; but should any company, from any unforeseen cause, fail to pay it, the State will have it to meet promptly and without fail, or permit her high character and credit to go down.

It is a matter of little consequence to our argument whether the interest be paid by the companies themselves, or directly by the State. In either case the amount to be paid, must come from the hard earnings of the people. This enormous drain upon the industry of the State of six hundred thousand dollars, the annual interest on ten millions, must and will be felt by the laboring or producing classes, who constitute a majority of the country; and should the bills that are now before the General Assembly become the law, with a pledge of the aid of the State to companies of seven million dollars more, increasing the annual interest to be paid by this State to foreign governments, to over one million dollars, it must be severely felt by every citizen of Tennessee, whether the amount be raised by the companies, or by taxation.

Your committee will not prophecy evil to their own loved State; but, in justice to themselves, they must be permitted to observe, that an inordinate zeal in the cause of internal improvement may induce the Legislature to overstep the bounds of judicious discretion; in which case your committee fear that the result will be repudiation and consequent dishonor.

To avoid the danger of a large foreign debt; to develop the mineral resources of the commonwealth; to relieve the mechanics of the State from the odious convict competition so much complained of by them, and to aid in the establishment of a system of internal improvement, your committee recommend the bill now before the Senate, or some other bill with similar provisions, be passed into a law.

In addition to the foregoing reasons for passing the bill under consideration, your committee beg leave further to suggest that by the Internal Improvement act of 1851-2, section 5, companies are bound to deposite the interest on their bonds in the Bank of Tennessee, at Nashville, at least fifteen days before the interest becomes due, and on default of the payment of interest, the State is to take possession of the whole road and all the assets thereof. This your committee consider a peculiar hardship upon a company honestly endeavoring to complete the second or third sections of their road; who, because they cannot complete the distance from one commercial point to another—may not be able to pay the interest on the bonds for ironing their first thirty miles. In such cases they would forfeit their road to the State, and it would be put into the hands of a receiver until the interest, exchange, &c., should be paid.

It will be seen by reference to the sixteenth section of the bill now under consideration, that such cases of peculiar hardship are provided for, and the Governor is authorized, on certain conditions, to extend time to the companies to pay their interest, from year to year, until their whole road in Tennessee will, no doubt, require prompt payment. It will, therefore, be to the interest of every company in Tennessee to buy their iron from the Penitentiary, because the State in that case, can grant the indulgence, which she could not do, were the bonds in the hands of foreigners.

It may be well here to remark, and your committee only do so by way of suggestion,—that companies are chartered and make some progress in constructing their roads, thinking only of the interest of the country of their section, without much regard to the immediate pecuniary interest of their stockholders; they trust that *in time* their roads may be profitable. In such cases, your committee consider that indulgence or extension of time to pay the interest, will, by all means, be good policy on the part of the State; and when companies, in their zeal in the cause of internal improvement, *in good faith*, have invested their own capital, as well as that of the State, and have bought their iron from the Penitentiary—instead of ruling them up to the strict letter of the law, would it not be well to give them the time proposed in the sixteenth action of the bill?

As to the practicability of the scheme, your committee can only say that they are assured by gentlemen of high standing and great practical ability, that it can with a moderate outlay be put in successful operation.

In regard to the cost of a site and erecting such an establishment, your committee, having but little experience themselves in such matters, can only venture an opinion that the amount proposed in the bill would be sufficient, and with the aid of as many convicts as could be advantageously employed upon it, they think the whole might be completed in a very short time.

Your committee are prepared to show from reliable data the following facts:

That convicts can be fed and clothed, one year with another, at sixty dollars each—in the neighborhood of a city; and in the country where provisions are generally cheaper, they may be kept for less.

We can also further show that persons not regular mechanics, but such as with a few years experience would be capable of overseeing convicts and conducting a forge or coal mine, can be employed at three hundred dollars per annum and possibly less. We presume that a principal manager could not be obtained for less than two thousand dollars or twenty-five hundred, and we estimate that the cost of assistant managers, clerks, guards, &c., &c., cannot possibly exceed ten thousand dollars.

Your committee have made estimates, and have received information and calculations from manufacturers of iron, and others upon whom they can rely, and they are satisfied that two hundred and fifty convicts with proper machinery, managed by thirty or forty hired workmen, can carry on an institution of this kind, and manufacture twenty tons per day or over six thousand tons per annum.

The annual earnings of the institution, would therefore amount at the present high price, to over four hundred and fifty thousand dollars.

Estimating the expense of carrying it on at forty thousand dollars a year, and deducting that sum from the proceeds of the labor, leaves a net balance of four hundred and ten thousand dollars in favor of the Penitentiary.

But supposing for argument, that the expenses were doubled, and the proceeds of the labor only one half of the above amount, we would still have the handsome sum of one hundred and twenty-five thousand dollars per annum clear profit from the institution.

After the State shall, by means of the penitentiary, become the owner of her own bonds, and shall be the recipient of the annual interest from the railroad companies—it seems to your committee that in course of time she might forgive the interest to such companies, and where a company was really meritorious, but unfortunate, she might generously forgive—not only the interest but the principal also."

The statistics presented by the committee appeared to the Senate to be either fantastic or unrealistic, for the bill was swamped by an adverse vote of 17 to 8.[49]

Referring at length to the Bill of Rights in his major Message, Governor Johnson bore down on what constituted at the time the *bete noir* (black beast) of the mechanism of the judiciary—the law's delay and the conflicts between law and equity. Andrew Johnson was too shrewd a man not to have observed a tendency in human nature to reverence

---

[49] *Ibid.*, 604.

with almost undeviating observance established practices and existing procedures; he also was cognizant of the opposition that would be registered against any innovation that would alter the plans adopted by "the founding fathers," for suggested changes would be met with inflated panegyrics of the present system. The crux of Johnson's recommendation was that the courts should be so organized "that law and equity can be administered by the same court, by the same judge and jury, and at the same time, and that, too, without 'sale, denial, or delay'."

Governor Johnson's reference to a bill pending before the Legislature was to a bill introduced about a week before the transmission of his Message. Whether by accident or design, the author of the bill was Democratic Senator B. F. Bell representing Johnson's home county of Greene. The bill [50] was captioned to abridge and simplify the pleadings, practice, and proceedings in the courts of justice,—the very things for which Johnson had entered a plea in his Message. The first snag encountered was a recommendation by the Senate Judiciary Committee that the bill be rejected.[51] After several minor amendments, the bill passed second reading, the recommendation of the Judiciary Committee having been withdrawn.[52] On January 27, 1854, the bill advanced to third reading and hurdled the barriers by a vote of 14 to 11.[53]

When the Senate-approved bill reached the House, consideration of the bill was set for special order [54] on February 2. After the second reading, Whig Representative Henry Cooper from the counties of Rutherford and Bedford moved indefinite postponement which was tantamount to rejection. Either adjournment or some other parliamentary procedure was invoked which action deferred a vote on Cooper's motion. Five more times the motion to postpone action indefinitely was made, and on an afternoon session on February 6, the above motion prevailed by a vote [55] of 35 to 31.

The above bill, which doubtless had the hearty approval of Governor Johnson, was the only real effort made to revamp court practices and procedures. The bill encountered considerable difficulty in the Democratic Senate, but finally was passed by that body. In the Whig House, the bill appeared doomed from the very beginning. Only parlia-

---

[50] *Ibid.*, 272.
[51] *Ibid.*, 432.
[52] *Ibid.*, 433.
[53] *Ibid.*, 444.
[54] *House Journal*, 1853, 717.
[55] *Ibid.*, 756.

mentary maneuvers were indulged in, the ultimate objective being the rejection of the measure.[56]

What must have been a rather inconsequential law [57] was enacted, the caption of which was "to prevent the law's delay." The statute merely provided that the party seeking a "discovery" must file his petition with the clerk of the court five days before the trial term of the cause. Another minor act [58] provided that no replication had to be filed in a Chancery Court, and that the clerk of the court was empowered to make up "the hearing docket."

Even prior to Governor Johnson's Message in which he pleaded for some reform in regard to court procedure, two strong editorials in a Nashville newspaper had advocated a need for drastic reform measures. Those editorials [59] presented a layman's point of view, but they doubtless appealed to the vast majority of his reading clientele, especially those who had been entangled in the meshes of legal technicalities. The editorials were as follows:

"THE LAW REFORM BILL.

We stated, in our previous notice, that we thought this bill best for the parties litigating, for the State as a body politic; and best for the professional interest of the practising attorney.

We will give some of the reasons which induce us to think so.

The system of oral examination in open court and the examination of parties and of persons interested, will result in the discovery of the truth and the consequent attainment of justice in almost every case. The knowledge of the true state of the facts in a vast number of cases is confined exclusively to the parties and persons interested, and can be obtained only by resorting to their evidence; and in regard to the oral examination of witnesses before the trying body, no Judge can be certain that he is doing justice in a large class of cases unless he sees the witnesses and hears them give evidence. The superiority of testimony given in open court is affirmed by BLACKSTONE and by almost every writer on evidence. The provision that the defendant in criminal cases shall have the privilege of meeting his witnesses 'face to face,' is to be found in the Constitution of the United States and in the Constitution of (we believe) every State in the Union. This affirms its superiority, because in cases of life and liberty it is guaranteed by Constitutional safeguards.

---

[56] Author's note. Unfortunately, the original bill was not located in the State Archives. There is internal evidence, however, that the bill was as long as the moral code in Deuteronomy! On page 433, *Senate Journal*, 1853, appears the following statement regarding the Bell bill: "On motion by Mr. Bell, the 163d section was amended by striking out 'prohibition, information'." It is a matter for interesting conjecture as to whether any law containing at least 163 sections could possibly be construed as being a statute that would "abridge and simplify" any type of procedure! Shakespeare's comment on verbosity would appear to have special application to Senator Bell: "He draweth out the thread of his verbosity finer than the staple of his argument."

[57] *Acts of Tennessee*, 1853, Chapter 28.

[58] *Ibid.*, Chapter 55.

[59] *Daily Union and American* (Nashville), November 26, 1853 and December 15, 1853, respectively.

If, however, it were not affirmed by a single law writer nor by a single constitutional safeguard, it is still a fact which every man of common sense and observation knows to be true.

If the object of courts of justice be to dispense justice, they should be organized upon the principle of oral examination in open court as far as practicable and by a resort to the knowledge of those who in almost all cases do know most about the controverted facts.

It will bring a much larger portion of controversies to be tried in the counties in which they arise, and where the parties reside. This will bring justice nearer home to each man's door, according to ALFRED'S maxim of judicial expediency. The personal expenses of parties will therefore be less.

It will remove all questions as to the court the suit is to be brought in, and most of those as to the mode of proceeding, as there will be but one court to sue in, and one mode of proceeding, instead of two. The cost of obtaining rights, and the loss from this source, will be removed, and a court will not be so terrible an affair as it now is.

It will reduce the cost of suits by reducing the length of pleadings and the consequent costs of transcripts, &c., &c., from court to court.

It will reduce the cost of suits by trying the entire matter in controversy, in one suit and in one court, instead of making two or three suits out of transactions which might better be settled in one; instead of trying half the case in one court, and half the case in another, or trying the same case in two courts, in order to settle legal rights in one and equitable rights in the other.

This great and crying evil of our system can never be removed but by abolition of all forms of action, and of the distinction between legal and equitable remedies.

It will diminish cost by the examination of parties and of persons interested, who in the very nature of things, know more about the matters in controversy than others. It will thus get clear in many cases of a host of witnesses, who can only testify to isolated facts and detached conversations remote from the matter in issue.

It will diminish cost by cutting off debate about jurisdiction, pleadings, amendments, and competency of witnesses, which now consume so much of the time of courts and ruin so many suitors by the cost of attending witnesses. Uninformed men abuse lawyers for their debates. There is, however, inherent difficulty in the questions, and discussion is absolutely necessary. The remedy is to remove the necessity which creates discussion on collateral questions as far as possible, and confine discussion to the merits of the controversies.

It will shorten much the duration of law suits.—Law suits will consequently consume less of suitors' time which is spent about the court houses, where, having nothing to do, they contract habits of gaming, drinking, idleness and vice.

It will diminish the cost of the judiciary system. Juries will not be so long in attendance when most of the debates about pleadings, evidence, jurisdiction, &c., are removed, and fewer Judges can do the business. The same judicial force can try a much larger number of cases in the same time, for in many cases the collateral questions consume more time and require more learning and legal research than the merits of the controversy.

Lastly. It will reduce the amount of labor which students and practising lawyers have to undergo to learn and learn again and again two systems of pleadings, practice, and proceedings; a vast volume of minute rules and regulations, made upon no general principle; dry, toilsome drudgery, which results in the acquisition of no principle of morals or of enlightened jurisprudence, and which, therefore, passes through the mind like the flight of a bird through the air, leaving no trace behind. But what is worse for the lawyer, seeking through honorable toil and labor to secure for his family a support, it is a toil which is not seen, not known, and not appreciated, and is hardly ever paid for but with the impression that downright extortion is practiced. When the defendant's lawyer drives the plaintiff out of court on a collateral question, he confers no permanent benefit on his client. He keeps him longer in court, and if the opposite party has the right on his side, he loads his own client with costs ultimately. On the other side, when the plaintiff's lawyer loses upon a collateral question he is frequently cursed as an ignoramus, is paid grudgingly, and is threatened with costs. The books of reports show that able lawyers everywhere are constantly defeated on such questions, and their clients subjected to costs. If they were made to pay the costs in such cases it would drive every lawyer out of the courts, and for the plainest of all reasons, lawyers cannot declare what the law is before there is any adjudicated case to guide them.

There is nothing which excites so much unjust prejudice against the profession as this very system, and they owe it to themselves to remove it by abolishing it at the earliest practicable moment.

When all the rubbish which now obstructs the path of the student, the practising lawyer and the Judge is removed, *the science of human rights* will be found a boundless field in which the labor of a quarter of a century by the stoutest frame and the most vigorous mind will accomplish little else, *than the power to investigate questions with facility*."

"LAW REFORM.

The present state of our judiciary and laws has been and is the subject of unceasing complaint by some of those who know the true remedy, and more especially by those who do not. The arbitrary division of rights into legal and equitable and the establishment of separate organic structures to maintain and perpetuate those idle and injurious distinctions; the investigation of one division of rights by oral testimony in one court and the other in another court by deposition; the inability of either court to do complete justice in many cases without the aid of the organization and process of the other; the constant mistakes as to the proper court in which relief is to be asked arising from the unsettled and changing boundaries of the jurisdictions; and the impossibility of determining the proper jurisdiction in many cases until the parties are heard in proof; the double set of costs accruing and double delay incurred; the frequent taxation of costs on the party entitled to a recovery and ultimately recovering; all tend to keep alive a perpetual discontent, which those who have been in the habit of a free association with the people at large know to be rankling in their minds. This dissatisfaction manifests itself in perpetual sarcasms against lawyers, judges, and courts, and 'the terrors of the law.' It shows itself in a constant effort to reduce the fees of officers below what is a proper compensation for the services rendered; by the constantly increasing current of justices' jurisdictions, to avoid the costs and delays of courts of record; and by the heavy minority always found in the General Assembly favorable to a mere abolition of chancery courts, under the belief that that measure alone would improve the grievances.

Plain men go into the courts and there hear almost endless discussions upon questions which they regard as utterly frivolous. They see their own and the public time consumed in settling questions about amendments, pleadings, jurisdiction, &c., and the cases taken up and reversed against the justice of the case, upon some point of which they cannot see the force when settled. They understand not much but the result, and they see the result disastrous to a speedy and cheap administration of justice.

This state of popular feeling has existed in different ages, and wherever these systems of common law and equity proceedings have been in existence. It results necessarily and inevitably in as great a delay and cost as any system which the wit of man can easily devise. If it were made on purpose to spin out every judicial controversy to the greatest possible length, it is not easy to see how it could be made more fully to accomplish that object. Every lawyer knows that the two separate systems had their origin in accidental and fortuitous circumstances many centuries ago; that it sprang out of an attempt to correct the crudities and absurdities of common law courts. The prolonged controversy between priests and common law lawyers built up two structures, which have now grown to be stupendous fabrics of complicated folly and absurdity. Multitudes of people have become so accustomed to the obstructions to justice existing in this deplorable system, that they have come to regard its continuance as one of the irremediable evils which Providence has inflicted on mankind for their sins and crimes. The great English poet, living under the operations of this system which our forefathers adopted by sweeping provisions, makes Hamlet repeat as amongst 'the thousand natural shocks that flesh is heir to—

> The oppressor's wrong, the proud man's contumely,
> The pangs of disprized love, *the law's delay*,
> The insolence of office, and the spurns
> That patient merit of the unworthy takes.'

The noble Dane thought 'the law's delay' one of the 'whips and scorns of time,' which he could only escape by passing 'that bourne from whence no traveller returns.' Whilst Hamlet talked thus on the English stage, that dry, hard old lawyer, COKE, delivered himself in these words: 'When I consider the course of our books and terms, I observe that more jangling and questions grow up upon the matter itself, and that infinite causes are lost or delayed thereby.' Yet we are told that any attempt to overthrow this stupendous pile of absurdities which our forefathers adopted under the pressure of circumstances will result in confusion, as if it were possible to produce greater confusion, cost, and delay than exist now. This is the stereotyped cry that one hundred lawyers, headed by Chancellor BROUGHAM, had to fight against in England.—This is the cry that the New York reformers had to hear from the Representatives of that State.—'to rest as we are,' said CURTIS, now one of the Supreme Court of the United States, 'to rest as we are is to continue to impose on the people of this State a burden of delays, expense, and vexation which in our judgment necessarily grows out of the present state of things.' The Legislature of Massachusetts, in 1851, abolished all the distinctions of actions, retaining only that between contracts and wrongs, and in 1853 passed a bill of five sections, applying equitable remedies in suits at law. The last of the mutilated system was swept by this statute to the 'receptacle of things lost upon earth.'

How can confusion be produced by the repeal of two thousand pages of CHITTY'S forms, and half a dozen other volumes containing regulations about as profound and sensible as those which occupied the minds of the monks of the dark ages, and the substitution of petition and answer sworn to and stating the facts just as they would be stated on the street in plain, concise language, without repetition? We pray to be informed on this subject. We beg for a ray of light to our benighted understanding. We cannot for the life of us see why it should take a sheet of closely written matter to charge that defendant had written or said that plaintiff had stolen his horse, or to demand a horse or lot of ground or negro, or to charge the defendant with beating plaintiff, or to demand a title for a lot of ground.—Our poor understanding has never been able to penetrate the philosophy of all this. Nor have we ever been able to divine why volume upon volume of forms one, two, three, and four centuries old should be laid down as *the absolute law language* in which the parties are to speak, on pain of costs and delay if not expulsion from the court.

We venture the assertion that so gross and shocking an outrage on the common sense of mankind, involving so great an obstruction to their true interests, is not to be found in the history of any other enlightened country. We are told, with a gravity that would seem to import earnestness, that these forms are intended to inform the parties of the claim and defence. One of the ablest of the late English law writers says of the records in common law cases, 'They contain an endless multitude of words from which if the real matter in dispute can be gathered at all, it is only guess work. Generally speaking, it may be said if the plaintiff tells us less in his plea.'

It would task human ingenuity to devise a scheme more effective to conceal the matter in dispute than the pleadings in the action of assumpsit. In fact, common law pleadings are a sort of ambush by which the parties conceal from each other the claim and defence. A trial is a great game, where there is a large stake up, and the pleadings prevent the parties from 'showing their hands.' We forget what French philosopher it was who said that words were given to men to enable them to conceal their ideas. In this light, we look upon pleadings. Of course, if a party were to swear to one declaration in ten in assumpsit, he would have to be indicted for perjury and handed over to the keeper of the penitentiary.

It is hard to tell which is the most ridiculous, the prescribed forms or a writ in criminal cases. The frivolous minuteness of detail, the involved sentences, the wretched transposition of language, the senseless repetitions and barbarous jargon, excite the dread and jealousy of the ignorant by the appearance of trick and mystery, and call forth the ridicule of the enlightened man. What intelligent man ever heard a declaration in libel, slander, or assumpsit, or an indictment for murder or perjury, read without a feeling of contempt for anti-reformers, who would desire to retain such foolery in the judicial proceedings of an age that claims to be enlightened? Yet, if it be proposed to require by law that the changes and defences in a court of justice shall be made in a language suited to the age in which we live and intelligible to those to whom it is addressed, some profess to consider it as a most unhallowed attempt to pull down the very temple of justice on the heads of the people, and to spread confusion and disorder through the land. They profess to consider those who bring forward such reforms as crack-brained projectors, who, in the classical language of an indictment for murder, do not have the 'fear of God before their eyes,' but 'are moved and seduced by the instigation of the devil.'

We have, however, consoled ourselves with the reflection that no system, whether it be the result of accident, ignorance, or charlatanism, or all of them combined, can produce greater uncertainty in the administration of the law, greater delay, or greater costs, than the present one; and that not many greater judicial calamities can befall a country than to have 'law and equity separated from each other.' "

Despite gubernatorial and neswpaper indorsement, the Legislature refused to heed their pleas for any significant simplification of court practices and court procedures. For the time being, legal legerdemain remained in vogue and the reign of technicalities prevailed.

The ninth recommendation of Governor Johnson received favorable action on the part of the Legislature. On March 3, 1854, a legislative resolution [60] was enacted calling upon the Governor to appoint a Superintendent of Weights and Measures who was directed to prepare a set of standard weights and measures for each county in the State. The measure seemed to have presented no difficulty in the Legislature, although passage of the above resolution was deferred to within three days of adjournment.

Governor Johnson made no specific recommendation in regard to the Consular Convention between representatives of the United States and the French Government, but merely advised the Legislature of such a meeting and officially left the matter in the hands of the Legislature for its "consideration." The official records disclose no action on the measure by the Legislature, not even the offering of a resolution upon the topic.

Likewise Governor Johnson's reference to the proposed amendments to the Constitution of the United States were allowed to lapse into oblivion so far as the Thirtieth General Assembly of Tennessee was concerned. The failure of the Legislature to take any action on this portion of the Governor's Message may have been due to the fact that the Legislature became entangled early in regard to amendments to the 1835 Constitution of Tennessee, a matter that will receive attention later on in this chapter.

As a sort of peroration to his Message, Governor Johnson bore down on a topic near and dear to his heart. In his second term as Congressman, 1845–1847, Johnson introduced his "Homestead Bill" which proposed to give to every head of a family a homestead of one hundred and sixty acres out of the public domain, provided the recipient of the donation settled upon the land thus granted. Congressman Johnson was unquestionably the promoter of the Homestead Policy and introduced the first bill in Congress on the subject, in 1846. Credit is sometimes given to Galusha Aaron Grow, a Free Soil Democrat from Pennsylvania, as being the father of the Homestead Act. The fact is that Grow did not enter Congress until 1851, and Johnson had been hammering away on his Homestead Bill during the five years preceding Grow's entering Congress. Grow's connection with the Homestead Act is due to the passage of the bill under his earnest advocacy and direction. Curiously enough, the only Tennessee Congressmen beside Johnson who ever

---

[60] *Acts of Tennessee*, 1853, 791–792.

voted for this measure were George W. Jones and Andrew Jackson Clements.

One month prior to the transmission of Governor Johnson's Message, Democratic Senator Godfrey Nave from Carter County introduced the following resolution:[61]

"Whereas, We, as members of the General Assembly, view the beneficent policy of granting to every head of a family, one hundred and sixty acres of public land, out of our immense public domain, as embraced in the homestead bill, which passed the United States House of Representatives by a majority of nearly two to one, on the 12th day of May, 1852, and which was then transmitted to the Senate of the United States, as calculated in an eminent degree to advance the wealth and prosperity of the whole nation, elevate and ameliorate the condition of the toiling thousands, and at the same time, increase, rather than diminish, the revenue from the public domain; and we, in common with all lovers of our kind, shall hail the day of its final consummation into a law as constituting one of the brightest epochs in our national annals, and as an unmistakable harbinger of the incalculable good which will descend to our children's children in the far distant future.

And whereas, in our opinion the safest and wisest disposition which could be made of the public domain, would be to set it apart permanently for the purpose of carrying out in good faith the homestead policy; and further that the General Government confine all further sales of the public lands to actual settlers, and to them in limited quantities; therefore,

Be it resolved, by the General Assembly of the State of Tennessee, That our Senators in the Congress of the United States be, and they are hereby instructed, and our Representatives most respectfully requested, to urge upon the consideration of Congress the importance of these measures, and to use all reasonable exertions to procure the passage of the Homestead Bill, as referred to in the foregoing preamble, or some one similar in its provisions.

Resolved, That it be the duty of the Governor of the State to forward to each of our Senators and Representatives in the Congress of the United States, a copy of the foregoing preamble and resolution."

Whig Senator Michael Carriger of Claiborne County proposed to amend the Nave resolution as follows:[62]

"*Resolved, by the General Assembly of the State of Tennessee,* That it is our opinion that if Congress in its wisdom should think proper to apply a certain portion of the public domain to the homestead purposes, the proceeds of the sales of the remainder of the public lands, or the public lands themselves, should be divided between the several States of the Union, according to their federal population, for the purpose of internal improvement and common school education, and that Congress can make no disposition of the public lands to any object whatever, so laudable and patriotic, or so much calculated to promote the general prosperity and happiness of the whole country; and thereby expand the intellect and enlarge its capacity to appreciate our civil and religious institutions, and the better fitting it for the enjoyment of a free government, adding thereto strength and durability in all time to come amidst the conflicting elements of sectional interest and civil discord, so peculiar to a free people, and will also increase our facilities in commerce,

---

[61] *Senate Journal*, 1853, 197.
[62] *Ibid.*, 203–204.

unite us together in interest and social intercourse by opening new avenues of trade and wealth, and identify us in all the business transactions of life, and give a new impulse to commerce, agriculture, manufactures, industry and enterprise of every kind and description, and thus strengthen the ties of the Union, and place it upon so firm a foundation that the wily tricks of the un-principled demagogue, abolitionist, or secessionist cannot in all time to come, prevail against it, and thereby establish the great principle that man is capable of self-government, in consideration whereof, our Representatives in Con-gress are requested, and our Senators are instructed to use all honorable means to cause a law to be passed making the above disposition of our public lands."

On February 7, 1854, the Committee on Federal Relations to which the Governor's Message and Resolution No. 56 had been referred sub-mitted a lengthy but rather illuminating report,[63] to-wit:

"The committee on Federal Relations have had under consideration that portion of the Executive Message, which recommends the adoption, by Con-gress, of a homestead policy, together with resolution, No. 56, and the amend-ment offered thereto, which were referred to your committee by order of the Senate, and after having given to these several papers that patient investigation which their importance demands, and which the results of such a policy nec-essarily impose, beg leave to make the following report:

In the survey and elucidation of a question of such magnitude and inter-est, and which, if adopted and engrafted upon the land policy of the Federal Government, looks to a thorough and radical change in that policy, your committee are naturally led into the history of the acquisition of our vast public domain—our present population—the means of peopling and cultivat-ing this great national inheritance—the evils to be remedied, and the want and suffering to be alleviated, and the benefits, both national and individual, which will result from the adoption of a system, at once calculated to popu-late and develope the vast resources of this unoccupied domain. With a popu-lation of twenty-six millions of inhabitants; with every variety of climate, and adaptation to the most varied production; and with a geographical posi-tion upon the globe that stimulates all the branches of agriculture and manu-factures, and gives the widest range to the exchanges and commerce of the world, your committee are of opinion that the Government should so shape its policy as to improve and give energy and force to all these natural ad-vantages. Your population is now chiefly confined to the eastern and western slopes of the Alleghany range, and a wilderness nearly as large as Europe, fertile in soil and rich in mineral wealth, lies vacant and unproductive west of the Mississippi. To engraft upon this extensive area of unoccupied land a policy that will give an impetus to settlement and production, and best con-duce to the permanent interests and progress of the country, 'is a consumma-tion devoutly to be wished' for. That legislation that looks to the freedom of labor and to the comfort and independence of the citizen, and, at the same time, subserves the highest and noblest ends of society, enriches and benefits, not only the citizen, but imparts strength and vigor to the Government.

'By a report made to Congress in December, 1850, by the Secretary of the Interior, we find the total receipts from the sale of public lands up to that date, amount to one hundred and thirty-five million, three hundred and thirty-nine thousand dollars ($135,339,000,) whilst the entire cost of the public lands, including the sum of fifteen millions of dollars ($15,000,000,) paid

---

[63] *Ibid.*, 496–504.

France for the purchase of Louisiana; five millions of dollars ($5,000,000,) paid Spain for the acquisition of the Floridas; the extinguishment of Indian titles, surveying, selling and managing the public domain in seventy-five millions of dollars (75,000,000.') There are other charges, however, that legitimately belong to the public lands, created by virtue of the treaty of Guadaloupe Hidalgo, and by the Act of Congress of 1850, settling and defining the boundary line of the State of Texas; but when all the items of expense properly chargeable to the public domain are summed up, the records show an excess of receipts over expenditures. Your committee, from the best evidence they have before them, assume the fact that the Federal Government has realized a larger amount of money by the same of the public lands, than she has expended in their acquisition and management; and the grave and delicate question arises, as to whether it is sound policy or in accordance with a true sense of political economy, to longer continue a system that monopolizes the very basis of all enlightened and refined society, hordes without profit, and withholds the means of subsistence and comfort from thousands of our needy and destitute population?

Civilization, order, government, all depend upon the bounties of agriculture for their incipient support; and commerce, not less dependent, gathers its earliest trophies from the product of the soil. Agriculture, in all ages of the world, has been the ally of thrift and independence, and the companion of contentment and all the noble virtues.

Congress has the power to make all needful rules and regulations respecting the territory of the United States, and your committee, within the meaning and legitimate construction of this provision, are of opinion that the Federal Government has clearly the right to establish a policy with reference to the public lands, which, whilst it enlarges the field of agriculture, and gives the widest scope to the industry and energies of thousands, will enlarge the revenues, elevate the patriotism, and add vigor and opulence to the commonwealth.

There is no axiom that commends itself more forcibly to the favorable consideration of Government, than that which has for its two-fold object the welfare of individuals as constituent elements of a general society, and likewise, so diffuses its benefits as to make government really a beneficiary of its own munificence. That political philosophy which upholds a system that hampers millions of population within our large cities and densely inhabited districts, that cripples their energies—that deadens the finer feelings of the heart, and to poverty and haggard want carries the incubus of misery and despair, is founded upon a false idea of the true relation between government and citizen. It is time in the opinion of your committee, that a different and a policy more American should be adopted, which, whilst it opens and superinduces the settlement and cultivation of the West, will pour its grateful tribute into the store-house of national wealth. 'It cannot be doubted that the early settlement of these lands constitute the true interests of the Republic. The wealth and strength of a country are its population, and the best part of the population are the cultivators of the soil. Independent farmers everywhere are the basis of society, and true friends of liberty.' Your committee heartily accord the sanction of their humble judgment to this text of political wisdom, and hope and believe that the day is not distant when the policy, which it foreshadows, will realize the fondest expectations of the public.

Why let this vast area of virgin soil lie unproductive, when you have a homeless population that would drive the ploughshare into its fertile bosom and turn it bare to the sunshine and the seasons, and make it yield an abundance of the comforts of life? A homestead of an hundred and sixty acres of land to every American citizen, who is the head of a family, who will settle and cultivate the same, or a portion thereof, for a period of years, rises above ordinary political questions, and is closely interwoven and identified with the highest and holiest interests of the Union in all the variety of its industrial pursuits, and the moral stamina and strength that it imparts to society and to Government; and your committee are not advised of any plan for the disposition of the public lands that commends itself so eloquently to the philanthropy and beneficence of the Government, as the one that looks to the glorious consummation of providing a home—fixed and permanent—for our sterling destitute population, where they may reap the entire earnings of their toil, and cultivate all the nobler affections that are inseparable from the domestic hearth-stone.

It may be insisted that, inasmuch as these lands were acquired by the common blood and treasure, it would be unjust to provide a home, free of charge, to the heads of families, because, from the very nature and organization of society, it would be utterly impossible for each and every American citizen to bring him or herself within the provisions of the law. In one sense the public lands may be regarded as belonging to every American citizen, and it does not appear to your committee that the adoption of a homestead policy would materially change or destroy this idea of common property in the public lands, but is really in accordance with, and comfortable thereto. This policy of giving it away to actual settlers, would clearly recognize, in all its force, the equality of American citizens in the dispensation of its bounties. Such a law would not discriminate between our citizens, but offers to all, who may be inclined to emigrate and bring themselves within its provisions, equal and impartial justice. The *apparent* injustice arises from the dissimilar circumstances and inclinations of persons themselves. Those around whom wealth had scattered its blessings, and were attached to the place of their nativity by the associations of childhood, would remain around the old family altar; whilst others, pressed by want and necessity, would avail themselves of the public bounty. Whilst such a system offers to all, it withholds from none. All are placed upon an equal footing, the millionaire as well as the homeless yeoman.

Earth is as indispensable an element in a well-balanced society as air is to the support of animal existence. In the retreat of rural industry, purity and simplicity find their appropriate abiding place. There is not that strife, nor jealousy, nor dependence that characterize the other vocations of life. Pass the homestead law and hundreds who now linger about your cities in idleness and in want, will migrate to the West, rear the cabin, clear the forests and rear around them all the comforts of home. You will send a thrill of joy and gratitude to the poor man, wife and children, whom poverty confines to the old States, where it is almost impossible to lease or rent lands. Take them by the hand, by a wise and salutary policy, and invite them as pioneers in a Western civilization. Aid and encourage him, for as he blazes the dim pathway through the forest and builds his cabin of logs, he becomes the nucleus around which will gather a society compact, energetic and intelligent. Give them the means to germinate, and as the forests shall gradually recede before the hard blows of the axe and give way to fields of corn and other products, you will realize, in the general thrift of these pioneers, a grateful requital for your bounty. With an independent freehold, where he is independent of imperious landlords, fixed in his own castle and beneath his own vine and fig-tree, and with a heart full of loyalty to his country, he feels a nobler and a better man. There is a motive; deep and fixed; a generous impulse to exertion, and an effort commensurate to the accomplishment of something that has for its object the elevation and education of his children. By frugality and economy he will husband the earnings of his toil, enlarge the limits of his freehold, and be enabled to give to his children that moral and intellectual instruction so essential to the enjoyment and happiness of life. There's a sweetness in the memory of the scenes of the family fireside; there cluster around it all the warmer affections of our nature, and the heart pours out its grateful offering upon the spot consecrated to our earlier pastimes, and to the recollections of maturer manhood. A consciousness in the freeholder that he is enabled to rear his fortunes upon the partial munificence of his country, and that he is indeed an American farmer, with all the dignity which that term implies, and all the obligations which this new relation impose, he aspires to the improvement and culture of all that is around him, and in turn to become a benefactor to society.

Land is worthless without the application of labor. Settlement and cultivation, production and profit, is the true touch-stone by which to ascertain the value of land. The government has some fourteen hundred millions of acres, peopled by a few nomadic hordes of savages, who, like the wild Tartar, scorning to till the earth, delights in the chase and the *cruelties* of the wild foray. The hum of industry is unknown in this vast domain; all is solitude, and the beast and the savage hold undivided sway. Would it not be more becoming our condition—the wants of our citizens, and the highest hopes of the country, agricultural, manufacturing, and commercial, that this worthless territory should be opened to settlement and cultivation? Let the destitute in —let them have the soil—and by your policy bid them subdue the wilderness; establish highways; erect churches, school houses, and academies, and all these will stamp value, real and permanent upon your otherwise worthless territory. And when the West shall have been settled; when its facilities for transporting its produce to the markets of the world, shall have been increased; when its population shall have become sufficiently dense and compact to develope the capabilities of its soil for production, its wealth, refinement, and power will be a glorious counterpart of the opulence, intelligence, and civilization of the seaboard States.

As a bonus for the public bounty, the daring pioneer encounters the dangers and difficulties incident to the settlement of a new country; he and his family undergo hardships and privations, and infuse the first dim light of order and civilization into the primeval wilds of the West. Such men should be encouraged and secured in the enjoyment of a little farm against all vicissitudes and in spite of all misfortune. In the opinion of your committee, the West is not to be the only beneficiary of a homestead policy; there are other and higher elements involved in the consideration of this question. The seaboard States have large investments in commerce and manufactures, and thousands of their population derive their subsistence from these branches of industry: and whilst this policy would open, and rapidly populate the West; it would open a large and profitable market for the manufactures of the East. And again, the transportation and exchanges of the vast produce of the West would give employment to commission houses, railroads, canals, and to your already large and increasing tonnage. The commercial, mechanical, and manufacturing industry of the old States, will thrive in proportion of the advancement and production of the new.—Your committee, then, apprehend no danger of such a policy operating injuriously upon the various industrial pursuits of any portion of our Union; on the contrary, they are satisfied that the production and wealth of the West will contribute to the advancement and prosperity of the whole confederacy. Ohio, Indiana, and all the States of the West have made wonderful progress in population, and the accumulation of all that makes commonwealths great, intelligent and opulent; whilst Massachusetts, New York, and the old States have been sharers of their thrift, and partakers of their fortune. The granaries and raw produce of the former have enlarged and given an impetus to the ship yards and ship building, and quadrupled the tonnage and carrying trade of the latter. Consumption must necessarily, to a certain extent, depend upon production, and whilst the government pursues a policy which stints the toiling man and his family, and withholds from him the means of a liberal consumption, it freezes up the very source of taxation, which is consumption, itself. Why not throw open this vast territory to destitute American citizens, and let there be freedom of labor for all who may constitute the vanguard in the glorious work of reclaiming a wilderness, and spreading a network of popular institutions, and civilization?—Let labor be unfettered of rents to landlords and tribute to government; give to it the reward of its own hard earnings, and it will be enabled to purchase more of the luxuries of life, and contribute to swell the revenues of your country.

Consumption being dependent upon production, the increase of the latter creates the ability to purchase a large amount of imported merchandise, and therefore, the augmentation of the former naturally enlarges the basis of your taxation. Such a policy, in the opinion of your committee, like blood in the physical system, would be sensibly felt throughout all the great arteries and channels of trade, elevating and ennobling the citizen, and lending the prestige of strength and progress to the country. That such a policy would, to some extent, depopulate the old States, is not in the estimation of your committee, a very sound or plausible objection, because, whilst it would enable the homeless to open and improve a farm, and secure them a larger reward for their labor, it will be the means of enhancing the wages of the landless who *may* remain in the old States. If the laborer, by such removal, can get more of the necessaries and comforts of life, it not only benefits him, but he has contributed just so much to national wealth. The thrift of one is, in one sense, the prosperity of the whole.

But it may be further urged that a homestead policy will virtually destroy an important source of the Federal revenue by opening the public lands, free of charge, to settlement, and that the necessary result would be an increase of the tariff upon imported goods. 'The Secretary of the Treasury in his report to the 31st Congress, says, by the various acts of Congress appropriating the public lands to objects which withdrew them from ordinary revenue purposes, it is quite certain that for several years to come, the treasury must be mainly, if not entirely, dependent for its receipts upon duties levied upon foreign merchandise. The warrants yet to be presented under these acts will require 80,000,000 of acres, valued at ($100,000,000) one hundred million dollars. At the average of five millions of acres per annum, it will require sixteen years to absorb and satisfy the warrants yet to be issued, as estimated, under the several bounty land acts now in force.' These bounty land warrants in addition to the heavy donations of swamp lands to the various States, in consideration of reclamation, together with the millions of acres that have been donated by Congress to various railroad companies, shut out the probability that the public lands can for a long period of years, be a source of revenue. The emigrant, instead of purchasing land from the Government, will purchase a land warrant and locate it upon the unappropriated land, for the very reason that he can get it cheaper. The disposition of the public lands is likely to be a vexed and complicated question, and your committee think it the best policy, of the Government to solve the difficult problem, by making the public lands free to every American citizen. As a source of revenue, the public lands have comparatively ceased. There are other competitors in the market who greatly undersell the Government. Your committee are of opinion that this policy would be consistent with public justice, and promotive of the general welfare, and whilst it would yield the greatest practical good to the people, largely increase the revenue of the Government. Instead of its cutting off, it would enhance the means of administering the Government, in its foreign and domestic affairs.

'The population of the West have contributed their equal share of taxation under our import system, and for the land now occupied, they have paid a large proportion of our entire revenues, whilst but a small proportion has been expended among them. When, to the disadvantage of their situation in this respect, we add the consideration that it is their labor alone which gives value to the public lands, and that the old States are relieved from the burdens of taxation, by enabling the great producing West to consume more foreign goods, and consequently to contribute to the aggregate revenue in proportion to her augmented consumption, it appears to your committee that justice and sound policy dictate that the public lands should be thrown open to free ingress and settlement of American citizens. Every man, woman, and child, who may avail themselves of the public largess, derives, *ipso facto*, the ability to pay more revenue to the Government, than can ever be realized by sale of such lands to those who purchase and horde them for speculation and profit.' Your committee then wholly eschew the idea of settlers upon the public lands becoming alms people; on the contrary, they become larger tax payers, and contribute their earnings to the general store of national thrift. The general principle of *quid pro quo* is clearly demonstrable, in the operations of such a policy. The Government dispenses its bounty, and reaps a rich harvest of principal and interest by increased production and consumption. Fixed and permanent upon his little farm, and encouraged by the general prosperity that rewards his industry, his energies, mental and physical, rise above the tyranny of poverty and want. The mother may plant the favorite shrub, or twine the delicate vine as it gathers in festoons around the cottage door, with the knowledge that her children may pursue their childish gambols, 'nor look with sorrow and regret for the last time upon the spot consecrated to the thrilling scenes and recollections of home.' Whatever may be their relations of prosperity or penury, there is a mentor within that speaks of the endearments of 'home,' and a talisman (homestead) without that frowns down despair. These adventurous pioneers become the great stays around which gather compact settlements, and extend the hand of generosity to those who come after them. Such men should be encouraged, and a homestead is but a partial requital for the dangers they must risk, and the privations they must suffer, in subduing the forests and reclaiming a country of wild beasts and savages.

Aside from considerations of profit, both to Government and to individuals, which would flow from this policy, your committee would for a moment pause and survey its moral results upon your border population. Presuming to carry out the argument, that the emigrant is fixed and identified with the soil; he feels that he has a common interest in all that looks to the development and honor of his country; the feelings of his soul expand to a comprehension of the great obligations of man to society, and aspire to the moral and intellectual culture of his children. He feels that he is a peer of the commonwealth, and is sensitive to her interests and jealous of her honor. By the munificence of his country, independence has supplanted poverty, and an active patriotism has supplanted the feelings of cold indifference. Whilst fulfilling a mission of peace, in the culture of his farm and in the society of his family, he is ready at all times to obey the behests of his country. Chatham said 'that the true strength and stamina of a country are to be looked for in the cultivators of the soil. In the simplicity of their lives is found the simpleness of virtue, the integrity and courage of freedom. These true, genuine sons of the soil are invincible.' This is but the truth of the history of the world. Wherever the fluttering ensign leads, or the din of battle is fiercest, you find the sturdy yeoman grappling with the enemies of his country. He stands against the inroads of the savage, and as the protector of your border settlements as a wall of fire, and he asks but for the poor largess of a little home to feed and clothe his children. Justice, self-interest, the general welfare and patriotism all demand the bounty.

The amendment offered to Resolution No. 56, has been considered by your Committee, and inasmuch as it looks to the welfare of Tennessee, we would be pleased to give to it the sanction of our approbation, if it did not, in our judgment, violate principle and establish a bad precedent. A local policy, such as is contemplated in the amendment, must become a national policy if the door is once opened. That policy would throw thirty-one land venders in the market—create the most complicated and vexatious relations between the States, and hold out larger inducements to monopoly and speculation in the public lands, than results from the present system. It would, perhaps, be a century before our State would dispose of such a donation, and the superintendence, survey, and management of it within half of that period, would absorb the larger portion of its entire proceeds. Your committee, therefore, recommend the rejection of the amendment, and commend to the favorable consideration and adoption by the Senate of resolution No. 56, with their preamble, with the exception of that portion which limits the sale to actual settlers, and in limited quantities, which your committee recommend to be stricken out.

If you would relieve the poor and unfortunate, and bring them to the knowledge and sympathies of the world; if you would alleviate suffering and distress; if you would recall the vicious and the vile to the paths of rectitude and virtue; if you would increase the stock of national wealth and enhance your revenues; if you would disgorge your almhouses and houses of correction, and make the destitute wiser and better, then give them a home. Give them the means to elevate the moral and intellectual influences of the family fireside, and impress upon the soul the insignia of truth and virtue in all their glorious relations to God, to Government, and to society, and when you have done this, the noblest impulses and energies of these pioneers will be dedicated to the best end of society. All of which is respectfully submitted.

J. J. JONES,
Chairman of the Committee on Federal Relations."

On February 24, 1854, the Senate resumed action on the resolution relative to the Homestead Policy, and by a vote of 22 to 3 the resolution was passed.[64]

---

[64] *Ibid.*, 625.

Two days before final adjournment, the Whig-controlled House took up the Democratic Senate-approved Homestead Resolution but an amendment in lieu of the original resolution was adopted by a vote of 34 to 23.[65] The in lieu amendment was by Whig Representative George McKnight of Rutherford County, and was as follows:[66]

"Resolved, That our Senators in Congress be instructed, and our Representatives requested, to use all laudable means to procure the passage of an act granting out of the public domain a Homestead of one hundred and sixty acres to every free white citizen of the United States, who at the time of his or her application for the same, may be the head of a family, and who by reason of poverty, may be unable to purchase a homestead; such homestead to be located in any of the Territories of the United States; to be granted upon condition for a term of years, and to be exempt from execution so long as it may remain in the possession of the original grantee, in order that it may inure to the benefit of those for whom it is intended, that is the families of indigent citizens."

The net result of the legislative action was that Governor Johnson could not report to Congress that the popular sentiment of the sovereign State of Tennessee had contributed "to the consummation of this great measure." Undoubtedly Governor Johnson was keenly disappointed in the legislative action of his own State in that no resolution was adopted by both branches of the Legislature, resulting in a defeat for Johnson's plea for indorsement of the Homestead movement which he had espoused and supported so vigorously while a member of Congress.

A summation of the legislative action upon Governor Johnson's recommendations to the Legislature discloses that that body acted favorably upon four of the twelve topics specified in the Message. In accordance with the Governor's suggestions, a halt was made upon rather careless appropriations and a decided brake was placed upon issuance of State bonds for Internal Improvements. The high-mark of Governor Johnson's first administration was the enactment of a law levying a public tax for the support of public education, the first such law in the history of the State. The fourth recommendation that received legislative sanction related to the establishment of standard weights and measurements.

On the opposite side of the ledger, seven of the Governor's recommendations were rejected. The topics in question were public roads, tax on merchants, Bank of Tennessee, penitentiary, judiciary, amendments to the Constitution of the United States, and the Homestead Policy. On one topic, the Consular Convention, Governor Johnson submitted no recommendation and the Legislature ignored the matter altogether.

In order that the record may be complete, attention should be called

---

[65] *House Journal*, 1853, 1085.
[66] *Ibid.*, 1082–1083.

to the fact that one branch of the Legislature did take cognizance of Governor Johnson's recommendation regarding proposed amendments to the Constitution of the United States concerning the method of electing the President of the United States by direct vote of the people, election of United States Senators by the people instead of by the Legislature, and making the tenure of office of the Judges of the United States Supreme Court twelve years instead of for life. On February 3, 1854, Democratic Senator Godfrey Nave submitted the following resolution:[67]

"*Resolved by the General Assembly of the State of Tennessee*, That the constitution of the United States ought to be so amended, as to carry the election of President and Vice President directly to the qualified voters of the several States, preserving the basis of the Electoral College, as it now stands in the constitution of the United States, and as recommended by President Jackson in his annual messages in 1829 and '30, and thereby dispense with all intermediate illegal Congressional caucuses and irresponsible National Conventions, which in fact, have for a series of years virtually taken the election of President and Vice President away from the sovereign people, the real and only source of all political power, and that too in violation of the combined will of the people as expressed in the letter and spirit of the constitution of the United States.

Resolved, That it is contrary to the genius and progressive spirit of a democratic republican form of government, to clothe any man or set of men, with a life tenure in office beyond the reach of popular will, the only and true corrective of all abuses in a free government. We therefore favor and recommend a modification of the constitution to the friends of free government, so as to change the tenure in office of the Supreme Court of the United States, to a term of not more than twelve years; to be classed similar to that of the Senate of the United States.

Resolved, That the qualified voters of the several States have given the most incontestible evidence of their honesty and capacity in the selection of their rulers or Representatives, and experience proves that the nearer the Representative is brought to the constituent the greater and more direct the responsibility. We therefore recommend a modification of the constitution of the United States, so as to transfer the election of Senators to the United States Senate, to a majority of the qualified voters of the several States, instead of the Legislators as now provided.

Resolved, That we view the policy as embraced in the 'Homestead Bill,' which passed the United States House of Representatives by a majority of two to one, on the 12th day of May, 1852, and then transmitted to the Senate of the United States, as calculated in an eminent degree to advance the wealth of the whole nation, elevate and ameliorate the condition of the toiling thousands, and at the same time, increase, rather than diminish, the revenue from the public domain, and we in common with all lovers of our kind, shall hail the day of its final consummation into a law, as constituting the brightest epoch in our National Annals, and as an inmistakeable harbinger of the incalculable good which will descend to our children's children in the far distant future.

Resolved, That retrenchment, industry and rigid economy should be car-

[67] *Senate Journal*, 1853, 478–480.

ried into all departments of the Government, as the surest guarantee to sound morals and the greatest protection against frauds and peculations on the people's Treasury, and extravagant and unnecessary appropriations of their money.

Resolved, That the farmers and mechanics of the country constitute the great productive power and principal source from which the nation draws its main support, and they should be made to occupy their true position as the first class of society; the laborer, the mechanic and farmer being the chosen men of God.

Resolved, That in the opinion of this General Assembly, the appointments of all persons to office, either by the President or the heads of Departments, should be made upon the basis of representation from the several States in the Congress of the United States, that is to say, the whole number of persons appointed to office, should be divided by the whole number of representatives; giving to each Congressional District in the Union, its fair ratio of officers under the Federal Government.

Resolved, That in the opinion of this General Assembly, every Congressional District in the Union, is more than competent to furnish its full quota of officers, upon the principle as laid down in the foregoing resolution, who would be honest, capable, and faithful to the constitution of the United States.

Resolved, That in the selection of individuals to fill all the offices under the Federal Government, due regard should be had to farmers and mechanics so as to give them fair opportunity to participate in the offices of the country.

Resolved, That the people, the principles of the constitution, the spirit of the times, and justice, all demand at the hands of the President and heads of the Departments, so soon as may be practicable, to carry into full and fair effect, the principles and doctrines as laid down in the foregoing resolutions."

Three weeks rolled by before the Senate took any action on Senator Nave's resolution and that action was brief indeed. The resolution was merely referred to the Committee on Federal Relations and in the hands of that committee the resolution was allowed to die.

The Thirtieth General Assembly had before it for consideration a question never before presented to any Tennessee Legislature. The question related to the amendments to the State Constitution of 1835. The method of amending the Constitution resolved itself into three steps: (1) passage of the proposed amendment by a majority vote of the Legislature; (2) passage of the same proposed amendment by the succeeding Legislature by a two-thirds vote; and (3) ratification by the people of the proposed amendment or amendments. These three constitutional requirements had been complied with in all respects. The General Assembly of 1849 and of 1851 had passed the proposed amendments in accordance with constitutional requirements. One week after the Legislature of 1853 had convened, the Secretary of State transmitted to that body the full returns of the popular vote on the proposed amendments to the 1835 Constitution, the tabulated votes showing that the people had ratified the amendments.[68]

Within minutes after the reading of the above report, Whig Sena-

---

[68] *Ibid.*, 49–51.

tor William O'Neill Perkins from the counties of Rutherford and Williamson introduced the following resolution:[69]

"*Resolved*, That the Senate meet the House of Representatives in Convention, on Wednesday the 19th instant, for the purpose of electing a Judge and Attorney General for the sixth Judicial Circuit."

The above resolution drew fire immediately from a Nashville newspaper, to-wit:[70]

"THE ELECTION OF JUDGES AND ATTORNEYS GENERAL BY THE PEOPLE.

We observe that a resolution has been offered in the House of Representatives that the Legislature go into the election of an Attorney General for the ———— district. We are surprised at this movement, inasmuch as the amendments to the constitution recently ratified by the people take away from the Legislature the power of electing Judges and Attorneys General, and confer it on the people. It is true that the vote upon these amendments has not yet been officially ascertained, but there can be no doubt as to the fact that they have been ratified, and it is the duty of the Legislature to ascertain this fact without delay, and before entertaining any motion to go into the election of an Attorney General. If an examination of the vote upon the amendments is postponed, and vacancies filled upon the pretext that the Constitution remains unchanged until the alteration is officially ascertained, the people will be justly indignant at such a flagrant outrage upon their rights. We do not apprehend, however, that such a suicidal policy will be seriously advocated by any one. We believe the members of the Legislature are sincerely desirous of getting at a correct understanding of this matter, and of legislating accordingly.

In compliance with the request of a number of the members of the Legislature, we shall to-morrow give our views upon this subject, which, view it as we may, is, to say the least, surrounded with perplexing difficulties.

—P.S.—We observe in the Senate proceedings that the Secretary of State yesterday made a report to the Senate of the vote cast for the proposed amendments to the constitution, and the vote cast for representatives. The aggregates, according to this report, are—

Whole No. of votes 118,270
For the election of Judges, &c., by the people, ... 68,676
For the new counties, ... 55,375

According to this statement, the amendment to elect Judges and Attorneys General by the people is adopted by a majority of 18,082. The amendment relative to new counties is defeated by 7520 majority.

The Secretary of State reported the vote for floating representatives separately from that of county representatives—unnecessarily as we think. Where the vote for floaters was larger than that for county representative, the former should have been counted instead of the latter. Where the vote for county representative was the largest, the vote for floater need not be reported. We find that the vote for floater exceeded that for county representatives in Jefferson, 3; Knox, 11; Davidson, 389; Maury, 64; Williamson, 172; Fayette, 7; Shelby, 172; in the aggregate, 818. Add this to the reported

[69] *Ibid.*, 51.
[70] *Daily Union and American* (Nashville), October 12, 1853.

whole number of votes, and we have the true 'whole number of persons voting for representatives' at the late election, 119,078. And the amendments are adopted by an actual majority of 17,964.

The amendments are adopted, and the fact officially reported to the Legislature. They are a part of the constitution. And members of the Legislature may now as well introduce a resolution to proceed to the election of a President of the United States as of a judge or attorney general. The people have taken the matter into their own hands, and have left the Legislature nothing to do but to pass a law to fix the time of election."

The Perkins resolution and others of a kindred nature stirred up a considerable ruckus in the General Assembly. Opinion in each legislative branch was divided over two basic questions: (1) whether the schedule attached to the constitutional amendments became a part of the Constitution, and (2) whether the present Legislature or that of 1855 should enact a law designating the date for the election by the people of all Judges and Attorneys-General.

The Schedule [71] to the amendments was as follows:

"Section 1. And that no inconvenience may arise from the proposed amendments, should the same be adopted by the people, it is declared that all judges of the courts and attorneys, contemplated in the proposed amendments, shall continue to hold their offices and exercise the duties and functions thereof, according to the true existing laws and constitution, until the election of their successors by the people to be held and made under a law to be passed by the General Assembly next elected after the ratification of the proposed amendments by the people, which law shall prescribe the times and places of holding said election, and which shall be passed without delay and in strict pursuance of said amendments: *Provided*, The legislature shall appoint a day for holding the election of judges and attorneys general separate and apart from the days already prescribed or hereafter to be prescribed by the legislature for holding the elections for State and county officers."

Numerous resolutions were introduced and motions were made that centered around the two above issues. In the Senate, perhaps the contrasting viewpoints were well-expressed by the majority and the minority reports from the Judiciary Committee to which the controversy had been referred. The majority report [72] was presented by Democratic Senator Joel J. Jones from the counties of Bedford and Marshall:

"The Committee on the Judiciary, to whom were referred certain resolutions touching 'the amendments to the constitution,' in reference to the election of Judges and Attorneys General by the people, and the legitimate effect thereof; and also as to the powers of the General Assembly as to the election of Judges and Attorneys General, &c., have had the same under consideration, and beg leave to report, that it is the unanimous opinion of the committee that said amendments are a part of the organic law of Tennessee. A majority of your committee are of the opinion that the schedule is a part of the Constitution of Tennessee, but differ in opinion as to the legal effect thereof. The difficulty in the way of your committee acting as an unit upon the ma-

---

[71] *Acts of Tennessee*, 1849, Resolution VI, 566–567.
[72] *Senate Journal*, 1853, 130–131.

terial question under consideration, is to be found in the words 'next elected,' which are a part of the schedule. A majority of your committee do not believe the words 'next elected' withhold the power from this General Assembly to fix the time and place for holding the elections for Judges and Attorneys General; for, to give these words their broadest significance and literal meaning, we find that meaning entirely controlled and destroyed by that portion of the schedule, which commands the General Assembly to pass a law fixing the time, &c., in strict pursuance of the amendments, without delay. The question then recurs, as to what the amendments were intended to remedy, and what ends were intended to be attained by them? These amendments provide for the election of Judges and Attorneys General by the people, and 'in strict pursuance thereof,' we are commanded to fix the time and place. To postpone the fixing of the time and place to a period two years hence, would, in the opinion of a majority of your committee, be clearly violative, and a perversion of the intent and meaning of the words 'in strict pursuance thereof, and without delay.' The words 'in strict pursuance' imply an effort and obligation to reach, or accomplish, something–a *continued* exertion to effect a consummation of the end desired. The end is clear and evident that is sought, but if the present Assembly fail to give these amendments vitality and operation, by prescribing the 'time and place,' it appears to a majority of your committee that the great object of the amendments has failed. The motive and intent, in the opinion of your committee, of these amendments should be looked to; the evil to be remedied and the object to be attained. What motive could there have been in a postponement of time for fixing the time and place for these elections? Why not postpone for half a century, as well as two years? There being no motive, nothing to be effected by such postponement, that cannot be effected by fixing the time and place 'without delay,' your committee think it the imperative duty of this Assembly to bring these elections before the people. Your committee are of opinion, that Judges and Attorneys whose terms of office expire before the time prescribed for the elections by the people, will go out of office, and that it is the duty of this Assembly, under the 4th section of the 7th article of the Constitution, to make provision for all vacancies that have or may occur, previous to the election by the people.

In accordance with these opinions, a majority of the committee have instructed me to report the following resolutions, to wit:

1. That this General Assembly has the power, and it is made their duty by the Constitution, to prescribe the times and places for the election of Judges and Attorneys General by the people, 'without delay.'

2. That it is the duty of this General Assembly to fill all vacancies that have occurred, or may occur, before the elections by the people.

3. That the schedule is a part of the Constitution of Tennessee.

All of which is respectfully submitted.

J. J. Jones, *Chairman*."

The minority report [73] was presented by Whig Senators John Reid of Davidson County and John R. Nelson representing the counties of Knox and Roane:

"Mr. Reid, from the minority of the Committee on the Judiciary, to which was referred sundry resolutions on the subject of the amendments to the Constitution, made the following report:

_____
[73] *Ibid.*, 134–141.

The undersigned being members of the Judiciary Committee, and disagreeing with the majority of said committee in their report upon the construction of the amendments to the Constitution, offer the following as their views by way of a counter report:

1. Does this Legislature, or does the next ensuing Legislature, appoint the day when the people are to elect the Judges and Attorneys General of this State?

The schedule says, that the Judges and Attorneys 'shall continue to hold their offices and exercise the duties and functions thereof, according to the true existing laws and constitution, until the election of their successors by the people, to be held and made under a law to be passed by the General Assembly (next elected, after the ratification of the proposed amendments by the people), which laws shall prescribe the time and places of holding said elections, and which shall be passed without delay, and in strict pursuance of said amendments: *Provided*, The Legislature shall appoint a day for holding the election of Judges and Attorneys General, separate and apart from the days already prescribed, or hereafter to be prescribed, by the Legislature, for holding the elections for State and county officers.'

In arriving at the meaning of this schedule, in other words, in putting upon it the proper construction, the undersigned will assume it as admitted, that the same mode, and the same principles, must be applied, whether we view it as a common ordinary statute, or as a part of the Constitution. Or, to speak more plainly, we construe a statute in the same way and by the same principles, that we construe the Constitution or any part of it.

How then do we arrive at the meaning of a statute Chancellor Kent, in the first volume of his Commentaries, page 461, lays this down as the mode? 'The true meaning of the statute is generally and properly to be sought from the body of the act itself.' And again, at page 462, of same vol., he says: 'The words of a statute, if of common use, are to be taken in their natural, plain, obvious and ordinary signification and import.' The same mode of construction is applied even to written contracts, in order to arrive at the meaning of the parties. Mr. Chitty, in his Treatise on Contracts, at page 99, says: 'Where there is no ambiguity in the terms used, the agreement, or instrument itself, shall be the only criterion of the intention of the parties,' and this 'although oral testimony would clearly show, that the real intention of the parties was at variance with the particular expressions of the written agreement.'

Adopting this mode of construing the schedule, (and the undersigned would be led to adopt the same mode without the weight of authority, from necessity, and from the principles of common sense,) the undersigned must be permitted to say, that, in their judgment, it is too clear for argument, that it will devolve upon the next and not upon the present General Assembly, to appoint the day when the people are to elect these officers—the Judges and Attorneys General.

The words used in the schedule are 'of common use,' and in no way ambiguous in their sense. The members of the present General Assembly were not '*next elected after* the ratification of the proposed amendments by the people,' but were elected on one and the same day, at one and the same time, as these amendments were ratified by the people. It is said by some, that it was not so understood either by the Legislature or by the people. But how do we arrive at this conclusion? The law tells us, that to arrive at their understanding and meaning, we must look to the 'body of the law (schedule) itself;' and we have just attempted to show, that if we are to interpret the words used, according to their 'natural, plain, obvious and ordinary signification and import,' that we will be led irresistibly to the conclusion, that both the Legislature and people did so understand it. It is true, that the schedule also says, that the law appointing the day when the people are to elect these officers, '*shall be passed without delay*,' but in the opinion of the undersigned, that has nothing to do with the present question. That simply says, that the Legislature *whose duty it is made to pass this law*, shall do so without delay, and does not in any way determine or aid in determining whether it is the province of this or the next Legislature to pass this law. When it is once ascertained which Legislature is to pass this law, appointing the day, then that part of the schedule will come in and direct *that* Legislature to pass the law without delay. In other words, if it shall become the duty of the next Legislature, which will meet in 1855, to pass this law, when the people are to elect these officers, then this part of the schedule will direct and command that Legislature to pass such law without delay. This is clearly the meaning of that part of the schedule, and no other construction can be fairly put upon it, if we are to give any force, any meaning to the words going before it. And the undersigned cannot see or feel the force of the reasoning, that, because it is made the duty of the Legislature, which is to appoint the day when these officers are to be elected by the people, to do so without delay, that therefore the schedule must have meant that the Legislature, which first met after the ratification, must appoint the day. Suppose the schedule had said, in so many words, that the Legislature, which met in 1855, should pass the law appointing the day when the people were to elect these officers, and should do so without delay, could any one be found, whose mind was so illogical as to contend that, therefore, the Legislature of 1853 was intended? That the words *without delay* were so potent as to override the previous part of the sentence, and to show that those who framed and adopted the schedule, must have intended that the Legislature of 1853, and not the Legislature of 1855, should pass the law, appointing the day when the people were to elect? And yet the undersigned believe, that the schedule as it is now worded, is as plain and strong, as it would have been if couched in the words supposed; that the words, 'the General Assembly *next elected after* the ratification of the proposed amendments by the people,' are as clear in their signification as if it had been said, 'the General Assembly elected in 1855.'

It is true, that it has been said by some, that the election of a member to the General Assembly is not consummated until after he has been qualified—that is, until after he has been sworn to support the Constitution of this State and of the United States, and has also taken an oath of office. The 2d sec. of article 10 says, that 'each member of the Senate and House of Representatives, shall, *before they proceed to business*,' take these oaths. And it is argued by those, who espouse this opinion, that it cannot be said that a person is elected to the General Assembly, until he has taken these oaths; that his induction into office is not completed until this is done; and until he is inducted into office he cannot be said to be elected. Hence they argue, that these amendments were ratified by the people before the members of the present General Assembly were elected, and that this General Assembly were 'next elected after the ratification of the proposed amendments by the people.' But, in the opinion of the undersigned, this position is utterly untenable, and evidences a disposition to twist and force the schedule into a particular meaning, rather than fairly to seek out what was intended by those who framed it. It confounds the election and qualification of a member, whereas they are wholly distinct, both in the meaning attached to them, in common parlance, and in the meaning attached to them by our Constitution and laws. To elect is to pick out or choose; and when we say, that an individual is elected to the

Legislature, we mean to say, that he is picked out or chosen from the mass of his fellow-citizens, or from those who offer themselves as candidates, to represent us. The moment he receives a majority of votes, and the polls are closed, that moment he is elected. We manifest our choice by our votes; and when the votes are counted, and it is ascertained that he has received a majority, we say, that he was elected on the day the votes were polled, and not that he will be elected when he presents himself on the day the Legislature is to meet, and the oaths of office are administered to him. Everybody so understands it. Our Constitution manifestly and incontrovertibly puts the same meaning upon the word. The 7th sec. of article 3d, is as follows: 'The first election for Senators and Representatives, shall be held on the first Thursday in August, one thousand eight hundred and thirty-five; and forever thereafter, elections for members of the General Assembly, shall be held once in two years, on the first Thursday in August; *and said elections shall terminate on the same day*.' By consulting our statutes, it will be found, that our Legislatures have invariably affixed the same meaning to the word, and used it in that sense alone. In using the words 'the General Assembly next elected after the ratification of the proposed amendments by the people,' the framers of the schedule must therefore have meant the same thing, as if they had adopted a different phraseology, and had said, 'the General Assembly whose members shall be next chosen by a majority of the people to represent them, after the ratification of the proposed amendments.'

But is the schedule a part of the amendments? It becomes important to decide this question, not because a different construction would be put upon it, but because, if it is, this Legislature would have no right to repeal or in any way to modify it. The undersigned believe that it is, and assign the following as their reasons for so believing:

The Constitution itself declares how it is to be amended. The third section of article 11, declares in substance that amendments may be proposed in either House of the Legislature, and if the same are agreed to by a majority of both Houses, they shall be referred to the General Assembly next to be chosen, and shall be published six months previous to the election of such General Assembly. And if the General Assembly next chosen after the General Assembly in which they were proposed, should, by a vote of two-thirds of all the members, approve of such amendments, they should then be submitted to the people for their ratification or rejection. The Constitution can be amended by taking these steps, but in no other way. The Legislature must submit the amendments to the people and the people must vote upon them as submitted. They would have no right to vote for amendments which had not been proposed, and for the same reason no right to vary, in any way, such as were proposed by the Legislature. They would have the physical power, but not the right under the Constitution.

And again: If the Legislature in which these amendments were proposed and approved, regarded the schedule as a part, they must have submitted it to the people, as such, for their ratification.

Now, how are the facts? These amendments and schedule were proposed and passed in the Legislature of 1849-50. These amendments and schedule were published in the Whig, on the 18th January, 1851—six months before the members of the next Legislature were chosen. These amendments and the schedule were approved by the Legislature of 1851-2, two-thirds of the members of both Houses voting in favor of both the amendments and schedule.

It is clear, therefore, that the Legislature regarded this schedule as a part of the amendments. If not, why was the schedule voted upon by two consecutive Legislatures? One Legislature alone can pass a law, and this is known to all. It would, therefore, have been idle, to say the least, in the Legislature of 1851-2, to have voted upon this schedule, and to have approved of it by a vote of two-thirds of all its members, after it had been passed by the Legislature of 1849-50, if it looked upon it as a mere act or statute. But there is still stronger evidence of the estimate put upon the schedule, by the Legislature of 1851-2. Mr. Starke, (who was at the time the Senator of Robertson county,) moved to strike out these words from the schedule: 'next elected after the ratification of the proposed amendments by the people,' and his motion was rejected. (See Journal of Senate for 1851-2, page 237.) The object of Mr. Starke was evidently to give to the present Legislature the power instead of the Legislature of 1855-6, to fix or appoint the day when the people were to elect the Judges and Attorneys General. Now, why was it lost? It must have been, because the schedule was regarded as a part of the amendments; and if in any way changed, it was known that it would thereby throw back the amendments two years. In fact, this is the recollection of one of the Senators of the present Legislature, who was also a Senator of the Legislature of 1851-2. He states, that when Mr. Starke made his motion, an eminent lawyer, then the Senator from Davidson, arose in the Senate, and stated it as his opinion, that the schedule was a part of the amendments, and thereupon the motion of Mr. Starke was unanimously rejected. From this statement, it is believed by the undersigned to be manifest, that the Legislature of 1851-2, regarded the schedule as a part of the amendments, and as such submitted it to the people.

But without this statement of facts, it is clear to the minds of the undersigned, that the schedule must be regarded as a part of the amendments. It is not only connected with them by the conjunction 'And,' but from its very nature is inseparable. It is clear, that it was intended to keep alive the old Constitution and laws until these amendments went into operation, and also to state the time when the amendments should go into operation. The name and form is nothing; we must look to the substance. It is the same, and it was intended to have the same effect, by attaching the schedule to these amendments, as if it had been stated in the amendments proper, when they should go into operation, and that, in the meantime, the Constitution and laws should remain in force. Suppose, instead of the schedule, the amendments had been submitted to the people for ratification alone, as they now are with this addition to the bottom of each: But the Judges (at the bottom of section 3, and Attorneys General at the bottom of section 5,) are not to be elected by the qualified voters as hereinbefore stated, until a day is fixed under a law to be passed by the Legislature of 1855-6, and in the meantime, the section, which this is intended to amend, is to remain in force as heretofore. Would any one contend that this addition was no part of the amendments? And yet the schedule was intended to perform the same office, and is, in substance, the same. It differs only in form. Indeed, without taking more time upon this point, its very style betrays its nature. It 'speaks like one having authority,' as one above the Legislature, and having the right to control it. It declares that the Legislature shall appoint a day for the election of Judges and Attorneys General 'separate and apart from the days already prescribed, or hereafter to be prescribed, by the Legislature, for holding the elections for State and county officers.'

But there is no difference between the undersigned and the majority of the Judiciary Committee on this point. We all, or nearly all, agree that the schedule is a part of the amendments. In fact, the undersigned are disposed to believe, that if the schedule were a mere legislative act, it would be a nullity; that the naked amendments would take effect as soon as they were ratified by the people, and all the acts of Judges and Attorneys General since that time and until these offices were filled by the people, would be void. Certainly, if no schedule had been attached, the amendments would go immediately into operation. If the schedule were a mere legislative act, could it suspend the operation of the amendments? If it could one day or two years, it could forever, and thus it would seem that an act of the Legislature could abolish a part of the Constitution, which is an absurdity. It would seem, that a Constitution, and consequently an amendment of the Constitution, must express upon its own face when it goes into operation, if it is intended that it should not go into operation on the day it is adopted, but on a future day. Hence all constitutions, on their face, provide when they are to go into operation. Hence the schedules attached to the two Constitutions of Tennessee, each of which, it is believed, has always been regarded as part of the one to which it was affixed.

The undersigned, therefore, believe, and so report to the Senate, that the schedule is a part of the amendments, and that, according to the true construction of this instrument, it will devolve on the Legislature of 1855-6 to pass the law appointing the day when the people are to elect the Judges and Attorneys General of this State.

2. Do these officers hold over by virtue of the schedule, or will the present Legislature have to elect such of them whose term of office would expire during the present Legislature under the Constitution, as it was before these amendments were proposed? The undersigned believe, that the present Legislature has the right to fill the vacancies, and that it is its duty so to do.

The schedule says, that the Judges and Attorneys General 'shall continue to hold their offices and exercise the duties and functions thereof, *according to the true existing laws and Constitution*, until the election of their successors by the people,' &c. Now, what was the object intended to be effected by this schedule? It has already been said, that its object was to say when the amendments should go into effect, and to declare, in the meantime, *that the Constitution and laws should remain as they were before the amendments were proposed*. 'And that no inconvenience may arise from the proposed amendments,' are the first words used in the schedule, and plainly show that it was the intention of the framers to avoid all confusion from the change, to effect which they provided that the Judges and Attorneys shall continue to hold their offices until the election of their successors by the people, '*according to the true existing laws and Constitution*,' that is, to hold them under and subject to the laws and Constitution, as they would have held them had no amendments been proposed. In other words, they desired that the Constitution and laws should remain as they were, until the amendments were put completely into operation. Now, if we were to hold that these officers were to hold over, by virtue of the schedule, this very object would be defeated, and confusion, and to some extent, probably anarchy, would prevail. Vacancies might, and out of so many offices, probably would, occur by the death, removal, resignation or otherwise, of some of the Judges and Attorneys General, and if neither the Legislature nor Governor had the right to fill them, confusion and anarchy (the very state sought to be avoided) would prevail. The Governor, under the Constitution, has no right to fill vacancies, except when they occur during the recess of the Legislature. All vacancies, therefore, which occur during the sitting of the Legislature, must be filled by the Legislature, or remain vacant. All of us concur upon this point, and if there were no other reason, necessity itself would force upon us this construction.

The undersigned have now finished their report. It is upon a subject of the highest importance to the people of this State. It has been drawn up hurriedly, and not as ably as they could have wished, and as the importance of the subject demanded. They have, however, attempted to arrive at the truth, and they console themselves with the thought, that, however weakly and confusedly they may have enforced and unfolded their opinions, they, nevertheless, occupy upon this subject the same ground as the best judicial minds of the State.

JNO. REID.
JOHN R. NELSON."

In the House of Representatives, opinion on the issues was as sharply divided as in the Senate. Whig Representative Alvin Hawkins of Carroll County (later elected Governor of Tennessee) propounded the following questions:[74]

"Whereas, Doubts are entertained as to the true construction of a part of the 3d section of the 11th article of the Constitution of the State of Tennessee, also as to the true construction of the schedule annexed to the recently proposed amendments; therefore,

Resolved, That this General Assembly respectfully solicit of the Supreme Court of Tennessee, or the several Judges thereof, an opinion upon the following propositions, to-wit:

1st. Is it necessary, in order that the proposed amendment shall become a part of the Constitution, according to the provisions of the 3d section of the 11th article thereof, that the same shall have been voted for by a majority of all citizens in the State entitled to vote for representatives, or is a majority of those actually voting for representatives sufficient for ratification?

2d. If the proposed amendments in reference to the election of Judges and Attorneys General have been ratified by the people according to the requirements of the Constitution, is the schedule annexed thereto a part of the Constitution, or is it only a legislative enactment?

3d. If said amendments have been ratified at the recent election, has this General Assembly the power, in any case, to elect a Judge or Attorney General?

4th. If said amendments have been ratified, is it the duty of this General Assembly, or has it the power to fix by law the time for holding the elections of Judges and Attorneys General?

Resolved, That a committee of three, upon the part of the House, be appointed to act in conjunction with a committee, upon the part of the Senate, to forward copies of these resolutions to each of the Judges of the Supreme Court, and solicit of them an early compliance with the same."

In the House the Joint Select Committee, composed of members from both branches of the General Assembly, submitted both a majority and a minority report on the issue involved. The majority report[75] was filed by Whig George Brown of Monroe County:

"The Joint Select Committee, composed of members from both Houses, who are required to investigate and report whether the proposed amendments to the Constitution, or either of them, have been ratified by the people,

---

[74] *House Journal*, 1853, 58–59.
[75] *Ibid.*, 74.

have had the subject under consideration, and they have directed me to report that the proposed amendment which provides for the election of Judges and Attorneys General by the people has been approved and ratified by a majority of all the citizens of the State voting for Representatives at the last election; and therefore, said amendment has been approved and ratified by the people of this State according to the requirements of the constitution. The proposed amendment of the constitution in relation to making certain new counties has been rejected, by a majority of all the citizens of the State voting for Representatives at the last election, and has not therefore been ratified and approved by the people according to the requirements of the constitution, &c.

GEORGE BROWN, *Chairman*."

The minority report was from a fellow Whig, Alvin Hawkins, who interjected into his viewpoint an issue not significantly raised in any other discussion, namely, whether a majority of those *voting* for representatives or a majority of those *entitled to vote* for representatives was the prerequisite for determining the ratification or non-ratification of the amendments. Let us view the reasoning put forth by Representative Hawkins in his minority report:[76]

"To the General Assembly of the State of Tennessee:

Being one of the Select Committee upon the part of the House of Representatives, to whom has been referred the resolution in reference to the adoption or rejection of the recently proposed amendments of the Constitution of the State of Tennessee, by the people at the election in August last, the undersigned would beg leave to state:

The enquiry now is, not as to the character of the proposed amendments of the Constitution, or whether or not they are demanded by the country; or whether or not they are founded in wise or unwise policy. These are questions with which it is apprehended we have nothing to do. The question to be considered, is one of more serious import, and one of vital importance to the country; not only so because of its reference to the amendments which have been proposed and voted upon, but more especially so, because of the principle involved and the effect which its settlement is destined to have upon the country—involving as it is believed it does, the very principles which lie at the foundation, and form the main pillar and support of all free governments, as declared and recognized by the 1st section of the Bill of Rights which is incorporated into, and made a part of, the Constitution of our State; and declares that 'all power is inherent in the people, and all free governments are founded upon this authority'; and involving as it is believed it does, the maintenance and preservation of the government, and the fundamental laws of the land, as they have been formed and spoken into existence by the voice and have for their basis the clearly expressed will of the majority of the people, against the assaults and opposition of the minority.

The 3rd section of Article 11, of the Constitution of the State, defines the means, or rather declares the mode by which that instrument may be amended; and the enquiry now is, have the recently proposed amendments thereto, been approved and ratified by the people in accordance with the provisions of that section; for it is to be apprehended, no one would wish to over-ride the Constitution of the State in his zeal for either or all of the amendments, or in his opposition thereto. Then the question depends upon the construction

---

[76] *Ibid.*, 83–86.

to be given to that part of said section which is in these words: 'And if the people shall approve and ratify such amendment or amendments, by a majority of all the citizens of the State voting for Representatives, voting in their favor, such amendment or amendments shall become a part of this Constitution.' Now let us, as becomes the Representatives of freemen, with unprejudiced and untrammelled minds, under a full sense of the imposing obligations resting upon us, and with a full appreciation of our duty to our country, calmly investigate, and dispassionately consider this question. And I may be permitted to express my trust, that this invocation will not be unheeded; for surely the subject is one which may command our attention, and upon which some of the ablest minds in the State are arrayed upon opposite sides. I believe that to constitute the proposed amendment a part of the Constitution, according to the provisions of the clauses in our Constitution before referred to, it is necessary that the same shall have been approved and ratified by a majority of all the citizens of the State entitled to vote for Representatives, voting in its favor. And this I believe to have been the intention of the framers of the Constitution, as the same appears upon the face of that instrument. It is true, there is at first blush a seeming plausibility in the argument of those who insist that a majority of those actually voting for Representatives, is all that is necessary for a compliance with the Constitution. But let it be borne in mind, that the qualification of electors, or voters, is fixed in no instance by our Constitution, except by the 1st section of Article 4th, which fixes the requisite qualifications of electors of members of the General Assembly. The 2nd section of Article 3rd, provides, 'That the Governor shall be chosen by the Electors of the members of the General Assembly;' thereby fixing the qualifications of the electors of the Governor by reference to the qualifications of electors of members of the General Assembly. Section 1st of Article 7th, provides: 'There shall be elected, in each county, by the qualified voters therein, one Sheriff, one Trustee, and one Register;' thereby, by use of the words 'qualified voters,' the qualifications of the electors of these officers, are fixed by reference to the same section, which fixes the qualifications of the voters in the election of the civil officers of the government. I am therefore constrained to believe that the words 'voting for Representatives,' as they are used in section 3, of Article 11, were only designed and intended to fix the qualifications of the electors, or voters, upon the proposition to amend, without any reference to those actually voting for Representatives.

If the true construction be that the constitution requires only that a majority of those actually voting for Representatives, shall vote for the proposed amendment, then we are driven into this absurd position, that none are entitled to vote even for the amendment, except those who actually vote for Representatives. And how can that question be determined. Although the citizen may desire to vote for the amendment, but not choosing to actually vote for representative, he is met at the polls and told that he is disfranchised, and not permitted to vote upon the proposed amendment. Can it be that such a construction is to prevail? If it does, it then becomes a matter of very grave enquiry, whether under the 2nd section of Article 3rd of the constitution, the qualifications of the electors of Governor, are not limited to those who shall actually vote for members of the General Assembly. I say it will be a matter of grave enquiry, and a question of a very doubtful character.

As a further argument to show the construction which I have given to sec. 3 of Art. 11, of the constitution, is the true one, it will be observed, there is nothing in the constitution which requires that the election for the proposed amendment shall be holden on the same day of the election for Representatives. Suppose, then, that the General Assembly at its last session, as it certainly had the power to have done, had fixed upon some day in August, 1852, for the election upon the proposed amendment, equi-distant in point of time from two elections for Representatives, then by which election of Representatives, the one in August, 1851, just one year before, or the one in August, 1853, just one year after the election upon the amendment, would the fate of the amendment be determined, if the construction that the constitution means a majority of those actually voting for Representatives is to prevail? The vote for Representatives in one election is larger than in the other; the vote for the amendment may have been in numbers between the two. Then I ask again, how will the fate of the amendment be determined? The friends of the amendment would insist upon comparing the vote upon the proposition to amend with the smaller vote, whilst those opposed to the amendment would with equal plausibility insist upon comparing the vote with the larger vote for Representatives; one party insisting that the amendment had been ratified; the other that it had been lost, and just here reference would be had to the Constitution itself, and if appealed to, to settle the question; but it is silent and refuses to speak, and wholly fails to guide to any conclusion; it does not point to one election any more than the other. Surely the framers of our constitution intended there should be some certain mode by which this question was to be settled, and they have as surely provided it, if the construction I have given to Sec. 3 of Art. 11, be the true one; which I believe to be so from the very necessity of the case, if for no other reason. If it be the true construction there will be no difficulty; but if the other be received as the true one, we are surrounded and hedged in upon all sides with insurmountable obstacles; upon every hand barriers rise up in our paths and say to us, 'thus far shalt thou come and no farther.' Again, if the construction that a majority of those actually voting for Representatives is all that is necessary to change, alter, reform or abolish the present constitution, prevails, is it not fraught with danger to the best interests of the Government and the institutions under which we have been happy and prosperous, and grown in our greatness as a people, and is it not calculated in its tendency to undermine the foundation of this fair fabric, and to dry up the fountain of the life-blood of the tree of liberty itself? Will it not be virtually declaring that a free Government, which is made by the majority for their peace, welfare and happiness, may be abolished by the minority?—and not only so, but a new one, or rather one of a different character, erected in its stead and over the heads and against the will of the majority?—and that radical changes may be made in the character of the Government, or of the fundamental laws of the land, without the consent of the majority, and against their will expressed by them in the only manner provided by law for them to do so? And in other words, will it not be placing the majority in a free Government at the mercy of the minority? To show that these deductions are true, it will be borne in mind that those only who are in favor of the amendment actually vote upon the proposition to amend, those who are opposed to it remain silent, and are counted, or ought to be counted, as voting against it. By remaining silent is the only mode they have appointed them by law of voting against the amendment. Then, if owing to indifference or apathy, or anyone of the other thousand causes which may lay hold of and influence the public mind in reference to the election of Representatives, the people fail to vote for Representatives, however much they may be opposed to the proposed amendment, they are virtually disfranchised, and have no means of voting against a proposition which they may believe to be most injurious to their rights, and in violation of the genius and spirit of a free Government; and radical changes are made in their Government and the fundamental laws of the land, by a minority of the people. Can it be that the framers of our constitution intended to place it in the power of the minority thus to overreach and set at defiance the will of the majority?

It is conceded by all that the recently proposed amendments have not been approved by a majority of all the citizens of the State entitled to vote for Representatives, by thousands, as is clearly shown to be true by comparing the vote for the proposed amendments with the census of 1850, even supposing our population not to have increased since that time. And being of the opinion, that in order the proposed amendment shall become part of the constitution, it must be approved and ratified by a majority of all the citizens of the State entitled to vote for Representatives, voting in favor of the amendment and the proposition to amend in reference to the election of Judges and Attorneys General, and the formation of certain new Counties having failed to receive that majority, with all due deference to the opinions of others, I beg leave to report, that said amendments have failed.

All of which is respectfully submitted.

ALVIN HAWKINS.

Nashville, Oct. 19, 1853."

On October 20, Senator Robert Farquharson introduced a resolution [77] the substance of which was that

"It is hereby declared that the amendments aforesaid: 'For the election of Judges and Attorneys General by the people' is now a part of the Constitution of the State of Tennessee."

Four days later, the Farquharson resolution was adopted in the Senate by a vote of 20 to 4.[78]

On November 3, after concurring in the report of the Judiciary Committee relative to the amendments to the Constitution by a vote of 58 to 14, the House concurred in the Senate-approved Farquharson resolution.[79] This action put an end to the controversy, for it was now an accepted fact that future elections of Judges and Attorneys-General would be by a vote of the people. There can be no serious doubt but that this constitutional change in the method of electing the above officials was a forward step. No longer would there be a waste of time and money by the Legislature in log-rolling tactics centering around the election of such officials; furthermore, much political sniping and assailment of private character would be likewise eliminated. So bitter had many such contests become that a number of eminent lawyers refused to allow their names to be considered, and thus the State was being penalized in some instances by having 'pot politicians' ensconced in the offices of Judge and Attorney-General instead of men of pronounced ability.

There remained, however, one knotty problem before the Legislature—was the Schedule attached to the amendments a part of the Constitution? If the Schedule was in fact a part of the Constitution,

---

[77] *Senate Journal*, 1853, 73.
[78] *Ibid.*, 92.
[79] *House Journal*, 1853, 197.

then the duty of the Legislature was to pass a law prescribing the time
and the places for holding said election. Moreover, the Schedule directed that such a law "shall be passed without delay." To get at this problem; Senator William O'Neill Perkins introduced the following resolution [80] on October 26, 1853, to-wit:

"*Resolved, by the General Assembly of the State of Tennessee*, That the
schedule attached to the amendments of the Constitution, and being part of
the amendments, has been ratified by the people, and is part of the Constitution."

Nearly two months rolled by before the above matter was taken
up by the Senate. On December 19, however, the Senate passed the
Perkins resolution by a vote of 15 to 9.[81] Another month passed by before the House took final action on the Perkins amendment, said action
being recorded by the following prosaic entry:[82]

"Joint Resolution No. 39, declaring the schedule a part of the constitution, was adopted in the House."

With the amendments to the Constitution having been declared
adopted and with the Schedule declared a part of the Constitution,
there now remained one other duty for the Legislature to discharge—
the enactment of a law setting the date for the election of Judges and
Attorneys-General by the people.

On January 5, 1854, as required by the Schedule to the amendments to the Constitution, a law [83] was enacted whereby the election
of all Judges and Attorneys-General was to be henceforth done by the
people. The fourth Thursday of May, 1854, was the date selected for
the election of the above officials. This date may be considered a red
letter day in the history of the Tennessee Judiciary, for this marked
the first time in the long course of more than half a century that the
people themselves had had bestowed upon them the privilege of electing their own judicial officers by a direct vote. A special provision in
the law required every voter to prefix to the name of each candidate for
Supreme Court Judge the words *Eastern, Western*, or *Middle* Division
to denote the Grand Division of the State for which he desired each
candidate to be elected.

Prior to the passage of the foregoing law, there were a number of
vacancies in judgeships and attorneys-generalships that were customar-
ily filled by the action of the Legislature. Now that the adoption of
the amendment to the Constitution had been declared, what about filling these offices? Tenures of office in numerous cases ended with the
convening of the Legislature; these officers could not be elected until

[80] *Senate Journal*, 1853, 96.
[81] *Ibid.*, 319.
[82] *House Journal*, 1853, 703.
[83] *Acts of Tennessee*, 1853, Chapter 32.

May, 1854, as decreed by statute. In the meanwhile, laws could not be carried into execution without Judges and Attorneys-General. The matter was resolved by proceeding with such elections as formerly, but with a proviso added in the case of each person elected. The proviso [84] was introduced by Representative William J. Sykes of Maury County and was as follows:

"Provided, that any Judges or Attorneys General elected by this General Assembly shall not hold their offices for any longer time than the election of their successors by the people and their qualification."

Six Judges and eight Attorneys-General were elected [85] by the 1853 General Assembly, but with the above proviso added. For example, when a Supreme Court Judge was elected, the official pronouncement [86] was as follows:

"The Convention proceeded to elect a Judge of the Supreme Court in place of the Hon. Nathan Greene resigned ... The Speaker of the Senate thereupon pronounced the Hon. Robert Caruthers duly and constitutionally elected Judge of the Supreme Court until the election of his successor by the people, under a law to be passed by the General Assembly."

The Thirtieth General Assembly has to its own credit the passage of a number of important laws. For example, a law [87] was enacted to create the State Agricultural Bureau together with County and District Agricultural Societies. In all probability, the movement was initiated by a memorial on the subject, the memorial [88] being presented by Senator Adrian Northcutt of Warren County. At first glance, the object of the memorial appeared to be doomed, for Senator Michael Carriger of the Committee on Agriculture and manufactures requested that his committee be discharged from any further consideration of the memorial, and that the matter be referred to the House of Representatives.[89] In the meanwhile, Whig Representative W. B. Dortch of Fayette County had introduced a bill to create the State Agricultural Bureau.[90] On January 19, 1854, the House Committee on Agriculture recommended that the bill be rejected,[91] and a month later, February 20, the bill was rejected by a vote of 36 to 28.[92] But the battle was not yet lost. A motion to reconsider the former action of the House was sustained, a committee amendment was accepted, and the bill passed third and

---

[84] *House Journal*, 1853, 198.
[85] *Senate Journal*, 1853, Appendix, 727.
[86] *Senate Journal*, 1853, 178.
[87] *Acts of Tennessee*, 1853, Chapter 255.
[88] *Senate Journal*, 1853, 416.
[89] *Ibid.*, 482.
[90] *House Journal*, 1853, 524.
[91] *Ibid.*, 628.
[92] *Ibid.*, 890.

final reading by a vote of 43 to 28.[93] The bill had easy sailing in the Senate, being passed on final reading by a vote of 17 to 6.[94]

Agitation of the liquor question was a constant item on the legislative agenda throughout most of the 1853 session. The recent enactment of what was known as "the Maine liquor law" prohibited the manufacture or sale of intoxicating beverages in that State, and anti-liquor advocates in Tennessee seized upon the idea of eliminating the legal sale of intoxicants in Tennessee. No less than sixty-four memorials upon the tippling question were poured into the legislative hopper.[95] For example, thirty such petitions were introduced into the House of Representatives in a single day.[96] Two typical petitions are inserted as showing something of the ideas entertained by their respective sponsors.

The Bethel College petition[97] is of special historical importance in that it contained the "germ" of the "four-mile" law of 1877 which prohibited the sale of intoxicating beverages within four miles of any incorporated institution of learning. Here was the language of the forerunner of the four-mile statute:

"To the Honorable Legislature of the State of Tennessee:

We your Humble Petitioners being members of the Board of Trustees of Bethel College together with near all the citizens of this vicinity, would most respectfully beg leave to represent to your Honorable Body, that said institution is situated in Carroll County, Tenn. eight miles west of Huntingdon, and now in a flourishing condition, & bids fair to be a blessing to our country and especially the rising generation. We would also represent that we believe it to be our duty in every way possible to guard the morals of the youth entrusted to our care and finding great difficulty to carry out our purposes while our vicinity is infested with those dins of desolution called grocerys allways ready to tempt and allure the unsuspecting youth. We therefore pray your Honorable Body to pass a special act for the benefit of Bethel College making it a penal offence to sell or keep for sale any spiritous or intoxicating liquors within two miles of said Institution except for medical purposes for which we will ever pray &c. &c."

The second petition[98] suggested the idea of ascertaining an expression of opinion from the people at large on the liquor question, and was couched in the following language:

"To the Honorable the Senate of Tennessee:

The Middle Tennessee Synod of the Cumberland Presbyterian Church composed of 174 official members and representing about 69540 population respectfully ask your honorable body to pass a law with suitable penalties an-

[93] *Ibid.*, 904.
[94] *Senate Journal*, 1853, 657.
[95] *Senate Journal*, 1853, 790–792.
   House Journal, 1853, 1172–1180.
[96] *House Journal*, 1853, 176–177.
[97] Original document in State Archives, Nashville. (72 signatures)
[98] *Ibid.*

nexed thereto prohibiting the trafic in intoxicating drinks except for medicinal and mechanical purposes in the State of Tennessee or at least to submit a bill prohibiting the same to be voted upon by the people on a day separate from all other elections, which vote shall be taken as instruction for the action of the next General Assembly of the State.

This prayer is made by this Synod in view of the following among other considerations.

1st. Your Penitentiary report shows that more than *five to one* of the 240 inmates of that prison were intemperate previous to the commission of the various crimes for which they were incarcerated, and that *more than one half were actually drunk* when their crimes were committed.

2d. The Revenue arising from Tippling licenses as shown by the Comptrollers report for 1851 & 2 amounted to $19,555.70 while the cost of *State Prosecutions* as shown by the same report amounted to $83,002.60 and we hesitate not to state that more than *five to one of all* these prosecutions have grown out of the tippling system as our observation and your Penitentiary report force this conviction upon us.

3d. It is further believed that the amount of Pauperism in the State is greatly increased by said trafic and consequently that the amount of taxes paid in the State is larger in the same proportion.

4th. The moral portion of the citizens of the State have for many years endeavored to relieve our land of these crying evils thus produced, of crime, pauperism and heavy taxation, by moral influences, and they have done much, and probably as much as can be done without the cooperation of the legal powers, but they have failed to accomplish the great work which all good and true men desire—the total extinguishment of the great evil of intoxication and its consequent crimes and results.

Therefore the above prayer is made to your honorable body, which we humbly request to be granted unto us, as good citizens of your commonwealth.

And we will ever pray.

ALPHA YOUNG
J. C. PROVINE
WM. L. LANGDON
Committee of Middle Tenn. Synod."

On November 15, 1853, Representative James J. Odell of Sullivan County, Chairman of the Joint Select Committee on Tippling, submitted a majority report[99] on the question of referring the liquor problem to an expression from the voters of the state.

"MAJORITY REPORT

The undersigned, members of the Joint Select Committee on Tippling, on the part of the House, to whom were referred sundry petitions and memorials from citizens of this State, asking the Legislature to pass a Resolution with suitable penalties and provisions contained therein, prohibiting the manufacture and traffic in intoxicating liquors, as a beverage, and submitting the same to a vote of the people of this State,—have had said petitions and memorials under consideration, and ask leave to make the following report:

---

[99] *Ibid.*

Author's note. Neither the majority nor minority report was printed in the *Senate Journal.* The minority report was not located in the State Archives.

Without entering into an examination, or giving an opinion in regard to the policy, and constitutional principles involved in a law prohibiting the traffic in, and manufacture of, intoxicating liquors, except for 'medical and mechanical purposes,' the Committee, in the first place, directed their attention, to questions connected with submitting this or any other Resolution to the people under similar conditions. The evident intention of the petitioners is, that if the Resolution is submitted, and a majority approve of the principles and provisions, contained therein,—such approval by the people, shall be instructions to the Legislature. Which Legislature? The present one, or to the one to be chosen two years hence? If to the Legislature chosen in 1855, then the propriety and binding authority of the instructions must be considered. The Committee think it would amount to no instructions *at all:*—for candidates for the Legislature—some in every county—would take the position before their fellow-citizens, that if elected they would oppose the passage of any prohibitory or Maine Law. If so elected, then here would be counter, and later instructions from the people. Suppose a majority of the voters of this state vote in favor of the Resolution (and we have no idea they would), and a majority of the members, elected to the General Assembly of 1855, are pledged to oppose prohibition, then the vote on the Resolution is useless and unnecessary and would have no binding obligation at all on the Representative.

If it is intended by the memorialists, that an approval of the Resolution by the citizens of this State, should be considered as instructions to the Legislature, now in session—to enact a prohibitory Law, then the grave question arises, ought Representatives to support a law which they in plain terms, pledged their constituents to oppose if elected? Certainly not, for the discussion of this prohibitory law entered into the canvass all over the State and every one knows that few or none advocating such a law were chosen to this Legislature. Again, a majority of the aggregate vote of the state might support the Resolution—but a large majority of a county or senatorial district, vote against it,—then the enquiry arises, should the representative or Senator, as the case may be, cast his vote in conformity with the instructions of the majority of the state—or in accordance to the wishes of a majority of his immediate constituents, those who elected him, whom he represents, and whose wishes and interests he is bound to promote. If the right of instruction, and to obey it, be admitted, then it is reasonable to conclude that the Representative will act out the will of his county or district. Consequently, the vote on the Resolution by the State, will accomplish little or nothing in the way of instructions—and besides cost the people time, money, trouble, and a great deal of excitement while the election is pending and after it is over, nothing definite is attained, no binding act is consummated that this Legislature or the one to be chosen two years hence could consistently recognize.

If the Legislature were to pass this resolution on the condition asked for and presented in the memorials, it would establish and encourage a precedent unknown in the legislative history of our state, at once dangerous, and not easily to be checked. Ours is a representative government, the purest and most perfect yet modeled by man. Once commence the example of submitting laws and resolutions to a popular vote, and the firmness, integrity, and cautiousness of the Legislature is shaken, every question that may come up, whether popular or unpopular, right or wrong, and even doing violence to the Constitution will be disposed of in the same way, by legislatures afraid to meet it; and thus duty and responsibility both would be avoided, and the Legislature virtually become a law proposing instead of a law making power, influenced by the capricious and restless will of a few agitators. Our Constitution vests the 'legislative authority in the General Assembly chosen by and representing the people;' and the Committee think the recent election in Tennessee has clearly shown that a large majority of her citizens are opposed to the enactment of a prohibitory law and even to a Resolution which was resorted to in order to throw the question out of the canvass, and to avoid taking a bold & decisive position.

In the second place, the Committee directed their investigations to the *contents* and object of the Resolution: to wit:—to prohibit the manufacture and sale of liquors as a beverage, (In some of the petitions to prohibit the sale only). This subject though an important one, embracing many valuable principles, will be briefly noticed and we cannot better express our opinions concerning it, than the following extract from a Report of a Joint Select Committee of the Connecticut Legislature:—

'A law similar to that of the State of Maine, is inconsistent with all the general principles that protect persons, property, possession, and domicil,—is inconsistent with the progress of liberty and free institutions in our republican nation,—is subject to extensive abuses for the gratification of private malice or the fanatical notions of extreme moral reformers, is not enjoined by any constitutional obligation to enact such a statute, and cannot obtain the general acquiescence or support of the community in its enforcement, that therefore it is calculated to unsettle the rights of property, the observance and respect for just and wholesome laws, and to bring into discredit the laws, the constitution, and the judicial tribunals of the country, without offering any practical and certain benefits, which are not better secured by laws made in accordance with those settled convictions of fundamental rights which have ever made the citizens of this eminent and enlightened state, a law respecting, and a law abiding people.'

For these and other considerations, the Committee recommend the rejection of the Resolution asked for, by the memorialists.

All of which is Respectfully Submitted.

JAMES J. ODELL
ABNER A. STEELE
W. S. MAXWELL
HORACE A. OVERALL
JOSHUA EASTERLY
Committee on the part of the House."

After a lot of parliamentary maneuvering, in which the decision of the Speaker of the House was challenged, the vote to non-concur with the majority report was defeated by a vote [100] of 46 to 29.

Over in the Senate, Senator John Reid of Davidson County introduced on November 28, 1853, a bill [101]

"To ascertain the will of the people of Tennessee in regard to the restraint of the sale of spirituous liquors."

Once more, various parliamentary "blocks" were interjected, among which was a request that the committee prepare a bill giving specific details as to how the matter was to be handled.[102] More than a month

[100] *House Journal*, 1853, 389–390.
[101] *Senate Journal*, 1853, 221.
[102] *Ibid.*, 284.

later, haggling over the liquor bill was still going on, as evidenced by the following excerpt from the official record:[103]

"Mr. Farquharson moved that fifty copies of the bill be printed.
Which motion was rejected.
Mr. Nixon moved that thirty-three copies be printed.
Which motion was rejected.
Mr. Bell moved that twenty-five copies be printed.
Which motion was rejected.
Mr. Bell moved that twenty-four copies be printed.
Which motion prevailed."

In another discussion of the bill, Senator Farquharson was successful in getting the following amendment adopted:[104]

"*Be it enacted*, That this act is not intended to be construed to prohibit the importation of liquors, or the sale of same in the original vessels or quantities imported, or to regulate or restrain commerce between the several States."

After the adoption of the Farquharson amendment, the bill passed second reading by a vote of 13 to 11. On third and final reading, the bill squeaked through by a vote of 12 to 11.[105]

When the bill came up in the House, its obsequies were performed quickly and quietly. The bill was rejected on first reading by a vote of 39 to 26.[106] The net result was that no liquor legislation whatsoever was enacted by the Thirtieth General Assembly. The guzzlers could still say with St. John Honeywood:

> "When Darby saw the setting sun,
> He swung his scythe and home he run;
> Sat down, drank off his quart, and said:
> 'My work is done, I'll go to bed'."

The Thirtieth General Assembly was the first to hold its meetings in the present State Capitol building, although the structure was not complete at the time. Governor Johnson made but slight reference in his Message to the building and his observations were a bit satirical. He was by no means favorably impressed with the idea of erecting out of public funds

"magnificent State edifices, with niches and rotundas accommodated to the reception of fine statues and gorgeous paintings—the exterior presenting all the grandeur of carved and massive columns which architectural ingenuity can invent or display ... to be studded over with monuments and works of statuary, in imitation of oriental splendor and folly. ..."

In the early part of the legislative session, quite a bit of fault-finding

---

[103] *Ibid.*, 368.
[104] *Ibid.*, 398.
[105] *Ibid.*, 414.
[106] *House Journal*, 1853, 809.

regarding acoustical annoyances was displayed by some of the legislators. At the end of the first week, a Senate Committee was appointed

"to confer with Mr. Strickland, the architect, to see if he can by any means remedy the difficulty of hearing in the Senate Chamber." [107]

On the next day, a committee was appointed to purchase window curtains primarily for the purpose of trying to reduce the echoes within the chamber, and to stretch some canvass or plain cloth around the Senate Chamber.[108] One further expedient seemed to have been somewhat effective:[109]

"THE STATE CAPITOL ... We are happy to be able to state that the difficulty which existed in regard to the reverberation of sound in the Senate Chamber has been remedied almost entirely. A layer of sawdust has been spread upon the floor, and a heavy carpeting over this; and the windows have been curtained with heavy drapery. The evil has not existed in the Representative Hall, though we presume the same appliances in that spacious room would greatly facilitate business."

With the noise somewhat abated in the Senate Chamber, matters rolled along rather routinely for several weeks. But a noise of another variety broke when the Report of the Capitol Commissioners was received on November 7, indicating that there was deficit of more than $32,000 in the expenditures incurred during the preceding biennium in erecting the State House.[110] Two years before, the Legislature had been assured by the architect and the commissioners that the $200,000 then appropriated would be adequate to complete the structure. But the present Report indicated that more money would need to be appropriated, for still unfinished were the basement, offices, cupola, and the terrace surrounding the building.

About two weeks after receipt of the above Report, Senator Godfrey Nave introduced a resolution[111] of the "down to brass tacks" variety:

"*Resolved*, That the Commissioners of the State Capitol are hereby requested to report as early as practicable, to the Senate of this General Assembly, the manner in which the two hundred and fifty thousand dollars, appropriated to the building of the Capitol by the last Legislature, was expended, how many of the Penitentiary hands were employed for the last two years, the value of their labor, the number employed receiving certain salaries, and the amount of each, the whole amount of money appropriated to said building, and the whole value of the Penitentiary labor on the same.

Also, whether the services of the Architect may not be dispensed with, and if not, if his salary may not be reduced, and how much money will be

---

[107] *Senate Journal*, 1853, 51.
[108] *Ibid.*, 54.
[109] *Nashville True Whig*, October 24, 1853.
[110] *Senate Journal*, 1853, Appendix, 105–107.
[111] *Senate Journal*, 1853, 196.

necessary to complete said building, by employing as much of the Penitentiary labor as can be done to advantage, and how it is that the Architect has reported to this General Assembly that it will yet take two hundred thousand dollars to complete said building, when the Commissioners reported two years ago to the Legislature that two hundred and fifty thousand dollars would complete the building."

An itemized report [112] of expenditures was presented by the President of the Board of Capitol Commissioners. The continuance of the services of the architect was recommended, although his former underestimate as to the amount of money necessary to finish the job had upset the Legislature. This "off the beam" estimate plus the resounding noises in the Senate Chamber, for which the Legislature held the architect responsible, placed Mr. Strickland in "hot water." A House Resolution [113] to remove him as architect was narrowly defeated, the vote being 34 to 33. But Time, the Great Healer, softened down the legislative opposition to Mr. Strickland. An appropriation of $200,000 for continuation of the work on the State Capitol was voted, and it was provided

"That the vault in the basement story of the capitol is hereby set apart as a burial place for the architect of the State Capitol, in honor of his genius in erecting so grand a work."[114]

Space limitations prevent any extended presentation of other important legislation by the Thirtieth General Assembly. Among such were the creation of the Office of State Librarian;[115] creation of the Office of State Geologist;[116] and the election of Dr. James Safford as State Geologist on the fifth ballot; [117] and the awarding [118] of a gold medal to Mark Cockrill of Davidson County, who had won first honors at the World's Fair in London, in 1851, for having "wrung from the assembled wool growers of the civilized world the reluctant confession that Tennessee produces the finest fleece known to man."

A few days prior to *sine die* adjournment of the Legislature, Governor Johnson transmitted to that body the following communication:

---

[112] *Senate Journal*, 1853, 141–144.

[113] *House Journal*, 1853, 731–732.

[114] *Acts of Tennessee*, 1853, Chapter 86.

Author's note. Five weeks after the passage of the above law, the renowned architect of the State Capitol died. His enfeebled state of health undoubtedly was a factor that tended to soften legislative criticism of him toward the end of the session.

[115] *Ibid.*, Chapter 41.

[116] *Ibid.*, Chapter 135.

[117] *House Journal*, 1853, 1004–1008.

[118] *Acts of Tennessee*, 1853, Resolution XV, 792.

Legislative Message,* February 23, 1854

"EXECUTIVE DEPARTMENT,
February 23rd, 1854.

GENTLEMEN OF THE SENATE AND HOUSE OF REPRESENTATIVES:

There has been transmitted by the Governor of the State of Georgia, to this department, through the Hon. John D. Stell, a Message of the Governor to the Legislature of that State, and two resolutions adopted in conformity with the recommendation thereof, together with a letter requesting that the Message and resolutions be laid before your honorable body at the earliest moment convenient—all of which is herewith most respectfully transmitted. The Message and resolutions will fully explain the nature and character of the object intended to be accomplished.

The Hon. John D. Stell, who has been appointed commissioner on the part of the State of Georgia, is here in person, and if desired, no doubt will give any explanation that may be required by the Legislature, outside of the Message and resolutions herewith transmitted.

It will be perceived by the Legislature, from an examination of the documents, that the question raised by the State of Georgia is one of no ordinary character, and demands the calm and deliberate consideration of the Legislature, in advance of any definite action which may be had. On the one hand, we should take great care to cultivate that amity which should always exist between members of the same confederacy, and especially so between two adjoining sovereignties, whose commercial and other relations are so closely and intimately identified. These should, and no doubt will be on your part, every disposition manifested in the settlement of this question, that comports with the honor and dignity of the State. On the other hand, we should be equally careful in not compromitting any right or privilege guaranteed to our citizens by the organic law of the land. Whether the Legislature is clothed with the power to transfer by law, a citizen of the State of Tennessee to the courts of

---

* *Senate Journal*, 1853, Appendix, 267–268.
House Journal, 1853, Appendix, 267–268.
Author's note. Four minor Messages, dealing with nominations for Bank Directors and Penitentiary Inspectors, are omitted in this treatise. They will be found in the *Senate Journal*, 1853, on pages 104–105; 321; 364; and 384, respectively.

the State of Georgia, for remedy for an injury done him in Tennessee, in his goods, lands, person or reputation, and if clothed with the power, the expediency or propriety of doing so, is a question of grave and important consideration, and your attention is therefore most respectfully called to the 17th section of the first article of the constitution of this State.

It is hoped that prompt and efficient steps will be taken on the part of the Legislature, to meet the State of Georgia in that spirit of comity which is indicated on her part, and which should always characterize two sister States in adjusting differences of opinion, arising out of any former legislation or intercourse, and which will lead to a satisfactory arrangement of all their existing difficulties, and a continuance of that friendship which will promote their commercial, agricultural and other relations so essential to their future peace and prosperity.

Very respectfully,

ANDREW JOHNSON."

"The following Message was transmitted to both branches of the General Assembly of the State of Georgia on the 9th day of February, 1854.

EXECUTIVE DEPARTMENT,
Milledgeville, Georgia, Feb. 9, 1854.

To the Senate and House of Representatives:

My immediate predecessor, in his last Message to the General Assembly called your attention to the fact 'That suits have been commenced against the Western and Atlantic Railroad, in the State of Tennessee.' Apprehending that you may adjourn without action upon this important subject, I respectfully urge it again upon your attention.

These suits are commenced by virtue of a special statute of Tennessee, designed, no doubt, to apply particularly to the road. I have not been able to obtain a copy of the Acts of 1852, in our library; but, I am furnished with a transcript from the law authorizing these suits, in a private letter, which I have no doubt is correct. It is as follows:

'Be it enacted, That when any railroad extends into this State from an adjoining State, and the president or head officer of said road resides beyond the limits of Tennessee, a right of action for the redress of any injury caused by, or for any claim, or demand against the corporation, company, proprietor, or railroad, shall exist in this State, in any court or judicial tribunal having jurisdiction thereof, against such road, proprietor or company, and process may be served upon any depot agent of such road residing in this State in the absence of the President or head officer of said road. And the judgment which may be rendered against the company or road, in the name by which it transacts its business, and the property, real and personal, belonging to such company or road within the limits of this State, shall be liable to the satisfaction of said judgment. The 8th section provides that no statute of limitations shall be a bar, where the head officer resides out of the State of Tennessee. Laws of Tennessee, 1851-2, 337.

Under this act many suits have already been commenced, and several more likely to be, involving large amounts, and necessarily leading to expensive, annoying and protracted litigation.

In Tennessee, the Magistrates' Courts have jurisdiction for sums as high as fifty dollars. Hence, you will perceive, that the road is liable to be impleaded even in Justice's Courts in Tennessee. Well might my predecessor say: 'We have a right to complain of this proceeding on the part of our neighbors, as it was principally to gratify them that the doors of our own courts were thrown open to claimants against the State Road.' I repeat the complaint, and would ask whether the causes that provoke it are to be perpetual? Can it be believed, that the fraternal and neighborly feelings which should characterize the intercourse of conterminous sister States are to be jeoparded without an effort to prevent it? Can it be possible that Tennessee will persist in a policy which presents the humiliating spectacle of a sovereign State impleaded at the tribunal of a Justice's Court in her own jurisdiction? She will not, if the subject shall be fairly represented before her enlightened representatives. Or, if she should, it is to be hoped that Georgia, animated by a proper sense of self respect, and a regard for her own rights, will adopt such measures of redress or prevention as will save her for the future, from further annoyance.

I would not suggest any harsh action on our part. I would not utter a word which could be construed into a menace. That would be as unworthy of Georgia as it would be unkind to Tennessee. I would advise to do nothing that would endanger our friendly relations with her; but, on the contrary, that we should exhaust every method of courteous negotiation. This is the spirit by which we should be actuated. But, still, this General Assembly should not adjourn, until, in its wisdom, it has adopted the initiatory steps for a friendly negotiation with Tennessee upon this important subject. I therefore, respectfully recommend to the Legislature to designate by law, the location of the head of the Western and Atlantic Railroad, and the place where all suits shall be commenced against it.

I would further submit, respectfully, to the Legislature, that it would be wise to authorize the appointment of one or more commissioners to repair immediately to the Legislature of Tennessee, now in session, with instructions to procure if possible, the repeal of the obnoxious law of February 26th, 1852, and in its place, such reciprocal legislation as would save us from future collision, and perpetuate our fraternal intercourse.

Tennessee has a line of railroad extending into Georgia, over as much or more territory than our State road traverses within her jurisdiction. It is believed, that this fact alone may be made the basis of a successful and happy negotiation. It suggests a very simple and it would seem, a just proposition to Tennessee. Let it be understood and agreed between the two States, that all suits that may be necessary, by the citizens of the one to enforce claims against a railroad, built or chartered by the other, shall be brought in the State that chartered or built the same reciprocally. This will settle the whole difficulty. If this view should strike your minds as sound and judicious, it is believed that it may be carried into effect, by the appointment of the suggested Commission.

This department, however, is wedded to no particular plan. I believe something must be done. It is a matter of paramount importance; and it will afford me great pleasure to co-operate in and zealously to carry into effect, any plan of adjustment with the State of Tennessee, which you in your wisdom may adopt.

HERSCHEL V. JOHNSON"

The Joint Select Committee to which the above Message and accompanying document were referred pleaded justifiably that lack of time before adjournment prevented full and proper consideration of the contents.[119] Upon recommendation of the above committee, the following resolution [120] was adopted:

"*Resolved by the General Assembly of the State of Tennessee*, That his Excellency, the Governor, be authorized to appoint a commissioner, learned in the law, whose duty it shall be to confer with the commissioner appointed by the Governor of Georgia, either here or in the State of Georgia, upon the subject of the intercourse by railroad between the two States, with instructions to report to the General Assembly of this State, all the legislative action that has been had by the two States in reference to this matter; and also, what further legislation, if any, is necessary to preserve the rights of the citizens of Tennessee, and to maintain our friendly relations with Georgia.

Resolved, That his Excellency, the Governor of this State, be instructed to forward a copy of this report to his Excellency, the Governor of Georgia.

WM. H. WISENER,
Speaker of the House of Representatives.
EDWIN POLK,
Speaker of the Senate."

Passed, March 3, 1854.

On March 6, 1854, the Thirtieth General Assembly adjourned *sine die*. The contact between the Executive and Legislative Departments of State terminated, and their respective records passed into history. The closing moments witnessed farewell speeches from Edwin Polk, Speaker of the Senate, and William H. Wisener, Speaker of the House of Representatives. At the conclusion of their remarks, the gavels pounded and the legislative members wended their respective ways homeward, some to return and some relegated to political oblivion. As for the Chief Executive, he remained at the new State Capitol executing the laws and directing the affairs of State. He would have but a short respite from exacting official duties, for within a few months he had to face a strong competitor brought forth by a recently-born political party, the KNOW NOTHING.

---

[119] *Senate Journal*, 1853, Appendix, 275–278.
   House Journal, 1853, Appendix, 275–278.
[120] *Acts of Tennessee*, 1853, Resolution XXII, 798.

The downfall of the Whig Party as a national organization was due to the passage of the Kansas-Nebraska Act and the sectional controversy over slavery in the territories. Out of this conflict arose two new political parties, the Republican Party and the American Party (better known to its contemporaries as the Know-Nothing Party). The Know-Nothing Party sprang from the outgrowth of a secret society called the *Supreme Order of the Star-Spangled Banner* which appealed to voters on the basis of prejudice against foreigners, especially Catholics. There were embodied in the set-up of the Know-Nothing Party a constitution, degrees, passwords, grips, oaths, etc. Only a native-born citizen of the United States and "a Protestant, either born of Protestant parents or reared under Protestant influence and not united in marriage with a Roman Catholic," was eligible for membership in the secret organization.[121] When a casual inquiry was made as to the nature of the organization, the reply was "I know nothing." The secrecy and mystery of its organization and movements lured crowds to its meshes. Free born, frank, manly men, decoyed into its secret conclaves, emerged from them with their souls in fetters and a padlock upon their lips.

The phenomenal growth of the organization was due partly to the charm of *secrecy* with which the party enveloped itself. But more accountable for its rapid growth and expansion was the period in which it thrived. Old party lines had been partially wiped out by the Kansas-Nebraska Act and many voters, unwilling to cast their lot either with pro-slavery Democrats or anti-slavery Republicans, sought and found refuge in the Know-Nothings. In the South, this fledgling party offered political hope to those Whigs who refused to support the new-born Republican Party but would not line up with the old-time Democratic Party. Inasmuch as the Know-Nothing Party was a secret outfit, its first council in Tennessee is not known, but midway of 1854 there was evidence of its political strength in the State. In June of that year, a Know-Nothing mayor and city council were elected in Memphis. In September of the same year, Nashville followed suit by electing a Know-Nothing mayor. Clarksville also elected as mayor an unannounced Know-Nothing.[122]

In 1855, the Know-Nothings threw down the gage of battle to the Democrats in Tennessee by marshaling their strength in a contest for the governorship. Inasmuch as the membership of the organization was secret, no State Convention was held for the nomination of a candidate for Governor. But the old-line Whig newspapers, bitterly opposed to the incumbent Governor, Andrew Johnson, lent aid and comfort to the

---

[121] Cluskey, M. W.: *The Political Textbook*, Twelfth Edition, Philadelphia, 1860, 57–58.

[122] Hamer, Philip M.: *Tennessee—A History*, Volume I, 496.

Know-Nothings by spreading the news throughout the State that Meredith P. Gentry was seemingly the choice of many people for the post held by Johnson. Without the benefit of any convention nomination, Gentry inserted in his local paper, the *Shelbyville Expositor*, the following announcement [123] which was widely copied and hailed with great joy by numerous Whig papers throughout the State:

"Hillside, Bedford County, Feb. 12, 1855.

TO THE PEOPLE OF TENNESSEE:

Fellow Citizens:

Grateful for the generous sentiments expressed for me in the newspapers and private channels, I deem it my duty to respond by announcing that I am a candidate for the office of Governor of Tennessee, at the next election.

Faithfully, your obed't serv't,

M. P. GENTRY."

As will be noted in Gentry's announcement, there was no mention of party or political principles. Not even a skeleton outline of any platform was so much as intimated. He just wanted the job, and was willing to be pitted against the man who had broken the political spear of the redoubtable "Eagle Orator" and had sent him back to Clarksville to private life in the preceding gubernatorial contest, in 1853.

The nomination of Governor Johnson unanimously for re-election was made by the State Democratic Convention which met in Nashville, March 27, 1855. Now that the opposing candidate had been "smoked out" of hiding and was forced to rely upon the support of the Know-Nothings, the Democratic platform turned its heavy artillery in that direction by the following resolves: [124]

"The representatives of the democratic party of Tennessee, in Convention assembled, faithful to the usages of their party, adhering with steadfast faith to the great principles, the successful enforcement of which have made the country powerful and prosperous at home, and honored and respected abroad, do—

Resolve, That the American democracy place their trust in the intelligence, patriotism and the discriminating justice of the American people; and that we regard this as a distinctive feature of our political creed, which we are proud to maintain before the world as the great moral element in a form of government springing from and upheld by the popular will; and we contrast it with the creed and practice of Federalism, under whatever name or form, which seeks to palsy the will of the constituent, and which conceives no imposture too monstrous for the popular credulity.

Resolved, That the democratic party has never hesitated or feared to make an open and candid declaration of its creed and principles; that we regard all secret political clubs as at war with the genius and spirit of our Repub-

---

[123] *The Republican Banner and Nashville Whig,* February 15, 1855.

[124] *Daily Union and American* (Nashville), March 28, 1855.

lican Institutions; that the secret oath bound political club, commonly called the 'Know Nothings,' in its attempts to abridge the rights of conscience and create religious tests in the selection of men for office, is violative of the Constitution and dangerous to the public liberty; that it is but a weak invention of the enemies of the democratic party; and that we will fight this secret enemy with the same energy and ardor which in times past has enabled us to defeat and drive from the field open and undisguised foes.

Resolved, That the democratic party reaffirm those noble truths which are stated in our declaration of rights: 'That all men have a natural and indefeasible right to worship Almighty God according to the dictates of their own conscience; that no man can of right be compelled to attend, erect or support any place of worship, or to maintain any Minister against his consent; that no human authority can, in any case whatever, control or interfere with the rights of conscience; and that no preference shall ever be given, by Law, to any religious establishment or mode of worship. That no religious test shall ever be required as a qualification to any office or public trust under this State."

As if "Americanism" were not a sufficiently "hot" issue in the forthcoming gubernatorial race, an attempt was made to inject the liquor question into the campaign. About a month before the opening of the campaign, the Temperance Committee submitted a questionnaire [125] to the two candidates, to-wit:

"TO THE PUBLIC

At a meeting of the State Temperance Committee, held in Nashville, April 24th, 1855, the following members were present, viz. W. B. Ewing, R. A. Lapsley, J. B. McFerrin, S. S. Hall, Hugh Carroll, J. H. Currey, and N. Davison Cross. The chairman laid before the Committee the following correspondence.

Nashville, March 29, 1855.

Hon. M. P. Gentry:

Sir:—The undersigned were appointed, by the State Temperance Convention, a Committee to propound the following interrogatories to the candidates for the office of Governor of the State of Tennessee, in the approaching canvass, viz:

1. Are you in favor of a law prohibiting the sale of intoxicating liquors as a beverage?

2. Will you, if elected, recommend, in your message to the Legislature, the passage of such a law at an early period in the session?

As you are announced as a candidate for said office we addressed you this note, requesting you to answer the above interrogatories at an early day.

A copy of the above has been sent to the Hon. Andrew Johnson.

W. B. Ewing,
H. Carroll,
S. S. Hall,
J. H. Currey,
J. B. McFerrin.

---

[125] *Daily Gazette* (Nashville), April 28, 1855.

MR. GENTRY'S ANSWER.

Hillside, April 3, 1855.

To Messrs. W. B. Ewing, Hugh Carroll, S. S. Hall, J. B. McFerrin, and J. H. Currey.

GENTLEMEN:—Yours of the 29th of March came to hand yesterday. You inform me that you were appointed by the State Temperance Convention a Committee to propound the following interrogatories to the candidates for the State of Tennessee, in the approaching canvass, viz:

1. 'Are you in favor of a law prohibiting the sale of intoxicating liquors as a beverage?

2. 'Will you, if elected, recommend, in your message to the Legislature, the passage of such a law at an early period in the session? And you request me 'to answer the above question at an early day.' I proceed promptly to comply with your request, by stating unequivocally what will be my recommendation to the Legislature, on the subject of your letter, in the event of my election to the office of Governor of Tennessee.

I will recommend the enactment of a law prohibiting the sale of intoxicating liquors, in small quantities, except license shall have been obtained for that privilege—which license shall be issued by the Clerk of the County Court, only in cases where application shall be made for the same in writing, signed by the person applying, and by a majority of the qualified voters of the civil district within which he proposes to retail spirituous liquors. A law founded upon this general principle, embracing in its details provisions for its efficient execution, would, in my opinion, speedily put an end to tippling in most of the civil districts of the State—and, at no distant day, in all of them; and would be more effective in repressing the evils resulting from the immoderate use of intoxicating liquors, than any other that has been suggested theoretically, or experimentally tested in this State.—Moral reform by this process, being accomplished by the people, acting for themselves in every civil district, would be in harmony with the spirit of our free institutions, and a beautiful illustration of the republican doctrine that man is capable of self-government; and would, therefore, be durable.

If all those who are aiming at a common object with respect to a remedy for the evils resulting from the immoderate use of intoxicating liquors, would concentrate their exertions during the approaching canvass in favor of this policy, I believe their efforts would be crowned with success, by the enactment, at the next session of the Legislature, of such a law as I have indicated; and great good would be accomplished. By aiming at more, it is highly probable that nothing will be achieved. But, gentlemen, you know full well that the Constitution of Tennessee does not confer upon the Governor of the State the power to veto acts of the Legislature; nor invest him with patronage to influence the deliberations of that body. I think, therefore, that the interrogatories propounded to me, by you, would be more appropriately addressed to candidates for the Legislature. I have responded only to exhibit my respect for you, and that numerous and highly respectable body of citizens whom you represent.

Respectfully, your obedient servant

M. P. GENTRY.

GOVERNOR JOHNSON'S ANSWER.

Nashville, April 29, 1855.

GENTLEMEN:—Your letter of the 20th ultimo, propounding two interrogatories to me, in reference to the passage of a law, by the next Legislature, prohibiting the sale of intoxicating liquors as a beverage, has been received.

The first of which is as follows:

'Are you in favor of a law prohibiting the sale of intoxicating liquors as a beverage?'

The second:—'Will you, if elected, recommend to the Legislature the passage of such a law at an early period in the session?

I am not sure that I understand the precise import of the first interrogatory; but if a resolution adopted by the Convention of the friends of Temperance in Davidson County on the 14th of February last, and by which Convention all of you were appointed delegates to the State Temperance Convention which was to sit on the 22d of February, is to be taken as a correct interpretation of the first interrogatory which you have propounded to me, and is as follows:

'Resolved, That as friends of temperance reform, and of the community in which we reside, we pledge ourselves to vote for no man; for either branch of the Legislature, who does not advocate and support the principles of the *Maine Law;* in other words, a law *prohibiting* the *manufacture* of, and traffic in alcoholic liquors, with the necessary provisions and penalties for the enforcement of the same, and the enactment of such a law at an early day of the next Legislature of Tennessee.'—

I understand you as asking me directly whether I am for or against a law commonly denominated the '*Maine Liquor Law.*' If this is the interrogatory which you have propounded to me, I answer directly and explicitly that I am not in favor of the '*Maine Liquor Law*' as the *mode* by which the excessive use and sale of intoxicating liquors are to be prohibited as a beverage; believing, as I do, that some of the leading provisions of that law are incompatible with the rights and privileges of freemen, and as coming in conflict with the spirit, if not the very letter of the Constitution of the State: and, if elected Governor of the State, cannot recommend the passage of such a law to the next Legislature.

I hope that I have succeeded in making myself understood, and that my answer may be entirely satisfactory.

I will add, that your letter would have been answered before this, but for the press of official and other engagements, which prevented me from reaching it in its proper order until the present date.

I have the honor to be, most respectfully,

ANDREW JOHNSON.

To W. B. Ewing, Esq., Hugh Carroll, Esq., S. S. Hall, Esq., Rev. J. B. Mcferrin, J. H. Currey, Esq., Committee, &c.

The Committee are free in stating that neither the answer of one nor the other of these gentlemen is satisfactory. The one opposes what is called the 'Maine Law'—a law by the way, which is not mentioned in our letter to him, or, as we understand him, he is opposed to a law prohibiting the sale of intoxicating drinks. The other, we think, advocates a system which, though good, does not go far enough—does not strike at the root of the evil. We advocate *total prohibition.* In view, however, of all the facts before us, and the circumstances surrounding us, we deem it inexpedient to call a Convention for the nomination of a separate candidate for Governor, but we recommend the friends of prohibition to nominate and vote for candidates for the Legislature who will pledge themselves, if elected, to vote for the enactment of a law prohibiting the sale of intoxicating drinks as a beverage.

W. B. EWING, *Chairman.*

Hugh Carroll, Sec'y."

The opening gun was fired on May 1, at Murfreesboro, with a tremendous and excited crowd on hand to witness the two giants lock horns in what proved to be in all probability the most bitterly contested gubernatorial race in the annals of Tennessee history up to that time. According to agreement, Johnson opened the speaking with a two-hour speech in which he twitted his competitor with having abandoned the Whig party by which he had been honored time and time again. Knowing full well that Gentry must rely largely upon old-line Whigs for support, Johnson recalled to his audience Gentry's former blast at the Whig Party:

"I am seeking to reform, purify, and nationalize the party; and when I have made an honest effort for that object and fail, then the next highest debt which I shall deem incumbent upon me will be to destroy it as thoroughly as I can. And I will perform it to the utmost extent of my power, and if the declaration which I have made be treason, make the most of it."

At the conclusion of the above quote from a Gentry speech, Johnson turned toward his opponent and tauntingly inquired:

"Has my competitor now come forward to thoroughly destroy the Whig Party?"

After Johnson had pronounced Gentry as a traitor to his party, as the advocate of a radical liquor law, and as the sponsor of the assumption of State debts by the Federal Government, he then turned his battery upon the Know-Nothings. Terrible invectives, sarcasm, and defiance were the ingredients of Johnson's characterizations of the *secret order*. In all Johnson's public career, he probably never surpassed his denunciations of the new-born organization which he maintained was at war with most fundamental principles of the democratic way of life. The Editor of the *Nashville Daily Union and American* was present and sketched the two-hour bombardment which Johnson delivered with devastating effect. The climax of Johnson's denunciations were thus reported by Editor E. G. Eastman:[126]

"But the watch-word of the Syren song now sung by this new Order is, that 'Americans must rule America.' Gov. J. said that he was not only for Americans ruling Americans, but he was for Americans ruling foreigners also. He had been taught to understand that in this government the people ruled, and that in filling the offices which they had created in the formation of their

---

[126] *Daily Union and American*, May 3, 1855.

Constitution, and the laws passed in conformity thereto, they were merely appointing agents or servants to transact and perform the duties which they had prescribed in the Constitution and laws, and in the selection of these agents, they had a right to elect those that they deemed most efficient and faithful to the law and the Constitution, whether native or foreign born. This he considered was Americans ruling America; or, in other words, the people controlling the action of the government according to their own will and judgment.

Gov. Johnson then took up the pretended opposition of the know-nothings to Catholicism, and contended that it was the veriest hypocrisy on their part. So far as he was concerned, on that occasion, it was not his intention to interfere with any of the numerous religious denominations that prevail in this country, but to leave them all where the Constitutions of the United States and the States had placed them, believing in and yielding his full credence to the doctrine that all men have a natural and indefeasible right to worship Almighty God according to the dictates of their own conscience. He was for no established religion—no Union of Church and State,—but for their remaining separate and distinct. He said that, if he understood correctly, and he thought he did, the position of the know-nothings, that there were but two inferences to be drawn from it: one was the Union of Church and State, the other was, the overthrow of all religion and the establishment of Atheism and infidelity upon its ruins. The know nothings assume the bold and broad proposition that a Catholic is disqualified from holding office on account of his religious tenets. If a Catholic is incompetent and disqualified on account of his religious tenets, the opposite of the proposition must be true and assumed at the same time, that the individual who is qualified must profess the religious tenets and principles necessary to qualify him to hold office, which was at once making a religious test the qualification. This being so, the party that is strong enough to put down one sect, on account of their objectionable tenets, would be strong enough to put up another on account of their acceptable and approved religious principles. This being so, is a practical union of church and State, and would in a short time be followed by legislative enactments making it the established church or religion of the land.

We will assume now that the Catholics have been disfranchised and excluded from any participation in the offices of the country. He put the question to the different branches of the Protestant church throughout the United States, which one of them would be the fortunate and favored church by this Know Nothing order. He said that as he had remarked in the introduction of this portion of the subject, there were but two inferences to be drawn from their position, and if the conclusion he had just reached was not a correct one, that they intended a union of Church and State, the other was inevitable, that is, the establishment of Atheism and Infidelity. And the means they were now adopting were not so bold and direct as they were in the French revolution. There the attack was directly upon the Bible, believing if the main trunk was struck in its most vital parts, that the scions would all fall to the ground, and thereby the religion of Christ and the teachings of the Bible become extinct. Here their mode of warfare is more insidious; they are afraid to attack the Bible direct and array all religious denominations against them, but attack that branch of the church, the Catholic, which they believe is most unpopular with all others, and against which deep-rooted prejudices exist. The war is now upon Catholicism, inviting all the branches of the Protestant church to unite with them in this crusade of persecution. We will suppose they have done so, and that Catholics are now out of the way. The crusade has commenced, but has it ended? Will the work of demolition stop here? The nostrils of the persecutor being once distended with the scent of the blood of the persecuted, will he stop at this point, or will the work progress? We say that it will go on, and the Methodist, Presbyterian, Baptist, or some other denomination will be selected as the next work of persecution. The Catholics having been prostrated will then join with the persecutor and help to perpetrate the same work upon others that has been perpetrated upon them; and so the work will progress, between the persecutor and the persecuted, or until the various churches have destroyed each other, and thereby the Know Nothings accomplish stealthily and covertly what they dare not attempt openly and boldly—the destruction of all the churches in the United States, leaving the Bible in existence, barren and unproductive. Atheism and Infidelity now having full sway, we may now prepare to see re-enacted the sanguinary scenes of the French revolution. He said there, when the Bible and religion had been put down, Atheism and Infidelity, sometimes called Reason, were in the ascendant. The Bible condemned and scouted as a fable and an idle tale, and to make the demonstration more perfect and complete, a female was selected as the Goddess of Reason, and seated upon a chair, festooned with ivy. She was attired in white, a sky-blue mantle gracefully thrown upon her shoulders, the chair borne by four of the most respectable and intelligent citizens, preceded and succeeded by a large concourse of females dressed in white, the mass moving along in thousands, until the Metropolitan Cathedral was reached, and then the Goddess of Reason was elevated to the throne and the crown was placed upon her head, 'with luxuriant ringlets hanging in graceful negligence around her neck and shoulders.' This, he said, was the triumph of Atheism and Infidelity.

Gov. Johnson said he could not believe that the Protestant church of this country would join in such an unholy crusade, which would result in the end of their own overthrow and carry us back to the revolutionary times of infidel France, when the hoof of the cavalry horse was saturated in human gore, and liberty went staggering from the struggle through carnage and blood.

The Know-Nothings were opposed to the Catholic religion because it was of foreign origin, and many of its members in this country were foreigners also. He said that if it was a valid objection to tolerating the Catholic religion in this country, because it was of foreign origin and many of its members were foreigners, we would be compelled to expel most of the other religions of the country for the same reason. Who, he asked, was JOHN WESLEY and where did the Methodist religion have its origin? It was in old England, and JOHN WESLEY was an Englishman. But if JOHN WESLEY, were alive to day, and here in this country, Know Nothingism would drive him and his religion back to England, whence they came, because they were foreign. Who, he asked, was JOHN CALVIN, and where did Calvinism take its rise? Was it not Geneva? And were CALVIN alive this new Order would send him and his doctrines back, whence they came. Who, he asked, was ROGER WILLIAMS? And would not ROGER WILLIAMS and the Baptists share the same fate? And so with MARTIN LUTHER, the great reformer. He would be subjected to the same proscriptive test.

If Know-Nothingism could be carried out as assumed by its authors it would expel every foreign religion beyond the limits of the United States; in fact, if its great aim was not the establishment of Atheism and infidelity, it would adapt some religion that was purely native in its origin and indigenous to our soil, which he supposed would be, *Mormonism*, as that was purely American. Mormonism, as he supposed, was to become the religious standard of the Government, by which the consciences of men were to be measured, and those that thought a little more than the Mormon standard would have to be cut off, and those that thought a little less would have to be stretched out and made to conform to this Mormon standard of *religion* and *morals*.

The ridiculous absurdity and inconsistency to which such doctrines lead must be apparent to all. This subject may be turned and twisted in every way that the inventive mind of man may suggest, and there was but one doctrine that was right and sound after all, and that was, let all men worship God in their own way, according to the dictates of their consciences. Men will differ in their religious feeling and opinions. It was as natural for them to do so, as it was for them to differ in the color of their hair, or in the expression of their countenances. These differences of opinion must be tolerated if we expect the mind and conscience of men to be free. Charles the Fifth, the Emperor of Germany, when tired of the cares of State, resigned his vast possessions to his son and retired to a Monastery, and there, to amuse the evening of his life, undertook the regulation of watches, and after many experiments, patience and perseverance, found it impossible to make any two of them keep precisely the same time. This led him to reflect upon the crime and folly he had committed while Emperor, in attempting to make men think alike. Hence, he said, he was disposed to tolerate all religions, leaving it a matter to be settled between the professor and his God.

Gov. J. said that he thought the danger apprehended by many from the toleration of the Catholic religion in a free government, was more imaginary than real. He said that *San Marino*, situated in Italy, is now the *oldest republic* in the world. This republic was founded by *Marino*, who was a stone mason by trade and a Catholic in religion, more than *fifteen hundred years* ago, and it has stood upon its rocky summit, two thousand feet above the elevation of the sea, undisturbed and composed amid the rising and falling of surrounding empires; and the Catholic had been the principal religion enjoyed by the people of that republic from its foundation by Marino to the present period of time.

For himself, he said, that he apprehended no very great danger from the few Catholics which were in this State, their whole number being some *fourteen hundred*, with *three* churches for their accommodation. The whole number of Protestants being some *six hundred and twenty four thousand two hundred and ninety-five*, with *two thousand and eleven* churches for their accommodation. He could not believe that there was any sane minded man in all the length and breadth of all Tennessee, who could think or believe for one moment that it was necessary to form and have *secret political* organizations, bound together by *terrible* and *penal oaths*, for the purpose of putting down *fourteen hundred* professors of the Catholic religion in the midst of a Protestant population numbering *seven hundred and fifty six thousand eight hundred and thirty-six*. The simple facts were so glaring in themselves that further remark upon this point was unnecessary.

Gov. Johnson demanded to know what was the religion of this know-nothing order? what religion did they profess? what system of morals did they teach? Were they believers in Jesus Christ? do they acknowledge the doctrine of the orthodox church? what right have they to make war upon the religion of others, when they profess none themselves? The Devil, his Satanic Majesty, the Prince of Darkness, who presides over the *secret conclave* held in Pandemonium, make war upon all branches of Christ's church. The know-nothings advocate and defend none, but make war upon one of the churches, and thus far become the allies of the Prince of Darkness.

A denomination like this, to set up as the guardian of the religion and morals of the country! A denomination bound together by *secret* and TERRIBLE OATHS, the first of which on the very initiation fixes and requires them to carry a lie in their mouths! They are solemnly sworn upon the Holy Bible, before Almighty God 'that they will not divulge any question proposed to them, whether they become members or not; that they will never under any circumstances mention the name of any person or persons they see present, nor that they know such an organization to be in existence.' If the question is asked of a member of this order whether such an order is in existence or not, or whether he is a member thereof, he is sworn not to divulge it, and lies if he omits to tell the omission, being an admission that it does exist and that he is a member; and if he admits that it does exist and that he is a member he tells which he has sworn not to divulge. This is the substance of the oath that the members of this order take on their first entrance into the *secret midnight conclaves.*

The applicant for admission is then asked the following questions:
'Were you born within the limits or jurisdiction of the United States?
'In religious belief are you a Roman Catholic?
'Have you or have you not, been reared under protestant influence?
'Are or were either of your parents Roman Catholics in religious belief?
'Is your wife a Roman Catholic?
'Are you willing to use your influence and vote only for native born American citizens for all the offices of honor or trust in the gift of the people, to the exclusion of all foreigners and aliens, and of Roman Catholics in particular, and without regard to party predilection?'

This is the ordeal through which the candidate has to pass. Having now made himself a slave by declaring under the solemn sanction of an oath, that he would use all his influence and vote as required without regard to party predilection. The candidate having advanced thus far, is prepared to take the second oath, a part of which is as follows:

'You will in all things political or social, so far as this order is concerned comply with the will of the majority, when expressed in a lawful manner, though it may conflict with your personal preference.'

We perceive, as the members of this Order advance in degrees, that they cease, in a corresponding proportion, to be freemen, and are compelled to obey the commands of a majority. The oath then continues:

'You furthermore promise and declare that you will not vote nor give your influence for any man, for any office in the gift of the people, unless he be an American born citizen, in favor of Americans ruling America, nor if he be a Roman Catholic, and that you will not, under any circumstances, *expose the name of any member of this Order, nor reveal the existence of such an Organization.*'

He then went on and stated that he would show the process by which these *secret conclaves* were convened for the purpose of disposing of public business.

He then read as follows from their Constitution:

'Public notice for mass meetings is given by means of a right angle triangular piece of paper, white in color. If information is wanted of the object of the gathering, or the place, &c., the inquirer will ask of an undoubted brother only, 'Have you seen SAM today?' The reply will be—'Go to...., at....o'clock.' A piece of paper, red in color, will signify suspected danger. If the color is red, with an equilateral triangular piece cut out, it will denote actual trouble; which requires that you come prepared to meet it. These notices, or calabistic signs are posted up or thrown out by the members, by the direction of the President, which is required to be done between *midnight and one hour before daybreak.'*

From midnight to one hour before day-break, is the time for these notices to be given. The time at which bats retire to their hiding places, and hyenas go forth in quest of dead bodies, upon which to prey. This is the party or order which assumes to take charge of the religion and politics of this country. These are the men who are to be seen in the night, some with, and others without, dark lanterns, winding their way through alleys and dark passages, with none but dim, glimmering lights to guide their steps to the places of their *secret conclave*, and there to determine upon the *religion* and *politics* of a free people! He could not believe that the freemen of Tennessee would ever consign their destinies to the hands and care of such an Order or party as that.

Gov. Johnson said that it was not his intention, as he had before remarked, to interfere with any one of the religious denominations of the country, but to leave them upon that basis where they had been placed by the Constitution and law; but he felt like calling upon all religious denominations, as well as those outside of the church, to unite with him in helping to expel from our midst this, the greatest of all political heresies that have ever been attempted to be imposed upon a free people. He called upon them now, to at once disarm these janizarian cohorts, or the day is not distant when they will have to prepare their necks for the bow-string and the scimeter.

Gov. Johnson continued, by saying that his remarks had been intended on that occasion, more for the purpose of presenting facts, and some of the positions he intended to occupy during the canvass, in obedience to the will of the people, as reflected through their delegates in convention, than to make a regular speech. The very fact of his being presented by them as their standard bearer, was strong proof that they relied more upon the correctness of their principles and the justness of their cause, than in his ability to advocate them. In compliance with what he believed was their wish, he accepted their ensign, upon which they had inscribed, 'the people are capable of self-government, and have the right and capacity to determine the *nature* and character of their own institutions in the formation of their State Constitution. No religious tests as a qualification to office. All men have a natural and indefeasible right to worship Almighty God according to the dictates of their own conscience.' 'Freedom of the press—liberty of speech—and the right of conscience.'

These principles, inscribed by the people upon their Standard, and by them placed in my hands, (said Gov. Johnson,) shall be defended by me from this day to the first Thursday in August next, with whatever of ability I may be possessed, physical and mental. I intend to stand by them in the heat and the dust—in the sun and the rain—though fatigued and wearied, I may become from the arduous task I have undertaken, yet I will not shrink from it, though the sword of my spirit cuts through the scabbard."

Posterity is not so fortunate as to have any detailed report of Gentry's speech in reply to Johnson's opening address of the campaign. Editor Henry Maney, of the Nashville *Daily Gazette*, was also present on the occasion, but his account is almost wholly a resumé of his own reaction. He admitted that "he lost sight of his duty as reporter," and as a consequence only a bird's-eye view of Gentry's speech is available in the form of "glittering generalities." A summation of the general tenor of Gentry's speech was chronicled by Editor Maney as follows:[127]

"As to his own past quarrels with any party he forgot and forgave them all—expected them to be forgotten and forgiven by those with whom he had quarrelled. He came out as the candidate of neither Whig nor Democratic party—but as the candidate of the people of Tennessee.

He then proceeded to the discussion of the cardinal principles of the American party, taking them up one by one and advocating them in a manner that for one hour held that vast assembly spell-bound with silent, eager attention. Seldom have we heard, or read, so able a vindication, or so able an advocacy.—The shouts of applause that had interspersed the previous portion of his speech were hushed, and a breathless interest seemed pervading the entire mass of his hearers. Our readers will forgive the omission of a sketch of his argument. So absorbed were we in the clear and lucid, eloquent and unanswerable exposition of the principles of the party, we lost sight of our duty as reporter.

His time being out, Governor Johnson arose to the privilege of his half hour's rejoinder. The straight jacket that Gentry had placed upon him, had stimulated the Governor to a high pitch of excitement, and the rejoinder was far better than the first speech, which, in our candid opinion, was an emphatic failure.

A heavy shower now came up, and as much of the crowd as could squeeze within the walls, entered the Court House to hear the reply of Col. Gentry. Some misunderstanding had occurred between the speakers, and an intense excitement ensued on the part of the audience. The discussion however was amicably closed, and the assembly dispersed.

We have waited with much patience, and with much expectation for the opening of the Gubernatorial canvass. We have maintained silence thus far, with regard to any preference as to who should be the candidate of the American party in this campaign. But having heard the advocacy of Col. Gentry, knowing him, in every personal and constitutional respect, qualified to run and to serve as the American Governor, we here approve his course, and in token thereof have this day set his name at the head of our columns. Disentangled from all association with any party, fearless as was ever Henry Clay himself, gallant, gifted and generous, no better selection could be made by the American party. Even his opponent has cut him off from co-operation with the old Whig party; and good democrats, not members of the American order, impressed with the high-bearing, the unbending integrity, the acknowledged talents of Meredith P. Gentry, will extend to him their cordial support. Opposed to a man, whose wild and ultra notions, whose domineering demagogueism, whose arrogant dictation has rendered him obnoxious, not only to his opponents, but to his former friends and supporters, who will, in point of fact, rejoice at any method of unburdening themselves of his political sins and party domination, what true man in Tennessee will not cheerfully rally to the standard of the American party, so well and so gallantly borne in the hands of Meredith P. Gentry? The one appeals to the intelligence, to the conservatism, to the patriotism of the people of Tennessee for his support. He is honest, he is faithful, he is efficient. The other appeals to the partizanship, to the prejudice, to the lowest instincts of the populace for his support. He is shrewd, he is cunning, he is ambitious, and, if he could, would be tyrannical. Look at the two men. The one of approved truth and magnanimity—wedded to principle and not to party—a sterling, honest, able man. The other of

_____

[127] *Daily Gazette*, (Nashville), May 3, 1855.

known demagogueism—wedded to faction and self-interest, a bold, determined dictator. Which will the people of Tennessee, without respect to party, support. The ballot box in August next will tell."

Slavery and prohibition were issues in the campaign, but the political gladiators spent a major portion of their time on Know-Nothingism. An agreed-upon list of sixty places for joint speakings were published in numerous newspapers throughout the State, the dates running from May 1 to August 1, inclusive. Many of the Whig papers featured Johnson's terrible attacks upon the Know-Nothings, frequently displaying them at the mast head of the editorial column, to-wit:[128]

"THE DEVIL, HIS SATANIC MAJESTY, THE PRINCE OF DARKNESS, WHO PRESIDES OVER THE SECRET CONCLAVE HELD IN PANDEMONIUM, MAKES WAR UPON ALL BRANCHES OF CHRIST'S CHURCH. THE KNOW NOTHINGS ADVOCATE AND DEFEND NONE, BUT MAKE WAR UPON ONE OF THE CHURCHES, AND THUS FAR BECOME THE ALLIES OF THE PRINCE OF DARKNESS. (Speech of Andrew Johnson, at Murfreesboro.)

A DENOMINATION LIKE THIS, TO SET UP AS THE GUARDIANS OF THE RELIGION AND MORALS OF THE COUNTRY! A DENOMINATION BOUND TOGETHER BY SECRET AND TERRIBLE OATHS, THE FIRST OF WHICH, ON THE VERY INITIATION, FIXES AND REQUIRES THEM TO CARRY A LIE IN THEIR MOUTHS! (Speech of Andrew Johnson, at Murfreesboro.)

SHOW ME THE DIMENSIONS OF A KNOW NOTHING, AND I WILL SHOW YOU A HUGE REPTILE, UPON WHOSE NECK THE FOOT OF EVERY HONEST MAN OUGHT TO BE PLACED. (Speech of Andrew Johnson, at Manchester.)

THEY ARE LIKE THE HYENA, AND COME FROM THEIR LAIR AFTER MIDNIGHT TO PREY UPON HUMAN CARCASSES. (Speech of Andrew Johnson, at Manchester.)

I WOULD AS SOON BE FOUND IN THE CLAN OF JOHN A. MURRELL AS IN A KNOW NOTHING COUNCIL. (Speech of Andrew Johnson, at Manchester.)"

At long last, the Ides of August rolled around and the battle came to a weary end. Johnson was victor over Gentry by a majority of 2,167 votes.[129]

The vote of counties gave the following results:[130]

---

[128] *Nashville True Whig*, May 15, 1855.

[129] *House Journal*, 1855, 85–86.

Author's note. The official majority for Johnson was given as 2,157, when the official count was made and declared in a Joint Convention of both branches of the Legislature on October 11, 1855. Later in the day, it was pointed out that an error of ten votes in favor of Gentry had been made in the returns from Giles County. When correction had been made, Johnson's actual majority was 2,167 votes. See *House Journal*, 1855, page 98.

[130] *Senate Journal*, 1855, 43.
House Journal, 1855, 85–86.

Counties	Andrew Johnson	Meredith P. Gentry	Counties	Andrew Johnson	Meredith P. Gentry
"Anderson	333	772	Lawrence	845	524
Bedford	1,293	1,630	Lewis	243	34
Benton	453	475	Lincoln	2,521	402
Bledsoe	361	404	Macon	424	540
Blount	789	1,069	Madison	788	1,448
Bradley	1,021	644	Marion	468	554
Campbell	383	507	Marshall	1,310	678
Cannon	859	458	Maury	1,793	1,444
Carroll	694	1,567	Meigs	588	97
Carter	238	768	Monroe	1,005	851
Claiborne	744	756	Montgomery	881	1,502
Cocke	422	929	Morgan	358	219
Coffee	880	294	McMinn	953	909
Davidson	1,783	3,132	McNairy	1,059	915
Decatur	429	353	Obion	865	407
DeKalb	738	560	Overton	1,528	290
Dickson	745	388	Perry	450	320
Dyer	483	442	Polk	676	385
Fayette	940	1,151	Rhea	415	298
Fentress	616	129	Roane	769	1,002
Franklin	1,302	394	Robertson	804	1,256
Gibson	1,213	1,618	Rutherford	1,288	1,435
Giles	1,439	1,312	Scott	259	121
Grainger	621	1,327	Sevier	120	964
Green	1,985	989	Shelby	1,477	1,831
Grundy	425	22	Smith	644	1,572
Hamilton	1,044	966	Stewart	785	563
Hancock	589	264	Sullivan	1,403	601
Hardeman	1,123	619	Sumner	1,740	780
Hardin	775	745	Tipton	566	424
Hawkins	1,158	887	Van Buren	228	90
Haywood	762	803	Warren	1,153	393
Henderson	734	1,230	Washington	1,338	847
Henry	1,738	871	Wayne	535	687
Hickman	1,053	223	Weakley	1,411	885
Humphreys	543	354	White	694	978
Jackson	1,131	1,122	Williamson	688	1,621
Jefferson	444	1,697	Wilson	937	2,290
Johnson	215	400			
Knox	695	2,560			
Lauderdale	297	354			
Total				67,499	65,343

Majority for Johnson, 2,157."

In comparison with the gubernatorial race in 1853, a survey discloses that Johnson had gained strength in Middle and West Tennessee
but had lost strength in East Tennessee. What were the factors that

contributed to the defeat of Gentry, unquestionably one of the ablest men in Tennessee at the time and one of its most polished orators? There can be no question but that Johnson's terrific attack upon Know-Nothingism and Gentry's relatively weak defense constituted the pivotal point upon which the campaign hinged. An exceedingly able commentator, who was a strong political opponent of Johnson, summed up the results of the first meeting of Johnson and Gentry at Murfreesboro as follows:[131]

"... The result, therefore, of this first debate was unfavorable to Gentry. His friends went away disappointed and discouraged.... With Johnson's fearful arraignment of the secret order and oath-bound party, and the apparently half-hearted defense made of it by Gentry, its friends became despondent and timid all over the State. On the other hand, Johnson's daring assaults had filled his friends with the highest courage and enthusiasm.... When Andrew Johnson began thundering his terrible denunciations against it (Know-Nothingism), calling upon all honest men to come out of the midnight dens of this wicked party, Democrats all over the State commenced hurriedly tumbling out of the order, so great was their haste to escape odium.... There is in the minds of a majority of men a widespread and deepseated prejudice against secret, oath-bound organizations. It was especially so at that time, and Johnson by his furious and vindictive denunciations intensified this feeling. Every Catholic in the State, as well as some foreign-born citizens not Catholics, voted against Gentry. These, with those who could not support a secret organization, must have amounted to at least three thousand votes...."

Another factor, the effect of which can not be determined, that contributed to Gentry's defeat was a public letter published in numerous newspapers throughout the State. The letter was by Whig Ex-Governor James C. Jones, who was at the time United States Senator. In the lengthy letter,[132] Jones expressed strong opposition to Know-Nothingism on account of its religious intolerance. "I will enter no crusade," said his letter, "against any religious denomination. Our boast is that this is a land of religious freedom and toleration. What sort of freedom is that which ostracises a large class of our citizens both native and foreign for mere religion's sake." Underneath and behind the motives that inspired the letter was the personal and political hostility existing between the two men. They had been "in each other's hair" politically for more than a decade, and "Lean Jimmy" did not forego the opportunity of taking a blast at an issue that would do damage to his foe. As intimated, there is no way whereby the effect of the Jones communication can be measured, but it is inconceivable that an expression from the man who had twice defeated James K. Polk for Governor and was at present a Whig United States Senator went unheeded by many of his thousands of Whig friends and supporters in Tennessee.

Although the Whigs had been defeated in the gubernatorial race,

---

[131] Temple, Oliver P.: *Notable Men of Tennessee*, 386–390.
[132] *Nashville True Whig*, June 5, 1855.

they salvaged a part of their efforts in the congressional and legislative
contests. Out of the ten Congressmen, the Know-Nothings elected six.
In the State Legislature, the State Senate was composed of thirteen
Know-Nothings and one Whig, while the Democrats could muster
up only eleven. The House of Representatives was a *melange* whose
political ingredients were difficult to determine. According to a contemporary newspaper,[133] the Democrats had thirty-eight members, the
Know-Nothings thirty-four, and the Whigs three. In a joint convention of both houses, the Democrats could muster but forty-nine votes,
while a combination of Whigs and Know-Nothings produced a total of
fifty-one. What contributed further to the confusion was that Senator
A. P. Hall, though listed among the Know-Nothings, was known to
be an old-line Whig, and Whig Representative M. J. Galloway was
classified as *anti* Know-Nothing. And there remained two members
definitely classified as WHIGS, M. M. Brien of DeKalb County, and
J. R. Rudd, of Monroe. With such a political mixture, nose-counting
was indeed a fine art and political prophecies were hazardous indeed!

The foregoing aggregation, comprising the personnel of the Thirty-
First General Assembly, convened in Nashville on October 1, 1855.
On the second ballot, Know-Knothing Senator Edward S. Cheatham
from the counties of Robertson, Montgomery, and Stewart was elected
Speaker.[134] In the House, it was quite a different story. Throughout
three days, forty-five ballots were taken for Speaker without any
election. On October 4, the following resolution [135] by Know-Nothing
Representative Robert Hatton of Wilson County was introduced and
adopted:

"Whereas, The interests of the State require the speedy organization of
this House, and a prompt discharge of the duties devolved upon us as Representatives of the people; and, whereas, three days have been spent in fruitless
efforts to elect a Speaker of this House, and forty-five ineffectual ballots have
rendered it wholly improbable that said officer can be chosen in accordance
with the practice heretofore prevailing, of requiring a majority of all the
votes cast to elect, Therefore, for the purpose of enabling this House to make
said election—
Be it Resolved, That the House will proceed immediately to the election
of a Speaker, *viva voce;* and if, after the roll shall have been called three
times, no member shall have received a majority of the whole number of
votes, the roll shall again be called, and the member who shall then receive the
largest number of votes, provided it be a majority of a quorum, shall be declared to be chosen Speaker."

The forty-sixth, forty-seventh, and forty-eighth ballots resulted

133 *Union and American* (Nashville), September 30, 1855.
Author's note. Most writers of Tennessee history have omitted or glossed over
the *political* complexion of the 1855 General Assembly. Its composition practically
defies analysis.
134 *Senate Journal,* 1855, 5.
135 *House Journal,* 1855, 24.

in no election. Thereupon, the House proceeded to ballot for the forty-ninth time whereupon Neill S. Brown, former Whig Governor of Tennessee, received a plurality of the votes cast and under the Hatton resolution was declared elected Speaker of the House. This was the first time in the history of Tennessee that a Speaker of either branch of the Legislature had been elected by a plurality vote instead of a majority vote.

Upon the forty-ninth and final ballot, the three Whig members, Brien, Galloway, and Rudd, joined the Know-Nothings and put Know-Nothing Neill S. Brown in the Speaker's chair.[136] And so, the Know-Nothings had succeeded in controlling the Speakership in each legislative branch.

On October 23, 1855, the inaugural ceremonies were conducted in the Hall of Representatives in the State Capitol. Governor Andrew Johnson, who was also Governor-elect, delivered a brief inaugural address,[137] after which the oath of office was administered by Honorable William R. Harris, one of the Judges of the Supreme Court. Governor Johnson has the distinction of having been the first Governor to be inaugurated in the State Capitol.

"Gentlemen of the Senate, of the
House of Representatives, and Fellow Citizens:

It is not my purpose on the present occasion to make an address to you. Two years ago I presented in the form of an Inaugural address my views in regard to National and State policy, which I thought then ought to be pursued, and would now, if it were necessary, reiterate and endorse them as sound and correct. They were my views and sentiments then, they are mine now, and I have been confirmed in them by reflection and experience. The leading and fundamental principles of Democracy were then laid down, constituting, as they do, the four great cardinals of my political creed. They are inherent and self-existing in the nature of man, and will cease to exist only with man's total annihilation from the earth. They were *taught* and *practised* by the founder of our holy religion, and they will have followers and advocates so long as His precepts and example are respected and received by the civilized world, as being of Divine origin.

The Democratic Party of the Nation is now passing through a severe and trying ordeal, contending with an enemy that comes as

---

[136] *Ibid.*, 27.
[137] *Nashville True Whig*, October 24, 1855.

a thief in the night, cautious and subtile in its approach, noiseless in its footsteps, and swift in its progress: in its transitory pause exerting an influence upon the morals, religion and politics of the country as withering and deadly in its effects as the poisonous emission of the Upas tree is upon all animal life. But Democracy has heretofore passed similar ordeals; and it will, as I confidently believe, as it has done on former occasions, rise from the present contest purer and stronger than at any former period of our country's history. The people have heard the struggle that has been going on; they have been aroused to a sense of the great danger that surrounds and threatens our instiutions; they are in their might coming up to the rescue, and will save the country and preserve the Constitution from a practical violation of some of its most essential provisions. Democracy knows, and it is to be expected, too, that every plan, effort, and undertaking that has a tendency to improve and to elevate the great mass of the people, is naturally inclined to excite the ill will and opposition of those in possession of considerable extra learning, wealth, and power, or those who contend for undue advantages over their fellow men. It is important, therefore, always to bear in mind, that whatever tends substantially to benefit the common people, will be generally viewed with hostility by the pseudo aristocracy of the country. Hence, genuine Christianity and Democracy, both originate with, and have mainly been supported by, men of humble origin, circumstances, and situations, whom those puffed up with undue wealth, assumed learning, power, rank, and authority, generally profess to despise for their low birth, poverty, and ignorance.

Everything which has a tendency to promote genuine civilization, Christianity and Democracy, is most in accordance with the interest and feelings of the mass of the people. We must, therefore, look to them chiefly for an impulse or true sense of equal justice and fellow feelings, and for whatever imports a common good or the promotion of justice, humanity, prosperity and happiness, to mankind in general.

Virtue and intelligence, talent and genuine learning, honest industry, economy and real merit, combined with a heart that loves its kind, of whatever clime, tongue or condition, constitute the only aristocracy that can ever command and receive the respect and admiration of the American people. An aristocracy like this has my profound respect, and no other has. It is principles and sentiments like these which enable the patriot and philanthropist to exclaim in sincerity and truth that *the world is my home, and that every honest man is my brother*.

In assuming the heavy responsibilities of a second Gubernatorial term, I must be permitted to state, that I have, or feel that I have, performed every duty which has been imposed on me by the law of the Constitution, with strict fidelity; and do now enter upon the second term, as I did two years ago upon the first, with a fixed and unalterable determination to discharge every duty growing out of my official station, with punctuality and strict justice to all. It is with no ordinary pleasure that I avail myself of this occasion to tender one time more, to the sovereign people of the State my unfeigned gratitude for this additional evidence of their confidence in me as a man and as a public servant. I will add, in conclusion, that the people have never deserted me, and *God being willing,* I will never desert them."

With the Legislature organized, Governor Andrew Johnson transmitted his Message to the Legislature just one week after its convening.

Legislative Message, October 8, 1855

"FELLOW CITIZENS OF THE SENATE AND
    HOUSE OF REPRESENTATIVES:

The organic law and long established custom in this State requires the Governor, from time to time, to submit to the consideration of both Houses of the General Assembly, such measures and suggestions as he may deem expedient and proper. I would, therefore, in the first place, most respectfully call your attention to the liabilities of the State.

The actual indebtedness of the State at this time is as follows:

Five and a quarter per cent bonds issued for
    stock in internal improvement companies .$ 227,416.66
Five per cent bonds issued for stock in internal
    improvement companies 1,824,440.00

---

* *Senate Journal,* 1855, 14–34.
  House Journal, 1855, 55–75.

Six per cent bonds issued for capital in the
  Bank of Tennessee 1,000,000.00
Six per cent bonds issued for building State
  Capitol 691,000.00
For stock in the Union Bank 259,000.00
                                          _____
           Amounting to $3,992,856.66

In addition to the above actual indebtedness, the State is liable for bonds loaned and endorsed, as follows:

To the East Tenn. and Georgia Railroad ....$ 870,000
To the Tennessee and Alabama Railroad   300,000
To the Memphis and Ohio Railroad   340,000
To the East Tennessee and Virginia Railroad   569,000
To the Memphis and Charleston Railroad   740,000
To the M'Minnville and Manchester Railroad ...   300,000
To the Mississippi and Tenn. Railroad   98,000
To the Mississippi and Dyersburg Plank Road ..   25,000
To the Manskers Creek and Springfield Turnpike,
  (endorsed)   10,000
To the Nashville and Chattanooga Railroad,
  (endorsed) 1,500,000
                                          _____
           Amounting to $4,752,000

Making the whole liabilities of the State for bonds issued for Stock, loaned and endorsed to Internal Improvement Companies, amount to eight million seven hundred and forty-four thousand eight hundred and fifty-six dollars and sixty-six cents (8,744,856.-66).

It will devolve on you to provide for the payment of one hundred and twenty five thousand dollars, (125,000) of the bonds which were issued for stock in the Union Bank, falling due first of January, 1858, and fifty thousand dollars (50,000) bonds issued for building the State Capitol, falling due first of April of the same year. It is for the Legislature to determine whether these bonds shall be paid by imposing additional taxes on the people or out of the Stocks owned by the State.

I lay before you for examination the original cost and present estimated value of the State Stocks, and also the value of the taxable property and number of taxable polls, made out by the Comptroller of the Treasury.

STOCK OWNED BY THE STATE.

Stock	Original Cost	Estimated Pres. Val.
Bank of Tennessee	$1,000,000	$1,000,000
Union Bank	650,000	650,000
East Tenn. and Georgia Railroad .	650,000	300,000
Franklin and Columbia Turnpike .	75,950	56,925
Lebanon and Nashville Turnpike .	80,000	48,266
Nolensville Turnpike	47,000	11,750
Nashville and Charlotte Turnpike	30,000	20,000
Lebanon and Sparta Turnpike ...	85,000	21,170
Columbia Central Turnpike	139,000	21,170
Nashville and Kentucky Turnpike	50,000	12,500
Clarksville and Russelville Turnpike	37,500	9,000
Columbia, Pulaski and Elkton Turnpike	126,600	12,233
Nashville and Murfreesboro Turnpike	66,666.66	30,530
Gallatin and Cumberland Turnpike	6,000	5,283
Gallatin Turnpike	130,000	26,000
Cumberland and Stone's River Turnpike	119,000	20,000
Total value	3,292,716.66	2,244,827

The above Turnpike Companies pay 6 per cent on the estimated value.

Total value of Taxable Property $219,011,047.81

Total number of Taxable Polls 100,011

State tax on $219,011,047.81 at ten cents on the hundred dollars 219,011.04

State tax on 109,011 polls at fifteen cents ... 15,001.65

At the last session of the Legislature, an act was passed directing the Governor and Comptroller to invest the dividends arising from the stock in the Union and Planters Banks in the six per cent bonds. We have received on account of said bonds one hundred and fifty-five thousand two hundred and forty-nine dollars and thirty-six cents; and have contracted with the Bank of Tennessee for the whole amount in bonds.

As it becomes your duty to appoint a committee to examine the accounts of the Comptroller and Treasurer, I would therefore suggest that you direct the same committee to examine and report as to the amount received and disbursed under the act of 1853-4, chapter 44.

For the details of the State debt and the true condition of the Treasury, I most respectfully refer you to the report which will be made by the Comptroller of the Treasury.

BANKS.

The condition of the Bank of Tennessee will be fully set forth and made known in a report which will be made and submitted to the General Assembly, by the President and Directors of that institution, at an early day. It will be seen from a careful examination of that report that the principal bank and branches have been conducted with great efficiency in the ordinary banking transactions, and especially so in collecting and securing a large portion of what is called the suspended debt. More of this debt has been collected and secured in the last two years than at any former period.

In regard to this institution, I still adhere to my former opinion, as submitted to the last Legislature, that the principal bank and its branches ought to be put into gradual liquidation, and that the present is an auspicious time for such gradual liquidation, giving ample and reasonable time to all persons indebted to the institution to make arrangements for paying the amount they may owe the principal bank and its branches. The process of winding up the institution at the present time can be made so gradual and easy as not to embarrass the indebted portion of the community in the smallest degree.

A number of banks have gone into operation under a law passed by the General Assembly of 1851-2, and others no doubt will soon commence. In addition to this, the last Legislature incorporated seven stock banks, which will more than supply the vacuum created by the withdrawal or the winding up of the Bank of Tennessee, and furnish all the banking facilities needed by the whole commercial and business portion of the country. As the capital of the bank is withdrawn from circulation, it can be profitably invested in the bonds of the State, thereby again making its way into the general circulation, and at the same time creating a home market for the bonds of the State equal to the entire assets of the bank. The bonds are bearing an interest of six per cent per annum, which will, in the end, yield a greater profit to the State, making it the safest and most judicious investment that can be made with the common school and other funds, which now constitute the capital of the Bank of Tennessee, and which is under the control of the Legislature.

If the State can in any reasonable time, dispose of the stock owned in the Union and Planters Banks, upon good and safe terms, and all other stocks owned by the State in turnpikes or railroads, it would be equally wise, safe and judicious to make a like investment with the proceeds of such stocks in the six per cent bonds of the State. The number of internal improvement works which have been commenced by the various companies, and which are entitled to aid by law from the State, and a number of others that in all probability will be commenced, which will require the issuance of a large amount of State bonds, amounting to many millions of dollars, will absorb the entire capital of the State Bank and the proceeds of all the stocks owned by the State, if they are invested in the bonds of the State as already indicated.

The Free Banking Law, as it is commonly called, requires revision and amendment, and should be so modified as to require all applicants for banking privileges under it to deposit, as a greater security to note holders, with the Comptroller of the treasury, twenty-five per cent more in bonds than they receive notes in exchange for circulation. The note holders are entitled to this additional security to meet any reasonable depreciation which may take place in the value and sale of the bonds of the State when thrown into market for sale. And, as a further protection to the community, there should be a law passed prohibiting the circulation of any bank note of a less denomination than five dollars, in the State. We have seen within the last few years gold and silver driven almost entirely out of circulation for all the ordinary business transactions of the country, by the excessive issue of small notes by the various banks throughout the State. The passage of such a law would in a short time restore to circulation, for all ordinary purposes, gold and silver, which cannot depreciate in the hands of the small and unsuspecting dealers, as is often the case with bank notes, by the depreciation of small notes or the breaking of banks. The necessity of the passage of such a law must be obvious to all, and it is wholly unnecessary for me to make any argument to the Legislature or to the country in its favor.

There is one other suggestion that I will make in regard to the Free Banking Law: the law should be so amended as to fix definitely the rates at which notes should be discounted by all persons banking under that law, thereby making the discounts equal and uniform in banking operations throughout the State.

TAX ON MERCHANTS.

In my message to the last Legislature, the attention of that body was called to the subject of merchants' taxes, and as no action was then taken upon it, I again submit that portion of my message to your consideration:

'There is some complaint with the mercantile interest, in consequence of the unequal and discriminating operation of our revenue laws regulating merchant's license. The complaint is not without some foundation and good cause on their part. The law, as it now stands, requires all wholesale and retail dealers in merchandise in this State to pay into the treasury of the State one half per cent on the invoice cost of goods vended by them. The main cause of complaint, as I understand it, is, that in the first place, the wholesale merchant, by the revenue law, is required to first pay into the treasury the half of one per cent, or fifty cents on the hundred dollars. After the tax is paid by him into the treasury, the retail merchant then purchases the same goods of him and takes them to another establishment, in or out of the county where purchased, as the case may be, and vends them again; for which he is required to pay one-half of one per cent, or fifty cents on the hundred dollars, into the treasury; which is one per cent paid to the State for the goods thus sold. By this process it will be perceived that the State lays a double tax on the goods purchased from the wholesale dealer within the limits of the State. The business retail dealer has no difficulty in understanding the operation, and finds it to his interest to go beyond the limits of the State to make his purchases, and thereby save the one-half of one per cent in the purchase of his goods, or fifty cents on every hundred dollars. It must be obvious to all business men, that if the wholesale dealer is required first to pay the tax into the treasury, that when the retail merchant buys of him he must pay it back, and then when he makes sale of the goods, he must pay a like amount into the treasury; which is practically compelling the country merchant to pay a double tax to the State on the same goods; which, as a matter of course, makes it his interest to go beyond the limits of the State to make his purchases, and become the customer of the foreign wholesale dealer, instead of the wholesale dealer at home; and to that extent operates against our own commercial cities and commercial men.

'It is most manifest to my mind that the practical effect of the revenue law, as it now stands, regulating merchants' license, is to discriminate against the merchant at home and in favor of the one abroad. The subject is, therefore, submitted to your consideration, with the hope that the law will be so modified as to place the mercantile interest of the State on an equal footing and in a field of fair competition with a like interest of the other States of the union.

NASHVILLE AND CHATTANOOGA RAILROAD.

By the sixth section of an act passed February the 8th, 1854, chapter 31, it was made the duty of the Governor to endorse and guarantee the bonds of the Nashville and Chattanooga Railroad Company in an amount not exceeding six hundred and fifty thousand dollars. Immediately after the passage of this law, the President of the company presented six hundred and fifty thousand dollars in bonds of the company, which bonds were endorsed and guaranteed as the law prescribed. The bonds, were then delivered to the President of the company, he executing his receipt for them. Sometime after this the President and Mr. Edwin H. Ewing made application to the Governor for the endorsement and guarantee of ninety five thousand dollars more in bonds of the said company. The reason given for this application was that the bonds had been destroyed to the amount of ninety-five thousand dollars, they having been through mistake burned for other bonds, and presented as proof of the fact a certificate of the Cashier of the Bank of the Republic of New York, together with the fragments of scraps of forty-three bonds, or that portion of them which contained the coupons; the body of the bonds containing the signature of the President of the company and the endorsement of the Governor, being entirely gone. The fragments of scraps of the bonds, presented as material proof of the fact of the bonds having been destroyed, were so discolored and charred by the action of the fire, that they afforded no proof that the Governor had ever seen or endorsed them, leaving no evidence before him but the certificate of the Cashier of the Bank of the Republic of New York, where the bonds had been burned through mistake. In this connection, however, it is due to state that there is no class of evidence that could have been presented proving the loss or destruction of the bonds that would have induced the Governor, as the law now stands, to endorse and guarantee any additional number of bonds on account of their loss or destruction, there being no law authorizing it to be done. The bonds had been once endorsed and guaranteed and delivered to the President of said company. This was deemed a complete execution of the law, leaving the Governor after its execution no control or discretion over the subject whatever. These is no law conferring power on the Executive where bonds have been misplaced or destroyed, upon application to him, to issue other bonds in their place, whether they have been endorsed or loaned, held by companies or individuals. The exercise of such a power on the part of the Governor, in the absence of law, would be setting a dangerous precedent, which might open the door wide to fraud and peculation by all unscrupulous persons into whose hands the bonds of the State might fall, which had been loaned to companies to aid in works of internal improvements, or those that had been endorsed or guaranteed for the same purpose. The second or third holder of bonds which had been transferred by any internal improvement company, in the event of the loss or destruction of the bonds in his hands, would have the same right to apply to the Governor for the issuance of new bonds in consequence of the loss or destruction of the old bond, so transferred, that the company had who first received the bonds from the State. It would be unsafe and dangerous to confer any such power on the Executive, thereby leaving it to his discretion to determine the nature and character of proof which would authorize him to issue bonds in all cases where they might be represented as being lost or destroyed. All questions of this character should be provided for by direct legislation, and not left to executive discretion.

Taking this view of the subject, the Governor declined to endorse and guarantee the ninety-five bonds already referred to. In reference to the actual destruction of the bonds in the present case, the Governor had no doubt of its having occurred as represented by the President of the company and Edwin H. Ewing, Esq., and at the time the application was made for the endorsement and guarantee of the bonds he felt more than anxious to accommodate them and the company, but declined doing so for the reasons already given. The whole subject is therefore submitted for your consideration and action, and will be disposed of as you may hereafter direct.

PUBLIC ROADS.

I would also call your attention to my former recommendation on this subject:

'Our whole system of public roads is exceedingly defective, perhaps more so than in any other State in the Union, imposing the burden of keeping it up upon that portion of our fellow-citizens least able to bear it, and who have the least use for it after it is kept up. Many persons are compelled to work on the public roads many days in the year, who have not the time to spare to do so, without pay, and the necessities of whose families need the proceeds of their entire labor for their support; while on the other hand there are many who are exempt by law from working on the public roads, who are either able, physically to work them, or pecuniarily to pay for having it done, and who derive the greatest benefit from good roads when they are made, by the enhanced value good roads impart to their property, and by increasing the comforts and facilities of traveling over them. In view of changing or modifying our present system, I most respectfully call your attention to the system of keeping up public roads in the States of Ohio and Pennsylvania, where property and other taxes are levied for the purpose of keeping up the public roads and highways, and thereby carrying out the principle, that the individual who derives the greatest benefit from having them kept up, and in proper condition for the traveling public, shall pay correspondingly for the benefits thus conferred. All persons should contribute to the support of the government under which they live, in proportion to the protection they may receive from it. Our present road system, it must be conceded by all, operates most unjustly and unequally upon the great mass of the people, and ought to be changed. I therefore recommend to your consideration the propriety of so changing or modifying the present system as to confirm it to the requirements of the public judgment and wants of the country, and that it be done during the present session of the Legislature.'

NATIONAL HOMESTEAD.

This important measure, by a large majority, has passed the popular branch of our national Legislature twice in succession, and was lost both times in the Senate, which is conclusive that the popular will demands the passage of such a law. I therefore call the attention of both branches of the Legislature to my recommendation upon this subject, which was made to the last Legislature:

'I feel that I cannot conclude this message without urging upon your consideration the importance and propriety of instructing our Senators in the Congress of the United States, and requesting our Representatives to use all reasonable exertion to procure the passage of a bill granting to every head of a family, who is a citizen of the United States, a "Homestead" of one hundred and sixty acres of land, out of the public domain, upon condition of the settlement and cultivation for a number of years. This is a measure of no ordinary consideration to the American people, and the correctness of its policy has been settled in the public judgment, and it would have been the law long before this time, had the popular will been carried out by the Congress of the United States. I therefore hope that you will take such action as will reflect the popular sentiment of the sovereign people of this State, and thereby contribute the weight of your influence to the consummation of this great measure.'

JUDICIARY.

I would most respectfully call your attention to my views upon this subject, as submitted to the last Legislature. I also transmit for examination a copy of the bill referred to in my message:

'The true foundation of our Judiciary is to be found in the Bill of Rights, which was adopted by the sovereign people in the year 1796, and was, in the year 1834, re-affirmed. In the 17th section they have declared in the most emphatic manner, "that all courts shall be open, and every man, for an injury done him, in his lands, goods, person, or reputation, shall have remedy by due course of law, and right and justice administered without sale, denial or delay." "Right and justice" is to be "administered without sale, denial or delay;" this is laid down as the basis—as the foundation of our whole system of jurisprudence; and it is imperative on the Legislature, in the organization of our courts, to conform them to the principles herein laid down. To a correct understanding of the kind of courts to be established, we should first determine what is meant by the terms "right and justice," as used in the bill of rights. The most approved authors define the term *right:* "Conformity to human laws, or other human standard of truth, propriety or justice." *"Justice*—the constant and perpetual disposition to render every man his due," &c. In this connection we might consider the meaning of *equity* also. In an enlarged and legal view, "Equity, in its true and genuine meaning, is the soul and spirit of the law." In this, "equity is made synonymous with justice." Right, justice and equity, according to common sense, and the best authorities, mean the same thing. When it comes to establishing a court or a tribunal, or it may be called by any other name, which is intended as a standard by which the precise difference can be determined between the contending parties, it is imperative on the Legislature to establish the standard which will accomplish the great end, as designed in the bill of rights, and if it were possible to so organize our courts, that when parties came into them to have their differences adjusted, for the court and jury to ascertain what is the precise equity between the parties, and then to determine that as the law of the case "equity being the soul and spirit of the law"—in other words, making the equity of the case, *the law of the case.* Taking the bill of rights as the foundation for our courts, the inquiry very naturally arises as to whether our courts, as now established, under the sixth section, first article of the constitution, are in conformity with the principles herein laid down. This article says: "The judicial power of the State shall be vested in one supreme court, and in such inferior courts as the Legislature shall ordain and establish." This provision of the constitution would seem to give great latitude to the Legislature in the organization of the courts. But the exercise of this power by the Legislature must be in strict conformity with the principles laid down, in the bill of rights. The bill of rights, being the better part of the constitution, is paramount.

'In all questions of apparent conflict between the bill of rights and the constitution, they should be reconciled and made to harmonize, if possible; but where there is a final repugnance, the constitution must give way, it bearing the same relation to the bill of rights that a law does to the constitution. Hence, in the organization of the courts, the Legislature has no authority, under the sixth article, to depart from this great and fundamental principle, as laid down in the bill of rights, or the better part of the constitution.

'Under the constitution of 1796, judges of the supreme and inferior courts were appointed by the Legislature to office during good behavior. The Legislature conferred upon the courts, chancery and law jurisdiction, which was exercised by them for thirty-eight years, or till 1835. The people, after making the experiment, became well satisfied that our judicial system was exceedingly defective, falling far short of carrying out the great principles, as contemplated in the bill of rights.

'In 1834, the people again, in convention, so changed the constitution as to make it more in conformity with the great idea of right and justice, by changing the tenure of all judicial officers from that of life to a term of years, and at the same time referring back many other elections to themselves which had been given up in the constitution of 1796.

'These changes in the constitution have been effected, in part, for the purpose of conforming the courts of the country, in their whole structure, to the wants and necessities of the people. There has been evident dissatisfaction with the courts of the country for a number of years past. The people find fault with the judges, complain of lawyers, and sometimes condemn jurors—affording conclusive evidence that there is a wrong somewhere: delay, expense and perplexity of mind on the part of the litigants—confidence in the courts much impaired in the public estimation. Under our present system, an individual goes into what is termed a court of law, to obtain justice in some matter of controversy; and after much time is spent and expense incurred, he comes out of law with a long bill of costs to pay; and if he complains of the proceeding, he is told that his case was a good one, but he was unfortunate in bringing his action in the wrong court; that his remedy is not in law, but in chancery. Another individual brings his suit in a court of chancery, and after a like delay of time and trouble in filing bills and hearing answers, he is turned out of court with a long bill of costs and charges to pay, and he is consoled in the same way by telling him his case is a good one, but his remedy is not in chancery, but in a court of law; and from a court of law to a court of chancery, until, in the end, if the end ever comes, the substance of the parties is in many instances consumed, and the gainer of the suit is frequently the loser, and the unfortunate party goes into immediate bankruptcy. This is the manner in which law and equity is administered under our present system of jurisprudence, which, in fact, is the great cause of complaint of the parties who go into our courts to obtain justice, and a want of confidence on the part of the people in the courts of law and chancery.

'Upon this subject I shall take high ground, and assume that the courts can be so organized, that law and equity can be administered by the same court, by the same judge and jury, and at the same time, and that, too, without "sale, denial, or delay." Let the courts of law and chancery be blended or converted into one court—(it is not material by what name you call it)—or, in other words, let the law and equity of the case be heard by the court and jury at the same time—let the parties, if necessary, be examined in open court—let all the restraints and barriers be removed—all false issues and collateral questions be thrown aside, and the cause tried upon the naked merits involved, and thereby administer "right and justice" to the contending parties, and let them go hence without delay.

'I feel well assured that the people throughout the State expect legislative action upon this subject before the close of your session. This is a most propitious time for bringing about the change in our judiciary, as indicated, the people having removed all constitutional difficulties that were in the way by the adoption of the recent amendments to the constitution. There is now a bill before your honorable body, entitled a bill *"To abridge and simplify the pleadings, practice and proceedings in the courts of justice in this State,"* which will, if passed into a law, accomplish much in conforming the practice in the courts to the requirements of the bill of rights and the wants of the people. In recommending this bill to your favorable consideration, or some one very similar in its provisions, I am not recommending a new and untried experiment, but one which has been tried and approved by many of our sister States. It will and can succeed with us as it has with them, if the experiment is fully and fairly made, and will, no doubt, give general satisfaction here, as it has there, by simplifying, cheapening and shortening the process by which litigants may obtain "right and justice".

'That the bill referred to has been prepared by its originator with great care and much labor, is manifest to all who will give it a careful examination; and it is believed, after passing the legislative ordeal, will be so improved as more closely to approximate the intentions and design of those who framed the constitution. The leading principles of the measure now recommended to your favorable consideration, have been advocated by me since my first entrance into public life, in the year 1835; and my reflection and observation, together with the successful experiment which has been made in other States of the Union, have tended to confirm me in the opinion that it ought to be adopted in this State, and that, too, before the adjournment of the present Legislature.'

AMENDMENTS TO THE CONSTITUTION OF THE UNITED STATES

'I will most respectfully call the attention of the General Assembly to the fifth article of the Constitution of the United States, which prescribes the mode and manner of amendment to that instrument, and also to three propositions to amend the Constitution of the United States, which are appended to, and made a part of this message, which is respectfully submitted for consideration and action by the General Assembly. In submitting this subject, I shall make no long or labored argument to the Legislature, or to the country, to prove the importance and necessity of adding these three amendments to the Constitution of the United States. All who are in favor of popularizing our free institutions as far as may be practicable, and bringing the general government nearer to the people, will receive and treat them as self-evident propositions.

'I will conclude by adding, that they were the doctrines of Jefferson, Jackson, Macon, and a number of other statesmen and patriots, whose opinions are at all times entitled to the respect and consideration of the American people.'

Since this recommendation was made to the last Legislature, I have become more thoroughly convinced in my own mind of the importance of making the proposed amendments to the Constitution of the United States. The last two popular elections in this State show the importance of electing United States Senators at the ballot-box instead of electing them by the Legislature. The popular will of the State, as reflected through the ballot-box, has, twice in succession, demonstrated most conclusively that the Legislature does not reflect the will of the people in the election of Senators; but, on the contrary, has elected Senators to the Senate of the United States who stand opposed to the public judgment, as twice recorded by the sovereign people of the State.

The great importance of amending the Constitution of the United States, so as to bring the election of President and Vice President of the United States directly before the people, as proposed in the amendment as hereunto appended, is becoming more and more manifest by every day's experience. In the next election of President and Vice President, it is highly probable that there will be three or more candidates, and, in that event, the chances are that the people of the several States will not have the privilege of choosing the President and Vice President through the electoral college, no one of the candidates receiving a majority of all the electoral votes, which will cause the election to be transferred from the electoral college to the United States House of Representatives, where the choice will be made by States, without regard to the electoral vote; which, in all probability, will result, as it did in 1824, by foisting men into office in utter disregard of the popular will. The proposed amendment to the Constitution will remove all apprehension and difficulty on this account, and cause the election to be made by the electoral college—some one of the candidates receiving a majority of all the electoral votes.

JOINT RESOLUTION
PROPOSING AMENDMENTS TO THE CONSTITUTION OF THE UNITED STATES

CONSTITUTION OF THE UNITED STATES
ARTICLE FIFTH—OF AMENDMENTS

'Congress, whenever two-thirds of both Houses shall deem it necessary, shall propose amendments to this Constitution, or the application of the Legislatures of two-thirds of the several States shall call a convention for proposing amendments; which, in either case, shall be valid to all intents and purposes, as part of this Constitution, when ratified by the Legislatures of three-fourths of the several States, or by conventions in three-fourths thereof, as the one or the other mode of ratification may be proposed by Congress; provided that no amendment which may be made prior to the year one thousand eight hundred and eight, shall in any manner affect the first and fourth clauses in the ninth section of the first article; and that no State, without its consent, shall be deprived of its equal suffrage in the Senate.'

JOINT RESOLUTION,

Proposing amendments to the Constitution of the United States.

'*Resolved by the Senate and House of Representatives of the United States of America in Congress assembled, two thirds of both Houses concurring,* That the following amendments to the Constitution of the United States be proposed to the Legislatures of the several States, which, when ratified by the Legislatures of three-fourths of the State, shall be valid to all intents and purposes as part of the Constitution:

That hereafter, the President and Vice President of the United States shall be chosen by the people of the respective States, in the manner following: Each State shall be divided, by the Legislature thereof, into districts, equal in number to the whole number of Senators and Representatives to which such State may be entitled in the Congress of the United States; the said districts to be composed of contiguous territory, and to contain, as nearly as may be, an equal number of persons entitled to be represented under the

Constitution, and to be laid off, for the time, immediately after the ratification of this amendment, and afterwards, at the session of the Legislature next ensuing the apportionment of representatives by the Congress of the United States; that on the first Thursday in August, in the year eighteen hundred and fifty-six, and on the same day every fourth year thereafter, the citizens of each State who possess the qualifications requisite for electors of the most numerous branch of the State Legislatures, shall meet within their respective districts, and vote for a President and Vice President of the United States, one of whom at least shall not be an inhabitant of the same State with themselves; and the person receiving the greatest number of votes for President, and the one receiving the greatest number of votes for Vice President in each district, shall be holden to have received one vote; which fact shall be immediately certified by the Governor of the State, to each of the Senators in Congress from such State, and to the President of the Senate and the Speaker of the House of Representatives. The Congress of the United States shall be in session on the second Monday in October, in the year eighteen hundred and fifty-six, and on the same day every fourth year thereafter; and the President of the Senate, in the presence of the Senate and House of Representatives, shall open all the certificates, and the votes shall then be counted. The person having the greatest number of votes for President, shall be President, if such number be equal to a majority of the whole number of votes given; but if no person have such majority, then a second election shall be held on the first Thursday in the month of December then next ensuing, between the persons having the two highest numbers for the office of President; which second election shall be conducted, the result certified, and the votes counted, in the same manner as in the first; and the person having the greatest number of votes for President, shall be President. But, if two or more persons shall have received the greatest, and an equal number of votes, at the second election, then the person who shall have received the greatest number of votes in the greatest number of States, shall be President. The person having the greatest number of votes for Vice President, at the first election, shall be Vice President, if such number be equal to a majority of the whole number of votes given; and if no person have such a majority, then a second election shall take place between the persons having the two highest numbers, on the same day that the second election is held for President; and the person having the highest number of votes for Vice President shall be Vice President. But if there should happen to be an equality of votes between the persons so voted for at the second election, then the person having the greatest number of votes in the greatest number of States, shall be Vice President. But when a second election shall be necessary in the case of Vice President, and not necessary in the case of President, then the Senate shall choose a Vice President from the persons having the two highest numbers in the first election, as is now prescribed in the Constitution.

SEC. 2. *And be it further resolved,* That article one, section three, be amended by striking out the word 'Legislature,' and inserting in lieu thereof the following words, viz: 'persons qualified to vote for members of the most numerous branch of the Legislature,' so as to make the third section of said article when ratified by three-fourths of the States, read as follows, to-wit:

The Senate of the United States shall be composed of two Senators from each State, chosen by the persons qualified to vote for the members of the most numerous branch of the Legislature thereof, for six years, and each Senator shall have one vote.

SEC. 3. *And be it further resolved,* That article three, section one, be amended by stricking out the words 'good behavior,' and inserting the following words, viz: 'the term of twelve years.' And further, that said article and section be amended by adding the following thereto, viz: 'and it shall be the duty of the President of the United States, within twelve months after the raification of this amendment by three-fourths of all the States as provided by the Constitution of the United States, to divide the whole number of judges as near as may be practicable, into three classes. The seats of the first class shall be vacated at the expiration of the fourth year from such classification; of the second class, at the expiration of the eighth year; and of the third class, at the expiration of the twelfth year, so that one-third may be chosen every fourth year thereafter.'

The article, as amended, will read as follows:

ARTICLE III.

SECTION 1. The judicial power of the United States shall be

vested in one Supreme Court, and such inferior courts as the Congress, from time to time, may ordain and establish. The judges, both of the supreme and inferior courts, shall hold their offices during the term of twelve years, and shall, at stated times, receive for their services a compensation, which shall not be diminished during their continuance in office. And it shall be the duty of the President of the United States, within twelve months after the ratification of this amendment by three fourths of all the States, as provided by the Constitution of the United States, to divide the whole number of judges, as near as may be practicable, into three classes. The seats of the judges of the first class shall be vacated at the expiration of the fourth year from such classification; of the second class, at the expiration of the eighth year; and of the third class, at the expiration of the twelfth year; so that one-third may be chosen every fourth year thereafter.'

'This is merely submitted as one plan amendment, to accomplish the contemplated change in the Constitution of the United States. Any other plan more perfect, and more in conformity with the whole structure of the Government, will be equally acceptable. It is expected that the amendments will be put in the most perfect form possible that can be devised by the exercise of your better judgment.'

WEIGHTS AND MEASURES.

By a joint resolution of the General Assembly, adopted March 3rd, 1854, the Governor was authorized to appoint a suitable person as superintendent of weights and measures. In compliance with this resolution, Mr. John Herriges has been appointed superintendent to take charge of the weights and measures, as furnished by the Federal Government, under a resolution passed June 14th, 1836. Since the appointment of the superintendent the weights and measures have been received, and are now under his control, and by him have been deposited in one of the rooms of the Capitol, set apart for that purpose by the commissioners. The weights and measures were all received in good order, and are now subject to the inspection of both branches of the Legislature. The resolution authorizing the appointment of superintendent of weights and measures, made no provision for any compensation for the time and labor necessary for taking the proper care of the weights and measures, which are now in his possession. It cannot be expected that the superintendent can lose his time and labor without some pay. The resolution also authorized the Governor to have made, under the direction of the superintendent, a set of standard weights and measures for each county of the State. This portion of the resolution, so far, has not been carried out by the Governor, believing, as he did, that, the cost would be much greater to procure a set of standard weights and measures for each county in the State, than the Legislature was aware of at the time the resolution passed. The cost of a set of standard weights and measures, such as would be suitable for the respective counties, from the most reliable sources of information, will not cost much less than two hundred dollars per set, which will make the aggregate cost near sixteen thousand dollars. Notwithstanding the aggregate cost may seem to be high, I am still of the opinion that sound policy and the best interest of the State require a law to be passed making the standard weights and measures for that purpose; and unless the Legislature repeal the resolution, the Governor will, at an early day, proceed, as authorized, to have each county furnished with a set of standard weights and measures, as authorized by law.

PENITENTIARY.

Upon this subject, my general views have undergone no change since the sitting of the last Legislature; and I would most respectfully call your attention to the suggestions and recommendations then made in my message to that body.

'This institution has, so far, failed in all the leading objects of its creation. The confinement of persons within the prison house or prison walls of a penitentiary, with the view of reforming them in their moral character, has been proven by all experience to be a great error; and it is not now contended for as a reforming institution by any one who has become at all familiar with the subject. There is not one in every thousand convicts whose moral condition is improved by such imprisonment; but, on the contrary, most of them, if not all, are made worse than they were before, and become more confirmed in crime.

'Upon the subject of convicts reformed by penitentiary imprisonment and association, Dr. John S. Young, former Secretary of State, in an able and elaborate report made on the 15th of September, 1845, to the Commissioners of Public Buildings, and by them submitted to the Legislature, used the following language: "I am entirely skeptical on the subject of reforming convicts by teaching them mechanical trades; little or no good results from it. When a convict leaves the prison, he lays down his cap, and with it his trade. He looks back upon both as the badges of his disgrace, and the companions of his imprisonment; he aims to something else which he considers better than his trade, or returns to the re-commission of crime. His trade, in most instances, as I believe, serves to better quality the villain without reforming the man. Those who would attempt the moral reformation of the felon, most employ other means. They must bear in mind that three-fourths of those stained with crime can neither read nor write. The mind must be cultivated in order to produce those genial influences which are calculated to remove vicious inclinations and base propensities, and give place to proper sensibilities and corrected feelings, from which altered intentions and virtuous actions must spring.

'The trial, conviction and sentence by the court of persons to the penitentiary for violation of the laws, has had no restraining influence whatever on immorality, and carried little or no terror to the mind of the evil doer. The announcement in the court-house yard that such a person has been sentenced for so many years imprisonment, is received with no alarm, but, on the contrary, with great indifference; and it is the frequent remark that it is better for the individual who has just been sentenced to so many year's confinement—it will be far better for him. He will, while there, be enabled to learn a good trade, and will live better there than he ever did before. The sheriff then prepares with his guards and starts with the convict for the penitentiary, making rather the impression, as he leaves, upon the mind of many spectators, that the prisoner has done well in obtaining a traveling trip of pleasure and a money-making business for the sheriff and his escort, and he in the end be made one of the mechanics of the country. In fine, on these two points, it will be readily perceived the penitentiary reforms no one after he is confined within its walls; and the sentence of the court, and confinement together, deters no one from a violation of the laws of the land.

'In the next place, the system has fallen far below the expenses incurred in the erection of the establishment, and the annual cost of carrying it on, up to the present time. Upon a close examination of the items properly chargeable to the institution, after giving it full credit for all that it is entitled to, there will still be found a deficit of not less than one hundred thousand dollars—probably much more. I have obtained sufficient data from Mr. Love, the principal book-keeper, who has appeared very accommodating, and much disposed to afford every facility in his power to remove all difficulty in getting at the true financial condition of the institution, together with a report recently made by the Comptroller to the Senate, showing how much has been paid out of the treasury for the conveyance of convicts to the penitentiary, to satisfy my mind that the State has incurred a heavy loss by the penitentiary. It will take but little investigation of this subject to satisfy any discerning mind that the penitentiary exerts no beneficial moral influence on society, in or out of the penitentiary, and that it is now, and has been, an incubus on the treasury, and will most likely continue so, unless the whole establishment undergoes a thorough change.

'While the institution has failed in all the leading objects of its creation, the manner in which it has been conducted has been made to operate injuriously upon the mechanical interest of the country. It has been made practically a *State mechanic institute*, fostered and sustained by the treasury of the State, and brought into direct competition with the mechanics of the country to the extent of its entire operation. The conditions upon which persons are admitted into this *State mechanic institute* are very discriminating and invidious in their character. Before the candidate can obtain admission to the high privilege of being employed in this institution, at any of the branches of business carried on there he must first commit the horrid crime of murder, arson, larceny, rape, or some other one of the offences violative of law. He must then stand a trial at some of our courts of justice, and then receive a certificate from the presiding judge that these facts are all true, and, in addition to this, he must be accompanied by the high sheriff of the county and his retinue to the *State mechanic institute*. Having arrived, his credentials are presented, and such other evidence as may be required, that he is a fit and worthy candidate, having passed through the ordeal necessary and proper to his qualification for admission. He is then received by the proprietor of the institute, and safely conducted to the stone mason's, sculptor's, or some other department, and there begins his new vocation of reducing the rough and unpolished marble to shape and fashion. The hands that are yet crimson with the blood of the unoffending, are made to ply the mallet and chisel, as did Socrates, the Grecian philosopher and statesman—perhaps, too, in the course of his servitude, with the same guilty hand, to engrave upon the tomb of the departed and illustrious dead the lines which are intended to indicate to the inquiring living their many virtues and exalted worth. And so, also, with all the other departments that are carried on in this institution. There might be similar illustrations made in reference to tailors, shoemakers, hatters, blacksmiths, wagon-makers, &c.

'The State, by the establishment of this institution, and the passage of laws to sustain it, gathers from every county in the State all the incorrigible offenders who are known to the law, and after collecting them within the walls of the penitentiary, embarks in all the branches of mechanism, and openly enters the field of competition with the mechanics of the country. The mechanics outside of the penitentiary are required, by all the obligations of good citizens, in peace as well as in war, to submit to taxation to sustain the government under which they may live, and at the same time compete with the State in their own branches of business. This policy of the State, in carrying on the branches of mechanism, and the employment of all the felons of the country at them, has a direct tendency to degrade the mechanics of the country as a body. Felon and mechanic, crime and mechanism, from their close association, become corresponding terms in the public mind. The felons, after having served out their time, are turned loose upon the country, to mix with the mechanics as best they may, and perchance to become inmates of their families, and companions in their shops. Is it right that this description of our population should be thrown upon, and associated with, the honest and industrious mechanics of the State, either in person or profession? There is an instinctive repugnance in the bosoms of all honorable men, and it is reduced to practice by

nearly all those who have charge of our cemeteries, by excluding the felon from being associated with us even in the grave. If
it is degrading to be associated with a felon after we are dead,
it must be much more so to be associated with them while we are
living.

'In conclusion upon this subject, I must be permitted to make
one earnest appeal, and that is, for the legislature to so direct the
future management of the affairs of the Penitentiary, by their legislation, as to protect this large and respectable portion of our fellow-
citizens from this degrading association and competition, by excluding, as far as possible, all the branches of mechanism from the Penitentiary.'

Since the sitting of the last Legislature, the Penitentiary has met
with a serious accident, and a very heavy loss, by fire. On the 29th
of March last, about 3 o'clock in the morning, the prison was discovered to be on fire in the north-east corner of the buildings; the
flames spread with great rapidity in both directions, until all the
inside buildings were nearly consumed, embracing the eastern end
of the main front building, which contained one-half of the cells
for the confinement of convicts at night. The most energetic efforts,
as I am reliably advised, were made by the Keeper and other officers connected with the prison, as well as some of the fire companies of this city, to arrest the devouring element; but, from the
great scarcity of water, and other means necessary in such an emergency, were found to be wholly unavailing. The prison was set on
fire by means of a slow match, which had been constructed by two
of the convicts the day before, and deposited by them in the north-
east corner of the building, a short time before they were taken by
their manager to their cells for confinement in the evening. The fire,
which proceeded from this slow match, and which communicated
to the building, was not discovered until 3 o'clock the next morning,
as before stated. At an early hour after the buildings were consumed
and lying in a pile of smoking ruins, the Inspectors of the Penitentiary, together with the Governor, had a consultation in reference to the most efficient steps necessary to be taken under the existing circumstances. The inside buildings were all burned down, or
nearly so; half of the cells destroyed in the east end of the main
building; tools of every description consumed, or so spoiled as to

make them unfit for use. The convicts, two hundred and thirty-seven in number, were divided into different companies and were marched and counter-marched about in the yard, for the purpose of preventing mutiny or an outbreak—all of them without employment. With these state of facts before them, the Inspectors and the Governor at once determined that it would be best, in view of safety and economy, to proceed, without delay, to repair the buildings so that the convicts could be employed profitably, and made more secure at night. They, therefore, concluded to borrow a sufficient amount of money from the various banks of this city, upon their own credit and responsibility, to refit and repair the prison in such manner as might be considered absolutely necessary. This course was deemed by the Governor the most efficient step that could be taken, because it dispensed with the necessity of convening the Legislature in extraordinary session, which would cause great delay before anything practicable could be done, leaving the whole Institution in a chaotic and unsafe condition. The Inspectors, by taking this course, have done all that the Legislature could have practically done in extra session, and by so doing have saved the expense of an extra session of the Legislature, which would have been much greater than the entire amount necessary to repair the Penitentiary.

The amount of money borrowed by the Inspectors from the various banks in this city, upon their own responsibility, and which has been applied to the refitting and repairing of the Penitentiary, is twenty thousand dollars. This sum, it is believed, has been profitably and economically applied to the purposes for which it was borrowed. A statement of the entire expense, giving all the items in detail, will be furnished by the Inspectors for your examination. For a more minute and detailed account of this whole affair, I refer you to the report of the Inspectors, which will be submitted to both branches of the Legislature, in a few days.

This heavy responsibility has been incurred by the Inspectors, and, by so doing, there has been saved to the State many thousands of dollars. It is, therefore, expected that the Legislature will take prompt and efficient action upon this subject, and relieve the Inspectors from the heavy responsibility which they have incurred for the refitting and repairing of the State prison.

AGRICULTURAL BUREAU.

The Legislature, at its last session, passed an act to establish a State Agricultural Bureau, with county and district societies subordinate thereto, &c. By this act, the Governor of the State was constituted President *ex-officio* of the Bureau. The Bureau was organized, according to law, on the 20th day of April, 1854. Full details of its action will be laid before you by the Secretary of the Bureau. From his report you will see that county societies have been chartered in seventeen counties; division Fairs were, last year, held in the Eastern and Middle Divisions of the State, and by the Sumner County Society, and that a new and beneficial interest has been awakened on the subject of agricultural improvements. Division Fairs, will, this year, be held in each division of the State, and the Biennial State Fair is now in progress near Nashville, under your own immediate inspection. The Agricultural interest has always been, and will probably long continue to be the leading interest of Tennessee. It is wise and proper that it should be fostered and encouraged by the Legislature, by all reasonable and legitimate means. I am of opinion that the law of 1854 was a wise and salutary step in the progress of Agricultural and Mechanical improvement and reform. Some slight modifications of the details of the law have been found necessary, not conflicting with its general scope and plan, to render it efficient in its practical operations. A committee of the Bureau, after its Biennial meeting on the second Monday in October, will suggest such modifications as may be thought advisable; and I doubt not that such suggestions will receive your careful consideration. Nature has been prodigal in her gifts to our State, and the Representatives of the people can render no service of greater value to their constituents, than by affording a judicious encouragement to associations having for their object the development of the agricultural and mineral wealth of the State, and stimulating the mechanical skill and industry of its citizens. When our people learn that the necessity for labor is a blessing, rather than a curse; that 'he who causes two blades of grass to grow, where but one grew before, is a greater public benefactor than he who conquers armies;' and that honor, fame and fortune may be as certainly earned in the workshop of the artisan, as in the offices of the learned professions, and as freely accorded by the public sense to the former as to the latter, then we shall have lived down an obstacle in the way of State progress, as absurd as it is injurious.

In bringing this communication to a close, I cannot forbear expressing with you, and, I hope, the whole country, heartfelt gratulations that all the elements of prosperity, designed to make a people great, contented and happy, continue to exist in our favored land. Every branch of industry has been amply rewarded. Our fields have teemed with rich and abundant crops, yielding plenty of all that is needful for man and beast. Our various works of internal improvement are steadily and constantly advancing by the timely and judicious aid of the State, developing our hitherto hidden and latent resources, and bearing off to the markets of the world, at cheap rates, the mechanical, agricultural, and other products of the country. Education has also received an impulse by legislation which, it is hoped, will be continued, and carried out, and cause our State ultimately to take a position upon this subject not inferior to that of any State in the Union. Under a beneficient and overruling Providence, we are still permitted to enjoy that sacred and greatest of all privileges, relating to man in social life, civil and religious liberty; making this one of the freest and happiest forms of government on the earth's broad surface. An efficient and pure administration of the laws, by all the departments of the government, Executive, Judicial and Legislative, together with a short session of the Legislature, and the enactment of necessary, wise and wholesome laws, will also add to the many blessings which have been bestowed upon our favored people, and will meet with their hearty approval, irrespective of parties, throughout the state.

ANDREW JOHNSON."

The above Message, with two minor exceptions, was an almost duplicate of the Message of 1853. In fact, Governor Johnson repeated *verbatim* much of the former Message. The two new items related to the Nashville and Chattanooga Railroad and the Agricultural Bureau. The repeated items dealt with

1. Liabilities of the State.
2. Banks.
3. Tax on Merchants.
4. Public Roads.
5. National Homestead.

6. Judiciary.

7. Amendments to U. S. Constitution.

8. Weights and Measurements.

9. Penitentiary.

After presenting a tabulation of the State indebtedness, Governor Johnson requested that provision be made for the payment of $125,000 for bonds issued for State stock in the Union Bank. Inasmuch as the bonds did not fall due until January 1, 1858, the 1855 Legislature by-passed the whole subject of payment, leaving that item for the consideration of the ensuing Legislature. No attention was paid to the handling of the State Capitol bonds in the amount of $50,000 which would fall due in April, 1858. That item, also, was bequeathed to the next Legislature. There was, however, an appropriation made of $150,000, in State bonds, for the completion of the State Capitol.[138]

Relative to the Bank of Tennessee, the Legislature ignored altogether the Governor's suggestion that it be put in gradual liquidation. A curb was placed upon the so-called Free Banks by requiring that $100,000 in lawful currency be paid in before any such bank could be lawfully established.[139] The above provision was made to apply to banks already organized, provided there was no infringement upon their "vested rights." This salutary law did away with most of the "wild cat" banking that had infected the State to a considerable exent.

Despite ten petitions[140] requesting some modification of the tax on merchants, the Legislature ignored the pleas as well as the Governor's recommendation by passing no remedial legislation on the subject.

The repeated recommendation of Governor Johnson to modifying the law in regard to keeping up the public roads so as to meet "the requirements of the public judgment and wants of the country" again fell upon leaden ears. No legislation whatsoever upon the subject was enacted.

In repeating his recommendation regarding the National Homestead movement, Governor Johnson was touching upon a subject close to his heart. While a member of Congress, he had introduced the first bill upon the subject. His recommendation was recognized by Democratic Senator D. W. Ballew who introduced the following resolution:[141]

"Resolved, by the General Assembly of the State of Tennessee, That our Senators in the Congress of the United States be instructed, and our Representatives requested, to use all reasonable exertion to procure the passage of a bill granting to every head of a family, who is a citizen of the United States,

---

138 *Acts of Tennessee*, 1855, Chapter 268.

139 *Ibid.*, Chapter 250.

140 *Senate Journal*, 1855, 755.

141 *Ibid.*, 38.

a homestead of one hundred and sixty acres of land, out of the public domain, upon condition of settlement and cultivation for a number of years."

The above resolution, which contained the very core of what Johnson had been advocating for a number of years, seems to have been "chloroformed" somewhere in the legislative quagmire. The Ballew resolution, after slumbering in committees and pigeon-holes for some three and one-half months, was finally supplanted by "a resolution in lieu" on January 24, 1856.[142] But the substitute resolution never emerged in the form of either a law or a resolution by the 1855 General Assembly. Its requiem was so silent that the final rites appear not to have been recorded in the official proceedings.

With an earnestness that amounted to almost an obsession, once more Governor Johnson pleaded for some reform in court procedures. A fellow Democrat, Senator J. W. Head from Sumner and Smith counties, from the Committee on Law Reform reported that his committee had considered all bills on the subject and had prepared a bill [143]

"To reorganize the judicial system of Tennessee, and to reform the code of practice."

After various hearings and the adoption of sundry amendments, the bill was rejected by a vote of 13 to 11,[144] the Senators ignoring party lines insofar as voting for or against the bill was concerned.

In regard to the Governor's request for an expression of legislative approval of proposed amendments to the United States Constitution, he was rebuffed as the following excerpt from an adopted resolution [145] on the subject discloses:

"... The amendments proposed and recommended by the Governor are unwise, inexpedient, and dangerous to our liberty and the perpetuity of this Union, and that the change is uncalled for by the American people, let it come from whatever source it may, and that our Senators in Congress be instructed, and our Representatives requested, to oppose, by all just and honorable means, any amendments offered to the Constitution of the United States."

As if to "rub it in a bit" on Governor Johnson, a portion of the preamble to the above resolution cited his similar recommendation of two years before, wherein it was alleged that such a recommendation

"... if adopted, would be dangerous to our liberties and the perpetuity of this glorious Union, as it would inevitably open the door for other changes, no doubt, that would be demanded, thereby causing it to lose that sacredness and reverence, and could no longer be held out as the work of our ancestry, but would be regarded as the work of demagogues and fanatics."

The above preamble and resolution passed in the Senate by a strict

[142] *Ibid.*, 430.
[143] *Ibid.*, 170.
[144] *Ibid.*, 320.
[145] *Acts of Tennessee*, 1855, Resolution 13, 576.

party vote, 14 to 11.[146] All eleven Democratic Senators opposed the passage of the measure, while the Know-Nothings and Whigs accounted for the fourteen favorable votes. In the House, the three Whigs joined up with the Know-Nothings and passed the resolution by a vote of 36 to 34.[147]

In compliance with Governor Johnson's recommendation, the Legislature enacted a law [148] to regulate weights and measures in the State. All that this meant was that the Standards of Weights and Measures approved by Congress in 1836 became the guide for use in Tennessee.

Two acts were passed with reference to the penitentiary. The sum of $20,000 for the biennium was appropriated for operational expenses of the institution.[149] The other law [150] provided for the sum of $22,000 to be paid to the Inspectors of the Penitentiary who had expended that sum in rebuilding the penitentiary which had been destroyed by fire in the early part of the year, the details of which were set forth in the Governor's Message.

Two new topics were included in Governor Johnson's Message, the other nine subjects having been specified in the Message of two years before. The Legislature passed a law [151] authorizing the Governor to indorse duplicate bonds in favor of the Nashville and Chattanooga Railroad in the amount of $95,000 as replacement of the original bonds which had been burned mistakenly for other bonds. Attention was called by the Governor to the two-year old State Agricultural Bureau which needed some slight modifications in the law governing its operations. The most important action by the Legislature in this matter was authority for the issuance of coupon bonds in the amount of $30,000 for the purpose of purchasing a suitable site for the Fair Grounds in the vicinity of Nashville and for the erection of necessary buildings and fixtures thereon.[152]

Insofar as his recommendations to the 1855 Legislature were concerned, Governor Johnson's "batting average" was very low. All of his major recommendations, merchant's tax, public roads, National Homestead, judicial reform, and proposed amendments to the United States Constitution, went down to signal defeat. Evidence that these recommendations were based upon *conviction* and not upon partisan views is the fact that Governor Johnson stressed the importance of remedial legislation regarding these topics in the last Message that he transmitted to the Legislature under date of October 6, 1857,—just a few days be-

---

[146] *Senate Journal*, 1855, 394.
[147] *House Journal*, 1855, 583.
[148] *Acts of Tennessee*, 1855, Chapter 73.
[149] *Ibid.*, Chapter 117.
[150] *Ibid.*, Chapter 265.
[151] *Ibid.*, Chapter 35.
[152] *Ibid.*, Chapter 95.

fore he retired from the Executive Office. The seer was without honor in his own State, so blinded by partisan fury was a majority of the Legislature. The ridiculous extent to which petty politics can drive otherwise sensible men may be seen in the 1855 Senate's refusing to confirm the Governor's nominations of Penitentiary Inspectors, although he submitted two lists of outstanding citizens.[153]

Another illustration of "spite" politics, which was in evidence throughout the session of the Thirty-First General Assembly, may be ascertained by noting the futile efforts made to fill the niches in the nearly-completed State Capitol with statues of famous men. On October 18, 1855, Mr. Speaker Neill S. Brown introduced

"A bill to provide for the erection of statues to Gen. Washington and Gen. Jackson in the Capitol of the State." [154]

A bill in lieu was next offered whereby the name of James K. Polk was added.[155] Almost a month later the bill came up for consideration, and the name of Hugh Lawson White was added.[156] In the meanwhile, friends of John Sevier, the first Governor of Tennessee, had succeeded in getting his name inserted in the bill, but Sevier's name was stricken out later on.[157] But the action of the House was reconsidered and Sevier's name restored to the bill. Thereupon a lot of squabbling ensued, one point of contention being whether a bronze or marble statue of General Washington should be selected. Finally, the bill was rejected by a vote of 37 to 31.[158]

Perhaps the prize legislative quibbling in 1855 over a mere picayune should be awarded to the actors participating in the following colloquy. On November 19, 1855, Representative J. M. Meek of Jefferson County introduced the following resolution:[159]

"Whereas, A firm reliance on, and implicit trust in the All-wise Ruler and Disposer of the events and destinies of Nations and States, is, at all times, fit and becoming a Christian nation and State, and characteristic of an enlightened people;

And, whereas, The custom, from the days of the Puritan Fathers to the present time, has obtained and received the universal sanction of setting apart, annually, a day of general thanksgiving; and whereas, General prosperity, peace, health, and the bounty of an abundant harvest, are the rich blessings

---

[153] *Senate Journal*, 1855, 469 and 500.

Author's note. A resolution for *sine die* adjournment on March 3, 1856, was adopted by both legislative branches on February 7. Despite this fact well-known to every member of the Legislature, Know-Nothing Senator A. J. Fletcher resorted to the despicable strategy of authoring a motion "to make the said nominations the special order for the first of April next." And the "sneak" attack upon the Governor was sustained.

[154] *House Journal*, 1855, 115.
[155] *Ibid.*, 197.
[156] *Ibid.*, 300.
[157] *Ibid.*, 390.
[158] *Ibid.*, 552.
[159] *House Journal*, 1855, 256.

and heritage of our State; and whereas, some day in the present month, (November,) has most usually been set apart by the Executive of most of the States of this Union, for the observance of such day; therefore,

Be it resolved, That a committee of three be appointed by this House, to wait on His Excellency Andrew Johnson, Governor of the State of Tennessee, and learn his pleasure, and request him to appoint some suitable day to be observed as a day of General Thanksgiving throughout this State."

When the resolution came up for consideration the following day, action on the measure was thwarted by a resort to the well-known strategy of obtaining an adjournment.[160] The next day, in considering the resolution, Representative N. Y. Cavitt of Weakley County offered the following [161] in lieu of the pending resolution:

"Resolved, that every member may fast or feast, and pray whenever it suits him."

A contemporary newspaper gave the following sketch of the "tempest in a teapot" scrap: [162]

"The unfinished business of yesterday was then taken up, being the resolution relative to a day of thanksgiving.

Mr. Cavitt moved to indefinitely postpone the resolution.

Mr. Dunnington thought it wholly unnecessary to pass such a resolution. If it had ever been customary to pass such resolutions, he would cheerfully vote for it, but he thought such a proceeding was without precedent, and that it was wandering far from the regular course of legislation, to interfere with the Executive Department. Perhaps some members were not aware that the Governor had been absent with the corpse of a deceased friend. He had lately returned, and would, no doubt, as he had on former occasions, appoint such a day without the interference of this legislature.

Mr. Meek said he had introduced the resolution in good faith, and was surprised to hear the accusation made, that it had been proposed in a party spirit, and with a view to cast any reflection upon Gov. Johnson. He appealed to his conduct since he had occupied a seat in the House, to vindicate him from any such insinuation.

He was not here he said to invoke party spirit, but to conduct the interests of the people.

He was surprised, he said, that the resolution should meet such opposition from the other side of the House. Seats filled with the admirers and followers of Gov. Johnson, who had expressed such peculiarly religious doctrines but a few weeks since in his inaugural address. Why, Mr. Speaker, has not that gentleman proclaimed to the world that democracy and theocracy are travelling side by side on converging lines, each seeking the redemption of mankind. And that democracy, in time, would supply the place of christianity, and do for the world what christianity now does.

Under these circumstances, he said, that he could not but feel surprised at the opposition manifested to the proposition to carry into effect one of the evidences of christian feeling in the country, which the Governor deemed so necessary to the furtherance of the principles of democracy.

---

[160] Ibid., 268.
[161] Ibid., 270.
[162] Union and American (Nashville), November 22, 1855.

Mr. Burch hoped after such a speech from the gentleman, that he would withdraw his resolution. When the resolution was introduced he was in favor of it, having a firm reliance in the ruling of the Supreme Judge, but when it became a question of party, when gentlemen brought forward a subject for the express purpose of casting reflection upon the action of Gov. Johnson, he thought it unwise for the gentleman to expect any gentleman on the democratic side of the House to vote for such a measure. He was surprised at the course of the gentleman. Such a proceeding was without a precedent, and he would be obliged to vote against the resolution.

Mr. Brown, of Madison, said that we had laid one resolution on the table this morning refusing to again call on the Clergymen, and he thought it would not look well to lay this one there also. He did not look upon it as casting a reflection upon any one. If such were the case he would heartily oppose it.

Mr. Cavitt offered a resolution in lieu, as follows:

Resolved, That every member may fast and pray whenever it suits him: Which he subsequently withdrew, but said that he did not withdraw his opposition to the resolution. He did not suppose any gentleman was in good faith until he heard the remarks of the gentleman from Madison, (Mr. Brown,) whose mind this morning seems to be replete with an unusual degree of reverence. If that gentleman would propose the election of a Chaplain, he would support it. If he would propose to have prayer here every morning by any clergyman who has not refused to perform those services, he would go for that also. But this resolution is going beyond our duties—it is without a precedent. And if we consume so much time on questions of this sort, we will fall far short of getting through with public business at the time we propose to adjourn. He was not particular whether there was a day of thanksgiving appointed or not, but thought the Governor ought to adopt his own pleasure, as he is accountable himself to the people of Tennessee, and his God. If the people desire to feast or fast and pray they can do so without any action of ours.—He hoped gentlemen on the other side of the House would reserve their political gas for more important questions.

Mr. Dunnington moved to indefinitely postpone.

Mr. Gleaves called the ayes and noes, as follows: ayes 23, noes 42; and the House refused to indefinitely postpone.

Mr. Galbreath offered a resolution in lieu, as follows:

Resolved, That the Governor is competent to discharge his duties. And if he fails to do so, the gentleman from Jefferson, (Mr. Meek,) be authorized to crack him on the head with a round of *Jacob's Ladder*. The Speaker ruled the resolution out of order.

Mr. Dunnington called the previous question, being the passage of the resolution. The call was sustained, and,

Mr. Gleaves called the ayes and noes, as follows: ayes, 31; noes, 34; and the resolution was lost.

During the calling of the ayes and noes, when the name of Mr. Dunnington was called, that gentleman arose and said:

Mr. Speaker: I think it necessary before casting my vote upon this resolution to state my reason for the manner in which I shall vote. In doing so, sir, I feel that it is a duty I owe to myself and to my constituency, to be set right upon this subject. There is no one, Mr. Speaker, who feels more sensibly than I do, the duty we owe for the blessings so bountifully showered upon us by the Giver of all Good Gifts, and no one appreciates, more highly than I, this time honored custom. The principles of the resolution are well enough but the action is unprecedented. Point me to the Legislature that has ever wandered so far from its legitimate course, as to interfere with, and prescribe the Gubernatorial duties! It cannot be done. This is the first attempt, and I hope, sir, it may be the last. This is a duty that has always devolved upon the Chief Executive—a duty that has always heretofore been performed; and I, for one, sir, have no fears but in this instance, it will be attended to in proper time, and the use of appointing such a committee as is proposed in this resolution, is more than I am able to see. What reason is there in it? The answer is obviously, none.

And again, Mr. Speaker, notwithstanding the declaration of gentlemen to the contrary, I cannot help thinking that it has been introduced in a wrong spirit. It is a reflection upon Gov. Johnson, and if gentlemen will look to the course pursued on the other side of the House, they can come to no other conclusion.

The resolution does not provide for the appointment of a day of thanksgiving by the Legislature. If such were the case, there would be more reason in it. But it is not so. This committee are to inform Gov. Johnson that he has neglected his duty. To tell him that he has 'left undone those things which ought to have been done.' What, Sir, is this, but a reflection? It certainly is intended for nothing else. If I wished for proof of this statement I would go no farther than to the speech of the gentleman from Jefferson, (Mr. Meek.)

Sir, it is not only a reflection upon Gov. Johnson, but it is a reflection on this body. We come here, to enact good and wholesome laws, that will be beneficial to our constituents, and to the State; and to bring up issues of this kind—to bring political strife within this hall, is, in my opinion, a reflection of no trifling character. Another reason, Sir,—a reason that I fain would sound, trumpet-tongued, to every one of my constituents, is, that these questions are calculated to retard the progress of legislation. Instead of bills being introduced and acted upon, we have resolution upon resolution offered, of a party character, that are wholly useless, and certainly ought to be dispensed with. A few days since, hours were consumed in the consideration of a scurrilous article that appeared in one of the city papers—then came the resolution in regard to the banks, upon which much time was spent; to-day, here is a special order, instructing our Senators in Congress. This morning the propriety of again inviting the Clergymen of the city to open our deliberations with prayer, was the subject of a lengthy discussion; and now here is a resolution, unknown in the history of all previous legislation, proposing to instruct the Chief Executive in the discharge of his duties. These, Sir, to me are strange proceedings. If a member introduces a resolution to economise or save time, the cry is at once raised of *buncome*, in which, if I mistake not, my friend from Jefferson partakes freely. But when a resolution is offered that consumes time and interferes with the legitimate business of the House, we hear no such cry. This is one great reason why these outside issues should be abated, and I hope that this one may be defeated together with all others of like nature that may come up hereafter.

Mr. Galbreath, when his name was called, said that in voting against this resolution he did not wish to be understood as being opposed to its principles. He was as much a believer in the ruling of Divine Providence as any one, but the course of gentlemen on the other side of the House had induced him to think that it was not introduced in the right spirit, and therefore he should oppose it. They seemed to want to strip Governor Johnson of all his powers. He thought him fully capable to discharge his duties, and had no doubt but he would do so.

State Capitol

Mr. Gleaves, said that in voting for the resolution, he did not do it as casting any reflection upon Gov. Johnson or any one else. He did not consider the resolution as conveying any such meaning. He knew that the Governor had been absent from the city; knew that he had sacred and solemn duties to perform; knew that he had been called to bear to their final resting place, the remains of a friend; and, such being the case, he presumed that the appointment of a day of Thanksgiving had escaped the memory of the Governor, and he could see no harm in reminding him of it. If he thought that any disrespect was meant to the Governor, he would be the last one to vote for it. He would always treat members of all parties courteously, and always stood ready to record his vote for principles irrespective of any party feeling.

Mr. White made some remarks, in which he referred to Gov. Johnson as believing that christianity was not essential to the salvation of man, but that it was as easy to ascend to heaven on his Jacob's Ladder, as to follow the teachings of the meek and lowly Jesus. He was interrupted, and took his seat. Upon the conclusion of the remarks of Mr. White, Mr. Wilson of Marshall, said that when the resolution was introduced, he was in favor of it. He had voted against the indefinite postponement, hoping the gentleman from Jefferson, (Mr. Meek,) would withdraw his political remarks. He had failed to do so, and the remarks of the gentleman from Knox, (Mr. White,) had fully convinced him, that the spirit in which the resolution was introduced was wrong, and he would therefore change his vote, and vote against the resolution."

The resolution was defeated, but there is valid evidence [163] that Governor Johnson did set apart a day of thanksgiving and that the strife-torn Legislature took due notice of the Governor's proclamation:

"Mr. Carlock moved
That the House adjourn till Friday morning, 9½ o'clock, in order to afford the members an opportunity of observing the day set apart by the Governor of the State as a day of Public Thanksgiving.
The motion prevailed."

Thursday, December 6, 1855, was, therefore, observed as Thanksgiving Day, the quibbling and pussyfooting of a partisan Legislature to the contrary notwithstanding.

Under date of October 1, 1855, Samuel D. Morgan, President of the Board of Commissioners of the State Capitol submitted a report [164] on the status of the building. A general breakdown of expenditures, delay caused by the burning of the stone-cutters' shops at the penitentiary, where stone materials for the Capitol were being prepared, and the resignation of two Board members were cited in the early part of the Report. Attention was also called to the death of the famed architect, William Strickland, whose death had occurred on April 6, 1854. His son, Francis W. Strickland, was employed to continue supervision of the completion of the Capitol at a salary of $1,200 per annum.

Attached to the Commissioners Report was a report by the newly-elected architect. The minute description of the building warrants the

---

[163] *House Journal*, 1855, 342.
[164] *Senate Journal*, 1855, Appendix, 41-45.

inclusion of his sketch of the State Capitol, perhaps the most detailed and accurate of any description on record. The Report [165] was as follows:

"ARCHITECT'S REPORT.

To Samuel D. Morgan, Esq., President of the Board of Commissioners for the building of the State Capitol:

SIR: I have the honor to report to you the progress which has been made in the building of the State Capitol, since the adjournment of the last Legislature. Although you are conversant with all the details of the labor and workmanship of which the building is composed, it is proper for me to report the amount of work yet to be done toward its final completion.

Since March, 1854, the tower has been carried up to its destined height from the first course of stone above the comb of the roof. There is 8,587 feet of dressed stone in the quadrangular basement above the arches, and 4,557 feet of dressed stone, double faced, in the circular part. The columns, of which there are eight, are thirty feet in length, including cap and base, and three feet in diameter, together with the cornice—the whole weighing about 4,000 tons.

The Rafters, which are of wrought iron, and the sheathing and copper which compose the roof, are all put in their places; and the cast iron leaves which form the crowning ornaments, upon which stands the tripod, are all in progress.

The cornice will be surrounded by an ornamental edge, usually termed a vitruvian scroll, which is of cast iron. They are all finished, and are being put up in their places. There is to be a cast iron stairway, supported by brackets, let into the interior wall of the tower, ascending to the roof.

The groined and segment arches in the tower are to be flagged over, together with over 2,000 feet of flagging to be laid in the main hall of the principal story immediately under the tower.

The upper floor of the tower which is supported by wrought iron joists, is to be plastered, and also the two arches below.

The library is to be fitted up with two rows of galleries, supported by wrought iron brackets let into the wall some eight inches, surrounded by a light cast iron railing, with shelving, alcoves, &c., with two circular iron stairways leading to the different galleries.

The stairway leading to the Senate gallery, together with private stairs to gallery of the House of Representatives, and to the tower, and also to the basement, are yet to be finished with cast iron ballusters. The Senate gallery has been completed with paneled ceiling, flooring, seats, iron rafters, &c.

The terrace is about one third completed. There are to be four flights of steps extending the whole width of the porticos on each front, as main entrances into the building. The work is in hand, and there is enough in progress to form the entrance on the west front. There is 3,064 feet of dressed ashlar for terrace, with about 700 perch of rubble masonry, as backing for terrace wall and support to flagging on terrace; 2,860 feet of which has been placed in position, and the balance in a state of progress.

Since October, 1853, there has been 22,370 feet of flagging laid; one main flight of steps, in main passage; twenty-four steps under the different porticos; five division walls in first story; 1,540 feet of double faced rubbed or polished ashlar, equal to 4,000 feet of ordinary character. The main halls in the base-

---

[165] *Ibid.*, 45–48.

ment story, East and West, North and South, are to be plastered. The surface of the hill at the eastern entrance will be cut down some eight feet, so as to form the terrace and make the ground nearly on a level all around the building. I would suggest the idea of terracing the ground, so as to form a gradual ascent to the building, with an avenue on each front. I have a plan in preparation, showing the shape of the grounds belonging to the State, together in the manner they may be laid out. The line of the State grounds on the North front is only 70 feet from the terrace of the building, and it would be necessary to extend them so that they might be laid out to advantage; and the whole plat should be enclosed with a stone wall, surmounted by a heavy cast iron railing, with four large entrance gates.

THE STATE CAPITOL OF TENNESSEE.

In plan and elevation, the design and whole character of the architecture is essentially Grecian, consisting of a Doric basement, supporting, on its four fronts porticos of the Ionic order, taken from the example of the Erectheum at Athens.

In the centre of the building rises a tower above the roof to the height of eighty feet, the superstructure of which is after the order of the Choragic monument of Lysicrates at Athens.

The whole structure is composed of fossillated limestone, hewn and chiseled from the quarries in the neighborhood of Nashville—the blocks of stone weighing from six to ten tons.

The various chambers, halls and porticos, are arched throughout. The rafters of the roof are of wrought iron, having a span of the whole width of the building, being supported by the interior walls at the North end and by the columns of the Southern division of the building, the whole covered by thick sheets of copper.

In plan, the basement story is intersected by longtitudinal and transverse halls of wide dimensions, to the right and left of which large and commodious rooms are appropriated to the uses of the Governor, Supreme Court, Secretary of State, Federal Court, &c., &c.

From the great central hall, you approach the principal story by a double flight of stairs, which leads to the chambers of the Senate and House of Representatives, to the library, and to the other rooms in connection therewith.

The committee rooms of the House are disposed on the same floor, to the right and left, communicating immediately with it and the lobbies; over these rooms the gallaries are placed.

Flanking the public hall, private stairways are constructed, leading from the crypt to the various stories, and to the roof.

The tower is built up from the foundation of solid stone, containing four niches in the basement, and eight in the principal story, with spacious halls leading to the right and left. A cast iron stairway leads from the level of the roof to the top of the tower, where you land upon a platform supported by wrought iron girders.

The Hall of Representatives contains sixteen fluted columns of the Roman Ionic order, two feet eight inches in diameter, and twenty-one feet ten inches in height, from the level of the galleries over the committee rooms. The shafts of these columns are all in one piece. A chief beauty and convenience in the design of the principal story, so much superior to the plan of the Capitol at Washington, is, that the committee rooms are on the same plane with and surrounding the Hall of Representatives. The dimensions of this room are one hundred feet by seventy; height of ceiling from floor, forty-two feet.

The Senate Chamber is of an oblong form, thirty-five by seventy feet, having pilasters of the Ionic order with a full entablature; the ceiling of this room is formed into radiating panels or lacunaria, and is forty-three feet in height; there is a gallery of twelve feet in width on three sides of the room, supported by twelve columns of variegated East Tennessee marble.

The Library is immediately opposite the Senate, and is thirty-five feet by thirty-five; on each side there are committee rooms, communicating. Over the arches of these rooms there will be alcoves for books, papers, and archives of the State; the doors and windows, which are of a large size, are of white oak, moulded, paneled, and ornamented with devices. The windows are all double, divided by stone pilasters, enriched with consoles, ovals and spears.

All the floors are groin arched and flagged with rubbed stone; hanging stone steps throughout the building.

The building stands on a rusticated basement eighteen feet in height, which is tooled on all fronts; and the superstructure is of rubbed stone inside and out; all the walls of the foundations are 7 feet in thickness, and those of the superstructure 4 feet 6 inches.

The building is in the form of a parallelogram, one hundred and forty feet by two hundred and seventy, surrounded by a terrace seventeen feet in width and seven feet in height, flagged with stone, with flights of steps extending across the four fronts.

There are twenty-eight fluted columns four feet eight inches in diameter, ornamenting the four porticos with the most elaborately wrought capitals; the North and South porticos are finished with pediments containing ceilings of stone, and the East and West porticos are surmounted by parapets; those of the North and South are octo style, and those of the East and West are hexa style.

The water is conveyed from the gutters of the roof, by means of cast iron pipes, into the reservoirs under the terrace, for the purpose of supplying the water closets.

The whole building will be heated with furnaces communicating with hot air flues within the walls.

Respectfully submitted by your ob't serv't,

FRANCIS W. STRICKLAND, *Arch't.*"

Before any final appraisal is made of Governor Johnson's low batting average in regard to his recommendations to two Legislatures, one should bear in mind that he had encountered bitter opposition on the part of the supporters of two powerful opponents in the gubernatorial races of 1853 and 1855, Gustavus A. Henry and Meredith P. Gentry. In the defeat of Henry, Johnson had broken the back of the Whig Party in Tennessee. His devastating attacks upon the Know-Nothings in the race with Gentry most assuredly did not win him friends in the ranks of that party. In addition, there were a number of Democrats who did not like Johnson. Furthermore, it should be remembered that Johnson never had a Legislature *in toto* of his own political faith. The 1853 Legislature had a Whig majority in the House of Representatives, with the Democratic majority in the Senate limited to just one vote. The 1855 Legislature, both House and Senate, was of political complexion at variance with that of Johnson. Politically speaking, Andrew Johnson had had to contend with the world, the flesh, and the Devil, and fight with the wild beasts at Ephesus. His undaunted courage in the face of tremendous odds, his ability as a "stump speaker," and his constant advocacy of the rights of "the common man" rendered him almost invincible when he presented his program to the general public. His three major Messages [166] to three Tennessee Legislatures stamp him as a man of real statesmanship caliber, a status that he maintained later as United States Senator and President of the United States.

Here was Andrew Johnson's final Message to a Tennessee Legislature, that of 1857.

"GENTLEMEN OF THE SENATE,
    AND OF THE HOUSE OF REPRESENTATIVES:

It has again become my duty, as Governor of the State, to submit for your consideration such measures and suggestions as may be deemed expedient and best calculated to promote the interest of the citizen and the general prosperity of the State. In the discharge of this high and solemn duty, permit me to congratulate you upon the arrival of a period so peculiarly favorable to the performance of such high and responsible duties by the representatives of the people. Much indeed will depend on what direction your legislation may take generally, and especially so in regard to the finances, actual indebtedness and liabilities of the State. Your action upon these measures, along with some others, will be vital to the future prosperity of the people of the whole State, and will merit your profound and deliberate consideration.

In the first place, I would most respectfully call your attention to the actual indebtedness of the State up to this time, which is as follows:

---

[166] Major Message to the 1853 Legislature, *Senate Journal*, 1853, 293–307; *House Journal*, 1853, 452–467.

Major Message to the 1855 Legislature, *Senate Journal*, 1855, 14–34; *House Journal*, 1855, 55–75.

Major Message to the 1857 Legislature, *Senate Journal*, 1857, 12–32; *House Journal*, 1857, 12–33.

Author's note. Four or five minor messages to the Legislature of 1855 have not been included in this volume. They dealt with nominations of personnel to relatively minor offices, and with a controversy with Georgia concerning railroad intercourse between the two States. The Message of 1857 was directed to a Legislature with which Johnson had official contact only a few days, his term of office having expired. This Message will receive proper attention in Volume V.

RAILROADS	Bonds Endorsed	Bonds Loaned	Total
Nashville and Chattanooga Railroad	$1,500,000		$1,650,000
Nashville and Chattanooga Railroad for Cleveland and Chat. Railroad	200,000	1,289,000	1,489,000
East Tennessee and Virginia Railroad	150,000	870,000	1,020,000
East Tennessee and Georgia Railroad			
East Tennessee and Georgia Railroad for Cleveland and Chattanooga R. R.	150,000		
Memphis and Charleston R. R.		1,100,000	1,100,000
Memphis and Ohio R. R.		670,000	670,000
Tennessee and Alabama R. R.	20,000	300,000	500,000
McMinnville and Manchester R. R.		372,000	372,000
Miss. and Tenn. R. R.		98,000	98,000
Miss. Central and Tenn. R. R.		574,000	574,000
Mobile and Ohio R. R.		706,000	706,000
Memphis and Little Rock R. R.	350,000		350,000
Edgefield and Kentucky and Lou. and Nash. Bridge		60,000	
Railroads, Total			$8,589,000

TURNPIKES	Bonds Endorsed	Bonds Loaned	Total	Grand Total
Carthage and Hartsville Turnpike Company		6,000		
Carthage, Alexandria and Red Sulphur Springs Turnpike Company		16,000		
Miss. and Dyersburg Plank Road		25,000		
Mansker's Creek and Springfield Turnpike Co.		10,000	57,999	
Agricultural Bureau		30,000	30,000	
		$8,676,000		$ 8,676,000.00
Total Liabilities			....	12,866,856.66

THE ACTUAL INDEBTEDNESS OF THE STATE.

Internal Improvement Bonds,
   bearing interest at the rate of 5 ¼ per cent .... $ 227,416.66
Internal Improvement Bonds,
   bearing interest at the rate of 5 per cent 1,824,440.00
Union Bank Bonds,
   bearing interest at the rate of 5 per cent 250,000.00
Bank of Tennessee,
   bearing interest at the rate of 6 per cent 1,000,000.00
State Capitol Bonds,
   bearing interest at the rate of 6 per cent 841,000.00
Purchase of Hermitage 48,000.00
                                                          _____
                                                          $4,190,856.66

State liability for Bonds endorsed for and loaned to Rail Roads, Turnpike Companies, and to the State Agricultural Bureau.

This exhibit shows the actual indebtedness of the State to be four million one hundred and ninety thousand eight hundred and fifty six dollars and sixty-six cents, [$4,190,856.66.] The stocks owned by the State, in Banks, Internal Improvement Companies, &c., amount to three millions two hundred and ninety-two thousand seven hundred and sixteen dollars and sixty-six cents, [$3,292,716.-66,] as will appear by reference to another part of this Message. These stocks, when reduced to their market or estimated value, will amount to two million two hundred and forty-four thousand eight hundred and twenty-seven dollars, [$2,244,827.] If this amount is applied to the liquidation of the actual indebtedness of the State, it will reduce that debt to one million forty-seven thousand seventy-nine dollars and sixty-six cents, [$1,047,079.66.] It is the opinion of some correct thinking and judicious persons, as well as my own, that it would be sound policy and economy to dispose of all the stock owned by the State, in Banks and Internal Improvement Companies, or otherwise, as soon as it can be done on advantageous terms, and to apply the proceeds of the sale of the same to the reduction of the actual indebtedness of the State, and for the State, as soon as practicable, to become entirely disconnected with all corporations whatever, either as partner or stockholder. The six per

cent which would be saved upon the Bonds, will amount to more
than all the dividends which will be paid upon the stock so long
as it is owned by the State.

The following tabular statement will show the amount of stocks
owned by the State, in Banks, Internal Improvement Companies,
&c., its original cost, and its estimated value at the present time.

STOCK OWNED BY THE STATE.

Stock	Original Cost	Estimated Present Val.
Bank of Tennessee	$1,000,000	$1,000,000
Union Bank	650,000	650,000
East Tenn. & Georgia Railroad	650,000	300,000
Franklin & Columbia Turnpike	75,950	56,925
Lebanon & Nashville Turnpike	80,000	48,266
Nolensville Turnpike	47,000	11,750
Nashville & Charlotte Turnpike ...	30,000	20,000
Lebanon & Sparta Turnpike	85,000	21,170
Columbia Central Turnpike	139,000	21,170
Nashville & Kentucky Turnpike ...	50,000	12,500
Clarksville & Russelville Turnpike ..	37,500	9,000
Columbia, Pulaski & Elkton Turnpike	126,600	12,233
Nashville & Murfressboro Turnpike.	66,666.66	30,530
Gallatin & Cumberland Turnpike ..	6,000	5,283
Gallatin Turnpike	130,000	26,000
Cumberland & Stone's River Turnpike	119,000	20,000
Total	$3,292,716.66	$2,244,827

The foregoing Turnpike Companies pay 6 per cent on the estimated value.

It will be perceived from the tabular statement that the actual
indebtedness and liabilities of the State for Internal Improvement
Companies and the Agricultural Bureau will make the State liable
for the sum of twelve million eight hundred and sixty-six thousand
eight hundred and fifty-six dollars and sixty-six cents, [$12,866,-
856.66] up to this time. And if all the Internal Improvement Com-

panies apply for the aid of the State which have been authorized to do so by the various acts of Assembly which have been passed to encourage works of Internal Improvements, it will swell the State debt up to not less than twenty million dollars, [$20,000,000.]

The Bonds of the State which have been already issued to the various Internal Improvement Companies have been and are now selling in the money markets at ruinous rates of discount; in fact, at a lower rate of discount than the Bonds of some of our sister States whose resources and financial ability are not superior, if equal, to those of Tennessee, to meet their public engagements. Tennessee Bonds are issued and thrown into market without any definite information as to what amount of Bonds can be, or will be, issued under existing laws, or as to whether future Legislatures will extend the amount to be issued. The want of this information on the part of those who are willing to invest their capital in State securities, as to the amount of Bonds that can and will be thrown into market, deters and prevents many who otherwise would make investments in Tennessee Bonds. It is believed that if the Legislature will fix upon some definite and known limit to which the State credit is to be extended, and especially so if that limit is clearly within the financial ability of the State, it will have an immediate influence upon the price and sale of the Bonds now in market, and those that are to be thrown upon it hereafter for sale; which will greatly relieve those Internal Improvement Companies which now have their Bonds hypothecated, and which are entitled to the issuance of Bonds hereafter. I would, therefore, recommend that the boundary of our prospective public debt be well defined, and that it be reduced to the lowest limit consistent with the interest and credit of the State. The credit of the State can be sustained by the aid of a little timely and judicious legislation in the manner already indicated. It would, also, add to the confidence and credit of the State, if the constitution was so amended as to inhibit any future Legislature from the creation of any public debt beyond a limited amount, without first submitting the proposition to the people for their approval or rejection, unless in some great emergency, such as insurrection, rebellion, or invasion. A proposition of this character at the present time, to amend the constitution of the State, would be an earnest indication to capitalists that the public mind was healthy and sound in regard to State indebtedness; and its ultimate adoption would secure the people in the future against improvident, log-rolling legislation, and the creation of heavy and excessive state indebtedness, without at least first obtaining the people's consent.

The total value of taxable property, according to the best data that can now be obtained, will aproximate three hundred million dollars $300,000,000

Total number of taxable polls	125,000
State tax on three hundred million dollars, at ten cents on the hundred dollars	300,000
State tax on one hundred and twenty-five thousand polls, at twenty-five cents	31,250

It will be perceived that from these two sources, alone, the State will derive a large revenue, amounting to three hundred and thirty-one thousand two hundred and fifty dollars, [$331,250.00] which, with the other receipts into the Treasury, ought to make a fund sufficiently large to defray the current expenses of the State, when judiciously and economically appropriated.

For a full and more detailed statement of the indebtedness of the State, and the true condition of the Treasury, I most respectfully refer you to the reports by the Comptroller and Treasurer.

By an act passed on the 27th day of February, 1854, it was provided that after paying the interest on the Bonds of the State, issued for stock in the Union Bank, the balance of the dividends and bonus shall be vested by the Governor and Comptroller in six per cent Bonds of the State. It was also made the duty of the Governor and Comptroller to cancel the Bonds purchased with the proceeds of the dividends of State Stock and bonds of the Union Bank, until the amount shall equal the sum paid out of the Treasury, for the redemption of Union Bank Bonds. Under the provision of this law, there has been paid over to the Governor and Comptroller, of the bonus and dividends of the Union Bank, one hundred and fifty-seven thousand one hundred and ninety-five dollars and ninety two cents, [$157,195.92.] Of this amount, there has been vested one hundred and five thousand one hundred and three dollars and fourteen cents, [$105,103.14,] in six per cent Bonds of the State, leaving a credit on the books of the Bank in favor of this fund of ninety-two dollars and seventy-eight cents. The Bonds which have been cancelled are on deposit in the Bank of Tennessee.

It is also provided by the second section of said act, that the dividends arising from the School Fund Stock in the Union and Planters' Banks shall be paid over to the order of the Governor and Comptroller for six per cent Bonds of the State. It is further made the duty of the Governor and Comptroller to deposit the Bonds purchased with the dividends from the School Fund Stock in the Union and Planters' Banks, in the Bank of Tennessee, and take the receipt of the President of the Bank for the same. There has been paid, of the dividends arising from the School Fund Stock, in the Union and Planters' Banks, upon the Governor and Comptroller's order, the sum of fifty-nine thousand dollars, [$59,000,] which sum has been vested in six per cent State Bonds, and the receipt of the President of the Bank of Tennessee taken for the same.

As it will become your duty to appoint a committee to examine the accounts of the Comptroller and Treasurer, I would, therefore, suggest that you direct the same Committee to examine and report as to the amount received and disbursed under the law referred to.

BANKS.

In my first two Biennial Messages to the Legislatures of 1853-4 and 1855-6, I submitted for their consideration the propriety of putting the Bank of Tennessee and its branches in a gradual course of liquidation; to which Messages you are referred for the reasons and arguments which induced these recommendations. These views were followed up and attained by the President and Directors of the Bank in their report made to the Legislature of 1855-6. The President and Directors, after having had the Bank two years under their control, closely observing it in all its practical operations connected with the finances of the Treasury, together with the monetary affairs of the State, with great unanimity of opinion recommended that it would be better for the State and the people generally to wind up the Bank, or to place it in a gradual course of liquidation; and in their report present the following irrefragable facts and arguments in support of their recommendations, to which I ask your earnest attention:

'The creation of so many new Banks at the last session of the

Legislature, in addition to those that existed before, produced so much competition between them as will, in all probability, reduce the business and profits of each to a point so low as not to justify the continuance of all of them; and in the conflicts likely to arise from such competition, an institution belonging to the State, organized as the Bank of the State is at present, is likely to be made the victim of the selfishness and cunning of others more interested and more skilful in their management than experienced citizens can be; and as the Legislature cannot now recall the charters granted to others, the Directors have come to the conclusion, with great unanimity, and from a settled conviction, that the best interests of the State require it, that the Bank of Tennessee should be put in liquidation, and its concerns closed at as early a period as the convenience of the citizens will allow.

'That non-resident stockholders should have no control over the moneyed institutions in this State; they have no interests in common with the people, and no sympathy for them in times of distress; their interests are indeed often antagonistic. Their investments in our stocks are made solely with a view to the per centum derived from them, and their control of them will be solely with a view to the profits that can be secured by them. That dealing in the circulating medium of the State, whether of the precious metals or paper currency, which regulates the value of property and the price of the productions of the State, should be prohibited as far as the Legislature has the authority to do so. The citizens have too deep an interest in the amount, as well as the quality of the circulating medium by which the trade and business of the country is carried on, to allow any intermeddling with it by stockjobbers, speculators, brokers, or bankers turned brokers.

'The Bank of Tennessee was established for the purpose of creating "a fund for Internal Improvements," and to aid in the establishment of a system of education.

'The operations of the bank in a few years seem to have convinced the General Assembly of the impracticability of accomplishing the great objects of its creation under the organization which had been given it; and an act was passed in 1849, directing the profits of the bank to be paid into the Treasury, and the payment of the interest on the bonds of the State and the School Fund to be made by the Treasury. By that time near a million of dollars had been taken from the capital by appropriations of the Legislature, and the debts lost by the bank. By the act of the 3rd March, 1854, the annual profits of the bank were directed to be applied to supply the deficiency of the capital occasioned by the bad debts. So that the bank cannot be regarded at this time in any other light than a financial project to aid the Treasury of the State. It can scarcely be doubted that an investment of the School Funds, composing in part the capital of the bank, in the bonds of the State, bearing an interest of six per cent would have been a more wise and judicious disposition of them, than in the stock of any corporation yielding nominally two or three per cent more; and especially in one which was subject, from its organization, to all the casualties arising from the change of its officers every few years, as the one or the other party prevailed in our elections, and to the carelessness, negligence, or frauds of those controlling it. The other portion of its capital belonging to the State, a million of dollars, was obtained by issuing bonds of the State, bearing six per cent interest, and upon which the State now pays interest, and will be compelled to pay whether the bank yields a profit or not.

'From the operations of the bank heretofore, there is strong reason to apprehend that losses of a similar character may occur hereafter, and that the profits, by the time the charter expires, may be required to reinstate the capital as now required by the act of 1854. Under such circumstances, it would seem to be the true policy of the State to pay the million dollars for the bonds of the State whilst it has the means under the control of the bank, and to invest the school funds in other bonds of the State bearing interest, and thus avoid the hazards incident to borrowing money to be reloaned under the control of any corporate body. The public is seldom benefited by such financial schemes.

'If the money has to be paid by the citizens, it makes but little difference whether it be done through the Treasury or by the profits on discounts, and loans made to them through such a corporation; the more direct the mode adopted, the better generally for the citizens. It is, in the opinion of the Board of Directors, no unimportant matter to avoid the danger, seriously apprehended by many, of subjecting the citizens to taxation for the payment of the debts created for the establishment of the bank, which would be the case in the event of any serious disaster happening to it before the expiration of its charter. The fund now belonging to the State, and now in bank, will go far toward extinguishing the present indebtedness of the State. The present time seems more favorable for the accomplishment of this object than any other for years past, or than may be expected for years to come. The circulation of this bank is now less than it has been for years, and if withdrawn, its place will be at once supplied by the numerous banks now in operation, and its loss will be scarcely felt by the community.

'The past season has been more favorable to the great interests of the State than for many years, and the surplus products will enable the debtors of the bank to meet the demands against them without serious embarrassment, if a reasonable time be allowed for that purpose.

'By closing the concerns of the bank, an end will be made of the competition for making money between the State and its own citizens, and especially with those corporations in which it has so large an interest. Such contests always result in the loss of money, as well as credit to the State; and the exciting contests for the control of its capital which is witnessed almost at every general election, will be avoided.'

This report of the President and Directors, of itself, seems almost conclusive upon the subject, well nigh superseding the propriety of offering any thing more in addition to what they have said. The necessity and expediency of longer continuing the bank as a fiscal agent for the Treasury, or, as a convenience for the people in their monetary affairs, would seem, after reading the able report made by the President and Directors of the bank, an utter absurdity; and it should be dispensed with, and thereby all connection between the State and Banks be dissolved. To carry on the business of banking is not one of the objects for which the State was created, no more than it was to go into the pursuits of agriculture or mechanics. It was not designed by those who framed the Constitution of the State, or of the United States, that the States should become either bankers, or brokers, or Moneychangers in any sense of the term, or to make any thing a tender in payment of debts except gold and silver. This is the currency intended by the framers of the Constitution of the United States and of the States, for the people. It may be assumed that this great principle has never been violated, so as to come in conflict with the letter of the organic law of the land, but it has been violated in spirit and practice since the creation of the first bank in the State, and the people have been made the sufferers in the end by every such violation of this fundamental principle of currency.

Within the last four years, not to go farther back in the history of banking in Tennessee, ten or twelve of the banks of the State have suspended specie payment. The failure of these banks will result in the loss of millions to the people, who had exchanged their produce for the worthless circulation. The time has arrived when the legislation of the country should be brought to bear upon all these spurious schemes and plans of originating what is commonly called money, a mere paper circulation, which passes for currency one day, and on the next becomes valueless in the hands of some innocent holder, who has exchanged the product of his field, or shop, or day's labor, for the worthless trash. To the extent that legislation can be made to bear upon currency, it should be in making the circulating medium uniform in quantity and value, and thereby give all the business transactions of the country uniformity and stability, and should studiously avoid all legislation which will expand or contract the circulating medium, or diminish it in value. As between the banks which have been incorporated in this State, the Bank of Tennessee is believed to be in as sound and healthy a condition as any other bank in the State, if not more so; and upon an exhibit of the business transactions of the bank since it has been under the control of the present able, efficient and honest Directory and President, it will be shown that the bank has realized greater profits made fewer bad debts, and has given more general satisfaction to the public than in any other period of four years since its incorporation. It is believed, however, notwithstanding the institution has been well that it would be safer and better, and more profitable in the end, to convert the entire capital of the bank, and all the real estate owned by it, into six per cent bonds, as recommended in my former Messages, and subsequently by the President and Directors of the bank. By converting the entire capital of the bank into State bonds, the whole machinery now necessary to carry it on successfully might be dispensed with, which would result in a saving of some thirty-five or forty thousand dollars per annum to the State.

It is the opinion of some, and it may be urged before the Legislature, that the capital of the Bank of Tennessee should be increased to an amount which would enable it to control the entire banking accommodations and circulating medium of the State, and at the same time giving to the President and Directory of the principal bank, located at Nashville, absolute control of all the branches throughout the State, establishing a kind of central power at the city of Nashville, which, according to their views of the business and wants of the country, could expand and contract the circulation at pleasure. The entire circulation of banks in the State on the first of January, 1857, in round numbers, was eight million dollars, ($8,-000,000.) A bank, with the capacity to furnish eight millions of circulation, must be under the control of a central regency; which central regency must always, to a greater or less extent, be governed by the influences which surround it. To increase the capital of the Bank of Tennessee, and confer these additional powers upon it, would be doing great injustice to the other commercial divisions of the State, each of which would be more competent to judge of its necessities and conveniences, as to the amount of the circulation required, than any Directory could be at the city of Nashville.

If banks are to be continued for the purpose of making and issuing paper circulation, it would be but just and fair to give to each commercial division the control of its own banking accommodations, and all the circulation issued by banks in each of these commercial divisions should be made redeemable at the counter of the bank where issued, and at the principal commercial point in each division. For instance, to suppose East Tennessee to constitute one division: let all the circulating medium, issued by the banks in that division, be made redeemable at the counter of the bank where issued, and at whatever point may be deemed the most commercial point in that division. And so with the Middle and Western divisions of the State: requiring each one of those principal commercial points to make arrangements with the other two for the redemption of their paper circulation whenever it passed beyond the commercial boundary in which it was issued. An arrangement by the banks, upon a principle of this kind, would exert a powerful and salutary influence in making the bank paper uniform in value and quantity, when thrown into circulation by each of the commercial divisions, and at the same time leave each to determine the wants and necessities in regard to banking accommodations in each commercial division.

I have stated that the circulation of banks in this State, on the first of January, 1857, was eight million dollars. I will now add, that the entire amount of specie in all the banks, great and small, with which this eight millions of bank paper was to be redeemed, in round numbers, was two million dollars. The bare statement of this fact must be conclusive to all minds, which are familiar with the operations of banks, that eight millions of bank paper, resting upon two millions of specie, cannot be sustained whenever there is a pressure or a derangement of the monetary affairs of the country.

A circulation in paper amounting to four dollars for one in specie, cannot afford a sound and uniform currency. A circulation which can be expanded from two to eight millions of dollars, as the interest and cupidity of the banks may suggest, can never be made uniform in quantity or value, but the whole country must be subjected to the increase and diminution of prices, for all the products of the country, just in proportion as their bank accommodations are expanded or contracted. This state of things is bad enough when brought about by all the banks, but to confer such a power upon any one institution, whether it be a State bank, or otherwise, embracing separate and distinct commercial divisions to be controlled by a Directory in the city of Nashville, is a state of things which I hope will never be brought about by the representatives of the people of Tennessee.

In recommending to your consideration the propriety of winding up the Bank of Tennessee, it will not be inferred or understood by any, that I am in favor of the creation or continuance of Stock or Free Banks. I would be in favor of winding them all up, so soon as it is practicable and consistent with the commercial, agricultural, and mechanical wants of the country to do so: believing as I do that the whole banking system in the United States is *founded in error*, and that all banks having their origin in such a system must necessarily contain the elements of their own destruction, and, as a general rule, will sooner or later result in ruin or fraud, producing great injury in all the business transactions and morals of the community wherever they may be located. But to attain this end will require time and the exercise of sound discretion. The work has to be commenced; and we had as well set the example by commencing with the Bank of Tennessee, constantly and steadily progressing, until there shall not be a bank incorporation left in the State. This being once accomplished here, hoping that a similar policy will be pursued and carried out by all the surrounding States, the vacuum created by their withdrawal will be supplied by the capitalists in furnishing exchange for the commercial wants of the community, and money, in the proper sense of the term, sufficient to purchase all the surplus product of the country. This will follow as naturally and as certainly as water will find its level, or the surrounding atmosphere supply and fill up a vacuum when created.

The strongest objection now urged to the winding up of the Bank of Tennessee is, that it is necessary as a fiscal agent for the State to receive its revenue and disburse the same, to pay the interest on State Bonds that have been issued, or may hereafter be issued. This objection, when examined and reduced to a practical test, ceases to have any force or solidity in it whatever. I would most respectfully suggest that all the duties now performed by the Bank of Tennessee as a fiscal agent in receiving and disbursing the revenue of the State and paying the interest upon State Bonds, can be performed by the Comptroller and Treasurer, the financial officers of the State proper, with equal convenience and safety, and at a far less expense than it now costs to carry on the machinery of the Bank of Tennessee.

It is a matter of great importance to the people of Tennessee that our State should be free from debt. If the policy I have recommended should be adopted, the debt which accrued under the acts of 1835-6, and 1837-8, would be liquidated in a very short time. We should then have no interest to pay in the Eastern cities, except on the bonds loaned to railroad companies, and would, therefore, need no bank or other fiscal agent to make payment at any place, other than at the office of the State Treasurer.

Under the act of 1851-2, by which the State credit was loaned to various railroad companies, provision was made that the interest accruing on the bonds loaned should be paid into the Bank of Tennessee fifteen days before it become due in New York. Surely any president of a railroad company having the money to pay the interest on the bonds issued to his road, could, in less than fifteen days, by buying exchange from a bank or broker, or by shipping coin, transfer the amount to New York, or any other point in the Union. This is often done now, as many of the roads have issued bonds which are endorsed by the State, and the interest has been promptly met, without any agency on the part of the Bank of Tennessee. Our merchants and manufacturers must necessarily have frequent payments to make in the Northern and Southern States. These payments are made by purchasing exchange from banks or brokers, and so long as capital is employed in any pursuit which requires the transmission of money from one point to another to pay for articles purchased, there surely will be, even in the absence of all banks, exchange brokers or factors ready to supply any demand for exchange.

In no event can there be any necessity for a fiscal agent, other than the Treasurer or State comptroller. Both of these officers should be well qualified for the important positions they occupy, and as competent to manage the finances of the State as a bank president or cashier. The Constitution of the State provides for the election of a Treasurer and entrusts to him the receiving and disbursing the entire funds of the State.

It may be said that a bank is better able than the Treasurer to tell the condition of other banks, and would not receive the notes of such Banks as would likely become insolvent. Such an argument would only prove that some former Legislature had chartered corporations for banking purposes, without requiring sufficient indemnity to protect the note-holder. In granting banking privileges to a company, the people have a right to expect of their representatives, that they should be fully protected from fraud in the circulation of any bank notes. If the Legislature would grant no banking privileges except when the note-holder was secure beyond any possible contingency, it would be simply discharging a duty which the electors have a right to demand of their representatives.

Within a period of about four years, as before remarked, many of the banks chartered by our Legislature have entirely failed, and

the money put in circulation by some of them will prove to be almost worthless to the note-holder. I am of the opinion that this evil
might have been prevented at the time the charters were obtained,
and I am clearly of the opinion that you have the power to guard
against any further fraud which may possibly be practiced by any of
the banks chartered by a previous Legislature. It will certainly not
be contended that any former Legislature can take out of your
hands the power to correct any evil, or prevent a fraud from being
practiced on the people you represent.

Our State, very properly, requires security of all its officers
having charge of any of the State money or property. Individuals
require security of each other in their daily money transactions, and
there is no reason why a corporation, chartered by our Legislature,
with the privilege of issuing notes, checks, and bills of credit, should
not be required to give ample security to the note-holder. The integrity and business capacity of bank officers is often the principal
capital of banks. Past experience has taught us that this is not a
sufficient guaranty to the note-holder, that he will be paid when he
presents to a bank its own issue. It becomes, therefore, a matter of
first importance for the safety of the funds of the State, the security
of the people, and for the prosperity of all branches of industry,
that in granting charters of incorporation, when special privileges
are guaranteed to the few, a credit should not be given such corporation until it is deprived of all power to do injury. I cannot see the
necessity of our State creating a Bank, or continuing one already in
existence, with 'power to emit bills of credit,' on the ground that we
require a fiscal agent to receive, disburse, and keep more safely the
funds of the State.

The losses sustained by the State on account of depredations of
officers, in the Bank of Tennessee, are large, compared with any
loss sustained on account of our State Treasurer.

In my last Biennial Message, I recommended the passage of a
law suppressing the issuance and circulation of bank notes or bills
of a less denomination than five dollars. An act passed by the last
Legislature, 'To regulate Banking,' the third section of which, it
seems, was intended to accomplish that purpose, has wholly failed to
do so. It merely prohibits the issuance of small notes by the banks,
but does not suppress the circulation of those already issued, and it

is believed that the amount in circulation on the passage of the law has not been materially diminished. The law has, no doubt, in many instances been evaded and violated in getting notes back into circulation which had been returned to the Banks by their holders. It is hoped that the Legislature will so amend the present law as to prevent the issuance of smaller notes than five dollars by all of the banks, and, after giving a reasonable notice, to suppress the circulation, among the people, of all those which have heretofore been issued, and especially those which have been issued by other States, and find their way here for circulation.

The vacuum created by the withdrawal of those change bills, which have been thrown into circulation by the numerous banks throughout the State, will at once, be supplied with gold and silver—the currency intended for the great mass of the people. Banks which cannot furnish the community with a gold and silver currency, from five dollars down, are not entitled to public confidence, and ought to be wound up, and the sooner it is done the better for the public good. In fine, let the law be so amended as to suppress the circulation of all bank paper of a less denomination than five dollars. The propriety of the passage of a law like this is so clear and obvious to all, that it is not necessary again to repeat the arguments in its favor.

WEIGHTS AND MEASURES.

By a joint resolution adopted March 3d, 1854, the Governor of the State was authorized to appoint a suitable person as Superintendent of weights and measures. In obedience to this resolution, Mr. John Heriges has been appointed Superintendent to take charge of the weights and measures, as furnished by the Federal Government, under a resolution passed June 14th, 1836. Since his appointment as Superintendent, the weights and measures have been received and are now under his control, and by him have been deposited in one of the rooms of the Capitol set apart by the Commissioners for that purpose. The weights and measures are all in good order, and are now subject to inspection by both branches of the Legislature. The resolution authorizing the appointment of Superintendent of weights and measures made no provision for any compensation to him for the time and labor necessary for their preservation, which are now in his possession. It cannot be expected that the superintendent can lose his time and labor without some reasonable consideration therefor.

The resolution also authorized the Governor to have made under the direction of the Superintendent a set of standard weights and measures for each county in the State. Not without some difficulty and trouble, the manufacture of a set of weights and measures for each county in the State has been commenced, and five sets have been completed, which in workmanship will most favorably compare with those furnished by the Federal Government. The five sets completed are deposited in the same room with those furnished by the Federal Government, and both branches of the Legislature are respectfully invited to examine and compare them with those furnished by the government and determine for themselves as to the accuracy and workmanship with which they have been prepared. Before the Superintendent commenced the manufacture of the weights and measures, he visited Washington City, where the originals were made, and several of the States which had prepared weights and measures, by the standard furnished them by the Federal Government, for the purpose of getting the best pattern and ascertaining the most economical terms upon which they could be made. It was then believed from the most reliable data that could be had, that it would cost two hundred dollars per set to manufacture them. After taking every step for the purpose of obtaining accurate information in regard to the cheapest and best mode of supplying all the counties in the State, as contemplated by the resolution referred to, it was believed that the weights and measures could be manufactured in Nashville of equal quality as to workmanship and material, and upon as economical terms as those which have been manufactured in any of the other States. Entertaining this opinion, steps have been taken, and the experiment has been fairly made in the five sets already manufactured, which has proven that the average cost will not be more than one hundred and fifty-nine dollars per set. Sound policy, and the urgent demand of almost every county, and the best interests of the State, require the completion of this work at the earliest day practicable, thereby bringing about uniformity in the weights and measures throughout the State. It is regretted that it has not been in the power of the Governor to have provided every county in the State with a set of standard weights and measures, as authorized, before this time. I will add that there should be a law passed, or the laws now in force should be so amended as to fix definitely and intelligibly what is the standard of weights and measures, and to annex such penalties as will most certainly insure a compliance with its provisions.

TAX ON MERCHANTS.

In my Message to the last Legislature, the attention of that body was called to the subject of merchants' taxes, and as no action was then taken upon it, I again submit that portion of my Message to your consideration:

'There is some complaint with the mercantile interest, in consequence of the unequal and discriminating operation of our revenue laws regulating merchants' license. The complaint is not without some foundation and good cause on their part. The law, as it now stands, requires all wholesale and retail dealers in merchandise in this State to first pay into the Treasury of the State one half of one per cent on the invoice cost of all goods vended by them. The main cause of complaint, as I understand it, is, that, in the first place, the wholesale merchant, by the revenue law, is required to first pay into the treasury the half of one per cent or fifty cents on the hundred dollars. After the tax is paid by him into the Treasury, the retail merchant then purchases the same goods of him and takes them to another establishment, in or out of the county where purchased, as the case may be, and vends them again; for which he is required to pay one half of one per cent, or fifty cents on the hundred dollars, into the Treasury; which is one per cent paid to the State for the goods thus sold. By this process, it will be perceived that the State lays a double tax on the goods purchased from the wholesale dealer within the limits of the State. The business retail dealer has no difficulty in understanding the operation, and finds it to his interest to go beyond the limits of the State to make his purchases, and thereby save the one-half of one per cent in the purchase of his goods, or fifty cents on every hundred dollars. It must be obvious to all business men, that if the wholesale dealer is required first to pay the tax into the Treasury, that when the retail merchant buys of him he must pay it back, and then when he makes sale of the goods, he must pay a like amount into the Treasury; which is practically compelling the country merchant to pay a double tax to the State on the same goods, which, as a matter of course, makes it his interest to go beyond the limits of the State to make his purchases, and become the customer of the foreign wholesale dealer, instead of the wholesale dealer at home; and to that extent operates against our own commercial cities and commercial men.

'It is most manifest to my mind that the practical effect of the revenue law, as it now stands, regulating merchants' license, is to discriminate against the merchant at home and in favor of the one abroad. The subject is, therefore, submitted to your consideration, with the hope that the law will be so modified as to place the mercantile interest of the State on an equal footing and in a field of fair competition with a like interest of the other States of the Union.'

PUBLIC ROADS.

In again calling the attention of the Legislature to this subject, I can do nothing more than substantially repeat what I have heretofore stated to preceding Legislatures. Our whole system of public roads is exceedingly defective, more so perhaps than in any of our sister States, which detracts materially from the facilities of travel and the transfer of the surplus products to the main channels of commerce, both as to the rivers and railroads which penetrate the country, bearing off the great staples of the State to distant markets. The condition in which our public roads are now kept depreciates materially the value of all property, real and personal, which is not situated immediately upon our navigable streams or line of railroads. Besides, the expense and burden of keeping up our public roads fall mainly upon that portion of our fellow citizens who are least able to bear it, and who have the least use for public roads after they have been put in repair. Many of our fellow-citizens are compelled to perform manual labor on the public roads, a number of days in the course of a year, who have not the time to spare from their other pursuits without pay. Their own condition and the necessities of their families are such, as to require the proceeds of their entire labor for their support; while, on the other hand, there are many who are exempt by law from working on the public roads, who are either able physically to work or pecuniarily to pay for having it done, and in fact who derive the greatest benefit from good roads when they are made, by the enhanced value good roads always impart to property. There are many of our fellow citizens who deal in thousands, and own in value large amounts of property, who never pay one farthing to keep our public roads in repair or to open new ones, while there are others who own no property, and whose pecuniary dealings are confined to their absolute necessities, and who have not even a vehicle of any kind, nor one single pound of surplus product to transport on them, but who under our present laws are required to toil many days in the year in repairing roads which are of little or no use to them. In view of changing or modifying our present system of public roads, I most respectfully invite your attention to the systems adopted in the States of Ohio and Pennsylvania, where property and other taxes are levied for the purpose of keeping them up, and thereby establishing and carrying out the principle that all persons who derive the greatest benefit from their being kept in repair and in proper condition for the travelling public, shall pay correspondingly out of their means for the benefits thus conferred. All persons should contribute to the support of the government under which they live, in proportion to the protection which they may receive from it. It is the physical power in a government, under the direction of law, which gives security, protection, and value to all the property owned by the citizen. The owners of property constitute but a very small portion who make up what is commonly denominated the physical power of the government; the non-property holder constitutes not less than three and perhaps four-fifths of those who make the aggregate of physical power. This is the population that is called upon in time of danger and need to suppress insurrection at home or to repel invasion from abroad. It will be perceived, though they are not property holders, they constitute one of the most important elements in the government; hence the conclusion, against oppressing that portion of the community which gives protection and security to all who own property, real and personal. Our present road system, it must be conceded by all who are reasonable and just, operates unequal and oppressive upon the great mass of the people, and it ought to undergo a radical and thorough change. I therefore most respectfully recommend to your favorable consideration the propriety and justice of so changing or modifying our common road system as to conform it to the requirements of the public judgment and wants of the country, and that it be done during the present session of the Legislature.

LAW REFORM.

On two former occasions, I called the attention of the Legislature to this all-important subject, so deeply interesting to the people throughout the State, and earnestly pressed the adoption of a system which has been so unmistakably indicated by the public judgment in the popular elections which have recently taken place, and will again refer the General Assembly to my views as then expressed upon this subject, with the earnest hope that the Legislature will conform their action to the popular will, in carrying it out at the earliest day practicable. I am advised that Messrs. Cooper and Meigs, who have been appointed by the Legislature to prepare a Digest of the Laws of this State, have with great care and much labor performed that service, and will at an early day submit their Digest to your inspection and consideration.

If our system of jurisprudence is so modified as to conform to the requirements of the public interest, during your present sitting, I am advised that the Digest which has been prepared, can be suited or adapted to the change which may be made in our system of jurisprudence, with but little labor and very slight alterations.

These are subjects that will merit your care and attention, which I have no doubt they will receive at an early day of your session.

AGRICULTURAL BUREAU

Under the act of 1854, establishing a State Agricultural Bureau, charters have been granted to Agricultural Societies in thirty-six counties, viz: Six in East Tennessee, fifteen in Middle Tennessee, and fifteen in West Tennessee. Of these, about twenty-five have complied with the law in regard to annual reports, thus entitling themselves to the bounty provided by the act, from the State Treasury, of two hundred dollars each. Fairs were held last year in twenty-one counties, in addition to the State and Divisions' fairs. Reports of these fairs, with specific statements of the manner in which the bounty of the State has been applied, will be laid before you in the Biennial Report of the Secretary of the Bureau.

The opening of works of Internal Improvements in different sections of the State, affording means for the more rapid and cheap transportation of the products of the field to market, and consequently enhancing the price which the producer realizes for his investment of labor and capital, has awakened a new interest in improved modes of cultivation and in those labor-saving machines by which harvests of large fields are speedily gathered and prepared for market, as well as in improved and more valuable breeds of domestic animals. A large portion of the soil of Tennessee is of exhaustless fertility when carefully and skillfully cultivated. Associations like those contemplated in the act establishing the State Agricultural Bureau, when wisely managed, are of vast importance to the State, by stimulating competition and constantly provoking comparisons of methods among enterprising farmers. I am satisfied that the bounty of the State in this direction has been wisely bestowed. Many of the wisest practical agriculturists are heartily engaged in the scheme inaugurated by the Legislature of 1854, and I confidently look to constantly increasing benefits to the people of the State as the reward of their labors, and as a return for the appropriations made from the Treasury to encourage them.

The development of the mechanical and manufacturing resources of the State is an object altogether worthy of your consideration, and which should engage the attention of every citizen, and arouse the energies of every capitalist, and such assistance ought to be given to aid in further developments as may be found consistent with judicious legislation. We are possessed of natural elements, if properly developed and successfully directed, which would give us a commanding position among our sister States, by supplying them with articles of manufacture and implements of husbandry. Instead, however, of furnishing supplies, the product of our natural resources, to the surrounding States, we are to-day dependent on them for the ordinary articles of mechanism, required by the farmer, the merchant, the mechanic and housekeeper.

The 'Mechanics' Institute' of Tennessee, has done much, it is believed, by its annual fairs, to stimulate the mechanical and manufacturing interest of the State, and to develop much talent peculiar to the successful prosecution of these branches of industry. The leading principle upon which this institution is established, is paramount, in directing the mechanical genius of the young men of the country, in that branch of mechanism to which it is best adapted. In brief, it is designed to stimulate and bring out the latent mechanical talent and excite a laudable ambition among mechanics, manufacturers, artizans and inventors, to excel, to foster and to encourage the arts in every way, and ultimately to establish a school of design for the benefit of the youth of the State, whose opportunities are limited for the want of pecuniary means, or otherwise. The institution is not established upon such a basis as desired by the Directors; though they have been struggling against many difficulties, it is believed they will ultimately succeed in its permanent establishment. They desire to erect a hall suitable for the institution, and have already leased a lot of ground convenient and favorably located for the erection of suitable buildings.

The Legislature with great liberality has aided other important interests in the State, such as railroads and agriculture. Will it not, therefore, extend similar aid to manufacturers and mechanics, and in so doing, place these great interests on an equal footing with the other industrial pursuits of the country, and thereby exonerate the Legislature from the charge of invidious and partial Legislation? *If you legislate for one, legislate for the whole.*

HERMITAGE.

It was made the duty of the Governor, by an act entitled 'An Act to purchase the Hermitage,' passed by the last Legislature, to purchase for the State of Tennessee, five hundred acres of the late residence of Andrew Jackson, deceased, including the Mansion, Tomb, and other improvements known as the Hermitage, and said act authorized him to issue six per cent Coupon Bonds to the amount of forty-eight thousand dollars, ($48,000,) in payment of the same.

In compliance with this law, the purchase has been made, the five hundred acres, including the Mansion, Tomb, and other improvements known as the Hermitage, has been run out and platted by a competent and skilful surveyor, and a title unencumbered has been made to the State, which title has been registered in the Register's office, of Davidson County, and is now on file in the office of the Secretary of State. It was also made, by said act, the duty of the Governor to tender the said property to the General Government of the United States, upon the express condition that it be used as a site for a branch of the Military Academy at West Point. This tender has been made by the Government in person to the Federal Government, through the President of the United States; the President transmitted the tender as made to both branches of Congress. The subject was there taken up and referred to the appropriate committees. In the Senate it was referred to the Committee on Military Affairs, which the committee, after consideration, made a favorable report, accompanied with a bill, accepting of the five hundred acres, upon the terms and conditions authorizing the tender to be made. The proposition at the time, so far as it could be ascertained, seemed to be favorably entertained by both Houses of Congress. But it being the short session, and much important business remaining to be disposed of, Congress adjourned on the fourth of March, without having any definite action upon the proposition, and it is still pending before the Federal Government for its final determination.

In the event the Federal Government should refuse to accept of the property tendered by the State, would it not be better to set it apart as a permanent residence for all future Governors of the State? In so doing, the property would be preserved from misuse and dilapidation, and the State hereafter saved from a heavy expenditure in the erection of an Executive Mansion. Would thus, furthermore, preserve, as the property of the people, the sacred spot of earth, which contains the mortal remains of her most gifted and distinguished son, whose renown as a patriot, as one who loved the people and the Union, as a statesman and a soldier, is co-extensive with the civilized world. His deeds, civil and military, are the property of the nation; his tomb belongs to the people of his adopted State, who venerate his name, and still love and cherish his memory, and who will witness the transfer of its ownership to other hands with deep regret and much dissatisfaction.

STATE CAPITOL.

It has now been more than twelve years since the corner-stone of the State Capitol was laid, and the work is still dragging along, and the Capitol in an unfinished condition. Progressing at this slow rate, it has already cost the State, including appropriations directly from the Treasury, labor performed by the Penitentiary convicts, and issuance of State bonds, &c., one million two hundred and four thousand and seventy-two dollars and twelve cents, ($1,204,072.12). To raise this amount in part, there has been issued eight hundred and forty-one thousand dollars, ($841,000,) of six per cent State bonds, the principal and interest to be paid out of the State Treasury. These bonds constitute a part of the State debt, and must, ultimately, be paid out of the people's taxes.

It would seem that the time had arrived, when the Capitol should be completed, and this source of expenditure have an end. It is believed if the work had, from the beginning, been pressed with energy and economy, that it would have been completed long before this time, and at a much less cost to the people. It is hoped that the Legislature will adopt some means by which its completion will be brought about at an early day, and this continued issuance of State Bonds, year after year, and the payment of interest thereon, be brought to a speedy and final close. I would suggest the propriety of adding to the present board of Building Commissioners, the Secretary of State, Treasurer, and Comptroller. These officers are, in most instances, from different portions of the State, and would feel themselves responsible to the people of the State for the manner in which they discharge their duty; and, furthermore, their offices are all in the Capitol, convenient to the work now being performed, and also for consultation in reference to the best mode of having it done, and as to the most vigorous means in its prosecution.

I have now laid before you such subjects for your consideration as the public interest seems to require, and will, therefore, conclude this communication with the sincere and confident hope that your labors will be distinguished for their harmony, prudence, and wisdom, and that retrenchment, reform, and rigid economy, may, by your legislation, be carried into every department of the Government, in such manner as will advance the best interests and welfare of the State.

ANDREW JOHNSON."

INAUGURAL CEREMONIES OF TENNESSEE GOVERNORS 1845-1857

Name	Date of Inauguration	Place	Oath of Office Administered by:	Term Ended
Aaron Venable Brown	Oct. 15, 1845	Nashville	Thomas Maney, Judge of Circuit Court	Oct. 16, 1847
Neill Smith Brown	Oct. 16, 1847	Nashville	Nathan Greene, Judge of Supreme Court	Oct. 16, 1849
William Trousdale	Oct. 16, 1849	Nashville	W. K. Turner, Judge of Criminal Court	Oct. 16, 1851
William Bowen Campbell	Oct. 16, 1851	Nashville	Thomas Maney, Judge of Circuit Court	Oct. 17, 1853
Andrew Johnson	Oct. 17, 1853	Nashville	W. K. Turner, Judge of Criminal Court	
	Oct. 23, 1855	Nashville	William R. Harris, Judge of Supreme Court	Nov. 3, 1857

APPENDIX

VOLUME IV

CONSTITUTION *of the* STATE OF TENNESSEE, 1835[1]

"WHEREAS, THE PEOPLE of the territory of the United States, south of the river Ohio, *having the right of admission into the General Government as a Member State thereof, consistent with the Constitution of the United States, and the act of cession of the State of North Carolina, recognizing the ordinance for the government of the territory of the United States, north west of the river Ohio, by their Delegates and Representatives in Convention assembled, did, on the sixth day of February, in the year of our Lord one thousand seven hundred and ninety-six,* ordain and establish a constitution or form of government; *and mutually agreed with each other to form themselves into a free and independent state, by the name of* 'THE STATE OF TENNESSEE'; *and whereas the General Assembly of said* State of Tennessee, *(pursuant to the third section of the tenth article of the Constitution) by an act passed on the twenty-seventh day of November, in the year of our Lord one thousand eight hundred and thirty-three, entitled* 'An act to provide for the calling of a Convention,' *did authorize and provide for the election, by the People, of Delegates and Representatives, to meet at Nashville, in Davidson county, on the third Monday in May, in the year of our Lord one thousand eight hundred and thirty-four,* 'for the purpose of revising, and amending *(or changing)* the Constitution':

WE, *therefore,* the Delegates and Representatives of the People of the State of Tennessee, *elected and in Convention assembled, in pursuance of the said Act of Assembly,* have ordained and established *the following* amended Constitution and form of Government for this State, *which we recommend to the* People of Tennessee *for their ratification; that is to say:*

---

[1] *Journal of the Constitutional Convention,* 1834, 389–411.

ARTICLE I.

DECLARATION OF RIGHTS.

SEC. I. That all power is inherent in the people, and all free governments are founded on their authority, and instituted for their peace, safety and happiness; for the advancement of those ends, they have, at all times, an unalienable and indefeasible right to alter, reform or abolish the government in such manner as they may think proper.

II. That government being instituted for the common benefit, the doctrine of non-resistance against arbitrary power and oppression, is absurd, slavish and destructive to the good and happiness of mankind.

III. That all men have a natural and indefeasible right to worship Almighty God according to the dictates of their own conscience; that no man can, of right, be compelled to attend, erect or support any place of worship, or to maintain any Minister against his consent; that no human authority can, in any case whatever, control or interfere with the rights of conscience; and that no preference shall ever be given, by law, to any religious establishment or mode of worship.

IV. That no religious test shall ever be required as a qualification to any office or public trust under this State.

V. That elections shall be free and equal.

VI. That the right of trial by jury shall remain inviolate.

VII. That the people shall be secure in their persons, houses, papers and possessions, from unreasonable searches and seizures; and that general warrants, whereby an officer may be commanded to search suspected places, without evidence of the fact committed, or to seize any person or persons not named, whose offences are not particularly described and supported by evidence, are dangerous to liberty and ought not to be granted.

VIII. That no free man shall be taken or imprisoned, or disseized of his freehold, liberties or privileges, or outlawed, or exiled, or in any manner destroyed or deprived of his life, liberty or property, but by the judgment of his peers, or the law of the land.

IX. That in all criminal prosecutions, the accused hath a right to be heard by himself and his counsel; to demand the nature and cause of the accusation against him, and to have a copy thereof; to meet the witnesses face to face; to have compulsory process for obtaining witnesses in his favor; and in prosecutions by indictment or presentment, a speedy public trial, by an impartial jury of the county or district in which the crime shall have been committed; and shall not be compelled to give evidence against himself.

X. That no person shall, for the same offence, be twice put in jeopardy of life or limb.

XI. That laws made for the punishment of facts committed previous to the existence of such laws, and by them only declared criminal, are contrary to the principles of a free government; wherefore no *ex post facto* law shall be made.

XII. That no conviction shall work corruption of blood or forfeiture of estate. The estate of such persons as shall destroy their own lives, shall descend or vest as in case of natural death. If any person be killed by casualty, there shall be no forfeiture in consequence thereof.

XIII. That no person arrested or confined in jail, shall be treated with unnecessary rigor.

XIV. That no free man shall be put to answer any criminal charge but by presentment, indictment or impeachment.

XV. That all prisoners shall be bailable by sufficient sureties unless for capital offences when the proof is evident or the presumption great. And the privilege of the writ of *habeas corpus* shall not be suspended, unless when in case of rebellion or invasion the public safety may require it.

XVI. That excessive bail shall not be required, nor excessive fines imposed, nor cruel and unusual punishments inflicted.

XVII. That all courts shall be open; and every man, for an injury done him in his lands, goods, person, or reputation, shall have remedy by due course of law, and right and justice administered without sale, denial, or delay. Suits may be brought against the State in such manner, and in such courts, as the Legislature may by law direct.

XVIII. That the person of a debtor, where there is not strong presumption of fraud, shall not be continued in prison after delivering up his estate for the benefit of his creditor or creditors, in such manner as shall be prescribed by law.

XIX. That the printing presses shall be free to every person who undertakes to examine the proceedings of the Legislature, or of any branch or officer of Government; and no law shall ever be made to restrain the right thereof. The free communication of thoughts and opinions is one of the invaluable rights of man, and every citizen may freely speak, write and print on any subject, being responsible for the abuse of that liberty. But in prosecutions for the publication of papers investigating the official conduct of officers or men in public capacity, the truth thereof may be given in evidence; and in all indictments for libels, the jury shall have a right to determine the law and the facts, under the direction of the Court, as in other criminal cases.

XX. That no retrospective law, or law impairing the obligations of contracts, shall be made.

XXI. That no man's particular services shall be demanded, or property taken, or applied to public use, without the consent of his representatives, or without just compensation being made therefor.

XXII. That perpetuities and monopolies are contrary to the genius of a free State, and shall not be allowed.

XXIII. That the citizens have a right, in a peaceable manner, to assemble together, for their common good, to instruct their representatives, and to apply to those invested with the powers of government for redress of grievances or other proper purposes, by address or remonstrance.

XXIV. That the sure and certain defence of a free people, is a well regulated militia: and, as standing armies in time of peace are dangerous to freedom, they ought to be avoided, as far as the circumstances and safety of the community will admit; and that in all cases the military shall be kept in strict subordination to the civil authority.

XXV. That no citizen of this State, except such as are employed in the army of the United States, or militia in actual service, shall be subjected to corporeal punishment under the martial law.

XXVI. That the free white men of this State have a right to keep and to bear arms for their common defence.

XXVII. That no soldier shall, in time of peace, be quartered in any house without the consent of the owner; nor in time of war, but in a manner prescribed by law.

XXVIII. That no citizen of this State shall be compelled to bear arms, provided he will pay an equivalent, to be ascertained by law.

XXIX. That an equal participation of the free navigation of the Mississippi, is one of the inherent rights of the citizens of this State: it cannot, therefore, be conceded to any prince, potentate, power, person or persons whatever.

XXX. That no hereditary emoluments, privileges, or honors, shall ever be granted or conferred in this State.

XXXI. That the limits and boundaries of this State be ascertained, it is declared they are as hereafter mentioned, that is to say: Beginning on the extreme height of the Stone mountain, at the place where the line of Virginia intersects it, in latitude thirty-six degrees and thirty minutes north; running thence along the extreme height of the said mountain to the place where Watauga river breaks through it; thence a direct course to the top of the Yellow mountain, where Bright's road crosses the same; thence along the ridge of said mountain between the waters of Doe river and the waters of Rock creek, to the place where the road crosses the Iron mountain; from thence along the extreme height of said mountain, to the place where Nolichucky river runs through the same; thence to the top of Bald mountain; thence along the extreme height of said mountain, to the Painted Rock, on French Broad river; thence along the highest ridge of said mountain, to the place where it is called the Great Iron or Smoky mountain; thence along the extreme height of said mountain, to the place where it is called Unicoi or Unaka mountain, between the Indian towns of Cowee and Old Chota; thence along the main ridge of the said mountain, to the southern boundary of this State, as described in the act of cession of North Carolina to the United States of America: and that all the territory, lands and waters lying west of the said line, as before mentioned, and contained within the chartered limits of the State of North Carolina, are within the boundaries and limits of this State, over which the people have the right of exercising sovereignty and the right of soil, so far as is consistent with the constitution of the United States, recognizing the articles of confederation, the bill of rights, and constitution of North Carolina, the cession act of the said State, and the ordinance of Congress for the government of the territory north west of the Ohio: *provided*, nothing herein contained shall extend to affect the claim or claims of individuals, to any part of the soil which is recognized to them by the aforesaid cession act: *and provided also*, that the limits and jurisdiction of this State shall extend to any other land and territory now acquired, or that may hereafter be acquired by compact or agreement with other States or otherwise, although such land and territory are not included within the boundaries herein before designated.

XXXII. The people residing south of French Broad and Holston between the rivers Tennessee and Big Pigeon, are entitled to the right of pre-emption and occupancy of that tract.

ARTICLE II.

I. The powers of the Government shall be divided into three distinct departments; the Legislative, Executive and Judicial.

II. No person or persons belonging to one of these departments, shall exercise any of the powers properly belonging to either of the others, except in the cases herein directed or permitted.

III. The Legislative authority of this State shall be vested in a General Assembly, which shall consist of a Senate and House of Representatives, both dependent on the people.

IV. An enumeration of the qualified voters and an apportionment of the Representatives in the General Assembly, shall be made in the year one thousand eight hundred and forty-one, and within every subsequent term of ten years.

V. The number of Representatives shall, at the several periods of making the enumeration, be apportioned among the several counties or districts according to the number of qualified voters in each; and shall not exceed seventy-five, until the population of the State shall be one million and a half; and shall never thereafter exceed ninety-nine; *provided*, that any county having two-thirds of the ratio, shall be entitled to one member.

VI. The number of Senators shall, at the several periods of making the enumeration, be apportioned among the several counties or districts, according to the number of qualified electors in each, and shall not exceed one-third the number of Representatives. In apportioning the Senators among the different counties, the fraction that may be lost by any county or counties, in the apportionment of Members to the House of Representatives, shall be made up to such county or counties in the Senate as near as may be practicable. When a district is composed of two or more counties, they shall be adjoining; and no county shall be divided in forming a district.

VII. The first election for Senators and Representatives shall be held on the first Thursday in August, one thousand eight hundred and thirty-five; and forever thereafter, elections for Members of the General Assembly shall be held once in two years, on the first Thursday in August; said elections shall terminate the same day.

VIII. The first session of the General Assembly shall commence on the first Monday in October, one thousand eight hundred and thirty-five; and forever thereafter, the General Assembly shall meet on the first Monday in October, next ensuing the election.

IX. No person shall be a Representative, unless he shall be a citizen of the United States of the age of twenty-one years, and shall have been a citizen of this State for three years, and a resident in the county he represents one year immediately preceding the election.

X. No person shall be a Senator unless he shall be a citizen of the United States, of the age of thirty years, and shall have resided thee [three] years in this State, and one year in the county or district, immediately preceding the election. No Senator or Representative shall, during the time for which he was elected, be eligible to any office or place of trust, the appointment to which is vested in the Executive or the General Assembly, except to the office of Trustee of a literary institution.

XI. The Senate and House of Representatives, when assembled, shall each choose a Speaker and its other officers, be judges of the qualifications and election of its members, and sit upon its own adjournments from day to day. Two-thirds of each House shall constitute a quorum to do business; but a smaller number may adjourn from day to day, and may be authorized by law to compel the attendance of absent members.

XII. Each House may determine the rules of its proceedings, punish its members for disorderly behaviour, and, with the concurrence of two-thirds, expel a member, but not a second time for the same offence; and shall have all other powers necessary for a branch of the Legislature of a free State.

XIII. Senators and Representatives shall in all cases, except treason, felony or breach of the peace, be privileged from arrest during the session of the General Assembly, and in going to and returning from the same; and, for any speech or debate in either House, they shall not be questioned in any other place.

XIV. Each House may punish by imprisonment, during its session, any person not a Member, who shall be guilty of disrespect to the House, by any disorderly or contemptuous behaviour in its presence.

XV. When vacancies happen in either House, the Governor for the time being, shall issue writs of election to fill such vacancies.

XVI. Neither House shall, during its session, adjourn without consent of the other for more than three days, nor to any other place than that in which the two Houses shall be sitting.

XVII. Bills may originate in either house, but may be amended, altered or rejected, by the other.

XVIII. Every bill shall be read once on three different days, and be passed each time in the House where it originated, before transmission to the other. No bill shall become a law, until it shall be read and passed on three different days in each House, and be signed by the respective Speakers.

XIX. After a bill has been rejected, no bill containing the same substance shall be passed into a law during the same session.

XX. The style of the laws of this State shall be, *'Be it enacted by the General Assembly of the State of Tennessee.'*

XXI. Each House shall keep a journal of its proceedings, and publish it, except such parts as the welfare of the State may require to be kept secret; the ayes and noes shall be taken in each House upon the final passage of every bill of a general character, and bills making appropriations of public moneys; and the ayes and noes of the members on any question shall, at the request of any two of them, be entered on the journal.

XXII. The doors of each House and of Committees of the Whole, shall be kept open, unless when the business shall be such as ought to be kept secret.

XXIII. The sum of four dollars per day, and four dollars for every twenty-five miles travelling to and from the Seat of Government, shall be allowed to the Members of the first General Assembly, as a compensation for their services. The compensation of the Members of the succeeding Legislatures, shall be ascertained by law; but no law increasing the compensation of the Members shall take effect until the commencement of the next regular session after such law shall have been enacted.

XXIV. No money shall be drawn from the treasury, but in consequence of appropriations made by law: and an accurate statement of the receipts and expenditures of the public money, shall be attached to and published with the laws at the rise of each stated session of the General Assembly.

XXV. No person, who heretofore hath been, or may hereafter be, a collector or holder of public moneys, shall have a seat in either House of the General Assembly, until such person shall have accounted for and paid into the treasury, all sums for which he may be accountable or liable.

XXVI. No Judge of any court of law or equity, Secretary of State, Attorney General, Register, Clerk of any court of record, or person holding any office under the authority of the United States, shall have a seat in the General Assembly; nor shall any person in this State hold more than one lucrative office at the same time: *Provided*, that no appointment in the militia, or to the office of Justice of the Peace, shall be considered a lucrative office, or operate as a disqualification to a seat in either House of the General Assembly.

XXVII. Any member of either House of the General Assembly shall have liberty to dissent from, and protest against, any act or resolve which he may think injurious to the public or to any individual, and to have the reasons for his dissent entered on the journals.

XXVIII. All lands liable to taxation, held by deed, grant, or entry, town lots, bank stock, slaves between the ages of twelve and fifty years, and such other property as the Legislature may from time to time deem expedient, shall be taxable. All property shall be taxed according to its value; that value to be ascertained in such manner as the Legislature shall direct, so that the same shall be equal and uniform throughout the State. No one species of property from which a tax may be collected, shall be taxed higher than any other species of property of equal value. But the Legislature shall have power to tax merchants, pedlars, and privileges, in such manner as they may, from time to time, direct. A tax on white polls shall be laid, in such manner and of such an amount, as may be prescribed by law.

XXIX. The General Assembly shall have power to authorize the several Counties and Incorporated Towns in this State, to impose taxes for county and corporation purposes respectively, in such manner as shall be prescribed by law; and all property shall be taxed according to its value, upon the principles established in regard to State taxation.

XXX. No article manufactured of the produce of this State, shall be taxed otherwise than to pay inspection fees.

XXXI. The General Assembly shall have no power to pass laws for the emancipation of Slaves, without the consent of their owner or owners.

ARTICLE III.

I. The Supreme Executive power of this State, shall be vested in a Governor.

II. The Governor shall be chosen by the electors of the Members of the General Assembly, at the times and places where they shall respectively vote for the members thereof. The returns of every election for Governor shall be sealed up, and transmitted to the seat of government, by the returning officers, directed to the Speaker of the Senate, who shall open and publish them in the presence of a majority of the members of each House of the General Assembly. The person having the highest number of votes, shall be Governor; but if two or more shall be equal, and highest in votes, one of them shall be chosen Governor by joint vote of both Houses of the General Assembly. Contested elections for Governor, shall be determined by both Houses of the General Assembly, in such manner as shall be prescribed by law.

III. He shall be at least thirty years of age, shall be a citizen of the United States, and shall have been a citizen of this State seven years next before his election.

IV. The Governor shall hold his office for two years, and until his successor shall be elected and qualified. He shall not be eligible more than six years in any term of eight.

V. He shall be commander-in-chief of the army and navy of this State, and of the militia, except when they shall be called into the service of the United States.

VI. He shall have power to grant reprieves and pardons, after conviction, except in cases of impeachment.

VII. He shall, at stated times, receive a compensation for his services, which shall not be increased or diminished during the period for which he shall have been elected.

VIII. He may require information in writing, from the officers in the executive department, upon any subject relating to the duties of their respective offices.

IX. He may, on extraordinary occasions, convene the General Assembly, by proclamation; and shall state to them, when assembled, the purposes for which they shall have been convened; but they shall enter on no legislative business, except that for which they were specially called together.

X. He shall take care that the laws be faithfully executed.

XI. He shall, from time to time, give to the General Assembly, information of the state of the government, and recommend to their consideration such measures as he shall judge expedient.

XII. In case of the removal of the Governor from office, or of his death, or resignation, the powers and duties of the office shall devolve on the Speaker of the Senate; and in case of the death, removal from office, or resignation of the Speaker of the Senate, the powers and duties of the office shall devolve on the Speaker of the House of Representatives.

XIII. No member of Congress, or person holding any office under the United States, or this State, shall execute the office of Governor.

XIV. When any officer, the right of whose appointment is by this Constitution vested in the General Assembly, shall, during the recess, die, or the office, by the expiration of the term, or by other means, become vacant, the Governor shall have the power to fill such vacancy, by granting a temporary commission, which shall expire at the end of the next session of the Legislature.

XV. There shall be a Seal of this State, which shall be kept by the Governor, and used by him officially, and shall be called the *Great Seal of the State of Tennessee.*

XVI. All grants and commissions shall be in the name and by the authority of the State of Tennessee, be sealed with the State Seal, and signed by the Governor.

XVII. A secretary of State shall be appointed by joint vote of the General Assembly, and commissioned during the term of four years: he shall keep a fair register of all the official acts and proceedings of the Governor; and shall, when required, lay the same, and all papers, minutes and vouchers relative thereto, before the General Assembly: and shall perform such other duties as shall be enjoined by law.

ARTICLE IV.

I. Every free white man of the age of twenty-one years, being a citizen of the United States, and a citizen of the County wherein he may offer his vote, six months next preceding the day of election, shall be entitled to vote for Members of the General Assembly, and other civil officers, for the County or District in which he resides: *provided*, that no person shall be disqualified from voting in any election on account of color, who is now by the laws of this State, a competent witness in a court of justice against a white man. All free men of color, shall be exempt from military duty in time of peace, and also from paying a free poll tax.

II. Laws may be passed excluding from the right of suffrage, persons who may be convicted of infamous crimes.

III. Electors shall in all cases, except treason, felony or breach of the peace, be privileged from arrest or summons, during their attendance at elections, and in going to and returning from them.

IV. In all elections to be made by the General Assembly, the Members thereof shall vote *viva voce;* and their votes shall be entered on the journal. All other elections shall be by ballot.

ARTICLE V.

I. The House of Representatives shall have the sole power of impeachment.

II. All impeachments shall be tried by the Senate; when sitting for that purpose, the Senators shall be upon oath or affirmation. No person shall be convicted without the concurrence of two-thirds of the Senators sworn to try the officer impeached.

III. The House of Representatives shall elect, from their own body, three Members, whose duty it shall be to prosecute impeachments. No impeachment shall be tried until the Legislature shall have adjourned *sine die,* when the Senate shall proceed to try such impeachment.

IV. The Governor, Judges of the Supreme Court, Judges of Inferior Courts, Chancellors, Attorneys for the State, and Secretary of State, shall be liable to impeachment, whenever they may, in the opinion of the House of Representatives, commit any crime in their official capacity, which may require disqualification; but judgment shall only extend to removal from office, and disqualification to fill any office thereafter. The party shall, nevertheless, be liable to indictment, trial, judgment and punishment, according to law.

V. Justices of the Peace, and other civil officers, not hereinbefore mentioned, for crimes or misdemeanors in office, shall be liable to indictment in such courts as the Legislature may direct; and upon conviction, shall be removed from office, by said court, as if found guilty on impeachment; and shall be subject to such other punishment as may be prescribed by law.

ARTICLE VI.

I. The Judicial power of this State, shall be vested in one Supreme Court, in such Inferior Courts as the Legislature shall from time to time ordain and establish, and the Judges thereof and in Justices of the Peace: The Legislature may also vest such jurisdiction as may be deemed necessary in Corporation Courts.

II. The Supreme Court shall be composed of three Judges, one of whom shall reside in each of the grand divisions of the State; the concurrence of two of said Judges, shall in every case be necessary to a decision. The jurisdiction of this Court shall be appellate only, under such restrictions and regulations as may from time to time be prescribed by law; but it may possess such other jurisdiction as is now conferred by law on the present Supreme Court. Said Courts shall be held at one place, and at one place only, in each of the three grand divisions in the State.

III. The General Assembly shall, by joint vote of both Houses, appoint Judges of the several Courts of law and equity; but courts may be established to be holden by Justices of the Peace. Judges of the Supreme Court shall be thirty-five years of age, and shall be elected for the term of twelve years.

IV. The Judges of such Inferior Courts as the Legislature may establish, shall be thirty years of age, and shall be elected for the term of twelve years.

V. The Legislature shall elect Attorneys for the State, by joint vote of both Houses, of the General Assembly, who shall hold their offices for the term of six years. In all cases where an Attorney for any district fails or refuses to attend, and prosecute according to law, the court shall have power to appoint an attorney *pro tempore*.

VI. Judges and Attorneys for the State, may be removed from office by a concurrent vote of both Houses of the General Assembly, each House voting separately; but two-thirds of all the Members elected to each House must concur in such vote: the vote shall be determined by ayes and noes, and the names of the Members voting for or against the Judge or Attorney for the State, together with the cause or causes of removal, shall be entered on the journals of each House respectively. The Judge or Attorney for the State, against whom the Legislature may be about to proceed, shall receive notice thereof, accompanied with a copy of the causes alleged for his removal, at least ten days before the day on which either House of the General Assembly shall act thereupon.

VII. The Judges of the Supreme and Inferior Courts, shall, at stated times, receive a compensation for their services, to be ascertained by law, which shall not be increased or diminished, during the time for which they are elected. They shall not be allowed any fees or perquisites of office, nor hold any other office of trust or profit under this State or the United States.

VIII. The jurisdiction of such Inferior Courts, as the Legislature may from time to time establish, shall be regulated by law.

IX. Judges shall not charge Juries with respect to matters of fact, but may state the testimony and declare the law.

X. The Judges or Justices of such Inferior Courts of law as the Legislature may establish, shall have power, in all civil cases, to issue writs of *certiorari* to remove any cause or transcript thereof, from any inferior jurisdiction, into said court on sufficient cause supported by oath or affirmation.

XI. No Judge of the Supreme or Inferior Courts, shall preside on the trial of any cause, in the event of which he may be interested or where either of the parties shall be connected with him by affinity or consanguinity, within such degrees as may be prescribed by law, or in which he may have been of counsel, or in which he may have presided in any Inferior Court, except by consent of all the parties. In case all or any of the Judges of the Supreme Court, shall be thus disqualified from presiding on the trial of any cause or causes, the Court, or the Judges thereof, shall certify the same to the Governor of the State, and he shall forthwith specially commission the requisite number of men of law knowledge, for the trial and determination thereof. In case of sickness of any of the Judges of the Supreme or Inferior Courts, so that they or any of them are unable to attend, the Legislature shall be authorized to make provision by general laws, that special Judges may be appointed to attend said Courts.

XII. All writs and other process shall run in the name of the State of Tennessee; and bear test and be signed by the respective clerks. Indictments shall conclude, '*against the peace and dignity of the State.*'

XIII. Judges of the Supreme Court shall appoint their Clerks, who shall hold their offices for the period of six years. Chancellor (if Courts of Chancery shall be established) shall appoint their Clerks and Masters, who shall hold their offices for the period of six years. Clerks of such Inferior Courts as may be hereafter established, which shall be required to be holden in the respective counties of this State, shall be elected by the qualified voters thereof, for the term of four years; they shall be removed from office for malfeasance, incompetency or neglect of duty, in such manner as may be prescribed by law.

XIV. No fine shall be laid on any citizen of this State, that shall exceed fifty dollars; unless it shall be assessed by a jury of his peers, who shall assess the fine at the time they find the fact, if they think the fine should be more than fifty dollars.

XV. The different counties in this State shall be laid off as the General Assembly may direct, into districts of convenient size, so that the whole number in each County shall not be more than twenty-five, or four for every one hundred square miles. There shall be two Justices of the Peace and one Constable elected in each district, by the qualified voters therein, except districts including county towns, which shall elect three Justices and two Constables. The jurisdiction of said officers shall be co-extensive with the County. Justices of the Peace shall be elected for the term of six, and Constables for the term of two years. Upon the removal of either of said officers from the district in which he was elected, his office shall become vacant from the time of such removal. Justices of the Peace shall be commissioned by the Governor. The Legislature shall have power to provide for the appointment of an additional number of Justices of the Peace in incorporated towns.

ARTICLE VII.

I. There shall be elected in each County, by the qualified voters therein, one Sheriff, one Trustee, and one Register; the Sheriff and Trustee for two years, and the Register for four years; *provided,* that no person shall be eligible to the office of Sheriff more than six years in any term of eight years. There shall be elected for each County, by the Justices of the Peace, one Coroner and one Ranger, who shall hold their offices for two years. Said officers shall be removed for malfeasance, or neglect of duty, in such manner as may be prescribed by law.

II. Should a vacancy occur, subsequent to an election, in the office of sheriff, trustee, or register, it shall be filled by the justices; if in that of the clerks to be elected by the people, it shall be filled by the courts; and the person so appointed, shall continue in office until his successor shall be elected and qualified; and such office shall be filled by the qualified voters at the first election for any of the county officers.

III. There shall be a Treasurer or Treasurers appointed for the State, by the joint vote of both Houses of the General Assembly, who shall hold his or their offices for two years.

IV. The election of all officers, and the filling of all vacancies that may happen, by death, resignation, or removal, not otherwise directed or provided for by this Constitution, shall be made in such manner as the Legislature shall direct.

V. The Legislature shall provide, that the election of the county and other officers by the people, shall not take place at the time that the general elections are held for Members of Congress, Members of the Legislature, and Governor. The elections shall commence and terminate on the same day.

ARTICLE VIII.

I. All Militia officers shall be elected by persons subject to military duty, within the bounds of their several companies, battalions, regiments, brigades and divisions, under such rules and regulations as the Legislature may, from time to time, direct and establish.

II. The Governor shall appoint the Adjutant General and his other Staff Officers; the Majors General, Brigadiers General and commanding officers or regiments, shall respectively appoint their Staff Officers.

III. The Legislature shall pass laws, exempting citizens belonging to any sect or denomination of religion, the tenets of which are known to be opposed to the bearing of arms, from attending private and general musters.

ARTICLE IX.

I. Whereas, Ministers of the Gospel are, by their profession, dedicated to God and the care of souls, and ought not to be diverted from the great duties of their functions; therefore, no Minister of the Gospel or Priest of any denomination whatever, shall be eligible to a seat in either House of the Legislature.

II. No person who denies the being of a God, or a future state of rewards and punishments, shall hold any office in the civil department of this State.

III. Any person who shall, after the adoption of this Constitution, fight a duel, or knowingly be the bearer of a challenge to fight a duel, or send or accept a challenge for that purpose, or be an aider or abettor in fighting a duel, shall be deprived of the right to hold any office of honor or profit in this State, and shall be punished otherwise, in such manner as the Legislature may prescribe.

ARTICLE X.

I. Every person who shall be chosen or appointed to any office of trust or profit, under this Constitution, or any law made in pursuance thereof, shall, before entering on the duties thereof, take an oath to support the Constitution of this State, and of the United States, and an oath of office.

II. Each Member of the Senate and House of Representatives, shall before they proceed to business, take an oath or affirmation, to support the Constitution of this State, and of the United States, and also the following oath: 'I, ..., do solemnly swear (or affirm,) that, as a Member of this General Assembly, I will, in all appointments, vote without favor, affection, partiality, or prejudice; and that I will not propose or assent to any bill, vote or resolution, which shall appear to me injurious to the people, or consent to any act or thing whatever, that shall have a tendency to lessen or abridge their rights and privileges, as declared by the Constitution of this State.

III. Any elector who shall receive any gift or reward for his vote, in meat, drink, money, or otherwise, shall suffer such punishment as the laws shall direct. And any person who shall directly or indirectly give, promise or bestow, any such reward to be elected, shall thereby be rendered incapable for six years, to serve in the office for which he was elected, and be subject to such further punishment, as the Legislature shall direct.

IV. New Counties may be established by the Legislature, to consist of not less than three hundred and fifty square miles, and which shall contain a population of four hundred and fifty qualified voters. No line of such county shall approach the court house of any old County from which it may be taken, nearer than twelve miles. No part of a county shall be taken to form a new County or a part thereof, without the consent of a majority of the qualified voters in such part taken off. And in all cases where an old County may be reduced for the purpose of forming a new one, the seat of justice in said old county shall not be removed without the concurrence of two-thirds of both branches of the Legislature, nor shall said old county be reduced to less than six hundred and twenty-five square miles: *provided*, however that the county of Bedford may be reduced to four hundred and seventy-five square miles; and there shall not be laid off more than one new county on the West, and one on the East, adjoining the county of Bedford, and no new county line shall run nearer than eleven and a half miles of the seat of justice of said county. The line of a new county may run within eleven miles of the seat of justice of Franklin county; *provided*, it does not reduce said county to less contents than six hundred and twenty-five square miles. The counties of Carter, Rhea, Tipton, Dyer and Sullivan are excepted out of the provisions of this section: the county of Humphreys may be divided, at such time as may be prescribed by the Legislature, making the Tennessee river the dividing line; a majority of the qualified voters of said county voting in favor of said division: the counties of Carter, Rhea and Humphreys, shall not be divided into more than two counties each; nor shall more than one new county be taken out of the territory now comprising the counties of Tipton and Dyer; nor shall the seats of justice in the counties of Rhea, Carter, Tipton and Dyer, be removed, without the concurrence of two-thirds of both branches of the Legislature. The county of Sullivan may be reduced below the contents of six hundred and twenty-five square miles, but the line of any new county which may hereafter be laid off shall not approach the county seat of said county nearer than ten miles. The counties of Marion and Bledsoe shall not be reduced below one thousand qualified voters each, in forming a new county or counties.

V. The citizens who may be included in any new county, shall vote with the county or counties from which they may have been stricken off, for members of Congress, for Governor and for members of the General Assembly, until the next apportionment of members to the General Assembly after the establishment of such new county.

ARTICLE XI.

I. All laws and ordinances now in force and use in this State, not inconsistent with this Constitution, shall continue in force and use, until they shall expire, be altered or repealed by the Legislature.

II. Nothing contained in this Constitution, shall impair the validity of any debts or contracts, or effect any rights of property, or any suits, actions, rights of action, or other proceedings in courts of justice.

III. Any amendment or amendments to this Constitution may be proposed in the Senate or House of Representatives; and if the same shall be agreed to by a majority of all the members elected to each of the two Houses, such proposed amendment or amendments shall be entered on their journals, with the yeas and nays thereon, and referred to the General Assembly then next to be chosen: and shall be published for six months previous to the time of making such choice. And if in the General Assembly next chosen as aforesaid, such proposed amendment or amendments shall be agreed to by two-thirds of all the members elected to each House, then it shall be the duty of the General Assembly to submit such proposed amendment or amendments to the people, in such manner, and at such time, as the General Assembly shall prescribe. And if the people shall approve and ratify such amendment or amendments, by a majority of all the citizens of the State, voting for Representatives, voting in their favor, such amendment or amendments shall become part of this Constitution. When any amendment or amendments to the Constitution shall be proposed in pursuance of the foregoing provisions, the same shall at each of the said sessions be read three times on three several days in each House. The Legislature shall not propose amendments to the Constitution, oftener than once in six years.

IV. The Legislature shall have no power to grant divorces, but may authorize the courts of justice to grant them for such causes as may be specified by law: *provided*, that such laws be general and uniform in their operation throughout the State.

V. The Legislature shall have no power to authorize lotteries for any purpose, and shall pass laws to prohibit the sale of lottery tickets in this State.

VI. The Legislature shall fix the rate of interest—and the rate so established shall be equal and uniform throughout the State.

VII. The Legislature shall have no power to suspend any general law for the benefit of any particular individual, nor to pass any law for the benefits of individuals inconsistent with the general laws of the land; nor to pass any law granting to any individual or individuals, rights, privileges, immunities, or exemptions, other than such as may be, by the same law, extended to any member of the community, who may be able to bring himself within the provisions of such law: *provided* always, the Legislature shall have power to grant such charters of corporation as they may deem expedient for the public good.

VIII. The Legislature shall have the right to vest such powers in the courts of justice, with regard to private and local affairs, as may be deemed expedient.

IX. A well regulated system of internal improvement is calculated to develop the resources of the State, and promote the happiness and prosperity of her citizens; therefore it ought to be encouraged by the General Assembly.

X. Knowledge, learning, and virtue, being essential to the preservation of republican institutions, and the diffusion of the opportunities and advantages of education throughout the different portions of the State, being highly conducive to the promotion of this end; it shall be the duty of the General Assembly in all future periods of this government, to cherish literature and science. And the fund called the *common school fund*, and all the lands and proceeds thereof, dividends, stocks, and other property of every description whatever, heretofore by law appropriated by the General Assembly of this State for the use of common schools, and all such as shall hereafter be appropriated, shall remain a *perpetual fund*, the principal of which shall never be diminished by legislative appropriation, and the interest thereof shall be inviolably appropriated to the support and encouragement of common schools throughout the State, and for the equal benefit of all the people thereof; and no law shall be made authorizing said fund, or any part thereof, to be diverted to any other use than the support and encouragement of common schools; and it shall be the duty of the General Assembly, to appoint a Board of Commissioners, for such term of time as they may think proper, who shall have the general superintendence of said funds, and who shall make a report of the condition of the same, from time to time, under such rules, regulations and restrictions as may be required by law; *provided*, that if at any time hereafter a division of the public lands of the United States, or of the money arising from the sales of such lands, shall be made among the individual States, the part of such lands, or money, coming to this State, shall be devoted to the purposes of education and internal improvements; and shall never be applied to any other purpose.

XI. The above provisions shall not be construed to prevent the Legislature from carrying into effect any laws that have been passed in favor of the colleges, universities or academies, or from authorizing heirs or distributees to receive and enjoy escheated property, under such rules and regulations as from time to time may be prescribed by law.

XII. The Declaration of Rights hereto prefixed, is declared to be a part of the Constitution of this State, and shall never be violated on any pretence whatever. And to guard against transgression of the high powers we have delegated, we declare every thing in the Bill of Rights contained, is excepted out of the general powers of government, and shall forever remain inviolate.

Schedule.

I. That no inconvenience may arise from a change of the Constitution, it is declared, that all officers, civil and military, shall continue to hold their offices; and all the functions appertaining to the same shall be exercised and performed according to the existing laws and Constitution, until the end of the first session of the General Assembly, which shall sit under this Constitution, and until the government can be re-organized and put into operation under this Constitution, in such manner as the first General Assembly under this Constitution shall be held in Nashville.

II. The General Assembly which shall sit after the first apportionment of representation under the new Constitution, to wit, in the year one thousand eight hundred and forty-three, shall, within the first week after the commencement of the session, designate and fix the seat of government; and when so fixed; it shall not be removed except by the consent of two-thirds of the members of both Houses of the General Assembly. The first and second sessions of the General Assembly under this Constitution shall be held at Nashville.

III. Until a land office shall be opened, so as to enable the citizens south and west of the congressional reservation line, to obtain titles upon their claims of occupancy, those who hold lands by virtue of such claims, shall be eligible to serve in all capacities where a freehold is, by the laws of the State, made a requisite qualification.

Done in Convention at Nashville, this thirtieth day of August, one thousand eight hundred and thirty-four, and of the Independence of the United States of America the fifty-ninth. In testimony whereof, we have hereunto subscribed our names.

WILLIAM B. CARTER, *President.*

ROBERT ALLEN,
HUGH C. ARMSTRONG,
ADAM R. ALEXANDER,
RICHARD BRADSHAW,
ROBERT M. BURTON,
WILLIE BLOUNT,
MACLIN CROSS,
JAMES GRAY,
NEWTON CANNON,
WILLIAM G. CHILDRESS,
TERRY H. CAHAL,
ROBERT L. COBBS,
RICHARD CHEATHAM,
BURCHETT DOUGLASS,
FRANCIS B. FOGG,
GRAY GARRETT,
JAMES GILLESPY,
BOLLING GORDON,
CALLAWAY HODGES,
ISAAC HILL,
ADAM HUNTSMAN,
WEST H. HUMPHREYS,
NELSON I. HESS,
JOHN KELLY,
ANDREW A. KINCANNON,
JOSEPH KINCAID,
PETER KENDALL,
BRADLEY KIMBROUGH,

WILLIAM LEDBETTER,
WILLIAM H. LOVING,
ABRAHAM MCCLELLAN,
ROBERT J. MCKINNEY,
JOSEPH A. MABRY,
JOHN MCGAUGHEY,
JOHN MONTGOMERY,
GEORGE W. L. MARR,
JOHN NEIL,
RICHARD NELSON,
THOMAS C. PORTER,
JOHN PURDY,
WILLIAM C. ROADMAN,
GEORGE W. RICHARDSON,
HENRY RIDLEY,
JULIUS C. N. ROBERTSON,
MATTHEW STEPHENSON,
WILLIAM T. SENTER,
JAMES W. SMITH,
WILLIAM C. SMARTT,
HENRY SHARP,
JAMES SCOTT,
ESSIE URY,
JOHN WHITSON,
ISAAC WALTON,
JOHN J. WHITE,
JONATHAN WEBSTER,
ROBERT WEAKLEY.

WILLIAM K. HILL, *Secretary.*"

MEMBERS OF THE GENERAL
ASSEMBLY OF TENNESSEE

TWENTY-SIXTH GENERAL ASSEMBLY

Held at Nashville, October 6, 1845-February 2, 1846.

SENATORS—Alfred Martin, Johnson, Carter, Sullivan, and Washington; Philip Critz, Greene and Hawkins; John F. Henry, Cocke, Sevier, and Blount; Montgomery Thornburgh, Grainger, Jefferson, and Claiborne; Thomas C. McCampbell, Knox; I. T. Lenoir, Morgan, Campbell, Anderson, and Roane; Granville C. Torbett, Monroe, McMinn, Polk and Bradley; Isaac Roberson, Hamilton, Marion, Bledsoe, Rhea, and Meigs; Samuel Turney, Fentress, Overton, Jackson, White, and Van Buren; H. M. Watterson, Coffee, Warren, DeKalb, and Cannon; John D. Fletcher, Lincoln and Franklin; Richard Warner, Bedford and Marshall; Abram P. Maury, Rutherford and Williamson; John Muirhead, Wilson; William Cullom, Sumner and Smith; John Trimble, Davidson; Jonas E. Thomas, Maury and Giles; John D. Tyler, Robertson and Montgomery; Jacob Voorheis, Dickson, Stewart, Humphreys, and Benton; Archibald G. McDougal, Hickman, Lawrence, Wayne, and Hardin; John A. Gardner, Henry, Weakley, and Obion; Valentine Sevier, Gibson, Carroll, and Dyer; John W. Harris, Madison, Haywood, Tipton, and Lauderdale; Hezekiah Bradbury, Henderson, Perry, and McNairy; James M. Williamson, Hardeman, Fayette, and Shelby.

REPRESENTATIVES—Samuel W. Williams, Carter and Johnson; John B. Hamilton, Sullivan; Brookins Campbell, Washington; Samuel Milligan, Greene; James M. Hord, Hawkins; L. C. Haynes, Washington, Greene, and Hawkins; Wilson Duggan, Cocke and Sevier; A. G. Watkins, Jefferson; Martin Cleveland, Grainger; William Houston, Claiborne; W. G. McAdoo, Campbell and Anderson; John Williams, Knox; D. W. Tedford, Blount; Henry Stephens, Monroe; Joel Henebree, Roane; Prince B. Anderson, McMinn; Robert S. Holt, Polk, McMinn, and Monroe; N. G. Frazier, Rhea and Meigs; James Lauderdale, Bradley; John Thomas, Bledsoe and Morgan; David Rankin, Hamilton; C. F. Huddleston, Overton; J. T. Quarles, Jackson; Anthony Dibbrell, White; J. G. Mitchell, Fentress, White, and Van Buren; Adrian Northcutt, Warren; John A. Fuson, DeKalb; Henry Trott, Cannon; Isaac H. Roberts, Coffee; Thomas H. Garner, Franklin; Henry Turney, Lincoln; John Buchanan, Giles; Thomas N. Jones, Lincoln and Giles; E. J. Frierson, Bedford; T. C. H. Miller, Marshall; Thomas Black, Bedford and Marshall; Powhattan Gordon, R. A. L. Wilkes, Maury; S. Venable, R. W. H. Bostwick, Williamson; J. E. Manlove, W. R. Elliston, Davidson; H. S. Frazier, Edwin Chambers, Wilson; H. B. Flippin, W. A. R. Hallum, Smith; J. C. Guild, M. C. Duffy,

Sumner; W. W. Pepper, Robertson; W. C. J. Burrus, J. W. Richardson, Rutherford; W. B. Munford, Montgomery; Thomas Shaw, Stewart; John Eubanks, Dickson; R. Yeates, Humphreys and Benton; Pleasant Walker, Hickman; Thomas M. Brashear, Perry; William B. Allen, Lawrence; Jonathan Morris, Wayne; Christopher H. McGinnis, Hardin; James Warren, McNairy; M. J. Galloway, Henderson; A. P. Hall, Carroll; John B. McFarland, Henry; E. Etheridge, Weakley; Hugh G. Bone, Gibson; Micajah Bullock, Madison; H. M. Clark, Haywood; Austin Miller, Hardeman; G. W. Fisher, Fayette; J. L. T. Sneed, Shelby; Augustus Pearce, Hardeman, Fayette, and Shelby; Philip B. Glenn, Tipton and Lauderdale; G. W. L. Marr, Dyer and Obion.

TWENTY-SEVENTH GENERAL ASSEMBLY

Held at Nashville, October 4, 1847-February 7, 1848.

SENATORS—Landon C. Haynes, Johnson, Carter, Sullivan, and Washington; James Britton, Greene and Hawkins; John F. Henry, Cocke, Sevier, and Blount; M. Thornburg, Grainger, Jefferson, and Claiborne; F. S. Heiskell, Knox; F. H. Bratcher, Campbell, Anderson, Roane, and Morgan; William H. Cook, Bradley, Monroe, McMinn, and Polk; J. M. Anderson, Bledsoe, Meigs, Hamilton, Marion, and Rhea; John A. Minnis, Fentress, Overton, Jackson, White, and Van Buren; James McGuire, Warren, DeKalb, Cannon, and Coffee; William Edward Venable, Lincoln and Franklin; Thomas Dean, Bedford and Marshall; John W. Richardson, Rutherford and Williamson; John Muirhead, Wilson; James L. McKoin, Sumner and Smith; Return J. Meigs, Davidson; Thomas M. Jones, Maury and Giles; John D. Tyler, Robertson and Montgomery; Thomas Shaw, Dickson, Stewart, Humphreys, and Benton; William P. Rowles, Wayne, Hardin, Hickman, and Lawrence; Isham G. Harris, Henry, Weakley, and Obion; Isaac I. Roach, Gibson, Carroll, and Dyer; Gayle H. Kyle, Tipton, Lauderdale, Madison, and Haywood; Hezekiah Bradbury, Henderson, Perry, and McNairy; James M. Williamson, Hardeman, Fayette, and Shelby.

REPRESENTATIVES—Samuel Williams, Johnson and Carter; Jesse Cross, Sullivan; James W. Duncan, Washington; William McDaniel, Greene; John F. White, Hawkins; Jacob Miller, Washington, Greene, and Hawkins; Wilson Duggan, Cocke and Sevier; C. T. P. Jarnagin, Jefferson; Hardin P. Shannon, Grainger; W. W. Greer, Claiborne; William Cross, Campbell and Anderson; John Williams, Knox; Calvin D. Anderson, Blount; James Ramsey, Monroe; John W. Wester, Roane; David W. Ballew, McMinn; James H. Stuart, Polk, McMinn, and Monroe; Caleb Muse, Rhea and Meigs; James Orme, Bledsoe and Morgan; James A. Whitesides, Hamilton; David Rankin, Marion and Hamilton; William Donaldson, Overton; Rodham Kenner, Jackson; A. S. Rogers, White; J. G. Mitchell, Fentress, White, and Van Buren; Adrian Northcutt, Warren; Jacob Adcock, Cannon; John A. Fuson, DeKalb; Willis Blanton, Coffee; F. T. Estill, Franklin; Coleman A. McDaniel, Lincoln; Archibald Wright, Giles; John M. Bright, Lincoln and Giles; Franklin Buchanan, Lawrence; W. H. Wisener, Bedford; T. C. H. Miller, Bedford and Marshall; Benjamin Williams, Marshall; R. A. Z. Wilkes, Barclay Martin, Maury; James Robinson, F. Hardeman, Williamson; Joseph E. Manlove, John Bell, Davidson; E. S. Smith, T. W. Davis, Wilson; Hugh B. Flippin, James Barnett, Smith; W. M. Blackmore, King Kerley, Sumner; H. Norman, W. C. J. Burrus,

Rutherford; W. W. Pepper, Robertson; E. P. McGinty, Montgomery; John Eubank, Dickson; James Wyley, Humphreys and Benton; Samuel B. Moore, Hickman; Thomas M. Brashear, Perry and Decatur; William Benham, Wayne; Daniel Smith, Hardin; James Warren, McNairy; Obed F. Hendricks, Henderson; Beverly S. Allen, Carroll; James T. Dunlap, Henry; Presley F. Glass, Weakley; Felix Parker, Gibson; John T. Herron, Madison; James A. Rogers, Haywood; Edwin Polk, Hardeman; William A. Jones, Hardeman, Fayette, and Shelby; Humphrey R. Bate, Tipton and Lauderdale; R. P. Caldwell, Dyer and Obion; James M. McCalla, Fayette; Samuel Bond, Shelby; A. Goodrick, Stewart.

TWENTY-EIGHTH GENERAL ASSEMBLY

Held at Nashville, October 1, 1849-February 11, 1850.

SENATORS—Abraham Tipton, Johnson, Carter, Sullivan, and Washington; Francis Britton, Greene and Hawkins; Samuel Pickens, Cocke, Sevier, and Blount; M. Thornburg, Grainger, Claiborne, and Jefferson; John F. Henry, Knox; William Tunnell, Campbell, Anderson, Roane, and Morgan; James Walker, Monroe, McMinn, Polk, and Bradley; James W. Gillespie, Hamilton, Marion, Bledsoe, Rhea, and Meigs; E. L. Gardenhire, Fentress, Overton, Jackson, and White; Adrian Northcut, Warren, DeKalb, Cannon, and Coffee; John McDaniel, Lincoln, and Franklin; John Laws, Bedford and Marshall; R. W. H. Bostwick, Rutherford and Williamson; James Hamilton, Wilson; Samuel M. Fite, Sumner and Smith; Felix K. Zollicoffer, Davidson; Richard A. L. Wilkes, Maury and Giles; H. S. Kimble, Robertson and Montgomery; Benton T. W. Shaw, Dickson, Stewart, Humphreys, and Benton; I. W. Whitfield, Wayne, Hardin, Hickman, and Lawrence; William S. S. Harris, Henry, Weakley, and Obion; M. R. Hill, Gibson, Carroll, and Dyer; Gayle H. Kyle, Madison, Haywood, Tipton, and Lauderdale; Thomas M. Brashear, Decatur, Henderson, Perry, and McNairy; George W. Fisher, Hardeman, Fayette, and Shelby.

REPRESENTATIVES—Hawkins P. Murphy, Carter and Johnson; James Odell, Sullivan; John Blair, Washington; George Kenney, Greene; Samuel Powell, Hawkins; Landon C. Haynes, Hawkins, Washington, and Greene; Wilson Duggan, Cocke and Sevier; Seburne W. Senter, Grainger; Michael Carriger, Claiborne; John Phillips, Campbell and Anderson; Joseph Parsons, Knox; David McKamy, Blount; William Heiskell, Monroe; Joel Henebree, Roane; Russell Lane, McMinn; William M. Biggs, Polk, McMinn, and Monroe; Pleasant Hollisman, Rhea and Meigs; Thomas Foster, Bledsoe and Morgan; John M. Harron, Marion and Hamilton; James R. Copeland, Overton; W. R. Kenner, Jackson; Thomas Snodgrass, White; J. Cummings, Fentress, White, and Van Buren; Samuel McGee, Warren; William B. Stokes, DeKalb; James Adcock, Cannon; James M. Sheid, Coffee; Hayden March, Franklin; Zadock Motlow, Lincoln; Thomas Buford, Giles; Nathan Adams, Lincoln and Giles; George H. Nixon, Lawrence; Edmund Cooper, Bedford; George W. Buchanan, Bedford and Marshall; William F. McGregor, Marshall; George Gault, W. J. Strayhorne, Maury; Elijah Thompson, P. G. S. Perkins, Williamson; C. W. Nance, G. E. Maney, Davidson; Erastus S. Smith, J. W. Benton, Wilson; Ro. B. Allison, J. W. McClanahan, Smith; W. B. Bate, James Butler, Sumner; J. B. Palmer, George W. Crosthwait, Rutherford; Wilie Woodard, Robertson; George A. Howell, Montgomery; William A. Moody,

Dickson; Sylvester Adams, Humphreys and Benton; Sam B. Moore, Hickman; Hartwell H. Barham, Perry and Decatur; William Benham, Wayne; Daniel Smith, Hardin; John H. Meeks, McNairy; Albert G. Shrewsbury, Henderson; Beverly I. Allen, Carroll; J. D. C. Atkins, Henry; J. E. R. Ray, Weakley; Marion J. Clay, Gibson; Alex. Jackson, Madison; James A. Rogers, Haywood; Edwin Polk, Hardeman; J. J. Neely, Hardeman, Fayette, and Shelby; H. R. Bate, Tipton and Lauderdale; Samuel C. Henry, Dyer and Obion; Andrew M. Campbell, Fayette; H. Valentine, Stewart; William Galbraith, Jefferson; Jonathan C. Tipton, Bradley; Granville D. Searcy, Shelby; Robert C. McKee, Hamilton.

TWENTY-NINTH GENERAL ASSEMBLY

Held at Nashville, October 6, 1851-March 1, 1852.

SENATORS—James W. Deaderick, Johnson, Carter, Sullivan, and Washington; John Bell, Greene and Hawkins; David W. Tedford, Cocke, Sevier, and Blount; Michael Carriger, Grainger, Claiborne, and Jefferson; Samuel McGammon, Knox; John W. Wester, Campbell, Anderson, Roane, and Morgan; Jacob Doyle, Bradley, Monroe, McMinn, and Polk; James W. Gillespie, Hamilton, Marion, Rhea, Bledsoe, and Meigs; Richard F. Cooke, Fentress, Overton, Jackson, and White; Caleb B. Davis, Warren, DeKalb, Cannon, and Coffee; Joseph W. Carter, Lincoln and Franklin; Wilson P. Davis, Bedford and Marshall; William C. J. Burrus, Rutherford and Williamson; Paulding Anderson, Wilson; William McClain, Sumner and Smith; Francis B. Fogg, Davidson; Ephraim R. Osborne, Maury and Giles; Joseph C. Stark, Robertson and Montgomery; Stephen C. Pavatt, Dickson, Stewart, Humphreys, and Benton; John W. Whitfield, Hickman, Lawrence, Wayne, and Hardin; James T. Dunlap, Henry, Weakley, and Obion; M. R. Hill, Gibson, Carroll, and Dyer; James A. Rogers, Madison, Haywood, Tipton, and Lauderdale; H. Bradbury, Henderson, Decatur, Perry, and McNairy; William C. Dunlap, Hardeman, Fayette, and Shelby.

REPRESENTATIVES—Calvin D. Anderson, Blount; Jesse Arledge, Franklin; J. D. C. Atkins, Henry; Alfred L. Baines, A. Bratton, Smith; Russell Hinton, Joel A. Battle, Davidson; Leonidas M. Bentley, Lawrence; John Bowles, Overton; Reese B. Brabson, Hamilton; Robert M. Bugg, Giles; Loyd Bullen, Greene; Brookins Campbell, Washington; D. Campbell, Frank Hardeman, Williamson; J. Burch Cook, McMinn; D. M. Currin, Hardeman, Fayette, and Shelby; F. M. Davis, Sullivan; Wilson Duggan, Cocke and Sevier; Robert Farquharson, Lincoln; E. A. Ferguson, Dyer and Obion; R. Fowler, Cannon; Monroe Gore, Jackson; W. W. Green, Claiborne; George M. Hamilton, Hardin; T. H. Hardin, Marshall; John M. Havron, Hamilton and Marion; O. F. Hendrick, Henderson; Ake Henry, Bradley; G. A. Henry, Montgomery; H. H. Hubbard, Jefferson; Granville C. Hurt, Carroll; Alexander Jackson, Madison; Frank H. Kimble, Perry and Decatur; Alvis Kincaid, Campbell and Anderson; Michael B. King, Gibson; G. W. Mabry, Knox; Barclay Martin, John L. Miller, Maury; R. W. McClary, Polk, McMinn, and Monroe; John McDaniel, Lincoln and Giles; Edward McDuffer, Roane; J. H. Meeks, McNairy; W. A. Moody, Dickson; Jonathan Morris, Wayne; Joseph R. Mosby, Fayette; Hawkins P. Murphy, Carter and Johnson; John W. Richardson, J. B. Palmer, Rutherford; Samuel Parker, White; William Phillips, Hickman; Edwin Polk, Hardeman; Levander Pope, Warren; Seburne W. Senter, Grainger; Thomas Shaw, Stewart; James M. Shied, Coffee; Cravens Sherill, Bledsoe and Morgan; Joel M. Simpson, Humphreys and Benton; Henry M.

Stephens, Monroe; John G. Stewart, Rhea and Meigs; W. B. Stokes, DeKalb; Jordan Stokes, R. E. Thompson, Wilson; G. W. Telford, Hawkins, Washington, and Greene; David Whitaker, Haywood; W. H. Wisener, Bedford; Willie Woodard, Robertson; M. B. Winchester, Shelby; William Simpson, White, Van Buren, and Fentress; J. E. R. Ray, Henry; John Netherland, Hawkins; Thomas Dean, Bedford and Marshall.

THIRTIETH GENERAL ASSEMBLY

Held at Nashville, October 3, 1853-March 6, 1854.

SENATORS—Godfrey Nave, Johnson, Carter, Washington, and Sullivan; J. M. Bewly, Hawkins and Jefferson; B. F. Bell, Greene, Cocke, Sevier, and Blount; Michael Carriger, Claiborne, Grainger, Anderson, and Campbell; John R. Nelson, Knox and Roane; John Bowles, Morgan, Scott, Overton, and Fentress; James H. Reagan, Meigs, McMinn, Polk, and Monroe; John M. Havron, Bledsoe, Bradley, Rhea, Hamilton, and Marion; Richard F. Cooke, White, Jackson, and Macon; J. G. Frazer, Smith and Sumner; Samuel W. Davis, Wilson and DeKalb; William O'Neill Perkins, Rutherford and Williamson; Joel J. Jones, Bedford and Marshall; Adrian Northcut, Coffee, Grundy, Van Buren, Warren, and Cannon; Robert Farquharson, Franklin and Lincoln; G. H. Nixon, Giles, Lawrence, and Wayne; Samuel B. Moore, Maury, Lewis, Hickman, and Dickson; John Reid, Hugh Robertson, Robertson, Stewart, and Montgomery; A. P. Hall, Benton, Humphreys, Perry, Decatur, and Henderson; Edwin Polk, Hardin, McNairy, and Hardeman; James T. Dunlap, Henry, Weakley, and Obion; A. Benton, Gibson, Carroll, and Dyer; James A. Rogers, Madison, Haywood, Lauderdale, and Tipton; William C. Dunlap, Fayette and Shelby.

REPRESENTATIVES—James J. Odell, Sullivan; I. E. T. Harris, Washington; Lloyd Bullen, Greene; W. F. Morris, Cocke; H. H. Hubbard, Jefferson; L. M. Ellis, Grainger; I. C. Lane, Claiborne; George W. Mabry, Knox; William Wallace, Blount; George Brown, Monroe; John A. Patton, Roane; J. B. Cooke, McMinn; W. H. Tibbs, Bradley; John Cowart, Hamilton; Joshua Easterly, Marion; Madison Williams, Franklin; E. I. Wood, Cannon; Thomas Mabry, Warren; Joseph Hord, White; B. C. Chowning, Overton; H. M. Clements, Jackson; H. W. Hart, Smith; H. Overall, DeKalb; G. W. Winchester, Sumner; George McKnight, Rutherford; W. H. Wisener, Bedford; A. A. Steele, Marshall; W. M. Nunn, Williamson; E. S. Cheatham, Robertson; John F. House, Montgomery; A. W. Winns, Stewart; Wilson Mathis, Dickson; William Phillips, Hickman; W. J. Sykes, Maury; Thomas Buford, Giles; S. A. Carroll, Lawrence; J. Morris, Wayne; C. S. Broyles, Hardin; W. B. Hall, Henderson; Alvin Hawkins, Carroll; W. E. Travis, Henry; N. Y. Cavitt, Weakley; B. L. Stovall, Obion; I. Richardson, Gibson; John C. Green, Madison; W. F. Brown, McNairy; R. H. Wood, Hardeman; W. B. Dortch, Fayette; R. E. Thompson, T. C. Martin, Wilson; W. H. Clements, J. Hugh Smith, Davidson; J. C. Farrington, G. C. Holmes, Shelby; John W. Hyder, Carter and Johnson; M. I. Temple, Greene, Hawkins, Hancock, and Jefferson; W. H. Chamberlain, Knox and Sevier; R. D. Wheeler, Anderson and Campbell; W. C. Wood, Scott, Morgan, and Fentress; J. M. Lillard, Polk, McMinn, and Meigs; N. M. Pope, Rhea, Bledsoe, and Hamilton; L. G. Stewart, Smith, Sumner, and Macon; Henry Cooper, Rutherford and Bedford; W. P. Chambliss, Lincoln, Marshall, and Giles; William E. Erwin, Williamson, Maury, and Lewis; H. R. Lucas, Benton and Humphreys; W. S. Maxwell, Perry and Decatur; L. M. Tharpe, Carroll, Gibson, Madison, and Henry; John N. Arnold, Dyer and Lauderdale; E. James Lamb, Tipton, Shelby, and Fayette; James White, Hawkins; George V. Hebb, Lincoln; James H. Baily, Davidson, Robertson, and Montgomery.

THIRTY-FIRST GENERAL ASSEMBLY

Held at Nashville, October 1, 1855-March 3, 1856.

SENATORS—H. C. Smith, Johnson, Carter, Washington, and Sullivan; B. F. McFarland, Jefferson, Hawkins, and Hancock; A. J. Fletcher, Greene, Cocke, Sevier, and Blount; Christopher Hitch, Claiborne, Grainger, Anderson, and Campbell; S. R. Rodgers, Knox and Roane; John Bowles, Morgan, Scott, Fentress, and Overton; D. W. Ballew, Meigs, McMinn, Polk, and Monroe; John M. Havron, Rhea, Bledsoe, Bradley, Hamilton, and Marion; Samuel Turney, White, Jackson, and Macon; J. W. Head, Smith and Sumner; W. B. Stokes, Wilson and DeKalb; R. G. Ellis, Rutherford and Williamson; Thomas Dean, Bedford and Marshall; J. M. Shied, Warren, Cannon, Coffee, Grundy, and Van Buren; Joseph W. Carter, Franklin and Lincoln; T. J. Brown, Giles, Lawrence, and Wayne; W. C. Whitthorne, Maury, Lewis, Hickman, and Dickson; A. W. Johnson, Davidson; E. S. Cheatham, Robertson, Montgomery, and Stewart; A. P. Hall, Benton, Humphreys, Perry, Decatur, and Henderson; J. D. C. Atkins, Henry, Weakley, and Obion; R. P. Caldwell, Gibson, Carroll, and Dyer; I. M. Steele, Haywood, Tipton, Madison, and Lauderdale; C. S. Palmer, Fayette and Shelby; O. L. Meeks, McNairy, Hardeman, and Hardin.

REPRESENTATIVES—F. D. Massengill, Sullivan; Lloyd Bullen, Greene; I. E. T. Harris, Washington; John Ball, Hawkins; W. A. Campbell, Cocke; J. M. Meek, Jefferson; J. C. Carmichael, Grainger; B. F. Cloud, Claiborne; Moses White, Knox; W. B. Colburn, Blount; J. R. Rudd, Monroe; H. J. Welcker, Roane; J. C. Carlock, McMinn; Eli Richey, Bradley; John C. Burch, Hamilton; Joshua Easterly, Marion; T. W. Newman, Franklin; E. J. Wood, Cannon; Thomas Mabry, Warren; Thomas Snodgrass, White; H. M. Colquitt, Overton; J. G. Galbreath, Jackson; W. G. Ward, Smith; M. M. Brien, DeKalb; D. S. Donelson, Sumner; J. M. Tompkins, Rutherford; William Little, Bedford; E. S. N. Bobo, Lincoln; E. A. Wilson, Marshall; E. C. Cook, Williamson; E. A. Fort, Robertson; M. D. Davie, Montgomery; A. J. Shemwell, Stewart; W. J. Mathis, Dickson; Robertson Whiteside, Hickman; F. C. Dunnington, Maury; G. H. Nixon, Lawrence; W. W. Pogue, Wayne; B. J. Brazelton, Hardin; M. J. Galloway, Henderson; J. W. Wilson, Carroll; W. E. Travis, Henry; N. Y. Cavitt, Weakley; B. L. Stovall, Obion; Smith Parks, Gibson; Henry Brown, Madison; J. B. Smith, McNairy; R. H. Wood, Hardeman; W. B. Dortch, Fayette; D. B. Thomas, Haywood; N. S. Brown, L. M. Temple, Davidson; Robert Hatton, J. F. Gleaves, Wilson; G. C. Holmes, G. M. Bartlett, Shelby; A. J. Tipton, Carter and Johnson; George Kinney, Greene, Hawkins, Hancock, and Jefferson; R. H. Armstrong, Knox and Sevier; William Wallace, Anderson and Campbell; E. Myatt, Scott, Morgan, and Fentress; J. B. Cobb, Polk, McMinn, and Meigs; N. M. Pope, Rhea, Bledsoe, and Hamilton; A. Northcutt, Grundy, Coffee, and Van Buren; W. H. DeWitt, Smith, Sumner, and Macon; H. Cox, Davidson, Robertson, and Montgomery; P. R. Runnels, Rutherford and Bedford; H. N. Cowden, Lincoln, Marshall, and Giles; A. M. Looney, Williamson, Maury, and Lewis; B. B. Gilbert, Benton and Humphreys; J. B. Algee, Carroll, Gibson, Madison, and Henry; A. T. Fielder, Dyer and Lauderdale; F. H. Kimble, Perry and Decatur.

BIBLIOGRAPHY

PRIMARY SOURCES

Manuscript

Bill by William Cullom *re* promotion of Education in Tennessee, 1845.

Memorandum of an agreement of William Strickland and Commissioners to build State Capitol, June 18, 1845.

Requisition for tools for construction of State Capitol by William Strickland, 1845.

Memorial of Miss Dorothea L. Dix *re* Hospital for the Insane, November, 1847.

Letter of January 31, 1848 to Tennessee Legislature from John McFall *re* grave of Meriwether Lewis.

Letter from Cave Johnson to James Buchanan, August 12, 1849.

Bill by G. D. Searcy *re* education, December 21, 1849.

Memorial from Marshall County *re* Common Schools, 1849.

Memorial from Jefferson County *re* Common School System, 1849.

Bill by R. D. Allison *re* education, January 4, 1850.

Memorial from Samuel Martin *re* common school fund, January 18, 1850.

Communication from Edward McMillan *re* "A Plan to Make the Common School Fund more Effective," 1851.

Letter from Cave Johnson to James Buchanan, September 15, 1851.

House Bill No. 70, *re* establishment of Public Schools, introduced on October 27, 1851.

Senate Bill to redistrict State into Congressional Districts introduced on January 21, 1852.

Letter from Andrew Johnson to S. Milligan, July 20, 1852.

Letter from William B. Campbell to David Campbell, March 23, 1853.

Report from Joint Select Committee *re* Tippling, November 15, 1853.

Memorial from McMinn County protesting against teaching trades to convicts, 1853.

Petition from Bethel College *re* liquor question, 1853.

Petition from Middle Tennessee Synod of Cumberland Presbyterian Church *re* liquor question, 1853.

Tennessee Historical Society Minute Book, 1880.

State Publications

Acts of Tennessee, 1815, 1823, 1843-1857, 1866, 1909.

Appendix (Legislative Documents), 1857.

Constitution of Tennessee, 1835.

Senate Journal (Tennessee), 1845-1857.

House Journal (Tennessee), 1845-1857.

Journal of the Constitutional Convention of the State of Tennessee, 1834.

U. S. Government Publications

Compendium of U. S. Census, 1850.
Congressional Globe, Second Session, Twenty-Ninth Congress.
Congressional Globe, First Session, Thirty-Second Congress.

Newspapers

Nashville Union, 1845, 1846.
The Daily Union (Nashville), 1847, 1849, 1851.
The Daily Union and American (Nashville), 1853, 1855.
Nashville Whig, 1845, 1847.
Politician and Weekly Nashville Whig, 1847.
Nashville True Whig, 1849, 1851, 1853, 1855.
The Republican Banner and Nashville Whig, 1855.
Weekly American Eagle, 1847.
Presbyterian Record (Nashville), 1849.
Nashville Gazette, 1850, 1855.

SECONDARY SOURCES

Books

ALEXANDER, THOMAS B.: *Thomas A. R. Nelson of East Tennessee.*
BROWN, AARON V.: *Speeches, Congressional and Political and Other Writings.*
CALDWELL, JOSHUA W.: *Bench and Bar of Tennessee.*
CLUSKEY, M. W.: *The Political Textbook.*
GILCHRIST, AGNES ADDISON: *William Strickland.*
HAMER, PHILIP M.: *Tennessee—A History,* Volume I.
MEIGS, RETURN JONATHAN: *Digest of all Decisions of the Former Superior Courts of Law and Equity and of the Present Supreme Court of Errors and Appeals in the State of Tennessee,* Volume I.
MILLER, CHAS. A.: *Official and Political Manual of the State of Tennessee.*
NICHOLSON, A. O. P. and ROWLES, W. P.: *The Life and Character of Captain William B. Allen.*
TEMPLE, OLIVER PERRY: *Notable Men of Tennessee.*
WHITE, ROBT. H.: *Messages of the Governors of Tennessee,* Volume III.
——— (Editor): *Tennessee: Old and New,* Volume I.

Magazines, Periodicals, Journals and Pamphlets

Speech of M. P. Gentry, of Tennessee, Vindicating his Course in the Late Presidential Election, Delivered to his Constituents at Franklin, Tennessee, November 20, 1852.
American Historical Association, 1914, Volume I.
Mississippi Valley Historical Review, Volume II, December, 1915.
Tennessee Historical Magazine, December, 1918.

INDEX

TOPICAL INDEX

OF

GOVERNORS' MESSAGES

1845—1857

(CHRONOLOGICALLY ARRANGED)

GENERAL INDEX

Agriculture: Survey recommended by Governor Campbell, 500; State Agricultural Bureau created, 603–604; slight defects in the law cited by Andrew Johnson, 658–659; bonds issued for purchasing suitable site near Nashvville, 662; report by Andrew Johnson *re* operations of Agricultural Bureau, 693–695.

Alexander, Thomas B.: Cited, 460.

Allen, Beverly S.: Resolution *re* preservation of the Union, 360–361.

Allen, William B.: Speech regarding erection of monument to Andrew Jackson, 90–94.

Allison, R. D.: Suggestions for improving education, 315–316.

Appendix: 698–720.

Apportionment: Resolution concerning Congressional and Legislative, 455; political composition of Redistricting Committee, 455–456; one principal objective of redistricting bill, 457; the "Whig-laden" redistricting bill passed, 457–458; one probable effect of redistricting bill, 1851 (footnote), 458; Congressional, 1851, 517–518.

Attorneys General: Proposed amendment to Constitution changing mode of election, 343–344; change in method of electing, 602; limitation placed upon tenure, 603.

Ballew, David W.: Proposed amendment to Constitution relative to changing mode of electing judicial officers, 333–334; *re* National Homestead, 660–661.

Bank of Tennessee: Certain branch banks discontinued, 84; Directors nominated and confirmed, 115; discontinuance opposed, 157–161; Di-

Bank of Tennessee (*Continued*)
rectors nominated and confirmed, 192–193; status of conditions and obligations, 194–197; statement of Governor Neill S. Brown concerning, 197–200; report of, 1847, 213–215; branch banks continued, 241; Directors made Board of Commissioners of Common Schools, 241; resources and obligations in 1849, 256–258; nomination of Directors, 289–290; legislative committee on banking "loaded", 290–291; nominees for Bank Directors unconfirmed, 292; second list of Bank Directors transmitted to Legislature, 293; legislative investigation of, 294; conditions and obligations of, 295–297; special message to Legislature concerning, 304–305; opinion of Attorney General regarding legal status, 306–312; special message of Governor and opinion of Attorney General ignored by Senate, 312; investigation recommended by Governor William Trousdale, 397–398; assets and liabilities enumerated by Governor William B. Campbell, 1851, 426–428; recommendation for "gradual liquidation" unheeded, 564; liquidation suggested by Andrew Johnson, 636; liquidation of ignored by Legislature, 660; prolonged argument by Andrew Johnson for liquidation of, 678–685.

Banking: Provisions of "Free Banking Law", 475; status of, 1853, 548–549; "Free Banking Law" needed revision, 637–638; Free Banks placed under restrictions, 660; recommendations concerning, 686–688.

Bate, William, B.: Resolutions regarding slavery, 345–347; amendment to

Bate, William B. (*Continued*)
Allen resolution, 360; resolution on death of James K. Polk, 362; resolution *re* publication of eulogy on James K. Polk, 363.

Bell, John: Elected United States Senator, 190; strategy employed in United States Senator race, 190–191.

Bethel College: Petition contained "the germ" of the "Four Mile Law" of 1877, 604.

Bibliography: 721–722.

Brabson, R. B.: Submitted majority report on "Compromise Measure", 463–465.

Brown, Aaron Venable: Biographical sketch, 1–3; Democratic nominee for Governor, 4; letter to A. O. P. Nicholson *re* nominee for Governor, 4; comments on his campaign speeches, 6–8; vote for Governor, 9; inaugurated as Governor, 12; inaugural address, 12–21; abolishment of capital punishment, 49; state prison management, 49–50; erection of State Capitol, 50–51; recommendations concerning Lunatic Asylum and Schools for the Blind, Deaf, and Dumb, 51; public education, 52–53; recommendations concerning internal improvements, 53–54; status of state indebtedness, 54–55; status of Bank of Tennessee, 56–58; suggestions for increasing common school fund, 59; cited inadequacy of school fund, 80–81; opposed taxation for support of public schools, 81; favored connection of Chattanooga and Nashville by railroad, 86; suggested plan for retirement of state debt, 89; summary of legislative action *re* recommendations, 89; suggested erection of monument to Andrew Jackson, 89–90; proclamation *re* raising troops for Mexican War, 120–124; notifying Col. William B. Campbell of transfer of troops under his command, 124–126; defeated for re-election, 146; recommendations concerning Lunatic Asylum, 147–148; appraisal of penitentiary conditions, 148; comments *re* education, 148–150; importance of railroad construction emphasized,

Brown, Aaron Venable (*Continued*)
150–157; opposed discontinuance of Bank of Tennessee, 157–161; proclamation and orders issued *re* putting state on war basis, 161–169; appraisal of legislative message, 170–171; valedictory address, 172–175.

Brown, Neill S.: Biographical sketch, 176–177; sketch of gubernatorial campaign against Aaron V. Brown, 178–179; elected Governor, 179–180; inaugural ceremonies, 180; inaugural address, 180–186; nomination and confirmation of Directors of Bank of Tennessee, 192–193; nomination and confirmation of Inspectors of Penitentiary, 193; financial condition of the state, 194–197; suggestions concerning construction of State Capitol, 197; comments upon Lunatic Asylum, 197; statement concerning Bank of Tennessee, 197–200; views upon education, 200–206; recommendations *re* internal improvements, 206–209; *re* Tennessee volunteers for Mexican War, 210; war with Mexico unwarranted, 210–212; war with Mexico ought to be prosecuted vigorously, 212–213; summary of legislative recommendations, 213; taxation for public schools recommended but later withdrawn, 247–248; slight legislative concurrence with recommendations, 248; minor legislative messages cited, 251; plea for increase in revenue, 251–252; Legislature declined to levy additional tax, 253; report concerning assets and liabilities of Bank of Tennessee, 256–258; views regarding public education, 259–260; additional railroad construction emphasized, 260–263; urged tax relief for merchants, 264; law regarding capital punishment defective, 264; views on slavery, 265–267; nominated by Whigs for re-election, 1849, 279–280; valedictory address, 283–286; views *re* public education, 318–319.

Caldwell, Joshua W.: Quoted, 109.

Campbell, Brookins: Speech favoring erection of monument to Andrew Jackson, 94–99; remarks upon ad-

Johnson, Andrew (*Continued*)
1857, 677; prolonged argument for liquidation of Bank of Tennessee, 678–685; recommendations concerning banking, 686–688; difficulties in administration of law *re* weights and measures, 688–690; recommendation repeated for reduction of tax on merchants, 690–691; previous recommendation repeated *re* public roads, 691–693; previous recommendations repeated concerning law reform, 693; report *re* operations of Agricultural Bureau, 693–695; report concerning purchase of Hermitage by the State, 695–696; slow progress toward construction of State Capitol cited, 696–697.

Jones, James C.: Elected United States Senator, 460.

Jones, Joel J.: Presented majority report *re* constitutional amendments, 590–591.

Judiciary: Report concerning digest of general laws and reports of Supreme Court, 116–117; recommended changes in method of electing judicial officers, 301–302; first proposed amendment to Constitution defeated, 333–334; newspaper support for changing method of electing judicial officers, 334–338; proposed amendment to Constitution by Abraham Tipton, 338–339; report of the committee on election of judicial officers, 340–342; legislative vote on amendment to Constitution, 343; passage of resolution proposing amendments to Constitution, 343–344; changes in judicial system recommended by Governor Campbell, 428; resolution calling for change in court procedure, 448–449; constitutional amendments proposed for changing mode of electing judicial officers, 450–451; proposal for constitutional amendment passed, 452; body of aforesaid resolution, 452–453; setting date for popular vote on legislative amendment to Constitution, 453–454; recommended increase of salaries for judges, 500–501; basic defects called for drastic remedy, 553–557; reform strongly advocated, 572–576; no

Judiciary (*Continued*)
remedial law enacted, 577; change in method of electing judicial officers, 602; important revision of court procedure recommended by Andrew Johnson, 643–646; no remedial legislation enacted, 1855, 661; previous recommendations by Andrew Johnson repeated, 693.

Know-Nothing Party: Origin of, 615; early development in Tennessee, 615; Meredith P. Gentry candidate for Governor in 1855, 616.

Labor: Report of legislative committee "to relieve the mechanic trades of Tennessee from moral, pecuniary, and social degradation", 388–390.

Lea, John M.: Report *re* equestrian statue of Andrew Jackson, 103–107.

Legislative Journals: Action regarding indexing, 253–254.

Legislature: Organization of, 1845, 9–12; some outstanding members, 1847, 253; political complexion of, 1849, 280–281; prominent members of, 1849, 281; 1849 Legislature a "divided house", 361–362; defeat of resolution proposing constitutional amendment requiring Legislature to meet once every four years, 391; political composition of, 1851, 414; summary of action on Governor Campbell's recommendations, 474–475; frivolous resolutions cited, 485; political complexion, 1853, 519; summary of legislative action upon Governor Johnson's recommendations, 586; creation of office of State Librarian and State Geologist, 610; political complexion of, 1855, 630; Neill S. Brown elected Speaker of House by plurality vote, 631; summary of recommendations to, 1855, 659–660; major recommendations of Governor Johnson defeated, 662–663; political complexion of, 1853 and 1855, 670–671; personnel of Twenty-Sixth to Thirty-First General Assemblies, inclusive, 715–720.

Lewis, Meriwether: Appropriation for marking burial site, 255; report of Lewis Monument Committee, 385–387; letter describing burial site of, 387.